HISTORY OF ECONOMIC ANALYSIS

BY

JOSEPH A. SCHUMPETER

EDITED FROM MANUSCRIPT BY

ELIZABETH BOODY SCHUMPETER

NEW YORK

OXFORD UNIVERSITY PRESS

Library of Congress Catalogue Card Number: 52-9434

sixth printing 1966

printed in the united states of america

Editor's Introduction

The *History of Economic Analysis*, upon which Joseph A. Schumpeter worked during the last nine years of his life and which he had not quite finished, was the result of his intention to translate, revise, and bring up to date the 'little sketch of doctrines and methods' (*Epochen der Dogmen- und Methodengeschichte*) written for the first volume of Max Weber's *Grundriss*, which was published in 1914.[1] This was a long essay (about 60,000 words) of a little more than a hundred pages which was divided into four parts or chapters. An examination of the table of contents will show that these four parts or chapters cover very briefly the same general topics that are treated in much more detail in Parts II, III, and IV of the 1200-page *History of Economic Analysis*. The first two, which are concerned with (1) the development of economics from the work of the philosophers and the popular discussion and (2) the discoveries in economics associated with the physiocrats, Turgot, and Adam Smith, are discussed in a single part in the present work (Part II: From the Beginnings to 1790). The third and fourth divisions in the two works are roughly parallel. The four main headings in the *Epochen* were as follows:

I. Die Entwicklung der Sozialökonomik zur Wissenschaft (The Development of Economics as a Science).
II. Die Entdeckung des wirtschaftlichen Kreislaufs (The Discovery of the Circular Flow of Economic Life).
III. Das klassische System und seine Ausläufer (The Classical System and its Offshoots).
IV. Die historische Schule und die Grenznutzentheorie (The Historical School and the Marginal Utility Theory).

The old essay had been out of print; it had never been translated from German into English; many people had been interested in it and had urged a translation. After herculean labor, J. A. S. had finished his monumental *Business Cycles* in 1938 and sought relaxation in *Capitalism, Socialism, and Democracy*, which he regarded as distinctly a 'popular' offering that he expected to finish in a few months. He completed it some time in 1941. In the meantime he began to give a half course in the History of Economic Thought at Harvard. He gave this course for the first time in the fall term, 1939 and for the last time in the spring term, 1948—giving it in every year except in

[1] *Grundriss der Sozialökonomik*, I. Abteilung, *Wirtschaft und Wirtschaftswissenschaft*, pp. 19-124, published by J. C. B. Mohr (Paul Siebeck), Tübingen, 1914; 2nd ed. 1924.

1940 when he was on leave. This last development was probably the decisive factor. He was once more teaching in a field which had always interested him. It was natural to think of writing in that field. He would translate, revise, and bring up to date the *Epochen.* In the beginning he did not stress so much the purely analytic element in the writings of the economists discussed in his course and about whom he wrote. In fact, for a long time I had the impression that he was writing a history of economic thought.

His original plan was not a very ambitious one. He certainly had no intention of spending nine or ten years on a history of economic analysis. At first he probably thought of giving his spare time for a few months or a year to a little book of three or four hundred pages. Later he thought of one large volume of six or seven hundred pages. His main interest was his work on theory and he planned to write his major contribution in this field. He worked constantly at his mathematics because he believed it to be an indispensable tool of modern theory. He envisaged a theory which might some day synthesize dynamic economics in the same way that the Walrasian system summed up static economics. Eventually he modified this program to the extent that he would first write a little Introduction to Theory which would be for this kind of theory what the *General Theory of Employment, Interest, and Money* was for Keynesian theory. He read the current theoretical literature (largely in periodicals), worked at his mathematics, and assembled voluminous notes. The results of this work are reflected in some of the later parts of the *History,* especially in those parts which sum up modern developments.

It is hard to say just why his work on the *History* constantly became more and more elaborate and took up more and more of his time. It was partly because his interests were constantly broadening, and he found it increasingly difficult to treat very briefly something which was to him a fascinating development. (For example, the scholastics and the philosophers of natural law became an absorbing interest in the early forties.) Here also he could weave together the threads of all his interests—philosophy, sociology, history, theory, and such applied fields in economics as money, cycles, public finance, socialism. I believe also that the war had something to do with it. I remember his telling one or two friends that he found work on the *History* a rather soothing occupation for wartime. It removed him temporarily from a grim reality which grieved him beyond measure because he was convinced it would destroy the civilization he loved.

As always he wrote out everything in his own hand and kept everything that he wrote. It is possible to see, therefore, how the early treatments became more and more elaborate. He probably began writing the *History* in 1941. During the years 1942 and 1943 he seems to have had typed a good many chapters and sections, most of which were subsequently revised. The only substantial parts of the *History* written in the early years which were not later rewritten are the chapter The 'Mercantilist' Literature, which was typed in June 1943, the chapter on Sozialpolitik and the Historical Method, part of which was typed in January 1943 and the rest in December 1943, and the section on Senior's Four Postulates at the beginning of Chapter 6 of Part III (General

Economics: Pure Theory). These, too, would probably have been revised or rewritten had J. A. S. lived to complete the *History*. Occasionally a few pages of an earlier version were incorporated in later versions. This process is described in some detail in the Appendix.

As time went on, he began to emphasize that this was a history of economic analysis and not a history of economic thought. He makes this clear in a brief description which he wrote early in 1949 for his English publishers, Allen & Unwin, in which he stated:

> This book will describe the development and the fortunes of scientific analysis in the field of economics, from Graeco-Roman times to the present, in the appropriate setting of social and political history and with some attention to the developments in other social sciences and also in philosophy. The ideas on economic policy that float in the public mind or may be attributed to legislators and administrators, whether or not embodied in elaborate systems, such as liberalism or solidarism and the like, which are commonly referred to as economic thought, come in only as part of that setting. The subject of the book is the history of the efforts to describe and explain economic facts and to provide the tools for doing so.
>
> Since the very possibility of treating the history of economics like the history of any other science is controversial, Part I of the book is devoted entirely to the methodological questions that this approach raises and especially to the question how far the distinction between scientific economic analysis and economic thought is valid in spite of the interaction between the two. Part II then tells the story of the growth of historical, statistical, and theoretical knowledge of economic phenomena from its beginnings in ancient Greece to the emergence of economics as a recognized special field and to the consequent appearance in the second half of the eighteenth century of systematic treatises, of which A. Smith's *Wealth of Nations* proved to be the most successful one.
>
> Part III covers the period between 1776 [later changed to 1790] and 1870, and Part IV the period between 1870 and 1914. Part V is to help the reader to relate the present state of economics to the work of the past. Throughout, an effort has been made to make the most important contour lines stand out without sacrificing correctness to simplicity of exposition.

I stated at the beginning that J. A. S. had been working on his *History of Economic Analysis* during the last nine years of his life. In a larger sense, he had been working on it all his life. Probably all of his writing and all of his teaching contributed to the final result. The lecture which he gave on leaving Czernowitz in 1911, for example, was entitled 'Vergangenheit und Zukunft der Sozialwissenschaften.' [2] This was a brief outline of what first became the

[2] 'The Past and Future of the Social Sciences.' A revised and enlarged version was published by Duncker & Humblot (1915) in the *Schriften des Sozialwissenschaftlichen Akademischen Vereins in Czernowitz*.

Epochen and finally the *History of Economic Analysis*. His Presidential Address before the American Economic Association in December 1948—'Science and Ideology'—was concerned with some of these problems of methodology which he takes up in Part I of the *History*. The course which he gave at Harvard on the History of Economic Thought covered essentially the period between A. Smith and A. Marshall, with special emphasis on the Ricardian system of economic theory. In the course on Advanced Economic Theory [3] he discussed many of the problems which are written about in Part IV, Chapter 7 (Equilibrium Analysis) and in Part V. He also taught at Harvard a course on Socialism and sometimes a course on Business Cycles and the course on Money. At the University of Bonn, J. A. S. held the Chair of Public Finance, but also conducted a seminar which was concerned largely with theory, including the theory of money, and with epistemology. While at Yale for a year, he taught the course in International Trade. Not only his courses, but also his many articles on almost every aspect of economics, his numerous book reviews, his biographical essays, his books—all were part of the preparation for writing the *History of Economic Analysis*. Even his reading for pleasure and recreation—he loved to read biographies, preferably those in many volumes—contributed to that fascinating knowledge of men, events, and backgrounds which is apparent throughout the *History* and which will liven for some readers sober discussions on fine points of economic analysis.

No part of the manuscript was in final form but some parts were more nearly complete than others. The three main Parts (II, III, and IV) were practically finished, with the exceptions noted in the Appendix; the introductory Part I and the concluding Part V were being written at the very end. The last thing written, at the close of 1949, was apparently the chapter on Keynes and Modern Macroeconomics at the end of Part V. This was left behind to be typed when he went to Taconic for Christmas and to New York for the meetings of the American Economic Association. On his return from the meetings, he started to write up his address, 'The March into Socialism,' and also to read the typescript of Part III of the *History*. He left several pages of notes for revisions in the first three or four chapters in this part on 'classical' economics. His death on January 8, 1950, made it impossible for him ever to carry out these revisions.

The entire *History* was first written in longhand. Some portions, such as the early chapter on Money (Part II, ch. 6) and much of the material on the

[3] At the beginning of the reading list for this course (Economics 203a) in the fall term of 1948-9 occurs the following brief description:

> The primary object of this course is to train the students in the art of conceptualizing the salient features of the economic process. But discussion of individual problems will give the opportunity of rehearsing critically large parts of traditional theory, old and new. The program for this term includes, first, a preliminary survey of certain fundamental notions, especially determinateness and stability; second, the general dynamics of economic aggregates; third, the general theory of the behavior of households and firms. Though some knowledge of the calculus and of differential equations is desirable, purely mathematical aspects will not be stressed.

Walrasian system of equilibrium (Part IV, ch. 7, sec. 7), existed only in longhand and had never been typed. In a few cases there were even several alternative versions in longhand. Other portions had been typed but not read by the author after typing. Still others had been read in typescript and corrected in pencil with notes and questions for subsequent revision. There were occasional references to be filled in, and J. A. S. told me that the references needed to be checked. I was to have helped at this task. The interested professional reader will find more detailed information on these points in editorial notes throughout the work and in the Editor's Appendix.

J. A. S. had no regular secretarial assistance during most of the period when he worked on this book, but he did have people who knew his handwriting and who typed for him. Occasionally he sent off a large batch of completed manuscripts to be typed. He wrote most of his letters in his own hand. This, of course, added immensely to the burden of his work and meant that his material was never filed as an efficient secretary might have filed it. He did not acquire a part-time secretary until the summer of 1948, when he was president of the American Economic Association and simultaneously carrying on all his other work. Even then he was reluctant to take the time to instruct her properly because the days and weeks were never long enough to do all the things he planned to do—his teaching, his consultations, his reading, his writing, his correspondence.

I conceived my editorial task to be the simple one of presenting as complete and accurate a version of what J. A. S. actually wrote as possible but not to attempt to complete what he had not written. No outline of the whole work existed, and I had read none of it before his death because J. A. S. wished me to begin with the introduction, upon which he was working, and to read the whole work in its proper order. The material was found in many places—some of it in file boxes, some of it piled on shelves—in the Cambridge study on Acacia Street, in the Taconic study, and a little of it in his office at Littauer Center. It took me two or three months to discover that the *History* was nearly completed, and sections or subsections kept turning up for some time. The initial fitting together of the pieces was made difficult by the fact that the manuscript pages were often not numbered at all, and that the typescript was not numbered consecutively from the beginning but only in small batches as typed. J. A. S. used only the first typescript for the publisher. He never bothered with a carbon copy for himself. Fortunately the various people who typed the manuscript kept a carbon copy, and these carbon copies were stacked in a room on the third floor of the Acacia Street house. Some of these—those done in 1943 and 1944 especially—were dated. I kept looking until I found manuscript and a first typescript to match the carbons. In a number of cases, the carbons represented early treatments subsequently discarded or partially incorporated in later versions. As I read the whole work over and over again I found that, though no outline or table of contents had been written out, such an outline existed within the text. There was a minor complication due to the fact that the number of chapters originally planned was reduced from eight to seven in the case of Part II and from ten to eight in the case of

Part IV. In the end, however, I had almost no difficulty in determining where each section or subsection belonged or in deciding which was the latest of two or more versions. These problems are discussed in the Appendix.

The task was immensely complicated by the length of the book. Even though I am an economist with some editorial experience, it was not easy to put together so long a work dealing with so many economists, writing in so many languages over so long a period. In general, the procedure was as follows: the sections still in manuscript were typed; then various assistants read the manuscript to me from beginning to end while I corrected the typescript; references were completed and checked; titles and subtitles were supplied where necessary; after the Oxford University Press edited the typescript, I went through it once more to pass on the changes made, to supply cross references to other parts of the work, to check against a card catalogue of authors; finally various assistants read the author's copy to me from beginning to end while I corrected the galley proofs. During each successive reading of the *History*, more and more minor inaccuracies and uncertainties were cleared up. Doubtless this process could have gone on indefinitely, but considerations of time imposed a reasonable stopping place. It seems appropriate at this point to acknowledge gratefully a gift from David Rockefeller and a grant from the Rockefeller Foundation which made possible much of the secretarial and editorial assistance outlined above.

One difficulty should perhaps be touched upon here. It applies especially to the unfinished portions of the *History*. J. A. S. often started and abandoned many treatments of the same subject. He kept all these trial efforts and his original notes together with the finished bits of manuscript so that it was not always easy to know what was a more or less final version. Sometimes the date of a reference or the incorporation of a page or two of an earlier version was a clue. Another difficulty is that his plans or his notes for revision were often in a mixture of English, German, and shorthand. Four pages of such notes are reproduced in the Appendix (the plan and the final page for the money chapter in Part II and two outlines for Part V). I made no effort to interpret or carry into effect either such shorthand revisions or brief suggestions as to revisions. I merely incorporated the straightforward corrections on the first typescript. The original manuscript, the alternative versions, the notes, and the first typescript with corrections and suggested revisions in the hand of J. A. S. will all be deposited in the Houghton Library at Harvard University, where they may be consulted by the interested scholar.

Material has been added by the editor only for clarity or consistency, and such additions are enclosed in square brackets. This applies especially to titles and subtitles, editorial notes in the text, and editorial footnotes. In the beginning, J. A. S. merely numbered his sections. As time went on, he added titles for both sections and subsections. Occasionally he left a blank where he had not made a final decision. The titles supplied by the editor were based on the text and are all enclosed in square brackets. There are both author's comments and editor's notes in square brackets, but it is almost always possible to distinguish between them. The author's comments are usually in the midst of quotations, whereas the editor's material occurs as complete sentences at the end of notes, as complete footnotes, or as a complete paragraph in the text printed in the footnote type. Where there is danger of confusion, the initials 'J. A. S.' or the abbreviation 'Ed.' are used.

There are some repetitions, of which J. A. S. was well aware, and some omissions of material promised 'above' or 'below.' For the most part, I did not attempt to eliminate repetitions except such as were very close together and obvious. When the same article was quoted several times in different connections or the same idea expressed several times in different parts of the text, I did not feel competent to remove some references and leave others, although the author himself would have done so. I have attempted to call attention in footnotes to the more important omissions, which were the consequence of some parts of the work being not quite complete. At the suggestion of Richard M. Goodwin, I also called attention in footnotes to some of the other writings of the author which had a bearing on problems under discussion, since J. A. S. hardly ever referred to his own work either in his teaching or in his writing. Other people could doubtless have done this better but no one else had the time to go through this long work again and again.

Occasionally it was impossible to read a word or a word was omitted or a sentence was incomplete. I dealt with such problems to the best of my ability. The vocabulary used was extensive and many an unusual English word had to be tracked down in the great Oxford Dictionary. Many of the foreign titles quoted were not to be found in any of the Harvard Libraries, nor were they listed by the Library of Congress. By using various foreign book lists and with the help of scholars in this country and in Europe, I was able eventually to verify almost all the authors and titles.

For the most part, J. A. S. was specific about the editions used where this was important, but occasionally there was a little difficulty in this connection, because the author had worked in so many places over such a long period that inevitably he had used different editions and printings of the works quoted. He undoubtedly used European university libraries and his own extensive library for his notes and writings before he came to Harvard in 1932. At that time his library was packed up and stored in Jülich near Bonn. It was not brought to the United States before the war because at first he did not have room for it and later there were various 'practical difficulties' (perhaps more imaginary than real). Then came the war. Eventually it was destroyed in the bombing of Jülich by the American Air Force. Only about a hundred books (mostly English biographies) were salvaged from the rubble. After 1932, J. A. S. used working books acquired in this country and my library of economics books in Taconic. He spent much time during the war working quietly in the Kress Library of Business and Economics at the Harvard School of Business Administration. (He also read extensively in the professional periodical literature, and he read the current books and reprints in many languages which scholars everywhere sent him.) This may help to explain why both earlier and later editions of the same work are listed in the *History* and why I found page references to two different English translations of Volume I of *Das Kapital* and to both English and American editions of Cairnes (*Some Leading Principles*) and Keynes (*Tract on Monetary Reform*). The original work on Turgot's *Réflexions* was obviously done before the publication of the Schelle edition.

There is no attempt to present a bibliography with this *History of Economic Analysis*. In a sense the whole history may be regarded as a bibliography. I do, however, present a list of books frequently quoted where the edition used is important and where this is not specifically mentioned on each occasion. J. A. S. used the fourth edition of Marshall's *Principles* (1898) because both he and I owned this edition. (He had many qualms about this and wondered if he shouldn't shift to a later edition.) This list of books (with the edition or printing used) is to be found at the end of the work, following directly after the Appendix.

The reader may be puzzled by the significance of the indented material which occurs in the first 566 pages of this work. It must be admitted at once that this is an error, the consequence of a misunderstanding between the printer and publisher on the one hand and the editor on the other. All the indented material should have been set in footnote type (not indented) as being supposedly of lesser interest to the average reader. It will be recalled that J. A. S. was attempting to write a history which could be published in one volume of possibly six or seven hundred pages. As time went on, however, his treatment became more and more elaborate, and he was aware of the fact that the book was getting too long—also that he was treating subjects which might not interest the average reader. He therefore decided to write the book on two levels, with the more or less technical material, the epistemological and philosophical discussions, and the biographical sketches set in small type so that they would take up less space and so that they could be easily skipped. He indicated this by having them typed in single space like the footnotes. The printer, having chosen an appropriate type for the book, decided that there would be too much of the small or footnote type and evolved the plan of putting this 'secondary' material in the text type but indented, thus reversing what the author had intended to be the relative importance of this material. Unfortunately this plan was not made clear to me and nearly half the *History* was in galleys before I saw any proof. Resetting all this would have involved both considerable expense and considerable delay. I therefore let it stand for the most part and had only small sections of incomplete or very technical discussion reset in small type. A glance at pages 414-18, 449-52, and 464-9, where Comte, Mill's *Logic*, and Longfield, Thünen, and John Rae are discussed, will illustrate the kind of material which the author intended to have subordinated. I am not sure that he was always right in his emphasis, especially with reference to the biographical sketches, which appeal to most people who have read them.

In the rest of the *History* (the last two chapters of Part III and Parts IV and V), I divided the 'secondary' material between the text type and the footnote type, with only two or three 'philosophical' discussions indented as had been done earlier. The biographical sketches, some of which were rather long, were almost all printed in the larger rather than in the smaller type, as originally intended. I did this because I was persuaded that it would be difficult to read so much material in the very small footnote type already chosen, although this change was, of course, contrary to my policy of publishing the *History* as nearly as possible as J. A. S. had written it. The manuscript and first typescript deposited in the Houghton Library will show what the author planned in this respect.

It is possible for me to mention here only a very small number of the people without whose advice or assistance I could not have prepared the work for publication. Arthur W. Marget was the first person to read the entire *History* in typescript, to advise me about the unfinished sections, and to discuss general editorial policy with me. He also put together and edited the chapter on Value and Money in Part II. This chapter had never been typed, the manuscript pages had not been numbered, and there was some uncertainty about the order of the pages in a few cases. Gottfried von Haberler also read most of the typescript and helped me check obscure references and any theoretical points which troubled me. Paul M. Sweezy read all of the proof, made many valuable suggestions, and caught several errors which had escaped me. Richard M. Goodwin first put together for me the material in Part IV, Chapter 7, and Part V, which were unfinished and upon which J. A. S. was working at the time of his death. This was the important material upon equilibrium analysis and upon modern developments. Alfred H. Conrad read some of the typescript and much of the proof and checked mathematical formulations. William J. Fellner read some of the typescript, and Alexander Gerschenkron read some of the proof. Frieda S. Ullian was both resourceful and indefatigable in tracking down obscure authors. Anna Thorpe has helped at every stage of this book from typing some of the early manuscript many years ago to helping me read proof and prepare an index. Her familiarity with J. A. S.'s somewhat difficult handwriting and his methods of work helped solve many a problem. My gratitude goes out to these people and to all the others who helped me in one way or another to edit this *History of Economic Analysis*.

ELIZABETH BOODY SCHUMPETER

Taconic, Connecticut
July 1952

NOTE: After Professor Schumpeter's death and up to the last weeks of her prolonged illness, Mrs. Schumpeter devoted most of her time to preparing this book for publication. At her death the author index was nearly finished, but the work on the subject index had been barely started. Dr. Robert Kuenne undertook the difficult and extensive task of preparing the subject index; he also completed the author index and co-ordinated the two.

The publishers are deeply grateful to Professor Wassily Leontief for his help in making publication possible.

Table of Contents

PART IV

FROM 1870 TO 1914 (AND LATER)

PART V

CONCLUSION

A SKETCH OF MODERN DEVELOPMENTS

PART I

INTRODUCTION

SCOPE AND METHOD

CHAPTER 1

[Introduction and Plan]

1. Plan of the Book

By History of Economic Analysis I mean the history of the intellectual efforts that men have made in order to *understand* economic phenomena or, which comes to the same thing, the history of the analytic or scientific aspects of economic thought. Part II of this book will describe the history of those efforts from the earliest discernible beginnings up to and including the last two or three decades of the eighteenth century. Part III will go on through the period that may be described, though only very roughly, as the period of the English 'classics'—to about the early 1870's. Part IV will present an account of the fortunes of analytic or scientific economics from (speaking again very roughly) the end of the 'classic' period to the First World War, though the history of some topics will, for the sake of convenience, be carried to the present time. These three Parts constitute the bulk of the book and embody the bulk of the research that went into it. Part V is merely a sketch of modern developments, relieved of some of its cargo by the anticipations in Part IV that have been just mentioned, and aims at nothing more ambitious than helping the reader to understand how modern work links up with the work of the past.

In facing the huge task that has been attempted rather than performed in this book we become aware immediately of an ominous fact. Whatever the problems that, to snare the unwary, lurk below the surface of the history of any science, its historian is in other cases at least sure enough of his subject to be able to start right away. This is not so in our case. Here, the very ideas of economic analysis, of intellectual effort, of science, are 'quenched in smoke,' and the very rules or principles that are to guide the historian's pen are open to doubt and, what is worse, to misunderstanding. Therefore, Parts II to V will be prefaced by a Part I that is to explain as fully as space permits my views on the nature of my subject and some of the conceptual arrangements I propose to use. It has further seemed to me that a number of topics should be included that pertain to the Sociology of Science—to the theory of science considered as a social phenomenon. But observe: these things stand here in order to convey some information about the principles I am going to adopt or about the atmosphere of this book. Though reasons will be given for my adopting them, they cannot be fully established here. They are merely to facilitate the understanding of what I have tried to do and to enable the reader to lay the book aside if this atmosphere be not to his taste.

2. Why Do We Study the History of Economics?

Well, why do we study the history of *any* science? Current work, so one would think, will preserve whatever is still useful of the work of preceding generations. Concepts, methods, and results that are not so preserved are presumably not worth bothering about. Why then should we go back to old authors and rehearse outmoded views? Cannot the old stuff be safely left to the care of a few specialists who love it for its own sake?

There is much to be said for this attitude. It is certainly better to scrap outworn modes of thought than to stick to them indefinitely. Nevertheless, we stand to profit from visits to the lumber room provided we do not stay there too long. The gains with which we may hope to emerge from it can be displayed under three heads: pedagogical advantages, new ideas, and insights into the ways of the human mind. We shall take these up in turn, at first without special reference to economics and then add, under a fourth head, some reasons for believing that in economics the case for a study of the history of analytic work is still stronger than it is for other fields.

First, then, teachers or students who attempt to act upon the theory that the most recent treatise is all they need will soon discover that they are making things unnecessarily difficult for themselves. Unless that recent treatise itself presents a minimum of historical aspects, no amount of correctness, originality, rigor, or elegance will prevent a sense of *lacking direction and meaning* from spreading among the students or at least the majority of students. This is because, whatever the field, the problems and methods that are in use at any given time embody the achievements and carry the scars of work that has been done in the past under entirely different conditions. The significance and validity of both problems and methods cannot be fully grasped without a knowledge of the previous problems and methods to which they are the (tentative) response. Scientific analysis is not simply a logically consistent process that starts with some primitive notions and then adds to the stock in a straight-line fashion. It is not simply progressive discovery of an objective reality—as is, for example, discovery in the basin of the Congo. Rather it is an incessant struggle with creations of our own and our predecessors' minds and it 'progresses,' if at all, in a criss-cross fashion, not as logic, but as the impact of new ideas or observations or needs, and also as the bents and temperaments of new men, dictate. Therefore, any treatise that attempts to render 'the present state of science' really renders methods, problems, and results that are historically conditioned and are meaningful only with reference to the historical background from which they spring. To put the same thing somewhat differently: the state of any science at any given time implies its past history and cannot be satisfactorily conveyed without making this implicit history explicit. Let me add at once that this pedagogical aspect will be kept in mind throughout the book and that it will guide the choice of material for discussion, sometimes at the expense of other important criteria.

Second, our minds are apt to derive new inspiration from the study of the history of science. Some do so more than others, but there are probably few that do not derive from it any benefit at all. A man's mind must be indeed sluggish if, standing back from the work of his time and beholding the wide mountain ranges of past thought, he does not experience a widening of his own horizon. The productivity of this experience may be illustrated by the fact that the fundamental ideas that eventually developed into the theory of (special) relativity occurred first in a book on the history of mechanics.[1] But, besides inspiration every one of us may glean lessons from the history of his science that are useful, even though sometimes discouraging. We learn about both the futility and the fertility of controversies; about detours, wasted efforts, and blind alleys; about spells of arrested growth, about our dependence on chance, about how not to do things, about leeways to make up for. We learn to understand why we are as far as we actually are and also why we are not further. And we learn *what succeeds and how and why*—a question to which attention will be paid throughout this book.

Third, the highest claim that can be made for the history of any science or of science in general is that it teaches us much about the ways of the human mind. To be sure, the material it presents bears only upon a particular kind of intellectual activity. But within this field its evidence is almost ideally complete. It displays logic in the concrete, logic in action, logic wedded to vision and to purpose. Any field of human action displays the human mind at work but in no other field do we get so near the actual methods of working because in no other field do people take so much trouble to report on their mental processes. Different men have behaved differently in this respect. Some, like Huyghens, were frank; others, like Newton, were reticent. But even the most reticent of scientists are bound to reveal their mental processes because scientific—unlike political—performance is self-revelatory by nature. It is for this reason mainly that it has been recognized many times—from Whewell and J. S. Mill to Wundt and Dewey—that the general science of science (the German *Wissenschaftslehre*) is not only applied logic but also a laboratory for pure logic itself. That is to say, scientific habits or rules of procedure are not merely to be judged by logical standards that exist independently of them; they contribute something to, and react back upon, these logical standards themselves. To convey the point by the useful device of exaggeration: a sort of pragmatic or descriptive logic may be abstracted from observation and formulation of scientific procedures—which of course *involve*, or merge into, the study of the history of sciences.

Fourth, it stands to reason that the preceding arguments, at least the ones that have been presented under the first two headings, apply with added force to the special case of economics. We shall attend presently to the implications of the obvious fact that the subject matter of economics is itself a unique historical process (see sec. 3 below) so that, to a large extent, the economics of different epochs deal with different sets of facts and problems.

[1] Ernst Mach, *Die Mechanik in ihrer Entwicklung: historisch-kritisch dargestellt* (1st ed., 1883; see Appendix, by J. Petzoldt, to the 8th ed.); English trans. by T. J. McCormack, containing additions and alterations up to the 9th (the final) ed., 1942.

This fact alone would suffice to lend increased interest to doctrinal history. But let us discard it for the moment in order to avoid repetition and to emphasize another fact. As we shall see, scientific economics does not lack historical continuity. It is in fact our main purpose to describe what may be called the process of the Filiation of Scientific Ideas—the process by which men's efforts to understand economic phenomena produce, improve, and pull down analytic structures in an unending sequence. And it is one of the main theses to be established in this book that *fundamentally* this process does not differ from the analogous processes in other fields of knowledge. But, for reasons that it is also one of our purposes to make clear, this filiation of ideas has met with more inhibitions in our field than it has in almost all others. Few people, and least of all we economists ourselves, are prone to offer us congratulations on our intellectual achievements. Moreover our performance is, and always was, not only modest but also disorganized. Methods of fact-finding and analysis that are and were considered substandard or wrong on principle by some of us do prevail and have prevailed widely with others. Although it is possible nevertheless—as I shall try to show—to speak for every epoch of established professional opinion *on scientific topics* and although this opinion has often stood the test of being proof against strong differences in political views, we cannot speak with as much confidence about it as can physicists or mathematicians. In consequence we cannot, or at least we do not, trust one another to sum up 'the state of the science' in an equally satisfactory manner. And the obvious remedy for the shortcomings of summarizing works is the study of doctrinal history: much more than in, say, physics is it true in economics that modern problems, methods, and results cannot be fully understood without some knowledge of how economists have come to reason as they do. In addition, much more than in physics have results been lost on the way or remained in abeyance for centuries. We shall meet with instances that are little short of appalling. Stimulating suggestions and useful if disconcerting lessons are much more likely to come to the economist who studies the history of his science than to the physicist who can, in general, rely on the fact that almost nothing worth while has been lost of the work of his predecessors. Why, then, not start in at once upon another story of intellectual conquest?

3. But Is Economics a Science?

The answer to the question that heads this section depends of course on what we mean by 'science.' Thus, in everyday parlance as well as in the lingo of academic life—particularly in French and English-speaking countries—the term is often used to denote mathematical physics. Evidently, this excludes all social sciences and also economics. Nor is economics as a whole a science if we make the use of methods similar to those of mathematical physics the defining characteristic (*definiens*) of science. In this case only a small part of economics is 'scientific.' Again, if we define science according to the slogan 'Science is Measurement,' then economics is scientific in some of its parts and not in others. There should be no susceptibilities concerning 'rank' or 'dignity' about this: to call a field a science should not spell either a compliment or the reverse.

For our purpose, a very wide definition suggests itself, to wit: a science is any kind of knowledge that has been the object of conscious efforts to improve it.[1] Such efforts produce habits of mind—methods or 'techniques'—and a command of facts unearthed by these techniques which are beyond the range of the mental habits and the factual knowledge of everyday life. Hence we may also adopt the practically equivalent definition: a science is any field of knowledge that has developed specialized techniques of fact-finding and of interpretation or inference (analysis). Finally, if we wish to emphasize sociological aspects, we may formulate still another definition, which is also practically equivalent to the other two: a science is any field of knowledge in which there are people, so-called research workers or scientists or scholars, who engage in the task of improving upon the existing stock of facts and methods and who, in the process of doing so, acquire a command of both that differentiates them from the 'layman' and eventually also from the mere 'practitioner.' Many other definitions would be just as good. Here are two which I add without further explanations: (1) science is refined common sense; (2) science is tooled knowledge.

Since economics uses techniques that are not in use among the general public, and since there are economists to cultivate them, economics is obviously a science within our meaning of the term. It seems to follow that to write the history of those techniques is a perfectly straightforward task about which there should be no doubts or qualms. Unfortunately this is not so. We are not yet out of the wood; in fact, we are not yet in it. A number of obstacles will have to be removed before we can feel sure of our ground—the most serious one carrying the label Ideology. This will be done in the subsequent chapters of this Part. Just now, a few comments will be presented on our definition of science.

First of all we must meet what the reader presumably considers a fatal objection. Science being tooled knowledge, that is, being defined by the criterion of using special techniques, it seems as though we should have to include, for instance, the magic practiced in a primitive tribe if it uses techniques that are not generally accessible and are being developed and handed on within a circle of professional magicians. And *of course* we ought to include it on principle. This is so because magic, and practices that in the relevant aspect do not differ fundamentally from magic, sometimes shade off into what modern man recognizes as scientific procedure by imperceptible steps: astrology was astronomy's mate until the beginning of the seventeenth century.

[1] We shall reserve the term Exact Science for the second of the meanings of the word Science enumerated above, i.e. for sciences that use methods more or less similar in logical structure to those of mathematical physics. The term Pure Science will be used in contrast to Applied Science (the French used the same term, for instance, *mécanique* or *économie pure*, but also the term *mécanique* or *économie rationnelle;* the Italian equivalent is *meccanica* or *economia pura,* the German *reine Mechanik* or *Ökonomie).*

There is however another and still more compelling reason. The exclusion of any kind of tooled knowledge would amount to declaring our own standards to be absolutely valid for all times and places. But this we cannot do.[2] In practice we have indeed no choice but to interpret and to appraise every piece of tooled knowledge, past as well as present, in the light of our standards, since we have no others. They are the results of a development of more than six centuries,[3] during which the realm of scientifically admissible procedures or techniques has been more and more restricted in the sense that more and more procedures or techniques have been ruled out as inadmissible. We mean this critically restricted realm only when we speak of 'modern' or 'empirical' or 'positive' [4] science. Its rules of procedure differ in different departments of science and, as we have already seen above, are never beyond doubt. Broadly, however, they may be described by two salient characteristics: they reduce the facts we are invited to accept *on scientific grounds* to the narrower category of 'facts verifiable by observation or experiment'; and they reduce the range of admissible methods to 'logical inference from verifiable facts.' Henceforth we shall put ourselves on this standpoint of empirical science, at least so far as its principles are recognized in economics. But in doing so we must bear this in

[2] The best way of convincing ourselves of this is to observe that our rules of procedure are, and presumably always will be, subject to controversy and in a state of flux. Consider, e.g., the following case. Nobody has proved that every even number can be expressed as the sum of two prime numbers, although no even number that cannot has been discovered so far. Suppose now that this proposition someday leads to a contradiction with another proposition which we agree to accept. Would it follow from this that *there exists* an even number that is not the sum of two primes? 'Classic' mathematicians would answer Yes, 'intuitionist' mathematicians (such as Kronecker and Brouwer) would answer No; that is, the former admit and the latter refuse to admit the validity of what are called *indirect proofs of existence theorems*, which are widely used in many fields and also in pure economics. Evidently, the mere possibility of such a difference of opinion on what constitutes valid proof suffices to show, among other things, that our own rules cannot be accepted as the last word on scientific procedure.

[3] This estimate refers to Western Civilization alone and in addition takes account of Greek developments only so far as they entered scientific thought in western Europe from the thirteenth century on, as an inheritance, but not of those developments themselves. As a landmark, we choose the *Summa Theologica* of St. Thomas Aquinas, which excludes revelation from the *philosophicae disciplinae*, that is, from all sciences except supernatural theology (*sacra doctrina*; natural theology is one of the *philosophicae disciplinae*). This was the earliest and most important step in methodological criticism taken in Europe after the breakdown of the Graeco-Roman world. It will be shown below how exclusion of revelation from all sciences except the *sacra doctrina* was coupled by St. Thomas with the exclusion from them of appeal to authority as an admissible *scientific* method.

[4] The word 'positive' as used in this connection has nothing whatever to do with philosophical positivism. This is the first of many warnings that will have to be issued in this book against the dangers of confusion that arise from the use, for entirely different things, of the same word by writers who themselves sometimes confuse the things. The point is important and so I shall mention instances at once: rationalism, rationalization, relativism, liberalism, empiricism.

mind: although we are going to interpret doctrines from this standpoint we do not claim any 'absolute' validity for it; and although, reasoning from this standpoint, we may describe any given propositions or methods as invalid—always of course with reference to the historical conditions in which they were formulated—we do not therefore exclude them from the realm of scientific thought in our original (broadest) sense of the word or, to put it somewhat differently, deny to them scientific character [5]—which must be appraised, if at all, according to the 'professional' standards of every time and place.

Second, our original definition ('tooled knowledge') indicates the reason why it is in general impossible to date—even by decades—the origins, let alone the 'foundation,' of a science as distinguished from the origins of a particular method or the foundation of a 'school.' Just as sciences grow by slow accretion when they have come into existence, so they emerge by slow accretion, gradually differentiating themselves, under the influence of favorable and inhibiting environmental and personal conditions, from their common-sense background and sometimes also from other sciences. Research into the past, clarifying those conditions, can and does reduce the time range within which it is in each case about equally justifiable to aver or to deny the existence of a body of scientific knowledge. But no amount of research can eliminate altogether a zone of doubt that has always been broadened by the historian's personal equation. As regards economics, bias or ignorance alone can explain such statements as that A. Smith or F. Quesnay or Sir William Petty or anyone else 'founded' that science, or that the historian should begin his report with one of them. But it must be admitted that economics constitutes a particularly difficult case, because common-sense knowledge goes in this field much farther relatively to such scientific knowledge as we have been able to achieve, than does common-sense knowledge in almost any other field. The layman's knowledge that rich harvests are associated with low prices of foodstuffs or that division of labor increases the efficiency of the productive process are obviously prescientific and it is absurd to point to such statements in old writings as if they embodied discoveries. The primitive apparatus of the theory of demand and supply is scientific. But the scientific achievement is so modest, and common sense and scientific knowledge are logically such close neighbors in this case, that any assertion about the precise point at which the one turned into the other must of necessity remain arbitrary. I use this opportunity to advert to a cognate problem.

To define science as tooled knowledge and to associate it with particular groups of men is almost the same thing as emphasizing the obvious importance of specialization of which the individual sciences are the (relatively late)

[5] All this is very inadequate and of course completely fails to do justice to the deep problems that we have been touching superficially. Since, however, it is all that can be done in the available space, I wish to add only that the interpretation above will be seen to be as far as possible removed from (a) a claim to professorial omniscience; (b) a wish to 'grade' the cultural contents of the thought of the past according to present standards; and especially (c) to appraise anything but techniques of analysis. Some related points will become clearer as we go along.

result.[6] But this process of specialization has never gone on according to any rational plan—whether explicitly preconceived or only objectively present—so that science as a whole has never attained a logically consistent architecture; it is a tropical forest, not a building erected according to blueprint. Individuals and groups have followed leaders or exploited methods or have been lured on by their problems, as it were, cross country, as has been already explained in Section 2. One of the consequences of this is that the frontiers of the individual sciences or of most of them are incessantly shifting and that there is no point in trying to define them *either by subject or by method.* This applies particularly to economics, which is not a science in the sense in which acoustics is one, but is rather an agglomeration of ill-co-ordinated and overlapping fields of research in the same sense as is 'medicine.' Accordingly, we shall indeed discuss other people's definitions—primarily for the purpose of wondering at their inadequacies—but we shall not adopt one for ourselves. Our closest approach to doing so will consist in the enumeration presented below of the main 'fields' now recognized in teaching practice. But even this epideiktic definition [7] must be understood to carry no claim to completeness. In addition we must always leave open the possibility that, in the future, topics may be added to or dropped from any complete list that might be drawn up as of today.

Third, our definition implies nothing about the motives that impel men to exert themselves in order to improve upon the existing knowledge in any field. In another connection we shall presently return to this subject. For the moment we only note that the scientific character of a given piece of analysis is independent of the motive for the sake of which it is undertaken. For instance, bacteriological research is scientific research and it does not make any difference to its procedures whether the investigator embarks upon it in order to serve a medical purpose or any other. Similarly, if an economist investigates the practices of speculation by methods that meet the scientific standards of his time and environment, the results will form part of the scientific fund of economic knowledge, irrespective of whether he wishes to use them for recommending regulatory legislation or to defend speculation against such legislation or merely to satisfy his intellectual curiosity. Unless he allows his purpose to distort his facts or his reasoning, there is no point in our refusing to

[6] Let me add at once that within such groups of fellow workers a specialized language is sure to develop that becomes increasingly un-understandable to the lay public. This effort-saving device could even be used as a criterion by which to recognize the presence of a science if it were not the fact that very often it is adopted, only long after a science in our sense has grown to respectable size, under pressure of the intolerable inconvenience incident to using concepts of everyday life that serve but ill the purposes of analysis. Economists in particular, much to the detriment of their field, have attached unreasonable importance to being understood by the general public, and this public even now displays equally unreasonable resentment toward any attempt to adopt a more rational practice.

[7] An epideiktic definition is the definition of a concept, say the concept 'elephant,' by pointing to a specimen of the class denoted by the concept.

accept his results or to deny their scientific character on the ground that we disapprove of his purpose. This implies that any arguments of a scientific character produced by 'special pleaders'—whether they are paid or not for producing them—are for us just as good or bad as those of 'detached philosophers,' if the latter species does indeed exist. Remember: occasionally, it may be an interesting question to ask *why* a man says what he says; but whatever the answer, it does not tell us anything about whether what he says is true or false. We take no stock in the cheap device of political warfare—unfortunately too common also among economists—of arguing about a proposition by attacking or extolling the motives of the man who sponsors it or the interest for or against which the proposition seems to tell.

CHAPTER 2

Interlude I: [The Techniques of Economic Analysis]

The last paragraph of the preceding chapter points toward momentous problems, which will, under the heading of Sociology of Science, be touched upon in Chapter 4. Now we break off our argument and turn aside in order to hunt two hares whose paths diverge sometimes in a disconcerting manner: on the one hand, it is necessary to define the relations of economics to some of the fields of tooled knowledge that have or have had influence upon it or have border zones in common with it [1] (ch. 3); on the other hand, it is convenient to use this opportunity to explain right now some of the concepts and principles that will govern our exposition of the history of economic analysis. This will be done in the current chapter.

Let us begin in a thoroughly common-sense manner. What distinguishes the 'scientific' economist from all the other people who think, talk, and write about economic topics is a command of techniques [2] that we class under three heads: history, statistics, and 'theory.' The three together make up what we shall call Economic Analysis. [Later in this chapter, J. A. S. added to these three a fourth fundamental field, Economic Sociology.]

[1. Economic History]

Of these fundamental fields, economic history—which issues into and includes present-day facts—is by far the most important. I wish to state right now that if, starting my work in economics afresh, I were told that I could study only one of the three but could have my choice, it would be economic history that I should choose. And this on three grounds. First, the subject matter of economics is essentially a unique process in historic time. Nobody can hope to understand the economic phenomena of any, including the present,

1 This clumsy phrasing has been chosen in order to avoid the unrealistic suggestion of sharp and permanent border lines.

2 The word 'technique' should be understood in a very wide sense: mere command of the facts of some field, systematically acquired and such as to be beyond the range of knowledge than can be gained by practicing in that field, is sufficient to constitute scientific level, even though cultivation of the field does not require any elaborate methods that the layman could not understand.

epoch who has not an adequate command of historical *facts* and an adequate amount of historical *sense* or of what may be described as *historical experience*.[3] Second, the historical report cannot be purely economic but must inevitably reflect also 'institutional' facts that are not purely economic: therefore it affords the best method for understanding how economic and non-economic facts *are* related to one another and how the various social sciences *should* be related to one another.[4] Third, it is, I believe, the fact that most of the fundamental errors currently committed in economic analysis are due to lack of historical experience more often than to any other shortcoming of the economist's equipment. History must of course be understood to include fields that have acquired different names as a consequence of specialization, such as prehistoric reports and ethnology (anthropology).[5]

Two ominous consequences of the argument above should be noticed at once. First, since history is an important source—though not the only one—of the economist's material and since, moreover, the economist himself is a product of his own *and all preceding* time, economic analysis and its results are certainly affected by historical relativity [6] and the only question is how much. No worth-while answer to this question can be got by philosophizing about it, but it will be one of our major concerns to work one out by detailed investigation. This is why sketches of 'the spirit of the times' and, in particular, of the politics of each period will preface our exposition of the economic analysis in the subsequent Parts. Second, we have to face the fact that, economic history being part of economics, the historian's techniques are passengers in the big bus that we call economic analysis. Derivative knowledge is always unsatisfactory. Hence, even economists who are not economic historians themselves and who merely read the historical reports written by others must understand how these reports came into being or else they will not be able to appraise the real meaning. We shall not be able to live up to the program that follows from this. In principle however let us remember: Latin palaeography, for instance, is one of the techniques of economic analysis.

[2. Statistics]

It stands to reason that for economics, statistics, that is, the statistical figure or series of figures must be of vital importance. In practice this has been

[3] This does not render 'theory,' in the sense to be explained below, either impossible or useless—economic history itself needs its help.

[4] Owing to the unreliability of 'theories' on this subject, I personally believe the study of history to be not only the best but the only method for this purpose.

[5] In this book, unless warning to the contrary is given, anthropology means physical anthropology only. Above it has the usual meaning which makes it synonymous with the study of primitive tribes, their behavior patterns, language, and social institutions. We call this ethnology.

[6] This is one of several meanings of that much misused word, relativity. Here we mean by it no more than (a) that we cannot use more material than we have and that in consequence some or all of our results may not stand up in the light of further experience (a fact that must of course be duly allowed for in the interpretation of the economists of the past); and (b) that economists' interests in the problems of their epoch and also their attitudes to these problems condition their *general* views on economic phenomena. See ch. 4. This has nothing to do with philosophic relativism.

recognized *at least* since the sixteenth and seventeenth centuries when a large part of the work of the Spanish *políticos*, for example, consisted in the collection and interpretation of statistical figures—not to mention the English econometricians, who were called political arithmeticians, and their fellow workers in France, Germany, and Italy.[1] We need statistics not only for explaining things but also in order to know precisely what there is to explain. But a comment has to be added that is analogous to the comment made in the preceding paragraph on the subject of history. It is impossible to understand statistical figures without understanding how they have been compiled. It is equally impossible to extract information from them or to understand the information that specialists extract for the rest of us without understanding the methods by which this is done—and the epistemological backgrounds of these methods. Thus, an adequate command of modern statistical methods is a necessary (but not a sufficient) condition for preventing the modern economist from producing nonsense, though very much more so in some fields than in others: our stake in these methods is too great for us to leave judgment on the virtues or shortcomings, say, of the variate-difference method to specialists, even if they were unanimous about it. Again, we shall not be able to live up to the program that follows from this. But again, we shall recognize, in principle at least: statistical methods are part of the tools of economic analysis even when not specially devised to meet its particular needs; and Jacques Bernoulli's *Ars conjectandi* or Laplace's *Théorie analytique* stand in the history of many sciences but they have their places also in the history of our own.[2]

[3. 'Theory']

The third fundamental field is 'theory.' This term carries many meanings but only two of them are relevant so far as our own usage in this book is concerned. The first and less important one makes theories synonymous with Explanatory Hypotheses. Such hypotheses are of course essential ingredients of historiography and statistics also. For instance, even the most fiercely factual historian, economic or other, can hardly avoid forming an explanatory hypothesis or theory, or several explanatory hypotheses or theories, on the origins of

[1] It is therefore only as a *curiosum* that we notice the fact that the simple and apparently unchallengeable statement in the first sentence of the paragraph above has been staunchly denied by some economists to this day.

[2] Lest the reader should throw up his hands in despair at the range of competence which the historical and statistical requirements seem to indicate, let me point out that these requirements can be easily fulfilled by every graduate student who has had a tolerably good undergraduate training in history *or* mathematics. Only the student without any training in either will have to realize that, as an all-round economist, he is suffering from a handicap and that he can move with assurance only within narrow portions of the science unless he is prepared to make up for his deficiencies by a heroic effort for which one or two years of graduate study are altogether inadequate. But it also takes more than that to become a scientifically competent lawyer or engineer or doctor.

towns. The statistician must form a hypothesis or theory, say, on the joint distribution of the stochastic variables that enter into his problem. All that needs to be said about this is that it is an error—though a widespread one—to believe that the sole or main business of the economic theorist consists in formulating such hypotheses (some may wish to add: out of the blue sky).

Economic theory does something entirely different. It cannot indeed, any more than can theoretical physics, do without simplifying schemata or models that are intended to portray certain aspects of reality and take some things for granted in order to establish others according to certain rules of procedure. So far as our present argument is concerned, the things (propositions) that we take for granted may be called indiscriminately either hypotheses or axioms or postulates or assumptions or even principles,[1] and the things (propositions) that we think we have established by admissible procedure are called theorems. Of course a proposition may figure in one argument as a postulate and in another as a theorem. Now, hypotheses of this kind are also *suggested* by facts—they are framed with an eye to observations made—but in strict logic they are arbitrary creations of the analyst.[2] They differ from the hypotheses of the first kind in that they do not *embody* final results of research that are supposed to be interesting for their own sake, but are mere instruments or tools framed for the purpose of *establishing* interesting results. Moreover, framing them is no more all the economic theorist does than framing statistical hypotheses is all that the statistical theorist or in fact any theorist does. Just as important is the devising of the other gadgets by which results may be extracted from the hypotheses—all the concepts (such as 'marginal rate of substitution,' 'marginal productivity,' 'multiplier,' 'accelerator'), relations between concepts, and methods of handling these relations, all of which have nothing hypothetical about them.[3] And it is the sum total of such gadgets—inclusive of strategically useful assumptions—which constitutes economic theory. In Mrs. Robinson's unsurpassably felicitous phrase, economic theory is a box of tools.

The rationale of this conception of economic theory is very simple and the same as in all other departments of science. Experience teaches us that the phenomena of a given class—economic, biological, mechanical, electrical, and what not—are indeed individual occurrences each of which, as it occurs, re-

[1] By 'principle' we shall mean in this book any statement that we (or the authors under discussion) do not propose to challenge. But it may be a proposition that we (they) have established as well as a proposition that we (they) have postulated or assumed. The same holds for the objectionable term 'law,' the emergence and use or misuse of which will have to be carefully considered: we speak of the 'law' of decreasing returns or of Keynes's 'law' of the propensity to consume, which are assumptions, but also of the Marxist 'law' of the falling rate of profit, which is a proposition that Marx thought he had established.

[2] To use J. H. Poincaré's simile: tailors can cut suits as they please; but of course they try to cut them to fit their customers.

[3] Example: theoretical mechanics proceeds upon a number of assumptions (or hypotheses in this sense); but evidently the list of these assumptions is not the whole of theoretical mechanics but only constitutes, where explicitly assembled, its first chapter.

veals peculiarities of its own. But experience also teaches us that these individual occurrences have certain properties or aspects in common and that *a tremendous economy of mental effort may be realized if we deal with these properties or aspects, and with the problems they raise, once and for all.* For some purposes it is indeed necessary to analyze every individual case of pricing in an individual market, every case of income formation, every individual business cycle, every international transaction, and so on. But even where this is necessary we discover that we are using, in each case, concepts that occur in the analysis of all. Next we discover that all cases, or at least large sets of individual cases, display similar features which, and the implications of which, may be treated for all of them together by means of general schemata of pricing, income formation, cycles, international transactions, and so on. And finally we discover that these schemata are not independent of one another but related, so that there is advantage in ascending to a still higher level of 'generalizing abstraction' on which we construct a composite instrument or engine or organon of economic analysis—though not the only one, as we have seen—which functions *formally* in the same way, whatever the economic problem to which we may turn [4] it. Richard Cantillon's [5] work is the first in which awareness of this last truth is clearly discernible, though economists took over a century to realize all its possibilities—Léon Walras was in fact the first to do so (see below Part IV, ch. 6, sec. 5b).

Although it is neither possible nor desirable for us to embark upon an epistemology of economics and although some of the topics pertaining to that field will receive attention both in the subsequent chapters of this Part and in all the subsequent Parts, it will be helpful to insert here a few additional remarks in the hope that they will do something to scale down possible barriers between myself and my readers.

First, then, a qualification should be added to the preceding argument about the nature and functions of economic theory. This argument ran in terms which are applicable, substantially at least, to all sciences that have any all-purpose apparatus of analysis. But there are limits to this parallelism and the most important of them are represented by the two following facts. Economics lacks the benefits that physics derives from laboratory experiments—when economists talk about experimenting they mean something quite different from experimenting under laboratory conditions—but enjoys instead a source of information that is denied to physics, namely, man's extensive knowledge of the *meanings* of economic actions. This source of information is also a source of controversies that will bother us repeatedly on our journey. But its existence can hardly be denied. Now, when we speak, for example, of motives that are supposed to actuate individuals or groups, our source of information may be roughly identified with knowledge of psychic processes, conscious or

[4] The statement above is a brief rendering of E. Mach's doctrine that every (theoretical) science is a device for effecting economy of effort (*Denkökonomie*).

[5] See below Part II, ch. 4, sec. 2.

subconscious, which it would be absurd not to use, although, as I shall never cease to emphasize, this is not the same thing as trespassing upon the field of professional psychology—any more than stating the 'law' of decreasing returns from land implies trespassing upon the realm of physics. There is, however, also another way of interpreting our knowledge of meanings which is more akin to logic. If I state, for example, that—under a number of conditions—instantaneous gains of a firm will be maximized at the output at which marginal cost equals marginal revenue (the latter equaling price in the case of pure competition), I may be said to be formulating the logic of the situation and a result that is true, just as is a rule of general logic, independently of whether or not anyone ever acts in conformity to it. This means that there is a class of economic theorems that are logical (not, of course, ethical or political) *ideals* or *norms*. And they evidently differ from another class of economic theorems that are directly based upon observations, for example, on observations as to how far expectations of employment opportunity affect workmen's expenditure on consumers' goods or how variations in wages affect the marriage rate. It would no doubt be possible to assimilate both types of theory by interpreting the logical norms also as 'purifying' generalizations from observational data, if need be, from observations that are subconsciously stored up by common experience. On the whole, however, it seems better not to do so but to recognize frankly that we have, or think we have, the ability to understand meanings and to represent the implications of these meanings by appropriately constructed schemata.

Second, the foregoing explanation may have done something toward exonerating me from the suspicion that I am tainted with Scientism. This term has been introduced by Professor von Hayek [6] to denote the uncritical copying of the methods of mathematical physics in the equally uncritical belief that these methods are of universal application and the peerless example for all scientific activity to follow. This history as a whole will answer the question whether there actually has been such uncritical copying of methods that have meaning only within the particular patterns of the sciences that developed them—*apart of course from programmatic utterances that have been numerous enough ever since the awe-inspiring successes of the physical sciences in the seventeenth century but mean next to nothing*. As regards the question of principle, there cannot be the slightest doubt that Hayek is right—and so were all who in the nineteenth century preceded him in uttering protests similar to his—in holding that the borrowing by economists of any method on the sole ground that it has been successful somewhere else is inadmissible,

[6] F. A. von Hayek, 'Scientism and the Study of Society,' *Economica*, August 1942, February 1943, and February 1944. This treatise—these articles are nothing less than a treatise—is strongly recommended both because of the profound scholarship of which it is the product and because it presents an excellent example of how near to each other, in discussion of this kind, dwell truth and error.

and that the rare and unimportant cases in which this has actually been done deserve what they get at his hands. Unfortunately this is not the real question. We have to ask what constitutes 'borrowing' before we can proceed to ask what constitutes illegitimate borrowing. And here we must beware of an optical illusion similar to the one that makes Marxists so reluctant to use such terms as price or cost or money or value of the services of land or even interest when speaking of a future socialist order: these terms denote concepts of general economic logic and seem to Marxists to be tainted with a capitalist meaning only because they are used also in capitalist society. Similarly, the concepts and procedures of 'higher' mathematics have indeed been first developed in connection with the physicist's problems, but this does not mean that there is anything specifically 'physicalist' about this particular kind of language.[7] But this also holds for some of the general concepts of physics, such as equilibrium potential or oscillator, or statics and dynamics, which turn up of themselves in economic analysis just as do systems of equations: what we borrow when we use, for example, the concept of an 'oscillator' is a word and nothing else. Two circumstances combine, however, to reinforce that optical illusion. On the one hand, physicists and mathematicians, when they hit upon those general concepts that occurred to us only later, not only baptized them but also worked out their logic. So long as this logic does not introduce anything 'physicalist' it would be waste of effort not to make use of it. On the other hand, students sometimes understand a physical analogy more readily than they do the economics of the case to be presented. Hence such analogies are often used in teaching. It therefore seems as though the things we are accused of borrowing are merely the reflexes of the fact that all of us, physicists or economists, have only one type of brain to work with and that this brain acts in ways that are to some extent similar whatever the task it tackles—the fact to which the Unity-of-Science movement owes its existence. This does not involve any mechanistic, deterministic or other '-istic' errors, or any neglect of the truth that 'to explain' means something different in the natural and in the social sciences, or finally any denial of the implications of the historical character of our subject matter.

Third, if economic theory is such a simple and harmless sort of thing as I have represented it to be, the reader might wonder where the hostility comes from that has followed it ever since it attracted any attention at all (which was roughly since the time of the physiocrats) to this day. I shall simply list the main headings for an answer which our story will amply verify:

(1) At all times, including the present, in judging from the standpoint of the requirements of each period (not judging the state of the theory

[7] Hayek's teachers, the Austrian utility theorists, by operating the concept of marginal utility, actually discovered the calculus. It cannot be a crime to formulate their reasoning correctly.

as it was at any time by standards of a later time) the performance of economic theory has been below reasonable expectation and open to valid criticism.

(2) Unsatisfactory performance has always been and still is accompanied by unjustified claims, and especially by irresponsible applications to practical problems that were and are beyond the powers of the contemporaneous analytic apparatus.

(3) But while the performance of economic theory was never up to the mark, that is, never what it might have been, it was at the same time beyond the grasp of the majority of interested people who failed to understand it and resented any attempt at analytic refinement. Let us distinguish carefully the two different elements that enter into this resentment. On the one hand, there were always many economists who deplored the loss of all those masses of facts that actually are lost in any process that involves abstraction. So far as application is concerned, resentment of this type is very frequently quite justified. On the other hand, however, there are untheoretical minds who are unable to see any use in anything that does not directly bear upon practical problems. Or, to put it less inoffensively, who lack the scientific culture which is required in order to appreciate analytic refinement. It is very important for the reader to bear in mind this curious combination of justified and unjustified criticism of economic theory, which will be emphasized all along in this book. It accounts for the fact that criticism of economic theory practically always proceeded from both people who were above and people who were below the level of the economic theory of their time.

(4) The hostility that proceeded from these sources was frequently strengthened by the hostility to the political alliances which the majority of theorists persisted in forming. The classical example for this is the alliance of economic theory with the political liberalism of the nineteenth century. As we shall see, this alliance had the effect of turning for a time the defeat of political liberalism into a defeat of economic theory. And at that time many people positively hated economic theory because they thought it was just a device for bolstering up a political program of which they disapproved. This view came all the easier to them because economic theorists themselves shared their error and did all they could to harness their analytic apparatus into the service of their liberal political creed. In this and many analogous cases, of which modern economic theory is another deplorable example, economists indulged their strong propensity to dabble in politics, to peddle political recipes, to offer themselves as philosophers of economic life, and in doing so neglected the duty of stating explicitly the value judgments that they introduced into their reasoning.

(5) Although really implied under one or more of the preceding headings, we may just as well list as a separate one the view that economic theory consists in framing unfounded, speculative hypotheses in the first of the two meanings that were distinguished above. Hence, the tendency

quite frequent among economists or other social scientists to rule out economic theory from the realm of serious science. It is interesting to note that a propensity [8] of this kind is by no means confined to our field. Isaac Newton was a theorist if he was anything. Nevertheless, he displayed a marked hostility toward theory and especially toward framing of causal hypotheses. What he really meant was not theory or hypothesis of our second kind but just inadequately substantiated speculation. Perhaps there was also something else in this hostility, namely the aversion of the truly scientific mind to the use of the word 'cause' that carries a metaphysical flavor. Newton's example may also be appealed to in order to illustrate the truth that dislike of the use of metaphysical concepts in the realm of empirical science does not at all imply any dislike of metaphysics itself. [J. A. S. intended to have these nine paragraphs of indented material set in small type so that it would be easy for the average reader to skip them.]

[4. Economic Sociology]

The reader will have observed that our three fundamental fields, economic history, statistics and statistical method, and economic theory, while essentially complementing each other, do not do so perfectly. In writing economic history, there are indeed statements that should not be added at all unless properly substantiated by pieces of reasoning that belong to economic theory: such a statement is, for instance, the one that links England's great economic development from the 1840's to the end of the nineteenth century to the repeal of the Corn Laws and of practically every other kind of protection. The schemata of economic theory derive the institutional frameworks within which they are supposed to function from economic history, which alone can tell us what sort of society it was, or is, to which the theoretical schemata are to apply. Yet, it is not only economic history that renders this service to economic theory. It is easy to see that when we introduce the institution of private property or of free contracting or else a greater or smaller amount of government regulation, we are introducing social facts that are not simply economic history but are a sort of generalized or typified or stylized economic history. And this applies still more to the general forms of human behavior which we assume either in general or for certain social situations but not for others. Every economics textbook that does not confine itself to teaching technique in the most restricted sense of the word has such an in-

[8] There is nothing to wonder at in the fact that on this ground alone the word economic theory, as used by some fellow economists, in itself implies derogation. To some extent, however, this attitude is simply a consequence of the fact that our intellectual tastes and aptitudes differ and that we naturally practice in our research according to our preferences. It is merely human nature that we overrate the importance of our own types of research and underrate the importance of the types that appeal to others. Perhaps it is not too much to say that we should never do what we are doing, both in science and in other pursuits of life, if we did not do this.

stitutional introduction that belongs to sociology rather than to economic history as such. Borrowing from German practice, we shall find it useful, therefore, to introduce a fourth fundamental field to complement the three others, although positive work in this field also leads us beyond mere economic analysis: the field that we shall call Economic Sociology (*Wirtschaftssoziologie*). To use a felicitous phrase: economic analysis deals with the questions how people behave at any time and what the economic effects are they produce by so behaving; economic sociology deals with the question how they came to behave as they do.[1] If we define human behavior widely enough so that it includes not only actions and motives and propensities but also the social institutions that are relevant to economic behavior such as government, property inheritance, contract, and so on, that phrase really tells us all we need. Of course, it should be observed that this distinction is one we make for our own purposes. It is not implied that this distinction has been made by the authors themselves whom we are going to encounter. The proof of any pudding is in the eating and hence I refrain from saying anything in its defense just now.

[5. Political Economy]

The sum total of the historical, statistical, and theoretical techniques that have been characterized above, together with the results they help to produce, we call (scientific) economics. This term is of relatively recent growth. A. Marshall's great treatise was the first to establish its use, from 1890 on, at least in England and the United States.[1] In the nineteenth century, the term commonly in use was Political Economy, though in some countries other terms competed with it in the first decades of that century. This unimportant matter will be attended to, as we go along, in the subsequent Parts. But it is just as well to note two points at once. First, political economy meant different things to different writers, and in some cases it meant what is now known as economic theory or 'pure' economics. A warning must therefore be issued right now that in order to interpret correctly what any given writer said about the scope and method of political economy, we must always make sure of the meaning he attached to this term—some propositions about those subjects that have outraged critics become perfectly harmless if this rule be borne in mind. Second, ever since our science or agglomeration of sciences was baptized political economy by a not very significant writer of the seventeenth century whose work owes an undeserved immortality to this fact, there has been the implicit or explicit suggestion that the exclusive concern of our science was with the economy of the state—though of course not only of the *polis*, the city-state of Greece—or, what is almost the same thing, with public policies of an economic nature. This suggestion, which was still more emphasized by the German term frequently used as a synonym of political economy, *Staats-*

[1] I believe that this phrase is due to Mr. Gerhard Colm.

[1] Later on, a parallel usage was introduced, though less firmly established, in Germany. The word was Social Economics, *Sozialökonomie*, and the man who did more than any other to assure some currency to it was Max Weber.

wissenschaft, implied of course an altogether too narrow conception of the scope of economics. Incidentally, it over-emphasized the largely meaningless distinction between economics and what is now called business economics. Let us therefore have it understood that we ourselves do not divorce the two and that all the facts and tools relevant to the analysis of the behavior of individual firms, past or present, come within our meaning of economics just as much as do the facts and tools relevant to the analysis of the behavior of governments, and therefore will have to be added to the contents of any narrower political economies of the past. We have, however, to notice a novel meaning of the term political economy that has asserted itself of late.

Some contemporaneous economists are of the opinion that modern economic theory (in our sense) hangs too much in the air and does not take sufficient account of the fact that no sensible application to practical questions or even to the analysis of given situations of an economy can be made of its results without reference to the historico-political framework within which they are to hold. This opinion is sometimes extended so as to imply criticism of any work that concentrates on the improvement of theoretical or statistical tools of analysis, and then it seems to me to mean nothing except a failure to realize the inexorable necessity of specialized work. But all the more justified is this opinion if it be formulated as it has been in the first sentence of this paragraph. In particular, an economics that includes an adequate analysis of government action and of the mechanisms and prevailing philosophies of political life is likely to be much more satisfactory to the beginner than an array of different sciences which he does not know how to co-ordinate—whereas, to his delight, he finds precisely what he seeks ready-made in Karl Marx. An economics of this type is sometimes presented under the title Political Economy. In partial recognition of the truth that seems to be contained in this program, we have set up our 'fourth fundamental field,' Economic Sociology.

Political Economy in the sense discussed in the preceding paragraph calls up still another meaning of the term, the one that occurs in a discussion of Systems of Political Economy. And this meaning in turn evokes, by association, the term Economic Thought. But it will be convenient to deal with these two concepts in Chapter 4. There we shall also try to clarify the relation of this History of Economic Analysis to any history of the systems of political economy and to any history of the thoughts on economic subjects that float in the public mind.

[6. Applied Fields]

Division of labor, in research as well as in teaching, has produced, in economics as elsewhere, an indefinite number of specialties that are usually described as 'applied fields.' In order to obtain a list of them (which does not claim to be complete) let us draw inspiration from the courses offered by the larger institutions of higher learning in the United States that teach economics.

In addition to general survey courses and courses in economic history, statistics, economic theory, and economic sociology,[1] we find, first, offerings in a group of fields which everyone considers part and parcel of 'general economics' and which receive separate treatment only in order to facilitate more intensive treatment of their subjects. Such are money and banking, business fluctuations (or cycles), foreign trade (international economic relations), and, occasionally, location. Second, we find a group of fields, such as accounting, actuarial science, and insurance, that, historically, have preserved altogether too much independence from general economics (which is slowly being surrendered in the case of accounting) but are useful or even indispensable for all or some economists, because they offer both instruments of economic analysis or opportunities for applying it—witness, for example, the subject of depreciation. Third, we find a group of standard fields that pivot on the old-established departments of public economic policy especially: agriculture,[2] labor, transportation and 'utilities,' the problems of manufacturing industry (and of *its* public control)—for which there is no generally accepted English name—and public finance ('fiscal policy'), to which most people will add (for the present) a number of other fields such as marketing ('commodity distribution') and social security (so far as not covered by insurance). Socialism and 'comparative economic systems' or again 'population' may stand for a fourth group, and the 'area studies' that have become so popular of late for a fifth. Inclusion of other fields or the subdivision of some of those that have been mentioned could swell impressively the number of passengers in what we have described as a big bus. But our list as it stands and the reader's general knowledge suffice to verify the three statements which it is relevant to our task to make.

First, there is evidently no permanence or logical order to this jumble of applied fields. Nor are there definite frontier lines to any of them. They appear or vanish, they increase or decrease in relative importance, and they overlap with one another as changing interests and methods dictate. And, as has been indicated already, this is as it should be. To undertake or to refrain from undertaking any interesting task out of respect for frontiers or tectonics would be the height of absurdity.

Second, *all* those special or applied fields, and not only the three that have

[1] Owing to the discredit that, for good reasons and bad, attaches to the word 'theory' in many minds, this word is occasionally replaced by the word 'analysis' which then carries a meaning that is more restricted than the one attached to it in this book. The field of economic sociology does not, so far as I am aware, appear under this title or separately, but topics belonging in it are treated in courses on history, theory, 'comparative economic systems,' the more institutionally oriented courses on labor, and in a number of others.

[2] The field of agriculture offers an interesting example of a department of economics that it is hardly possible to treat without a considerable command of agricultural technology. In principle, though mostly to a lesser extent, this is true also in other departments and, so far as this is so, there is no point in drawing any sharp line between, say, the economics of banking, marketing, or manufacturing industry and the corresponding 'technologies.'

been mentioned as constituents of our first group, are mixtures of facts and techniques that form what we have described as the four fundamental divisions of economic analysis in our sense. The mixtures differ greatly from one another because there are wide stretches of ground on which there is much less need or opportunity for elaborate statistical or theoretical tools than there is in others or even none at all, though the historical element can hardly ever be entirely neglected with impunity. In addition, the mixtures also differ for another reason: the specialist workers in the various fields are, individually and groupwise, very differently grounded in the fundamental fields, and so mix techniques in a manner that differs considerably from what their chosen specialties might be thought to require—a fact that we must keep in mind if we are to understand why economics is what it is. In principle, however, it is impossible to divorce any of the applied fields from the fundamental ones.

But, third, such divorce is also impossible because the applied fields not only apply a stock of facts and techniques that lies ready for their use in general economics but also add to it. These fields may accumulate 'private' stocks of facts and methods that are of little or no use outside their boundaries. Beyond this, however, they have repeatedly developed accumulations of facts and conceptual schemata that should be recorded as contributions to general economic analysis, even though the appointed wardens of the latter have sometimes been slow to welcome them. Modern agricultural economics affords some examples, the fields of transportation and public finance afford others. It follows that we cannot confine ourselves to the history of 'general' economic analysis but shall have to keep an eye on developments in applied fields as best we can.

CHAPTER 3

Interlude II: [Contemporaneous Developments in Other Sciences]

From time to time, we shall look up from our work in order to view a piece of intellectual scenery. Slightly less perfunctorily, we shall, for every one of our periods, register some contemporaneous developments in other sciences (in our sense of the term) that were relevant or might, for one reason or another, be expected to have been relevant to the development of our own. What has to be said now about this aspect of our exposition is so preponderantly concerned with 'philosophy' that I might as well have entitled this chapter: Economics and Philosophy. The rest will be disposed of in the two paragraphs that follow.

[1. Economics and Sociology]

After what has been said in the preceding chapter about the paramount importance for economic analysis of history—and all the sciences and branches of sciences that this term stands for [1]—and of statistics, it goes without saying that we must try to keep some contact with them; the reason why this will be done in a fragmentary manner is not that a more systematic treatment would not be desirable but that such treatment is impossible within the space at our disposal and within the limits of my own knowledge—and even if it were possible, it would drown our own story in an unfathomable ocean. Similarly, it goes without saying that we cannot afford, subject to the same restrictions, to neglect the developments of sociology. This term we shall use in the narrow sense in which it denotes a single though far from homogeneous science, namely the general analysis of social phenomena such as society,

[1] Amplifying what has been said about this point, I want to point out that all the historical sciences and branches of sciences that specialization (mainly of philological competence to deal with particular bodies of material) has produced are to some extent relevant for us even where they do not treat of specifically economic facts. For instance, the Graeco-Roman civilization is the subject of research by three clearly distinguishable groups of scholars, namely historians proper, philologists, and jurists. All three of them deal with many things that do not concern us. But even when they do so they contribute to the cultural picture of that world which as a whole is not a matter of indifference to us; and even where they describe military history or the history of the arts, they use the same techniques that they use in describing economic or social events and institutions, so that there is no hard and fast frontier at which our interest could be definitely said to stop.

group, class, group relations, leadership, and the like. And we shall use the term in this sense throughout, that is, for developments that antedate by centuries the introduction of the word. In a wider sense it means the whole of many overlapping and unco-ordinated social sciences—which is the term we prefer and which includes, among other things, our own economics, jurisprudence, hierology, 'political science,' ecology, and descriptive ethics and aesthetics (in the sense of sociology of moral behavior patterns and of art). In the footnote below the kinds of relations that may make developments in these and other fields relevant to a history of economic analysis are illustrated by the example of jurisprudence.[2]

The closeness of some of these relations has been recognized by our setting up the 'fundamental field' of Economic Sociology in which neither economists nor sociologists can get very far without treading on one another's toes. But it does not follow *either* that the co-operation between the two groups has actually been particularly close or fertile; *or* that either of them would have got along better if there had been more co-operation. As regards the first point it is the fact that ever since the eighteenth century both groups have grown steadily apart until by now the modal economist and the modal sociologist know little and care less about what the other does, each preferring to use, respectively, a primitive sociology and a primitive economics of his own to accepting one another's professional results—a state of things that was and

[2] The science or sciences (in our sense) whose subjects consist of statutory or customary 'law,' of legal practice, and of legal techniques are relevant to a history of economic analysis, first of all, because, to a considerable extent, economists have been lawyers (or, as we prefer to say, jurists) who brought to bear the habits of the legal mind upon the analysis of economic phenomena. For instance, the sociological and economic systems of the scholastic doctors of the sixteenth century (the literature *de jure et justitia*) cannot be understood if we do not realize that they were primarily treatises on the political and economic law of the Catholic Church and that their technique was derived primarily from the old Roman law as adapted to the conditions of the time. Second, the legal framework of the economic process, and the shaping influence of either upon the other, are, to say the least, of considerable importance for economic analysis. Third, the historical roots of the concept of 'economic law' are in the purely legistic concept of 'natural law' (see below Part II, ch. 2). Fourth, certain nineteenth-century economists professed to have derived inspiration for a historical view of the economic process from a school of jurisprudence that called itself the 'historical school' and whose emergence and position must be understood more completely than economists usually do if the elements of truth and error in that view are to be disentangled. I take the opportunity to add that the sociological analysis of law as a social phenomenon is one thing; that the study of the techniques of legal practice—the sort of thing that is taught in American law schools—is quite another thing; and that historical jurisprudence is still another thing: so we must distinguish at least three different 'sciences' of the law that differ in material, tools, and aims and are cultivated (though there are overlappings) by different groups of workers, and similarly in the fields of religion, ethics, and aesthetics. Confusion becomes almost excusable under these circumstances and great battles about principles and 'methods' have been fought on issues (e.g., in the sciences of art) that clear themselves up automatically as soon as it is realized that the contestants aim at different targets.

is not improved by mutual vituperation. As regards the second point it is by no means certain that closer co-operation, so often clamored for by laymen who expect great things from 'cross-fertilization' with a certainty untroubled by professional competence, would have been an unmixed blessing. For it could certainly not have brought *net* gains because there would have been some loss of that efficiency which is the result of strict or even narrow specialization. This holds even for the division of economics and of sociology (in the wider sense) into departments that have developed into what are, to all intents and purposes, semi-independent sciences. This is precisely why we prefer to speak of social sciences rather than to speak of sociology in the wider sense. As an eminent economist once observed, cross-fertilization might easily result in cross-sterilization. This does not affect what has been said about the necessity of following up, at least in a fragmentary fashion, the developments of all the 'neighboring fields' in this book. It was only to avoid a possible misunderstanding that I thought it necessary to write the last sentences.

[2. Logic and Psychology]

For the rest we are particularly interested in logic and psychology. The former claims our attention because economists have made a not inconsiderable contribution to it but especially because of their propensity to dogmatize and to quarrel about 'method': economists who enjoy this sport are apt to be influenced by the writings of the logicians of their time which therefore, though more apparently than really, gain some influence, legitimate or otherwise, upon our work. As regards psychology, there is the view that came first to the fore in the eighteenth century, and hence has been sponsored intermittently, that economics like other social sciences deals with human behavior. Psychology is really the basis from which any social science must start and in terms of which all fundamental explanation must run. This view, which has been defended as strongly as it has been attacked, we shall denote by the term Psychologism. Actually, however, economists have never allowed their analysis to be influenced by the professional psychologists of their times, but have always framed for themselves such assumptions about psychical processes as they thought it desirable to make. On the one hand, we shall note this fact occasionally with surprise because there exist problems in economic analysis that might be attacked with advantage by methods worked out by psychologists. On the other hand, we must avoid a very natural delusion. If we use an assumption the contents of which seem to belong to a particular field, this does not necessarily mean that we actually invade that field. For instance, the so-called law of decreasing returns from land refers to what might be termed a physical fact. But, as has been pointed out already, this does not mean that in formulating this assumption we are entering the field of physics. Similarly, when I state the assumption that as I go on eating successive pieces of bread my desire for further such pieces decreases, I may be said to be stating a psychic fact. But, in doing so, I am not borrowing anything from professional psychology, good or bad; I am simply formulating what rightly or wrongly I believe to be a fact of common experience. If we place ourselves on this standpoint, we shall find that there is much less of psychology about economic propositions than one might think at first sight. To speak of psychological laws, such as the Keynesian law of the propensity to consume, is a flagrant abuse, because this practice suggests justification for our assumptions, which, in effect, do not exist. Nevertheless, it is necessary to glance occasionally at the developments in the field of professional psychology, and this necessity arises, though less often, also with respect to a number of other sciences. For the moment, we confine ourselves to mentioning biology as an example. There is, or has been, such a thing as social and economic Darwinism. If we are to appraise this phenomenon, it is just as well to make sure of what Charles Darwin actually said and of the methods and materials that induced him to say it.

[3. Economics and Philosophy]

Now we turn to the subject of the relations between economics and philosophy. Or, to put it more precisely, to the question, how far economic analysis has experienced influences from philosophy.[1] Owing to the many meanings that have been assigned to the word philosophy, some care is needed in order to avoid confusion.

There is first a meaning for which our question is very easy to answer, or rather, for which no problem exists. The Greek 'philosopher,' who shaded off into the rhetor and sophist, was simply the man of intellectual pursuits. Taken in this sense, which was transmitted to the Middle Ages and survived right into the eighteenth century, philosophy meant the sum total of all scientific knowledge. It was simply the universal science, of which metaphysics formed a part not less than did physics, and physics not less than mathematics or any 'philosophy' on the nature of society and of the *polis*. This usage was bound to maintain itself so long as the stock, both of analytic tools and facts, remained small enough for one brain to encompass. More or less, this was the case until, very roughly, the middle of the eighteenth century, when the time of the polyhistors was definitely over.[2] As we have seen, St. Thomas Aquinas

[1] For reasons that will appear presently, we shall not go into the large literature on this subject any more than we can help. For the moment, it is sufficient to mention the English standard work, James Bonar, *Philosophy and Political Economy* (1st ed., 1893; 3rd ed., 1922).

[2] Of these polyhistors, or universal scientists, Gottfried Wilhelm Leibniz (1646-1716) was perhaps the most famous. His thought ranged from pure mathematics to political economy and back again to physics and to the metaphysical speculation of his monadology. His views on economics that have been collected with loving care by W. Roscher are too insignificant to be mentioned again. But Giambattista Vico (1668-1744) was a sociologist of outstanding importance, and in advertising for pupils he promised to teach everything that is knowable (*tutto lo scibile*). And never forget: Adam Smith wrote—and brilliantly—on the development of astronomy. It is true, of course, that many or most polyhistors excluded certain specialties from their universal competence. Thus, most of the great historians were nothing but historians; most of the great physi-

fell in with this use of the word philosophy, except that he excluded the sacred doctrine which was a science apart. All the others were 'philosophical disciplines.' It is interesting to note that St. Thomas made no attempt to assign to the former any other prerogative but that of super-mundane dignity and did not give it any authority over the latter.

When we look over those comprehensive systems[3] of science, we cannot fail to make a discovery of the utmost importance for the problem in hand. Neither Aristotle nor any of the later polyhistors succeeded in unifying, or even attempted to unify, the various departments of his teaching and, in particular, to assert in each of them his views on the 'last causes,' the 'ultimate meaning' of things, and the like. The physical theories of Aristotle, for instance, are entirely independent of his views on those 'fundamentals' and could, so far as these are concerned, just as well have been different from what they were. And this is as true of his political sociology (for example, his investigations into the constitutions of Greek city-states) as it is of his physics. Similarly, Leibniz' views on foreign trade have nothing whatever to do with his fundamental vision of the physical and the moral world and he could, so far as these are concerned, just as well have been a free trader. Therefore, we had better speak of a compound of sciences rather than a universal science. This compound broke to pieces as the exigencies of the division of labor asserted themselves. It was then in the seventeenth and eighteenth centuries that philosophy was usually divided into natural and moral philosophy, a division that foreshadowed the German one between *Natur- und Geisteswissenschaften.*[4] There is another sense of the word philosophy in which no question arises of its influencing economics. This is the case if philosophy is conceived of as a science, like any other, that asks certain questions, uses certain materials, and produces certain results. Examples of the problems that arise, if we then define philosophy in this sense, would be: what is meant by matter, force, truth, sense perception, and so on. This conception of philosophy, which ap-

cians were nothing but physicians. The Greek philosophers kept aloof from the utilitarian ('banausic') arts.

[3] The reader is warned that the term System—which in fact carries no more a definite meaning than did its Greek prototype—is used in this book in a variety of different senses which should not be confused, for instance: a set of more or less co-ordinated principles of political action (e.g. liberal system, free-trade system); an organized body of doctrine (e.g. the scholastic system, Marshall's system); a set of quantities between which certain relations are assumed to exist (e.g. system of prices); a set of equations expressing such relations (e.g. the Walrasian system).

[4] For the sake of brevity we neglected a development that culminated around 1900 and produced philosophy in a sense that has some affinity with the sense in which philosophy simply means science in general: namely, the sense that makes philosophy an attempt to construct a consistent picture of the empirical world from the contributions made by the individual scientists. This conception will be mentioned in its place, but all that we need to say about it here is that it does not create any difficulty or problem concerning the relation between philosophy and economics. A philosophy in this sense evidently does not undertake to restrict the autonomy of any of the individual sciences.

peals to many who are not philosophers, makes philosophy completely neutral as regards any particular proposition in any other science. It comes near to making philosophy synonymous with epistemology, the general theory of knowledge.

But a problem, and a very important one, does arise if we define philosophy to mean all theological and non-theological systems of beliefs ('speculative systems') concerning ultimate truths (realities, causes), ultimate ends (or values), ultimate norms. Ethics and aesthetics enter into such systems, not as sciences of certain sets of phenomena (behavior patterns) which they seek to describe (explain) but as normative codes that carry extra-empirical sanctions.[5] One may well ask whether economics does not also enter in the sense that a writer's 'philosophy' determines, or is one of the factors which determine, his economics.

In order to prepare the ground for our answer I shall first mention a few illustrative cases from the history of other sciences. For any worker whose philosophy includes Christian belief, research is research into the works of God. For him, the dignity of his vocation flows from the conviction that his work is revealing a part, however small, of the Divine order of things. Thus, Newton expressed Christian beliefs in a purely scientific work. Leibniz went readily from matters of pure physics and mathematics to matters of theology—he evidently saw no difference of methodological principle between the two, and theological aspects suggested themselves to his mind with the utmost ease. Leonhard Euler (1707-83) argued for his 'method for finding curves that enjoy certain extremal properties' on the ground that the world is the work of the most perfect Creator and *hence* must be amenable to description in terms of maximum and minimum propositions. James P. Joule (1818-89), the co-discoverer of the fundamental principle of modern thermodynamics, the principle of the mechanical equivalent of heat, adduced the argument that, in the absence of the equivalence between heat and motion, something (energy) could be lost in the physical universe which it would be contrary to the dignity of God to assume. The last two instances might even be construed as proving direct influence of Euler's and Joule's beliefs upon their analytic work. Nevertheless nobody doubts that there was no influence of this kind, that is, (a) that the scientific work of the four authors mentioned was not deflected from its course by their theological convictions; (b) that it is compatible with *any*

[5] This also applies to materialism in its technical philosophical sense, that is, to the doctrine that has not changed from the days of Leucippus and Democritus to this day and holds that 'matter' is the ultimate reality and exists independently of experience. I take the opportunity offered by the need for an illustrative example of the text above to bring home to the reader that the word 'materialism' means many things that have nothing to do with the technical meaning just defined. The 'idealist' philosophy that turns around the proposition (equally devoid of meaning for me personally) that in the last analysis reality (or the 'world') is 'spirit' would have served both purposes equally well: it would have given an example of philosophy in the sense in which it raises a problem of influence upon economics; and it would have served as another example of a word of many meanings that are commonly confused, the word Ideal.

philosophical positions; and (c) that there would be no point in trying to explain its methods or results by their philosophical positions. They simply co-ordinated their methods and results with their live Christian belief as they would co-ordinate with it everything else they did. They put their scientific work in a theological garb. But, so far as the content of this work is concerned, the garb was removable.

I hold that the garb of philosophy is removable also in the case of economics: economic analysis has not been shaped at any time by the philosophical opinions that economists happened to have, though it has frequently been vitiated by their political attitudes. But this thesis, as it stands, is open to so many misinterpretations that we must now spell it out carefully. The best method of doing so is to state explicitly what it does *not* involve.

First, it does not involve 'scientism' (see above ch. 2, sec. 3). That is, I am not arguing that because the philosophical or theological garb is removable from propositions belonging to the physical sciences, it must therefore also be removable from propositions belonging to the social sciences. Our examples have been presented merely in order to illustrate what I mean by saying that the theological or philosophical creeds of a scientific worker need not exert any definite influence upon his analytic work, but not in order to establish my thesis. So far as those examples go, it is still an open question whether or not it also applies to the sciences of human action.

Second, my thesis does not imply of course that human action itself and the psychic processes associated with it—motives or methods of reasoning, whether political or economic or of any other type—are uninfluenced by, or uncorrelated with, philosophical or religious or ethical convictions. It so happens that it is part of my own social psychology to hold that this correlation is far from perfect—a robber baron may have professed quite sincerely a creed of meekness and altruism—but this is an entirely different matter. We are now concerned with the propositions of the sciences of human behavior *about* this human behavior and are not questioning that religious or philosophical elements must indeed enter into any explanations *of* this behavior whenever they aim at completeness or realism. *And this also applies to the scientific economist's 'politics' and to any advice or recommendation he may tender with a view to influencing 'policies.'* All that our thesis involves is that it does not apply to his tools and 'theorems.' [6]

Third, my thesis does not involve reliance on general considerations about the logical autonomy of the economic proposition or theorem from philosophy. This would be still compatible with the latter's influences creeping into the procedures of analytic work in a logically illegitimate manner. It might indeed be made plausible that such propositions, as that towns frequently developed

[6] If the reader finds this a difficult distinction to make, I sympathize with him. It is in fact this relation between an economist's political preferences and his analysis and the relation of the former with his philosophy—particularly evident if we extend 'philosophy' to include the sum total of a man's views on what is 'fair,' 'just,' 'desirable,' and so on—which do prevent most economists from accepting the argument above, which is after all only simple common sense if correctly understood.

from meeting places of merchants, do not carry any particular philosophical connotation; or that such propositions, as that ordinary significance tests are useless in the case of correlation between time series. are valid alike for the deist and the atheist; or that propositions, such as that increase in the rate of remuneration of a factor of production may decrease its supply, are compatible with *any* philosophy and imposed by none. But I am not asking my readers to put their trust in any arguments of this kind, however convincing they may seem to some. At the moment I am not making any attempt to establish my thesis. I am only announcing it and explaining its meaning. The proof will be supplied in the subsequent Parts, when it will be shown that even those economists who held very definite philosophical views, such as Locke, Hume, Quesnay, and above all Marx, were *as a matter of fact* not influenced by them when doing their work of analysis.

The reason why so much emphasis has been placed upon the thesis that philosophy in any technical sense of the term is constitutionally unable to influence economic analysis and actually has not influenced it, is that the opposite thesis is one of the most important sources of pseudo-explanations of the evolution of economic analysis. These pseudo-explanations have a strong appeal for many historians of economics who are primarily interested in philosophical aspects and therefore attach an undue weight to the references to such aspects which in fact abound in the literature and are not always easy to recognize for what they are—frills without importance that nevertheless obliterate the filiation of scientific ideas.

CHAPTER 4

The Sociology of Economics

[The Chapter is unfinished. There is no treatment of the last two sections outlined at the beginning of the chapter, namely:

We have already referred to a department of science that we called the Science of Sciences (*Wissenschaftslehre*). This science, starting from logic and to some extent also from epistemology, treats of the general rules of procedure in use in the other individual sciences. But there is another science about science which is called the Sociology of Science (*Wissenssoziologie*) [1] and treats of science as a social phenomenon. That is, it analyzes the social factors and processes that produce the specifically scientific type of activity, condition its rate of development, determine its direction toward certain subjects rather than other equally possible ones, foster some methods of procedure in preference to others, set up the social mechanisms that account for success or failure of lines of research or individual performances, raise or depress the status and influence of scientists (in our sense) and their work, and so on. Our emphasis upon the fact that the workers in the fields of tooled knowledge are apt to form distinct vocational groups qualifies particularly well for conveying to the reader the reasons why, and the extent to which, science constitutes a proper subject of sociological research. Our interest in this subject is of course confined, primarily at least, to the topics that may usefully figure in an introduction to a history of economic analysis. Of these the problem of ideology is by far the most important and will be dealt with first (1); under a second heading we shall consider the motive forces of scientific endeavor and the mechanisms of scientific development (2); and finally we shall discuss some topics concerning the personnel of science in general and economics in particular (3).

[1] [J. A. S. left space for this note but did not write it. In *Capitalism, Socialism and Democracy* (New York, 1950), p. 11, he explains the term Sociology of Knowledge as follows: 'The German word is *Wissenssoziologie*, and the best names to mention are those of Max Scheler and Karl Mannheim. The latter's article on the subject in the German Dictionary of Sociology (*Handwörterbuch der Soziologie*) can serve as an introduction.']

1. Is the History of Economics a History of Ideologies?

[(a) *Special Nature of 'Economic Laws.'*] The historical or 'evolutionary' nature of the economic process unquestionably limits the scope of general concepts and of general relations between them ('economic laws') that economists may be able to formulate. There is indeed no sense in denying, a priori, as has been done sometimes, that any such concepts or relations can be formulated at all. In particular it is not necessary that the concepts we use in the study of social groups should be familiar to the members of these groups themselves: the fact, if it be a fact, that the concept of income was not familiar to the people of the Middle Ages before the fourteenth century is no reason for not using it in an analysis of their economy.[1] But it is true that 'economic laws' are much less stable than are the 'laws' of any physical science, that they work out differently in different institutional conditions, and that neglect of this fact has been responsible for many an aberration. It is also true that whenever we attempt to interpret human attitudes, especially attitudes of people far removed from us in time or culture, we risk misunderstanding them not only if we crudely substitute our own attitudes for theirs, but also if we do our best to penetrate into the working of their minds. All this is made much worse than it would be otherwise by the fact that the analyzing observer himself is the product of a given social environment—and of his particular location in this environment—that conditions him to see certain things rather than others, and to see them in a certain light. And even this is not all: environmental factors may even endow the observer with a subconscious craving to see things in a certain light. This brings us up to the problem of ideological bias in economic analysis.

Modern psychology and psychotherapy have made us familiar with a habit of our minds that we call rationalization.[2] This habit consists in comforting our-

[1] Let me make this quite clear. Sociologists like Max Weber who stand for the interpretative method of social states or changes—that is, who believe that it is our main or sole business to try to understand what things meant to the people concerned—may easily drift into the position that the use of any concepts not familiar to the people under study involves the error of assuming that their minds functioned just like ours. Now this error may be involved but it need not be: using a concept that carries meaning for us but not to the people that we observe is one thing; postulating that the concept carried meaning also for the latter is another thing. We need not go to primitive tribes in order to illustrate this: if, in terms of concepts of our own, we formulate the conditions for maximizing profits, we need not assume that the businessman himself uses these concepts; our 'theory' is perfectly meaningful even if we know that he does not.

[2] 'Rationalization' in the sense I am about to explain must be carefully distinguished from other meanings of the same word, and especially these two: (1) We sometimes speak of rationalization when we mean action that aims at improving something, e.g. an industrial concern, to make it conform to standards of which consulting specialists approve. (2) In research work we sometimes speak of rationalization when we mean the

selves and impressing others by drawing a picture of ourselves, our motives, our friends, our enemies, our vocation, our church, our country, which may have more to do with what we like them to be than with what they are. The competitor who is more successful than we are ourselves is likely to owe his success to tricks that we despise. As likely as not, the leader of a party not our own is a charlatan. The beloved girl is an angel exempt from human frailties. The enemy country is the home of monsters, our own the home of wholly admirable heroes. And so on. The importance of this habit for the health and happiness of the normal mind is obvious [3] and so is the importance of a correct diagnosis of its verbal manifestations.

[(b) *The Marxian Exposition of Ideological Bias.*] Half a century before the full importance of this phenomenon was professionally recognized and put to use, Marx and Engels discovered it and used their discovery in their criticisms of the 'bourgeois' economics of their time. Marx realized that men's ideas or systems of ideas are not, as historiography is still prone to assume uncritically, the prime movers of the historical process, but form a 'superstructure' on more fundamental factors, as will be explained at the proper place in our narrative. Marx realized further that the ideas or systems of ideas that prevail at any given time in any given social group are, so far as they contain propositions about facts and inferences from facts, likely to be vitiated for exactly the same reasons that also vitiate a man's theories about his own individual behavior. That is to say, people's ideas are likely to glorify the interests and actions of the classes that are in a position to assert themselves and therefore are likely to draw or to imply pictures of them that may be seriously at variance with the truth. Thus, the medieval knights fancied themselves as protectors of the weak and defenders of the Christian faith, whereas their actual behavior and, still more, other factors that had produced and kept in existence the social structure of their world are bound to look very different to an observer of a different time and class. Such systems of ideas Marx called ideologies.[4] And his contention was that a large part of the economics of his time was nothing but the ideology of the industrial and commercial bourgeoisie. The value of this great contribution to our insight into the processes

attempt to link a set of empirical findings to some theoretical principle that is to explain them. Thus, we say that we rationalize observed business behavior by the principle of profit maximization. These meanings have nothing to do with the one under discussion.

[3] This seems to me the essential point about rationalizations: they supply a sort of self-defense for our psychic organisms and make many a life bearable that would not be so without them. Let me add, however, that there is also another side to them that accounts for their role in psychoanalytic practice.

[4] The term is of French origin and at first meant simply the analysis of ideas, especially with reference to Condillac's theory. Occasionally it seems to have been used in much the same sense as the term Moral Philosophy, i.e. as roughly equivalent to social science. In this sense it was used by Destutt de Tracy. Napoleon I also used it but in a different sense that carried a derogatory connotation: he described as *idéologues* those opponents of his government, such as Lafayette, whom he considered unrealistic dreamers.

of history and into the meaning of social science is impaired but not destroyed by three blemishes, which it is as well to notice at once.

First, while Marx was so much alive to the ideological character of systems of ideas with which he was not in sympathy, he was completely blind to the ideological elements present in his own. But the principle of interpretation involved in his concept of ideology is perfectly general. Obviously we cannot say: everywhere else is ideology; [5] we alone stand on the rock of absolute truth. Laborist ideologies are neither better nor worse than are any others.

Second, the Marxist analysis of ideological systems of thought reduces them to emulsions of class interests which are in turn defined in exclusively economic terms. According to Marx the ideologies of capitalist society are, to put it crudely, glorifications of the interests of what he styled the capitalist class, whose interests are made to turn on the hunt for pecuniary profits. Ideologies that do not glorify the behavior of capitalist man in business but something else, for instance the national character and behavior, must hence always be reducible, however indirectly, to those economic interests of the dominant class. This however is not implied in the principle of ideological interpretation but constitutes an additional and much more doubtful theory. The principle itself implies only two things: that ideologies are superstructures erected on, and produced by, the realities of the objective social structure below them; and that they tend to reflect these realities in a characteristically biased manner. Whether or not these realities can be completely described in purely economic terms is another question. Without entering upon it here, we merely record the fact that we are going to attach a much wider meaning to the concept of Ideological Influence. Social location undoubtedly is a powerful factor in shaping our *minds*. But this does not amount to saying that our minds are exclusively shaped by the economic elements in our class position or that, even so far as this is the case, they are exclusively shaped by a well-defined class or group *interest*.[6]

Third, Marx and especially the majority of his followers assumed too readily that statements which display ideological influence are ipso facto condemned thereby. But it cannot be emphasized too strongly that, like individual rationalizations, ideologies are not lies. It must be added that statements of fact that enter into them are not necessarily erroneous. The temptation is great to avail oneself of the opportunity to dispose at one stroke of a whole body of propositions one does not like, by the simple device of calling it an ideology. This device is no doubt very effective, as effective as are attacks upon an opponent's personal motives. But logically it is inadmissible. As pointed out already, explanation, however correct, of the reasons why a man says what he says tells us nothing about whether it is true or false. Similarly statements that proceed from an ideological background are open to suspicion, but they may still be perfectly valid. Both Galileo and his opponents may have been swayed by ideologies. That does not prevent us from saying that he was

[5] [J. A. S. put a pencil note 'delusion?' beside this reference to ideology and the one in the next to the last sentence in the paragraph above.]

[6] [This problem is touched upon at intervals throughout the *History*.]

'right.' But what logical warrant have we for saying so? Is there any means of locating, recognizing, and possibly eliminating the ideologically vitiated elements in economic analysis? And does enough remain when we have done so?

It will be understood that our answers, though illustrated by examples, will for the moment be provisional and that the validity or otherwise of the principles I am about to formulate can be judged only by their applications in this book as a whole. But before we embark upon this task we must clarify a preliminary matter.

Unfortunately we have to bar a fire escape by which some of the strongest exponents of the doctrine that economics, and in principle all science, is vitiated by ideological delusions have tried to escape from the apparently inevitable conclusion concerning the possibility 'of scientific truth.' Professor K. Mannheim taught that, though ideological delusion is the common fate of mankind, there are nevertheless 'detached intelligences,' floating freely in space, who enjoy the privilege of being exempt from this fate. Slightly more realistically, everyone is a victim of ideological delusion except the modern radical intellectual who stands indeed upon the rock of truth, the unbiased judge of all things human. Now, if anything can be called obvious in this field, it is the fact that this intellectual is just a bundle of prejudices that are in most cases held with all the force of sincere conviction. But this apart, we cannot follow Mannheim down his fire escape because we have fully accepted the doctrine of the ubiquity of ideological bias and therefore cannot see anything else in the belief of some groups in their freedom from it but a particularly vicious part of their own system of delusions.[7] Now we turn to our task.

First, ideological bias, as defined above by our amended version of the Marxist definition, is obviously not the only danger that threatens economic analysis. In particular there are two others that should be mentioned specifically because they are easily confused with ideological bias. One is possible tampering with facts or with rules of procedure by Special Pleaders. All we have to say about this has been said already: here I only wish to warn the reader that special pleading is not the same thing as ideologically vitiated analyzing. Another danger proceeds from the inveterate habit of economists to pass value judgments upon the processes they observe. An economist's value judgments often *reveal* his ideology but they *are not* his ideology: it is possible to pass value judgments upon irreproachably established facts and the relations between them, and it is possible to refrain from passing any value judgments upon facts that are seen in an ideologically deflected light. We are not going to discuss the problem of value judgments here. It will be more

[7] Some groups, like bureaucracies, are more given to this ideology, which among other things involves the clearly ideological denial of any group interest of their own or at least of its influence on the policies that they originate or assist in shaping. This may be used as a first example of the influence of ideologies upon analysis. For this ideology of bureaucracies is an important factor in the unscientific habit of economists of using a clearly ideological theory of the state that raises the latter into a superhuman agency for the public good and neglects all the facts about the realities of public administration that modern political science provides.

convenient to do so on other occasions, especially when I shall have to report upon a full-dress debate on the subject in Part IV, Chapter 4.[8]

[(c) *How Does a History of Economic Analysis Differ from a History of Systems of Political Economy; from a History of Economic Thought?*] The distinction above between ideologically biased statements and value judgments should not, however, be interpreted as a denial of their affinity. This affinity is even the main reason why I think it important to distinguish this history of economics—economic analysis—from either a history of Systems of Political Economy or a history of Economic Thought. By a system of political economy I mean an exposition of a comprehensive set of economic policies that its author advocates on the strength of certain unifying (normative) principles such as the principles of economic liberalism, of socialism, and so on. Such systems do come within our range so far as they contain genuinely analytic work. For instance, A. Smith's *Wealth of Nations* was, in fact as in intention, a system of political economy in the sense just defined and as such it does not interest us. All the more does it interest us by virtue of the fact that A. Smith's political principles and recipes—his guarded advocacy of free trade and the rest—are but the cloak of a great analytic achievement. In other words, we are not so much interested in *what* he argued for as we are in *how* he argued and what tools of analysis he used in doing so. His political principles and recipes themselves (including ideology—revealing value judgments) were no doubt what mattered most to himself and to his readers and, furthermore, what accounts primarily for the success of his work with the public and, in this sense, for its proud position in the history of human thought. But I am prepared to surrender them all as mere formulations of the ideology of his epoch and country, without validity for any other.

The same applies to what we define as Economic Thought, that is, the sum total of all the opinions and desires concerning economic subjects, especially concerning public policy bearing upon these subjects that, at any given time and place, float in the public mind. Now the public mind is never an undifferentiated or homogeneous something but is the result of the division of the corresponding community into groups and classes of various natures. In other words, the public mind reflects more or less treacherously, and at some times more treacherously than at others, the class structure of the corresponding society and the group minds or attitudes that form in it. Since these group minds have different opportunities of asserting themselves and especially of leaving their marks upon the literature which comes under the observation of later generations, questions of interpretation arise that are always difficult and sometimes impossible to solve. The public mind of a time and place is in particular not only differentiated sectionally, but also according to the position and intelligence of the individuals that form the same horizontal or vertical section. It is one thing with politicians, another with the shopkeepers, farmers, and laborers that are 'represented' by these politicians. And it may be

[8] [Unfortunately, there is only an unfinished version of this chapter, written in 1943. It was one of the sections that J. A. S. had taken out to rewrite and amplify.]

formulated into systems of political economy by writers who belong, or who attach themselves, to particular sections. On the other hand, it may border on, or overlap with, analytic work as it has often done in treatises written by members of the commercial or industrial bourgeoisie. So far as it does do the latter, it will of course be our task to pick out as best we can such analytic performances from the common run of verbalizations of the humors of the times that are unconnected with any effort to improve our conceptual apparatus, and hence without interest for us. However difficult it may be to carry out this program in any particular case, the distinction between different masses of thought which we are trying to draw is quite clear on principle.

It would, I suppose, be possible to write alongside a history of economic analysis another history of the popular views on economic subjects. By the same token it is possible to write a history of economic thought that traces out the historical change of attitudes, mentioning analytic performances in passing. Such a history would indeed display the close association that exists within the attitudes of the public mind in the sense defined, with the kind of problems that at any given time interest analysts and form the general attitude or spirit in which they approach their problems. Our own plan is exactly the opposite one. We shall, of course, never neglect the general environment of economic thought in which, at various times, analysts did their work. But these environments and their historical changes are never our main object of interest. They come in as favorable or inhibiting influences upon analytic work, which shall remain the hero throughout our play. In trying to disentangle analytic work from its popular background, even though this background incessantly asserts its influence, we shall make a discovery which it is just as well to notice at once.

The development of analytic work, however much disturbed it may have been by the interests and attitudes of the market place, displays a characteristic property which is completely absent from the historical development of economic thought in our sense and also from the historical succession of systems of political economy. This property may best be illustrated by an example: from the earliest times until today, analytic economists have been interested, more or less, in the analysis of the phenomenon that we call competitive price. When the modern student meets the phenomenon on an advanced level of his study, for instance in the books of Hicks or Samuelson, he is introduced to a number of concepts and problems that may seem to him difficult at first, and would certainly have been completely un-understandable to so relatively recent an author as John Stuart Mill. But the student will also discover before long that a new apparatus poses and solves problems for which the older authors could hardly have found answers even if they had been aware of them. This defines in a common-sense and at any rate a perfectly unambiguous manner, in what sense there has been 'scientific progress' between Mill and Samuelson. It is the same sense in which we may say that there has been technological progress in the extraction of teeth between the times of John Stuart Mill and our own.

Now our ability to speak of progress in these cases is obviously due to the fact that there is a widely accepted standard, confined, of course, to a group of professionals, that enables us to array different theories of competitive price in a series, each member of which can be unambiguously labeled superior to the preceding one. We further observe that this array is associated with the lapse of time, in the sense that the later theory of competitive price almost always holds higher rank in the array of analytic perfection: whenever this is not the case, it is possible to assign this fact to extra-analytic and, in this sense, disturbing influences. But while it is thus possible to speak of analytic progress and impossible to deny the facts that this word is to denote, there is nothing corresponding to this in the field of economic thought or even in any historical array of systems of political economy. For instance, there would be no sense in speaking of a superiority of Charlemagne's ideas on economic policy as revealed by his legislative and administrative actions over the economic ideas of, say, King Hammurabi; or of the general principles of policy revealed by the proclamations of the Stuart kings over those of Charlemagne; or of the declarations of policy that sometimes preface acts of Congress over those Stuart proclamations. We may of course sympathize with some of the interests favored in any of those cases rather than with the interests favored in others, and in this sense array such documents also in a scale of preference. But a place of any body of economic thought in any such array would differ according to the judge's value judgments, and for the rest we shall be left with our emotional or aesthetic preference for the various schemata of life that find expression in those documents. We should be very much in the same position if we were asked whether Gauguin or Titian was the greater painter. That is, the only sensible answer to such a question is that there is no meaning to it. And the same thing applies of course to all systems of political economy if we exclude from them technical excellences or deficiencies. We may, indeed, prefer the world of modern dictatorial socialism to the world of Adam Smith, or vice versa, but any such preference comes within the same category of subjective evaluation as does, to plagiarize Sombart, a man's preference for blondes over brunettes. In other words, there is no objective meaning to the term progress in matters of economic or any other policy because there is no valid standard for interpersonal comparisons. It should be superfluous to add that this argument seems to clarify satisfactorily the differences between historians of economics on this point. Some of them think of technical analysis and an increasing command of facts; these are quite right in speaking of scientific progress in our field. Others are speaking of the changing humors, themselves the product of changing social conditions, that produce changing opinions about policies and desirabilities; these are quite right in denying that there is such a thing as progress in our field. Either group may err only in overlooking that there is an aspect of man's thought on economic subjects other than the one they are considering exclusively. Only those err without qualification who either see in the development of economic analysis nothing but a reflex of the changing humors of the public mind, or else indulge in the enviable but childish belief that political attitudes are a function of nothing except progressive insights.

[(d) *The Scientific Process: Vision and Rules of Procedure.*] We are now ready to take the second step in our inquiry into the dangers of ideological bias, namely, to ask the question how far it threatens the validity of results in that narrower field that we have described as Economic Analysis. Some readers may think even that there is no second step to take: since we have already surrendered, as ideologically conditioned, all the systems of political economy, and since, in addition, we have recognized as ideologies the less completely systematized sets of opinions on economic subjects that, at any time and place, 'float in the public mind,' we seem in fact to have admitted all there is to admit. And those readers in particular whose primary interest is in the history of the ideas that shape or, at all events, are closely associated with policies or with people's ideas about what is to be considered as fair or desirable in the management of economic affairs and whose interest in the development of technical economic analysis is secondary only are quite likely to grant—perhaps with a shrug of the shoulders—that our box of tools may well be as far removed from the influence of ideologies as are the techniques of any other science. Unfortunately we cannot take this for granted. Let us therefore analyze the scientific process itself in order to see where ideological elements may enter it and what are our means of recognizing and perhaps eliminating them.

In practice we all start our own research from the work of our predecessors, that is, we hardly ever start from scratch. But suppose we did start from scratch, what are the steps we should have to take? Obviously, in order to be able to posit to ourselves any problems at all, we should first have to visualize a distinct set of coherent phenomena as a worth-while object of our analytic efforts. In other words, analytic effort is of necessity preceded by a preanalytic cognitive act that supplies the raw material for the analytic effort. In this book, this preanalytic cognitive act will be called Vision. It is interesting to note that vision of this kind not only must precede historically the emergence of analytic effort in any field but also may re-enter the history of every established science each time somebody teaches us to *see* things in a light of which the source is not to be found in the facts, methods, and results of the pre-existing state of the science.

Let us illustrate this at once by an outstanding example from our own field and time. Critics and admirers of the scientific performance of the late Lord Keynes will agree to the statement that his *General Theory of Employment, Interest, and Money* (1936) was the outstanding success of the 1930's and that it dominated analytic work for a decade after its publication, to say the least. The *General Theory* presented an analytic apparatus which the author summed up in Chapter 18. If we follow his exposition step by step (see especially pp. 249-54) we observe that this apparatus had been designed in order to give convenient expression to certain facts of 'the world in which we live'—although, as Keynes himself emphasized, these facts are attributed to his fundamental schedules (propensity to consume, attitude to liquidity, and marginal efficiency of capital) as special characteristics and not as 'logically necessary' properties. This analytic pattern will be discussed in the proper place,[9] where it will also be shown that the special characteristics in question are the characteristics of England's aging capitalism as seen from the standpoint of an English intellectual. There can be no question of their having been established by antecedent factual research. They are 'plausibly ascribed to our [the English] world, on our general knowledge of contemporary human nature' (p. 250). This is not the place to discuss the merits or demerits of this conception. All that matters here and now is that it *is* a conception or vision in our sense, and that it antedated all the analytic efforts that Keynes and others bestowed upon it. The process stands out in this case with such unsurpassable clearness because we can read a formulation of the vision, as yet analytically unarmed, in a few brilliant pages of Keynes's *The Economic Consequences of the Peace* (1919). So far as this line of endeavor of a man of many interests was concerned, the whole period between 1919 and 1936 was then spent in attempts, first unsuccessful, then increasingly successful, at implementing the particular vision of the economic process of our time that was fixed in Keynes's mind by 1919 at latest. Other examples, from our field as well as from others, could be adduced in order to illustrate this 'way of our mind.' But it would hardly be possible to find a more telling one.

Analytic effort starts when we have conceived our vision of the set of phenomena that caught our interest, no matter whether this set lies in virgin soil or in land that had been cultivated before. The first task is to verbalize the vision or to conceptualize it in such a way that its elements take their places, with names attached to them that facilitate recognition and manipulation, in a more or less orderly schema or picture. But in doing so we almost automatically perform two other tasks. On the one hand, we assemble further facts in addition to those perceived already, and learn to distrust others that figured in the original vision; on the other hand, the very work of constructing the schema or picture will add further relations and concepts to, and in general also eliminate others from, the original stock. Factual work and 'theoretical' work, in an endless relation of give and take, naturally testing one another and setting new tasks for each other, will eventually produce *scientific models*, the provisional joint products of their interaction with the surviving elements of the original vision, to which increasingly more rigorous standards of consistency and adequacy will be applied. This is indeed a primitive but not, I think, misleading statement of the process by which we grind out what we call scientific propositions. Now it should be perfectly clear that there is a wide gate for ideology to enter into this process. In fact, it enters on the very ground floor, into the preanalytic cognitive act of which we have been speaking. Analytic work begins with material provided by our vision of things, and this vision is ideological almost by definition. It embodies the picture of things as we see them, and wherever there is any possible motive for wishing to see them in a given rather than another light, the way in which we see things can hardly be distinguished from the way in which we wish to see them. The more honest and naïve our

[9] See Part v, ch. 5. [This appraisal of Keynes's *General Theory* was apparently the last thing written for the *History of Economic Analysis*.]

vision is, the more dangerous is it to the eventual emergence of anything for which general validity can be claimed. The inference for the social sciences is obvious, and it is not even true that he who hates a social system will form an objectively more correct vision of it than he who loves it. For love distorts indeed, but hate distorts still more. Our only comfort is in the fact that there is a large number of phenomena that fail to affect our emotions one way or the other, and that therefore look to one man very much as they do to another. But we also observe that the rules of procedure that we apply in our analytic work are almost as much exempt from ideological influence as vision is subject to it. Passionate allegiance and passionate hatred may indeed tamper with these rules. In themselves these rules, many of which, moreover, are imposed upon us by the scientific practice in fields that are little or not at all affected by ideology, are pretty effective in showing up misuse. And, what is equally important, they tend to crush out ideologically conditioned error from the visions from which we start. It is their particular virtue, and they do so automatically and irrespective of the desires of the research worker. The new facts he is bound to accumulate impose themselves upon his schema. The new concepts and relations, which somebody else will formulate if he does not, must verify his ideologies or else destroy them. And if this process is allowed to work itself out completely, it will indeed not protect us from the emergence of new ideologies, but it will clear in the end the existing ones from error. It is true that in economics, and still more in other social sciences, this sphere of the strictly provable is limited in that there are always fringe ends of things that are matters of personal experience and impression from which it is practically impossible to drive ideology, or for that matter conscious dishonesty,[10] completely. The comfort we may take from our argument is therefore never complete. But it does cover most of the ground in the sense of narrowing the sphere of ideologically vitiated propositions considerably, that is, of narrowing it down and of making it always possible to locate the spots in which it may be active.

[J. A. S. did not complete his introductory part and stopped at this point. The following three paragraphs were found untyped among the notes and manuscript of this Part.]

While it is hoped that the foregoing treatment of the ideology problem will help the reader understand the situation within which we have to work, and put him on his guard without imbuing him with a sterile pessimism concerning the 'objective validity' of our methods and results, it must be admitted that our answer to the problem,

[10] The role of what above is meant by conscious dishonesty is greatly enhanced by the fact that many things that do amount to tampering with the effects of logic do not in our field necessarily present themselves as dishonesty to the man who practices such tampering. He may be so fundamentally convinced of the truths of what he is standing for that he would rather die than give new weight to contradicting facts or pieces of analysis. The first thing a man will do for his ideals is lie. Now we do not interpret this element in the case as we do when speaking of ideological bias, but of course it reinforces the baleful influence of the latter.

consisting as it does of a set of rules by which to locate, diagnose, and eliminate ideological delusion, cannot be made as simple and definite as can the usual glib assertion that the history of scientific economics is or is not a history of ideologies. We have had to make large concessions to the former view, concessions that challenge the scientific character of all those comprehensive philosophies of economic life—such as the Political Economy of Liberalism—which are, to many of us, the most interesting and most glamorous of the creations of economic thought. Worse than this, we have had to recognize, on the one hand, that although there exists a mechanism that tends to crush out ideologies automatically, this may be a time-consuming process that meets with many resistances and, on the other hand, that we are never safe from the current intrusion of new ideologies to take the place of the vanishing older ones. Under these circumstances, examples that may do something toward teaching the use of our rules may usefully complement the discussion above. We shall arrange our example in four groups.

First, when we look at the contents of our box of theoretical or statistical tools, we discover many items that are, and are known to be, ideologically neutral. For instance, we find a concept that is called the marginal rate of substitution, which has, since about 1900, been increasingly used in the theory of value instead of the older concept, marginal utility. Those who accepted the former in preference to the latter, have done so for purely technical reasons that are completely irrelevant to any ideology of economic life, and, as a matter of fact, nobody has ever asserted the contrary. Similarly, the question whether or not the ordinary significance tests are applicable to the case of correlation between time series is a very important one for economic analysis. But it would be waste of time to investigate the arguments that have been used in establishing the negative answer for ideological bias, because it is clear from the outset that they are impervious to it by nature. The results that we produce by means of reasoning that makes use of such stainless-steel concepts or theories may still be ideologically vitiated. But we can at least be sure that the ideological bias, if there be any, must be sought for among the other elements of our reasoning.

Second, there are tools or theories that, though they can be shown to be actually neutral, yet acquire a putative ideological importance because people erroneously believe that they are relevant to their ideologies. We have just noticed the unchallenged fact that the transition from the marginal utility theory of value to a theory of value based upon the concept of marginal rate of substitution was ideologically neutral in the sense that either can be shown to be equally compatible with any ideology whatsoever. But this was not so with the preceding phase of the development of the theory of value. Among the opponents of the marginal utility theory of value were the Marxist sponsors of a labor theory of value who believed—as did many marginal utility theorists also—that the choice between labor and marginal utility 'explanations' of economic value depends upon our vision of the economic process and is ideologically relevant. Specifically, the Marxist notion that value is congealed labor was the first link in what Marxists considered to be a proof that the source of all incomes except wages is exploitation. However, as will be shown in Part III, the ideology . . .

[J. A. S. had nearly finished Section 1 of Chapter 4 (Is the History of Economics a History of Ideologies?). For a further discussion of some of these problems, the reader is referred to the presidential address (by J. A. S.) before the American Economic Association, 'Science and Ideology,' *American Economic Review*, March 1949.

Chapter 4 was apparently to have been the last chapter of the introductory Part. There were to have been two more sections (2. The Motive Forces of Scientific Endeavor and the Mechanisms of Scientific Development, and 3. The Personnel of Science in General and of Economics in Particular). These subjects are discussed at intervals throughout the *History* (see Index under these headings) and in connection with the author's concept of 'schools.' About the Ricardians, for example, he said: 'Moreover, the group was a genuine school in our sense: there was one master, one doctrine, personal coherence; there was a core; there were zones of influence; there were fringe ends.'

A few preliminary paragraphs (probably dictated), which deal to some extent with the personnel of science, were found among the author's notes and are printed below.]

The reader will have no difficulty in perceiving the relation which exists between the definition of a science as a technique that develops in a social group professionally devoted to its cultivation and the ideological aspects of the methods and results that emerge from the 'scientific' activities of such a group. Evidently there must be a certain amount of cohesion between its members, at least when the group has attained a sufficiently definite existence, a corporative spirit that produces explicit or subconscious rules according to which the members recognize each other and admit certain individuals and exclude others. In noticing a few of the phenomena to which these facts give rise we shall complete the little that can be said here on the subject of the sociology of science.

If it be possible at all to imagine an individual who no matter for what reason embarks for himself and by himself upon the investigation of any of those sets of phenomena that have ever become the objects of scientific efforts, it should also be possible to realize a very simple yet very fundamental truth. Our individual must first recognize the phenomena on which he is going to work and he must recognize them as being somehow connected with one another and distinct from others. This recognition is a cognitive act. But it forms no part of the analytic work. On the contrary, it supplies the object or material on which analysis works and is therefore a prerequisite of it. The analytic work itself then consists of two different though inseparable activities. The one consists in conceptualizing the contents of the vision. By this we mean the fixing of its elements into precise concepts that receive labels or names in order to retain their identity, and in establishing relations (theorems or propositions) between them. The other consists in hunting for further empirical data (facts) with which we enrich and check the ones originally perceived. It stands to reason that these two activities are not independent of one another but that there must be an incessant give and take between them. Attempts at conceptualization invite the hunt for further facts and the new facts discovered must themselves be inserted and conceptualized. In an endless sequence both activities improve, deepen, and correct the original vision and also each other's results. We do try at any given stage of our scientific endeavors to construct schemata or systems or models by which to describe as best we can the set of phenomena we are interested in, which are then developed 'deductively' or 'inductively.' But they are provisional by nature and are always relative to the stock of facts we command. This is indeed a very imperfect description of scientific procedure but it brings out a fact that will be emphasized again and again in these pages: there is not and there cannot be any fundamental opposition between 'theory' and 'fact finding,' let alone between deduction and induction. It will be one of our tasks to show why the appearance of such opposition has emerged nevertheless.

In practice, of course, no scientific worker ever goes through all the stages of the work beginning with an independent vision of his own. Intuitive perception of novel aspects is indeed never absent so long as a science is really alive. But vision of the kind that produces novel methods or propositions or else leads to the discovery of novel facts—which then enter the science in the form of new hypotheses or restrictions—only adds to and perhaps partly displaces existing scientific structures, the bulk of which is handed from generation to generation as a matter of course. And practically always it isn't society as whole or even a random collection of members that hands on the stock of scientific knowledge but a more or less definite group of professionals who teach the rising generations not only their methods and results but also their opinions about the direction and the means of further advance. In a majority of cases competence in doing scientific work cannot be acquired, or can be acquired only by individuals of quite exceptional originality and force, from any source other than the teaching of recognized professionals. Let us briefly glance at some of the consequences of this fact.

First of all, it should be observed that this social mechanism is tremendously labor-saving. By means of it any beginner who follows the advice received and who does the work assigned to him acquires knowledge of facts, grasp of problems, mastery of methods with an economy of energy that should set the bulk of his force free for exploration of lands that lie beyond the boundary line at which the competence of the teacher ends. There should be no reasonable doubt about it, therefore, that primarily the social mechanism glanced at is not only favorable to the development of conceptual apparatus and to the accumulation of factual knowledge but even that it supplies the most potent motive power of what is usually referred to as scientific progress. Obviously, however, there is also another side to the medal. Teaching in any established science stereotypes the mind of the tyro and may stunt such originality as he may have. This has another and less obvious consequence. Owing to the resistance that an existing scientific structure offers, major changes in outlook and methods, at first retarded, then come about by way of revolution rather than of transformation and elements of the old structure that might be permanently valuable or at least have not yet had time to yield their full harvest of result are likely to be lost in the process. There is thus plenty of justification, just as there is for the resentments of the revolutionary, for the propensity of a certain type of mind to emphasize continuity and to defend old insights against new ones. Many examples of this will be noticed in this book.

Second, the fact that existing structures once established tend to persist accounts in the field of scientific endeavor as it does in others for a phenomenon that is not easy to explain, the phenomenon of 'generations.' Consider a population with constant age distribution in which moreover the number of people that enter scientific vocations are equal to the number of people who retire. A given profession, say the profession of scientific economists, would then also display a constant age distribution. It is no doubt possible to construct sub-groups whose outlooks and methods may be expected to develop and there is no problem whatever in the antagonism of these age groups that we might observe. But this is not the problem of scientific generations for we also observe that at any given time a majority of the people in all the age groups display certain similarities of attitude so that, for example, it is possible to speak of a generation of 1880-1900 and to contrast it with the generation of 1920-1940 although younger and older men presumably differed in the first period as much as they did in the second. There would be no point in this if change in methods and results proceeded at an even rate. In the case of economists one might be tempted to explain this phenomenon by the change in social and economic conditions and by the consequent change in the practical problems that attracted attention in the two periods. But we find the same phenomenon in sciences that work on invariant environments. It is precisely this which gives us the clue to the nature of the problem and at the same time to its solution. Problems and methods not only change because environments change. They also change in consequence of the [fact that the] analytic work that is embodied in a given structure of a science has a way of resisting change.

Third, the professionals that devote themselves to scientific work in a particular field and even all the professionals who devote themselves to scientific work in any field tend to become a sociological group. This means that they have other things in common besides the interest in scientific work or in a particular science per se. In most cases they teach the science which they are trying to bring up and to make their living by teaching. Naturally, this will tend to evolve a social and economic type. The group accepts or refuses to accept co-workers also for reasons other than their professional competence or incompetence. In economics this grouping took long to mature but when it did mature it acquired much greater importance than it did in physics. We shall see how in most countries writers on economic topics hail from all the sectors of society. There were indeed factors that made for grouping at an early time, the most important instance being the Catholic scholastic doctors, but all the rest consisted of types that came from anywhere in the scales of social rank or of income brackets. In England, this was so even in the first half of the nineteenth century. In such cases we must use the word profession with a proviso. In England there was at the time indeed a profession of economists in the sense that there were writers on economic topics who mutually recognized their professional competence. But later on the association of scientific work with teaching produced an economic profession in a fuller sense of the word and this economic profession developed attitudes to social and political questions that *were similar also for reasons other than similar scientific views*. This similarity of conditions of life and of social location produced similar philosophies of life and similar value judgments about social phenomena. It would be unnecessary to dwell on the consequences of this were it not for the fact that it was closely associated with the phenomenon of scientific schools. Since this concept will inevitably play a considerable role in our story we had better stay for a moment in order to investigate its meaning.

Part II

FROM THE BEGINNINGS TO THE FIRST CLASSICAL SITUATION

(To About 1790)

CHAPTER 1

Graeco-Roman Economics

1. Plan of the Part

It has been explained in Part I that no science, in the sense there defined, is ever founded or created by a single individual or group. Nor is it in general possible to assign any precise date to its 'birth.' The slow process by which economics, as we now call it, rose into recognized existence ran its course between the middle of the seventeenth and the end of the eighteenth centuries. However, a concept that has been introduced in Part I may help us to be somewhat more precise, at least so far as the exigencies of exposition are concerned: the concept of Classical Situations.[1] Such a classical situation emerged

[1] [J. A. S. did not complete the sections of Part I in which he would have discussed his concept of Classical Situations (and the difficulties inherent in periodizing) with special reference to his reasons for arranging the subject matter of the history of economic analysis in the three main divisions covered by Parts II, III, and IV. The reader will, however, find references to these problems at intervals throughout this book, especially in Part III, ch. 1 and again in Part IV, ch. 1.

As J. A. S. points out, the term classic in this book has three meanings which should be distinguished from one another. Formerly it referred to the economic literature of the period from Adam Smith to J. S. Mill. 'It retained this label until, at a time when the word "classic" had lost its eulogistic connotation and was beginning to stand for "obsolete," Lord Keynes used the word in order to denote the teaching of A. Marshall and his immediate followers (or simply, pre-Keynesian economics).' J. A. S. himself uses the term Classical Situation to describe the achievement of substantial agreement after a long period of struggle and controversy—the consolidation of the fresh and original work which went before. When he wishes to use the term classic in the first sense (Adam Smith to J. S. Mill), he puts it in quotes 'to prevent confusion' (Part III, ch. 1, sec. 1).]

in the second half of the eighteenth century and no such classical situation had ever emerged before. Availing ourselves of this, we might be tempted to start somewhere between 1750 and 1800, perhaps with the peak success of that epoch, A. Smith's *Wealth of Nations* (1776). But every classical situation summarizes or consolidates the work—the really original work—that leads up to it, and cannot be understood by itself. Therefore, we shall try to cover in this Part, as best we can, the whole span of more than 2000 years that extends from 'beginnings' to about twenty years after the publication of the *Wealth of Nations*. This task is much facilitated by the further fact that, so far as the purposes of this history are concerned, many centuries within that span are blanks.

The classical situation of the second half of the eighteenth century was the result of a merger of two types of work that are sufficiently distinct to justify separate consideration.[2] There was the stock of factual knowledge and the conceptual apparatus that had slowly grown, during the centuries, in the studies of philosophers. And, semi-independent of this, there was a stock of facts and concepts that had been accumulated by men of practical affairs in the course of their discussions of current political issues. These two sources of nascent economics cannot be separated strictly. On the one hand, there were numerous intermediate cases that cannot be classified without cutting many a Gordian knot. On the other hand, right into the time of the physiocrats, the scholar's technique was so very simple that most of it was within the reach of ordinary common sense and easily rivaled by unlearned practitioners, whose writings, therefore, cannot be dismissed as irrelevant to our purpose: on the contrary, they frequently rose to what we call in this book the scientific level. Broadly, however, our distinction is valid all the same.

Let us recall our distinction between Economic Thought—the opinions on economic matters that prevail at any given time in any given society and belong to the province of economic history rather than to the province of the history of economics—and Economic Analysis—which is the result of scientific endeavor in our sense. The history of economic thought starts from the records of the national theocracies of antiquity whose economies presented phenomena that were not entirely dissimilar to our own, and problems which they managed in a spirit that was, in fundamentals, not so very dissimilar either. But the history of economic analysis begins only with the Greeks.

Ancient Egypt had a kind of planned economy that turned upon her irrigation system. The Assyrian and Babylonian theocracies had huge military and bureaucratic establishments and elaborate legal systems—of which the code of Hammurabi (about 2000 B.C.) is the earliest legislative monument; they pursued an activist foreign policy; also they developed monetary institutions to a high degree of perfection, and knew credit and banking. The sacred books of

[2] Like periodization, the setting up of such types is an expository device. Though certainly based upon provable facts, neither must be taken too seriously or else what is intended to be a help for the reader turns into a source of misconceptions. Periods and types are useful only so long as this is remembered.

Israel, especially the legislative portions of them, reveal perfect grasp of the practical economic problems of the Hebrew state. But there is no trace of analytic effort. More than anywhere else we might expect to find such traces in ancient China, the home of the oldest literary culture of which we know. We find in fact a highly developed public administration that dealt currently with agrarian, commercial, and financial problems. These problems are frequently touched upon, mainly from an ethical standpoint, in the remains of Chinese classical literature, for instance in the teaching of Kung Fu Tse (551-478 B.C.), who was himself at two stages of his life a practical administrator and reformer, and of Mêng Tzû (Mencius, 372-288 B.C., works trans. by L. A. Lyall, 1932), from whose works it is possible to compile a comprehensive system of economic policy. Moreover, there were methods of monetary management and of exchange control that seem to presuppose a certain amount of analysis. The phenomena incident to the recurrent inflations were no doubt observed and discussed by men much superior to us in cultural refinement. But no piece of reasoning on strictly economic topics has come down to us that can be called 'scientific' within our meaning of the term.[3]

The obvious inference is of course highly uncertain. There may have been analytic work, the records of which failed to survive. But there is reason to suppose that there was not much of it. We have seen before that common-sense knowledge, relative to scientific knowledge, goes much farther in the economic field than it does in almost any other. It is perfectly understandable, therefore, that economic questions, however important, took much longer in eliciting specifically scientific curiosity than did natural phenomena. Nature harbors secrets into which it is exciting to probe; economic life is the sum total of the most common and most drab experiences. Social problems interest the scholarly mind primarily from a philosophical and political standpoint; scientifically they do not at first appear very interesting or even to be 'problems' at all.

[2. From the Beginnings to Plato]

So far as we can tell, rudimentary economic analysis is a minor element—a very minor one—in the inheritance that has been left to us by our cultural ancestors, the ancient Greeks. Like their mathematics and geometry, their astronomy, mechanics, optics, their economics is the fountainhead of practically all further work. Unlike their performance in these fields, however, their economics failed to attain independent status or even a distinctive label: their *Oeconomicus* (οἶκος, house, and νόμος law or rule) meant only the practical wisdom of household management; the Aristotelian *Chrematistics* (χρῆμα, possession or wealth), which comes nearest to being such a label, refers mainly to the pecuniary aspects of business activity. They merged their pieces of economic reasoning with their general philosophy of state and society and rarely

[3] See, however, E. D. Thomas, *Chinese Political Thought* (1927); S. Y. Ly, *Les grands courants de la pensée économique chinoise dans l'antiquité . . .* (1936); and Huan Chang Chen, *The Economic Principles of Confucius and His School* (1911).

dealt with an economic topic for its own sake. This accounts, perhaps, for the fact that their achievement in this field was so modest, especially if compared with their resplendent achievements in others. Classic scholars as well as economists who rate it more highly think of that general philosophy and not of technical economics. Also they are prone to fall into the error of hailing as a discovery everything that suggests later developments, and of forgetting that, in economics as elsewhere, most statements of fundamental facts acquire importance only by the superstructures they are made to bear and are commonplace in the absence of such superstructures. Such as they were, the scientific splinters of Greek economic thought [1] that are accessible to us may be gleaned from the works of Plato (427-347 B.C.) and Aristotle (384-322 B.C.).

Greek thought, even where most abstract, always revolved around the concrete problems of human life. These problems of life in turn always centered in the idea of the Hellenic city-state, the *polis*, which was to the Greek the only possible form of civilized existence. Thus, by virtue of a unique synthesis of elements that with us dwell in different worlds, the Greek philosopher was essentially a political philosopher: it was from the *polis* that he looked into the universe, and it was the universe—of thought as well as of all other human concerns—that he found reflected in the *polis*. The Sophists seem to have been the first to analyze this universe very much as we do now: they are, in fact, the forefathers of our own methods of thought, our logical positivism included. But Plato's aim was not analysis at all but extra-empirical visions of an ideal

[1] We are not concerned with economic conditions and with public opinion about them. But the reader can with little trouble get an instructive glimpse of both from G. M. Calhoun, *The Business Life of Ancient Athens* (1926). This book may also bring home to him, among other things, the curious affinity that exists between our own reactions to business practice and those of the ancient Greeks. The works of Greek poets and historians are relevant only from this standpoint and need not be considered here though some of the latter, especially Thucydides and Polybius, are of absorbing interest to any student of society. Nor is it necessary to discuss Xenophon, whose *Oeconomicus* is precisely the sort of treatise on household management that went under similar titles until the sixteenth century, and whose *Poroi*, a treatise on Attic public finance, is of course very interesting for the economic historian (as is also the pseudo-Xenophontic treatise on the Athenian commonwealth, the survivor of what may have been a large literature written mainly by opponents of the radical regimes in post-Periclean Athens). Among 'philosophers,' Plato and Aristotle are of such commanding importance that reference may be confined to them, in a sketch like this. The huge literature about them naturally pays but little—and sometimes dilettantic—attention to the topics that matter to us. The purposes of the general reader will be served adequately by the perusal of M. L. W. Laistner, *Greek Economics* (1923), which also contains translations of portions of representative works. See also Auguste Souchon, *Les Théories économiques dans la Grèce antique* (1898). It seems, however, impossible not to mention such classics as Fustel de Coulanges' *La Cité antique* (12th ed. of the English trans. by W. Small, 1921); T. Gomperz' *Griechische Denker* (trans. by Magnus and Berry, 1901-12), and U. von Wilamowitz-Moellendorp's *Staat und Gesellschaft der Griechen und der Römer* (2nd ed., 1923)—masterly pictures of the cultural backgrounds from which sprang, among so many more important things, also the beginnings of economic analysis.

polis or, if we prefer, the artistic creation of one. The picture he painted of the Perfect State in his *Politeia* (*The Republic* [2]) is no more analysis than a painter's rendering of a Venus is scientific anatomy. It goes without saying that on this plane the contrast between what is and what ought to be loses its meaning. The artistic quality of the *Politeia* and of the whole literature—mostly lost—of which the *Politeia* seems to have been the peak achievement is well brought out by the German term for it, *Staatsromane* (literally: state novels). In default of a satisfactory English synonym we must use the word Utopia. The reader presumably knows that more or less under the influence of the Platonic example, this type of literature again found favor in the Renaissance and then continued to be produced, sporadically, to the end of the nineteenth century.[3]

But analysis comes in after all. There is a relation between the painter's Venus and the facts described by scientific anatomy. Just as Plato's idea of 'horseness' obviously has something to do with the properties of observable horses, so his idea of the Perfect State is correlated with the material furnished by the observation of actual states. And there is no reason whatever to deny the analytic or scientific character—remember: we do not attach any complimentary meaning to either of these words—of such observations of facts or relations between facts as are enshrined, explicitly or by implication, in Plato's construction. Reasoning of an analytic nature is still more prominent in a later work, the *Nomoi* (Laws). But nowhere is it pursued as an end in itself. Consequently it does not go very far.

Plato's Perfect State was a City-State conceived for a small and, so far as possible, constant number of citizens. As stationary as its population was to be its wealth. All economic and non-economic activity was strictly regulated—warriors, farmers, artisans, and so on being organized in permanent castes, men and women being treated exactly alike. Government was entrusted to one of these castes, the caste of guardians or rulers who were to live together without individual property or family ties. The changes introduced in the *Nomoi* are considerable—chiefly they are compromises with reality—but they do not touch the fundamental principles involved. This is all we need for our purpose. Though Plato's influence is obvious in many communist schemes of later ages, there is little point in labeling him a communist or socialist or a forerunner of later communists or socialists. Creations of such force and splendor defy classification and must be understood in their uniqueness, if at all. The same objection precludes attempts to claim him as a fascist. But if we do insist on forcing him into a strait jacket of our own making, the fascist strait jacket seems to fit somewhat better than the communist one: Plato's 'constitution' does not exclude private property except on the highest level of

[2] The standard English translation by B. Jowett includes introductory essays on Plato's life, writings, and philosophy, and an analysis of the work.

[3] The best interpretation of Greek *Staatsromane* that I know of—and one that is itself a work of art—is Edgar Salin's *Platon und die griechische Utopie* (1921). This literature naturally reflects the social movements of its time, a subject into which it is impossible to enter here. See Robert von Pöhlmann's *Geschichte der sozialen Frage und des Sozialismus in der antiken Welt* (1912).

the purest ideal; at the same time it enforces a strict regulation of individual life, including limitation of individual wealth and severe restrictions upon freedom of speech; it is essentially 'corporative'; and it recognizes the necessity of a *classe dirigente*—features that go far toward defining fascism.

The analytic background, such as it is, comes into view as soon as we ask the question: why this rigid stationarity? It is difficult not to answer (however pedestrian such an answer may sound to the true Platonist) that Plato made his ideal stationary because he disliked the chaotic changes of his time. His attitude to contemporaneous events was certainly negative. He hated the Sicilian *tyrannos* (though we must not translate this word by tyrant). He almost certainly despised the Athenian democracy. Yet he realized that tyranny grew out of democracy and was, in any case, the practical alternative to it. Democracy, in turn, he interpreted as the inevitable reaction to oligarchy, and this again he traced to inequality of wealth, the consequence, as he thought, of commercial enterprise (*Politeia* VIII). Change, economic change, was at the bottom of the development from oligarchy to democracy, from democracy to tyranny (of a popular leader), that was so little to his taste. Whatever we may think of Platonic stationarity as the remedy, is there not a piece of—almost Marxian—economico-sociological analysis behind that diagnosis?

We need not stay to consider the numerous economic topics that Plato touched upon incidentally. It will suffice to mention two examples. His caste system rests upon the perception of the necessity of some Division of Labor (*Politeia* II, 370). He elaborates on this eternal commonplace of economics with unusual care. If there is anything interesting in this, it is that he (and following him, Aristotle) puts the emphasis not upon the increase of efficiency that results from division of labor per se but upon the increase of efficiency that results from allowing everyone to specialize in what he is by nature best fitted for; this recognition of innate differences in abilities is worth mentioning because it was so completely lost later on. Again, Plato remarks in passing that money is a 'symbol' devised for the purpose of facilitating exchange (*Politeia* II, 371; Jowett translated σύμβολον by 'money-token'). Now such an occasional saying means very little and does not justify the attribution to Plato of any definite view on the nature of money. But it must be observed that his canons of monetary policy—his hostility to the use of gold and silver, for instance, or his idea of a domestic currency that would be useless abroad—actually do agree with the logical consequences of a theory according to which the value of money is on principle independent of the stuff it is made of. In view of this fact it seems to me that we are within our rights if we claim Plato as the first known sponsor of one of the two fundamental theories of money, just as Aristotle may be claimed as the first known sponsor of the other (sec. 5b below). It is highly unlikely, of course, that these theories originated with them, but it is certain that they taught them and that they attached exactly the same meaning to them as did the authors who again took them up from the late Middle Ages on. We may assume this with confidence because those authors display both Platonic and Aristotelian influences clearly enough. In fact, filiation can be strictly proved.

The dialogue *Eryxias*, which was not written by Plato but has been transmitted to us among his writings and contains nothing that clashes with any of his known opinions, is mentioned here because it is the only extant piece of work that is wholly devoted to an economic subject and indeed treats it for its own sake. Otherwise, the contents of the dialogue—substantially an inquiry into the nature of wealth, which is related to wants and carefully distinguished from money—do not present any great interest.

[3. Aristotle's Analytic Performance]

Aristotle's performance is quite different. It is not only that in his works Platonic glamour is conspicuous by its absence, and that instead we find (if such a thing may be said without offense of so great a figure) decorous, pedestrian, slightly mediocre, and more than slightly pompous common sense. Nor is it only that Aristotle much more than Plato—in any case, much more frankly than Plato—co-ordinated and discussed pre-existing opinions that prevailed in what must have been a copious literature. The essential difference is that an analytic *intention*, which may be said (in a sense) to have been absent from Plato's mind, was the prime mover of Aristotle's. This is clear from the logical structure of his arguments. It becomes still clearer when we observe his method of work: for instance, his political concepts and doctrines were drawn from an extensive collection he laboriously made of constitutions of Greek states. Of course, he also looked for the Best State,[1] which was to realize the Good Life, the *Summum Bonum*, and Justice. He also overflowed with value judgments for which he claimed absolute validity (as do we). He also gave normative form to his results (as do we). And finally he also went hortatory on Virtue and Vice (as we do not).[2] But, however important all this may have been to him and, for more than 2000 years, to all his readers, it does not concern us at all; as I have said already and shall use every opportunity to repeat again and again, all this affects the goals and motives of analysis but it does not affect its nature.[3]

[1] It is interesting to note that he, too, philosophized primarily about the Greek city-state which, in spite of the exploits of his illustrious tutee, was and remained for him the only form of life worthy of serious attention. That Alexander's stupendous experiment in political construction completely failed to stir his imagination and to set his mind working on the vast vistas opened up by that experiment is highly characteristic of the man.

[2] He therefore refused assent to the pleasure-and-pain doctrines about behavior that were gaining ground in the Greece of his day. But though he did not give a utilitarian definition of happiness, he placed the concept of happiness in the center of his social philosophy. Whoever does this has taken the decisive step and has committed the original sin: whether he then emphasizes virtue and vice or pleasure and pain is secondary—the way is smooth from the one to the other.

[3] If any doubt were possible concerning Aristotle's analytic intention, it would be removed by his programmatic statement: 'As in other departments of science, so in politics, the [given] compound [of phenomena] should always be resolved into the simple elements or least parts of the whole' (*Politics* I, 1). To be sure, the term 're-

But only a small part of his analytic performance is concerned with economic problems. His main work as well as his main interest, so far as social phenomena are concerned, was in the field we have decided to call economic sociology or rather it was in the field of political sociology to which he subordinated both economic sociology and technical economics. It is as a treatise or textbook on state and society that his *Politics* must be appraised. And his *Nicomachean Ethics*—a comprehensive treatise on human behavior presented from the normative angle—also deals so preponderantly with political man, with man in the city-state, that it should be considered as a companion volume to the *Politics*, making up together with the latter the first known systematic presentation of a unitary Social Science. The reader presumably knows that up to, say, the times of Hobbes, all that went under the name of political science and political philosophy fed upon the Aristotelian stock. For our purpose, it must suffice to note: (1) that not only was Aristotle, like a good analyst, very careful about his concepts but that he also co-ordinated his concepts into a *conceptual apparatus*, that is, into a system of tools of analysis that were related to one another and were meant to be used together, a priceless boon to later ages; (2) that, as is indeed implied in his 'inductive' approach alluded to above, he investigated processes of change as well as states; (3) that he tried to distinguish between features of social organisms or of behavior that exist by virtue of universal or inherent necessity (φύσει) and others that are instituted by legislative decision or custom (νόμω); (4) that he discussed social institutions in terms of purposes and of the advantages and disadvantages they seemed to him to present, and that he himself thus gave in, and led followers to give in, to a particular form of the rationalist error, namely, the teleological error.[4] Deferring consideration of his concept of Natural Law, we confine ourselves to three characteristic samples of his analysis.

solving' is but a literal equivalent to 'analyzing' and actually identifies only a particular type of the activity we mean to indicate by analysis. It is, however, the spirit of the passage that counts and not its particular wording. The passage as a whole clearly expresses the fact that Aristotle consciously applied an analytic method.

[4] Teleology, or the attempt to explain institutions and forms of behavior *causally* by the social need or purpose they are supposed to serve, is obviously not always erroneous: many things in society can be, of course, not only understood in terms of their purpose but also causally explained by it. In all sciences that deal with purposive human actions, teleology must always play some role. But it must be handled with care; and there is the ever-present danger of making improper use of it. Mostly, this improper use consists in exaggerating the extent to which men act, and shape the institutions under which they live, according to clearly perceived ends that they consciously wish to realize in the most rational way. This is why the teleological error may be called a particular instance of the wider category of rationalist errors. It is interesting to note, however, that Aristotle was quite free from the teleological error in matters outside of his social science. In *Physicae auscultationes* (II, 8) he recognized, for instance, that our teeth are adapted to chewing food, not because they were made for this purpose but, as he thought, because individuals who are by accident endowed with serviceable teeth have a better chance of surviving than those who have not. What a curious piece of Darwinism!

[4. On the Origin of the State, Private Property, and Slavery]

Contrary to a widespread impression, Aristotle did not accept Plato's idea that the state developed from the patriarchal family or *gens*. Neither did he fully accept the idea of a Social Contract which seems to have been current among Sophists, but it always hovered around his path. Occasionally, he even talked about an original covenant so that the idea came easily to any disciple of his. This is interesting for two reasons. First, in the seventeenth and eighteenth centuries the social contract became the centerpiece of a line of thought whose exponents would have greatly resented being called Aristotelians. Second, Aristotle's handling of this subject is characteristic of his general attitude toward ideas of the Sophists. Much in Aristotle is strongly suggestive of Sophist influences. Yet he consistently argued against them, or rather against the views that we know to have been held by them. Perhaps it is not difficult to explain such an attitude; it is by no means rare. In any case, however, we must not allow it to obliterate the fact that he absorbed some of their thought and that it was mainly through his works that some Sophist influences reached the Middle Ages.

In the second Book of the *Politics*, Aristotle discussed private property, communism, and the family, mainly by way of criticizing Plato, Phaleas, and Hippodamus. His criticism of Plato—the only one of the three whose text we can compare with the criticism—is strikingly unfair and, moreover, misconceives completely the nature and meaning of Plato's creation. But the arguments he adduced for private property and the family and against communism were all the more successful—they read almost exactly like the arguments of middle-class liberals of the nineteenth century.

Aristotle lived in a society and breathed the air of a civilization to which slavery was essential. However, he also lived in a time when this essential institution was under fire from social critics. In other words, slavery had become a problem. This problem Aristotle attempted to solve by positing a principle that was to serve both as an explanation and as a justification. It stated what he thought was an indubitable fact, the 'natural' inequality of men: by virtue of inborn quality, some men are predestined for subjection, others for rule. He saw the difficulty of identifying this proposition with the quite different one that the former class of men actually furnishes the slaves of real life, and that the latter class of men actually furnishes the masters of real life. But he eliminated this difficulty by admitting 'unnatural' and 'unjust' cases of slavery such as would arise from indiscriminate enslavement of (Hellenic) prisoners of war. Most of us will see in this theory a peerless example of ideological bias coupled with apologetic intention (as we know, the two do not necessarily coincide). All the more important is it to make quite clear precisely *what* it is that justifies this impression. Our dislike of the proposition that slavery is due to a congenital inferiority—of some sort—in the enslaved would certainly not justify it. Nor is it sufficient that Aristotle's theory involves several non sequiturs. This would establish faultiness of analysis but not ideological bias. At the same time, if the mistakes committed in an argument all point in the same direction and if this direction agrees with what we may conceive the analyst's ideology to be, we are probably within our rights in suspecting ideological bias. Even so, it is not the suspicion of bias but the proof of the mistakes that should motivate rejection.

[5. Aristotle's 'Pure' Economics]

Keeping these principles of interpretation in mind, we now turn to Aristotle's embryonic 'pure' economics, the elements of which are to be found mainly in *Politics*, I, 8-11, and in *Ethics*, V, 5. Nothing would be easier than to show that he was primarily concerned with the 'natural' and the 'just' as seen from the standpoint of his ideal of the good and virtuous life, and that the economic facts and relations between economic facts which he considered and evaluated appear in the light of the ideological preconceptions to be expected in a man who lived in, and wrote for, a cultivated leisure class, which held work and business pursuits in contempt and, of course, loved the farmer who fed it and hated the money lender who exploited it. These things are just as interesting but not more so than are the corresponding though different value judgments and ideologies of the modern intellectual. The points that really matter for us are these. Aristotle based his economic analysis squarely upon wants and their satisfactions. Starting from the economy of self-sufficient households, he then introduced division of labor, barter, and, as a means of overcoming the difficulties of direct barter, money—the error of confusing wealth with money duly coming in for stricture. There is no theory of 'distribution.' This—presumably the extract from a large literature that has been lost—constitutes the Greek bequest, so far as economic theory is concerned. We shall follow its fortunes right to A. Smith's *Wealth of Nations*, the first five chapters of which are but developments of the same line of reasoning. Let us therefore look at the bequest more closely.

(a) *Value*. Aristotle not only distinguished value in use and value in exchange as clearly as did any later writer but he also perceived that the latter phenomenon derives somehow from the former. But in itself this is not only common sense but also commonplace, and further than this he did not advance. His failure to do so was made good by the later scholastics, who are entitled to the credit for having developed the theory of price which he himself cannot be said to have had. It has been held that this was due to his preoccupation with the ethical problem of justice in pricing—'commutative' justice—which diverted his interest from the analytic problem of actual pricing. Nothing could be farther from the truth. Preoccupation with the ethics of pricing, as the example of the later scholastics suffices to show, is precisely one of the strongest motives a man can possibly have for analyzing actual market mechanisms. Several passages show, as a matter of fact, that Aristotle tried to do so and failed.[1] He considered, however, the case of Monopoly (*Politics*,

[1] The most characteristic of these passages occurs in *Ethics*, V (1133), which I interpret like this: 'As the farmer's labor compares with the shoemaker's labor, so

I, 11 and *Ethics*, v, 5), which he defined as it has been defined ever since, namely, as the position in a market of a Single Seller (μόνος, alone or standing alone; πωλεῖν, to sell).[2] He condemned it as 'unjust.'

These facts seem to yield the solution of a problem that has exercised some historians of the theory of value. Aristotle no doubt sought for a canon of justice in pricing, and he found it in the 'equivalence' of what a man gives and receives. Since both parties to an act of barter or sale must necessarily gain by it in the sense that they must prefer their economic situations after the act to the economic situations in which they found themselves before the act—or else they would not have any motive to perform it—there can be no equivalence between the 'subjective' or utility values of the goods exchanged or between the good and the money paid or received for it. And since Aristotle did not offer any theory of exchange value or price, those historians concluded that he must have had in mind some mysterious Objective or Absolute Value of things that is intrinsically inherent in them and independent of circumstances or human valuations or actions—a metaphysical entity most welcome to people with philosophical propensities and most distasteful to people of a more 'positive' type of mind. But surely this does not follow. Failure to explain exchange value is not failure to recognize it as a fact. And it is much more reasonable to assume that Aristotle simply thought of the exchange values of the market, as *expressed* in terms of money, rather than of some mysterious value substance *measured* by those exchange values. But does not this imply that he accepted the actual commodity prices as the standard of his commutative justice and thereby lost the means of pronouncing upon their justice or injustice? Not at all. We have seen that he condemned monopoly prices. It is not farfetched to equate, for Aristotle's purpose, monopoly prices with prices that some individual or group of individuals have set to their own advantage. Prices that are given to the individual and with which he cannot tamper, that is to say, the *competitive* prices that emerge in free market under normal conditions, do not come within the ban. And there is nothing strange in the conjecture that Aristotle may have taken normal competitive prices as standards of commutative justice or, more precisely, that he was prepared to accept as 'just' *any* transaction between individuals that was carried out at such prices—which is in fact what the scholastic doctors were to do explicitly. If this interpretation be correct, his concept of the just value of a commodity is indeed 'objective,' but only in the sense that no individual can alter it by his own action. Moreover, his just values were social values—expressive, as he almost certainly thought, of the community's evaluation of every commodity[3]—but only in the sense that they were the super-individual result of

the product of the farmer compares with the product of the shoemaker.' At least, I cannot get any other sense out of this passage. If I am right, then Aristotle was groping for some labor-cost theory of price which he was unable to state explicitly.

[2] Joan Robinson added the corresponding concept, Monopsony, the position in the market of a Single Buyer (ὀψωνεῖν, to buy).

[3] This idea kept on turning up throughout the ages. We also find it in J. B. Clark (see below, Part IV). But though it seems to have had a strong appeal for some minds,

the actions of a mass of reasonable men. In any case, they are nothing more metaphysical or absolute than quantities of commodities multiplied by their normal competitive prices. The reader will have no difficulty in perceiving that, if values are defined in this way, the Aristotelian requirement of commutative justice acquires a sound and perfectly simple meaning. It will be fulfilled by their equality in every act of exchange or sale: if *A* barters shoes for *B*'s loaves of bread, Aristotelian justice requires that the shoes equal the loaves when both are multiplied by their normal competitive prices; if *A* sells the shoes to *B* for money, the same rule will determine the amount of money he ought to get. Since, under the conditions envisaged, *A* would actually get this amount, we have before us an instructive instance of the relation which, with Aristotle himself and a host of followers, subsists between the logical and the normal ideal and between the 'natural' and the 'just.'

We have expended such care on this argument because it disposes once for all of metaphysical speculations about objective or absolute value wheresoever and whensoever they might occur. Dismissing for good what we have seen to be a spurious problem, we shall henceforth understand by objective value of a commodity the magnitude defined and nothing else. Similarly, we shall not bother about any possible metaphysical meaning of the concept of Intrinsic Value since it is always possible (and in most cases very easy) to attach to it an entirely unmetaphysical one—as, for instance, in the most important case, where an author speaks of the intrinsic value of a coin.

(b) *Money*. The theory of money that Aristotle sponsored in conscious opposition, so it seems to me, to the alternative one sponsored by Plato was this: the very existence of any non-communist society involves the exchange of goods and services; this exchange, at first, 'naturally' takes the form of barter; but the people who want what other people have may not have what the latter want; therefore it will often be necessary to accept in exchange what one does not want in order to get what one does want by means of a further act of barter (indirect exchange); obvious convenience will then induce people to choose, tacitly or through legislative action, one commodity—Aristotle did not consider the possibility that people might choose more than one—as a Medium of Exchange. Aristotle briefly mentioned the fact that some commodities—such as the metals—are better fitted for this role than others, thus foreshadowing some of the tritest passages in nineteenth-century textbooks about homogeneity, divisibility, portability, relative stability of value,[4] and so on. Moreover, the requirements of his rule of equivalence in exchange naturally led him to observe that the Medium of Exchange will also be used as a Measure of Value. And finally he recognized, implicitly at least, its use as a Store of Value. Three of the four functions of money traditionally listed in those nineteenth-century

there is very little to it: there is no realistic sense in which it can be averred that any non-socialist society as such evaluates commodities, though it is true of course that social influences shape the subjective valuations of individuals that govern their behavior and thus produce prices and 'objective values.'

[4] He recognized, however, that the value of gold and silver was not immutable.

textbooks—the fourth is to serve as the Standard of Deferred Payments—can therefore be traced to Aristotle.

Essentially, this theory embodies two propositions. The first is that, whatever other purposes money may come to serve, its fundamental function, which defines it and accounts for its existence, is to serve as a medium of exchange. Therefore, this theory belongs to what Professor von Mises has described as 'catallactic' theories of money (καταλλάττειν, to exchange). The second proposition is that in order to serve as a medium of exchange in the markets of commodities, money itself must be one of these commodities. That is to say, it must be a thing that is useful and has exchange value independently of its monetary function—this is all that intrinsic value means in this connection—a value that can be compared with other values. Thus the money commodity goes by weight and quality as do other commodities; for convenience people may decide to put a stamp on it (χαρακτήρ) in order to save the trouble of having to weigh it every time, but this stamp only declares and guarantees the quantity and quality of the commodity contained in a coin and is not the cause of its value. This proposition, which, of course, is not either identical with the first or implied by it, will identify what we shall henceforth call Metallism or the Metallist Theory of Money in contrast to the Cartal Theory of which Plato's is an example.[5]

Whatever may be its shortcomings, this theory, though never unchallenged, prevailed substantially to the end of the nineteenth century and even beyond. It is the basis of the bulk of all analytic work in the field of money. Therefore, we have every motive to make sure of our interpretation of Aristotle, whose personal influence in this matter is recognizable at least as late as A. Smith. No passage in the *Politics* will bear any other interpretation unless we attribute to Aristotle certain views that he mentioned but clearly attributed to others. But in the *Ethics*, playing upon the Greek word for current coin (νόμισμα), he did state that money exists not by 'nature' but by convention or legislation (νόμῳ), which seems to point in another direction. The fact, however, that he added, by way of explaining his meaning, that money might be changed or demonetized by the community suggests that he meant no more than that convention or legislation decides the material to be used for coining money and on the particular form to be given to the coins.[6]

Attention should finally be called to an interesting point of method. Aristotle's theory of money is a theory in the ordinary sense of this term, that is to say, an attempt to explain what money is and what money does. But, he presented it in a genetic form, as was his habit in dealing with any social institution: he lets money develop in what purports to be a historical sequence that

[5] See ch. 6 of this Part.

[6] We cannot enter, as we should, into a discussion of other passages. It must suffice to say that, at worst, they weigh but lightly as against the clear implications of Aristotle's emphasis on the necessity that money should consist of a material that is a commodity in its own right. Either the phrase that money is ὑπάλλαγμα τῆς χρείας κατὰ συνθήκην (*Ethics*, v, 5, 11) means that money is a means of exchange [used] according to convention or else I do not understand it.

starts from a condition or 'stage' in which there was no money. Of course, we need not see more in this than an expository device. In fact, the reader should remember this possible interpretation, which will redeem from sheer absurdity many an argument that presents itself in the garb of purely imaginary 'history,' as do, for instance, those theories of the state that use the idea of an original social contract. Even A. Smith's 'early and rude state of society' may benefit from an interpretation that refuses to take it seriously. But the case of money is different because the Aristotelian theory of the *logical* origin of money may pass muster—at a push—as a verifiable theory of its *historical* origin. Such instances as the Semite shekel or the tea-money of Mongolian nomads suffice to show this. It is in such cases that our point of method arises. Is it valid procedure to trace as far back as we can the history of an institution in order to discover its essential or its simplest meanings? Clearly not. Primitive forms of existence are as a rule not more simple but more complex than later ones: the chieftain who is judge, priest, administrator, warrior all in one is evidently a more complex phenomenon than are any of his specialized successors of later times; the medieval manor is conceptually a more complex phenomenon than is the U.S. Steel Corporation. Logical and historical origins must, therefore, be kept distinct. But this distinction presents itself only in advanced stages of analysis. The unsophisticated analyst invariably confuses them.[7] This confusion is undoubtedly implied in Aristotle's theories of money and also of other social institutions. He bequeathed it to the whole line of thinkers that descends from him, the English utilitarians included. And it survived, in spots, until today.

(c) *Interest.* The rest of Aristotle's 'pure' economics, *considered from our standpoint,* is hardly worth mentioning. Many, if not most, of the things that were to become problems for the economist of later times he took for granted in the spirit of prescientific common sense; and he passed his value judgments upon a reality large stretches of which he failed to explore at all. The chiefly agrarian income of the gentleman of his time evidently presented no problem to him; the free laborer was an anomaly in his slave economy and was disposed of perfunctorily; the artisan, except so far as the just price of his product was concerned, fared little better; the trader (and shipowner), the shopkeeper, the money lender were mainly considered with a view to the ethical and political appraisal of their activities and their gains,[8] neither of which seemed to call

[7] It should be observed, however, that identification of historical and logical evolution does not necessarily involve confusion. But if it does not involve confusion then it requires *either* proof of coincidence in every particular case *or* acceptance of an evolutionary or 'emanatistic' logic, such as Hegel's.

[8] Observe: I am not arguing against Aristotle's ideal of life or against any particular value judgments of his. Still less am I arguing for glorification of economic activity. On the contrary, I applaud the philosopher for having refused to identify rational behavior with the hunt for wealth. All I want to establish is that Aristotle, who in political matters was so alive to the necessity of analyzing and fact-finding as a preliminary to judging, never seems to have bothered about this preliminary in 'purely' economic matters except in the matters touching value, price, and money. For instance,

for explanatory analysis. There is nothing surprising or blameworthy in this. It is by slow degrees that the physical and social facts of the empirical universe enter the range of the analytic searchlight. In the beginnings of scientific analysis, the mass of the phenomena is left undisturbed in the compound of common-sense knowledge, and only chips of this mass arouse scientific curiosity and thereupon become 'problems.'

For Aristotle, interest was no such chip. He accepted the empirical fact of interest on money loans and saw no problem in it. He did not even classify loans according to the various purposes they are capable of serving and does not seem to have noticed that a loan that financed consumption is something very different from a loan that financed maritime trade (*foenus nauticum*). He condemned interest—which he equated to 'usury' in all cases—on the ground that there was no justification for money, a mere medium of exchange, to increase in going from hand to hand (which of course it does not do). But he never asked the question why interest was being paid all the same.[9] This question was first asked by the scholastic doctors. It is to them that the credit belongs of having been the first both to collect facts about interest and to develop the outlines of a theory of it. Aristotle himself had no theory of interest. In particular, he should not be hailed as the forerunner of the monetary interest theories of today. For though he linked up interest with money, this was not due to analytic effort but to the absence of it: analysis that eventually leads back to a preanalytic view, that earlier analysis seemed to have disproved, imparts a different meaning to it.

[6. Greek Philosophy]

So far as economics in the technical sense is concerned, we do not lose anything by leaving Greek thought at this point. Unfortunately, we lose a lot in another respect. There is hardly an idea in the realm of philosophy that does not descend from Greek sources, and many of these ideas, while not directly relevant to economic analysis itself, are all the more relevant to the general attitude and spirit of the analyst, though, as I have been careful to point out, such background influences should not be overemphasized. The various post-Aristotelian schools in particular, such as the Skeptics, Stoics, Epicureans, and then the Neo-Platonists, all not only influenced the Roman eclectics such as Cicero and Seneca but also helped to shape directly medieval as well as more modern thought. It goes without saying, for instance, that the Stoic idea of a rational universe [1] governed by immutable laws reflects an atti-

---

the fundamental difference he finds between the trader's and the producer's gains is essentially preanalytic. This fact has nothing to do with the other fact that he disapproved of the former and approved of the latter.

[9] In order to make this point quite clear, let us compare Aristotle's attitude toward interest with that of Karl Marx, who condemned the phenomenon at least as strongly as did Aristotle. But the analytic problem of interest was all the more important to him.

[1] On the meaning to be assigned in this connection to the term rational, see below. ch. 2, sec. 5c.

tude of mind that is not without significance for us. We must be content, however, to cast a glance at the message of Epicurus (about 341-270 B.C.).[2]

Epicurean philosophy might serve as a standard example for the truth that what a set of ideas comes to mean in the course of time is but distantly related to what the originators meant to convey. Epicurus lived in the Hellenistic period that witnessed the rapid decay of the *polis*. Active life, to the Greek, had meant active participation in the administration and politics of the city-states. For a man of culture such a life was then no longer possible. And Epicurus', like many other people's, answer to the resulting ethical problem—the problem of what might be called spiritual unemployability of the refined mind—was to leave the world alone and to try to achieve detached serenity (αταραξία) by *understanding resignation*. The causes that produced this particular attitude—there is no good equivalent for the German *Lebensstimmung*—were historically unique and so is really that attitude itself—or has been until today. But three elements of Epicurus' system of thought kept on turning up in the later Middle Ages, in the Renaissance, and also later on. The first of these elements is his atomistic materialism that tallies with, and perhaps influenced, later mechanistic philosophies of the universe. The second is this: Epicurus' attitude to the social environment may indeed be described as a highly sublimated egocentric hedonism or eudaemonism; and though his hedonism and eudaemonism was something very different from the hedonism and eudaemonism of later ages and in particular defined pleasure and pain quite differently, there is still a connecting line that leads from Epicurus to Helvetius and Bentham. Bentham's boisterous and vulgar utilitarianism would no doubt have shocked the old sage. But, much as we may dislike associating them, we must call both of them hedonists in a wider sense. The third element is the social contract, of which Epicurus, though not the originator, was an important exponent. But the idea was handed to the philosophers of natural law, who adopted it in the seventeenth and eighteenth centuries, by their scholastic predecessors, and this fact does not point to Epicurus.

[7. The Contribution of the Romans]

Let us now consider the still smaller contribution of the Romans. The doctrine that practical need—and not, as I hold, the lure of intellectual adventure—is the prime mover of scientific endeavor can be put to the test in the case of ancient Rome. Even in the earliest time when Rome was substantially a community of peasants, there were economic problems of first-rate importance that produced violent class struggles. By the time of the first Punic War important commercial interests had developed. Toward the end of the Republic, trade, money and finance, colonial administration, the plight of Italian agriculture, the food supply of the capital, the growth of *latifundia,* slave labor, and so on all presented problems that, in an artificial political setup created

[2] See C. Bailey, *Epicurus, the Extant Remains* (1926); W. Wallace, *Epicureanism* (1880).

by military conquest and by all the consequences of incessant warfare, might have fully employed a legion of economists. At the height of cultural achievement, at the epoch of Hadrian and Antoninus Pius, when many of those difficulties were temporarily in abeyance and peace and prosperity reigned for a time in the vast realm, its able rulers and the galaxy of brilliant generals and administrators around them could have made use of a brain trust. Yet there was nothing of the kind—nothing beyond the occasional utterance of groans about the empire's unfavorable balance of trade or about *latifundia perdidere Italiam.*[1]

[(a) *Absence of Analytic Work.*] But this is not difficult to understand. In the social structure of Rome, purely intellectual interests had no natural home. Though its complexity increased as time went on, we may, for our purpose, put the case in a nutshell by saying that there were the peasants, the urban *plebs* (including traders and artisans), and the slaves. And above them all, there was a 'society' that no doubt had its business stratum (more or less represented by the order of the *equites*) but consisted mainly of an aristocracy that, unlike the Athenian aristocracy in the times after Pericles, never retired into opposition to lead a life of refined leisure, but threw itself wholeheartedly into public affairs both civil and military. The *res publica* was the center of its existence and all its activity. With widening horizons and increasing refinement, it cultivated an interest in Greek philosophy and art and developed a (largely derivative) literature of its own. These things were touched upon lightly, however, and were definitely considered as pastimes, essentially nugatory in themselves. There was little steam left for serious work in any scientific field, as Cicero's (106-43 B.C.) representative writings are sufficient to show.[2] And this deficiency was not, and could not be, made up by encouraging foreigners and freedmen who were directed primarily toward utilitarian tasks.

Of course, a society of this structure was bound to be passionately interested in history, mainly its own history. This was in fact one of the two main outlets for such scientific curiosity as the Roman mind harbored. But this curiosity was characteristically confined to political and military history. Sociological and economic backgrounds were hastily sketched—such sketches occur even in Caesar—social upheavals were reported with the utmost economy of general considerations. The one great exception is Tacitus' (*c.* 55-120) *Germania.*

[(b) *Importance of Roman Law.*] The only other outlet was the law. In order to understand the nature of the Roman achievement in this field and

[1] This phrase—that the large landed estates were the cause of the decline of Italy—was the elder Pliny's (23-79). The very fact that he saw nothing but the obvious, and in particular that he failed to see that the *latifundia* were as much the consequence as they were the cause of that decline, in itself shows what sort of economics was deemed adequate by a very able and highly civilized Roman (though it was not worse than is our own popular economics).

[2] *De re publica* is the one to come nearest to our field. Yet there is in it very little that could interest the economist, apart of course from what it tells us, directly and indirectly, about the economic conditions of that epoch. That applies still more to the *Letters to Atticus.*

the reason why, unlike other legal systems, the Roman law plays a role in the history of economic analysis, we must recall a few facts about it. The reader is familiar, perhaps, with the English division of legal material into common law and equity. A somewhat analogous division existed in ancient Rome. There was the old and formalistic civil law (*jus civile, jus quiritium*), which, however, unlike the English common law, applied only to the affairs of the citizens (*quirites*) who until A.D. 212 formed but a part of the free population of the empire. This civil law [3] was developed by 'interpretation' through the agency of a college of priests (*pontifices*) and also through the agency of an officer of state in charge of judicial administration (*praetor urbanus*). This additional legal material bears some similarity to the English law of equity. But the bulk of what, to some extent, may be likened to English equity grew from another root, namely, from the relations, commercial and other, between non-citizens (*peregrini*) or between citizens and non-citizens. The body of legal rules that applied to these was called *jus gentium*. Note that this term, as used in Roman times, has nothing to do with the meaning it began to acquire from the seventeenth century on, namely, the meaning of Law of Nations (*droit des gens, Völkerrecht*). Since this body of law was formulated, and largely created, by another officer of state, who was in charge of a separate department of public administration (*praetor peregrinus*), it was also, together with the legal rules formulated or created by the *praetor urbanus*, referred to as 'officers' law' (*jus honorarium*): every *praetor* codified and promulgated it for his year of office in his *edictum*. Of course, there was also a steady stream of special enactments of various types. Comprehensive codification or even compilation was not attempted before the fourth century, though those praetorian *edicta* were fused, and stereotyped in an enactment, in the reign of Hadrian. We have, however, a second-century textbook, the *Institutiones*, by a jurist whose given name (*praenomen*) was Gaius.

Anglo-American jurisprudence, that is to say, the sum total of the techniques of legal reasoning and of the general principles to be applied to individual cases, is largely the work of the superior courts, whose decisions together with the motivating arguments, as everyone knows, have an authority that approaches that of an enactment. In Rome, the same practical needs produced a similar achievement but in a different way. English and American judges of the highest ranks are professional lawyers and, in principle at least, very eminent lawyers—leaders of the legal profession of great personal authority. The Roman judges were laymen—like our jurors—who had to be told what the law was. And the practicing lawyers were also laymen except for a group of professional pleaders (*causidici*) who had not much standing. This deficiency was made up in a way for which there is no analogy. Men of position and leisure became interested in legal questions almost as a hobby (unless they

[3] The reader should not confuse Civil Law in this sense with Civil Law in the sense used by modern Anglo-American lawyers: in their parlance it simply means the whole of the Roman law preserved in the *Corpus juris civilis* (see next footnote), as developed by medieval and modern practice.

taught; the first to lecture on jurisprudence was, so far as we know, M. Antistius Labeo; the first to establish a school, Masurius Sabinus, *c.* A.D. 30). And they were interested not so much in the individual cases as such as in the logical principles relevant for their solution. They did not plead or do any other kind of legal work except one: they gave opinions on points of law whenever consulted by parties or attorneys or judges. So great was their authority that it may well be compared to that of English judges. It was first officially recognized by Augustus, who granted to the more eminent of these 'jurists' a special privilege of giving such opinions, the *jus respondendi*. These opinions were little monographs which together with more comprehensive works (such as the commentaries *ad edictum*) piled up to an extensive literature of which the remains, most of them preserved in the extracts made for Justinian's *Corpus* (528-33),[4] have been the object of admiration ever since.

The reason we have for referring to this literature is its genuinely scientific character. Those jurists analyzed facts and produced principles that were not only normative but also, by implication at least, explanatory. They created a juristic logic that proved to be applicable to a wide variety of social patterns—indeed to any social pattern that recognizes private property and 'capitalist' commerce. So far as their facts were economic, their analysis was economic analysis. Unfortunately the scope of this analysis was strictly limited by the practical purposes they had in view, which is why their generalizations yielded legal principles but not also economic ones. Mainly, we owe to them definitions—for example, of price, money, of purchase and sale, of the various kinds of loans (*mutuum* and *commodatum*), of the two types of deposits (*regulare* and *irregulare*), and so on—which provided starting points for later analysis. But they did not go beyond these starting points. Any theorems—for example, about the behavior of prices or about the economic importance of the 'irregular' deposit that creates no obligation to return the individual things deposited but only the obligation to return 'as much of the same kind' (*tantun-*

[4] A word on that compilation may be welcome to some readers. In A.D. 528, the emperor Justinian appointed a committee of jurists, presided over by his minister of finance (*quaestor sacri palatii*), Tribonianus, in order to trim into a manageable shape the exuberant foliage of both enactments and legal literature. Apart from subsequent imperial statutes (*Novellae*), that were added to it, the *Corpus juris civilis*, as the compilation was called, contains first, the *Institutiones*, a textbook for beginners based upon that of Gaius; second, the *Digestae* or *Pandectae*, which consist of a mass of extracts or quotations from the works of those consulting jurists; third, the Codex, which reproduced all the imperial statutes that were still in force. We are interested only in the *Digestae*. Unfortunately, Justinian ordered the destruction of everything that was not included in them. But the committee had at least the sense to refrain from mutilating the fragments included. Thus, the *Digestae*, though invested with the force of law, do not contain pulverized gems—pulverized into paragraphs of a code of law—but the gems themselves, a unique method of codification. Let us bow to the greatest of the authors included: Julius Paulus, Celsus, Papinianus, Ulpianus, Modestinus, Africanus, and Salvius Julianus—the order expressing a personal scale of preference that I cannot expect everybody to share.

dem in genere)—would have been irrelevant digressions. It is therefore not quite correct to speak of an economic theory of the *Corpus juris* [5]—not, in any case, of an articulate one—though it may be said with truth that the Roman jurists, by clarifying concepts, did preliminary work.[6]

The importance of this work—and also of the training in clear thinking that everybody undergoes who studies the literature—is greatly enhanced by the curious fact that the law of the *Corpus juris* was again taught from the twelfth century on and that subsequently it recovered its authority with the courts of most European countries ('reception' of the Roman law). Now, to the end of the eighteenth century, most of the writers on economic questions were, if not businessmen, either clergymen or lawyers by profession: the scholarly training of these two types of economists was largely provided by the Roman and the canon law and so there was a natural avenue by which the concepts, the spirit, and even, perhaps, some mannerisms of the Roman jurists entered the field of economic analysis. Among these concepts was the fundamental one of Natural Law. Once more, however, we defer its consideration, as we did when we met it in Aristotle: it will be more convenient to give later on a connected account of its development.

[(c) *Writings on Agriculture*.] We now turn for a moment to a minor matter, the Roman writings on agriculture (*De re rustica*). This branch of economic literature that seems to have been cultivated rather extensively by the Romans is more interesting for the economic historian than it is for us. It dealt with the practical principles of farm or rather estate management but rarely touched upon questions that come within our province. For instance, the elder Cato's advice that the landowner should sell aging slaves before they become useless and that he should show himself as hard a taskmaster as possible when inspecting his estate is no doubt very revealing in many respects but it does not involve any economic analysis. Some of those writers, of whom

[5] See, however, Paul Oertmann, *Die Volkswirtschaftslehre des Corpus juris civilis* (1891), which, though obsolete in parts, is still the standard work on the subject.

[6] One point may, however, be worth mentioning. Julius Paulus (1, *Dig.*, XVIII, 1) explained the nature of money much as had Aristotle (from the inconvenience of direct barter). The passage is quite straightforward and calls for no comment until he adds that the stamped material of which the money is made (*materia forma publica percussa*), *usum dominiumque* (this may be safely translated by purchasing power) *non tam ex substantia praebet quam ex quantitate*. This passage has puzzled many a commentator and was the subject of a controversy in the eighteenth century. It seems, in fact, to renounce the metallist theory clearly indicated in the preceding sentence. But I do not think that such an 'aside' should be taken very seriously. In addition, there is the word *quantitas*, which has induced some writers to credit Paulus with a quantity theory of money. But there is no indication in the passage of an *inverse* relation between the quantity of money and its purchasing power. Moreover, the word *quantitas* is much more likely to mean 'nominal value' than quantity. This was its meaning in the literature on money in the Middle Ages and in the sixteenth century. All that Paulus probably meant was that people, in handling money in everyday transactions, usually take a coin at its nominal value without any conscious thought of the commodity value of its materials.

only Varro and Columella need be mentioned, occasionally made some remarks that suggest later developments, such as that the most profitable use of a piece of land depends, among other things, upon its distance from the center of consumption. But it is as true in these cases as it is in others that the mere statement of facts that are known to us from common experience is of no scientific importance, unless they become the starting point of an analysis that distills from them more interesting results.[7]

[8. Early Christian Thought]

We do not leave the Graeco-Roman world when we now turn for a moment to the Christian thought of the first six centuries. After what has been said about the nature of our aims, it is obvious that there would be no point in looking for 'economics' in the sacred writings themselves. The opinions on economic subjects that we might find—such as that believers should sell what they have and give it to the poor, or that they should lend without expecting anything (possibly not even repayment) from it—are ideal imperatives that form part of a general scheme of life and express this general scheme and nothing else, least of all scientific propositions.

But neither is there anything for us to garner in the works of those great men who during these centuries laid the foundation of the Christian tradition. And this does call for a word of explanation. For we might expect that, so far as Christianity aimed at social reform, the movement should have motivated analysis in the way in which, for example, the socialist movement did in our own time. Yet there is nothing of the kind either in Clement of Alexandria (about 150-215) or in Tertullian (155-222) or in Cyprian (200-258) to mention a few of those who did concern themselves with the moral aspects of the economic phenomena around them. They preached against wanton luxury and irresponsible wealth, they enjoined charity and restraint in the use of worldly goods, but they did not analyze at all. Moreover, it would be quite absurd to suspect mercantilist theories behind Tertullian's advice to content oneself with the simple products of domestic agriculture and industry instead of craving for imported luxuries, or a theory of value behind his observation that abundance and rarity have something to do with price. The same is true of the Christian teachers of the subsequent period. They lacked nothing in refinement and did develop techniques of reasoning—that partly hailed from Greek philosophy and from the Roman law—for the subjects that seemed to them worth while. Yet neither Lactantius (260-340) nor Ambrosius (340-97) —who might have elaborated a little on his statement that the rich consider as their rightful property the *common goods of which they have possessed*

[7] M. Terentius Varro (116-27 B.C.) was a man of some eminence who, in his long life, turned out an almost incredible quantity of literature on all sorts of subjects. Among his extant remains are *Rerum rusticarum libri tres* in which the remark above occurs. Much less interesting is *De re rustica* by L. Junius Moderatus Columella (1st century A.D.), which deals mainly with the cultivation of vegetables, trees, flowers, and so on, and with the rearing of animals.

themselves—nor Chrysostomus (347-407) nor St. Augustine (354-430), the accomplished author of the *Civitas Dei* and of the *Confessiones*—whose very *obiter dicta* reveal analytic habits of mind—ever went into economic problems though they did go into the political problems of the Christian state.

The explanation seems to be this. Whatever our sociological diagnosis of the mundane aspects of early Christianity may be, it is clear that the Christian Church did not aim at social reform in any sense other than that of moral reform of individual behavior. At no time, even before its victory, which may be roughly dated from Constantine's Edict of Milan (313), did the Church attempt a frontal attack on the existing social system or on any of its more important institutions. It never promised economic paradise or, for that matter, any paradise this side of the grave. The How and Why of economic mechanisms were *then* of no interest either to its leaders or to its writers.

CHAPTER 2

The Scholastic Doctors and the Philosophers of Natural Law

1. The Great Gap

The Eastern Empire survived the Western for another thousand years, kept going by the most interesting and most successful bureaucracy the world has ever seen. Many of the men who shaped policies in the offices of the Byzantine emperors were of the intellectual cream of their times. They dealt with a host of legal, monetary, commercial, agrarian, and fiscal problems. We cannot help feeling that they must have philosophized about them. If they did, however, the results have been lost. No piece of reasoning that would have to be mentioned here has been preserved.

In the Germanic states of the West, similar problems arose even before the time of Charlemagne, and we know fairly well from literary sources as well as from documents how they dealt with them. But Charlemagne's vast empire presented problems of internal administration and international economic relations that had been unknown to any Germanic ruler before him. Practical wisdom, however, not inferior to that of any other age, is all that his measures reflect. The historians and philosophers who adorned his court touched upon economic questions incidentally, if at all.[1] So far as our subject is concerned we may safely leap over 500 years to the epoch of St. Thomas Aquinas (1225-74), whose *Summa Theologica*[2] is in the history of thought what the south-western spire of the Cathedral of Chartres is in the history of architecture.

2. Feudalism and Scholasticism

St. Thomas' life extended over the crest of feudal civilization. This term suggests the idea of a particular type of warrior society, namely, of a society dominated by a warrior stratum that was organized, on the principle of vassalage, in a hierarchy of fief-endowed lords and knights. From the standpoint of this hierarchy of warriors, the old distinction between men of free status and men of unfree status had lost much of its original significance. What mattered was not whether a man was free or not, but whether he was a knight or not. Even the Emperor of the Holy Roman Empire of German Nationality—to use the official phrase—who was in theory recognized as the feudal overlord of all Christianity, primarily was, and felt himself to be, a knight; and even the unfree man was a knight as soon as he had got hold of a horse and arms and had learned how to use them—which was at first a very simple matter, though in St. Thomas' age it had become a highly skilled occupation. This warrior class enjoyed unrivaled power and prestige, and hence impressed the stamp of its own cultural pattern upon the civilization of feudal times.

The economic base of this social pyramid consisted of the dependent peasants and manorial craftsmen on whose work the warriors lived. We thus seem to behold what at first sight looks like a structural unit in the sense that the phrase Social Pyramid is indeed meant to convey. But this picture is quite unrealistic. Societies, with the possible exception of primitive tribes and full-fledged socialism, are never structural units, and half the problems they present arise from the fact that they are not. The society of feudal times cannot be described in terms of knights and peasants any more than the society of capitalist times can be described in terms of capitalists and proletarians. Roman industry, commerce, and finance had not been destroyed everywhere. Even

1 The reader will find an instructive description of the intellectual situation of these times in M. L. W. Laistner, *Thought and Letters in Western Europe*, A.D. *500 to 900* (1931).

2 New edition: S. *Thomae Aquinatis, Doctoris Angelici, Summa Theologica, diligenter emendata de Rubeis, Billuart et Aliorum* (Taurini, 1932). The work, though unfinished, has acquired unrivaled authority in the course of the centuries. But it contains much that was revolutionary in St. Thomas' day, and shortly after his death a number of propositions were declared heretical, though only locally. The canonization of the author in 1323 marks the turning of the tide. It was not, however, until the sixteenth century that Catholic thought definitely rallied round his teaching. Pope Leo XIII's encyclical *Aeterni Patris* (1879) made it the official teaching of the Church.

where they had been destroyed or where they had never existed, they—and consequently classes of bourgeois character—had developed or developed again before St. Thomas' day. In many places these classes had outgrown the framework of the feudal organization and, helped by the fact that a well-fortified town was normally impregnable to the knights' arts of warfare, they had successfully challenged the rule of the feudal lords—the most conspicuous instance being the victorious resistance of the towns of Lombardy. As a historical reality, therefore, feudalism means the symbiosis of two essentially different and largely, though not wholly, antagonistic social systems.

But there was another factor of nonfeudal origin and character that the warrior class failed to absorb or to conquer, for us the most important of all, the Roman Catholic Church. We cannot enter into a discussion of the extremely intricate relations of the medieval Church with the feudal powers. The one essential point to grasp is that the Church was not simply an organ of feudal society but an organism distinct from feudal society that always remained a power in its own right. However closely allied with, or dependent upon, feudal kings and lords it may at times have been, however near it may have come to defeat and to being harnessed into the service of the warrior class, it never resigned its own authority and never became the instrument of that or any other class. Since the Church was always able not only to assert itself but also to wage successful war upon the feudal powers, this fact should be too obvious to require explicit statement, were it not that historiography, inspired by a popular version of Marxian sociology, may easily create the impression—to put it in the crudest possible way—that medieval thought was merely the ideology of a landholding warrior class, verbalized by its chaplains. This impression would be wrong not only from the standpoint of those who refuse to accept the Marxian sociology of ideas, but also from the standpoint of Marx himself, even if we chose to interpret the Catholic system of thought as an ideology, it would still remain the ideology of the clergy and never merge with that of the warrior class. It is important to keep this in mind because of the practically complete monopoly of learning that the Catholic Church enjoyed until the Renaissance. This monopoly was due primarily to the spiritual authority of the Church. But it was greatly reinforced by the conditions of those ages in which there was neither room nor security for professional scholars except within a convent. In consequence, almost all 'intellectuals' of those times were either monks or friars. Let us briefly consider some implications of this.

All those monks and friars spoke the same unclassical Latin; they heard the same Mass wherever they went; they were formed by an education that was the same in all countries; they professed the same system of fundamental beliefs; and they all acknowledged the supreme authority of the Pope, which was essentially international: their country was Christendom, their state was the Church. But this is not all. Their internationalizing influence was strengthened by the fact that feudal society itself was international. Not only the Pope's but also the Emperor's authority was international in principle and, to some varying degree, in fact. The old Roman Empire and that of Charlemagne were no mere reminiscences. People were familiar with the idea of a temporal as well as of a spiritual superstate. National divisions did not mean to them what they came to mean during the sixteenth century; nothing in the whole range of Dante's political ideas is so striking as is the complete absence of the nationalist angle. The result was the emergence of an essentially international civilization and an international republic of scholars that was no phrase but a living reality. St. Thomas was an Italian and John Duns Scotus was a Scotsman, but both taught in Paris and Cologne without encountering any of the difficulties that they would have encountered in the age of airplanes.

In fact as well as in principle, practically everybody who wished to do so was allowed to enter a monastic order and also to join the ranks of the secular clergy. But advancement within the Church was open to everybody in principle only, since the claims of members of warrior-class families in fact absorbed the greater part of bishoprics and abbotcies. But the man without connection was never entirely excluded from the higher dignities, not even from the highest; and, what is much more important for us, he was not debarred from becoming an idea-shaping and policy-shaping 'keyman.' The regular clergy (the monks) and the friars supplied, as it were, the general staff of the Church. And in the monasteries men of all classes met on equal terms. Naturally, the intellectual atmosphere was often charged with social and political radicalism, though this was, of course, much more the case at some times than at others and much more with the friars than with the regular monks. In the literature that we are going to survey we get this radicalism in a highly rarefied form but we do get it.

But how can a radical—hence also critical—attitude of mind be imputed to a social group whose members were bound to obey the dictates of a supreme and absolute authority? This apparent paradox is easily resolved. The lives and the faith of the monks and friars were indeed subject to authority that was, in theory at least, absolute and spoke immutable truth. But beyond the sphere of discipline and fundamental religious belief—beyond the matters that were *de fide*—that authority did not undertake to direct their thought, nor did it prescribe results.[1] In particular, it had not, in general, any motive for doing so in the department of political and economic thought, that is to say, for compelling the clerical intellectuals to expound and defend or to represent as immutable any given temporal order of things. The Church was *judge* of all things human; conflict with temporal authority was an ever-present possibility and very often the actual fact; the monastic orders were important instruments of Papal authority: these were no reasons for preventing them from looking upon temporal institutions as historically mutable works of man. I am far from wishing to belittle the importance of Christian ideals and precepts per se. But we need not invoke them in order to realize that monastic subordination to authority in matters of faith and discipline was compatible with extensive freedom of opinion in all other matters. We must go even further. Not only did the monks' sociological location—outside, as it were, of the class

[1] Facts that apparently contradict this statement will be discussed later on.

structure—make for an attitude of detached criticism of many things; there also was a power behind them that was in a position to protect that freedom. So far as treatment of political and economic problems is concerned, the clerical intellectual of that age was not more but less exposed to interference from political authority and from 'pressure groups' than was the laical intellectual of later ages.

The indictment that unquestioning acceptance of ecclesiastic authority invalidated the reasoning of those monastic scholars from a scientific standpoint is thus seen to be without foundation. We have, however, still to consider a particular form of it. The analytic nature of their reasoning has often been denied on the ground that their arguments can have been only arguments from authority: subject to the authority of the Pope as they were, they had no other method left of establishing or refuting a proposition than to adduce for or against it literary authorities recognized by that supreme authority. But this is not so. The point can be cleared up by a reference to St. Thomas. He taught indeed that authority was of decisive importance in matters involving Revelation—namely, the authority of those to whom the revelations had been made—but he also taught that in everything else (and this includes, of course, the whole field of economics) any argument from authority was 'extremely weak.' [2]

With the monopoly of learning went the monopoly of 'higher' teaching. In the schools that were founded from the seventh century on, by temporal and spiritual lords, it was clerics who taught the tatters of Graeco-Roman science as well as theology and philosophical doctrines of their own—great teachers like Abelard attracted students and caused, occasionally, a lot of trouble for the controlling authorities. In some cases from these schools, in others independently, the self-governing 'universities' developed in the twelfth and thirteenth centuries—incorporated associations [3] of either teachers, as in Paris, or students, as in Bologna, who before long grouped themselves into theological, philosophical, legal, and medical 'faculties.' At first, princes and bishops had no more to do with them than what was implied in the granting of corporative privileges and in religious supervision. Accordingly, the universities enjoyed a large measure of freedom and independence; they gave more scope to the individual teacher than do the mechanized universities of today; they were a meeting ground of all classes of society; and they were essentially international. But from the fourteenth century on, government foundations became increasingly frequent. Governments also acquired control of previously independent institutions. Eventually, this changed everything. Government influence not

[2] 'Nam licet locus ab auctoritate quae fundatur super ratione humana, sit infirmissimus . . . ,' *Summa* I, quaest. I, art. 8, *ad secundum*. Of course, the scholastics all quoted copiously, but so do we. They deferred to authority—where they agreed with it—more than we do because they emphasized co-operative rather than individual opinion and attached great importance to continuity of doctrine. But this is all.

[3] *Universitas* originally meant nothing but corporation. Many people enrolled merely for the sake of the legal privileges that membership in such a self-governing corporation entailed. The meaning of *universitas litterarum*, which we attach to the term University, is of later origin.

only made for the assertion of purely utilitarian aims but also for restriction of freedom, particularly, of course, in matters of political doctrine. But, precisely because of the power that stood behind the clerical teachers, the universities held their own fairly well until the religious split in the sixteenth century.

The opportunities offered by the universities naturally reinforced the old tendency of scholars to become teachers. And since the public was then as prone as it is now to overemphasize the teaching at the expense of the production of what is being taught, medieval men of science were and are usually referred to as Schoolmen or Scholastics (*doctores scholastici*). In order to disabuse himself of prevailing preconceptions, the reader had better see in these scholastic doctors simply college or university professors. St. Thomas, then, was a professor. His *Summa Theologica* was, as he informs us in the preface, conceived as a textbook for beginners (*incipientes*).

3. Scholasticism and Capitalism

The processes that eventually shattered the social world of St. Thomas Aquinas are usually summed up in the phrase Rise of Capitalism. Though infinitely complex, they yet admit of a description in terms of a few broad generalizations that are not too hopelessly wrong. Also, though there was of course no break anywhere, it is possible to date developments at least by centuries. Capitalist enterprise had not been absent before, but from the thirteenth century on it slowly began to attack the framework of feudal institutions that had for ages fettered but also sheltered the farmer and the artisan, and to evolve the contours of the economic pattern that still is, or until quite recently was, our own. By the end of the fifteenth century most of the phenomena that we are in the habit of associating with that vague word Capitalism had put in their appearance, including big business, stock and commodity speculation, and 'high finance,' to all of which people reacted much as we do ourselves.[1] Even then these phenomena were not all of them new. Truly unprecedented was only their absolute and relative importance.

The growth of capitalist enterprise, however, created not only new economic patterns and problems but also a new attitude toward all problems. The rise of the commercial, financial, and industrial bourgeoisie of course altered the structure of European society and in consequence its spirit or, if you prefer, its civilization. The most obvious point about this is that the bourgeoisie acquired power to assert its interests. Here was a class that saw business facts in a

[1] Owing to the importance of the financial complement of capitalist production and trade, the development of the law and the practice of negotiable paper and of 'created' deposits afford perhaps the best indication we can have for dating the rise of capitalism. Around the Mediterranean both emerged in the course of the fourteenth century, though negotiability was not fully established before the sixteenth. See A. P. Usher, *The Early History of Deposit Banking in Mediterranean Europe* (1943), and R. de Roover, 'Money, Banking, and Credit in Medieval Bruges,' *Journal of Economic History*, Supplement, December 1942.

different light and from a different angle; a class, in short, that was *in* business, and therefore could never look at its problems with the aloofness of the schoolman. But this point is second in importance to another. As we have seen in the first part of this book, it is more essential to realize that quite irrespective of the assertion of his *interests*, the businessman, as his weight in the social structure increased, imparted to society an increasing dose of his *mind*, just as the knight had done before him. The particular mental habits generated by the work in the business office, the schema of values that emanates from it, and the attitude to public and private life that is characteristic of it, slowly spread in *all* classes and over *all* fields of human thought and action. Results burst forth in the epoch of cultural transformation that has been so curiously misnamed Renaissance.[2]

One of the most important of these results was the emergence of the laical intellectual,[3] and hence of laical science. We may distinguish developments of three different kinds. First, there always had been laical physicians and lawyers; but in the Renaissance they began to crowd out the clerical element. Second, starting from their professional needs and problems, laical artists and craftsmen —there was really no sociological distinction between them—began to develop a fund of tooled knowledge (for example, in anatomy, perspective, mechanics) that was an important source of modern science but grew up outside of scholastic university science: such a figure as Leonardo da Vinci will illustrate this point; and the figure of Galileo will illustrate another point, namely, how this kind of development produced the laical physicist. It had its analogue in economics; the businessman and civil servant, also starting like the artist-craftsman from his practical needs and problems, began to develop a fund of economic knowledge which will be surveyed in the next chapter. Third, there were the Humanists. Professionally, these were classical scholars. Their scientific work consisted in the critical editing, translation, and interpretation of the Greek and Latin texts that became available in the fifteenth and

[2] The 'revival' of the interest in the thought and art of ancient Greece and Rome was so powerful a factor in the intellectual life of those times only because ancient forms provided convenient vessels for new needs and meanings. The real cultural achievement of that period did not consist in reconditioning old heirlooms.

[3] The word 'laical' has been chosen after some hesitation. 'Secular' would not do because it derives another connotation from the distinction: secular clergy—regular clergy. 'Laymen's science' conflicts with our use of the term layman (a man not trained in scientific method). 'Laicist' conveys the idea of an antagonism to the Church (cf., for instance, the phrases 'laicist state' or 'laicism'). So 'laical' will have to serve in order to denote people or any activity (scientific or propagandist) of people who are not in holy orders. The noun shall be 'laics.' There is a more serious difficulty, however. On the one hand, the educational system of the Catholic Church proved so strong that many laical intellectuals continued to be shaped by it. Many of them retained habits of mind that did not differ essentially from those of the intellectuals in holy orders. On the other hand, an increasing number of the latter renounced allegiance to the scholastic system of thought as completely as any laic could have done: Erasmus of Rotterdam (1467-1536) affords an early instance. Our distinction though based upon a real difference is therefore not an easy one to handle. It is not simply a question of the cloth.

sixteenth centuries. But they loved to believe that a command of Greek and Latin would make a man competent in everything; and this together with their social location—also outside of the scholastic universities—turned these critics of texts into critics of men, manners, beliefs, and institutions, as well as into all-round *littérateurs*. They did not, however, contribute to technical economics. For us they are important only so far as they influenced the general intellectual atmosphere of their age.

The Catholic Church had little reason to object to the laical physician or lawyer as such and actually did not object to them; it was the most liberal patron of the artist-craftsman, whose art in fact remained primarily religious for a long time to come; it employed humanists in the Papal chancery and elsewhere, and the Renaissance Popes and Cardinals, some of whom were distinguished humanists themselves, invariably encouraged humanistic studies. The conflict that arose nevertheless is therefore a problem. And diagnosis of its nature is not facilitated by painting the picture all in black and white. There is little if anything to the saga of a new light that had flashed upon the world and was bitterly fought by the powers of darkness, or of a new spirit of free inquiry that the henchmen of hidebound authoritarianism vainly tried to smother. Nor is our understanding of the conflict helped by mixing it up with the related but quite different phenomenon of the Reformation—the intellectual revolution and the religious revolution reinforced each other but their sources are not the same; they do not stand to each other in any simple relation of cause and effect.

There was no such thing as a New Spirit of Capitalism in the sense that people would have had to acquire a new way of thinking in order to be able to transform a feudal economic world into a wholly different capitalist one. So soon as we realize that pure Feudalism and pure Capitalism are equally unrealistic creations of our own mind, the problem of what it was that turned the one into the other vanishes completely.[4] The society of the feudal ages con-

[4] This problem is a typical instance of what may be termed Spurious Problems, that is to say, of those problems that the analyst himself creates by his own method of procedure. For purposes of abbreviated description, we construct abstract pictures of social 'systems' that we endow with a number of well-defined characteristics in order to contrast them sharply. This method of (logically) Ideal Types (discussed below) has, of course, its uses, though it inevitably involves distortion of the facts. But if, forgetting the methodological nature of these constructions, we put the 'ideal' Feudal Man face to face with the 'ideal' Capitalist Man, transition from the one to the other will present a problem that has, however, no counterpart in the sphere of historical fact. Unfortunately, Max Weber lent the weight of his great authority to a way of thinking that has no other basis than a misuse of the method of Ideal Types. Accordingly, he set out to find an explanation for a process which sufficient attention to historical detail renders self-explanatory. He found it in the New Spirit—i.e. a different attitude to life and its values—engendered by the Reformation (*The Protestant Ethic and the Spirit of Capitalism,* trans. by Talcott Parsons, 1930; see also, R. H. Tawney, *Religion and the Rise of Capitalism,* 1926, and, *contra,* H. M. Robertson, *Aspects of the Rise of Economic Individualism; a Criticism of Max Weber and His School,* 1933). The

tained all the germs of the society of the capitalist age. These germs developed by slow degrees, each step teaching its lesson and producing another increment of capitalist methods and of capitalist 'spirit.' Similarly, there was no such thing as a New Spirit of Free Inquiry whose emergence would call for explanation. The scholastic science of the Middle Ages contained all the germs of the laical science of the Renaissance. And these germs developed slowly but steadily within the system of scholastic thought so that the laics of the sixteenth and seventeenth centuries continued rather than destroyed scholastic work. This applies even where it is most persistently denied. Even in the thirteenth century Albertus Magnus observed, Roger Bacon experimented and invented—he also insisted upon the need for more powerful mathematical methods—while Jordanus the Nemore theorized in an entirely 'modern' spirit.[5] Even the heliocentric system of astronomy was not simply a bomb thrown at the scholastic fortress from outside. It originated in the fortress. Nicolaus Cusanus (1401-64) was a cardinal. And Copernicus himself was a canon (though he did not actually take orders), a doctor of canon law, lived all his life in church circles, and Clement VII approved of his work and wished to see it published.[6]

---

historical objections to this construction are too obvious to detain us. Much more important is it to see the fundamental methodological error involved.

[5] See, e.g., Pierre Duhem's *Les Sources des théories physiques* (1905) and *Les Origines de la statique* (1905-6); also *Études sur Léonard da Vinci* (1906-13).

[6] The subsequent struggle about the Copernican system of astronomy should be briefly noticed, both in order to display the element of truth in the traditional saga and in order to reduce it to its true dimensions. Nicolas Copernicus (1473-1543) completed his manuscript in or about 1530. For decades his idea spread quietly without let or hindrance. It met indeed with opposition and even ridicule from professors who continued to hold on to the Ptolemaic system, but this is only what we should expect in the case of a new departure of such importance. It was this ridicule and not the Inquisition that Galileo feared when, toward the end of the sixteenth century, he became a convinced adherent of Copernicus' theory. The execution (1600) by the Inquisition of another adherent of it, Giordano Bruno, is no proof to the contrary because he also held purely theological views of a heretical nature and, moreover, frankly expressed contempt for the Christian faith. But when Galileo finally decided to come out in support of it (1613 and 1632), the theory was indeed declared heretical by a group of theological advisers of the Inquisition—not, however, by Cardinal Bellarmine—and he was forbidden to hold or teach it; when he failed to keep his promise to submit, he was forced to abjure it and was imprisoned for a fortnight. The point is not only that in this case a purely physical theory was considered theologically obnoxious and that its scientific sponsor was made to suffer for it but also that such an occurrence was an ever-present possibility in an age that interpreted scripture more or less literally. This is the element of truth in the saga. But it is clear that the case was quite exceptional; for the bulk of scientific work, that possibility hardly existed at all. Moreover, Galileo's case was complicated by his impulsiveness and his unfortunate talent for personally antagonizing people who were in a position to make their resentment felt. The case of Copernicus himself, and indeed the whole history of the fortunes of his theory up to 1613, suggest that more tactful handling of the matter might have avoided prosecution.

Nor is this at all surprising because, as we have seen, the authority of the Church was not the absolute bar to free research that it has been made out to be. The prevalent impression to the contrary is due to the fact that until recently the world has been content to accept the testimony of the enemies of the Church, which was inspired by unreasoning hatred and unduly dramatized individual events. During the last twenty years or so a more impartial opinion has been gaining ground. This is fortunate for us because it makes it much easier to appreciate scholastic scientific performance in our field.

If, then, we remove a coating of partisan colors, the true picture of the conflict appears without further difficulty. It was primarily political in nature. The laical intellectuals, Catholics no less than Protestants, were often opposed to the Church as a political power, and political opposition against a church very easily turns into heresy. It was this spirit of political opposition and the incidental danger of heresy that the Church sensed—sometimes wrongly, more often rightly—in the works of the laical intellectuals and which made it react even to writings that had nothing to do with either church government or religion and would have passed unnoticed had they been published by a cleric of whose political and religious allegiance the Church was sure. There was, however, another point of limited but, for us, considerable importance. It would seem that the scientific profession does not always absorb novelties with alacrity. Moreover, professors are men who are constitutionally unable to conceive that the other fellow might be right. This holds for all times and places. In Galileo's day, however, the universities were in the hands of monastic orders, except in the countries that had become or were becoming Protestant. These orders welcomed novices and readily opened the scientific career to them. But they did not welcome the scientific work of people who did not want to join them: hence a conflict of interest between two groups of intellectuals that stood in each other's way. And professional resentment against a scientific opponent, of which all ages afford amusing examples, sometimes acquired a connotation that was not amusing under circumstances in which the universities, though they had not always the ear of the Pope, always had the ear of the Inquisition. But this does not mean that those professors themselves did nothing but rehearse Aristotelian texts.

4. Scholastic Sociology and Economics [1]

St. Thomas divided the field of tooled knowledge into the sciences that work by the light of human reason only (*philosophicae disciplinae*), including Natural Theology (*illa theologia quae pars philosophiae ponitur*), and Supernatural Theology (*sacra doctrina*). The latter was also a science but a science

[1] During the last half-century, research in medieval economic conditions and processes has grown to proportions that are unmanageable for anyone but the specialist. This literature contains frequent references to economic thought or even analysis, which are, however, made in a spirit and from a standpoint that render them almost useless for our purpose. By far the most serviceable work of this kind that I know, outdated but excellent in its way, is W. J. Ashley's *Introduction to English Economic History and*

sui generis by virtue of the fact that, unlike all other sciences, it makes use not only of human reason but also of revelation. (*Summa* I, quaest. I.) [2] In this schema which seems to have been generally accepted, sociology and economics had no separate compartments of their own. At first, they formed parts of moral theology or ethics, which was itself a part of both supernatural and natural theology. Later on, especially in the sixteenth century, sociological and economic topics were treated within the system of scholastic jurisprudence. Individual questions, mainly about money and interest, were occasionally dealt with separately. So were political questions. But economics as a whole never was. For our purpose, it will be convenient to distinguish three periods in the historical evolution of scholastic thought, according to the degree to which economic problems received attention.

[(a) *From the Ninth Century to the End of the Twelfth.*] The earliest of our periods extends from the ninth century, in the course of which scholastic thought first gathered momentum, to the end of the twelfth. Apart from purely theological questions, it was mainly problems of the theory or philosophy of knowledge which attracted the thinkers of those times. So far as I am able to

---

Theory (1888 and 1893; especially Book I, ch. 3, and Book II, ch. 6). The standard work on scholastic economic *doctrine*, though marred by serious defects, is still W. Endemann's *Studien in der romanisch-kanonistischen Wirtschafts- und Rechtslehre* (1874 and 1883). Still older and still useful is G. A. L. Cibrario, *Dell'economia politica del Medioevo* (1839). V. Brants' *L'Économie politique au Moyen-Age. Esquisse des théories économiques professées par les écrivains des XIIIe et XIVe siècles* (1895) and H. Pirenne's *Economic and Social History of Medieval Europe* (English trans. 1936), taken together, complement Ashley's history for the Continent. J. W. Thompson's *Economic and Social History of the Middle Ages* (300-1300) and (1300-1530) [1928 and 1931] does the same. Also see: G. A. T. O'Brien, *An Essay on Mediaeval Economic Teaching* (1920); E. Schreiber, *Die volkswirtschaftlichen Anschauungen der Scholastik . . .* (1913); M. Beer, *Early British Economics from the XIIIth to the Middle of the XVIIIth Century* (1938); H. Garnier, *L'Idée du juste prix* (1900); and B. Jarrett, *Social Theories of the Middle Ages* (1926); some other works will be mentioned later. For 'background' see especially M. de Wulf, *Histoire de la philosophie médiévale* (English trans. by Messenger, 1925-6) and, since the scholastic renaissance in our own day is a phenomenon nobody can afford to neglect, also his *Introduction à la philosophie néo-scolastique* (1904; English trans. by Coffey, 1907). I make no claims for this selection, except that it will suffice to start off further study.

[2] There are two points about this that deserve to be noticed. First, Aristotle defined each science by its subject. But St. Thomas realized that different sciences often deal with the same things (*de eisdem rebus*) and that it is not the subject but the cognitive process (*ratio cognoscibilis*) which identifies a science. Second, St. Thomas did not, of course, deny that Supernatural Theology also used logical procedure (I, quaest. I, art. 8). The real difference is in the source of the starting points (*principia*) which, like other sciences, it takes for granted. These are derived from revelation in the case of Supernatural Theology but in all other sciences, with the possible exception of the purely formal ones, they are derived either from other sciences or else from direct observation of facts. The latter proposition St. Thomas did not state explicitly. But it is clearly implied. If he had stated it explicitly, much misunderstanding of scholastic thought might have been avoided.

make out, no piece of reasoning that could be claimed for the province of economic *analysis* occurs in any of the works of such leaders as, to mention a few, Erigena, Abelard, St. Anselm, or John of Salisbury. Our program, therefore, debars us from considering their performance, though this will fatally limit our conception of the general stream of scholastic thought. But two things must be mentioned nevertheless. We shall call them (I) the Platonic streak and (II) the individualist streak.

I. In the slow and laborious task of intellectual reconstruction that had to be undertaken after centuries during which Europe had been ravaged by barbarian hordes, the remains of ancient learning naturally acquired paramount importance. Most of these remains were, however, not available before the twelfth century and much of the rest was beyond the scholars of the time or was available only in bad translations. Within the little stock, Platonic and Neo-Platonic influences predominated both directly and, through the mediation of St. Augustine's philosophy, indirectly. But Platonic influence will inevitably bring to the fore the problem of Platonic ideas, the problem of the nature of general concepts (*universalia*). Accordingly, the first and most famous of all scholastic discussions in pure philosophy was about this problem; and until the end of the fifteenth century it kept on flaring up again and again. We shall not wonder at this or accept it as proof positive of the sterility of scholastic thought. For it should be clear that this problem represents but a particular form of positing the general problem of pure philosophy. To say that the scholastics never ceased to discuss it therefore means no more than that, while interested in a great many other things, they never ceased to be interested in pure philosophy. On the whole, it may be averred that the 'realistic' view—the view according to which only ideas or concepts, as such, have real existence, and which is therefore the exact opposite of what *we* should call a realistic view—prevailed more or less until the fourteenth century when the battle turned in favor of the opposite, the 'nominalist,' view.[3] But Abelard's (1079-1142) compromise seems to have enjoyed a great, though varying, amount of popularity throughout: the ideas or universals exist independently of any individuals corresponding to them in the mind of God (*universalia* are *ante res*, in this sense); but they are embodied in individual things (*universalia* are therefore also *in rebus*); and the human

[3] It is important to keep in mind that, in scholastic times, schools of thought tended to be identified, and even to identify themselves, with individual monastic orders. The Franciscan order was, for example, a stronghold of nominalist philosophy. This phenomenon is readily understandable, and I do not think I need explain it. But there is need for emphasizing its importance, for it also shows in other matters: the reason why the late scholastics were so severe on the economics of Duns Scotus—a fact that is not easy to motivate—may perhaps be sought in the antagonism of orders, just as in later ages it is sometimes necessary to invoke the explanatory virtue of antagonisms between national groups of economists—a not unimportant piece of the sociology of science.

mind gets a glimpse of them only by observation and abstraction (in which sense they are *post res*).

This controversy was purely epistemological in nature and has no bearing whatever upon the practice of economic or any other analysis. But it had to be mentioned because, in our own time, the Realism and Nominalism of the scholastic doctors have been linked with two other concepts, Universalism and Individualism, which are held by some writers to be relevant to analytic practice. These writers went so far as to represent Universalism and Individualism as two fundamentally different views of social processes, the conflict between which runs through the whole history of sociological and economic analysis and is indeed the essential fact behind all the other clashes of opinion that occurred throughout the ages.[4] Whatever argument it may be possible to adduce for this doctrine from the standpoint of economic thought or, conceivably, also from the standpoint of a philosophical interpretation of analytic procedures, there is nothing in it that concerns these analytic procedures themselves: the rest of the book will establish this point. Just now we are interested merely in showing that Universalism and Individualism have nothing to do with scholastic Realism and Nominalism. Universalism as opposed to Individualism means that 'social collectives,' such as society, nation, church, and the like, are conceptually prior to their individual members; that the former are the really relevant entities with which the social sciences have to deal; that the latter are but the products of the former; hence that analysis must work from the collectives and not from individual behavior. If, then, we choose to call these collectives sociological universals, then the doctrine in question may indeed be said to oppose universals to individuals. But scholastic Realism opposed universals to individuals in quite a different sense. If I were to adopt scholastic Realism, then my idea of, say, society would claim logical precedence over any individual empirical *society* that I observe but not over individual *men;* the idea of these men would be another universal in the scholastic sense, claiming logical precedence over the empirical indi-

[4] The doctrine of Universalism is usually associated with O. Spann, who is in fact responsible for its success in Germany (for his and his group's publications, see *Encyclopaedia of the Social Sciences*, 'Economics, Romantic and Universalist Economics'). But it is really due to K. Pribram (e.g. Die Entstehung der individualistischen Sozialphilosophie, 1912), who also linked Universalism with scholastic Realism, and Individualism with scholastic Nominalism. I do not hold that the categories Universalist-Individualist are useless for purposes other than ours. Important aspects of economic thought, particularly in its ethico-religious aspects, can perhaps be described by means of them. And the term Universalist is better than the term Socialist, which has acquired a more restricted meaning. Objection is raised only to the improper extension of the field of application of these concepts, which is precisely due to failure to distinguish between economic thought and economic analysis. It is this failure to recognize the epistemological barrier between these two which is to be blamed for the talk about universalist *methods* and even a universal *science* that can only produce confusion.

viduals. Manifestly, this would imply nothing about either the relation between the two scholastic universals or the relation between any empirical society (a universal in the sense of universalist doctrine) and the empirical individuals comprising it. In particular, I could in this case still be as strong an individualist, politically or in any other sense, as I please. The opposite opinion is thus seen to rest on nothing but an error induced by the double meaning attached to 'universal' and 'individual.'[5]

II. In surveying the history of civilizations, we sometimes speak of objective and subjective cases. By an objective civilization we mean the civilization of a society in which every individual stands in his appointed *niche* and is subject, without reference to his tastes, to superindividual rules; a society that recognizes as universally binding a given ethical and religious code; a society in which art is standardized and all creative activity both expresses and serves superindividual ideals. By a subjective civilization we mean a civilization that displays the opposite characteristics; in which society serves the individual and not the other way round; in short, a society that turns upon, and implements, subjective tastes and allows everyone to build his own system of cultural values. We need not enter into the general question of the analytic standing of such schemes. But we are concerned with the sweeping assertion so often met with that, in the sense explained, medieval civilization was objective and modern civilization is (or until recently was) subjective or individualist, because this touches, or may be supposed to touch, upon the 'spirit' in which people conducted or conduct their economic analysis. There cannot be any doubt that some of the characteristics fit—religious life in the age of 'One God, One Church,' as compared to religious life in the age of hundreds of denominations, is the standard example. But neither can there be any doubt that as a whole those abstract pictures are ludicrously inadequate. Is it possible to imagine a fiercer individualist than a knight? Did not the whole trouble that medieval civilization experienced with military and political management (and which largely accounts for its failures) arise precisely from this fact? And is the member of a modern labor union or the mechanized farmer of today really so much more of an individualist than was the medieval member of a craft guild or the medieval peasant? Therefore, the reader should not be shocked to learn that the individualist streak in medieval thought also was much stronger than is commonly supposed. This is true, both in the sense that opinion was much more differentiated individually and in the sense that the individual phenomenon and (in speculations about society) the individual man were much more carefully attended to than we are apt to think. Scholastic sociology and economics, in particular, are strictly individualist, if we understand this to mean that the doctors, so far as they aimed at description and explanation of economic facts, started invariably from the indi-

[5] By the same token, we must not label Abelard as individualist on the ground that he seems to have coined the phrase: *nihil est praeter individuum.*

vidual's tastes and behavior. That they applied superindividual canons of justice to these facts is not relevant to the logical nature of their analysis; but even these canons were derived from a moral schema in which the individual was an end in himself and the central idea of which was the salvation of individual souls.

[(b) *The Thirteenth Century.*] Our second period, speaking roughly, covers the thirteenth century. There is justification for calling it the classic period of scholasticism so far as theology and philosophy are concerned. Theological and philosophical thought was indeed not only revolutionized but also consolidated into a new system that was all that the term Classic implies. Chiefly, this revolution was the work of Grosseteste, Alexander of Hales, St. Bonaventura, and Duns Scotus (Franciscan school) on the one hand, and of Albertus Magnus and his disciple, St. Thomas (Dominican school), on the other. The consolidation, that is, the creation of the classic system, was the towering achievement of St. Thomas alone. But in other respects, there was only revolution and no consolidation. That century, indeed, gave birth to scholastic science as distinguished from theology and philosophy; it produced work that initiated and laid the foundations for further work, but it did not establish anything beyond starting points. This holds for the social as well as for the physical sciences. It should be particularly noticed that, as the example of Grosseteste shows, interest in mathematical and physical research was widespread even among men who did no such research themselves. Roger Bacon was a peak, but not a solitary peak; and plenty of men, without and within the Franciscan order, stood ready to go on in his line of advance. The reason why this does not stand out as it should is that the scholastic physicists and mathematicians of the subsequent four centuries tended to become specialists in their particular fields and their scholastic background is easily lost from sight. For instance, we look upon Francesco Cavalieri (1598-1647) simply as a great mathematician. It does not occur to us to associate the origins of the integral calculus with scholasticism in general or with the Jesuit order in particular, though as a matter of fact Cavalieri was the product of both.[6]

In itself, that theologico-philosophical revolution is no concern of ours. But one aspect of it is of considerable importance for the history of sociological and economic analysis, namely, the resurrection of Aristotelian thought. During the twelfth century more complete knowledge of Aristotle's writings filtered slowly into the intellectual world of western Christianity, partly through Semite mediation, Arab and Jewish.[7] To the scholastic doctors this meant two

[6] Roger Bacon (1214?-92), the *doctor mirabilis* of scholastic tradition, affords another case that illustrates the nature and the causes of the troubles that were experienced by some eminent physicists. He was still more aggressive than was Galileo 400 years later. In all ages people react unfavorably to being called fools. In rough ages they react roughly.

[7] Avicenna (Ibn Sina, 980-1037), the Arab physician-philosopher, and Averroës (Ibn Rushd, 1126-98), the lawyer-philosopher of Cordoba, and Moses Maimonides (1135-1204) the Hebrew theologian-philosopher (especially his *Guide of the Perplexed*, Eng-

things. First, Arab mediation meant Arab interpretation, which was unacceptable to them in some matters of epistemology as well as of theology. Second, access to Aristotle's thought immensely facilitated the gigantic task before them not only in metaphysics, where they had to break new paths, but also in the physical and social sciences, where they had to start from little or nothing.

The reader will observe that I do not assign to the recovery of Aristotle's writings the role of chief *cause* of thirteenth-century developments. Such developments are never induced solely by an influence from outside. Aristotle came in, as a powerful ally, to help and to provide implements. But perception of the task and the will to rush forward were, of course, there independently of him. An analogy will clear up this point. We have had occasion to refer to the partial adoption or 'reception' of the *Corpus juris civilis* in the later Middle Ages and the Renaissance. This phenomenon cannot be causally explained by a lucky discovery of a few old volumes coupled with the naïve belief of uncritical minds that these volumes contained legal material that was still in force. The economic process was evolving patterns of life that called for legal forms, especially for a system of contracts, of the type that the Roman jurists had worked out. There can be no doubt but that the lawyers of the Middle Ages would have eventually worked out similar forms for themselves. The Roman law came in usefully, not because it brought something that was foreign to the spirit and needs of the age—so far as it did this, its reception was in fact an unmitigated nuisance—but precisely because it presented, ready made, what without it would have had to be produced laboriously. Similarly, the 'reception' of Aristotle's teaching was principally a most important time- and labor-saving device, particularly in those fields that were as yet waste lands. It is in this light—and not in the light of the theory that there was passive acceptance of a lucky discovery—that we must see the relation between Aristotelism and scholasticism.

But so soon as the scholastic doctors realized that in Aristotle's writings they had all, or nearly all, they could hope for at the moment and that with the help of his doctrines they might accomplish what it would have cost them a century's work to do by themselves, they naturally made the most of this opportunity. Aristotle became for them *the* philosopher, the universal teacher, and most of their work took the form of expounding him to students and to the public at large, and of commenting upon him. Moreover, his writings served admirably for didactic purposes since they were in fact summarizing and systematizing textbooks. In consequence, it was in the role of expounders of, and commentators on, Aristotelian doctrine that Grosseteste, Albertus Magnus,

lish trans. by Friedländer, 1881-5) should be mentioned in this connection. The problem of reconciling Aristotle's teaching with Hebrew theology presented itself to Maimonides in much the same manner as the analogous problem presented itself to the Christian doctors.

and the other leaders mentioned above appeared to the public of their own and of later times. St. Thomas himself became, for many people, simply the man who had succeeded in harnessing Aristotle for the service of the Church. This misconception of the revolution of the thirteenth century and, in particular, of St. Thomas' performance was not corrected but, on the contrary, was fostered by the scientific practice of the next 300 years. For Aristotle's work continued to provide the systematic frame for the growing scientific material and to supply the need for nicely pedestrian texts; everything, therefore, continued to be cast in the Aristotelian mold—nothing so completely as scholastic economics, which also illustrates the way in which, by this convenient practice, the scholastic doctors were likely to lose the credit for their original contributions.

This explains not only the otherwise quite incomprehensible success of Aristotelian teaching through these 300 years but also the penalty the ancient sage was eventually to pay for this success. We may just as well complete the story which is so full of interest to the student of the tortuous ways of the human mind. We have seen that there was nothing in the scholastic system to bar new developments within it or even developments away from the ground taken by its classic works. Descartes' philosophy may exemplify such a development.[8] He displayed no hostility to the old scholastic philosophy and, among other things, accepted St. Anselm's proof of the existence of God—rejected by St. Thomas—as the basis of his own theory of the *cogito*. There is plenty of room for doubt as to how much this amounts to. But it certainly suffices for speaking of peaceful evolution from scholastic backgrounds. We have also seen, however, that scholasticism became a bugbear, as the influence of laical intellectuals asserted itself. And wherever hostility to scholasticism asserted itself, hostility to Aristotle asserted itself also: because Aristotelism was the vessel of scholastic thought, hostility to Aristotelism became the vessel of hostility to the doctors. There were even anti-scholastic and anti-Aristotelian scholastics of whom Gassendi is the outstanding example.[9] His mathematical and physical work, entirely neutral in itself, acquired a critical connotation by the way in which he advocated the cause of experimental—'empiricist' or 'inductive'—methods rather than by this advocacy as such. In philosophy he replaced the Aristotelian basis (substantially) by one essentially Epicurean. However, it was of course among the laical enemies of the Catholic doctors that it became the fashion to represent Aristotle

[8] René Descartes (1596-1650). For the purpose in hand, only his *Essais philosophiques* (1637) is relevant. He was the mediator between medieval and modern philosophy, and was the product of Jesuit education.

[9] Pierre Gassendi (1592-1655) was a philosopher, mathematician, and physicist, a professor in holy orders whom, on his actual work, nobody would think of excluding from the scholastic circle. But he went out of his way to distance himself from it. Of his works those most important for us are: *Exercitationes paradoxicae adversus Aristoteleos* (1624); *Syntagma philosophiae Epicuri*, 1649 (works ed. by Montmort, 1658); see also G. S. Brett, *The Philosophy of Gassendi* (1908).

as the incarnation of old dust and of futility. Paracelsus had Aristotelian books solemnly burned before starting his medical lectures; Galileo, in the famous dialogue on the heliocentric system that gave so much offense, made a comic figure of the inept Aristotelian objector; Francis Bacon, in espousing the cause of 'inductive' science, contrasted it with both scholastic and Aristotelian speculation. All this was unfair to the scholastic doctors. But it was still more unfair to the old sage. For if there is any general message at all that speaks to us from his pages, it is surely the message of empirical research.[10] So true is it that, in science as elsewhere, we fight for and against not men and things as they are, but for and against the caricatures we make of them.[11] However, let us return to the classic period, the thirteenth century, in order to search for elements of sociological and economic analysis.

We find small beginnings only—little of sociology, still less of economics. In part this was doubtless due to lack of interest. St. Thomas, in particular, was indeed interested in political sociology but all the economic questions put together mattered less to him than did the smallest point of theological or philosophical doctrine, and it is only where economic phenomena raise questions of moral theology that he touches upon them at all. Even where he does we do not feel, as we do elsewhere, that his powerful intellect is all there, passionately resolved to penetrate into the core of things but rather that he is writing in obedience to the requirements of systematic completeness. More or less, this applies to all his contemporaries. In consequence, Aristotle's teaching sufficed for them and they hardly ever went beyond it. There was indeed a difference in moral tone and cultural vision and also a shift of emphasis that is accounted for by the different social patterns they beheld. But neither is so important as we might have expected. Since these things are of no great moment in a history of economic analysis, it will suffice to note that the scholastic doctors looked upon physical labor as a discipline favorable to Christian virtue and as a means of keeping men from sinning,

[10] Theophrastus Bombastus von Hohenheim, who called himself Paracelsus (1490?-1541), was a physician and chemist of eminence though not without an element of charlatanism. Francis Bacon (1561-1626; works ed. by Spedding, Ellis, and Heath, 1857-62) presumably needs no introduction. The tremendous success of his writings—not so much in his day but during the Enlightenment and then during the nineteenth century—is amply accounted for by the fact that he expressed with supreme ability what a rapidly increasing number of people actually came to believe. He was the very type of a 'representative man.' But precisely because he was and because in consequence his figure stands out so clearly, his ideas now seem much more novel and much less in keeping with previous developments than they were. Therefore, his writings inculcated into the public mind the unreal contraposition of inductive research and scholasticism in which, along with his contemporaries, he himself was so fond of believing, the more so because he probably knew very little about the work of the scholastics. More than any other individual, he helped to foster the delusion that to this day distorts the history of thought.

[11] Outstanding examples from the history of economics are A. Smith's criticism of the 'mercantilists' and Schmoller's criticism of the English 'classics.' Both cases will be discussed in their places.

which implies an attitude entirely unlike that of Aristotle; that with them slavery was no longer a normal, let alone fundamental, institution; that they gave their blessings to charity and to voluntary poverty; that their ideal of a *vita contemplativa* carried, of course, a meaning that was quite foreign to Aristotle's corresponding ideal of life, though there are important similarities between the two; that they repeated but qualified Aristotle's views on commerce and commercial gain.

While all the other points apply to scholastic doctrine of all ages, the one mentioned last holds fully only for the classic period. After the thirteenth century a significant change occurred in the attitude of the scholastic doctors to commercial activity. But the thirteenth-century scholastics undoubtedly held the opinion expressed by St. Thomas, namely, that there is 'something base' about commerce in itself (*negotiatio secundum se considerata quandam turpitudinem habet, Summa* II, 2, quaest. LXXVII, art. 4), though commercial gain might be justified (a) by the necessity of making one's living; or (b) by a wish to acquire means for charitable purposes; or (c) by a wish to serve *publicam utilitatem*, provided that the lucre be moderate and can be considered as a reward of work (*stipendium laboris*); or (d) by an improvement of the thing traded; or (e) by intertemporal or interlocal differences in its value; or (f) by risk (*propter periculum*). St. Thomas' wording leaves some room for doubt about the conditions in which he was prepared to admit considerations (d)-(f), and it may be true that others, especially Duns Scotus (1266-1308) and a doctor whom I have not mentioned so far, Richard of Middleton (1249-1306), went somewhat further, especially as regards justifying the social usefulness of the practice of buying in a cheaper market and selling in a dearer one. However, even qualifications (b) and (c) go beyond Aristotle's teaching. The emphasis all these authors place upon the element of remuneration of some socially useful activity has given rise, on the one hand, to the opinion, which may be correct, that the source of the (moral) 'right to the produce of one's labor' may be found in the scholastic literature, and, on the other hand, to the error that the scholastic doctors held a (analytic) labor theory of value, that is, that they *explained* the phenomenon of value by the fact that (most) commodities cost labor. For the moment, the reader should only notice that there is no logical relation between mere emphasis upon the necessity, moral or economic, of remunerating *labor* (no matter whether we translate the Latin word by the English 'labor' or by 'activity' or 'effort' or 'trouble') and what is technically known as the labor theory of value.

St. Thomas' sociology of institutions,[12] political and other, is not what readers will expect who are in the habit of tracing the political and social doctrines of the nineteenth century to Locke or to the writers of the French Enlightenment or to the English utilitarians. Considering that, in this respect, the teaching of St. Thomas not only was representative of that of his contemporaries but also was accepted by all the scholastic doctors of later times, its main points should be briefly indicated. There was the sacred precinct of the Catholic Church. But for the rest, society was treated as a thoroughly human affair, and moreover, as a mere agglomeration of individuals brought

[12] Our main source for St. Thomas' political sociology is a tract entitled *De regimine principum*, widely used throughout the Middle Ages, and a letter to a Duchess of Brabant. But only part of the former is certainly by St. Thomas himself; the rest may be the work of another Dominican, Ptolemy of Lucca (d. 1327).

together by their mundane needs. Government, too, was thought of as arising from and existing for nothing but those utilitarian purposes that the individuals cannot realize without such an organization. Its *raison d'être* was the Public Good. The ruler's power was derived from the people, as we may say, by delegation. The people are the sovereign and an unworthy ruler may be deposed. Duns Scotus came still nearer to adopting a social-contract theory of the state.[13] This mixture of sociological analysis and normative argument is remarkably individualist, utilitarian, and (in a sense) rationalist, a fact that it is important to remember in view of the attempt we are going to make to link this body of ideas with the laical and anti-Catholic political philosophies of the eighteenth century. There is nothing metaphysical about this part of scholastic doctrine. Nor did the Catholic doctors countenance political authoritarianism. The divine right of monarchs, in particular, and the concept of the omnipotent state are creations of the Protestant sponsors of the absolutist tendencies that were to assert themselves in the national states.

The individualist and utilitarian streak and the emphasis upon a rationally perceived Public Good run through the whole sociology of St. Thomas. One example will suffice: the most important one, the theory of property. Having disposed of the theological aspects of the matter, St. Thomas simply argues that property is not against natural law but an invention of the human reason,[14] which is justifiable because people will take better care of what they possess for themselves than of what belongs to many or all; because they will exert themselves more strenuously on their own account than on account of others; because the social order will be better preserved if possessions are distinct, so that there is no occasion for quarreling about the use of things possessed in common—considerations that attempt to define the social 'function' of private property much as Aristotle had defined them before and much as the nineteenth-century textbook was to define them afterward. And since he

[13] This theory was not, of course, applied to the government of the Catholic Church. When this was done by Marsilius of Padua (*c.* 1270-1342; *Defensor pacis*, 1326), it spelled heresy. From our standpoint two observations suggest themselves: first, the case illustrates how implicit acceptance of supermundane authority in some respects may in practice be complemented by extreme freedom of thought and action in other respects; second, the case also shows why the question of the influence of supermundane authority upon analysis cannot be answered once for all, but must be answered separately for every individual argument. Since too much care cannot be expended on clearing up this point, let us, by way of supplementing previous argument, introduce the following tripartite distinction which applies to all authorities that ever did or do attempt to direct opinion. First, as the case in hand shows, there were matters in which the Catholic Church prescribed opinion and barred analysis that led to any other results. Second, there were many matters in which, being indifferent to both opinion and analysis, it did not interfere in any way. Third, there were matters (such as interest) in which it prescribed opinion in the sense of moral judgment but did not bar analysis of facts.

[14] *Summa* II, 2, quaest. LXVI, art. 2: *proprietas possessionum non est contra jus naturale, sed juri naturali superadditur per adinventionem rationis humanae*. On the meaning to be attached to *jus naturale*, see next section.

found in Aristotle all he wished to say, he referred to him and accepted his formulations.

This holds with added force for St. Thomas' 'pure economics' (*oeconomia* with him means, however, simply household management). It was embryonic and really consists of only part of his argument on Just Price (*Summa* II, 2, quaest. LXXVII, art. 1) and on Interest (*Summa* II, 2, quaest. LXXVIII). The relevant part of the argument on just price—the price that assures the 'equivalence' of commutative justice—is strictly Aristotelian and should be interpreted exactly as we have interpreted Aristotle's. St. Thomas was as far as was Aristotle from postulating the existence of a metaphysical or immutable 'objective value.' His *quantitas valoris* is not something different from price but is simply normal competitive price. The distinction he seems to make between price and value is not a distinction between price and some value that is not a price, but a distinction between the price paid *in an individual transaction* and the price that 'consists' in the public's evaluation of the commodity (*justum pretium . . . in quadam aestimatione consistit*), which can only mean normal competitive price, or value in the sense of normal competitive price, where such a price exists.[15] In cases where no such price exists, St. Thomas recognized, as coming within his concept of just price, the element of the subjective value of an object to the seller, though not the element of the subjective value of the object for the buyer—a point that is important for scholastic treatment of interest. Beyond this he did not go in the article referred to. But other passages, perhaps, support the opinion that, by implication at least, he did take a step beyond Aristotle which was more explicitly taken by Duns Scotus, Richard of Middleton, and possibly others. Duns Scotus, at all events, may be credited with having related just price to cost, that is, the producers' or traders' expenditure of money and effort (*expensae et labores*). Though he presumably thought of nothing beyond providing a more precise criterion of scholastic 'commutative justice'—which was rightly rejected by the later scholastics—we must nevertheless credit him with having discovered the condition of competitive equilibrium which came to be known in the nineteenth century as the Law of Cost. This is not imputing too much: for if we identify the just price of a good with its competitive common value, as Duns Scotus certainly did, and if we further equate that just price to the cost of the good (taking account of risk, as he did not fail to observe), then we have ipso facto, at least by implication, stated the law of cost not only as a normative but also as an analytic proposition.

Following Alexander of Hales and Albertus Magnus, St. Thomas condemned

[15] This interpretation is supported by the fact that the *quaestio*, in which the theory of just price is presented (quaest. LXXVII of II, 2) is entitled *De fraudulentia* and, in fact, mainly deals with frauds perpetrated by sellers. If the just price were something else than the normal competitive price, practices other than fraud would be more important. But if St. Thomas was thinking of what we call normal competitive price, fraud becomes the chief phenomenon to be dealt with. For if there exists a competitive market price, individual deviations from it are hardly possible except through fraudulent representations about the quantity and quality of the goods.

interest as contrary to commutative justice on a ground that proved a conundrum for almost all his scholastic successors: interest is a price paid for the use of money; but, viewed from the standpoint of the individual holder, money is consumed in the act of being used; therefore, like wine, it has no use that could be separated from its substance as has, for example, a house; therefore charging for its use is charging for something that does not exist, which is illegitimate (usurious). Whatever may be thought of this argument, which among other things neglects the possibility that 'pure' interest might be an element of the price of money itself—instead of being a charge for a separable use [16]—one thing is clear: exactly like the somewhat different Aristotelian argument, it does not bear at all upon the question why interest is actually paid. Since this question, the only one that is relevant to economic analysis, was actually raised by the later scholastics, we defer the consideration of the clues for an answer, which St. Thomas' reasoning nevertheless suggests.

[(c) *From the Fourteenth Century to the Seventeenth.*] The last of the three periods into which we have decided to divide the history of scholasticism extends from the beginning of the fourteenth century to the first decades of the seventeenth. It comprises practically the whole of the history of scholastic economics. But, having already fully explained the setting and the nature of scholastic work, we can now afford to be brief. In particular, no further explanation seems to be needed for the ease with which the economics of the doctors absorbed all the phenomena of nascent capitalism and, in consequence, for the fact that it served so well as a basis of the analytic work of their successors, not excluding A. Smith.

In order to achieve the maximum of economy, I shall mention only a very few representative names and then attempt to draw a systematic sketch of what I conceive the state of scholastic economics to have been about 1600. Other names, of course, would have to be mentioned for other purposes; we are artificially narrowing down what was a very broad and deep stream.

For the fourteenth century we choose Buridanus and Oresmius as representatives.[17] The latter's treatise on money is usually described as the first

[16] The reason why St. Thomas did not consider this possibility was obviously that he placed implicit confidence in the proposition that the price of any commodity that is chosen for the standard of value is unity by definition. Reasoning on from this, we may easily arrive at the conclusion that any 'pure' premium cannot be anything else but a fraudulent charge for a nonexistent use, since the price of the substance or 'capital' must necessarily be equal to the capital itself.

[17] Joannes Buridanus (Jean Buridan, fl. 1328-58), professor in the University of Paris. Of his many works, all drawn up on the Aristotelian frame, the most important for us are: *Quaestiones in decem libros Ethicorum Aristotelis* (ed. used, 1637) and *Quaestiones super octo libros Politocorum Aristotelis* (ed. used with notes by G. Baterel, 1513). His theory of volition (*Summula de dialectica*, 1487, and *Compendium logicae*, 1487) led up to the familiar paradox of the logic of choice that is illustrated by the perfectly rational ass that starves between two equally attractive bundles of hay owing to his inability to make up his mind which to consume first. Nicole Oresme (1320?-82), Bishop of Lisieux, was a man of polyhistoric interests who also wrote on theology, mathematics, and astronomy. The work in question, *Tractatus de origine et jure nec nor*

treatise entirely devoted to an economic problem. But it is mainly legal and political in nature and really does not contain much strictly economic material—in particular, nothing that was not current doctrine among the scholastics of the time—its chief purpose being to combat the prevalent practice of debasing money, a topic that was treated later on in a copious literature to be briefly noticed presently. Our fifteenth-century representatives will be St. Antonine of Florence, perhaps the first man to whom it is possible to ascribe a comprehensive vision of the economic process in all its major aspects, and Biel.[18] For the sixteenth century we select Mercado and, as representatives of the literature on Justice and Law (*De justitia et jure*) that in the sixteenth century became the main scholastic repository of economic material, the three great Jesuits whose works have been recently analyzed by Professor Dempsey—Lessius, Molina, and de Lugo.[19]

---

et de mutationibus monetarum, was written between 1350 and 1360 (ed. used 1605). An extract is included in Monroe's *Early Economic Thought*, pp. 79-102. After having met with great success in its own time, it seems to have falllen into oblivion from which it was rescued by F. Meunier, *Essai sur la vie et les ouvrages de Nicole Oresme* (1857) and especially by W. Roscher ('Ein grosser Nationalökonom des vierzehnten Jahrhunderts' in *Zeitschrift für die gesamte Staatswissenschaft*, 1863), who extolled its merits, particularly its originality, beyond all reason, as discoverers of forgotten worthies are apt to do—which naturally induced a reaction. There is quite a literature on Oresme. Let us single out C. A. Conigliani, *Le dottrine monetarie in Francia durante il medio evo* (1890).

18 St. Antonine (Antonio Pierozzi, also called Forciglioni; 1389-1459), Archbishop of Florence, *Summa theologica* (ed. used: for the first and second parts, Lyons, 1516; for the third, Venice, 1477); also *Summa moralis* (Verona, 1740). See B. Jarrett, *S. Antonino and Mediaeval Economics* (1914). Gabriel Biel (1425?-95), professor in the University of Tübingen, another discovery of Roscher's (*Geschichte der Nationalökonomik in Deutschland*, 1874). His *Tractatus de potestate et utilitate monetarum* (1541; English trans., 1930) does not, however, contain anything that cannot be found in earlier writers. Why he should have been called the last of the scholastics I am unable to understand. But I have chosen him for reference because perusal of his work is particularly effective in destroying prejudices concerning the spirit of scholasticism. Really more important seems to be Panormitanus (Nicolaus dei Tedeschi or Tudeschi, Archbishop of Palermo, 1386-1445) to judge from quotations in the later scholastic literature.

19 The choice was a difficult one and may give rise to valid objection particularly against the exclusion of such men as John Major (d. 1549; cf. the comments of Ashley in *Economic History* I, Part II), Navarrus (Martinus de Azpilcueta, d. 1586), Domingo de Soto (*De justicia et jure*, 1553), and Gaetanus (Cardinal Cajetan, Tommaso de Vio, 1468-1534) all of whom we shall have to mention, and others. Tomás de Mercado, author of *De los tratos de India y tratantes en ellas* (1569; enlarged ed. of 1571, the only one known to me, under the title *Summa de tratos y contratos*), has been included only because of his 'quantity theory of money' and cannot be put on the same level with Lessius, Molina, and de Lugo in any other respect. But I am positive that the latter three must be included in any history of economics, though there was a further motive for selecting them: Professor Dempsey's book (B. W. Dempsey, *Interest and Usury*, 1943, chs. VI-VIII) contains a full exposition of their economics; this book com-

All that need be said about the sociology of the later scholastics is that they developed, in greater detail and with a fuller perception of implications, the ideas that had crystallized in the works of their thirteenth-century predecessors. Their political sociology in particular retained the same method of approach to the phenomena of state and government and also the same 'radical' spirit.[20] Their economic sociology, especially their theory of property, continued to treat temporal institutions as utilitarian devices that were to be explained—or 'justified'—by considerations of social expedience centering in the concept of the Public Good. And this social expedience might, according to historical circumstances, sometimes tell in favor, and sometimes tell against, private property. They no doubt believed that in civilized societies, that is, in societies that were past the early or natural state in which all possessions were common to all (*omnia omnibus sunt communia*), these considerations told in favor of private property (*divisio rerum*); but there was neither a theoretical nor a moral principle to prevent them from arriving at the opposite result whenever new facts should suggest it.[21] Some methodological aspects of this will be dealt with in the next section. But another point should be briefly mentioned.

The scholastics were not primarily concerned with the problems of the national states and their power politics. This is precisely one of the most important links between them and the 'liberals' of the eighteenth and even the nineteenth centuries. But some of the phenomena that accompanied the rise of these states were, nevertheless, bound to attract their critical attention, and among them was fiscal policy. I mention this here, and not in connection with their economics, because they hardly went at all into the specifically economic problems of public finance, such as incidence of taxation, economic effects of government expenditure, and the like: even when they did discuss government borrowing (which, following the lead of St. Thomas, they mostly condemned) or the question of the relative merits of taxes on wealth and taxes on consumption (Molina, Lessius, and de Lugo, among others, touched upon

---

bines to a degree that is quite exceptional, thorough familiarity with scholastic thought and with economic theory, so that the interested reader may be referred to it with confidence. Lessius (Leonard de Leys, 1554-1623), Luis Molina (1535-1600), and de Lugo (Juan de Lugo, 1583-1660) all wrote treatises *de justitia et jure*. Our chief guide will be Molina. His treatise appeared in instalments in 1593, 1597, and in and after 1600; (ed. used *De justitia et jure*, 1659).

[20] Any doubt about this may be dispersed by a single reference: Juan de Mariana, *De rege et regis institutione*, 1599. But even scholastics who did not go so far never worshiped at the shrines of either absolute monarchs or omnipotent bureaucracies, see e.g., Molina, *Tractatus secundus, disp.* 22 and 26. The scholastic doctors, following their own earlier tradition, must therefore be considered as the most important of the 'monarchomachs' of the sixteenth century. On these, see especially J. W. Allen, *A History of Political Thought in the Sixteenth Century*, 1928.

[21] The reader will find a very characteristic quotation from Lessius in Dempsey's *Interest and Usury*, p. 132. It does not follow, of course, that Lessius, were he alive today, would embrace political communism. The point is that in good logic he would be *free* to arrive at the conclusion that private property no longer fulfils the requirements of social expedience and that economic communism does.

this question), they produced nothing that qualifies as economic analysis. What they were most interested in was the 'justice' of taxation in the widest acceptance of the term—such questions as whether and when taxes might be rightfully imposed, by whom and on whom, for what purposes, and to what extent. And below their normative propositions there was some sociological analysis of the nature of taxation and of the relation between state and citizen. Both these norms and this analysis, along with the rest of their political and economic sociology, went into the work of their laical successors though the later science of public finance grew mainly from other roots.[22]

But while the economic sociology of the scholastic doctors of this period was, in substance, not more than thirteenth-century doctrine worked out more fully, the 'pure' economics which they also handed down to those laical successors was, practically in its entirety, their own creation. It is within their systems of moral theology and law that economics gained definite if not separate existence, and it is they who come nearer than does any other group to having been the 'founders' of scientific economics. And not only that: it will appear, even, that the bases they laid for a serviceable and well-integrated body of analytic tools and propositions were sounder than was much subsequent work, in the sense that a considerable part of the economics of the later nineteenth century might have been developed from those bases more quickly and with less trouble than it actually cost to develop it, and that some of that subsequent work was therefore in the nature of a time- and labor-consuming detour.

In what may be described as the applied economics of the scholastic doctors, the pivotal concept was the same Public Good that also dominated their economic sociology. This Public Good was conceived, in a distinctly utilitarian spirit, with reference to the satisfaction of the economic wants of individuals as discerned by the observer's reason or *ratio recta* (see, below, next section)—and is therefore, barring technique, exactly the same thing as the welfare concept of modern Welfare Economics, Professor Pigou's for instance. The most important link between the latter and scholastic welfare economics is the welfare economics of the Italian economists of the eighteenth century (see below, ch. 3). So far as appraisal of economic policy and business practice is concerned, the scholastics' idea of what is 'unjust' was associated—though never identified—with their idea of what is contrary to public welfare in that sense. To give at least one example: Molina declared that monopoly was in general (*regulariter*) unjust *and* harmful to the public welfare (*tract.* II, *disp.* 345); though he did not identify the two, their juxtaposition is nevertheless significant.

The welfare economics of the scholastic doctors linked up with their 'pure' economics through the pivotal concept of the latter, Value, which also was

[22] The fact should, however, be recorded, that Nicolaus Cusanus (already mentioned in connection with the heliocentric theory) framed a comprehensive plan for the reform of the finances of the German Empire, based upon a general income tax (actually introduced, for the Empire as distinguished from the component states, in 1920).

based upon 'wants and their satisfaction.' Of course, there was nothing new in this starting point itself. But the Aristotelian distinction between value in use and value in exchange was deepened and developed into a fragmentary but genuine subjective or utility theory of exchange value or price in a manner for which there was no analogue in either Aristotle or St. Thomas, though there was in both what we may describe as a pointer. First, by way of criticizing Duns Scotus and his followers, the late scholastics, particularly Molina, made it quite clear that cost, though a factor in the determination of exchange value (or price), was not its logical source or 'cause.' [23] Second, they adumbrated with unmistakable clearness the theory of the utility which they considered as the source or cause of value. Molina and Lugo, for instance, were as careful as C. Menger was to be to point out that this utility was not a property of the goods themselves or identical with any of their inherent qualities, but was the reflex of the uses the individuals under observation proposed to make of these goods and of the importance they attached to these uses. But a century before that, St. Antonine, evidently motivated by the wish to divest the relevant concept of undesirable 'objective' meanings, had employed the unclassical but excellent term *complacibilitas*—the exact equivalent of Professor Irving Fisher's 'desiredness,' which also is used to express the fact that a thing is actually being desired and nothing else. Third, the late scholastics, though they did not explicitly resolve the 'paradox of value'—that water though useful has normally no exchange value—obviated the difficulty by making their utility concept, from the first, relative to abundance or scarcity; their utility was not utility of goods in the abstract, but utility of the *quantities* of goods available or producible in the individual's particular situations. Finally, fourth, they listed all the price-determining factors,[24] though they failed to integrate them into a full-fledged theory of demand and supply. But the elements for such a theory were all there and the technical apparatus of schedules and of marginal concepts that developed during the nineteenth century is really all that had to be added to them.

There are two more aspects of this theory of exchange value that deserve to be noticed. On the one hand, the late scholastics identified their just price not, as Aristotle and also Duns Scotus seem to have done, with *normal* competitive price but with any competitive price (*communis estimatio fori* or *pretium currens*). Wherever such a price existed, it was 'just' to pay and to accept it, whatever the consequences might be for the trading parties: if mer-

[23] This statement, I think, renders fairly the meaning of Molina's argument in *tract.* II, *disp.* 348, if proper attention is paid to the analytic kernel in the word 'just.' Still less than a cost theory of value can a labor theory of value be imputed to them, though this has been done. We shall see later that the emotional appeal of the latter has induced some historians to interpret as many authors as possible in this sense. It should be borne in mind, therefore, that mere emphasis on the importance in the economic process of the element of labor or effort or trouble does not amount to sponsorship of the proposition that expenditure of labor *explains*, or is *causal* to, value—which is what is meant by labor theory of value in this book.

[24] Cf. especially a passage in Lessius, quoted by Dempsey, op. cit. p. 151.

chants, paying and accepting market prices, made gains, this was all right, and if they suffered losses, this was bad luck or else a penalty for incompetence *so long as gain or loss resulted from the unhampered working of the market mechanism though not if it resulted, for example, from price fixing by public authority or monopolistic concerns.*[25] Molina's disapproval of price fixing, though qualified, and his approval of gains arising from high competitive prices in times of scarcity are no doubt ethical judgments. But they reveal a perception of the organic functions of commercial gains and of the price fluctuations that are responsible for them, a fact that marks a considerable step in analysis. This should be borne in mind, for we are not as a rule in the habit of looking to the scholastics for the origin of the theories that are associated with nineteenth-century laissez-faire liberalism.

On the other hand, the late scholastics analyzed economic activity itself—St. Antonine's *industria*—and particularly commercial and speculative activity, from a standpoint that was diametrically opposed to Aristotle's. The Economic Man of later times put in an appearance in the conception of 'prudent economic reason'—a Thomistic phrase which acquired an entirely un-Thomistic connotation by de Lugo's interpretation, which was to the effect that this prudence implies the intention of gaining in every legitimate way. This did not spell moral approval of profit hunting. As far as that goes, it is safe to assume that neither de Lugo's nor any other scholastic doctor's feelings differed from Aristotle's; St. Antonine, for example, was very explicit on this point. But it spelled an improved analysis of business facts that was, of course, partly induced by observation of the phenomena of rising capitalism. This realistic character of the work of the late scholastics should be particularly emphasized. They did not simply speculate. They did all the fact-finding that it was possible for them to do in an age without statistical services. Their generalizations invariably grew out of discussions of factual patterns and were copiously illustrated by practical examples. Lessius described the practice of the Antwerp exchange (*bursa*). Molina sallied forth from his study to interview businessmen about their methods. Some of his investigations into the economic conditions of his time and country, such as his study of the Spanish wool trade, amount to little monographs.

As regards money, it will suffice to record the four following points. First, reasoning on Aristotelian lines, the doctors presented, practically to a man, a strictly metallist theory of money which, in fundamentals, did not differ from that of A. Smith; we find the same genetic or pseudo-historical deduction from the necessity of avoiding the inconveniences of direct barter, the same conception of money as the most saleable commodity, and so on. Second, they were not only theoretical but also practical metallists, disapproving, with varying degrees of severity, of debasement and of any gain that accrued from it to princes. As mentioned before, the outstanding authority on this matter, Oresmius, only formulated the doctors' common opinion, which in this case

[25] See, e.g., Molina, *tract.* II, *disp.* 348 and 364.

was evidently shared by most people.[26] The modern student of monetary theory, who may possibly sympathize with those princes and feel inclined to regard them as worthy predecessors of the governments of his own day, should observe that the doctors went but a very short way into the economic effects of devaluation. They saw the effect on prices and felt that creditors and holders of money were being defrauded but that was about all. Even in these matters their analysis did not go beyond the obvious, and the idea that devaluation—and other methods of increasing the amount of circulating monetary units—might stimulate trade and employment was quite foreign to them; it first occurred to those businessmen who wrote on monetary policy in the seventeenth century (see below, ch. 6). Since this idea was almost entirely lost on the

[26] Oresme, op. cit. ch. xv: *Quod lucrum quod provenit Principi ex mutatione monetae sit injustum.* Cf. Jean Bodin's precept in the sixth Book of his *De re publica* (Les six livres de la République): *princeps a nummorum corruptela debet abstinere.* This adage and similar ones resound from a large chorus of voices that were raised in protest against governmental malpractices during those centuries of almost incessant monetary disorders. But some writers who joined that chorus were not theoretical metallists. To quote an example, François Grimaudet (*Des Monnoyes*, 1576), though he insists that the nominal value of a coin should not surpass the value of the material except for the 'fraiz de façon et quelque petit proffit,' yet states explicitly that the 'essence of money' is in that nominal value *et non en la matière.* On the whole, I think, *valor impositus* should be translated by nominal value, *valor intrinsecus* by value of material, and *valor extrinsecus* by purchasing power (which is, however, also called *potestas*). *Quantitas* also means nominal value, and not quantity. Devaluation is denoted by *mutatio, corruptela,* or *augmentum.* The last term corresponds to the English usage of the sixteenth and seventeenth centuries (and even later times) when 'raising' money meant debasement or devaluation.

In that large chorus of protesting voices, I cannot hear any note worth recording. But I shall mention names of a few authors—not all of them scholastics—who seem to have gained considerable contemporary reputation: C. A. Thesaurus' *Tractatus novus et utilis de augmento ac variatione monetarum* (1607), and M. Freher's *De re monetaria* (1605), do display some traces of the distinction between devaluation and depreciation, and may on this account be assigned a special place. Also ran (among many others, doctors and laics): René Budel, Joannes Aquila, Martinus Garratius, Franciscus Curtius, Ioannes Regnandus, Joachimus Mynsinger, Didacus [Diego] Covarruvias (the famous jurist), Henricus Hormannus, Franciscus de Aretio, Joannes Caephalus. There is some difference, partly explained by the fact that they had different situations in mind, in their solutions of the problem of the repayment of debts contracted in a currency that was subsequently debased. This is the problem that really interested the public and is responsible for the unending stream of publications of this kind. But the answers are practical shifts and of no interest for us. One author should be added, however, because his argument on usury secured him one of those places in the history of economics that remain occupied indefinitely for no other reason than that nobody bothers to revise the occupant's claims. Charles Dumoulin (Carolus Molinaeus, 1500-1566) was a French lawyer of reputation whose *Tractatus commerciorum et usurarum redituumque pecunia costitutorum & monetarum* (I have used the 1st ed., 1546) was a great success and enjoyed international reputation. There is nothing in it, however, that could be described as a new contribution to economic analysis.

English 'classics' of the nineteenth century, we have here another of those curious doctrinal affinities that exist between J. S. Mill and Father Molina. Third, we note for future reference that some of the doctors, among whom Mercado is the most important instance, adumbrated more or less clearly what came to be called the quantity theory of money, at least in the sense in which Bodin can be said to have held it. And, fourth, they dealt with a number of problems in coinage,[27] foreign exchange, international gold and silver movements, bimetallism, and credit in a manner that would merit more attention and that compares favorably in some points with much later performance.

Contrary to an opinion that has some adherents, the scholastic doctors did not work out any theory of the physical aspect of production ('real capital'), though they did eventually—since St. Antonine—block out a theory of the role in production and commerce of monetary capital. Nor did they possess any integrated theory of distribution, that is to say, they failed to apply their embryonic demand-supply apparatus to the process of income formation as a whole. Moreover, the rent of land and the wages of labor had not as yet become analytic problems to them. In the case of rent, this was perhaps due to the facts that, with farmers who tilled their own soil, the element of rent does not readily display its distinctive character, and that rents paid to landlords were in the times of the doctors so mixed with dues of a different nature that the economic rent, which was moreover traditionally fixed, did not show up very distinctly even in this case. In the case of wages, too, they did not ask the theoretical question; presumably they felt that nobody needs to be told what it is wages are paid for. They proffered indeed moral considerations and recommendations as to policy. However, even St. Antonine's recommendations, noteworthy because of the broad social sympathies that inspired them, do not rest on any analytic foundations of the kind we are interested in. The same applies to the considerable literature that developed in the sixteenth century on relief of the poor, unemployment, mendicancy, and the like, to which the doctors contributed copiously.[28] Much more important were their contributions to the theories of the two types of income that they did feel to be analytic problems, business profits and interest. The risk-effort theory of business profit is undoubtedly due to them. In particular, it may be mentioned that de Lugo—following a suggestion of St. Thomas—described business profits as 'a kind of wage' for a social service. No less certain is it that they launched the theory of interest.

So far, our sketch of scholastic economics has been drawn without much attention to its methodological philosophy, which will be discussed in the next section, and also without much attention to the logical processes involved in unwrapping the analytic

[27] The eminence of Copernicus in other fields suggests special notice of his *Monetae cudendae ratio* (1526).

[28] De Soto's *Deliberacion en la causa de los pobres* (1545), and Juan de Medina's *De la orden que . . . se ha puesta en la limosna . . .* (1545), are examples of those scholastic contributions. The subject will be briefly mentioned again (see below, ch. 5).

element in the reasoning of the doctors from the normative considerations in which it was embedded. In order to exhibit these processes and to show precisely how it was that they came to ask the question which they were the first to ask—namely, the question why interest is actually paid—we shall, in the case of interest, be more careful in doing the unwrapping.

The motive of scholastic analysis was manifestly not pure scientific curiosity but the desire to understand what they were called upon to judge from a moral standpoint.[29] When the modern economist speaks of 'value judgments,' he refers to moral or cultural appraisal of institutions. As we have seen, the scholastic doctors also passed value judgments of this kind. Primarily, however, and so far as their practical task was concerned, it was not the merits or demerits of institutions that mattered to them, but the merits or demerits of individual behavior within the frame of given institutions and conditions. More than anything else, they were directors of individual consciences or, rather, teachers of directors of individual consciences. They wrote for many purposes but principally for the instruction of confessors. In the first instance, therefore, they had to expound moral precepts that were immutable on principle. Secondly, they had to teach the application of these precepts to individual cases arising in an almost infinite variety of circumstances.[30] But this was not enough. In order to secure something approaching uniformity of practice among the numerous confessors, it was necessary to work out concrete decisions for the more important types of cases that occur in practice. Moreover, one of the considerations that are most helpful in deciding whether, from the standpoint of a given individual, a given act is a sin, and if so, how serious a sin it is, is whether or not it is common practice in the individual's environment. For both these reasons it was necessary for the doctors to investigate typical forms of economic behavior and also the actual practices prevailing in the environments under their observation—a task that was often so simple as not to call for special effort, but was exceedingly difficult when it came to the complex phenomenon of interest.

Thus the normative motive, so often the enemy of patient analytic work, in this instance both set the task and supplied the method for the scholastic analysts. Once set, the task was strictly scientific and logically independent of the moral theology whose purposes were to be served. And the method was also strictly scientific; in particular,

[29] For our purpose, the history of legislation on interest, whether proceeding from temporal or spiritual authority, is not of any great importance. Moreover, the reader will find in the *Encyclopaedia of the Social Sciences* or in *Palgrave's Dictionary* all he may wish to have in the way of general orientation. Nevertheless, a few facts about the policy of the Catholic Church may be welcome at this point. In the times of the Roman Empire the Catholic Church dealt very cautiously with interest, Aristotle and St. Luke notwithstanding. The Council of Nicaea (325) did not go beyond a prohibition addressed to the clergy, though more general disapproval was expressed. The decisive step, which also included the declaration that secular legislation to the contrary was invalid (St. Thomas had not thought so), was not taken until 1311. Prohibition was then reaffirmed many times and is still in force. But its practical importance decreased along with the decrease in importance of the cases that came under it, as will be explained in the text. Some notice of this was eventually taken in the encyclical *Vix pervenit*, 1745. In 1838 a circular instructed confessors not to disturb penitents who accept interest at current rates.

[30] The theory of this was given, e.g., by St. Thomas (*Summa* II, 1, quaest. VII). The chief reference, so far as moral theology is concerned, for what follows in the text is to St. Alphonso de'Liguori (1696-1787; *Theologia moralis*, see *Works*, English ed., 1887-95.)

it was eminently realistic, since it involved nothing beyond observation of facts and their interpretation: it was a method of working out general principles from 'cases' somewhat akin to the method of English jurisprudence. Moral theology came in only after the analytic work was done in each case, to subsume the result under one of its rules.

It is not surprising, however, that to unsympathetic critics of scholastic work, scholastic research into interest appeared in the light not only of 'casuistry' in a derogatory sense of the term but even of a series of attempts to cover the retreat of the Catholic Church from an untenable position by logical tricks or subterfuges, and to justify *ex post* each *fait accompli*. The reader may judge for himself. But it is as well to point out a fact that will seem to support that opinion. On the one hand, moral precept, however immutable, will yield different results if applied to different circumstances; and capitalist evolution did create circumstances in which the cases that came under the prohibition of usury rapidly decreased in importance. On the other hand, such an evolution will be inevitably paralleled by subterfuges of interested parties, who will try to avail themselves of all the possibilities offered by a system of rules and exceptions that grew increasingly complex; perhaps the most famous of these subterfuges was the abuse of the element of *mora* presently to be mentioned in the text, but there were many of them. This parallelism cannot fail to impress the superficial observer, particularly if he is not very well versed in either scholastic literature or economic theory. Moreover, we are speaking of scholastic doctrine at its highest. It is of course not denied that the ordinary clerical practitioners, like any bureaucracy, committed a great many mistakes and fostered resort to subterfuges both by unintelligently restrictive interpretation of the rules they were directed to apply and by well-meaning connivance at evasions.

Usury, then, was sinful. But what is usury? On the one hand, it does not necessarily involve the exploitation of the needy: this element is morally relevant in other respects but was not a constituent of the scholastic concept of usury. On the other hand, usury is not always present when more than repayment of the sum lent is stipulated: simple exegesis of St. Thomas' teaching sufficed to justify compensation for the lender's risk or trouble—particularly evident in the purchase below par of notes—or compensation in cases where the lender was deprived of his money against his will, as in cases of forced loans, or of the debtor's failure to repay at the stipulated time (*more debitoris*). Thomistic teaching even suggested Molina's proposition that, since the lender of any commodity is in any case entitled to receive back its full value at the time of lending, more units might have to be repaid than were given (*esto plus in quantitate sit accipiendum*), though no application was made of this, so far as I know, to money loans. From all those cases emerged the principle that a charge was to be considered as normal or unobjectionable whenever the lender incurred any loss (*damnum emergens*). Some doctors argued that the lender in temporarily giving away his money always and inevitably suffers such loss. But most of them refused to accept this view. Nor did the majority admit that the gain the lender foregoes by lending (*lucrum cessans*) is in itself a justification for making a charge. They did admit, however, that, as we may put it, gain foregone turns into actual loss when the opportunity for such gain is part of a man's normal environment. This meant two things. First, merchants themselves who hold money for business purposes, evaluating this money with reference to expected gains, were considered justified in charging interest both on outright loans and in cases of deferred payment for commodities. Second, if the opportunity of gain contingent on the possession of money is quite general or, in other words, if there is a money market, then everyone, even if not in business himself, may accept the interest determined by the market mechanism. This proposition had to be handled with care, for it evidently opened the door to all sorts of evasions. But it is no more than a special case of the principle that everyone may, in justice, pay and ask the current price for everything, and was not invented ad hoc: if it is not in evidence in the thirteenth century and much in evidence in the sixteenth, this is merely due to the fact that money markets had been uncommon in the former century and became quite common in the latter.[31] Observe that whenever alternative opportunities of gain are normally available to everyone, the argument from gain foregone will coincide with the argument from 'privation': foregoing gain is in this case precisely what the privation consists in. Observe further that in *all* the cases mentioned justification rests on circumstances that, however frequently or even generally they may prevail in a given environment, are logically accidental to the pure loan contract (*mutuum*), which in itself was never held to justify interest. And observe finally that justification was never, or hardly ever, based upon the advantages that the *borrower* might reap from the loan; it was exclusively based on the disadvantages that lending brought to the *lender*.

Dropping now the normative garb of scholastic interest analysis and the moral *doctrines* that motivated their research, we may restate as follows the causal *theories* their research unearthed, on the understanding that the picture cannot be quite satisfactory because the scholastic doctors did not much more agree on the theory of interest than do we.

1. Interest, though construed on the more general model of loans of 'con-

[31] This is no doubt a very imperfect account of a rich doctrinal development. Considerations of space, however, make it impossible to present a more satisfactory one which the interested reader will find in Professor Dempsey's book. Also see A. M. Knoll, *Der Zins in der Scholastik* (1933). But a much discussed construction, associated with the name of the famous Dr. Eck (1486-1543) and also favored by Navarrus and Major, should be noticed, the triple contract, *contractus trinus*. It is, of course, licit to enter into a partnership and to draw an income from it. Nothing prevents the partner in a business from insuring his capital against loss; hence he may also do so with his other partners in which case the price of the insurance will amount to a reduction of his share in the profits. Finally, he may legally convert this reduced share in variable profits into a constant annuity that will represent pure interest. This construction is interesting from an analytic point of view because it exhibits the connection between interest and business profits in a very instructive way. As a defense of usury it was, however, rightly condemned. For either we accept the argument that the partner in question has alternative business opportunities of the kind that justify the charging of interest; then the construction is superfluous. Or we do not accept that argument; then the failure of the second contract to reduce that partner's share to zero (apart from a remuneration of his work) would spell usury. The logical slip involved in Eck's argument is worthy of the reader's attention.

sumptibles,' is essentially a monetary phenomenon. There was no analytic merit in this. The scholastic doctors simply accepted a surface fact exactly as had Aristotle. They did sometimes relate interest on money to the returns of income-bearing goods, land, mining rights, and the like that may be bought for money. But this point—though used in some interest theories of the seventeenth and eighteenth centuries—was without analytical value because the price of income-bearing goods and therefore the net return from them already presupposes the existence of interest.

II. Interest is an element of the price of money. Calling it a price for the use of money does not explain anything and at best restates the problem in an unenlightening way. In itself, it is an empty phrase. Nor is the analogy of interest with interlocal premia or discounts on money more than a restatement of the problem. For these interlocal premia and discounts are explained by risks and costs of transfers whereas pure interest, as distinguished from compensation for risks and costs, is an intertemporal premium which the analogy does not help to explain. The uncritical appeal to mere lapse of time per se is valueless—circumstances are easily conceivable in which it would fail to produce a deviation from zero interest. Though negative only, these propositions are of great analytical value. They clear the ground and prove that the scholastic doctors—in this respect much superior to nine-tenths of the interest analysts of the nineteenth century—saw the real logical problem involved. In fact, these propositions define it. This is why they should be credited with having launched the theory of interest.

III. Hence deviation of interest from zero is a problem the solution of which can be found only by analysis of the particular circumstances that account for the emergence of a positive rate of interest. Such analysis reveals that the fundamental factor that raises interest above zero is the prevalence of business profit—all the other facts that may produce the same results are not necessarily inherent in the capitalist process. This proposition constitutes the main positive contribution of scholastic interest analysis. Adumbrated before, it was first clearly stated by St. Antonine, who explained that though the circulating coin might be sterile, money capital is not so because command of it is a condition for embarking upon business.[32] Molina and his contemporaries, while rightly insisting that money was 'in itself' not productive and no factor of production, yet accepted a similar view: they coined the significant phrase that money was the Merchant's Tool. Moreover, they quite understood

[32] This, of course, was a frontal attack on Aristotle's 'sterility of money.' It is interesting to note that St. Thomas' argument proffered a clue for this. After having taught that there was no reason why money should ordinarily carry a premium, he went on to say that there were secondary employments of money in which something might be charged for it. This would be the case, for instance, if somebody lent money for the purpose of enabling the borrower to deposit it as a pledge or guarantee (*loco pignoris*). St. Thomas certainly did not mean to include business loans in these 'secondary uses,' of money. But this was done in Jacobus Ferrarius' *Digressio resolutoria* . . . (1623), where the author went so far as to include all loans made for any legitimate purposes whatsoever.

the mechanism by which this premium, if capitalist business be sufficiently active and—relative to the rest of the environment—sufficiently important, will tend to become an all-pervading normal phenomenon. And their ideas on *lucrum cessans* and *damnum emergens* complement their analysis as regards the supply side of the money market.

Further than this they did not go. Their theory of business profits in particular was not sufficiently developed to allow them to reap the full benefit from the insight that led them to trace interest to profit as its source. Also, being the first in this field, they groped for their generalizations rather than stated them. In this prolonged process of groping they slipped up frequently and used many inadequate and even faulty arguments. But if we are to treat them as we treat other groups of analytic workers, merits prevail greatly over shortcomings, especially if we give them credit, as we ought to, for much of what successors and even opponents learned from their analysis.

But what, if that be so, becomes of the great battle on interest between scholastic and anti-scholastic writers that is supposed to have raged in the sixteenth and seventeenth centuries? So far as the history of economic analysis is concerned, the only answer is that there was no battle. No analytic progress was made and no new analytic ideas on interest were proffered for a long time to come. Even the most famous leaders on the anti-scholastic side such as Molinaeus or Salmasius [33] had nothing new to say: Molinaeus and Navarrus—contemporaries roughly speaking—were about on a par in theoretical grasp of the interest problem. Salmasius only reformulated the scholastic theory about *lucrum cessans* from available business opportunities that we find in Molina. So far as the moral issue was concerned, the Protestant theologians and the laic lawyers differed among themselves on the subject of interest, but were also content to repeat arguments forged by the scholastics, whichever side they espoused.[34] But, in addition there was a legislative or administrative issue, and it is this that accounts for the controversy in question. As we have

[33] Molinaeus (Charles Dumoulin) has been discussed above. Salmasius (Claude de Saumaise, 1588-1653) wrote a number of tracts on interest, of which it is sufficient to mention two: *De usuris* (1638; but there seems to have been a previous ed., 1630) and *De foenore trapezitico* (1640).

[34] We may as well dispose of this matter once for all. Scholastic doctrine was taught by Richard Baxter (1615-91; see, e.g., his *Christian Directory*). On a lower level, the same holds for the considerable literature on interest that, representing the popular reaction to the financial aspects of rising capitalism, denounced usury on purely moral grounds. Here are a few English samples which, I think, are fairly representative: Thomas Wilson, *Discourse upon Usurie* (1584, but there was an earlier ed., in 1572, according to the Kress Library Catalogue; new ed., with introduction by R. H. Tawney, 1925). Philippus Caesar, *General Discourse against the Damnable Sect of Usurers* (1578), purely moral invective; Anon., *Death of Usury or the Disgrace of Usurers . . .* (1594); Anon., *Usurie Arraigned and Condemned* (1625). There were, of course, plenty of sermons that I have not investigated. Roger Fenton (*Treatise of Usurie*, 1612) may stand for the defense of interest on a ground that was known to the scholastics but not accepted by them as relevant to the *moral* issue, viz. the advantage that accrues to the borrower.

seen, the scholastics held that interest had to be justified on grounds not inherent in the loan contract (*mutuum*) as such. But this amounted to saying that each case, or at least each type of case, was on trial and not to be approved without investigation. Though they did not always object to secular legislation that permitted interest,[35] it is easy to imagine what inconvenience this principle must have caused after interest had become a normal phenomenon. The question naturally arose, that was in the end answered affirmatively by Popes Pius VIII and Gregory XVI, whether in such circumstances an over-complicated set of rules, however correct logically, should not be replaced by admitting a sweeping presumption that the acceptance of a market rate of interest was all right. This is really all that a steadily increasing number of laical and even clerical writers demanded. But they did not put it this way, partly because they were not able to understand the finely spun logic of the scholastics and therefore set it down as mere sophistry, and partly because, most of them being enemies of the Catholic Church or the scholastic doctors for political and religious reasons, they could not bring themselves to argue the question of policy without sneers or invective. This created the impression that there was a battle between old and new *theoretical* principles which, since it distorts the picture of a phase in the history of economic analysis, it seemed worth while to dispel.

5. The Concept of Natural Law [1]

We must now attend to a subject the consideration of which we have twice deferred. It is beset with difficulties and an inexhaustible source of misunderstandings which cannot be straightened out entirely in the available space. An appeal for the patient co-operation of the reader is, however, justified by its fundamental importance for the origins and early history of all social sciences. For the first discovery of every science is the discovery of itself. Awareness of the presence of a set of interrelated phenomena that give rise to 'problems' is evidently the prerequisite of all analytic effort. And in the case of the social sciences, this awareness shaped itself in the concept of natural law. We shall try to disentangle its various meanings and to catch their subtle changes and associations.

[35] St. Thomas even went so far as to say (loc. cit. *ad tertium*) that, in the condition of imperfect man, many useful things would be impeded (*multae utilitates impedirentur*) if all sins were strictly forbidden by human law.

[1] From the large literature on the subject, I select for the reader's general information Sir Frederick Pollock's 'History of the Law of Nature' (in his *Essays in the Law*, republ. 1922). Also see P. Struve, 'L'Idée de loi naturelle dans la science économique,' *Revue d'économie politique*, July 1921. The only study I can commend for correct appraisal of the work done under the auspices of the natural-law idea (though of the work of the successors of the scholastics rather than of the scholastics themselves) is O. H. Taylor's 'Economics and the Idea of Natural Laws,' *Quarterly Journal of Economics*, November 1929. Vinogradoff's well-known *Outlines of Historical Jurisprudence* (1920-22) may prove helpful.

(a) *The Ethico-Legal Concept.* The scholastic doctors themselves traced their concept of natural law back to Aristotle and the Roman jurists, although, as we shall presently see, they made of it something totally different. Aristotle, speaking of justice, distinguished the 'naturally just' (φυσικὸν δίκαιον) from the 'institutionally just' (νομικὸν δίκαιον) (*Ethics* v, 7). But in that passage, the term Natural must be understood in a very narrow sense. Aristotle there means to refer only to forms of behavior that are enforced by very general necessities of life that man shares with other animals. But elsewhere he used the term Natural in a much wider sense, in fact in all the senses it ever acquired without distinguishing, let alone defining, them clearly. And the Natural in the wider senses, also, he associated with the Just, thus setting an example for ages to come—even the English 'classical' economists sometimes mixed up the natural and the just—though he was not quite consistent about it: he sometimes approved of what he did not call natural; but he never disapproved of anything to which he affixed this label.

The Romans, not much given to philosophizing, simply accepted the Aristotelian definition: Gaius (*Instit.* I, 2) said naïvely that natural law (*jus naturale*) 'is what nature has taught all animals' (*quod natura omnia animalia docuit*). Ulpian said the same thing. They simply accepted this Natural Law as a source of legal rules that was just as good as, and in fact superior to, any of the sources of positive law, statutory and other. But there are two important points to be noticed in addition. First, there developed a tendency among Romans of literary propensities, such as Cicero, to affix the term *jus naturale* to what was officially called *jus gentium*. The reason was that the latter, embodying as it did rules of equity, seemed somehow more 'natural' than the formalistic civil law. The reader should observe that this sense of natural law, the sense that ultimately prevailed (while, as we have seen, the term *jus gentium* acquired in the seventeenth century the meaning of Law of Nations) is not identical with the sense defined by Aristotle in *Ethics* v, 7, though it has more to do with the other senses in which Aristotle actually used the word Natural. Second, the Roman jurists also associated different meanings with the words Nature and Natural, of which one is important for us: [2] the *rei natura* or the nature of the case. For instance, when we are confronted by a legal question arising out of a contract, we must first find out what the 'nature of the business' was that the parties to the contract intended to effect. At first sight, this nature of the case seems to have nothing to do with natural law in any sense—as many legal treatises try to explain that are written by jurists who, under the influence of the historical school, have come to hate the very phrase Natural Law. But we shall presently see that it has a lot to do with it.

St. Thomas [3] accepted the Aristotelian definition in the legalist formulation

[2] Other meanings are embodied in such terms as *naturale negotii* and *naturalis obligatio* with which I do not want to bother the reader. All of these and other meanings, though distinct, are of course related.

[3] What may be termed the Thomistic theory of law, natural and positive, is presented in *Summa* II, 1, quaest. XCIV, XCV, and XCVII; II, 2, quaest. LVII, art. 2 and 3. Interpretation is not easy. My thesis of the mutability of natural law is gleaned from

of the Roman jurists but merely as a matter of form. Actually, his attempt to put logical order into Aristotle's various uses of it produced something that was neither Aristotelian nor Roman.[4] In the first place, natural law or the 'naturally just' (*lex naturalis, justum naturale*) may be the set of rules that nature imposes upon all animals and also may be, in the sense of Aristotle's definition, immutable on principle. But since these rules work out differently in different conditions of time and place and with different people, and since it is possible to add to them or to subtract from them, even this natural law became historically variable in practice (see, especially, *Summa* II, 1, quaest. XCIV, art. 4 and 5). In the second place, there was another meaning of natural law that St. Thomas explains only by examples but which really equates natural law to the set of rules that conform (*habet quandam commensurationem*) to social necessity or expedience, the historical relativity of which St. Thomas never tired of stressing. Natural law in *this* sense is almost, though not quite, identified with *jus gentium* in the Roman official sense. In the third place, it is held that human positive law necessarily consists either in deductions from this natural law or in adjustments of its rules to particular conditions. An enactment that violates any rule of *this* natural law does not make valid law at all. The reader will notice the political implications of this doctrine.

To make a long story short, we leap from St. Thomas to Molina. Molina clearly identified natural law, on the one hand, with the dictates of reason (*ratio recta*), and with what is socially expedient or necessary (*expediens et necessarium*), on the other. These propositions, in themselves, are nothing but Thomism formulated more pointedly. But he took a further step (*tract.* I, *disp.* 4): after repeating the Aristotelian definition he added, apparently by way of explaining its meaning: 'that is to say,' the naturally just is that which obligates us by virtue of the nature of the case (*cuius obligatio oritur ex natura rei*). But this is not at all what Aristotle meant. Molina does not interpret his meaning but adds a new one: he definitely married natural law to our rational diagnosis, with reference to the Common Good, of the cases—whether individual contracts or social institutions—which we observe in research or practice. Molina's

---

an argument that purports to prove the contrary but so qualifies and hedges in the principle that the subsequent statement in the text seems warranted. St. Thomas also argued that natural law was the same *apud omnes* and again the practical upshot is relativity: his emphasis upon what is *loco temporique conveniens* suffices to establish this, though different interpretations may very well be appropriate from philosophical or theological standpoints.

[4] Many critics will disagree. They will point to the references to Aristotle and Ulpian by which St. Thomas supported his exposition. Very likely, these critics and I will have to agree to differ, because no agreement can be expected in matters into which the personal equation of interpreters must inevitably enter. The personal equation in this case refers to the importance we attach to passing remarks, *obiter dicta*, hints. I admit that pointers to St. Thomas' teaching can be found in Aristotle and the Roman jurists (also in Cicero). But their weight appears to be so great only because it is precisely such passages that St. Thomas brought together. Taken independently of what he made of them they amount to very little.

view about 'the nature of natural law' is mentioned only as an example of what was the general opinion of the doctors in his and even an earlier time. De Soto's concept of the Command of Reason (*rationis ordinatio*) amounts to the same thing.

One way of putting this result is to say that all speculative or metaphysical or non-empirical elements had evaporated from Molina's natural-law concept, and that there was nothing left but reason applied to particular facts, though, so far, applied from the normative standpoint. Unfortunately, however, the subject is more complicated than this. The doctrine of the scholastics also contains the sources of two currents of thought that are the very opposites of sober matter-of-factness. These must be mentioned because they contributed substantially to the prevailing confusion about natural law. First, there is the association of natural law with primitive conditions. We have seen that, following Aristotle, the doctors, like A. Smith, frequently made use of a pseudo-historical method of exposition: they liked to start, in explaining a social phenomenon such as property or money, from an imaginary 'early state' of society. They did not, so far as I can see, make any improper use of this construction. But the Natural was the Just and if the Natural is particularly clearly revealed in primitive conditions, as that method of exposition implies, then primitive conditions become just as well as natural. From this standpoint starts an uninterrupted line that runs right into Rousseau's glorification of the natural, in the sense of primitive, state of humanity —an association that is entirely immaterial but did not add to the standing of the concept. The scholastics themselves, needless to say, displayed no tendency to glorify primitive conditions.

Second, there is a relation between the scholastic natural law and the Rights of Man, *droits de l'homme*, and similar eighteenth-century constructs including the laborer's natural right to his product. The existence of this relation cannot be doubted. For the natural law of the doctors was considered as a source of valid legal rules about rights and duties, and all the framers of the *droits de l'homme* pretended to do was to draw on this source for the Command of Reason or *rationis ordinatio* with respect to the political rights of civilized man. Moreover, some items in the list of these rights are clearly recognized by scholastic writers. And yet, the speculative character of these and similarly conceived rights is a commonplace. It is precisely this sort of thing, more than anything else, which accounts for the distaste many of the best economists have felt for the concept of natural law, and which has made it a byword for unhistoric and unscientific metaphysics. So much is this the case that, with some of us, a proposition need only be linked up with natural law in order to be put out of court; in fact, one of the most common reasons for wholesale rejection of economic theory to this day is that it is nothing but an offshoot of unscientific natural-law philosophies. We have, therefore, every motive for looking more closely at the indictment. This will be done under the next heading.

(b) *The Analytic Concept*. So far we have been inquiring into the development of the natural-law concept in its role within the ethical and legal sphere or, what amounts to the same thing, of natural law considered as a source of morally and legally valid imperatives. After what has been said in preceding sections of this chapter, it is easy to find the bridge to the natural-law concept in its analytic role. In fact, we need only generalize our findings in the special case of the theory of interest. For this purpose, let us ask the question: why should Aristotle have called certain forms of behavior 'naturally just' in the narrow sense of his definition? Evidently because these forms of behavior were necessary conditions of the survival of (as he thought) animal life in general. A similar answer will hold true for the 'naturally just' in the wider sense that covers the necessities of social life in the actual historical circumstances of any given human society. Therefore, in order to find out what is naturally just in any particular case, it is first necessary to analyze these circumstances. The generalizations that we may derive by so doing can be called natural law in the analytic sense: *the normative natural law presupposes an explanatory natural law*. The former is nothing but a particular kind of value judgment passed upon the facts and the relations between facts unearthed by the latter. The two are logically as distinct and practically as distinguishable as are the value judgments and analytic propositions of any economist. For instance, A. Smith had a theory of wages that consists of statements of fact and of generalizations derived from them. But he also said (*Wealth*, Bk. I, ch. 8) that 'the produce of labour constitutes the natural recompence or wages of labour.' Since by produce of labor he there meant the whole product, and since, on his own showing, the wages do not normally amount to that, we have here clearly a natural-law proposition in the philosophical or value-judgment sense. But when we are interested in scientific analysis only, we have no difficulty in discarding this sentence. Or, a modern economist may both analyze the phenomenon of price discrimination and pass a value judgment upon it. If he does the latter by calling it unjust, he is adopting a natural-law rule that does not differ, in this case, from that of the scholastics. If he approves of the Robinson-Patman Act, which forbids discrimination, he does what the scholastics would have done in their day by saying that this act is valid law because it conforms to an imperative of natural law. We may indeed call this, or any value judgment of any kind, unscientific or extrascientific. But there is no point in throwing out the analytic baby with the philosophic bath-water. And this is precisely what is being done by those who dispose of the economics of the scholastic doctors or their laical successors merely by pointing to its associations with a system of moral and legal imperatives—of natural laws in the analytic sense because of its association with a system of natural laws in the normative sense.

The main objection raised against natural-law jurisprudence and economics by the historical school was, however, not this but a different though related one: natural law was supposed to be entirely divorced from historic reality. We have seen that this objection is unfounded so far as the scholastic doctors, who always stressed the historical relativity of social phenomena, are concerned. It is better founded in the case of some of their successors. But it should be observed that, whether well or ill founded, this objection touches only the use of the concept and not the concept itself. Any concept can be faultily used. Moreover, any theory may be inadequate or wrong. In particular, it may claim for its propositions an undue amount of generality. The theoretical views associated with the *droits de l'homme,* for instance, certainly did. But an inadequate—or even wrong—scientific theory is still a scientific theory. On the other hand, we shall understand that the absolute claims made in the eighteenth century on behalf of certain legislative programs, without due reference to conditions of time and place, fostered all sorts of misunderstandings of the true character of natural-law analysis.

I have said that social science discovered itself in the concept of natural law. This will be particularly clear if we visualize it in the form of Molina's definition—as distilled from the 'nature of the case,' the *rei natura.* Taken in this sense, the ideal of natural law embodies the discovery that the data of a social situation determine—in the most favorable case, uniquely—a certain sequence of events, a logically coherent process or state, or *would do so if they were allowed to work themselves out without further disturbance.* This is putting it in modern terms. But the reason why we may attribute this idea, in however rudimentary a form, to the scholastic doctors is in their concept of justice. This (Aristotelian) concept of justice St. Thomas explained by relating the word 'justice' to adjustment and the word 'just' to adjusted. Just is what is adjusted, or conforms, to—what? The only answer we can give if we take the clue proffered by Molina's *rei natura* is: to the social pattern involved, as viewed from a utilitarian Common Good or social expediency. Hence the equations between just and natural, natural and normal.[5] Hence also the ease with which *they* passed from normative doctrine to the analytic theorem and vice versa, and with which *we* can pass, for example, from their just price to the price of (short- or long-run) competitive equilibrium. Hence, finally, the relation—not, of course, amounting to identification—that subsists with them between justification and explanation. Therefore, while it is true, as a matter of

[5] This relation between natural in the sense of normal and natural in the sense of just explains why the term Natural survived so long—almost until Marshall—in the former sense and also why some authors, who had certain philosophical ideas about 'natural liberty,' continued to link it with the just. But this is not all of it. The proviso about absence of disturbance that occurs in our text a few sentences earlier indicates a somewhat different but related meaning of such phrases as natural prices, natural wages, and so on: in these phrases Natural simply means that disturbances other than such as may have been included in the data are assumed to be absent, or that we intend to investigate a process or state as it would be if left to itself. Also, it is, of course, absurd to look for natural-law philosophies wherever the word Natural occurs: 'naturally' in particular simply means the same as 'obviously.' We do not commit ourselves to any philosophy when we state that a man is 'naturally' offended after having been called a fool. It seems worth while adding that the term Normal must not be understood in the statistical sense but rather in the sense in which we speak of normal eyesight: a physiologist, from his grasp of the *rei natura,* in this case of the structure of the human eye, may arrive at a concept of normality that may be far removed from any statistical measure of the actual eyesights observable in any given population.

history, that modern economics stems from the scholastic writers, as its critics hold, it is also true that this fact does not constitute an objection.[6]

(c) *Natural Law and Sociological Rationalism.* I. *A comment on philosophical rationalism.* In order to exhibit a point that is important for us, we select the following meaning of the protean word Rationalism. We call Philosophical Rationalism the belief not only that our mind ('natural reason') is the source of truths that are antecedent to experience, but also that our mind is able to produce results about supermundane subjects, such as the existence of God.[7] In this sense, St. Thomas was a metaphysical rationalist because, unlike other (mainly Scotist) scholastics, he believed that the existence of God can be logically proved. He was not a metaphysical rationalist in the sense in which this phrase came to be used in the seventeenth and eighteenth centuries, namely, that human reason was the *only* admissible source of knowledge in matters of theology, for he also admitted revelation. Now, if a man believes that, also by the unaided powers of his own logical apparatus, he can prove that God does not exist, he is indeed, in this particular matter, contradictorily opposed to St. Thomas. But there is a point in which they are nevertheless brothers in the spirit: the rationalist deist and the rationalist atheist are both rationalists in the sense defined and allies against anyone who does not trust his reason to soar as high as that, in particular against any logical positivist of today. Of course, there is nothing surprising in this. It is a most common occurrence that people who hold different views, nevertheless recognize, and appeal to, the same authority. But it was necessary to advert to this fact because it will help us to see continuity in doctrinal development where, without its help, we should see nothing but break and antagonism.

II. *Sociological rationalism.* Scientific activity is often looked upon as the standard instance of rational activity in the sense that the worker, whatever his ultimate aim, allows himself to be guided by the rules of logical inference. This is indeed not quite accurate: precisely the strongest achievements in science proceed not from observation or experimentation and orderly logic-

[6] Some historians of economics have believed that the normative element acquired added significance owing to its theological nature (observe, by the way, the meaning of 'nature' in this sentence). This has been held to be relevant even for an appraisal of the physiocrat system (see below, ch. 4, sec. 3). This, however, is another error. For the scholastic order of things, physical and social, is entirely autonomous within the scholastic theology, the only influence of which—beyond ethical imperatives—concerns the problems of miracles and of creation. Apart from miracles and creation, this order is to be understood entirely by the light of human reason. No doubt, in analyzing it, reason is analyzing part of God's works. But since God's plan in any case includes any amount of 'evil,' not even evaluation is seriously restricted by association with theology, and analysis is left entirely free. For discussion of an exactly opposite error of interpretation, see the next section.

[7] I have to apologize for the innumerable shortcomings of this definition. It is, however, brief and it is sufficient for the purpose of making the one point that is relevant to our subject.

chopping but from something that is best called vision and is akin to artistic creation. Still, results have to be 'proved' by the logical or rational procedure dictated by professional standards and this suffices to impress rationality in this sense—which has nothing to do with the sense discussed above—upon the stock of scientific knowledge that we possess at any time. But this concept of scientific rationality refers only to the attitude of the analysts and not to the behavior of the object analyzed. The alienist may 'rationally' investigate the reactions of madmen, the sociologist may rationally investigate war psychologies or the behavior of maddened crowds, without implying that the words and actions observed 'make sense.' So far as this goes, we are all of us, including the scholastic doctors no less than their worst enemies, of necessity Methodological Rationalists, that is, we all believe that *some* rational methods are applicable to the description of social phenomena. Generalizations resulting from the application of such methods may be called natural laws, and this is the only *indispensable* relation that exists between the natural-law concept and the 'right reason' or *ratio recta.*

But Sociological or Economic Rationalism means something else. Just as we may look upon the physical universe—in the way first made fashionable by the Stoics—as a logically consistent whole that is modeled upon an orderly plan—so we may look upon society as a cosmos that is possessed of *inherent* logical consistency. For us, it matters little whether this order is imposed upon it by divine will—directed to some definite ends by an invisible hand—or is inherent merely in the sense that the observer discovers in it plan and purpose that are independent of his analytic rationality, because in either case nothing is allowed to enter that 'rational' cosmos but what comes within the grasp of the light of reason. We must, however, further distinguish Objective Sociological or Economic Rationalism which does not, and Subjective Sociological Rationalism which does, postulate that this order or plan is or can be realized by the rational action of the individuals or groups that compose society. Both must evidently be attributed to the scholastic doctors as well as to most of their successors down to our own time. And this lends additional color to their concept of Natural Law and establishes another relation between it and their *ratio recta* that is quite distinct from the one established in the preceding paragraph—the relation formulated for all times by St. Thomas: *rationis autem prima regula est lex naturae* (*Summa,* II, 1, quaest. XCV, art. 2).

This, of course, is inacceptable from the standpoint of modern positivism. It constitutes in fact the one justification for finding 'speculation' not only in the normative but also in the analytic concept of natural law. All the more important is it to repeat that sociological or economic rationalism bears only upon the interpretation of natural-law propositions and not necessarily upon their content. We may drop the former and retain the latter. It is true, however, that the postulate of subjective rationalism embodies an exaggerated opinion of the explanatory value of rational action and tempts us into placing undue confidence in teleological arguments and into similar errors. This is especially serious if associated with a habit economists have of setting themselves up as judges of the rationality not only of means but of ends (motives), that is to say, if they approve, as rational, of ends (motives) that seem 'reasonable' to themselves and dispose of all others as irrational. The scholastic doctors are guilty on all these counts. But it is interesting to note that so are we: in this respect, too, as in so many others, we are their heirs. No better example can be found to illustrate this point than Alfred Marshall.

III. *Ratio recta* and *la raison*. Observe that sociological or economic rationalism need not lead to 'conservative' attitudes in practice. Like metaphysical rationalism it cuts both ways. We may indeed infer from our belief in the existence of an economic order or cosmos that all is always for the best in the world as it actually is—the view that Voltaire ridiculed in the figure of Dr. Pangloss (in *Candide*). But we need not assume that the rational order of things actually exists in the things as they are. It is sufficient to believe in a rational order that exists only in the realm of reason and that reason itself calls upon us to assert as against a deviating reality. This is the meaning sociological or economic rationalism carries with all reforming groups who propose 'to apply reason to social phenomena'—with the men of the Enlightenment whose cult of *la raison* was of this type, with the Benthamites, and with most liberals, radicals, and socialists of today. *And all of them descend from the scholastics.* For the political sociology of the doctors is by itself sufficient to prove that they held the second and not the first view concerning the social cosmos or the natural law. All the differences in the results of the application of the 'light of reason'—amply accounted for as they are by differences of standpoints and circumstances—are immaterial so far as the point under discussion is concerned. It is the same methodological principle that pervades all sociological and political thought that is not anti-intellectualist. The Greeks were the first to give it articulate expression. But the scholastics were the first to do so in the Germanic world. Whatever *la raison* revolted against in the eighteenth century, it was not a mode of thought. Epistemologically, there is perfect continuity, and *ratio recta* (equal to *naturalis ratio*) is the mother of *la raison*.

This need not surprise or shock anybody. The sword that was forged by angels might easily fall into the hand of devils. And the sword that was forged by devils might be wrenched from them by angels—only that, in this case, the devils are entitled to the kind of recognition that every civilized socialist extends to the achievements of capitalism.

6. The Philosophers of Natural Law: Natural-Law Analysis in the Seventeenth Century

We now part company with the scholastic doctors in order to consider the work of their immediate successors. The eternal questions about the government of mankind continued to be asked, of course, and others arose during the seventeenth century from the welter of new political patterns and problems. Especially in England, these produced a torrent of pamphlets of all types that ranged all the way from closely reasoned argument—I suppose that the writings of (George Savile, Marquess of) Halifax, the 'trimmer,' will always stand out as the peak achievements of this literature—to rantings nourished on apocalyptic quotations. But the craving for answers was also satisfied, on the level of general principle, by a group of writers whom we shall call Philosophers of Natural Law.[1]

(a) *The Protestant or Laical Scholastics.* Though separated from the scholastics by the religious split and by the change in the political scene, they were of the same professional type as the scholastics and they went about the same task, by the same method, in much the same spirit—so much so, in fact, that the best way of characterizing them is to call them Protestant (or laical) scholastics. They would not, of course, have agreed with this diagnosis. Nor is the characterization likely to appeal to modern students of either Catholic or Protestant or 'liberal' sympathies. They all emphasize the differences in religious and political beliefs or doctrines and, from their standpoints, are quite right in seeing contrast where we see similarity. It cannot be too often repeated that in this book we are concerned only with the methods and results of analysis and that everything else comes in only so far as it sheds light on them. And these methods and results do not differ substantially from those of the late scholastics. This does not mean that the philosophers of natural law copied the scholastics without saying so. Though in many cases scholastic influence is clear beyond reasonable doubt, there presumably was also rediscovery or development from the same sources—the Roman jurists in particular.

The current of thought that the philosophers sponsored was much too important to leave any educated person untouched. Moreover, as will become clear presently, they were but a link in a sequence that runs far into the nineteenth century. For both reasons it is impossible to speak of them as a definitely delimited group. Just now we shall exclude not only all those authors whom it is usual to appraise as mere economists but also all those contributions that do not bear any relation to the philosophy of natural law, even though the men who wrote them belonged to the group. On this understanding, it will suffice to mention a very few representative seventeenth-century names: Grotius, Hobbes, Locke, Pufendorf.

Hugo Grotius or Huigh de Groot (1583-1645, *De jure belli ac pacis*, 1st ed., 1625; 2nd rev. ed., 1631) was first and last a great jurist whose fame rests upon his outstanding performance in international law. He dealt but briefly with economic subjects, such as prices, monopolies, money, interest, and usury in Book II, ch. 12—very sensibly no doubt but without adding anything of note to the teaching of the late scholastics.

Thomas Hobbes (1588-1679; besides the *Leviathan* (1651), *De cive* (1642) and *De corpore politico* (1650) should be mentioned; Sir Leslie Stephen's biography may be recommended as one of the best sketches of the cultural backgrounds of that time) was an Oxford man of the private-tutor type and, first and last, a political sociologist. He was not more interested in economics than was Grotius, though he also touched upon economic subjects, especially money. His importance for us is due not so much to the powerful originality of his political philosophy (which really fits in better with the subject of the next chapter) but rather to the fact that, more than any other philosopher of natural law, he was open to the incipient mechanistic materialism of his time and

[1] This term I have adopted on the advice of Professor A. P. Usher.

that he transmitted its influence, particularly through his ethical and psychological (sensationalist) teaching, to the social sciences. It is relevant to note that though he was not a good, let alone creative, mathematician and physicist, he took a more than dilettantic interest in both these fields; and that all this did not prevent him from making several excursions into speculative theology besides using theological arguments and biblical quotations within his sociological analysis.

John Locke, the philosopher (1632-1704; a first and incomplete collection of his works appeared in 1714, a nine-volume one in 1853; there are many lives), was also a product of Oxford. He started his career by tutoring and lecturing and then entered the civil service, in which, under the wings of Whig protectors (whom he furnished with advice and ideologies), he eventually rose to a seat in the Board of Trade. His work is of first-rate importance for us on a number of counts. First, as a philosopher in the narrow sense of the word, he led the empiricist tendency to victory first in England and then on the Continent, especially in France, as against Cartesian rationalism (the decisive work was his *Essay concerning Human Understanding,* publ. 1690). This was indeed a break with the scholastic tradition (Aristotle) and a quite decisive one. The reader should reflect, however, that this *does not imply that there was a similar break in political or economic theory:* it is essential to keep these things distinct. Second, as an advocate of (qualified) tolerance, of the liberty of the press, and of extended education, Locke was instrumental in building up the general scheme of later political liberalism, which fact must be mentioned in passing because of its relation to economic liberalism. Third, as a political theorist (see especially his *Two Treatises of Government,* publ. 1690) Locke may claim a front-rank place among the philosophers of natural law, though he added little to Grotius and Pufendorf. Fourth, as an economist (see below, ch. 6) he made significant contributions which will, however, be dealt with in another connection because they stand in no relation to either his philosophy or his political theory. Finally, we must again note his theological interests (see especially his *Reasonableness of Christianity,* 1695).

Samuel von Pufendorf (1632-94) was a jurist of the academic type and successively professor at the Universities of Heidelberg, Lund (Sweden), and Berlin. He was not much more than a follower of Grotius. But he wrote a treatise that became a textbook of international reputation and sums up and represents the whole structure of the social science of the philosophers of natural law much better than do the works of the greater men mentioned before: *De jure naturae et gentium, libri octo* (1st ed. [the one used], 1672); more important than his earlier *Elementa jurisprudentiae universalis* (1660). It is the work to consult to get a general idea of the range and level of that type of social science. Moreover, Pufendorf went much further into economics than did Grotius (Book v, chs. 1-8), though he still does not seem to me to have added much to the stock of knowledge and to the analytic apparatus of the late scholastics. But he presented the material in a systematic form. Characteristically enough, he also wrote a theological tract: *De habitu christianae religionis ad vitam civilem.*

Other names might be mentioned, among them some the reader is likely to miss. But the great name of Leibniz and that of his faithful henchman, Christian Wolff, are left out advisedly: they were polyhistors, of course, and greatly interested, among other things, in the economic events and policies of their day; but they made no contribution to our subject. However, perhaps I should have mentioned Thomasius (1655-1728) because his writings shed interesting light on the concept of natural law as used by the group.

Exactly like the scholastics, the philosophers of natural law aimed at a comprehensive social science—a comprehensive theory of society in all its aspects and activities—in which economics was neither a very important nor an independent element. This social science of the philosophers first appeared in the form of systems of jurisprudence that were similar to the scholastic treatises *De justitia et jure:* Grotius and Pufendorf were primarily lawyers and their treatises are primarily treatises on law. They dealt with legal and political principles for which very general validity was claimed on the ground that they were natural in the sense that they derived from general properties of human nature and not, like positive law, from the particular conditions of individual countries.[2] And all the rest of what has been said in the preceding section about the methodological character and the various meanings of natural law of the late scholastics, particularly on the relation between its normative and its analytic aspect, would now have to be repeated for the natural law of the laical philosophers. But though it is grossly inaccurate either to ascribe to the latter the conception itself and its exploitation for purely analytic purposes, or to style them as innovators who rose against scholastic methods of thought, there are several contributions of theirs to record, some of them more felicitous than others.

(b) *Mathematics and Physics.* The philosophers of natural law lived in the heroic age of mathematics and physics. Spectacular discoveries in what for the general public—though not for us—was the 'new experimental philosophy' were attended by no less spectacular popularity of physics, even with mere men of letters and great ladies. First in Italy, then everywhere else, experimenters and mathematicians gathered in order to discuss results and fight out differences; but their meetings drew the curious who wished to have things explained and were welcomed because of the assistance they were able to render financially and otherwise.[3] Those successes and this fashion were not lost upon the philosophers of natural law. They—or some of them—looked at their tools and wondered whether they did not after all bear some similarity

[2] Hobbes, *Leviathan,* I, chs. 14 and 15, enumerated 19 such principles which he called natural laws. The 'science' of these laws he called Moral Philosophy, a term that will presently be introduced in a different sense.

[3] For our purpose, it will suffice to mention the example of the English Royal Society, chartered, after having existed informally for about twenty years, in 1662—King Charles II took a dilettantic but intelligent interest in it. For a century to come, it was precisely such a gathering of professional physicists and interested laymen. Sir Isaac Newton (1642-1727) was president from 1703 to his death and published his *Philosophiae naturalis principia mathematica* (1687) under its auspices. Its organ, the *Philosophical Transactions,* began to appear shortly after the granting of the charter. The term Natural Philosophy was used to denote what we call the physical (as distinguished from social) sciences until the first decades of the nineteenth century. This use of the word 'natural' further contributed to confusion.

It was, I believe, the curiosity awakened by the achievements of the physical sciences which, spreading beyond its original habitat, created a demand for a type of work that was substantially new, the encyclopaedia. The first achievements in this field were Pierre Bayle's (1647-1706) *Dictionnaire historique et critique* (1697)—the forerunner of the much more comprehensive work of the *encyclopédistes* of the eighteenth century whom we shall mention later on—and John Harris' *Lexicon technicum* (1704).

to those of the victorious physicists; Pufendorf professed to use a *methodus mathematica*, though actually he did not do so. Hobbes declared that 'civil philosophy'—a term clearly used for the sake of the parallelism to natural philosophy in the sense of physical science—dated from the publication of his own book, *De cive* (1642), and that he was the first to apply to this civil philosophy the methods of Copernicus and Galileo (which he, however, conceived of as deduction from an abstract and universal 'law of motion'). This sort of thing, mere talk though it was, had a most unfortunate consequence.

We have seen that later critics, mainly those in sympathy with the historical school, attacked the natural-law concept on the ground that it was metaphysical and speculative. Other nineteenth-century writers who took that talk at its face value, as critics are apt to do, condemned it as too 'naturalist,' that is to say, as implying an attempt to copy physical methods of analysis. It even happened that the same critic raised both objections, which, in addition to being unfounded, are mutually exclusive. So the unfortunate concept of natural law eventually met disaster under fire from two opposite quarters. Or rather, the phrase did; for the idea lived on.

It cannot even be asserted that the laical philosophers were less theology-minded than the late scholastics, though theirs was, of course, a different theology. They wrote books on theological questions. They quoted scripture in support of their arguments. The fourth Part of Hobbes's *Leviathan* (1651) is entitled 'Of the Kingdom of Darknesse' and contains a chapter on Daemonology, though the demons are no doubt reduced to a symbolic existence as are angels in the third Part.

(c) *Economic and Political Sociology*. Into this conception of human nature the philosophers of natural law introduced elements which, though not entirely new, received an emphasis that was. The more important of these are due to Hobbes. The scholastic doctors had implied that private property owes its origin, in part, to the necessity of avoiding a chaotic struggle for goods, and government its origin to the necessity of enforcing peace and order. But they did not go as far as to speak of an original war of all against all (*bellum omnium contra omnes*) or of every man's being a wolf to every other man (*homo homini lupus*). This sort of thing did not become general doctrine and can hardly be called an analytic improvement. Similarly, the social contract, more delicately adumbrated by the doctors and by Grotius, came out with brutal naïveté in Hobbes's system. In the *Leviathan* (II, chs. 17 and 18) he lets a commonwealth or *civitas*, 'that great Leviathan,' actually be generated by an agreement or covenant, which everyone enters into with everyone else for the purpose of transferring each one's right to govern himself to a man or an assembly of men. This doctrine, restated in its baldest as well as most influential form by Locke, did command almost general assent. But the omnipotence with which Hobbes invested this government did not; Locke in particular was in no mind to argue that the subjects cannot change the form of government, and that the power of the government cannot be forfeited. In any case, the thesis of governmental omnipotence has no analytic standing. For it is not, like some of the juridical arguments of the doctors and the philosophers, the cloak of an analytic proposition, but just a juridical argument and nothing else; Hobbes simply deduced it from the imaginary covenant by arbitrarily interpreting it in such a way as to imply unconditional surrender of the citizen. Finally, we may note that Locke 'justified' private property from everyone's right to his own person, which includes the right to one's labor, which includes the right to the results of one's labor—again a purely juridical argument and an obviously inadequate one at that. It hardly needs to be added that this argument has nothing whatever to do with a labor theory of value.

If this were all, then the contribution of the philosophers to political and economic sociology would be indeed a poor one. But there is something else, namely, a contribution to what we may call Metasociology or Philosophical Anthropology: some of the philosophers probed into that human nature from which their natural laws were to be derived.[4] Again, Hobbes is the outstanding example. The first Part of the *Leviathan*, entitled 'Of Man,' which leads up to the natural-law concept, blocks out a whole philosophy of the human mind and deals with the psychology and social psychology of thought, imagination, speech, religion, and the like. Much of this has Aristotelian and scholastic roots, though Hobbes adopted the all but general practice of indicating antagonism where there was development. But, in a definite direction, he actually went much further than either Aristotle or the scholastics had gone. He defined 'thought'—an individual thought, the same thing as Locke's 'idea'—as the 'representation of an external object' and let the human mind be furnished by sense impression. It may indeed be asserted that he anticipated the substance of Locke's empiricism as well as the principle of associationist psychology that was to become so closely allied to economics in the times of the two Mills, father and son (see below, Part III, ch. 3, sec. 5).

By Philosophical Empiricism we mean the doctrine, adumbrated by the Greeks (Aristotle, Epicureans, Stoics) but developed mainly by English thinkers of the seventeenth and eighteenth centuries (especially by Hobbes, Locke, and Hume), that (a) all knowledge of the individual is derived through experience during his own life; (b) that this experience may be equated to the sense impressions to which his mind is exposed; (c) that prior to this experience his mind is not only a complete blank but even without 'conative' activity of its own and also without innate ideas in the sense of categories by which the sense impressions are marshalled—so that it would perhaps be logical to say that, as such, 'mind' does not exist at all; (d) that the impressions are the ultimate elements into which all mental phenomena may be resolved, not only remembrance, attention, reasoning—including the construction of causal sequences—but also the affective ones, the 'passions': all these are but

[4] Metasociology, then, denotes investigations into human nature or human behavior or, more generally, into the wide realm of all the facts that, though relevant for sociology, do not belong to it in a professional sense but lie beyond or behind it, such as investigations into the formation of habits or into the properties of physical environments. Analogously, we may speak of Metaeconomics. The term Philosophical Anthropology denotes the same thing as Metasociology, the adjective distinguishing it from Anthropology in the usual sense (study of physical characteristics).

agglomerations of elemental impressions and produced by their random 'associations.' This resolution of the human 'mind' or 'soul' into atomic impressions may be likened to the reduction of all physical phenomena to atomistic mechanics, a much employed analogy that made empiricism popular to some and hateful to other people. The reader will please observe that the term Empiricism is here used in what is only one of its many meanings, which is why the adjective Philosophical is added. It has, in particular, *nothing whatever to do* with Scientific Empiricism, a term that merely denotes the attitude that extols the roles of experiment and observation at the expense of that of 'theory.' More specific labels are Sensualism or Sensationalism.

As a philosophy, Empiricism or Sensualism or Sensationalism, although brilliantly defended by Hume in the eighteenth century and by J. S. Mill in the nineteenth, and although it always had a considerable vogue among English nonphilosophers, did not wear well. Leibniz raised the obvious though not decisive objection—what is it?—at the beginning of the eighteenth century. Bishop Berkeley, a little later, produced a different argument that amounted to rejection (*Principles of Human Knowledge*, 1710), and even in England, let alone Scotland or Germany, the battle among professional philosophers went mostly against it. But Associationist Psychology fared much better and in fact commanded the explicit or implicit allegiance of English economists and their continental allies until about 1900 and beyond. A distinguished economist, James Mill, is even responsible for its most uncompromising nineteenth-century exposition. By Psychological Associationism we mean exactly the same doctrine that we called Philosophical Empiricism before. The difference that calls for a separate term is this. Whereas the latter is, or pretends to be, a philosophy in the strict sense of the term and also an epistemology or theory of knowledge, the former denotes the same doctrine, but considered as a fundamental hypothesis in the study of the various problems that come within the professional field of psychology, such as the theory of imagination, or attention, or language, and so on. The reader is requested to keep all this in mind for future reference.

Another point cannot be too strongly impressed upon the reader. The scholastic doctors had taught the doctrines of natural liberty and natural equality of men. With them, however, this natural equality was not an assertion about facts of human nature but a moral ideal or postulate: it rested on Christian beliefs such as that the Saviour died for the salvation of all. But Hobbes, when explaining the conditions that produce his original state of war of all against all, asserted *as a fact* (*Leviathan*, ch. 13) that man's faculties of mind and body are about equal in the sense that the range of their variations is so narrowly limited as *to make complete equality a permissible working hypothesis*. And this was the general opinion of the philosophers. Henceforth we denote this proposition by the phrase Analytic Equalitarianism in order to distinguish it from the Christian ideal, which we shall call Normative

Equalitarianism. Now, first, it should be obvious that analytic equalitarianism is of immense importance, not only for economic sociology and not only for the wider implications of economics proper, but also for many problems of economic theory itself. We need only replace it by the opposite assertion of fact in order to realize that this would change the whole picture of the economic process. Second, with few exceptions and with little qualification, most economists have accepted, and are accepting to this day, analytic equalitarianism. But they never made any serious attempt to verify it, though one would think that they had every reason for making sure of the reliability of such a pillar of their analytic structures. We shall return to this most curious fact in our survey of the *Wealth of Nations*.

(d) *Contribution to Economics*. The economics of the philosophers could have been taken from Molina. It will suffice to advert to the well-rounded presentation in Pufendorf's treatise. Distinguishing value in use and value in exchange (or *pretium eminens*), he lets the latter be determined by the relative scarcity or abundance of goods and money. Market price then gravitates toward the costs that must normally be incurred in production. His analysis of interest (in which he proves himself not averse to biblical quotations) is distinctly inferior to that of the late scholastics. He goes on to discuss various problems of public policy, such as the repression of luxury by sumptuary laws, the regulation of monopolies, craft guilds, inheritance, entails, population. Good sense and moderation are invariably in evidence as is also a sense of the historic flux of things. The welfare aspect is always kept in view. Again, we behold an embryonic *Wealth of Nations*.

7. The Philosophers of Natural Law: Natural-Law Analysis in the Eighteenth Century and After

By 1700, developments that are to be surveyed in the next chapter had already outdistanced the economics of the philosophers of natural law. It will prove helpful, however, to stay for a moment in order to follow the subsequent fortunes of that little body of economic truth until it loses its individuality and, merging with a broader stream, vanishes from our sight (see below, subsec. g).

The sixty or seventy years that preceded the French Revolution are commonly referred to as the Enlightenment. This phrase is meant to indicate quickened advance on many fronts, or rather a quickened sense of advance—general enthusiasm for progress and reforms. Applying reason to what appeared to be the heap of nonsense inherited from the past was the program of the epoch. A wave of religious, political, and economic criticism that was pathetically uncritical of its own dogmatic standards swept over the intellectual centers of Europe. French society in particular was rapidly disintegrating, but as yet felt perfectly safe. Like all disintegrating societies that do not want to face their danger, it delighted in protecting its enemies and thus provided a milieu of unique charm for a literature that will attract even those of us who sense a flavor of decay—and sometimes, what is worse, also a flavor of mediocrity—

when they turn to these old volumes that harbor so much complacency. The best antidote to the compliments that the men of that self-styled Age of Reason were in the habit of paying to themselves is to read them. Fortunately, there are better performances to record than those of Voltaire and Rousseau. It is, however, impossible to convey, in the space available, a picture of either that intellectual situation or its social background.[1] We can only touch upon the irreducible minimum of essential points.

[(a) *The Science of Human Nature: Psychologism.*] The only fact that need be noticed in matters of theology is that a Natural Theology as distinguished from the *sacra doctrina*—remember that this distinction goes back to the thirteenth century—definitely established itself as a separate field of *laical* social science. Its properly theological contents tended to shrink to an insipid Deism.[2] But more interesting was the development of a sociology of religion—a theory of the origin and social practice of religious ideas—the first substantial beginnings of which we located with Hobbes. The most important fact about philosophical thought is the victorious progress of English empiricism or sensationalism—of Hobbes's and Locke's teaching—which is all the more remarkable because, methodologically, it does not agree as well as does philosophical rationalism with all the claims that were being made, in theology and

[1] Both have been described innumerable times. It is very difficult, however, to present a helpful selection. Perhaps the best advice to give is that the reader turn to Hippolyte Taine's famous book, *Les Origines de la France contemporaine* (1876-93) or to Henri Sée's *Les Idées politiques en France au XVIIIe siècle* (1920). But the portrait not only of an individual but of a civilization is so excellently drawn by Lytton Strachey in a brief essay on Morellet (*Portraits in Miniature,* 1931) that half an hour invested in reading it plus another half-hour of pondering over it will do more for the reader than would many hours spent on heavier works. For England, Sir Leslie Stephen's old standard work, *History of English Thought in the Eighteenth Century* (1876), or his *English Literature and Society in the Eighteenth Century* (1904), and H. J. Laski's *Political Thought in England from Locke to Bentham* (1920) may be recommended. J. Bonar's *Philosophy and Political Economy* (3rd ed., 1922) is always a stand-by, of course.

[2] This statement illustrates well the difficulties inherent in the drawing of any sketches such as this. It had to be made in order not to miss an important background fact, and it is of course true. Nevertheless, it is quite misleading in its effects. On the one hand, it misses the affinity of mere Deism with frank philosophical materialism and hence its true nature. Therefore, let us note the fact that philosophical materialism also developed in a form in which it was not known in the Middle Ages. Holbach's *Système de la nature* (1770) may stand as an example. On the other hand, the statement in our text neglects the fact that in the eighteenth century there were a number of religious revivals which are the symptoms of currents that perhaps sum up to more than the Deism and materialism combined. This holds even for France: the intellectual activity within the French Church is, of course, not wholly represented by infidel abbés whose cloth was important to them chiefly as a title to prebends. In this connection, the activities of the Société de l'abbaye de Saint-Germain-des Prés, of which Jean Mabillon was the center, should be mentioned. We must hurry on, however.

elsewhere, on behalf of *la raison*. This, of course, greatly favored the success of associationist psychology. Let us call a halt in order to glance at three figures who are not only of outstanding importance for us but also representative of the spirit of the age at its highest, Condillac, Hume, and Hartley. The first two we shall meet again in the role of simple economists. The third points directly to James Mill's performance of 1829.[3] All three did not philosophize simply for the sake of philosophizing but in order to develop the Science of Man or of Human Nature that was to be the basis of the science —or the sciences—of society: more than anything else, they were metasociologists or philosophical anthropologists. No doubt, they were convinced that both in aim and method—the 'experimental' method, for which they invoked

[3] Étienne Bonnot de Condillac (1714-80; *Oeuvres complètes*, 1821-2; see, for general information, R. Lenoir's *Condillac*, 1924), worked out Locke's sensationalism into an elaborate system (*Essai sur l'origine des connaissances humaines*, 1746; *Traité des sensations*, 1754), which constitutes the most important continental response to the English lead, both in its philosophical and in its psychological aspects. But the achievement does not consist in systematic elaboration only, for the work presents many original elements, and some of them, such as the theory of the role of language and other symbolisms (*Langue de calculs*, 1798), point far into the future, in spite of the introspective method used, even to the Watsonian behaviorism of our time.

David Hume (1711-76)—who, among other things, exerted formative influence on A. Smith—claims our attention in three quite different and almost unconnected incarnations: as an economist, in which incarnation he swam outside of the natural-law current now under discussion; as a historian, in which incarnation he will be noticed presently; and as a philosopher and metasociologist, which is the incarnation that matters just now. The work of his youth—strikingly illustrative both of the truth of Ostwald's thesis that original creation is the privilege of men under thirty and of the other truth that part of this subjective originality is due to the young author's blissful ignorance of the previous development of his subject—the *Treatise of Human Nature: being an Attempt to introduce the Experimental Method of Reasoning* [*sic, J. A. S.*] *into Moral Subjects* (1st two vols., 1739, 3rd vol., 1740), remodeled (infelicitously) into the *Philosophical Essays* of 1748 (republished as *Enquiry concerning Human Understanding*, 1758) is the most important stepping-stone between Locke and Kant, far above the former and almost on the intellectual level of the latter. The most important contribution was Hume's theory of causality. This also was Hume's opinion, for it is this topic he singled out for relatively full treatment in the *Abstract of a Treatise of Human Nature* which he published in 1740 and which was retrieved and republished in 1938 with an introduction by J. M. Keynes and P. Sraffa. *Works* (modern ed. by Green and Grose, with introduction and bibliography); *Life and Correspondence* by J. H. Burton (1846); *Letters to Strahan*, ed. by J. Birkbeck Hill (1888). Further *Letters* of great interest, ed. by J. Y. T. Greig (1932).

David Hartley (1705-57) was not, any more than was Condillac, the father of associationist psychology. But his *Observations on Man* . . . (1749) did for it what, to use an economic analogy that the reader will appreciate later, Malthus' *Essay on Population* was to do for the theory contained in it. Also he imparted to it a slant that was new, so far as I know: he linked sense impressions and their associations with 'nerve vibrations' and thus psychology with physiology. Finally, he worked out a theory of ethics and even of natural theology on this basis.

the authority of Francis Bacon—their work meant a new departure. All the more important is it to realize that this was not the case. In aim as well as in method they had been clearly anticipated by Hobbes. But we know that Hobbes, though original in a number of important individual points, was a philosopher of natural law like Grotius or Pufendorf and that in fundamental aim and method he did not differ from them. Condillac, Hume, and Hartley were certainly more articulate; with clearer purpose, they developed this science of human nature more fully. The idea of this science itself, however, and the program of deriving from it the basic propositions of the individual social sciences are the idea and the program of the philosophers of natural law and indirectly of the scholastics. The affinity shows in many details: for instance, the germs of associationist psychology are to be found in Aristotle's concepts of similarity and contiguity and in the corresponding concepts of scholastic psychology. Moreover, the methods actually used by the eighteenth-century men were exactly the same as, and in particular not more 'experimental' than, those of their predecessors. Therefore, just as we expressed an important aspect of the work of the philosophers of natural law by calling them laical scholastics, so we may now express an important aspect of the work of the Condillacs, Humes, and Hartleys by calling them eighteenth-century philosophers of natural law.[4] Two points about this science of man are of special interest for us.

First, the metasociology of Condillac, Hartley, and Hume was essentially psychological. And their associationist psychology was essentially introspective, that is to say, it admitted the analyst's observation of his own psychic processes as a valid source of information. Both these features are of obvious significance for the history of economic analysis but we are now particularly interested in the first. Those authors and most of their contemporaries evidently believed that psychological considerations will explain not only the psychological mechanisms of individual and group behavior, and the ways in which social facts are reflected in, and interpreted by, individual or group minds, but also these social facts themselves. They would not have denied, of course, that in order to explain any actual event, institution, or process we must also take account of facts other than psychological. But they did not develop any general theories about them or admit them into their metasociology: the only stock of general knowledge needed in all the branches of science that have anything to do with human actions or attitudes was psychology and all these branches of science were nothing but applied psychology.

[4] The affinity I wished to exhibit may be underlined by a contrast: modern specialists in the various social sciences never think of looking to a mother science of human nature for guidance. They just attack the facts and problems of their special fields directly, using the methods and making the hypotheses that seem most useful for their particular purposes. In fact, if there be any particular 'modernity' about such authors as Hume—apart from their hostility to metaphysics—it would have to be found in the facts that they failed to carry out their program and that, as economists, for instance, they actually reasoned without much reference to their science of human nature. This is one of the reasons why their economics will be dealt with separately.

This view is, however, not the only possible one. We may think that other than psychological data, for instance, geographical, technological, biological facts. are much more important in the practical work of analysis than anything a psychological science of human nature has to contribute. Hence metasociology should be built up from materials other than psychological; and even—which was, for instance, the opinion of Karl Marx—that social processes are governed by a super-individual logic of their own, to the understanding of which the psychology of individuals and groups has nothing to contribute except the knowledge of surface phenomena for the sake of which, moreover, it is not necessary to go very far into psychology. No matter which of these two views of the nature and method of the social sciences we make our own, we must never forget that the one sponsored by our representative authors cannot simply be taken for granted. In order to emphasize this we will give it a distinctive label, Psychologism.

Second, the sociology that was based upon that science of man tended to overstress, just as Aristotle's had overstressed, the element of rationality in behavior. It is therefore interesting to note that the best brains began to react against this. For instance—curious lag phenomenon!—while the *contrat social* was carried to the high-water mark of its popularity by such writers as Rousseau, Hume already denounced it as a completely imaginary and, moreover, unnecessary construct. In addition, he fired another shot at a similar target when he penned the pithy sentence: ''tis not, therefore, reason which is the guide of life but custom' (*Abstract*, p. 16).

[(b) *Analytic Aesthetics and Ethics*.] The way in which that fundamental science of man—of human nature, human knowledge, and human behavior—produced all sorts of 'natural laws' may be illustrated best by what may be described as the English 'natural aesthetics' and the 'natural ethics' of the eighteenth century. Of course, not all speculations on aesthetics and ethics were offshoots of that science, even in England, but we are interested only in those that were, because these present highly revealing analysis by methods that were to serve economic analysis for more than a century to come.

Natural aesthetics and ethics were, first, analytic aesthetics and ethics: though the normative purpose was never discarded, it was not allowed to interfere with the primary task of explaining actual behavior. This analytic point of view had been brought to the fore already during the seventeenth century, for aesthetics, by a number of Italian writers and, for ethics, by Hobbes and Spinoza.[5] Second, the analytic task was tackled in the spirit of

[5] Baruch Spinoza (1632-77). The two works relevant to the subject in hand are his *Ethics* and his *Tractatus politicus* (both of which appeared posthumously, 1677). The purely scientific program in question is obscured by the fact that Spinoza's ethics eventually weld into a highly metaphysical system. But he did emphasize the necessity of analyzing human passions as they are instead of preaching about them. Since this is our only opportunity of saluting that great thinker, let me quote here a sentence of his which, though it refers to politics and ethics, every economist ought to be able to repeat on his deathbed: *ut ea quae ad hanc scientiam spectant, eadem animi libertate, qua res mathematicas solemus, inquirerem sedulo curavi* (I have sedulously tried

what was defined above as psychologism: not only was psychology to provide the approach to the aesthetical and ethical phenomena, but it was to explain all there was to explain about them. Third, the psychology actually used, though not always strictly associationist, was always individual psychology, introspective, and of the most primitive kind, rarely if ever involving anything beyond some simple hypothesis about the reactions of the individual psyche from which everything else followed by deduction. Aesthetical and ethical values were thus explained in a manner suggestive of that in which Italian and French economists in the eighteenth century, and the majority of economists of all countries in the nineteenth, explained economic values. This procedure was called empirical and in a sense it was, but only in the sense in which, for example, the Jevons-Menger-Walras theory of marginal utility is. There was nothing 'experimental' or inductive about it and it was in fact not very realistic, notwithstanding all the programmatic utterances, war cries, and appeals to Francis Bacon.

Aesthetics, then, tended to shrink, so far as this school of thought is concerned, to an analysis of the pleasurable sensations evoked by a work of art, the psychology of the creative effort of the artist receiving less attention.[6] In order to exhibit the analogy that interests us, we shall compare the objective fact that a work of art is considered as 'beautiful' in a given social group with the objective fact of market price. The aesthetic theory in question will then be seen to explain the former fact by subjective valuations of the members of the group, much as the analogous economic theory explains the latter fact by subjective valuations of the individuals participating in a market. In both cases subjective valuation creates the objective value—we know that this had been taught, in the case of commodities, by the scholastic doctors—and not the other way round: a thing is beautiful because it pleases, it does not please because it is 'objectively' beautiful. Of course, we may go on to ask why certain things please certain people and we may probe into the origins of our ideas about the beautiful. But however far we may get in these and similar problems, we always move within the range of a particular conception of the meaning of things, even if we introduce, by special hypothesis, a 'sense' of the beautiful. Different authors went to different lengths in 'subjectivizing' aesthetics. Nevertheless, it was this subjectivization that constituted the main contribution of the school in question and which, moreover, its members felt to be the particularly realistic or 'experimental' or nonspeculative element in it. The principal English authors to mention are Shaftesbury, Hutcheson, Hume, and Alison. The first three are much more important for ethics.[7]

---

to deal with the subject of this science with the same serene detachment to which we are accustomed in mathematics).

[6] This is only broadly true, and even so only for the English theory envisaged. The psycho-sociological meaning of artistic creation was touched upon by Hobbes and subjected to searching analysis by Vico.

[7] A. Ashley Cooper, third Earl of Shaftesbury (1671-1713), the grandson of the politician of doubtful fame. The work that co-ordinates his earlier publications, and hence the only one that needs to be mentioned, is *Characteristicks of Men, Manners,*

The preceding argument fully applies also to ethics but must be supplemented, in this case, by some additional considerations. So far as analytic ethics—analysis of actual conduct—is concerned, the main points of the story are quickly told. Hobbes had described actual conduct, by means of what he supposed to be its determining factor, individual and hedonist egotism. This may have appeared to him as the acme of realism but is, as a matter of fact, nothing but a postulate or hypothesis and an obviously unrealistic one at that. Shaftesbury countered this theory by another hypothesis, the hypothesis of altruism: he explained that for man who habitually lives in society it is just as natural to develop fellow feelings and hence to value the good of other people as it is to develop self-interest and to value his own good. On this he superimposed still another hypothesis, also derived from introspection, according to which the virtuous experience pleasure from doing good irrespective of their appreciation of its effects. This is what is specifically known as Shaftesbury's moral-sense theory, which, though its explanatory value is evidently not great, met with considerable success precisely because of the extreme simplicity of the 'psychology' involved. Shaftesbury's position was systematically elaborated by Hutcheson. And Hume, under the influence of all three, created the moral type of the amiable, easy-going, humane, soberly pleasure-loving egotist that summed up the sort of person he was himself: no asceticism or any other 'monkish' virtue for him—no indeed!—and hence, *of course*, not for anyone else. That unprejudiced analysis of these monkish virtues might, perchance, unearth the true key to the ethical phenomenon was quite beyond his range of vision. Abraham Tucker (1705-74) [8] similarly posited satisfaction of individual desires as the ultimate goal and universal motive of action. I do not think I am wrong in attributing the Hume-Tucker opinion also to Bentham, who held that the only interests an individual can be relied on to consult are his own, but added a qualifying note by emphasizing reasonable or enlightened self-interest that does take account also of other people's interests, feelings, and reactions.

The English moralists of the eighteenth century were, however, no more prepared to do without a normative standard of conduct and judgment than any other moralists ever have been. Some were content to fall back upon a moral law that men know and accept intuitively, an idea that foreshadowed

---

Opinions, Times (1711). Francis Hutcheson (1694-1746), owing to his having been the teacher (and a predecessor in the Glasgow chair) of A. Smith, is for us a 'key man.' A vital and most successful teacher—perhaps all the more successful because he seems not to have despised occasional phraseological fireworks—he exerted widespread influence. His chief work embodies the harvest of years of lecturing: *A System of Moral Philosophy* (publ. posthumously in 1755; see below subsec. e). For the subject in hand, as well as for some subjects that are to follow, we must mention his *Inquiry into the Original of our Ideas of Beauty and Virtue* (1725). See W. R. Scott, *Francis Hutcheson . . .* (1900). Archibald Alison's *Essays on the Nature and Principles of Taste* (1790), is particularly characteristic of the possibilities and limitations of the psychologistic approach.

[8] *Light of Nature Pursued* (1768-77, republ. 1805).

the moral imperative of Kant. Even Locke appealed to such intuition, though this was a bad lapse from grace for an empiricist. But solutions of this type would never have done for Hume or Bentham. To their way of thinking all that was empty metaphysics. At the same time they were quite ready to turn their humane egotism into an ideal, that is to say, to convert their theory of conduct into a source of norms for conduct. We have seen that Hume modeled the moral world to his own image.[9] It is plain that, with delightful naïveté, he thoroughly approved of this image: the schema of his own preferences was the reasonable schema. On the other hand, reason had eliminated all superpersonal values except the good of society. But, in view of that philosophy of human values, what else could this good of society consist in but the sum total of all the satisfactions accruing to all individuals from the realization of their hedonic schemes of preference? If this be so, have we not discovered, at one stroke, the rationale of social values, the relation between them and individual values, and also the only norm of morality that can possibly be meaningful? Affirmative answers to these questions had been suggested already in the seventeenth century, especially by Bishop Cumberland[10] and, less distinctly, by Grotius, who did not go far beyond the common-good concept of the scholastics. The eighteenth-century writers, especially those between Hume and Bentham, only elaborated the fundamental canon of Utilitarian Ethics: good is every action that promotes, bad is every action that impairs, social welfare. Before we consider this canon in its wider aspects, we must glance at a work of particular interest to the economist, that of A. Smith.[11]

With the possible exception of Shaftesbury's this performance must, I think, be placed far above all others. First, he distinguished, like Hutcheson but more clearly than anyone else, between ethics as a theory of behavior and ethics as a theory of people's judgments about behavior, and resolutely concentrated on the latter. Second, this theory of ethical judgment is based upon our ability to place ourselves, as it were, in the other man's place ('sympathy')

[9] This tendency of the social philosopher to exalt his own schema of life's values into an ethical norm from which to judge the habits and tastes of all other men deserves attention because it runs through the whole economic literature and explains a great part of the value judgments of economists. Marshall, for instance, had a very definite conception of the Noble Life (see below, Part IV). It does not take much trouble to realize that this conception was shaped on the model of the typical life of a Cambridge professor. Tastes, pursuits, levels of comfort widely different from it, he at best viewed with indulgence but without ever embracing them with full understanding. It hardly needs to be emphasized how important this is for an appreciation of economists' attitudes to the social worlds they live in.

[10] *De legibus naturae* (1672).

[11] *The Theory of Moral Sentiments*; or, *An Essay towards an Analysis of the Principles by which Men naturally judge concerning the Conduct and Character, first of their Neighbours, and afterwards of themselves. To which is added,* A *Dissertation on the Origin of Languages*. This is the title of the 6th ed., 1790. The 1st appeared in 1759 under the title of *The Theory of Moral Sentiments*. The differences between the two, though considerable, are (apart from the *Dissertation*) not of any great importance.

and to understand him, the judgment of our own acts being then derived from our principles of judging others. Third, the natural is conceived of as that which is psychologically normal—to be analyzed realistically—and not identified with, but distinguished from, the ideal rule of reason (see vol. I, p. 128, 6th ed.). Fourth, the influence of utility upon aesthetic and ethical approbation is not treated simply as a postulate but as a problem in the actual practice of judging (Part IV). Fifth, custom and fashion are not only recognized as relevant factors but systematically investigated (Part V). 'Systems of Moral Philosophy,' that is, theories other than A. Smith's own, come in for criticism that is occasionally trite but on the whole strikingly successful (Part VII). Plan and performance are quite similar to the plan and the performance of the *Wealth of Nations*.

[(c) *Self-Interest, the Common Good, and Utilitarianism.*] We know that both Self-Interest and the Common Good were old stagers. But around the middle of the eighteenth century, they asserted themselves with a new energy, not only in ethics, but over the whole field of social thought. In particular, they were, or were supposed to be, the basic and unifying principles of all the social sciences, practically the only ones 'reason' had espoused. Helvétius[12] (1715-71) compared the role of the principle of self-interest in the social world to the role of the law of gravitation in the physical world. Even the great Beccaria[13] went to the length of asserting that man is wholly egotistic and egocentric and does not trouble at all about any other man's (or the common) good. It should be observed once more that this individual self-interest was oriented on rational expectation of individual pleasure and pain,[14] which must, in turn, be defined in a narrowly hedonist sense. It is true that the eighteenth-century authors added qualifications and recognized pleasures that are not usually classed as hedonist, such as pleasures from malevolence, from the acquisition of power, and even from religious belief and practice. In consequence, defenders of that doctrine have been to some extent successful in their attempt to redeem it from the allegation that has made human behavior turn on beefsteaks. But this success—apart from the fact that it does not touch all the other objections that may be raised against any theory that overstresses rationality in behavior—was more apparent than real. For if we go very far beyond

[12] *De l'Esprit* (1758), Discours II, ch. 2. The book, one of the continental forerunners of English utilitarianism, enjoyed a sweeping success. Few writers have ever professed more naïve and more unconditional belief in education and legislation—that work, of course, upon a perfectly malleable human material which reacts mechanically to physical experience.

[13] The work that is relevant for us at the moment is his famous treatise *Dei delitti e delle pene* (1764), which, a beacon light in the history of the emergence of modern criminal law, illustrates the truth that analytic and practical merit do not necessarily go together.

[14] The standard reference on this subject is Verri's essay on the nature of pleasure and pain published, long after it had circulated and influenced minds, in his *Discorsi di argomento filosofico* (1781). Systematic classification and analysis of the various pleasures and pains is due to Bentham.

idea was of ancient origin and grew so slowly as to defy dating, the slogan itself may be dated more precisely: so far as I know, it occurs first in Hutcheson (op. cit. 1725), then in Beccaria (op. cit. 1764, *la massima felicità divisa nel maggior numero*); after that in Priestley (op. cit. 1768), to whom Bentham gives the credit for what to him was a 'sacred truth.' Hume does not have the slogan, but should be included in this series all the same. The word Utilitarianism is Bentham's.[16]

The essential point to grasp is that utilitarianism was nothing but another natural-law system. This holds not only in the sense that the utilitarians were the historical successors of the seventeenth-century philosophers of natural law; nor only in the sense that the utilitarian system developed from the system of the philosophers which, though evident, can be proved in detail from the history of ethics, on the one hand, and from the history of the common-good concept, on the other; but it holds also in the much more significant sense, that in approach, in methodology, and in the nature of its results utilitarianism actually was another, the last, natural-law system. The program of deriving, by the light of reason, 'laws' about man in society from a very stable and highly simplified human nature fits the utilitarians not less well than the philosophers or the scholastics; and if we look at this human nature and the way in which it was supposed to work, as we did above, we realize that the affinity goes much further than that.

Like the systems of the philosophers or the scholastics, utilitarianism presents a threefold appeal. First it was a philosophy of life, exhibiting a scheme of 'ultimate values.' It is here that we must look for the source of the ineradicable impression that utilitarianism, Bentham's especially, was something new and fundamentally antagonistic to the older systems. But, as the reader should know by now, the difference was not great so far as the philosophy of the current business of everyday life is concerned.

---

a church historian of note and a famous controversialist on theological matters, was also a recognized research worker in electricity and chemistry. That essay may be called the bridge between Locke's theory of government and James Mill's unfortunate exploits in this field. Neither Paley nor Priestley, however, contributed much that cannot be found in earlier writings, e.g. in Cumberland's work already referred to. Of continental 'precursors' it is sufficient to mention again Beccaria, Verri, and Helvétius. With Beccaria, the relation, to be presently discussed, of utilitarianism to earlier natural-law systems is particularly clear.

From the large literature on English utilitarianism and on the Philosophical Radicals, J. S. Mill's essay on *Utilitarianism* (publ. 1863) deserves the reader's first attention. Also see: Sir Leslie Stephen's work, *The English Utilitarians* (1900), H. J. Laski's *Political Thought . . .* already referred to, W. L. Davidson's *Political Thought in England: The Utilitarians from Bentham to J. S. Mill* (1915), and Graham Wallas' charming book on *Francis Place* (1898).

[16] The interesting note of skepticism sounded by A. Smith in a famous dictum of his should be recorded here: he remarked in passing that, so far as conscious happiness is concerned, there is not much difference between any state that we accept as permanent and any other.

For the sphere of stable, barn, shop, and market, the scholastic doctors were utilitarian enough. The real difference was that the doctors confined the utilitarian point of view to purely utilitarian activity where it is (nearly—not even there wholly) adequate, whereas the utilitarians reduced the whole world of human values to the same schema, ruling out, as contrary to reason, all that really matters to man. Thus they are indeed entitled to the credit of having created something that was new in literature—for it cannot be attributed to Epicurus—namely, the shallowest of all conceivable philosophies of life that stands indeed in a position of irreconcilable antagonism to the rest of them.

Second, utilitarianism was a normative system with a strong legal slant. It was, like the scholastic system, a system of moral imperatives, on the one hand, and of legislative principles, on the other. Bentham considered himself primarily a moralist and legislator,[17] and it was as a criterion of 'good' and 'bad' legislation that the principle of greatest happiness of the greatest number acquired for him paramount importance. Observe once more the equalitarian element in it which was as essential as the element of happiness. And these two together with the belief not only that any individual was very much like any other, but also that every individual was nondescript and malleable material with few or no innate characteristics of his own, then produced the fundamental political 'plank' of Benthamism: educate people and let them vote freely and everything else will take care of itself.[18]

But, third, again like the natural law of the philosophers and the scholastics, utilitarianism also was a comprehensive system of social science embodying a uniform method of analysis. And this aspect of it is separable from the two others in the same sense in which the analytic work of the scholastics and the philosophers is separable from the rest of their thought. In other words, it is logically possible to despise utilitarianism,

[17] Before Bentham, the catalogue of utilitarian moralists does not quite coincide with the catalogue of utilitarian legislators, and in a more complete exposition it might be advisable to distinguish the histories of moral and political utilitarianism. Most of the important names, however, would occur in both, and in view of the close relation we need not insist further on that distinction.

[18] It should be observed that these political principles do not uniquely determine a man's allegiance to a political party or the position he will take on any practical political question. Bentham impressed his personal preferences upon a group of personal adherents—the Philosophical Radicals already mentioned—and the strong coherence of this group accounts for a definite program (in substance laissez-faire combined with universal suffrage) and the impression that this program followed inexorably from analytic premisses. But in other times and countries, the Benthamites might have been conservatives—Hume was, and most of the Italian utilitarians were—or else socialists. There is nothing surprising in this so soon as it is realized that preference plays so large a part in arriving at conclusions as to practical policy that it bends almost any analytic structure to its dictate. A man may accept Marx's analytic work entirely and yet be a conservative in practice.

root and branch, both as a philosophy of life and as a political program and yet to accept it, as an engine of analysis, in all or some of the departments of the social sciences. But since, on the one hand, utilitarianism may be not much more valuable as an engine of analysis than it is in the other two respects and since, on the other hand, many economists have not hesitated to declare that it is basic to economic theory—Jevons even defined economic theory as 'a calculus of pleasure and pain'—the extent of its influence upon analytic work should be cleared up at once.

It is the common failing of laymen, philosophers, and historians of thought to pay exaggerated respect to whatever presents itself as a fundamental principle. Actually, people do not always make use, in scientific work any more than in the practical concerns of life, of the fundamental principles to which they profess allegiance. Utilitarianism being a set of such fundamental principles, we must therefore inquire in every case what role it was allowed to play. So far as economics is concerned, we may, however, return broad answers for four types of cases. First, utilitarian hypotheses are completely valueless in questions of interpretations of history or in questions touching the moving forces of economic history. Second, utilitarian hypotheses are worse than valueless in all problems involving questions of actual schemes of motivation, for example, in such a problem as the economic effects of inheritance. Third, utilitarian hypotheses are in fact basic to that part of economic theory that is usually referred to as Welfare Economics—the heir to Italian eighteenth-century theories on *felicità pubblica*. We adopt these hypotheses habitually when discussing such problems as the effects of 'transfers of wealth from the relatively rich to the relatively poor.' And this is precisely the reason why the propositions of welfare economics never convince anyone who is not already convinced beforehand and irrespective of any argument. For though there is, of course, an aspect of these problems to which the utilitarian approach is appropriate—provided we believe it to be methodologically admissible—this aspect is evidently not the only one: we have proved very little, when we have proved that transferring a rich man's dollar to a poor man increases welfare in the utilitarian sense. Fourth, in the field of economic theory in the narrowest sense of the term, utilitarian hypotheses are unnecessary but harmless. For instance, we can state and discuss the properties of economic equilibrium without introducing them. But if we do introduce them, results are not materially affected, hence not impaired. This makes it possible for us to salvage much of economic analysis that at first sight seems hopelessly vitiated by utilitarian preconceptions.

[(d) *Historical Sociology*.] The writers of the eighteenth century have often been blamed for lack of 'historical sense,' a disability that went in fact so far with some of them as to make them blind to the values of bygone civilizations. All the more necessary is it to point out that the antidote developed along with the disease. If we find, in some instances, the most foolish contempt for

Greek art—Voltaire being put above Homer, for instance—we also find the origins of its modern cult. If we sometimes find a perfectly stupendous absence of interest in history, we also find a rich crop of serious historical work that laid the foundations of nineteenth-century developments. We cannot do more than list five essential points: a good beginning was made with systematic collection of materials; new methods of interpretation and criticism of documents were worked out;[19] economic and cultural history began to divert some of the attention previously all but monopolized by political and military history; the (relatively speaking) detached report that renders documentary evidence began to prevail over epics or preachings (Hume, William Robertson, Gibbon);[20] and the awakening of interest of the public is attested by the success of popular universal and national histories. Of course, there is such a thing as unhistorical history, that is to say, a man may do historical work without ever getting the specifically historical angle. But Hume's *History of England* (8 vols., 1763) was not of this kind. Though hopelessly out of date by now, it will always be a landmark of historiography—which shows that he, at least, was not a slave to his utilitarianism.

Still more noteworthy from our standpoint is the emergence of Historical Sociology—sometimes called Philosophy of History[21]—that is to say, of sociological theories that, on the one hand, used historical material in order to arrive at generalizations and were, on the other hand, intended to explain individual historical states and processes. The greater part of this kind of work was dilettantic and of a nature to disgust serious historians. Some of it was, moreover, unhistorical in the sense just defined: historical fact was often twisted to fit the preconceptions of *la raison*. Nevertheless, there were also considerable and even path-breaking performances. By way of example, I may mention Condorcet, Montesquieu, and one who was one of the greatest thinkers to be found in any age in the field of the social sciences—Vico.[22] Condorcet's

[19] F. A. Wolf's (1759-1824) seminal *Prolegomena ad Homerum* appeared in 1795, but was the result of earlier work.

[20] To this day historians have not ceased to preach, to bestow praise and blame, and to air their personal, social, and national prides and hates. What I mean to convey is that substantial progress was made toward presentation of facts in something like a scientific spirit and away from the epic.

[21] See Robert Flint, *History of the Philosophy of History* (1893).

[22] The Marquis de Condorcet (1743-94; *Oeuvres*, ed. 1847-9; English readers are perhaps best referred to Lord Morley's essay on him, republ. in *Critical Miscellanies*, 1886-1908, vol. II), one of the *encyclopédistes* (see below, sub e), roamed over almost all fields of science and policy. Among other things, he was a trained mathematician; his ventures in the application of the calculus of probabilities to legal and political judgments, though not wholly felicitous, gave an important impulse; he propagated 'natural rights,' popular sovereignty, and equal rights for women, and was a great hater of Christianity—in all of which, ardor completely extinguished his critical faculty. His contributions to economics are not worth mentioning. The work relevant here is *Esquisse d'un tableau historique des progrès de l'esprit humain* (1795; English trans. 1802).

Montesquieu (1689-1755) presumably needs no introduction beyond the remark that

Esquisse presents a definite theory of historical evolution or 'progress': its goal is equality[23] and its motive force is the ever-increasing knowledge that the indefinitely perfectible human mind keeps on acquiring. This, of course, is very poor sociology. But the work is the outstanding example of an uncompromisingly 'intellectualist' view of the historical process. In sharp contrast, Montesquieu's *Esprit des lois,* despite inadequate workmanship—especially inadequate as to critical use of material—is serious sociology. The chief virtue of the latter work, both as regards method and performance, is that it envisaged historical states of societies and their changes in the light of a number of objective factors,[24] which yield realistic explanations and in this sense analytic theories but no simple, in particular no rationalist, general formula. This was indeed a new departure and methodologically spelled a significant break with natural-law ideas: it was sociology based upon actual observation of individual temporal and local patterns, not merely of general properties of human nature. For our purposes, this was Montesquieu's essential achievement, foreshadowed in this treatment of the particular case of ancient Rome. His success, at the time and later, was of course due to the appeal of his 'constitutional' theories—*contrebalance des pouvoirs* and the like—which are of no interest to us.

---

he was one of the most influential thinkers of all times and that in particular, though his economics is insignificant—without originality, force, or scholarship—he greatly influenced A. Smith in other respects. The three works to mention are the—also insignificant—*Lettres persanes* (1721), the *Considérations sur les causes de la grandeur des Romains et de leur décadence* (1734), and of course his magnum opus, *De l'Esprit des lois* (1748), which is so much more than mere '*esprit sur les lois.*'

Giambattista Vico (1668-1744; *Opere,* newest ed. Nicolini, 1911-31; bibliography by B. Croce, 1904; revised, enlarged ed. 1947-8). Part of the extensive Vico literature is impaired by attempts of authors to claim the great name for tendencies of their own, but see Croce's essay (English trans. by Collingwood, 1913), R. Flint's *Vico* (1884), and a few beautiful pages on Vico in Tagliacozzo's *Economisti napoletani* (1937); there are several good German books, especially those by Werner and Klemm. Vico was professor in Naples, professing to teach 'all the knowable' (*tutto lo scibile*). The fact that, among other things, he was a lawyer and always stressed legal aspects (the history of law was to him the history of the human mind) is important because it brings out his relation to the philosophers of natural law. The influences that contributed to shaping his thought and the problems raised by the various cases of earlier occurrence of ideas similar to his own are much too complex for us. The Greeks, the Roman jurists, Grotius, the English empiricists, Descartes (by way of antagonism), the scholastics, and many other groups would have to be mentioned, among them also the Arab historian Abu Said Ibn Khaldun (1332-1406; see de Slane's French trans. of the first introductory part of his history, 1863-8, all I know). The only work of Vico's that need be mentioned specifically is *Principii di una scienza nuova . . .* (1725; almost rewritten for the 2nd ed. of 1730).

[23] The sociologist of thought will, of course, see in this a secularized scheme of salvation.

[24] The emphasis upon the influence of geographic environments that may have hailed from Thucydides and may have inspired later anthropogeographical researches such as that of Vidal de la Blache deserves to be speciallv noticed.

Vico's achievement was quite different and met with little success until late in the nineteenth century. His New Science (*scienza nuova*) is best described by the phrase 'an evolutionary science of mind and society.' But this must not be interpreted to mean that the evolution of the human mind shapes the evolution of human society; nor, though this would be nearer the truth, that the historical evolution of societies shapes the evolution of the human mind; but that mind and society are two aspects of the same evolutionary process. Reason, in the sense of the rational or logical operations of the human mind, is no causal factor in this process which Vico conceived in a thoroughly anti-intellectual spirit. Neither has reason, in the sense of goals or meanings perceived by the observer's reason, anything to do with it: Vico's theory of recurrent processes (*corsi e ricorsi*) emphatically denies any tendency toward, and in fact the existence of, any such goals and meanings. In this scheme philosophy and sociology had become one—thought and action had become one—and this unit was essentially historical in nature.[25] And, after all, though the common currents of eighteenth-century waters did not reach up to his knees, Vico too was eighteenth century.

[(e) *The Encyclopédistes.*] We have had occasion to notice the increase in the demand for dictionaries or encyclopaedias during the seventeenth century. Further increasing during the eighteenth, this demand was satisfied by ever more ambitious ventures (Chambers' *Cyclopaedia*, Zedler's *Universal-Lexicon*, and others). All of these were surpassed by the great French *Encyclopédie* (from 1751 on),[26] which, among other things, excelled the other works of its type and time by the number and quality of its articles on economic subjects. But it is mentioned here for an entirely different reason: whoever believes at all in the concept of the 'spirit' of an age will be inclined to look upon the *Encyclopédie* as the very incarnation of the eighteenth-century spirit. So far as this is correct, the work itself is an important part of the cultural background of which we are trying to reconstruct some patches. But how far is it correct? Like all encyclopaedias of such range, this one contained articles that differed widely not only in quality but also in point of view. The economic articles referred to, for instance, were written by writers as far apart from one another as were Quesnay and Forbonnais, while the bulk of the articles—physics and technology were particularly attended to—left no scope for difference of point of view in the philosophical or political sense. Nevertheless, the strong personality of the editor-in-chief, Diderot, succeeded in imparting some uniformity to what was called the Tower of Babel by hostile critics. In order to realize this, it is sufficient to name a few of the leading

[25] This scheme, very obviously, points forward toward Hegel and, less obviously, toward Husserl. This fact explains both his comparative failure in his own day and his success after nearly two centuries. But it should not be allowed to obliterate the purely analytic aspects of his work which parallel (i.e. anticipate) some feature of the less spacious and profound work of Montesquieu, especially as regards emphasis upon environmental factors.

[26] The reader will find more than enough information in the *Encyclopædia Britannica's* article 'Encyclopædia.'

members of the circle that gathered round Diderot: d'Alembert, Voltaire, Condorcet, Holbach, Helvétius—all vowed to the service of *la raison* in the particular sense in which it meant enmity to the Christian faith and especially to the Catholic Church. With varying measures of reserve, the opportunity afforded by the articles on history, philosophy, and religion was exploited for purposes of propaganda in that respect. But this was all. In other respects not much uniformity was either aimed at or achieved. The philosophy is mainly empiricist, but not wholly so. The politics reflects the opinions about state, public administration, and policy that were carried far beyond the specifically encyclopaedist circle. Beyond this there was no definite program. In particular, there was no revolutionary program: those intellectuals no doubt had their dig at the regime of Louis XV and occasionally aimed at its special features; on the whole, however, they felt too comfortable to long for a violent upheaval; some of them saw points in the enlightened despots of their time who reformed—and paid well; those who lived to witness the realities of revolution were not very happy about it. Thus, though it remains true that the great French venture may be taken as a symbol of an important current of thought, its importance for us is not as considerable as it seemed to its contemporary enemies, who insured its success by fighting it.

There is one point, however, that should be emphasized or emphasized again (see above, sec. 5), namely, the relation of the thought of the *encyclopédistes* to that of the seventeenth-century philosophers of natural law. The teaching of the latter fared quite well at the hands of the former. The *encyclopédistes*—and all the writers whom this term, in a wider sense, may be said to cover—did not always give credit to the philosophers as they should have done. But they displayed no hostility to the natural-law system and in fact developed its ideas. Nor is this surprising. Was not natural law derived, by reason, from human nature and hence the very embodiment of their own program? And the Natural Rights of the philosophers were, of course, thoroughly to their taste. The religious barrier hid from them the true origin of these ideas: they could not have quoted St. Thomas' statement that the natural law was *rationis regula*. But no such barrier existed in the case of the philosophers who were, at least, no Catholics. And so the *encyclopédistes*, within and without the volumes of the encyclopaedia, and many other men, such as Quesnay, who were not *encyclopédistes* in the strict sense (even if they were contributors), continued to use the philosophers' analytic schema and, sometimes, even their most dubious arguments. Quesnay's *ordre naturel* would be recognizable as an offshoot of the natural-law stem, even if Quesnay had never written his article on *droit naturel*. The Abbé Morellet, an ardent free trader, was quite content to argue that, since man is naturally free and since this implies that he can buy and sell where he pleases, protection stands condemned for violation of natural law—which argument occurs also in other writings of the time and must evidently have impressed some people,[27] a most interesting comment upon the age of reason.

[27] The Abbé André Morellet (1727-1819) was, it is true, a very minor light among the *encyclopédistes*—not more than an effective pamphleteer. We need not mention his economic works. But he is interesting as a type, which is why perusal of Lytton Strachey's essay on him has been recommended above. However, he collected materials that went into Peuchet's *Dictionnaire universel de la géographie commerçante* (1799-1800), which is an important link in the long chain of economic or semi-economic dictionaries.

[(f) *The Semi-Socialist Writers.*] It has been stated that, as a body, the *encyclopédistes* were not politically revolutionary. Neither were they socialists. The equalitarianism of the time—both normative and analytic—suggested the criticisms of inequalities, especially great inequalities, of wealth that we find in Helvétius and many other writers. And the obvious weaknesses of natural-law philosophies about the natural right to property that were expounded either on the lines of Locke or in the special form adopted by the physiocrats (see below, ch. 4), invited criticism that sometimes went from attack upon particular arguments in defense of property to attack upon property itself. But though the historian of socialist ideas is no doubt able to compile a lengthy list of socialist or communist or near-communist publications that were not without influence on nineteenth-century socialism, the historian of economic analysis has little of interest to record: he can only agree with Karl Marx's opinion about that literature. It should be observed, however, that socialist or semi-socialist writers, when arguing against conclusions drawn from natural-law premisses by natural-law methods, almost invariably used these premisses and methods themselves. Thus, exactly as the votaries of *la raison* fought scholasticism while remaining its pupils so far as methods and results of analysis are concerned, so the socialist or semi-socialist writers of the eighteenth century remained natural-law philosophers in their way of thinking: the concepts of natural law and of natural rights were quite capable of serving opposite practical aims, and few if any writers thought of attacking the method they embodied. Rousseau, Brissot, Morelly, and Mably are illustrative examples. For the sake of convenience, we add here a very different figure, Godwin, whose only contribution to economic analysis will, however, have to be considered later.

J. J. Rousseau (1712-78), in spite of his glorification of the natural state of society and of equality, can hardly be called a socialist—he was typically what our term 'semi-socialist' is meant to convey. But neither can he be called an economist. His article on political economy in the *Encyclopédie* contains next to no economics. His essay on the origin of inequality (1755) is not a serious effort to account for the phenomenon. In particular, despite some superficial similarities in phrasing, he was not a physiocrat or a forerunner of the physiocrats. Such ideas as he entertained on economic subjects were, however, of considerable influence with the public. J. P. Brissot de Warville (1754-93), a Girondist politician executed in 1793, holds a place among reformers of criminal law. The work relevant for our subject, the *Recherches philosophiques sur le droit de propriété et sur le vol . . .* (1780), is pure natural-law speculation of the kind that made later critics of natural-law sociology and economics completely overlook its serious achievements. The nonexistence of the right to private property is the *thema probandum.* Brissot seems to have been unaware of practically all the realistic and really damaging arguments that may be forged against it. The doctrine that Property is Theft, made famous in the nineteenth century by Proudhon is the centerpiece of the book. Morelly's *Code de la nature* (1755) is a program of full-fledged state communism of considerable merit: it presents, in minute detail, solutions of the practical problems of the structure and management of a communist society, many of which turn up, mostly without acknowledgment, in the nineteenth-century literature of socialism and most of which reflect a sober sense of 'workability.' The doctrine, much more often implied than frankly stated, that all the deviations from normal behavior that are felt to be immoral are caused by the conditions of life in capitalist society, was, so far as I know, first stated in this book. We cannot go beyond pointing out that this book, too, is pure natural-law philosophy: strictly state-controlled communism is the form of existence that corresponds ideally to natural laws discerned by reason. Gabriel Bonnot de Mably (1709-85), though he was not a communist from the beginning, and though in the end he resigned himself to practical programs that did not go beyond rather commonplace reforms, must also be classed as a straight communist on the strength of the implications of the only work that can be mentioned here, *Doutes proposés aux philosophes économistes sur l'ordre naturel et essentiel des sociétés politiques* (1768). This work contains an elaborate attack not only upon the physiocrat theory of private property but also upon private property itself, which is held to be an almost unmixed evil. But though one-sided and otherwise defective analysis, Mably's argument is still analysis of facts and not merely a discussion of 'rights.' The theory that property in land is the ultimate cause of all inequalities of wealth—repeatedly espoused in the nineteenth century and, by F. Oppenheimer in the twentieth—may be wrong, but is still an analytic proposition or theory. The authors mentioned as well as many others have received considerable attention from historians of thought, including economists primarily interested in the history of thought. See, for example, A. Lichtenberger, *Le Socialisme au XVIIIe siècle* (1895).

The French ideas of the Enlightenment were good sailors (crossing the Channel easily), the more so because they had important English—especially empiricist and associationist—roots. High above the common run of enthusiasm rose the book that is to represent this literature for us, William Godwin's *Enquiry concerning Political Justice* (1793). It is only semi-socialist and even this only by virtue of its dogma that property in the product of other people's labor is 'unjust.' Perhaps those are right who, on the strength of Godwin's extreme distaste for violence and compulsion of any kind, class him as an anarchist. In any case, the view of human nature, according to which man's mind is a blank—but indefinitely perfectible—to be filled in by experience conditioned by social institutions has hardly ever, before or after, been made to serve absolute equalitarianism so uncompromisingly. Godwin was indeed goaded into doing a piece of analytic work by the attack of Malthus. But his work itself is essentially nonanalytic and therefore beyond the range of scientific criticism. It expounds a creed that is impervious to argument and at the present time counts more adherents than it ever did.

[(g) *Moral Philosophy.*] All the facts presented above about eighteenth-century thought go to show that the natural-law approach to sociology and economics held its own to a considerable extent and that the notion that a new 'experimental' spirit rose victoriously against it—or else that the cult of *la raison* was something fundamentally new—is as illusory as is the analogous notion that the work of the seventeenth-century philosophers of natural law spelled a violent break with scholastic analysis. In other words, these facts teach a lesson of continuity in development. Nevertheless, the natural-law system of thought disintegrated or, at least, underwent a transformation. We know that, originally, it had been a system of jurisprudence and that all nonlegal material had been fitted into the legal framework in an ancillary role. But in the eighteenth century, the increase of this material and the addition of new fields of research burst that framework. From having been in the position of a governing holding company that unified and co-ordinated everything, 'natural jurisprudence' became merely a specialty of a new comprehensive unit that was no longer primarily legal in character.[28] This new unit was called, especially in Germany and Scotland, Moral Philosophy—the word philosophy being taken in its old sense of the sum total of sciences (St. Thomas' *philosophicae disciplinae*), so that, roughly, moral philosophy means the social sciences (the sciences of 'mind and society') in contrast to Natural Philosophy that denoted the physical sciences plus mathematics. It was the subject of a standard course offered within the university curricula and consisted, mainly, of natural theology, natural ethics, natural jurisprudence, and policy (or 'police') which included economics and also public finance ('revenue').[29] Francis Hutcheson, the teacher of A. Smith, was professor of moral philosophy in this sense at the University of Glasgow, and so was A. Smith. Both the *Moral Sentiments* and the *Wealth of Nations* are blocks cut out from a larger systematic whole. Thus the old universal social science of the scholastic doctors and of the philosophers of natural law survived in the new form. But not for very long. Though the moral-philosophy course figures in university curricula even

[28] As we already know, the Historical School of Jurisprudence was very hostile to this natural jurisprudence and saw nothing in it but entirely unscientific speculation. This view was very influential; it was in fact from the lawyers of this school that people learned to despise everything that was in any way connected with the concept of natural law. It should be repeated, however, that this view, while quite understandable considering the abuse of the idea of natural rights of all kinds, neglects an important nonspeculative core of natural-law analysis. The natural jurisprudence of which I speak in the text was an inadequate but still scientific theory—or general logic—of law for which it is possible to make out a case similar to that which can be made out for economic theory.

[29] The contents of the course varied, however. Also, the division of all sciences into moral and natural philosophy was neither complete nor invariable. Pure philosophy in the narrow sense stood outside and so did logic, philology and literature, history, and other fields.

in the first half of the nineteenth century—universities are conservative—it was rapidly losing, in most places, its old meaning and position toward the end of the eighteenth.

This was due to the same cause that burst the natural-law system. The accession of material in the individual branches of moral philosophy tended to bring them into the hands of specialists, every one of whom had inevitably to concentrate on his own branch and to neglect both the other branches and the comprehensive principles. This applies with particular force to economics because in this case the new material came from outside (see next chapter). It is highly significant that A. Smith found it impossible to do what Hutcheson had done as a matter of course, namely, to produce a complete system of moral philosophy or social science at one throw. The time for doing this had passed: absorption of the new material—both facts and analyses—had become a full-time job.

As long as this absorption was not consummated, the little body of scientific economic knowledge that had been inherited from the scholastics and nursed along by the philosophers of natural law retained not only independent existence but also a distinctive character of its own. Owing to the greater intellectual refinement of the men who had created it, and to their detachment from the immediately practical issues of economic policy, their economic analysis was different from the analysis of other people. Beholding it we cannot fail to notice more correct formulation of fundamentals and a wider view of practical problems, both anticipating much later opinions. But so soon as that absorption was consummated, we naturally lose sight of it, though we do not lose its contribution. This happened, roughly speaking, between 1776 and 1848: the latest natural-law system, utilitarianism, getting under sail when the economic specialists had established their claim to autonomy, was not, as were its predecessors, able to exert effective control over them.

CHAPTER 3

The Consultant Administrators and the Pamphleteers

1. More Facts from Social History

We know already that, as the eighteenth century wore on, economics settled down into what we have decided to call a Classical Situation, and that, mainly in consequence of this, it then acquired the status of a recognized field of tooled knowledge. But the sifting and co-ordinating works of that period, among which the *Wealth of Nations* was the outstanding success, did not simply broaden and deepen the rivulet that flowed from the studies of the schoolmen and of the philosophers of natural law. They also absorbed the waters of another and more boisterous stream that sprang from the forum where men of affairs, pamphleteers, and, later on, teachers debated the policies of their day. In this chapter we shall take a bird's eye view of the various types of economic literature produced by these debates, reserving for subsequent chapters fuller treatment of works and topics that seem to require it.

This literature is not a logical or historical unit. The men who wrote it, unlike the philosophers of natural law, form no homogeneous group. Nevertheless there is a link between them all which it is necessary to emphasize: they discussed immediately practical problems of economic policy, and these problems were the problems of the rising National State. Therefore, if we are to understand the spirit that animates those writers, their lines of reasoning, the data they took for granted, we must for a moment digress into the sociology of those states whose structure, behavior, and vicissitudes shaped European history—thought as well as action—from the fifteenth century on. The important point to grasp is that neither the emergence nor the behavior ('policies') of those states were simply manifestations of capitalist evolution. Whether we like it or not, we have to face the fact that they were the products of a combination of circumstances that, viewed from the standpoint of the capitalist process as such, must be considered as accidental.[1]

[(a) *Incidental Factors in the Emergence of the National States.*] First, it was an accident that the rise of capitalism impinged upon a social framework of quite unusual strength. 'Feudalism' no doubt gave way, but the warrior classes that had ruled the feudal organism did not. On the contrary, they continued to rule for centuries and the rising bourgeoisie had to submit. They even succeeded in absorbing a great part of the new wealth for their own purposes. The result was a political structure that fostered but also exploited the bourgeois interest and was not bourgeois in nature and spirit: it was feudalism run on a capitalist basis; an aristocratic and military society that fed on capitalism; an amphibial case very far removed from bourgeois control. This pattern produced problems and—'militarist'—angles from which to look at them, which were completely different from what the mere logic of the basic process would lead us to expect.[2] Thus, for the majority of economists, monarchs that were primarily warlords and the class of aristocratic landowners, remained the pivots of the social system as late as the middle of the eighteenth century, at least on the continent of Europe. The reader should therefore apply the requisite qualification to what he has read in the preceding chapter on the increasing social weight of the bourgeoisie.

Also, it was an accident that the conquest of South America produced a torrent of precious metals. The growth of capitalist enterprise might presumably have been expected to produce inflationary situations in any case, but this torrent made a lot of difference to the course of events. In a way that is too obvious to need elaboration, it speeded up capitalist development, but much more important are two other facts about it that point in the opposite direction. On the one hand, this access of liquid means greatly strengthened

[1] Like all theorists, theorists of social history are reluctant to admit not only the importance of causal factors other than the ones emphasized by their own theories but also the importance of chance in the evolution of actual patterns. But the historical processes that produced the situations, created the problems, and shaped the attitudes reflected in that literature cannot be interpreted as many observers, Marxists especially, would like to interpret them, viz., as effects of the rise of capitalism. Even so far as they are traceable to capitalist evolution, they worked out in a way that differed radically from that prescribed by either capitalist interests or the capitalist mind. Let us note in passing how important this is not only for our own limited purpose but also for our diagnosis of the nature and *modus operandi* of the capitalist system in general—and even for our philosophy of history in general.

[2] I tried to illustrate this by a short analysis of an outstanding instance, the state of Louis XIV, in *Capitalism, Socialism, and Democracy*, ch. xii.

the position of those rulers who were able to get hold of them. Under the circumstances of the times, this conferred a decisive advantage in the planning of military ventures on lines that often, as for instance in the case of the Spanish Hapsburgs, were quite unconnected with bourgeois interests in the component parts of their farflung empire or with the logic of the capitalist process. On the other hand, the price revolution that ensued [3] spelled social disorganization, and hence was not only a propelling but also a distorting factor. Much that might have been gradual change, if nothing but the basic process had been at work, became explosive in the feverish atmosphere of inflation. Particular notice must be taken of the effect on the agrarian world. By the time that inflation set in, the greater part of the dues that continental peasants owed to their lords had been converted into terms of money. With the purchasing power of money rapidly falling, the lords attempted in many countries to raise the monetary values of those dues. The peasants resisted. Agrarian revolutions were the consequence, and the revolutionary temper thus engendered was an important factor in the political and religious upheavals of that epoch. But, owing to the strength of the top feudal stratum, these revolutions did not, as we might have expected, accelerate social developments in accordance with the basic process. The risings of the peasants and of the other groups that had revolted in sympathy were put down with ruthless energy. The religious movements met with success only so far as they were sponsored by the aristocracies and in the most important cases quickly lost such social or political radicalism as had been originally associated with some of them. Princes and barons, armies and clergies, emerged from the trial with enhanced prestige and power whereas the prestige and the political power of the bourgeoisie declined, especially in Germany, France, and Spain. The great exception, on the Continent, was the Netherlands.

A third historic event of prime—and lasting—importance was the breakdown of the only effective international authority the world has ever seen. As has been pointed out, the medieval world was a cultural unit and, in principle at least, professed allegiance both to the Empire and to the Catholic Church. Although widely different views were held as to their true relation to one another, these two together formed a supernational power that was not only ideologically acknowledged but also politically invincible so long as they were united. According to the traditional view, this power was bound to wane as soon as the acids of capitalism began to dissolve the basis of medieval society and its beliefs. This is not so. Whatever those acids might have eventually done to that dual power, they had nothing to do with the actual breakdown that occurred long before those beliefs were impaired, simply because of the fact—which, from the standpoint of the basic process, was again accidental—that, for reasons which cannot be analyzed here, the empire was unable either

[3] This price revolution set in before the impact of the new gold and silver had made itself felt, and was at no time a function of their inflow alone. For our purposes, however, the popular opinion that it was may be allowed to stand as an approximation.

to accept the supremacy of the Popes or to conquer them. A prolonged struggle that shook the Christian world to its foundations ended in a Pyrrhic victory of the Popes in the time of Frederick II (1194-1250). But in this struggle both parties had so thoroughly exhausted their political resources that it is more correct to speak of a common defeat of both: the Popes lost authority, the empire disintegrated. In consequence. medieval internationalism was at an end and the national states began to assert their independence from that supernational authority which had been formidable only so long as the Roman church co-operated with the 'temporal sword' of Germany.[4]

[(b) *Why the National States Were Aggressive.*] It must be left to the reader to develop the implications of all this. But it should be clear that it was the persistence of aristocratic rule, the access of ideally disposable wealth, and the breakdown of the supernational power of the Middle Ages—rather than anything derivable from the capitalist process itself—that explain not only the emergence but also the political physiognomy of the modern state. In particular, those facts explain why the modern state was 'national' from the first, and refractory to any supernational consideration; why it insisted and was compelled to insist on absolute sovereignty; why it fostered national churches even in Catholic countries—as instanced by Gallicanism in France; and above all why it was so aggressive. The new sovereign powers were warlike by virtue of their social structures. They had emerged in a haphazard way. None of them had all it wanted; each of them had what others wanted. And they were soon surrounded by new worlds inviting competitive conquest. Because both of this situation and the social structure of the epoch, aggression —or, what is the same thing, 'defense'—became the pivot of policy. In this fermenting world, peace was but armistice, war the normal remedy for political disequilibrium, the foreigner ipso facto the enemy—as he had been in primitive times. All this made for strong governments; and strong governments, chronically suffering from political ambitions that went beyond their economic means, were driven to increasingly successful attempts to make themselves still stronger by developing the resources of their territories and harnessing them into their service. This in turn explains, among other things, why taxation

[4] Perhaps it is misleading to stress the national element in this change. Though it shows well enough in the most important cases, those of France, Spain, and, earlier than anywhere else, in England, the true nature of the phenomenon will be more clearly visualized if we take account of the fact that in Germany and Italy, the countries that had been immediately subordinated to the imperial power, such states or 'principalities' emerged on a nonnational basis: it was not, at first, national feeling that welded those units but rather the interest of feudal princes who were strong enough to organize, to defend, and to rule a territory. Frederick II's own kingdom of Naples and Sicily is the earliest example, the Prussian state of another Frederick II the most telling. Popular support that might be linked up with capitalist interests and national sentiment came later and was as much the consequence of habit-forming conditions as it was a causal factor in subsequent developments. Nevertheless we shall, for convenience, go on speaking of the National State.

assumed not only a much greater but a new significance (see sec. 6 of this chapter).

These facts, though fundamentally the same all over Western and Central Europe, produced somewhat different results according to the circumstances of different nations. Neglecting smaller countries, we find the main difference was between England and the Continent. In Germany, economic and political trends were broken by the course of events centering in the Thirty Years' War (1618-48), which created an entirely new situation and changed the political and cultural pattern of Germany for good. On the ravaged soil and in a population that had in places been reduced to less than 10 per cent, the princes, their soldiers, and their bureaucracies were, in the greater part of the national territory, practically all that was left of the political forces of the past. In Italy, alien rule and also devastation were responsible for a situation that differed from the German one only in degree. France and Spain did not have to go through experiences like these, but religious troubles and unending war efforts produced similar impoverishment in Spain and similar political and administrative conditions in both France and Spain.

In most of these countries—one exception is instanced by Switzerland and another by Hungary—the prince came to personify the state and the nation from the sixteenth century on. He succeeded in subjecting all classes to his authority—the nobility and the clergy not less than the bourgeoisie and peasantry, though the two former on the understanding that they should continue to hold a position of social and economic privilege. The wealth and power of this state was the unquestioned object of policy: maximum public revenue—for the court and the army to consume—was the purpose of economic policy, conquest the purpose of foreign policy. There should be no need for showing how concern for the welfare of the classes on which that social system fed entered into that policy: this welfare was not looked upon simply as a means to an end; it was an end in itself for many a great monarch or administrator, exactly as the welfare of his workmen was and is an end in itself for many a great industrialist; but it had to fit in with the given political pattern and with the given social system. All this—precisely where concern for the welfare of manufacturers, farmers, and laborers was most real—meant management of everything which in turn meant the rise of modern bureaucracy, a fact that is no less important than is the rise of the business class. The resulting economy was a Planned Economy; and it was planned, primarily, with a view to war.[5]

[5] This might be illustrated by the careers and policies of many great administrators of international and historical reputation. Comparative study of these men and their measures also brings out interesting differences and, above all, the fact that precisely the greatest of them cannot be said to have followed any consistent system of principles at all. One aspect of this will be mentioned presently in our text. We must confine ourselves to a brief comment upon Colbert, who has been and still is considered by many historians as the typical representative of that imaginary entity, the 'mercantilist system'—so much so that Colbertism is often used, especially in Italian, as a synonym of mercantilism. Jean Baptiste Colbert (1619-83), of bourgeois origin, was a civil servant who rose to be minister of finance (this, although various other

In England we observe the same tendencies. But there they were weaker and resistance to them was stronger because she was saved from the experiences that elsewhere broke the backbone of aristocracies and bourgeoisies alike. This was perhaps not merely a matter of a few miles of channel; but we may for brevity's sake adopt a theory which is only inadequate not untrue, namely, that it was the absence of actual foreign invasions and the rarity of serious threats of invasion that reduced the necessity for a military establishment—a navy of course carries much less political weight—and, in consequence of this, the power and prestige of the crown and of all the administrative agencies dependent upon the crown. The most obvious symptom of the difference this made, the survival in England alone of the old semifeudal constitution, is not in itself important for us. But all the more so is the fact that, throughout, the English state did not succeed in taking hold of national life as did the states elsewhere and that in particular the economic sector of national life, colonial venture included, remained relatively autonomous. Planning, if not absent, was more limited in scope—concerned principally with the relations of the English economy to Ireland and the colonies, and with foreign trade—and, what is still more to the point, was less strictly enforced than it was in most continental countries. But for the writers on economic topics this made less difference than we might expect. Some of them nevertheless reveled in visions of planning. And while some voiced the businessman's views, others voiced those of the bureaucrat. Also, we must never forget, if we wish to understand them, that practically all of these writers, in spite of what has just been said, consistently wrote with war and conquest in their minds. After all, notwithstanding her own relatively sheltered position, England was then going through the buccaneering stage of her imperialism.

[(c) *Influence of Special Circumstances on the Contemporary Literature.*] Unfortunately, the literature to be surveyed cannot be understood from the

---

offices were added from time to time, is the best way in which to describe his main function, which must, however, be understood to cover the affairs of industry, commerce, and agriculture as well) in the first period of Louis XIV's reign. He was an honest, able, and energetic administrator who knew how to raise money, intimidate creditors, improve administrative and accounting methods, stimulate industry, build palaces and harbors, develop the navy, and so on, though he was distinctly unlucky in the execution of his larger plans, e.g. colonial enterprise, the history of which shows that the wastes of public planning may easily surpass anything that, on the score of wastefulness, can be charged to private enterprise. There is no reason to extol his achievement, especially to see in him the oversized champion of some great principle, as did some of his admirers. See on Colbert and his immediate successors, C. W. Cole, *Colbert and a Century of French Mercantilism* (1939), and *French Mercantilism, 1683-1700* (1943). In his review of the former book, in *Economic History* (February 1940), Sir John Clapham voiced a reaction against unintelligent admiration that is almost amusing in its vehemence: according to him, Colbert had 'no single original idea' (which is true but beside the point in the appraisal of an administrator) and was a 'big stupid man,' tyrannical, brutal, fussy. For the period preceding his administration, see J. U. Nef, *Industry and Government in France and England,* 1540-1640 (1940).

facts referred to alone. Much of it is conditioned by individual situations in individual countries that writers took for granted, and by individual issues that arose from these situations. Even books and pamphlets that do not deal with questions raised by an individual bill or practice can hardly be appreciated without full knowledge of the particular national patterns as seen by their authors. A lengthy list of mistakes in interpretation and appraisal that were committed, especially by nineteenth-century 'liberal' critics of that literature but also by later ones, could be compiled to illustrate this truth. But there is nothing we can do about it here [6] beyond offering the following generalities. A few other facts will be added where necessary as we go along.

I. All the economics of those times—with the possible exception of the Dutch branch of it—was written in and for countries that were poor. This holds without exception if 'poor' is equated with 'undeveloped.' All European countries stood at the beginning of their industrial and even of their agricultural careers and everybody realized this. With us, economic expansion is primarily linked with new wants and methods; that age, however, had practically inexhaustible possibilities before it with existing wants and technologies, in addition to what it was coming to expect from technological progress and from conquest. But our proposition applies in a different sense and with added force to the great continental countries that in the second half of the seventeenth century were faced also with an immense reconstruction problem. They were poor even relatively to what they had been in the sixteenth century. It should be clear that in such conditions policies and reasonings may have had meaning that seemed mere nonsense to observers who viewed them from the standpoint of nineteenth-century conditions.

II. Throughout, all countries—even England—were predominantly agrarian. Their economic problems were primarily agrarian problems, the masses of their people were agrarian masses—peasants, farmers, agrarian laborers. In the sixteenth, seventeenth, and eighteenth centuries, this agrarian world underwent changes that revolutionized it completely: economic historians rightly speak of an agrarian revolution, or rather of several agrarian revolutions. This phrase indicates two distinct, though of course related, types of change that reinforced each other and would have broken down the framework of medieval society even if nothing had happened in the industrial sector. On the one hand, there was a long series of changes in the technologies of all branches of agrarian production—this process gained momentum in the eighteenth century but started at the beginning of the sixteenth. On the other hand, there was, in sympathy with the technological revolutions, a process of organizational change that turned medieval manors into grain, wool, and meat factories and destroyed the old relations between lords and peasants or farmers.

[6] It is impossible, even, to give an annotated reading list, for it would fill a volume. Going to the other extreme, therefore, I shall mention but two well-known standard works which in any case are, or ought to be, in every student's hands: E. F. Heckscher's *Mercantilism* (1931, English trans. by M. Shapiro, 1935) and P. Mantoux's *The Industrial Revolution in the Eighteenth Century* (rev. ed., 1927, English trans. by M. Vernon). These works contain the bulk of what the reader ought to know.

It must suffice to mention the chief English form of this type of change, Enclosures. Governments and, accordingly, writers took two characteristically different attitudes to this change. On the Continent, and especially in Germany, governments made a determined and largely successful effort to save the peasants and to turn them eventually into a class of small landowners. In England, the land-owning and land-tilling yeomanry was allowed to disappear and, deserted-village emotionality notwithstanding, the large estate prevailed, not however as a producing unit but as a unit of administration that left production to the workman-capitalist, the farmer.

III. But it is by no means surprising that manufacturing and international trade, comparatively insignificant though they were, attracted more literary attention than did agriculture. They were the young children and, moreover, the children on whom the future of the family was mainly felt to depend. Also, they had more motive and opportunity than had the landowners and farmers to spill ink on their own behalf. For economics this simply meant that there were more 'industrial and commercial' than 'agricultural' economists. But the existence of these two groups of writers was primarily a phenomenon of division of labor as it is now: their very natural antagonisms should not be sublimated into antagonisms between philosophies either of life or of economics except in cases—the only important one is that of the physiocrats (see below, ch. 4)—where there is some provable warrant for it.

Large-scale enterprise—large relatively to environmental standards—emerged, to a significant extent, in the fourteenth century in Italy, in the fifteenth in Germany, in the sixteenth (under Elizabeth) in England, first in the financial and commercial sphere and then in the sphere of production. But, substantially, the manufacturing industry that economists beheld and reasoned about was all along the manufacturing industry of the artisan (still organized in craft guilds), of the 'master' of domestic industry, and of the owner-manager of factories that were few and mostly quite small. In Western Europe, especially in England, this changed (significantly but not fundamentally) in the Industrial Revolution of the last decades of the eighteenth century, but the full consequences did not reveal themselves before the first decades of the nineteenth. Many authors, occasionally even A. Smith, class the manufacturer with the workman. No author, not even A. Smith, had any very clear idea of what the processes really meant that led to what economic historians have dubbed the Industrial Revolution. A. Smith felt that the corporate form of industry was an anomaly except in such cases as canals and the like. To him and his contemporaries big business still meant commercial and financial big business—colonial enterprise particularly. And they looked upon it much as modern economists look upon any kind of largest-scale business, namely, with feelings of resentful distrust.

IV. This industrial and commercial evolution was characterized, almost until the end of the period under discussion, by 'monopolistic' policies and business practices that were one of the chief topics of the economic literature of that period and have been visited with sweeping condemnation by economists and economic historians from A. Smith to this day. By 'monopolistic' public policy and private business practice, we mean measures and forms of behavior intended to secure profitable 'vent' for the products or services of an individual or group by (1) keeping the foreigner out of national and international markets—which, so long as national territories had not become economic units, often included keeping out the producers and traders of the neighboring town or district; (2) keeping out of a trade, so far as possible, all connationals other than the favored individual or group—for instance, keeping retailers out of the merchant's business; (3) restricting the output of the favored individual or group itself and regulating its distribution between markets. Let us stay for a moment in order to analyze, in the light of the preceding considerations, the reasons for the prevalence of this policy and practice.

First, we might expect that, if fullfledged capitalism had suddenly burst upon the world and if it had been permitted to unfold without being distorted by the factors referred to, both business behavior and public policy would have been from the first what they became in fact, for a time, in the nineteenth century. That is to say, we might expect that in this case there would have been, in countries that were so poor in goods and so rich in possibilities, an onward rush of competitive enterprise. This expectation would be, however, only in part justified. Poverty is a bad customer, and normal risks of doing business are greatly increased in an environment where the wealth from which demand is to proceed has not only to be attracted but created. In business as elsewhere, forward strategy very often requires defensive tactics as a complement, though most economists of all ages stubbornly refuse to see this. But under conditions in which long-run advance was inevitably slow, each stage had to be safeguarded with particular care in order to gain means and time for advancing beyond it. It is quite natural that the observing historian should be much more impressed by the practices and policies that aimed at protective restriction, which dominate the scene at every point of time, than by the picture of the process over time.[7] But it is true nevertheless that even an ideally rational government, actuated by the sole motive of fostering industrial development, would have had to grant privileges of monopoly in many cases in which enterprise would not have been possible at all without it, and that, in others, it would have had to permit monopolistic practice on the part of the businessmen concerned. This holds, of course, with added force for those countries that had been ravaged by war, such as Germany, where only prospects of abnormal gain could call forth entrepreneurial effort from a population immersed in misery and despair.

Second, however, capitalism did not burst upon a world that was a blank: it grew by slow degrees from a pre-existing pattern dominated, in the respect under discussion, by the spirit, institutions, and practice of craft guilds. New

[7] There is no better illustration for this attitude than the late George Unwin's brilliant essay on the Merchant Adventurers in *Studies in Economic History* (1927). Professor Heckscher (op. cit.), with less reluctance to penetrate beyond that short-run view, formalized the situation into the two polar concepts of 'hunger for goods' and 'fear of goods,' which do not express well the economics of it.

products, new methods of production, and new forms of enterprise are resisted by any environment; but in these centuries there was in existence a legal machinery of resistance that worked automatically. This bears upon our topic in two ways. On the one hand, legislation and administration in all countries, under pressure from craft guilds and in their interest, subjected the newer 'free' enterprise to various regulations that spelled restriction of output. On the other hand, though these regulations have no roots in the capitalist system, but spell distortion of it, the merchants, masters, and so on who were affected by them naturally made the best of a bad business and organized themselves in a similar way. There were several reasons—besides the gains to be expected from restrictive regulation—why this came easily to them: the merchants and masters were themselves the products of a world in which organization and corporate action was the recognized thing and they had no objection to accepting 'ethical' and religious codes, enjoining standardized behavior, prayer meetings included. They lacked standing and political weight so long as they acted as individuals, whereas each Worshipful Company was a political power; and, in the most important case of overseas trade, the need of providing for physical protection and aggression—there were such things as joint stock companies formed for no other business than piracy—was a motive that was bound to throw traders together and to invite corporate action in other respects also. The Chartered Company, not a trading company itself but rather the organizational shell for the trade of its members, was, partly in opposition to, and partly in alliance with, the medieval Staple System (*jus emporii*), the obvious answer to all these needs and the natural instrument for making the most of the opportunities afforded by the protectionism of the age.[8]

Third, the governments of the national states had particular motives of their own for creating or favoring more or less 'monopolistic' organizations or positions. One of these motives has been mentioned already, the reconstruction motive. Another was the prospect of personal gain for the rulers—Queen Elizabeth participated personally in the gains (and losses) of 'monopolistic' ventures, even in the proceeds of downright robbery. The same great monarch offers outstanding examples of the method of providing for favorites by granting them letters patent of monopoly. Also, 'monopolist' organizations were sponges, which it was much easier to squeeze than it would have been to

[8] It is unfortunate that we cannot go more fully into the meaning and structure of both. Reference to Professor Heckscher's work must suffice. One point must be mentioned, however. The staple system has been called medieval because it grew out of the pattern of craft-guild industries in the thirteenth century (it had spread to England by the time of Edward III, as his ordinance on staples shows). But, adapting itself to changing conditions, it survived, as a general method of regulating international trade through the greater part of the period under survey, in Venice even until the Napoleonic occupation. In England, the loss of Calais in 1558 killed one form of it but in another form it continued to prevail: in fact, it was fully developed only by the Navigation Act of 1660 (for the policy of the Navigation Acts is but a special type of staple policy) and by the Staple Act of 1663.

squeeze a large number of independent entrepreneurs. And, finally, given strong governments, such organizations are not only easier to exploit but also easier to manage: their own administrative organs are so many ready-made handles for governments to seize. This aspect will appear in its full importance if we remember the nature of the policy of those governments for whom measures concerning trade were just one of the instruments of aggressive power politics: to force trade in one direction, to stop it entirely in another, was in some cases almost as effective as was a campaign; moreover, colonial companies of different nations might wage war upon each other while the respective national governments were officially at peace.[9]

Very naturally, the public at large resented being exploited in any of those ways and for any of those purposes without troubling to distinguish between them and without asking the question whether or not there were any compensating advantages to those practices in some cases, for instance, in cases where certain articles could not have been provided at all without them. The copious literature on the subject—the reader knows most of it if he knows the corresponding popular literature of today—simply reflected this resentment and rarely [10] went beyond denouncing favored individuals and groups, the East India Company and the Merchant Adventurers being, in England, the most popular targets. Even the businessmen joined the fray against restriction and privilege in almost every case that was not the writer's own: everyone was the sworn enemy of everyone else's privilege. Thus, most search-

[9] Again we may appeal to Dr. Unwin's lectures (op. cit.) for illustration of a kind of 'liberal' criticism of such attitudes and policies that tends to obstruct historical understanding even where it asserts nothing that is not correct. He offers strong reasons for believing that England did not net any national advantage from either her 'monopolistic' policies or her buccaneering (though it is going rather far to assert that robbery of treasure was not nationally remunerative because it destroyed the essential thing, credit) and, so far as this goes, errs only by ignoring the long-run aspects of 'monopolistic' restriction and 'monopolistic' gains. But his case, were it even stronger than it is, must remain inconclusive precisely because it is the case of the nineteenth-century liberal. The pattern of sixteenth and seventeenth-century behavior must be considered from the standpoint of sixteenth and seventeenth-century data *and men*. If we do this, even from a purely economic angle, irrationality is not so obvious. But in a situation of perennial warfare, where harming the other fellow is an end in itself, purely economic considerations are obviously inadequate. And there is something else. In discussing historical situations we must always distinguish between the principles underlying a form of behavior and the efficiency with which they are acted upon. This is very important. A. Smith, for instance, argued as much against the corruption and mistakes incident to the state management of his own and earlier times as he argued against state management per se. And so do we: the present-day argument against socialism or against extension of bureaucratic control is as much an argument from inefficiency to be expected in the application of the principles of socialism or control as it is an argument against these principles themselves. Both types of argument have their place but they must be kept separate.

[10] The most important instance is the 'discovery' of oligopoly (see below, ch. 6, sec. 3c).

ing analysis was produced principally by 'special pleaders' who defended individual cases.[11] Let us recall, however, from Part I that the motives of the analyst are not relevant to the question whether his facts or arguments are or are not true, valuable or not valuable, and that the presence of 'interested motive,' however effective its revelation may be in popular discussion, no more invalidates the reasoning that proceeds from it than its absence avails to validate a man's reasoning. For us, the special pleader's facts and argument are just as good or bad as those of the 'detached philosopher,' even if he exist.

Explanations too obvious to detain us may be offered for the fact that the public's reaction to restrictive practice was much stronger in England than it was on the Continent: to mention a symptom, free trade, which in the seventeenth century meant, among other things, abolition of the staple system or abolition of the chartered companies or at least every trader's right to become a member of the latter, found support in parliament and a fairly sweeping bill against restrictions of trading—not, of course, for free trade in the later sense of the term—was introduced, though not carried, as early as 1604. But there is another point of difference that is of considerable interest to us. The reader may have observed that, however objectionable to the man in the street most of the restrictive practices and legislative measures may have been, they did not create monopolists in the strict sense of Single Sellers,[12] and did not result in specifically monopolistic pricing. Nevertheless, the general outcry against them all was against monopoly. The reason is not far to seek. Though the English public of Queen Elizabeth's time can hardly have been influenced by the fact that monopoly had been stigmatized already by Aristotle and the scholastics, it harbored old resentments, dating from the Middle Ages, against corners and the like. These resentments flared up into fury when Elizabeth and James I adopted the practice of creating in large numbers what were in fact genuine monopolies and, moreover, monopolies that presented, in most

[11] One of the best of those performances may be mentioned by way of example: John Wheeler's *Treatise of Commerce, Wherein are shewed the Commodities arising from a well ordered and ruled trade, such as that of the Societie of Merchants Adventurers is proved to be. Written principally for the better Information of those who doubt of the Necessarinesse of the said Societie in the State of the Realme of England* (1601), and, so we may add, in view of impending hostile legislation.

[12] Monopoly in the strict sense denotes the position of a single (individual or corporate) seller, who faces a demand schedule that is given to him independently of his own action and of the action of sellers of competing goods. The exclusive right to sell port wine may, in the conditions of sixteenth and seventeenth-century England, be considered as a good practical approximation to strict or genuine monopoly, although, in general, a seller of port wine could not expect the demand schedule to stay put when the prices of similar beverages varied. But the big trading companies such as the Merchant Adventurers were not monopolies in this sense, for though they regulated the business of their members they did not in general fix prices. The reason why economists should confine the term Monopoly to the 'genuine' case defined is that their theory of monopoly price applies to this case only—or, to put it differently, because specifically monopolistic price policy is possible in this case only—so that nothing but confusion can result from any wider definition.

the grossest gratifications of the simplest appetites, we come dangerously near to identifying expectation of 'pleasure' with all possible motives whatsoever, even with intentional suffering of pain, and then, of course, the doctrine becomes an empty tautology. Worse still, if we allow too much scope to such 'pleasures' as may be afforded by exertion, victory, cruelty, and the like, we may get a picture of human behavior and of society that differs totally from the one those men actually envisaged. Thus, if we are to derive the conclusion *they* derived from their ideas about pleasure and pain, we have after all no choice but to adopt a definition of the latter that may indeed allow some freedom for going beyond beefsteaks, but only a limited one; that is to say, we have no choice but to adopt a theory of behavior that is at variance with the most obvious facts. Why, then, was it so readily adopted by many good brains? The answer seems to be that these good brains belonged to practical reformers who fought a historically given state of things that seemed to them 'irrational.' In such a struggle, simplicity and even triteness are the chief virtues of an argument, and beefsteak philosophies the best answer to a system of supermundanely sanctified rights and duties. Not that these authors were insincere: we all of us quickly convince ourselves of nonsense that we habitually preach.

We have seen above how the common good or social expediency of the scholastic doctors was harnessed into a particular shape by the eighteenth-century votaries of reason. Let us repeat and reformulate. The pleasures and pains of each individual are assumed to be measurable quantities capable of being (algebraically) added into a quantity called the individual's happiness (*felicità*); a frequently used German term was *Glückseligkeit*. These individual 'happinesses' are again summed up into a social total, *all of them being weighted equally:* 'everyone to count for one, nobody to count for more than one.' Finally, that social total is substituted for, or identified with, the common good or welfare of society, which is thus resolved into individual sensations of pleasure or pain, the only ultimate realities. This yields the normative principle of Utilitarianism, namely, the Greatest Happiness of the Greatest Number, which is chiefly associated, in recognition of ardent advocacy, careful elaboration, and extensive application, with the name of Bentham.[15] If the

[15] Jeremy Bentham (1748-1832), trained as a lawyer, though he early retired to a life of research and propaganda, became the undisputed leader of the utilitarian circle and the central figure of a group usually described as Philosophical Radicals. His performance in the field of economics will be noticed elsewhere. Here he interests us as a philosopher, sociologist, and theorist of legislation. The only one of his many voluminous works (ed. John Bowring, 1838-43) that need be mentioned is *An Introduction to the Principles of Morals and Legislation* (1789), which widely influenced thought and legislative practice though, on the Continent, similar ideas spread from domestic roots particularly in Italy and France.

The essentials of the utilitarian system had, however, been presented before in the *Principles of Moral and Political Philosophy* (1785) by William Paley (1743-1805), and some of them in the *Essay on the first Principles of Government* (1768) by Joseph Priestley (1733-1804), the versatile theologian and scientist who, besides being

cases, no redeeming features. In the struggles over these, the word Monopoly became loaded with emotion, a bugbear for all time to come, that was in the mind of the average Englishman associated with royal prerogative, favoritism, and oppression; and Monopolist became a term of opprobrium. But once a word has acquired an emotional value, positive or negative, that guarantees automatic reaction from almost anyone who hears or reads it, speakers and writers will try to exploit this psychic mechanism by applying the word as extensively as possible. And so monopoly came to denote almost anything that a man disliked about capitalist practice. This emotional attitude naturally spread to the United States the more readily because a large percentage of English emigrants to this country were, for other reasons, strong opponents of the Tudor-Stuart regime. It has survived, and has powerfully influenced public opinion, legislation, and even professional analysis to this day, both in England and the United States.[13]

Most of what has been said in this section indicates definite patterns of behavior that seem to invite sublimation into 'principles.' This has in fact been done, and the phrases Mercantilism, Mercantile System, Mercantilist Policy have been coined, first by hostile critics, to denote the result. Nevertheless, I have tried to avoid using them so far. The reason for this will be explained in Chapter 7, where we shall make Mercantilism—phrase and reality—our central theme. Meanwhile I wish to ask my readers to forget all they may know about it and to peruse what follows with an open mind, that is, with a mind unbiased by unhistoric preconceptions.

[2. The Economic Literature of the Period]

We shall now try to classify the unwieldy material from which we are to extract more or less significant products of analytic effort. This is a difficult task. Even in our own day economists are not always of one mind as to which performances do and which do not measure up to professional standards. But we are dealing with a formative period in which there were no professional standards, not, at all events, before the Classical Situation at the end of it. Moreover, the field itself was undefined and, by virtue of this fact alone, much wider than it is now: it covered, for instance, technology. However, in order to reduce our task to manageable proportions, we shall right away exclude from consideration certain bodies of literature that are also excluded

[13] This explanation seems to be more convincing than the usual general references to a specifically English love of freedom and fair play or to a specifically continental propensity to accept regimentation and the like. An English example that will illustrate both the phenomenon to which I wish to draw attention and its persistence is afforded by the nineteenth-century English champions of free trade in foodstuffs, who loved to refer to their opponents as 'monopolists' although neither the English farmers nor the English landowners were monopolists in any meaningful sense of the term. Even Sir Robert Peel, who occasionally displayed a sense for demagogical values, used the phrase in his speech in the Commons delivered on the defeat of his great ministry in 1846.

by modern practice, though we must not conceal from ourselves that, in so doing, we may be excluding pieces of analysis that are not inferior to some we include without question. This operation on our material is performed in the four paragraphs which follow.

[(a) *The Material Excluded.*] I. In the sixteenth century and even later, *Oeconomia* still meant household management. This type of literature seems to have been extremely popular. The no doubt unreliable method of browsing among books of this sort did not yield anything that would qualify for notice in this history. But two samples may be mentioned: first, the famous *Oeconomia ruralis et domestica* (1593-1607) by Johann Colerus, which lived for over a century and contains all sorts of advice about housekeeping, including farming, gardening, and domestic medical practice; second, *L'Economo prudente* (1629) by B. Frigerio, who defined *economia* as 'a certain prudence with which to govern a family' (ch. IX, for instance, deals with the *governo* of one's wife) and might conceivably interest some economists because it attempts to describe national economic behavior—in fact its concept of the *economo* is a common-sense forerunner of the concept of the Economic Man. Similarly, B. Keckermann, *Systema disciplinae politicae* (1606) defined *Oeconomia* as *disciplina de domo et familia recte dirigenda.*

II. Much more important is the literature on accounting and commercial arithmetic, which shades off into the neighboring literature on business management, business law, commercial geography, and business conditions in various countries. A few examples will characterize the contents of these literatures, which we exclude, although little pieces of purely economic analysis do occur in them. Fra Luca Paccioli's *Summa de arithmetica, geometria, proportioni e proportionalità* (Venice, 1494) contains, besides the ordinary commercial calculations of interest, bills, exchanges, and so on, also an exposition of double-entry bookkeeping. The first German book on double-entry bookkeeping that I have seen is W. Schweicker's *Zwifach Buchhalten* (1549). Such texts became common in the sixteenth and seventeenth centuries. So did guides to commercial practice in the trading centers of Europe. One of the earliest and most famous of these which the reader may look up in Cunningham's *Growth of English Industry and Commerce* (5th ed., vol. I, pp. 618 et seq.) was F. B. Pegolotti's *La Pratica della mercatura* (about 1315). The seventeenth-century publications of this type often contain rudimentary economic arguments. See, for example, John Roberts, *The Trades Increase* (1615), and Lewes Roberts, *The Merchants Mappe of Commerce* (1638). In the seventeenth and eighteenth centuries we find, on the one hand, a rich crop of monographs, especially on banks, some of which will have to be noticed later on, and, on the other hand, comprehensive compilations. We must mention Jacques Savary's *Le parfait negociant* (1675), which proved its vitality by going through new editions until 1800 and seems to me to repeat, on a larger scale, the performance of G. D. Peri, *Il Negotiante* (1638-65) and the still earlier one of B. Cotrugli Raugeo, *Della Mercatura e del mercante perfetto* (1573); and Savary's son's (Jacques Savary des Bruslons) *Dictionnaire universel du commerce* . . . (finished and published by his brother Philémon-Louis, 1723-30). Malachy Postlethwayt's *Universal Dictionary of Trade and Commerce* (1751-5), though based upon the latter, is by no means a mere translation of it, as has sometimes been asserted (on the differences, see E. A. J. Johnson, *Predecessors of Adam Smith*, 1937, Appendix B. The same author, in the same work, Appendix C, also reduced to its proper proportions the charge of plagiarism that has been frequently leveled against Postlethwayt, though the case remains bad enough). Neither of these dictionaries is, however, primarily concerned with what we call economics. Both were meant to serve the merchant's practical needs and deal with economic problems only incidentally. This is the difference in principle that, apart from the statistical complement, separates these ventures from later similar ones, especially from McCulloch's *Dictionary, Practical, Theoretical, and Historical of Commerce and Commercial Navigation* (1832).

III. It is with misgivings that I also exclude the literature on husbandry (farm management, agrarian technology) and forestry; the exclusion of other technological material need not cause qualms, though some writers, for instance writers on the technological aspects of mining, also dealt with economic subjects (see G. Agricola, *De re metallica*, 1556, later translated into German, an apparently highly successful treatise). The development of the literature on husbandry during the period may be briefly sketched as follows. In the thirteenth century there was a group of English writers—nobody has so far been able to link them up with either predecessors or immediate successors—who produced several remarkable works on estate management and farming (translated from Norman French and critically edited for the Royal Historical Society by Miss Elizabeth Lamond, 1890); it suffices to mention a treatise on *Husbandry*, written before 1250 and attributed to Walter of Henley. Disregarding this group, we find active interest in these matters from the fifteenth century on, when new editions of the Roman agriculturalists (*Scriptores rei rusticae*, the earliest edition I have seen is dated 1472), Columella in particular, seem to have been eagerly demanded. A new spirit of commercialism in agriculture—associated with the upheavals in the social structure of the countryside—then produced everywhere a literature that aimed at teaching those new methods of production, the introduction of which is usually referred to as the Agrarian Revolution. In England, there is a continuous development from Fitzherbert's *Boke of Husbondrye* (1523), to Weston's *Discours of Husbandrie used in Brabant and Flanders* (1650), to Worlidge's *Systema agriculturae* (1669), Mortimer's *Whole Art of Husbandry* (1707), and Jethro Tull's *Horse-Houghing Husbandry* (1731), which stands at the fountainhead of an outburst of literary activity that lasted throughout the eighteenth century and, in a sense, culminated in Arthur Young's copious writings (see, e.g., his *Rural Economy*, 1770, and his periodical, the *Annals of Agriculture*). This literature dealt with a wide range of topics from enclosures to drainage, drilling, crop rotation, turnips and clover, and cattle breeding. On the Continent, the Dutch led in agricultural practice, but the Italians in the literature of the subject. Let us notice as a forerunner, as yet substantially under the influence of the ancients, P. de Crescenzi (*Opus ruralium commodorum*, I only know the edition of 1471) and then A. Gallo (*Dieci giornate della vera agricoltura*, 1566), G. B. della Porta (1583), and especially the strikingly original Camillo Tarello (*Ricordo di agricoltura*, 1567, but I only know an edition of 1772), who in important points anticipated the development of almost two centuries. Of German contributions, we shall notice Heresbach's *Rei rusticae libri quatuor* (1570, first translated into English, 1577) and the work of Colerus (see above). Developments were then interrupted, but were resumed by the end of the seventeenth century to run on steadily to the writings on rural economy of J. C. Schubart (1734-87), whom Emperor Joseph II ennobled with the significant title of 'Cloverfield.' The Spaniard, G. A. de Herrera (*Libro de agricultura* . . . new ed. 1563), and the Frenchmen, Charles Estienne (*L'Agriculture et maison rustique*, 1570; Italian trans. 1581; I do not know the original) and Oliver de Serres (*Théâtre d'agriculture*, 1600) should also be mentioned. This attempt to locate the early landmarks must suffice, although this literature contributed considerably to the formation of some of the habits of thought that are most characteristic of modern economics. The same is true of the literature on forestry, into which I have not been able to go at all. It is worth noting, however, that forestry remained a recognized division of German treatises on general economics right into the nineteenth century.

IV. Description by travelers of the economic conditions they observed in foreign and even in their own countries forms an important part of the economic literature in the period under discussion, owing to the absence of regular reporting by permanent agencies. This method of reporting on facts and interpreting them was done on very different levels that range from stray observations to careful analyses, occasionally involving considerable bits of theory. Neglect of this literature is apt to distort seriously our picture of the economics of those centuries and in particular to hide the full extent of the fact-finding work that was actually done. Nevertheless, we have no choice but to exclude this literature. It must suffice to mention two famous English samples which will repay perusal: Sir William Temple's *Observations upon the United Provinces* (1672; 3rd augmented ed. 1676), which presents conditions in the Netherlands from the standpoint of a definite philosophy of wealth (that centers on 'frugality and industry'), and Arthur Young's reports on his various tours and travels (most important in this connection: *Travels . . . with a view to ascertaining the Cultivation, Wealth Resource, and National Pros-*

perity of the Kingdom of France, 1792), which contain a lot of what might be termed 'theory in action.'

[J. A. S. intended to have this discussion of the Excluded Material set up in small type as being of interest only to the specialist. Many of the books mentioned he examined in the Kress Library (Harvard School of Business Administration), which seemed both to him and to the Editor to be a kind of scholars' Paradise.

To Professor Alexander Gerschenkron I owe the information that Georg Agricola's *De re metallica* (mentioned above, III) was translated into English by Herbert Clark Hoover and Lou Henry Hoover (1912; new ed. 1950).]

[(b) *The Consultant Administrators*.] The authors of the remaining material we shall divide into two clearly, if only broadly, distinct groups. We shall call them the Consultant Administrators [1] and the Pamphleteers. Among the Consultant Administrators, teachers and writers of more or less systematic treatises form a subgroup that is relatively easy to delimit. In that paradise of bureaucracy there was, of course, a steady demand for the instruction of young men who were preparing themselves for the public-service career—or of older men who wished to improve their equipment—particularly in Germany and Italy. In the course of the eighteenth century, professorial chairs began to be provided for the teaching of what was described, in Germany, as Cameral Science or Science of the State (*Staatswissenschaft*) and what may be more accurately described as Principles of Economic Administration and Policy (in German, *Polizeiwissenschaft*).[2] Thenceforth those treatises were to

[1] This term roughly covers the same type as does the Spanish term *políticos*. In the German literature the word in general use is *Cameralist* or *Kameralist* (derived from the territorial treasuries, the *camerae*). But it carries a misleadingly narrow association and in addition would not serve our purpose, which is to label a group that includes the German type but is not confined to it. Histories and bibliographies of German Cameralist literature were published as early as 1758 by J. J. Moser and 1781-2 by K. G. Rössig (*Versuch einer pragmatischen Geschichte der Ökonomie, Polizei und Kameralwissenschaft*). Much help has been derived from R. von Mohl, *Geschichte und Literatur der Staatswissenschaften* (1855-8) and from the comprehensive bibliography, *Bibliographie der Kametalwissenschaften* (1935-7) by Miss Magdalene Humpert, who lists about 14,000 items, most of which fortunately do not come within the range of this history. Also see K. Zielenziger, *Die alten deutschen Kameralisten* (1914), and Louise Sommer, *Die österreichischen Kameralisten* (1920-25). An American book may be added: A. W. Small, *The Cameralists* (1909).

[2] See especially Wilhelm Stieda, *Die Nationalökonomie als Universitätswissenschaft* (1906). We may mention the foundation of the chairs in the Universities of Halle (1727; which immediately evoked derogatory comment as regards the competence of the newly appointed professors), of Uppsala (1740), and of Naples (1754, chair of 'economia e commercio' founded for Genovesi). We know, of course, that the teaching of economics must not be dated from these. The scholastic and the natural-law philosophers had taught economics before, both in law and in moral-philosophy courses. And the training of civil servants also antedates the eighteenth century. In the Universities of Naples (founded 1224), Oxford, Prague, Cracow, Vienna, Salamanca, and others its beginnings go back to the thirteenth and fourteenth centuries, and in the sixteenth it was second in importance to the training of clergymen in Marburg, Königs-

a large extent simply textbooks and the products of academic lectures. The same need, however, had asserted itself much earlier, and systematic treatises of pedagogical interest had been written in all continental countries long before economics as a distinct field received the official recognition implied in the foundation of those professorships.

But from the fifteenth century on, first in Italy then elsewhere, public administrators of all ranks and types—great noblemen as well as humble drudges—began to put on paper their ideas about how the government and the economy of their countries should be run and especially how their finances should be managed. These administrators were practitioners, familiar with the business of governing, and most of them were laics. Their books, reports, and memoranda thus differ characteristically from the works of the schoolmen and the philosophers of natural law. It is true that they also differ from those of the teachers.

The practitioners lacked the systematic habit and the erudition of the academic professional, though they made up for these shortcomings by their command of facts and the freshness of their outlook. Nevertheless we shall include them with the teachers in our group of Consultant Administrators. After all, they were mostly public servants writing for other public servants. We must, however, go still further. We must also include a number of men who were not public servants but who made, in the same spirit as did these, the public cares their own or, doing still better, wrote in the genuine spirit of scientific analysis—businessmen, professors of sciences other than economics, private individuals of the most varied backgrounds and stations. Thus we get, alongside of the professional subgroup, another one that forms a unit not in any sociological sense but by virtue of the nature of its performance. From it proceeded much of the most important—especially the most original—work of the period. And this work, though rarely systematic in form, was very often systematic in substance. In England, such publications became so numerous in the seventeenth century that they constitute an easily recognizable standard type; there was also a standard title for them, *Discourse of Trade*. But they were not confined to England, though elsewhere there was no standard title except, perhaps, in the case of the French *Éléments du Commerce* of the eighteenth century. We shall call these books Quasi-systems. It was in them that 'general economics' first took *independent* shape.

[(c) *The Pamphleteers*.] The Pamphleteers were a mixed crowd—projectors of banks, canals, industrial and colonial ventures; special pleaders for or against some individual interest, such as the Company of Merchant Adventurers or the East India Company; advocates or foes of a particular measure or policy; planners—often cranks—with pet ideas; and men who do not come within

berg, Würzburg, and Graz. Moreover, there were professorships of 'statistics' in the seventeenth century. It may be of some interest to note that in England and Scotland no chairs of economics per se were founded in the eighteenth century. Professors of agriculture were, however, appointed in Edinburgh, 1792—where the chair of Political Economy actually dates from 1871—and in Oxford, 1796—where it dates from 1825.

any of these categories but simply wished to clear up some issue or to present a piece of analysis. All of them flourished in all countries owing to the rapid increase of the opportunities for printing and publishing. Newspapers also, rare ventures in the sixteenth century, became plentiful in the seventeenth and, for the eighteenth, 170 papers and periodicals that published economic material have been listed for Germany alone.[3] But England was the classical home of the pamphlet, as we should expect. For nowhere else was there so strong an incentive for anyone with an axe to grind to try to influence public opinion.

It is with these pamphleteers that the difficulty pointed out at the beginning of this section becomes most serious. So far as their writings simply reflect the conditions, humors, struggles, and idiosyncrasies of their day, they are of course very interesting for the economic historian and the historian of economic thought, but of no interest for us. In a report on the present state of economics nobody would think of including the 'popular' or what Marx termed the 'vulgar' economics of our own time. But up to, say, 1750 no such distinction is possible. All the 'scientific' economics there was consisted in the small nucleus contained in the systems of the philosophers of natural law, and with this any intelligent businessman who knew his facts was able to compete successfully without having to acquire any particular technique. Moreover, the Pamphleteers slowly evolved the primitive technique they needed. Some of them produced tracts of strictly scientific character. And the economics of the First Classical Situation owes a considerable debt to them. So we cannot afford to neglect them. But every one of us must, within his individual command of the material,[4] rely upon his own fallible judgment of quality.

3. Sixteenth-Century Systems

Again we take the *Wealth of Nations* as our point of orientation. In the preceding chapter we looked upon A. Smith as a philosopher of natural law. In this one we shall look upon him as a Consultant Administrator. On our way toward him I shall try to avoid confusing and empty enumerations and introduce as few names as possible. But a small number of major or particularly representative performances will, either in this or in the subsequent chapters,

[3] This is, of course, a total for the century. Many of these papers and periodicals were very short-lived. Perhaps not more than 10 per cent of that total existed at any one time. Nor were they equal to the French in quality. The specifically economic journal is in fact a French achievement. The first of this type was the *Journal Oeconomique* (1751); then followed the *Gazette du Commerce* (1763), which the government bought and supplemented by the *Journal de l'Agriculture, du Commerce et des Finances* (1764), which became for a time the organ of the physiocrats.

[4] So far as I know it, and so far as contributions to economic analysis are concerned, the European pamphlet literature of the sixteenth, seventeenth, and eighteenth centuries can be reduced to less than two dozen items. The reader must not overlook, however, that we class with the Consultant Administrators several names that other writers would class with the Pamphleteers.

be discussed in sufficient detail to give an idea of their nature and significance. Taking the period as a whole, I think that first honors should go to Italy. If there could be any point in such a statement, we might say that economics was primarily an Italian science until the last quarter of the eighteenth century. Spain, France, and England divide second honors, though in very different proportions at different times. The rest of this chapter is devoted chiefly to the first, or professorial, of the two subgroups into which we have divided the Consultant Administrators, though it will be necessary to cast some glances also at authors of quasi-systems. The reason for this arrangement is not that the works of the former type are of commanding interest or importance. On the contrary, no other group produced, among more inspiring ones, books of such unspeakable tedium. Rather we deal with them first in order to get them out of our way.

[(a) *The Work of Carafa.*] In the late Middle Ages economic history already affords ample evidence of what, in view of our own performances, we are bound to call a high level of insight into the practical problems of economic policy. An often-quoted English instance [1] will suffice to show this. What we should call 'hearings' on the outflow of money from England and other currency problems were held in 1382. The reader can easily satisfy himself that what the experts examined had to say makes perfectly good sense and does not differ substantially from what we should expect to hear from similar experts under similar conditions, though it would no doubt be couched in more sophisticated phraseology. If documents such as these reveal the presence of a certain amount of analytic power, there are also indications of the presence of interest in the collection of facts: Étienne Boileau's *Livre des métiers* (about 1268),[2] a compilation of the regulations concerning the trades of Paris, is a landmark of this type of research which gathered momentum from the sixteenth century on. Literary effort of the type to be discussed in this chapter also goes far back—in a sense to St. Thomas' *De regimine principum* and to the *English Speculum regis* (ed. by Moisant, 1894) and other works of the thirteenth and fourteenth centuries, such as Aegidius Colonna's *De regimine principum libri*, or Fra Paolino's *Trattato* (ed. Mussafia, 1868), or Petrarch's *De republica optime administranda.*

From this literature emerged, in the fifteenth century, a work so superior to all that had been written before that we may fittingly head our list of Consultant Administrators with its author, though he was primarily a practical one, the Neapolitan count and duke, Carafa.[3] The range of his ideas may be

[1] See 'Opinions of the Officers of the Mint on the State of English Money, 1381-2' in *English Economic History: Select Documents* (compiled and ed. by A. E. Bland, P. A. Brown, and R. H. Tawney, 1914), pp. 220 et seq.

[2] Edited by Depping in *Documents inédits sur l'histoire de France* (1837).

[3] Diomede Carafa (1406-87), *De regis et boni principis officio . . .* (ed. used, 1668; I have not seen the original, written in Italian in the seventies of the fifteenth century). Carafa's contemporary, Mattheo Palmieri (1405-75), wrote a treatise entitled *Della vita civile* published in 1529 (posthumously) that is much more definite as to matters of taxation (especially in developing the doctrine that taxes are paid in con-

indicated by some of his recommendations. He wanted to see a balanced budget that would have plenty of room for welfare expenditure and avoid the necessity of resorting to forced loans—which he compared to robbery and theft—and the like; definite, equitable, and moderate taxes that would not drive capital from the country or oppress labor. which is the source of wealth; business left alone, though he added that industry, agriculture, and commerce alike should be encouraged by loans of money and in other ways; foreign merchants made comfortable because their presence is most useful to the country. All this is no doubt excellent sense and remarkably free from any definite errors and prejudices. But it is equally free from any attempt to analyze. The normal processes of economic life harbored no problem for Carafa. The only problem was how to manage and improve them. In particular we must not suspect a theory of value behind that passage about labor's being the source of wealth. Such questions exercised the nimble minds of his scholastic contemporaries. But they never occurred to that soldier-statesman.

Nevertheless his performance holds a prominent place in the history of economic analysis. His systematic arrangement alone would suffice to show this. The first part of his book discusses the principles of general policy and of defense—compare A. Smith's lectures on arms—the second the administration of justice. The third is a little treatise on public finance and within measurable, though of course long, distance from the Fifth Book of the *Wealth of Nations*, 'Of the Revenue of the Sovereign or Commonwealth.' The fourth and last part presents Carafa's views on economic policy proper, and many an eighteenth-century treatise reads like an expansion of these views. There is no evidence that later writers took his book as a model and that, in this sense, he created the systematic form in which an important part of the work of the Consultant Administrators was to be cast. But as a matter of fact, he was, so far as I know, the first to deal comprehensively with the economic problems of the nascent modern state, and during the next three centuries a host of writers, adopting the same systematic ideas and defining their field similarly, followed in his wake and wrote in the spirit that he represented at its best. They no doubt learned to plough more deeply as well as to take new land under the plough. But they did not alter the general layout. In particular they not only adhered to, but in time also developed, the fundamental idea that Carafa clothed in his conception of the Good Prince (and which Sir James Steuart was to personify in his Statesman). This anthropomorphic entity is the embryo of their concept of a National Economy (in German, *Volkswirtschaft* or *Staatswirtschaft*), which reflects so well the historic process we have tried to visualize in the first section of this chapter. This National Economy is not simply the sum total of the individual households and firms or of the groups and classes within the borders of a state. It is conceived as a sort of sublimated business unit, something that has a distinct

---

sideration of the help and protection extended by the state to individuals in their economic activities, from which he deduced the principle of proportionality) but seemed to me, on the whole, to be inferior to Carafa's as a representative performance.

existence and distinct interests of its own and needs to be managed like a big farm. This was the way in which that epoch conceptualized the key position that governments and bureaucracies actually acquired, and also the way in which a distinction was drawn between political and business economy that survived to our own day, although, from a purely analytic standpoint, there is little to be said for it.

[(b) *Representative Performances: Bodin and Botero.*] In the sixteenth century this type of economics flourished in all continental countries. As representative performances—that were also outstanding in their influence on contemporary and later writers—we shall choose two works by Bodin and by Botero.[4] Both works are primarily treatises on 'political science'—written in the spirit of Aristotle's *Politics*—and as such are important stepping stones between Machiavelli and Montesquieu. Their economics is, like Carafa's, the economics of public policy and administration, taking its place beside all other branches of political knowledge. The economic analysis in the Sixth Book of Bodin's *République* is, however, hardly above the ideas that were current in its time and indeed does not go far beyond Carafa's, though his principles of taxation do mark further progress toward the Fifth Book of the *Wealth of Nations.*[5] Botero, who in some other respects may be classed as a follower of Bodin, made a much more important contribution to economic analysis that will be noticed in a subsequent chapter on population. Here, another remark suggests itself. Botero's treatise, especially if considered in connection with his other works, displays remarkable fact-mindedness. He was an able analyst. But the bulk of his labors went toward the collection, co-ordination, and interpretation of past and contemporaneous fact—economic, social, political. In this he was no exception. We have seen that the scholastic doctors of the sixteenth century were eager fact hunters and that they reasoned much

[4] Jean Bodin or Baudin (Bodinus, 1530-96), *Les six livres de la République* (1576; 2nd ed. 1577; the one used, 1580). On the author and his works, see Henri Baudrillart, *Jean Bodin et son temps* (1853), a book which the lapse of nearly a century has not deprived of its authoritative position. This is the only one of Bodin's works that need be mentioned here; the other that is relevant to our subject will be noticed later (ch. 6). Lest the reader find that our text fails to do justice to the author, I want to emphasize that we consider only his contribution to economic analysis, which I believe to have been but modest, and not his much greater importance in other fields, the theory of sovereignty in particular.

Giovanni Botero (1544-1617), *Della ragion di stato* (1589, many editions and translations; recent ed. with introduction by C. Morandi, 1930, in the series *Classici del Pensiero Politico*). In order to appreciate the full significance of the work of this great man, two other publications must be mentioned: first, his *Delle cause della grandezza delle città* (1588), suggestive, in some points, of Montesquieu's *Grandeur des Romains* and also of Book III of the *Wealth of Nations;* and second his universal reports (*Relazioni universali*), compiled on his travels, on the power and resources of the states of Europe and Asia, which were published 1591-6.

[5] They would, I think, have to be Exhibit A in any proof of the continental, mainly French, origins of A. Smith's ideas on public finance.

more from observation and much less from abstract premisses than one might suppose. This was, however, still more the case with the literature now under discussion, whose greater part as well as main value may be said to consist in 'factual' investigations: then *as always, throughout the history of economics*, fact-finding was the chief care of the overwhelming majority of economists. Besides Botero's theory of population, Italy produced during the sixteenth century several other works that are much more important than the systematic literature we are now surveying, especially in the field of money (Davanzati, Scaruffi see below, ch. 6).

[(c) *Spain and England*.] The very high level of Spanish sixteenth-century economics [6] was due chiefly to the scholastic contributions. But we may note what I believe to have been an early 'quasi-system,' the work of Ortiz,[7] mainly a well-reasoned program for industrial development of a type that was to be so prolific in the seventeenth century, both in Spain and in England. For Germany there is little to record. Two quasi-systems that seem to have met with success are, however, mentioned in the footnote below.[8]

At first sight one might conceive the impression that in sixteenth-century England there was little to correspond to the type of work surveyed so far. But this is not so. Corresponding work there was, only it took other forms owing to the different political structure of the people to which it was addressed. Discussion of the economic problems of the day, encouraged and

[6] See E. Castelot, 'Coup d'oeil sur la littérature économique de l'Espagne au XVIe et au XVIIe siècle' (*Journal des économistes*, vol. 45, 1901); Manuel Colmeiro, *Historia de la economia politica en España* (1863) and *Biblioteca de los economistas españoles* (1880); another anthology is helpful, Juan Sempere y Guarinos' *Biblioteca española economico-politica* (1801-21), the Spanish counterpart of the Italian Custodi collection; A. V. Castillo, *Spanish Mercantilism* (1930); E. Hamilton, 'Spanish Mercantilism before 1700' (*Facts and Factors in Economic History* by former students of E. F. Gay); and José Larraz López, 'La Época del Mercantilismo en Castilla, 1500-1700' (Real Academia de Ciencias Morales y Politicas, 1943), and the review of this address in the *Economic History Review*, 1944, by J. Márquez. Señor Larraz speaks of a Spanish school—the 'school of Salamanca'—of sixteenth-century economists. There is indeed some justification for this. But the core of this school was made up of late scholastics, many of the most eminent of whom happened to be Spaniards; and there was nothing specifically Spanish about their teaching; the rest of Spanish sixteenth-century economists, though most of them were also clerics, do not form a school.

[7] Luiz Ortiz, *Memorial al Rey para que no salgan dineros de estos reinos de España* (1558; see Colmeiro's *Biblioteca*). Never mind the title, which might bring the work under ban on the score of 'mercantilism.' It has little to do with the true import of the argument and was presumably chosen by the author in order to attract the attention of laymen.

[8] Melchior von Osse's (*c.* 1506-57) *Politisches Testament*, written 1556, though published under the title *De prudentia regnativa* (1607), was reprinted by Thomasius for classroom use, as late as 1717. Georg Obrecht's (1547-1612) tracts on economic subjects (he is of more importance as a jurist) were posthumously published in 1617 as *Fünff underschiedliche Secreta Politica*. Bodin's influence is much in evidence.

also disciplined by the ritual of parliamentary and government inquiries, greatly improved throughout that century and occasionally rose to 'scientific' significance. From evidence given before royal commissions—such as the Royal Commission on Exchange, 1564—speeches, petitions, pamphlets on enclosures, guilds, companies, the staple system, monopolies, taxation, currency, customs, poor relief, wages, regulation of industry, and so on, a manual of economic analysis and policy might be compiled that would compare favorably with contemporaneous systematic efforts on the Continent.[9] Instead of attempting to do this we shall, however, follow a much easier course that is fortunately open to us. There are a number of publications that may be considered as general surveys of the economics of the time. In part, at least, they supply what we need. We shall confine ourselves to the most widely known of these treatises.[10]

The *Discourse of the Common Weal* contains three dialogues that deal with a wide variety of topics. The author regrets 'that younge studentes be alwayes over hastye in utterynge theire Jugementes,' and the 'scysme in matter of relygyen'; recommends better training all round, going so far as to consider superiority in 'lernynge' as one of the reasons for Julius Caesar's victory over Pompey; condemns enclosures in so far as they turn arable land into pasture; criticizes the rising business corporations and their monopolistic practices; disapproves of debased currency and of inflation that hurts people whose

[9] The best way for the reader to satisfy himself of this quickly is to glance through the source book already mentioned, Bland, Brown, and Tawney, *English Economic History: Select Documents* (1914), and through the still more useful compilation, Tawney and Power, *Tudor Economic Documents*, being select documents illustrating the economic and social history of Tudor England (3 vols., 1924), the third volume of which contains 'pamphlets, memoranda, and literary extracts.'

[10] This is a book entitled A *Compendious or briefe examination of certayne ordinary complaints, of divers of our countrymen in these our days: which although they are in some part iniust & frivolous, yet are they all by way of dialogues throughly debated & discussed.* To Miss Elizabeth Lamond we owe an excellent critical edition under the title A *Discourse of the Common Weal of this Realm of England* (1893), which besides the text presents the results of careful researches into the nature and the origin of the work. She attributed it to John Hales, a public official who also served in parliament and on the commission on enclosures of 1548, and assumed that it was written in 1549. Both statements have been questioned. But for us it is more important to note that the edition printed in 1581, and from which were made all the later editions (1751, 1808, 1813, 1876), differs from an earlier one (1565), the most important difference being the addition of a passage on the causes of the rise in general prices: whereas the edition of 1565 speaks only of the deterioration of the coinage, the later one also mentions the increase in the supply of the precious metals. Whoever made this addition therefore *may* be entitled to a share in such credit as this 'discovery' deserves, though Bodin's priority (*Response aux paradoxes de Monsieur de Malestroit*, 1568; see below, ch. 6), not only as to publication but also as to the discovery itself, is of course established beyond doubt by the existence of the volume of 1565. On the works of Clement Armstrong or Armeston that would have served our purpose equally well, see S. T. Bindoff's paper in the *Economic History Review*, 1944

incomes do not react promptly, such as the laborers,[11] landlords, and even the King's Highness; recommends the fostering of young industries as well as the accumulation of a monetary fund for emergencies ('sodeyne eventes')—money being as it were a 'storehouse of any commodity' and *nervus bellorum;* does not favor the export of raw materials, especially of wool; frowns upon these 'straungers' who sell nothing but frivolous stuff that costs them little though the English pay dearly for it, and buy in return good honest English goods, if indeed they do buy anything and do not take 'monye currant' outright, which they prefer to do of late; feels that foreign commodities should be taxed so that domestic producers *might be able to compete;* wants to see the nation's money kept in the country and to recover that which has already left it. And so on.

From these indications, the reader should be able to draw a picture of our author's economics. Of course, it was popular—preanalytic—economics. But most of it was sound common sense. The 'doctor' of the dialogues was evidently a thoroughly reasonable man and never said anything that would seem absurd to the intelligent layman or politician of today. In one respect, however, he was especially reasonable for his time. He distrusted regulation less than did the liberals of the nineteenth century but more than we do ourselves. He did not like compulsion. He wished to work with and not against the profit motive, which he considered quite essential. Moreover, he sometimes saw below the surface of things. For instance, he saw quite correctly that the encroachment of sheep runs upon the arable land had much to do with the policy that aimed at keeping wheat cheap by means of price fixing and export prohibitions, and thus defeated its purpose by altering the relative profitability of wheat and wool production in favor of the latter. This piece of reasoning (analoga of which are frequently met with in the writings of the Consultant Administrators) goes beyond the obvious. In its implications, it approaches the status of analytic work.

4. The Systems, 1600-1776

[(a) *Representatives of the Earlier Stages.*] The richer developments of the seventeenth and eighteenth centuries are much more difficult to convey. Keeping in mind our plan of campaign we shall, in this section, provisionally disregard everything else and go through with our survey of the 'systematic' literature of those two centuries until we reach the neighborhood of the *Wealth of Nations.* The earlier stages of this type of work will be represented by Montchrétien for France, by Bornitz and Besold for Germany, and by Fernández Navarrete for Spain.

Antoyne Montchrétien, Sieur de Watteville (c. 1575-1621), *Traicté de l'oeconomie politique* (1615), seems to have been the first to publish a book under the title of

[11] The Elizabethan Statute of Apprenticeship, 1562/3 (5 Eliz. c. 4), introduced, however, what we should call index wages: that is to say, wage rates were to be adjusted annually according to the changes in the cost of living.

Political Economy. This was, however, his only merit. The book is a mediocre performance and completely lacking in originality. Though there is a rough common sense about its recommendations, it abounds in elementary slips of reasoning that indicate a level of competence rather below than above its own time. For a thoroughly different appraisal, see T. Funck-Brentano's introduction to his edition of the work (1889), and also P. Lavalley's study, *L'Oeuvre économique de Antoine de Montchrétien* (1903).

Jacob Bornitz, *Tractatus politicus de rerum sufficientia in republica et civitate procuranda* (1625), an ill-digested compilation of economic facts; Christoph Besold's (1577-1638) *Collegium politicum* (1614), *Politicorum libri duo* (1618), and, to mention another of his numerous works, *Synopsis politicae doctrinae* (1623), moved on the higher level of the polyhistoric learning of this famous teacher, though he was inferior to Bornitz in factual knowledge; his treatment of interest anticipated that of Salmasius; Bodin's influence is unmistakable.

Pedro Fernández Navarrete, *Discursos* (first 1621; later edition under the title *Conservación de monarquías,* 1626). This author, an officer of the Inquisition, displays a remarkable freedom from the tendency of his (and our own) time to overstress the importance of the monetary factor and a not less remarkably sound judgment in maintaining that a normal process of industrialization would have gone far toward remedying the ills from which Spain was suffering (the value added to raw materials by human labor being much more important than gold and silver, see the sixteenth of his fifty *Discursos*) and that this process was capable of being accelerated by removing obstacles. I feel fairly confident that I am right in preferring Fernández Navarrete's performance to that of the equally well-known Moncada (*Discursos,* 1619, republished as late as 1746 under the title *Restauración politica de España*) so far as ability to analyze is concerned.

Four further names will suffice to characterize what may be considered a more advanced stage: Martinez de la Mata, who developed a program of industrial policy on the lines of Fernández Navarrete; Seckendorff, who wrote the first outstanding treatise on the public administration and policy of German principalities; the great name of Sully, whom we neglect as we must; and Du Refuge (Philippe de Béthune), who went much beyond either Bodin or Montchrétien.

Francisco Martinez de la Mata is known for his *Memorial ó discursos en razón del remedio de la despoblación, pobreza y esterilidad de España* (1650; the *Epitome de los discursos* . . . 1701, is all I know; Sempere y Guarinos, op. cit. vol. III contains extracts). This work of the self-styled 'servant of the afflicted poor' (*siervo de los pobres afligidos*) must have been a great success. The fundamental soundness of its main thesis —the same as Navarrete's—is, in fact, beyond doubt and was to be repeated by a chorus of later economists.

Veit Ludwig von Seckendorff (1626-92), himself a distinguished administrator, published in 1656 the *Teutscher Fürstenstaat,* the classic work of its genus. Behind the descriptive and pedagogic program there is a definite social vision and a definite policy. The given end being a numerous and well-employed population, protection and internal freedom of industry and trade—which will of itself eliminate obsolete craft guilds—compulsory elementary education, and a system of taxation based upon the excise—which by bearing lightly on the higher incomes will increase employment—are the principal means envisaged. We shall presently see that this was, and continued to be, the typical program—and, by implication, the typical analysis of the German and Italian 'cameralists' throughout their careers, that is, up to the first decades of the nineteenth century. The man who first formulated it definitely and correctly, and in doing so anticipated, in some points, the developments of more than a century to come, was no second-rater. On the contrary, he towers high, as a man and as an intellect, above many a writer who figures much more prominently in these pages. But explicit analysis, that is, conscious efforts to state relations of causation or interdependence, is hard to find in his work. And what there is of it, is not up to much.

Maximilien de Béthune (1560-1641), created Duke de Sully by Henry IV, the latter's minister of finance, was a much greater and especially stronger man than was the most famous of his successors, Colbert. He reformed the fiscal system of France most successfully and saw much beyond the range of what he actually accomplished. Moreover, he knew—which is the criterion of greatness in a fiscal administrator—how to make fiscal policy an element and tool of general economic policy. His *Économies royales* (first publ. 1638; a selection, which is all I know, has been republished in Guillaumin's *Petite bibliothèque économique*) are substantially memoirs of his administration and make, in their quaint form, charming and most instructive reading. But there is no point in calling him a forerunner of the physiocrats, on the strength of his preoccupation with the welfare of the agrarian population and of his saying that husbandry and pasture were the two *mamelles* of France. Nothing can be more obvious than that this man was entirely innocent of any theory whatever.

Eustache Du Refuge's * work, *Le Conseiller d'estat ou recueil général de la politique moderne* (1645), descends from that of Bodin. The first forty chapters deal with the various forms of government, tolerance, the duties of magistrates, conscription, and so on; Chapters 41 to 44 are to all intents and purposes a treatise on economics and economic policy in outline; the rest includes, among other things, public finance, especially taxation, and marks another step toward A. Smith's Fifth Book. Du Refuge's economics is remarkable in several respects. In particular he was the first author I know of to distinguish and at the same time to co-ordinate the effects of 'parsimonie' (ch. 44) which conserves wealth and of *l'espargne* (hoarding, ch. 49) which interferes with commerce. In this and in other points he made a creditable effort to analyze.

Throughout the rest of the seventeenth and practically the whole of the eighteenth century the same type of work was turned out by an increasing number of writers, among whom academic teachers rapidly gained the majority. In some countries, especially in Germany, it was the main domestic source of economic teaching even in the first decades of the nineteenth century. Much of it was, however, so distressingly unoriginal and so obviously written in response to demand rather than to creative impulse that there would be no point in following its history in any detail. For our purposes, that is to say, in order to get an idea of its general character and to see how far it had advanced at the threshold of the Smithian age, it will suffice to introduce two eighteenth-century authors of international reputation, Uztáriz and Justi, and to take up for discussion one of the works of the latter.

* [This work, *Le Conseiller* . . . (published anonymously), was attributed to Du Refuge when J. A. S. used it in the Kress Library; recently it has been attributed to Phillipe de Béthune, Comte de Selles de Charost. There is an English translation as early as 1634 which implies an earlier date for the original French publication.]

Gerónimo Uztáriz (1670-1732) wrote a treatise entitled *Theórica y práctica de comercio y de marina* (1st ed. 1724, two other editions improved by the author himself), which may be said to be related to Martinez de la Mata's as the latter's treatise is to Fernández Navarrete's. It was translated into English and French and widely read and admired. The title is misleading in two respects. First, it suggests limitation to topics of international trade, whereas it deals comprehensively with practically all the problems of taxation, monopoly, population, and so on that come within the range of 'applied' economics. Second, the title also suggests theoretical analysis, though none is to be found in the treatise: what he, like so many later economists, means by theory is criticism and recommendation as distinguished from the presentation of facts. The care and space bestowed on the latter (he reprinted or extracted so many documents as to make his treatise serve the purposes of a source book) is what strikes the reader first. The recommendations acquire for us additional historical interest when we remember that Uztáriz held public office of the policy-making kind at the time when Cardinal Alberoni was at the head of affairs: the latter followed—not without considerable success—exactly the policy of armament and industrialization that Uztáriz recommended in the treatise which appeared five years after the Cardinal's fall. Whatever this fact may mean—the reader's guess is as good as mine—our author must certainly be commended, considering the then situation of his country and the standpoint from which he viewed it, for the correctness of such analysis as may have been behind his recommendation.

[(b) *Justi: the Welfare State.*] Johann Heinrich Gottlob von Justi (1717-71) was a professor for part of his life and an administrator of public enterprises for another part. His intellectual equipment covered all the natural-law philosophy of his and the preceding epoch but was enriched by practical experience in a way in which the two were rarely combined. Of course, we must grant the professor a fair ration of ponderous triviality, and also allow for his way of arriving at common-sense conclusions by a circuitous route that leads through questionable political philosophies. An example will illustrate the latter point: freedom is absolute by virtue of natural law; only, as the professor has somewhere learnedly shown, it consists in freedom to obey the laws and the rulings of the bureaucracy; but the latter as taught by Justi is so very reasonable that after all we come out of the woods with the result to be presented in the text. Of Justi's numerous works his *System des Finanzwesens* (System of Public Finance, 1766) has been chosen by Professor Monroe for partial publication in *Early Economic Thought* (1924). Our sketch in the text is based upon *Die Grundfeste zu der Macht und Glückseeligkeit der Staaten oder ausführliche Vorstellung der gesamten Polizeywissenschaft* (The Groundwork of the Power and Welfare of States or Comprehensive Presentation of the Science of Public Policy, 2 vols., 1760-61). We are concerned with the first volume only. The second contains, in the spirit of that science of administration, dissertations on religion, science, the government of the private household, civic virtues, fire brigades, insurance—of which Justi was a fervent advocate—regulation of dress, and the like. His *Staatswirtschaft* (1755) would have served equally well.

Instead of Justi, I might have chosen Joseph von Sonnenfels (1732-1817; *Grundsätze der Polizey, Handlung, und Finanzwissenschaft*, 1765-7), who was in several respects superior to Justi, though in substance he moved on the latter's and Forbonnais' lines. The son of a Berlin rabbi, he became, after emigrating to Vienna, one of the lights of that 'age of reason' and took part, both as an academic teacher (being the first professor of policy and cameral science in Vienna) and as a civil servant in many of the legislative reforms of his time: he was a member of what may be described as Joseph II's brain trust. His book remained the official textbook within the Austro-Hungarian monarchy until 1848. The subject of his inaugural lecture (1763) deserves to be noticed. It was on the Inadequacy of Mere Experience in Economics.

The subject of Justi's inquiry is what German historians call the Welfare State (*Wohlfahrtsstaat*) in its historic individuality and in all its aspects. That is to say, he dealt with economic problems from the standpoint of a government that accepts responsibility for the moral and economic conditions of life—just as modern governments do—in particular for everyone's employment and livelihood, for the improvement of the methods and organization of production, for a sufficient supply of raw materials and foodstuffs, and so on through a long list of topics that include beautification of cities, fire insurance, education, sanitation, and what not. Agriculture, manufactures, commerce, money, banking—all come in for discussion from this point of view, technological and organizational aspects receiving much attention. But having thus pinned his faith to a principle of comprehensive public planning, he, like Seckendorff and most of the writers between these two, did not arrive at the practical conclusions this principle might lead us to expect. On the contrary, he was by no means blind to the inherent logic of economic phenomena, and did not wish to replace it by government fiat. Price fixing, for instance, was a measure to which the government had the right and duty to resort for particular purposes in particular circumstances, but it was to be avoided as much as possible. He took Mirabeau to task for teaching, among other 'false, nonsensical, and monstrous doctrines,' that the lowering of interest depends upon the will of government whereas actually 'nothing is so little subject to it.' Nor was he blind to the potentialities of free enterprise, on which he looked with detachment but without hostility. In fact, notwithstanding his approval of government regulation, which goes so far as to make him admit the expediency of enforcing the production of certain things by government decree, he stated as a general principle that all industry and commerce really needed was freedom and security. Though he would not advise the liquidation of artisans' guilds—because they were there and might just as well be used for filling some administrative functions he considered useful —he nevertheless looked upon them as a nuisance and advised governments not to be hard on outsiders. And, though he taught that high protective duties and even import prohibitions and compulsion to buy domestic products might 'sometimes' be in the public interest, he nevertheless declared it to be his opinion that 'in general' there should be no impediment to imports beyond an ad valorem duty of 10 per cent—a condition which none of us would be able to distinguish from unrestricted free trade.

Many other instances could be adduced for what to nineteenth-century liberals simply spelled discreditable inconsistency, which they were inclined to attribute to the fact that Justi lived in a transitional age: while still a victim of exploded error, he could not quite shut his eyes to the new light. But if we look more closely at the particular cases to which he applied his principle of planning, a very different explanation suggests itself. He saw the practical argument for laissez-faire not less clearly than did A. Smith, and his bureaucracy, while guiding and helping where necessary, was always ready to efface itself when no guidance or help seemed needed.[1] Only he saw much more clearly than did the latter all the obstacles that stood in the way of its working according to design. Also, he was much more concerned than A. Smith with the practical problems of government action in the short-run vicissitudes of his time and country, and with particular difficulties in which private initiative fails or would have failed under the conditions of the German industry of his time. His laissez-faire was a laissez-faire plus watchfulness, his private-enterprise economy a machine that was logically automatic but exposed to breakdowns and hitches which his government was to stand ready to mend. For instance, he accepted as a matter of course that the introduction of labor-saving machinery would cause unemployment: but this was no argument against the mechanization of production because, also as a matter of course, *his* government would find equally good employment for the unemployed. This, however, is not inconsistency but sense. And, to us who are apt to agree with him much more than we do with A. Smith, his vision of economic policy might look like laissez-faire with the nonsense left out.[2] But two Spanish examples show still better than does Justi's how well the best brains of that time knew their 'applied economics': I am referring to Campomanes and Jovellanos,[3] who rose

[1] This was not merely a dream. It will be pointed out below that the bureaucracy of the typical German principality actually tried to behave like this.

[2] Such views, which were extremely common at the time, naturally assumed an anti-Smithian garb that exaggerates the difference. This was the case, e.g., with Justus von Möser (*Patriotische Phantasien*, 1774-86), whose name I also mention for another reason. His interest in the description of individual historical patterns—a sort of historical miniature painting—has induced some historians of thought to assign to him the position of early romanticist or forerunner of the historical school: an example of those unrealistic attributions that, once made, keep on distorting our views of groups and developments. He was an excellent man, no doubt, but he was no economist at all.

[3] Pedro Rodriguez, Count Campomanes (1723-1802) was by training a jurist-economist of the continental type. A man of wide culture and great ability, he tried his

to prominence in the reform era of Charles III. They were practical reformers in the line of economic liberalism, and neither bothered about nor contributed to the progress of analysis. But they understood the economic process better than did many a theorist. And, in view of the date of Campomanes' *Discurso* (1774) it is not without interest to observe how little, if anything, he stood to learn from the *Wealth of Nations*.

This covers, and indeed sums up, a large part of continental seventeenth- and eighteenth-century economics. The reader should realize, however, that though in practical insight and practical usefulness, it was—at least as it came to be taught eventually—hardly inferior to the *Wealth of Nations*, it also was, with the exception to be noticed presently, completely outdistanced by the latter as regards analytic achievement. Justi's work exemplifies this weakness as clearly as it exemplifies those merits. I have said that he was not blind to the inherent logic of economic phenomena. But this was mere prescientific intuition. He did nothing to show how they hang together and how they determine each other, which is where scientific economics begins. He was not alive to the necessity of proving propositions—for instance, his proposition that mechanization creates unemployment—or of using any tools not at the layman's command. His arguments were the arguments of untutored common sense; it was only when he argued against another author that he attempted any analysis at all. And when he did so, he occasionally slipped up badly. To quote an instance, he was not above pulling the following atrocious boner: suppose that two countries, A and *B*, are exactly alike in every respect except that A holds twice as much monetary silver as *B*; while their states of welfare will be exactly equal, prices in A will be twice as high as prices in *B*; but owing to the double quantity of money, A's rate of interest will be half of *B*'s rate of interest and therefore A, producing more cheaply, will undersell *B* and keep on drawing money from it, which will increase employment in A, and so on (*Die Grundfeste*, p. 611)—and all that in spite of the facts that his reasoning on interest was otherwise quite sensible, that in general he did not at all overrate the advantages that accrue to a country from an abundance of metals, and that he emphasized the basic importance of consumption not less than did A. Smith.

---

hand, both in office and out of it, on all the great economic problems of his time and country. Of his writings, the one most relevant to our purpose is his *Discurso sobre el fomento de la industria popular* (1774), which was to move McCulloch to fervent eulogy. The *Respuesta fiscal* (1764), concerning the grain trade, should also be mentioned.

Gaspar Melchor de Jovellanos (1744-1811), a man of similar type but of a less prosperous career, among many other things wrote two reports, one on the liberty of the industrial arts (1785), and another, on behalf of the Royal Economic Society of Madrid, on agrarian legislation (1794), in both of which the principles of economic liberalism are expounded, but judiciously tempered by practical considerations. They were published (1859) in the *Biblioteca de Autores Españoles*. However, their dates reduce their importance, as compared with Campomanes' tracts, for the historian of economic thought.

[(c) *France and England.*] The French civil servant was educated as an abbé or else as a lawyer. Economics was not taught, as a distinct subject, until during and after the revolution. Could it be that this great disadvantage carried some compensation? In any case, the much less voluminous French literature of the systematic type rose in the eighteenth century to a level far and away above the German. Since we reserve such peaks as Boisguillebert, Cantillon, Turgot, and, of course, the physiocrats for discussion in the next chapter, we may content ourselves with the five following names—Forbonnais, Melon, Mirabeau, Graslin, and Condillac. Forbonnais,[4] who might be compared with Justi or Sonnenfels, is the prototype of the 'useful' or 'sound' economist of whom the public approves. No historian will ever sing his praises; for the historian who is interested only in what policy a man was for or against will not be satisfied and will put down Forbonnais as an eclectic without originality; and the historian who looks for contributions to our analytic apparatus will also be dissatisfied, for he will not find it, and he will notice clumsy and pedestrian behavior whenever Forbonnais did venture upon theoretical ice. But few economists ever said or implied so little that is definitely and provably wrong in either fact or logic. He is an outstanding example by which to illustrate the truth that to be an economist or physician is one thing and that to be a theorist or physiologist is quite another thing.

Markedly inferior to Forbonnais in these respects and but little above him in analytic proficiency, Melon [5] has fared somewhat better at the hands of later critics. But his performance, which, so far as 'principles' are concerned, partly anticipated Forbonnais', is of much the same nature. His contribution to mone-

[4] François Véron de Forbonnais (1722-1800) was a businessman and civil servant and, being a Frenchman, addressed a different public and envisaged different conditions, so that the similarity between his and Justi's performances does not stand out at first sight. Fundamentally, however, he did—very successfully—the same kind of thing. His practical grasp of the social and economic situation confronting him was his, as it was Justi's, chief merit. He is at his best in his analyses of definite sets of historic facts such as the finances of France from 1595 to 1721 (1758) or the finances of Spain (1753). For us the most interesting of his works are: *Élémens du commerce* (1754 and 1766) and *Principes et observations économiques* (1767; the latter is available in the Guillaumin collection, reading recommended: not below the average nineteenth-century textbook and superior to a good many). His recommendation of an ad valorem import duty of 15 per cent may be mentioned as one of several instances of parallelism between his views and those of Justi, whom the first volume of his *Élémens* may have influenced. That he influenced Sonnenfels as much as did Justi is obvious from acknowledgments.

[5] Jean François Melon (1675-1738) was a public servant who worked with John Law during the short career of the latter's 'system' and thus had first-hand knowledge of it. His *Essai politique sur le commerce* (1734, English trans. 1738) was a great success in France and abroad and exerted considerable influence. The misleading term Neo-Mercantilism is sometimes used to designate the views on foreign trade and finance that he and other eighteenth-century writers espoused (see below, ch. 7). See G. Dionnet's *Le Néomercantilisme au XVIIIe siècle et au début du XIXe siècle* (1901) and also L. de Lavergne's *Les Économistes français du dix-huitième siècle* (1870).

tary theory will be noticed in a subsequent chapter. The elder Mirabeau [6] is primarily known as the head, in succession to Quesnay, of the physiocrat group, but he had independently established himself before that by a work that may be called a systematic treatise on all the problems of applied economics written from a very personal standpoint—systematic unity being achieved by making those problems pivot on Population and Agriculture. Its analytic merit is negligible, but all the greater was its success. Graslin's [7] reputation never was what it should have been because he put so much emphasis upon criticism of the physiocrats—which is in fact the best ever proffered—that his readers were apt to overlook his positive contribution. Actually, his *Essai analytique* presents the outlines of a comprehensive theory of wealth as a theory of total income rather than of income net of all producers' expenses including wages—a not inconsiderable improvement considering the role the latter was to play later on. Also he was above his contemporaries in insight into the problem of incidence of taxation. Finally, Condillac's work [8] does not indeed quite merit the eulogies of W. S. Jevons, who called it 'original and profound' and of H. D. Macleod, who called it 'infinitely superior to A. Smith's.' The eulogies are amply accounted for by the enthusiasm of those two authors for what they

[6] Victor Riquetti, Marquis de Mirabeau (1715-89), called the elder to distinguish him from his son, the Mirabeau of the Revolution, was an eccentric aristocrat of exuberant vitality and irrepressible impulses. It is difficult to understand—except on the hypothesis that force of temperament and glowing phrases will always carry everything before them—how it was that this man, whose unquestioned ability was completely spoiled by lack of judgment, could have enjoyed, though only for a few years, an international and national fame much greater than that of any other economist before or after, not excluding A. Smith or K. Marx. This happened in the first part of his career, that is, before he had joined the physiocrats, and on the strength of a performance that cannot be called impressive in anything except passionate phraseology. This performance, anonymously published in three parts under the title *L'Ami des hommes, ou traité de la population* (1756), will have to be mentioned again in our chapter on population. Of all the other works of Mirabeau—he left dozens of volumes besides a quantity of unpublished material—only the subsequent parts (4-6) of *L'Ami* (1758 and 1760), the *Philosophie rurale* (1763), and the *Théorie de l'impôt* (1760) call for notice in this book. The last two are, however, physiocratic, at least in principle, and therefore need not detain us here. See L. and C. de Loménie, *Les Mirabeau* (1879-91) and L. Brocard, *Les Doctrines économiques et sociales du Marquis de Mirabeau dans L'Ami des hommes* (1902).

[7] Jean J. L. Graslin (1727-90), *Essai analytique sur la richesse et sur l'impôt* (1767; new ed. by A. Dubois, 1911). See J. Desmars, *Un précurseur d'A. Smith en France, J. J. L. Graslin* (1900). His correspondence with Baudeau is of considerable interest (2 vols., 1777-9).

[8] *Le Commerce et le gouvernment* . . . (1776) by the sensationalist philosopher and psychologist we have already met above. The relation between his psychology and his utility theory of value should not be overstressed. As we know already and as we shall see more fully later on, the latter has a quite independent history of its own that harks back to the scholastics rather than to Hartley. Condillac's relation to the physiocrats should not be overstressed either. Rather he had learned from Turgot. See, however, A. Lebeau, *Condillac économiste* (1903).

believed to be an early formulation of their own theory of value. But there was nothing original about it and, considering all the predecessors on that path, we should wonder at Condillac's inefficient handling of it rather than at his sponsorship of it. Still, the book is a good if somewhat sketchy treatise on Economic Theory and Policy and much above the common run of its contemporaries.

England was still more immune to 'systemitis' than was France. Excepting the *Wealth* itself, there is but one book of the strictly systematic type to mention, but this one is of first-rate importance, Steuart's *Principles*.[9] It was intentionally and laboriously systematic: what he wanted was to consolidate the factual and analytic knowledge of his time into a 'regular science,' that is to say, he clearly aimed at the same goal as A. Smith. Comparison with the *Wealth of Nations* is rendered difficult by two facts. In the first place, Steuart's work did not ride, like Smith's, on the wave of a single and simple policy that was rapidly conquering public opinion. On the contrary, he grouped all that really interests the public around the old-fashioned figure of an imaginary patriot statesman who in infinite wisdom watches the economic process, ready to interfere in the national interest—a conception that recalls Justi's and was quite out of contact with England's humor. But this should not weigh with us. In the second place, when one surveys (as the reader should) the five books into which the work is divided—Population, Trade and Industry, Money and Coins, Credit and Debts, and Taxes—one cannot fail to be struck by the number of points that indicate more originality and deeper thought than does the *Wealth of Nations*; but also by the number of definite mistakes and infelicitous formulations. In the theories of population, prices, money, and taxation Steuart went much below the smooth surface on which A. Smith happily sailed his course. But only in the first of these did he make a significant contribution, which will be discussed below in Chapter 5; in the others it is a hard job to get the wheat out of unpromising chaff or even, in some instances, to be quite sure that there is any wheat at all.

[(d) *High Level of the Italian Contribution.*] But the honors of the field of pre-Smithian system production should go to the eighteenth-century Italians. In intent, scope, and plan their works were in the tradition that has been

[9] Sir James Steuart (1712-80), the scion of a family that held a prominent position in the Scottish magistracy, was educated as a lawyer, and, being an adherent of the Stuarts, lived in exile from 1745 to 1763—three facts that go some way toward explaining both the nature and the reception of his performance; on the one hand, there is something un-English (which is not merely Scottish) about his views and his mode of presentation, the latter being stiff and embarrassed in the bargain; on the other hand, he was, and even after he had regained the rights of citizenship remained, distinctly under a cloud. Such things count. In particular, they make it easy for competitors to pass a man by in silence, which is precisely what A. Smith did. *An Inquiry into the Principles of Political Economy* . . . 1767, accordingly was never much of a success in England even before it was completely overshadowed by the *Wealth of Nations*. But it received rather more than its due from some of the Germans. Other writings by Steuart will be mentioned later. His collected *Works* were edited by his son (1805).

illustrated by the examples of Carafa and Justi; they were systems of Political Economy in the sense of welfare economics—the old scholastic Public Good and the specifically utilitarian Happiness meeting in their concept of welfare (*felicità pubblica*). But whereas in zeal for fact-finding and in grasp of practical problems they were not inferior to the Germans, they were superior to most of their Spanish, English, and French contemporaries in analytic power and achievement. Most of them were professors and civil servants and wrote from the standpoint of professors and civil servants. The regionalism of Italian life [10] divides them into groups. But I can discern only two 'schools' in the strict sense of the term which implies both personal contact and similarity of doctrine due to mutual influence: the Neapolitan and the Milanese. Genovesi and Palmieri represent the former; [11] other members, particularly its brightest star, Galiani, will be introduced later.

The representative figures of the Milanese school are Verri and Beccaria. We take, however, this opportunity to introduce a man who stands quite by himself, Ortes the Venetian.

10 This regionalism accounts for the existence of Italian histories of 'provincial' economics, a phenomenon for which there is no analogy in any other country except Spain. Two examples may be mentioned: Augusto Graziani's *Le idee economiche degli scrittori Emiliani e Romagnoli sino al* 1848 (1893), and T. Fornari's *Delle teorie economiche nelle provincie Napoletane dal secolo XIII al MDCCXXXIV* (1882), the complement of which will be cited in the next footnote.

11 Antonio Genovesi (1712-69), professor, first of ethics and moral philosophy, then of economics and commerce, in the University of Naples, was first and last a great teacher whose prodigious success in this capacity even his detractors have been unable to deny. It was I think F. Ferrara who set the example of speaking of Genovesi in derogatory terms, possibly because he never could see any merit in anyone who was not a thoroughgoing free-trader. For a list of prominent economists who were his pupils see G. Tagliacozzo, *Economisti Napoletani* (p. xxvi n.). The same author, moreover, draws a picture of Genovesi's scientific personality and background (on these also see A. Cutolo, *Antonio Genovesi,* 1926) and gives a judicious appraisal of his performance. Genovesi was a prolific writer. We are concerned, however, only with his *Lezioni di economia civile* (1765; republ. in P. Custodi's *Scrittori classici Italiani di economia politica,* 50 vols., 1803-16), which may be described as an unsystematic system of the whole range of his economic thought. These lectures do indeed display the influence of contemporaneous and earlier writers and, what is worse, the argument frequently lacks rigor. But nobody had, when they appeared, published as comprehensive a presentation of the utilitarian welfare economics that the epoch was evolving. The 'mercantilist' elements in Genovesi's teaching only prove the realism of his vision.

Giuseppe Palmieri, Marchese di Martignano (1721-94?), was one of that brilliant band of Neapolitans in which Filangieri (see P. Gentile, *L'Opera di Gaetano Filangieri,* 1914) was perhaps the most widely known figure. Palmieri (there is a life by B. De Rinaldis, 1850; also see T. Fornari, *Delle teorie economiche nelle provincie Napoletane,* 1735-1830, 1888) was primarily a practical administrator. But the welfare economics of the eighteenth-century Consultant Administrators can perhaps be best appreciated by reading his *Riflessioni sulla pubblica felicità relativamente al regno di Napoli* (1787) or his *Pensieri economici . . .* (1789) or his *Della ricchezza nazionale* (1792).

Count Pietro Verri (1728-97), an officer in the Austrian administration of Milan—but not a teacher—would have to be included in any list of the greatest economists. But though it would be easy to survey his various recommendations as to policy—which for him were the important things; in the preface to his main work, he exclaimed: *potessi io dire qualche cosa di utile, potessi io farla* (how I wish to say something useful, nay, to do it!)—it is less easy to convey an idea of his purely scientific achievement; some aspects of it will be mentioned later. Here we need to mention only two of his many publications, the *Elementi del commercio* (1760), which established him, and the *Meditazioni sull' economia politica* (1771; republ. in the Custodi collection; there are French and German translations) into which the former was expanded. Besides presenting a powerful synthesis, these works contain a number of original contributions (among them his constant-outlay demand curve). Among other things, he had a clear if undeveloped conception of economic equilibrium based, in the last instance, upon the 'calculus of pleasure and pain' (he anticipated Jevons' phrase) and was, as far as this goes, rather above than below A. Smith. It is important to emphasize his fact-mindedness. Not only did he do historical research of importance (*Memorie storiche,* posthumously published) but he was a true econometrician—for example, he was one of the first economists to figure out a balance of payments—that is to say, he knew how to weave fact-finding and theory into a coherent tissue: the methodological problem that agitated later generations of economists he had successfully solved for himself. On the man and his career, see E. Bouvy, *Le Comte Pietro Verri* (1889), and M. R. Manfra, *Pietro Verri* . . . (1932). The best exposition and appraisal of Verri's work is, however, to be found in Professor Einaudi's masterly introduction to his new edition of Verri's *Bilanci del commercio dello stato di Milano* (1932).

Giammaria Ortes' (1713-90) main title to fame is in his contribution to the 'Malthusian' theory of population (see below, ch. 5). His systematic venture (*Economia nazionale,* 1774; republ. in the Custodi collection) will always stand out in the history of the theories that look upon consumption as the limiting factor of *total* output and derive from this set-up their economic diagnosis—this is another link between him and Malthus. In this as in some other respects his performance is certainly original in the sense that it does not lie on the main road of advance. But little else can be said for it. Critics and historians have been, on the one hand, puzzled by it and, on the other hand, reconciled by his attack on the 'mercantilist confusion' (see below, ch. 6) of money and wealth and his free-trade views. Thus, a tradition has developed of dealing with him in an attitude of diffident admiration. It is worth while adding that he seems to have learned much from Sir James Steuart. From the Ortes literature it will suffice to mention A. Faure, *Giammaria Ortes* . . . (1916), the old book by F. Lampertico, G. *Ortes* . . . (1865), and C. de Franchis, G. *Ortes, un sistema d'economia matematica* . . . (1930), though I cannot myself find much mathematics in Ortes.

Cesare Bonesana, Marchese di Beccaria (1738-94), was a Milanese and the product of Jesuit education. His international fame as a penologist, won at the age of about thirty (the year of his birth is not quite certain), and the place he incidentally acquired in the history of utilitarianism have been mentioned already. Mainly on the strength of this success—he had as yet done little as an economist—the Austrian Government (Prince Kaunitz) appointed him to a chair of economics in Milan founded for the purpose (1768). After only two years of tenure, he exchanged this chair for employment in the Milanese administration, in which he continued to serve until his early death, rising by degrees to the highest rank open to a man not qualifying for governor, taking part in, and in some instances initiating, the reforms of the period, busily writing a great many reports and memoranda—on grain storage, monetary policy, the metric system, population, and what not—and roaming over a wide realm of intellectual interests at the same time. Among other things, he was cofounder of, and a contributor to, *Il caffè*, a periodical modeled on the example of the English *Spectator*. In 1770 he published the first and only volume of his aesthetics (on *Style*). Moreover, he seems to have been a fair mathematician.

The bulk of his economic writings consisted of those government reports. The only piece of economic reasoning that he published himself (in *Il caffè*, 1764) was an essay on smuggling, which presents two features of interest, first, the algebraic treatment of the problem and, second, the analytic device embodied in the question he made basic to his pure theory of smuggling: given the proportion of the goods smuggled that will on the average be seized by the authorities, what is the total quantity that smugglers must move in order to be left without either gain or loss? This spells the discovery of the idea that underlies modern indifference-variety analysis. Beccaria's argument was developed by G. Silio, 1792 (see Augusto Montanari's *La matematica applicata all 'economia politica*, 1892). Here, we are concerned with Beccaria's lectures (written 1769-70). These he did not publish himself: he left them in his files for nearly a quarter of a century. They were first published in Custodi's collection, under the title: *Elementi di economia pubblica* (1804).

The sweeping success of his *Dei delitti e delle pene*, *An Essay on Crimes and Punishments* (1st ed. 1764; English trans. 1767) has in a way obliterated the greatness of the man: ever since he has been considered primarily as a penologist. The Beccaria literature deals with little else and is therefore only peripherically interesting for us. Reference should be made, however, to P. Custodi's life (*Cesare Beccaria*, 1811) and to P. Villari's edition of his works (*Opere*, 1854).

For the moment, we concentrate upon Beccaria, the Italian A. Smith. The similarity between the two men and their performances is indeed striking. There is even some similarity in their social backgrounds and locations. There is similarity in their lives—and in those attitudes that are conditioned by one's pursuits—though Beccaria was much more of a public servant than A. Smith, who only held a subordinate position without creative possibilities, and A. Smith was much more of a professor than Beccaria, who taught for only two years. Both were sovereign lords of a vast intellectual realm that extended far beyond what, even then, was possible for ordinary mortals to embrace. Beccaria presumably knew more mathematics than A. Smith, but A. Smith seems to have known more astronomy and physics than Beccaria. Neither was merely an economist: A. Smith's life work contains no match for *Dei delitti e delle pene*, but his *Moral Sentiments* are more than a match for Beccaria's aesthetics. Both swam joyfully in the river of their time, but with a difference: whereas Beccaria not only accepted all utilitarianism stands for but also was a leading force in shaping it, A. Smith quite clearly showed some critical coolness toward it; and whereas A. Smith not only accepted (almost) all that free trade and laissez-faire stand for but also was a leading force in their victory (so far as economic literature is concerned), Beccaria clearly showed some critical coolness toward them. Splendid figures both of them. But, at least after 1770, Beccaria, almost certainly more richly endowed by nature, gave to the public service of the Milanese 'state' what A. Smith reserved for mankind.

Beccaria's *Elementi*, after defining the subject of economics in the same normative way as did A. Smith in the introduction to the Fourth Book of the *Wealth of Nations*, starts with considerations about the evolution of technology, division of labor, and population (the increase of which he made a function of the increase in the means of subsistence). As the principle of economic action, we know already, he embraced without qualification the utilitarian doctrine of hedonist egotism, which he himself had done much to develop, and which later on proved so embarrassing an ally to economics. The second and third parts of the lectures deal with agriculture and manufactures, and the fourth, on commerce, is made the repository of the theory of value and price: barter, money, competition, interest, foreign exchanges, banks, credit, and public credit follow each other in a sequence that is as suggestive of nineteenth-century textbook practice as is the framework as a whole. In detail, Beccaria's argument—particularly as to the theories of cost and of capital—is not always faultless or logically rigorous. But all the essential problems are seen, and seen in co-ordination. Some points will be mentioned in subsequent chapters. There are several contributions, however—such as the indeterminateness of isolated barter, the transition from this case to that of a determinate competitive market and thence to the case of indirect exchange—which we are in the habit of associating with much later, especially with post-Smithian, times. Physiocrat influence is in evidence but does not go very deep. Was the Scottish Beccaria the greater economist of the two? If we judge by their works as they lie before us, he certainly was. But to do so would not be fair to the men. It is not only that we must take into account priority and also that the years between 1770 and 1776 were very significant ones in the march of economic ideas; much more important is it that the *Wealth of Nations* was the mature result of a life's work whereas the *Elementi* are lecture notes and, moreover, lecture notes *which the author refused to publish*.

So far as subjective performance is concerned, they should not be matched with the *Wealth of Nations* but rather with the economic part of A. Smith's Glasgow lectures—where Beccaria would win hands down—or else the *Wealth of Nations* should be compared with what we might conceive Beccaria would have done with his lectures if he had emigrated to Kirkcaldy and spent another six years on them instead of immersing himself in the problems of the Milanese state. That the *main* cause of the difference we perceive consists in the amounts of labor invested is, in any case, an important clue to the secret of A. Smith's success.

[(e) *Adam Smith and the* Wealth of Nations.] [12] So often have we mentioned Adam Smith, so often shall we have to mention him again, that the reader might well wonder whether there is need for a comprehensive survey of his performance in any one place. For our purpose, the references to it that are scattered all over this history are in fact more important than what will be said in this section. Nevertheless, it seems proper to stay for a moment in order to look at the figure of the most famous of all economists—to form an idea of what stuff he was made—and at the most successful not only of all books on economics but, with the possible exception of Darwin's *Origin of Species*, of all scientific books that have appeared to this day. Moreover, it will again be useful to present a brief Reader's Guide.

Few facts and no details are needed about the man and his sheltered and uneventful life (1723-90).[13] It will suffice to note: first, that he was a Scotsman to the core, pure and unadulterated; second, that his immediate family background was the Scottish civil service—in order to understand his outlook on social life and economic activity (very different from what has been often imputed to him), it is important never to forget the gentility, the intellectuality, the critical attitude to business activity, the modest yet adequate means that characterized the environment which produced him; third, that he was a professor born and bred, not only while he lectured at Edinburgh (1748-51) and

[12] [There is no indication as to where this sketch of Adam Smith followed by a Reader's Guide to the *Wealth of Nations* belongs, but it seems appropriate to place it here at the end of the discussion of 'The Systems, 1600-1776.' This section was originally written for the *History* but was withdrawn by J. A. S., possibly at a time when he was attempting to reduce the length of the book or possibly because he felt that there was too much duplication in view of 'the references . . . that are scattered all over this *History*.' It is a first draft that was not even typed. Since, however, similar biographical sketches of other famous economists are presented throughout the book, it seemed appropriate to restore this account of Adam Smith and the *Wealth*. A reference to the Reader's Guide will be found below in ch. 6, sec. 3d (Codification of Value and Price Theory in the *Wealth of Nations*).]

[13] Of the many lives of Adam Smith the interested reader is referred to the one by John Rae (1895). Of all the books containing supplementary material on and interpretations of Smith the man, by far the most important is Professor W. R. Scott's *Adam Smith as Student and Professor* (1937), which will be referred to in the text and from which the reader will derive much instruction and, perhaps, some amusement. The minimum of references concerning the *Wealth* will be given later.

Glasgow (1751-63) but always and by virtue of *character indelebilis;* fourth—a fact which I cannot help considering relevant, not for his pure economics of course, but all the more for his understanding of human nature—that no woman, excepting his mother, ever played a role in his existence: in this as in other respects the glamours and passions of life were just literature to him. In 1764-6 he traveled in France, acting as 'tutor' to the young Duke of Buccleuch, to whom economics owes the subsequent leisure and independence that produced the *Wealth of Nations*. His appointment to a quasi-sinecure (1778) added ample comfort for the rest of his life. He was conscientious, painstaking to a degree, methodical, well-poised, honorable. He acknowledged obligation where honor required it, but not generously. He never uncovered the footprints of predecessors with Darwinian frankness. In criticism he was narrow and ungenerous. He had the courage and energy that exactly fit the scholar's task and go well with a good deal of circumspection.

The day of polyhistoric knowledge was not yet over: a man could then roam over the whole of science and art and even do work in widely distant fields without meeting disaster. Not less than Beccaria or Turgot, A. Smith held sway over a wide domain of which economics was only a part. We have already had the opportunity to notice his *Theory of Moral Sentiments* (1759), to which was appended (3rd ed. 1767) A *Dissertation on the Origin of Languages*—his first great success, which matured, from beginnings in the material of the Edinburgh lectures, during the first half of his tenure of the Glasgow chair, and should be recalled to make the reader immune to the silly criticism that A. Smith gave inadequate attention to the importance of ethical forces. Moreover, Smith's *philosophy* of riches and of economic activity is there and not in the *Wealth of Nations*. To this and to his work in natural law, 'natural theology,' and belles lettres must, however, be added six essays,[14] some of which are the crystallized fragments of the grandiose plan of a 'history of the liberal sciences and elegant arts' which he abandoned 'as far too extensive.' The pearl of the collection is the first essay on the 'Principles which lead and direct Philosophical Enquiries; illustrated by the History of Astronomy.' Nobody, I venture to say, can have an adequate idea of Smith's intellectual stature who does not know these essays. I also venture to say that, were it not for the undeniable fact, nobody would credit the author of the *Wealth of Nations* with the power to write them.

We know already that the skeleton of Smith's analysis hails from the scholastics and the natural-law philosophers: besides lying ready at hand in the works of Grotius and Pufendorf, it was taught to him by his teacher Hutche-

[14] *Essays on Philosophical Subjects by the late Adam Smith* . . . ed. by his executors, Black and Hutton, to which was prefixed an *Account of the Life and Writings of the Author by Dugald Stewart* . . . (1st ed. 1795). Stewart, by the way, who held the Edinburgh chair of moral philosophy, 1785-1810, though he can hardly be said to have made any mark by his published writings, was so strong a personality and so effective a teacher that a more complete history of our subject could not pass him by as we must.

son.[15] It is true that neither the scholastics nor the natural-law philosophers ever evolved a completely articulate scheme of distribution, still less the misleading idea, which was to play so great a role in the theory of the nineteenth century, of a social product or National Dividend distributed among the agents that take part in its production. But they had worked out all the elements of such a scheme, and Smith was no doubt equal to the task of co-ordinating them without further help from anyone. According to Cannan, the Glasgow Lectures—which show no great advance beyond Hutcheson in any direction—contain 'no trace whatever . . . of the scheme of distribution which the

[15] On Francis Hutcheson, see above, ch. 2, sec. 7b. Also see W. R. Scott, *Francis Hutcheson* (1900). The lineage of Smith's economics has been, as we might expect, the subject of much research. A great event was the discovery and subsequent publication by E. Cannan of the *Lectures on Justice, Police, Revenue and Arms, delivered in the University of Glasgow by Adam Smith, reported by a student in* 1763 (1896), to which I shall refer as Glasgow Lectures; another was the discovery, and publication in Scott's book mentioned above, of what may be called an early draft of the *Wealth of Nations,* which, according to Professor Scott, antedates by but little Smith's departure for France and thus presumably reflects the general state of Smith's work before he came into personal contact with the French economists. It will be referred to as Draft. To Professor Cannan we owe by far the best of the many editions of the *Wealth of Nations* (1904; republished many times, 6th ed. 1950) which contains a most valuable introduction, which sheds much light on some questions of lineage. Publication of *A Catalogue of the Library of Adam Smith* (1st ed. 1894; 2nd ed. 1932) with introduction was one of the many services rendered to 'Smithology' by James Bonar.

Space forbids our dealing with matters of editions, translations, summaries, paraphrases of, and excerpts from the *Wealth of Nations,* a fact that I regret the more because the Vanderblue Memorial Collection of Smithiana in the Kress Library (see pamphlet published by the Kress Library, containing a special catalogue of this collection by Homer B. Vanderblue, prefaced with an essay by Charles J. Bullock, 1939) gave me an excellent opportunity for investigating them. Nor is it possible to do justice to the extensive literature that deals with the *Wealth of Nations.* The most valuable comments, expository and critical, are scattered all over the economic treatises and papers of the nineteenth century: it is they that make up the true monument to Smith, the scientific economist. Those economists and non-economists who wrote on Smith and 'Smithianism' per se, particularly the Germans, were usually not, or not primarily, interested in his analytic performance, but rather in his views on practical issues, his philosophical backgrounds, his social sympathies. Neglecting the comments that are, of course, to be found in all general histories of economic thought, we must however notice the analyses of Smith's work by Marx, in the *Theorien über den Mehrwert,* and by Cannan, in the *History of the Theories of Production and Distribution.* In addition we may mention: J. F. Baert, *Adam Smith, en zijn Onderzoek naar den Rijkdom der Volken* (1858); A. Delatour, *Adam Smith* (1886); W. Hasbach, *Untersuchungen über Adam Smith* (1891); S. Feilbogen, *Smith und Turgot* (1892); G. R. Morrow, *The Ethical and Economic Theories of Adam Smith* (1923); W. Bagehot, *Adam Smith and Our Modern Economy* (*Works,* ed. by Mrs. Russell Barrington, vol. 7); Edwin Cannan, 'Adam Smith as an Economist,' *Economica,* June 1926; and the sesquicentennial Chicago *Lectures* (1928).

Wealth of Nations sets forth.' It is not necessary to infer from this, however, that Smith was under heavy (and largely unacknowledged) obligation to the physiocrats, whom he met (1764-6) and presumably read before he settled down to work at Kirkcaldy. The Draft discovered by Professor Scott proves that this may go too far: the Draft clearly foreshadows the scheme of the *Wealth*. On the other hand, however, it must not be forgotten that the heritage of the natural-law philosophers and the achievements of A. Smith's French contemporaries were not all he had to work with. There was the other of the two streams that meet in the *Wealth of Nations,* represented by the Consultant Administrators and the Pamphleteers. Smith knew Petty and Locke; he presumably made acquaintance with Cantillon, at least through Postlethwayt's *Dictionary,* at an early stage of his work; he laid Harris and Decker under contribution; his friend Hume's writings and Massie's must have been familiar to him; and in the long list of writers whom he affected to despise because of their 'mercantilist errors,' there are some who might have taught him a lot, for example, Child, Davenant, Pollexfen, not to insist on such 'anti-mercantilists' as Barbon and North.[16] But no matter what he actually learned or failed to learn from predecessors, the fact is that the *Wealth of Nations* does not contain a single *analytic* idea, principle, or method that was entirely new in 1776.

Those who extolled A. Smith's work as an epoch-making, original achievement were, of course, thinking primarily of the *policies* he advocated—free

[16] Two authors should be mentioned, if only because they are mentioned so frequently. Adam Ferguson (1723-1816), professor first of 'natural' then of 'moral' philosophy in Edinburgh, was primarily a historical sociologist. His *Essay on the History of Civil Society* (1st ed. 1767), the only one of his works that need be noticed, hails from Montesquieu (to whom also Smith was indebted) and met, on a reduced scale, with the same kind of success as did the *Esprit des lois*. In Germany, partly under the influence of Marx, it enjoyed considerable—and, as it seems to me, unmerited—reputation in the nineteenth century. There is hardly any reason to believe, as did Marx, that Smith owed any considerable debt to it or, as others have held, that Ferguson owed much to Smith's lectures or conversation: the parallelisms that are adduced in support of either view concern ideas—on division of labor and taxation—which were common currency at that time and could have been drawn from a number of older authors.

Bernard de Mandeville published a didactic poem entitled *The Grumbling Hive* (1705; better known under the later title, *The Fable of the Bees: or, Private Vices, Publick Benefits,* 1714), in which he endeavored to show that the individual motives that produce socially desirable actions are not unlikely to be morally objectionable. Adam Smith, like other virtuous people, was hard on this piece of work. It contained indeed a eulogy on spending and an indictment of saving, as well as certain 'mercantilist errors' that must have displeased him. But there was more than that to his hostility. Smith cannot have failed to perceive that Mandeville's argument was an argument for Smith's own pure Natural Liberty couched in a particular form. The reader will have no difficulty in realizing how this fact must have shocked the respectable professor—particularly if it should be the case that he learned something from the offending pamphlet.

trade, laissez-faire, colonial policy, and so on. But, as should be clear by now and as will become still clearer as we go along, this aspect would not lead to a different conclusion even if it were relevant to our subject. Smith himself, according to Dugald Stewart, indeed laid claim (in a paper drawn up in 1755) to priority concerning the principle of Natural Liberty on the ground that he had taught it as early as 1749. By this principle he meant both a canon of policy—the removal of all restraints except those imposed by 'justice'—and the analytic proposition that free interaction of individuals produces not chaos but an orderly pattern that is logically determined: he never distinguished the two quite clearly. Taken in either sense, however, the principle had been quite clearly enunciated before, for example, by Grotius and Pufendorf. It is precisely for this reason that no charge of plagiarism can be made either against Smith or on his behalf against others. This does not exclude the possibility of course that, in stating it with greater force and fullness than anyone before him, Smith experienced subjectively all the thrill of discovery or even that, some time before 1749, he actually made the 'discovery' himself.

But though the *Wealth of Nations* contained no really novel ideas and though it cannot rank with Newton's *Principia* or Darwin's *Origin* as an intellectual achievement, it is a great performance all the same and fully deserved its success. The nature of the one and the causes of the other are not hard to see. The time had come for precisely that kind of co-ordination. And this task A. Smith performed extremely well. He was fitted for it by nature: no one but a methodical professor could have accomplished it. He gave his best: the *Wealth* is the product of labor ungrudgingly bestowed during more than twenty-five years, exclusively concentrated upon it during about ten. His mental stature was up to mastering the unwieldy material that flowed from many sources and to subjecting it, with a strong hand, to the rule of a small number of coherent principles: the builder who built solidly, regardless of cost, was also a great architect. His very limitations made for success. Had he been more brilliant, he would not have been taken so seriously. Had he dug more deeply, had he unearthed more recondite truth, had he used difficult and ingenious methods, he would not have been understood. But he had no such ambitions; in fact he disliked whatever went beyond plain common sense. He never moved above the heads of even the dullest readers. He led them on gently, encouraging them by trivialities and homely observations, making them feel comfortable all along. While the professional of his time found enough to command his intellectual respect, the 'educated reader' was able to assure himself that, yes, this was so, he too had always thought so; while Smith taxed the reader's patience with his masses of historical and statistical material, he did not tax his reasoning power. He was effective not only by virtue of what he gave but also by virtue of what he failed to give. Last but not least, argument and material were enlivened by advocacy which is after all what attracts a wider public: everywhere, the professor turned his chair into a seat of judgment and bestowed praise and blame. And it was Adam Smith's good fortune that he was thoroughly in sympathy with the humors of his time. He advocated the things that were in the offing, and he made his analysis serve them. Needless to insist on what this meant both for performance and success: where would the *Wealth of Nations* be without free trade and laissez-faire? Also, the 'unfeeling' or 'slothful' landlords who reap where they have not sown, the employers whose every meeting issues in conspiracy, the merchants who enjoy themselves and let their clerks and accountants do the work, and the poor laborers who support the rest of society in luxury—these are all important parts of the show. It has been held that A. Smith, far ahead of his time, braved unpopularity by giving expression to his social sympathies. This is not so. His sincerity I do not for a moment call into question. But those views were not unpopular. They were in fashion. A judiciously diluted Rousseauism is also evident in the equalitarian tendency of his economic sociology. Human beings seemed to him to be much alike by nature, all reacting in the same simple ways to very simple stimuli, differences being due mainly to different training and different environments. This is very important considering A. Smith's influence upon nineteenth-century economics. His work was the channel through which eighteenth-century ideas about human nature reached economists.

Now for the Reader's Guide: *An Inquiry into the Nature and Causes of the Wealth of Nations* by Adam Smith, LL.D. and F.R.S., formerly Professor of Moral Philosophy in the University of Glasgow, in two volumes, London 1776, defines scientific economics quite well by its title and hardly less felicitously, though less concisely, in the last paragraph of the Introduction. But in the introduction to Book IV we read that Political Economy 'proposes to enrich both the people and the sovereign,' and it is this definition which expresses both what Smith wanted above everything and what interested his readers more than anything else. It makes economics a collection of recipes for the 'statesman.' All the more important is it to remember that the viewpoint of analysis is not absent and that *we*, whatever A. Smith himself may have thought, can separate the analysis from the recipes without doing any violence to his text.

There are five Books. The fifth and longest—taking 28.6 per cent of total space—is a nearly self-contained treatise on Public Finance and was to become and to remain the basis of all the nineteenth-century treatises on the subject until, mainly in Germany, the 'social' viewpoint—taxation as an instrument of reform—asserted itself. The length of the book is due to the masses of material it contains: its treatment of public expenditure, revenue, and debts is *primarily* historical. The theory is inadequate, and does not reach much below the surface. But what there is of it is admirably worked in with the reports on general developments as well as on individual facts. Further facts have been amassed and theoretical technique has been improved but nobody has to this day succeeded in welding the two—plus a little political sociology—together as did A. Smith. The fourth Book, nearly as long,[17] contains the famous indictment of the 'commercial or mercantile system'—the patronizingly benevolent criticism of physiocrat doctrine in the ninth and

[17] The fourth and fifth Books account for nearly 57 per cent of the total space.

last chapter does not call for comment—from the ashes of which rises, phoenix-like, Smith's own political system. Again: the reader beholds masses of facts painstakingly marshalled, very little of very simple theory (no advance whatever in this over even distant 'predecessors'), which is, however, most successfully used in lightening up the mosaic of details, in heating the facts till they glow. The facts overflow and stumble over one another: two monographs are inserted by way of digressions (on Banks of Deposit and on the Corn Trade) where they do not belong. The great and justly famous chapter 'Of Colonies' (which should be compared with the last pages of the work) falls out of line, but nothing matters: we have a masterpiece before us, a masterpiece not only of pleading but also of analysis. Book III, which occupies less than 4.5 per cent of total space, may be described as a prelude to Book IV, filling in general considerations of a primarily historical nature on the 'natural progress of opulence,' the rise and the commerce of towns as distorted—hampered or propelled—by the policies sponsored by various interests. This third Book did not attract the attention it seems to merit. In its somewhat dry and uninspired wisdom, it might have made an excellent starting point of a historical sociology of economic life that was never written. Books I and II—respectively about 25 and 14 per cent of the whole—also overflowing with illustrative fact, present the essentials of A. Smith's analytic schema. They can indeed be perused by themselves. But the reader who, more interested in theory than in 'application,' refuses to go beyond them will miss much that is indispensable for a full understanding of the theory itself.

The first three chapters of Book I deal with Division of Labour.[18] We are in the oldest part of the building, the part already completed in the Draft. Also, presumably because in his teaching Smith had so often gone over this subject, it is by far the most polished part of the whole. Though, as we know, there is nothing original about it, one feature must be mentioned that has not received the attention it deserves: nobody, either before or after A. Smith, ever thought of putting such a burden upon division of labor. With A. Smith it is practically the only factor in economic progress. *Alone* it accounts 'for the superior affluence and abundance commonly possessed even by [the] lowest and most despised member of Civilized society, compared with what the most respected and active savage can attain to' in spite of so much 'oppressive inequality' (Draft, see Scott, op. cit. p. 328). Technological progress, 'invention of all those machines'—and even investments—is induced by it and is, in fact, just an incident of it. We shall consider this feature of A. Smith's analytic schema at the end of this Reader's Guide.

Division of labor itself is attributed to an inborn propensity to truck and its development to the gradual expansion of markets—the extent of the market at any point of time determining how far it can go (ch. 3). It thus ap-

[18] The reader will please bear in mind that all the more important points of A. Smith's analysis that can be touched upon at all in this history will be dealt with in their proper places, excepting a few which there is no opportunity to mention elsewhere. This is nothing but a jejune and desperately brief Reader's Guide.

pears and grows as an entirely impersonal force, and since it is the great motor of progress, this progress too is depersonalized.

In Chapter 4, A. Smith completes the time-honored sequence: division of labor-barter-money and, falling far below the level reached by many older authors and particularly by Galiani, severs 'value in exchange' completely from 'value in use.' In Chapter 5 (which starts with Cantillon's definition of *richesse*) he undertakes to find a measure of the former that is more reliable than is price expressed in terms of money. Equating value in exchange to price and observing that 'price in money' fluctuates in response to purely monetary changes, Smith replaces for purposes of interlocal and intertemporal comparisons this monetary or 'nominal price' of each commodity by a real price in the same sense in which we speak, for example, of real wages as distinguished from money wages,[19] that is, by price in terms of all other commodities. And these real prices he in turn replaces, in ignorance of the index-number method already invented in his time, by prices expressed in terms of labor (after having considered corn for the role): in other words, he chooses the commodity labor instead of the commodity silver or the commodity gold as *numéraire*—to use the phrase brought into general use by L. Walras. This may or may not be helpful, but there is no logical objection to it. But Smith flounders so badly in conveying the idea and, moreover, confuses it with philosophies concerning the nature of value and real price in a different sense—see the famous doctrines about 'toil and trouble' as the real price of everything (paragraph 2 of ch. 5) and about labor alone 'never varying in its own value' (paragraph 7)—that his fundamentally simple idea was misunderstood even by Ricardo. Accordingly, he was credited with a labor theory of value—or rather with three incompatible labor theories [20]—whereas it is quite clear from Chapter 6 that he meant to *explain* commodity prices by cost of pro-

[19] See, e.g., the 9th paragraph of ch. 5.

[20] Though it will be necessary to return to A. Smith's view on value both in ch. 6 of this Part and in the third Part, a brief clarification of the matter in this place may prove helpful. In itself, the choice of hours or days of labor as units by which to express commodity values or prices—on the (invalid) ground that labor never varies in its own value or on any other ground—no more implies any particular theory of exchange value or price than the choice of oxen as units by which to express commodity values or prices implies an ox theory of exchange value or price. But Smith (just as R. Owen and other sponsors of the plan to make labor notes the medium of circulation) does not seem to have seen this clearly and undoubtedly argued in several places as if his use of labor as *numéraire* did imply a theory of value. Moreover, he repeatedly seems to confuse the quantity of labor a commodity will exchange for with the quantity of labor this commodity costs to produce—which is what Ricardo criticized. The quantity a commodity costs to produce then comes to the front in the famous beaver-deer example at the beginning of ch. 6, though it is but just to add that Smith confines the proposition that this quantity 'regulates' price expressly to that 'early and rude state of society' in which there are no other distributive shares to take into account. Finally, there is the 'toil and trouble' which is the 'real price of everything' and which, at least if interpreted as equivalent to the later concept, disutility of labor, agrees with neither of the two other measures. These, then, are

duction, which in this chapter he divides up into wages, profit, and rent—the 'original sources of all revenue as well as of all exchangeable value.' This is no doubt very unsatisfactory as an explanation of value but serves well as an avenue both to a theory of equilibrium price and to the theory of distribution.

The rudimentary equilibrium theory of Chapter 7, by far the best piece of economic theory turned out by A. Smith, in fact points toward Say and, through the latter's work, to Walras. The purely theoretical developments of the nineteenth century consist to a considerable degree in improvements upon it. Market price, defined in terms of short-run demand and supply, is treated as fluctuating around a 'natural' price—J. S. Mill's 'necessary' price, A. Marshall's 'normal' price—which is the price that is sufficient and not more than sufficient to cover 'the whole value of the rent, wages, and profit, which must be paid in order to bring' to market that quantity of every commodity 'which will supply the effectual demand,' that is, the demand effective at that price. There is no theory of monopoly price beyond the meaningless (or even false) sentence that the 'price of monopoly is upon every occasion the highest which can be got,' whereas 'the price of free competition . . . is the lowest which can be taken' in the long run—an important theorem though Smith does not seem to have had any notion of the difficulties of a satisfactory proof. Chapters 8 to 11 complete the self-contained argument of the first Book, whose contour lines, though hidden by the luxuriant foliage of illustrative fact that often degenerates into digression, are not without beauty. They deal with 'the circumstances which naturally determine' the rate of wages and the rate of profit and 'regulate' the rent of land (p. 56).[21] These chapters, summing up and co-ordinating, handed down the theory of distribution of the eighteenth century to the economists of the nineteenth, who found it all the easier to start from them because the very looseness of Adam Smith's doctrines invited development on many different lines: Smith's very weaknesses conspired to qualify him for his type of leadership. It must suffice to draw the reader's attention to the following points.

---

the three labor theories of value or price which A. Smith is supposed to have held. However, since the first is logically incapable of serving as an *explanation* of the phenomenon of value—the reader will perceive that, considered as such, it spells circular reasoning—and since we may neglect the third, because A. Smith made no effort to develop the theme of disutility, we are really left with the second or labor-quantity theory of value. And, finally, since A. Smith—unlike Ricardo and Marx—claimed no validity at all for this except in a special case, we come to the conclusion that, in spite of his emphasis on the labor factor, his theory of value is no labor theory at all. The fact that the first sentence of the introduction makes the whole of the National Dividend a 'produce of labor,' does not affect this conclusion as a little reflection should show.

21 [The page references in this Reader's Guide are to the Everyman's Library Edition published by J. M. Dent, London, and E. P. Dutton & Co.., New York (1910), of which there was a copy in the library in Taconic. Elsewhere J. A. S. used the Cannan edition referred to in note 15.]

Chapter 8 on wages contains not only the rudiments of both the wage fund (p. 61) and the minimum-of-existence (pp. 71, 76) theories, which might have been derived from Turgot and the physiocrats and which have been made the most of by A. Smith's English successors, but also another element, the full importance of which these successors failed to see. This is enshrined in his pithy sentence that the 'liberal reward of labour' is both 'the necessary effect' and 'the natural symptom of *increasing* [J. A. S.'s italics] national wealth' (p. 65) which, though inadequately motivated, sheds a light on the problem of wages quite different from that in which Ricardo saw it. Chapter 9 on profit offers many points about the factors that determine the rate of profit (for instance on p. 83), especially relatively to wages, but fails to face the fundamental problem. So far as Smith can be credited with having had a theory of 'profit' at all, it must be pieced together from indications, mostly vague and even contradictory, that are scattered over the first two Books. First, he definitively sanctioned and helped to victory the doctrinal tendency that was to prevail in nineteenth-century economics, particularly in England: profit, treated as the basic income of the capitalist class, is (substantially) the return from the use in business of physical goods (labor's means of subsistence included) which that class supplies; and interest on loans is simply a derivate from it. Excepting the case of the mere lenders ('monied men'), there is no distinctive function of the entrepreneurs—though Smith does speak of the 'undertaker'—or industrialists, who, 'inspection and direction' being brushed aside, are fundamentally capitalists or masters 'setting to work industrious people' and appropriating part of the product of 'their work' (ch. 6). The Marxist implications of this, which moreover Smith goes out of his way to underline, are obvious. Nevertheless, it cannot be said that Adam Smith held an exploitation theory of profit, though it can be said that he suggested it. For he also emphasized the element of risk and spoke of employers' *advancing* 'the whole stock of materials and wages' (p. 42), which points in an entirely different direction. Moreover, nobody who thought as highly of the social importance of saving as did A. Smith can complain if he be associated with abstinence-theory ideas.

In treating of the differences 'Of Wages and Profits in the different Employments of Labour and Stock' (ch. 10), Smith, reveling in facts and arguments of a somewhat trite sort, improved upon Cantillon and succeeded in creating a standard chapter of the nineteenth-century textbook. Chapter 11, 'Of the Rent of Land'—Smith, and following him, practically all the English economists to Marshall's epoch, confined the concept of rent to land and mines—is swollen by a gigantic digression (or a cluster of digressions or monographs) that makes up about 7.6 per cent of the whole work. If the vast materials and the almost innumerable disquisitions on particular points be boiled down, a mosaic of ideas emerges of which these are the outstanding elements. First, reasoning from his cost theory of value, Smith not unnaturally—though wrongly—arrives at the conclusion that the phenomenon of rent can be due only to a 'monopoly' in land (p. 131), thus starting on its career an idea that was to find sponsors again and again and has not even yet died out. But second, we find (p. 132) the statement that, whereas 'high or low wages and profit are the causes of high or low price; high or low rent is the effect of it,' which fits but ill with the monopoly theory and points in the Ricardian direction: the so-called Ricardian theory of rent *might* have emerged from an effort to put logical order into the Smithian jumble. And, third, there is even a suggestion that might have induced a disciple to straighten out that jumble by means of a productivity theory (see, e.g., p. 133). All this is intermingled with other ideas, good and bad—for example, the old idea which was as persistent as it was useless and which we encounter again in Malthus, that the production of foodstuffs holds a unique position in that it creates its own demand because people will multiply as it expands —that enter and leave the stage much as does the Falstaff crowd in *Henry IV*. Even before the reader gets to the digressions on the value of silver and on the relation between the values of silver and gold, the chapter contributes much to Smith's theory of money, which cannot however be fully mastered without reading the whole work (see especially ch. 2 of the second Book and the important Digression Concerning Banks of Deposit in ch. 3 of the fourth). Two more points should be added: at the end of the digression on silver Smith tries to show why, at least on the whole, the price—the real price— of agrarian products will rise in consequence of the Progress of Improvement (pp. 198 et seq.) and, in an additional digression (pp. 224 et seq.), that the real price of manufactures will fall. In a sense, this foreshadows the nineteenth-century doctrine of decreasing returns in agriculture and increasing returns in industry toward which he may be said to have cautiously felt his way and which *might* have been distilled from his pages. Furthermore, he arrived at the Ricardian conclusion (p. 229), though it does not follow cogently from his muddled argument, that landowners benefit in the process directly, both because the real value of the products of the land rises and because they receive a larger relative share of these products; and in addition indirectly, owing to the fall of the real price of manufactures. Laborers also benefit (p. 230) because their wages rise and the prices of part of the commodities they buy fall. But the third class, the 'merchants and master manufacturers' (p. 231), suffer, because, as A. Smith said, the *rate* of interest tends to be low in rich countries and high in poor countries, so that the interest of this class conflicts both with the interests of the other two and with the 'general interest of the society.' This was evidently intended for a schema of economic class interests such as many later economists tried to construct, possibly inspired by A. Smith's example and by a desire to correct his mistakes.

The second Book presents the theory of capital, saving, and investment that, however much transformed by development and criticism, remained the basis of practically all later work until, and partly even beyond, Böhm-Bawerk. It certainly looks like a new wing added to an old structure. In spite of the weak attempt made in the introduction to link it to the first Book by means of another and quite unconvincing appeal to 'division of labour,' there is no reason to believe that any essential part of it was either written or planned before A. Smith's stay in France. Specifically physiocrat influence is much more definitely recognizable than it is in any part of the first Book, both in many details and in the conception as a whole. This statement must not be misunderstood, however. A. Smith was not in the habit of accepting passively what he read or heard: he read and listened judicially, criticized vigorously, and in so doing arrived at a conception of his own. This is why I have spoken of physiocrat influence only, and not also of his being influenced by Turgot. Turgot holds priority in essential points, but it does not follow that Smith derived his views from him. For these views are such as would naturally emerge in Smith's mind from a creative criticism of Quesnay's teaching so that, in the absence of cogent evidence to the contrary, it seems more just to speak of parallelism than of dependence. Space forbids our presenting more than a single illustration. The Scotsman's common sense took offense at Quesnay's statement that only agricultural (and extractive) labor was productive. From Turgot he might have learned how to shrug his shoulders at this vagary and to pass on with a graceful bow. This, however, was not his way. He took things not only seriously but also literally. He had to embark upon ponderous refutation. But in his meditations on the subject it may have occurred to him that there was something to the distinction between productive and unproductive labor.[22] And so he worked out his own interpretation of it and substituted it for Quesnay's. In a sense it was suggested to him by Quesnay—this is indicated by the fact that there is no hint of it in the first Book though it would naturally belong there—but in another sense it was his own.

Chapter 1 of the second Book distinguishes that part of a man's—and society's—total stock of goods that is to be called capital (not only physical goods, since 'the acquired and useful abilities of all the inhabitants' are capital) from the rest; introduces the concepts of fixed and circulating capital; and classifies the goods that are to come under both headings, including in circulating capital money but not the means of subsistence of productive laborers, although Smith's argument calls for and actually implies inclusion of the latter. The long Chapter 2, one of the most important of the work,

[22] It may be just as well to state at once what that something was, because both A. Smith's clumsy and inconsistent handling of it and the nineteenth-century controversy on this distinction have needlessly obscured its meaning. Productive laborers reproduce the value of the capital that employs them with a profit; unproductively employed laborers either sell their services or else produce something that does not yield profit. This may be considered as the embryo of Marx's theory of surplus value. Interpreted in this sense, this distinction is not irrelevant. But Smith himself has to take the blame if this meaning of it, which is quite clear from the first paragraph of ch. 3, did not stand out from all the irrelevancies with which he associated it. From another but cognate standpoint the distinction is between labor that does and labor that does not produce something that must be sold in order to complete the transaction: when a personal servant has sold his services to his employer and has received payment *out of the latter's income*, there is no further step in the process; if the same man secures employment in a shoe factory, he is paid out of capital and the process in which his work is an element is not completed until the shoes have found a buyer.

contains the bulk of A. Smith's theory of money. It is much above Chapter 4 of the first Book and certainly the result of a late stage of A. Smith's labors. But it displays no physiocrat influence—all recognizable influence is English. Chapter 3 (which introduces the distinction between productive and unproductive labor), with its tremendous emphasis on the propensity to save as the true creator of physical capital ('Parsimony, and not industry, is the immediate cause of the increase of capital,' p. 301; 'every prodigal appears to be a public enemy, and every frugal man a public benefactor,' p. 304), marks the victory for more than 150 years to come of a pro-saving theory. 'What is annually saved is as regularly consumed as what is annually spent, and nearly in the same time too; but it is consumed by a different set of people' (p. 302), namely, productive laborers whose wages and employment are thus positively related to the rate of saving which is identified or at least equated to the rate of increase of capital, that is, investment. In this chapter, revenue means profit plus rent, exactly as it does with Marx. Chapter 4 tackles the problem of interest. Since, as indicated above, profit is treated as the fundamental phenomenon and this is taken for granted here, interest simply follows from the fact that money—but, as Smith holds, really the producers' goods and services that can be bought for it—always meets with demand at a premium motivated by the expectation of profits. Smith as well as all his successors until recent times simply saw no difficulty in explaining interest per se: the difference between him and his nineteenth-century successors was only that he did not see much of a problem in business profit either, whereas, as time went on, an increasing number of the latter began to worry about it. There are thus but three points to mention: first, his unconvincing explanation of the tendency of the rate of interest to fall by the increasing competition between increasing capitals; second, his vigorous, and for 150 years successful, argument against the monetary theories of interest that attempt to explain that tendency by the increase in the quantity of monetary metals; third, his moderate and judicious argument about legal maxima which called forth an entirely unjustified attack from Bentham.

[The Reader's Guide was not completed. There is, for example, no discussion of ch. 5 (Of the different Employment of Capitals), the concluding chapter of the second Book. The final paragraph was on a separate sheet with no indication as to its intended position.]

Before the century was out the *Wealth of Nations* had run to nine English editions, not counting the ones that appeared in Ireland and the United States, and had been translated (so far as I know) into Danish, Dutch, *French*, *German*, Italian, and Spanish (italics indicate more than one translation; the first Russian translation appeared 1802-6). This may be taken to measure the extent of its success in the first stage of its career. For a work of its type and calibre—which entirely lacked the graces of the *Esprit des lois*—it can, I think, be called spectacular. But this was as nothing compared with the really significant success that is not so easy to measure: from about 1790 on, Smith became the teacher not of the beginner or the public but of the professionals, especially the professors. The thought of most of them, including Ricardo, started from him and most of them again never got beyond him. For half a century or more, roughly until J. S. Mill's *Principles* (1848) started on its career, Adam Smith supplied the bulk of the ideas of the average economist. In England, Ricardo's *Principles* (1817) meant a serious check. But outside of England, most economists were not quite up to Ricardo, and Smith continued to hold sway. It was then that he was invested with the insignia of 'founder'—which none of his contemporaries would have thought of bestowing on him—and that earlier economists moved into the role of 'precursors' in whom it was just wonderful to discover what nevertheless remained Smith's ideas.

5. Quasi-Systems

Lest the reader should conceive an entirely wrong impression—which if it be allowed to settle in his mind the subsequent chapters might be powerless to dispel—it is necessary to supplement without delay the story told in the preceding section by at least some account of the parallel stream of quasi-systems. Most of them, as we know, were programs of industrial and commercial development. Their authors recommended or fought policies appropriate or inimical to those programs, and reasoned in terms of individual problems. But their ideas were not unsystematic in the sense of lacking coherence. They knew how to relate one problem to another and to reduce them to unifying principles—*analytic* principles, not merely principles of policy. If these analytic principles were not always stated explicitly, they were nevertheless often worked out effectively in a way that suggests the development of English law. In this section, we shall confine ourselves to a selection of seventeenth-century writers, all of whom will have to be mentioned again as we go along. Many more will be introduced in the next and later chapters.

The honors of this literature—for the seventeenth century—belong to English businessmen and civil servants but the list is headed by an Italian, Serra.[1]

[1] Antonio Serra, *Breve trattato delle cause che possono far abbondare li regni d'oro e argento dove non sono miniere* (1613; republ. in the Custodi collection and in A. Graziani's *Economisti del cinque e seicento*, 1913; by extract also in G. Tagliacozzo's *Economisti Napoletani dei secoli XVII e XVIII*, 1937, with summary and appraisal, English trans. in A. E. Monroe's *Early Economic Thought*). Nothing is known of the author except that he wrote the treatise in a Neapolitan prison, perhaps in the hope of regaining his freedom thereby, for it is dedicated to the Spanish Viceroy. Again—as in the case of L. Ortiz, who might be claimed as a predecessor of Serra as might also another Spaniard, Gonzáles de Cellorigo (*Memoriales. De la politica necesaria . . . á la república de España*, 1600), both of whom, however, lacked Serra's grasp of principle—the reader is asked to forget the title, which evidently was chosen in order to interest the Viceroy and does not express the gist and importance of the argument at all well. However, there was some justification for it: the author argued at length against the exchange-control policy advocated by De Santis—not entirely successfully—so that the treatise has also a place in the history of the 'mercantilist' controversies (see below, ch. 7). On Serra and his work, see R. Benini, '*Sulle dottrine economiche di Antonio Serra*,' *Giornale degli Economisti*, 1892. Further references in Tagliacozzo's edition.

This man must, I think, be credited with having been the first to compose a scientific treatise, though an unsystematic one, on Economic Principles and Policy. Its chief merit does not consist in his having explained the outflow of gold and silver from the Neapolitan Kingdom by the state of the balance of payments but in the fact that he did not stop there but went on to explain the latter by a general analysis of the conditions that determine the state of an economic organism. Essentially, the treatise is about the factors on which depend the abundance not of money but of *commodities*—natural resources, quality of the people, the development of industry and trade, the efficiency of government—the implication being that if the economic process as a whole functions properly, the monetary element will take care of itself and not require any specific therapy. And this argument contains several contributions to the nascent stock of theoretical tools that will be noticed later.[2]

For several decades, there was nothing like this anywhere. But in the second half of the century we behold a rich crop of works of a similar type in England, the standard title of which was, as mentioned already, *Discourse of Trade*. Gradually their authors discovered for themselves pieces of the logic inherent in the economic process: the things which they could have learned from the scholastics and their successors and which, under different circumstances and, accordingly, from the standpoint of different political aims, were to become the rationale of the doctrines of laissez-faire liberalism. A landmark on this way was Child's *Discourse*.[3] This outstanding performance was and is usually disposed of as one of the many 'mercantilist' writings—which was and (to some extent) still is sufficient to prevent many historians from seeing any

[2] Almost immeasurably inferior to Serra in grasp of economic principle and analytic power, but not dissimilar from him in views on the issues of practical policy, was B. de Laffemas, who wrote around 1600 (for a list of his writings see F. Hayem, *Un Tailleur d'Henri IV, Barthélemy de Laffemas*, 1905; also see H. Hauser, 'La liberté du commerce et la liberté du travail sous Henry IV,' *Revue historique*, 1902).

[3] Sir Josiah Child (1630-99). That work eventually appeared in its final form under the title *New Discourse of Trade* (1693), but to do justice to its historical merit we must take into account the fact that it took decades to mature into that form. The first draft, *Brief Observations concerning Trade and Interest of Money* and also *A Short Addition* were published in 1668. Ten chapters were added, 1669-70. Those years are the relevant ones for questions of priority, because the *Discourse about Trade* that was published in 1690 did not add or alter very much. The *New Discourse* of 1693 contains still fewer alterations and adds nothing except a new introduction. A minor publication written in defense of the trade of the East India Company also merits notice. Child's reputation as an economist, besides suffering from the general prejudice against 'mercantilist' writings, also suffered from a fact that is of great interest to the sociologist of science. Child was a leading businessman, in fact the very incarnation of the most hated big business of that age: he was chairman and for some years the undisputed leader of the East India Company, besides being personally very wealthy. Accordingly, he was unpopular in his time, and so he has remained for over 250 years, historians being careful to clear their skirts of the 'monopolist' and 'special pleader' (*scilicet* for his personal interest).

merit in it. But quite independently of whether or not that label fits, it should be recognized that this *Discourse* deals with the practical problems of its time—employment, wages, money, exchanges, exports and imports, and so on—in the light of clearly adumbrated 'laws' of the mechanism of capitalist markets; though not explicitly worked out, the tool that we call equilibrium theory is, as it were, present behind the scene. This performance was matched and in many individual points surpassed by such men as Barbon, Davenant, North, Pollexfen, and others.[4] In every one of these cases we see more or less awareness of the existence of an analytic apparatus that runs on in essentially the same manner, whatever the practical problem for the sake of which it is set working, and more or less willingness and ability to use it. For us this is what matters: whether we like or dislike the practical recommendations that are supposed by the authors to follow from their analysis is entirely immaterial.

I take this opportunity to mention a remarkable though little-known treatise on foreign trade which Professor Foxwell (see Kress Library of Business and Economics, Harvard Graduate School of Business Administration, Catalogue) described as 'one of the earliest formal systems of political economy, and stating one of the most forcible practical arguments for free trade,' though the latter part of Foxwell's statement seems to me more true than the former: Isaac Gervaise, *The System or Theory of the Trade of the World* (1720). Professor Viner (see below, ch. 7) has done full justice to this remarkable contribution to the theory of international trade whose author outlined in addition—all in the space of 34 pages—the topics of general theory germane to his particular subject, though of course not in any 'formal' layout.

The common run of these discourses was, however, far below that level. Most of them were merely motivated programs for the industrial and commercial development of England. Since foreign trade occupied the place of honor and most of the space in those programs, a selection of works of this type will be noticed in the last chapter of this Part. For the moment it will suffice to mention by way of example the tracts of the overrated Mun (his title was, however, not Discourse of Trade but *England's Treasure by Forraign Trade*, 1664), of

[4] References will be given in subsequent chapters. However, Charles Davenant's contribution must not be appraised from his *Discourses on the Publick Revenues, and on the Trade of England* (1698), but rather from all his many publications taken together: they sum up to a comprehensive quasi-system. And Pollexfen will be commented on at once. John Pollexfen was a merchant and M.P., who also served on the Board of Trade. In addition to his principal work, A *Discourse of Trade, Coyn, and Paper Credit* (1697, reprinted 1700), he also wrote *England and East India Inconsistent in their Manufactures* (1697), a tract that, besides attacking his *bête noire*, the East India Company, in reply to Davenant's *Essay on the East-India-Trade* (1696), complements part of the argument of the *Discourse*. The latter is an excellent piece of work, precisely as regards analytic ability. It is therefore a question of some interest to ask why he has received so little recognition and especially why such recognition as he received has been tempered in most cases by derogatory comments upon his supposed lack of originality and upon his various 'mercantilist errors.' The latter indictment seems without foundation, and concerning the former it is sufficient to ask: if we define eminence in an economist solely by the presence in his writings of entirely new results, where will A. Smith be, or Ricardo, or J. S. Mill?

Cary, and of Petyt.[5] There was no lack of unity about them as to political vision. And this vision was quite comprehensive, embracing all the economic problems of the nation. But there was no analytic work, and faults of reasoning abound. Cary, for instance, besides discussing carefully the conditions and possibilities of English trade with each foreign country, with Ireland, and with the colonies (the most valuable part of the tract) also concerns himself with monopolies (that is, the monopolies of the great trading companies), the causes of and remedies for unemployment, coinage, credit, and many other subjects down to the problem—or was this Mrs. Cary's contribution?—of how to make maid servants 'more orderly and governable than now they are' (p. 162). But every attempt he makes to carry analysis beyond the obvious is a failure. High rents, for instance, are made responsible for England's being undersold in foreign markets. High interest is held to be another cause of this but without recourse to any argument that might raise this theory above the status of a popular observation. In spite of the emphasis on export surpluses, high prices and high wages are commended on grounds that tax the reader's capacity for generous interpretation. And so on. Yet there is plenty of shrewd sense about it all—shrewd, narrowly nationalistic, and naïvely brutal (compare, for example, his enthusiasm for the slave trade, England's 'silver mine,' p. 76, or his views about the treatment to be dealt out to Ireland, *passim*).

Once we have learned to discern 'quasi-systems' in or behind writings that profess to deal only with particular problems, we find the genus everywhere. In the Netherlands, for instance, Graswinckel's and de la Court's[6] writings belong to it, although the former dealt only with the grain trade. Many historians will place them above their English contemporaries on account of their 'liberal' views on national and international trade—though de la Court lapsed from grace as to the latter—government interference, medieval corporations, and so on. But we shall arrive at a substantially similar estimate because of those authors' clear perception of causes and effects in all matters of the price mechanism. A man who in 1651 recognized the economic function of 'forestalling' and speculation, as did Graswinckel, knew something that could have

[5] John Cary, merchant in Bristol, *An Essay on the State of England in Relation to its Trade, its Poor, and its Taxes . . .* , 1695, the edition used. There were several others—the one of 1745 bearing the title *Discourse on Trade*—which points to considerable success. For Locke's praise of the performance I can only account by the fact that Cary favored recoinage of the currency at the old standard of weight and fineness and that, in 1695, Locke would have welcomed *any* writer who did so (see below, ch. 6). Perhaps, however, he was also attracted by Cary's careful discussion of England's trade with various countries. The other work, *Britannia Languens, or a Discourse of Trade . . .* (1680), appeared under the pseudonym Philanglus and is attributed to William Petyt on Professor Foxwell's authority (see Catalogue of the Kress Library).

[6] Dirck Graswinckel (1600-1666), a lawyer and public servant, wrote a treatise on the economics of the food trade under the unpromising title: *Placaetbook op het stuk van de Leeftocht* (Compilation of regulations concerning food, 1651). Pieter de la Court (1618-85) was a manufacturer. Of his works it is only necessary to mention the *Interest van Holland . . .* (1662; 2nd ed. under the title *Aanwysing . . .* 1669).

been presented as a discovery in 1751—not that it would really have been one—though it was a commonplace in 1851 and will sound altogether wrong now.

German seventeenth-century writings of this genus, besides taking, of course, a different view as to policy, were not on this level but there were many of the Cary type or better. We shall be content with an Austrian representative, the well-known Hornigk,[7] who, like the much more important Becher and some others, figures in every history of economics. His book is another program for a policy of fostering economic development, written this time for a poor country, perennially threatened by Turkish invasions and lacking both the resources and the possibilities of England. If, however, we take due account of this fact, the family likeness of the recommendations with those of Hornigk's English contemporaries—or even with those of the doctor in the *Discourse of the Common Weal*—is striking: waste lands and other unused resources are to be exploited; the efficiency of labor is to be increased by better training; domestic industry should be helped, among other things, by directing consumers' demand toward its products; exports of manufactures and imports of necessary raw materials should be favored, exports of the latter and imports of the former restricted; trade should be balanced bilaterally with every individual foreign country (see last chapter of this Part); and so forth—sound sense all or most of it and very interesting as a monument of the intelligent bureaucrat's thought, but sound sense that did not even suspect that it might be usefully reinforced by analysis.

As regards the United States, there is nothing to record in the way of systematic endeavor before the nineteenth century. This is as we should expect from environmental conditions that were unlikely to produce either a demand for or supply of general treatises. But discussion of current practical problems was active even in colonial times, and for the eighteenth century, reports, pamphlets, and tracts abound, especially on questions of paper money, coinage, credit, trade, and fiscal policy.[8] And some of these performances

[7] *Oesterreich über Alles wann es nur will* (1684). Philipp W. von Hornigk (1638-1712) was a civil servant. Extracts from the book are included in A. E. Monroe's *Early Economic Thought*.

[8] The late Professor Seligman's essay, 'Economics in the United States,' reprinted as ch. 4 of his *Essays in Economics* (1925), gives a selection of titles (unfortunately little more than titles) on which I cannot hope to improve. Such reading as I have done was primarily guided by this selection. Also see C. F. Dunbar, 'Economic Science in America, 1776-1876,' in the *North American Review*, 1876, and the reprints of a number of the more important pamphlets by the Prince Society, 1911 (ed. McFarland Davis). American economists seem on the whole to have been too ready to discount the importance of that early literature from a scientific standpoint, and most of the attention it has received is confined to the policies or particular measures advocated or attacked. The critical historian then commends or blames according to his personal views on those policies and measures. The specifically analytic contribution of a writer as a rule goes by the board, especially in those cases where, as often happens in the field of money, 'unsound' practice goes with sound theory and vice versa. However,

answer to our idea of 'quasi-systems.' Here are three examples which the American reader is advised to look up for himself. First, Hamilton's famous *Report on Manufactures* (1791),[9] though no doubt intended as a description with a program, is really 'applied economics' at its best and reveals quite clearly essentials of the analytic framework that was to be made explicit by D. Raymond and F. List and in turn points back to the work of such men as Child and Davenant. Second, Coxe's work comes near to actually being a systematic treatise.[10] Third, Benjamin Franklin's (1706-90) various tracts on economic subjects [11] present material enough to enable us to reconstruct his system—on the practical side, substantially of a laissez-faire type—though there is little to commend for purely analytic virtues.

6. Public Finance Once More

In the first section of this chapter, the fact was emphasized that in the rising national states public finance acquired not only paramount importance but also a new significance. There would be little exaggeration in saying that,

within the plan of this book, very little can be done to remedy this state of things. [J. A. S. wrote this chapter before the publication of Joseph H. Dorfman's work, *The Economic Mind in American Civilization,* the first two volumes of which cover the period 1606-1865. J. A. S. read the first volume and made notes which he intended to use in revising the chapter.]

[9] Alexander Hamilton's (1757-1804) brilliant figure is so familiar to the reader that it would be absurd to tell him who and what Hamilton was. Nor is there any need to refer to the Hamilton literature. All that needs to be said from the standpoint of our purpose is that he was one of those rare practitioners of economic policy who think it worth while to acquire more analytic economics than that smattering that does such good service in addressing audiences of a certain type. He knew Smithian economics well—not only A. Smith himself—so well in fact as to be able to mold it to his own visions of practical possibilities or necessities and to perceive its limitations. All his reports—not only the one mentioned in the text but also the ones on the import duty (1782), public credit (1790 and 1795), the establishment of a national bank (1790) and of a mint (1791)—are much more than untutored common sense. Perusal of the volumes of the *Federalist,* the periodical in which he co-operated with Madison and Jay, is strongly recommended: the American reader will get much more out of it than mere economics. For guidance in starting a study of Hamilton's writings, see P. L. Ford, *Bibliotheca Hamiltoniana* (1886), and the life by H. C. Lodge (1882).

[10] Tench Coxe (1755-1824), Commissioner of Revenue, *A View of the United States . . .* (1794), in form a collection of essays and addresses.

[11] Particularly, *Modest Inquiry into the Nature and Necessity of Paper Currency* (1729); *Observations concerning the Increase of Mankind . . .* (1751); *Positions to be Examined concerning National Wealth* (1769; the work responsible for the opinion that this great realist was a physiocrat). But though these are, with the possible exception of his *Reflections on the Augmentation of Wages,* his only works that come at all within the category of economic research, other essays and much material that he contributed in a popular form to popular publications (such as *Poor Richard's Almanack*) help to round off our knowledge of his opinions and analytic efforts (*Works,* ed. by John Bigelow, 1887-8). Of course, it would be still more absurd than it would

at least for the continental branches of the literature that have been surveyed, it was the central topic around which revolved most of the rest. Let us therefore retrace our steps and look more closely at the financial problem of these centuries.

Public finance in our sense, and especially modern taxation, first developed in the course of the fifteenth century in the Italian city-republics, Florence in particular, and in the German free towns (*Reichsstädte*). More important for us is, however, the development of the fiscal systems of the national states and the Italian and German principalities. For the sake of both brevity and concreteness we shall think primarily of the case of the latter or, still more precisely, of the development of public finance in a typical *temporal* principality of Germany. Of course, people always recognized the existence of some interests that were common to all members of a political unit—recognition of the *res publica* was fostered, among other factors, by scholastic teaching. Nevertheless, public affairs were in legal principle the affairs of the territorial ruler. Wars in particular were his personal quarrels (compare the English official phrase that still survives, 'the King's enemies'). Hence, so far as the military service that his vassals owed to him proved inadequate—and this resource petered out in the course of the sixteenth century—he had to finance them from his own means. These consisted, first, of the feudal income from his own lands and, second, of a number of customary fiscal rights that went with the lordship of a principality, such as seigniorage, tolls, and customs, the right of charging for safe conduct of travelers and caravans of merchants, the right to levy taxes from Jewish communities for the protection extended to them, and rights to a wide variety of fees of all sorts (*regalia*).

The rise in prices, the cost of mercenaries and later on of standing armies, profuse expenditure on court nobilities and bureaucracies, and other causes, all related to the political ambitions of those princes or else to the social structure of their territories, rendered these customary sources of revenue inadequate and led to a rapidly mounting burden of debt. In the untenable situations that ensued the princes appealed to their Estates on the plea that, for instance, a Turkish invasion was after all not only the private affair of the prince. The Estates thereupon granted subsidies which, apart from the contributions of the towns, they levied upon their own *feudal* income, that is, upon the dues their peasantries owed to them—land in their own management remaining free. At first they insisted each time that they were making the grant of their own free will in response to a humble request and only for the particular emergency in question; but they actually bore the burden. Very soon, however, regular recurrence of these direct taxes had to be recognized. But, while accepting the fact, the Estates, on the one hand, set up their own administrations for levying them and expending the proceeds and, on the other hand, no longer bore them themselves but collected them in turn from their dependent peasantries.

have been in the case of Hamilton to dilate on the life and achievements of this household figure, particularly in view of the recent publication of a masterly life by Carl Van Doren.

This arrangement, besides being inadequate, was of course not at all to the taste of the princes and their bureaucracies. A tug of war between them and the Estates ensued for the control of this new fiscal apparatus that had grown up alongside of their own. The reader knows that the English parliament succeeded in keeping its hold on these purse strings which eventually in the seventeenth century throttled the power of the king. In most other countries, however, kings and princes, or rather their bureaucracies, won out in the course of the eighteenth, though the French *ancien régime* broke down in the attempt to secure fiscal reform.

Meanwhile, that is to say, until the bureaucracies had conquered the fiscal stronghold of the Estates, the growing Leviathan had to feed on the old sources of revenue. Accordingly, development of these, especially of all the fiscal rights, became a major task of governments and their henchmen. This meant eventually the disproportionate growth of indirect taxation, especially in the forms of the General Excise on the one hand, and of the General Turnover Tax—the Spanish *alcavala* is the outstanding instance—on the other. For though the introduction or increase of indirect taxes, too, was in principle dependent upon the consent of the Estates, it proved, nearly everywhere except in England, easier to get round this requirement in the case of indirect than it was in the case of direct taxation. Princes and bureaucracies had also another motive for preferring the former. We are accustomed to looking upon indirect taxation as contrary to the interests of the relatively poor. But in the seventeenth and eighteenth centuries the 'social' argument told in favor of indirect taxation: for indirect taxes were at least *also* borne by the nobility and the clergy whereas these classes contributed hardly anything at all to the proceeds of direct taxation. However, since it was not easy to introduce or reform indirect taxes either—which, by the way, shows how far those monarchies were from being 'absolute'—revenue from this source had to be increased according to opportunity rather than to any rational plan. And since, furthermore, governments were rarely in a position to abandon revenue from old fiscal rights however irrational, burdensome, or vexatious, the result was an almost unbelievable—the only word is 'mess,' the mere straightening out of which was an extremely difficult task which, when taken in hand in the seventeenth and eighteenth centuries, exercised the ingenuity of administrators and writers alike. The literature that blossomed forth in response to these conditions contains some analysis on such problems as incidence of taxes, which will be briefly noticed later on, and also analysis of a kind that had better be noticed right now, along with those much larger parts of that literature which are not relevant to a history of analytic economics and have to be mentioned only to be dismissed.

First, the tug of war referred to produced innumerable books and pamphlets on the right to tax, the 'justice' of taxation, and the constitutional questions germane to taxation. We have already remarked on the important prelude to this that is contained in the scholastic writings. The laical literature of this type displays a characteristic difference in tendency between its English branch and its continental branches: most of the continental writers sided with the bureaucracies and often saw benighted and antisocial resistance of class interest where the vast majority of English writers—particularly in the struggle over the ship money of Charles I—saw a meritorious stand for liberty. All this was, however, either simple politics or 'political philosophy' and is of no interest to us. Second, pure description of sources of public revenue and administrative practice dates far back. There is an English instance for the twelfth century.[1] This literature developed greatly from the sixteenth century on, especially on the Continent, but needs no further attention for our purposes.[2] Third, the necessity of making the most of existing fiscal rights produced in the public service a special type of lawyer whose task it was to safeguard, extend, and systematize those rights by appropriate interpretation and who naturally also taught and wrote, creating what is known as Fiscal Jurisprudence.[3] A fourth category consisted of the fiscal planners—the numerous writers who advocated schemes of fiscal reform: every financial emergency or controversy since the fifteenth century naturally produced clusters of them. In the light of their ideas it would be possible to write not only a history of public finance but also a history of political society, for everything that happens in the political sphere reflects itself more truly in the prevailing ideas about fiscal policy than it does in anything else. Most of the planners did no analytic work, however. This is especially true of some of the most eminent ones among them, such as Cardinal Cusanus, who proposed a scheme that would in fact have rescued the German Empire from the decay into which it was falling in the fifteenth and sixteenth centuries. But some did analyze. They analyzed the nature of taxation—an early example, Mattheo Palmieri's theory, has been mentioned already; its economic effects; the severity of pressure exerted by different systems; the effects of public expenditure; the relative merits of direct and indirect taxation and of financing of wars by taxation, borrowing, and inflation; and so on. Spanish discussion of the seventeenth and eighteenth

[1] Richard Fitzneale *Dialogus de scaccario* (exchequer), ed. by Hughes, Crump, and Johnson (1902).

[2] By way of example we may mention Anon., *Traicté des finances de France* (1580); N. Froumenteau, *Le Secret des finances de France* (1581), more interesting for the finances of the temporal and spiritual magnates than for the finances of the king; Jean Combes, *Traicté des tailles et autres charges . . .* (1586); Jean Hennequin, *Le Guidon général des finances* (1585, re-edited repeatedly, even as late as 1644); J. Matthias, *Tractatio methodica . . . de contributionibus* (1632); H. Conring (whom we shall meet again), *De vectigalibus et aerario* (1663). The last two are not merely descriptive, however, though all their interest lies in the description.

[3] This branch of public-finance literature, which in the nineteenth century swelled to dimensions beyond the range of anyone but the full-time specialist, should really not be dismissed so cavalierly. But we have no choice. In my—very likely erroneous—opinion, the classic of the genus is Caspar Klock's *Tractatus juridico-politico-polemico-historicus de aerario* (1651). Its quaint title has the merit of expressing exactly what it is. C. Besold's (see above, sec. 4) earlier *De aerario publico discursus* (1615) should, however, not go unmentioned. It contains, as does Klock's, quite a lot of sound wisdom on tax policy that is as trite as, alas and alack, sound wisdom mostly is.

centuries would be particularly interesting to follow,[4] English discussion on seventeenth and eighteenth-century war finance or on Sir Robert Walpole's excise scheme is no less so. But from the mass of this literature we shall select only two works of first-rate importance. Petty's treatise on taxes and contributions (discussed in the following chapter) is not one of them because the interest it presents, though great, belongs in the field of general economics rather than in that of fiscal policy.

The first is one of the works that were called forth by the economic situation of France during the last twenty years of the reign of Louis XIV. The War of the Spanish Succession following upon the War of the Grand Alliance was turning impoverishment into nationwide misery when one of the great figures of the state and the army, the soldier-engineer Vauban, committed the indiscretion of publishing an old idea of his, the *Projet d'une dixme royale* (1707).[5] This is one of the outstanding performances in the field of public

[4] It turned mainly on the remedy to be applied to the grievances concerning the *alcavala*, the *cientios*, and the *millones*. Bautista Dávila (*Resúmen de los medios prácticos para el general alivio de la monarqúia*, date of writing unknown, publ. 1651; see Colmeiro's *Biblioteca*) seems to have been one of the earliest economists—ignorance prevents me from being more precise—to look upon a single tax as the wand by which to conjure up the benign spirits of fiscal order. In any case his *Resúmen* is a milestone on the road to single-tax ideas. In his case, it was to be a graduated capitation tax, evidently meant to be a rough approximation to a proportional income tax. Similar ideas were discussed during the subsequent hundred years. The minister Ensenada (A. Rodriguez Villa, *Don Cenon de Somodevilla, Marqués de Ensenada*, 1878) made a modified version of this program his own and carried an income and property tax in 1729 (for Catalonia). But elsewhere and particularly in Germany, seventeenth-century discussion favored the general excise against direct taxes, precisely on the ground that it would relieve the pressure of taxation. An interesting symptom of this trend of opinion was the success of a book by an author who styled himself Christianus Teutophilus: *Entdeckte Gold-Grube in der Accise* (a gold mine discovered in the excise, 1685, of which the 5th ed. came out in 1719). Among English advocates of the excise Davenant was first in eminence. But he thought that the burden would fall on the land. For a similar reason, F. Fauquier (*An Essay on the Ways and Means . . .* 1756) later on advocated a house tax, namely on the ground that, since indirect taxes so far as they are paid by the poor will be transferred to the rich by means of a rise in money wages, taxes should be laid on where they will rest without giving rise to the losses incident to the process of transference. Observe that this anticipates much of what A. Smith and Ricardo had to say on the subject. In appraising attitudes toward the taxation of land it must not be forgotten that, before the eighteenth century, no efficient methods of surveying were available. Taxation of agricultural land entered a new phase of its history when these were improved. The *Censimento Milanese*, at the beginning of the eighteenth century was one of the first results.

[5] Sébastien le Prestre, Seigneur de Vauban (1633-1707), Maréchal de France and a favorite with Louis XIV (until that publication), had previously written a tremendous number of memoirs on fortifications, war, naval matters, public finance, religion, money, agriculture, and colonization that fill an imposing series of manuscript volumes. In 1698 he had instigated orders for a census of the population, and in 1695 he had first suggested the project that he published in 1707. Somewhat like Étienne Boileau

finance, unsurpassed, before or after, in the neatness and cogency of the argument. The recommendation itself does not greatly matter here. Essentially it was that the unwieldy and irrational welter of taxes that had grown up in an entirely unsystematic way should be scrapped—excepting a rationalized salt tax, certain excises, and export and import duties—and replaced by a general income tax that was to apply to all kinds of income, though at varying rates, of which the highest was to be 10 per cent (hence the word *dixme*); similar ideas had occurred before. The features that do matter are these. First, Vauban rose fully to those heights, trodden by so few, from which fiscal policy is seen to be a tool of economic therapeutics, the ultimate result of a comprehensive survey of the economic process. With Gladstonian vision he realized that fiscal measures affect the economic organism right to its cells and that the method of raising a given amount of revenue may make all the difference between paralysis and prosperity. Second, he based his conclusions in every detail on numerical fact. His engineer's mind did not guess. It figured out. Purposeful marshalling of all the available data was the essence of his analysis. Nobody ever understood better the true relation between facts and argument. It is this that makes him an economic classic in the eulogistic sense of the word, and a forerunner of modern tendencies, though he contributed nothing to the theoretical apparatus of economics.[6] His case affords another illustration of

---

four centuries and a half before him, he had a passion for collecting and arranging economic facts and figures. Accordingly, he has had his partisans, who claimed for him the title of *Créateur de la Statistique* (E. Daire in his edition of the *Dixme royale*, in *Economistes-financiers du XVIIIe siècle*, 1843, which is the edition used). The *Dixme* has been translated into English. There is a bibliography of Vauban by F. Gazin (1933). Also see D. Halévy, *Vauban* (1923); J. B. M. Vignes, *Histoire des doctrines sur l'impôt en France* (1909); and F. K. Mann, *Der Marschall Vauban . . .* (1914).

In his effort to secure fiscal reform Vauban had two allies whose relation to him however is not clear. The one was Boisguillebert, who was much more of an economist than was Vauban and whose performance will be considered in chs. 4 and 6 of this Part. Here we need only record, first, that his proposal, though differing from Vauban's, was yet conceived in the same spirit and expressed the same economic and fiscal vision; and, second, that Boisguillebert's outspokenness or rather bitterness—witness the subtitle of his first book, *Le Détail de la France. La France ruinée sous le règne de Louis XIV*—and his inability to appreciate practical difficulties—witness another subtitle, *Moyens très-faciles* [!] *de faire recevoir au Roy 80 millions par-dessus la capitation, praticable par deux heures de travail des Messieurs les Ministres* [!!]—naturally annoyed the poor slaves whose bad luck it was to serve at that time as ministers of finance (Pontchartrain, Chamillart, Desmarets). The other ally therefore found it easier to get on terms with them. This was the Abbé de Saint-Pierre (1658-1743), famous as moralist, all-round reformer, sponsor of the League-of-Nations idea, whose considerable performance as a practical economist is gradually emerging into the light of day (*Ouvrajes*, 1733-41). See P. Harsin, 'L'Abbé de Saint-Pierre, économiste,' *Revue d'histoire économique et sociale* (1932).

[6] He has been called a forerunner of the physiocrats. There is not the slightest foundation for this. As has been pointed out before, concern with agricultural conditions does not make a writer a physiocrat.

the truth that a man can be an excellent economist without being a good theorist. The reverse also holds true, unfortunately.

The second work to be mentioned, Broggia's[7] treatise on taxation, is of an entirely different nature and has been selected for entirely different reasons. It also outlines an 'ideal' system of taxation that might have been derived by critically developing that of Vauban: the main practical ideas, barring one, are roughly similar. But Italian sources, both earlier and contemporaneous ones, can be indicated for every particular, among others for the 'canons of taxation' (ch. 1) that, further expanded in Verri's *Meditazioni* (1771), essentially anticipate those of A. Smith. Thus the freshness—the 'subjective' originality—that makes Vauban's *Projet* such delightful reading is lacking here. Nor is there anything to correspond to the chief merit of Vauban's work, the facts and figures. Instead, however, we find systematic completeness and more searching analysis: the result is—at least—a digest of all that was best, not only in the public-finance literature of the eighteenth century but also in most of that of the nineteenth. There is the fifteenth-century rationalization of taxes as payments for security and as equivalents for the services rendered by the government. There is the principle that direct and indirect taxation are necessary complements of each other, the two hands of finance (Gladstone might have said that: actually, he spoke of two sisters so nearly alike that one hesitates in deciding which one to court). A proportional tax (10 per cent) on *certain* incomes (*entrate certe*, mainly from land, houses, including owner-inhabited ones, and public funds; compare A. Smith's predilection for land and house taxes) that will not be transferred, is combined with a system of indirect taxes (*gabelle*) that are supposed to be transferred to buyers, whereas all *uncertain* incomes (profits, wages, and so on) are to be left free. The interesting thing about this is the underlying diagnosis of the economic situation: Broggia's finance was to foster the increase of wealth through industrial and commercial activity; for this purpose, acquired wealth was to be taxed to force people into business pursuits, whereas both wealth in the making

[7] Carlo Antonio Broggia's (1683-1763) *Trattato de' tributi, delle monete e del governo politico della sanità* (treatise on taxes, money, and the policy of public health, 1743) was planned as a comprehensive textbook-like treatment of the three topics indicated in the title. The edition in the Custodi collection separated them and we are interested only in the first which forms a self-contained unit (though there was considerable merit also in Broggia's ideas on money and public health). We know almost nothing about the man—he seems to have been a businessman, or a retired businessman, of considerable acquirements. As a Neapolitan, he may be included in what we have called the Neapolitan school. The most interesting parts of the treatise on taxes are reprinted in the *Economisti Napoletani* of Tagliacozzo, who also presents us with a summary and appraisal of the work that contains references to immediate Italian predecessors of Broggia, especially Pascoli and Bandini—important links in the evolution of fiscal doctrine and analysis that must be neglected, to the fatal injury of the resulting picture, in a sketch like this. A fuller though, perhaps, not quite satisfactory picture both of Broggia's work and of the development in which it was an element may be found in G. Ricca-Salerno, *Storia delle dottrine finanziarie in Italia* (1881).

and labor were to be touched gently. This is why he recommended that money loans to business or monetary business funds (money *impiegato a negozio*) be left untaxed, and why even his direct taxes were not on personal incomes but on 'real' or 'objective' returns—he did give weight to considerations of administrative convenience in this, as Bodin and Botero had done already, but the essential point was to avoid fettering business activity and oppressing 'struggling poverty.' There are three aspects to this: first, a scheme of aims and valuations with which we are not more concerned than we are with all his talk about 'justice'; second, a vision of social and economic conditions and their possibilities which went far below the surface; and, third, analysis, though not made entirely explicit, of economic causes and effects. It is this third point that constitutes the scientific merit of the work.[8]

7. Note on Utopias

A few words will be inserted here on sixteenth- and seventeenth-century state novels (*Staatsromane*)[1] which derive their name—Utopias—from the title of the peak success of the genus, the *Utopia* of Thomas More. This meaning of the term Utopia must be distinguished from the meaning that the Marxist phrase Utopian Socialism is intended to convey. F. Engels (1892) defined 'utopian' in contrast to 'scientific' socialism to denote socialist ideas that are (a) unconnected with an actual mass movement and (b) not based upon any proof of the existence of observable economic forces that tend to realize those ideas. In this sense, Morelly's *Code de la Nature* (1755) is certainly utopian socialism. We have not called it a Utopia, however, not only because this would have restricted the concept to socialist utopias but also because in this book we wish to use the term, except when notice to the contrary is given, for something entirely different—for a distinctive literary type—for artistic creations of a nature that the term state novel suggests and Plato's *Republic* exemplifies. In this sense, description of the blueprint of a socialist or any other kind of society, even though it does not exist, like the one drawn by Morelly, is not a utopia. This type, which, no doubt under Greek influence, was fairly popular in the epoch under review,[2] is difficult to interpret. A literary form may enshrine anything—from a day dream cast into a prose poem to the most realistic analysis. Fortunately it is always possible

[8] Professor Luigi Einaudi credits the physiocrats with having 'created' the pure theory of taxation (*Atti, Reale Accademia delle Scienze di Torino*, 1931-2). But with due deference to Professor Einaudi's authority, I am inclined to think that in Broggia and the literature behind him there seem to be much more valuable elements of such a theory if, indeed, on the strength of the fact that neither he nor any other eighteenth-century writer produced a satisfactory analysis of incidence, we refuse to find in him that theory itself.

[1] [See explanation of *Staatsromane* in ch. 1, sec. 2 of this Part.]

[2] The reader presumably knows, however, that it has never died out, witness the great success of Bellamy's *Looking Backward*, 2000-1887 (1888). But we shall have no occasion to mention any of these more modern Utopias in this book.

to recognize the presence and especially the absence of the latter element, though it is not always possible to say whether what presents itself as a statement of fact or as an imperative is to be understood as 'poetry or as truth.' Only four instances need be mentioned, the works of Francis Bacon, Harrington, Campanella, and More. And the first three may be dismissed at once as irrelevant to our purpose: Bacon's *New Atlantis* (1627), a fragment—a singular deviation from the creed of 'inductive science' preached by its author —and Harrington's *Oceana* (1656) are of no interest at all; to Campanella's *Civitas solis* (City of the Sun, 1623) Platonic rays playing around rather commonplace matter do lend a glamour not its own; [3] but the case of More's *Utopia* is different.[4]

This rich book is full of mature wisdom and has naturally been the object of many different interpretations which, since we are concerned only with one of the many aspects it presents, and with a very minor one at that, we need not stay to discuss. Nor need we enter into More's social criticisms or the general features of his communist scheme of life that facilitates the solution of most economic problems by the postulate of simple and invariant tastes in a population that is kept stationary or almost stationary by regulated or rather enforced emigration—one of the many points of similarity with Plato's *Politeia*. Two things have relevance to analysis, however. First, the general plan of production and distribution of goods: tastes being given, the quantities currently produced, according to government regulations, by all adults except a privileged class of 'learned' men—not quite Plato's guardians, because there is an elected king—are distributed so as to put all districts on a footing of equality on the basis of statistics of current production and by means of a system of public storage. This, whatever else it may mean, is not a bad method to put into evidence the essentials of the functioning of *any* economic organism. In particular, a serviceable theory of money may be derived from this conception, and More hints at this theory by pouring out the vials of humorous wrath on the fetishism of gold and silver, which, unless required for paying for excess imports, Utopia uses only for purposes indicative of More's contempt. Criticism of the popular economics of his day may well have been

[3] Tomaso Campanella (1568-1639); in his preface to Plato's *Politeia*, Jowett presents an abstract. There is also a translation (in H. Morley's *Universal Library*). All works on state novels and most histories of socialist and communist ideas, as well as several monographs, deal with Campanella more or less fully.

[4] Sir Thomas More (1478-1535), the English Lord Chancellor who was beheaded by Henry VIII and canonized 400 years later, was a man of penetrating intelligence, comprehensive (classic) learning, and wide experience, none of which ever killed his good-natured humor; and all of these four qualities went into the making of his *Utopia*, published in Latin in 1516, translated into English (after German, Italian, and French translations had appeared) in 1551. The considerable literature on More, so far as a perfunctory examination permits me to judge, is for the most part not relevant to our purpose. Bonar's *Philosophy and Political Economy* will tell the interested reader all that has any bearing upon economics as such. Reference may, however, be made also to E. Dermenghem, *Thomas Morus et les utopistes de la renaissance* (1927).

one of the major aims of this construction. Second, his criticism of economic conditions, though most weighty in legal and especially penological matters, were interspersed with diagnoses and formulations some of which may be ranked as contributions to analysis. The tracing of unemployment to enclosures, though always a half truth, was not, in 1516, the commonplace it became soon afterwards. And he introduced the word and concept of oligopoly in exactly the same sense in which we use it now.

CHAPTER 4

The Econometricians and Turgot [1]

The individuals and groups to be discussed in this chapter were also Consultant Administrators, though not of the academic type, and some of them qualify in addition as philosophers of natural law. Nevertheless, it was not only to relieve a chapter already overloaded with names that they have been reserved for separate treatment. Except for the great figure of Turgot, which is to come in at the end of the chapter, they have something in common that makes it desirable to marshal them into a connected array—the spirit of numerical analysis. They were Econometricians. In fact their works illustrate to perfection what Econometrics is and what Econometricians are trying to do.[2]

1. Political Arithmetick

Repeatedly we have had occasion to observe that, with economists of all types but especially with the Consultant Administrators, factual investigation was the primary task that absorbed most of the available manpower and progressed more satisfactorily than did such 'theory' as there was. This was so from the first, as such representative examples as Botero and Ortiz suffice to show. However, in the seventeenth and eighteenth centuries, a type of teaching developed, especially at the German universities, that specialized in purely descriptive presentation of the facts relevant to public administration. A German professor, Hermann Conring (1606-81), is usually credited with having been the first to give lectures of this kind. Another, Gottfried Achenwall (1719-72), who did the same, introduced the term Statistics. These 'statistics'

[1] [J. A. S. had originally entitled this chapter 'The Econometricians'; on the typescript he added 'and Turgot?' in pencil.]

[2] The word Econometrics is, I think, Professor Frisch's, and it has been coined by analogy with Biometrics, statistical biology. A distinctive name, embodying a program, is perfectly justified in this case (see the first number of *Econometrica*, January 1933, on the foundation and aims of the Econometric Society). And so we may leave it at that, though the term is exposed to objection on philological grounds: it ought to be either Ecometrics or Economometrics.

did not present figures primarily but rather non-numerical facts, and therefore had nothing to do, in the hands of those professors, with what we now call statistical method. But the purpose of this information was much the same as that which our figures, treated by somewhat more refined methods, are calculated to serve. The definition of statistics adopted as late as 1838 by the Royal Statistical Society—to give it its present title—still turned upon 'illustration of the conditions and prospects of society,' and thus covered the work of Conring and Achenwall quite well.[1] But—alas for the academic profession! —the really interesting development did not start from it.

The decisive impulse came from a small English group led and inspired by Sir William Petty.[2] The nature both of what he called Political Arithmetick and of his personal contribution to it has been formulated with unsurpassable fairness by one of his ablest followers, Davenant[3] (*Of the Use of Political Arithmetick*, *Works*, I, p. 128): 'By Political Arithmetick we mean the art of reasoning by figures upon things relating to government. . . The art itself is

[1] Since statistics came to mean sometimes various bodies of facts, and sometimes various types of methods, there is nothing surprising in the number of different definitions that have been proposed by different workers from their different standpoints. The German statistician Engel, whom we shall meet again on a more important occasion, once put that number as high as 180. See G. Loyo, *Evolución de la definición de estadistica*, Publicación 44 of the Instituto Panamérico de Geografia e Historía (1939).

[2] Petty (1623-87) was a self-made man—physician, surgeon, mathematician, theoretical engineer, member of parliament, public servant, and businessman—one of those vital people who make a success of almost everything they touch, even of their failures. Though he paid the price of his versatility, his is one of the great names in the history of economics. But as regards his posthumous fame, luck lent its aid to merit. Marx's decree to the effect that Petty was the founder of economics added socialist applause to bourgeois eulogies initiated by Roscher in 1857. Thus, economists whom no other topic could unite, among them many who were complete strangers to the real meaning of Petty's message, have ever since joined forces in extolling him, Germans even more than Englishmen. Perusal of Lord E. Fitzmaurice's *Life* (1895) is recommended. Of Petty's writings the following are of prime importance for us: *A Treatise of Taxes and Contributions* (1662); *Verbum Sapienti* (written 1665, publ. 1691); *Political Anatomy of Ireland* (1672); *Political Arithmetick* (written 1676, publ. 1690); *Quantulumcunque concerning Money* (written 1682); *Essays on Political Arithmetick* (written 1671-87); all republished in *The Economic Writings of Sir William Petty*, by C. H. Hull (1899). This edition also contains the celebrated *Natural and Political Observations . . . upon the Bills of Mortality*, originally published (1662) by John Graunt. A long and inconclusive controversy has been waged on the question of Petty's share in this performance, which may be looked upon as the fountainhead of modern demography, though Graunt should not, on this account, be called the 'founder' of statistics. Lord E. Fitzmaurice's *Life* has been supplemented by the Marquis of Lansdowne's editions of the *Petty Papers* (1927) and of the *Petty-Southwell Correspondence*, 1676-87 (1928).

[3] The name of Charles Davenant (1656-1714) moves slowly into the front-rank position that belongs to him but it has not quite arrived there as yet. He was a public servant but also a politician, thrice elected M.P., and, as such, a violent enemy of the Whigs rather than a violent Tory: perhaps it is this and the effects of this on some

undoubtedly very ancient. . . [But Petty] first gave it that name and brought it into rules and methods.' It will be seen that the 'methods'—which of course he did not invent either but, as it were, helped into consciousness—do not consist in replacing reasoning by the assembling of facts. Petty was no victim of the slogan: let facts speak for themselves. Petty was first and last a theorist. But he was one of those theorists for whom science is indeed measurement; who forge analytic tools that will work with numerical facts and heartily despise any others; whose generalizations are the joint products of figures and reasoning that are never allowed to part company. The relation of this procedure to that of the physical sciences—and to Newtonian principles, in particular—is so obvious as to make it necessary to emphasize that Petty displayed no propensity to borrow from them or even to strengthen his case by doubtful analogies with them. He simply proposed 'instead of using only comparative and superlative words and intellectual arguments . . . to express [himself] in terms of number, weight and measure.' No less obvious is it that he was acutely aware of the polemical aspects of his methodological creed. He was quite ready to fight for it and to start what would have been the first controversy on 'method.' But nobody attacked. A few followed. Many admired. And the vast majority very quickly forgot. That is to say, economists did not forget the name; they even remembered individual views of Petty's on various practical issues and some of his theories—precisely those that were couched in mere

---

of his writings that interfered with his recognition. There also was something else. Those historians who ask 'What does a man stand for?' did not quite know what to make of him. On the one hand, the 'liberals' among them were delighted when they hit upon such phrases as that trade is by nature free, that it finds its own channels, that laws which limit or regulate it are seldom advantageous to the public (though they may serve individual interests), and that money was a mere counter. On the other hand, they were grieved to find in him so much about regulative policy that they had to class him as an adherent of a (nonexisting) 'mercantilist theory.' Some accounted for what they took to be a self-contradictory attitude by the hypothesis that in those earlier writings in which the 'liberal' passages occur, Davenant spoke his mind freely whereas, later on, in office especially, he turned opportunist. We shall see later (below, ch. 7) that there is another explanation, viz., that he was a good economist. His *Works* have been (incompletely) edited by Sir Charles Whitworth (1771). Additional ones have since emerged, the latest find being published under the title *Two Manuscripts by Charles Davenant*, 1942 (A *Reprint of Economic Tracts*, ed. by Professor G. Heberton Evans, Jr., with an instructive introduction by Professor Usher). Also see Y. Ballière, *L'Oeuvre économique de Charles Davenant* (1913). His contributions to economic analysis amount to an impressive total and may be classified as follows: (1) there is, implicit but clear, behind all his writings the awareness of the logic of the relations by which things economic hang together, a merit that is somewhat, but not necessarily much, reduced by the priority of Child, Barbon, and also others; (2) he substantially improved, though only by what may be called a case method, his epoch's acquirements in the theories of money and of international trade and finance; (3) he was one of the first authorities of his time on public finance—taxes, debts, and so on; (4) he was one of the few who understood, and co-operated in, the work of Political Arithmetick. Individual points will be noticed in subsequent chapters.

slogans. It was the inspiring message, the suggestive program, which wilted in the wooden hands of the Scottish professor and was practically lost to most economists for 250 years: A. Smith took the safe side that was so congenial to him when he declared (*Wealth*, Book IV, ch. 5) that he placed not much faith in Political Arithmetick.

Not lost, however, was the impulse given to vital statistics and thus indirectly to statistics in general. In this, the chief or even sole merit is now usually attributed to Graunt (see footnote 2 above).

In the next chapter we shall touch upon the controversies of that period on the subject of the growth (or decline!) of population which until the census of 1801 was, in England at least, a matter of conjecture. This, however, was only one of the problems that Graunt's or Petty's achievement put into a more promising shape by means of the 'bills of mortality' drawn from parish registers. Computations of the chance of survival with application to insurance, of the influence of inoculation on longevity, of the relation of the sexes at birth, and of the average duration of marriage in relation to the ages of husband and wife are examples taken at random from a large field of research that was to be taken into cultivation within the subsequent hundred years on the lines chalked out by Graunt's book. Nor is his merit adequately characterized by calling him the 'Columbus of the mortality bills.' It is perhaps still more to his credit that he displayed a sense of the methodological nature of those mass phenomena that may be described by 'laws' although the individual elements of them are fortuitous. It must suffice to mention the main stepping stones of further progress. The first to inquire with exactness into the problem of chances of survival was E. Halley (*An Estimate of the Degrees of the Mortality of Mankind*, 1693). J. P. Süssmilch (*Die göttliche Ordnung in den Veränderungen des menschlichen Geschlechts . . .* , 1740) may be said to have put vital statistics definitely on its feet by developing and systematizing the work of his English predecessors. The theory of probability, the basis of statistical method, was developed by Jacques Bernoulli (1654-1705; *Ars conjectandi*, 1713) and still further by his nephews Nicholas (1687-1759) and Daniel Bernoulli (1700-1782), who also worked out further applications. In view of the close alliance between modern economics and not only the material but also the methods of statistics, it is highly regrettable that we cannot follow this line of advance any further. The reader may, however, glean most of what is wanting here from a study of H. L. Westergaard's excellent *Contributions to the History of Statistics* (1932).

More important for economics proper was another performance that illustrates the curious obtuseness (just lamented) of economists: Gregory King's (1648-1712) law of demand for wheat.[4] It refers to deviations from an assumed

[4] *Natural and Political Observations and Conclusions upon the State and Condition of England in* 1696 (sec. VII). This work, a pioneer of quantitative economics and one of the best examples of what Political Arithmetick stood for, was not published by the author. Davenant incorporated some parts of it in his *Essay upon the Probable Methods of Making a People Gainers in the Ballance of Trade* (1699), but the whole was not presented to the public before 1804, when George Chalmers published it with a life of the author. The first five sections deal with the number of inhabitants, ingeniously inferred from hearth-tax returns, age distribution, marital status, mortality in cities and the country, and cognate matters. Sections VIII-XIII are devoted to matters

normal and states that if the harvest falls short of this normal by 1, 2, 3, 4, or 5-tenths, the price will rise above what we should call its trend value—which King, however, assumed to be constant, at least, for many years together—by 3, 8, 16, 28, or 45-tenths. From this an equation, explicitly giving the law of demand implied, can easily be derived.[5] The remarkable thing is that King, though he did not attempt any further refinements, evidently understood the problem perfectly; that he worked with deviations from a normal is a particularly interesting touch. Still more remarkable is it that, in spite of the general notoriety that 'King's law' was to gain, it did not occur to economists either to improve upon it—though all that was required was to proceed further on a line unmistakably chalked out—or to apply the same method to other commodities until the work of H. L. Moore, 1914 (see below, Part IV, chs. 5 and 7) released the avalanche of statistical demand curves of our own time—a lag of over 200 years. Do not let us forget, however, the econometric work done elsewhere, for example, in Italy, by such men as Verri or Carli.

To return to Petty. All or most of his writings were prompted by the practical problems of his time and country—problems of taxation, of money, of the policy of international trade particularly with a view to getting the better of the Dutch, and so on. The superior quality of his mind shows in all his comments and suggestions, but there is nothing very striking or very original or very distinctive about them: they represented the views that were then current, or rapidly becoming current, among the best English economists. Nor is there anything distinctive in the fact itself that Petty no doubt reasoned from a more or less clearly perceived set of principles or theoretical schema; several of his contemporaries did that, and his schema was no more articulate than were theirs. There was something, however, that was specifically his own and in which his mental energy and theoretical talent asserted themselves conspicuously: as already observed, he hammered out concepts from, and in connection with, statistical investigations, and in doing so he got further at some points than did any of his contemporaries. His concept of velocity of money is—rightly—the most famous example and will be mentioned again in Chapter 6. Another example is his work on national income: he did not bother about its definition, but he recognized its analytic importance and he tried to figure it out. Modern income analysis may be said, in this sense, to start with him, though it seems on the whole better to trace it to Quesnay (see below, sec. 3). A third example is this: everyone knows the phrase that has been repeated *ad nauseam*, 'labor is the father . . . of wealth, as lands are

---

of public finance. From our standpoint, sections VI and VII are the most important. Besides the famous demand schedule, they contain other noteworthy contributions, such as his estimates of the income and expenditure of the nation in 1688, of meat consumption, and of the quantity of gold and silver in England and other countries.

[5] It has been calculated by G. U. Yule ('Crop Production and Prices: A Note on Gregory King's Law,' *Journal of the Royal Statistical Society*, 1915, p. 296 et seq.) at $y = -2.33x + 0.05x^2 - 0.00167x^3$.

the mother.' This means that he put on their feet the two 'original factors of production' of later theorists. Illogically dropping the mother, he declared elsewhere that capital (the 'wealth, stock, or provision of the nation') is the product of past labor—which brings to mind James Mill's blundering reformulation of Ricardo.[6] But it cannot be repeated too often that in themselves, and without the developments that make them valuable, such suggestions amount to very little. What does amount to something is his research on a 'natural par' between land and labor, that is to stay, his attempt, foreshadowing the much more thorough-going one of Cantillon, to relate the values of land and labor by equating a piece of land that will produce a 'day's food of an adult man' (with certain corrections) to the day's labor of such a man. If technological and all other conditions of production and consumption remained severely the same, this procedure might give us the economic philosopher's stone—the unit of measurement by which to reduce the available quantities of the two 'original factors,' land and labor, to a homogeneous quantity of 'productive power' that could be expressed by one figure, and the unit of which might serve as a land-labor standard of value. As it is, this interesting venture, like all similar ones, proved to be a blind alley.

Of course, this was no explanation of the phenomenon of value, still less a labor theory of value—if anything, it was a land theory of value. On division of labor, however, we find all the essentials of what Adam Smith was to say about it, including its dependence upon the size of markets. Pricing is dealt with sketchily. Contrary to Marxist opinion, there is no theory of wages (unless we choose to dignify by this name the proposition that laborers 'should' never get more than a subsistence minimum because if they got double as much they would reduce their work to half!) and no exploitation theory of surplus value or of rent (unless we choose to dignify by these names the trivial propositions that there would be no surplus if the laborers claimed the whole product, that the rent of land is what is left after costs of production have been defrayed, and that it increases as, with increasing demand, corn must be brought from greater distances).[7] There is, however, at least in a particular instance that is not too well framed, a perception of the tendency toward equalization of returns as between industries.[8] Although it lacks the reference to margins,

[6] See below, Part III, ch. 6.

[7] *Treatise of Taxes*, ch. 5. This 'discovery' of the rent of location zealous admirers may easily construe so as to imply decreasing returns and, in the end, the *whole* of the Ricardian theory. Only, this would be quite unhistorical.

[8] The argument, a rather interesting illustration of the ways of primitive analysis, is simply this: if, *by the same amount of labor*, one man produces corn and another man produces silver, then both will in general be left with some corn or silver after the usual deductions have been made (he also deducts the necessary consumption of the producers or, alternatively, assumes that the silver producer, besides producing silver, has also supplied himself with the means for that necessary consumption). Now Petty holds that the values of these two net returns must necessarily be equal and, since silver is the monetary metal, this equality determines the money price of corn, hence the monetary value of the corn 'rent.' As a useful exercise, the reader should work out precisely

which would be necessary to make the theorem tenable, we have here in fact a contribution toward the explanation of the business mechanism.

Finally, Petty's theory of interest, so far as he can be said to have had one, points back to the scholastics. Direct influence is not quite impossible, since he received part of his education at the Jesuit college at Caen. There is, on the one hand, his statement that foreign exchange is 'local interest,' which suggests, though he does not say so quite explicitly, that he would have agreed to the phrasing that interest is 'exchange over time'—the scholastic doctors considered, though they did not accept, an explanation on this line. And there is, on the other hand, Petty's explicit statement to the effect that interest is a compensation 'for forbearing the use of your own money for a term of time agreed upon whatsoever need you may have of it meanwhile." This, especially if considered in the light of his disapproval of interest on money that the lender may claim at any time, is simply late scholastic doctrine. His various and not always felicitous considerations about the relation between interest and the rent of land—where he conspicuously failed to make an obvious contribution, namely, to derive the value of land by means of discounting its net return by the prevailing rate of interest—also recall scholastic arguments, although no outside influence need be invoked in order to understand why this problem should obtrude itself to any analyst.

2. Boisguillebert and Cantillon

Though, as a leader in the field of public finance, we have met Boisguillebert already and though, as a leader in the field of money, we shall meet him again before long, it is desirable not to miss him in the scenery we are trying to visualize now [1] as an important figure in the field of 'general theory.' He

why this argument is unsatisfactory and especially why it does not explain anything about the rent of land. This argument has sometimes been used in support of an attempt to credit Petty with a labor theory of value—the values of corn and silver being compared by means of the labor hours they embody. Our opinion on this matter will depend on the weight we are prepared to attribute to incidental use of such a standard of comparison. Petty's father-and-mother slogan does not point in this direction.

[1] Pierre le Pesant, Sieur de Boisguillebert (1646-1714), was a public-spirited member of the semi-hereditary civil-service gentry of prerevolutionary France (*noblesse de robe*) and lived mostly in Normandy removed from all the Paris influences that might have interfered with the originality of his ideas. Though, as we know, chiefly preoccupied with the problems of French fiscal policy and nearly as fact-minded as was Vauban, he differed from the latter not only in the much wider scope of his interests but also in the fact that he was theoretically articulate—perhaps more so than any writer before Cantillon. His chief works (*Le Détail de la France; Le Factum de la France; Traité de la nature, culture, commerce et interêt des grains; Causes de la rareté de l'argent; Dissertation sur la nature des richesses, de l'argent et des tributs*) were re-edited, by Eugène Daire, in *Économistes financiers du XVIIIe siècle* (*Collection des principaux économistes*, publ. by Guillaumin, 1843). Daire's prefatory note to this edition, so far as I know, is the first document of that Boisguillebert cult, the manifestations of which contrast so curiously with (and are in fact only explainable by) the persistent neglect

has been called a precursor of the physiocrats, and it is easy to see why: on the one hand, he was an energetic sponsor of the agricultural interest; on the other hand, we find in his pages such phrases as: all that is necessary is *laissez faire la nature et la liberté*. But though these facts do suffice to put him into line with the political thought of the physiocrats, they do not suffice to make him the ancestor of specifically physiocrat analysis. There is analytic affinity between his and Quesnay's views on money (see below, ch. 6) but on the whole, it seems better not to stress the relation too much. He was one more of those authors who saw the economic organism as an equilibrium system of interdependent economic magnitudes and who constructed this system from the angle of consumption—getting further, perhaps, than anyone before Cantillon. His economic sociology turned, in an almost Marxist spirit, upon two social classes, rich and poor, the existence of which he explained in a way that was to become quite common as the eighteenth century wore on. The stronger individuals, by *crime et violence*, get hold of the means of production and then do not want to work any more; also—a very modern touch that the reader will not fail to appreciate—these strong robbers, who have become rich, tend to stock money rather than goods (*hoarded* money, the 'moloch of the world'!), and thereby depreciate real wealth and disturb the current of economic life. The economic principle of order he found in competition quite as clearly as did A. Smith more than half a century later. From the standpoint of analysis, this is decisive. That, on the strength of this, he did not (as did A. Smith) espouse unconditional free trade is immaterial, for into this practical conclusion enter so many other considerations and, in addition, so many personal preferences that its acceptance or rejection per se proves nothing for or against a man's analysis. But though his conception of competitive 'proportionate equilibrium' was as definite as A. Smith's, it was not more so: it did not occur to him to define it or to investigate its properties. Defining *richesse*, as Cantillon was to do, as the *jouissance* of everything that can give satisfaction (*plaisir*), he declared, as had Petty, that this wealth had no other sources

---

of Boisguillebert's performance by the vast majority of economists. Daire considered him to be the first in the 'learned chain,' the further links of which are Quesnay, Smith, Ricardo, and Rossi (!); Boisguillebert was the Columbus *du monde économique*, and so on and so forth. In a more reasonable manner, this cult was revived by Professor H. W. C. Bordewijk in his excellent *Theoretisch-historische Inleidingtot de Economie* (1931). But Miss Roberts, in an otherwise very meritorious book (*Boisguilbert: Economist of the Reign of Louis XIV*, 1935), displays a bad case of what Lord Macaulay called the illness of biographers or lues Boswelliana. It was, however, a rebuke administered to me by Professor A. Gray in a review of Miss Roberts' book (*Economic History*, 1937) for not having, in an old essay of mine, paid due respect to Boisguillebert that sent me back to Boisguillebert's writings and in fact changed my own opinion of him. Also, see F. Cadet, *Pierre de Boisguilbert, précurseur des économistes* [i.e. of the physiocrats] (1870); A. Talbot, *Les Théories de Boisguilbert et leur place dans l'histoire des doctrines économiques* (1903); R. Durand, *Essai sur les théories monétaires de Pierre de Boisguilbert* [which is, perhaps, the more correct spelling] (1922).

but land and labor,[2] and then simply went on to say that the process of incessant transformation of land and labor into consumers' goods will normally function without hitches if all commodities and services are produced on the unfettered initiative of competing producers—as if this did not require any proof. The first to attempt a (primitive) mathematical definition of equilibrium and a (also primitive) mathematical proof of that proposition was Isnard, who has as yet to conquer the position in the history of economic theory that is due him [3] as a precursor of Léon Walras.

Cantillon's great work [4] fared better both because of its well-rounded sys-

[2] Petty, nevertheless, considered capital as accumulated labor. Boisguillebert's set-up, however, is an early case of the 'resolution' of produced means of production into services of natural agents and labor that was to be a central feature of Böhm-Bawerk's theoretical scheme (see below, Part IV, ch. 6), but Boisguillebert did not try to exploit this conception analytically.

[3] Achille Nicolas Isnard, an engineer about whom practically nothing is known, not even the exact dates of his birth and death, and who does not rate an article in the *Encyclopaedia of the Social Sciences,* wrote, besides another work that does not concern us, a *Traité des richesses* (1781) that seems to have been rescued from oblivion by a lucky chance: Jevons included it in his list of writings on mathematical economics that he appended to his *Theory of Political Economy.* The (almost) complete neglect of Isnard's work is understandable, however, because the historic performance mentioned in the text is embedded in a conventional argument against physiocrat doctrines and other neither very original nor very interesting matter. Owing to the weakness in our field of the specifically scientific interest, progress on this fundamental line was almost unbelievably slow.

[4] Richard Cantillon (the date of his birth is uncertain, but is usually given as 1680; he died, presumably murdered, in 1734) was a Paris banker of Irish extraction. He influenced French economists much more than English ones. He was indeed plagiarized by some Englishmen and recognized by others, among the latter being A. Smith. But he had to be practically rediscovered by W. S. Jevons ('Richard Cantillon and the Nationality of Political Economy,' *Contemporary Review,* 1881), whereas in France he was never quite lost sight of. Thus, his influence is obvious in Canard's *Principes d'économie politique* (1801), which, with apologies to the *Académie* that 'crowned' it—the same *Académie* that ignored Cournot and Walras—we shall only briefly mention again. On these grounds I class him as French, but I admit that anyone interested in such questions as the 'nationality' of a science can make out a strong case for claiming this Irish Frenchman as an English economist because of his descent from Petty. The *Essai sur la nature du commerce en général* is supposed to have been written about 1730 and was, though in a very unconventional sense, 'published' soon after; that is to say, the manuscript circulated and exerted influence soon after. (This meant a lot in a small and highly concentrated professional circle.) The date of its actual (posthumous) publication, 1755, therefore has not the usual significance; there is a Harvard University reprint (1892) and an English trans. under the auspices of the Royal Economic Society (1932). See H. Higgs, 'Richard Cantillon,' *Economic Journal,* June 1891. I do not know of any other good study on our author unless it be the very useful article in *Palgrave's Dictionary.* Jevons' estimate fails by overstatement. In particular nothing could be more infelicitous than to call the *Essai* the 'cradle' of Economics: this is precisely what it was not. There is a brief 'Biographical Note on Richard Cantillon' in the *Economic Journal,* April 1944, by Joseph Hone.

tematic or even didactic form and because it had the good fortune to gain, long before its actual publication (see footnote 4), the enthusiastic approval and the effective support of two very influential men, Gournay and Mirabeau. What Petty failed to accomplish—but for what he had offered almost all the essential ideas—lies accomplished before us in Cantillon's *Essai*. True, it was not accomplished in the style of a pupil who at every step looks back over his shoulder for the master's guidance, but in the style of an intellectual peer who strides along confidently according to his own lights. Likewise, Quesnay strode on according to his own lights and was no more a mere pupil of Cantillon than Cantillon was of Petty. Nevertheless, few sequences in the history of economic analysis are so important for us to see, to understand, and to fix in our minds, as is the sequence: Petty-Cantillon-Quesnay. Cantillon's econometric zeal derived its direction from Petty. The supplement to his *Essai* which contained his computations has unfortunately been lost. But, as we shall presently see, the results presented in its text suffice to show that it was Petty's problems—mainly the 'par' between land and labor—and Petty's methods which inspired them. Moreover, dependence or possible dependence—there can be no certainty about it—extends beyond such important individual points as the theory of velocity of circulation or the theory of population to the fundamental features of the general theoretical set-up. Exactly the same conclusion will be seen to apply to the relation of Quesnay's work to Cantillon's. Affinity is obvious, differences being not less revelatory of it than are agreements: for a man may learn from another by criticizing him just as well as by accepting his teaching, and some of Quesnay's views look indeed as if they had been derived from Cantillon by the former method. And, again, it is precisely the fundamental features of Quesnay's analytic set-up that are unmistakably foreshadowed in Cantillon's work. An analogy may be helpful: Cantillon was to Quesnay, and Petty was to Cantillon, what Ricardo was to Marx. This leaves out Boisguillebert, though there are important affinities between him and Cantillon and, as regards money, between him and Quesnay. But just now it seems important to focus the reader's attention on one strong and simple line of development. The only way to raise all this above vague generalities is to take a bird's-eye view of Cantillon's work or, to phrase it differently, to present a Readers' Guide. This is what I proceed to do.

The First Part contains the fundamentals of the analytic structure. In the first chapter we get the general layout by means of the key concepts—land, labor, and wealth. Exactly as with Petty, and just as misleadingly, land, the source of material, and labor, the form-giving or productive agent, enter on equal terms to turn out wealth which *n'est autre chose que la nourriture, les commodités et les agrémens de la vie* (Boisguillebert's definition). Chapters 2-6 present what to all intents and purposes is an economic sociology. We get first a theory of social classes: ownership of land—itself based upon conquest and violence as with Boisguillebert—creates the three fundamental 'natural' classes of landlords, farmers, and laborers (traders and entrepreneurs do come in, along with artists, robbers, lawyers, beggars; but they are added to this schema, not really fitted into it). Then we get a very interesting theory of the origin of villages, the emergence of townships (Cantillon adopted a 'market theory' of towns, the theory that makes them develop first from periodical, then from permanent markets), cities, and capital cities. Besides creating the form in which many a nineteenth-century textbook was cast (in a sense even Alfred Marshall's treatise), Cantillon thus clearly proved his awareness of the fact, which smaller minds so often failed to grasp, namely, that the problems of any analytic social science necessarily divide up into two methodologically different groups: the group that centers in the question how the actual behavior of people produces the social phenomena we observe, and the group that centers in the question how that behavior came to be what it is. In Chapter 3 we also learn something about location—this is perhaps the first attempt (if we neglect embryonic considerations in the agricultural literature) at making some headway in this field.

Transition to pure economics—the economics that deals with behavior within the social framework described—is effected in Chapters 7-9 where Cantillon, for future reference, settles a number of preliminary questions concerning (a) differences in remuneration as between laborers and artisans and as between artisans in different employments, and (b) population. The former subject was to be a favorite with later writers, particularly A. Smith, and became a standard topic in the standard text of the nineteenth century. The latter subject will have to be dealt with in the chapter on population, wages and employment which follows. But it is just as well to record here, by anticipation, that Cantillon (clearly developing views of Petty) lets population, on the one hand, adapt itself to the demand for labor and, on the other hand, be regulated by a law of minimum-of-existence wages, so that his authority might be claimed for a Malthusian view were it not for the fact that he also (in this still more like Petty) looked upon labor as the 'natural riches' of a nation (ch. 16). This last points in a different direction, though there is really no contradiction between the two ideas. Both had become common doctrine in the seventeenth century.

Having thus prepared the ground, our author presents (ch. 10) a cost theory of normal price or value (*valeur intrinsèque*: never mind the objectionable word, it is quite harmless). This, if anything, falls short of the theory of the scholastics except that Cantillon, going through with Petty's theory, defined his cost in terms of the quantities of land and labor which enter into the production of each commodity. The obvious problem thus raised—we might call it Petty's problem—which Ricardo tried to dodge by eliminating land (see below, Part III, ch. 6) so as to be left with one factor only, Cantillon tackles in Chapter 11 by the alternative expedient: labor is reduced to land by the consideration that the labor *du plus vil Esclave adulte vaut au moins . . . la quantité de terre* that must be employed to provide for his needs. Or, rather, since according to Halley's tables about half the children died before reaching the age of 17 (and also for other reasons) it was roughly double that quantity. Other laborers get more than the *plus vil Esclave,* but this is either because their labor costs more land to produce or because their remuneration is subject to risk. The figures on workmen's budgets that Cantillon held to justify this estimate were in the lost supplement, but we must in any case credit Cantillon with having made the first important step in this particular field of research that was to develop considerably before the century was over. For the rest, it is not necessary to enter here into criticism either of the land-labor theory of value itself (if such it may be called) or of the particular attempt to make it numerically operative. As far as this goes, it must suffice to say that the latter is not what it seems to be, that is, complete nonsense, and that success on this line is not out of the question at some distant future. Let us repeat, however, first, that the really important thing is the message of econometric research that comes to us from this attempt—the message that *numerical* calculations must be at the basis of any science, however 'theoretical,' that is quantitative by nature; and, second, that the *arpents* of land per year (1 arpent = 330 sq. ft.) played exactly the same role in Cantillon's analysis that days of labor played in Ricardo's. And let us add that we have here the positive kernel of Quesnay's theory of normal value: his philosophies about the value-creating powers of nature added as little to the operative content of the Petty-Cantillon theory as Marx's philosophies about the value-creating power of labor added to the operative content of the Ricardo theory.

With the deviations of actual prices from this norm—that he reduced from cost in terms of land and labor to cost in terms of land alone—Cantillon dealt very carefully. There is nothing in the *Essai* that could rank as a theory of monopoly, which is the more serious because, as will be evident from the rest of our narrative, Cantillon reasoned on the hypothesis of the most perfect of perfect competitions so that any imperfections in it naturally acquire particular importance. But there is a lot about temporary deviations because of other reasons, that is, Cantillon paid much attention to the problem of market price as distinguished from normal price—exactly as did A. Smith later on. One feature of his treatment is worth noting because it persisted practically to J. S. Mill. Like all 'classics' of the nineteenth century, Ricardo especially, Cantillon never asked the question *how* market price is related to normal price and precisely *how* the latter emerges—if indeed it does emerge—from the supply and demand mechanism that produces the former. Taking this relation for granted, he was led to treat market price as a separate phenomenon *and to restrict the supply and demand explanation to it.* Thus emerged the superficial and, as the later development of the theory of value was to show, misleading formula—normal price is determined by cost, market price is determined by supply and demand—of which we shall see more in Part III.

Going on, we see Quesnay's figure still more clearly looming in the future, and Boisguillebert's no less clearly looming in the past. All the classes (*ordres*) of society and all the men in a state subsist or enrich themselves at the expense of the landowners (ch. 12). In the light of Chapter 14, this will be seen to mean no more than that, whereas every other income item is being balanced by a cost item, including in costs the necessary living expenses of the receiver, the landowners' rent is the only one that is not so balanced because, to use a later phrase, it is a return to a 'costless,' that is, non-produced, natural factor. Therefore, income from land, not being bound to certain more or less predetermined uses, can be spent in any way that the whims of the landowners may suggest. Its expenditure is the undetermined and, precisely because of this, the determining and active factor in the total of national consumption—hence also in the total of national production, so that everyone's economic fate depends upon *les humeurs, les modes et les façons de vivre* of the prince and the landowning aristocracy. These *humeurs* determine *les usages auxquels on emploie les terres*, and, in particular, how many people will be employed and able to make a living in a country (ch. 15), and how its balance of trade will look if both sides of it are measured in terms of land—which is the criterion he applied for judging the advantage or disadvantage a country derives from foreign trade. Not all of this reappears in physiocrat writings, not, for example, the last-mentioned point. But most of it does, and it is therefore desirable to make it quite clear what we are to think of it. Several aspects must be distinguished. First there is the theorem that pure rent is a net return that is explained by the productivity of scarce natural agents: this is a true and valuable proposition to which, after many wanderings, theory returned about 1870. Second, there is the statement that this net return is the only one, and that it is therefore agriculture which produces the whole net income of society, no other economic activity producing any of it. This, on the face of it, is wrong but—like the labor theory of value—it can be made true by the introduction of a sufficient number of auxiliary assumptions or postulates—such as absolutely perfect competition, stationary state, absence of urban rent, minimum-of-existence wages so that labor becomes a product of what the laborer consumes, and others [5]—which, however, destroy the statement's practical value. Third, there is the emphasis upon the importance of this net income's being promptly spent in order to keep the economic process going. This point played a small role with Cantillon but more with Boisguillebert before him and with Quesnay after him. And fourth, there is the emphasis—that is specifically Cantillon's—upon the way in which the net income is spent. A common-sense case can obviously be made out for this, especially for the society that stood before Cantillon's eyes.

Now, the *produit de la terre* is, so Cantillon asserted, divided into

[5] The reader will derive benefit from working them out fully.

three approximately equal parts (*les trois rentes*), one-third replacing the farmer's outlays, including his own necessary keep, another third going to him as 'profits,' and the last third to the *seigneurs*. These landlords spend the equivalent of their third of the product of land in the towns where approximately half of the total population is supposed to live. The farmers also spend something on the manufactures produced in the towns, namely, one-fourth of their two-thirds. Thus, the equivalent of one-half ($\frac{1}{3} + \frac{1}{6}$) of the total product of agriculture finds its way to the towns, into the hands of the *marchands et entrepreneurs*, who expend it in turn on foodstuffs and raw materials and so on. Interpretation of this schema, for which Cantillon himself claims no more than the value of a very rough thumb-nail sketch, presents various difficulties into which we cannot enter. But it also presents many points of interest, of which we shall mention two.

First, Cantillon had a clear conception of the function of the entrepreneur (ch. 13). It was quite general, but he analyzed it with particular care for the case of the farmer. The farmer pays out contractual incomes, which are therefore 'certain,' to landlords and laborers; he sells at prices that are 'uncertain.' So do drapers and other 'merchants': they all commit themselves to certain payments in expectation of uncertain receipts and are therefore essentially risk-bearing directors of production and trade, competition tending to reduce their remuneration to the normal value of their services. This, of course, is scholastic doctrine. But nobody before Cantillon had formulated it so fully. And it may be due to him that French economists, unlike the English, never lost sight of the entrepreneurial function and its central importance. Though presumably Cantillon had never heard of Molina and though there is nothing to show that he actually influenced J. B. Say, it is none the less true that 'objectively' his performance on this point—and this was not suggested by Petty nor developed by Quesnay—is the link between those two. Second, if we look once more at Cantillon's sequence of payments and deliveries, which starts from the tripartite division of the gross product or revenue of farming—the *trois rentes*—and, through a number of definite stations, takes us back again to its starting point, the farmers, we immediately feel that we are beholding something that is novel, something that is not explicitly present in the schemes of Cantillon's predecessors or contemporaries—not even in Petty's—or in fact in the schemes of most theorists of any time. From them, we get indeed statements of general principles that govern the economic process. But they leave it to us to visualize this process itself as it runs its course between social groups or classes. Cantillon was the first to make this circular flow concrete and explicit, to give us a bird's-eye view of economic life. In other words, he was the first to draw a *tableau économique*. And, barring differences that hardly affect essentials, this *tableau* is the same as Quesnay's, though Cantillon did not actually condense it into a table. Cantillon's priority is thus beyond question as regards the 'invention' that Mirabeau, indulging as usual his generous ardors, compared in importance to the 'invention' of writing. But since Quesnay's formulation is so much more famous we shall add what there is to add in connection with his work.

It stands to reason that the *tableau* method offers special opportunities for investigating monetary phenomena, especially velocity of circulation—this is one of its chief advantages. In fact, Cantillon is at his best in this field. Chapter 17 of Part I, which presents the fundamentals of monetary theory, is not particularly original: we get pretty much the old stuff, including the divisibility, portability, et cetera, of gold and silver that recommend them for the monetary function. But the whole of Part II (which, however, also includes the theories of barter, market price, and so on) is devoted to money, credit, and interest, and so is much of Part III (mainly on foreign trade), where we find Cantillon's analysis of banks, bank credit, and coinage. Consideration of the main items of this brilliant performance, which in most respects stood unsurpassed for about a century—the automatic mechanism that distributes the monetary metals internationally is, for example, almost faultlessly described, an achievement usually credited to Hume—will however be reserved for subsequent chapters.[6]

3. The Physiocrats

[(a) *Quesnay and the Disciples.*] The small group of French economists and political philosophers who were known in their own day as *Les économistes* and are known to the history of economics as Physiocrats presents strongly characteristic features to even the most perfunctory backward glance. But, when seen from our standpoint, the group really reduces to one man, Quesnay, to whom all economists look up as one of the greatest figures of their science. I know of no exception, though there are no doubt some differences in the reasons which different people would proffer in motivation of their individual agreement with the unanimous vote. Of the other members of the group we need to notice only Mirabeau, Mercier de la Rivière, Le Trosne, Baudeau, and Dupont. They were all of them disciples, nay, pupils of Quesnay in the strictest and most meaningful sense these terms will bear—disciples who absorbed and accepted the master's teaching with a fidelity for which there are but two analogues in the whole history of economics: the fidelity of the orthodox Marxists to the message of Marx and the fidelity of the orthodox Keynesians to the message of Keynes. They were a school by virtue of doctrinal and personal bonds, and always acted as a group, praising one another, fighting one another's fights, each member taking his share in group propaganda. They would in fact illustrate the nature of that sociological phenomenon to perfection had

[6] A. Marshall (*Principles*, p. 55, n. 1) states that Cantillon was in important respects anticipated by Barbon (see below, ch. 7). Unless this refers to a certain (but not at all close) similarity between Cantillon's and Barbon's views on foreign trade—which both of them had in common with many other writers—I fail to see what Marshall can have meant.

they not been something more than a scientific school: they formed a group united by what amounted to a creed; they were indeed what they had been called so often, a Sect. This fact naturally impaired their influence upon every economist, French or foreign, who was not prepared to take the vows to One Master and One Doctrine: moreover, it invited wholesale rejection of their teaching even by people who agreed with them on many points of theory as well as of policy or even by people who were under obligation to them. Some serious foreign scholars, particularly the leading Italians—among them Genovesi, Beccaria, and Verri—were indeed friendly. But so far as analysis and not policy is concerned, this friendliness meant little more than occasional lip service to specifically physiocrat tenets and should not mislead us into calling them physiocrats. Enthusiastic adherents of any importance are to be found in Germany only: it will suffice to mention the Margrave of Baden, Schlettwein, Mauvillon, and the Swiss, Herrenschwand. The necessary minimum of facts about the men so far mentioned is assembled below.

François Quesnay (1694-1774), the son of a moderately successful lawyer, was above all else a surgeon-physician. His distinguished professional career absorbed the bulk of his energy and never left more of it for economics than a man may be able to reserve for a passionately beloved hobby. He wrote a medical treatise on bleeding, became General Secretary of the Academy of Surgery and editor of its journal, surgeon and eventually first physician to the king. Actually, he was medical adviser to Mme de Pompadour, in whom he found a protectress who was not only extremely kind but also intelligently understanding, a fact that assured to him a strategic position in the intellectual life of Versailles and Paris and should assure to the lady the lasting gratitude of economists. He was pedantic and doctrinaire to a degree and must have been an awful bore. But he had all the force of character that often goes with pedantry. It is pleasant to add that he was also thoroughly upright and honest. His loyalty to his protectress and his imperviousness to the typical temptations of his environment are amply established by an anecdote related by Marmontel that is more amusing than proper. The fact that he was the only creative force in his circle is somewhat obscured by his inability or unwillingness to work out his ideas fully and systematically. We will notice of his economic writings (his only voluminous work was the *Essai physique sur l'économie animale*, 1736) the *Encyclopédie* articles 'Fermiers' (1756), 'Grains' (1757), 'Hommes' (1757); the *Tableau économique* (1758; see below, sub d); the article 'Droit naturel' (1765) and the dialogue 'Du Commerce' (1766), both in the *Journal de l'agriculture, du commerce et des finances*; also the article 'Despotisme de la Chine' (*Éphémérides*, 1767), which has given rise to speculations on the subject of Chinese influence upon the physiocrats. (See, e.g., the article under this title by L. A. Maverick, *Economic History, Supplement to the Economic Journal*, February 1938.) Finally, there are Quesnay's *Maximes*, a highly revealing supplement to, or political commentary on, the *Tableau*

(1758), and the *Oeuvres économiques et philosophiques* edited by August Oncken with an interesting introduction (1888). All histories of economics deal with Quesnay, of course, the treatment in Gide and Rist calling for special notice. See H. Higgs, *The Physiocrats* (1897); G. Schelle, *Le Docteur Quesnay* (1907); G. Weulersse, *Le Mouvement physiocratique en France de* 1756 *à* 1770 (1910), and *Les Physiocrates* (1931); M. Beer's *Inquiry into Physiocracy* (1939) is, quite rightly, almost entirely devoted to Quesnay himself.

Mirabeau we have met already (see above, ch. 3). After his conversion by Quesnay he devoted himself wholeheartedly to the cause of physiocracy, without however completely surrendering independent judgment. Two of his works already mentioned, the *Théorie de l'impôt* and the *Philosophie rurale,* may have been written in collaboration or consultation with Quesnay but are certainly not pure Quesnayism and contain things of which Quesnay cannot have approved. Nevertheless, the *Philosophie* (1763) was generally accepted as the first of the four textbooks of physiocrat orthodoxy. The sixth Part of *L'Ami* presented among other things Mirabeau's explanation of the *Tableau.*

Pierre-Paul Mercier de la Rivière (also known as Lemercier; 1720-93), whose impulsiveness or bad manners made him more conspicuous than he deserved to be, was responsible for the second of those textbooks, namely, *L'Ordre naturel et essentiel des sociétés politiques* (1767, reprint with useful introduction by E. Depitre, 1909), which Dupont de Nemours republished, in abstract, with a title that is revelatory of the group's frame of mind: it read *De l'origine et des progrès d'une science nouvelle* (1768). The first thirty-five chapters of Mercier's work are devoted to topics of political theory, which was what primarily interested him—Quesnay's scheme of *despotisme légal* that was really no despotism at all. The economics that occupies the remaining nine chapters is negligible. Both Diderot and A. Smith, however, thought highly of the book.

G. F. Le Trosne (1728-80) was a much abler man. But he was a lawyer and mainly interested in the natural-law aspects of the physiocrat system. In the field of economics he embraced physiocrat orthodoxy with some reservations. His *Liberté du commerce des grains* (1765) and his *De l'interêt social . . . ,* second volume of *De l'ordre social* (1777), are meritorious performances, though they are not more than that.

The Abbé Nicolas Baudeau (1730-92) began as an enemy but had his day of Damascus in 1766 and from then on proved a most useful popularizer and controversialist as well as an efficient editor. His *Première introduction . . .* (1771; reprint with instructive introduction by A. Dubois, 1910) is the third of the group's textbooks, perhaps the weakest of all.

The fourth and best of these textbooks was the short *Abrégé des principes de l'économie politique* (publ. first in vol. I of the *Éphémérides,* for 1772) by Karl Friedrich von Baden-Durlach.

Pierre S. Dupont de Nemours (1739-1817), who entered adult life as an all-round literary free lance, was by far the ablest of the lot. Napoleon I once described Marshal Villars as a 'fanfaron d'honneur.' Similarly we can describe Dupont as a 'go-getter' who never forgot honor and principle and who, in particular, retained both a genuine interest in purely scientific questions and loyalty to the physiocrat creed throughout a career that offered every excuse for dropping them. He was won over to the cause of physiocracy by shrewd old Quesnay himself, who knew perfectly with whom he was dealing and never pulled the curb too sharply. Dupont immediately began to write copiously and effectively, publishing, among other things, a free-trade tract on grain exports and imports, 1764. On the strength of his success as a writer and editor, he secured various important employments under Turgot and later on under the last great minister of the *ancien régime,* Vergennes. We need not follow him through the ups and downs of life which, through the *Constituante* and the *Directoire* finally landed him—a Roman would say, with the loss of his shield—in the United States. Nor need we record his numerous publications, all of which bear witness to the brilliance of his talents, though these talents were those of the pianist and not those of the composer. The interested reader finds all except his letters in G. Schelle's *Dupont de Nemours et l'école physiocratique* (1888); also see Weulersse's work previously quoted.

As already mentioned, the school was thoroughly alive to the importance of propaganda and some of its members, Baudeau and Dupont especially, were very good at it. They founded discussion groups, worked upon individuals and agencies in key positions (the *parlements* especially), and produced a large quantity of popular and controversial literature. Their exploits in economic journalism, however interesting in themselves, would not have to be mentioned here were it not for the fact that, rising above it, they also produced the bulk of the material that went into the pages of the first scientific periodicals in the history of economics. The *Journal Oeconomique* (1751-72) had from the first kept a highly creditable level, rendering such services to scientific economics as the publication of translations of Hume (an important fact to keep in mind) and Josiah Tucker. The *Journal d'agriculture, du commerce et des finances* (1764-83) was intended from the first to supplement the *Gazette* by taking care of 'heavier' articles. The physiocrats partly controlled, partly had ready access to, this journal in 1765-6 and 1774-83. In 1765, however, Baudeau founded the famous *Éphémérides du citoyen* ('the citizen's daily records' would render this title, though it was a weekly), which, after Baudeau's conversion (from protectionism) in 1766 became identified with physiocracy. In 1768 Dupont took over. It was suppressed, owing to its strong hostility to the policy of the Aiguillon-Maupeou-Terray government, but recalled to life by Turgot (1774), whose policies it of course supported and some of whose enemies it attacked. The *Nouvelles éphémérides* died in 1776, and several efforts at resuming publication ended speedily in failure. But in a sense the short-lived *Journal d'économie publique, de morale et de politique* (founded 1796), though neither physiocrat nor the equal of the physiocrat journal, was the same kind of thing—as was in fact the later *Journal des économistes*. In more than one respect, therefore, the *Éphémérides* should be remembered by the student of the history of economics as one of the major achievements of Quesnay and his group. The reader will find an excellent sketch of this journal's career, giving all the essential facts in a short compass, in Palgrave's *Dictionary of Political Economy*, article 'Éphémérides' by Professor S. Bauer. I. Iselin founded a German replica, not equal to the prototype (*Ephemeriden der Menschheit*, 1776-82).

The impressions a reader gets as he wades through the volumes of the *Éphémérides* (I have been able to do so only to 1772) will of course vary from one reader to another. Personally, I have been greatly struck by a certain similarity they display to the scientific journals of late nineteenth-century Marxist orthodoxy, especially the *Neue Zeit:* the same fervor of conviction, similar controversial talent, quite the same inability to take any other but the orthodox view of anything, comparable capacity for bitter resentment, and equal absence of self-criticism. This shows particularly in the review articles. But solid merit all but obliterates these blemishes. Even apart from Turgot's *Réflexions*, which are, of course, in a class by themselves, and the explanations of the *Tableau*, there is a lot of thoroughly good stuff. Dupont, for example, contributed what is to my knowledge the first genuine history of economics. Masses of historical material are presented. Contemporaneous events from all corners of the globe are currently reviewed, though always from a narrowly sectarian point of view. All in all, the first of the long series of scientific journals of economics set a high standard for a long time to come. Its international success was well deserved.

The three Germans mentioned above need not detain us long. As regards the Margrave of Baden-Durlach (later Grand Duke of Baden, 1728-1811), who politically was one of the ablest public men of his time, we need add only a reference to his correspondence with Mirabeau and Dupont (edited, with introduction by K. Knies, 1892), which will repay perusal. J. A. Schlettwein (1731-1802) was the Margrave's executive collaborator in the experiment on the practical application of the physiocrat recipe to the village of Dietling which he reported in *Les moyens d'arrêter la misère publique . . .* (1772). Neglecting his later and fuller account of this experiment, we shall be content to mention his *Grundfeste der Staaten oder die politische Oekonomie* (1778). His almost turbulent activity in the service of physiocracy, considered as a practical scheme of agrarian reform, made a stir wherever he went and secured him one of those traditional positions in the history of scientific economics for which no analysis of published performance can unearth a justification. In one respect only can this man interest us, excellent though he no doubt was in his way. He illustrates to perfection the type of economist who will, I fear, never die out and who will forever discredit economics in the eyes of men whose approval is worth having. This is the type that says: here is the patent medicine that will cure all ills, 'the most important thing for the public' (these words are the title of one of his publications); in fact, the only thing that is important for humanity, is to swallow it. Jakob Mauvillon (1743-94) was a still more excellent man in many respects, but still weaker as an economist. His essay on luxury included in his *Sammlung von Aufsätzen* . . . (1776-7) is negligible. His *Physiokratische Briefe an den Herrn Professor Dohm* (1780) is in or near the center of a German controversy on physiocracy, for the sake of which alone this publication deserves to be mentioned. But this controversy itself needs to be mentioned only because some interest attaches to the fact that the physiocrat doctrine, though very little understood in its true scientific importance and mainly discussed in its practical aspects, could raise a full-dress debate around 1780. However we use the opportunity to refer to the best performance on behalf of physiocracy, K. G. Fürstenau's *Apologie des physiokratischen Systems* (1779). Of opponents it will suffice to mention C. K. W. von Dohm (*Kurze Vorstellung des physiokratischen Systems,* 1778) and J. F. von Pfeiffer (*Antiphysiokrat,* 1780). The latter's voluminous systematic works of the Justi type, no doubt marked by strong practical sense, have earned for him high praise from several historians. Jean (Johann) Herrenschwand (1728-1811), was a late physiocrat. Perhaps he should not be called a physiocrat at all, for he was not orthodox. But he was an able economist. His chief works were *De l'économie politique moderne* (1786); *De l'économie politique et morale de l'espèce humaine* (1796); *Du vrai principe actif de l'économie politique* (1797). There is a German monograph: A. Jöhr, *Jean Herrenschwand* (1901).

A sect with a creed and a political program naturally presents many aspects and calls for interpretative analysis from many standpoints other than ours: we shall first glance at some of these, then consider the bare bones of Quesnay's economic analysis, and especially the *Tableau économique.*

[(b) *Natural Law, Agriculture, Laissez-Faire, and l'Impôt Unique.*] Physiocracy [1] was nonexistent in 1750. *Tout Paris* and still more Versailles talked about it from 1760 to 1770. Practically everybody (excluding professed economists) had forgotten it by 1780. This meteoric career will be readily understood as soon as we realize the nature and extent of this success, that is to say, as soon as we realize precisely *what* it was that, for about two decades, succeeded so conspicuously, *how* it succeeded, and *why.*

Above (in Chapter 2) we have interpreted Quesnay as a philosopher of natural law. In fact, Quesnay's theories of state and society were nothing but reformulations of scholastic doctrine. The motto, *Ex natura jus, ordo, et leges* might have been, though it presumably was not, taken from St. Thomas. The

[1] The term means Rule of Nature and was used by Dupont as a book title in 1767. But according to Oncken it was used earlier by Baudeau and is perhaps due to Quesnay himself. The question is of no importance.

physiocrat *ordre naturel* (to which there corresponds in the world of real phenomena an *ordre positif*) is the ideal dictate of human nature as revealed by human reason. What difference there is between Quesnay and the scholastics is not to the former's credit. We have seen that St. Thomas and still more the late scholastics, such as Lessius, were perfectly aware of the historical relativity of social states and institutions and that they always refused to commit themselves, in mundane affairs, to an invariable order of things. But Quesnay's ideal order is invariable. Moreover, in his paper on *Droit naturel,* he defined Physical Law as the 'regulated (*réglé*) course of all physical events which is evidently the most advantageous to mankind,' and Moral Law as 'the rule (*règle*) of every human action conforming to the physical order evidently most advantageous to mankind': these 'laws' form together what is called 'natural law,' and they are all immutable and the 'best possible ones' (*les meilleures lois possibles*). In the case of the scholastic doctors, such principles were confined to the realm of metaphysics and not directly applied to historically conditioned patterns. In the case of Quesnay they were directly applied to particular institutions, such as property. And Quesnay's political theory—*both* analytically and normatively—turned upon a monarchical absolutism in an uncritical and unhistoric manner that, as we have seen, was also quite foreign to the scholastics.[2] Now, we know how well the old natural-law system fared in the eighteenth century and how acceptable it proved to be, in its essential features, to *la raison.* Therefore, Quesnay's particular form of it, some non-essential frills excepted, fell in with the intellectual fashion of the hour: everybody readily understood this part of his teaching, sympathized with it from the start, and felt at home when discussing it. And, unlike other votaries of *la raison,* Quesnay harbored no hostility either to the Catholic Church or to the monarchy. Here, then, was *la raison,* with all its uncritical belief in progress, but without its irreligious and political fangs. Need I say that this delighted court and society?

Again, agriculture held a central position in Quesnay's program of economic policy as well as in his analytic scheme. And this feature of his teaching, too, fell in with the fashion of the hour. Just then everybody was raving about agriculture. This enthusiasm had two different sources that reinforced each other, though they were really quite independent. First, the revolution of agrarian technique gave a novel actuality to agricultural problems. It amounted to less in France than it did in England, but it produced just as much drawing-room talk in Paris as it did in London. Second, the illogical association of the natural rights of men with a glorified primitive state of society and the not less illogical association of the latter with agrarian pursuits gave to agriculture a drawing-room popularity that had, to be sure, no relation to Quesnay's serious

[2] It should be observed, however, that in Quesnay's time and country there was perhaps much practical wisdom in this. For in the actual situation of eighteenth-century France, the reforms advocated by the physiocrats could have been carried (without revolution) only by the strong hand of a despotic monarch. The hostility of the physiocrats against 'privilege' of any kind was therefore not, as one might think, in contradiction to their allegiance to monarchy but on the contrary the very reason for it.

teaching but nevertheless blew wind into his sails. We have the picture if we add one more touch. The dogmatizing doctor's apartment in the entresol of the palace of Versailles was not far from the well of all preferment, Mme de Pompadour's suite. The ambitious on the lower rungs of the ladder could hardly fail to perceive this fact, and some of them may have thought that an hour's boredom in the former was a cheap price to pay for a good word dropped in the latter. Marmontel was quite frank about this, and it is safe to assume that he was not the only one to make the discovery.

Such things do matter at all times though different environments have different methods of favoring doctrines without absorbing, or caring for, their real scientific import, if any. Expressed in terms of that particular environment, Quesnay's success was primarily a *succès de salon*. Polite society talked physiocracy for a time but very few people outside took much notice of it except by way of sneering at it. There was thus a physiocrat fashion but there was no physiocrat movement in the sense in which there was (and is) a Marxist movement, especially not one rooted in agrarian class interests. But what about the political influence of the physiocrats of which we read so much? What about their historic role in combating privilege, abuses, and all the horrors of protection? The reader would completely misunderstand the drift of the argument presented, as well as the reasons why it was thought necessary to present it, if he concluded from what has been said so far that this influence should be equated to zero. No group so well disciplined and so bent upon propaganda as the physiocrats were can fail to exert some influence. For instance, such a group as our own League of Women Voters is a cog in our political engine that no realistic analysis of our time can afford to neglect entirely. The point is that the physiocrat group exerted this kind of influence and no other, and that their importance as a motive power of politics was small. A brief examination of Quesnay's recommendations will establish this.

These recommendations may for our purposes be reduced to two: laissez-faire, including free trade, and the single tax on the net income from land. In order to arrive at a true estimate of Quesnay's competence as a 'practical' economist, it is necessary with regard to both to distinguish doctrinal frills from underlying common sense. Thus, Quesnay taught laissez-faire and free trade as absolute norms of political wisdom. But these imperatives must be viewed in the light of the physiocrats' hostility to all kinds of privileges and to a great many things that seemed to them to be abuses, monopoly positions among others. Since these could not have been abolished without a good deal of governmental 'interference,' Quesnay urged upon government what really was an activist policy, and not at all one of doing nothing. Moreover, in spite of his wholesale condemnation of government regulation or control, it is relevant to observe that what he actually faced were regulations that were inherited from the past and no longer fitted current conditions: the absolute norm of laissez-faire acquires in such a case a relative significance that differs greatly from what its absolutism suggests. Finally, we must not forget that

French agriculture in 1760 was not interested in protection: there was no 'danger' of large wheat imports as a normal phenomenon; and free trade in agricultural products would have, if anything, increased their prices. We shall presently discover reasons for doubting whether Quesnay would have been a thorough-going free trader if he had written in 1890. Similarly, as regards his single tax, we must distinguish the common-sense idea from the trappings that made it an object of ridicule. To simplify and rationalize the French system of taxation by basing it upon a tax on net income was evidently a sensible idea. To base it *exclusively* on such a tax was a doctrinaire's way of putting this idea. To base it exclusively on a tax on the net rent of land was Quesnay's way of applying his theory that the net rent of land was the only kind of net income in existence and that any tax must ultimately fall upon it in any case. This theory may be untenable. Even if it were tenable as an abstract proposition, its application to the practical question of taxation would be indefensible because the mere presence of friction in the system would be enough to produce net returns other than the rent of land. But the value of the fundamental idea is not entirely destroyed by this particular twist. Moreover, the suggestion to tax the pure rent of land, in view of the fact that it was then not directly taxed at all, carried sense whatever the frills in which it was presented—sense that cannot be claimed for later proposals of a similar nature, such as Henry George's. The physiocrat contribution to public finance in fact stands out well in the group's textbook on it, Mirabeau's *Théorie de l'impôt* (1760). This work—Dupont called it 'sublime'—relieved the stress upon the single-tax panacea by properly emphasizing the importance of administrative reforms, of revenue from the *domaine*, the mint, the post office, a special tax on tobacco production, and a salt tax: all of this helps to remove the stigma of freakishness that has been put upon the *impôt unique*.

But observe that there was nothing in the physiocrat general program that was substantially new. The traditional assertion to the contrary may be traced (1) to the understandable desire of historians of the group to protect its priorities against A. Smith, in which they were, of course, quite right; (2) to the optical illusion that will victimize any historian of doctrine who concentrates his vision upon a particular group and pays inadequate attention to what lies around and, historically, before it; (3) to Quesnay's way of quaint and distinctive formulation, which separates his views from similar ones by overaccentuated but all the same artificial dividing lines. Thus, the single-tax idea was as we know an old one; if Quesnay can be said at all to have done something novel with it, then his contribution consists in his having given it that particular twist which few of us will hail as an improvement. In matters of free trade it may indeed be held that the physiocrats were the first *group* to advocate unconditional free trade though they had been anticipated by individuals such as Sir Dudley North. But for us this is not important. Much more important is it that as regards grasp of the scientific principles involved, many of their contemporaries, including their professed enemies such as Forbonnais, were their equals. It cannot be too often repeated that sponsorship of a particular practical conclusion proves nothing for or against a man's insight into economic causes and effects. In fact, if equality of insight be doubted at all, the doubt should be raised against Quesnay. For 'whole-hog' positions, though there are many other explanations for them, usually point to some defect in insight rather than to the contrary.

Nevertheless, Quesnay's views about the economic process and his policies being what they were, it is of course possible to trace to him practically the whole arsenal of nineteenth-century liberal argument. But all those ideas floated toward nineteenth-century writers and politicians in a much broader stream, in which the physiocrat element was but a small part. This also applies to the politicians of the *Constituante* and of the Revolution in general. Nor is there more justification for the claim that physiocrat influence was responsible either for Turgot's appointment or for his policy (see below, sec. 4). The only instances of practical influence were the experiments with the *impôt unique* made by Karl Friedrich of Baden-Durlach and by Peter Leopold, Grand Duke of Tuscany. However, it has been remarked already that Quesnay, if he got rather more than his due as a patron saint of economic liberalism, has to this day been receiving less than his due as a scientific economist, if we neglect the glowing eulogies of his immediate disciples. Especially that kind of recognition—the only serious one—that consists in the acknowledgment by competent workers of obligation, or at least of priority, in definite points, has been dealt out to him rather sparingly. One reason for this was that his analytic work was little understood and that in consequence later economists actually did not owe as much to him as one might think. Another was the presence in his teaching of what people felt to be an element of oddity. In the case of A. Smith both reasons seem to have been operative: almost certainly he did not fully grasp the importance of the *tableau économique;* quite certainly he was overanxious to avoid associating himself with anything that was in any way odd. Karl Marx was the only first-rank economist to give Quesnay his due.

[(c) *Quesnay's Economic Analysis.*] Recall Quesnay's definition of Natural Law. As soon as we realize all its implications we shall understand what those historians mean who, pointing to a theological bent in Quesnay's thought, either deny the analytic character of his work or, if they go not quite as far as that, at least hold that Quesnay's religious beliefs must have been a factor in shaping his economics.[3] There may be some truth in this as far as Quesnay's views on economic policy and his value judgments are concerned. But there is no truth in this as regards his economic theory. It is not decisive of course that Quesnay himself repeatedly claimed that he was faithfully describing facts.[4] But application of our own test yields the same result and establishes

[3] This point will stand out particularly if we compare Quesnay's definition with Montesquieu's, whose natural laws are nothing but *rapports nécessaires qui dérivent de la nature des choses,* a definition that cannot be commended too highly.

[4] Two references may be useful: first, in the dialogue *Du commerce* (1766), where Quesnay expounds part of his theory of capital, he invites his readers to visit farms and factories in order to satisfy themselves of the realism of his theory; second, speaking of the economic relations between classes he tells us: *La marche de ce commerce*

the validity of that claim: the reader will presently see that no economic proposition of Quesnay's rests upon any theological premisses or would be affected by discarding what we know about his religious beliefs. This proves ipso facto the purely analytic or 'scientific' nature of his economic work and leaves no room for extra-empirical influences. Let us now consider briefly the salient features of his theoretical set-up.

1. All reasoning on economic topics necessarily implies recognition of an Economic Principle of some sort. Precisely because of this it is difficult to say when and by whom such a principle was first formulated. But if we wish to stress explicitness of formulation, then, I think, priority (as against the Italians) belongs to Quesnay's rule of conduct: greatest satisfaction (*jouissance*) to be attained with the smallest expense or, as he goes on to say, labor-pain. The importance of this rule or principle, considered as a contribution to formal theory—or, as we may also call it, to the pure logic of economics—consists primarily in bringing out the fact that the fundamental problem of that theory is a maximum problem. The importance of the hedonist garb in which Quesnay presented it consists in the fact that, considering dates, it gives him a prominent place in the history of utilitarian social philosophy: he certainly was one of the founding fathers of utilitarianism though he did not state the greatest-happiness principle in so many words.

But he also is the most important of all the founding fathers of the doctrine that will henceforth be referred to as the Maximum Doctrine of Perfect Competition (see A. Marshall, *Principles*, p. 531). That is to say, he held that maximum satisfaction of wants for all members of society, taken together, will result if, conditions of perfect competition prevailing, everyone be allowed to act freely upon his own individual self-interest. This doctrine was taught throughout the nineteenth century, unconditionally or with some qualification, by most nonsocialist theorists of standing, including many who refused to accept the utilitarian philosophy: serious, though at first very cautious, criticism really starts with A. Marshall. All the more necessary is it to point out how weak its foundations were from the first. The doctrine is of course never strictly true under any circumstances. But, for certain historical environments, a case can be made out for it under assumptions that are restrictive indeed, but not so restrictive as to deprive it entirely of practical value. The point to which I wish to call the reader's attention is, however, that Quesnay did not make any attempt to prove it. It did not seem to him to stand in need of explicit proof. He manifestly thought that if every individual strives to realize maximum satisfaction, then all individuals will 'of course' achieve maximum satisfaction. The fact that one of the best brains of our science could have been content with such an obvious non sequitur is indeed food for thought: low standards of rigor and sloppiness of thinking have been worse enemies of scientific economics than has been political bias.

Observe, however, that the physiocrat slogan—'the interests of individuals

---

entre les différentes classes et ses conditions essentielles ne sont point hypothétiques. Quiconque voudray réfléchir, verra qu'ils sont fidèlement copiés d'après la nature.

are the servants of the public interest'—is not per se open to our objection. It may mean no more than that, as A. Smith was to put it, we owe our bread not to the benevolence of the baker but to his self-interest, a pedestrian truth which it is worth while to repeat again and again in view of the ineradicable prejudice that every action intended to serve the profit interest must be antisocial by virtue of this fact alone. A. Smith was careful not to build too much on this. In particular, he was keenly aware of the antagonism between social classes. But Quesnay went on, from asserting universal compatibility—or, indeed, complementarity—of individual interests in competitive society, to asserting universal harmony of class interests, which makes him the forerunner of nineteenth-century Harmonism (Say, Carey, Bastiat). In this case, however, we have an attempt at proof: the *tableau économique* shows how every class, as it were, lives upon every other class, and in particular how the prosperity of the landowners conditions the prosperity of the other classes. The proof—which hails from Cantillon—is open to obvious objections and even to ridicule, but nevertheless Quesnay's harmonism does not simply hang in the air. Nor is it necessary to appeal to belief in providential ordinance in order to explain it.

II. Quesnay possessed a very comprehensive analytic schema, though he presented it by means of disconnected sketches. Some parts of it, especially those concerning population, wages, interest, and money, will come in for notice in subsequent chapters. In order not to leave the present picture incomplete, however, I shall indicate his positions on these subjects: his theory of population anticipated that of Malthus in all essentials; his theory of wages centered in a minimum-of-existence proposition; his theory of interest may be said to be almost nonexistent and he entirely failed to account for the phenomenon; his theory of money, unlike Cantillon's, was what we have decided to label cartalist.

Barter and pricing he analyzed on strictly 'subjective' lines—basing his theory resolutely upon the fact of consumers' wants. This is of some importance—though he added nothing to the price theory of the late scholastics—because his treatment of the problem (like Condillac's) must be counted among the influences that kept this theory alive in France: it points directly to J. B. Say. There is, however, another point to be recorded in this connection. A. Marshall may have been right in denying that the theory of consumption is the scientific basis of economics. But it was certainly the basis of Quesnay's economics. 'Liberal' economists of the nineteenth century were in the habit of commending eighteenth-century free traders, especially A. Smith, for having duly emphasized the truth that consumption is the 'sole end and purpose of production' and for having thereby abolished one of the 'errors of mercantilism.' There is very little to this: the truth, so far as it is a truth, is trivial and the error is largely imaginary. However, Quesnay also attended to consumption in a different sense that would have been very little to the taste of those 'liberal' economists and is, if anything, suggestive of 'mercantilist' lines of thought:[5] unlike Turgot and A. Smith, he made it an explicit condition for the economic process to function smoothly *that everybody should promptly spend his net receipts upon consumers' goods* or, to use a phrase that has gained currency in Washington in the last years, that everybody should 'utilize' his income fully. If this were not done, he thought, and especially if some people saved *in order to increase their individual stocks of money*, all classes would decay and total output would shrink, since anybody's refusal to spend necessarily destroys somebody else's income. This 'Keynesian' aspect of Quesnay's teaching will be considered later.

III. Particularly significant as a creative contribution was Quesnay's theory of capital. Cantillon and other precursors notwithstanding, he may be said to have laid the foundations of this part of economic theory. The performance is an interesting illustration of the way in which, in the mind of the born theorist, *analytic generalization may grow out of observation induced by preoccupation with practical problems*. Quesnay's agricultural program, which to him was practically equivalent to the sum total of economic policy, was geared to the needs of fairly large-scale farming: like Cantillon, he never considered seriously any agrarian world other than one that turned on, and was propelled by, the enterprise of an intelligent and active farming class in full possession of all the technological and commercial opportunities of its time. These intelligent farmers he did not visualize as owners of their land, but as free from all interference from landlords, from whom they would rent, for long periods, large lots of land—cleared and equipped with buildings—in order to do with them as they pleased. Commons should be dissolved and let to individuals like the rest of the land; feudal rights and duties—in particular the right to hunt on farm land—should be abolished; so should internal and external customs that hamper disposal of products, and taxes that discourage effort (one of the practical reasons for the single tax that was to be paid by the landlord); the countryside, as it were, was to dissolve into a swarm of prosperous enter-

[5] Quesnay's free-trade recommendations are, of course, responsible for the tradition that put him into a position of uncompromising hostility to 'mercantilist' doctrine. We have seen, indeed, that even in those recommendations there is an element that distinguishes his free trade from the free trade of the nineteenth-century 'liberals'; viz., the emphasis upon the *bon prix*, the high price, of agricultural products. But in itself this might be interpreted as an insertion, for reasons of political preference, of a practical consideration into a doctrinal structure to which it was thoretically extraneous. Looking more closely, however, we discover that there was more than that to the *bon prix*. Unlike A. Smith, who carried the cheapness-and-plenty doctrine to victory (and therefore was, if we adopt Lord Keynes's view, a victim of the 'fallacy of cheapness'), Quesnay sponsored, *as a matter of analytic principle*, the dearness-and-plenty view (see below, ch. 6, sec. 1). And this, taken together with the point to which I am about to call attention in the text, makes him a brother in spirit, as far as analysis and not policy is concerned, of writers that are usually classed as 'mercantilists' and distances him from the nineteenth-century writers who were to follow A. Smith and from A. Smith himself, at least in one very important respect.

prises, left to their own devices, selling at high prices, buzzing with energy themselves, and energizing the whole of the national economy.[6]

Now, if the reader visualizes this particular type of program, he will immediately see that its success presupposed fulfilment of three conditions: first, that these farmer-entrepreneurs should actually buzz with energy, a condition that Quesnay took lightly because, being a typical child of his age, he did not attach much importance to the problem of innate qualities of personnel; second, that this farmer's paradise should not be undersold from abroad, a condition about which, in eighteenth-century France, it was not necessary to worry; and third, that there should be plenty of capital—cheap capital—available for these essentially capitalist farmer-entrepreneurs. Quesnay did worry about this last condition. He had every reason for doing so, because his realistic studies, which went into all the details of the technology and business policy of farming, had given him a true idea of what the capital requirements of this kind of farming actually are. And it was from these investigations that, conceptualizing his findings, he developed his theory of capital. The immediate result is embodied in his classification of the farmer's capital requirements into *avances foncières*, initial expenditures on clearing, draining, fencing, building, and the like that do not recur at all or recur only in long periods, *avances primitives*, expenditures on equipment including cattle and horses and the *avances annuelles*, the current expenditures on seed, labor, and the like.[7]

Quesnay did not bother much about generalizing these concepts: their extension to include industry does not present any difficulty. But what do these *avances* consist in? It is no doubt the drainage, buildings, oxen, ploughs, seed and labor, and the like, that the farmer needs. A stock of goods and services, then? But if so, what are we to do with the facts that 'capital required' or 'capital invested' is, at the very least, *expressed* in terms of money, and that, as a matter of fact, it is also *bought* for money, which is really what landlord (for the *avances foncières*) and farmer need in the first instance? Quesnay ran up against all the problems that lurk behind these questions, and his rudimentary attempts at solving them may have been—even if they were not actually, for it is impossible to be certain about this—the starting points of all further work upon them. We shall discuss below the reasons that have been adduced for believing that A. Smith's capital theory grew out of critical absorption of Quesnay's, which would in fact make the latter the ancestor of

[6] By way of supplementing what has already been said about the common sense of much of Quesnay's economic philosophy, it may be observed that a policy of this kind seems indeed a more reasonable thing to recommend, in the domestic and international situation of France around 1750 or 1760, than throwing away means on colonial ventures which, even if successful, would only provide prizes for the English fleet, or on financial enterprise that might end as John Law's had ended, or on military establishments that might produce another Rossbach. This psychology of the thoroughly disappointed nation that Quesnay was addressing must be understood.

[7] There are in addition the *avances souveraines*, public expenditure on roads, et cetera.

practically all the capital theories down to J. S. Mill's. And since the man who first tackles a subject will often throw out all sorts of suggestions that point in many more directions than he himself is aware of, we might even be tempted to trace back to Quesnay such later developments as are associated with the names of Walras and Irving Fisher, on the one hand, and of Jevons and Böhm-Bawerk, on the other. This, however, is hardly permissible, for the logical possibility of doing so simply results from the rich and indefinite possibilities—of truth as well as of error—that are enshrined in the word *avances*. Of course, no writer on economic subjects can ever have doubted the simple fact that what 'capitalists' do is to provide either goods or money with which to start and carry on production; and 'capitalists' themselves always knew that what they were doing was to 'advance' money for these purposes. But one of the fundamental types of analytic achievement precisely consists in raising some simple fact (for example, that apples, severed from the branches of the apple tree, will fall to the ground) *into the light of theoretical consciousness*. This is what Quesnay's contribution to capital theory consists in: impressed by the fact that his farmer-entrepreneurs could not start upon their careers unless they were provided with all sorts of things *beforehand*, he introduced capital into economic theory as wealth accumulated previous to starting the production under consideration. But more than this he did not do, and widely divergent paths may open out from this starting point. In particular, he did not analyze the formation and behavior of money capital as a thing distinct from 'real' capital—a thing, moreover, that plays tricks of its own. And he accepted the Janus-face of nonmonetary capital, which is value on one side (*valeurs accumulées*) and physical goods on the other, without straightening out the problems involved, particularly that of the carrying charges which enter the value concept but do not enter the physical one.

IV. The third chapter of Book II of Marshall's *Principles* opens with the sentence, 'Man cannot create material things.' This statement hails from J. S. Mill and Rae and many earlier writers. Since economics is concerned with the 'creation' or production of either utilities or market values, it is difficult to see the relevance of such a statement, of which, in fact, none of those writers ever made any use. But, as everyone knows, the physiocrats did put it to analytic use: following Cantillon they derived from it their theory of the *produit net*. This is the only reason why the subject crosses our path again. For neither their statement of what they believed to be a physical fact nor the philosophies in which they indulged in connection with it are in themselves worth our while to discuss. Nor would there be anything particularly interesting in Quesnay's terminological decision to call, on the strength of that fact, agricultural activity 'productive' (the farmer's activity, not that of the farm laborer) and every other activity 'sterile' (which, of course, does not mean useless), though it is precisely this which was felt to be odd and attracted an undue amount of critical attention. Let us, however, observe that it is really not so very odd to look upon an economy as an engine that is fed materials drawn from the womb of nature and that simply works up these materials without adding to them: the only question that arises is whether or not the analogy is useful. After what has been said on the subject in our survey of Cantillon's work, we can dispose of it quickly.

We have seen in that survey that the theory of Cantillon's *produit de la terre*—and Quesnay's *produit net* is the same thing—is a method, though certainly not the most correct or convenient one, of expressing the fact that the rent of land is, or contains, a net return. But, as we have also seen, the theory goes further than this. It holds that the rent of land is the only net return in existence, and that it is coextensive with the whole of society's disposable net income, all other returns being balanced by cost items in the sense that they are not more than sufficient to replace what production uses up. The workman gets no more than is necessary to reproduce his ability to work. The capitalist, taking account of risks, gets no more than is necessary to replace his stock and *his* ability to work: labor, management, and capital are 'sterile' in the sense that, though they produce utilities, they do not produce any Surplus Value.

In general conception this theory bears a striking similarity to that of Marx. Exactly as Quesnay let land alone be productive of surplus value, so Marx let labor alone be productive of surplus value. Neither construction allows any productivity to capital—meaning plant, equipment, and material—which is indeed a conductor or embodiment of a surplus value created, respectively, by land or labor but does not add to it. So far Marx's theory looks as if it were the result of switching Quesnay's schema from one of Petty's two original factors of production to the other. There seems, however, to be a fundamental difference between the two. Marx's way of carrying out his postulate of productivity's being inherent in labor alone is, as we shall see, open to objection. But, with him, labor's productivity is from the first a value productivity, and he attempted to show, on the basis of his law of values, how surplus value emerges from the mechanism of competitive markets. Quesnay made no such attempt. His starting point was physical productivity, that is, 'creation' of stuff and not of values. He took it for granted that the fact of physical productivity implied value productivity, and he shifted in midstream from the one to the other. On the face of it, this seems to be a definite error of which Marx was not guilty. But we have seen above that, by means of suitable assumptions, it is nevertheless possible to make the proposition that the rent of land is the only net return formally valid. And this means in turn that if we grant these assumptions—which are, after all, not much worse than those which it is necessary to grant in order to validate the labor theory of value—it is possible to transpose Quesnay's irrelevant argument from physical productivity into a relevant one from value productivity: the scarce natural agent, by hypothesis operating in agriculture alone, produces a value surplus over the other factors there employed, and manufacture adds nothing to it because competition will reduce what it does add to the value of the materials to the level of the value of the agrarian products that the manufacturers and their workmen consume. If we be grimly resolved to go through with this argument, even interest could be explained as a derivate of the *produit net*. This would complete the analogy with Marx.

(d) *The Tableau Économique*. The analytic structure we have been surveying is logically quite complete, and he who knows how to piece it together—which Quesnay did not do—will not miss any of the essentials that go into a comprehensive treatise on pure and applied economics. The over-all description of a stationary economic process which Quesnay embodied in his *tableau* is not, as his pupils and practically all critics believed, the centerpiece of that structure but an addition to it that is separable from the rest—painted, as it were, on a separate canvas—and therefore can be dealt with separately. What it depicts is the flow of expenditures and products between social classes, which here become the actors in the economic play—which they are not in the rest of Quesnay's work.

Economists, of course, always had some schema of the class structure of society at the back of their minds. Cantillon seems, however, to have been the first to construct such a schema explicitly and to use it as a tool of analysis. This schema was adopted by Quesnay. Accordingly, he distinguished landowners (*classe des propriétaires,* or *classe souveraine* or, what is significant, *classe distributive*), farmers (*classe productive*), and all the people engaged in nonagricultural pursuits, roughly equivalent to the bourgeoisie (*classe stérile*). Labor may either be treated as a fourth class or added in proper proportions to the second and third. The latter seems preferable in order to bring out the nature of the schema, which is not so much a schema of classes as sociological entities, but of economic groups of the kind we meet in the familiar statistics of people 'attached' to, say, agriculture or mining or manufacturing industries. In any case, however, labor plays an entirely 'passive' role with him exactly as it did with Cantillon. The flow of expenditures and products, then, is between a 'farmer basin,' a 'landowner basin,' and a 'sterile-class basin.' It is not necessary to reproduce Quesnay's picture of it or to enter into its details.[8] All the reader needs to retain is this.

Suppose that in the unit period *t*-1 the landowners have received and ac-

[8] As already stated, the *Tableau économique* ('picture' would render the meaning better than does the more usual 'table') was first printed in Versailles, 1758, with much pomp and circumstance—Louis XV himself, so we are told, correcting the proofs. This original, lost for over a hundred years, was recovered and reproduced in facsimile for the British Economic Society (as the Royal Economic Society then was called) in 1895 with a valuable introduction by H. Higgs, and has been repeatedly reprinted since. But Quesnay himself published another simplified version in the *Analyse* (see *Oeuvres*), which Dupont used in his *Physiocratie*. The reader finds a translation of Quesnay's commentary in A. E. Monroe's *Early Economic Thought*. Mirabeau, in the sixth Part of *L'Ami* presented a version of his own. There are thus at least two *tableaux* (disregarding variants that differ but little), which not only use different figures but also differ somewhat in theoretically relevant features. We shall not, however, go into these matters. The best way to get the essential idea with a minimum of trouble is to look up the excellent presentation by Shigeto Tsuru in Appendix A to P. M. Sweezy's *Theory of Capitalist Development* (1942).

cumulated in many instalments the rent due them by the farmers, so that, at the beginning of period *t*, they hold in cash all the net national income (in Quesnay's sense) while everybody else stands ready to sell and to produce. We are to follow the meanderings of that rent or net income through the economy. Let its amount be 1000 units of money. The landowners, so we will further assume, spend 500 of this on farm products and 500 on manufactures, the products of the sterile class, that is, the class that does not produce surplus value. The 500 units that the farmers get back in this way (for these units came out of their payments in *t*-1) are first of all doubled in their hands in consequence of their surplus value-producing activity so that they swell up to 1000. Half of this then goes to the landlords for rent (not to be spent until period $t + 1$), one quarter is 'consumed' within the agrarian sector, the last quarter goes to the 'steriles' in payment of manufactures for the farmers' use. The 'steriles' do not add any value but only reproduce it. Of the 500 they received from the landlords, 250 units are absorbed by their and their workmen's consumption of their own products. For the other 250 they buy food and raw material from farmers in whose hands these 250 again swell up to 500. And the same happens with the 250 and any later amounts they get from farmers. Whatever the farmers receive is always doubled and used for payment of rent to the landlords to be spent in period $t + 1$ for consumption in the agrarian sector and for further purchases from the 'steriles.' It will be readily seen that, if the length of the unit period be properly chosen, we shall find at the end of it that the 1000 units of net income are back again in the hands of the landowners, who will, at the beginning of period $t + 1$, spend them and so start the whole process again. The reader will realize that all this, apart from the pictorial form, amounts to no more than a development in fuller detail of Cantillon's schema.[9] But what is the use of this picture, and what is the nature of the analytic achievement it embodies?

It should be observed at the outset that so far as the idea of such a schema is concerned the specifically physiocrat features in the Cantillon-Quesnay

[9] The question how 'credit' should be distributed between Cantillon and Quesnay is both difficult and, from the standpoint of the sociology of scientific invention and scientific success, interesting. Cantillon no doubt felt the scientific need for some such tool, had the idea of how to construct one, *and* actually pointed the way toward doing so. If one of these three criteria for attributing inventions to individuals had been absent, the case would be much easier to deal with: as it is, Cantillon did for the *tableau* method what *both* Newcomen and Watt did for the steam engine. Yet I frankly confess to a reluctance toward attributing to Quesnay no more than the merit of sharpening Cantillon's concepts and putting results into the *tableau* form which puzzled and attracted. Such deep understanding and wholehearted absorption of another man's work is rare unless it is propelled by original perception of the same thing. Moreover, as will presently be pointed out in the text, an essential part of the achievement was the circuit-flow idea. It is tempting to assume that this idea came independently to Quesnay, the physician, through analogy with the circulation of the blood in the human body. William Harvey's (1578-1657) discovery of the latter was then a century old but had lost nothing of its freshness (*Exercitatio anatomica de motu cordis et sanguinis,* 1628).

tableau are irrelevant. Having dealt with these already, we are therefore no longer interested in the central position Cantillon and Quesnay assigned to landowners and their expenditure: we could just as well start from one of the two other 'basins.' Nor are we any longer interested in what was of primary importance to Quesnay, namely the principle that every sum that goes to farmers increases (doubles) in their hands and that sums that go to manufacturers do not. Every analyst can arrange these points so as to suit his theoretical set-up. What we are now interested in is the *tableau* idea considered as a tool, the *tableau* method itself. Three aspects of it call particularly for attention.

First of all, the *tableau* method achieves a tremendous simplification. Actually the economic life of a nonsocialist society consists of millions of relations or flows between individual firms and households. We can establish certain theorems about them, but we can never observe all of them. But if we replace them by relations between classes or by flows of class (or other) aggregates, the unmanageable number of variables in the economic problem suddenly reduces to a few which are easy to handle and follow up. Reserving this aspect for later discussion, we take the opportunity of noticing a cognate though different point. A glance at the *tableau* suggests the idea of a Social Product or Total Output that is produced in one series of steps and 'distributed' in another. We are so familiar with this idea that we rarely if ever realize how very unrealistic an abstraction it is. Production and distribution are indeed different processes in a socialist society. But in capitalist society they are but different aspects of one and the same process: the bulk of capitalist incomes is formed in the course of the transactions that constitute production in the economic, as distinguished from the technological, sense. Nevertheless, the realistic idea of income formation—the realistic virtue of which moreover does not carry any disadvantage that might justify its neglect—has come to the fore only sporadically.[10] With the French economists, the physiocrat idea of distribution prevailed throughout and the same holds true of English economists who adopted it, perhaps, under the influence of J. B. Say, at the beginning of the nineteenth century. The concept of total annual output and its value (*valeur de la reproduction annuelle*) has, of course, its uses independently of this. It was adopted by A. Smith.

Second, the simplification of the analytic pattern achieved by the *tableau* method opens up great possibilities for numerical theory. Quesnay was more alive to these possibilities than had been Cantillon and, in this particular respect, he carried the latter's work much further. He troubled himself about statistical data and actually tried to estimate the values of annual output and other aggregates. That is to say, he did genuinely econometric work. This aspect, too, has acquired new actuality in our time through the great work of Leontief,[11] which, entirely different though it is from Quesnay's in purpose

[10] The first to urge the case for income formation vs. distribution was, I believe, E. von Philippovich (in the later editions of his textbook, *Grundriss der politischen Oekonomie*, 1st ed., 1893-1907).

[11] Wassily W. Leontief, *The Structure of the American Economy* (1941; new rev. ed., 1951).

and technique, nevertheless revived the fundamental principle of the *tableau* method. Marx, who stands between the two, did not attempt to make his schema statistically operative.[12]

Third and most important, the Cantillon-Quesnay *tableau* was the first method ever devised in order to convey an *explicit* conception of the nature of economic equilibrium. It would seem impossible to exaggerate the importance of this achievement if admiring disciples had not actually succeeded in doing so. Economics, like every other science, started with the investigation of 'local' relations between two or more economic quantities, such as the relation between the price of a commodity and the quantity of it that is available in a market; in other words, it starts with Partial Analysis (see below, Part IV, ch. 7, sec. 6). Disconnected efforts of this type were directed toward points that happen to be of some practical interest or to attract our curiosity for other reasons. It was but slowly that the fact began to dawn upon analysts that there is a pervading interdependence between all economic phenomena, that they all hang together somehow. We have seen that the best of the seventeenth-century Discourses of Trade, such as Child's or Pollexfen's or, still more, the writings of Davenant, display unmistakable symptoms of a growing awareness of this. But they never bothered to investigate *how* things hang together. They took it for granted and either were unable to raise this interdependence to the plane of explicit formulation or did not see the necessity for doing so. They were very far from realizing that this all-pervading interdependence is the fundamental fact, the analysis of which is the chief source of the additions that the specifically scientific attitude has to make to the practical man's knowledge of economic phenomena; and that the most fundamental of all specifically scientific questions is the question whether analysis of that interdependence will yield relations sufficient to determine—if possible, uniquely—all the prices and quantities of products and productive services that constitute the economic 'system.' I have said on a previous occasion that the first discovery of a science is the discovery of itself. But this does not spell discovery of its fundamental problem. That comes much later. In the case of economics, it came particularly late. The scholastics had an inkling of it. The seventeenth-century businessmen-economists came nearer to it. Isnard, A. Smith, J. B. Say, Ricardo, and others all struggled or rather fumbled for it, every one of them in his own way. But the discovery was not fully made until Walras, whose system of equations, defining (static) equilibrium in a system of interdependent quantities, is the Magna Carta of economic theory—the technical imperfections of that monument of constitutional law being an essential part of the analogy (see below, Part IV, ch. 7, sec. 7). The history of economic analysis or, at any rate, of its 'pure' kernel, from Child to Walras might be written in terms of this conception's gradual emergence into the light of consciousness.

Now Cantillon and Quesnay had this conception of the general interdependence of all sectors and all elements of the economic process in which—so Dupont actually put it—nothing stands alone and all things hang together.

[12] On Marx's reproduction schema see P. M. Sweezy, op. cit. Appendix A.

And their distinctive merit—shared, to some extent, by Boisguillebert—was that, without realizing the possibilities of the method later on adumbrated by Isnard, they made that conception explicit in a way of their own, namely, by the *tableau* method: while the idea of representing the pure logic of the economic process by a system of simultaneous equations was quite outside their range of vision, they represented it by a picture. In a sense, this method was primitive and lacking in rigor—which is, in fact, why it fell out of the running and why analysis historically developed on the other line. But in one respect it was superior to the logically more satisfactory method; it visualized the (stationary) economic process as a circuit flow that in each period returns upon itself. This is not only a method of conveying the fact that the economic process is logically self-contained, a distinct thing that is complete in itself, but it is also a method of conveying features of it—definite sequences in particular—that do not stand out equally well in a system of simultaneous equations. Of course, there is also the simplification of the theory of general equilibrium adverted to already: Quesnay identified general equilibrium, that is, equilibrium in the economy as a whole in distinction to the equilibrium in any particular small sector of it, with the equilibrium of social aggregates—exactly as do the modern Keynesians.[13]

4. Turgot

Although Turgot was no econometrician, his great name has been assigned this place in our gallery because he is so often classed with the physiocrats, though mostly with qualifications. At first sight, this seems reasonable enough, for his main work abounds in passages that are evidently intended to emphasize allegiance to specifically physiocrat tenets. We read that land is the *only* source of *richesses;* that the *cultivateur* produces not only his own compensation but also the income that serves to remunerate the class of artisans and other *stipendiés;* that the farmer's activity is the prime mover of the social engine, whereas the manufacturer's only transforms; that the farmer supports and feeds all other classes; and so on. But, if we look more closely, we make a surprising discovery. Those passages are then seen to be strangers to the argument into which they are inserted. We can suppress them without affecting the rest. In fact, the rest gains in consistency thereby. Therefore, if we adhere to a principle that is uniformly applied in this book to the interpretation of such professions of faith, namely, the principle of relevance to analytic procedure and results, we have no choice but to neglect those passages. What are we to think of this? First of all, commonly accepted rules of criticism would lead us to suspect those passages if we were dealing with an ancient text. And it so happens that in this particular case such distrust is not completely unwarranted. For we know that there was a not quite amicable discussion between Dupont and Turgot on the subject of the publication of the latter's manuscript, and we do not know exactly what the result was. However, I will waive

[13] See in particular Joan Robinson, 'The Theory of Money and the Analysis of Output,' *Review of Economic Studies*, October 1933.

this point. But quite independently of it, there is, considering what we know of Turgot's generous character, no difficulty in understanding why, writing for publication at that particular time, he should have gone out of his way to pay respect to a group with which he agreed on many points of scientific economics—from which he had, perhaps, learned a good deal, for example, in matters of capital theory—and with which he agreed wholeheartedly on all the immediately practical points of economic policy, though he disagreed with them on some points of their political philosophy. According to this hypothesis, which puts him, morally, high above all those who emphasize points of difference in order to distance themselves from fellow workers to whom they owe obligation, he should not be classified as a physiocrat with reservations, but as a nonphysiocrat with physiocrat sympathies. This seems, in fact, to meet the case.

We went to the trouble of disentangling Turgot from the physiocrats not only in order to make his figure stand upon its own pedestal, as it should, but also in order to put this pedestal into the right place. For more closely than with the physiocrats was he associated with another group, if 'group' is the word for a very loose connection that was no school in the proper sense of the term. It centered in a strong and influential man, who was no doctrinaire, however, and no exponent of any 'system'—Gournay.[1] This fact throws

[1] Jacques C. M. Vincent de Gournay (1712-59) was a bourgeois businessman (the 'de Gournay' came from an estate that was left to him by a business connection) who later in life made himself a public servant by the purchase of the office of intendant of commerce. He was an altogether superior sort of person of a type that is rare outside England. But his great services to economics are by no means easy to characterize. They are not embodied in publications (he wrote reports, though, and also notes to translations of English economic works). Nor are his letters and various utterances (one of which has become famous: *laissez faire, laissez passer* has been attributed to him) adequate to convey what he means to the history of our science. We know pretty well his role in shaping opinion on economic policy by exerting formative influence upon some of the best minds of the age, and we also know in a general way what it was he advocated: relaxation of the fetters of public control, moderate protection, and that sort of thing. But we can only *sense,* or reconstruct from a few indications, the formative influence upon analytic work. He appointed himself, as it were, tutor to his friends, whom he knew how to choose and, like a good tutor, he effaced himself in order to give stimulating pointers to other people's teaching. His two provable claims to our gratitude are his successful propaganda for Cantillon's work and his contribution to Turgot's education as an economist. But below these two peak achievements there must have been broader middle ranges. In the highest sense of the word Teacher, this man who never taught in the technical sense may have been one of the greatest teachers of economics that ever lived. Therefore it seems that the traditional place that practically every textbook on the history of economics or economic thought accords to him is well merited, however slender the direct evidence that justifies it. The whole literature on physiocracy deals with him. G. Schelle's *Vincent de Gournay* (1897) is still the standard work. See also Turgot's '*Éloge de Vincent de Gournay*' in the latter's *Oeuvres,* and A. Oncken's *Die Maxime: Laissez faire et laissez passer . . .* (1886).

much light on Turgot's background as an economist. Gournay had traveled extensively and was an intelligent observer of English developments. Much of what we know about his views has a distinctly English flavor. And among his writings are several translations, in particular one of Child's *New Discourse*. Turgot was his personal friend and was also interested in the works of English economists, especially Hume and Josiah Tucker, whom he translated. If the obvious inference may be trusted, we have here an instance of the way in which not only political but also scientific ideas crossed and recrossed the Channel. The possible filiation Child-Hume-Turgot is particularly interesting—still more so in case we have to add the name of A. Smith after that of Turgot.[2] In the French part of his background, the most important figure is Cantillon.

Turgot's brilliant achievements, his unchallenged place in the history of our science, and his evident title to membership in the triumvirate in which Beccaria and A. Smith are his colleagues are sufficient reasons why it is desirable to look for a moment at the man and his career. Anne Robert Jacques Turgot, Baron de l'Aulne (1727-81; referred to, by his contemporaries, as M. de Turgot; before 1750, he was known as Abbé de Brucourt), came from a Norman family that was of old, if not high, nobility and fairly well to do, if not rich. The sociological type is rendered by the English word 'gentry' and by the German word 'Junker.' He was, as a third son, educated for the Church, and this clerical education, which gave full scope to his brilliant and precocious gifts, ought to receive recognition, though it usually does not, in an enumeration of the factors that made for his achievements. He emerged full of great plans and master of wide horizons (scientifically and otherwise) as an abbé at the Sorbonne, where he became quite a figure, writing, discussing, experiencing the second formative influence of his youth, that of the 'secte encyclopédiste,' though he very soon moved away from it. Then he exchanged the career of churchman for the civil service, and a civil servant he remained for the rest of his active life. The bureaucracies of all times and countries may be proud of him, for not only was he an ornament of the French bureaucracy of the *ancien régime*, but this bureaucracy also was the third of the environmental influences that helped to form him. He was a great success as *intendant* (general administrator) of the district (généralité) of Limoges, 1761-74, where his zeal, resourcefulness, and public spirit showed up to best advantage. On the strength of this success he was appointed, in 1774, Minister of the Navy and, a few months later, *Contrôleur Général des Finances* (which means Minister of Finance and Commerce and Commissioner of Public Works), a position he held for twenty months, much of the time tortured by gout. After his fall, he lived in retirement until his death.

Except for the just pride we economists may take in so brilliant a fellow worker, the main importance of this career for a history of economic

[2] See below, ch. 6, sec. 6.

analysis is that it explains why Turgot's scientific work did not come to full fruition. Biographers and historians of economic thought, however, have always allocated most of their space to his exploits as a minister of finance and, in dealing with them, have propagated two sagas that have a bearing upon the sociology of our science and must therefore be briefly noticed. Before doing so I wish, however, to disclaim any intention of 'debunking' the fame of one of the none too numerous significant figures of which the history of economics can boast: it goes without saying that nobody would think of writing a volume on Great Ministers of Finance without including Turgot. The first of those sagas might be entitled: 'The Economist in Action.' It depicts the man who, from scientific analysis, derives recipes for curing the ills of the state and, on attaining power, rushes to carry them into effect. There is nothing whatever in this. Turgot was, first and last, a great civil servant, who looked upon state and society with the eyes of a civil servant. So, when he attained cabinet office—'power' would be a misleading term to use—he set about to improve the financial administration and the all but desperate situation of the royal finances. In both these respects he succeeded remarkably—in fact almost unbelievably—well, and these were his main achievements. He also established, by royal decree, internal free trade in grains and—the only other measure relevant for us—abolished the *jurandes*, the craft guilds. These and some minor measures were not successes in the political sense mainly because of his failure to consider tactical aspects: they immediately elicited violent resistance, the one concerning the grain trade through a piece of bad luck—its coincidence with a bad harvest. The point to be observed is, however, that nothing Turgot actually did or showed any intention of doing has any particular relation to any doctrine, scientific or other. It was all in the line of an unusually able civil servant who perceived the currents of his time and tried to serve them in a practical spirit. He was so little given to obeying abstract principles—which of course is all to his credit—that, in one instance, he actually introduced a protective duty, and, in another, embarked upon state enterprise (in the chemical industry). The physiocrats applauded him, of course, and made propaganda for him, but they had little to do with his policies and nothing to do with his advent to office, for in 1774 they were in no position to exert any influence. By the same token, his fall was not a defeat of any doctrine that was specifically their own.

The other saga derives from the saga of the French Revolution. Since most of the writers on Turgot were and are in sympathy with the latter, they were and are inevitably driven to exalting into 'heroes that fought for the light in the darkness of despotism' a chosen few of the servants of the *ancien régime*. Turgot is the chief beneficiary of this tradition that was initiated by the revolutionaries themselves, who, even officially, sometimes referred to Turgot as *ce bon citoyen*. And some writers have added the touch that Turgot was raised to office by the voice of the people and dismissed at the behest of an intriguing court. As a matter of fact, Turgot was appointed *Contrôleur* by a thoroughly well-meaning monarch who looked around among his bureaucrats for the best man for the job. If there was any other influence, it was that of the Minister de Maurepas. As soon as he was in office Turgot, no doubt with the most meritorious intentions, began to lean heavily on the royal prerogative. Now it is very easy, when a minister is supported by a monarch, to draw up excellent decrees and to force them down the throats of *parlements* who refuse to register them. The difficulty, since government is carried on among living people and groups, is to make those decrees accepted. Louis XVI at first lent his wholehearted support, but the trouble with him, who had many good qualities, was precisely that he was no despot and quite unwilling to use force. And though Turgot was also the target of court and other intrigues—of the former, mainly owing to his policy of retrenchment—it was the popular resistance of the rural proletariat and of craft guilds that became after a time the dominant factor of the situation: there were even local revolts which Turgot suppressed with a firm hand. It would not be true either, but it would be nearer the truth than is the opposite, to say that Turgot was raised to ministerial office by the king and overthrown by the people. For our purpose, the relevance of this is in the light it sheds on the personality of one of the greatest scientific economists of all times. The interpretation submitted makes the king come off better than does the usual one but, what alone matters here, it does not make Turgot come off worse. It only makes him come off differently. We see the excellent civil servant who is a good administrator and (perhaps) adviser but no leader or tactician. We also see honesty and firmness (quite as much as do other interpreters) and (what does not, perhaps, impress these other interpreters quite as much) loyalty to his king. The answer to the academic question that has been raised, whether or not, had he stayed in office, he might have prevented the Revolution, depends on what we mean by revolution. If we mean the overthrow of the monarchy and the sanguinary excesses, the answer should be in the affirmative: no more, however, because of the reforms he might have carried in that case than because of his willingness to call out the troops. No cap of liberty will fit Turgot.

His chief work, the *Réflexions sur la formation et la distribution des richesses*, was written for the benefit of two Chinese students in 1766, and published (as has been stated above, not without some friction that arose from Dupont's attempts at editorial interference, presumably made in the interest of physiocrat orthodoxy) in the *Éphémérides* (1769-70; English trans. 1898). Of minor publications that usefully supplement this work, the most important are the *Éloge de Gournay*, the letter on paper money to the Abbé de Cicé (his first economic publication, 1749), the *observations* on the essays by St.-Péravy (1767) and Graslin (1767) on indirect taxation, and a paper on loans of money (1769). His contributions to the *Encyclopédie*, including such topics as 'existence,' 'expansibility,' and 'etymology,' and his criticism of Berkeley's philosophy—and many others—are interesting as so many proofs of the breadth of his range. The *Oeuvres* of Turgot were edited by Dupont de Nemours (1808-11) and again by G. Schelle (1913-23), the latter edition being the one to use. Léon Say's *Turgot* has been translated into English by M. B. Anderson (1888). Also see Alfred Neymarck, *Turgot . . .* (1885); S. Feilbogen, *Smith und Turgot* (1892); W. W. Stephens, *The Life and Writings of Turgot* (1895); and especially G. Schelle, *Turgot* (1909).

If we now try to compare Turgot's scientific personality with those of Beccaria and A. Smith, significant similarities strike us first: all three were polyhistoric in learning and range of vision; all three stood outside the arena of business and political pursuits; all three displayed single-minded devotion to the duty in hand. Turgot was undoubtedly the most brilliant of the three, though his brilliance was somewhat tinged with superficiality, not in economics, but in his outlying intellectual domains. The main difference, from the standpoint of their scientific achievement, is that A. Smith expended very little of his energies on nonscientific work, Beccaria very much, and Turgot, from 1761 on, almost all he had. During the thirteen years at Limoges, Turgot can have had but scanty leisure; during his (nearly) two years of ministerial office, practically none: his creative work must have been done between the ages of 18 and 34. And this explains all there is to explain, not indeed about the comparative merits of the three works in question, but about the different degrees to which they were finished works at all.

Turgot was much too able a man to write anything insignificant. Nevertheless, only the Turgot specialist needs to go beyond the *Réflexions*, and with one exception we shall confine ourselves to this. The slender work was evidently written in hot haste and never thoroughly revised. It looks as Marshall's *Principles* would look if text, notes, and appendices were destroyed and only the marginal summaries—and not all of those—were preserved. In fact, it is not much more than a very elaborate analytic table of contents written for a bulky but nonexistent treatise. Such as it is, however, Turgot's theoretical skeleton is, even irrespective of its priority, distinctly superior to the theoretical skeleton of the *Wealth of Nations*. In order to arrive at this opinion, it is not necessary to impute to Turgot anything he did not actually say or to credit him with any implications of what he did say that he may possibly not have seen himself. He actually delivered the goods. In calling the work unfinished or a skeleton, I do not mean to say that there is need for uncertain conjecture or generosity of interpretation in order to finish it. It presents a complete system of economic theory. What is lacking any competent economist could supply without adding (except criticism) from his own stock of knowledge. Of course, nobody admires the *Wealth of Nations* for its theoretical skeleton alone. It owes its position to its mature wisdom, its luxuriant illustrations, its effective advocacy of policies. And there is, also, something to be said for the ponderous creation of the academic professional: it was the product of patience, of meticulous care, of self-discipline—and we cannot be sure that Turgot would ever have produced something comparable to it, even if he had had all the leisure in the world. Still, a lesson does follow from the very different success of both works: in economics, at least, intellectual performance is not enough; finish counts; and so do elaboration, application, and illustration; even now the days are far off when it will be possible, as it is in physics, to shape international thought by an article that covers less than one page. Turgot's contribution fared as well as it did because of his eminence in another walk of life. Even so it never bore the fruits that it easily might have borne.

Since the only satisfactory way of summarizing that summary is to transcribe it, and since, moreover, the most important points will be touched upon in subsequent chapters, only a few general comments will be offered here instead of a Reader's Guide. Roughly the first third of the treatise—the first 31 sections [3]—presents the groundwork including the Cantillon-Quesnay schema of classes and an analysis of their relations in production and distribution that is splashed with physiocrat colors. Certain fundamental propositions, like the proposition that competition always reduces wages to the minimum-of-existence level, are insisted on from the first. Sections XXXII-L contain a theory of barter, price, and money that, so far as it goes, is almost faultless, and, barring explicit formulation of the marginal principle, within measurable distance of that of Böhm-Bawerk. The rest of the treatise is devoted mainly to a capital theory that anticipates most of the nineteenth-century work, and to the subjects of interest, saving and investment, and capital values. Originality in individual points is difficult to assert or to deny, the more so because Turgot does not quote—which is no reproach in the case of such a sketch. But comprehensive vision of all the essential facts and their interrelations plus excellence of formulation are in evidence to a degree that would make the whole of the work an original contribution even if no individual point had been exclusively Turgot's own. And there are practically no definite errors to be found in this first of all the treatises on Value and Distribution that were to become so popular in the later decades of the nineteenth century. It is not too much to say that analytic economics took a century to get where it could have got in twenty years after the publication of Turgot's treatise had its content been properly understood and absorbed by an alert profession. As it was, even J. B. Say—the most important link between Turgot and Walras—did not know how to exploit it fully.

[3] [Apparently, the numbering of the sections in the Schelle edition of the *Oeuvres* differs slightly from the original version in the *Éphémérides* where one (or more) of the sections was suppressed. See ch. 6, sec. 7, n. 5.]

CHAPTER 5

Population, Returns, Wages, and Employment

1. The Principle of Population

The problems of population, that is to say, the questions what it is that determines the size of human societies and what the consequences are that attend the increase or decrease in the number of a country's inhabitants, might well be the first to occur to a perfectly detached observer as soon as he looks at those societies in a spirit of scientific curiosity. The view that the key to historical processes is to be found in the variation of populations, though one-sided, is at least as reasonable as is any other theory of history that proceeds from the prejudice that there must be a single prime mover of social or economic evolution—such as technology, religion, race, class struggle, capital formation, and what not. Thus it is quite understandable that population problems should have received attention in the very beginnings of economic analysis; that they should have loomed large in the thought of all leading writers of the period under discussion; and that they should have been given a place of honor in the one great pre-Smithian system of economics that England produced, Sir James Steuart's *Principles*.

But there was also a practical reason for this prominence of population problems. Ever since primitive tribes had solved theirs by abortion and infanticide, people in general and social philosophers in particular never ceased to worry about them. Roughly speaking until the end of the sixteenth century, the trouble arose from a relation between birth rates and death rates that was incompatible with stationary or quasi-stationary economic environments: the problem of population was one of actual or threatening overpopulation. It was from this angle that it presented itself to Plato and Aristotle. The opposite type of trouble was quite exceptional—the outstanding example is the decay of the native Roman stock in the last century of the Republic and throughout the epoch of the Empire. In the Middle Ages the dwelling places of the lower stratum of the warrior class, the simple knights, suffered from overcrowding whenever there were no crusades, wars of the Roses, epidemics, and so on to reduce numbers; and the artisans' guilds offered livelihood for restricted numbers only and experienced perennial difficulties with ever-lengthening 'waiting lists.' But all this changed during the seventeenth and eighteenth centuries. We have seen that the practical economic problems of those centuries were the problems of countries that were poor in goods but rich in possibilities. Seen against these possibilities, the population problem became one of underpopulation. Moreover, some countries, particularly Germany and Spain, had actually experienced depopulation for decades together.[1] And, as we have also seen, these conditions prevailed when ideas of national or territorial power and expansion filled everybody's thought and heart.

[(a) *The Populationist Attitude.*] Accordingly, governments began to favor increase in population by all means at their command. Measures differed from time to time and from country to country but were in some cases—for instance in France under Colbert—as energetic as any that have been resorted to by modern dictators. Economists fell in with the humors of their age. With rare exceptions they were enthusiastic about 'populousness' and rapid increase in numbers. In fact, until the middle of the eighteenth century, they were as nearly unanimous in this 'populationist' attitude as they have ever been in anything. A numerous and increasing population was the most important *symptom* of wealth; it was the chief *cause* of wealth; it *was* wealth itself—the greatest asset for any nation to have. Utterances of this kind were so numerous as to render quotation superfluous. In England, in particular, the first-flight men who go on record as leaders of populationist sentiment, such as Child, Petty, Barbon, Davenant, were joined by almost all the rank and file.[2] That German and Spanish writers went further than any others is amply explained by the conditions of their countries. Since Italy had a comparatively dense population and was least favored as regards opportunities for national expansion, the Italian economists went less far in this direction and, later on, less far in the opposite one than did their English and French brethren. As always, the one question that interests us is: what was the economic rationale of all this, if indeed economic analysis had anything to do with it at all? The answer should be obvious. The analytic complement of the populationist attitude boils down to one proposition: *under prevailing conditions,* increase in heads

[1] German and especially Spanish writers may have exaggerated the extent to which there was depopulation. The fact itself is nevertheless beyond doubt.

[2] Most of those writers came within the traditional category of 'mercantilists,' who as a group have been charged with the famous 'confusion' between wealth and money or gold and silver which will have to be noticed later on. It is interesting to note, therefore, that some of the writers who seem to be most guilty of that confusion, such as the author of *Britannia Languens* (W. Petyt), at the same time 'confuse' wealth with size of population. That author, for instance, expressly stated that 'people are . . . the chiefest, most fundamental, and precious commodity.' Should not this make us pause before we take either of these 'confusions' too literally? But there were also dissenting voices. One of the earliest of them was that of Malynes, who already pointed to the 'positive checks' that increase would eventually bring into operation.

would increase real income per head. And this proposition was manifestly correct.

With unimportant exceptions, these conditions did not substantially change in the eighteenth century or even in the first decades of the nineteenth. Therefore, it is quite a problem to explain why the opposite attitude—which might be called anti-populationist or, to associate it with the name of the man who made it a popular success in the nineteenth century, Malthusian—should have asserted itself among economists from the middle of the eighteenth century on. Why was it that economists took fright at a scarecrow! The first step toward a solution of this problem is to localize the emergence of the Malthusian attitude. German and Spanish economists were not afraid of the scarecrow. In fact there never was any native Malthusianism either in Germany or Spain: such Malthusianism as there ever was in those countries was the product of English teaching during the first half of the nineteenth century. The Italians, as stated above, had some real reason to be (mildly) frightened, and were. But the cradle of the genuinely anti-populationist doctrine was France. The second step toward a solution is therefore to find out whether there was not something in the economic and political situation of France that might, 'objective' opportunities notwithstanding, suggest pessimism as regards the economic future of the country and thus explain that change in attitude. As a matter of fact, there was. During practically the whole of the eighteenth century France was fighting a losing battle with England. Many of her leading spirits began to accept this defeat by 1760 and to discount the opportunities for national expansion. Moreover, the outworn institutional pattern of the last half century of the monarchy was not favorable to vigorous economic development at home. Thus, thought turned from bold venture to the possibilities offered by agriculture, from dreams of evolution to the picture of a 'mature' or quasi-stationary economy. The third and final step, then, is to explain why anti-populationist sentiment gained a hold on the English mind in spite of the fact that exactly the opposite state of things prevailed in England. In order to understand this we have to realize that the long-run trend of an evolution is one thing, and the sequence of short-run situations through which it fights its way is quite another thing. Thus, the English populationists of the seventeenth and eighteenth centuries may have been quite right in considering rapid increase as motor, condition, and symptom of economic development, and equally right in worrying at the same time, as most of them actually did, about the short-run vicissitudes, the unemployment in particular, which accompanied that development; this does not convict them of contradiction either in their analysis or in their recommendations. But in the Industrial Revolution of the last decades of the eighteenth century, these short-run vicissitudes grew more serious than they had been before, precisely because the pace of economic development quickened. And some economists—as will be pointed out in a moment, a minority only—were so impressed by them as to lose sight of the trend. The resulting anti-populationist mood then produced the set of analytic propositions that came to be known, in the nineteenth century, as the Malthusian principle or theory of population. Before considering its early history, we must attend to another matter.

[(b) *Growth of Factual Knowledge*.] In the United States the first census was taken in 1790; in England in 1801. In Canada and in some countries of continental Europe there had been earlier ones, but it was only in the first decades of the nineteenth century that reliable information about the numerical facts of population became available at regular intervals. The writers of the seventeenth and eighteenth centuries, therefore, theorized about population in ignorance of statistical facts. All they had to go on, if we except the rare cases in which local observation yielded definite results, were untrustworthy indications and vague impressions: thus, it was possible for English writers to disagree on such a question as whether the English population had increased or decreased during the century between 1650 and 1750. Hence, the investigations that were undertaken in order to dispel this fog and the resulting controversies exemplify a peculiar type of theory. Ordinarily, theoretical analysis is concerned with facts that are, or are supposed to be, known: it marshals, interprets, explains, establishes relations between, and generalizes from given facts or 'data.' This, of course, is also what the theory of population was to do in the nineteenth century. But in the seventeenth and eighteenth centuries, the main task of research on population was not to analyze given facts but, so far as possible, to find out what the facts actually were: it was the kind of theory that, unlike other kinds, retreats before advancing factual knowledge and must eventually be replaced by it. But the work done by those investigations—first by the Political Arithmeticians—also laid the foundations of the later theory of population. For many of the considerations that were originally developed in order to form an idea of the facts, served later on to interpret them. This is why examples of those controversies are presented below.

Sir William Petty's *Essay concerning the Multiplication of Mankind* (2nd ed. rev. and enl., 1686) is the standard example of seventeenth-century speculation about the facts. Sir Matthew Hale's *Primitive Origination of Mankind* (1677; partly republ. in 1782 under the title of *Essay on Population;* on the author see J. B. Williams, *Memoirs of the Life, Character and Writings of Sir Matthew Hale*, 1835) may also be mentioned. Both authors infer facts, on scanty observations, mainly from 'laws' derived from general considerations.

Of eighteenth-century controversies we shall first notice one that arose from Montesquieu's statement in the *Lettres persanes* that the ancient world was more populous than was the Western world of his time. In his essay 'Of the Populousness of Antient Nations' (*Political Discourses*, 1752), Hume proffered reasons for the opposite opinion that were criticized by Robert Wallace in the Appendix to his *Dissertation on the Numbers of Mankind* (1753), in which he upheld Montesquieu's thesis. Wallace found a follower in William Bell, who expanded the discussion on numbers into a discussion of causes and effects: in his dissertation *What Causes principally Contribute to Render a Country Populous?*

And what Effect has the Populousness of a Nation on its Trade? (1756) he presented the theory that the development of manufacture and trade, by diverting resources from the production of foodstuffs, tends to produce a decrease in population (which he took to be a fact and of which he disapproved); accordingly, he advocated fostering agriculture and an equal distribution of land among farm families. This tract called forth another, *A Vindication of Commerce and the Arts* (1758) by W. Temple (a clothier, not to be confused with Sir William Temple, the seventeenth-century statesman and writer). No great importance attaches to either Bell's or Temple's works. They are mentioned here because of a similar discussion on a similar subject that took place half a century later and is much better known: opinions not unlike those of Bell, having been re-asserted by Thomas Spence, elicited a reply by James Mill that established his reputation as an economist.

Another controversy was more interesting. In 1779, Richard Price, now mainly remembered on account of his proposal to establish a sinking fund that would extinguish the national debt, published an *Essay on the Population of England* in which he stated that population had decreased by one-fourth since the revolution of 1688 and that urban agglomeration was responsible for it. Naturally this was attacked by a number of writers, especially by W. Wales (*An Inquiry into the Present State of Population in England and Wales*, 1781), John Howlett (*Examination of Dr. Price's Essay* . . . 1781), and others, A. Young among them. Howlett's contribution is the most interesting one, not only because it is a good example of the art of reasoning on inadequate facts but also because, like Bell, he launched out into an analysis of related economic phenomena. In particular, he interpreted enclosures as a consequence of the increase in population and as a 'cause' of some of those improvements in agriculture that were called for because of that increase —a theory in which there was an important element of truth.

[(c) *Emergence of the 'Malthusian' Principle.*] The theory of population as understood in the nineteenth century, however, that is to say, a theory of the factors—or 'laws'—that determine numbers and rates of increase or decrease, emerged much earlier than that.[3] Divested of nonessentials, the 'Malthusian' Principle of Population sprang fully developed from the brain of Botero in 1589: populations tend to increase, beyond any assignable limit, to the full extent made possible by human fecundity (the *virtus generativa* of the Latin translation); the means of subsistence, on the contrary, and the possibilities of increasing them (the *virtus nutritiva*) are definitely limited and therefore impose a limit on that increase, the only one there is; this limit asserts itself

[3] See especially: René Gonnard, *Histoire des doctrines de la population* (1923); J. Bonar, *Theories of Population from Raleigh to Arthur Young* (1931); C. E. Stangeland, *Pre-Malthusian Doctrines of Population* (1904); J. J. Spengler, *French Predecessors of Malthus* . . . (1942); F. Virgilii, *Il Problema della popolazione* (1924). Readers are referred to these works for details of a story that cannot be presented here.

through want, which will induce people to refrain from marrying (Malthus' negative check, prudential check, 'moral restraint') unless numbers are periodically reduced by wars, pestilence, and so on (Malthus' positive check). This path-breaking performance—the only performance in the whole history of the theory of population to deserve any credit at all—came much before the time in which its message could have spread: it was practically lost in the populationist wave of the seventeenth century. But about two hundred years after Botero, Malthus really did no more than repeat it, except that he adopted particular mathematical laws for the operation of the *virtus generativa* and the *virtus nutritiva:* population was to increase 'in geometric ratio or progression'—that is, in a divergent geometric series—food in 'arithmetic ratio or progression.' [4] But the 'law of geometric progression,' though not in Botero's work, was suggested by Petty in his *Essay concerning the Multiplication of Mankind* (1686), by Süssmilch (1740), by R. Wallace (1753), and by Ortes (1774), so that, within this range of ideas, there was nothing left for Malthus to say that had not been said before. Of the eighteenth-century authors who, without committing themselves to this particular mathematical form, stated that population will always increase to the limit set by the supply of means of subsistence, it will suffice to mention Franklin [5] (1751), Mirabeau (1756)—who expressed himself in his picturesque manner: men will multiply to the limits of subsistence like 'rats in a barn'—Sir J. Steuart (1767), Chastellux (1772),[6] and Townsend (1786).[7] Steuart, whose priority Malthus was to acknowledge, was particularly explicit. Exactly as Botero did, he took the 'generative faculty' as a constant force to be compared to a spring that is held down by a weight and is certain to respond to any decrease in this weight. Townsend defined the limiting factor as 'hunger, not as directly felt or feared by the individual himself, but as foreseen and feared for his immediate offspring.' As far as I know, Ortes was the only writer to admit that 'reason' may have more influence than is implied in the anticipation of want—an influence that he illustrated by the celibacy of the Catholic clergy.

Botero, then, was the first to sound that note of pessimism which was to become so famous a bone of contention in the days of Malthus: as we have seen, he associated increase of population with actual or potential misery. But most of the authors who believed that populations tend to increase without

[4] If an initial value be denoted by a and another constant by b, then a geometric series runs like this: $a, ab, ab^2, ab^3, \ldots$ The series is divergent, i.e. the sum of its elements soars above any figure we care to name, if b is equal to, or greater than, unity. An arithmetic series runs like this: $a, a + b, a + 2b, a + 3b \ldots$ It is always divergent.

[5] Benjamin Franklin, *Observations concerning the Increase of Mankind.* Still more than others Franklin treated the case of human populations in the light of the general case of all animal species. On the other hand, he emphasized 'room' and 'enemies' as limiting factors rather than food.

[6] François Jean, Marquis de Chastellux, soldier by profession, published a treatise *De la félicité publique* that is not without merit.

[7] Joseph Townsend, see especially his *Dissertation on the Poor Laws,* 1786.

assignable limit did not share Botero's pessimism but were on the contrary in sympathy with the populationist sentiments of their times and countries. Petty and, before their conversion to the Botero-Malthus view of he matter, Mirabeau and Paley may serve as examples.[8] This position involves, of course, no error of reasoning. For the fact that a population *is physically capable* of multiplying until it lacks not only food but also ground to stand on is no cause for worry unless complemented by the additional proposition that *it actually will* tend to do this instead of merely responding to an expanding economic environment by growing along with it (or even, possibly, by a decrease in the birth rate). In other words, population must actually tend to 'press against' the food supply. But even if such a tendency be admitted, it need not cause any worry about the calculable future or, what is more important for us, have any relevance to the explanation of contemporaneous phenomena. For this to be the case it is evidently not sufficient to believe that population will or may 'press against' food supply at some indefinitely distant time: we must believe the pressure to be either actually present or actually imminent. Unless this can be established, belief in that tendency is compatible with the opposite belief as regards any given situation or as regards the outlook *ex visu* of any given situation. The reader may well think that I am placing unnecessary emphasis upon these obvious distinctions, but their neglect is responsible for the futility of many of the controversies that arose about population both in the eighteenth and in the nineteenth centuries.

A work by R. Wallace[9] will, however, illustrate the way in which mere belief in pressure of population at some indefinitely remote future may after all be made relevant to economic analysis. Wallace considered equalitarian communism as the absolutely ideal form of society. Nevertheless, he rejected it. And the only reason he adduced for doing so was that in such a society there would be no check to the operation of mankind's physical powers of multiplication, so that the career of a communist society would eventually have to end in overcrowding and misery—a standpoint that evidently did not imply any opinion about the situation that actually prevailed in Wallace's

[8] Petty listed populousness among the main assets of the Netherlands which made them such formidable competitors of England. Mirabeau, in those parts of *L'Ami des hommes ou traité de la population* that were published in 1756, declared that a large population is a blessing and the source of wealth: agriculture should be encouraged precisely because this would make people multiply like rats. It was Quesnay himself who induced Mirabeau to reverse the causal relation between wealth and population. William Paley (*Principles of Moral and Political Philosophy*, 1785, Book VI, ch. 11) held the same opinion. He was converted by Malthus' *Essay* and recanted in his *Natural Theology* (1802).

[9] *Various Prospects of Mankind, Nature, and Providence*, 1761. This work was criticized by Godwin and, since Malthus' work in turn started from a criticism of the latter's ideas, Wallace may have had more influence upon what became known as Malthusianism than any other of the writers who anticipated Malthus' doctrine. Malthus did full justice to Wallace's work but made it quite clear that, unlike Wallace and like Quesnay, he believed that pressure was an actual and indeed ever-present fact.

time. Whatever we may think of the merits of the argument, it presents two characteristic features that cannot be underlined too strongly. First, if the proposition about unchecked multiplication were valid, it would evidently come near to being a 'natural law' in the strict sense of the term. Most of the English economists of the subsequent hundred years accepted it as such—as formulating an inexorable quasi-physical necessity. The same economists were in the habit of claiming similar necessity and universal validity, not only for those economic propositions that are nothing more than applied logic, but also for others such as their 'law of wages.' It is evidently not unreasonable to suspect that this habit of the English economists had something to do with their belief in that biological 'law.' If this be so, the question of the classic 'eternal laws of economics' should not be treated as a question of the philosophy of scientific method but simply as a question of the validity or relevance of an individual proposition. Second, it never seems to have occurred to Wallace to look for obstacles to human perfection other than mankind's power of multiplication: except for the dangers that threatened from this he had no more doubt about human perfectibility than had Condorcet. This was in keeping with the superficial sociology of the Enlightenment, but it is interesting to note that Malthus and in fact all the 'classics' seem to have been of the same opinion. I know of only one writer who at least sounded the eugenic note. It was Townsend. In the work mentioned above he argued that provision for the 'idle and vicious' would put a burden on the 'more prudent, careful, and industrious' that would restrain them from marrying: 'the farmer breeds only from the best of his cattle; but our laws choose rather to preserve the worst. . .'

The outstanding authority for the other opinion, that is to say, for the opinion that pressure of population was actually present around 1750—and is in fact an ever-present phenomenon—was Quesnay. Unlike Cantillon, from whom he broke away in this point,[10] he held not only that propagation has no other limits than those of subsistence but also that it tends *always* to go beyond them. The only justification he proffered for this dogmatic statement was that, always and everywhere, there are people who live in poverty or want (*indigence*). This overpopulation theory of poverty is of the essence of 'Malthusianism.' But before the publication of Malthus' *Essay* it had so few adherents that to this day most historians attribute it to him. Populationism did not indeed hold its own—not, at least, outside Germany and Spain. But everywhere economists refused to accept the opposite view. Most of them seem to have agreed with Bishop Berkeley, who delighted in the vision of joyfully bustling multitudes, or with Hume, who called the happiness of society and its populousness 'necessary attendants.' Accordingly, A. Smith summed up by reducing the principle of population to a stale truism, preserving however its character as a natural law: 'every species of animals naturally multiplies in proportion to the means of their subsistence, and no species can ever multiply beyond it.'

[10] Substantially, Cantillon was populationist. But he touched in passing upon the problem 'whether it is better to have a great multitude of poor people or a smaller number of more prosperous ones.'

(*Wealth*, Book I, ch. 8.) And at the same time he declared, in the spirit of the old populationists, that 'the most decisive mark of the prosperity of any country is the increase of the number of its inhabitants' (ibid.). Beccaria discounted both the enthusiasms and the pessimisms of economists about increasing numbers: he recognized that increase was not always a blessing to be prayed for at all times; but also that there was no reason for being afraid of it at all times. In fact he seems to have been the one authority to teach explicitly the obviously sensible view. Genovesi went further than this, however, in effecting a synthesis between the two opposites. He saw that, from the standpoint of a population living under given conditions, numbers are capable of being either too small or too great in the sense that increase or decrease would produce greater 'happiness.' This led Genovesi to reassert the old idea of optimum population (*popolazione giusta, Lezioni*, Part I, ch. 5) that was to be sponsored again by Knut Wicksell. This concept is difficult to handle and perhaps not very valuable. But it has the merit of bringing out the truth that populationism and Malthusianism are not the mutually exclusive opposites they seemed to be to so many people.

2. Increasing and Decreasing Returns and the Theory of Rent

[(a) *Increasing Returns.*] We have seen that the populationist attitude, so far as it is economically motivated, implies a belief that increase in population will (within limits) increase per capita wealth or, as we may also put it, a belief in Increasing Returns. So does, in most cases, the protectionist attitude that went with populationism (see below, ch. 7). The idea of increasing returns in this sense—that is to say, increasing returns with reference to a national economy as a whole, and irrespective of any well-defined reason why returns should be increasing and of whether it is physical returns or returns in terms of money that are meant—is no doubt a hazy one and does not amount to more than an 'inkling' of any of the various meanings that the concept was to acquire. But beyond such inklings, which were of course very frequent, we also find here and there more precise arguments such as Petty's argument that expenditure on what may be termed social overhead—expenditure on government, roads, schools, and so on—does not, other things being equal, increase proportionately with population: this puts increasing returns into the not quite equivalent form of decreasing cost per unit of service, but nevertheless identifies a definite phenomenon that can be observed in every society and in every individual firm. Before this, a general law of increasing returns in manufacturing industry, also in the form of a law of decreasing unit cost, had been stated explicitly and in full awareness of its importance by Antonio Serra,[1] much as it was to be stated in the nineteenth-century text-

[1] *Breve trattato* (1613), Part I, ch. 3: *nell' artefici vi può essere moltiplicazione . . . e con minor proporzione di spesa* (in manufacturing industry, output may be increased at less than proportional increase in expense). Serra does not tell us to what this fall in cost is due. It may be plausibly assumed, however, that he thought of the same facts that A. Smith was to enumerate.

book. The restriction of increasing returns to manufacturing should be particularly noticed. Serra did not indeed assert that agrarian production was subject to decreasing returns. But the idea that industrial and agrarian production as such follow different 'laws' was as clearly expressed by him as if he had. Thus he foreshadowed an important feature of nineteenth-century analysis that was not completely abandoned even by A. Marshall. In the seventeenth and eighteenth centuries, however, most economists said nothing about this. But many implied, or even explicitly said, that increasing returns prevailed also in agriculture. We shall presently discuss the most important example of this position. At the moment let us notice that A. Smith, more than a century and a half after Serra, took a view that was closely similar to his. He clearly, though loosely, stated a law of increasing returns for manufactures: first, in connection with division of labor (Book I, ch. 1) and, second and more fully, in the digression on the 'Effects of the Progress of Improvement upon the Real Price of Manufactures,' which he inserted into Part III of his huge chapter on the rent of land (Book I, ch. 11), where he attributed the fact that 'a much smaller quantity of labour becomes requisite for executing any particular piece of work' 'in consequence of better machinery, of greater dexterity, and of a more proper division and distribution of work.' [2] But nowhere did he state a law of decreasing returns, though he repeatedly brushed against it, especially in Chapter 11. In fact, in Chapter 1, he merely noted a difference between agricultural and industrial production in the scope they offer for ever increasing division of labor, and his text is compatible with the interpretation that he meant to assert increasing returns also for agriculture but to a lesser degree. And this in spite of the fact that the two cases of decreasing (physical) returns, which West and Ricardo were to recognize, had been fully described before him by Sir James Steuart (1767) and Turgot (1767).[3]

[(b) *Decreasing Returns: Steuart and Turgot.*] Steuart in his *Principles* (1767)—and after him Ortes in his *Economia Nazionale* (1774)—presented what the late followers of Ricardo were to call the case of the Extensive Margin: as population increases, poorer and poorer soils have to be taken into cultivation and, applied to these progressively poorer soils, equal amounts of productive effort produce progressively smaller harvests. Turgot discovered the other case of decreasing physical returns, the one that the same followers of Ricardo were to refer to as the case of the Intensive Margin: as equal quantities of capital (*avances*)—amounts of labor would, however, do just as well in this

[2] Observe that this statement mixes up two entirely different things: 'better' machinery seems to point to an effect of the widening of knowledge—the Technological Horizon—that occurs in the course of economic development. Improved division of labor, on the other hand, is one of the consequences of mere increase in output and may occur within an unchanging technological horizon or an unchanging state of the industrial arts.

[3] Observations *Sur le Mémoire de M. de Saint-Péravy*, included in the editions of the *Oeuvres* (mentioned in ch. 4, sec. 4). The date given in the text is not absolutely certain; moreover, it is the date of writing. We do not know how wide or narrow a circle of readers the paper reached at the time.

case—are successively applied to a given piece of land, the quantities of product that result from each application will first successively increase up to a certain point at which the ratio between increment of product and increment of capital will reach a maximum. Beyond this point, however, further application of equal quantities of capital will be attended by progressively smaller increases in product, and the sequence of these decreasing increases will in the end converge toward zero. This statement of what eventually came to be recognized as the genuine law of decreasing returns cannot be commended too highly. It embodies an achievement that is nothing short of brilliant and suffices in itself to place Turgot as a theorist high above A. Smith. It is much more correct than are most of the nineteenth-century formulations—Turgot's formulation was indeed not surpassed until Edgeworth [4] took the matter in hand.

A particularly felicitous feature is the insertion of an interval of increasing returns before the interval of decreasing returns; that is to say, the recognition of the fact that decreasing returns do not prevail right from the application of the first 'dose' of some variable factor but set in only after a certain point has been reached. This should have disposed, once for all, of the erroneous opinion that he who asserts that extension of production will, under given circumstances, be attended by increasing returns therefore denies the validity of the 'law of decreasing returns.' Moreover, Turgot's increasing returns are defined with unsurpassable neatness: they are the increasing returns that attend the application of a variable factor to one that is given in a fixed quantity—or to a set of factors whose quantities are held constant—*before the optimum combination of factors is attained.* Thus, Turgot may be said to have formulated a special case of what American economists around 1900 were to call the Law of Variable Proportions.[5]

[4] See below, Part IV, ch. 6, sec. 5b.

[5] The same thing may be expressed, by means of a different concept, in a somewhat different way. This concept, which emerged toward the end of the nineteenth century (see below, Part IV, ch. 7, sec. 8), is now being called the Production Function. This function expresses the technological relation that exists between the quantity of product and the quantities of the 'factors' that co-operate in varying proportions to produce it. Reducing, for the sake of simplicity, the number of these factors to two, we may mark off the quantities of the product and of the two factors on the axes of a system of rectangular space co-ordinates. Every point in space that corresponds to any positive and finite values of those three quantities will then represent that quantity of product that can (at best) be produced by the corresponding quantities of factors, and the set of all these points will identify a surface in three-dimensional space, the production surface. Now let one of the factor quantities be held constant, and cut this surface by a plane at right angles to this factor's axis and go through the point on this axis that corresponds to the constant. The curve of intersection between the surface and the plane will represent Turgot's law of first increasing and then decreasing returns. Though Turgot did not discover either the production function or its geometric picture, the production surface as such, we may say that he discovered a property of it, viz., the form of one of its contours, and hence that he got hold of something, possession of which (with ordinary care and competence prevailing in our science) should

And finally it must be recorded to Turgot's credit that he stated his law in terms of successive increments of product and not in terms of average product (per unit of the variable factor). This means that he actually used marginal analysis and that command of modern technique could have improved only the form of his statement. There is really nothing to criticize in it except inadequate awareness of the necessity to specify both the product for which his law is to hold and also the variable factor that is to be applied: the basketful of disparate things that hide behind his *avances* does not meet the latter requirement but merely dodges it.[6] To the further objection that he did not emphasize the fact that his law made sense only with a given state of technological knowledge, or a given technological horizon, or a given production function—as we should say—he would probably have replied that this goes without saying. But we are about to see that this is not so. Another point must, however, be noticed before we go on.

Both Steuart and Turgot spoke of agriculture only. Fifty years ago this would not have astonished anybody, since it was then established practice to restrict decreasing returns to agriculture. But we who take it for granted that neither increasing nor decreasing returns are restricted to any particular branch of economic activity but may prevail in any branch, provided certain general conditions are fulfilled, are in a position to realize how surprising that actually was. Explanation seems to lie in the fact that, to the unsophisticated mind, there is something particularly compelling in the limitations imposed upon human activity by an inexorably 'given' physical environment. It takes prolonged effort to reduce the analytic importance of these limitations to their proper dimensions and to divorce them from the soil and the industry that works the soil. Yet it should not have taken so long to see that there is really no *logical* difference between trying to expand output on a given farm and trying to expand output in a given factory, and that if farms cannot be indefinitely multiplied or enlarged, neither can factories. The additional explanation required is provided by the belief of practically all eighteenth-century authors—a belief that carries over to the 'classics' of the nineteenth century—that while the factor land was given once for all, the other original factor, labor, would always increase to any amount required if allowed to do so. If we adopt this view, we shall at once sympathize with the reluctance of those authors to treat labor and land alike and to apply the laws of physical returns impartially to both. Then we shall also sympathize with the lopsided analytic structure they set up.

---

have brought out the production function of today before the eighteenth century was out. The reason why this argument is being inflicted upon the reader at this stage is that the case is so revelatory of the 'ways of the human mind,' which rarely discovers the obvious and fundamental first. More often it gets hold of some particular aspect of an idea and then works back to the conceptions that hold priority in logic.

[6] Unless the factor applied is such a definite physical thing as a fertilizer of invariant kind and quality or even labor of a given kind and quality, difficulties arise that threaten the meaning of the law.

[(c) *Historical Increasing Returns.*] As we have seen above, asserting that, in a given situation, increasing returns prevail in a country's agriculture, that is, that increase of input would be attended by more than proportional increase in output, does not imply denial of the validity of the law of decreasing returns. This fact must now be brought to bear upon the interpretation of the views of those English economists and politicians who actually did make that assertion. Whether right or wrong in point of fact, their position was logically defensible if they meant no more than either or both of two things. They were all right as to logic (though possibly wrong as to their facts) if they meant that in the last decades of the eighteenth century English agriculture [7] was moving in an interval of increasing returns, that is to say, that land had not yet received its optimum complement of other factors. They were not less right in logic (and, to some extent, in fact) if they meant that there were looming in the future possibilities of improving agricultural methods of production that would materialize if additional resources ('capital') were made available to agriculture—in the same way in which this was actually happening in industry. Observe, however, that this is something quite different from the increasing returns we have been discussing. We can indeed, if we so choose, speak of increasing returns' attending increased application of resources also in this case. But these spells of increasing returns, unlike the others, do not occur within the given pattern of technological practice. Like A. Smith's improved machines they involve a change in this pattern. If we visualize Turgot's intervals, first of increasing and then of decreasing returns, as a curve that ascends, reaches a maximum, and then descends,[8] then we see that the increasing returns in the previous sense are depicted by a section of the curve, but that increasing returns in the sense now under discussion are not. They can, however, be represented by shifting the whole curve upward (altering its shape or not as the case may require) into a new position: the old curve breaks off and is replaced by a new one that keeps a higher level (though not necessarily all along its course) but again displays both an interval of increasing returns in the previous sense and an interval of decreasing returns. The increase in returns in the new sense occurs as the curve shifts from its old to its new position. It should be added that, if the curve shifts again and again, there is no reason why the differences between these successive levels should grow

[7] Those authors and politicians always spoke of returns to agriculture as a whole just as nineteenth-century economists were in the habit of doing. Strictly, however, the laws of returns in the sense of Turgot are defined only for the individual farm. It is an additional merit of Turgot that he so envisaged them. Transition to a whole industry, let alone the national economy as a whole, is not quite such plain sailing as primitive analysis assumes.

[8] See footnote 5 above. To repeat, the abscissae of the curve there described represent successive equal 'investments' of some resource, say, labor of a given quality, the ordinates the corresponding amounts of total product. But we may also let the ordinates represent the *increments* in total product that successively result from each additional dose of 'investment.' Of course, this 'derived' curve (of marginal products) will reach its maximum before the other does.

smaller: *there is no law of decreasing returns to technological progress.* In order to avoid confusion between two entirely different phenomena, we had better restrict the term Increasing Returns to Turgot's case. This we shall accordingly do. When we wish to retain the association between the two, misleading though it is, we shall use, for the phenomenon now explained, the phrase Historical Increasing Returns. The phrase has been chosen in order to indicate that these historical increasing returns cannot, like the genuine ones, be represented by any curve or 'law,' least of all by a curve on which we can travel back and forth. For new levels of technique are reached in the course of an irreversible historical process and are hidden from us until they are actually reached.

An example will illustrate this situation. One of the most interesting English economists of the late eighteenth century, Anderson,[9] boldly asserted that man's power to increase the productiveness of his fields was such 'as to make it keep pace with his population whatever that might be.' [10]

This has been interpreted to spell denial of the law of decreasing returns, Malthus being the first of Anderson's critics to misunderstand him in this sense. But Anderson's emphasis was not upon the *product* but upon the *productiveness* of land. And this, together with his reference to 'discoveries' which occurs in the same passage, should be sufficient proof that all he was thinking of was what we have just decided to dub Historical Increasing Returns. In Anderson's case, it is particularly easy to satisfy ourselves that his no doubt exaggerated ideas concerning these possibilities were compatible with the recognition of the law of decreasing returns. Though it is true that he nowhere mentioned Turgot's case, it is equally true that he accepted Sir James Steuart's case. For he actually invented the 'Ricardian' theory of rent which presupposes it.

[(d) *Rent of Land.*] We have seen that the explanation of the rent of land was not one of the problems that attracted attention in the early stages of economic analysis. Cantillon and, after him, the physiocrats, may be said to

[9] James Anderson (1739-1808) was a Scottish gentleman farmer. His numerous writings are as important for an appreciation of the course of the corn-law controversy as they are for the history of economic analysis. The most important ones are: *Observations on the Means of exciting a Spirit of National Industry . . .* (1777); *An Enquiry into the Nature of the Corn Laws* (1777); and several essays in his 6 volumes of *Recreations in Agriculture, Natural History, Arts, and Miscellaneous Literature* (publ. 1799-1802). He had to an unusual degree what so many economists lack, Vision.

[10] *Recreations,* Vol. IV, p. 374; the passage has been quoted by Cannan, *A History of the Theories of Production and Distribution* (3d ed., 1917, p. 145), in order to prove that the law of decreasing returns was unknown to the agriculturalists of that time. It is of course beyond doubt that they were thoroughly confused about it and that, since Turgot's performance had passed unnoticed, professional and political opinions of the time sometimes read like unalloyed nonsense. But it should not be asserted without qualification that they actually were unalloyed nonsense or that they were always vitiated by the ignorance of that law.

have been the first[11] to entertain a distinctive view of the phenomenon: it simply amounted to the proposition, if we may couch it in terms of a later time, that land yields rent because it is a scarce factor of production (or even the only 'original' one), and that this rent is partly an interest payment on investments made by the landlord and partly a payment for the 'natural and indestructible productive powers of the soil.' This theory was primitive and not fully articulate but nevertheless superior to many later speculations. In addition to the merit of saying or implying nothing that is definitely wrong, it had another one that raises it above triviality: whoever holds this theory thereby proves his awareness of the fact that productiveness and scarcity, in the case of a costless factor, are sufficient to account for its yielding a net return so that there is no point in looking for other explanatory circumstances. But this is precisely what most economists failed to realize, then, and throughout the first half of the nineteenth century. Accordingly, they engaged in speculations that produced, before the eighteenth century was out, both the theories of rent that were to prevail during the subsequent epoch (roughly to the last quarter of the nineteenth century). The one may be associated with the name of Adam Smith, the other with the name of James Anderson.

A. Smith's theory of value, which will be discussed in the next chapter, yields the result that, under conditions of competition, a costless thing really cannot have a price. The services of land are costless: A. Smith explained at length that these services are not to be identified with the services of the capital that may have been invested in the land. Nevertheless, they fetch a price. Hence 'the rent of land . . . considered as the price paid for the use of land, is naturally a monopoly price' (*Wealth*, Book I, ch. 11). If this were true, rent would have to 'enter into the composition of the price of commodities' exactly as do profit and wages, which A. Smith explicitly denies on the next page. But of course it is not true: the landed interest is not a single seller and therefore its income cannot be explained by the theory of monopoly. The poverty of this rent analysis is overlaid by a plenty of materials and detailed comment that made the eleventh chapter burst the framework of Book I. Many of these details deserve recording but we must confine ourselves to three. First, A. Smith placed much emphasis upon the rent of location. Second, he worked out a theory that was to enter Malthus' stock in trade, and that kept on cropping up in the lower strata of the nineteenth-century theory, namely, the theory that 'Human food seems to be the only produce of land which always and necessarily affords some rent to the landlord' (ch. 11, Part II) because, by virtue of the principle of population, food production is the only kind of production which, as it were, will always create its own demand—mouths always increasing in response to every increase in the supply of food.

11 This disregards the comments that Petty made on the subject—which do not amount to much—and also something else. Those authors who, like Locke, explained—or 'justified'—property in land by labor invested in it might be interpreted to have held a labor theory of rent. Such attributions are, however, unsafe and I prefer not to stress this point.

Though comment is, I trust, superfluous concerning the merits of this proposition, it is not superfluous to point out that this sort of thing goes far toward justifying the animosity to *theory* harbored by institutionalist and historical economists. It is for the same reason that I mention a third theory (presented in the Conclusion of ch. 11): believing that *every* increase in the real wealth of society tends, directly or indirectly, to raise the real rent of land, he concluded that the class interest of the landowners 'is strictly and inseparably connected with the general interest of society' so that, unlike 'those who live by profit,' landowners when speaking from the standpoint of their class interest 'never can mislead' the public in its search for measures that promote the general welfare. A truly unbelievable piece of reasoning—the premiss could be shown to be wrong from material and argument within the covers of the *Wealth*, and the conclusion would not follow even if the premiss were right.[12]

As has been stated, we need nothing beyond the productiveness and the scarcity of land in order to explain why there is such a thing as rent. Neither the fact to be explained nor the explaining facts have anything to do with decreasing returns. However, the association of rent with decreasing returns, which was to be one of the most characteristic features of the Ricardian system, was established by Anderson. In his *Observations* of 1777 he arrived at the conclusion that the rent of land is a premium paid for the privilege of cultivating soils that are more fertile than others, and in his *Enquiry* of the same year he formulated more precisely the conditions which Cannan stated established the formula: 'The rent paid in respect of any particular boll is equal to the difference between the expense of raising the most expensive boll raised and the expense of raising that boll,' explaining fully how the competition among farmers will secure exactly this amount for the landlord.[13] In a later essay, included in the *Recreations* (Vol. v), he presented another aspect of the same idea by saying that rent was a 'contrivance' for equalizing the profits on lands of different fertility—an emphasis upon the 'law of the average rate of profit' that makes him a forerunner of Ricardo in still another sense. Except for the claim that it explained rent, all this was quite correct so far

[12] Reasoning such as this indicates certain limitations of a man's judgment once for all. But we are also within our rights to suspect such an argument of ideological bias, precisely because of the obviousness of its faults. Therefore, it is interesting to note that as a matter of fact A. Smith harbored an ideological bias *against* the landed interest (see below, ch. 6) so that no explanation can be derived on this line.

[13] I fail to understand why the late Professor Cannan, who quoted the passages (op. cit. pp. 371-3) should have thought it necessary to warn his readers that 'Anderson's anticipation of particular points in the Ricardian theory must not be mistaken for an anticipation of the whole theory.' It is true that Ricardo also noticed the Turgot case of decreasing returns. But his reasoning practically runs in terms of the Steuart case, just as does Anderson's. Like Anderson, moreover, Ricardo seems to have thought that there would be no rent if there were no decreasing returns, thus confusing the latter with scarcity of land. Hence, as far as the *theory* (to which Cannan specifically refers) is concerned—and not the diagnosis of the actual conditions of English agriculture or the political recommendation—I cannot see any difference whatsoever between Anderson and Ricardo, or, for that matter between Anderson and West.

as it went. But the achievement of anticipating a century's thought on this subject would have been a noteworthy one, even if all of it had been wrong.

3. Wages [1]

The most obvious analytic use to which the principle of population can be put is surely the theory of wages. Many writers—among the leaders, especially Quesnay and Turgot—might be cited to show how easy it was, starting from an uncritical acceptance of that principle, to arrive at a minimum-of-existence theory of wages as an equally uncritical conclusion. Since, moreover, the physiocrat theory of capital—the idea of the *avances*—was of a nature to suggest the concept of a 'wage fund,' another pillar of Ricardian economics was thus erected by pre-Smithian writers, mainly French.

But the proposition that wages per head tend toward a minimum-of-existence level (however defined) is no more a theory of wages than the quantity theory is a theory of money. Both are propositions about the values certain economic quantities assume in a state of long-run equilibrium and form part of a comprehensive theory of wages or money—that is, if we believe in them—but are not the whole of it. No such comprehensive theory was worked out before A. Smith. But many pre-Smithian economists contributed fragments. The most important of these contributions was Child's, discussed above in Chapter 4. It had nothing to do with the principle of population. Child, as we know, was a populationist who declared that 'most nations in the civilized parts of the world are more or less rich or poor proportionable to the paucity or plenty of people.' This paucity or plenty he made dependent upon 'employment,' so that we may interpret him to have meant that the wage rate is determined, on the one hand, by the demand for labor and, on the other hand, by the supply that this demand calls forth. This was a good beginning, the more so because Child said nothing about the particular level at which the forces of demand and supply would fix wages. In particular, he kept clear of any minimum-of-existence law. Instead, he said that high wage rates are the consequence and 'infallible evidence' of the riches of a country. Davenant went a little further in his statement that in a poor country interest is high and land and labor cheap. Also other writers got as far as this. But nowhere do we find more than this until we reach the minimum-of-existence theorists mentioned above.

This does not mean, of course, that people were not interested in wage questions. On the contrary, economists debated them eagerly and practically every one of them left us his opinion about wage policy. But most of these

[1] The works on the history of population doctrines all take some account of the history of wage doctrines as well, but Spengler's should be particularly mentioned. Facts as well as views the reader finds in Heckscher and Mantoux. Also, see E. S. Furniss, *The Position of the Laborer in a System of Nationalism* (1920), which work, however, concentrates on the task of bringing out one particular aspect of the picture and does not aim at presenting the whole; and R. Picard, 'Etude sur quelques théories du salaire au XVIIIe siècle' in *Revue d'histoire des doctrines économiques* (1910).

utterances were preanalytic in nature. They reveal sentiments and evaluations that reflect important aspects of social history and are a legitimate object for the application of the Marxist theory of ideology, provided that it be handled without unintelligent dogmatism. For us, however, these sentiments mean only an additional difficulty of interpretation: we are driven to unraveling elements of analysis from the various recommendations of our authors—or such reasons as they give for their normative statements—and in doing so we are in constant danger of mistaking for an analytic proposition what may have been no more than a profession of sympathies. Thus Child, though he interpreted high wages as a symptom of wealth, did not proffer any high-wage theory in the sense that high wages are in themselves a factor that makes for prosperity. But he was evidently in sympathy with high wages and hence *seems* to have held a high-wage theory in this sense. That this was not the case we can see from the way in which he behaved when confronted with a low-wage argument. He did not really argue but simply got angry and hurled defiance at the obnoxious doctrine: 'a charitable project and well becoming a userer!' Other authors offer hints at motivating analytic propositions. Some—including Cary—looked upon high wages as a part in the mechanism of brisk business and adumbrated the purchasing-power argument. Others were of the opinion that high real wages are conducive to better performance.[2] But this did not amount to much. Neither did the reasoning of the low-wage men. Petty's argument was that high wages would only encourage sloth and that if wages were doubled the supply of labor hours would be reduced to half. The most important argument on this side of the question was, of course, the argument from competition in international trade. It was because high wages would impair the competitive situation of the country that Sir James Steuart held that wages 'should' be kept at the level of physical necessities.[3] D. Hume also believed

[2] For example, Daniel Defoe (*c.* 1659-1731) in *Plan of the English Commerce* (1728); B. Franklin, in his *Reflections on the Augmentation of Wages*, also distinguished high wages from high cost of labor per unit of product.

[3] There cannot be any doubt, of course, that many declarations in favor of low wages simply and naïvely voice class interest and are not the result of any attempt at appraising causes and consequences in a scientific spirit. Not only did low-wage opinions fit the social structure and the resulting national spirit of those times, but also whatever low-wage opinions were held were quite freely uttered because the labor interest was not yet a political factor and intellectuals therefore did not side with it. So opinions were held with regard to labor—and voiced without inhibitions—that sometimes recall the opinions held by the Romans with regard to their slaves as voiced, e.g., by Cato. That the welfare of the laborers, or 'laboring poor,' or simply the poor, should have been, by implication, denied the status of an end in itself—in the economic literature roughly until Beccaria and Smith—does not necessarily mean what it seems to mean. For such statements also occur with respect to the merchant class and are only what we should expect in a nationalist civilization. But opinions could be cited to the effect that workmen 'should' be kept poor, and ignorant as well as poor, that they 'should' be strictly disciplined and, in order to facilitate this, kept at work from early youth and continually, so that they should never know what it is to be at leisure and so on. Such views, like the opposite ones, naturally tended

that high wage rates are detrimental to a country's foreign trade, though he did not draw the same conclusion; on the contrary, he went on to say that this disadvantage weighs lightly as compared with 'the happiness of so many millions.'

A. Smith's performance in the field of labor economics [4] is highly characteristic and in fact a fair sample of his work as a whole. Moreover it acquires additional importance by virtue of its having been the first fully systematic treatment of the subject. He no doubt followed the available leads but, scaling off edges here and developing there, he made a well-rounded whole of it that was qualified to serve, as in fact it did serve, as a basis of further analysis. First of all, he worked out a comprehensive theory of wages. Borrowing a natural-law proposition that was widely accepted in his time, namely, that 'the produce of labour constitutes the natural recompense or wages of labour,' he proceeded to explain how it came to pass that labor has to surrender part of 'its' product—meaning the entire result of the productive process—to landlords and another part to 'masters.' Observe that this indeed posits the fundamental problem of wages but that it does so in a peculiar way: A. Smith's argument starts from a pseudo-historic background of a natural state in which, on the one hand, there are no landlords and no 'masters' and in which, on the other hand, labor is the only scarce factor of production; confusing these two quite different facts, he reduced the problem of wages at once to the problem of the two other distributive shares which thereby became 'deductions from the produce of labour.' Rent is a deduction from 'natural' wages that is motivated not by the productivity of land but by the emergence of private property in it which tallies nicely with his monopoly theory of rent: some people monopolize land exactly as they might monopolize air, were it technologically possible to do so. And profit is another deduction motivated not by the productivity of capital—stock 'advanced' to the laborer—but solely by the power of its owners [5] to insist on it, a power that is much enhanced by the ease with which these owners can combine against the poor and helpless laborers who 'must either starve or frighten their masters into an immediate compliance with their demands.' The reader should realize both the obvious weaknesses that this argument presents when considered as a piece of analysis and the appeal it was bound to have. It foreshadowed, in fact, all the exploitation and bargaining-power theories of wages that the nineteenth

---

to reflect themselves in the analytic work emanating from their sponsors or in the way in which its results are formulated; and if that analytic work is rudimentary, it becomes still more difficult than it is in the case of elaborate theories, to separate what for brevity's sake we may call the logic and the class interest served by that logic. This political aspect is also important for the topics to be touched upon in sec. 4, which follows.

[4] The substance of it is to be found in chs. 8 and 10 of Book I of the *Wealth of Nations*. But additional facts and comments are scattered all over the work.

[5] It is only here, within the theory of wages, that A. Smith adopts this view. Elsewhere he leaves room for other elements, such as risk and trouble.

century was to produce, and also suggested the idea that labor is the 'residual claimant.'

A. Smith went much further than that, however. Since the laborer cannot live without the advances of the 'masters,' the latter can, strictly speaking, reduce his wages to the physical minimum of existence. But the masters' competition for labor will, with increasing national wealth, force them to 'break through the natural combination of masters not to raise wages' and will raise wage rates above that level for indefinite periods of time. Accordingly, A. Smith denied vigorously that wages in Great Britain were anywhere near the minimum-of-existence level or that they fluctuated with the price of provision as they would have had to do in that case.[6] For practical purposes this amounts to denying the validity of the physiocrat theory of wages. In principle, however, A. Smith accepted it. This reconciliation of two apparently contradictory opinions he achieved by emphasizing not so much the absolute level of the wealth from which the demand for labor proceeds but 'its continual increase'—it was not great wealth as such but increasing wealth which, outstripping increase in population, causes wage rates to rise in monetary as well as real terms. But wealth that does not increase, however great it may be, is no guarantee against low wages: the hands will 'in this case naturally multiply beyond their employment,' so that Quesnay would be right in the end. A. Smith also accepted the wage-fund theory, which he restated in the form that was to be the object of both elaboration and attack in the nineteenth century. When dealing with the demand for labor, he stated what reads like a harmless truism: this demand 'it is evident, cannot increase but in proportion to the increase in the funds which are destined for the payment of wages.' The joker that lurks behind the word 'destined' was responsible for many a headache later on. But A. Smith lightheartedly concluded that the demand for labor, since it comes either from the income of the well-to-do, who demand personal service, or from the stock of businessmen, who demand productive services, and since 'the increase of revenue and stock is the increase of national wealth,' will increase with the increase of wealth, 'and cannot possibly increase without it.' There is no more fertile source of error than apparently trivial premisses.

This theory of wages was copiously illustrated by all sorts of facts, which is why it gives the reader the impression of fullness and realism. Critical—and often wise—comments on the labor legislation and the poor laws of that and earlier times are freely inserted. And A. Smith's interest in the concrete phenomena of practical life is responsible for many analyses of particular questions, one of which may be mentioned. Abstract theory reasons about an imaginary wage rate, the counterpart of which in real life is a structure of widely varying wage rates. In order to make sure that a theory working with a single rate has any relevance at all to the explanation of real phenomena, we must

[6] This seems, however, to have been the prevalent popular opinion. Galiani in his *Dialogues* (see below, ch. 6) attributes it to *Le Marquis* whose role it is to voice popular opinions.

analyze the nature of the differences in the wages—and profits—earned in different employments and places. This is the kind of thing in which A. Smith both delighted and excelled. The lead had been given by Cantillon. But A. Smith went much more deeply into the matter, thus creating an important if not exactly exciting chapter of the nineteenth-century textbook.

4. Unemployment and the 'State of the Poor'

In principle, medieval society provided a berth for everyone whom it recognized as a member: its structural design excluded unemployment and destitution. Actually, the threat of involuntary unemployment was not completely absent. The journeymen who worked under the masters within the craft guilds were often, and the agricultural laborers (*mercenarii*) were always, hired workers whose employment was not guaranteed. But as a rule neither group had much difficulty in finding jobs. In normal times unemployment was quantitatively unimportant and confined to individuals who had broken loose from their environment or had been cast off by it and who in consequence had become beggars, vagrants, and highwaymen. The highwaymen were treated with brutal yet ineffective energy; with the other types, the charity enjoined and organized by the Catholic Church was perfectly able to cope. It is important to keep this pattern in mind because it formed an attitude toward unemployment and the unemployed that persisted for centuries after medieval conditions had passed away. Let us remember in particular that mass unemployment, definitely unconnected with any personal shortcomings of the unemployed, was unknown to the Middle Ages except as a consequence of social catastrophes such as devastation by wars, feuds, and plagues.

This changed in and after the fifteenth century. The breaking up of the medieval world, attended as it was by social upheavals, is in itself sufficient to account for the widespread suffering and destitution we observe. The agrarian revolution not only destroyed environments that might have sheltered fugitives from distressed areas but also caused the landless proletariat to increase more rapidly than did the effective demand for labor. The resistance to change offered by the organized crafts, while it protected some elements of the population, made things worse for others. The rising capitalist industry in the long run absorbed rather than created unemployment. But there were many bottlenecks that impeded the development of the new opportunities and the flow of labor into them. Moreover, when the pace of industrial development quickened in the second half of the eighteenth century, technological unemployment put in an appearance as a mass phenomenon and frequently overshadowed that long-run effect. This explains why the rise of the factory system was associated with so much misery: for many years labor was not attracted to the factories by higher wages and better living conditions, but driven into them in spite of lower real incomes and worse living conditions. The old protective regulations broke down not so much under the influence of laissez-faire philosophies as under the weight of actual or threatening unemployment. For a time, though not everywhere to the same extent, all barriers to the deterioration of the worker's lot were giving way. Thus it is not difficult to understand the paradox already noticed, namely, that governments and writers who were enthusiastically populationist never ceased to worry about how 'to set the poor to work' or how to combat 'idleness.' [1]

But the first problem that confronted European governments from the beginning of the sixteenth century was an administrative one. Everywhere the swelling numbers of destitute beggars and vagrants outgrew the possibilities of private charity and everywhere public organization of relief had to take its place. In England, earlier measures were systemized by the Elizabethan Poor Law of 1601, which definitely established the compulsory poor rate on a permanent basis. The poor rate was a tax that was levied in every parish for the maintenance of its own destitute inhabitants. The burden was considerable and above all very visible. Principles and results were evidently debatable. Accordingly, amendments were suggested, discussed, and actually enacted in an unending stream until the advent of modern security legislation. Because of the importance for the history of economics of the corresponding stream of books, pamphlets, and articles which for more than three hundred years were to deal with those problems, we had better note the two main questions at issue. The Elizabethan enactment had left the administration of the funds raised by the poor rate to honorary local officers elected for the purpose, a highly inefficient arrangement which was not radically changed until the Poor Law Amendment Act of 1834; thus the first question was one of central versus local control. The second question, which is more interesting from our standpoint, was Outdoor Relief versus Maintenance in a Workhouse. Outdoor relief was the original method which, owing to a variety of administrative abuses that were only in part inherent in its principles, elicited the criticisms that brought the workhouse method steadily to the fore, and thus prepared the ground for its temporary victory in 1834.[2] To repeat, legislation and administration in the seventeenth and eighteenth centuries did little to supplement existing systems of unemployment relief by measures for the protection of the employed with respect to hours, working conditions, and so on (not even in the case of women and children). In some continental countries we find the beginnings of factory legislation within our period, in Austria, for instance, under the reign (1781-90) of Joseph II. But in England there was next to nothing before the (ineffective) Health and Morals of Apprentices Act of

[1] Those conditions have been described numberless times with widely varying degrees of competence and accuracy. Reference to the works of Heckscher and Mantoux must again suffice for our purpose.

[2] The reader will find a sufficiency of relevant facts in almost any economic history. Three books, however, should be particularly recommended: E. M. Hampson, *The Treatment of Poverty in Cambridgeshire*, 1597-1834 (1934); S. and B. Webb, *English Poor Law History* (1927-9); and Dorothy Marshall, *The English Poor in the Eighteenth Century* (1926). An eighteenth-century history will be mentioned presently. The outstanding nineteenth-century history is Sir George Nicholls' *History of the English Poor Law* (1854), complemented by his histories of the Irish and the Scotch Poor Law (1856).

1802.[3] In another line, however, we may note the Friendly Society Act of 1793, which mitigated the legislation against corporative action by the workers.

The chief remedies for unemployment consisted in measures intended to foster manufacturing industry. We shall see later (in ch. 7) that concern about employment opportunity was one of the chief motives of 'mercantilist' policies. In some continental countries, especially in Germany, protection of the peasant holding was an important safeguard against pauperization of the industrial workers. And the deficit financing of continental governments, though not motivated by this purpose, certainly had some alleviating effects. England came much nearer to balancing her budgets. But some English writers, though they did not recommend deficits, were more alive to the possibilities of monetary remedies for unemployment than were their continental brethren.[4]

The late scholastics,[5] like their predecessors, had emphasized the role of charity and defended the beggar against the rough reactions of the environment. In particular, they had defended the 'right to beg.' But they came to realize that unemployment was growing beyond the possibilities of private benevolence and therefore entered upon a discussion of the possibilities offered by legislation and public administration, touching, first incidentally, later on more systematically, upon problems of causation. This discussion was taken up by laic writers, mainly the Consultant Administrators, all over Europe. In Germany, *das Armenwesen* naturally became a standard subject within the 'cameralist' literature. German governments accepted the state's responsibility for employment and maintenance as a matter of course. The same principle was repeatedly asserted in England, for example, by the Berkshire magistrates in 1795. But there is not much to record for the historian of economic analysis.[6]

In the first place, a great many writers on the poor laws argued on the explicit or implicit 'theory' that, barring misfortune, and especially sickness, the destitute unemployed was personally to blame for his fate. In appraising this view, contempt for its inadequacy as a theory of the social phenomenon to be

[3] See, e.g., B. L. Hutchins and A. Harrison, *History of Factory Legislation* (1903).

[4] The question how far economists of the seventeenth and eighteenth centuries may be credited with what we should call a monetary theory of employment will be briefly considered in the next chapter.

[5] The tracts by de Soto and de Medina (sixteenth century) mentioned already (see above, ch. 2), may again serve as examples from a large literature which continued to pour forth, especially in Spain and Italy, throughout the seventeenth and eighteenth centuries. We confine ourselves to noticing one of its latest and most successful products, Giovanni Battista Vasco's (1733-96) *Mémoire sur les causes de la mendicité et sur les moyens de la supprimer*, 1790 (republ., with other works of his, in the Custodi collection). Vasco was a Piedmontese priest who, under the influence of Turgot and A. Smith, developed into a thoroughgoing 'liberal' in the laissez-faire sense.

[6] For further information, see especially T. E. Gregory, 'The Economics of Employment in England, 1660-1713,' *Economica*, 1921. There is no equally valuable survey for any other country. Reference should, however, be made to the interesting article by G. Arias on Ortes' theory of unemployment, *Giornale degli Economisti*, September 1908.

explained, and indignation at the callousness of which it may be the symptom, must not blind us to the element of truth in it which has come to be as much underrated in our own time as it was overrated then. It was at the basis of the argument of the defenders of the workhouse system and survived, in various nuances, until 1914. The principles that relief should be confined to maintenance in the workhouse and that life and labor in the workhouse should be made less eligible than the least eligible employment may merely aim at testing the presence of destitution; actually, however, they were often associated with punitive intent that can be explained only on the theory in question. In the second place, writers who went beyond this mentioned a number of factors that were all of them more or less relevant to the explanation of either unemployment or substandard conditions among employed workers but without subjecting them to any elaborate analysis. The most important ones were foreign competition, high rates of interest, taxes and regulations that hampered enterprise, enclosures, and, mainly in connection with enclosures, property in land. It is very difficult to tell how much insight any such statement reveals. To mention one example, Child listed high interest as a cause of unemployment. But the reason he adduced was not that high interest may restrict investment but that it facilitates premature retirement from business, which, though not quite indefensible, looks very much like an analytic blunder. Machinery as a cause of unemployment (or of low wage rates) was mentioned with increasing frequency as the eighteenth century wore on. But nobody attempted to develop a theory of the mechanization of the productive process. On the whole, the opposite view prevailed, namely, that the introduction of machinery tends to increase employment and to raise wages. This opinion, already held by Cary, seems to have been shared by A. Smith. In the third place, during the last quarter of the eighteenth century a tendency asserted itself to explain unemployment by means of the 'principle of population.' The analytic nature of this line of reasoning can be best conveyed by an analogy. One of the familiar phenomena we observe in every depression is that producers cannot sell their wares at prices that will cover cost; hence nothing is easier than to jump at the conclusion that the root of the trouble is 'overproduction.' This is the most primitive of all theories of crises or depressions. And the most primitive of all theories of unemployment is that people cannot find work at living wages because there are too many of them. It was almost always at the bottom of arguments to the effect that more generous provision for the 'able-bodied poor' would make matters worse for the working class as a whole, or even that the poor law as it then stood was breeding poverty by fostering increase in population.[7] Observe that this theory, as far as there is anything to it at all, ap-

[7] Such arguments were freely and effectively used against the legislation proposed by William Pitt which would have favored large families. The outstanding performance in this discussion was Jeremy Bentham's *Observations on the Poor Bill . . .* [*of*] *Mr. Pitt* (1797), which foreshadowed the opinion of the 'classical' economists of the nineteenth century on what, speaking from their standpoint, we might describe as the Fallacy of Relief. See *Works*, vol. VIII.

plies equally well to the relief granted to unemployed persons, and to the subsidies that the poor-law authorities were in the habit of granting to persons employed at less than living wages. The latter practice was severely criticized on account of the administrative abuses to which it gave rise—it made it possible for local potentates to shift part of their wage bill on to the poor rate. This is probably the reason nobody produced anything that could pass for a tolerably adequate theory of wage subsidies. But the fundamental similarity between unemployment and employment at substandard conditions stood out all the more clearly. Both entered into the concept of 'poverty' or 'indigence,' which, as we know, Quesnay had been the first to explain by overpopulation.

The discussion on the related problem of child labor was still less productive of analytic performance. Children had always worked with their parents on the farm and, under the system of domestic industry, in the home. The spread of factories merely created new opportunities for the employment of children at a very early age in the tending of simple machines and induced a new practice of binding out the children of paupers to cotton manufacturers in order to reduce the poor rate. Those writers who were impressed by the incidental horrors or by the obvious consequences for the health of the race were few indeed. The large majority accepted child labor, not only as a matter of course but with approval—as a sound discipline and as a solution of many of the worker's problems. Some seventeenth-century writers hailed it as a boon to the masses and seem to have considered the children's earnings as a net addition to the family income of workers, without taking account of the effects that the competition of the children must produce on the wages of adults. This theory, which was held by Yarranton,[8] qualifies well as an example of ideological distortion of vision. But it also qualifies as an example of early economic reasoning that in spite of its crudity contained an element of truth. If we choose to disregard everything except money income, then it is likely that in the conditions of that time child labor did result in a gain to the working class—though this gain was certainly less than the amount of the children's earnings—and did promote Yarranton's ideal of cheapness and plenty. This attitude changed but slowly in the eighteenth century, and humanitarian feelings had more to do with it than had economic analysis. Many instances could be adduced of writers who mention full employment of children at as early an age as possible—at six or even four years—with unqualified satisfaction; or who at least accepted it unquestioningly as the normal state of things.[9] Arthur Young's estimates of the normal budget of a rural laborer's family take it for granted that

[8] Andrew Yarranton (1616-84), *England's Improvement by Sea and Land* (1677). Both the man and the book we shall meet again in ch. 7. It is of some interest to note that in his advocacy of extensive employment of children Yarranton pointed to German practice as an example to be followed.

[9] To quote at least one instance, in his *Tour thro' . . . Great Britain* (1724-7), vol. III, Daniel Defoe noted that in some English villages through which he traveled there were no children to be seen—inferring with pleasure that they were all at work as they should be. The same attitude is in evidence in his *Plan of the English Commerce* (1728).

the chief breadwinner could not have provided a minimum of existence for his family without the earnings of his wife and children.

But fact-finding activity was in a much better situation, and its results constitute, in the field of labor economics, the most important achievement of that epoch. The outstanding performance was Eden's,[10] which in scope and method has no equal in the English or any other literature of the period. Of particular interest for us is the fact that the author, although he disclaimed any intention beyond what fact-finding implies (he offers some interesting discussions, nevertheless), was fully aware of the importance of his facts, not only for the purpose of legislative and administrative practice but also for economic analysis. He worked, as he said himself, as one of the 'hewers of stone and drawers of water' without whom 'the edifice of political knowledge cannot be reared.' It is of the utmost importance to bear in mind, if the history of economics is to be understood, that, though the greatest figure, he was not alone in that field. Davies' collection of family budgets of agricultural laborers and his careful analysis of his data were conceived in the same spirit,[11] and so was Richard Burn's *History of the Poor Laws*, 1764. Work of this type paved the way toward the legislative developments of the nineteenth century.

[10] Sir Frederick Morton Eden (1766-1809), *The State of the Poor: or an History of the Labouring Classes in England from the Conquest to the Present Period; in which are particularly considered their Domestic Economy . . . ; and the various Plans which, from time to time, have been proposed and adopted for the Relief of the Poor . . .* (3 vols., 1797; abridged ed. by A. G. L. Rogers, 1928). The price and wage data and the budget study in the third volume are particularly important.

[11] David Davies, *The Case of Labourers in Husbandry stated and considered, in three Parts: Part* I. *A View of their Distressed Condition. Part* II. *The Principal Causes of their Growing Distress and Number . . . Part* III. *Means of Relief Proposed.* The budgets are given in the Appendix. The work was (partially) published in 1795.

A few more titles of English books that are of some interest from either the factual or the analytic standpoint may serve as pointers for the interested reader. Their choice must be understood, however, to be the result of very unsystematic browsing: L. Lee, *Remonstrance . . . touching the Insupportable Miseries of the Poore of the Land* (1644)—a scheme of re-employment by means of semipublic workshops; Roger North, *A Discourse of the Poor . . .* (1753); Anon., *Observations on the Number and Misery of the Poor . . .* (1765); Anon., *Observations on the Present State of the Poor of Sheffield . . .* (1774); Anon. [R. Potter], *Observations on the Poor Laws, on the Present State of the Poor, and on Houses of Industry* (1775). John Howlett's (see above, sec. 1) interesting argument concerning enclosures should be particularly noticed: *Enquiry into the Influence which Enclosures have had upon the Population of this Kingdom*, 1786, and *The Insufficiency of the Causes to which the Increase of our Poor and of the Poor's Rates have been Commonly Ascribed* (1788).

CHAPTER 6

Value and Money[1]

1. Real Analysis and Monetary Analysis

We have already touched upon this subject in Chapter 4 when discussing Quesnay's work. It is now time to go a little more deeply into it in order to visualize as clearly as we can a doctrinal development that has acquired additional interest for the student of modern economics owing to the fact that Monetary Analysis has once more conquered in our own time. Let us first of all re-define the meaning of these two approaches.

[1] [Although this chapter was apparently written rather early, it was unfinished and not typed at the death of J. A. S. The manuscript pages were unnumbered and sometimes there were two or three versions of the same page. This chapter was put together with the assistance of Arthur W. Marget.]

Real Analysis [2] proceeds from the principle that all the essential phenomena of economic life are capable of being described in terms of goods and services, of decisions about them, and of relations between them. Money enters the picture only in the modest role of a technical device that has been adopted in order to facilitate transactions. This device can no doubt get out of order, and if it does it will indeed produce phenomena that are specifically attributable to its *modus operandi*. But so long as it functions normally, it does not affect the economic process, which behaves in the same way as it would in a barter economy: this is essentially what the concept of Neutral Money implies. Thus, money has been called a 'garb' or 'veil' of the things that really matter, both to households or firms in their everyday practice and to the analyst who observes them. Not only *can* it be discarded whenever we are analyzing the fundamental features of the economic process but it *must* be discarded just as a veil must be drawn aside if we are to see the face behind it. Accordingly, money prices must give way to the exchange ratios between the commodities that are the really important thing 'behind' money prices; income formation must be looked upon as an exchange of, say, labor and physical means of subsistence; saving and investment must be interpreted to mean saving of some real factors of production and their conversion into real capital goods, such as buildings, machines, raw materials; and, though 'in the form of money,' it is these physical capital goods that are 'really' lent when an industrial borrower arranges for a loan. The specifically monetary problems can then be treated separately, much as we treat many other things separately, for example, insurance.

Monetary Analysis, in the first place, spells denial of the proposition that, with the exception of what may be called monetary disorders, the element of money is of secondary importance in the explanation of the economic process of reality. We need, in fact, only observe the course of events during and after the California gold discoveries to satisfy ourselves that these discoveries were

[2] The phrase is not very felicitous. In particular, it invites confusion with another of the many meanings of the word 'real.' Real Analysis stands for emphasis upon real in the sense of non-monetary processes. But we commonly use the word 'real' for monetary quantities that have been 'corrected' for changes in some price level. For instance, we speak of real income when we mean money income divided by a cost of living index. Such 'corrected' monetary quantities are, however, still monetary quantities and are, along with uncorrected ones, used also in Monetary Analysis. Therefore our distinction must not be identified with the distinction between analysis in terms of dollars of constant purchasing power and analysis in terms of 'current' dollars. Moreover, we are defining both Real and Monetary Analysis as pure types in order to convey an important truth. In actual practice, neither type is ever pure. Hence the contrast between them is less sharp than we are forced to make it. There are many midway houses. And neither Real nor Monetary Analysis can ever get along without using concepts and arguments that strictly speaking belong to the other. Sponsors of Real Analysis have often used a monetary capital concept; sponsors of Monetary Analysis always use the essentially 'real' concept, Employment.

responsible for a great deal more than a change in the significance of the unit in which values are expressed. Nor have we any difficulty in realizing—as did A. Smith—that the development of an efficient banking system may make a lot of difference to the development of a country's wealth. To some extent, these and other things can be, and have been, recognized within the pale of Real Analysis. We may even hold monetary theories of business cycles or of interest without leaving its precincts. The reader should observe, however, that one cannot go very far on this route without becoming aware of the fact that the monetary processes that account for conspicuous 'disturbances' do not cease to act in even the most normal course of economic life. We are thus led, step by step, to admit monetary elements into Real Analysis and to doubt that money can *ever* be 'neutral' in any meaningful sense. In the second place, then, Monetary Analysis introduces the element of money on the very ground floor of our analytic structure and abandons the idea that all essential features of economic life can be represented by a barter-economy model. Money prices, money incomes, and saving and investment decisions bearing upon these money incomes, no longer appear as expressions—sometimes convenient, sometimes misleading, but always nonessential—of quantities of commodities and services and of exchange ratios between them: they acquire a life and an importance of their own, and it has to be recognized that essential features of the capitalist process may depend upon the 'veil' and that the 'face behind it' is incomplete without it. It should be stated once for all that as a matter of fact this is almost universally recognized by modern economists, at least in principle, and that, taken in this sense, Monetary Analysis has established itself.

[(a) *Relation of Monetary Analysis to Aggregative or Macroanalysis.*] Monetary Analysis, as usually understood, means more than this: in the third place, it means in addition Aggregative Analysis or, as it is sometimes called, Macroanalysis,[3] that is to say, analysis that attempts to reduce the variables of the economic system to a small number of social aggregates, such as total income, total consumption, total investment, and the like. Quesnay's *tableau* is the outstanding example for the alliance between Monetary and Aggregative Analysis. The alliance is not a logical necessity but is nevertheless close: it is possible, as we have put it, to introduce money on the ground floor of general economic analysis without adopting the aggregative view. But monetary aggregates are homogeneous, whereas most nonmonetary ones are but meaningless heaps of hopelessly disparate things; and if we wish to work with a small number of variables, we can hardly help resorting to monetary ones. And since this alliance with the aggregative approach actually runs through the whole history of Monetary Analysis, we shall henceforth restrict this term to analysis in terms of aggregates[4]—mainly, as we have seen in our study of the *tableau*,

[3] This term is due to Professor Ragnar Frisch.

[4] Some readers may welcome illustration from the leading system of Monetary Analysis of today, the Keynesian system. Readers entirely unfamiliar with the latter are requested to neglect this note. The chief variables of that system are quantity of money (sum total of cash balances demanded and supplied), national income, con-

streams of expenditure. It was pointed out there that analysis of this type does not do away with real analysis, but only confines it to the description of the behavior of individual households and individual firms. The point is, to repeat, that the social totals that result from this behavior are then dealt with as such and without referring back again, at every step, to the individual acts or decisions behind them. For instance, investment as a social total is the algebraic sum of a great many individual—positive or negative—investments. Monetary Analysis leaves the explanation of these to the Theory of Individual Households and Firms, and concerns itself only with that algebraic sum on the hypothesis *that this is all that matters for the economic process as a whole* and that all the effects on the economic process as a whole that emanate from the multitude of individual investment decisions are measured by their algebraic sum.[5] It cannot be emphasized too strongly that Monetary Analysis that accepts this hypothesis is not in as safe a position as is Monetary Analysis that does not. For it can be strictly proved that this hypothesis is in general contrary to fact. For our purpose, it is, however, sufficient to illustrate this by the example just mentioned. Suppose that, for any given year, the investment decisions of all firms sum up to zero. It stands to reason that the course of events to be expected from this will not depend solely on this fact but also on the component individual decisions: the effect will be different, for instance, if all firms have actually decided to invest nothing, that is, to leave their capital commitments unchanged, from what it would be if some of them had decided to make positive investments while others had decided to reduce their capital commitments by the same amounts. Moreover, effects—on the economic process as a whole—will differ according to the 'real' nature of the investments of the individual concerns and, in particular, according to whether these investments are complementary to, or competitive with, each other. It is

---

sumption, and investment, all measured either in money or in wage-units (the money wage of an ideal unit of labor). To these monetary aggregates correspond equal aggregative 'schedules' that embody assumptions about the behavior of households and firms in the aggregate: the schedule of marginal propensity to consume, the schedule of liquidity preference, and the schedule of marginal efficiency of capital (see below, Part v, ch. 5). Individual prices do not enter explicitly, apart from the rate of interest. It will be observed, however, that, though rate of interest is not an aggregative quantity, it fits well into a system of aggregative quantities because, unlike any other individual price, it can be readily put into a meaningful relation to them: a relation between the price of wheat and total investment does not, in general, make sense; but the relation between the interest rate and sum total of net investment does. *We must hence extend our idea of aggregative variables so as to cover any nonaggregative ones that may have to be introduced into an aggregative system.* The wage rate is the most important other instance.

[5] This point of view has been formulated by Joan Robinson, with unsurpassable energy and brilliance, in 'The Theory of Money and the Analysis of Output,' *Review of Economic Studies*, October 1933. From the standpoint defined in the text, the 'theory of money'—what we call Monetary Analysis—in fact becomes identical with the theory of social aggregates and, ultimately, of total output in terms of the monetary values of consumption and investment.

true that, so far as the immediate effects of firms' expenditure as such are concerned, our algebraic sum still tells us something. This is precisely why Monetary Analysis is not valueless. But it is not more than a part of the theory of the economic process as a whole and becomes seriously misleading if applied alone.[6]

[(b) *Monetary Analysis and Views on Spending and Saving.*] In the fourth place, as we have also seen in the case of Quesnay, Monetary Analysis is associated, not by logical necessity but nevertheless closely, with a characteristic set of views about Spending and Saving and, in connection with these, about monetary and fiscal policy. In fact, so soon as we see the economic process—primarily or exclusively—as a system of streams of expenditures, we shall be tempted to expect all sorts of disturbances from any obstruction to the even flow of these streams and, vice versa, to attribute any disturbance we observe in the economic process to such obstructions—as at least its proximate cause. The way in which households and firms handle their money and react to monetary magnitudes will thus acquire importance independently of the commodity aspect of their actions. In particular, we may be led to attach more importance to people's 'making full use of the income they receive from firms,' that is, to their spending it promptly on products of these firms than to the commodities they acquire in so doing and the prices at which they acquire them. By the same token, we may be led to identify Saving with obstruction to that flow of expenditure and, in the limiting case, to see it in the role of economic Disturber General. Thus, Monetary Analysis not only qualifies well as a tool for economists who are 'spenders' and 'anti-savers' independently of any theory but also tends to produce in the minds of its votaries the 'spending' and 'anti-saving' attitude by focusing attention on the process of the generation of monetary income behind which everything else disappears from sight.

Having cleared the ground, we must now follow the fortunes of Real and

[6] In partial recognition of this, modern votaries of Monetary Analysis, and in particular its leading exponent, Lord Keynes, frequently introduce a most significant restriction: they assume the organization and technique of production *and* the capital equipment as given (in the short run), thus reducing the problem before them to the question what determines (in the short run) the degree of utilization of a given industrial apparatus; and, in further simplification, they identify this greater or smaller degree of utilization with greater or smaller employment of labor so that increase or decrease of industrial investment simply means a greater or smaller wage bill. It is easy to see that, in this special case, plus and minus investments are much more nearly compensatory in their effects than they are in the general case and that hence their algebraic sum comes much nearer to expressing adequately this total effect on the economic process. But the reader should observe (a) that the restrictive assumption in question excludes the very essence of capitalist reality, all the phenomena and problems of which—including the short-run phenomena and problems—hinge upon the incessant creation of new and novel capital equipment, and (b) that, because of this, a model framed upon this restrictive assumption has next to no application to questions of practical diagnosis, prognosis, and, above all, economic policy unless reinforced by extraneous considerations.

Monetary Analysis during the epoch under consideration. Let us face at once the chief difficulty of this task. It arises from the circumstance that we meet the ideas underlying, or associated with, Monetary Analysis, as it were, on two levels—on a prescientific and on a scientific one. Ever since wages began to be paid in money, every servant girl has felt that all would be well if only her employers spent their money freely enough; and ever since trading began to mean taking in money, every trader has felt that he would be able to sell whatever it was he wished to sell, if only there were money enough or if the people who had it could only be persuaded to part with it. With exceptions that prove the rule—in nineteenth-century Europe they almost ousted the rule—this is and always has been a major item of the economics of the man in the street who never really believed in the gospel of thrift even when he paid lip service to it. The first thing that analytic effort does is to dispel some of these 'monetary illusions.' But other analytic efforts keep on creating and re-creating a Monetary Analysis on a scientific level which is sometimes just as successful in its attacks upon Real Analysis as the latter has been in its attacks upon those 'popular prejudices.' These two levels, however, are not unconnected, and this is where the historian's trouble comes in. On the one hand, popular sentiments about money and spending proved invincible. They always survived and always manifested themselves in a literary current that ran sometimes outside and sometimes inside of 'recognized' economics. And they always lent powerful support to attempts to establish Monetary Analysis on the scientific level: just as the popular success of socialist arguments forged by trained economists is not due to their scientific merits but to the fact that they fall in with cravings of the human heart that defy rational formulation, so the popular successes of scientific Monetary Analysis cannot be explained without taking into account the fact that its arguments fall in with extra-rational sentiments and therefore are likely, particularly in times of stress, to be greeted with many a sigh of relief.[7]

The most effective propositions of scientific Monetary Analysis are, in fact, those in which the public is able to discover a pointer toward the easy way out of difficulties and which bear a family likeness to what growling professionals call popular errors. On the other hand, these popular prejudices, like others, contain elements of scientifically provable truth so that association with them does not constitute a *prima facie* case for rejecting scientific Monetary Analysis. However, the exponents of Real Analysis thought that it did: not only did they neglect those elements of truth, to the disadvantage of their own teaching, but they also used the opportunity in order to represent the results of Monetary Analysis simply as new versions of what indubitably were popular fallacies. Later on, whenever they were in a position to do so, the votaries of Monetary Analysis retaliated in kind, the more zealously so because, in part, they actually did serve up exploded error in new dressing. No indictment of subjective honesty is intended. Such mix-ups will, however, arise as long as economists continue to analyze with an eye on practical programs they wish

[7] The case of the United States illustrates all this to perfection.

to recommend or to combat, as most of them did and do. For any effort of this kind will inevitably partake of the characteristics of political warfare in which the most primitive tactical wisdom precludes any admission to the effect that there may be something in the opponent's standpoint—with the result, in the case in hand, that both 'real' and 'monetary' analysts invariably overbid their hands. But in order to complete the analogy, it is necessary to add that they also committed all sorts of mistakes in playing them. However, we shall now try, so far as seems possible, to straighten out the tangle, first, by visualizing some broad contours of doctrinal development and, second, by mentioning a few representative names.

The history of economic analysis *begins* with Real Analysis in possession of the field. Aristotle and the scholastic doctors all adhered to it. This is perfectly understandable, since there was nothing to face them except the pre-analytic sentiments of the public. But, as we know, there is an important qualification to be made: they offered monetary explanations for the phenomenon of interest. *Very roughly*, this state of things prevailed until the beginning of the seventeenth century. Again, the history of economic analysis in the period under survey *ends* with a victory of Real Analysis that was so complete as to put Monetary Analysis practically out of court for well over a century, though one or two efforts were made on its behalf in the court of scientific economics, and though it continued to lead a lingering life outside of that court, in an 'underworld' of its own.[8] This victory is also understandable. It was, of course, greatly facilitated by vivid memories of monetary troubles—medieval and more recent ones—of spectacular mismanagement of banking methods—John Law's doings (see below, sec. 5) were still in everybody's mind—and by the antagonism to 'mercantilist' teachings. But powerful though they were, these factors[9] should not be overemphasized to the point of making us forget that Real Analysis was also the result of analytic advance and instrumental in bringing about further advance.

[8] The men who stand out from the conquering host are Turgot and A. Smith, who were to find, in the subsequent period, the ally who completed the conquest, J. B. Say. Lord Keynes (from whom I have borrowed the word 'underworld' that expresses so well the status of Monetary Analysis during the nineteenth century) dates the victory of Real Analysis from the controversy between Ricardo and Malthus (*General Theory*, p. 32). This is not correct, but there is truth in his statement that the views on policy associated with Real Analysis 'conquered England [and the rest of the world, J. A. S.] as completely as the Holy Inquisition conquered Spain.' In fact, anything savoring of Monetary-Analysis ideas was disapproved of, not only as erroneous but also as not quite all right morally: it was—and, needless to say, not always without reason—associated with advocacy of dilettantic and frivolous policies and, especially in the United States, with sponsorship of loose banking practice and the silver interest.

[9] They are good examples of ideological influence if we define ideologies in a sense that is both broader and more useful than the Marxist one. Any obsession that limits our range of vision and enslaves our thought then comes within that concept. And the idea, e.g. that nothing that writers tinged with 'mercantilism' had ever written *could* be true and that anything that we should call inflationism *must* be fought at any price, may well be called an obsession.

[(c) *Interlude of Monetary Analysis* (1600-1760): *Becher, Boisguillebert, and Quesnay.*] But between, say, 1600 and 1760, there was an important interlude of Monetary Analysis. The businessmen, civil servants, and politicians, who then took up their pens, attended to the monetary aspects of their troubles as a matter of course. They would as soon have doubted that they got wet when it rained as that more money spelled more profit and more employment, or that high prices were a boon, or that high interest was just a nuisance. But though this literature unmistakably took off from the preanalytic level of Monetary Analysis and never quite lost contact with the servant girl's economics, it did not stay there but eventually produced, barring technique, practically everything that has come to the fore again during the thirties of this century. Deferring consideration of the specifically 'mercantilist' tenets and, for the moment, also of all other matters, we shall now notice the emergence of Monetary Analysis in its most significant sense, that is, in the sense of a theory of the economic process in terms of expenditure flows. Though Quesnay's example suffices to show that, in strict logic, it has nothing to do with protectionism, the first document that presents such a theory with a clearness that is beyond the possibility of doubt was a strongly 'mercantilist' tract, Becher's *Politische Discurs* (1668).[10] This tract contains the rudiments of an analytic schema that turns upon people's expenditure on consumption—the prime mover or, as Becher said, the 'soul' of economic life. In itself the observation that one man's expenditure is another man's income—or that consumers' expenditure generates income—is as old as it is trivial. But it can be turned into a principle of analysis—the principle that Quesnay, a century later, was to embody in his *tableau*—just as can the old and trivial observation that a body at rest remains at rest unless some external force acts on it. We shall call it Becher's Principle, because he seems to have been the first to realize its theoretical possibilities. He did little to develop any *system* of Monetary Analysis and, of course, left plenty for Lord Keynes to do.[11] But so far as rec-

[10] *Politischer Discurs von den eigentlichen Ursachen dess Auff- und Abnehmens der Städt, Länder, und Republicken, in specie, wie ein Land folckreich und nahrhafft zu machen und in eine rechte Societatem civilem zu bringen* (i.e. how to make a country rich and populous and to develop it into a real society). Johann Joachim Becher (1635-82) was something of an adventurer. Professionally a physician and a chemist, he came to Vienna brimming over with plans and projects, and there played a certain role until he had to flee from his creditors. But his vigor and originality were universally recognized even by men like Leibniz and Stahl.

[11] Lord Keynes (*General Theory*, ch. 23) is not only generous but overgenerous in his recognition of the 'mercantilist' contribution. While this is admirable from a moral or aesthetic standpoint and appropriate in a man who cares more for the cause he espouses than for his own claims to originality, it is apt to convey a somewhat misleading picture and to obscure the amount of preanalytic wisdom and error that went into those works. Becher he does not mention. Instead he mentions W. von Schröder (1640-88; main work: *Fürstliche Schatz- und Rentkammer*, 1686), a less important, especially less original, contemporary of Becher, who seems to have been influenced both by the latter and by Thomas Mun.

ommendations may be trusted at all to reveal an author's analytic schema, there is practically complete concordance between the two (excepting their views on population),[12] among other things, in the matter of domestic investment.

It is not surprising that Becher found successors in Germany. The German Consultant Administrators were far indeed from understanding the analytic importance of his principle. But Monetary Analysis, in the sense defined, works with concepts which, though actually very abstract and indeed unrealistic, carry a surface meaning that is perfectly familiar to everyone. This surface meaning they absorbed readily because it fitted in excellently with the rest of their thought—so much so that it is not even necessary to assume dependence. Many of their diagnoses and recommendations may in fact be co-ordinated and rationalized with reference to Becher's Principle. Thus, many of them believed in the pivotal importance of high-level mass consumption or, to put the same thing into their normative way of expressing themselves, in measures that would stimulate mass consumption. For some of them, Justi for example, this was the main reason for putting so much emphasis on increase in population—as a means of expanding demand—rather than the other way round. Becher himself perceived the interaction of the two. His principle was of course relevant, as it is today, to the appraisal of the effects of high prices, saving, and luxury.

In England, neither Becher's Principle nor anything closely related to it was, so far as I know, explicitly formulated. All the more often was it implied. For instance, Potter's argument (1650) to the effect that an increase in the supply of money will increase the rate of spending and production proportionately points in this direction, and so does the analogous though more guarded argument of Law (1705).[13] The French literature offers, among others, the most noteworthy example of all—Boisguillebert's (*Dissertation sur la nature des richesses*, see ch. 4 above), which is the more interesting because, like Quesnay, he was in principle a free trader and laissez-faire advocate. He did not invoke state management to secure the steady flow of monetary values (expenditures), but on the contrary pointed to the state-made impediments to it: the export duties, the internal barriers to trade, regulative interference with agriculture and manufactures, the vicious operations of the most important direct tax, the *taille*—all of which desolated the countryside and impoverished the towns

[12] Becher's posthumous fame has been fostered by the eulogies of many German historians. Following the lead of Roscher (*Geschichte der Nationalökonomik in Deutschland*, 1874, p. 270), they have kept on listing a number of more or less interesting points in Becher's teaching, for instance, his concept of three market configurations of which he strongly disapproved, *monopolium*, *propolium* (forestalling), and *polypolium* (perfect competition). But there is not much in this. His lack of enthusiasm for perfect competition and his almost Keynesian dislike of laissez-faire will no doubt be judged more favorably now than it was in the nineteenth century, but it is likely that his analytic grasp was below rather than above the free-competition argument of a later time.

[13] On Potter and Law, see below, sec. 2 and 5.

because they restricted consumers' expenditure. Also, while we look upon the wage earners as the most dependable spenders, Boisguillebert, in the social pattern of his time, assigned this role to the landowners. But these differences serve only to emphasize the fundamental similarity both of his theory and his outlook upon practical problems with those of our own time. Consumers' expenditure was the active principle of economic life. Equilibrium was an equilibrium of reciprocal demand, in terms of money, of all groups for the products or services of all other groups; it would realize itself if and only if every seller promptly became a buyer.[14] Anything that interfered with prompt expenditure on consumers' goods would induce a fall in prices, hence a fall in incomes, then in turn another fall in consumers' expenditure, and thus result in cumulative deflation. Therefore his horror, never surpassed by anyone's outside the United States Senate, of that worst of all disasters—cheap bread. With delightful naïveté he warned lawyers, physicians, actors, and so forth not to clamor for low prices of agricultural products: in doing so they were 'digging their own graves'; for the landowners, who are nothing but intermediate spenders, would then find their incomes reduced and have to reduce their expenditure, and where would those lawyers, et cetera, be? Thus, his idea of a prosperous society did not involve Cheapness and Plenty but Dearness and Plenty. He did not use the phrase Fallacy of Cheapness of which modern 'spenders' are so fond, but it is evident that he meant exactly the same thing. Since this question has never ceased to arouse interest—at least in that no-man's land that lies between professional and popular economics—we had better take this opportunity to comment upon it.

[(d) *Dearness and Plenty versus Cheapness and Plenty.*] First of all, it is quite clear that both of the opinions envisaged are strongly rooted in the public mind and that the politicians, legislators, and administrators who took action in order to give effect to the one or the other simply responded to popular demands. This is as true today as it was for the price edicts of the later Roman Emperors, and explains not only the contradictions in professed motives and in actual measures that we observe but also the many insincerities in the use of apparently general arguments for what was meant to improve the relative position of some particular group. Broadly speaking, the workman always wanted low prices of *commodities*, the businessman high prices, and both assumed uncritically the absence of any further effects of either cheapness or dearness. Early analysis, here as elsewhere, proceeded from those popular sentiments and rationalized and reshaped them into doctrines. But in doing so, writers—

[14] This involves the concept of aggregate demand, in terms of money, for output as a whole and may hence be said to anticipate the Malthusian (and Keynesian) concept of aggregate demand which will be discussed on a later occasion. It has been observed already that, almost a century after Boisguillebert, essentially the same idea was sponsored by G. Ortes (see above, ch. 3, sec. 4d): to say that total consumers' demand is the limiting principle of production (employment) comes to the same thing as saying that it is the active principle of production.

again: here as elsewhere—usually sided with the one or the other and hence were slow, and often unwilling, to see the elements of truth in the other. The scholastic doctors associated prosperity with cheapness; dearness they associated with famine and mass misery. The English businessmen-economists of the seventeenth century, quite naturally in the conditions of their environment, inclined to the opposite position but not always: some, for example Roger Coke, made a case for Cheapness and Plenty; but the majority associated Dearness and Plenty—and, so we may add, a low rate of interest—with brisk trade and high levels of employment. It will be seen that the difference between them, as well as the difference between their majority and the scholastic doctors, was entirely due to differences in the situations that different writers and groups of writers envisaged, so that there really was no logical incompatibility between what at first blush looks like diametrically opposed views. But nobody saw or admitted this, for everyone wanted to teach a practical lesson. And this remains true for the more refined analysis of the eighteenth century. The high-price argument proved difficult to beat and was, at least in some respects, upheld by front-rank men, such as Boisguillebert and Quesnay, but it was beaten eventually, the tenable and even suggestive parts of it no less than the really fallacious ones. A. Smith cast his vote for Cheapness and Plenty, and practically all nineteenth-century economists of standing followed him. Again, it is to be observed that all that the Cheapness-and-Plenty school really did was, first, to assert such trivial truths as that any general level of prices and monetary expressions to which the economic process is adapted is, so far as a closed economy is concerned, as good as any other and that, so far as this goes, it is only the relations between some prices and others that matter, for instance, the relation between commodity and factor prices; second, to interpret cheapness in terms of effort rather than in terms of money; third, to accept the fall in money prices that occurs in consequence of accumulation and improvement as the natural method for giving effect to the increasing cheapness of things in terms of effort; and, fourth, to make light, on the one hand, of the disturbances that are inseparable from falling prices and, on the other hand, of the possibilities of stimulation, inherent in policies of rising prices. There was really nothing in all this that can properly be called a fallacy. In important respects, the victory of the Cheapness-and-Plenty advocates spelled analytic advance. But it was a one-sided advance that neglected many promising suggestions of the Dearness-and-Plenty men.

But, second, it should be observed that the slogan of Dearness and Plenty is not necessarily connected with Monetary Analysis in the sense of analysis in terms of monetary aggregates. Evidently, there is nothing in the latter to prevent us from associating prosperous conditions with cheapness. On the face of it, then, the connection between Monetary Analysis in that sense and dearness is historical only and therefore calls for special motivation in each case. In the case of Boisguillebert, this requirement can be easily met. His high-price argument was really an argument about high prices of agricultural products, and the effects of these on welfare were motivated by the consideration that they meant high incomes for the landowners on whom Boisguillebert principally relied for doing the spending: just as modern economists identify high wage rates with a high total income of the working class and this with liberal expenditure by consumers, so Boisguillebert identified high prices of agricultural products with high rents, high rents with liberal expenditure, liberal expenditure with high levels of employment and welfare. Here, then, we have a logical relation between Monetary Analysis and a high-price philosophy. But Verri's argument to the effect that an increase in the supply of money, owing to its stimulating effects on production, may induce a fall in prices (Verri is the most important pre-Smithian authority on Cheapness and Plenty) could be worked up into a piece of Monetary Analysis that would be allied to a low-price philosophy.

Quesnay was of the same opinion in regards to prices (see, especially, his *Maximes générales*, 1758). He also thought that, whereas plenty and low value are not riches, and scarcity and dearness spell misery, abundance and dearness spell opulence: prices must not be allowed to fall because *telle est la valeur vénale, tel est le revenu* (XVIII). One must not think that cheapness is advantageous for the poor—it only makes their wages fall. And the means (*aisance*) of the lowest classes must not be diminished (XIX), for then their consumption (that is, total demand in terms of money or spending) will be reduced, and this in turn will reduce production and income. But nothing is so characteristic of this type of theory, which can be so easily translated into modern language of familiar ring, as is the attitude to saving, adumbrated by Boisguillebert, fully developed by Quesnay. In this analytic schema the prompt onward flow of purchasing power is everything. Saving is believed to interrupt it. Hence saving is a sort of public enemy. Quesnay makes it one of his *maximes: que la totalité des sommes du revenu rentre dans la circulation annuelle et la parcoure dans toute son étendue* (VII). There must be no formation of *fortunes pécuniaires* (accumulations of actual cash?). Landowners and those who practice lucrative professions must not retain 'le pécule du royaume au préjudice de la rentrée des avances de la culture . . . : cette interception du pécule diminuerait la reproduction des revenus et de l'impôt.' *Le pécule* may no doubt be interpreted in the sense of uninvested savings. Even so, the similarity with Keynesian views is striking: in itself, saving is sterile and a disturber; it must always be 'offset,' and this offsetting is a distinct act that may or may not succeed. A fairly strong anti-saving tradition thus acquired additional support shortly before it almost vanished into thin air. This is all that need be said about the monetary theory of the physiocrats.

How was it then that Real Analysis conquered so easily and completely? This question will be answered in the last two sections of this chapter, where two of the chief battlefields of its victorious campaign will be surveyed, the theory of saving and the theory of interest. A general answer may, however, be given at once: the reason for the defeat or rather the collapse of Monetary Analysis in the last decades of the eighteenth century was its weakness. Even if, for the sake of argument, we grant without qualification that the principle of monetary analysis is sound and that the modern development of it is an improvement upon the real analysis of the nineteenth century, it should be clear that the latter was not less superior to the monetary analysis of the eighteenth. Such spirals of advance are, I believe, not uncommon: theories that it is an achievement to displace may return to displace those by which they had been displaced, and both the displacement and the return may benefit that strange thing, scientific knowledge.

2. Fundamentals [1]

We now turn to the theory of money in the narrower and still more usual sense—let us say, briefly though imperfectly, the theory of money as a technical device. For this purpose, it is convenient to introduce a few terms that will facilitate exposition throughout the rest of this book.

[(a) *Metallism and Cartalism: Theoretical and Practical.*] By Theoretical Metallism we denote the *theory* that it is logically essential for money to consist of, or to be 'covered' by, some commodity so that the logical source of the exchange value or purchasing power of money is the exchange value or purchasing power of that commodity, considered independently of its monetary role. It is true that in principle any commodity can be chosen to serve as money. But the term Commodity Theory of money has also another meaning. This is why, availing ourselves of the fact that in modern times only gold and silver have been normally chosen for that role, we prefer the term Metallism, though it is not strictly correct. It is also true that the 'standard' chosen may consist of more than one commodity: the singular is used merely in order to avoid adding 'or commodities' each time. By Practical Metallism we shall denote sponsorship of a principle of monetary policy, namely, the principle that the monetary unit 'should' be kept firmly linked to, and freely interchangeable with, a given quantity of some commodity. Theoretical and Practical Cartalism may best be defined by the corresponding negatives. Thus, we shall speak of theoretical cartalism wherever we find denial of the proposition that it is logically essential for money to consist of, say, gold, or to be promptly convertible into gold; of practical cartalism wherever we find sponsorship of the principle of policy that the value of the monetary unit 'should' not be tied to the value of any particular commodity.[2]

[1] [J. A. S. had tentatively suggested 'Ground Theory' (*Grundlagenforschung*) as the title of this section, but he used 'Fundamentals' as the title of the corresponding sections in Part III (ch. 7, sec. 2) and Part IV (ch. 8, sec. 3).]

[2] The words Metallism and Cartalism are borrowed from G. F. Knapp's *State Theory of Money* (see below, Part IV, ch. 8, sec. 3). Since, according to the metallist view, the theory of money derives directly from the logically prior theory of barter, metallist theories are (roughly or exactly, I am not quite sure) what L. von Mises has called

These distinctions owe their importance for us to the fact that theoretical and practical metallism need not go together. An economist may, for instance, be fully convinced that theoretical metallism is untenable, and yet be a strong practical metallist. Lack of confidence in the authorities or politicians, whose freedom of action is greatly increased by currency systems that do not provide for prompt and unquestioning redemption in gold of all means of payment that do not consist of gold, is quite sufficient to motivate practical metallism in a theoretical cartalist; this does not involve any contradiction. But the reader will realize that this fact may cause great difficulties in interpreting authors who are in the habit of confusing theoretical and practical considerations. Nor is this the only reason why it is not always easy to tell whether or not a man should be classed as a theoretical metallist. For, without being one, he may still believe that 'the most salable commodity' constitutes the historical as distinguished from the logical source of the phenomenon of money.[3] Again, he may wish to stress the role of government in choosing the commodity that is to serve as money and its power to alter this decision in various ways. In doing so he may easily, if not very sophisticated or careful, use language that will tempt us to class him as a cartalist. We remember that this difficulty arose in the case of Aristotle (ch. 1, above). Finally, basic theories are malleable and writers are often inconsistent, still more often vague. When we find that a writer compares money to a ticket—a ticket that admits the bearer to the great social store of all goods—we feel inclined to register him as a cartalist. But the phrase need not mean much, and both J. S. Mill, who used it in the nineteenth century, and Berkeley, who used it in the eighteenth, are more properly called metallists. There is no denying that views on money are as difficult to describe as are shifting clouds.[4]

[(b) *Theoretical Metallism in the Seventeenth and Eighteenth Centuries.*] Theoretical metallism, usually though not always associated with practical metallism,[5] held its own throughout the seventeenth and eighteenth centuries

---

catallactic theories of money (καταλλάττειγ, to exchange). But the word Metallism conveys the essential point more tellingly, besides offering easy transition to Monometallism and so on.

[3] Here we brush against a highly interesting question of methodology. [J. A. S. wrote: please leave rest of page for note.]

[4] [The next few pages were inserted by J. A. S. from an earlier version typed in March 1944 (see Appendix).]

[5] I am taking it for granted that theoretical metallism is untenable, i.e. that it is not true that, as a matter of pure logic, money essentially consists in, or must be backed by, a commodity or several commodities whose exchange value as commodities are the logical basis of their value as money. The error involved consists in a confusion between the historical origin of money—which, in very many cases, although perhaps not universally, may indeed be found in the fact that some commodities, being particularly salable, come to be used as the medium of exchange—and its nature or logic—which is entirely independent of the commodity character of its material. This type of error occurs very frequently in all fields of social analysis, especially in its early stages: it requires considerable analytic experience to perceive that primitive forms of social institutions may be more complex than modern ones and that they

and prevailed victoriously in the 'classical situation' that emerged in the last quarter of the latter. Adam Smith substantially ratified it. And for more than a century to come it was almost universally accepted—by nobody more implicitly than by Marx—so much so, in fact, that the majority of economists came to suspect not only unsoundness of reasoning but something very like obliquity of purpose behind every expression of antimetallist views.

This development, as we know, was in accordance with established tradition. The philosophers of natural law and those Consultant Administrators who were directly influenced by them simply repeated and developed the teaching of Aristotle and the scholastic authors. But the majority of those writers on money who cannot be proved to have experienced any influence from that quarter—for instance the English merchant economists—also fell in with that tradition. Examples abound for all countries. For England it will suffice to mention, first, some economists of the first rank, such as Child, who clearly identified money with those parts of the stocks of gold and silver that fill the monetary function and held that in spite of this function gold and silver, coined or uncoined, still remained commodities exactly like 'wine, oil, tobacco, cloth and stuff'; Petty, who also reasoned about money in terms of its material; and Locke,[6] who did likewise, though he was more ready to admit

may hide, rather than reveal, logical essentials. We shall have to return to this before long.

But one may realize all this and yet be a practical metallist, i.e. believe that in some or all cases effective association of the monetary unit with, say, gold is the best or even the only way to establish a monetary system or to make it function. This is not a matter of pure theory, however, and may be right or wrong according to circumstances and individual or group standpoints and interests. But although theoretical and practical metallism are logically independent, the reader will not be surprised to find that they are not always easy to distinguish. Few authors are quite explicit on the subject; the majority is to this day in the habit of confusing them; but practical metallists and practical antimetallists often display a tendency to strengthen their arguments, concerning the practical expediency of associating the monetary unit with a quantity of metal, by a metallist or antimetallist theory. Two additional facts further increase the difficulties of interpretation: on the one hand, metallist and antimetallist opinions are not so strictly incompatible as one would expect but admit of a great many nuances; on the other hand, turns of phrase—such as 'money is a ticket'—that do seem to point clearly toward one of the alternatives may mean very little if not followed up. Such difficulties we have met already in the case of Aristotle. I am by no means absolutely sure that I was right to class him with the theoretical metallists. Galiani, whom we shall meet presently, interpreted him in the opposite sense. In the case of tracts written without minute attention to fundamentals, these difficulties often become the more insuperable the deeper we probe into an author's ideas. What follows in the text must be read in the light of these considerations. I prefer putting my doubts frankly before the reader to dogmatizing with a confidence I do not feel.

[6] The wide horizon of the author of the *Essay concerning Human Understanding* and his sustained interest in economic facts and problems (of which his journal gives ample proof) should make it possible to construct a comprehensive system of his economic thought. This has in fact been attempted more than once, most successfully, perhaps, by W. Roscher (*Zur Geschichte der englischen Volkswirthschaftslehre*, 1851)

that the monetary function makes a diffierence; Hume,[7] whose teaching on this particular point differs from Child's only in explicitness and polish; Cantillon (op. cit. Part I, ch. 17), whose theoretical metallism exerted considerable influence in France; and, second, the authors of what may be considered as the two standard English works on money of the seventeenth and the eighteenth centuries, Rice Vaughan [8] and Joseph Harris.[9]

---

and J. Bonar (*Philosophy and Political Economy*, 1893). Nevertheless, though we have had, and shall have again, to mention his name in other connections, his claim to a place in the history of economic analysis rests exclusively on his work on money (mainly in *Some Considerations of the Consequences of the Lowering of Interest, and Raising the Value of Money*, 1692; the *Further Considerations* . . . 1695, add but little), which, though date and form of its publication were prompted by current controversies, yet embodies the thought of decades and amounts to much more than a tract for the day, to much more also than the title conveys, by virtue of the energy with which the author digs down to fundamental principles. Even so, however, we cannot speak of a great, still less a faultless, contribution to monetary analysis. Slips are frequent and, whatever the degree of 'subjective originality,' there is little that was not said as well or better by other writers at about the same time. The influence exerted was considerable also on the Continent.

Our right to class him as a metallist can be fully established from the structure of his argument. Doubts might be raised, however, on the strength of Locke's statement that money exists by virtue of common 'consent.' The question is the same as that which arises in connection with Aristotle's συνθήκη (see above, ch. 1), and may, I think, be answered in the same way: on the one hand, even though money evolves from the habit of using one commodity for the purposes of indirect exchange of the others—in order to facilitate barter—this might be expressed by saying that people 'agree' on the choice of that commodity; on the other hand, even though the monetary commodity acquires a 'price' through the market mechanism, this price may be said to arise from 'consent' as indeed may any other.

[7] David Hume's 'Of Money' is one of the major contributions contained in his *Political Discourses* (1752). Its position in the history of economics, while not undeserved, is due to the force and felicity with which it formulated the results of previous work rather than to any novelties. However this does not necessarily exclude 'subjective originality.' The main items will be mentioned in the text.

[8] Rice Vaughan, *A Discourse of Coin and Coinage* (about 1635, publ. 1675), reprinted in McCulloch's *Select Collection of Scarce and Valuable Tracts on Money* (1856). Perusal of this creditable performance may serve usefully as an antidote for all those who have learned to look upon seventeenth-century thought on money as unrelieved nonsense. But it may also serve as an illustration for the difficulties of interpretation alluded to in footnote 6 above. Vaughan falls in promptly with a typically metallist line of reasoning, but when explaining the nature of money, he uses phrases which taken by themselves would also admit of antimetallist interpretation.

[9] The *Essay upon Money and Coins* (two parts 1757 and 1758) by Joseph Harris (1702-64) has some claim to being considered one of the best eighteenth-century performances in the field of monetary analysis. Its importance for us does not, of course, consist in his various recommendations that account for the survival of his name (his monometallism, his views on foreign trade, which were not very far removed from those of Hume and Smith, and so on) or in his copious historical references but in what might be termed the theoretical anchorage of this theory of money and of foreign ex-

For the rest, we shall confine ourselves to instances from the Italian literature on money, which throughout the period kept a higher level than any other. Practically all the leading men were uncompromising metallists. The most important names are Scaruffi, Davanzati, Montanari, Galiani, and Carli. Beccaria and Verri should be added as examples of the treatment accorded to the subject of money in the comprehensive treatises on general economics.

Almost all the works of these authors have been republished in the Custodi collection (see above, ch. 3). In this note an attempt will be made to convey a general idea of the performance of each author excepting those of Beccaria and Verri, which are characterized elsewhere (ch. 3, sec. 4d above). Verri's and Carli's contributions, moreover, will again be met with in another connection (ch. 7, Mercantilism). Verri's monograph *Dialogo sulle monete* (1762) should not go unmentioned, however.

Gasparo Scaruffi (1515?-84), a banker of Reggio in the Emilia, published in 1582 a monograph on money entitled *Alitinonfo*, which admirably illustrates the range of sixteenth-century thought—starting from the functions of money and dealing with problems of coinage in a strongly metallist vein: money is a stamped piece of metal, the stamp has only declaratory importance. His proposal of international bimetallism (somewhat marred by an irrational faith in an invariable relation of 1:12) with an international unit to be issued (without seignorage) by an international authority *implies* a lot of fairly advanced theory. But very little of it comes out explicitly. Thus the step is great indeed to Bernardo Davanzati (1529-1606), 'un mercante letterato Fiorentino,' as Montanari called him. Davanzati's *Lezione delle monete* (1588; see also *Notizia de'cambi*, 1582) is the 'all-time high,' also as regards literary elegance, of the metallist theory of the origin and the nature of money.

About a century later, Geminiano Montanari (1633-87), a professor of mathematics and astronomy in Bologna and Padua, wrote a *Breve trattato del valore delle monete in tutti gli stati* (1680); followed by *La zecca in consulta di stato* (later title, *Della moneta*, 1683-7), which presents the same teaching in a more fully developed form but without adding anything essential to it.

The Neapolitan, Ferdinando Galiani (1728-87), a typical eighteenth-century *abbé*, sparkling with esprit, did for his time what Montanari had done for the seventeenth, and Davanzati for the sixteenth, century in his treatise *Della moneta* (1751; first book: *De'metalli;* second book: *Della natura della moneta;* third book: *Del valore della moneta;* fourth book: *Del corso della moneta;* fifth book: *Del frutto della moneta*—not only on interest, however, but also on public debts and exchange), which would have been received with respect if it had appeared in 1851. Another work of Galiani's will be mentioned in the next chapter. One point about his thought must be emphasized before we tear ourselves away from one of the ablest minds that ever became active in our field: he was the one eighteenth-century economist who always insisted on the variability of man and on the relativity, to time and place, of all policies; the one who was completely free from the paralyzing belief—that then crept over the intellectual life of Europe—in practical principles that claim universal validity; who saw that a policy that was rational in France at a given time might be quite irrational, at the same time, in Naples; who had the courage to say: 'Je ne suis pour

---

changes; he put the subject into a wide framework of general economic principles of which he never loses sight. His treatment thus contrasts favorably with that of all those authors, old and new, who fail to see that any satisfactory theory of money implies a theory of the economic process in its entirety.

rien. . . Je suis pour qu'on ne déraisonne pas' (*Dialogues sur le commerce des blés*, 1769, first dialogue); and who properly despised all types of political doctrinaires, including the physiocrats. There is quite a Galiani literature, and there are several reprints of, and selections from, his works. They are listed in Giorgio Tagliacozzo's *Economisti Napoletani dei sec. XVII e XVIII* (pp. lxv and lxvi), which also contains an essay on Galiani and extracts from *Della moneta* and the *Dialogues*.

Gian Rinaldo (Conte) Carli (1720-95), professor of astronomy at Padua, later on president of the Board of Finance in the Milanese state (then a part of the Habsburg monarchy), in which capacity he, among other things, reformed the coinage according to a plan of his own, a most versatile writer whose comments on the United States in *Delle lettere Americane* (1st ed. 1780; 2nd ed., in 4 vols., 1786) deserve mention even in a sketch like this, must be listed here because of his work entitled *Delle monete . . .* (first instalment, under the title *Dell'origine e del commercio della moneta . . .* 1751, the whole work in 3 vols., 1754-60), which includes the essay *Del valore e della proporzione dei metalli monetati con i generi* [commodities] *in Italia*, which contains the contribution to be mentioned below. Other economic writings of his will be noticed in the next chapter.

It is but natural that most of such advance as the analysis of monetary processes made links up with metallist foundations, even where, in strict logic, antimetallist starting points would have been more appropriate. This should not surprise us, however: in spite of its shortcomings, theoretical metallism, properly handled, gets us almost as far as would a more correct theory—which is precisely one of the reasons why it proved so hardy a plant.

[(c) *Survival of the Antimetallist Tradition.*] There was also, however, an antimetallist tradition, weaker no doubt but equally ancient, at least if we choose to trace it to Plato. It received impetus from governments in financial difficulties, and from inflationists, 'reflationists,' and bank promoters of the period—though the proponents of bank schemes were not all either inflationists or antimetallists,[10] and though there is no necessary relation between inflationism and theoretical antimetallism—but its survival during our period must not be wholly attributed to this factor. Of continental writers it will be enough to mention Ortes and Boisguillebert.[11] Corresponding English in-

10 Examples of metallist sponsors of national-bank schemes are numerous. The author of the proposal of 1576 was one. John Cary (*An Essay, on the Coyn and Credit of England*, 1696 and *An Essay towards the Settlement of a National Credit*, same year) was another. The writers who stood for the foundation of the Bank of England were all metallists so far as I know.

11 Ortes, *Economia Nazionale* (1774). His theoretical antimetallism—money defined as a symbol of wealth and expressly excluded from the items that constitute wealth itself—is another one of the striking parallelisms with the work of Sir James Steuart. Boisguillebert was antimetallist in the sense that he did not consider gold and silver—or, so we may obviously add, any other commodity—to be the essential material of money. The question why, if that be so, money should ever have been made from a material that could serve other uses he answers correctly by pointing to the fact that money so made is a pledge or security (*gage*) for the future delivery of whatever the payee really wants to have and that such a pledge is practically necessary where the payer's credit is not beyond all doubt. To deny that the concept of money requires a

stances are Potter, Barbon, Berkeley, Steuart, and, if we claim for England that Scotsman who became a Frenchman, Law.

William Potter's *The Key of Wealth*, published (anonymously) 1650 and followed by two interpretative publications, recommends a plan, namely the foundation of a corporation of tradesmen (to be strengthened by another body 'insuring' the credit of these tradesmen) which was to accept—or, what in this case amounts to the same thing—to issue 'bills' secured by land, buildings, and other assets and intended to circulate like legal tender money. This plan for mobilizing physical property not only puts Potter in the position of a forerunner of the land-bank projectors (sec. 5) but also obscures the analytic work behind it, which is of considerable interest. The antimetallist character of both the plan and the analysis is beyond doubt, though Potter does not entirely sever the connection of his bill currency with gold and silver, because, if such a plan were adopted, that connection would reduce to one of historical origin only: though money would have originated in the form of a commodity, its value and behavior would no longer be governed by that commodity.

The reputation of Nicholas Barbon, a physician who embarked upon various business enterprises, suffered in his own time as well as later on, from the many freakish elements not only in his plans but also in his analytic arguments. In addition, he was one of the land-bank projectors. In spite of this, he must, I think, be ranked with, say, the top half-dozen English seventeenth-century economists. We shall also meet him in another connection, but his main importance for us is in the field of money and interest. His *Discourse of Trade* (1690) has been republished by J. H. Hollander. Reference must also be made to: *A Discourse concerning Coining the New Money Lighter* (1696).

George Berkeley's (1685-1753)—Bishop Berkeley's—contribution to economic analysis is not on a level with his contribution to philosophy. It is chiefly contained in his *Querist* (1st ed., 1735-7). The idea of putting a prolonged argument into an endless string of wearying questions may not be to everyone's taste. But the forceful common sense, which is the strong point of his philosophic thought, is conspicuous in almost every one of them.

Sir James Steuart we have met already. For the subject of money it is necessary to add other publications to his *Principles*, especially the *Principles of Money applied to the Present State of the Coin of Bengal* (1772).

John Law (1671-1729), I have always felt, is in a class by himself. Fi-

---

commodity element in order to be logically complete and then to introduce the latter on the score of (good or bad) reasons of practical convenience is the very definition of theoretical antimetallism, combined (if these reasons are held to be valid) with practical metallism. But the term 'pledge' is also used by writers of metallist persuasion. It occurs, e.g., in R. Vaughan's explanation of the nature of money.

nancial adventurers—but is it fair so to call that administrative genius?—often have a philosophico-economic system of sorts. The Pereires of Crédit Mobilier fame had one (of St. Simonist complexion). But Law's case is different. He worked out the economics of his projects with a brilliance and, yes, profundity, which places him in the front rank of monetary theorists of all times. And this is all that matters for us. Since it is plain, however, that his analysis has been condemned, for about two centuries, primarily on the strength of the failure of his Banque Royale, it is pertinent to point out, first, that its predecessor, the Banque Générale, founded 1716, was a perfectly orthodox bank that was to issue notes and to receive deposits payable on demand and to discount commercial paper—no antimetallism about that—and that the Banque Royale and the Compagnie des Indes, which it absorbed, failed because the colonial ventures combined in the latter did not, for the time being, prove to be the source of anything but losses. If these ventures had been successful, Law's grandiose attempt to control and to reform the economic life of a great nation from the financial angle—for this is what his plan eventually amounted to—would have looked very different to his contemporaries and to historians. Even as it was, that gigantic enterprise was not simply a swindle and it may well be doubted whether France was the worse for it, on balance. However, economists not only fell in with the popular opinion that the scheme was nothing but swindle but also pointed to certain technical defects in it that were in fact important subsidiary causes of its failure. Thus that event acquired considerable influence on the evolution of what eventually became the classic theory of banking.

Law's performance as a monetary theorist is contained in his tract: *Money and Trade considered, with a Proposal for supplying the Nation with Money* (1st ed. 1705, 2nd ed. 1720; republ. in Somers' *Tracts*, 1809; French version, together with other writings including interesting *Mémoires justificatifs*, in the Guillaumin edition of *Économistes-financiers du XVIII*^{e} *siècle*, under the title of *Considérations sur le numéraire et le commerce*). The reader who wishes further information about that colorful personality is referred to A. W. Wiston-Glynn, *John Law of Lauriston* (1907), and P. Harsin, *Étude critique sur la bibliographie des oeuvres de John Law* (1928).

One of his plans was concerned with a land bank that was to issue legal tender paper money up to a certain proportion of the value of land and to receive as deposits *for placement* money that would otherwise lie idle, so that money would never be either too cheap or too dear. In this he followed the English land-bank projectors who must now be mentioned briefly.

The landed gentlemen in the House of Commons were no more, than were and are any other agrarians, able to see why they should not borrow as easily and cheaply as traders or financiers, and they did not take kindly to arguments about the difference between a bill and a mortgage. A land bank that, among other things, might satisfy these longings eventually became a Tory plank when the foundation of the Bank of England was in the offing. At the right time (1693) an intellectual, Hugh Chamberlen, an obstetrician by profession, presented a plan of a land bank where landowners would get loans at 4 per cent and the government would get more money than it had got from the Bank of England. The plan, which failed through lack of financial support, need not detain us. But there were supporters who attempted to supply it with an analytic background. Barbon, as we already know, was one. John Asgill (*Several Assertions Proved* . . . 1696, republ. in the Hollander series) was another; his tract illustrates the truth, which I try incessantly to emphasize, that the fact that *we* may be able to see some point in that scheme does not in itself salvage every devious argument that may have been put up for it. But John Briscoe (*Discourse on the Late Funds* . . . 1694; abstract of it in the same year), who claimed to have been plagiarized by Barbon and Asgill and was himself accused of having plagiarized Chamberlen, did provide some analytic groundwork with respect to which all those accusations are meaningless. Many economists would call him a metallist because he attributes importance to a stock of gold and silver. On reflection it will be realized, however, that a man's belief in the usefulness of a stock of universally acceptable commodities proves nothing about his views concerning the nature of money.

We cannot, and need not, go into the literature pro and con the foundation of the Bank of England. Not uninteresting in other respects, it was, so far as I know, sterile in the one that interests us here.

Barbon was more definite than anyone else in renouncing theoretical metallism on the ground that 'money is a value made by law,' to which the value of its material is not essential. John Law implies rather than states the same thing when emphasizing the virtues of paper money, which consist in its quantity's being amenable to rational management. Berkeley is, as far as I know, the author of the ticket analogy: 'Whether the true Idea of Money, as such, be not altogether that of a Ticket or Counter?' (*Querist*, no. 23). The only effort at building a theory of money on an antimetallist basis stands to the credit of Sir James Steuart. But he made so little headway and slipped up so often that the promising beginning was lost in the metallist current.

The point is this. The practice of the epoch, especially the practice of the four great clearing and deposit banks,[12] had familiarized economists with the idea of a money of account which was defined by quantities of metal and which existed only as a bookkeeping device for the purpose of facilitating large-scale trade and finance in a world of numberless and ever-changing currency systems. In this sense the money of account also entered monetary theory of the metallist type. Galiani called it *moneta ideale* or *moneta immaginaria*,[13] and distinguishes it from *moneta reale*, which consists of actual *pezzi di metallo*. Steuart (*Principles*, Book III) makes the same distinction between 'money

[12] Of Amsterdam, Hamburg, Genoa, and Venice.

[13] If there be any difference between these two phrases, it has escaped me.

of accompt' and 'money-coin,' but with him this distinction acquired a different meaning. Having previously (*Principles*, Book I, p. 32 of the edition of 1767) *defined* money as 'any commodity which purely in itself is of no material use to man but which acquires such an estimation from his opinion of it as to become the universal measure of what is called value . . .'—a faulty way of defining a pure *numéraire* of which he thus may be called the discoverer[14]—he then starts from a money of account, considered as an 'arbitrary scale' for measuring values and, unlike the money of account of practice and also of metallist theory, devoid of any commodity connotation. He tries unsuccessfully to find primitive instances of such a unit,[15] and does not succeed in explaining how such a unit can be theoretically constructed and how it might function in practice. But he had the idea and he also saw metallic money in its true light, namely, in the light of a very special case.

Every writer who went into fundamentals at all recounted and developed, as the scholastics had done, the particular virtues that explain why the precious metals proved so universally acceptable as to acquire their monetary role (their divisibility, mobility, and so on). Somewhat less trivial was the listing of the four functions of money that were to gain such prominence in the nineteenth-century textbook: the Aristotelian 'measure of (exchange) value' and 'medium of exchange' were supplemented by 'store of value'—an element much emphasized by the specifically mercantilist writers (see next chapter)—and by 'standard of deferred payments,' though I know of no case where these four functions appear neatly side by side—some writers even stressed the first only and others the second only. It was gradually realized that these two functions are separable and that their theories are different.

The economists of that period had before their eyes, as had the scholastics, almost all the forms of bimetallism that it is possible to conceive and hence all the practical problems that are incident to this system. It is the more surprising that so little progress was made with its analysis. In particular, the essential point about the legal ratio of the two metals does not seem to have been noticed: theorists realized, of course, that the metal which this ratio overvalues with respect to the other will tend to drive out the one it undervalues; they had discussed this phenomenon at least from Molina's time—one may in fact, if one so desires, subsume it under Gresham's law; but they failed to see that, so long as both metals are in circulation, this mechanism will tend to increase the market value of the one and to decrease the market value of the other and thus tend, within limits, to stabilize the market values

[14] It will be observed that the use of the word commodity does not make him a metallist. For a commodity that, by definition, is incapable of serving any purpose outside of its monetary function is not a commodity in the relevant sense of metallist theory.

[15] He mentions the *macute,* a unit that is supposed to have been current among West African tribes. Perhaps this was suggested to him by Montesquieu (*Esprit des lois,* Book XXII, ch. VIII), who was also an antimetallist and used the *macute* as an instance of a monetary unit that was a *signe* [of value] *purement idéal.* But the instance is of doubtful validity.

of both, which is the most interesting property of bimetallism. Locke, who was monometallist on principle, even argued on general grounds that there should be no legal ratio at all—no more than a legal rate of interest or a legal exchange rate—without observing that in this case the system becomes indeterminate.[16] Beccaria and others are not more satisfactory on this matter.

It will be convenient, before going on, to touch briefly upon a number of topics, some of them of great importance in themselves, that cannot be dealt with fully in a history of economic analysis.

First, questions of coinage were bound to be eagerly discussed under circumstances in which the state of the currency continued to give trouble. The large literature on technique, principally Italian, contains little that is of interest to us. But we may mention the question of seignorage. The old feudal privilege of kings and princes to coin money and to levy a tax in doing so, often in addition to a fee (brassage as it was sometimes called), was onerous even when it did not lead to frequent recoinage and produced an irresistible popular demand for free coinage. Accordingly, in England seignorage was abolished in 1666, while in other countries the tendency was to reduce it to the cost of coinage. There are two points about this that are relevant to the theory of money. One is that some writers, among them Sir William Petty, maintained that free coinage was essential for gold and silver to fill the function of money: if any charge at all were made for coining, they would no longer be true measures of the value of other things—which looks like a theoretical slip. The other is that the act which introduced free coinage was motivated by a desire to attract gold and silver—the costs to be defrayed by import duties on other commodities—and therefore was a typically 'mercantilist' measure. Economists were by no means in love with it and practically the entire free-trade chorus from North to Smith and from Smith to Mill recommended a cost-covering charge as did most continentals, though in the case of the German economists we might be tempted to attribute this to the fact that they were advising poor governments.

This naturally leads, secondly, to the discussion of devaluation or debasement ('raising the coin'). The old arguments, characteristic of strict metallism, that to debase was to defraud continued to be repeated: we find them in a host of writers, including Locke, Justi, and A. Smith.[17] But economists came

[16] I know of no clear recognition of this fact until Walras pointed it out, but Galiani recognized it implicitly. For he argued for the legal—though variable—ratio on practical grounds, one of which looks very much like it. A similar claim may be made for Massie.

[17] If economists were more given to clear statement than they are, the question what this fraud precisely consists in might well serve as a test for the presence or absence of metallist belief. If the fraud be held to consist in depriving the creditor of part of the metal that is due to him, we behold a metallist. If the fraud be held to materialize only, if, as, and when debasement or devaluation increases the money in circulation and hence decreases the creditor's potential share in the things that may be bought for money, then we behold a cartalist. The logical justification for this distinction is too obvious to require comment, but it may be well to point out that there is also a prac-

increasingly to take another and much more interesting view of the matter: they began to attend less to rights and wrongs and more to the effects of debasement upon the economic process. Sporadically, we find considerations of this type even in the sixteenth century, when people discussed whether debasement was advantageous or disadvantageous for the public finances. In the second half of the seventeenth and in the eighteenth century, discussion turned to the effects on the foreign trade and on the economic development of a country. Let us take cursory notice of a few beacon lights on this route. First, the English currency (silver monometallism with an increasing actual circulation of gold), having fallen into bad repair in the last decades of the seventeenth century, William III's Whig government, in which Charles Montague managed financial affairs, carried a bill (1698) according to which the silver coins were to be restored to their old weight and fineness at the public expense, this expense to be covered by a window tax, an operation that was completed by 1699. The debate on the measure is glorified by the name of Locke, who was the literary protagonist on the side of the government, and its interest to us reduces to the light his contribution sheds on the extent of his comprehension of monetary phenomena. Unfortunately, it is a sorry picture that unfolds itself before the eyes of Locke's reader. It is not only that he mainly worked the fraud line—this is a moral judgment and is his affair, not ours—but he failed to see (a) that recoinage at an average of the actual silver content of the silver coins could not be called debasement or could be called so only with the qualification that the economic situation was already adapted to it, so that in effect he was advocating overvaluation of the coin and undervaluation of the silver contained in it; (b) that in consequence, unless all prices adapted themselves promptly—which was not to be expected and would have, if it had happened, greatly accentuated the prevailing depressive conditions—silver would emigrate, as in fact it did; (c) that the presence of gold coins in actual circulation was at all relevant to the problem. He even went so far as to hold that what he called debasement was futile—in fact impossible—on the ground that an ounce of silver could never be worth more than an ounce of silver! His case and his defense of it was below that of his chief opponent, Lowndes—this is what happens to the man 'who gives up to party what was meant for mankind.' It is curious and melancholy to note that both the measure and Locke's advocacy of it have been eulogized, sometimes in extravagant terms, for more than two centuries.

Next we shall note, from the French discussion of the monetary troubles during and after the last wars of Louis XIV, the duel between Melon and Dutot [text breaks off at this point].

---

tical difference: devaluating governments need not and often do not inject the corresponding amount of money into circulation. They may hold it—wholly or in part—or use it for payments to foreign creditors, and there are other reasons why this access of money need not act upon prices. It even may be used in ways that benefit creditors. In fact, modern experience clearly shows that devaluation and depreciation are different things, and they are universally distinguished by now.

3. Digression on Value

Work in this field also proceeded from the scholastic background. We know that the scholastic doctors had developed the essentials of a realistic analysis of value, cost, and price—including a rudimentary concept of equilibrium—that needed only to be elaborated in content and perfected in technique. To some extent this is exactly what was done during the period under discussion. This work was powerfully propelled by the preoccupation with the problem of the value (purchasing power) of money. The metallist theory, as a theory of money, may not be much good in itself. But it certainly leads the economist who accepts it to inquire more closely into the problem of value in general. We shall therefore not be surprised that a great part of the best work in this field was done by students mainly interested in monetary phenomena. This is why this section stands where it does. We are going to try to bring out, by means of a brief survey of outstanding performances, the points that are most important for subsequent developments.

[(a) *The Paradox of Value: Galiani.*] The Italians from Davanzati on (*Lezione delle moneta*, 1588) were the first to realize explicitly how the Paradox of Value—the paradox that many very 'useful' commodities such as water have a low exchange value or none at all whereas much less 'useful' ones such as diamonds have a high one—can be solved and that it does not bar the way toward a theory of exchange value based upon value in use. The astounding fact that both Smith and Ricardo thought it did is, however, seen in its full significance only if we add that, for the century and a half after Davanzati, a lengthy list of writers might be compiled who understood quite well precisely how the element of utility enters into the process of pricing and that there were several Englishmen among them. John Law, in particular, in the tract quoted above (*Money and Trade considered* . . . 1705), gave a short but excellent account of the matter—actually using the examples of water and diamonds. However, we shall confine ourselves to the economist who carried this analysis to its eighteenth-century peak, Galiani.[1] Unlike Law, he was so uncompromising a metallist that he felt compelled to inquire into the value of gold and silver considered as commodities and therefore into the value of all commodities. In doing so he displayed sure-footed mastery of analytic pro-

[1] This, of course, involves injustice to his predecessors, to whom, in fact, he was unbelievably unfair himself. For instance, in developing Davanzati's argument, he writes in a vein of quite unwarranted superiority. Moreover, it must not be forgotten that the theory he developed was really that of the scholastics. It was not only in this matter that Galiani—like other economists—failed to acknowledge indebtedness properly. In his sociology—or, if readers prefer, social philosophy—he leaned heavily on Vico without acknowledging this debt either. See Tagliacozzo, op. cit. pp. xv (the most beautiful page in the whole Vico literature, so far as I know it) et seq., and F. Nicolini ('Giambattista Vico e Ferdinando Galiani,' *Giornale storico della letteratura italiana*, 1918, and the Note to his edition of Galiani's *Della Moneta*, 1915; but, being a philosopher, Nicolini is inclined to exaggerate the dependence, which amounted to little, so far as technical theory is concerned).

cedure and, in particular, neatness in his carefully defined conceptual constructions to a degree that would have rendered superfluous all the nineteenth-century squabbles—and misunderstandings—on the subject of value had the parties to these squabbles first studied his text,[2] *Della moneta*, 1751 (outlined in the preceding section of this chapter).

Having resolutely (first Book, ch. II) defined the term Value to mean a relation of subjective equivalence between a quantity of one commodity and a quantity of another—the objective equivalences on the market are treated as a special case of this, but he did not work out the transition from subjective to objective values in this sense—so that the phrase Value of a Commodity has no meaning except with reference to a given quantity of another, Galiani answers the question on what this value depends by Utility and Scarcity (*utilità e rarità*), and proceeds to develop these concepts in much the same way in which I suspect they are explained in many an elementary course today. Utility is not usefulness as understood by the observer—'useful' in the economist's sense is everything that produces pleasure (*piacere*) or procures welfare (felicità). Fashion, prestige value, and altruistic components are all trotted out in due course. And scarcity is the relation between the existing quantity of a thing and the uses one has for it and explains why a golden calf is valued more highly than a natural calf. To repeat, all that was not original with Galiani. The famous 'paradox of value,' which was gravely discussed again in the nineteenth century—the fact that obviously useful things fetch a low price and much less 'necessary' ones a high price—had been resolved several times before. But never before, or for more than a century to come, was this theory put forth so completely and with so full a sense of its importance. What separates Galiani from Jevons and Menger is, first, that he lacked the concept of marginal utility—though the concept of relative scarcity comes pretty near it—and, second, that he failed to apply his analysis to the problems of cost and of distribution. The first shortcoming is perhaps a reason why he stops short of a satisfactory theory of price, though he could have got further than he did in spite of it, as Isnard's later success suffices to show. Even so, however, he left his mark upon the subject. Having indicated how price derives from utility and scarcity, he ran up against the fact that this price, by limiting the quantity of the commodity consumers can procure, reacts in turn upon scarcity as felt by these consumers. It at the same time regulates, and is regulated by, demand (*consumo*). He knew perfectly how to deal with this phenomenon of interde-

[2] There was another Italian writer on money, Giovanni Ceva (*De re nummaria, quoad fieri potuit* [!] *geometrice tractata* . . . 1711), an engineer in Mantua, who did not, so far as I can see, add anything new to the theory of money, but whom no history of economic analysis can afford to pass by because of his insight into the nature of economic theory: real phenomena are always obscure and unmanageably complex; practice is always *minus exacta*; to understand the principles of things we must hence construct rational models by means of assumptions (*petitiones*) or else we must always move in the darkest of nights (*versari in obscurissima nocte*); and the proper way of dealing with these models is by mathematics, a methodology that took two centuries to assert itself.

pendence. And in the three pages he devotes to the subject he actually discovered the concept of long-run equilibrium and sketched out the profit mechanism that works to bring it about, visualizing a country, hitherto Mohammedan and teetotal, that suddenly embraces Christianity and thereupon develops a demand for wine. There is a Mandeville flavor about these pages that perhaps detracts a little from what otherwise would have to be considered as a remarkable display of originality. But this does not alter the fact that but little care and patience would have been sufficient to evolve from this a much more perfect body of theory than was to be presented by A. Smith.

While Galiani thus foreshadowed much later developments (marginal utility), he also anticipated the value theory of the next hundred years (Ricardo and Marx). For, with surprising abruptness, he turns from *rarità,* by way of quantity of commodities, to labor (*fatica*) and forthwith enthrones it as the only factor of production and the only circumstance *che dá valore alla cosa.* In one sense this spoils his theory of value, but in another it is highly interesting. *Fatica* means quantity of labor—corrected for the social habits that determine how many days a year and how many hours a day a man actually works and for the differences in natural ability (*talenti*) which account for the different prices of the *fatica* of different people—and, with a qualification for the monopoly price of unique things (*Venere de' Medici,* for instance), equilibrium value is made proportional to that quantity (temporary fluctuations being duly attended to). But this is in all essentials and in many details the theory of Ricardo and Marx, and more satisfactory—if we place ourselves on a Ricardian standpoint—than that of A. Smith.[3]

[(b) *Bernoulli's Hypothesis.*] But let us bear in mind that it was the 'subjective' or 'utility' theory of price that had the wind until the influence of the *Wealth of Nations*—and especially of Ricardo's *Principles*—asserted itself. Even after 1776, that theory prevailed on the Continent, and there is an unbroken line of development between Galiani and J. B. Say. Quesnay, Beccaria, Turgot, Verri, Condillac,[4] and many minor lights contributed to establishing it more and more firmly. They all linked price and the mechanism of pricing *directly* to what they conceived to be the fundamental purpose of economic activity, the satisfaction of wants. They all accepted Cantillon's definition of *richesse,* not only as a phrase to be forgotten as soon as stated, or, as in the case of Smith, to be remembered only in order to recommend policies favorable to consumers, but as the starting point of price analysis. Moreover, with all of them, the price phenomenon was rooted in the calculus of pleasure and pain, exactly as it was with Jevons: in this respect they were Benthamites by anticipation, and stronger Benthamites than were to be Bentham's adherents among English economists. Thus, they were not only the forerunners of the 'subjectivists' of the second half of the nineteenth century, but they

[3] Quantity of labor in turn is, in one place, equated to the expense of the laborer's subsistence (*spesa del nutrimento*). Though not Ricardian in form, this passage can be interpreted in a Ricardian sense. But it rather harks back to Cantillon.

[4] *Le Commerce et le gouvernement* (1776), see above, chs. 2 and 3.

also sealed that unfortunate alliance between the theory of value and utilitarianism that was to prove so embarrassing a century later.[5] For the moment, however, we shall not go into this any further but instead notice a performance that, besides presenting a number of other points of interest, anticipated the theory of marginal utility still more definitely.

In a paper [6] written in 1730 or 1731, Daniel Bernoulli, the eminent scientist whom we have already had occasion to mention, suggested the hypothesis that the economic significance to an individual of an additional dollar is inversely proportional to the number of dollars he already has. Referring this to income rather than, as Bernoulli did, to the monetary value of the total net assets of an individual, we readily identify this additional dollar with what, in the terminology of a later epoch, was to be the marginal dollar, and its significance with what, in the same terminology, was to be its marginal utility, the statistical measurement of which has been attempted by Fisher and Frisch in our own time.[7] No less interesting are the applications to business practice

[5] See below, Part III, ch. 3, sec. 1a.

[6] 'Specimen theoriae novae de mensura sortis,' publ. 1738 in the *Commentarii academiae scientiarum imperialis Petropolitanae.* The German translation by Professor Alfred Pringsheim (*Die Grundlage der modernen Wertlehre: Daniel Bernoulli* . . . 1896) contains instructive notes by the translator as well as a very useful introduction by Ludwig Fick. It is, however, highly characteristic of the haziness of our knowledge of doctrinal developments that Mr. Fick not only hailed Bernoulli as a precursor of Gossen, Jevons, Menger, and Walras, but also as one of the first, if not the first, to recognize that value is not an inherent property of things but a relation between a valuating person and the things valued—though *this* was perfectly clear to the scholastic doctors and, in any case, to dozens of eighteenth-century writers who did not know of Bernoulli's paper.

[7] This will be particularly clear on exact formulation. Let x denote an individual's income and y the 'satisfaction' derived from it. Bernoulli's hypothesis then says that

$$dy = K\frac{dx}{x}, \quad \text{or} \quad \frac{dy}{dx} = \frac{K}{x},$$

the factor of proportionality (K), being a constant for every individual, but different for different individuals—the range of variation in the individual K's taking account of individual differences of tastes or intensities of feeling (Bernoulli seems to have attributed the same K to all individuals excepting uninteresting abnormalities, but never mind)—dy/dx is obviously the marginal or final degree of utility, which therefore put in explicit appearance in 1738. As stated by Bernoulli, his fundamental idea was anticipated (1728) by the mathematician Cramer, who offered, however, a different hypothesis about the form of the marginal utility function, viz.,

$$dy = K\frac{dx}{\sqrt{x}},$$

but Bernoulli's hypothesis is, within moderate intervals, quite reasonable though it fails to make use of all we know, or think we know, about the behavior of this function (see below, Part IV, ch. 7).

Since even believers in the measurability of utility or satisfaction will not think it safe to say anything about its behavior in desperate situations, for instance, for in-that Bernoulli made of his hypothesis (op. cit. §§ 15, 16). The underlying idea is that even where the probabilities of gains and losses are strictly calculable—as are, for instance, the chances of loss in sea transport if long experience affords sufficient material—rational action is not determined by the value of these probabilities alone. It is also necessary to take into account the importance to the individual businessman of given gains and losses, which differs of course according to the individual's means, and Bernoulli's hypothesis supplies a method for effecting this. Thus he deduces a criterion by which to decide whether or not it is advantageous for a man to pay a given sum for insuring his cargo, and also a rule by which to evaluate the advantage to be derived from transporting a given quantity of wares in several ships, or from investment of a given sum in several securities instead of in one—important suggestions for a theory of business risks and of investment that even now are not fully exploited. And there may be point in recalling a sentence from Bernoulli's text (op. cit. § 17): 'Precisely because these results agree so well with observed business behavior, it does not seem right to neglect them like unproven statements that are based on insecure hypotheses.' I lament the impossibility of discussing other points [8] about this paper that are of absorbing

comes below which the individual cannot survive, we had better exclude such a 'minimum of existence' from consideration. If we call it a, total satisfaction derived from an income of the amount b may then be represented by the definite integral

$$y = \int_a^b K \frac{dx}{x} = K(\log b - \log a) = K \log \frac{b}{a}.$$

[8] Brief allusion to two of them may be permissible, however. The first is that it remained practically unknown to economists until it was noticed by some *who had arrived by themselves at the same or similar ideas.* Fick mentions Hermann (1832), F. A. Lange, *Die Arbeiterfrage* . . . (1865), and especially Jevons, and I have no names to add. This neglect is remarkable owing to Laplace's sponsorship of the Bernoulli formula in his *Théorie analytique des probabilités* (1812), which was of course widely known. The second fact is that Bernoulli's attempt to solve the paradox of the St. Petersburg game is not among the many valuable contributions of his paper, *although it was the primary object of it.* The problem is this. A coin is to be tossed n times. X promises Y to pay $1 if heads turns up on the first throw; $2 if heads, having failed to turn up the first time, turns up the second time; $4 if heads, having failed to turn up the first two times, turns up the third time, and so on. The series of Y's *possible* gains is hence $1, 2, 2^2, 2^3, \ldots 2^{n-1}$. We derive his mathematical expectation of gain by multiplying each of the possible gains by its probability, that is, if the coin be perfect, ½, ¼, ⅛, and so on. It is seen that this multiplication reduces each item to ½ so that, summing up, we get for Y's total mathematical expectation $n/2$, and if n is allowed to increase beyond any assigned limit, an expectation greater than any sum we care to mention. Nevertheless, it is the fact that nobody will pay X any considerable sum for it, as the reader can easily find out for himself. Why? Bernoulli thought that all we need to do in order to answer this question is to correct the possible gains by applying his hypothesis to them, which would in fact produce a finite 'moral' expectation in the place of the 'infinite' mathematical one. But this procedure, though not in itself meaningless, does not solve the problem. Neither do, for that matter, the points made by Professor Pringsheim in a footnote to his trans-

interest to the student of the ways of the human mind and of the mechanism of scientific progress.

[(c) *The Theory of the Mechanism of Pricing.*] As regards the theory of the *mechanism* of pricing, there is very little to report before the middle of the eighteenth century. The contributions of even the brightest lights, such as Barbon, Petty, Locke, do not amount to much, and the vast majority of the Consultant Administrators and Pamphleteers of the seventeenth century were content with the kind of theory they found or could have found in Pufendorf. They attended to practical problems of regulative policy, but the analytic side they took largely for granted and were slow to realize the need of rigorous conceptualization and proof. A few examples will illustrate the situation. People were quite familiar with the pattern of monopoly, on which they bestowed an impulsive hatred, and with competition, which they conceived to be the normal pattern without bothering to define it. But as early as 1516, it occurred to Sir Thomas More (*Utopia,* see ch. 3 above) that for competition to prevail it is not necessarily sufficient that a commodity be sold by more than one seller. Prices may fail to fall to the competitive level also if sellers are few, *quod . . . si monopolium appellari non potest . . . certe oligopolium est.*[9] Thus More introduced the concept of oligopoly. We might expect that this hint would have led to closer analysis of the concepts of monopoly and competition, especially in England, where the interminable discussion of monopolies of various types and of restraints of trade of all types—both the restraints that competitors agree on in order to further their common interest, and the restraints monopolists impose upon other people—that preceded and again followed the Statute of Monopolies of 1623/4, furnished all the motive and material one can desire. But there was hardly anything of the kind. Politicians, lawyers, and some businessmen fought 'monopolies' passionately, much as they do today—particularly those of the chartered trading companies—and the attacked interests defended themselves as best they could, also much as they do today. Intellectually, both sides made a poor show, once more much as they do today. Though practical results were achieved and

lation, although they, too, are by no means irrelevant. We cannot go further in this subject. But the reader would be much mistaken if he thought that it is without interest to the economist. The theory of games of chance is on the contrary highly important for many problems of economic logic. If proof were needed, a recent book by Professors Morgenstern and von Neumann would supply it (*Theory of Games and Economic Behavior,* 1944). And the first pointer in this direction still stands in Bernoulli's name. In economics it may take 206 years from a first step to the second—just about the same length of time as in the case of the statistical demand curve.

[9] I am indebted to Mr. E. Marz for having drawn my attention to this passage. The fact is curious. Sir Thomas did not only use—and so far as I know coin—the term (oligopoly) that plays so great a role in modern theory, but he used it in order to denote exactly the same thing, and he at once pointed to a feature of it that modern theory was to emphasize—after a lag of about 410 years. Yet the thought is no doubt suggestive and important. And the *Utopia* was very widely read. It is true, however, that this passage does not occur in the English translation of the Latin original.

though the historian of economic thought and policy finds plenty to record,[10] the historian of economic analysis goes from that literature almost empty-handed. Not to neglect any crumbs, however, let us notice, first, the tendency to extend the concept of monopoly beyond the case of a single seller [11] and, second, the rudiments of the argument that monopoly while striving to maximize profits—as we should say—changes the conditions with reference to which this maximization is attempted and so need not necessarily set a higher price than would prevail under competition working under different conditions.[12] We may also mention again Becher's attempt to classify—illogically —market patterns into *monopolium, propolium,* and *polypolium,* that is, monopoly, forestalling, and unregulated competition—which according to him is productive of disorganized markets in which every participant is proletarized.

But better things were to follow in the eighteenth century. We shall confine ourselves to the peak achievements of Beccaria, Turgot, and Isnard, and then consider the manner in which the *Wealth of Nations* codified the whole of the value and price theory of the epoch.

Beccaria dealt with value and price in Part IV, Chapter 1 ('Del commercio') of his *Elementi* (publ. posthumously, 1804): the subject stands there pretty much where it was to stand in J. S. Mill's *Principles.* He explains the phenomenon of value, as mentioned already, by utility and scarcity, and then proceeds to investigate the *modus operandi* of a hypothetical market in which wine is bartered for wheat (cf. Marshall's apples and nuts).[13] He recognized clearly

[10] The reader is referred to Professor Heckscher's *Mercantilism* I, pp. 269 et seq., for a masterly interpretation of that struggle for 'free trade' in the seventeenth-century sense. If he follows this advice, he cannot fail to be impressed by the distressing observation that popular and political discussion of this matter—as of others—shows practically no progress at all.

[11] See Heckscher, op. cit. pp. 273-4, especially the argument of Sir Edwin Sandys (an ardent trust-buster) put forth in the House of Commons debate in 1604, to the effect that the 'name of monopoly . . . is fitly extended to all improportionable paucity of sellers. . . If ten men had the only sale of all the horses in England, this were a monopoly.' Viewed as an analytic effort, this is of course somewhat short of admirable. But it is clear that there is something in what Sir Edwin unsuccessfully strove to express.

[12] Other arguments used for defense turned either on denials of the presence of monopoly—mostly quite true if monopoly be defined strictly, but inconclusive precisely because of this—or on the assertion that in certain cases—especially those of trade with uncivilized countries where protection was an important consideration—monopolistic organization was a practical necessity, or on other points that, whatever their practical weight may have been, are of no interest from the standpoint of analytic technique. One of the best, if not the best, expositions of 'defensive' arguments I have come across is John Wheeler's *A Treatise of Commerce. Wherein are showed the Commodities arising by a well ordered and ruled trade* . . . (1601). This was no doubt 'special pleading' on behalf of the Merchant Adventurers, of which company Wheeler was an attorney. But there is, from our standpoint, no reason for ruling it out on that account.

[13] I hope that we need not take too seriously his proposition that the exchange value of one commodity relatively to the other (the exchange ratio) will be *in ragione reciproca*

that the exchange ratio is indeterminate in the case of isolated exchange (between two individuals) and that determinateness is brought about by competition through the 'higgling of the market': fluctuations must eventually lead to the price at which *quantity demanded equals quantity supplied*. His careful treatment of the exchange of three commodities against one another, in which he insists on the phenomenon (and necessity) of indirect exchange, is particularly satisfactory. This is about as much as the average economist had to say a century later.

Beccaria's performance has been chosen for comment because of its comparative fullness, but it had been strikingly anticipated by Turgot's *Réflexions*, XXXIII-XXXV (written in 1766, published in 1769-70). After having deduced trading (commerce) from *besoins réciproques*, Turgot, too, touches upon the case of isolated exchange and then introduces the determining force, competition. His description of the market mechanism is very similar to that of Böhm-Bawerk (see below, Part IV, ch. 5, sec. 4). The resulting market price (*prix courant*) is then made to vary under the impact of forces acting through demand or supply. The crowning achievement of the epoch in this line of analysis is Isnard's.[14] In his not otherwise remarkable book there is an elementary system of equations that—barring the difference in technique—describes the interdependence within the universe of prices in a way suggestive of Walras.

[(d) *Codification of Value and Price Theory in the* Wealth of Nations.] A. Smith's 'chief work was to combine and develop the speculations of his French and English contemporaries and predecessors as to value.' [15] Also, it is

---

delle loro quantità. Possibly there is a connection between this and his friend Verri's hyperbolical demand law, which however is not open to the same objection but, on the contrary, must be recorded as the first attempt to give a precise form to the demand curve: if p be price (in money), q quantity, and c a constant, then, according to Verri's law, $pq = c$.

[14] Achille Nicolas Isnard's *Traité des richesses* appeared in 1781, and thus forms no part of the material 'codified' by A. Smith. There is, however, a question of the latter's influence upon the former. Isnard's treatise, also the contribution mentioned in the text, *could* have arisen from a perusal of the *Wealth of Nations*. Isnard does not mention A. Smith, however, unless, indeed, I have overlooked the reference. The title of the book is included in Jevons' list of mathematical writings, which is how I came to know of it. I have found no traces of its influence.

[15] A. Marshall, *Principles*, 4th ed., p. 58. The reader will realize that the opinion of a workman such as Marshall is worth a ton of philosophizing by less workmanlike people, and we cannot do better than use that dictum of a master of economic theory as a motto. Also, the reader will realize that even Marshall, whose admiration for Smith was unbounded, does not go beyond what our own term 'codification' implies. Though he was far from attributing to Smith any original ideas, he nevertheless arrived at an estimate of the performance that seems much higher than ours. One reason for this may be that he was speaking of a brother—for as has been and will be emphasized, there are many similarities in the performances and in the historical positions of the two. Another may be that he was speaking of a countryman—for Marshall was very insular. A third one may be that he was speaking of a fellow liberal—for Marshall, too, was a strong free trader. But whatever the reason, the reader should

quite true that he made 'a careful and scientific inquiry into the manner in which value measures human motive,' that is to say, I take it, that he made exchange value (price or, at all events, relative price) the centerpiece of a primitive system of equilibrium. But he was not, as Marshall held, the first to do so; moreover, in codifying, he dropped or sterilized many of the most promising suggestions contained in the work of his immediate predecessors. Of course, he may not have known Turgot's *Réflexions,* and he cannot have known Beccaria's *Elementi:* Pufendorf and then Cantillon, Harris, Locke, Barbon, Petty—these last five are mentioned by Marshall—and Quesnay were presumably his principal guides so that his 'subjective' performance was greater than was his 'objective' achievement. But he 'developed' this material less successfully than had Turgot and Beccaria. The blame is at his door for much that is unsatisfactory in the economic theory of the subsequent hundred years, and for many controversies that would have been unnecessary had he summed up in a different manner.

The reader should refresh his recollection of the Reader's Guide presented above.[16] A. Smith's exposition in the first Book surges purposefully up to the phenomenon of price and down again into the component parts of commodity prices, which components are the cost and income categories, wages, profit, and rent. This is, to repeat, a primitive way of describing the universal interdependence of the magnitudes that constitute the economic cosmos; but it is an effective way. Critics who did not understand that the theory of price is but another name for theory of economic logic—including, among other things, all the principles of allocation of resources and of formation of incomes—blamed him for having adopted the narrow point of view of the businessman. Other critics who did not understand the nature of a system of interdependent magnitudes accused him of circular reasoning. His shade easily wins out against these and other criticisms. It is this part of his performance that constitutes his chief merit in this field. There are others. As primitive but as distinctly visible as is his concept of universal interdependence is his concept of equilibrium or 'natural' price. This equilibrium price is simply the price at which it is possible to supply, in the long run, each commodity in a quantity that will equal 'effective demand' *at that price*. This again is the price that will, in the long run, just cover costs. And these, in turn, are equal to the sum total of the wages, profits, and rents that have to be paid or imputed at their '*ordinary or average rates*.' Thus, we also get a glimpse of Marshall's distinction between short-run and long-run phenomena, A. Smith's market price being essentially a short-run phenomenon, his 'natural' price a long-run phenomenon

---

observe that, so far as Marshall's very brief comments enable us to judge, there is no difference as to the facts of the case except this: Smith may certainly be said, in a sense, to have 'developed' existing doctrines of value and price; but whereas Marshall approved unconditionally of the manner of this 'development,' I have some fault to find with it.

[16] [After writing this, J. A. S. apparently removed several pages on A. Smith, including the Reader's Guide, from the manuscript. This material has been restored by the editor and is to be found in ch. 3, sec. 4e.]

—Marshall's long-run normal. 'It is all in A. Smith' was a favorite saying of Marshall's. But we may also say: 'It is all in the scholastics.' There is no theory of monopoly. The proposition (Book I, ch. 7) that 'the price of monopoly is upon every occasion the highest which can be got' might be the product of a not very intelligent layman—taken literally, it is not even true. But neither is the mechanism of competition made the subject of more searching analysis. In consequence, A. Smith fails to prove satisfactorily his proposition that the competitive price is 'the lowest which the sellers can commonly afford to take'—to the modern reader it is a source of wonder what kind of argument he took for proof. Still less did he attempt to prove that competition tends to minimize costs, though it is evident that he must have believed it.

But what was A. Smith's theory of value in the narrow sense of the phrase, meaning his views on the problem of causal explanation of the phenomenon of value? Since during the subsequent century economists were much interested in that problem, they eagerly discussed Smith's views about it and for this very reason we cannot pass it by. In itself, the answer is plain enough.

First of all, if the reader will look up the last paragraphs of Book I, Chapter 4, he will be able to satisfy himself of two things. On the one hand, A. Smith declares there that he is going to inquire into the rules which 'men naturally observe in exchanging' goods 'either for money or for one another.' This means that he was not primarily interested in the problem of value in the sense just defined. What he wanted was a price theory by which to establish certain propositions that do not require going into the background of the value phenomenon at all. Evidently this was also Marshall's opinion. On the other hand, having distinguished value in use and value in exchange, he dismisses the former by pointing to what has been called above the 'paradox of value'—which he evidently did believe to be a bar to progress on this line—thereby barring, for the next two or three generations, the door so auspiciously opened by his French and Italian predecessors. No talk about his 'recognizing the role of demand' can alter this fact. Second, in Book I, Chapter 6, A. Smith expressly states: 'Wages, profit, and rent, are the three *original* [my italics] sources of all revenue as well as of all exchangeable value.' If words mean anything, this is conclusive. His theory of value was what later on came to be called a cost-of-production theory. This is indeed the opinion of many students. But, third, the matter is complicated by the fact that a very large number of passages in the *Wealth of Nations* seem to point to a labor theory of value or rather to several.[17]

In Book I, Chapter 5, of the *Wealth of Nations* occurs the proposition: 'The real price of everything, what everything really costs to the man who wants to acquire it, is the toil and trouble of acquiring it'—one of those treacherous platitudes that may mean anything and nothing. On the face of it, however,

[17] It is still not sufficiently recognized that the term labor theory of value covers several distinct meanings. The subject has, however, been exhaustively dealt with by H. J. Davenport, *Value and Distribution*, 1908.

it indicates a tendency to base the value phenomenon upon the irksomeness or disutility of work, or to adopt a labor-disutility theory of value. This theory, however, may be discarded, because A. Smith makes no use whatever of it. Again, at the beginning of Book I, Chapter 6, Smith produces the famous example about the beaver: 'if . . . it usually costs twice the labour to kill a beaver which it does to kill a deer,' one beaver would naturally sell for as much as two deer. There it is quantity of labor that 'regulates' value and not toil and trouble, which is, of course, not the same thing. No doubt is possible but that this passage is the root of Ricardo's and Marx's labor-quantity theories of value. But A. Smith limits this theory to 'that early and rude state of society which precedes both the accumulation of stock and the appropriation of land,' which, interpreted charitably, means that competitive prices of commodities will, in equilibrium, be proportional to the labor entering into their production if the labor is all of the same 'natural' quality and if there are no other scarce means of production. This is true but does not in itself constitute a labor-quantity theory, or any labor theory, of value, because, for this special case, all theories of value would arrive at the same result. Finally, as we have already had occasion to notice, A. Smith (Book I, ch. 5) considers the quantity of labor a commodity can command in the market the most useful substitute for its price in money, that is to say, he chooses labor for *numéraire*. On principle, there can be no objection to this decision, which in itself no more commits him to a labor theory of value than the choice of oxen for *numéraire* would commit us to an ox theory of value. But he tries to motivate his decision by so many arguments that seem to claim deeper meaning for it—such as that 'labour alone . . . never varying in its own value, is alone [sic] the ultimate and real standard' of the values of all commodities or that 'it is their real price' or 'the only universal as well as the only accurate measure of value,' which are all wrong—and seems himself so little clear about what is and what is not implied in choosing something for *numéraire* that it is almost excusable if many later economists misunderstood what he actually did mean and that they, among them Ricardo,[18] accused him of having confused the quantity of labor that enters a commodity with the quantity of labor it will buy. This indictment fails, however, and it is important that it does, for it amounts to accusing Smith of an absurdity: taking what a commodity exchanges for, no matter what it is, as the *explanation* of its value would be one of the worst slips in the history of theory. It should be added that, if choosing an hour's or day's labor as the unit in which to express prices does not imply accepting a labor theory of value, no more does emphasis upon labor's role in production or upon labor's claims or wrongs. As has been mentioned already, there is plenty of this in the *Wealth of Nations*, much of it, perhaps, inspired by Locke. 'The produce of labour constitutes the natural recompence or wages of

[18] Ricardo did not misunderstand him always, however. Ricardo also argued that the exchange value of labor is no more exempt from fluctuations than is the exchange value of anything else. But this is relevant only with regard to making labor a *numéraire* that is to function over time.

labour' (Book I, ch. 8). It is the laborer who raises the crop and the landowner, having appropriated the land, demands a share of it. Profit makes a second deduction from the 'produce of labour.' To this day, it has remained difficult to make the philosophy-minded see that all this is completely irrelevant for a theory of value—considered not as a profession of faith or as an argument in social ethics, but as a tool of analysis of economic reality.

4. The Quantity Theory

It will not surprise the reader to learn that the *effects* of the violent price revolutions of the fifteenth, sixteenth, and seventeenth centuries should have been zealously discussed. But it might surprise him to learn that there was any question about their causes. For debasement of the currency—devaluations by governments as well as fraudulent clipping of coins by individuals—and the torrent of American gold and especially silver were before everyone's eyes; and not even the most sophisticated theorist of today could find fault with the obvious diagnosis, seeing that the monetary units newly created by either the debasement of the coinage or the influx of the American silver were very promptly spent, while the very wars on which they were mainly spent greatly interfered with production. Nevertheless, though it is probably possible to find early arguments that more or less distinctly imply this obvious diagnosis,[1] it seems to be the fact that no explicit, full, and—so far as it went—theoretically satisfactory presentation of it appeared before 1568, when Bodin published his *Response* to the *Paradoxes sur le faict des Monnoyes* (1566) of M. de Malestroict. (There is a translation of Bodin's *Response* in A. E. Monroe's *Early Economic Thought.*) On the strength of this, he is universally voted the 'discoverer' of the Quantity Theory of Money. Since the matter has received attention quite out of proportion to its importance, we shall go into it briefly ourselves.

[1] I say 'probably' because I do not myself know of any clear instances. The cases mentioned by Professor Seligman (article, 'Bullionists,' *Encyclopaedia of the Social Sciences*) are not convincing. Some historians who trace this kind of 'quantity theory' to the Middle Ages and even to the Roman jurist Paulus have misunderstood the word *quantitas*, which must not be translated by 'quantity' (see above, ch. 1). The best example I can mention—but it followed by a year Bodin's work, which I am about to mention in the text—is in the *Summa de tratos y contratos* of Tomás de Mercado (1st ed. 1569; ed. used 1571). By the end of the century, recognition of the effects on prices of the American silver was widespread, if not universal, as well it might have been. Luíz Valle de la Cerda (*Fundación*, 1593; *Desempeño*, 1600) called the price rise the 'efecto muy natural de la rapida multiplicacion de los signos y moneda.' The words 'very natural' in this passage have nothing to do with natural law but simply stand for 'indubitable' or 'obvious.' The contrary impression, voiced by Professor Hamilton, viz. that the influence of the inflow of silver upon prices was being persistently ignored or denied, seems due to the facts that many later authors had reasons for emphasizing the other factors in the price rise which were operative, especially in the case of Spain, and also that the common run of writers was then, as it is now, quite impervious to even the simplest economic truths.

[(a) *Bodin's Explanation of the Price Revolution.*] Jehan Cherruyt de Malestroict had argued that the universal rise in prices was due to debasement and that, expressed in full-weight coin, prices had not risen. Bodin replied—and then repeated in *Les six livres de la République,* 1576—that this argument overlooked the influence of American silver. The price revolution, according to him, was due to (1) the increase in the supply of gold and silver; (2) the prevalence of monopolies; (3) depredations that reduced the stream of available commodities; (4) the expenditure of kings and princes on the objects of their desires; and (5) the debasements that were the only factor considered by his opponent. He added, moreover, that the first cause was the most important one. The reader will observe that this analysis needs but little readjustment or generosity of interpretation to be a correct diagnosis of the historical case as it presented itself in 1568. Even as regards general theoretical content, it is superior to much later work. In fact, Bodin's analysis escapes several of the typical objections that were to be raised against the quantity theory in the nineteenth century. But does it state or imply this theory?

The question may seem surprising, but it is well worth asking. Let us embrace, for a moment, uncompromising metallism and consider the case of perfect gold monometallism—gold metallism such that gold can move freely in and out of the monetary system—from this standpoint. Gold being a commodity like any other, the value in terms of commodities of the golden monetary unit will fall, other things being equal, if gold production increases, just as the price of eggs will fall, other things being equal, if egg production increases. Any rise in prices in terms of gold that may occur is here explained as a consequence of increased supply. Let us note that the extent of this fall (in the value of gold) will simply depend upon the shape of the demand schedule for gold as a commodity in terms of some other standard, and that the operative 'quantity' in question is the total amount of the increase. In consequence, there is no reason to suppose that, however equal the other things, the fall will be proportional to the increase. It will be seen that no special hypothesis enters into the argument, which flows smoothly from the metallist basis and would have been accepted by the scholastics as a matter of course. But recognition of the relevance of 'quantity' to the value of money in this sense and for this reason has no more to do with the Quantity Theory of Money than that the word quantity occurs in both arguments. And no more than this is required for Bodin's argument or, let us add at once, for that of A. Smith.

[(b) *Implications of the Quantity Theorem.*] In order to make this clear, let us look at the same case from the standpoint of the quantity theory. To facilitate exposition we shall assume that there is an absolutely fixed collection of goods that must be sold for whatever money buyers have, and that these buyers feel compelled to spend promptly all of whatever money they have upon that collection of goods. Also we shall henceforth speak, instead of the quantity *theory,* of the quantity *theorem,* because it is not a complete theory of money but merely a proposition about the exchange value of money. Keeping, then, everything else severely as it is, we let gold production increase. As in the simple metallist argument, we infer that this will make the unit of gold less valuable, that is, raise all prices in terms of it. The reason for this is the same as before so far as that part of the increase is concerned that goes into industrial uses. But that part of the increase which spills over into circulation now operates in a different way and produces a fall in the exchange value of the monetary gold—a rise in commodity prices—for a different reason: the fall, under our highly artificial assumptions, is exactly proportional to the increase in the quantity of the *monetary* gold stock; and the immediate reason for this is not the fall in the commodity value of the gold—which is relevant indeed but only at one remove, that is, by virtue of the fact that it will determine the extent to which the quantity of monetary gold will be increased—but the increase of the quantity of coins per se. It is the increase in *this* quantity which, the purchasing power of the total monetary stock remaining constant, is the immediate cause of the resulting fall in the exchange value of the monetary unit. And this fall will be the same as if this stock, without being increased, had been split into units of smaller gold content, *because* in either case there is now less of every commodity per coin. Operation of the new gold in the *commodity* use may be likened to the effects of adding workers of the same skill to a given plant and equipment. Operation of the new gold in the *monetary* use may be likened to the effects of replacing the working force operating a given plant and equipment by more workers of proportionately less skill. Thus the quantity theorem does three things: first, it recognizes the fact that the monetary function will affect the value of the commodity chosen for money and is a logically distinct—though not independent—source of the exchange value of gold (this, of course, we can recognize without committing ourselves to the next steps); second, it recognizes that the mechanism that determines the value of gold in circulation is different from the mechanism that determines the value of the industrial gold or of any other commodity; third, it offers a specific schema—very primitive but also very simple—of that mechanism. The apparent difficulty of this really simple matter is due to the facts that in the case of perfect gold monometallism the two different mechanisms must, of course, produce the same values of gold in the monetary and in the industrial sphere; and that the influences of an increase in gold production upon the commodity value and upon the monetary value of gold so intertwine that we do not see either quite clearly. But it is one of the strong points of the quantity theory that it can be applied to the case of paper money without any auxiliary construction. And in this case—when there is no commodity value of the material to cause ambiguity about what quantity we mean and what *modus operandi* we attribute to it—all becomes perfectly clear. This logical affinity of the quantity theorem with theoretical cartalism should be borne in mind: the theorem essentially amounts to treating money not as a commodity but as a voucher for buying goods, though not everyone who does consider money in this light need accept the specific schema offered by the quantity theorem. It is the more important to remember this point because later developments tended to obliterate it.

There is no trace of considerations of this type in Bodin. But there is in

Davanzati (1588, see above, sec. 2), who confronted the mass of commodities with the mass of money—stock with stock—and would have to be credited with superior formulation of the quantity theorem in its most primitive form even if we interpreted Bodin's argument in the same sense. Subsequent advance on this line was slow. Mere recognition of the effect upon prices of American gold and silver imports or of any increase in a country's stock of gold and silver, of course, soon became commonplace. It is not always easy to tell from the uncouth writings of the less literate 'mercantilists' what it was they had in mind, but some of them, especially Malynes and Mun (see below, ch. 7), tried, I think, to convey the genuine quantity-theory idea—though in a quite rudimentary form—while others, perhaps the majority, were content with 'simple metallism.'[2] However, Davanzati at long last found a successor in Montanari (1680), and in England instances become frequent in the second half of the seventeenth century. Among these Briscoe (1694) deserves special notice,[3] because he was the first, so far as I know, to write an equation of exchange in the unsatisfactory form: stock of money equals prices times real income.[4] In the course of the eighteenth century it was the genuine quan-

[2] Malynes says categorically: 'Plentie of money maketh generally things deare' (*Tudor Economic Documents* III, 387), which at least admits the interpretation above. Mun's case is similar. An illustration of a recognition of the effect of increased 'treasure' that does not imply the genuine quantity-theory idea is in Sir Robert Cotton's speech on the 'Alteration of coine,' 1626: 'Gold and silver . . . are Commodities valuing each other according to the plenty or scarcity; and so all other Commodities by them' (Reprinted in McCulloch's *Scarce and Valuable Tracts on Money*). It should be observed, however, that what we have called the theory of 'simple metallism,' i.e. theoretical metallism without the specifically quantity-theorem element in it, is sufficient to protect 'mercantilists' from the indictments that in general they failed to perceive the effect of their beloved gold and silver imports upon prices and that, whenever they did, they really refuted their argument for export surpluses. The specific or genuine quantity theorem is not necessary for perceiving that effect. And the proposition that export surpluses are desirable because they will bring 'treasure' into the country, whatever its demerits may be, is not refuted by the argument that this inflow of gold and silver will raise prices and thus stop the exports. For, first, much treasure can be collected on the way to this consummation. Second, the treasure imported would have that effect only if it entered circulation, which was not always the idea. There are also other possible lines of defense that will appear as we go along.

[3] Montanari and Briscoe are discussed in sec. 2, above.

[4] Since this is the first time that we meet this analytic tool, it is convenient to make at once a few comments that will be of help to the beginner. Other comments will be added later (Part IV, ch. 8). The equation of exchange (also called the Fisher equation after the most eminent of those modern economists who used it as a starting point of the theory of money) is now usually written: $MV = PT$, where M means quantity of money, V velocity, P price level, and T physical volume of transactions. Briscoe's equation becomes identical with this by putting $V = 1$. The first thing to note is that M, V, P, T can each of them be given any of a number of different meanings, which must, of course, be made to correspond; for instance, M may mean only full-weight coin, or only legal tender (including government paper), or only legal tender plus bank notes minus the reserves held against them, or legal tender plus

tity theorem that, sometimes in the crudest possible form, became a commonplace for many of the leaders. It is taken for granted by Genovesi, Galiani, Beccaria, and Justi, and Hume reasserted it with an emphasis that was hardly necessary (1752). All the more significant is it that A. Smith did not definitely commit himself to more than simple metallism.

But Briscoe's equation of exchange was already obsolete when he published it: [5] a major step forward had been taken before. The most primitive way of looking at the relation between quantity of money and prices, but to the primitive mind the most natural way, is to compare a stock or fund of money with a stock or fund of goods that are supposed to be exchanged against one another. The next idea to occur to one's mind, when one comes to think of it more carefully, is that this stock of goods is a rather doubtful entity: the total of the coins may indeed be thought of as a definite stock of pieces that, unless demonetized or exported, are also permanent; but the commodities that are being currently exchanged for these coins are not each time the same individual pieces—the individual units of bread and wine and cloth and so on disappear from the market for good and are currently replaced by other units to meet, on the next market day, the same coins again. Therefore, comparison is between a stock and a flow. The obvious way to reduce them to comparability is to choose a unit period and to multiply the stock by a coefficient that tells us how often in this period the stock meets the flow, that is, how often per period the money does what the goods can do only once. The problem is greatly simplified, though its solution loses much in value, if we assume that all the coins are spent—none held back—and spent only once each market day—equal quantities of all goods being offered on each day—and that there are no other transactions: then the 'velocity' or 'rapidity of circulation' of money will equal the number of market days per unit period. If this number be 12 per year, the stock of money will support the same price level that a stock 12 times as great would support with but a single market day per year. *Taken in this sense,* 'velocity' is peculiar to money and neither has nor can have any analogue in the world of commodities.[6]

---

bank notes plus demand deposits minus the reserves of all banks. Similarly, T may mean all transactions, or only the transactions incident to production and distribution, or only the transactions consisting of income payments and income expenditure on consumers' goods—the last being the definition adopted by Briscoe. Second, in the case of V, there is a distinction of a different kind to be made that is of the utmost importance. On the one hand, we may put $V = PT/M$ *by definition.* If we do this, then the equation of exchange must evidently hold always and under all circumstances. It is, as we say, a mere tautology or identity and should really be written $MV \equiv PT$. But we need not do this. We can also define V independently of the three other magnitudes, for instance, by the number of times a dollar *can* on the average be paid to an income receiver in the institutional arrangements of a given society.

[5] Still more obsolete was, of course, a similar equation published in 1771 by H. Lloyd in his *Essay on the Theory of Money.* Of this essay I only know the Italian abstract appended to Verri's *Meditazioni* in Custodi's *Scrittori Classici.*

[6] I have taken space I can ill afford to spare to explain this matter in its most elementary aspect because it is essential for the reader to realize how it presented itself

Perception of this fact and its insertion into the analytic engine was mainly the achievement of three men—Petty, Locke, and Cantillon. Its importance warrants an inquiry into the manner in which the 'discovery' was made.

Neither Petty nor Locke proceeded in the logical way, that is to say, by deducing the phenomenon of velocity from the nature of money—the way adumbrated above. They ran up against it in the course of their attempts to answer a practical question which they thought important. This question was: what is the quantity of money that a given country needs? Hume ('Of Money' in *Political Discourses*, 1752) seems to have been the first to show clearly and explicitly that on the level of pure logic this question has no meaning—on the one hand, any quantity of money, however small, will do in an isolated country; on the other hand, with perfect gold currency all round, every country will always tend to have the amount appropriate to its relative position in international trade. But in the sixteenth century people thought differently, and practical sense may in fact be imparted to that question by adding: at the prevailing level of prices. Thus amended, the problem was to determine the requirements of internal circulation under given conditions of time and place with a view *either* to support up to a point *or* to combat beyond that point the 'mercantilist' policy of enforcing gold and silver imports.

The task was primarily of a statistical nature. Petty tackled it from the angle of income payments, that is to say . . . [unfinished; the two following paragraphs are taken from the brief early treatment on money described in the appendix and hence do not connect exactly with what precedes.]

There is one more point. From the standpoint of the theorist it is always a 'major event' when an important concept is made explicit and workable, although it was—this is the usual case—implicitly present in previous arguments. The shadow of Velocity of Money may be detected in Davanzati. But it did not acquire substance until the last decades of the seventeenth century. This was a purely English achievement. We know already of Sir William Petty's exploit in the field. The other sponsor was Locke (in *Some Considerations*, 1692). He approaches the phenomenon by way of the cash balances which various classes of people are under the practical necessity of holding. The effects of variations in the velocity on prices are not pointed out directly, though they may be said to come in indirectly through the action of the rate of inter-

---

in the beginnings of analysis: every further step leads into mist, ambiguity, difficulty, but that first one is perfectly clear and simple. I take the opportunity to add two points to our knowledge about the equation of exchange. Look again at our example: a definite number of coins settling by payment in specie the commodity transactions of the twelve market days. Now, first, these twelve market days represent a social custom, an institutional arrangement that individuals are powerless to alter. No coin can, under our assumption, have a greater velocity. But what if holders of some of the coins, on any given market day, refuse to spend all the coins they hold? We may then say, of course, that the coins that are not spent on any given market day or are not spent on any of them have a smaller velocity or even the velocity zero. But we may also say . . . [note unfinished].

est on idle balances.[7] Cantillon, who, so far as I know, was the first to speak of *vitesse de la circulation,* was also the first to state in so many words that increase in the velocity of money was equivalent to increase in its quantity. He also drew the conclusion that measures calculated to decrease velocity will counteract the effects of inflation. Neither Hume nor Smith added anything of importance.

It will be seen that the concept evolved from the first on both the lines that were followed in its later development. Petty and Locke used the cash balance approach, Cantillon the turnover approach. Locke and Cantillon clearly envisage not only velocity in the strict sense but also the rate of spending. Owing to the prominence that the related concept of Propensity to Consume has gained in connection with the multiplier analysis, it may be interesting to add two examples to show that this concept, too, was perfectly familiar to the economists of that epoch. As we already know, Boisguillebert (*Dissertation sur la nature des richesses*) pointed out that a coin in the hand of a very small trader is spent much more promptly than a coin in the hand of a rich man who is more likely to shut it up in his *coffres*—the hoarding rich are evidently no discovery or invention of the last ten years. And Galiani (in the second *Dialogue sur le commerce des blés*) drew a distinction between the propensity to consume of the farmer, who saves and hoards, and of the artisan who promptly spends (*dissipe*).

5. Credit and Banking

We know that the late scholastics were familiar with practically all the essential features of capitalism. In particular, they were familiar with stock exchanges and money markets, with lending and banking, with bills of exchange and other instruments of credit.[1] So far as the phenomena to be interpreted are concerned, the bank note is the only one that was added in the course of the sixteenth century—thrusting into the background for about two centuries the oldest form of what came to be called 'bank money,' the transferable deposit: even Hume, as late as 1752, spoke of 'this new invention of paper.' Yet the bank note, at least in one of its early forms, should not have struck him as a novelty: the note that was a goldsmith's receipt for gold actually deposited was really nothing but a device for increasing safety and convenience in handling one's money, and fitted in perfectly with older ideas. New, however, were the practices of which the bank note became the chief vehicle, and the importance it acquired in consequence. Daniel Webster, in 1839, made note issue

[7] On this point as well as on this subject as a whole, see M. W. Holtrop, 'Theories of the Velocity of Circulation of Money in Earlier Economic Literature,' *Economic History, Supplement to the Economic Journal,* January 1929, and Professor Marget's *Theory of Prices,* vol. I, *passim.*

[1] See above, ch. 2. The reader's attention is once more called to Professor Usher's book there mentioned (*The Early History of Deposit Banking in Mediterranean Europe,* 1943). Also see Van Dillen, *History of the Principal Public Banks* (with extensive bibliography), 1934.

the defining trait of a bank. These practices and the phenomena attending them quickly produced an interesting *analytic* development.

The point to grasp is this. When beholding the nascent institutions of capitalism, the scholastic doctors and their laical successors did not experience any difficulty in interpreting them and in fitting them into their metallist theory of money. This analytic task was facilitated by their command of the conceptual apparatus of the Roman law. Observing sales contracts that provided for deferred payment, they readily analyzed them into a sale proper and a loan of money. The deposit of money, being a *depositum irregulare,* conferred ownership on the receiver of the deposit: the scholastic fathers might even have deduced that the receiver was not bound in law or morals to keep deposits of this nature in a vault, because he owed only *tantumdem in genere,* that is, as much of the same kind as he had received. Moreover, if a business connection made *A* the debtor of *B* and concurrently *B* the debtor of *A*, they might—within limits—'compensate,' and were to be held responsible only for the difference; and this principle might then be extended to multilateral and interlocal clearing of debts without the use of actual cash. The upshot is that for the scholastics neither lending in the usual sense of the word nor the giving or receiving of credit in the course of commodity trade or any other transactions had really anything to do with the monetary system and its working: these things involved the use of money, no doubt, but in no other sense than does buying for money or making a gift in money or paying taxes in money.

But this of course is not so. 'Credit' operations of whatever shape or kind do affect the working of the monetary system; more important, they do affect the working of the capitalist engine—so much so as to become an essential part of it without which the rest cannot be understood at all. This is what economists discovered in the seventeenth century and tried to work out in the eighteenth: it was then that capitalism was analytically discovered or, as we may also say, discovered or became analytically conscious of itself. Let us see how this discovery came about and how far it went. Two lines of advance are distinctly visible.

[(a) *Credit and the Concept of Velocity: Cantillon.*] The first of these might have been taken by the scholastic doctors themselves, had scholastic economics developed from its own bases throughout the seventeenth and eighteenth centuries. That is to say, a strictly metallist conception of money invited, if it did not absolutely enforce, the attempt to draw a sharp dividing line between money and the legal instruments that embody claims to money and operations in money, *and to bring the latter into the picture by means of auxiliary constructions* for which the legal concepts alluded to above offered suggestions. To some extent such a course is always possible,[2] in our case even more so than

[2] To quote two instances of incomparably greater importance: the so-called Ptolemaic system of astronomy was not simply 'wrong.' It accounted satisfactorily for a great mass of observations. And as observations accumulated that did not, at first sight, accord with it, astronomers devised additional hypotheses that brought the recalcitrant facts, or part of them, within the fold of the system. Again, classical physics accounted satisfactorily for all the known facts until it received a severe jolt through

usually. The auxiliary construction that is needed consists in an extension of the concept of velocity. The banker who issues notes in excess of his cash holding is not thought of as creating or increasing means of payment, let alone 'money.' All he does is to increase the velocity of that cash, which by proxy, as it were, effects many more payments than it could settle by going from hand to hand; and the same applies, of course, when he directly lends part of the cash deposited with him. The clear perception of the truth that a bank note and a checking deposit are fundamentally the same thing is in fact one of the strong points of this theory. Thus money remains very strictly defined. Credit, particularly bank credit, is merely a method of using it more efficiently. I cannot stop to show, but the reader may easily see for himself, that most phenomena that go under the heading of credit *can* be described in this way. Government paper money may then either be included with full-weight coin in the total of the quantity of money or else construed as a government debt—that is, as a promise to pay in coin at some time or other. The latter view predominated, and throughout the nineteenth century there are instances of governments issuing notes with the legend: 'This note is part of the government's floating debt,' suggesting an analogy with treasury bills, especially when the notes carried interest, as they not infrequently did.

The outstanding authority for this theory is Cantillon, who carried it out in detail and with as much common sense as brilliance. His bankers are essentially intermediary lenders of other people's money. They lend the deposits they receive, and by so doing speed up things and lower the rate of interest. The logical difficulties that lurk in this apparently simple statement are somewhat reduced by his emphasis upon the case in which bankers only lend what depositors, for the time being, do not need—the case of time deposits, as we should say—so that a given sum of money only does one service at a time. Moreover, we must not forget that Cantillon lived in an environment where, wholesale trade apart, payment in specie was the overwhelming rule, so that people incessantly fetched and brought bags of coin to and from the bank; and where it was as usual to acquire a deposit by actually depositing coin as it is now to acquire one by borrowing or by transfer from another borrower. At any rate his teaching stands at the fountainhead of what remained official banking theory practically up to the First World War. Galiani and Turgot—independently or not—held the same doctrine. So did innumerable minor lights, such as Justi, and 'business economists,' such as Marperger.

But, to say the least, this is not the only way of interpreting the facts of banking practice. Even the banker who lends by paying out actual money deposited with him does more than collect it from innumerable small puddles, where it stagnates, in order to hand it to people who will use it. He lends

---

the negative result of Michelson's experiment (1881). But this did not induce physicists to abandon the classical system at once. Instead, the Michelson effect was built into it by means of a special hypothesis *ad hoc* (H. A. Lorentz, 1895); and this hypothesis satisfied the profession until the emergence of Einstein's theory about a quarter of a century after Michelson's experiment. *Si licet parva componere magnis*. . .

the same sums over and over again *before the first borrower has repaid:* that is to say, he does not merely find successive employments for the sum entrusted to him, but many employments which that sum then fills simultaneously. If he lends by paying out notes—or by crediting the sum lent to the borrower in a checking account—for which his cash holding acts merely as a reserve, the same fact stands out still more clearly. And so it does if he lends coins he received as a deposit, which the depositor proposes to use exactly as he would have used the coins had he kept them.[3] There surely must be other ways of expressing these practices than by calling these bank notes embodiments of velocity of circulation—a velocity so great that it enables a thing to be in different places at the same time. More important than this terminological inconvenience is the fact that the velocity of circulation in the technical sense of the word is not increased at all: the banker's loans do not alter the 'stations' through which a unit of purchasing power has to pass, or abridge the time it takes in passing them, or—in themselves—affect people's habits of holding certain amounts of what *they* consider to be ready cash. Therefore it may, perhaps, seem more natural to say that bankers increase not the velocity but the quantity of money—or of those means of payment that, within limits, serve as well as money if one wishes to reserve this term for coin or coin and government paper. This accords perfectly with practice—borrowers do feel that they get additional liquid means that are normally just as good as money. Banks are no longer said to 'lend their deposits' or 'other people's money,' but to 'create' deposits or bank notes: they appear to manufacture money rather than to increase its velocity or to act—which is a completely unrealistic idea—on behalf of their depositors. In any case, it is clear and actually beyond dispute that what the banker does with money cannot be done with any other commodity—or, as some of us would prefer to say, with a commodity—for no other commodity's quantity or velocity can be increased in this way. The only answer to the question why this is so is that there is no other case in which a

[3] Professor Rist (*History of Monetary and Credit Theory from John Law to the Present Day,* 1940, ch. 1), who may be cited as, perhaps, the leading modern exponent of the Cantillon view, rightly insists that there is no 'mystery' about credit and that talking about the 'mystery of credit' is often indicative of hazy thinking. But there is a question of interpretation and there is a point requiring elucidation. Suppose it occurs to the check-room attendant of a restaurant to rent out the coats deposited with him while their owners are having their meal. This may, upon occasion, cause a difficult situation for the attendant, but there is no *logical* difficulty about it. But suppose he is a wizard, and performs the feat of making it possible for two people—the owner and the hirer—to wear the same coat at the same time. Surely this would stand in need of explanation—and this is exactly what happens in the case of banking, if bank notes and bank deposits are really, as Professor Rist says, nothing but 'material embodiments of the velocity of circulation.' May I use this opportunity to add that, so far as any implications as to policy are concerned, I quite agree with him; that personally I feel nothing but admiration and gratitude for the brilliant services he has rendered in more than one country to the cause of what, like him, I believe to be sound finance? I hold no brief for land-bank schemes or any of their modern counterparts. I am interested in a mere point of theory and, at most, a few points of past history.

claim to a thing can, within limits to be sure, serve the same purpose as the thing itself: you cannot ride on a claim to a horse, but you can pay with a claim to money. But this is a strong reason for calling money what purports to be a claim to legal money, provided it does serve as means of payment. As a rule, an ordinary bill of exchange does not so serve; then it is not money, and belongs to the demand side of the money market. Sometimes, however, certain classes of them do; then, according to this view, they are money and form part of the supply on the money market. Bank notes and checking deposits eminently do what money does; hence they are money. Thus credit instruments, or some of them, intrude into the monetary system; and, by the same token, money in turn is but a credit instrument, a claim to the only final means of payment, the consumers' good. By now this theory—which of course is capable of taking many forms and stands in need of many elaborations—may be said to prevail.

[(b) *John Law: Ancestor of the Idea of a Managed Currency.*] Manufacture of money! Credit as a creator of money! Manifestly, this opens up other than theoretical vistas. The bank projectors of the seventeenth century, especially the English land-bank projectors and Law, who was one of them originally, had glimpses, varying in degree of distinctness, of the theory adumbrated above. But they fully realized the business potentialities of the discovery that money—and hence capital in the monetary sense of the term—can be manufactured or created. Their reputation, at the time and later, suffered greatly from the failure of their schemes—Law's schemes in particular—just as, in the nineteenth century, the reputation of fundamentally similar ideas suffered from association with wild-cat banking and with the failures of schemes that turned out badly without being fraudulent or nonsensical, such as the *Crédit Mobilier* of the brothers Pereire. But since there is a far cry from an economic principle to a banking project, these failures are not evidence in the court of theory.

Interpretation of John Law's theoretical position in matters of money and credit (on his theory of value, see above, sec. 2) presents difficulties quite apart from the fact that some of his arguments may have been no more than tactical moves. From the way in which he deduces the phenomenon of money—which, in the first instance, makes money a commodity—it seems that he must be classed as a theoretical metallist. This diagnosis derives support from his antagonism to debasement or devaluation—which he called an unjust tax, on the doubtful ground that it tends to hurt poor people more than the rich—and also from his practice, for he kept up redemption of his notes as long as he could. Since this seems to clash rather badly with the rest of his views, historians have brushed aside this evidence. But it is quite possible to arrive from the metallist principle at conclusions that seem to violate it, as the American example of our own time suffices to show. Law's argument admits of the following reconstruction: he first observed—a clear gain to analysis—that the use of a commodity as a means of circulation affects its value; from this it follows that the exchange value of the monetary commodity as money can no more be explained by its exchange value as a commodity than the latter can be explained by the former—although, of course, so long as the monetary commodity can freely move between its monetary and its industrial uses, the two must be equal; therefore he explained, quite logically, the exchange value of silver as money on the lines of the quantity argument (*abondance* of money as compared with *abondance des produits*); but since silver that serves as money has no other use than to buy goods, it might just as well be replaced by a cheaper material, in the limit[ing case] by one that has no commodity value at all, such as printed paper, for 'Money is not the Value *for* which Goods are exchanged, but the Value *by* which they are exchanged' [J. A. S.'s italics]. This, however, cuts the cable that so far [has tied money to a commodity having] 'intrinsic' value. Now he draws the conclusion that there is an advantage other than cheapness and absence of worry about how to get and keep [an adequate supply of money]—it is that the quantity of money is fully manageable.

[The preceding paragraph was unfinished with notes at the end which were filled in by Arthur W. Marget.]

This, then, seems to have been the work that gave birth to the idea of Managed Currency, which was subsequently lost to the large majority of economists until it forced itself upon them after 1919. The evident importance of the event makes it worth our while to stay for a moment to consider it. First, the relevant passages in Law's tract (*Money and Trade Considered . . .* 1705) acquire additional meaning by his practice, or rather by one aspect of it. We are not concerned with his particular schemes, from that of the *Banque Générale* (1716), which looks so innocuous and almost orthodox, to those of the *Compagnie des Indes* (1719), which look more and more visionary, and finally those of 1720, which were the ultimate resort of the strong swimmer in his agony. But one great plan was behind all this, in fact well advanced on the road to success: the plan of controlling, reforming, and leading on to new levels the whole of the national economy of France.[4] This is what makes Law's 'system' the genuine ancestor of the idea of managed currency, not only in the obvious sense of that term but in the deeper and wider sense in which it spells management of currency and credit as a means of managing the economic process. And this is what interprets and glorifies the modest passages of the tract.[5]

6. Capital, Saving, Investment

The word Capital had been part of legal and business terminology long before economists found employment for it. With the Roman jurists and their successors, it denoted the 'principal' of a loan as distinguished from interest

[4] The failure was not due to this idea. . . [Footnote incomplete.]

[5] It is not suggested that Law had no forerunners. First, the idea of managed currency lurks in the reasoning of most of the bank projectors who preceded him. However, the case seems to be one of those in which it is right to link 'priority' with fullness and depth of comprehension. Secondly, in a sense every currency is always managed. Moreover, currencies had been tampered with for ages. But this is not what I mean . . . [breaks off, unfinished, at this point].

and other accessory claims of the lender. In obvious relation with this, it later came to denote the sums of money or their equivalents brought by partners into a partnership or company, the sum total of a firm's assets, and the like. Thus the concept was essentially monetary, meaning either actual money, or claims to money, or some goods evaluated in money. Also, though not quite definite, its meaning was perfectly unequivocal, and there was no doubt about what was meant in every particular case. What a mass of confused, futile, and downright silly controversies it would have saved us, if economists had had the sense to stick to those monetary and accounting meanings of the term instead of trying to 'deepen' them! Before the eighteenth century, however, they hardly used it at all. Waiving such questions as whether or not St. Antonine of Florence evolved a capital theory, we merely note that in the seventeenth century terms like Wealth, Riches, Stock were often used where we should use Capital, and that throughout the eighteenth—and even in the first decades of the nineteenth—Stock was favored for use in the nascent capital theory.

Stock, more or less in the sense of either durable or productive wealth—the latter exemplified by Child's stock of tools and materials—was, of course, the object of attention and of recommendations. But when I said that economists were late in finding employment for it, I meant employment in articulate analysis involving a 'theory' of the nature and functions of capital. Of this there were only rudiments before Cantillon and the physiocrats. It may surprise the reader to find Quesnay credited with laying the foundations of a capital theory, considering his emphasis on the role of natural agents. We must, however, go further than this and simply recognize the presence of one of those cases—they are as frequent in science as they are in politics—where a man achieves if not the opposite of, yet something quite different from, what he intends to achieve: the physiocrats were even responsible for one of the later theories of the productivity of capital. The whole process described by the *tableau* starts from given 'advances' and, moreover, runs on in terms of the annual advances. These advances are goods—to live on or to produce with—though their quantity may be expressed in terms of money, and they are precisely what capital means in one of the many senses of the word. This idea is so important for the general character of any theoretical scheme that adopts it that we may well form a group of all the schemes that do so and call it 'advance' economics.[1]

This point was almost immediately seized upon by Turgot, who sketched out the corresponding theory of capital. He emphasized—one may almost say, he 'rubbed in'—that wealth other than natural agents (*richesse mobilière amassée d'avance*) is a *préalable indispensable* for all production (*Réflexions*, LIII), which amounts to offering his shoulders for future attempts to treat capital in this sense as a factor of production. In his own way, A. Smith did

[1] The reader will observe, of course, that for a theoretical schema to qualify for inclusion in that group it is not sufficient to recognize the trivial facts that in order to produce, one must have tools and materials and that producing takes time—just as, in order to accept Newtonian physics it is not sufficient to recognize that, if severed from its branch, an apple will fall to the ground.

the same thing. But one of the reasons for believing that he did not know the *Réflexions* (publ. in the *Éphémérides*, 1769-70) is that his exposition, though infinitely more prolix, falls far short of Turgot's. It looks to me as if Chapter 1 of Book II of the *Wealth* represents what he himself made of Quesnay's suggestion. The 'advance' idea is there and so is a hint of the productivity (necessity) of capital, but instead of a theory of interest, as in the case of Turgot (see below, sec. 7), only a 'taxonomy' of capital comes from it—Quesnay's primitive advances may have suggested the concept of 'fixed capital,' Quesnay's annual advances may have been transformed into 'circulating capital,' and A. Smith then proceeds to enumerate the various categories of goods that form the one and the other and to discuss what should and what should not be included in each category. It has often been pointed out that, owing to his different confusing points of view, this taxonomy is not quite satisfactory. We need not go into this. All that matters is that a physical or 'real' capital concept—which, however, included money, the 'acquired and useful abilities of all the inhabitants,' and also, though this is not obvious from Smith's catalogue, the means of subsistence of 'productive' laborers—was handed down to the theorists of the nineteenth century and, with but minor criticisms, accepted and further developed by most of them.

And so was the Turgot-Smith theory of saving and investment. With tremendous emphasis, A. Smith lays it down (ch. 3 of Book II) that 'parsimony, and not industry, is the immediate cause of the increase of capital'; that 'it puts into motion an additional quantity of industry'; that it does so 'immediately' (without lag) for 'what is annually saved is as regularly consumed as what is annually spent,' that is, the saver spends as promptly as the prodigal, only he does so for different purposes and the consuming is done by other people, that is, 'productive' laborers; and 'every frugal man is a public benefactor.' Turgot, only with a lighter touch, had written all this before.[2] But not Quesnay, nor Cantillon, nor Boisguillebert. Turgot evidently broke away from an anti-saving tradition established in his circle. Nor do I know of any earlier French economists—with the possible exception of Refuge—who could be credited with genuine 'predecessorship.' Among English economists only Hume had any claim. No doubt a host of writers, in the seventeenth century and before, declaimed against luxury (and the mischief of idleness), especially against imports of luxuries, called for or approved of sumptuary laws, and commended economy, at least for the bourgeois and the workman.[3] Among Span-

[2] In comparing the *Wealth* and the *Réflexions*, some doubt may assail us concerning the value of the indication previously mentioned about Smith's independence. For Turgot also says that, at least in the case of entrepreneurs, savings are converted into capital *sur-le-champ* (his italics). But Smith's 'immediately' certainly is the exact translation of *sur-le-champ*. And this is not unimportant; on the contrary, as will be seen in a moment, it is an essential feature of both theories and indeed their most serious shortcoming. That such a slip should occur independently in two texts is indeed quite possible; but it is not likely.

[3] To some extent, the confusing and confused mass of contradictory opinions on luxury may be straightened out, first by discarding, as not relevant to our subject, how-

ish and English economists this was, in fact, quite a fashion. The latter in particular held that inadequate propensity to save was one of the reasons that made it so difficult for Englishmen to oust the Dutch—for whom they felt so much resentful admiration and who were supposed to be so frugal—from their leadership in international trade. But this linked up with a conception of saving and investment that stopped in most cases at the accumulation of stocks of durable goods, gold and silver in particular, and at a favorable balance of trade—the mercantilist angle to be considered in the next chapter. Nobody saw, or at any rate bothered about, the *modus operandi* of saving and capital formation per se. Turgot, then, must be held responsible for the first serious analysis of these matters, as A. Smith must (at the least) with having it inculcated into the minds of economists.

Two points should be noted for future reference. First, in the face of frequent criticism, Turgot's theory proved almost unbelievably hardy. It is doubtful whether Alfred Marshall had advanced beyond it, certain that J. S. Mill had not. Böhm-Bawerk no doubt added a new branch to it, but substantially he subscribed to Turgot's propositions. Second, the theory was not only swallowed by the large majority of economists: it was swallowed hook, line, and sinker. As if Law—and others—had never existed, one economist after another kept on repeating that only (voluntary) saving was capital creating. And one economist after another failed to look askance at that word 'immediately.'

---

ever interesting from other standpoints, opinions that are (a) primarily morally motivated, in which case a writer may be 'against luxury' even if his economic argument leads him to attribute 'favorable' effects to it, (b) clearly traceable to bourgeois resentment against 'high living,' especially in the 'aristocratic' stratum; second, by distinguishing the different meanings that were attached to the word. During the eighteenth century, the plural Luxuries came more and more exclusively to denote nonnecessary commodities, the necessary ones including 'not only the commodities which are indispensably necessary for the support of life, but whatever the custom of the country renders it indecent for creditable people, even of the lowest order, to be without' (*Wealth of Nations*, Book v, ch. 2), so that luxury would be consumption exceeding what was later called the 'social minimum of existence.' Appraisal of opinion on the effects of luxury in this sense is complicated by two types of considerations extraneous to the fundamental problem: (a) so far as these luxuries were imported they come in for vituperation on balance-of-trade grounds (see below, next chapter); (b) so far as consumption of these luxuries presupposes relatively high wages, it was held by many writers, especially English ones, to be a handicap in the struggle for foreign markets, an argument that runs parallel to (a) and merges into the more general argument on wages that has been touched upon already. Apart from these two types of considerations, however, luxury in this sense was primarily viewed from the high-level consumption standpoint discussed in the text (above, sec. 1), even by later writers, who emphasized the role of saving, such as Hume, who added also the argument that industries producing luxury goods may prove a 'store of labor' for government to draw upon in emergencies. 'Vicious' luxury was commended by Mandeville as an important motive force and, though with qualification, by Hume. Typical for this line of thought was Butel-Dumont (*Théorie du luxe*, 1771). There is very little truth in the widespread belief that either A. Smith's own contemporaries or the economists of the seventeenth century needed his reminder that 'consumption is the sole end and pur-

But in effect—whatever else benevolent interpretation might make of it—this came to mean that every decision to save coincides with a corresponding decision to invest so that saving is transformed into (real) capital practically without hitch and as a matter of course or that, to put it differently, saving practically amounts to supplying (real) capital. The reader need not strain his imagination unduly in order to realize what a difference it would have made to doctrinal history if the possibility and, in depressive situations, likelihood of the occurrence of hitches had been pointed out from the first—of hitches that may paralyze the mechanism described by Turgot and cause saving to become a disturber of the economic process, hence possibly a destroyer instead of a creator of industrial apparatus. Not only would such an admission have broken off the spearhead from modern attacks upon the theory but it would also have made it a more effective analysis within the situations *for which it is quite true*. There was the less excuse for refusing to recognize the necessary

pose of all production' (Book IV, ch. 8). The reader should observe that, with Smith, this statement is no more than a platitude and entirely stripped of any connotation hostile to saving. But this meaning of luxury was not the only one.

Besides, there was a meaning in which luxury was associated with unproductive consumption. There were, from the middle of the seventeenth century on, several discussions on the latter, which, as we know, also greatly preoccupied A. Smith. The two elements that this meaning combines are exceedingly difficult to disentangle and space forbids us to enter into this—not very interesting—matter. Then there was the meaning in which luxury is the opposite to parsimony—luxury in this sense (Hume would have called it 'excessive' luxury) was bemoaned already by Thomas More, and this meaning, more or less distinct, runs through the whole literature on the subject; it was to be reasserted by Malthus. Again, there was the meaning that has perhaps more right than any other to be called the original one, viz. luxury as a style of life above one's station. The wish to protect distinctive class standards—spiced with the resentment of poor magnates against rich financiers—was an important factor in the policy that produced sumptuary laws (though there were others, such as the wish to compel people to reserve means for military uses). Since we shall not expect this point of view to play any great role in our literature, it is not uninteresting to note that some slight indication of it is to be found in the *Wealth of Nations*. Finally, there is the meaning that associates luxury with *ruinous* expenditure (dissaving). The wish to prevent people and in particular leading aristocratic and bourgeois families from ruining themselves was another important factor that made for the passing of sumptuary laws. In societies that center in a court and whose style of life derives its pattern from the 'magnificence' of the feudal household, fashion is much more compelling—for *all* except for the poorest classes—than it is in bourgeois society. And sumptuary laws, if effective, are perhaps the most obvious way of excusing the courtier or the leading officer of state from having to live beyond his means, and of preventing the rising merchant from setting a compelling example. This also explains why many Consultant Administrators who otherwise argued on the lines of Becher's principle, thought themselves in duty bound to frown upon luxury in this sense. From the large literature of the subject, it will suffice to mention: Juan Sempere y Guarinos (1754-1830) *Historia del luxo y de las leyes suntuarias de España* (1788). [J. A. S. was in doubt as to where to place this note on luxury. On the last page of the ms. of sec. 1 appeared the question: here * luxury?]

qualifications because they could have been taken from earlier as well as contemporaneous economists, especially from Quesnay's *Maximes*.

If saving is allotted such a part in the drama, the 'prince' (that is, public expenditure, hence public debts) cannot be expected to escape the role of the villain, or one of the villains, of the piece. The topic of public debts, though interesting from the standpoint of economic sociology and also from the standpoint of financial technique, is of little moment for us, because judgment and advocacy greatly prevailed over analysis. Therefore it will suffice to say that many authors tried hard to discover desired effects that might be attributed to public borrowing. Some indeed went so far as to make them a factor in national prosperity.[4] The opposite tendency prevailed, however—votaries of ideological interpretation are welcome to trace this to the increasing influence of the bourgeois mind, which in fact had more reasons than one to dislike cavalier finance. It was strongly sponsored by Hume and Smith. From their theory of saving—embryonic in Hume, developed in Smith—it follows indeed that public (or any) borrowing for nonproductive purposes spells setback in the growth of wealth. It is less easy to see why both should have been of the opinion that the public debts of their time were crushing burdens likely to produce bankruptcy and ruin. They hardly did more, however, than to express current opinion on the subject. The English public was in fact so nervous that the Pitt government in 1786 resumed, on a larger scale and more seriously, the policy of paying an annual sum into a Sinking Fund.[5]

7. Interest

The most significant development to notice in the interest theory of the period is the emergence, and all but universal acceptance, of the propositions (1) that interest on business loans is nothing but normal business profit transferred to lenders, and (2) that normal business profit itself is nothing but the return on the physical means of production, labor's means of subsistence included. So essential is it for us to grasp the full importance of this development which was to shape the subsequent history of interest theory that, in order to make it stand out clearly, we shall neglect side issues and cross currents as far as possible. In particular, we shall neglect discussions of interest on loans for purposes of consumption: for this . . . [incomplete].

[4] This was done, e.g., by Isaac de Pinto, *Traité de la circulation et du crédit*, 1771. But this line of thought had many adherents, especially in France.

[5] The plan adopted is usually attributed to the suggestion of Richard Price (1723-91; *An Appeal to the Public on the Subject of the National Debt*, 1772; *The State of the Public Debts and Finances in* 1783). The idea itself must be distinguished from the bold claim put forth by Price for his plan, according to which 'a State may, without difficulty, redeem all its debts by borrowing for this purpose,' which brought upon him much undeserved ridicule. Sir Nathaniel Gould (*An Essay on the Publick Debts* . . . 1726) had published similar views before. Both publications produced lively controversies into which we cannot—and need not—go.

[(a) *Influence of the Scholastic Doctors.*] We start again from the work of the scholastic doctors and their Protestant successors to which the reader had better refer before perusing this section. Their influence asserted itself in two ways. On the one hand, they provided one of the main topics of discussion: the controversy on the legality of charging and paying interest went on. In the second half of the eighteenth century, it flagged but it did not quite die out, and even Turgot wrestled, in his tract, *Mémoire sur les prêts d'argent*, with the Aristotelian position. Into this we need not go again. But a cognate point demands our attention. In most countries the moral issue was partly ousted by a purely economic issue, which turned not on the old question of principle, but on the question of the expediency of reducing the rate of interest by legislation. English merchants especially, looking with resentful admiration on commercial conditions in the Netherlands, embraced the theory that will naturally occur to the untutored practitioner, namely, that one of the causes, perhaps the main cause, of the flourishing state of Dutch trade in the seventeenth century was the low rate of interest that prevailed there, and they insisted that legal regulation could confer the same advantage upon England. It will suffice to mention Child as the most eminent among the many exponents of this theory and to glance in the footnote below at what seems to me to be the better part of the ensuing controversy from which the opposite theory, namely, that a low rate of interest is the consequence and not the cause of wealth, emerged victoriously—not to be seriously challenged again until our own time.[1] From this it does not follow, of course, that legal regulation of the rate of interest can have no sense at all. In fact, neither Locke nor A. Smith went so far as this. But in the end this view prevailed.[2]

On the other hand, scholastic doctrine also provided the theoretical (explanatory) ideas about interest from which the analysis of the seventeenth and eighteenth centuries started. Neglecting minor points, we shall concentrate upon these two: the monetary conception of interest and the proposition en-

[1] Child may be said to have argued on the lines first worked out in a presentable manner in Sir Thomas Culpeper's *Tract against the High Rate of Usurie*, 1621 (enlarged ed., 1641). This tract, together with another not printed before, was reprinted and prefaced by his son, another Sir Thomas (1668). The latter also published in 1668 what is the classic treatment of this side of the controversy: *A Discourse shewing the many Advantages which will accrue to this Kingdom by the Abatement of Usury together with the Absolute Necessity of Reducing Interest of Money to the lowest Rate it bears in other Countreys.* The opposite view is well stated in a pamphlet entitled, *Interest of Money Mistaken, Or, a Treatise, proving that the Abatement of Interest is the Effect and not the Cause of the Riches of a Nation* that appeared in the same year and in Thomas Manley's *Usury at Six per Cent Examined . . .* (1669). To this Culpeper junior replied with *The Necessity of Abating Usury Re-asserted . . .* (1670). Petty, North, Locke, and Pollexfen, with varying degrees of emphasis, are the principal names associated with the victory over the Culpeper-Child position.

[2] The first economist of real authority who held that view was Petty. The next to go even further was Turgot. The one to make it prevail definitively, Bentham. But it was held also by Justi, at least in principle.

shrined in Molina's pithy saying that 'money is the tool of the merchant's trade.' The scholastics did not indeed restrict the concept of interest to interest on loans of money, but the latter naturally commanded their attention more than anything else; they never agreed on or developed the idea that prospective profits are the source of the demand for business loans, but some of the most eminent of them adumbrated it with unmistakable clearness.

During the seventeenth century and far into the eighteenth, the large majority of economists looked upon interest—as many of us do again now—as a monetary phenomenon. In particular, this is true of the Culpepers, Manley, Child, Petty, Locke, and Pollexfen, not to mention any continental writers. In the case of Petty, direct scholastic influence is not inconceivable, since he had received part of his education at a Jesuit college. Looking, quite in the spirit of the scholastic fathers, for a special reason independent of, and additional to, the mere act of transferring money to the borrower, that would explain a premium, he hit upon, or rather resuscitated, the 'inconvenience' (a *damnum*) suffered by the lender who bound himself not to call for his money during a stated time. In any case—and in spite of the fact that he related this inconvenience to the rent of so much land as the same sum would buy—it is always money he is thinking of, and it is the quantity of money which is held to determine the rate of interest without there being any indication of the ceteris-paribus provisoes that would be required in order to make this true. Locke goes somewhat deeper than this. Owing to his clumsy way of expressing himself, it is extremely difficult to do him justice, but if I have caught his meaning, he may be credited with having introduced explicitly and having developed the second of the two ideas mentioned above. Again interest is a price for *money* lent. But the 'supply' on the money market must be seen in relation to the debt situation and the state of trade—high profits raising, low profits reducing, the rate. Though we cannot stay to prove it, still less to consider objections, I think that, at a push, this may be interpreted as an embryonic form of what is now known as the Swedish loanable-funds theory: interest is explained and determined by a demand proceeding from expected profits and meeting a supply of 'loanable funds.'

[(b) *Barbon: 'Interest is the Rent of Stock.'*] But further development did not take this line. There is no bridge between Locke and the monetary interest theories of today. Instead, there was a new departure, which was to be so successful that even now we find it difficult to be as surprised at it as we ought to be. There are, so far as I know, only the most elusive indications of it before 1690, when Barbon (*Discourse of Trade*) wrote the momentous statement: 'Interest is commonly reckoned for Money . . . but this is a mistake; for the Interest is paid for Stock,' it is 'the Rent of Stock, and is the same as the Rent of Land; the First is the Rent of the Wrought or Artificial Stock; the Latter, of the Unwrought or Natural Stock.' [3] If the reader is to under-

[3] Locke, also, compared interest to rent but in a quite different sense, which adds nothing to the monetary view of interest and is without deeper meaning: the lender of money, according to him, receives interest as the landlord receives rent.

stand the history of interest theory during the nineteenth century, and some part of it even during the first four decades of the twentieth, it is absolutely necessary to realize fully what this means.

At first sight, Barbon's statement might well sound trivial: of course, the borrower does not normally want the money in order to look at it; what he really wants, if we neglect the purpose of refinancing other obligations, are the goods and services that he actually buys with it. Neither do we want, for its own sake, the knife with which to cut our food, and yet it does not follow that the price we pay for the knife is 'really' paid for the food. For certain purposes we may indeed, for instance by means of the theory of imputation (discussed below, Part IV) adopt such a view of the matter. But it would be a most astounding as well as important result if it were permissible to adopt it for all purposes. Granting even that business loans are normally used for purchasing or hiring real capital in the sense of producers' goods and services, it does not follow that the interest paid for the former is 'really' an element of the price of the latter: interest may bear a particular relation to 'money' as distinct from the goods that are bought with it, or it may be a price for something else—the sacrifice involved in saving, for instance—that cannot be simply *identified* with 'real capital.' To aver that it is possible to brush aside the monetary element without losing anything essential in the process is therefore an extremely bold step—which neither the scholastics nor Petty nor Locke thought of taking, though the triviality above cannot have been unknown to them; in particular, it was the decisive step toward the 'real' analysis of the nineteenth century, according to which money was just a 'veil' that it was the business of analysis to lift, which is precisely the center of the analytic difficulties created by Real Analysis.

In addition to the service or disservice that Barbon rendered by the impulse he gave in the direction of Real Analysis, there is another aspect to his performance that is hardly less important. If interest is the return on 'wrought stock'—produced means of production—exactly as rent is the return on 'unwrought stock'—natural agents of production—then it is goods of some kind or other that the lender 'really' possesses. As a matter of fact, it is the manufacturer or trader who possesses such goods, and he gets them either by producing them himself or by buying them from other producers and not from the capitalist or lender. To neglect this and to reason as if the latter lent goods is another stroke of analysis, the boldness of which is hidden to us only by our familiarity with it. But then the return on these goods materializes in the hands of the businessman who uses them and constitutes the main—and theoretically basic—part of his profit, at least if we choose to make light of his 'trouble and risk.' Thus we easily slip into a position that may be characterized by the equivalent propositions that the business firm earns interest or that the lender receives profit—not, as would seem more natural to the unprejudiced mind, an income sui generis of which profit is merely the most important source.

[(c) *Shift of Analytic Task from Interest to Profit.*] For the whole of the nineteenth century and beyond, this shifted the analytic task from interest to profit. With the partial exception of abstinence and psychological-discount theories, the phenomenon to be explained was the net surplus of business, which, in turn, was essentially a surplus arising from the use of an assemblage of certain physical goods; that this surplus, cleared of accessories such as compensation for trouble and risk, had to be handed to some other person, if this person and not the business manager was its real (though not legal) owner, hardly required independent explanation. This applies also to Böhm-Bawerk and Wicksell, though the latter made the first step beyond this theory and must even now be kept in mind when we compare such a theory as Keynes's with other interest theories: the object of analytic endeavor is different.

It is not too much to say that this was to be the dominant feature of the theorist's general picture and even of economic sociology for everyone: the businessman became the 'capitalist.' Fundamentally his income was income from ownership of goods, an impersonal return.

[The two preceding paragraphs were on a single page with notes (both shorthand and longhand) to indicate how the argument was to be continued. This section on interest was more fragmentary than any other part of this unfinished chapter. It was obviously an outline that would have been filled in and completed, had the author lived.]

A. Smith substantially accepted this theory of interest and of the capitalist process. The nineteenth century in turn accepted it from him. However, before considering the precise form which he gave it, we must glance briefly at its development between 1690 and 1776.

Barbon's *Discourse*, on this point at all events, did not meet with success. The tract seems indeed to have been forgotten very soon. Thus, Barbon's fundamental idea remained in abeyance until 1750, when it was again expounded—for all we know, independently rediscovered—by Massie,[4] whose analysis not only went further than Barbon's but also gathered force from its criticism of the views of Petty and Locke. Two years later, in his volume entitled *Political Discourses*, Hume published two essays ('Of Interest' and 'Of Money') that do not seem to have received due tribute from recent historians. It is indeed true that, on the surface, we see little more than synthesis and effective re-exposition of ideas that had been put forth before. This impression is particularly strong with authors who attend primarily to certain practical results he drew from his analytic set-up, such as that interest is not simply a function of the quantity of money, that low interest is a consequence and not a cause of wealth, that it cannot be determined by legislation, that it is correlated with profits in a relation of mutual interaction, and that it is a 'barometer of the state,' low interest being 'an almost infallible sign of prosperity' (which, of course, is not true in every sense of 'prosperity')—none of which were novel. But the analytic set-up with which Hume backed all this, though sketchy, can be called synthetic only in the sense in which synthesis may transcend coordination and be creative. It amounts to accepting Locke's explanation of the demand for loans—definitely *loans* this time, not 'money'—by the needs of

[4] Joseph Massie, *Essay on the Governing Causes of the Natural Rate of Interest* (1750).

spendthrift landowners and by the profit expectations of businessmen, and to replacing Locke's supply of money by the supply of savings. This allows for the close relation between profit and interest without identifying them, and admits the monetary aspect—particularly as regards short-run effects of variations in the quantity of money on the rate of interest that were also recognized by Ricardo—without making it dominant. In short, we have here a schema that need only have been worked out in order to produce a much better and more complete theory of the interest phenomenon than can be found in either Ricardo or Mill. But precisely the most valuable points were lost.

[(d) *Turgot's Great Performance.*] Turgot's[5] contribution is not only by far the greatest performance in the field of interest theory the eighteenth century produced but it clearly foreshadowed much of the best thought of the last decades of the nineteenth. Like Hume, Turgot argued that the quantity of money does not determine the rate of interest, very nicely emphasizing the conceptual independence of the two meanings of the phrase 'value of money'—its value in the money market and its value in the markets of commodities—and even going so far as to assert that an increase in the quantity of money that raises commodity prices might conceivably *increase* the rate of interest. Also like Hume, he substituted supply of savings for supply of money. And there are other points that Hume made before him. But his theory goes much deeper than all that and is quite different in content as well as in background.

[5] As in the case of Hume, critical analysis does not seem to have done full justice to the essential point in Turgot's performance. This applies in particular to by far the most eminent of his critics, Böhm-Bawerk (*Capital and Interest*, Book I, pp. 61-9 of English trans. of 1932), who pinned him down to a 'fructification theory' of interest, an interpretation that does not do justice even to the letter, let alone the spirit, of Turgot's treatment. Cassel's analysis (*Nature and Necessity of Interest*, 1903) is much more satisfactory. This 'fructification theory' was, in fact, quite frequently used in the eighteenth century and even before in order to counter the Aristotelian argument about the sterility of money: since it is possible to use money for the purchase of land, which does yield a net return, therefore money will yield—most authors would have said: therefore it is 'just' that money should yield—a net return, whatever the purpose for which it is lent. Hutcheson argued like this, and Petty might perhaps be accused of having done so. It is obvious that this reasoning, as an *explanation* of interest, is, or at least may be, circular, because the value of land itself depends upon the rate of interest. But Turgot, though he stated the equilibrium proposition that a sum of money will be equivalent in value to a piece of land that produces the same net revenue (*Réflexions*, LIX), was so far from treating this fact as a datum from which to start, in explaining interest, that he made an elaborate attempt to determine the exchange ratio between land and *richesses mobilières* (LIII et seq.) and to deduce from it the value of lands in terms of money.

[The reader's attention is called to the fact that the numbering of the sections of the *Réflexions* in the *Oeuvres* edited by G. Schelle (1913-23) differs from the original numbering in the *Éphémérides*. For example, XXI, XXII, and XXIII became XXI in the Schelle edition and LXXIII in Schelle had been entirely suppressed in the *Éphémérides*. Apparently J. A. S. used the original numbering in the *Éphémérides* (1769-70), which is also the numbering used by Dupont de Nemours in vol. V of his edition of the *Oeuvres de M^r. Turgot* (1808-11).]

Canonist influence, as we might expect, is much in evidence—though, of course, scholastic ideas are sometimes made to serve exactly opposite practical conclusions—and one essential feature of Turgot's scheme, the identification of capital with 'advances,' goes back to Quesnay or Cantillon. The *hommes industrieux* share their profit with capitalists who supply the funds (*Réflexions*, LXXI). The share that goes to the latter is determined like all other prices (LXXV) by the play of supply and demand among borrowers and lenders (LXXVI), so that the analysis is from the outset firmly planted in the general theory of prices. At first blush and on the surface, interest is the price paid for the use of money (LXXII, LXXIV). But why does the use of money command a price or, to put it differently, why does the mechanism of supply and demand work out in such a way as to produce normally a premium on present as compared with future money? Turgot realized that it is not enough to answer that money lent is money saved. His answer was that the *fonds* supplied by the capitalist represent *richesse mobilière* or advances, which are an indispensable prerequisite of production (LIII): capital yields interest because it bridges the temporal gap between the productive effort and the product (LIX, LX). By now, this idea has become as stale as a quotation from Hamlet. Moreover, many of us have ceased to believe in its explanatory value. For both reasons, the reader may find it difficult to admire as he should the brilliance of the stroke by which Turgot, exploiting Cantillon's or Quesnay's conception of capital, tied the phenomenon of interest to a most elementary fact about production. The propositions that the rate of interest is the *thermomètre* of the (relative) abundance or rarity of (real) capital (LXXXVIII)—in other words, that the rate of interest is negatively correlated with the rate of saving—and that it measures the extent to which production can be carried (LXXXIX) also acquire additional meaning in the light of this theory. The first remained practically unchallenged until our own time, the second stands unchallenged even now.

As has been stated before, A. Smith stereotyped the doctrinal situation. But in doing so he dropped precisely the most promising suggestions proffered by Hume and (if he knew the *Réflexions*) by Turgot—still more those that he might have found in Locke—so that his successors started from a formulation that was much more Barbonian than that of any of these writers. In the *Wealth*, the monetary aspect of the interest problem is definitely reduced to a matter of form or technique. 'What the lender really supplies . . . is not the money but . . . the goods which it can purchase' (Book II, ch. 4), and there is *nothing* in the views of 'Mr. Locke, Mr. Law, and Mr. Montesquieu' that an increase in the quantity of gold and silver lowers the rate of interest (*ibid.*). The tendency of interest to fall he explained in exactly the same way as the tendency of profit to fall (Book I, ch. 9, which really deals with the same topics as Book II, ch. 4), both of which A. Smith seems to accept—with a qualification about 'acquisition of new territory or of new branches of trade'—as unquestionable facts. And this is quite logical for, as should be clear by now, they are, in A. Smith's schema, really one and the same thing. A. Smith does distinguish them: profit also includes compensation for 'trouble' and 'risk,' whereas the lender receives his interest without such trouble and risk. But these are relegated to a secondary position. Essentially, profit is 'profit of stock,' and interest which goes to the capitalist employer is received for 'stock' (goods) lent. Whether the stock be his own or borrowed from some other person, to supply the workmen with stock is the businessman's basic function. First and foremost, he is the 'capitalist' and *as* capitalist he is the typical employer of labor, whose basic function it is to supply this stock to the workmen though that capitalist employer need not always do the employing himself, in which case . . .

[This paragraph was written on a yellow sheet still adhering to a pad and was obviously unfinished. The page, which was crowded with notes in Austrian shorthand and in English longhand, is reproduced in the Appendix.]

CHAPTER 7

The 'Mercantilist' Literature [1]

Questions of international economic relations loomed so large on the horizons of all the authors of this epoch that we have already had to refer more than once to their propositions about these problems. It is nevertheless necessary to return to the charge and to examine some of these propositions more closely in order to introduce another batch of writings and to extract from them what contributions to analytic economics they may contain. I shall group those propositions under the headings of Export Monopolism, Exchange Control, and Balance of Trade. Doctrines concerning the second and third, particularly the third, are usually considered the core of that imaginary organon, the 'mercantilist system' of traditional teaching. To many economists, they mean in fact the whole of it. This tradition was established by Adam Smith, whose famous attack upon what he called (following, perhaps, the lead of the physiocrats) the Commercial or Mercantile System (*Wealth*, Fourth Book) centered in an argument about the balance of trade, although he was not blind to other aspects.

[1. Interpretation of the 'Mercantilist' Literature]

The reader presumably knows that these specifically 'mercantilist' doctrines have given rise to a controversy among historians of thought on which it is worth while to comment before embarking upon our task. This will not only

[1] [This chapter, though completed and typed at an early date (June 1943), had only a tentative title and no section titles. In reporting on the progress of the *History* in 1946 or 1947, J. A. S. told me that this chapter could be published substantially as it stood but that a good deal of work remained to be done on other chapters in Part II.]

clarify the issues involved but also afford an interesting illustration of the principles of interpretation outlined in Part I.

The opinions the 'mercantilist' writers held about those topics—so far as they can be said to have held uniform opinions at all [2]—came to be looked upon not only with disapproval but also with contempt by the large majority of the economists of the nineteenth century. They could see nothing but error in them and, in dealing with their predecessors, developed a practice according to which it was all but sufficient for putting a work out of court to attach to it the slightest tinge of 'mercantilism.' This can be verified, in an almost amusing way, by consulting the relevant articles in *Palgrave's Dictionary of Political Economy*.[3] Next, an opposition to this free-trade view arose; voiced mainly though not exclusively by German writers, it went practically to the other extreme. This opposition also succeeded in establishing a tradition, though a less general one, which of late seems to have elicited a reaction that, joining forces with the surviving elements of the 'liberal' tradition, in turn bids fair to overshoot the mark. Professor Jacob Viner's monograph may perhaps be cited as an instance.[4]

Now the first thing to observe about this prolonged campaign is that both the antimercantilists and the promercantilists were primarily interested in mercantilist *practice* and that the opinions of both hence were and are primarily a matter of political preference. The English critics were out of sympathy with what had been *done* in the mercantilist age. The German sympathizers were not in favor of all the aspects of mercantilist practice, but they were in favor of some measure of national autarky, of state management, and above all of state building. All this is completely irrelevant to our purpose, and the only thing that needs to be said about it is this: Both critics and sympathizers were victims of the belief, so dear to that rationalist epoch, that their opinions about policy were scientific inferences from premises that had been laid down in a scientific spirit. Especially the English utilitarians, such as John Stuart Mill, looked upon their recommendations concerning policy as an engineer would look upon his recommendation about the construction of an engine. Their present was invariably 'this enlightened age.' Hence practical and theoretical 'error' was for them equally definite and indeed the same thing.

[2] This is in fact the first issue involved.

[3] Let us notice, in passing, that for the same reasons exactly the same thing is happening now to the economists of the liberal epoch.

[4] Jacob Viner, 'English Theories of Foreign Trade before Adam Smith,' republished, in revised form, as chs. 1 and 2 of his *Studies in the Theory of International Trade* (1937). I wish to acknowledge my indebtedness to this excellent piece of work. In perusing it I have sometimes wondered, however, whether Professor Viner is prepared to pass the same peremptory judgments on certain measures and arguments of our own time that are exactly similar to those of the mercantilist age. Another book that must be mentioned here is *The Theory of International Prices* by James W. Angell (1926; chs. 2 and 8). See also Viner's review of this book in *The Journal of Political Economy*, October 1926.

This standpoint, which partly accounts for their pontifical attitude, is of course wholly untenable as we need not stay to prove once more.

Second, the promercantilists held what the antimercantilists by implication denied, namely that mercantilist policies were not only understandable in the sense in which everything is, crime and folly included, but also in the much more significant sense that, taking account of the circumstances and opportunities of the times, they constituted adequate means for securing what with the same proviso were rationally defensible ends. Here, as previous argument suffices to show, the promercantilists score, though not to the extent they themselves believed.[5] At all events, this must be admitted by all those who are not willing to condemn modern commercial policies of a similar type, which in fact enjoy the support of many who know all about their Smith, their Ricardo, and their Marshall. For the sake of future reference, let us call this the Practical Argument.[6]

[5] In the thicket of 'mercantilist' measures it is easy to find many that did not serve the ends their promoters had in view or that produced other effects besides those that were desired, which would have prevented their being taken if they had been foreseen. Adam Smith's common sense revelled in instances of this (Book IV, ch. 8), which might easily be multiplied. It is however possible to separate off 'mistakes' and to carry the discussion up to a plane of principle on which they may be assumed away, though it must not be forgotten that any system of management is prone to produce a goodly crop of them. This in fact would have been Smith's defense if somebody had accused him of unfairly using 'mistakes' in a discussion of 'principles.'

[6] At this point, a sideline branches off which we see immediately if we reflect that both the ends to be served by a policy and the means to be considered rational, in other words, the questions concerning the wisdom or unwisdom of a policy, are relative to schemes of value that are themselves relative not only to the national situation, but also to the kind of men who face it and thus, among other things, to the class structure and to group interests. The statement in the text that, to some extent, mercantilist policies admit of rational defense (which, mind, never amounts to 'justification' in any absolute sense) must be understood to imply this. Many policies of the mercantilist age may in fact be traced to the interests of, or to the pressure exerted by, groups that can be definitely identified and from whose standpoints they may acquire a character of rationality that would otherwise be lacking. Adam Smith had an eye for this as he showed in Book IV, ch. 8. I will emphasize again that this has nothing to do with the truth or value of any given proposition or line of reasoning. The most stubborn class interest may induce true and valuable analysis, the most disinterested motive may lead to nothing but error and triviality. I hope I have made this quite clear in Part I. Also, I want to repeat that considerations of the class now envisaged do not per se entitle us to attribute conscious or even subconscious interested motive to any *individual*. Apart from the fact just mentioned, viz. that motive has nothing to do with the objective nature of a proposition, it is unsafe to talk about individuals' motives. The only mind accessible to us is our own. In talking about motives of individuals we may be revealing nothing but our own propensities. Wheeler was secretary to the Merchants Adventurers. Mun and Child were connected with the East India Company. Milles was a disgruntled bureaucrat. Perhaps none of them has a claim to be included among the Consultant Administrators. But little more than triviality results from stressing this.

But, third, this does not prove anything for the analysis, the results of which have been used in order to defend those policies. A man may do what, from his standpoint and in his circumstances, is for him the right thing and yet do it for reasons that are complete nonsense.[7] The promercantilists, in particular the German ones who cared little and knew less about economic theory, were therefore wrong in thinking that they had proved anything for what they conceived to be mercantilist doctrine when they had succeeded in making out, in the sense defined above, a partial case for mercantilist practice. Moreover, it should be borne in mind that it is not enough to show that a proposition we find in a mercantilist pamphlet makes sense *to us,* that is to say, that *we* can prove it to be correct. For many modern propositions bear a striking surface resemblance—let us hope that the resemblance does not go below the surface—to quite primitive ones which can be easily disproved. To read our meaning uncritically into old texts amounts to betrayal of the historian's duty as much as does overemphasis on every mistake in formulation. This class of considerations we shall, for purposes of reference, call the Theoretical Argument. Armed with these distinctions we now proceed with our task.

[2. Export Monopolism]

To begin with, the practical argument is strongly in favor of those writers of that age who held that monopoly and quasi-monopolistic co-operation, no matter what their effects may have been on domestic industry and trade, filled an essential function in foreign commerce. This is what I mean by export monopolism. At all times people have judged differently monopolistic practice that was directed against foreigners. Thus, the American Congress, otherwise so hostile to anything that may be made to look like monopoly, was easily persuaded to relax antimonopolist legislation for the benefit of export trade by the Webb-Pomerene Act. The proposition involved is as simple as it is—so far as it goes and if only immediate effects are considered—correct: monopoly gains from foreign trade are net gains to a nation because the items that would have to be subtracted if these gains were made in the domestic market are equated to zero. Moreover, until the middle of the eighteenth century and in many parts of the world until much later, trading was only possible within protective *ad hoc* arrangements that the traders had largely to provide themselves. This did not necessarily involve monopolistic action. But it spelled organization and co-operation that could easily extend to price and general business policy, not only to facilitate exploitation but also to regulate it and to defend standard practice against substandard connationals. Of this,

[7] The reverse is also true—particularly in economics—in the sense that it is possible to reason correctly on a model constructed in an unexceptionable way and yet to arrive at wrong diagnoses concerning a reality that fails to conform to the model. We shall encounter instances of this. To top it all, scientifically interesting theories may be associated with quite uninteresting practice, interesting practice with uninteresting theories.

the Society of Merchants Adventurers affords a telling example.[1] Finally, it seems too obvious to require explicit statement but is surprisingly often left out of account by critics of 'mercantilist theories' that that age was the age of buccaneering imperialism and that trade was associated with colonization, with uninhibited exploitation of the colonies founded,[2] with private warfare for which the governments, especially the English, frequently declined responsibility, and with conditions permanently verging on war. The classic example of all this is the East Indian; the only modern instance, the Rhodesian case. This explains many things perfectly rationally that were bound to vanish under the influence of different conditions, even if there had not been any progress at all in the grasp of the logic of economic phenomena: in fact this progresss presumably had very little to do with the change in practice.

The two main sources of the large stream of literature on the subject of export monopolism—including colonization—flowed from the one fact that the policies of the great companies affected domestic interests also, and from the other fact that their success aroused the envious hatred of both the squire and the common man against the 'nabobs.' Attacks elicited replies, of which it may be worth while to notice the best example that has come to my notice: John Wheeler's defense of the Merchants Adventurers—among other things against the bureaucratic spokesmen for regulation who know nothing about business (*tout comme chez nous*). This work mentioned before in Chapters 3 and 6, entitled *A Treatise of Commerce, Wherein are shewed the Commodities arising by a well ordered and ruled Trade, such as that of the Societie of Merchants Adventurers is proved to be: Written principally for the better Information of those who doubt of the Necessarinesse of the said Societie in the State of the Realme of England* (1601), was also written, as we may add, with impending hostile legislation in view. In my opinion Mr. Wheeler did extremely well, and his argument successfully disposes of some of the points that are invariably raised in discussions about monopoly. His economics is not a bit below the level that we observe in similar popular or political or forensic arguments today. But he contributes nothing to our collection of scientific tools. His analytic economics was, on the whole, not wrong. There was very

[1] It is hardly possible to understand the circumstances that conditioned the economic thought of that period and in particular to appreciate the points made—and to be made—in the text without a pretty extensive command of the relevant chapters of economic history. Let me therefore again recommend a study of Professor Eli F. Heckscher's volumes: *Mercantilism* (first publ. in Swedish, 1931; German ed., 1932; English trans. by Mendel Shapiro, 2 vols., 1935).

[2] The lack of inhibition displayed by Spaniards, Frenchmen, and Englishmen alike is a very important element of the case. The economic reasoning about colonies runs on completely different lines and may, without involving contradiction, lead to completely different results according to the practice visualized by different men. Warren Hastings' practice—to wit: shameless robbery—is one thing. William Bentinck's practice—to wit: benevolent administration—is another thing. And the economic advantages differ accordingly. A rough dividing line can be discerned by studying the evolution of the attitude toward the slave trade.

little of it, however. Because of its prominence, the East India Company attracted the lion's share of public attention and hostility. This accounts for a large part of the literature in question. So far as I can see, however, there is nothing in it to interest us except the arguments and counter-arguments about the company's exportation of monetary metal and about the competition which—though harassed by legislation and administration—it offered to English woolens by its imports of Indian wares. However, these arguments and counter-arguments enter into the general discussion concerning the balance of trade (see sec. 4). Attention is invited to the footnote below.[3]

[3. Exchange Control]

Next let us see how the practical argument stands in the matter of Exchange Control. War, as we know from experience, inevitably induces government control of economic life and, not less inevitably, creates bureaucracies to

[3] Monopolistic policies were related to, though of course not congruent with, the Staple (*jus emporii*), which will be touched upon in connection with the two other topics we have singled out for discussion. But it is convenient to make its acquaintance right now. For our purposes we must carefully distinguish three different aspects of it. First, corporatively organized *traders* sometimes hit upon the device of making certain towns centers or entrepots of their trade in order the better to regulate it. The Merchants Adventurers may again serve as an example. John Wheeler in fact argued the advantages of 'mart towns.' Second, the towns themselves, which were in a position to do so or to prevail on their territorial governments to help them to such a position, tried to exercise staple rights, that is to say, to force traders to pass through them, to offer their wares for sale, and to submit to other restrictions that were, or were thought to be, profitable to those *towns:* here the foreign traders did not engineer the staple, but were the victims of it, sometimes in ways that to us look like the acme of irrationality and vexation. This is the type that is usually associated with the term Staple. It spread in the thirteenth century and after—all over Italy (Genoa and Venice being the most powerful centers of it) and then over the rest of Europe, including Russia. It also spread to England, as Edward III's Ordinance of the Staple shows. Professor Heckscher's statement to the contrary is not quite understandable to me. From this arose, third, the practice of forcing international trade into prescribed channels for the real or putative benefit of a *country* as a whole and for the purpose of injuring the foreigner. It is this type that was mainly discussed in the English literature. England—improving on the Spanish example—in fact developed it beyond all precedent. Her participation in the staple policy of the second variety practically ceased, of course, with the loss of Calais in 1558, whereas, e.g. in Venice, it continued to exist until Napoleon's conquest of that city. But her staple policy of the third type was then in its beginning and a whole century had still to elapse before its legislative bases were completed by the Navigation Act of 1660 and the Staple Act of 1663. The statement one meets so often, to the effect that, so far as England is concerned, the staple system died in 1558, is therefore misleading and a serious bar to the understanding of a considerable part of the mercantilist literature. Of course, the system gradually shaded off into ordinary protectionism in the modern sense, but this does not justify us in overlooking its peculiar features that were so important a part of the politico-economic scene of those times.

administer it which then not merely cling to their powers but automatically strive to expand them. Imports, exports, and foreign exchanges are obviously among the most important of the things to be controlled. The argument for control also applies to conditions permanently verging on war. Moreover we must take into account the spirit induced by war and the incessant threat of war, the frame of mind in which injury to a foreign nation is almost as welcome as gain to one's own, or, to put it differently, in which the policy of international economic relations merges with a policy of economic warfare and becomes just one of the weapons in the perennial game of power politics. If it be conceded that all this holds true for that epoch, the rationale for its practice in the matter of foreign exchange should be obvious, especially if we do not lose sight of the expansive tendency inherent in all bureaucratic practice. Embargoes on coined and uncoined gold and silver we simply subsume as a necessary complement under exchange control, although in more primitive cases they were the main measure to be taken or even all that it was possible to do.[1]

It may be useful, however, to present that rationale in a more general form, that is, without reference to the particular conditions of war economy. In doing so I shall consider perfect exchange control only, that is, the case in which a public authority, holding an effective monopoly of exchange transactions, can requisition and allocate foreign exchange as it pleases. Then, this authority can (a) tide over temporary shortages of foreign exchange which, if not attended to, may produce disproportionate consequences, especially through cumulative processes; (b) facilitate the orderly discharging of debts in situations in which automatic adjustment is impossible owing to inhibitions in the functioning of the international market; (c) prevent or defeat bearish speculation in an exchange market that lacks its normal resilience; (d) prevent undesired (depressive) effects of automatic adjustment that may ensue even where such automatic adjustment is possible; (e) prevent certain imports or exports and encourage others and thus powerfully influence national production; (f) improve a country's terms of trade within limits, which may be widened by complementary restrictions, by introducing a monopoly element into its transactions with foreign merchants.

[1] The practice of exchange control, as well as the discussion about it, was at the highest level in England. But the former reached its culmination much before the latter, viz. in the reign of Elizabeth in which, under the influence of a persistently favorable course of events, the decline set in also. It then consisted of a control over transactions in foreign exchange, administered by a special public officer, the Royall Exchanger, and was supplemented by an embargo (lifted definitively, after various ups and downs, in 1663 for everything except English coins) and by the Statute of Employment, 1390, which, a member of quite a family of similar measures enacted in many countries, attempted to enforce importers to employ the proceeds of their sales in purchasing English goods. After the First World War there were instances of similar measures in several European countries, e.g., Austria. The Royall Exchanger of course has found plenty of successors in present-day Europe whose practices no doubt differ from his in technique but do not differ at all in principle.

Two points remain to be added. First, in order to prove itself the sharp weapon it is capable of being, exchange control not only requires attention to the net result of all the transactions that cross a country's frontier or to the net results of a country's transactions with every other country taken separately—the bilateral trade principle of today—but it also requires attention to the transactions in every individual commodity and of every individual trader. This is particularly necessary if full advantage of the discriminatory possibilities of the method is to be reaped. Second, in order to be fully effective as a tool of comprehensive planning, exchange control (plus embargoes on monetary metals) must be implemented by other controls that act directly on the individual transactions themselves. Many such controls have been used at various times but that epoch had a *specificum* of its own, the institution of the Staple.[2] It is obviously much easier to control exchanges when trade is already controlled by being forced into prescribed channels; and the staple towns with their apparatus of mints, comptrollers, and hostelers (practically jailers of foreign merchants) offered unrivaled administrative opportunities for controlling the exchange market. It should be borne in mind, however, that the two policies while primarily complementary were also to some extent capable of being substituted for one another.[3]

Now, whatever we may think of the more remote effects of any such policy, especially if practiced by all countries, and whatever we may think of the way in which it was actually worked—legislation was (and is), of course, at all times a highly irrational heap of contradictory measures—it was not simply nonsense in principle and no writer who advocated it under the conditions of that time can be accused of having stood for nonsense. This certainly holds so far as the practical argument is concerned and hence for the practitioners, among whom Sir Thomas Gresham (1519-79) stands out without a peer.[4] John

[2] See footnote 3.

[3] There is thus nothing astonishing, and especially no contradiction, in the fact that some writers advocated both the staple system *and* exchange control and others exchange control instead of the staple system. Let us note in this connection that, roughly up to 1600, Free Trade as a program meant developing the staple system and fettering or even breaking up the merchants' companies. After 1600 it meant forcing the doors of those companies so as to make it possible for every trader to enter them. In both cases free trade meant a sort of 'trust busting.'

[4] He was a type that can no doubt be found everywhere but of which the English specimens are to this day so much more frequent and so much superior that it may well be called English: the businessman who is just as much a public servant as he is businessman and who, though perfectly successful in looking after his own advantage, serves the state in ways that are beyond the competence of the mere public servant. As a businessman he was a mercer, banker, entrepreneur (paper-milling), and public benefactor. As a public servant he was first 'factor' (fiscal agent) for the English crown in the Netherlands—keeping up its credit, managing the course of the English exchange, negotiating loans, acting as buyer of war materials, getting hold, by hook or by crook, of bullion to ship to England, and so on—and then, at home, exchange dictator (Royall Exchanger) and financial expert to Elizabeth—among other things, forcing merchants to lend to the crown by methods that were akin to holdups yet

Stuart Mill himself could not have suggested a workable alternative, and if he rose from the dead to deny this, we should reply that he did not know enough about the conditions of the time and that it was he who laid himself open to the charge of erroneous reasoning by denying it. But this does not alter the fact that those defensible practical views are generally believed to be associated with inadequate or even downright nonsensical theories. However, the question arises whether there was any theoretical argument at all.

In fact practically all the writers who discussed the possibilities of protecting the national exchange and securing an influx of gold and silver money or bullion without reference to the balance of trade or of payments should not be credited or charged with *any* theory.[5] Precisely in order to be just to them, we must realize how innocent they were of analysis. This will clear them of some accusations which it has become a tradition to direct at them for no better reason than that we take their utterances too seriously and insist on pinning them down to theories these utterances seem to imply. But they did not analyze at all. They had no conception of any but the most obvious relations between economic phenomena. Living at a time when nations braced themselves to match their fighting power, they impulsively resented imports of unnecessary luxuries—that does not imply considered rejection of Adam Smith's grand commonplace that consumption is the 'sole end and purpose

were so handled as to enhance instead of annihilate public credit: the interested reader should refer to J. W. Burgon's *The Life and Times of Sir Thomas Gresham* (1839). [See also Raymond de Roover, *Gresham on Foreign Exchange* (1949).]

We may use this opportunity to notice the two analytic achievements that have been placed to his credit. First, he described correctly enough the rules that apply to the movements of the rate of exchange with reference to the specie points, and he holds priority over Davanzati, who however did a much better job in 1582. To make scientifically articulate a piece of business practice, however well known in the business community, is a service that always deserves recording. Second, there is Gresham's Law, the proposition that if coins containing metal of different value enjoy equal legal-tender power, then the 'cheapest' ones will be used for payment, the better ones will tend to disappear from circulation—or, to use the usual but not quite correct phrase, that bad money drives out good money. This phrase occurs in the Royal Proclamation 'decrying' base silver coin in 1560, when Gresham is known to have been the government's chief adviser in such matters. There is also a memorandum of his (1559) which argues this case. The so-called 'law' can be found in many earlier writings. Considering its trivial nature, the question of priority is, however, without interest.

5 It would be apt to call them Primitives (Richard Jones, 'Primitive Political Economy of England,' *Edinburgh Review*, 1847), provided we bear in mind that the primitivity was in the analysis rather than in the practice. The usual term is Bullionists, which I want to avoid because it suggests—as well as do others that have been offered (see E. R. A. Seligman, article 'Bullionists' in the *Encyclopaedia of the Social Sciences* —that there were doctrinal nostra by which to identify them as a distinct group. They were not really a group. Such views as they had in common are also to be found, on a somewhat higher level, among writers with whom nobody would include them.

of all production.' They looked at the antics of exchange rates and attributed them to the machinations of speculators—exactly as the politicians and the public did in France and Germany after 1919. They felt it was nice for a nation as well as for individuals to have money—and said so without thinking any more about it. They were staunch nationalists—and the foreigner, of course, was an object of aversion and distrust. They were most of them what may be termed naively critical of business and of the doings of merchants—as public opinion always was and is. The reader will have caught the point and will excuse me from going on with this argument. Nor would it serve a useful purpose to present examples.[6]

There were, however, exceptions.[7] The only one to call for specific attention is Malynes [8] whom we have met before. Behind his recommendations—mainly higher import duties, prohibition of bullion exportation, the staple system, and resurrection of the office of Royall Exchange for the purpose of fixing exchange rates officially—there is more serious theory than has been admitted by a long series of critics who have treated his views with contempt. That he does not merit this, is proved by the fact that, as we shall see, during the whole of that century no other writer surpassed him in clear and full understanding of the international mechanism of foreign exchanges that works through price levels and gold and silver movements—the 'automatic mech-

[6] The reader who feels any inclination of this kind is referred to the articles by R. Jones and Professor Seligman quoted in the preceding footnote and to Professor Tawney's introductory essay in his edition of Thomas Wilson's *Discourse upon Usury* (1925). Still it may be well to mention one name at least: Thomas Milles, the customs official, who like a good bureaucrat craved for the regulated trade of the staple, which he describes as the 'first steppe towards heaven,' and for the import of bullion, which he describes as the sun, the pilot, and the 'chylus' of economic life. His least immature work: *The Mysterie of Iniquitie* (1611).

[7] Such were Marc' Antonio De Santis (*Discorso intorno agli effecti che fa il cambio in regno*, 1605), who owes survival to Antonio Serra's attack upon his theory (see T. Fornari, *Studi sopra Antonio Serra e Marc' Antonio De Santis*, 1880); Sir Thomas Culpeper, who in his *Tract against Usurie* (1621), which has been mentioned already, approached exchange transactions *per analogiam* of usury as did others and as the scholastic writers had done; the anonymous author of *Cambium Regis: or, the Office of His Majesties Exchange Royall* (1628); Miguel Caxa de Leruela (*Restauración de la antigua abundācia de España*, 1631); and quite a number of other Spanish writers. None of these, however, went below the surface or beyond the mere mechanics of the regulation of exchanges.

[8] Gerard de Malynes (fl. 1586-1641): *A Treatise of the Canker of England's Commonwealth* (1601); *Saint George for England, Allegorically described* (1601); *England's View, in the Unmasking of two Paradoxes: With a replication unto the answer of Maister John Bodine* . . . (1603)—a contribution to the controversy between Bodin and Malestroit, in which without really attacking Bodin's argument, Malynes reasserts the importance of his argument about 'overballancing.' Mainly these three publications (and, perhaps his big compilation of legislative material, *Consuetudo, vel, Lex Mercatoria*, 1st ed., 1622) are of importance at the moment, but I may just as well add the two by which he crossed swords with Misselden: *The Maintenance of Free Trade* . . . (1622), and *The Center of the Circle of Commerce* (1623).

anism' to be discussed presently under the heading Balance of Trade. In the Second Part of his treatise, *Canker of England's Commonwealth*, he nicely explains how, if a country's currency falls below its mint par and coin flows out in consequence, then prices will fall in that country and rise abroad 'where our mony concurring with the monies of other countries causeth plenty, whereby the price of forreign commodities is aduanced.' This is a considerable theoretical contribution. We must go to the eighteenth century in order to find the argument carried to the conclusion to which it points. Why then did Malynes fail to draw this conclusion himself? I think because he was much more impressed with the shortcomings of that mechanism than he was with the mechanism itself. In particular he complained that, in the small and inhibited markets of his time, operations in exchange so worked out for England that she was selling her goods more cheaply and paying for foreign goods more dearly than was necessary—that is, that her terms of trade were unnecessarily unfavorable—'wherein chiefly consisteth the . . . overballancing.' He perceived the possibility of improving those terms by exchange control (our point (f) above), and further proof that he reasoned correctly upon the matter is provided by the fact that, in considering the objections to his plan (*Canker of England's Commonwealth*, Third Part), he mentions first the effect on sales that might be expected from better terms of trade and promptly replies 'how necessarie our commodities are and what request thereof is in all places'—which means that, in his opinion, foreign demand for English goods was inelastic. Now he may have been wrong in his factual appraisal of the situation. It is even certain that he overestimated both what speculation in exchange can do to harm the interest of a country and what exchange control can do to further it. Overstatement of his point is obvious in the controversy with Misselden. But that is not the point. We are not concerned with the question whether England 'should have' accepted his advice. We are concerned with his reasoning. And this, though of course not above criticism, must be primarily listed as a contribution. If we label him a 'bullionist,' then the balance of the theoretical argument is not clearly against bullionism. Nor is it true that, so far as his theoretical position is concerned, he was dislodged by Misselden.

[4. The Balance of Trade]

Turning, finally, to the third topic, the proposition that a favorable balance of trade [1] (excess of exports over imports) is a highly desirable or even neces-

[1] The term turns up during the first decades of the seventeenth century (Francis Bacon used it in 1615; see Spedding's ed., *Letters and Life*, 1872, vol. VI, pp. 22-3, a reference I owe to Professor Seligman's article; see also W. H. Price, 'The Origin of the Phrase "Balance of Trade,"' *Quarterly Journal of Economics*, vol. XX, November 1905, p. 157). In Italy it seems to have been used before; see C. Supino, 'La scienza economica in Italia della seconda metà del secolo XVI alla prima del XVII' (*Memorie della Reale Accademia delle Scienze di Torino*, 1888). However, there were several synonyms in use before that. The earliest instance of the concept's playing any role in an argument occurs so far as I know in the important tract (to which reference

sary thing at which to aim, we first observe that, as regards the practical argument, much of what has been said before applies with equal force to this case. This is as true if we look at the commercial policies of that age merely under the aspect of protectionism as it is if we choose to emphasize specifically the balance-of-trade aspect. For, as has been stressed sufficiently, I hope, the war-economy and the power-politics elements in those policies would in themselves be quite sufficient to remove any tinge of *irrationality* from a wish to secure as large as possible an influx of universally acceptable money. Therefore the only question to raise is the one concerning the theoretical argument. Let us split it into two parts: (a) how far did the 'mercantilist' economists themselves take account of that association of both their recommendations and their arguments with the conditions of their time which imparts logically defensible meaning to the latter, though it does not of course—never forget this—'justify' them in any other sense; and (b) what did they contribute to economic analysis or else what provable errors did they commit in their reasoning?

[(a) *The Practical Argument: Power Politics.*] There cannot be any doubt concerning the first question. 'Mercantilist' writers—least of all the Italians, of course—were keenly alive to the power-politics element, as in fact they could not have helped being. In England in particular, the City from which most of the leading writers hailed was a pillar of aggressive foreign policy which, as is abundantly clear from what has been said before, suited the business interests to perfection even where it was not directly inspired by them. Of course this is not always explicitly stated. Imperialist urges rarely are. But it lurks behind the concern of our authors about the wealth of the king, behind their talk about the decay of the English power,[2] behind their fears for

will be made again): 'Polices to Reduce this Realme of Englande unto a prosperus Wealthe and Estate' (1549), publ. in *Tudor Economic Documents*, ed. R. H. Tawney and E. Power, Vol. III (1924), p. 311 et seq. The term used is 'overplus.' Professor Viner, op. cit., p. 9, mentioned also several others; but I do not think that Malynes' 'overballancing' refers to the same thing. How could it, since Malynes, when confronted with it in the controversy with Misselden, thought it an innovation and a valueless one to boot?

A difficulty should be mentioned here. Balance of trade in many instances stands for balance of commodity trade. Very early however, as will be explained in the text, a full list was produced of all the items of the balance of payments and it is safe to say that much of the reasoning of those authors referred to the latter. They were surprisingly slow, however, in inventing a separate term—Sir James Steuart has 'balance of payments' in 1767, though Pollexfen has 'balance of accompts' in 1697 (see Viner, op. cit. p. 14)—and meanwhile often spoke of balance of trade when they meant balance of payments. We shall always assume this when the argument requires it. There is a special reason why we may do this: under the circumstances of the time, the balance of trade was the most important item and also the one most amenable to management. Hence an author whose real concern was the balance of payments may well have concentrated on the balance of trade.

[2] Complaints about that decay were so frequent as to constitute a most interesting phenomenon of political psychology. Little of what we may term social psychoanalysis

England's safety, behind the attitude that Hume was to criticize in his essay *Of the Jealousy of Trade* (1752), behind their insistence on the vital importance of the navy and, in connection with it, of shipping and shipbuilding. Of special interest, however, are those cases in which the power (or safety) argument is not only put forth unmistakably but is also opposed to the profit argument: for whatever we may think of this from other angles, it marks progress in economic insight. Two well-known examples will suffice. In his *Discourse about Trade* (1690) Child defends the policy of the Navigation Acts by the power argument while admitting that, from a purely economic point of view, there may have been a strong case against them. In his *Discourses on the Publick Revenues and on the Trade of England* (1698), Davenant goes further still.[3]

[(b) *The Analytic Contribution.*] To answer the second question—the one about contributions to, and errors in, analysis—is not so easy. Some contributions there are. They will present themselves in the proper light if we look at them, as it were, *ex ante,* and not, as critics invariably do, from the standpoint of later analysis for which it was the most important contribution of the 'mercantilist' writers to have paved the road and which in fact grew out of their work. But as soon as one dives into that literature, one cannot fail to be struck by two things.

---

is required in order to understand what it meant. Parallel with them went complaints about a wholly imaginary economic decay—in the mind of the merchant class, power and prosperity were of course inextricably associated—which were characteristic of a large group of writers: Fortrey, Coke, 'Philanglus,' Bellers, and Pollexfen may be mentioned as examples.

[3] The nature of that antagonism between power and profit does not seem to have been always understood. Some critics, especially those who see nothing in the writings of the English 'mercantilists' except 'special pleading' for class or even personal interests, have argued that the power argument can only have been introduced to camouflage the profit interest and that the scribbling merchants must therefore have believed in the balance-of-trade argument independently of the power element. I think that this is bad sociology—we only impair our diagnosis by shutting our eyes to the fact that the imperialist urge is a stark reality that roots in other soil than that of the economic self-interest of the individual. But even disregarding this, we must distinguish two quite different things *within* the argument inspired by business interest: power and profit may conflict as regards immediate results and yet power may eventually lead to still higher profits, especially in an age of buccaneering imperialism. Hence there is no contradiction between the perception that the balance-of-trade argument, on the first plane of reasoning, needs support from the power argument, and the proposition, on the second plane of reasoning, that the power argument issues in *another* profit argument in the long run. I can see no point in sneering at Child's formula: 'foreign trade produces riches, riches power, power preserves our trade and religion' (with Louis XIV on the other side of the channel), but the argument can, if critics so wish, be made purely economic and still remain tenable, with the balance of trade in no other role than that of an intermediate link. [A long essay by J. A. S., 'Zur Soziologie der Imperialismen' (*Archiv für Sozialwissenschaft und Sozialpolitik,* 1919), bearing on this subject, is now available in English: *Imperialism and Social Classes* (ed. with introd. by Paul M. Sweezy, 1951).]

First, though pieces of genuine analytic work can be found occasionally and attempts at analysis more frequently, the bulk of the literature is still essentially preanalytic; and not only that, it is crude—the work of unprofessional or even uneducated minds that frequently lacked the rudiments of the art of exposition: much of that literature was popular in the most distressing sense of the word. Perception of this fact, of which some of those writers were themselves painfully aware, should not only teach us forbearance, particularly with respect to individual *dicta*—on the strength of which an author should never be condemned until we have satisfied ourselves that he actually makes improper use of them—but should also warn us that we are in constant danger, reasoning from our own sublime heights, of misunderstanding what those simple fellows really wanted to say. To be sure there are a considerable number of writers to whom this does not apply. But this only leads up to another difficulty. If we want to be just to the age, we must clearly separate substandard chaff from valuable wheat. How will the economics of our own age come off two or three hundred years hence, if critics take it into their heads to judge it by everything that has been written on economic subjects during the last decade? But what, beyond a rather small group of performances on which we may all agree, is the wheat? Here, every one of us must rely on his personal evaluations of analytic quality—the only kind of value judgments that are both permissible and unavoidable in a history of scientific economics—a matter in which often the only agreement attainable will be the agreement to differ.

Second, we have had ample opportunity already to observe that the views of the economists of that period—if indeed it be permissible to speak of economists at all for a period in which the profession was in process of emergence but had not really emerged as yet—were as uniform as are those of the economists of any other period but that they were not more so: individuals and groups differed from one another, in fundamentals and in details, as much as economists always have, and they fought one another's views and methods accordingly. The widespread opinion to the contrary has resulted in another injustice. The critical historian, after having set up a 'uniformed' man of straw, misses the fact that much of what is most objectionable from the standpoint of later analysis (or politics) had been rejected or corrected within the period. The historian has indeed a method of dealing with this fact when it stares him in the face: those who took what to him seems to be a more correct view are either visited with more lenient strictures or else they are excluded from that imaginary unit under the heading of heretics or forerunners. But this method is a doubtful one to say the least.

We have noticed, and tried to understand, the protectionist current of the times; we have also encountered the opinions that a number of writers held on the subject of protection. We shall naturally expect the writers we are considering under the heading of Balance of Trade to have completed the list of protectionist arguments. This expectation is not disappointed. We find the infant-industry argument, which, excepting perhaps the case of English woolens, must in the circumstances of the period be assumed to underlie any recommendation of protection to domestic industry that is not expressly motivated in a different way. We find the military, the key-industry, and the general-autarky arguments. We find the employment argument. We find the argument that today has come into such prominence in connection with the multiplier approach, namely, that so far as protection succeeds in producing an excess of exports it will stimulate the business process by increasing domestic expenditure. Foreign investment plays no role, or next to none, in their analysis except in a short-run sense: some of them pointed out that a temporary export of coin may be a necessary link in a series of transactions that eventually nets an export surplus. English instances—we shall confine ourselves to English ones although the Continent would also furnish a crop—are given below. They will also add to our modest collection of names.

As we should expect, the infant-industry argument turns up in the times of Elizabeth, when England experienced her first industrial boom, and pervades the literature under discussion to the end, that is, to the threshold of the industrial revolution, when Sir James Steuart put considerable emphasis on it. We are primarily interested in cases where protection is recommended only for a limited time or where the element of 'infancy' is otherwise stressed in such a way as to remove any possibility of doubt about the character of the argument. Thus, Arthur Dobbs in *An Essay on the Trade and Improvement of Ireland* (1729-31), Part II, expressly stated that 'premiums are only to be given to encourage manufactures or other improvements in their infancy' and that further help would be in vain 'if after their improvement they cannot push their own way.' Yarranton (*England's Improvement by Sea and Land, to Outdo the Dutch without Fighting, to Pay Debts without Moneys, to Set at Work all the Poor of England* . . . 1677, 2nd part, 1681) recommended protection to linen manufacture but only for a period of seven years. Andrew Yarranton found a biographer enthusiastic enough to call him 'the genuine founder of political economy in England' (see P. E. Dove, *Elements of Political Science*, 1854, App.). Although this is of course absurd, it was perhaps a healthy reaction against the neglect that had fallen upon his name. Yarranton was a versatile man of many trades and cannot, in some of the lines of his activity, agricultural technique in particular, be rated higher than as a popularizing projector. But in economics he was more than that. Though there are no analytic conquests to his credit, many of his suggestions and many of his comments on German and Dutch conditions imply a theoretical schema; so does the fact that, even in his most daring flights, he consistently stops short of nonsense. He paid little court to the balance of trade. He believed that the prosperity of neighboring countries was a gain to England. Improvement of credit facilities would reduce the rate of interest from 6 to 4 per cent (observe the limits which guard the statement against an indictment that without them would be dangerously near at hand). Employment and cheap food (the latter being sure to make cheap products [he says 'cloth']) are the goals to aim at. In fact we can herewith quote him as an authority for all the arguments mentioned in the text, as we have quoted him and shall quote him on other topics.

The military argument has been dealt with already. The key-industry argument is present in the discussion on foodstuffs and the production and exportation of wool. The general-autarky argument was developed in Germany rather than in England (for France, see J. Nowak, *L'Idée de l'autarchie économique*, 1925). For the employment argument we have just had an example in Yarranton. It occurs from the first (see Clement Armstrong, 'A Treatise Concerning the Staple and the Commodities of this Realme,' *c.* 1519-35, *Tudor Economic Documents*, III, pp. 90 et seq., especially p. 112; see also John Hales, *Discourse of the Common Weal*, 1549?). Protectionist legislation, motivated by the unemployment argument, is of course still older by at least a hundred years and is rarely absent from the more considerable books. Malynes, Misselden, Child (who makes it the criterion of the advantage that accrues to the mother country from colonies), Barbon, Locke, Petty—all have it. Let us notice in addition: John Cary, *Essay on the State of England . . .* (1695), which to judge from its being reissued a number of times and from Locke's commendation must have been a considerable success; John Pollexfen, whose whole case for prohibiting the exportation of wool and the importation of manufactured goods is based upon the employment argument; John Bellers, *Essays About the Poor, Manufactures, Trade . . .* (1699); and 'Philanglus' (W. Petyt), *Britannia Languens or A Discourse of Trade* (1680). Some of the 'mercantilist' writers went to surprising, in fact to Keynesian, lengths. There is nothing startling in Sir William Petty's saying that it is better to produce useless things than not to produce at all: this only shows his concern about the conservation of the efficiency of labor. But others sometimes expressed themselves as if they thought that the national advantage to be reaped from foreign trade consists exclusively in the employment it gave. And this in turn logically led to that position which looks so absurd when judged from the assumptions of the nineteenth-century 'liberals,' and has in fact been called absurd by Professor Viner (op. cit. p. 55; the reader finds examples on the two preceding pages), namely, that a trade is the more advantageous to a country the *higher* is the total labor cost of the exports as compared with the total labor costs of the corresponding imports. To one aspect of this we shall return.

The employment argument was not only advanced per se, but also in its indirect form, via the stimulus which inflowing cash will give to business. Here we are not concerned with all those writers who considered the possibility of imparting this stimulus by the creation of papei money, but only with those who thought of lubricating the wheels of business by means of the importation of coin and bullion. If the reader observes how very popular this idea is and always has been with the man in the street, he will expect that it is practically ubiquitous, so much so that it often is implied rather than explicitly stated. The only obstacle to its absolute sway was the treasure aspect of bullion importation—the idea that the imported bullion should be hoarded against the requirements of war. Malynes and Misselden, the two antagonists, may however both be quoted as instances of this 'lubrication argument.' Both saw the stimulus in connection with rising prices, Malynes' shade—after having been, for three centuries, the object of practically universal vituperation—drawing applause from Lord Keynes (*General Theory of Employment, Interest, and Money*, p. 345) for being aware of 'the fallacy of cheapness' and the danger of 'excessive competition' and for having associated increasing sales with rising, instead of falling, prices. But, as we have seen, other writers did not stress this relation of the stimulus with rising prices: they either looked upon higher rising prices with misgivings or else they believed that bullion importation would stimulate trade without raising prices. That it is by no means foolish to hold the latter opinion will be shown later in a footnote.

Child, Mun, and others afford examples of the proposition that foreign investments are inevitable in the short run—if they said so from interested motives, what of it?—but I am unable to quote instances of arguments in favor of permanent investment abroad before Sir James Steuart and, what is more, neither is Professor Viner (op. cit. p. 16).

So far as these arguments are concerned, there is little serious error to record. Considering the pattern to which they were to apply, they were all more or less capable of logical defense—more, in some respects, than are the similar arguments of today. Moreover, certain weaknesses should not be judged too severely. It is true, for instance, that most of those writers do not seem to have been aware of the extent to which the validity of their arguments, at least of the purely economic ones among them, depended upon the condition of underemployment or *underdevelopment* of productive resources.[4] But the reverse reproach may be addressed to their critics and successors in the nineteenth century, in part even to Marshall himself.[5] Finally we shall see that many of the necessary qualifications and many of those counterarguments that are complementary rather than competitive were worked out not by a few isolated 'heretics,' but by the 'mercantilist' writers themselves.

But neither is there much analytic merit to record. Whether right or wrong, those arguments were in most cases put forth on the strength of their common-sense appeal. The common man at all times believed in them as a matter of course, and the economists of that age believed in them along with him. They tried to rationalize the practice of their time, both in the sense that they tried to voice what they conceived to be the aims and needs of their times and countries, and in the sense that they tried to put some logical order into the irrational heap of actual measures and practices. But they did not

[4] Compare, however, Arthur Young, *Political Essays concerning the Present State of the British Empire* (1772), who (p. 533) explicitly refers to 'unemployed poor and unpurchased commodities.' I owe this reference to Professor Viner (op. cit. p. 54).

[5] Marshall, and also Pigou, did relax on the 'absolutism' of traditional free-trade doctrine, especially in their contribution to the controversy about Joseph Chamberlain's tariff-reform proposals. But they hardly made it sufficiently clear to others, and may not have sufficiently realized themselves, that the usual propositions about free trade are only valid under conditions that often fail to be fulfilled or, alternatively, only on a high level of abstraction.

We may use the opportunity to touch upon another point that has been made. It has been held that, as is indeed obvious, the 'mercantilist' writers presented short-run views and it has been admitted 'that some of the mercantilist doctrine would not be quite so absurd if appraised from the short-run point of view' (see Viner, op. cit. p. 111). But there is no 'evidence that the mercantilists intended their analysis and proposals to be regarded as holding true for the short run only, and there is abundant evidence that they were ordinarily not aware of any distinction between . . . desirable . . . practice to meet a temporary situation . . . and . . . permanent policy.' (ibid.) This is hardly fair. The distinction alluded to is a result of prolonged analytic work; it would be easy to mention examples of its violation from later and even from modern work. The mercantilist writers wrote for the situation that confronted them much as did Lord Keynes. This was, to be sure, not a temporary situation in the narrow sense—it was the situation of an age which was a sequence of emergencies and in which analysis of long-run equilibria could have interested only the purest of pure theorists. But they did not talk about any 'permanent' policy either. They were too practical-minded to believe in any such thing or rather this idea had not entered their heads at all. Apart therefore from passages (e.g. in Thomas Mun's *England's Treasure*, to be quoted later) which indicate that some of them did have an inkling of the fact that, as we should say, their argument did not apply in the longest run, let alone to a state of long-run *equilibrium*, it should be enough for us to judge their argument as it stands, whatever their own opinion of its methodology may have been.

probe below the surface to depths where the need for analytic technique asserts itself. They posited their arguments and hurried on to specific recommendations, for example, as to which industries were the most promising ones to foster—for England, they suggested fishing or iron or linen or the improvement of waterways or the development of crown lands—and how the government should go about fostering them: many of their works are just full of projects—Yarranton's are a good example. But as a rule they did what our own planners mostly do: they left off where analysis begins. This is what I meant when I said that the bulk of that literature was pre-scientific, which from our point of view is much more important than whether we like or dislike 'mercantilist' policies and their nationalist spirit. How very pre-scientific the reasoning of most writers was can be seen most clearly where they did make attempts at analysis and nowhere better than in the way they handled the one analytic tool that hostile historiography has singled out for criticism, the balance-of-trade concept.

[(c) *The Balance-of-Trade Concept as an Analytic Tool.*] The first thing to observe about this concept is that it is in fact an analytic tool. The balance of trade is not a concrete thing like a price or a load of merchandise. It does not obtrude itself upon untrained eyes. A definite analytic effort is required to visualize it and to perceive its relation to other economic phenomena, however insignificant that effort may be. The history of theoretical physics shows that achievement of this kind is difficult and takes much more time than we should expect: ideas have for centuries been within what to us seems easy reach, and they have even been uttered in some sterile form from time to time without really coming fully within anyone's grasp. If we reflect upon this difficulty we shall cease to make light of that particular achievement.

Nor does the concept lack importance. The balance of *payments* in the sense defined in the footnote below [6] is an important datum in the diagnosis

[6] I take it that the kind of statement that we refer to by this term (Balance of Payments) is familiar to the reader and that he properly distinguishes it from the balance of indebtedness. But there is one point about it on which it may not be superflous to comment. The statement might be drawn up according to ordinary bookkeeping principles. In this case, there is for every item that enters the balance sheet another item that will balance it as a matter of bookkeeping technique. Such a balance would always 'balance,' not only necessarily, but tautologically. But even if we simply confront the sum total of credit items with the sum total of debit items, the two totals must eventually be equated somehow, if necessary, by carrying forward, or defaulting on, the difference. In this sense the balancing is still necessary though it is no longer tautological. There is, however, a third sense in which credit and debit need not balance in either of these two meanings, but are made to balance by forces which their failure to do so will automatically set into motion—so that (but in a third sense) we may still say that they will balance 'necessarily.' The households and firms of countries A and B, which for simplicity's sake are now both assumed to be on a perfectly free gold standard and to have no other dealings except sales and purchases of commodities, may send out orders to each other that will at any given point of time sum up to different amounts. But as these orders are being carried out and paid for, any such difference will, in the absence of credit arrangements, have to be settled in

of the economic condition of a country and an important factor in its business processes. In the seventeenth and eighteenth centuries the *balance of trade* in commodities and services may well have been the operative part of the *balance of payments* and, thus, have had all the importance that may be attributed to the latter. The trouble with it is that, as a tool of general economic analysis, it does not work by itself: if we know nothing except the figures of exports and imports (always including figures for services), we cannot make any inferences from them. Thus, an 'unfavorable' balance may be the symptom of increasing wealth but also of a process of impoverishment; a 'favorable' one may mean prosperity and employment, but just as well the reverse. It is only in connection with other data that the balance of trade acquires both its symptomatic and its causal meaning. This should perhaps be qualified by the admission that, even taken by itself, the net of the balance of current debits and credits—which sometimes *may* be approximately indicated by the current net of the balance of trade—is an important factor in the monetary processes of a country, hence an important factor in the decisions of monetary authorities. But broadly speaking, reasoning as well as action that turns on nothing or next to nothing but the balance of trade cannot be correct except by accident. These considerations will help materially in appraising both the contributions and the errors of the 'mercantilist' writers. Let us keep in mind, however, that now we are not concerned with a plank in an economic platform but with the handling of an analytic tool.

[(d) *Serra, Malynes, Misselden, Mun.*] This analytic tool has a long prehistory into which we need not go.[7] Credit for having had a clear conception

---

specie, and this flow of monetary metal will (or would eventually, if there are absolutely no hitches, if prices are flexible, etc.) so act upon prices and incomes (to neglect everything else)—and these variations in prices and incomes will in turn so affect the orders, hence the commodity flows—as to bring about 'automatically' equality of debit and credit items and a distribution of the gold that will be adequate to support the prices resulting from the process. This primitive schema represents what we mean by the Automatic Mechanism, which was, as we have seen, described—partly at least—by Malynes and which will presently be used as one of the guiding stars in our travel through part of the 'mercantilist' literature. If we have sufficient confidence in its strength—miraculous though such confidence would be in people who have been witnesses to the world depression—we may be so little impressed with the danger of its failure to function as to hold that it will always insure that equality. This may then be expressed by saying (rather misleadingly) that balances of payment will 'necessarily' balance if we include the balancing gold flow. Note, for the time being, that in the text the term balance of payments should be understood to exclude this (or any other) balancing item, so that there is no *need* for debits and credits to balance.

[7] An instance of its use at the middle of the sixteenth century has been given in footnote 1, at the beginning of this section. Other instances could be mentioned even from much earlier times. Thus in 1381 an official of the name of Richard Aylesbury expressed the opinion that no money would flow out of England if not more 'strange merchandise' were allowed to enter England 'than to the value of the denizen merchandise which passes out of the realm.' He also supported the policy of prohibiting exportation of coin (and importation of debased foreign coin) and, displaying aware-

of it and for having been the first to use it fully and, in substance, correctly belongs to Antonio Serra.[8] It is not only that he paid due attention to the invisible items, in which he seems to have anticipated all writers of his own century; or that he fully realized the nature of exchange-control policies; or, as it is usual to put it, that he 'refuted the bullionist doctrine of the exchanges'; or that he expounded (as had Laffemas before him) the views about the prohibition of gold and silver exports which in England were to become general, at least among the writers of first rank,[9] as the century drew to its close; or that he introduced the quantity-theory element into the discussion concerning the proposal to stop the outflow of gold and silver by devaluation—although these were important contributions. Nor should we allow ourselves to be too much impressed by the fact that, though not the first to see the relation between gold and silver movements and the balance of trade (or payments), he was the first to elaborate it. For though this does carry analysis one step further, in itself it does not mean more than a rather obvious observation, which moreover is just as likely to suggest wrong or at least inadequate inferences as it is to suggest true ones. The really important point is not that he explained the outflow of gold and silver from the Neapolitan Kingdom by the state of its balance of trade, but that he did not stop at this but went on to explain both the outflow and the balance of trade by the economic conditions of the country. Essentially, the whole treatise is about the factors on which depends the abundance of *commodities*—natural resources, the quality of the people, the development of industry and trade, the efficiency of the government—the implication being that if the economic process as a whole functions properly, the balance of trade will take care of itself and not require any specific. In this schema monetary phenomena are consequences rather than causes, and symptomatic rather than important in

---

ness of the importance of the invisible items of the balance of payments, further suggested that the payments to Rome should be effected in kind rather than in money—the same suggestion that was to some extent adopted in the case of German reparation payments in and after 1919. All this is (contrary to M. Beer's opinion in *Early British Economics*) perfectly in keeping with sixteenth-century views. Source of quotation: 'Opinions of Officers of the Mint on the State of English Money' in Bland, Brown, and Tawney, *English Economic History, Select Documents*, pp. 220 et seq., a most helpful compilation, perusal of which cannot be recommended too strongly.

[8] *Breve trattato delle cause che possono far abbondare li regni d'oro e argento dove non sono miniere, con applicazione al regno di Napoli* (1613). The title, as will be seen from my comments, is somewhat misleading and the exposition of what I conceive to be his fundamental idea is somewhat impaired by this concentration on the narrow polemical purpose of refuting De Santis' exchange-control views (see above, sec. 3, n. 7) in which, if we judge him from the standpoint of present-day views, he also went too far. (On Serra, see above ch. 3, sec. 5.)

[9] For the benefit of some historians of economics, it may be well to add that Serra was not a director of the East India Company, but a poor devil who wrote his tract in a Neapolitan prison.

themselves.[10] And the author (in his discussion of the case of Venice, ch. x, Part 1) brushes against, though he does not explicitly state, the proposition that a prosperous country—that is to say, a country whose economic process is not disintegrating—can have all the gold and silver money it may require.[11] From this, however, the way should not have been very far to Hume.

There are two reasons why this has never been adequately recognized. First, Serra stopped short of pointed formulation, and there were no immediate successors to develop his analysis. Second, the vision of critics, whether friendly or hostile, has been so blurred by slogans about 'mercantilism' that they hardly bothered to ask what precise role a man's protectionism played in his schema of thought and in what sense the balance of trade seemed important to him —though, from the standpoint of economic analysis, these questions are much more interesting than is the question how far removed that man may have been from free trade.

In England, a controversy not dissimilar to that between De Santis and Serra arose between Malynes and Misselden. We have already glanced at it from the side of Malynes. To a lesser extent, Edward Misselden (fl. 1608-54) [12] is entitled to credit on a par with Serra. He did not fail to state the proposition that exportation or importation of bullion is in the last analysis to be explained by the 'plenty or scarcity of commodities' and therefore cannot be accused of having missed the point entirely.[13] Nor is it as easy as generations of critics believed it to be to convict him of erroneous reasoning if, on the

[10] The first sentences of the first chapter of Part 1 of Serra's *Breve trattato* cannot be adduced against this statement, because they are amply accounted for by the occasion and by the wish of the author to be read by the captain general, who was just then worrying about the state of the exchanges and the drain of money. I do not think that anyone who considers the book as a whole will wish to disagree.

[11] It is one of the weaknesses of 'mercantilist' literature that it never—not even at its peaks, such as Petty—got beyond the idea of a required amount of money, any excess or deficit being in the nature of a disadvantage. Serra did not even get as far as that, but merely speaks of 'abundance.'

[12] At first, that controversy was in the nature of a family quarrel between exponents of different monetary policies, for in his first publication, *Free Trade: or the Meanes to Make Trade Florish* (1622), Misselden expounded views not entirely different from those of De Santis (the meaning of Free Trade, as pointed out before, had little to do with the meaning the term acquired in the eighteenth century). Misselden meant no more than the removal of certain monopolistic restrictions, especially by the great companies, including the Merchants Adventurers to which at that time he belonged himself. But he developed, and in 1623, published his attack upon Malynes, in which he not only used the term balance of trade but placed the concept in the center of his argument: *The Circle of Commerce; or the Ballance of Trade* . . . 1623. On Misselden, see particularly E. A. J. Johnson, *Predecessors of Adam Smith* (1937).

[13] The reader will however recall what has been said above on behalf of Malynes. To that extent, commendation of Misselden must be tempered, as it must in Serra's case, by taking account of the fact that he entirely overlooked the elements of truth in his opponents' argument.

one hand, we fully allow for inadequacies of exposition and, on the other hand, for whatever may be said in his favor from the point of view of recent theories. Unquestionably, however, he came much nearer than did Serra to those definite errors which stand out so glaringly in Mun's book,[14] perhaps only because there the argument is more fully developed.

Mun's book is generally looked upon as the classic of English 'mercantilism.' This prominence is unfortunate, but it is not wholly unmerited. In fact we already have had to mention it several times. A wide variety of questions—from fishing to the gold and silver embargo—are dealt with sensibly (though without particular depth or originality) in its spacious frame, the connecting thread being what in Professor Johnson's felicitous phrase we may call concern for 'generating productive power.'[15] This aspect is, however, covered by previous comments, particularly on the protectionist argument. It is only in order to avoid misunderstanding that I wish to emphasize once more that the economics behind Mun's arguments on practical questions was, if primitive, yet substantially sound—which statement, to risk another repetition, has nothing to do with approval or disapproval of imperialist goals or any other 'ultimate standpoints.'[16] Those arguments are in fact very little affected by the analytic errors to be mentioned. Even the particular emphasis placed upon the export surplus is, as we know, in itself not incapable of defense. Finally, not only are the erroneous propositions removable, but they are in most cases, and especially in Mun's, associated with others that qualify and sometimes even contradict them. The two most important instances in his case are his recognition of the necessity of occasional gold and silver exports,[17] and his

[14] Sir Thomas Mun (1571-1641) was a prominent businessman—as modern critics never fail to emphasize, he was, among other things, a member of the committee of the East India Company—who by virtue of his ability and force of character acquired considerable authority that reached far beyond the business community. If in this book we were interested in doctrines and policies for their own sake, we should have to rank him very high. Let us note his *Discourse of Trade from England unto the East Indies* . . . (1621; an important contribution to the controversies about the East India Company, reprinted by the Facsimile Text Society, 1930) and the book mentioned in the text: *England's Treasure by Forraign Trade: Or, The Ballance of our Forraign Trade is the Rule of our Treasure*, an imperfectly systematized collection of papers written presumably about 1630, and posthumously published by his son, John Mun, in 1664. There were several reprints, one in Ashley's *Economic Classics* (1895).

[15] E. A. J. Johnson, *Some Origins of the Modern Economic World* (1936), p. 98.

[16] It should perhaps be explained why, in apparent contradiction to my programmatic explanations in the First Part, I constantly refer to policies and recommendations. I shall do so less and less as we go on. But in the case of the 'mercantilist' writers recommendations and 'practical' arguments offer the only possibility of probing into an embryonic fund of theoretical knowledge.

[17] This, of course, critics found it easy to dispose of by pointing out that all he thought of was to defend silver exportation by the East India Company. It is more to the point, however, that his argument about this exportation—based as it is on re-exportation of imports from India and other factors which would tend to reverse the flow, possibly more than reverse it—does not amount to more than a qualification

recognition—which seems to have escaped some critics—of the fact that in the end of ends a policy aiming at persistent export surpluses must defeat itself through the rise in domestic prices it would eventually produce.[18]

The errors in question all center in a single proposition, which may, however, be stated on three different levels: (1) that the export surplus or deficit *measures* the advantage or disadvantage a nation reaps or suffers from its international trade; (2) that the export surplus or deficit is what the advantage or disadvantage from international trade *consists in;* (3) that the export surplus or deficit *is the only* source of gain or loss for a nation as a whole.

All three statements have been made. None of them is defensible. The idea that a certain quantity measures another quantity that cannot be measured directly is not one that occurs readily to the untutored mind. Therefore, we shall not expect to find explicit instances of proposition (1) and I have inserted that statement only because it affords a mitigating interpretation, justifiable in some cases of what really reads like (2). Fortrey and Coke[19] may,

that leaves the principle intact. We also know that the analytic progress involved was anticipated by Laffemas and Serra.

18 Thus, Mun used the quantity theory fully as much as was requisite for his purpose. In the face of this and of what I said before in connection with Malynes' work, nothing more need be said about the indictment (which does hold for the Spanish *politicos* of the first half of the seventeenth century) that the English 'mercantilist' writers as a group, Bodin notwithstanding, had not yet discovered that theory. It is also interesting to note that, unlike some of the nineteenth-century economists who felt so superior to them, the 'mercantilists' were aware of the importance of that time interval during which increase in liquid means would assert its stimulating influence on business activity without as yet raising prices. An explicit statement about this may be found in a tract which it is not possible to commend in any other respect: J. Hodges, *Present State of England* (1697), *passim.*

19 Samuel Fortrey, a thoroughly insignificant writer, attracted much attention by his pamphlet: *England's Interest and Improvement* . . . (1663), in which he published (quite spurious) figures about England's trade with France according to which England had exported to France to the extent of £1,000,000 and imported to the extent of £2,600,000. This he called a 'loss' to England of £1,600,000, which we may, I think, take as a fair example of (1)—provided that any clear idea can be attributed to that author. But even a writer of very different caliber, who will be mentioned again, Roger Coke (the works most important for us are *A Discourse of Trade* . . . 1670, and *England's Improvements* . . . 1675), allowed himself, in an unguarded moment and scared by Fortrey's figures, to make the same statement, viz., that 'where consumption of things imported, does exceed in value the things exported, the loss will be as the excess is.' Of course, the error in question must not be assumed in every instance of the occurrence of the words 'loss' and 'gain.' For, first, they may have no other meaning than they have when we say, e.g., that the Bank of England 'suffered a loss of gold.' This is especially likely to be the case where gain and loss expressly refer to 'treasure,' which term often, though not always, means only gold and silver. Second, it should not be forgotten that, though our proposition is not valid in general, there are particular cases and meanings in which it is valid or in which the error involved is not very serious. In this connection it is especially important to bear in mind that the 'mercantilist' writers, more than their successors, actually did have particular situations in mind.

however, be quoted by way of illustration. The second statement—which of course we must not suspect behind every proposition about the advantages, real or fancied, of an export surplus—is not very easy to find in writers who count. Both Misselden and Mun seem to be among them, however—perhaps even Petty if we choose to take at face value a certain most infelicitous passage. With the small fry, such utterances as that all exports are gain, all imports are loss, are almost as common as they were with protectionist United States senators in the nineteenth century and even later. The third statement is the worst. Since no fair-minded person will lightly attribute such nonsense to any writer who displays any traces at all of ability to reason, and since inadequate formulation may easily make it indistinguishable from the harmless assertion that expansion of her foreign trade was, for seventeenth-century England, an important avenue to greatness (purely rhetorical overstatement was much more usual in the times of Euphuism, Marinism, and Gongorism than it is today), it would be tempting to deny the existence of convincing cases. The reason why this is not possible does not so much lie in the fact that some instances would prove rather refractory to benevolent interpretation, but rather in the fact that such attempts at analysis as were undertaken would, if they had been successful, have established the third statement along with the two others.

The most common of these attempts proceeded by way of analogy. Its most influential, though not its first, sponsor was Mun (and it was repeated by Cary). If an individual adds part of his annual income to the ready money in his chest—provided, so we must add, the others do not do the same thing—he will grow richer every year; if a nation realizes an export surplus and draws it in gold and silver, it is doing the same thing; *ergo* the nation will be enriched by the exact amount of this surplus. Let us remove some of the most obviously objectionable features of this piece of reasoning by choosing a somewhat different analogy. Suppose we look upon a nation as a business concern. A private firm may be said to grow richer or poorer every year by the amount of the profit or loss item of its balance sheet. Suppose further that the balance of payments is for the nation what the ordinary balance sheet is for the individual firm, so that its net corresponds to the latter's profit-and-loss item. If the balance of payments contains nothing except the elements that make up the balance of trade, the nation would grow richer or poorer every year by the amount of its export or import surplus. Two things are clear: first, that there is no sense whatever in this argument; second that, if it be taken seriously, then all three of our statements would follow and not only the first two.[20]

[20] Attention should be called to the fact, overlooked by at least one critic, that the phrase 'a nation is not enriched by what is purchased for consumption at home' does not necessarily involve statement (3). For it *may* mean no more than this: if A buys from his connational B some goods for his own consumption, then, in a central bookkeeping agency of the nation, A would be debited and B would be credited with equal amounts; if however B sells the goods to the foreigner C, then B would still be credited but there is no compensating debit—a triviality which may invite, but does not in itself spell, error.

Even if not explicitly stated, some such confusion must be suspected whenever the favorable-balance element is stressed in the absence of a special motivation, such as the argument about monetary stimulation of the business process. There is, however, another line of reasoning that may lead up to the first two statements and even entangle an author in the third. Several authors of high rank, such as Coke and Petty,[21] adopted it, but it was most clearly developed by Locke.[22] If we define national advantage to mean increase of the relative share of a nation in the world's real wealth, and if we suppose that all countries use an unfettered silver standard, the total amount of silver in existence being approximately constant, then the nation's relative share in the world's wealth will tend to be proportional to, or represented by, its relative share in the existing stock of silver. 'Riches do not consist in having more Gold and Silver, but in having more in proportion than the rest of the World,' which is why a certain quantity of silver, if acquired by means of a favorable balance of trade, increases the riches of a nation more than would the same quantity if newly mined. Disregarding the latter possibility, we may even say that a favorable balance of trade is the only means of increasing that share in the world's wealth or, for any nation, the only possible source of additional 'relative wealth,' a proposition that is not worse than many that are taught today. It is strikingly illustrative of the ways of the human mind that Locke of all men should have committed himself to this argument. That Colbert[23] should have been addicted to it is much less surprising.

[(e) *Three Erroneous Propositions*.] Before we go on, it is necessary to touch briefly upon three points of minor importance. First, if the argument just presented were acceptable, it would provide a rationalization for the idea that one nation's gain is another nation's loss. In fact this idea would simply follow from it. However, much as we stand in need of such a rationalization of an idea that was current at that time and has never been absent at any time, we are under no compulsion to assume that it was rationalized in that way. Bearing in mind the primitivity of all the economic reasoning of the period, we may perhaps more plausibly connect that idea with its counterpart in the realm of individual economics, the idea that in every exchange one man's gain is another man's loss. From Aristotle on, philosophers refined upon it by defining more precisely what the gain was that thus came under a ban, namely, the surplus above the just price. But however it was defined, the people always felt, as they do now, that the kind of gain that made the merchant rich resulted from their being somehow cheated or exploited. In the writings of the Consultant Administrators of all types, symptoms abound both that they more or less subscribed to that view and that gradually they were getting rid of it. Few subscribed as explicitly as did Montchrétien, who states it as an

[21] I do not think, however, that Petty (*Verbum Sapienti*, ch. x) meant anything to which very strong objection need be taken.

[22] *Some Considerations* . . . (1692), see above, ch. 6, sec. 2. He also uses the analogy just discussed.

[23] See Heckscher, op. cit. vol. II, p. 27.

axiom (Heckscher, op. cit. vol. II, p. 26); few got over it as completely as did Barbon: the bulk of the literature is between these extremes. This slow disintegration of one of the oldest elements of popular economic thought is one of the most important points to remember concerning the history of analysis in the seventeenth century.

Now, if we take hold, on the one hand, of the principle that 'one man's gain is another man's loss' and, on the other, of the habit of the period of reasoning on national trading by analogy with individual trading, we arrive immediately at another faulty rationalization of the belief that one nation's gain must be another nation's loss.

Second, from this follows immediately a possible explanation of another erroneous proposition that may be suspected behind many versions of the balance-of-trade argument. If we identify the gain that is somebody else's loss with profit in the businessman's sense, then all such gains will cancel out in a combined balance sheet of all firms and households in the country, *except* the gains that are made in foreign trade. These will not cancel out, because foreigners' losses do not count. Making the further wild assumption that these gains add up to the export surplus, we may cap a pyramid of nonsense by asserting that the latter represents the sum total of net—that is, uncompensated—private profits in a nation.

But I am not prepared to charge this to the account of any of those 'mercantilist' writers who were on a level sufficiently high to warrant the discussion of their views, even if some of them did come dangerously near to saying or implying it. My reason is that the Consultant Administrators did not primarily write—whatever they may have thought—about individual profits. Even when they used terms such as 'profits' from international trade, they meant national advantage. And this national advantage was not identified with the profit interest. Nor was it held that individual action on the profit motive, necessarily or normally, promotes the social or national interest. This laissez-faire proposition was at first quite foreign to their scheme of thought. They used the principle that business behavior turns upon profit—for instance, their recommendations mostly aim at influencing profit expectations—but they not only admitted the possibility of clashes with the public interest, they even considered clashes to be normal and concordance to be exceptional. This is precisely why most of them took the necessity of government regulation for granted and only discussed the aims and methods of it. It is true that they slowly worked their way toward a different point of view—as we shall see presently, one of their achievements consists in this. But fundamentally they were planners, planning precisely in order to avoid what they conceived to be the antinationalist effects of unregulated enterprise, irrespective of how profitable such enterprise might be to individuals: when they recommended that the importation of currants via Venice should be stopped, they did not bother about the profits that might be destroyed by so doing. Under these circumstances it is hardly necessary to insist on fastening upon them the responsibility for that particular analytic miscarriage.

Third, nothing has been said so far about the famous 'confusion of wealth (or riches) with money.' None of the errors of analysis that have been mentioned amount to, or imply, any such confusion. Moreover there is, so far as I know, no proposition to be found in 'mercantilist' writers that cannot be explained—however erroneous it may be—without assuming that they thought that wealth was the same thing as money or bullion or 'treasure,' or that they confused money with what money can buy. We have thus little reason to waste space on a completely uninteresting question. But readers may feel entitled to a comment on what has become a standard topic in the historiography of economics ever since Adam Smith, by his unintelligent criticism of the 'commercial or mercantile system,' [24] set the bad example.

As early as 1549, an anonymous author,[25] setting out to 'declare the means and polices howe to reduce this Realme to a prosperus and floreshing state,' finds it necessary to define in what this flourishing state consists. In his judgment, it consists 'cheifly in being stronge against thinvasion of eneymies [that this comes first is interesting to us from another standpoint, J. A. S.], not molested with cyvile warres, *the people being wealthie* [author's italics] and not oppressid with famyn nor penury of victualles,' the last words being clearly intended to illustrate the 'wealthie.' Yet he wants an export surplus in order to get an import of bullion. Of seventeenth-century authors, Serra, Misselden, Mun ('riches consisteth in the possession of those things which are needful for a civil life'), Child ('many tools or materials'), Cary, Coke, Yarranton, and of course, Barbon, Davenant, and Petty, not to mention the advocates of paper money and of bank schemes, can all be cited in support of the thesis that, whatever their shortcomings may have been and however much they may have overstressed the importance of an increase in 'treasure,' wealth was defined —explicitly or by implication—much as we define it ourselves. A *locus classicus* occurs in a tract signed by Papillon: [26] 'It is true that usually the measure of

[24] *Wealth of Nations*, Book IV, ch. 1. Adam Smith's criticism is open to a still more serious indictment. Obviously conscious of the fact that this particular charge cannot be made good, he does not strictly speaking make it, but he insinuates it in such a way that his readers cannot help getting the impression, which has in fact become very general. Excluding writers, German writers especially, who might be called either postmercantilists or neomercantilists, we may date the beginning of the reaction to it by W. Cunningham's article, 'Adam Smith und die Mercantilisten,' *Zeitschrift für die gesamte Staatswissenschaft* (1884).

[25] We have met him before. 'Polices to Reduce . . . ,' *Tudor Economic Documents*, vol. III, p. 313.

[26] Thomas Papillon, *The East-India Trade a Most Profitable Trade to This Kingdom* (1677), quoted from Heckscher, op. cit. II, p. 191. I have not read the book. Professor Viner (op. cit. pp. 17-18) offers a list of quotations to establish his contention that confusion actually existed 'between quantity of money, on the one hand, and degree of wealth, riches, prosperity, gain, profit, poverty, loss, on the other.' In justice both to the writers whom he quoted and to Professor Viner himself, it must be pointed out that he aims at a wider target. Nevertheless it is significant that, as the reader can easily satisfy himself, not a single one of the quotations establishes confusion (or identification) of wealth with money or bullion, though some of them *suggest* the presence of other errors such as we have embodied in our three statements.

Stock or Riches is accounted by Money, but that is rather in imagination than in reality: A man is said to be worth Ten thousand pounds, when possibly he hath not One hundred pounds in ready Money; but his Estate, if he be a Farmer, consists in Land, Corn, or Cattle, and Husbandry Implements . . .'

Yet turns of phrase like Wealth is Money do occur frequently.[27] Sometimes they can be easily disposed of as *façons de parler*. Why, Milles even says that 'Though money were the beames and exchange the very light, yet bullion is the sonne' (quoted by Seligman in his article, 'Bullionists'). Shall we infer that he thought bullion and the sun were the same thing? In other cases, it may be necessary to remember that, while we are dealing with pieces of analysis or attempts at analysis, we are dealing with primitive analysis, the methods of which differ but little from, and on the lower levels readily shade off into, those of the popular mind that still harbored vestiges of the cult of hoards of gold and silver, though the British navy had already ousted the protecting dragon from the place he used to hold. But this is all.

[5. Analytic Progress from the Last Quarter of the Seventeenth Century: Josiah Child to Adam Smith]

Let us return to the main road which, as we already know, rose sharply in the second half, especially the last quarter, of the seventeenth century. Bearing in mind what has been said before about other aspects of the analytic work of those decades, we shall now add what remains to be said about the specifically 'mercantilist' aspect. The work that remains to be noticed under this heading is much more important than that of the preceding decades and consisted largely in a critical revision of the latter—a revision which constitutes the main analytic effort of the mercantilist writers. It seems to me that credit for having given the lead must go to Child.[1] Of other names it will suffice to

[27] The reader who wishes for instances can find a little collection in Heckscher, op. cit. II, pp. 186 et seq., which even includes Bodin. Of particular interest is his discussion of *Britannia Languens* (1680), quoted before, because the case of its author differs from the usual case in which such turns of phrase appear occasionally and which we can leave out without changing anything in the argument. He insists again and again that wealth is *not* goods but only treasure and that poverty is nothing but lack of treasure. Even in the face of this, however, it is necessary to insist (a) that his arguments, or some of them, make sense independently of it; (b) that the book is a poor performance not up to the standard of Mun's or Child's; (c) that, though I defer to Professor Heckscher's authority, my own experience of the literature would not justify me in considering it as 'entirely typical' (Professor Heckscher qualifies this, it is true, by adding: 'of a large part of mercantilist literature' and therefore *may* mean what I should not deny); (d) that allowance must be made for the tendency of prevailing schemes of thought to produce freaks—for which thesis the economic literature of the last ten years provides ample verification.

[1] Sir Josiah Child (1630-99) was no systematic writer. His contributions are so scattered over a great many topics that it is easy to miss their combined import. In fact, it has been missed. The additional misfortune of having been a prominent businessman and very rich seems to have sealed his fate as an economist. More than anyone

mention Barbon, Cary, Coke, Davenant, Petty, Pollexfen,[2] Yarranton, and one which I expect some readers will be shocked to find in this list—North, the free trader! [3] The main points to note are these.

First, Child—and others about the same time but mainly after him (chief instance, Pollexfen)—drew the consequence of his theory of money, that money, being a commodity like 'wine, oil, tobacco, cloth or stuff' may often be exported as much to the national advantage as any other commodity.[4] This, if properly developed, knocks the bottom out of any position that attaches primary importance to the balance of trade per se. Child did not however proceed to frontal attack, which was, so far as I know, left to Barbon. But he made it inevitable. Similarly, he led up to the two corollaries of his proposition, but failed to state them. The one, that if exportation of gold and silver is nothing to worry about, their importation (the increase in the supply of money) is nothing to exult about, was also developed by Barbon. The other, that the importation of bullion does not add any more to the wealth of a nation than does the importation of raw materials, or even less (observe, however, that this is not in every sense above question), was developed, though somewhat *post festum* (1696) by Cary. The process of analysis that these instances illustrate also did away with the errors discussed before. This may be said to have been accomplished by the end of the seventeenth century. It is true that they were shaken off rather than explicitly renounced, which accounts for the fact that turns of phrase suggestive of them continue to occur even with such

else he has been voted 'a special pleader' whose views may be interesting as 'evidence of contemporary business life and opinion,' but have no place in a history of scientific economics. This appraisal may be found in a most typical form in the article 'Child,' in the *Encyclopaedia of the Social Sciences*. The author, Henry Higgs, should really have known better.

[2] John Pollexfen, *A Discourse of Trade, Coyn, and Paper Credit, and of Ways and Means to Gain and Retain Riches* (1697) and *England and East India Inconsistent in their Manufactures* (also 1697). The titles of the relevant publications of the others have all been given before.

[3] Sir Dudley North (1641-91), *Discourses upon Trade* (1691), ed. J. H. Hollander (1907). It is interesting to note how acutely he was conscious of the difference between results of analysis and 'ordinary and vulgar conceits, being meer Husk and Rubbish' (preface); but he was a merchant and, later on, a public servant—no professor.

[4] This must not be confused with the apparently similar argument of Mun's that has been mentioned before. Child's proposition not only went further, but it meant something entirely different. It was not, as it was in the case of Mun's, exclusively motivated by the possibility that such exportation would eventually result in still larger importation. On the other hand, we must guard against a possible misinterpretation: one might read into that passage an anticipation of the principle of gold movements that was sponsored by Ricardo—gold will flow if it is the relatively cheapest commodity. But Child does not envisage the element of commercial advantageousness of gold or silver exports, but only states that the national interest will not suffer if gold and silver are exported. (On Child's monetary theory, see above, ch. 6, sec. 2b and sec. 7a.)

writers as Cary, Davenant, Petty, Yarranton, and later ones, such as Harris, who in substance were quite free from those errors.[5] It is also true that, on what has been referred to as the lower levels, all this lived until it was replaced by 'liberal' slogans—which, on those levels, were of no better grain intellectually.[6]

[5] It is amusing to note that the 'mercantilist' writers became so alive to the dangers of overemphasis on money that they began themselves to use the slogan about the identification of wealth and money. Thus, in a pamphlet that has been ascribed to Davenant, Pollexfen was attacked on this ground, although in the *Discourse* he clearly defines wealth in terms of goods and although in *England and East India* he condemns the import trade of the company merely on the ground of the frivolous nature of those imports, which he does not believe were re-exported to a degree to justify Davenant's (and others') argument for that trade. This, whether good or bad economics, has nothing to do with that identification. The same Pollexfen was arraigned by Professor Viner (op. cit. p. 18) for having said that 'gold and silver is the only or most useful treasure of a nation.' But why should this mean more than that gold and silver are 'stores of value,' and best fitted for that role, a statement one can read in the majority of nineteenth-century textbooks on money? This interpretation is entirely adequate to take care of the meaning of his text: of course, as far as that store of value goes, only bullion can make up for loss of bullion.

Pollexfen, serving as he does as one of the standard instances for the views expounded in the text, should be cleared of what I conceive to be unjustified aspersions. We may refer to another point in which he was so unfortunate as to give umbrage to free-trade critics. He 'still' held that it is meaningful to balance trade with each individual country, a standpoint that, to the relief of those critics, Child and Barbon and even Mun had at last abandoned. But provided one does want to regulate and plan—the rationale of wishing to do so is another matter—Pollexfen's opinion is, as has been pointed out in our discussion of Malynes, perfectly sensible as is also his recommendation to set an upper limit to the export of money to India. There is hence no reason whatever to wonder at the survival of this or cognate ideas: anon., *Short Notes and Observations in Point of Trade* (1662) was, from the planner's standpoint, perfectly justified in denouncing the importation of vain and unnecessary commodities; and so was Ralph Maddison (*Englands Looking In and Out*, 1640) in holding that control should be extended to 'every particular trade.'

[6] By way of illustration, both of the statement made in the text and of the rationale of our method of appraising and 'placing' mercantilist (and also other) writers, let me give a late example of the occurrence of what most people will consider typically mercantilist errors. L. A. Muratori, in his *Della pubblica felicità* (1749), ch. XVI, lays it down as the principal maxim that ought to govern economic policy that as little money as possible be let out of the state (*fare, che esca dallo Stato il men Danaro, che si può*) and that as much of it as possible be imported (*e che ve ne s'introduca il più che si può*), a conclusion which was soon (1751) attacked by Galiani. See also A. Graziani, *Le Idee economiche degli scrittori emiliani e romagnoli* (1893). Now I do not try to palliate this by an 'understanding' interpretation. I should agree with every one of Professor Viner's crisp epithets if they were to apply only to cases like this. But I think it essential for a proper grasp of the history of economics to emphasize their low level (which of course is relative to dates). The case derives additional illustrative value from the fact that Muratori was a very eminent man in other fields. Even as an economic historian he stands high. But he did not know how to

[(a) *Concept of the Automatic Mechanism.*] Second, we have seen that the conception of the Automatic Mechanism—the mechanism which, if allowed to work and if conditions are not too much disturbed, may be held to guarantee in the long run an equilibrium relation between the money stocks, price levels, incomes, interest rates, et cetera of different nations [7]—was not entirely outside the range of vision of any of the 'mercantilist' writers one cares to quote: Serra saw much of it, Misselden and Mun, a little, Malynes, nearly the whole of it. The contributions that have just been discussed above, so one might think in retrospect, should have made the full-fledged theory of that mechanism an easy matter of co-ordinating and amplifying restatement. But—as the history of any science again shows: a particularly good instance is afforded by thermodynamics—such definitive formulation is surprisingly difficult to achieve and the first attempts at it are always likely to be failures. None of the authors mentioned did achieve it. North tried. He saw that there is such a mechanism as a result of which every country will draw to itself a 'determinate sum' of money that will just suffice to carry on its economic process (at, and after adjustment to, the appropriate level of prices, a qualification which, however, he does not add). But he went off the rails completely in his attempt to describe it. Locke was more fortunate. He even used the device later on adopted by Hume of trying to describe what will happen, if half of the money in existence in a country be suddenly removed, and realized that this will restrict imports and increase exports, and yet he does not draw the conclusion that to us seems obvious (or seemed so until twenty years ago). But in order to get things into the right historical perspective, it should be realized that this fortress, though it was not completely reduced before the middle of the eighteenth century, was eventually entered, not by means of a new attack from a different side or by a new method of attack, but simply by pressing on through the breach that the 'mercantilist' writers had made. This can be easily shown by a brief survey of subsequent developments, which will at the same time serve the purpose of carrying us not only to the *Wealth of Nations* but beyond it to the threshold of discussion raised by the suspension of specie payments (Bank Restriction, 1797).

The next substantive advance was made by Gervaise.[8] He added the propo-

wield the kind of analytic apparatus the evolution of which is the subject of this book, and hence he wrote commonplaces or nonsense when he touched subjects that cannot be successfully treated without it. And this nonsense was not typical of the works of those writers of his time who had command of such analytic apparatus as there was. It would only serve to blur the picture if his views on such subjects were allowed to figure in it.

[7] With regard to this mechanism, see the footnote on the balance of payments (above, sec. 4, n. 6).

[8] I have not mentioned Simon Clement, A *Discourse of the General Notions of Money, Trade, and Exchanges* . . . (1695), whose contribution has been strongly commended by Angell (op. cit. pp. 21 et seq.). But there was little merit in describing the specie-point mechanism that had been perfectly well understood more than a hundred years before. There was, however, merit in Clement's correct description of

sition, never before stated with unmistakable clearness, that an increase in 'credit' (say, banknotes) will increase income and consumption, hence decrease exports and increase imports, and thus produce, just as would an increase in the quantity of the monetary metals, an outflow of these metals that will eventually enforce credit restriction—an important contribution, particularly meritorious in its emphasis upon the 'income approach.' Of course this proposition implies full understanding of the fundamental mechanism we are talking about, since it merely develops a particular consequence of it. But Gervaise's actual account of the automatic mechanism, though superior to any that had been published before, is yet far from satisfactory. It would, however, be sufficient to insert a few passages from Malynes in order to make it so. Successive marksmen, however, came nearer and nearer to hitting the bull's-eye of the old target. Of those who did hit it, the most eminent were Cantillon and Hume.[9] The fact that Hume's essay aroused some opposition testifies to his

---

the sequence of events that devaluation will produce as long as domestic prices do not respond to it: bullion will flow, exports increase, imports decrease. He was not the first to see that, but his is the first compact statement, so far as I know, of the particular piece of mechanism, made with a full sense of its importance. The same claim may perhaps be made for the book as a whole, and if we add it to the contribution of the authors under discussion, it becomes still clearer that *all* the elements for what was to become a 'classical' theory were worked out before 1700.

Isaac Gervaise, *The System or Theory of the Trade of the World. Treating of the Different Kinds of Value. Of the Ballances of Trade. Of Exchange. Of Manufactures. Of Companies. And Shewing the Pernicious Consequences of Credit, and that it Destroys the Purpose of National Trade* (1720). This remarkable little book, the merit of which is only slightly impaired by slips and clumsinesses (for instance, Gervaise lets the precious metals be distributed among countries according to their population, but meets the obvious objection by a fairly satisfactory explanation), has I believe been discovered by the late Professor Foxwell, who called it 'one of the earliest formal systems of political economy, and stating one of the most forcible practical arguments for free trade.' It will be Professor Viner's merit, however, if henceforth these 34 pages take the place in the history of our science that belongs to them (see Viner, op. cit. pp. 79 et seq.).

I take the opportunity to call attention to Professor Viner's section on 'The Self-regulating Mechanism of Specie Distribution' (p. 74), which, the best part of an excellent work, is not only much richer in material than my exposition but also one of the most interesting essays ever written on the fascinating theme of *how a theory struggles into existence*. It is a pity that, in this section as well as in the other parts of his work, he failed to distinguish between progress in analysis and progress toward free-trade opinions, or to put it somewhat differently, between what an author understood of economic processes and what he thought of them. The same common confusion we shall presently encounter again when dealing with the general theory of international trade.

[9] R. Cantillon, *Essai sur la nature du commerce en général*, which, as has been mentioned before, was written (and circulated) about 1730 but did not appear in print until 1755. D. Hume, 'Of the Balance of Trade' in *Political Discourses* (1752), included in *Essays, Moral, Political and Literary* (ed. 1875, vol. I, pp. 330 et seq.). Comparison with other writers, who may also be said to have hit the bull's-eye, only serves

merit as do the further facts that he added several points which were new, as far as I know, and that, unlike some economists of the nineteenth century, he did not trust the automatic mechanism unconditionally, though he failed to emphasize the frictions and disturbances that may attend its working. Essentially, however, his achievement consisted in shaking off the dust of mistakes from pieces of the 'mercantilist' inheritance and in assembling these pieces into a neat and well-rounded theory.[10] And this is all. Nothing of major importance was added during the rest of the century. In the *Wealth of Nations,* Adam Smith did not advance beyond Hume but rather stayed below him. In fact it is not far from the truth to say that Hume's theory, including his overemphasis on price movements as the vehicle of adjustments, remained substantially unchallenged until the twenties of this century.

[J. A. S. left note: 'please leave rest of page' and added in pencil as a reminder the three names Melon, Dutot, Galiani.]

[(b) *Foundations of a General Theory of International Trade.*] A third point remains to be noticed about the work of our group of writers. Just as they paved the way toward the theory of that automatic mechanism of gold and silver movements, so they also paved the way toward the theory of the automatic mechanism of commodity movements. In other words, they pulled out of that prescientific stage in which the protectionist arguments had *no* theoretical basis, rather than a faulty one, and began to lay the foundations of the general theory of international trade that was to take shape in the last decades of the eighteenth and the first decades of the nineteenth centuries. Logically, though not historically, we may distinguish two steps in their advance.

The first step consisted in the qualification and elaboration of the primitive arguments. They perceived the fact that the immediate and visible advantages that protectionist measures aim at securing are never net advantages or, as we may also put it, that there is to every proposition about those advantages a

---

to make his merit stand out still more clearly. Two may be mentioned: Jacob Vanderlint, who preceded him (*Money Answers all Things,* 1734, p. 15 of the new ed. in J. H. Hollander's reprints) and Joseph Harris (*Essay upon Money and Coins,* I), who followed him, at least if we go by date of publication, 1757. That these two sound but certainly not first-flight men should have also 'done the trick' seems to strengthen the thesis of the text.

[10] No one who knows anything about the history of science in general will suspect me of a wish to underrate the importance of an achievement of this kind. Moreover, the performance may have been quite original 'subjectively' in the sense in which, e.g., Menger's was (see below, Part IV, ch. 5, sec. 1), all the forerunners notwithstanding. All major discoveries have to be repeated again and again. Finally, there is room for fair difference of opinion concerning the question how far the authors of the seventeenth century had really advanced. In any case, there is no justification for Professor Angell's statement that Hume 'at a single stroke wrecked the balance-of-trade theory' (op. cit. p. 26). This only amounts to repeating an old nineteenth-century error.

counterproposition about ulterior or invisible effects, many of which are in the nature of costs. Such complementary propositions are implied in Cary's argument about the importation of raw materials or Coke's argument about the importation of both raw materials and manufactured goods, or Coke's and Yarranton's argument on cheapness and plenty, or Yarranton's argument about the advantages that accrue to a nation from its neighbors' prosperity, or Barbon's argument—it occurs frequently, but it was not, I think, definitely set on its legs before Barbon—that regulations and restrictions always destroy some element of potential wealth. It is, or was, the common practice of critics to say that by introducing such arguments our authors contradicted or partially recanted their 'mercantilist' views, or that they became 'eclectics.' But whatever may be true from other standpoints, from ours those arguments and the qualifications they implied are simply the inevitable consequence of increasingly successful attempts to see more than one side of the case.

Similar conquests were made by continental writers of the same type. It will in particular not surprise us to learn that the Dutch were in the van of advance. The two outstanding examples are Graswinckel and Pieter de la Court.[11]

Thus, additional and less obvious aspects were gradually revealed, though in a wholly unsystematic manner. But among the disjointed pieces of economic reality that were being unearthed, there was one of sufficient power to coordinate all the others and to support the structure of a comprehensive theory of international trade or even trade in general. Child seems to have been the first to arrive (1668-70) at a clear idea of the explanatory value of the simple fact that commodities tend to seek the most advantageous market. To use the phrase of Davenant, who worked out the idea in the nineties, there are definite 'channels' which, under the stimulus of profit expectations, trade finds of itself; or, to put it still differently, the profit motive supplies a regulatory principle for 'unregulated' business activity, international and national, and produces results which we may like or not but which are determined and not chaotic. Propositions that imply this discovery or even expressly refer to that

[11] Dirck Graswinckel, *Placaetbook op het stuk van de Leeftocht* (Compilation of regulations concerning foodstuffs, 1651), the second part of which contains a critical analysis of the policies represented by the legislative material compiled in the first. Graswinckel's views on the harm done by prohibiting the exportation of grains, a practice which had become practically universal in the eighteenth century, were not new in 1651—we have encountered similar views in the *Discourse of the Common Weal,* and they cannot have been strikingly novel even then. But Graswinckel had a keener sense of the price mechanisms involved, especially of the function of forestalling. Pieter de la Court, *Interest van Holland . . .* (1662; 2nd ed. under the title: *Aanwysing der heilsame politike Gronden en Maximen van de Republike van Holland en West-Vriesland,* 1669; English trans., *Political Maxims . . .* falsely attributing the work to John de Witt, 1743; I know only the latter), presents mainly an argument for industrial freedom plus moderate duties—comparable and in some respects superior to Coke's of 1670 and 1675—the merit of which consists chiefly in its freedom from errors of reasoning. Both authors would have to be ranked very high in a history of economic thought or policy. Concerning their contributions to analysis, however, it is hardly possible to say more than this.

principle in particular cases occur in the sixteenth century and earlier. It was of course quite familiar to the scholastics. On the other hand, it was not fully developed until Léon Walras. But the mercantilist writers helped to place it in its key position in the theory of international trade.

Neither Child nor Davenant proceeded very far with it. Barbon, however, understood the mechanism sufficiently well to adumbrate the theory of equilibrium in international commodity trade, at least in the form of the proposition—stated without the necessary qualifications—that restrictions on imports will restrict exports to a corresponding amount. Much more than this I cannot find in any seventeenth-century author. In particular very little was made of the argument about territorial division of labor. In its most primitive form it cannot, of course, have ever been unknown to anyone. Armstrong and Hales in the sixteenth century based international trade on the fact that different nations, living under different conditions, produce different commodities, the superfluous parts of which may be exchanged with advantage to all parties concerned. Even North thought of international trade in quite the same spirit as the 'exchange of superfluities,' much as had Grotius (1625). Recognition of the much more interesting fact that this exchange will alter the economic organisms of the trading nations is, to be sure, implied in many practical suggestions, especially on the economic relations between England and Ireland and also in more general considerations of Davenant's (e.g., in his *Essay on the East-India Trade*, 1696), but nobody seems to have realized fully its significance as a starting point of analysis or to have had any inkling of the principle of comparative costs. North in particular did nothing but sum up, incompletely but effectively, the contribution of the 'mercantilist' writings to 1691.

But none of the others were thoroughgoing free traders. North alone was. And to interpreters of the history of economic analysis who were interested in nothing but free trade and knew of no canon of criticism except the distance that separates an author from free trade, this was of course the all-important fact. For them, there is, on the one side, the darkness of 'mercantilist' error and, on the other side, the eternal light of 'liberalism'; the light rose against the darkness and dispelled it so thoroughly that there was nothing left of it except the pious wonder of liberals how anyone could ever have been so benighted. Now this way of looking at the history of that time under the aspect of a sharp antithesis is totally wrong. And it is so essential for a proper understanding of the evolution of our science to grasp this that we must stay for a moment, even at the risk of some repetition, in order to clarify the nature of the confusion from which that view arose.

Even if we were studying the history of political doctrines, it would be necessary to point out that free-trade forces did not simply assemble outside of the mercantilist citadel and storm it—this is only true of the agrarian Tory component, which at that time was strongly antagonistic to big business and protection—but to a much greater extent formed up inside it. This should appeal to Marxists, for the decisive support of English free trade came after all from the same bourgeois class that had previously supported protection. But the advance of analysis that alone interests us here was not a matter of free trade and nascent liberalism at all. It could have occurred without anyone's being converted to free trade and liberalism, and free trade and liberalism could have gained their political victory without any help from that advance. Of this we can satisfy ourselves by the reflection that, for example, none of the old protectionist arguments listed above is affected by the later analysis that, in the hands of liberals, was made to serve free-trade policy. That analysis only established the existence of an 'automatic mechanism.' Knowledge of this mechanism is indeed not irrelevant for practice. When fully developed, it will prevent people from embracing protectionism or free trade for erroneous reasons. But beyond this it is not the master but the servant of the decisions we arrive at. It can serve—and rationalize—protectionist decisions just as well as free-trade decisions, but it does not in itself suffice to enforce either.

It is easy to apply this to the particular case of North. His allegiance to the Tory party had probably much more to do with his free-trade opinions than had his analysis. So far as the latter is concerned, in order to realize that he might have arrived at 'mercantilist' conclusions without any error or inconsistency, we need only suppose that he adopted one of those protectionist arguments or simply that he saw that an individual nation may gain by a well-devised system of protective duties. Therefore, we can discard his free-trade convictions as irrelevant in an appraisal *of his analytic apparatus*. But if we look at the latter, we have no difficulty in recognizing, first, its affinity to Barbon's [12] and, second, the fact that for the rest it is made up of quite old elements: wealth consists of whatever satisfies wants; money is a commodity of which there may be too much as well as too little; there is no sense in prohibiting its exportation or in taking any measures in order to secure an adequate supply of it; sumptuary laws blunt the spurs to trade; and so on. Clearly it is more correct to say that his analytic work grew out of that of the 'mercantilist' than to say that the relation was one of head-on clash.

[(c) *General Tendency toward Freer Trade.*] Let us again follow developments to the publication of the *Wealth of Nations*. It will be convenient to distinguish sharply the development of free-trade *policies* and free-trade *doctrines* from the development of *analysis* that was associated with both.

If due account be taken of all the obstacles that stood in the way, a general tendency toward freer trade is, I think, discernible. In England this tendency had already asserted itself in the growing opposition to the Navigation Acts and other 'mercantilist' measures, for example, in the Committee on Trade of 1668. Much more significant was the assault on the system that the Tories, under Harley and St. John, made in 1713: the eighth and ninth clauses of the peace treaty of Utrecht went a long way toward free trade with France. The

[12] The only point in which North definitely goes beyond Barbon is the proposition already mentioned on another occasion (see above, ch. 6, sec. 7) viz. that low interest is not the cause but the consequence of increasing wealth. Perhaps his rudimentary theory of gluts should also be mentioned. But it is so very primitive that there is no point in insisting on it.

assault ended in defeat. The Tories failed to carry those clauses and the subsequent Whig regime (Walpole first, the Pelhams after) kept strictly on the protectionist tack. The governments from Bute's to North's had other worries, but Shelburne and especially the younger Pitt led the way toward fewer and lower duties—the latter's crowning achievement being the commercial treaty with France, 1786. Further progress was checked for nearly thirty years by the revolutionary and Napoleonic wars, after which Pitt's policy was resumed in the twenties of the nineteenth century (by Huskisson). As we can see from this, France moved substantially in step. Only, there were two additional problems: even internal free trade was not achieved until the Revolution, though successive administrations tried to establish it, and the agrarian situation brought to the fore the particular question of free trade in grains, especially free exportation of grains.[13] In the German and Italian states we see at first glance nothing except further development of the 'mercantilist' system. But its rationalization led in many instances to a reduction of the burdens on interterritorial trade, especially in raw materials and semifinished products. In the Netherlands, as we should expect, a much more definite tendency toward freer trade already had asserted itself in the seventeenth century.

Doctrine moved more quickly. Free-trade conviction began to spread as part of a general laissez-faire code. With the bourgeois public, the operative impulse was simply surfeit with bureaucratic overadministration, which became so strong that even direct self-interest failed occasionally to counteract it. With the writers, or some of them, a similar impulse took on a philosophic flavor: free trade was increasingly considered as a part of the autonomy of the individual, which was held to imply a 'natural right' to trade as he pleased. This argument, which had been used already by Hugo Grotius and can be followed through the various natural-law groups, including the physiocrats and even the English utilitarians, is of course perfectly devoid of scientific meaning.[14] But it is relevant for us, first, because it was practically always associated with positive statements about economic effects, which do have scientific meaning and must be considered independently of it; second, because we have here (scientifically speaking) an illegitimate influence which blunted the edge of the critical faculty and imparted a bias to the economic reasoning of the best writers.

As we shall see more clearly later on, weaknesses that are not easy to explain in any other way may be traced to this influence, which understandably allied itself with the doctrine of the Invisible Hand, even in the cases of Quesnay and Smith. It counted of course still more in the popular opinions favoring laissez-faire that conquered coffeehouses and salons and foreshadowed the

[13] In England, an export bounty had been introduced in 1689 which naturally played a role in contemporaneous discussion. Otherwise English agrarian policy did not clash much with the general tendency described above until 1815.

[14] I hope I have made it quite clear before that my defense of the natural-law concept as an instrument of analysis does not cover its use as a means of deriving imperatives of the type of the *droits de l'homme*.

free-trade dogmatism of nineteenth-century liberals, which has not much more to do with scientific insight than had any of the popular dogmas of mercantilism.

Analytic progress, however, was slow. The controversies that arose about political issues, which happened to attract public attention, proved surprisingly sterile in this respect. The one raised by the French grain policy,[15] for instance, though it engaged the interest of some of the brightest stars of economic analysis, François Quesnay included, did not produce any results that we should have to notice.[16] Still there was some advance, though advance that led to new error as well as to new truth.

[15] We may notice another. When the freer-trade clauses of the peace treaty of Utrecht became known, the protectionists flew to arms. Among other things, a short-lived periodical was founded, *The British Merchant* (republ. 1743), the contributors to which throw an interesting light on the state of protectionist opinion. Among them, Joshua Gee should be mentioned in particular. He also wrote other protectionist tracts, e.g. *The Trade and Navigation of Great Britain considered* (1729), and his protectionism mainly turns upon the employment argument. On the whole, the performances of Gee and of the other contributors were by no means discreditable and, intended as they were for popular consumption on an issue of the day, may well be offered in refutation of the common belief that eighteenth-century 'mercantilism' was just a heap of nonsense. But as far as I can see, there was nothing in them to interest us here. The Tory counterblast was *Mercator, or Commerce Retrieved,* which appeared three times a week from May 1713 to July 1714 and was more of a one-man show. That man was Daniel Defoe of *Robinson Crusoe* fame, a most brilliant and prolific writer. But even his most ambitious efforts in our field remained in the sphere of economic journalism. In particular, his case for those clauses of the Treaty of Utrecht did not contribute anything new to economic analysis, though they rank high in the history of free- or freer-trade opinion. The reader who takes the trouble to peruse some of his writings (e.g. his *General History of Trade,* 1713) may well think that I am being unjust to him, especially if he recalls my comments upon Yarranton. But merit in such matters is to a large extent a matter of dates.

I take this opportunity to mention a somewhat later writer, Malachy Postlethwayt, but only to give an instance of the interesting phenomenon of the survival of names associated with substandard performance. The sole reason that I can see why this name should still be familiar to every student preparing for a course examination in the history of economic thought is a certain reputation he made in his own time by his *Universal Dictionary of Trade and Commerce* (1751-55), which was largely a compilation from unacknowledged sources. His other writings, mainly on the South African trade, are narrow and pedestrian, though not devoid of a certain crude common sense. His *Great Britain's true System* . . . (1757), which proves that he was intelligent enough to see the importance of Cantillon's book, contains a passage that interprets interest as a payment to hoarders by those who stand in need of it, i.e. as a payment necessary in order to overcome people's reluctance to part with cash. This reads like a clumsy version of Lord Keynes's own-rate theory of interest. To put him in a representative position as has recently been done by Fay . . . [note unfinished].

[16] That discussion has, however, some indirect importance for us owing to the general stimulus it gave to the interest in economic analysis, even though it did not add much to it directly. This is why it will have to be mentioned again. At the

[(d) *Benefits from Territorial Division of Labor.*] The one major accomplishment that I can see consisted in a technically superior formulation of the benefits from territorial division of labor that went some way toward anticipating the most important element in the nineteenth-century theory of international values. It stands to the credit of two English authors to whom we shall confine ourselves, though others could also be cited. An anonymous writer, in 1701, published a tract entitled *Considerations on the East-India*

---

moment let us note that all the authors to be mentioned were, in this matter, anticipated by Graswinckel, 1651 (if not in the *Discourse of the Common Weal*, 1549) and more immediately by Boisguillebert. After Boisguillebert there was a lull. It seems that the discussion was started afresh by Claude Dupin (*Oeconomiques*, 1745, of which the part entitled *Mémoire sur les bleds* was republ. separately in 1748), who presented once more the argument for internal free trade in grains. C. J. Herbert followed with his *Essai sur la police générale des grains* (1753). The fact that he still retained an export duty (of the English sliding-scale type) is immaterial here; it is more relevant that the argument about the adequacy of the *normal* supply that will be automatically forthcoming is fully developed by him, though without anything amounting to theoretical proof. Quesnay followed in an essay that will be mentioned later, and so did others, especially after the declaration of 1763 and the edict of 1764 which established free exportation. Galiani's spirited criticism of the dogmatic beliefs that were being developed (*Dialogues sur le commerce des blés*, 1770) is particularly worthy of notice.

These *Dialogues* grew out of the corresponding discussion among Italian economists, which began later and lasted longer and is really more interesting than the French one —though participants in the latter may claim priority as to such fundamental ideas as were involved—because the particular patterns of the situation in the Italian states, especially in the Neapolitan Kingdom, suggested both factual studies of considerable interest and arguments on particular points that were absent in the literature of the more fortunate nations. Since, however, it is impossible to go into these results, none of which, so far as I know, were of major importance to the development of the economic apparatus, it must suffice to mention some of the more significant of those performances which, as pointed out in the text, soon began to indicate the influence of the *Wealth of Nations*. For instance, Domenico Cantalupo published in 1783 a tract on free trade in grains (republ. in Custodi's *Scrittori classici Italiani*), in which he analyzed grain policy since 1400 and wielded the modest analytic apparatus at his command effectively and judiciously. Another Neapolitan noble, Domenico Caraccioli, followed him in 1785, interpreting his observations during a famine in Sicily (republ. in the same collection). Biffi Tolomei, in his *Confronto della ricchezza dei paesi che godono libertá nel commercio frumentario* (1795), attempted a factual proof of the importance of free trade in grains for the wealth of a country that is methodologically not without interest. There is appended to this book a memorandum entitled *Riflessioni sopra le sussistenze* by Saverio Scrofani, an out-and-out free trader of the physiocrat type whose other works need not concern us here. All these authors were, so far as the principle of free exportation of grains is concerned, anticipated by Verri, *Memorie storiche sull' economia pubblica dello stato di Milano* (written, 1768; publ. posthumously 1797) and *Riflessioni sulle leggi vincolanti, principalmente nel commercio de' grani* (written 1769, printed 1796). As an example of the success—for it was success and not eclectic weakness—with which conflicting, yet ineluctable, considerations were combined to fit Italian situations, I will mention Ferdinando Paoletti who, though

Trade,[17] in which he treated international trade as a method of acquiring goods with an amount of labor smaller than would be necessary to produce them at home. He does not seem to have been aware of the relation of this to the principle of comparative cost, but even so we have here a predecessor of Ricardo, though possibly a quite uninfluential one.

Now producing instead of a commodity A for domestic consumption, another commodity B, the export of which will fetch in commodity A at more advantageous terms, is obviously a matter of allocation of productive resources. From this angle the problem was considered by Gervaise, who inferred like Marshall[18] that tariffs, spelling as they do interference with the most advantageous allocation, must net a disadvantage to the nation as a whole, however great the immediately visible advantage to the protected industries might be. It has been mentioned that Gervaise's tract has but 34 pages and if, on the strength of this, we give him credit for what he might have had to say in ten times as many, then this proposition must indeed be looked upon as a considerable contribution to the apparatus of economic theory. It may, in fact, be said to give, in the guise of an application, one of the earliest glimpses of the theory of general equilibrium.

But there was hardly anything else. Hume, in spite of the many wise things he had to say in his essays on commerce, on the jealousy of trade, and on the balance of trade,[19] hardly carried this part of our subject any further. Neither did Adam Smith, who seems to have believed that under free trade all goods would be produced where their absolute costs in terms of labor are lowest, though he no doubt co-ordinated, rounded off, emphasized, and illustrated. In fact there is nothing of importance to report for the rest of the century in spite of the mounting flood of popular literature, most of which was of free-trade or freer-trade complexion and strongly influenced the *Wealth of Nations*.[20] And even that advance in the analysis of territorial specialization was

---

also one of the group of Italian physiocrats, inserted into his scheme of things agrarian protection (*Pensieri sopra l'agricoltura*, 1769; I only know the part included in the Custodi collection) and export bounties on goods not of prime necessity (*Veri mezzi di render felici le società*, 1772)—a sort of rudimentary Agricultural Adjustment Program that is not without interest to the theorist. It would be quite wrong to think that general principles of thought or action separate us from an author like Paoletti. What does separate us from him is exclusively our statistical and theoretical technique.

[17] [In J. R. McCulloch, ed., *A Select Collection of Early English Tracts on Commerce*, 1856.]

[18] *Official Papers*, published for the Royal Economic Society (1926), p. 391.

[19] Compare, however, the chapter on Hume in E. A. J. Johnson, *Predecessors of Adam Smith* (1937).

[20] The opinions on foreign trade of some important writers, such as the physiocrats or certain authors of comprehensive systems, may be of interest without involving 'contributions.' So far as necessary these will be mentioned or have been mentioned in connection with the works in which they occur. It is, however, convenient to supplement the exposition in the text in two ways. First, it is worth while to point out that in the twenty-five years or so preceding the publication of the *Wealth of Nations*, the majority of competent economists had reached what amounted to substantial agree-

not an unmixed gain. Both the anonymous author and Gervaise were much too ready to arrive at conclusions agreeable to their free-trade opinions [21] and

---

ment, the physiocrats and the writers directly influenced by them being the most important group in the minority. Representative of this *communis opinio* at its best were Josiah Tucker and Sir James Steuart in England, Justi and Sonnenfels in Germany, Beccaria, Genovesi, Verri, and Palmieri in Italy, and Forbonnais in France. Briefly, since they agreed in accepting public regulation as a normal, in fact inevitable, feature of the economic process, protectionism followed simply as a special case. But the mercantilist emphasis upon the balance of trade was reduced to small proportions, partly in consequence of valuable critical work (e.g. Verri in his *Meditazioni*, 1771, and Carli in his *Breve ragionamento sopra i bilanci economici delle nazioni*, 1770, which made short work of the idea that national wealth can be measured by exports). Moreover, protectionism in their hands became a much more delicate instrument than it had been, one of the consequences of which was the emphasis upon moderate rates, which modern eyes can hardly distinguish from no duties at all: Forbonnais suggested 15 per cent *ad valorem* and Justi 10 per cent. There was a tendency, however, widespread and inspired by very old practice, to believe in differentiating duties upon imports in inverse proportion to their distance from finished consumers' goods (Tucker, Verri)—a principle that proved a hardy growth and is often met with in the nineteenth century. Finally, though (as the uncritical acceptance of this rule by many writers is in itself sufficient to show) they frequently committed the kind of erroi that results from inadequate technique and places too much reliance on *prima facie* common sense, they rarely went wrong in matters of fundamental *analytic* principle.

Again, we shall readily understand why those critics who accepted the free-trade creed should have been unable to see anything in this except inconsistency or, at best, an uninteresting eclecticism characteristic of a transitional stage between old error and new truth. But from any other standpoint, there was no inconsistency (in the sense of logical incompatibility) in that quasi-common opinion, which not only reflected progress of analysis but also, as will be more generally re-emphasized in the text, might have been a better starting point for further research than was the narrow dogmatism of the free-trade doctrine that replaced it.

Second, by way of illustrating the preceding sentence, let us consider a single instance from a very large class of propositions. In his *Ways and Means* . . . (1757), Massie argues (as others had before him) that Port should be less heavily taxed than French wines, on grounds that suggest the following proposition. If a country, A, trades with countries B and C, and B's purchases of A's products are more elastic *with respect to the revenue that B draws from its sales to* A than are C's purchases of A's products with respect to C's revenue from C's sales to A, then it will benefit country A to treat B's products better than C's. Never mind how far this is true. True or false, this proposition is at least interesting, and its discussion is much more likely to enrich our understanding of international trade and our analytic apparatus in general than are any number of free-trade platitudes, however meritorious an attitude the latter may reveal and however conducive to wise, humane, peaceful, and so on policy they may be. Several additional instances could be adduced from Massie alone, who excelled in this eminently useful kind of analysis, also in fields other than that of international trade (see e.g. his *Observations on the New Cyder-Tax, so far as the same may affect our Woollen Manufacturies, Newfoundland Fisheries* . . . 1764).

[21] On Professor Viner's authority (op. cit. p. 92), it may be stated that besides those two and North, there were, before 1776, only two other English free traders (William

in so doing associated their achievement with errors of reasoning that were to become typical in the free-trade literature of the nineteenth century. Gervaise did not realize that his theorem about the allocation of resources cannot tell against any of those protectionist arguments, such as the infant-industry or the underemployment argument, which visualize conditions to which that theorem does not apply. By neglecting this Gervaise moved away from many valuable truths that had been unearthed by the mercantilist writers and, like North, adopted an attitude that, though permissible in pure theory, was bound to produce error when uncritically adhered to. The case of the anonymous author is still worse. He leans heavily on the argument that, *because* international trade consists of voluntary transactions, which therefore must necessarily be to the advantage of both contracting parties, nothing but advantage to the nation as a whole can result from it. North had also reasoned like this. And Adam Smith, after pointing *more suo* to an obvious fact, namely, that every individual will turn to that occupation for which he feels himself best adapted, goes on to declare that 'what is prudence in the conduct of every private family, can scarce be folly in that of a great kingdom.' From the standpoint of analytic technique, this was quite as bad as anything that can be charged to the debit of the 'mercantilist' account. However, the error involved will have to be discussed fully later on.

We have seen that, as far at least as economic analysis is concerned, there need not have been any spectacular break between 'mercantilists' and 'liberals.' Without any prejudice to their political ideals or interests, economists of the latter persuasion might have succeeded the economists of the former persuasion at the analytic task, much as one team of workmen succeeds another in order to carry on the job. To some extent this is what happened. But to the extent to which it did not happen, there was not only scrapping of outmoded error but also needless waste—comparable to the waste that would result if successive teams of workmen smashed the products of their predecessors, whenever they disliked the latter's politics. If Smith and his followers had refined and developed the 'mercantilist' propositions instead of throwing them away, a much truer and much richer theory of international economic relations could have been developed by 1848—one that could not have been compromised by one set of people and treated with contempt by another.

Paterson, the founder of the Bank of England, *Writings* edited with biography by Saxe Bannister, 2nd ed. 1859; and George Whatley, *Reflections on Coin in General*, 1762, reprinted in revised form as an appendix to the 2nd ed. of his *Principles of Trade*, 1774, the only one I know) and one author who came near to being a free trader (J. Jocelyn, *An Essay on Money and Bullion*, publ. 1718 but dated 1717). In a history of free-trade doctrine they are all of them entitled to prominent places. But Paterson's advocacy of free trade moved on a popular level and Whatley and Jocelyn, though not without merit, did not, so far as I can see, add anything to what had been said before them.

Part III

From 1790 to 1870

CHAPTER 1

Introduction and Plan

1. Coverage

This part is to cover the history of economic analysis from the 1790's to the end of the 1860's or the beginning of the 1870's. For a decade or two after the publication of the *Wealth of Nations* there is little to report *as far as analytic work is concerned,* and most of what there is has been fitted into Part II. I can see no point in insisting on a particular year, but if we did so insist, we might start a new period of analytic activity with Malthus' first *Essay on Population* (1798). Publication of the first volume of Marx's *Das Kapital* (1867), of Jevons' *Theory* (1871), of Menger's *Grundsätze* (1871), and the foundation of the Verein für Sozialpolitik (1872) are some of the events that clearly mark the advent of another period.

Periodizing, as we know, is a necessary evil. There is first an objection of principle to it that applies independently of the particular way in which a writer periodizes: historical developments are always continuous and they can never be cut into pieces without arbitrariness and loss. By refusing to date by years, we do not solve the problem but only mitigate the consequences of our inability to solve it. Second, our particular way of periodizing, dictated as it is by our concentrating on the history of economic analysis, will inevitably fail to satisfy those who are interested in something else. And, third, even from the standpoint of fellow students of the history of analysis, there are well-founded objections to a method that puts A. Smith near the end of the preceding period instead of at the beginning of the one that might be said to have been dominated by his influence. Our recognition of all this will show in many ways, for example, in the fact that we do not deal in this Part with all the authors who belong in it chronologically—the most important instance is Cournot—and that we include some who do not belong in it chronologically—an instance is Cairnes. But I hold, nevertheless, that our periodization brings out essential truth. This will be for the reader to judge. But we may mention at once two facts that go some way toward justifying our procedure. First, many historians before us have felt that this period formed a real unit. The feeling has expressed itself in a distinctive name: it was called the 'classic' period of economics—in a sense quite different from that in which the term is used in this book.[1] It retained this label until, at a time when the word

[1] Let me recall that whenever the term is used in this different sense in this book, it is put into quotes in order to prevent confusion. There are three meanings to be kept

'classic' had lost its eulogistic connotation and was beginning to stand for 'obsolete,' Lord Keynes used the word in order to denote the teaching of A. Marshall and his immediate followers (or simply, pre-Keynesian economics). Second and more important, the time between the 1790's and the end of the 1860's does answer our criteria of a period: there was, first, fresh activity that struggled hopefully with the deadwood; then things settled down and there emerged a typical classic situation in our sense, summed up in the typically classic achievement—again, in our sense of the term—of J. S. Mill, who underlined the fact by his attitude of speaking from the vantage ground of established truth and by the naïve confidence he placed in the durability of this established truth. Then followed stagnation—a state that was universally felt to be one of maturity of the science, if not one of decay; a state in which 'those who knew' were substantially in agreement; a state in which, 'the great work having being done,' most people thought that, barring minor points, only elaboration and application remained to be done.

2. Paraphernalia

Something that is very like envy comes in to spoil the smile with which we are apt to greet the numerous passages in the writings of this period that breathe immense complacency. Economists, or most of them, were evidently as pleased with the results of their handiwork as some of them were to be again in the 1930's. We shall make an effort later on to understand that happy state of mind in which economists saw a solid house where they had erected nothing better than a flimsy shack: [1] we still underrate pre-Smithian achievement; we still overrate the achievement of the 'classics.'

The conditions under which this work was carried on may be briefly characterized as follows. I hesitate to say that professional economics definitively established itself during this period. It certainly cannot be said that economics as a profession established itself, for the study of economic phenomena was not yet a full-time job and few people were economists and nothing else: many were businessmen, or public servants, or journalists, and even the academic teachers of economics, in many if not in most cases, also taught cognate —or even completely different—subjects. Nevertheless, we have a right to speak of a rapid process of professionalization that went on during that period: from the first, economics had established its claim to a definite field of research; it had become a definite specialty; it used definite methods; its results gained in definiteness; and economists, even though fractional personalities, recognized one another, and were recognized by the public, more definitely than before. New political economy societies were founded; new journals, new dic-

distinct: the old meaning in which 'classic' denotes the economic literature of the period under discussion plus A. Smith; Lord Keynes's meaning; and our own. [J. A. S. intended to treat this subject more fully in the unfinished Part I. See also Part IV, ch. 1.]

[1] See, especially, the often ridiculed passage on value theory in Mill's *Principles*, Book III, ch. 1, §2.

tionaries, and new bibliographies appeared—all of which, however, meant only continuation of previous practice.[2] The study of the history of economic thought made a vigorous start [3] and there was, of course, a rising tide of textbooks, a few of which we shall mention as occasion arises.

[2] Of the societies, the Political Economy Club of London (1821) was the most important; of the journals, the French *Journal des économistes* (1842); of the dictionaries, the French *Dictionnaire de l'économie politique* (Coquelin et Guillaumin, 1853-4). It is interesting to note that no journal exclusively devoted to scientific economics was founded in England until 1890. In part, however, this was owing to the existence of those excellent serious magazines, such as the *Edinburgh Review*, the *Quarterly Review*, the *Westminster Review*, which accepted even strictly professional stuff—a great compliment to the period's reading public. Beyond using a very limited number of articles that I found quoted in the 'professional' literature, I have not examined the contents of these periodicals—a serious lacuna in my work. I have examined the *Dictionnaire* but only perfunctorily.

[3] Historical references on individual points of doctrine date far back, of course. In the eighteenth century appeared also several bibliographies but no histories that I know of, except a few on the physiocrat school by Dupont and others. From the beginning of the nineteenth century, however, an increasing interest in doctrinal history manifested itself. The sketches of McCulloch (1824-5) and J. B. Say (1829; in the 6th vol. of the *Cours complet*) are the only publications of this kind that need be mentioned here for the time until 1837 when the first edition of J. A. Blanqui's *Histoire de l'économie politique . . .* (with a *bibliographie raisonnée*) appeared. A number of others, some of them confined to individual countries, followed to 1870. By 1858 this literature had grown sufficiently to induce Robert von Mohl (1799-1875) to insert in the third volume of his *Geschichte und Literatur der Staatswissenschaften* (1855-8) a chapter on Writings on the History of Political Economy. I shall mention only: (1) McCulloch's *Literature of Political Economy* (1845); (2) Ferrara's prefaces to *Biblioteca dell' Economista* (in 1850-68, Francesco Ferrara edited two series of Italian translations of foreign works which he prefaced by elaborate analyses that form the bulk of his theoretical contribution and really sum up to a history of economics; most of them were separately published in 1889-90); (3) Roscher (a great part of W. Roscher's work was in the field of doctrinal history. Within the period he wrote his *Zur Geschichte der englischen Volkswirthschaftslehre im sechzehnten und siebzehnten Jahrhundert*, 1851-52; *Über die Ein- und Durchführung des Adam Smith'schen Systems in Deutschland*, 1867; and he poured out his enthusiasm about Oresmius [see above, Part II, ch. 2] in *Ein grosser Nationalökonom des vierzehnten Jahrhunderts*, 1863; we add, immediately, his later *Geschichte der Nationalökonomik in Deutschland*, 1874, the fruit of enormous labor); (4) Manuel Colmeiro's *Historia de la economia politica en España* (1863), which does not strictly belong here but, together with his *Biblioteca* (1880), still forms the best starting point for a study of Spanish economics. I acknowledge the help derived from Dr. E. Schams's excellent study, 'Die Anfänge lehrgeschichtlicher Betrachtungsweise in der Nationalökonomie,' *Zeitschrift für Nationalökonomie* (September 1931), and his and Professor O. Morgenstern's 'Eine Bibliographie der allgemeinen Lehrgeschichten der Nationalökonomie,' ibid. (March 1933), which, however, excludes articles and also all work in doctrinal history that was incidental to theoretical investigations of primarily nonhistorical scope. Dr. Schams dates the beginning of a 'scientific' epoch of doctrinal historiography from E. K. Dühring's (see below, ch. 4) *Kritische Geschichte der Nationalökonomie und des Socialismus* (1871).

Research was largely financed by the research workers themselves: Tooke's achievement, for example, was possible only because he was a wealthy man; in some cases, of course, the proceeds from commercial publication of results proved adequate. Teaching was wholly inadequate, however. Even in those countries where there had been provision for regular lectures before, such as Germany, Italy, Spain, and Scotland, the intention was to provide a complement to other lines of study—law, for instance, or philosophy—rather than an independently organized curriculum of training in economics per se. In the United States a professorship of Moral Philosophy and Political Economy was founded at Columbia in 1818, and a professor of chemistry was commissioned to lecture on economics at South Carolina College in 1824. Teaching of sorts had, however, been done before that at various places by people of the most varied qualifications. In England, very few professorships or lectureships antedate the subsequent period. The one at Oxford was founded in 1825—the first incumbent was Senior—the one at University College, London, in 1828—the first incumbent was McCulloch—the one at Dublin in 1832—the first incumbent was Longfield—and there was a chair of history, commerce, and finance at the East India College in Haileybury to which Malthus was appointed in 1805.[4] But stipends and other conditions of tenure amply prove that founders and administrations did not even wish that people should hold appointments for long, let alone that they should make them their life jobs. In England a National Association for the Promotion of Social Science was founded in 1857 in order to remedy this state of things, but it took decades to achieve perceptible success.

This must be taken into account in any appraisal of the period's performance and still more in any appraisal of an individual's performance. On another occasion I shall have to emphasize that funds and chairs are not everything, but here I have to emphasize that neither are they nothing. Under those circumstances, men of brilliant ability and wide culture touched upon our field so lightly that all their abilities and acquirements did not prevent them from making insignificant economists—which is why, in our field and for that period, a given appraisal of the performance does not necessarily imply appraisal of the man.[5]

Barring a few lonely peaks abroad, England easily comes out first in that period's performance. In fact, that period was the specifically English period in the history of our science. The unrivaled prestige that English economists then enjoyed was only in part due to the glory that was irrationally reflected upon them from the economic success of their country. Mainly, that prestige was due to the quality of the work done by them, not only by a small number

[4] In France, some provision was made, temporarily, in the 1790's and then again after the Napoleonic Wars, but only in Paris (see below, ch. 4, sec. 4).

[5] If the reader will look up a biography of such a man as Pellegrino Rossi, he will immediately realize the force of this remark. But even in such a case as that of J. S. Mill, it is obvious that much of what strikes us as unsatisfactory in his *Principles* is easily accounted for by the fact that this work was largely written in an office with Mill's mind disturbed by the calls of current duties.

of masters, but also by a large number of able writers, who were not in the front rank but whose combined efforts amounted to a great deal.

3. Plan of the Part

We are going to change our method of presentation. In Part II we had not only to cover a vast span of years but also to contend with the difficulty that there was no generally accepted system to describe. Strictly speaking, no such system existed in the period covered by Part III. But there was something that was almost though not quite as good. That is to say, the great majority of the people who, as we have put it, recognized one another as economists agreed sufficiently about the fundamentals of subject matter, method, and results to make it possible to systematize their contributions, although they disagreed—individually or groupwise—on practically every individual problem within that frame of fundamentals. There was even more of common ground and, as between successive decades, of continuity than the individual writers would have been prepared to admit. For, then as now, most economists were apt to stress differences more than agreements, though there were important exceptions to this, the most important being J. S. Mill. It is true that there were many dissentients *toto coelo*, men who condemned the growing quasi-system of 'classical' economics root and branch. But most of these do not meet our test of analytic competence. And others objected on nonanalytic, that is, mainly on political, moral, or cultural grounds, so that their objections are not necessarily [1] relevant for us, even where we sympathize with them.

Availing ourselves of these facts, we shall be able to do in this Part what we were not able to do in Part II, namely, after having recalled the salient features of the political and intellectual scenery (Chapters 2 and 3), to draw a picture of analytic *developments* with reference to a cross section. This cross section will be represented (in Chapter 5) by J. S. Mill's *Principles*. But in order to simplify matters, we shall relieve Chapter 5 of some of its burden, by introducing ourselves to the most important individuals and groups beforehand (Chapter 4) and by reserving the details of pure theory and of money, as much as possible, for two separate chapters (6 and 7). Chapter 7 will also take care of the little that must be said on banking and cycles.

4. Concerning the Marxist System

Our plan is simple and works well in all cases save one: the case of the Marxist system. The difficulty is not, as might be supposed, that Marxist economics stands aloof in splendid isolation and is incommensurable with the rest of the work to be discussed. We shall see, on the contrary, that it is part and parcel of that period's general economics, which is precisely why it must be fitted in here. I was not thinking of Marx when I spoke of dissentients

[1] The reader will understand, of course, that a moral objection may constitute a motive for finding factual or logical objections that *are* relevant for us.

toto cælo in the preceding section, and he can and will be treated in this book exactly as are other economists.[1] Nor does the difficulty arise from the fact that he was also a sociologist. For his sociology can be fitted into its appropriate place just as well as can his economics. The difficulty is that in Marx's case we lose something that is essential to understanding him when we cut up his system into component propositions and assign separate niches to each, as our mode of procedure requires. To some extent this is so with every author: the whole is always more than the sum of the parts. But it is only in Marx's case that the loss we suffer by neglecting this [2] is of vital importance, because the totality of his vision, as a totality, asserts its right in every detail and is precisely the source of the intellectual fascination experienced by everyone, friend as well as foe, who makes a study of him. The way in which I propose to meet this difficulty cannot be satisfactory to the orthodox Marxist for whom Marx is the central sun of social science. Nor can it be satisfactory to him who wants artistic pictures of individual thinkers. But it is perfectly satisfactory for every reader who wants the picture of the evolution of technical economics that this book is intended to present. We recognize fully, but do not mean to duplicate, the distinct task of Marxology. We shall not disturb our plan. We shall take Marx's work to pieces and shall use, with strict economy, only what is relevant to our purpose, in the places indicated by our purpose. But we shall use the rest of this section in order to comment on the whole.

1. Marx figures in this book only as a sociologist and an economist. Of course, that creed-creating prophet was much more than this. And his creed-creating activity, on the one hand, and his policy-shaping and agitatorial activity, on the other hand, are inextricably interwoven with his analytic activity. So much is this the case that the question arises whether he can be called an analytic worker at all. This question may be answered in the negative from two very different standpoints. The orthodox Marxist, for whom the prophet's every word is eternal truth and for whom dissent spells not only error but sin, will return a negative answer, but in this particular sense: on Marx's Hegelian eminence, acting and reasoning, reality and thought, become identical; analysis cannot, on that level, be divorced from practice; therefore, if we do call Marx's thought analytic, we ought to add at once that it was analytic in a sense that

[1] Since this point is both very important and likely to cause surprise to some readers, I wish, besides referring them to what they will read in subsequent chapters, to state at once that this surprise is entirely due to the atmosphere of prophetic wrath in which Marx presented his economic analysis and which, to layman and philosopher, makes it look like something entirely different from any other. It is true, in addition, that the Anglo-American professional literature, both in this and the next period, treated him as an outsider. But in that literature other foreign economists of first rank fared no better in this respect.

[2] We never neglect this *quite*. In all the more important cases, economists are 'introduced' to the reader and these introductions give us the opportunity to look at personal performances as a whole. But I cannot go too far in this, for theorems and not persons are the heroes of our story.

differs essentially from the usual one; hence, his work is not analytic in the usual sense, and the author of this book, congenitally incapable of doing justice to it, ought to keep his unholy hands off it. Some anti-Marxists would agree in the result, though they might formulate it differently by advising me to keep my hands off the unholy thing: for them, Marx's work is a series of essentially unscientific diatribes, penned by a man congenitally unable to see a fact or to reason straight.

My answer to our question is, however, in the affirmative. The warrant for this affirmative answer is in the proposition that the bulk of Marx's work *is* analytic by virtue of its logical nature, for it consists in statements of relations between social facts. For instance, the proposition that a government is essentially an executive committee of the bourgeois class may be entirely wrong; but it embodies a piece of analysis in our sense, acceptance or refutation of which is subject to the ordinary rules of scientific procedure. It would be absurd indeed to describe the *Communist Manifesto,* in which this proposition occurs, as a publication of scientific character or to accept it as a statement of scientific truth. It is not less absurd to deny that, even in Marx's most scientific work, his analysis was distorted not only by the influence of practical purposes, not only by the influence of passionate value judgments, but also by ideological delusion.[3] Finally, it would be absurd to deny the difficulty that in some cases rises to impossibility of disentangling his analysis from its ideological element. But ideologically distorted analysis is still analysis. It may even yield elements of truth. To sum up: we shall not chant O *Altitudo* each time Marx's name turns up in the following pages; but neither do we put him out of court *a limine;* we simply recognize him as a sociological and economic analyst whose propositions (theories) have the same methodological meaning and standing and have to be interpreted according to the same criteria as have the propositions of every other sociological and economic analyst; we do not recognize any mystic halo.[4]

[3] On the difference between these three kinds of distortion, see above, Part I.

[4] Let me repeat this: due account being taken of differences in definitions and in degree of abstraction, every Marxist proposition is to carry the meaning which it would carry if penned by, say, Ricardo. This formulation takes care of a claim often, and sometimes justly, made by Marxists, viz. that critics (and even followers) of Marx are likely to miss his meaning by failing to attend to the facts that (1) Marx's terminology differs from that of other economists (the word Value e.g., simply means different things with Marx and J. S. Mill); and (2) that he reasons, in different parts of his work, on widely differing levels of abstraction. At the same time, that formulation spells refusal to admit another claim, noticed above, that is sometimes made by Marxists and is implied in their answer to the question concerning the logical nature of Marx's analysis, namely, the claim that Marxist propositions have, as it were, an astral body that is exempt from the ordinary rules of scientific procedure. Our reply to this is: Marx reasons about the empirical world by the methods of empirical analysis; hence his propositions—as every Marxist who discusses criticisms at all, recognizes by implication—have the usual empirical meaning or none. On the influence on him of Hegelian philosophy, see below, ch. 3, sec. 1b.

11. Since Marx counts for us only as far as he was a 'scientific' sociologist and economist, we need not consider any aspects of his career, activities, or personal character that are not relevant to his 'scientific' work. I wish to disclaim any intention to 'size him up' as a man, and this also applies to his friend and faithful ally, Engels. Some facts, however, are necessary in order to see the work of each in its proper light. They are presented in the footnote below.[5] Let us underline a few of them. First, nobody will understand Marx and

[5] Karl Heinrich Marx (1818-83) was the product of a thoroughly bourgeois environment that failed to provide economic independence, and of a thoroughly bourgeois education that made him (as it makes so many) an intellectual, a radical, and a scholar—the radicalism being of the bourgeois brand of his time and the scholarship being of the historico-philosophical, as distinguished from the mathematico-physical, type. As much by choice as by necessity, he took to journalism rather than to the academic career and in 1843 went to Paris, where he met Engels and economics (which he had touched only peripherically before) and where he made his position definitively socialist. In 1849, he settled in London for good and, for such a voracious reader, this is almost equivalent to saying that he settled in the British Museum library for good. Active revolutionism—such as he had practiced in 1848 in Germany—was finished, and his research work was for the rest of his life interfered with only by the necessity of earning his bread (in part by journalistic work), by his activity in the First International (1864-72), and later on also by failing health. The standard biography is still F. Mehring's (1918). Though in some respects less marred by narrow prejudice than are other works of this writer and in general commendable, it calls for a protest on behalf of Marx in one respect: it entirely failed to do justice to the scientific element in Marx's work. We ourselves may find in his works abundant proofs of ideological bias, but Mehring goes too far when he credits Marx with *nothing* but an intention to formulate proletarian ideology (of course he means to be complimentary).

Friedrich Engels (1820-95) interspersed a fairly successful business career with revolutionary activities until 1869, when he retired from business in order to serve the cause of Marxist socialism for the rest of his life. Among other things he became the warden of Marx's literary remains after the latter's death and, in addition, something of an oracle and elder statesman (hence the object of attack by a younger generation) to the German Social Democratic party. His self-effacing loyalty cannot but command our highest respect. Throughout he aspired only to be the faithful henchman and mouthpiece of the Lord Marx. It is therefore only from necessity that I point out—for it is necessary to do so to enable the reader to understand our situation with respect to the Marxist manuscripts that Engels edited—that he was not Marx's intellectual equal and that, while fairly up to the latter's philosophy and sociology, he was particularly deficient in technical economics. Of his own economic publications, *Die Lage der arbeitenden Klasse in England* (1845) will be mentioned again: however biased, it is a creditable piece of factual research, nourished by direct observation. The 'Umrisse zu einer Kritik der Nationalökonomie' (in Ruge's and Marx's *Deutsch-französische Jahrbücher*, 1844) and his *Herrn Eugen Dühring's Unwälzung der Wissenschaft* (1878; English trans. *Anti-Dühring*, 1907) are distinctly weak performances. His philosophical and sociological publications, though not original, keep a higher level. We shall have no occasion to mention either again. But these remarks, let me repeat, should not induce us to think less of the man whose name is fully entitled to the honorific position it holds in the history of German socialism. In par-

Engels who does not properly weigh the implications of their bourgeois cultural background, which is one of the reasons, though not the only one, why Marxism must be considered as a product of the bourgeois mind, a product that grew from eighteenth and early nineteenth-century bourgeois roots. The belief that it ever meant or could mean anything to the masses or in fact to any group, except a limited number of intellectuals, is one of the most pathetic elements in the personal ideology of Marx and Engels.[6] Second, our information enables us to form a pretty clear idea of Marx's opportunities for concentrated work. At times, he indulged in activities and lived under conditions that are bound to get on a man's nerves and to be more destructive of his scientific work than we might infer from the hours actually absorbed. Nevertheless, he had, on the average, an amount of time 'to himself' that compares favorably with the amount that is left, also on the average, to the typical American professor of our own day. And he used it to the full. Again, nobody will ever understand Marx and his work who does not attach appropriate weight to the erudition that went into it—the fruit of incessant labor that, starting from primarily philosophical and sociological interests in his early years, was concentrated increasingly on economics as time went on, until his working hours were all but monopolized by it. Nor was his the kind of mind in which scholarly coal puts out the fire: with every fact, with every argument that impinged upon him *in his reading,* he wrestled with such passionate zest as to be incessantly diverted from his main line of advance. On this I cannot insist too strongly. This fact would be my central theme were I to write a Marxology. Perusal of his *Theorien über den Mehrwert* suffices to convince one of it. And, once proved, it serves to establish in turn another fact and to solve a much discussed riddle: it serves to establish that he was a born analyst, a man who felt impelled to do analytic work, whether he wanted to or not and no matter what his *intentions* were; and it serves to solve the riddle why he failed to finish his work but instead left us heaps of disorderly manuscripts that no labor of love availed to put into an acceptable shape.

Third, our information warrants the statements that he was very much a philosopher dabbling in sociology and politics (as do so many philosophers) until he went to Paris; that there he quickly made headway and found his

---

ticular nothing is further from my mind than a wish to suggest that he was Marx's slave. In the 1840's he may even have helped to educate Marx in economics and in socialism, for at that time he was much further along. There are several biographies. It suffices to mention D. Ryazanov's *Karl Marx und Friedrich Engels* (English trans., 1927, Russian original unknown to me); there is a bibliography of works on both Marx and Engels in Marx-Engels Institute (later the Marx-Engels-Lenin Institute), *Marx-Engels Archiv,* vol. I, 1926. [The first two volumes of the *Marx-Engels Archiv* were published in German and in a parallel Russian edition; subsequent volumes have been published in Russian only.]

[6] Marx took himself in and helped to foster the same delusion in his followers by building into his structure a sufficient number of phrases—very coarse ones among them—which indeed everyone can understand and which are what Marxism means to the vulgar, perhaps even to people who are not covered by this term.

feet as an economist; and that by the time he and Engels wrote the *Communist Manifesto* (1847; published 1848); that is to say, at the age of 29,[7] he was in possession of all the essentials that make up the Marxist Social Science, the only important lacunae being in the field of technical economics. For the rest, the main line of his intellectual life may be described as a series of efforts to work out that Social Science and to fill those lacunae—*tasks which, I believe, Marx did not expect would involve any insurmountable difficulties, though he did expect that a great deal of further work would be required to straighten out and co-ordinate everything that was to find a place within the vast structure.*

This interpretation is not the usual one. It attributes to Marx an early conception of all that is fundamental in his scheme of thought and, barring points of comparative detail, a large amount of consistency in developing it, springing from a theoretical purpose and plan that never varied in essentials. Even Marxists, who may be expected to sympathize with this view, will find it too simple; but Marx critics will declare it to be downright wrong. Accordingly some defense is necessary. The relevant facts are these. In 1859, Marx published *Zur Kritik der politischen Ökonomie,* which evidently was to be the first installment of a comprehensive exposition and therefore constitutes proof that he must have thought himself equipped to write one. The fact that he abandoned this torso proves that he was not, and that he felt he had made an unsatisfactory beginning. But what of it? This is exactly what must be expected to happen in an enterprise of such magnitude—which, moreover, involves, on the economic side, a large amount of detail, theoretical still more than factual—and cannot be taken as proof that something had gone wrong with fundamentals. He started afresh and, after struggles that are most instructively reflected in some of the manuscript material eventually published in three volumes by Kautsky (*Theorien über den Mehrwert,* 1905-10), brought out a new first installment (*Das Kapital,* first vol., 1867).[8] The fact that no second volume followed during Marx's lifetime and that Engels had to edit the second volume (1885) and to compile a third one (1894), both from unfinished manuscripts, is interpreted by anti-Marxists to mean confession of failure: Marx, so they said, became conscious of the presence in his system of irreconcilable inconsistencies (especially in his value theory), and therefore refused to go on. From the *Theorien über den Mehrwert* it can be shown, however, that Marx, when he published the first volume, was perfectly aware of, and had planned for, what to his critics appeared to be irreconcilable inconsistencies. His correspondence, it is true, establishes the fact that he deferred

[7] If this be so, it would afford another illustrative instance for Ostwald's theory that thinkers conceive their truly original ideas before they are 30.

[8] This is all I have to say on the question whether and why Marx changed his plan. The question, interesting as it is for Marxology, is quite irrelevant to my interpretation. Any changes of plan are readily understandable in all cases of protracted efforts. See, however, H. Grossmann: 'Die Änderung des ursprünglichen Aufbauplans des Marxschen "Kapitals" und ihre Ursachen,' *Archiv für die Geschichte des Sozialismus und der Arbeiterbewegung,* 1929.

the completion of the second volume for reasons that do not read too convincingly. But surely this can be explained by the growing resistance of an aging organism that was afraid of new efforts. Thus, the facts mentioned cannot be held to disprove my interpretation. The positive reasons I have for preferring it are his method of work that has been alluded to above, and my theorist's knowledge of what Marx's theoretical difficulties were—from his standpoint, they were not insurmountable. This is, of course, quite compatible with my conviction that Marx's system is seriously at fault. I mean only that he could have presented a comprehensive economic theory without violating logic—he would always have had to do violence to facts.

III. Since we have decided to do what Marxists—perhaps rightly—resent, namely, to take the Marxist structure to pieces and to discuss each of these pieces in the places in which they belong, we shall not get an over-all view of it anywhere. The following comments are intended to offer a partial substitute for such a view.

The 'pieces' divide up into two groups, one sociological and the other economic. The sociological pieces include contributions of the first order of importance such as the Economic Interpretation of History, which, as I shall argue, may be considered as Marx's own, quite as much as Darwin's descent of man is Darwin's own. But the rest of Marx's sociology—the sociological framework that, like every economist, he needed for his economic theory—is neither objectively novel nor subjectively original. His preconceptions about the nature of the relations between capital and labor, in particular, he simply took from an ideology that was already dominant in the radical literature of his time.[9] If, however, we wish to trace them further back, we can do so without difficulty. A very likely source is the *Wealth of Nations*. A. Smith's ideas on the relative position of capital and labor were bound to appeal to him, especially as they linked up with a definition of rent and profits—as 'deductions from the produce of labour' (Book I, ch. 8, 'Of the Wages of Labour')—that is strongly suggestive of an exploitation theory. But these ideas were quite common during the enlightenment and their real home was France. French economists, ever since Boisguillebert, had explained property in land by *violence*, and Rousseau and many philosophers had expanded on the subject. There is, however, one writer, Linguet, who, more explicitly than others, drew exactly the picture that Marx made his own: the picture not only of landlords who subject and exploit rural serfs, but also of industrial and commercial employers who do exactly the same thing to laborers who are nominally free, yet actually slaves.[10]

[9] It is in this field that Mehring's interpretation of Marxist doctrine (as a verbalization of proletarian ideology) comes nearest to being true. Our quarrel with him is only that he extended this interpretation to the whole of Marx's work.

[10] S. N. H. Linguet (1736-94), a barrister and journalist, was a prolific and bellicose writer, who is difficult to classify. He criticized the physiocrats (*Réponse aux docteurs modernes . . .* 1771) and took part in many controveries of his day without making any mark. But one of his books is of great interest for us, his *Théorie des loix civiles* (1767), neither because of its attack upon Montesquieu nor because of Morellet's biting

This sociological framework offered most of the pegs that Marx needed in order to have something upon which to hang his glowing phrases. And since historians are primarily interested in these, no matter whether they admire them or are shocked by them, it is difficult to gain assent to what is the obvious truth about the nature of the purely economic pieces of the Marxist system. This obvious truth is that, as far as pure theory is concerned, Marx must be considered a 'classic' economist and more specifically a member of the Ricardian group.[11] Ricardo is the only economist whom Marx treated as a master. I suspect that he learned his theory from Ricardo. But much more important is the objective fact that Marx used the Ricardian apparatus: he adopted Ricardo's conceptual layout and his problems presented themselves to him in the forms that Ricardo had given to them. No doubt, he transformed these forms and he arrived in the end at widely different conclusions. But he always did so by way of starting from, and criticizing, Ricardo— *criticism of Ricardo was his method in his purely theoretical work.* Only three outstanding illustrations can be mentioned here: Marx substantially accepted the Ricardian theory of value (see below, ch. 6) and defended it by the Ricardian arguments but, recognizing that Ricardian values cannot be expected to be proportional to prices, tried to work out a different theory of the relation between the two; Marx, following Ricardo's lead, ran up, as Ricardo did, against the problem of surplus value but, recognizing that Ricardo's solution really was no solution at all, developed his exploitation theory from the Ricardian set-up; Marx wholly accepted, down to details, Ricardo's theory of technological unemployment but, finding it inadequate for his purposes, tried to turn into a general 'law' what with Ricardo was no more than a possibility. It is hoped that these points will become clearer as we proceed (chs. 5 and 6). Here they are mentioned by way of anticipation to give definiteness to the meaning of my statements that Ricardo was Marx's master, and that Marx, though he transformed the theoretical material he found, yet worked with tools that he

---

reply, but because it unfolded a quite elaborate historical sociology, the central theme of which was the enslavement of the masses. I do not know that the book had much influence. But, as a symptom at least, it stands at or near the fountainhead of the ideology that Marx and many others, nonsocialists among them, have substituted for capitalist reality, and on which sophomoric enthusiasms feed even today. Linguet supplied not only the picture but also the characteristic spirit with which to look at it. An example will illustrate. Linguet adopts the theory that in the dawn of civilization there were agrarian populations, living in substantially equalitarian conditions, and that a kind of feudal society arose through the subjection of those populations by warlike tribes who established themselves as their lords. There is much to be said for this theory, which is in fact accepted by some modern prehistorians. Now, however, among the results of this subjection that created lords and serfs is everything we include in the term 'culture.' But Linguet has no eye for this. It is the fact of subjection that matters to him and nothing else. And his conclusion is moral indignation and nothing else.

[11] Observe that, so far as theory is concerned, this makes Marx an English economist. And he was one.

found and not with tools that he created. This is only another way of expressing that, however 'secular' a phenomenon Marx may have been in some respects, he was essentially period-bound as a theoretical technician—a fact that later on created many a difficulty for followers who felt unable to admit that Marx could ever grow out of date in any respect.

However, in order to drive home a point that seems important, I have strictly confined myself in the preceding paragraph to Marx's theoretical technique. But there are two features of Marxist theory that transcend technique. And these were not period-bound. The one is his *tableau économique*. In his analysis of the structure of capital, Marx developed Ricardo once more. But there is an element in it that does not hail from Ricardo but may hail from Quesnay: Marx was one of the first to try to work out an explicit model of the capitalist process.[12] The other is still more important. Marx's theory is evolutionary in a sense in which no other economic theory was: it tries to uncover the mechanism that, by its mere working and without the aid of external factors, turns any given state of society into another.[13]

IV. This is all that our space permits us to say about the Marxist system in general and about the manner in which the component parts of it will be taken into account in this book.[14] A reader's guide should follow now. But I feel unable to produce one. Marx was so diffuse and repetitive a writer, and, barring the first volume of *Das Kapital*, his theoretical works reflect so unfinished a state of his argument, that it is impossible to point out what is most signifi-

[12] The next economist to try his hand at this task was Böhm-Bawerk (see below, Part IV, chs. 5 and 6). The affinity between the two is hidden by phraseology and by trappings, but is nevertheless real and close.

[13] Marxologists sometimes speak of Marx's methods' being essentially 'historical.' This phrase carries in this connection two different meanings: it means, first, that different parts of Marxist theory may have been intended by Marx to apply to different states of society; and it means, second, what is meant above by the word 'evolutionary.' Both meanings are capable of defense. But the phrase is infelicitous all the same, because it also carries other meanings—among them the one that is most naturally associated with the word 'historical'—that do not apply to Marxist theory. (On the evolutionary aspect of Marx's theory, see below, ch. 3, sec. 4b.)

[14] The reader need not, perhaps, be told again how incomplete all this is. But there is one point that merits explicit notice. I have emphasized the influence that Smith and Ricardo exerted upon Marx. I have mentioned the influence of Quesnay only as a possibility, because Marx's model might have been developed independently from the Ricardian base. But some other possible influences I have not mentioned at all. Many have been asserted by other historians and, since Marx's knowledge of literature was very nearly exhaustive, the possibility that they are right cannot be excluded. But there is no *cogent* reason for assuming other influences more specific than what is inevitably implied in his having read, analyzed, and criticized very many other people. I have therefore economized space by not mentioning any of the suggestions that have been offered. In fact, as soon as one has grasped the importance of Ricardo's influence, which Marx did nothing to hide, and, in addition, the caliber of Marx's mind, one will automatically cease to be interested in those suggestions, let alone accusations of plagiarism.

cant with any confidence. Instead of attempting an impossible task, I shall refer my readers to a book by Dr. Sweezy (the work of an accomplished theorist and a monument of unswerving loyalty) which presents Marx's economics in the most favorable light and, in addition, is the best introduction to Marxist literature I know.[15] Relying on this reference, I shall confine myself to tendering the following pieces of advice.

There is no point whatever in perusing selected bits of Marx's writings or even in perusing the first volume of *Das Kapital* alone. Any economist who wishes to study Marx at all must resign himself to reading carefully the whole of the three volumes of *Das Kapital* and of the three volumes of *Theorien über den Mehrwert*.[16] Further, there is no point whatever in tackling Marx without preparation. Not only is he a difficult author but, owing to the nature of his scientific apparatus, he cannot be understood without a working knowledge of the economics of his epoch, Ricardo in particular, and of economic theory in general. This is all the more important because the necessity for it does not show on the surface. Again, the reader must be on his guard against being misled by traces of Hegelian terminology. It will be argued below that Marx did not allow his analysis to be influenced by Hegelian philosophy. But he sometimes uses terms in their specifically Hegelian sense, and a reader who takes them in their usual sense misses Marx's meaning. Finally, a reader who wishes for anything other than indoctrination must, of course, learn to distinguish both facts and logically valid reasoning from the ideological mirage. Marx himself helps us in this: sometimes, becoming semiconscious of ideological delusion, he rises, in defense, to the heights of his vituperative rhetoric, which therefore serves to indicate the spots at which there is something wrong.

[15] Paul M. Sweezy, *The Theory of Capitalist Development* (2nd ed., 1946). My recommendation does not imply agreement with all of Sweezy's interpretations, especially with his attempt to make a Keynesian of Marx. Attention is drawn to the well-chosen entries in the bibliography, to which I have only one item to add: W. Lexis [J. A. S. here inserted the title of Böhm-Bawerk's criticism of Marx, *Zum Abschluss des Marxschen Systems* (1896)—obviously a slip. He probably intended to refer to a review article written by Lexis after the publication of vol. III of *Das Kapital*, namely, 'The Concluding Volume of Marx's "Capital"' in the *Quarterly Journal of Economies*, October 1895]. The importance of Bortkiewicz's contribution has been abundantly emphasized in Sweezy's text.

[16] The *Communist Manifesto* is also indispensable, of course. But for any purpose short of becoming a Marxologist, I think that nothing need be added except the *Class Struggles in France*, articles written in 1848-50, published as a book, with an introduction by Engels in 1895. Only the Marxologist need go into Marx's correspondence.

CHAPTER 2

Socio-Political Backgrounds

During the last decade or so before the French Revolution, some of the traits became visible of a social and political pattern that, after the revolutionary and Napoleonic Wars and their immediate consequences were over, more or less established itself for the rest of the nineteenth century. It seems desirable to touch upon a few of its essential features, if only to correct some misapprehensions the reader's mind may harbor and to soften the unrealistically definite colors in which the various ideological traditions have painted it.

In doing so we shall have to struggle with a difficulty that is not new to us. We are going to try to visualize an economic and social structure—in process of incessant change, of course—and the cultural superstructure that was either associated with it or, according to Marxist doctrine, generated by it: we call it the civilization or the spirit of the times, or the *Zeitgeist*.[1] But this *Zeitgeist* is never a structural unit. It is always an imperfect synthesis of warring elements and can never be described truthfully in terms of a few consistent 'principles.' The most obvious reason for this is that at any given time both the economic and social structure of a society and its *Zeitgeist* contain elements that hail from historically prior states. But there are other and more fundamental reasons, less easy to explain, which make it impossible to analyze what happens in a social organism in terms of processes that conform to the immanent logic of its state and in terms of processes that are induced by the resistance of survivals or, still more superficially, as 'progress' and 'reaction.' The conceptual arrangement we are going to use bears witness to this difficulty.

On the whole, however, it may be averred that, though the peak of bourgeois *ascendancy* occurred in the subsequent period, it was in the period under survey that the *ascent* of the business class was most nearly unimpeded, most nearly unchallenged. In the great nations, the bourgeoisie did not rule politically, the most important exceptions being the United States and, for the seventeen years of Louis Philippe's regime, France. But in all countries the gov-

[1] The Marxist term *Überbau* is satisfactorily rendered by its literal translation, superstructure. But for the German word *Zeitgeist* there is no perfect equivalent. Hence I am going to use it (as I do other foreign terms that are hard to translate exactly) just as American physicists use *Eigenschwingung* and American philosophers, *Weltanschauung*.

ernments, however unbourgeois in origin and structure, not excluding those that have been voted most 'reactionary' by bourgeois oppositions, backed the economic interests of the business class almost without question and did their best to protect them.[2] Still more important, they did so in a spirit of laissez-faire, that is to say, on the theory that the best way of promoting economic development and general welfare is to remove fetters from the private-enterprise economy and to leave it alone. This is what will be meant in this book by Economic Liberalism. The reader is requested to keep this definition in mind because the term has acquired a different—in fact almost the opposite—meaning since about 1900 and especially since about 1930: as a supreme, if unintended, compliment, the enemies of the system of private enterprise have thought it wise to appropriate its label.

By Political Liberalism, which must be distinguished from economic liberalism as our footnote amply shows, we mean sponsorship of parliamentary government, freedom to vote and extension of the right to vote, freedom of the press, divorce of secular from spiritual government, trial by jury, and so on, including retrenchment and pacific, though not necessarily pacifist, foreign policy. This was the program [3] of the first phase of the French Revolution. A tendency to carry it out eventually asserted itself everywhere. But the rates of speed differed widely as between different countries and so did the combinations of forces and circumstances that were responsible for each step.

The rate at which the business class itself was converted to political liberalism also differed widely, and not only as between different countries, but also as between different subgroups of the bourgeoisie. Not even economic liberalism was welcomed everywhere and by the whole business class; political liberalism came to large sectors of it like an undesired child. The adherents of the Spanish Constitution of 1811, who were the first to call themselves *liberales*, had not the whole bourgeoisie behind them. Neither had the French *libéraux* of the 1820's. It was a wing only, which was but semirecognized and received also nonbusiness support from intellectuals and the masses, that forced the pro-

[2] The Prussian government of the Stein-Hardenberg era, the Austro-Hungarian government from 1849 to 1859, and the Russian government throughout, are the most striking examples of governments that, though surely autocratic enough, adhered, so far as the principles and tendencies of their economic policy is concerned, to what I am about to call economic liberalism. This may read surprisingly. But the reason why it does so is only that these countries were, at the beginning of the period, so far removed from a state of individual freedom in the economic sphere, and that, in their conditions (especially in the conditions of Russia), progress toward this state had to be so slow that the tendency does not show so spectacularly as it does in England. Perusal of any economic history of Europe and, to some extent, the comments that are to follow in the text will, however, convince the reader. In order to understand the economic literature of the period, this fact is of prime importance. Both Prussian and Russian Smithianism was not just a literary fad indulged in by oppositions: its stronghold was in the conservative bureaucracies.

[3] Certain items of it are disputable. For example, men whose right to be called political liberals cannot be denied opposed free public education. Not all liberals sponsored extension of the franchise; some conservatives did.

gram of political liberalism upon a not-quite-willing majority, though this majority was converted in the end. In England, this shows quite clearly in the way in which first the Whigs and then the Palmerstonians were pushed along by a small group that was known as 'radical.' This group, or at least its intellectual core, the Philosophical Radicals, is of particular interest to us because some of the most important English economists belonged to it or sympathized with it. But unlike their successors of a later day, these radicals were not at all what we should call radical in matters of economic policy. Some of them, J. S. Mill in particular, visualized indeed a different organization of economic activity for a more or less distant future. For the time being, however, they were economic liberals in the sense defined above, or what we should now call conservatives. Their radicalism found plenty to do in the purely political sphere. Moreover, at the beginning of the period, laissez-faire—and in particular free trade—was not as yet established policy. It was something to be fought for, fresh not stale, and something that was felt to be 'progressive.' It attracted the majority of intellectuals instead of disgusting them. Their idea of reform was to clear the economic system of what they regarded as nonessential 'abuses' in order to allow laissez-faire to work itself out fully.[4] They were supporters of the new Poor Law and no friends to Chartism, still less to any of the socialist groups that were in existence then.[5]

Thus the correlation between the interests and attitudes of the business class and liberalism was anything but perfect. In addition, as we have already observed, it was by no means only its own left wing that pushed the bourgeoisie along. Conservative governments—and not only the autocratic ones, but also the English conservative governments—had a decisive share in the progress toward economic liberalism. Moreover, groups, strata, parties, and attitudes of noncapitalist origin, though they had to yield occasionally, held their own on the whole. The period's political history bears witness to this. So does its religious history. The period indeed begins and ends with a decade in which indifference or even actively hostile laicism prevailed. But between the Napoleonic Wars and the 1860's, the Catholic Church experienced a marked revival of activity and power that was paralleled in Protestant countries, especially in England (evangelical movement on the one hand, Oxford movement on the other). Nor do the period's currents of thought outside the religious sphere fit into any simple schema. Tory democracy put in an appearance.

[4] It is, therefore, understandable that Marx and the Marxists should have professed contempt for bourgeois radicalism—though they transferred their contempt also to the radicalism of a later time—that they should have looked upon it as a sham that was really meant to preserve what it pretended to reconstruct. But understandable though such an opinion is in people who felt themselves to be the competitors of bourgeois radicalism, it is nevertheless quite wrong (1) because radicals and, drawn along by them, simple liberals helped labor to gather in a harvest of considerable value even in the economic field; and (2) because their work in the political field created the conditions under which socialist parties were able to grow to numerical importance.

[5] On the *Chartist Movement*, see the book with this title by M. Hovell (1918).

Naïve radicalism—and the philosophical radicals were nothing if not naïve—certainly did interpret all these things as survivals. Only the subsequent period was to show that, when they thought they fought the past, they were really fighting the future.

A bird's-eye view of the intellectual scenery of the period and of some developments in fields of particular interest to the economist will be presented in the next chapter. The rest of this one will be devoted to a survey of the policies of the period. For brevity's sake, we shall confine ourselves almost entirely to economic policies and to the English paradigm.

1. Economic Development

The liberal intermezzo was everywhere, but most spectacularly in England, associated with an economic development which, so far as we can judge, was unprecedented—all the achievements of the early and middle railroad age. It was easy to attribute that impressive sequence of undeniable successes to the policy of economic liberalism as its main or even only cause. The reader will understand that, however inadequate, this theory was far from being wholly wrong. It cannot reasonably be doubted that, in the historical conditions of that epoch, the removal of fetters from the energies that crowded into business pursuits, together with a policy that guaranteed to the businessman secure enjoyment of success and at the same time made it clear to him that he had no help to expect in case of failure, must in fact have had the energizing influence that was extolled until the argument got stale through repetition. Thus the system kept on justifying itself in the eyes of most contemporaneous observers, even of those who, like J. S. Mill, bore it no love. Such complacent registration of 'progress' seems strange to us who look back upon that age from different standpoints and in a different humor and abhor the atmosphere of the hard-driven homes of rising industrialists almost as much as the squalid dwellings of their workmen. But let us remember that much of all that offends us now was in the nature of childhood diseases—some of which were passing even at the time of Marx's glowing indictments—and that the economic promise, which the system of free enterprise held out *to all*, was not an empty one: the standard of living of the masses remained low, but it rose steadily almost all the time; ever-growing numbers were absorbed at increasing real wages; the 'free breakfast table' of the English free traders was perhaps the least misleading slogan that politicians ever forged. Also, contemporaneous and later critics, both conservative and socialist, have never adequately realized the extent to which the welfare policies of the next period were rendered possible by the developments of the first three quarters of the nineteenth century and by the policies that fostered them. So far as this goes, there is no reason for discounting either the honesty or the competence of the economists of that time, or for voting them victims of ideological delusion.

2. Free Trade and Foreign Relations

The English advocates of free trade claimed perfect generality for their argument. For them, it was absolute and eternal wisdom for all times and places; he who refused to accept it was a fool or a crook or both. But as has been pointed out many times, England's individual historical situation in which a free-trade policy was clearly indicated had probably more to do with her conversion than had the element of general truth in the free-trade argument. The hope that a spectacular example would convert other nations also may have played some role. The decisive factors and arguments, however, were quite independent of any such hope. The superiority of England's industry in 1840 was unchallengeable for the calculable future. And this superiority had everything to gain from cheaper raw materials and foodstuffs. These were no delusions: so satisfied was the nation with what it took to be the results of this policy that criticism was almost silenced until the depression of the eighties. Even that hope did not prove illusory for several decades. Though England remained the only great nation to embrace free trade wholeheartedly, all the other nations displayed tendencies toward free trade for longer or shorter periods and to a greater or lesser degree. Thus Prussia and then the German Empire, from the Prussian Tariff of 1818 to the Caprivi treaties of 1891-4, moved on a line that never departed very far from free-trade principles.[1] The Anglo-French treaty of 1860 (Cobden-Chevalier Treaty) marked an important if short-lived interruption in the generally protectionist policy of France. It should be observed, however, that on the Continent free-trade or quasi-free-trade policy was never supported by public opinion as strongly as was the case in England: it was imposed by bureaucracies—as in Germany—or by rulers—such as Napoleon III—who were doctrinaire liberals in these matters. Those economists who, like the majority of the French, were free traders elicited little response from the public. In the United States, too, free trade was never popular except with economists and not with all of them. Different national conditions of course amply account for this, and they also enable us to put a more favorable construction on the views of protectionist economists in these countries than ardent free traders were wont to put upon them. The dramatic story of England's conversion to free trade need not be retold here. But there are two aspects of it that we cannot afford to neglect.

First, from a parliamentary point of view the adoption of the free-trade policy stands wholly to the credit of the conservative party. The first effective steps in the direction of free trade were taken before the outbreak of the French Revolution by Lord Shelburne and the younger Pitt. Advance toward it

[1] The fact is somewhat obscured by the moves and countermoves that preceded the conclusion of the Customs Union (*Zollverein*) of 1834 and by concessions made from time to time to individual protectionist interests. On the whole, however, the policy of the Customs Union and, for the rest of the century, of the Empire is adequately described by the sentence above. Bismarck's mild protectionism had mainly fiscal reasons.

was resumed in the 1820's by Huskisson. And free trade was (substantially) carried, the most difficult point—removal of the import duties on grains—included, by the conservative government of Sir Robert Peel. Though his cabinet and party foundered on the rocks, it still remains true that a government largely composed of landowners carried a policy that was obviously contrary to their own economic class interests as well as to the economic interests of the class with which they were most closely allied, the farmers. Interpret it as you please, but do not forget to ponder over this most interesting phenomenon of political sociology. The manufacturers and merchants who provided political steam are another matter. The Merchants' Petition of 1820 must be mentioned because it was drawn up by one of the leading scientific economists of the age, Thomas Tooke. And this is our only opportunity, in a history of *analysis* to mention the two heroes of the Anti-Corn-Law League, Richard Cobden and John Bright.[2]

But, second, free-trade policy means much more than a particular way of dealing with questions of foreign trade. In fact, it could be argued that this is the least important aspect of it and that a man might be a free trader, even if he thinks little of the purely economic case for free trade per se. It is easy to see—to some extent we shall see presently—that free-trade policy is related to other economic policies in such a manner that, for political as well as economic reasons, these other policies are difficult to pursue without free-trade policy, and vice versa. In other words, free trade is but an element of a comprehensive system of economic policy and should never be discussed in isolation. Nor is this all. The really important point to make is that this system of economic policy conditions, and is conditioned by, something that is more comprehensive still, namely, a general political and moral attitude or vision that asserts itself in all departments of national and international life and *may* indeed be linked up with utilitarianism.[3] This attitude, which has come to be called *Manchesterism* by its enemies, was in fact Cobden's and Bright's. Among its many manifestations, colonial and foreign policies are particularly important for us. Colonies used to be acquired for the sole purpose of being ruled and exploited in the interest of the mother country and of keeping other nations from doing the same thing. From the Manchester school standpoint there is not even an economic argument in favor of doing this. Still less is there a political one. Colonies exist for themselves just as do any other countries; they should be self-governing; and they should neither accord to, nor be accorded by, the mother country any particular commercial advantages. Nor did all this remain in the realm of either philosophy or agitation. Some practical progress was made toward the goal. England's Canadian policy, as out-

[2] It may seem incongruous, in spite of all I might say, that this book accords but a perfunctory notice to those great names. But there is nothing I can do about it except refer the reader to the two masterly lives that he will peruse with pleasure and profit: the *Life of Richard Cobden* by Lord Morley and the *Life of John Bright* by G. M. Trevelyan.

[3] In England, this affiliation was obvious. But it is not necessary—there are other systems of thought that yield the same attitudes.

lined in the Durham Report, was for the time being the most important step.[4] There were many backslidings, of course.

The foreign policy of the period, both at the time of the Holy Alliance and later, cannot be analyzed briefly. So far as England is concerned, we may, however, point to a few facts which, though hardly representative of prevailing practice, do indicate the existence of a tendency that was in accord with the wider implications of free trade. The most important of these facts was the actual practice of the second Peel administration, the one that repealed the Corn Laws: its sober and responsible management of foreign affairs, its refusal to see English interests in whatever happened anywhere on the globe, was an important sign of the times. Another was the adoption of the principle (Canning) to side with nations 'rightly struggling to be free' or even, with some reservation in the German case, with nations that strove for national union. nationalism did not have the connotation it later acquired and was an ally, not an enemy, of bourgeois liberalism or else of something to the left of it (Mazzini). Furthermore, though the period witnessed a number of wars, others were prevented by the new attitude: English relations with the United States during the Civil War afford an example. Most important of all, attempts at sowing the seeds of war by arousing a spirit of either aggression or suspicion, which of course continued throughout, were also under criticism throughout: as an example I mention Cobden's highly characteristic struggle for a better understanding of France and his not less characteristic struggle with Urquhart.[5] In parliament, Gladstone became—and remained—the most powerful spokesman of the new attitude which he invested with all the glories of his rhetoric.[6]

3. Domestic Policy and Sozialpolitik [1]

We must remember that conditions differed sufficiently in different countries to produce different policies and also different attitudes on the part of economists even where the guiding principles were the same. Thus the abolition of serfdom in Russia and the agrarian reforms in Germany and Austria—the so-called Liberation of the Peasants—were certainly conceived and car-

[4] See Charles P. Lucas, ed., *Lord Durham's Report on the Affairs of British North America* (1912). Lord Durham (1792-1840) submitted his report in 1839.

[5] David Urquhart, a former member of the diplomatic service, founded in 1835 a periodical, the *Portfolio,* and, later on, foreign-affairs committees that made vigorous propaganda for an activist foreign policy. Cobden subjected to destructive criticism the possible advantages from such a policy, made fun of arrogant and ignorant diplomatists and political busybodies, and on the whole counteracted Urquhart effectively.

[6] Perhaps the best, certainly the most pleasant, way for the reader to satisfy himself as regards this point is a perusal of Lord Morley's great Gladstone biography (*Life of William Ewart Gladstone,* 3 vols., 1903). This is also perhaps the best reference to make for the rest of this chapter.

[1] As I said before, I prefer a word that everyone understands, even though it is a foreign one, to one that would need explanation. Hence we shall use the word *Sozialpolitik* throughout.

ried out in the spirit of economic liberalism: the idea of making the peasant the free proprietor of a free holding and of leaving him to his own devices was even surprisingly—and indeed absurdly—radical. But in France this had been done in the Revolution; the land system of England presented for the moment no pressing problems at all; and the agrarian problems of Ireland were of an entirely different nature. Similarly, the regulations that fettered or sheltered the craft guilds and also other sectors of industry had withered away in England before this period; in France it was again the Revolution that had destroyed them; elsewhere they were removed at different times and in some places much more completely than in others: in Prussia, for example, by the Stein-Hardenberg reforms after the battle of Jena. These differences were, however, not a matter of different economic principles, although writers may sometimes have rationalized them in this way. They were merely a matter of different social conditions, of differences in the economic structures that existed in different countries at the beginning of the period. Again, England completely reconstructed her law of joint stock companies. To some extent this was done everywhere, and everywhere the tendency asserted itself to 'liberalize' company laws and to reduce public control (until after the crash of 1873 when some of the steps taken were retraced). But the results differed widely.

Differences of principle as well as of existing conditions account for the widely different policies we find in such matters as religion, the press, criminal and civil justice, education, and so on, within the same country at different times as well as between different countries. In England, for example, the old civil liberties having been restored after the Napoleonic Wars, it was Catholic emancipation, parliamentary reform—at first a liberal patent, later infringed on by the Disraeli conservatives [2]—and Ireland which supplied the daily bread of current politics in the noneconomic field. But we are mainly interested in the English [3] *Sozialpolitik* of that period.

[2] In England, the running fight for the ultimate enfranchisement of the masses was carried on entirely between upper-class groups: the masses themselves had nothing to do but to stand by and cheer or boo. This interesting phenomenon illustrates well a characteristic difficulty of political interpretation. Tactics had much to do with the attitudes taken by Whigs and Tories: Catholic emancipation 'drove the Whigs back upon parliamentary reform' and the Whig parliamentary reform in turn drove the Tories back upon further parliamentary reform. But tactics are not all of it. There is something in Disraeli's contention that conservatism of his type (Tory democracy) represents the true interests and feelings of the masses and hence should look to the masses for support.

[3] As the reader might expect, the paternalistic tendencies of the preceding period survived better in some continental countries. But there is something else. In France, before the accession to power of Napoleon III, socialist movements had had little practical effect except that of eliciting violent hostility. But there were nevertheless some writers who visualized with perfect clarity the governmental *Sozialpolitik* of later times. By far the most eminent of these was Charles Dupont-White (1807-78); see his *Essai sur les relations du travail avec le capital* (1846) and his *L'individu et l'état* (1857). Napoleon III and some of his advisers entertained fairly advanced ideas on the subject of social reforms that were to be imposed by authority (*socialisme autoritaire, so-*

English labor legislation developed along three lines. First, there was the factory legislation—protection being, however, substantially confined to women and children.[4] Second, the various acts prohibiting combinations of workmen were repealed in 1824, though complete legalization of trade unions was deferred until 1871 and 1875. Third, a Poor Law Amendment Act was passed in 1834, which is important for us, among other reasons, because it was based on a report written by Edwin Chadwick in collaboration with one of the leading economists of the age, Senior. Two aspects of this act must be carefully distinguished. On the one hand, it greatly improved the administrative machinery of poor relief and stopped a number of practices that would be considered abuses even now. This was almost universally recognized, though some critics found fault with the act's administrative scheme. In any case, this aspect does not concern us here. On the other hand, the act adopted certain economic principles that do concern us. They were by no means new. In fact, they were as old as the poor-law controversy: the act simply adopted the views of one party to the controversy. That is to say, it confined poor relief to maintenance in the workhouse and prohibited outdoor relief on principle,[5] the idea being that the able-bodied unemployed, who were in distress, should not indeed be left to starve but should be maintained in semipunitive conditions.

Interpretation of these policies is an extremely delicate matter. We cannot do much more than visualize the various groups of problems that arise. First of all, these policies must not be considered in isolation. They were part of a system that offered other things to the working class. If we assign its proper weight to the effects on the real wage bill of the free-trade policy and to all that the 'free-breakfast table' implies, we shall conceive a wholly different idea of the period's performance in *Sozialpolitik*. Second, it is by no means clear how these policies fit in with economic liberalism. As regards the factory legislation, for example, it is as easy to argue that it was part of the logic of economic liberalism as it is to argue that it spelled deviation from this logic. I suggest that, as far as protection for women and children is concerned, we adopt the former opinion. Third, it must not be forgotten that though this type of factory legislation enjoyed some liberal or radical support—Cobden came out strongly on behalf of the children—the bulk of the political forces that carried it was supplied by conservatives (Lord Ashley, seventh Earl of Shaftesbury), who approached this whole range of problems in a quite different spirit. This fact is significant, no matter how we answer the question of compatibility of social legislation with the logic of economic liberalism.

Contemporaneous and later critics, German exponents of *Sozialpolitik* in particular, have accused the English 'classic' economists of cold indifference

---

cialisme d'état), and some practical measures were actually taken. Dupont-White may be considered the literary exponent of this type of *étatisme*.

[4] A reference must be substituted for information that cannot be presented here: Hutchins and Harrison, A *History of Factory Legislation* (new ed., 1907).

[5] It soon proved impossible to enforce this principle where there was serious resistance.

to the fate of labor. The first thing to be said about this is that the indictment reveals a lack of historical sense that is particularly strange in critics associated with the German historical school: the man who disapproved of a ten-hour bill in 1847 might easily be a New Dealer in modern America without our having any right to impugn his consistency. But we can go further. Most 'classic' economists supported the factory legislation, McCulloch especially. The repeal of the Combination Acts was vigorously pushed by a member of the Benthamite circle (Place [6]). And the Poor Law Amendment Act, which was almost unanimously supported by economists, has other aspects besides what seems to us harsh treatment of people in distress. At the same time, we must not go too far. The support that 'classic' economists gave to this act acquires additional significance from the fact that the theory underlying it tallied well with their general scheme of economic and political thought, their scheme of Natural Liberty. It also tallied well with their views on population and wages. It tallied still better with their almost ludicrous confidence in the ability of individuals to act with energy and rationality, to look after themselves responsibly, to find work, and to save for old age and rainy days. This, of course, is Benthamite sociology, hence bad sociology. On this point, the critics were right, however wrong they were in imputing to the 'classics' a defective social conscience.[7]

4. Gladstonian Finance

In the field of fiscal policy, we are more prone than we usually are to give the jockey credit that is really due the horse. P. J. Cambon was an able financier, yet all the reader is likely to know about the finances of the French Revolution is the breakdown of its paper money.[1] F. N. Mollien was a master of the art, but under the conditions of the Napoleonic regime he had no chance to produce 'great' fiscal policy [2]—and there are several others who deserve our respect though they have left a checkered record. Yet there was one man who not only united high ability with unparalleled opportunity but also knew how to turn budgets into political triumphs and who stands in history as the great-

[6] On this interesting man, see Graham Wallas' *Life of Francis Place* (1898), one of those books that bring past milieus back to life.

[7] Nor is it quite true that all the 'classics' were liberals in the party sense; Malthus was not a liberal. But most of the others were; and there is some truth in speaking of an 'alliance' of 'classic' economists with the liberal party. Therefore, by virtue of psychological, though not of logical association, the later decline of political liberalism *contributed* to the decline of the prestige of 'classic' economics. Observe, however, that there is a long way between recognizing this and identifying 'systems' and their fortunes with the political humors of the hour.

[1] This gives me the opportunity to call the reader's attention to the important bibliography on the finances of France in the eighteenth century by René Stourm (*Bibliographie historique des finances de la France au dix-huitième siècle*, 1895).

[2] François N. Mollien's *Mémoires d'un ministre du trésor public*, 1780-1815 (1845), however, rise in places to the level of scientific analysis.

est English financier of economic liberalism, Gladstone.[3] We cannot do better than consider him alone.

The greatest feature of Gladstonian finance—the feature that it shares with, and which may be said to define, all 'great finance'—was that it expressed with ideal adequacy both the whole civilization and the needs of the time, *ex visu* of the conditions of the country to which it was to apply; or, to put it slightly differently, that it translated a social, political, and economic vision, which was comprehensive as well as historically correct, into the clauses of a set of co-ordinated fiscal measures. This applies both to the measures themselves and to the intuition that bore them, but not to the talk of the day, Gladstone's own included, which was highly doctrinaire. We are not interested in the details of these measures but only in the principles involved. Let us try to state them.

Gladstonian finance was the finance of the system of 'natural liberty,' laissez-faire, and free trade. From the social and economic vision that this implies—and which we must now understand historically, irrespective of all general arguments pro and con—the most important thing was to remove fiscal obstructions to private activity. And for this, in turn, it was necessary to keep public expenditure low. Retrenchment was the victorious slogan of the day and was even more popular with radicals—such as Joseph Hume, the 'sleepless watchdog of finance'—than it was with either Whigs or Tories. Retrenchment means two things. First, it means reduction of the functions of the state to a minimum; this was referred to by later, especially German, critics as the policy of the 'night-watchman state.' For instance, within that social vision there is hardly any place for public expenditure on art or science: the way to further art and science—and powerfully furthered they were—is to allow people to earn so that they have the money to buy pictures or to enjoy leisure for research.[4] Second, retrenchment means rationalization of the remaining func-

[3] The most spectacular of those triumphs was won by the budget of 1853. The reader will do well to familiarize himself with its main features. He finds these described, in the whole political setting and in all their rhetorical glory, in Lord Morley's Gladstone biography already referred to.

[4] In a well-known passage, Ruskin (see below, ch. 3) upbraided English governments for refusing, unlike continental governments, to spend money for the encouragement of the arts. This is an interesting instance of a type of social criticism that always fails to see a social system as a whole. It was Ruskin's *right* to prefer other methods of encouraging art. But it was his *duty*, as an analyst of social phenomena, to realize that the English method of doing so, even if inadequate, was a method and not just nothing. Independently of this, he should have further recognized that inadequacy of the English method was not obvious from results. This also holds for the sciences and, among others, for economics. If we view results in historical perspective and in particular attach due weight to *originality* of research, we shall not find it easy to aver with confidence that this social system was less productive of artistic and scientific achievement than is the modern system that uses different and more direct methods. I emphasize this because the principle involved is very important in the field of technical economics: for instance, present-day Keynesians are within their rights, logically,

tions of the state, which among other things implies as small a military establishment as possible. The resulting economic development would in addition, so it was believed, make social expenditures largely superfluous. Observe once more that all this, wholly wrong if cast into terms of timeless general principles, did contain a large element of truth for England in 1853.

Equally important was it, from the same vision of economic opportunities and mechanisms, to raise the revenue that would still have to be raised in such a way as to deflect economic behavior as little as possible from what it would have been in the absence of all taxation ('taxation for revenue only'). And since the profit motive and the propensity to save were considered of paramount importance for the economic progress of *all* classes, this meant in particular that taxation should as little as possible interfere with the net earnings of business. Therefore, so far as direct taxation is concerned, no progression. In principle, if not in practice, Gladstone went even further than this in 1853. The Napoleonic Wars had brought the income tax (in the English sense). It had been abolished promptly when the emergency was over (1816), but had been reintroduced by Peel (1842) in order to make good the deficiency expected from his reductions of import duties.[5] But Gladstone proposed in 1853 to abolish it again in seven years.[6] As regards indirect taxes, the principle of least interference was interpreted by Gladstone to mean that taxation should be concentrated on a few important articles, leaving the rest free. This opinion prevailed throughout against that of Sir George Cornewall Lewis, the Chancellor of the Exchequer during the Crimean War, who preferred a system of numerous duties that would bear lightly on every point touched.[7]

Last, but not least, we have the principle of the balanced budget or rather, since debt was to be reduced, the principle that Robert Lowe, one of the

when they aver that the capitalist mechanism that tends to equilibrate *ex ante* saving and investment is weak and apt to stall; but if they aver that it does not exist, they are simply committing a definite and provable mistake.

[5] The same policy was adopted by the Wilson administration in 1913.

[6] In fact, he kept to this idea throughout. In his electoral manifesto of 1874 he pronounced again in favor of total repeal. The question how far this is consonant with the creed of economic liberalism is difficult. An income tax so high as to change distribution of income substantially certainly is not. This would clearly conflict with the principle of 'taxation for revenue.' But an income tax of a few per cent, even if progressive, seems to me to fit the Gladstonian vision better than does the course he actually took.

[7] Economically—though perhaps not administratively—Lewis was right, I think. Gladstonian orthodoxy overlooked another point also. It was strongly against taxing 'necessities.' In fact, this principle, together with the free-trade policy, was the greatest *direct* contribution of Gladstonian finance to social welfare (though we must, in order to appraise its total contribution, keep in mind that this direct contribution was not its only one: in addition it did something toward helping into existence the wealth that later proved so easy to tax in the interest of the masses). But this exclusive emphasis on the distinction between 'necessaries' and 'luxuries' fails to do full justice to the implications of the distinction between commodities that are elastic and commodities that are inelastic in demand.

Chancellors of the Exchequer of the Gladstonian era, embodied in his definition of a minister of finance: 'an animal that ought to have a surplus.' Again, there is no point whatever in criticizing either the policy of balancing the budget or the policy of debt redemption from modern standpoints. Even if we grant all that modern advocates of deficit financing claim, we should admit that in a world bursting with 'investment opportunities' neither policy can be set down as unalloyed nonsense.

5. Gold

The little that need be said for our purposes on the currency and banking policies of that period will be more conveniently reserved for the last chapter of this Part. In consequence, there is only one point to make here. After the monetary disturbances—the inflation—incident to the Napoleonic Wars, all countries struggled back to what was considered normalcy. This took many decades in such countries as Austria, but was achieved promptly and with comparative ease in England and France. On the Continent, normalcy meant silver or a bimetallic standard, but England, after having legalized the de facto gold standard established in the eighteenth century, resumed gold redemption of Bank of England notes within a few years of Waterloo, much as she returned to gold at prewar parity (though in a somewhat different form) after the First World War of our time. Moreover, it was a perfectly 'free' or 'automatic' gold standard that allowed for no kind of management other than is implied in the regulatory power of any central bank that is 'a lender of last resort.' Our question is: why? The measure drew fire from many quarters, even from some economists. Powerful agrarian interests attributed to it—never mind now whether rightly or wrongly—the depression that plagued them. There was enough unemployment to induce the government (Castlereagh, 1821) to propose public works—an almost Rooseveltian program—as a remedy. Merchants do not relish losses, nor bankers frozen assets—and there were plenty of both. Also, we shall see that many competent people advocated a managed paper currency. Nevertheless, the gold-standard policy was never in real danger politically, and if it was not, until much later, adopted by all industrialized countries, this was not a matter of their choice: in spite of all counterarguments, the 'automatic' gold standard remained almost everywhere the ideal to strive for and pray for, in season and out of season. Again: why?

At present we are taught to look upon such a policy as wholly erroneous—as a sort of fetishism that is impervious to rational argument. We are also taught to discount all rational and all purely economic arguments that may actually be adduced in favor of it. But quite irrespective of these, there is one point about the gold standard that would redeem it from the charge of foolishness, even in the absence of any purely economic advantage—a point from which also many other attitudes of that time present themselves in a different light. An 'automatic' gold currency [1] is part and parcel of a laissez-faire and

[1] Of course, it is never quite automatic and this phrase is misleading. I use it here for the sake of brevity and do not mean by it more than that all other means of pay-

free-trade economy. It links every nation's money rates and price levels with the money rates and price levels of all the other nations that are 'on gold.' It is extremely sensitive to government expenditure and even to attitudes or policies that do not involve expenditure directly, for example, to foreign policy, to certain policies of taxation, and, in general, to precisely all those policies that violate the principles of economic liberalism. *This* is the reason why gold is so unpopular now and also why it was so popular in a bourgeois era. It imposes restrictions upon governments or bureaucracies that are much more powerful than is parliamentary criticism. It is both the badge and the guarantee of bourgeois freedom—of freedom not simply of the bourgeois *interest*, but of freedom in the bourgeois *sense*. From this standpoint a man may quite rationally fight for it, even if fully convinced of the validity of all that has ever been urged against it on economic grounds. From the standpoint of *étatisme* and planning, a man may not less rationally condemn it, even if fully convinced of the validity of all that has ever been urged for it on economic grounds.

---

ment should be redeemable in gold and that everyone should have the right to import and export, monetize or demonetize, gold at will.

CHAPTER 3

The Intellectual Scenery

1. The Zeitgeist of the Period and Its Philosophy

The truth of our proposition that the *Zeitgeist* of a period can never be defined in terms of a single system of mutually consistent ideas or beliefs is brought home to us when we turn to the philosophical currents of that time in order to discover the philosophical affiliations, if any, of the social sciences.

(a) *Utilitarianism.* The most obvious of these affiliations is with English utilitarianism.[1] This was indeed a product of the eighteenth century. But it ran the best part of its career in the first half of the nineteenth. No philosophy at all in the technical sense,[2] unsurpassably shallow as a 'philosophy of life,' it

[1] See Sir Leslie Stephen, *The English Utilitarians* (1900).

[2] Evidently, the 'calculus of pleasure and pain' and the principle of 'greatest happiness for the greatest number' do not, in themselves, assert anything about specifically philosophical or epistemological problems, though they are capable of producing an ethical doctrine. The reason why this speculative deficiency of utilitarianism was not

fitted to perfection the streak of materialistic (antimetaphysical) rationalism that may be associated with liberalism and the business mind. Actually, however, the majority of the English business class did not accept it but, whether Anglican or nonconformist, kept to the religious philosophy of either Church or Chapel. The utilitarian leaders evidently knew why they were so careful not to affront religion openly.[3] And all leading politicians knew why they left utilitarianism severely alone. Its appointed apostles, the philosophical radicals,[4] were at first a very small circle that gathered around Bentham and James Mill. J. S. Mill cannot be called a utilitarian without qualification. In some respects he outgrew the creed; in others he refined it. But he never renounced it explicitly, and it was through his influence upon the rising generations in the 1850's and 1860's that a more sophisticated utilitarianism established itself in the intellectual centers, especially in Cambridge. But it did not not become dominant. This seems to be clear from an analysis of the position of the men who were then or later became leaders of Cambridge life and thought, particularly of Sidgwick.[5]

It will be maintained later that there is no point in calling Ricardo a utilitarian, though he was personally connected with the group and may have professed sympathy with its creed. Bentham, James Mill, and (with qualification) J. S. Mill were the only prominent economists who were also prominent and militant utilitarians, as Beccaria and Verri had been in the eighteenth century. It was natural for Bentham and the Mills to see themselves in the role of philosophical patrons of economics and to assume responsibility for an alliance between economics and utilitarianism that was acquiesced in by many later economists, such as Jevons and Edgeworth; but it was neither necessary nor useful. This alliance is the only reason why utilitarianism looms so large in the economist's picture of nineteenth-century thought, much larger than is

---

more keenly felt was that utilitarians found what they wanted ready at hand in the empiricist tradition of the Locke-Hume type.

[3] J. S. Mill's *Three Essays on Religion* appeared posthumously in 1874. The views on religion that are contained in his elaborate *Examination of Sir William Hamilton's Philosophy* (1865) probably did not filter through to the general reading public.

[4] See e.g. C. B. R. Kent, *The English Radicals* (1899); E. Halévy, *La Formation du radicalisme philosophique* (1901-4; English trans. 1928).

[5] Henry Sidgwick (1838-1900) really has claim to more attention than we can bestow upon him. His work in economics will be noticed in passing where it belongs chronologically, but there is little in his eminently reasonable rendering of 'classic' doctrine to call for comment in a sketch like this. Nor, I am afraid, would a historian of ethics or politics—the other two fields in which he produced major work—be able to say more. But he was one of the greatest English university men all the same: milieu-creating, milieu-leading, soul-shaping to an extraordinary degree. Perhaps lack of originality is one of the conditions for this particular type of academic achievement. Of all the Cambridge leaders, he was—with his antimetaphysical mind that was so lucid and so wingless—the one most favorably disposed to accept utilitarian starting points. Nevertheless, his ethics cannot be called straight utilitarianism, and this is the test, for it is here that a utilitarian creed, *qua* philosophy, would have to assert its sway.

justified by its importance either as a philosophy or as a factor of the *Zeitgeist*. We must digress for a moment in order to consider the effects of that alliance upon economics. The reader will recall that, for earlier epochs, we have dealt with this question already.

Since economists, especially nontheorists, are and always have been apt to entertain exaggerated notions about the importance of philosophical backgrounds upon the positive work of economic analysis, we shall understand that this alliance made English economic theory unpopular in many quarters. Especially with some German writers the utilitarian garb was quite sufficient for wholesale condemnation of the theory that appeared in this guise. More interesting than this attitude, which rested upon nothing but an obvious misunderstanding, is, however, the question of the real influence of utilitarian philosophy upon the contents of 'classic' economics. We must distinguish influence upon policy recommendations, economic sociology, and economic analysis proper. As regards the 'classic' recommendations, there are no doubt many that are wholly neutral with respect to any philosophy of life: one need not be a utilitarian in order to recommend peasant proprietorship for Ireland, or in order either to recommend or condemn return to the gold standard after the Napoleonic Wars. But there are others—unconditional free trade, for example—that did imply views of general policy and attitudes to life that do seem, to say the least, to link up with utilitarianism better than with any other philosophy of life. As regards economic sociology, utilitarianism can only be described as a complete failure since its rationalistic conception of individual behavior and of social institutions was obviously and radically wrong. But as regards that part of economic analysis which works with rational schemata, utilitarian philosophy, though superfluous, does no harm. And this fact, as critics would have recognized if they had been competent economists, salvages the bulk of the work in economic analysis done by the utilitarians.[6]

Professional philosophy in England, mainly the philosophy of the Scottish common-sense school, was but moderately affected by utilitarianism and was, on the whole, hostile to the utilitarian way of disposing of specifically philosophical problems. But there was during that period no leader of English philosophical thought strong enough to counteract the able and vigorous propaganda of the philosophical radicals. Leaders of thought that did counteract it to some extent were produced by the romantic (see below, sec. 2) and several religious movements. A leader of still another type might be mentioned here, Carlyle.[7] For economists he is one of the most important and most char-

[6] Of course, this should not be understood to mean that this work was not open to objection on other grounds.

[7] Thomas Carlyle's (1795-1881) fame rests on the solid basis of his historical works that are too well known to be mentioned here. But one should not call him a historian without adding that, besides being much else, he was a historian *sui generis*. He

acteristic figures in the cultural panorama of that epoch—standing in heroic pose, hurling scorn at the materialistic littleness of his age, cracking a whip with which to flay, among other things, our Dismal Science. This is how he saw himself and how his time saw and loved to see him. Completely incapable of understanding the meaning of a theorem, overlooking the fact that *all* science is 'dismal' to the artist, he thought he had got hold of the right boy to whip. A large part of the public applauded, and so did some economists who understood no more than he did what a 'science' is and does. But the digression above on utilitarian economics shows that he was not wholly in error. The utilitarian economists did advocate policies indicative of a philosophy of life that fully deserved all the stripes that Carlyle administered. And the reader should for a moment stop to ponder over the difficulty that has so much to do with the futility of so many of our controversies, namely, the difficulty that both the professional and the public mind experience in disentangling the analytic aspect of such cases from the cultural philosophy that goes with it, and in realizing that adverse criticism of the former is perfectly compatible

---

painted portraits in the style and spirit of the artist. Though these portraits rest on sound and often minute research, they render artistic not scientific interpretations. The modern reader will be amazed to miss economic and social facts almost completely. And he will turn away with something like disgust from the overemphasis on the personal element that he finds everywhere. Yet this is not quite what he should do. By itself Carlyle's 'hero worship,' which seems to make history a tissue of individual biographies, is not indeed acceptable sociology. But in times when the personal element and its explanatory value are in danger of being drowned in statistics and when the 'common man' holds the stage, Carlyle's hero worship, by stressing the forgotten factor, personality, comes in as a useful antidote. Directly relevant to the history of economics are his *Chartism* (1840), *Past and Present* (1843), and *Latter-Day Pamphlets* (1850).

Carlyle's emphasis upon the element of personality (the contrast with Bentham, who was individualist without being a 'personalist,' should suffice to show that the two are entirely distinct) calls up the name of R. W. Emerson (1803-82), who was, to use his own phrase, another Representative Man. With him, that emphasis did not amount to hero worship, and to this extent his contribution to a sociological schema of the historical process is sounder though less original than is Carlyle's. Emerson did not cross swords with 'classic' economics. But from another angle he is still more important for us: his thought, the focus of many currents and the source of others, *was the adequate expression of the civilization of that age as it mirrored itself in the particular conditions of the New England environment*. This I conceive to be his claim to eminence in the history of thought. I am sorry this sounds involved. However, since it is impossible to describe that (New England) intellectual and moral environment in the available space, we must leave it with this sentence. Nor can we afford to stay to look at the Concord and Cambridge (or Boston) circles with which, directly and indirectly, Emerson and his associates were connected. This is all the more regrettable because they are the sources of an important component of a specifically American radicalism that influenced the attitudes of American economists long after those circles themselves had disappeared, and accounts for much that a European finds hard to understand. A study of Thoreau's writings might prove particularly enlightening. (On the 'social science movement,' see below, sec. 6a.)

with admiration for the latter and vice versa. Something, however, may be said for Carlyle even from the analytic point of view: he had the vision, though he had not the means to make it analytically articulate, of an economic sociology that was much more realistic than was the utilitarian. What a nation is and really wants and what are the real determinants of its fate, he saw much more clearly than did Bentham; the analysis that might be distilled from his pages would take account of a number of important facts that Bentham ignored or, at all events, brushed aside, because from the standpoint of his creed they were simply irrelevant aberrations. J. S. Mill sensed this to some extent. He grew to realize that the scheme of utilitarian rationality is quite inadequate beyond a limited range of problems. But he was not the man to make anything of it, and so the vision of one man and the analytic power of another never met to work together. Carlyle influenced another but (for us) much less important prophet, Ruskin, who, though his writings on economic subjects belong to the subsequent period, shall therefore be mentioned here.

Almost throughout the period under discussion, John Ruskin (1819-1900; any work of reference will give the reader all that is needed to appreciate the points to be made in this paragraph) was one of those creative interpreters of art—painting, architecture, sculpture, and also poetry—whose interpretations are themselves works of art, works that have a life of their own and elicit admiration even in those who (like myself) do not believe in them *as interpretations*. For us, it is particularly important to note his contributions to a general sociology of art, his attempts to analyze the social conditions that produce, or are favorable to the production of, great works of art. From the end of the 1860's on, he turned, however, to the mission that was to make him so popular with the crowd as well as with economists of radical propensities—wrathful and dilettantic criticism of the sins of capitalism: the reader will quickly acquire an adequate notion of this criticism by dipping into *Unto this Last* (1862), *Munera Pulveris* (1872), and *Fors Clavigera* (1871-84), all in *The Works of Ruskin.* I have only one point to make. There is a definite reason for objecting to Ruskin's way of handling economic problems (I am not speaking, of course, of his generous and not unsuccessful practical work in the interest of the welfare and civilization of the masses): he failed to do in this field what he did as a matter of course in the field of art. We know that he prepared himself most sedulously for his career as an interpreter of art; that he mastered techniques and studied historical detail according to the canons of scholarship. It is 'genius' that speaks from his interpretations, but genius tutored and made effective by learning. In the field of economics he did nothing of the sort; all he did was to add generous indignation to half-understood observations and undigested pieces of reading. It is this and *not* his evaluations (with which many of us will sympathize) that puts him out of court, except for such writers as J. A. Hobson. The judgment I pass on him—and he stands for so many—is exactly the same that he himself would have passed on any writer who undertook, for example, to criticize Turner's paintings without having previously acquired, by morally neutral study, an adequate mastery of the relevant facts and techniques.

(b) *German Philosophy.* The reader presumably knows that the first part of the period under discussion witnessed the peak achievements of German speculative philosophy, and the names of Kant, Schelling, Fichte, Hegel, and Schopenhauer will immediately turn up in his mind. But, no matter whether he knows much or little about them, it is impossible to enter here into the purely philosophical aspects of their work. All I can say without proof about Kant, Schelling, and Schopenhauer is this. First, their creations are striking examples of autonomous philosophical thought: it would be hopeless to try to link their teaching with the attitudes that may be associated with the class position of the bourgeois or any other element.[8] Second, Kant was the only one of the three to exert significant international influence; [9] but in Germany, all three of them wielded powerful influence upon the thought of generations in whose mental pattern the philosophical component then counted for still more than it did during the subsequent period. Nevertheless, whatever else this influence may have touched or shaped, it did not extend to the professional work of German—let alone of other than German—economists. Many of them no doubt would have described themselves as Kantians. But their professional methods and results were just as compatible with any other philosophy. This question of influence posits itself somewhat differently in the cases of Fichte and Hegel.

Fichte [10] calls for comment, because he associated with his speculative philosophy, in the technical sense of the term, a social and political philosophy that trespassed freely on the economics field and must be noticed for two reasons. He blocked out a plan for a particular economic organization of society that will be considered below in the section on socialism. And he has been assigned a key position in the early development of O. Spann's 'universalist economics.' [11]

[8] Some Marxists have tried it, fortified by the conviction that it *must* be possible to do so. Such a conviction will always insure some measure of spurious success that means nothing: everything can be *forced* into correlation with everything else.

[9] Kantian ideas spread in particular to England. Even James Mill grappled with them, but the nonutilitarians, Hamilton especially, and also philosophy-minded divines, put them under heavy obligation, which, considering the elements of English origin that we find in Kant, will not surprise us. A. Marshall's enthusiasm for Kant—highly significant of the intellectual atmosphere of his early days—will be noticed in the appropriate place.

[10] The works of J. G. Fichte (1762-1814) that are particularly relevant to us are his *Reden an die deutsche Nation* (1808), his *Grundlage des Naturrechts* (1796-7), and *Der geschlossene Handelsstaat* (1800), all in his *Sämmtliche Werke* (ed. by I. H. Fichte, 1845-6). Difficulties of interpretation are greatly increased by the fact that his ideas underwent, in several essential respects, changes of two different types: his philosophy changed, in the course of his life, in consequence of his own work upon it; his general outlook changed in consequence of a German's typical experiences during the Napoleonic period that turned the cosmopolitan—who had defined a man's country as that country which happens at any time to stand 'at the height of civilization'—into an ardent patriot.

[11] As has been mentioned already, the idea that the history of economics may be described in terms of the struggle between two 'systems' of thought, an individualist and a universalist one, is really Professor Pribram's. But it was Professor Spann who founded what is known in Germany as the universalist school. On Fichte's relation to it, as conceived by the latter, see O. Spann, *Haupttheorien der Volkswirtschaftslehre*

Fichte was, to be sure, no individualist in the Benthamite sense and no laissez-faire man. If this constitutes a 'universalist,' then he was one, and the only thing to be said is that this species will then grow uncomfortably numerous. If this is not enough to constitute a universalist, we are left with Fichte's conception of a superindividual and 'superconscious' group mind—in which the individual consciousnesses participate. The mere fact that he emphasized the autonomy of the phenomenon Society as against the phenomenon State, besides being as old as scholasticism, has certainly nothing specifically 'universalist' about it. It is true that this conception is in the 'universalist' line, but it is also in many other lines, for example, in the entirely positivist line of Durkheim. Perhaps it is somewhat less unrealistic to assume a connection, via romanticism, between Fichte and Spann than it is to trace Durkheim's thought to Fichte. Confidence in such purely phraseological relations is in any case misplaced and only serves to prevent perception of more substantial ones.

Hegel [12] calls for comment on three counts: first, because of his stupendous success; second, because of his theory of the state and because his philosophy constitutes an important branch of what we shall term evolutionism; third, because of his formative influence on the thought of Karl Marx.

All that I can say about the first point is that it makes Hegel's philosophy one of the factors in the *Zeitgeist* we are trying to survey. More than this I cannot say because the success was beyond anything I might be able to account for. I could explain temporary success in Germany of the philosopher who is credited with the saying: 'Of all my pupils one only has understood me; and this one has misunderstood me.' Perhaps I could also explain, partly by the fact that Hegelian philosophy is capable of widely different interpreta-

(1st ed., 1911, many later ones; English trans. 1930). The reader who wishes to have a further and more sympathetic first introduction to universalist economics than I am able to provide is referred, once for all, to Professor Salin's exposition in the *Encyclopaedia of the Social Sciences* (article, 'Economics,' section on 'Romantic and Universalist Economics'), where all the works of Spann are mentioned.

If the reader will carefully go over Professor Salin's exposition (op. cit. vol. v, pp. 386-7), he will immediately see the reason for lack of sympathy on my part. If universalists were content to preach a 'holist' meta-economic or philosophical interpretation of both economic reality and economic theory, there would be no objection; in fact I should actually sympathize with their meta-economics, though I might interpret it to myself in terms of *Gestalt* psychology. In any case, their philosophy would be as irrelevant for us as was Quesnay's theology. But they make larger claims, viz. claims to having developed a new and different method of analysis. They actually 'reject' propositions about pricing and money, for example. And all they do after rejecting them is to reformulate them in a clumsy and inadequate way. For instance, after rejecting the concept of equilibrium, Professor Spann introduced the concept of equi-importance (at margins), which is to do exactly the same things.

[12] G. W. F. Hegel (1770-1831). For us, the most important of his works are: *Phänomenologie des Geistes* (1807; 2nd ed. of English trans. 1931), his most 'realistic' performance that may serve to elucidate some of his more 'abstract' phases; *Wissenschaft der Logik* (1812-16, English trans. 1929) and *Vorlesungen über die Philosophie der Geschichte* (ed. 1837, from lecture notes; rev. English ed. 1899).

tions, why Hegel's influence on German thought not only proved durable but also experienced a strong revival in the twentieth century. But what is beyond my power of comprehension is the great influence he exerted in England, France, Italy, and the United States, that is, on soils that should not have been favorable to this plant. The fact itself is indubitable, however. The second point will be dealt with in section 4 of this chapter. The third, Hegel's influence on Marx, constitutes our immediate concern.

> Many Marxists, and not only those of philosophical bent of mind, have come near to stating that Marxism is rooted in Hegelism and that, the relation being one of dependence, acceptance of the 'dialectic method' constitutes part of Marxist orthodoxy. Marx himself was of a different opinion. In the preface to the second edition of the first volume of *Das Kapital*, he tells us that as a philosopher he had been a Hegelian; that he never lost his early preference for Hegel's philosophy; and that what he considered superficial criticisms of it only served to strengthen his taste for 'coquetting' with it; but that he never allowed himself to be guided by it in his positive research into the facts of capitalist society. I suggest that this statement be accepted. Authors often misinterpret their own procedure and there is the possibility that Marx was mistaken. But it can be shown that he was not. For every proposition of his, economic and sociological, as well as his vision of the capitalist process as a whole, may be either traced to sources other than philosophical—such as Ricardo's economic theory—or else understood as results of strictly empirical analysis of his own. The Hegelism of his exposition is not more than a form that we can discard in all cases without affecting the substance of his argument. The only case that could possibly be considered doubtful will be discussed below.

'Idealistic' (that is, metaphysical) philosophy never ruled unchallenged. As the period wore on, the streak of materialism that we associate with bourgeois rationality asserted itself independently of the utilitarian current. Among other things, it encouraged a materialistic interpretation of Hegel: some people discovered that his metaphysical concepts are not really necessary for his general mode of reasoning, which can stand without them, and dropped them accordingly. Perhaps the most important of the Hegelians who, in doing so, developed into straight materialists was Ludwig Feuerbach.[13] The poor lot of 'free thinkers' (exponents of mechanist or sensationalist materialism), who published in the last decades of that period and are significant only because

[13] L. A. Feuerbach's (1804-72) most important work, *Das Wesen des Christenthums* (1841; English trans., 2nd ed., 1877), holds a key position in two respects: first, it attacked the foundations of that part of Hegel's metaphysics that irked its 'free-thinking' followers most, the part that seemed to lend support to religious beliefs; second, it attacked, though less directly, Hegel's metaphysics altogether and turned—a most significant sign of the times—philosophy into a sociology of sorts. (On Marx's violent hostility to Feuerbach's system of thought—that of course does not exclude his being influenced by it—see below, sec. 3c.)

their popular success was an important sign of the times, owe something to him but less than we might suppose and less than many historians have supposed. Once more: in analyzing broad currents of ideas we are too prone to assume relations between the bubbles that bubble up from the same crater.

(c) *Comtist Positivism.* Of course, that period's pattern of philosophic thought was very much richer than our survey suggests. But we shall take from it only one more strand that not only embodies another of the main components of that period's *Zeitgeist*, but also is particularly important for economists. In France professional philosophy continued to keep up a Cartesian tradition, curiously interwoven with ideas that hailed from the English empiricists, from Condillac, and, in reaction against Condillac, from Scottish 'common sense.'[14] The antimetaphysical component, which, disregarding any other possible meaning of the word, I shall call *positivist*, asserted itself in many ways. But it found its most nearly adequate expression in a suggestion thrown out by Saint-Simon and carried out by Auguste Comte (1798-1857), a theoretical physicist by training, in his *Cours de philosophie positive*, which was to satisfy two distinct and logically independent needs: first, the need for a general body of thought that would fill the void left by receding metaphysical speculation, the need for a *substitute* for philosophy (or religion); second, the need for a general body of thought that would put some order into the tropical growth of specialized research. Herbert Spencer's *Synthetic Philosophy*—'synthetic' indeed!—that appeared in installments from 1862 on (*First Principles, Biology, Psychology, Sociology,* and *Ethics*) was, in a sense, another attempt to satisfy both needs.

Comte's *Cours* appeared, 1830-42, in six volumes. Of Comte's other writings only his letters to J. S. Mill (*Lettres d'Auguste Comte à John Stuart Mill,* 1841-1846, publ. 1877) come within our orbit. As regards the rest, the less said the better. It should be kept in mind that, in speaking of Comte and his work, I am referring exclusively to those two publications, for Positivism and Comtism were to acquire also, from the aberrations of his declining years, quite different meanings.

As explained above, the *Cours* presents two aspects which must be carefully distinguished. First, it expounds the doctrine that all our knowledge is knowledge of invariant relations between given phenomena on whose nature or causation there is no sense in speculating. This positivism brought earlier tendencies to a head and anticipated, in some respects, the much more interesting empiriocriticism of the next period. It is a philo-

[14] That group is usually referred to, with a value judgment, as eclectics, which perhaps does not do full justice to its most important member, Victor Cousin. It is associated with another group of political theorists and practitioners (and historians) that gathered around the strong personality of Royer-Collard (the 'doctrinaire' party as it was called; Guizot, the historian and prime minister belonged to it—more or less). Both groups are important elements in the Paris picture of the epoch between 1815 and 1848, and their thought displays parallelisms with that of the period's economists But I can mention them only in order to apologize for my inability to insert them.

sophical doctrine in the technical sense of the term—though a negative one—and as such did not exert, and was incapable of exerting, any influence upon research in any particular science.

But, second, Comte's primary concern was not really with this philosophy. The *Cours* starts with the question how, in an epoch of inevitable specialization, we might salvage that organic unity of all human knowledge that was so vital a reality in the times of the polyhistors. His answer was that we should create for this purpose another specialty, the specialty of *généralités*. This plan has meaning quite independently of whatever philosophic opinions one might entertain and comes to the fore again later on. The *Cours* is an attempt to carry this plan into effect in a particular way and with a particular slant.

Comte's particular way was this: he tried to arrange the total of all scientific knowledge (knowledge from other than scientific sources he did not recognize) into a hierarchy of sciences or, to change the simile, into a building, every floor of which was to be occupied by a different science and which was to rise from foundations in logic and mathematics toward the problems of human society. The six floors were respectively assigned to Mathematics, Astronomy, Physics, Chemistry, Biology, and—Psychology being conspicuous by its absence—Sociology, the science of society. And he actually proceeded, if I may keep to the analogy, to furnish every floor with what he conceived to be those elements in every science that were most important for the science located on the next floor. Nothing can or need be said about the grandeur and the shortcomings of the plan or of its execution.

Comte's influence upon the social sciences in general, and upon economics in particular, was considerable and gathered momentum as the century wore on. This was not because of his 'philosophy,' but because he did sociological work himself. We shall have to touch upon contributions of his—constructive and critical—both in the rest of this chapter and in later chapters. It will be convenient, however, to list the four most important ones, and to dispose of two of them at once: (I) Comte baptized nascent sociology and sketched out a research program for it that foreshadowed later developments in Social Psychology; (II) this sociology is geared, as we shall see, to an eighteenth-century conception of social evolution; (III) he introduced into the social sciences the concepts of Statics and Dynamics; (IV) he developed a methodology that led him to attack the procedure of 'classic' economics in a manner that anticipated many later criticisms. I shall proceed to comment on (III) and (IV).

(III) Comte was primarily concerned with social evolution (see below, sec. 4d). But he fully realized that the idea of evolution does not cover all the problems presented by social organisms. There are also nonevolutionary phenomena or aspects that require a different treatment. Therefore he assembled another body of facts and propositions about 'social instincts,' which act and react upon one another so as to produce by means of an equilibrating process the 'spontaneous order of society'; and this body of facts and propositions he laid alongside the evolutionary compound, or, as he styled it, the theory of 'natural progress.' Adopting, as he tells us, the terminology of the zoologist H. de Blainville, he called the former Statics and the latter Dynamics. J. S. Mill, the author who introduced these terms into economic theory, was well acquainted with Comte's thought, and it is natural to assume that he took them from Comte, though he did not say so. If this was the case, then Mill was wrong in speaking (*Principles*, Book IV, ch. 1) of 'a happy generalization of a mathematical phrase.' Since many people who failed to appreciate the importance of that distinction have tried to stigmatize it as an illegitimate derivate of a mechanistic way of thinking, it is time to state the fact that, so far as there is sense at all in talking about borrowing—as regards the words that is, not as regards the distinction itself which forces itself upon us in any case—the ultimate lender was not mechanics but zoology. We shall return to the subject more than once. It should, however, be mentioned that Mill's definitions of statics and dynamics correspond to Comte's, as far as I can see; but these terms subsequently acquired several different senses and are now being used in a still different one.

(IV) Methodologically, Comte's plan was to observe historical and ethnological facts and to build his science of society from such generalizations as these facts would suggest. This is, of course, a very familiar program that was, then and later, espoused by numerous writers, especially by historical economists. All the more important is it to realize a paradoxical fact: while it was perfectly natural for historical economists to adopt this plan, it was not at all natural for Comte to do so. The historian, and hence the historical economist, distrusts any theory that tries to 'isolate' the economic element in social life. Theory is for him indeed speculative and unrealistic. It is even something still worse: it is speculative construction that borrows its methods from the physical sciences. Only the real phenomenon in *all* its historical facets—with the economic, ethical, legal, and cultural facets all simultaneously considered—is for him the true object of social research, whose methods must therefore differ *toto cælo* from any used by the physicist. But Comte could not argue like this. On the contrary, he wanted to adopt the methods of the physicist. When *he* accused 'classic' economists of unscientific speculation, he meant exactly the opposite of what the economists of the historical school were to mean. And there, as J. S. Mill realized, he was completely in error. But in addition to being in error as regards his criticism, he was also in error as regards his own choice of method. For physical science does not accept unanalyzed fact: either in the laboratory or (where laboratory experiment is not possible) by mental experiment, physicists do separate or isolate individual aspects and then theorize about them with a boldness that far surpasses anything that economists ever ventured to do. Had Comte wished to be 'scientific' in *this* sense, he could not have adopted any method other than that followed by Bentham, Say, and later by J. S. Mill. He adopted the one he did adopt (generalization from unanalyzed historical or ethnological fact) by mistake and, if he anticipated some of the later arguments of the historical school, he anticipated them, again, by mistake—honest ignorance of economics and Saint-Simonian prejudice against it being, of course, the psychological sources of both. The comedy of errors will be complete when we realize that, on top of it all, he indulged in *genuinely* metaphysical speculation himself. This clarification reduces considerably our conception of Comte's influence: the later historical economists of the Schmoller school were not Comtists at all; their philosophical and methodological affiliations were quite different; they arrived at their arguments against 'classic' theory from the logic of their own intellectual position and would have arrived at them even if Comte had never lived; it is merely a coincidence that, as it was, these arguments, or some of them, look Comtist to the historian.[15] With other exponents of historicism, Comte's influence is more in evidence. (On Ingram, for example, see below, Part IV, ch. 4.)

2. Romanticism and Historiography

We might learn a lot about the *Zeitgeist* from surveying the literary currents of that period were it possible to do so. Very interesting inferences could be drawn, for example, from the success of the novels of Dickens, Thackeray, or Flaubert, which are also really sociological treatises—highly colored by ideologies that we do not usually attribute to the people who read them. Or to mention but one other and far distant example, we might also learn a lot by analyzing the burst of German enthusiasm for Greek art that started in the eighteenth century [1] but survived well into the nineteenth. We must refrain. But there was one literary movement, Romanticism, that we cannot afford to pass by, partly because of its real importance for the development of the social sciences, partly because of the importance that has been wrongly attributed to it.

(a) *Romanticism.* Like its cultural antipode, utilitarianism, the romantic movement started in the eighteenth century: we, who are primarily interested in its analytic performance, cannot do better than to choose as our landmark the great name of Herder.[2] Unlike utilitarianism, romanticism was not a philosophy, or a social creed, or a political or economic 'system.' It was essentially

[15] This is not true for sociology: many sociologists, especially French ones, did descend from Comte (de Roberty, Durkheim, and others). But as regards the economists who faced each other in the Battle of Methods, Menger, the theorist, was much more Comtist than was Schmoller, the historian.

[1] J. J. Winckelmann's *Geschichte der Kunst des Altertums*, a book, both symptomatically and causally important, appeared in 1764.

[2] J. G. von Herder (1744-1803): *Fragmente über die neuere deutsche Litteratur* (1767), the most definitely romanticist of his works; *Über den Ursprung der Sprache* (1772); *Ideen zur Philosophie der Geschichte der Menschheit* (1784-91), for us the most important of his writings. But Herder's thought transcends romanticism: influence from and influence on romanticism is but one aspect of his work. As a sociol-

a literary fashion that linked up with a certain attitude toward life and art: on the one hand, the movement was entirely confined to intellectual circles—there are no romanticists who were not also literati; on the other hand, the movement gained international importance primarily in the field of belles lettres and in the neighboring fields of literary criticism and philology. For painting, architecture, and music it meant less—though it also set fashions there, witness, for example, some 'Gothic' horrors—and it influenced but peripherically whatever else it touched. But from the history of literature it is indeed possible to compile an impressive list of names, such as Byron, Alfieri, Shelley, Wordsworth, Coleridge, Scott, Longfellow, Chateaubriand, Gautier, Hugo, Hölderlin, Novalis, Brentano, Arnim, and the two Schlegels.[3] It is there that we must look for the achievement of romanticism and for the serious work of the romanticists. They no doubt sallied forth from that stronghold, as literati will, and roamed all over those parts of philosophy and social science that happened to attract them. It is with their exploits on these excursions that we are concerned here. But we must bear in mind that in dealing with these we are not dealing with the core of romanticist achievement and that we must expect any grain we may find to be mixed with dilettantic chaff.

However, even as regards belles lettres we cannot help being struck by a fact that is indeed evident from our little list of names and would stand out still more clearly in any more extended one: works and men that in one sense or another may be labeled romanticist often have very little in common and look strange in juxtaposition. This will cease to surprise us as soon as we make an attempt to define what the romanticist attitude consisted in. On the surface, it spelled revolt against classic canons of art, for instance, against Aristotle's three dramatic unities (of time, place, and action). But below this surface, there was something much more important, namely, revolt against convention, particularly against rationalized convention: feeling (possibly genuine) rose against cold reason; spontaneous impulse against ultilitarian logic; intuition against analysis; the 'soul' against the intellect; the romance of national history against the artefacts of the Enlightenment. Let us call this attitude anti-intellectualism, although this term will also be used in a different sense below. Remembering that the romantic movement was confined to in-

ogist he also experienced and exerted influence of an environmentalist type (see below, sec. 3c); he fought Kant's aesthetics in an almost empiricist spirit, and there are passages in his *Ideen* on cultural change that have a Spencerian ring; his theories of language, literature, art, religion, mythology—including the methodological suggestions in the direction of comparative philology and comparative mythology and hierology—make him the precursor of several important modern, as they make him the heir to several important eighteenth-century, tendencies, including tendencies enshrined in the Hobbes-Locke-Hume tradition. If we cannot go into these cross currents of ideas that elucidate many features of the nineteenth-century *Zeitgeist*, our comfort must be that they entirely failed to fertilize economics.

[3] Goethe is too great to be pigeonholed and, moreover, disliked the romanticists intensely. But his work, both at dawn and at sunset, displays many romanticist elements. It is only in between that Goethe was, or tried to be, severely 'classic.'

tellectuals—and therefore was something quite different from what we may term the common man's anti-intellectualism—we should not flinch at the apparently paradoxical designation, intellectual anti-intellectualism. Viewed like this, the phenomenon of romanticism really comes within a well-known class: like other workmen, intellectuals seem from time to time to get disgusted with their tools and to be possessed with a desire to 'down' them and to use their fists instead.

This diagnosis explains, among other things, why it is impossible to systematize romanticism into a coherent whole and to develop rules that would enable us to identify romanticist ideas or programs as easily as we can identify, for example, utilitarian ideas or programs. The movement was in the nature of a shake-up. Its fertility was principally due to this fact. The individual who experienced its impact was left free to walk in any direction after having been shaken up. This applies particularly to the political and economic views of individual romanticists which later historians have tried to unify in directions of which they themselves approved if they were sympathetic, and in directions of which they disapproved if they were hostile. The resulting picture was unrealistic in both cases. Romanticism has been identified with political 'reaction'; it is true that many romanticists, following the tendencies of their time, turned conservative or 'reactionary' when their environments did, and that some of them even sold their services to 'reactionary' governments; but the essentially revolutionary character of the movement was never quite lost, as may be gathered from the case of that powerful leader of opinion, Joseph von Görres. Romanticist ideology has been contrasted with Benthamite ideas about liberty and democracy; again it is true that romanticist liberty was not the liberty of J. S. Mill's essay and that romanticist democracy was not Bentham's mechanistic thing; but it might be urged that some romanticists had a deeper understanding of what liberty and democracy meant to people *as they are and think and feel* than had the utilitarians or than has anyone who tries to impose a logical scheme of his making on existing social patterns. Romanticism has also been credited with a strong taste—taste is the right word, since we are speaking of literati—for the Roman Catholic faith; it is true that the romanticists, with their sense for live realities, were bound to look upon that mighty structure with feelings very different from those of the utilitarians; it is also true that, at least in the early nineteenth century, their movement went parallel with and was related to, a Catholic revival; but it is quite wrong to confuse the two. Few of the true leaders of the Catholic movement (Görres is the most important instance, Chateaubriand a doubtful one) were prominent in the romantic movement; most of them stood to it on a footing of cool and reciprocated indifference. Finally, if romanticism has been associated with 'universalist' social philosophies, this was only because romanticists were opposed to rationalist individualism of the utilitarian type; but the feeling, the intuition, the impulse they extolled were subjective and *individual* feeling, intuition, and impulse—this extreme subjectivism, which knew no binding rule, was precisely what set Goethe against them.

What, the reader may well ask, can have been contributed to economics by a movement such as this? The answer will, of course, read differently according to whether we think of attitudes to practical problems, ideological haloes, humors, and so on, or of technical analysis. A romanticist or any writer influenced by the romantic attitude would, of course, look upon industrial life and its problems in a nonbourgeois spirit and take views quite different from the Benthamite ones. More generally, he would feel a healthy disgust at the utilitarian tendency to reduce the colorful variety of social patterns and processes to a few bald generalizations about thoroughly rationalized hedonic interests. And he would build where utilitarianism leaves a void—or else provides a dump for what is simply nonsense from its standpoint—a shrine for the historically unique and for the values of the extrarational (though, as the discussion above shows, these values differed greatly from one romanticist to another). As voiced by some romanticist writers, much of this does not quite ring true. It should be clear, however, that not all of it was literary fake. The standpoint that is appropriate for a history of the search for scientific truth is not appropriate for a comprehensive appraisal. Nevertheless, we may list definite contributions to positive analysis.

There are *none* to be recorded so far as technical economics is concerned. Considering the nature of the movement, this is only what we should expect and does not even amount to a criticism. Enthusiastic lovers of romanticism seem to me to have committed a tactical mistake by insisting on the presence of contributions of this nature, especially because it forced them to make a hero of such a man as Adam Müller (1779-1829). As far as this goes, it should be frankly admitted that there never was such a thing as a 'romantic school of economics' at all.

It was, I think, W. Roscher who gave currency to that phrase by his paper, 'Die romantische Schule der Nationalökonomik in Deutschland,' *Zeitschrift für die gesamte Staatswissenschaft,* 1870, and who covered Müller with unmerited praise. Modern 'universalists,' having been hard put to it to find other members for this 'school,' have resorted to three devices: first, they included men such as F. Gentz and K. L. von Haller (the interested reader is invited to look them up in any work of reference), who were no economists at all; second, they claimed for the school famous men who had but the most tenuous relation to it, if indeed any, such as F. List; third, they applied themselves to the task of unearthing additional members who were duly dubbed geniuses, such as Franz von Baader (*Sozietätsphilosophie,* in his *Sämtliche Werke,* 1854), who may pass for a sociologist. As to Adam Müller himself (mainly: *Elemente der Staatskunst,* 1809, new ed., 1922; *Versuche einer neuen Theorie des Geldes . . . ,* 1816, new ed., 1922; *Von der Notwendigkeit einer theologischen Grundlage der gesamten Staatswissenschaften,* 1819; a selection of papers has been edited by Dr. Jacob Baxa, who also wrote a life of Müller with complete bibliography, 1930), it is sufficient to state that his economics consists in a negative revaluation of part of A. Smith's facts and arguments—of laissez-faire, free trade, division of labor, and so on—which is his and not our affair, and in the introduction of a number of wholly inoperative metaphysical conceptions.

Suppose even that there is any sense in saying, for instance, that money is money only in the moment it changes hands and that in this moment it is not private (*allod,* as he called it) but public property (*feod*), or that it is the expression of 'national value' or 'national force'—what of it? Such interpretations of metaphysical meanings are by nature incapable of telling us anything that we do not already know about the relations subsisting in the empirical world. On the other hand, I do not wish to go further than this. I have no intention of paralleling the ignorance that fails to appreciate the tasks and methods of analysis by equally ignorant failure to appreciate the tasks and methods of philosophic vision or interpretation of meanings. It is enough for me if I can make the reader understand that these are two different worlds that do not touch anywhere and neither of which can tell us anything about the phenomena —or whatever the word should be—in the other without reducing its own arguments to futility. In order to make this point stand out strongly, I refrain from asking the question how good or bad A. Müller's speculations are when considered as philosophies.[4]

It seems possible, however, to speak of a romanticist sociology or at least of definite contributions of romanticist writers to economic, political, and general sociology. One has been mentioned already: we may restate it by saying that it consists in the insertion, into the analysis of institutions and of behavior within institutions, of the compound of nonrational—not necessarily irrational—human volitions, habits, beliefs, and so on, which largely make a given society what it is and without which a society and its pattern of reaction cannot be understood. The names of Herder and Novalis[5] may be mentioned as illustrations. The artistic component in romanticism is, in particular, responsible for emphasis upon psychological relations and reactions, a fact which lends some color to the view that the romanticists were forerunners of modern social psychology.[6] The outstanding example of contributions of this kind are the concepts of a National Soul (*Volksseele*), a National Character, and a National Fate. Such concepts came readily to literati and they acquired with them an emotional connotation. But the sentiments, as well as any philosophical visions, may be dropped, whereupon the National Soul reveals itself as a catch-all for a number of very important facts. Even as an entity it has appealed to many later sociologists of the group-mind type. How very 'positive' a thing can be made of it is shown by the fact that we also find it in so thoroughly unromanticist a writer as Comte.

But the chief importance of the romanticist movement for analytic economics consists in the impulse it gave to all kinds of historical research. It taught us better understanding of civilizations other than our own—the Mid-

[4] It is on this question only that meaningful difference of opinion is possible between us and the modern universalist admirers of A. Müller. And with this statement they should really agree—especially as I am also prepared to concede political value judgments—because they have always affected to despise the field for which I claim autonomy from romantic or any other metaphysical speculation.

[5] Novalis was the pseudonym of Friedrich von Hardenberg (1772-1801), German poet. A fragmentary theory of society may be compiled from his unsystematized writing (*Gesammelte Schriften*, ed. Obenauer, 1925). There is an essay on him by Carlyle, which does not, however, go much beyond artistic aspects.

[6] I do not share this view without qualification (see below, Part IV, ch. 3, sec. 3e).

dle Ages, for example, and extra-European cultural worlds as well. This meant new vistas, wider horizons, fresh problems, and, above all, the end of the stupid contempt that Voltairians and utilitarians professed for everything that preceded 'this enlightened age.' [7] Let us glance at the most important of the cases where romanticist influence, national soul and all, shows unmistakably, on the surface at least: the emergence of the Historical School of Jurisprudence. This school acquires additional significance for us because it helped to produce a similar movement in economics.[8]

After the Wars of Liberation, national exhilaration asserted itself in many proposals that, more or less directly, pointed toward a unified Germany. Among them were proposals for codifying the German law. One of these—by a prominent jurist, Thibaut—was adversely criticized in a pamphlet by Savigny that attracted nationwide attention.[9] Its argument rose high above the particular occasion and amounts to a general sociology of law: the legal institutions of a nation are part of its individual life as a nation and the expression of the whole of it, and of the whole of its historically determined situation; they embody all the intimate relations and necessities of this life which find in them more or less adequate formulation; they fit as does the skin of the human body; to replace them by a rationally excogitated code is like tearing off a body's skin in order to replace it by a synthetic product. Hence—this is what matters to us—the necessity of studying law not from the standpoint of a few rational principles, but within the framework of all its bearings on the national soul or character. Hence the conclusion—in exact opposition to the

[7] Théophile Gautier occasionally used the phrase *moyennagiste* as a synonym for romanticist, and the two phrases seem in fact to have meant much the same for the whole romanticist *cénacle* in Paris. This cult of medieval civilization did not fail, of course, to elicit liberalist sneers, the more so because it involved unhistorical idealizations as well as (in the case of Gautier) red waistcoats. But we must see through and condone the inevitable pranks of literati: if ignorance entered into this cult, much more ignorance had entered into that of *la raison*.

[8] The influence of the historical school of jurisprudence is particularly evident in the case of Roscher, who took arguments from the jurists and attached importance to what he considered to be a close parallelism between the situations in the legal and the economic fields. In other cases, that of R. Jones for instance (see below, ch. 6), no such influence can be proved.

[9] *Vom Beruf unserer Zeit für Gesetzgebung und Rechtswissenschaft* (1814), by Friedrich Karl von Savigny (1779-1861), an academic jurist of established reputation, who had, by an earlier work of striking originality (*Recht des Besitzes*, 1803), rejuvenated the decadent jurisprudence of his day. By the foundation, with Eichhorn (who represents the Germanist element in the alliance, as Savigny represents the Romanist), of the *Zeitschrift für geschichtliche Rechtswissenschaft* (1815), by his *Geschichte des römischen Rechts im Mittelalter* (1815-31), and by his *System des heutigen römischen Rechts* (1840-49), he rose to a position of recognized leadership in the German legal world of his day, both in the academic and (in Prussia) in the official sense. This leadership meant the victory, for the time being, of the historical school. But he should not be called its 'founder.' As could be shown had we space, he brilliantly led and developed a tendency, all the seeds of which had been sown before.

Benthamite view—that the only method for scientific jurisprudence to pursue is the historical one.[10] This, in a nutshell, was the creed and program of the historical school of jurisprudence. Owing to the use of the concept of a national soul and character, the relation between this historical sociology of law and specifically romanticist thought stands out strongly, perhaps more strongly than it should. For common sense tells us that there would have been historical jurisprudence even if there had not been any romanticism. This also applies to those German economists who, having undergone legal training or having what by a later American term we may call an institutionalist bent, were no doubt influenced by the example of the historical school of jurisprudence.

(b) *Historiography.* The extent to which the rich developments in that period's professional historiography are to be credited to romanticist ideas is still more debatable. It is true that the romanticist mood stimulated interest in historical research and increased the public's receptiveness to its results. Beyond this it is not safe to go without more specific reasons than a general belief in the all-pervading influence of romanticism. But it seems to me that one such reason does in fact exist. The period had indeed a large number of historians who pleaded a cause, the cause of a country or of a political system or a party, or made it their business to grade—yes, as a schoolmaster grades his pupil's books—the men and events reported on, according to moral or cultural standards of their own.[11] A tendency toward taking a different line as-

[10] These points must be kept in mind if misunderstanding is to be avoided: (1) This sociology of law is *not* quietist or hostile to reform. It only sponsors 'organic' reform from 'organic' necessities as against reform from speculative principles. Savigny himself, as Grand Chancellor, carried reforms. (2) This sociology, by virtue of its emphasis upon historically given conditions, has a side that might be described as 'national.' But it has no 'nationalistic' implications whatsoever. (3) Even reforms carried out in the historical spirit presuppose certain general principles and deductions from them. Savigny overlooked this and his program was therefore, however great its merits, scientifically inadequate. From our standpoint as economists, it is very important, on the one hand, to notice this error and, on the other hand, to realize that it does not necessarily impair the usefulness of the historical method.

[11] Thus, Lord Macaulay pleaded the causes not only of England, but also of the Whig party: he made no effort to understand any other standpoints. Michelet glorified France; Droysen, Prussian policy; Dahlmann and von Rotteck pleaded for liberalism and constitutionalism; Grote for Athenian democracy (George Grote, *History of Greece,* 1st ed., 1846-56, is of particular interest to us because he was an orthodox Benthamite and one of the most important members of the philosophical-radical circle); G. Bancroft for Jacksonian democracy. In all such cases there is, irrespective of any conscious intention of the authors, obvious danger of ideological distortion of facts. But even if all facts are reported with scrupulous impartiality, they will still stand, as it were, in an artificial light—the light of the writer's convictions or creed—and not in their own. Consider an additional example of a somewhat different type: W. E. H. Lecky (especially *History of the Rise and Influence of the Spirit of Rationalism in Europe,* 1865), one of the relatively few nineteenth-century exponents of the eighteenth-century *raison.* To begin with, he wrote from a definite sociology of history that makes ideas the prime movers of the historical process. In addition, he re-

serted itself, however: to present facts in their own light, to let events appear as they might have appeared to the people who experienced them, to preserve the color and the spirit of time and place. This 'immanent interpretation' of historical processes evidently raises very serious methodological problems as regards the nature of the intuitive understanding of the individuals and civilizations it involves. For us it is of particular interest because of the close affinity of its principles to those of Max Weber. It is primarily associated with the name of Leopold von Ranke.[12] A French sponsor of it was Augustin Thierry. The work of these and other men was, in its scholarly aspects, neutral to romanticism and, in other aspects, even hostile to it. But their respect for the autonomy of every culture and for its individual color constitutes an affinity with romanticist ideas that we must not overlook.

For the rest, since it is impossible to report on that period's historiography so as to convey an adequate impression, we must confine ourselves to a brief survey of those features of it that are most relevant for economics. In the first place, there were the new materials and the new standards of criticism. It was during this period that historiography definitely stepped out of the range of literary sources and—systematically and on a large scale—began to use original documents and the information that is enshrined in monuments, inscriptions, coins, and the like. Cuneiform writing (Grotefend) and hieroglyphs (Champollion) yielded their secrets. Techniques for the exploitation of source materials were taught, and comprehensive publications of such materials were undertaken: the École des Chartes, the English Rolls Series, and the *Monumenta germaniae historica* are examples of a purposeful and systematic activity, for which there was no parallel in our own field. Criticism of sources attained new levels, and it was this plus the new materials that produced the achieve-

---

duced the march of ideas to a scheme that is unaware of anything but an increasingly successful struggle of reason with religion. He thus produced a report that stands and falls with a definite creed and has no meaning irrespective of it. I use this opportunity to advert to the problems that arise from the naïve habit of historians who have no axe to grind or cause to plead but set themselves up as judges of all things human, who know all motives and are in possession of all standards of behavior. An example will illustrate. The great Mommsen was a conspicuous victim of the self-delusion involved: he knew how the Roman legions should have been handled in the battle on the Trebbia; he knew how Cicero ought to have dealt with Catilina's conspiracy; he knew what motives swayed Julius Caesar. He never displayed any awareness of the dangerous extent to which he relied on his intuitive comprehension—the comprehension of a no doubt able and respectable middle-nineteenth-century bourgeois mind. This has some obvious bearings also upon procedures of economists.

12 Without presuming to proffer my own opinion, I may state that a majority of historians of all countries would agree to call him the first historian of that period. His international influence—also on historiography in the United States—rests mainly on the new standard of historical scholarship that his famous seminar was the means of establishing. His mastery in exploiting new source material and in applying new canons of criticism was of a piece with his refusal to accept the guidance of philosophical (especially Hegelian) ideas. If we notice the romanticist element in his work, it should be added that he himself was careful to distance himself from romanticism.

ments of Niebuhr [13] and Mommsen. But the emphasis upon the original document was quite general. It constitutes the main *scholarly* merit of Michelet. We find it also in writers whom we do not value primarily as scholars, for example, Thiers, the politician. We find it even in the creators of the realistic novel, for example, the brothers Goncourt.

In the second place, historians developed a bent for sociological analysis that benefited from its proximity to facts. Niebuhr's attention to institutions and to the question of the effects of policies and reforms and Thierry's attention to racial factors may serve as examples. This hardly ever amounted to explicit theorizing, but it very often implied sociological theories though, needless to say, they were none the better for not being properly articulated. Moreover, much more than before, we observe interest in economic phenomena per se. This interest manifested itself even where we should least expect it, in the field of ancient history,[14] on the one hand, and in the 'pictorial' history of the period, on the other. Lord Macaulay's *History of England* (1848-61) illustrates to perfection what I mean by pictorial history—history that concentrates on the picturesque military or political events and narrates them with an eye to stirring effect. But Macaulay has chapters descriptive of economic and social conditions that are indeed effective pictures but entirely different ones. An analogous statement holds for L. A. Thiers' *History of the French Revolution* (1st French ed., 1823-7; English trans. 1838).

In the third place, there was a literature, important by virtue of achievement but still more important as the basis of later developments, that may be described as the product of the purely scientific wing of the historical school of jurisprudence or as the product of the institutionalist wing of the historians. I shall illustrate this by the names of four eminent men whose lines of research, widely though they differed from one another, all come within the category envisaged. Maurer [15] was the leading though not unchallenged authority on the social organization of medieval Germany, and his theories exerted influence far and wide throughout the nineteenth century—even after they had become obsolete. Fustel de Coulanges' famous book, which penetrated

[13] I wish I could stay to sketch the personality and work of this civil servant, scholar, banker, teacher, and ambassador (B. G. Niebuhr, 1776-1831), whose *Römische Geschichte* (1811-32) placed research in Roman history on a new footing. Among other things, he holds two claims to being considered an economist also: he was an authority on currency policy; he wrote *Forschungen zur internationalen Finanz- und Bankgeschichte* (A. Trende ed., 1929). Theodor Mommsen's famous *Römische Geschichte* appeared 1854-6.

[14] Examples are, *Die Staatshaushaltung der Athener*, a study of Athenian finance by August Böckh (1817) and, still more significant, the *Ideen über die Politik, den Verkehr, und den Handel der vornehmsten Völker der alten Welt* (1793-1812, English trans. 1833-4) by A. H. L. Heeren. The influence of this great scholar and teacher extended over a wide domain that also included political geography.

[15] G. L. von Maurer (1790-1872), *Geschichte der Markenverfassung in Deutschland* (1856); *Geschichte der . . . Hofverfassung in Deutschland* (1862-3); *Geschichte der Dorfverfassung in Deutschland* (1865-6); *Geschichte der Städteverfassung in Deutschland* (1869-71).

into the general reading of the educated (but not, so far as I can see, into that of economists), arranged the fruits of scholarly work around a theory to the effect that religion is the most important factor in shaping the legal and political institutions of a society, a theory that, owing to the close correlation between the various departments of national life, will never be contradicted by facts, even though it should be wrong or inadequate.[16] Sir Henry Maine's (1822-88) leadership belongs to the next period, but the work that spread his fame belongs to this. It presents a most instructive piece of a historian's theorizing.[17] Finally, the historico-ethnological work of J. J. Bachofen [18] must be mentioned, though its influence also belongs in the next period.

Finally, in the fourth place, *Kulturgeschichte*,[19] though not of course a new phenomenon, established itself as a recognized specialty. Its bearings upon our subject are obvious. It may paint murals or it may paint miniatures. The footnote below mentions the outstanding masters of the two forms, Burckhardt and Riehl.[20]

16 N. D. Fustel de Coulanges (1830-89), *La Cité antique* (mainly the Greek city state or *polis*), 1864; English trans. 1874.

17 Sir Henry Maine, *Ancient Law* (1861). Students of economics should know more about Maine's work than the slogan 'from status to contract.'

18 That is, the one work of Bachofen's that I shall mention: *Mutterrecht* (1861), the fountainhead of a whole literature on matriarchy.

19 Another word that is refractory to translation except by the un-English phrase, history of culture. History of civilization is not quite right. History of civil society would be still more misleading.

20 Of Jakob Burckhardt's (1818-97) imposing works, it will suffice, for our purpose, to mention *Die Kultur der Renaissance* (1860; English trans. 1878). The nature of the performance, which I trust is familiar to every reader, is difficult to define in general terms. Perhaps this phrase will come as near to defining it as it is within my power: a vision of an epoch's life in terms of art and politics (both taken in the widest possible sense). The essential point that differentiates such a structure from the history of any of the things that furnish the material for it—from the history of art and literature per se, or science per se, or economic, social, or any other politics per se—is that these things do not stand in the structure for their own sake, but for the sake of expressing, *functionally*, some larger and deeper reality. Jakob Burckhardt's place in the history of thought transcends this performance, and the influences (Ranke's among them) that helped to form him and the influences that emanated from him would be interesting to analyze. But the popularity of the work I mentioned must not deceive us concerning his influence as a social philosopher or political thinker. He was too far removed from the liberal slogans of his time and then again too far removed from any prophetic wrath about them to wield much influence.

W. H. Riehl (1823-97) might have been included in the next section's report. For his work is still more definitely relevant to professional sociology than is Burckhardt's. But the elements of his sociology (some of them anything but bombproof) would have to be picked out from what, fortunately, always remained *historical* work. I do not think that his influence went much beyond Germany's frontiers. But perusal of his *Kulturstudien aus drei Jahrhunderten* (1859) would do a lot of good to students of economics. This book might be an excellent substitute for some of the items on our current reading lists.

3. Sociology and Political Science: Environmentalism

We know that sociology dates from the scholastics and even from the Greeks. But the status of a recognized field of research it did not acquire before the next period (see Part IV, ch. 3). In the period under discussion sociology was indeed, as we have put it above, baptized by Comte, but no great importance should be attributed to this fact. It is true that there was plenty of important sociological work. But it remained unco-ordinated and unsystematized. Most of it we have noticed already. We may speak of a philosopher's sociology, a lawyer's sociology, a historian's sociology. Each of them took many forms that differ widely from, and stand in the most varied relations to, one another. It is dangerous to force these forms into large categories. But, for the purpose of a summary review, they may be divided into an 'abstract' and a 'historical' compound. In practical importance, Benthamite utilitarianism stands first among the former,[1] historical jurisprudence first among the latter. In this section we shall adopt, as far as possible, this schema. In addition an attempt will be made to supplement our sociological harvest by whatever we can glean from the period's literature on government and politics, for which the phrase Political Science then came increasingly into use, and by a brief glance at a line of thought that should interest economists particularly, Environmentalism.

(a) *The Natural-Law Sociology of Government and Politics.* Let us recall three results that have been established previously at various turns of our way. First, the historical origin of all social science is in the concept of Natural Law, which was from very early stages associated with more or less definite concepts of 'community' or 'society.' The Greeks *may* have confused the latter with the concept of government. It would have been natural for them to do so under the conditions of the *polis*. But the scholastic doctors were proof against this analytic mistake, because the practical problems of their age and their own position in the social organism could not fail to make it clear to them that the State or the Government—or the 'Prince'—is a distinct agent with interests of its own that do not necessarily coincide with the interests of the people or the community (the Common Good). That 'society' was a discovery of the philosophers of natural law, of the romanticists, or of still later groups is one of the legends of the history of sociology.[2] Second, we have seen that utilitarianism was a natural-law system. Like all natural-law systems, it was all-

[1] Other types of sociologies, or fragments of sociologies, that were abstract in the sense that they proceeded from a few 'first principles,' are to be found chiefly in the writings of speculative philosophers. Thus, Kant presented what he described as Metaphysical Elements (*Anfangsgründe*) of the Theory of Law (*Werke* IX, pp. 72 et seq.). This theory was 'abstract' and nonhistorical enough. But it was, of course, anything but utilitarian.

[2] If there is a writer who actually can be accused of confusing the State with Society, that writer is the romanticist A. Müller, for he called the state the 'totality of human affairs' (*Elemente*, vol. I, p. 60).

embracing in principle and very nearly so in actual practice. It was conceived as a unitary social science that was both normative and analytic and, among other things, included ethics, government, and legal institutions down to all the details of judicial procedure and criminological practice—in both of which Bentham himself was at least as intensely interested as he was in any economic question. Third, we know that this unitary social science of utilitarianism was individualist, empiricist, and 'rationalist,' the last term meaning here simply that the system, both in its analytic and in its normative aspects, strictly excluded everything that would not pass the test of utilitarian or hedonist rationality. The reader will save himself much trouble and greatly improve his understanding of doctrinal history if he gives due consideration to two vital facts. First, individualism does not necessarily involve empiricism or rationalism in this sense; [3] empiricism does not necessarily involve individualism and rationalism in this sense; and rationalism in this sense does not necessarily involve individualism and empiricism. But, second, so powerful a synthesis as Bentham's was bound to create, in the minds of foes as well as friends, an association between all the elements that enter into it which gave the impression of logical connection even where none existed.[4]

Now, by virtue of its very nature, this system is incapable of taking account of the facts of political life and of the way in which states, governments, parties, and bureaucracies actually work. We have seen that its fundamental preconceptions do little harm in fields such as that part of economics where its 'logic of stable and barn' may be considered as a tolerable expression of actual tendencies. But its application to political fact spells unempirical and unscientific disregard of the essence—the very logic—of political structures and mechanisms, and cannot produce anything but wishful daydreams and not very inspiring ones at that. The freely voting rational citizen, conscious of his (long-run) interests, and the representative who acts in obedience to them, the government that expresses these volitions—is this not the perfect example of a nursery tale? Accordingly, we shall expect no contributions to a serviceable sociology of politics from this source. And this expectation is almost pathetically verified. Strong common sense redeems, to some extent, Bentham's philosophy of government as presented in the *Fragment on Government* (1776) and, of course, very many of his practical recommendations on judicial procedure and the like. But James Mill's 'Essay on Government' [5] can be described only as unrelieved nonsense though, so it seems, also ineradicable nonsense. Moreover, its purely speculative character—so unlike the character of

[3] This sense of the term rationalism has, of course, nothing to do with the sense which we attributed to it in another place (II, ch. 1, sec. 6). But all along, these two and other meanings have been confused by many writers—a fertile source of mutual misunderstandings and of pointless antagonisms and controversies.

[4] Actually, the situation was and is further complicated by the fact that, of the terms mentioned, only 'empiricist' (in the sense of antimetaphysical) has a fairly stable meaning. The preceding footnote shows that this is not so in the case of 'rational' or 'rationalistic.' The case of the term 'individualism' is still worse.

[5] *Encyclopaedia Britannica* (suppl., 1823).

the same author's no doubt abstract argument in his book on economic theory [6]—is obvious. This was realized at the time by many non-utilitarians such as Macaulay. But much more important is it that J. S. Mill (without mentioning his father's name) applied to the political theory of the Benthamite school the unflinching epithet 'unscientific' (*Logic*, VI, ch. 8, § 3) and that in addition, his sentences vibrating with suppressed impatience, he said practically everything else that needs to be said about it. In this, as in so many respects, he rose above his early Benthamism. But he never shook off its shackles entirely: though his essays *On Liberty* and *Considerations on Representative Government* are no doubt redeemed, in part, by wider horizons and deeper insight, they are still 'philosophical radicalism.' It will thus remain forever a matter of the historian's personal equation whether J. S. Mill's theory spells abandonment or improvement of that of his father.[7]

Non-utilitarian and anti-utilitarian philosophers also continued to produce systems of natural law—and corresponding philosophies of the state—but of much more restricted scope, most of which reflect the influence of the romantic mood or else the influence of Kant or Hegel.[8] The harvest to be gathered for our purposes from this field is small indeed. Lawyers, too, continued to produce natural-law speculations. The most valuable ones were, however, in special fields, such as constitutional or criminal law.[9] More comprehensive enterprise of this type was being rapidly discouraged by the rising prestige of the

[6] After all that has been said above, the difference should be obvious. But the point is important both for our immediate object, which is to show why general objections against utilitarian premisses do not necessarily constitute objections in the particular case of economic theory, and for our wider aim, which is to understand why general objections against any philosophy do not in themselves dispose of any particular theory that, actually or apparently, links up with that philosophy. Therefore, let me restate the argument in still a different form: any theory involves *abstractions* and therefore will never fit reality exactly, hence economic theory is inevitably unrealistic *in this sense;* but its premisses are induced from realistic observation of the profit-seeking and calculating businessman; the premisses of political theory (style James Mill) are not induced from observations of the agent of politics, the politician, but *postulated* from a completely imaginary agent, the rational voter; therefore these premisses, hence results that are derived from them, are not merely abstract but also unrealistic *in a different sense.*

[7] Exactly as in the case of the theory of value, as we shall see more fully later on; in all parts of his wide domain, J. S. Mill's intellectual situation and character asserted themselves in precisely the same way.

[8] A fairly long list, chiefly of German performances—for England, T. H. Green's would have to be mentioned—could be compiled. We merely recall one of the earliest and most influential that has been mentioned already, Fichte's *Grundlage des Naturrechts* (1796-7). Hegel's glorification of the state as the embodiment of Absolute Reason is mentioned as a *curiosum* only. No wonder he was popular with the Prussian bureaucracy.

[9] As an example, I mention P. J. A. von Feuerbach's (not to be confused with the philosopher L. A. Feuerbach) criminology: *Kritik des natürlichen Rechts* (1796).

historical school.[10] An extremely influential performance of this kind, Stahl's, must however be noticed.[11] For the rest, lecturers displayed a significant tendency to turn their lectures on philosophy of law into lectures on the *history* of the philosophy of law.[12]

(b) *The Historians' Sociology of Government and Politics.* Writers who were professional historians or at least had an eye for historical reality were bound to do better than utilitarian or other theorists as far as politics is concerned, for it is more difficult for historians to neglect facts that stare them in the face. Edmund Burke, for example, was a man who saw the concrete situation with passionate energy—whether indulging in bursts of wrath or proffer-

[10] But let the reader keep this in mind: the historical school fought abstract speculation of either the Benthamite 'empiricist' or the German 'idealistic' types, because these were the types with which natural law had become identified; they fought natural law as such. From our standpoint, however, there is no point in doing this, and any generalization produced by jurists of the historical school should also be included in the corpus of natural law, just as the historical economist's generalizations are still economics and may even enter the concept of economic theory (e.g. in the case of 'theories' of the origins of markets).

[11] F. J. Stahl (*Philosophie des Rechts nach geschichtlicher Ansicht*, vol. I, 1830; vol. II, 1837) was a sort of Lutheran Filmer and rose to be a power in the intellectual life of Prussia in the era of Frederick William IV. The title of that work is justified in the case of vol. I by its attack upon utilitarian natural-law rationalism (and, incidentally to this, by sympathy with the standpoint of the historical school of jurisprudence) but is a misnomer for vol. II, where Stahl, having found his bearings, attacked the historical school of jurisprudence and based himself squarely upon Lutheran theology. Informed readers will miss the name of K. Frantz (*Naturlehre des Staates*, 1870), as they will many others, e.g. that of Joseph de Maistre, and the whole contiguous literature on Church and State. In defense, I can only point to the particular purposes of this fragmentary sketch.

[12] It is with reluctance that I leave a topic that was a close neighbor of economics on the continent of Europe and in whose province the explanation may be found of many a peculiarity of continental economics, among other things, of the proficiency of German economists on the institutionalist side of their science: links that had to be fought for elsewhere, especially in the United States at the time of the institutionalist controversy, were a matter of course for the products of many, if not most, continental universities. The continental student of economics absorbed a sociology of legal institutions—that meant much for his intellectual equipment—in many cases before he had had a word of technical economics. I shall therefore mention the names of two eminent men, who were no doubt jurists first and last but who nevertheless helped to form many an economist. Their influence belongs in the next period rather than in the one under discussion, but both published their most characteristic work before 1870. Rudolph von Gneist (1816-95) was a typically Anglophile German liberal, an authority in many fields but especially in constitutional and administrative law. See *Das heutige englische Verfassungs- und Verwaltungsrecht* (1857-63). Rudolph von Jhering (1818-92), *Geist des römischen Rechts* (1852-65). Neither has been translated so far as I know, although later works of both of them were (e.g. Gneist's *Englische Verfassungsgeschichte*, 1882, English trans. 1889; Jhering's *Zweck im Recht*, 1877-83, English trans. 1913).

ing sober advice—and knew how to distill generalizations from them that have established the reputation of his writings as a storehouse of political wisdom even with people who bore no love to his politics: it might be said that he taught politics by the case method and, as everyone knows, very effectively.[13] Again, nobody has ever commended Lord Macaulay for profundity of thought. But as regards insight into the nature of political processes, he was immeasurably superior to James Mill, and his criticism of the latter's presentation of the political theory of utilitarianism in the *Edinburgh Review* (1829) was perfectly adequate as far as it went although it did not go very far. Politics was still a 'science' to him (not the object of a science) though an 'experimental' [14] one—by which he simply meant that the utilitarian principles of politics were out of contact with political reality and that generalizations could be arrived at only by observations of political reality. He did not try to formulate such generalizations explicitly. Had he done so, they would, we may be sure, have turned out to be idealized Whig politics. This was the case also with those historians who did try their hands at political generalization.[15] Finally, let us

[13] Edmund Burke's (1729-97) name—no particulars are necessary—cannot be omitted from any survey, however sketchy, of the intellectual scenery of the period, though chronologically his most characteristic performances belong to the preceding one. Students of economics should peruse his writings carefully to learn not only how people should reason on political questions but also how people do reason in these matters. As the reader sees, I find it difficult to join the general chorus of admiration for Burke as a thinker. In fact, the man who defined a political party as a group of people who co-operate in order to further the public interest on some principles on which they are all agreed was certainly no profound analyst; moreover, he was clearly infected by the tendency of his time to take rationalizations for analytic explanation. The reader can easily satisfy himself of the lack of realism in Burke's definition by trying to apply it, e.g., to the two great American parties.

[14] It is amusing to observe this use of the term 'experimental.' The utilitarians, being empiricist philosophers and believers in the application of the methods of physics, specifically claimed that *their* procedure was 'experimental.' These attempts by both 'theorists' and 'antitheorists' to appropriate a term that, through the successes of physical experimentation, had acquired a eulogistic connotation also runs through the whole history of economics from the seventeenth century as will be noted again and again. Actually the term as applied to social phenomena is next to meaningless; what the writers who use it mean to convey must be ascertained separately in each case.

[15] The subject being very important for us, I shall mention a few examples: the *Grundzüge der Politik* (1862) by the historian Georg Waitz is by far the most creditable one I know, though not free from intellectualist fallacies; the *Politik auf den Grund und das Maass der gegebenen Zustände zurückgeführt* (1835) by the strongly partisan (liberal) historian F. C. Dahlmann is an able piece of analysis; the *Lehrbuch des Vernunftrechts und der Staatswissenschaften* (1829-35) by the still more partisan (radical) historian K. W. R. von Rotteck is an illustration of the truth that, given sufficiently close-fitting blinkers, a man may completely lose that sense for historical reality which is the main practical advantage to be derived from historical study. Finally, it is convenient to mention in this place a book that belongs chronologically in the next period but is an excellent example of the Political Science of the best historians of the period under discussion: J. R. Seeley's *Introduction to Political Science*

recall what I believe to be the finest flower of the period's literature of political analysis: de Tocqueville's *De la Démocratie en Amérique* (1835-40).[16] What is the nature of the performance that produced one of the 'great books' of the period? It conveyed no discovery of fact or principle; it did not use any elaborate technique; it did nothing to court the public (especially the American public). An extremely intelligent mind, nurtured on the fruits of an old civilization, took infinite trouble as to observations and brilliantly subdued them to serve an analytic purpose. This was all. But it is much. And I know of no other book that would train us better in the art of succeeding in this particular kind of political analysis.

But the period's great performance in the field of political sociology stands in the name of Karl Marx. We are not yet in possession of the facts that are necessary to establish this. They will be supplied in the next section (4b). Here I wish merely to say by way of anticipation that Marx's theories of history, of social classes, and of the state (government) [17] constitute, on the one hand, the first serious attempts to bring the state down from the clouds and, on the other hand, the best criticism, by implication, of the Benthamite construct. Unfortunately, this scientific theory of the state, like so much else in Marxist thought, is all but spoiled by the particularly narrow ideology of its author. What a pity, but at the same time, what a lesson and what a challenge! Two examples will illustrate another type of political analysis that, from negligible beginnings in the eighteenth century, made some advance during that period, though it did not get very far. As soon as political analysis becomes alive to the claims of scientific methods, it is bound to run up against problems of criticism—in the logical, not in the political sense: criticism of political concepts and of political reasoning—and of mechanisms. The book of a man who was himself an eminent politician, Sir George Cornewall Lewis (1802-63) illustrates that

(first edited by H. Sidgwick in 1896—the gleanings from Seeley's 'conversation classes' on the subject that were so interesting a deviation from the current practice of formal lectures).

[16] Alexis de Tocqueville (1805-59) needs no introduction, for his name and work have penetrated into secondary schools—a success only the more difficult to explain because it was so thoroughly deserved. Attention is invited to the rest of his writings. See *Oeuvres complètes* (ed. Beaumont, 1860-65).

[17] Marx's truly sociological, i.e. nonspeculative, theory of the state is contained, in a nutshell, in the *Communist Manifesto* and is there summed up in the pithy sentence that a government is a committee for the management of the common interests of the bourgeoisie. There is, therefore, no such thing as a socialist state—the state as such dies in the transition to socialism, a proposition that has been taken over and much emphasized by Lenin(!). It is impossible to say here all that should be said about this theory of the state and of politics. That central sentence is, of course, a half-truth at best. But it suggests indirectly something that is much more important than is that half-truth, viz. the idea that the state (government, politicians, and bureaucrats) is not something to philosophize on or to adore but something to be analyzed as realistically as we analyze, e.g., any industry.

awakening to critical consciousness.[18] The later book of another man who also was something of a politician, though primarily an academic leader, Franz von Holtzendorff (1829-89), illustrates a growing sense of the necessity of analyzing the mechanism of public opinion.[19]

(c) *Environmentalism.* A *Zeitgeist* that contains a component of mechanist—or what amounts almost to the same thing, sensationalist—materialism will, in exact proportion to the relative strength of this component, favor sociological theories that emphasize the explanatory value of environmental factors. Accordingly, we find a streak of environmentalist thought that may be described as a vulgarized form of Montesquieu's.[20] Two examples will suffice. Feuerbach, the philosopher (not the lawyer), made man a product of his physical environment. If we add those qualifications that are necessary in order to raise this proposition to the level at which it becomes possible to discuss it at all, we have here a theory that has, explicitly and implicitly, come to the fore again in our own time. His emphasis, within environmental factors, upon food [21] is also in evidence in our second example, Buckle.[22] If space allowed us to do so, we should have to consider his work under three aspects which, as it

[18] *Treatise on the Method of Observation and Reasoning in Politics* (1852)—a forgotten book by a half-forgotten man. Yet both deserve to survive. The former is strongly recommended to the reader because economists greatly need instruction of the kind it imparts. The latter we have had occasion to mention in passing (above, ch. 2).

[19] *Wesen und Wert der öffentlichen Meinung* (1879). Von Holtzendorff also wrote *Principien der Politik* (1869), which does not seem to me to amount to much. None of the other works of this prolific writer (though some of the fruits of his editorial activities) are known to me.

[20] Montesquieu does not seem to me to have overrated the explanatory value of environmental factors. How far environmentalist arguments that occur fairly frequently in the sociological literature of the second half of the eighteenth century—e.g. in Herder's writings—should be traced to his influence, I do not feel able to say. The *Esprit des lois* was one of the most famous and most extensively read books of that century. On the other hand, there were so many other sources from which a man might have drawn environmentalist inspirations that it is difficult to make positive assertions even in cases where Montesquieu was quoted.

[21] L. A. Feuerbach (*Sämmtliche Werke*, 1903-11, vol. x, p. 22) coined the phrase: 'Der Mensch ist was er isst.' The pun loses in translation: 'Man is what he eats'—one of those phrases that express a whole mental world. Feuerbach's writings were part of a literary current that popularized what Marx and Engels so well described as 'vulgar materialism.' Let us notice in passing this very significant fact: many if not all ideas of Feuerbach should have appealed to Marx for they agreed well with one aspect of Marx's work. Nevertheless, Marx fought them in season and out of season (see e.g. *Marx-Engels Archiv*, I, 1926, and Engels' *Ludwig Feuerbach . . .*, 1888; English trans. by A. A. Lewis, 1903), often with arguments that, coming from him, were not very convincing. The explanation is simple, however: whatever else he was, Marx was a highly civilized man; it was beyond him to swallow that sort of thing.

[22] H. T. Buckle, *History of Civilization in England* (2 vols., 1857-61). The work is a torso; in fact it is not more than an introduction to what was conceived as a huge enterprise. There is a considerable Buckle literature.

is, can only be indicated. First, there is an *idea:* to reduce history to a science by arriving, through 'induction' from observed facts, at 'laws' of the same kind as what Buckle conceived the 'laws' of physics to be. In intention, Buckle's interpretation of history, and not Marx's, is the truly 'materialistic' one—which is, of course, all to the credit of Marx. Nothing is more obvious, however, as soon as one delves into Buckle's work, than the fact that this idea is purely ideological in nature: it is what he wished to carry into effect, whereas he was actually swayed by pure speculation that from first to last forced facts into a preconceived schema. Second, there is the conceptual *implementation* of the idea, consisting of three types of 'laws' that determine social states and their changes—physical, moral (i.e., propositions on human behavior), and intellectual. The latter (mainly growth of technological control over physical environments) supply the motive power of 'progress,' a principle that links up with what we shall presently describe as Condorcet-Comte evolutionism. As far as these aspects are concerned, namely, the analytic ones, even the little we have said about the book is too much: its importance consists wholly in providing a case study in analytic miscarriage, which may teach us to look out for speculative propensities behind a nonspeculative program and for dilettantism behind an apparently large scientific apparatus. But there is, third, the almost unbelievable success this book has had with all types of people, rich and poor, educated and uneducated, English and foreign. It is this success only that raises the book to significance: it was one of the items of the layman's reading, one of the educators of that period's public mind. As such its teaching is an important element in the intellectual scenery we are trying to visualize.

Like other 'theories,' environmentalism can easily be carried to a point where it becomes obvious nonsense. But within its sphere, it is an indispensable helper of the analyst of social phenomena—as it proved to be, for example, for Michelet. The case may be illustrated by the (in this respect) similar case of 'racialism.' It is a melancholy but very important observation to make that in the social sciences factors are always at work that will drive such theories to the point of nonsense and—what is very much the same thing—turn them into bones of contention for ideological and political parties. Both environmentalism and racialism suit so many books that neither is allowed to make its contribution to our understanding of social processes—their friends and their foes alike join forces to prevent this consummation. Let us notice again a work of the period which, with remarkable freedom from bias, succeeded in balancing the environmentalist and racial element in a way that was quite satisfactory as far as it went: F. T. (*not* Georg) Waitz's *Anthropologie der Naturvölker* (1859-64)—especially the first volume.

4. Evolutionism

Social phenomena constitute a unique process in historic time, and incessant and irreversible change is their most obvious characteristic. If by Evolutionism we mean not more than recognition of this fact, then all reasoning about social phenomena must be either evolutionary in itself or else bear upon evolution. Here, however, evolutionism is to mean more than this. One may recognize the fact without making it the pivot of one's thought and the guiding principle of one's method. The utilitarian system may serve to illustrate this. James Mill would have smiled at a questioner who asked him whether he was aware of the occurrence of social changes, and he would have, in addition, conceived a poor opinion of the questioner's intelligence. Yet his various systems—in economic, political, and psychological theory—were not evolutionary in the sense that his thought in any of those fields *turned* upon evolution. And it is this that shall be the criterion of evolutionism for us, both as regards philosophy—comprising also purely metaphysical speculation—and as regards any 'scientific' field. Evolutionism in this sense asserted itself in the course of the eighteenth century but reached and passed its high-water mark in the nineteenth.

Attention is drawn to the presence of a disturbing factor, the influence of which will be felt in many ways and not only in this section. In itself, the concept of evolution is perfectly free from any valuation except within well-defined standards.[1] As far as this goes, we merely recognize that people will describe a change as progress if they like it, and as retrogression or degeneration if they dislike it. But in the eighteenth century evolution was naïvely identified with progress—toward the rule of *la raison*—that is to say, it carried a value judgment by definition. And this naïve association of ideas persisted throughout the nineteenth century, though signs of its gradual dissolution appeared in serious research work as time went on. The bourgeois whose business and class position prospered had any amount of confidence in 'progress' of certain types, and he and the literary exponent of the bourgeois mind displayed a lamentable tendency to link this confidence in a certain set of desired changes with some ineluctible forces that move civilizations or even the universe. But we must try to keep clear of such infantilisms, however important they are as features of the *Zeitgeist*.

For clarification and illustration, it will be useful to distinguish five different—though often overlapping—types of evolutionist thought, all of which loom large in the intellectual scenery of this period and also in that of the subsequent one: what follows refers to both periods, though instances are taken only from the one under survey.

(a) *Philosophers' Evolutionism*. Hegel is the outstanding example. With every apology for the temerity involved, I shall put the one point that is relevant for the purposes of this book as follows. Let us postulate the existence of a metaphysical entity—no matter what we call it—that *is* ultimate and absolute reality, and let us thus place ourselves on the standpoint of an ultra-idealistic philosophy.[2] Let us, *at the same time and in the same sense*, define

[1] Thus, within the range of the accepted standards of the dental profession, it is a meaningful proposition to aver that at the present time teeth are being extracted 'more efficiently' than a century ago and even that dentist A extracts teeth 'more efficiently' than does dentist B. An analogous statement applies to technical economic theory. But obviously this is no longer so when it comes to comparisons of social structures or civilizations and outside of the range of specified standards in general.

[2] Idealism as applied to German philosophy from Kant to Hegel has, of course, nothing whatever to do with idealism in the ethical sense.

the *same* reality as the totality of all actual and potential observational facts. How is this possible? It is possible, if, as, and when we see in these observational facts, as it were, runes that embody (manifestations of) that entity [3]—in much the same way in which we should do so if we adopted straight pantheism in the ordinary sense. Now, that entity is supposed to undergo an immanent evolution in an essentially logical process of theses, antitheses, and syntheses.[4] And so does the observational reality. This is the kind of thing that will always appeal to one type of mind and never to another. We pass on with a definition and a comment. The definition: reasoning from the conception of a metaphysical entity, which in unfolding its own contents produces a sequence of changes in the reality of experience, we call *emanatist*. The comment: the reader will observe that of Hegel's emanatist conception of evolution something remains, even if we drop its metaphysical trappings, namely, the idea or perhaps discovery that reality, as we know it from experience, may be in itself an evolutionary *process*, evolving from inherent necessity, instead of being a set of phenomena that seek a definite state or level, so that an extraneous factor—or at least a distinct factor—is necessary in order to move them to another state or level as the analogy with Newtonian mechanics suggests. This idea, if tenable, is of course extremely important. As regards philosophy, it renders it possible to proceed, for example, from Hegelianism in its original acceptance to what may be termed Hegelian materialism, which many of the so-called Young Hegelians did. As regards sociology, it suggests a novel approach to the facts of social change.

Before going on, we may notice two other methods by which philosophers sometimes contrived to impart to their philosophies an evolutionary slant. 'Progress' was in the air and, like other people, philosophers enjoy being up to date. The agnostic or materialist, especially of the semi-popular variety, was apt to substitute intellectual progress for the entities that he discarded, that is to say, he was apt to raise a loan from what will be described below (d) as Condorcet-Comte evolutionism; or else he was apt to exploit biological evolu-

[3] This is what Hegel's famous phrase was meant to convey (if we equate our metaphysical entity to reason): whatever is, is rational (conforms to reason) and whatever is rational (thinkable), is. As meant, this does not lend any support to conservative attitudes. But the reader will have no difficulty in realizing how easily it can be made to do so. Moreover, Hegel's phrasing invites such an interpretation. This was even an important factor in his success.

[4] The irreverent did not fail to notice that here was an opportunity of proving Hegel's system to be nonsense. Misguided by their inability to rise to Hegelian heights, they pointed—with a vicious smile—to the fact that this piece of philosophizing cannot be readily translated into English. The German verb *aufheben* means both to cancel and to raise. Hegel averred that a thesis, A is B, and its antithesis, A is not B, *aufheben* each other into something higher, a synthesis that comprises the content of both. But contradictory statements do not *aufheben* each other in the sense of *raising* each other into something more comprehensive: they simply *cancel*, i.e. annihilate, each other—which would be rather serious for Hegel and evolution. It is, of course, possible to save the situation. A warning to us remains, however.

tionism (e) for philosophical purposes. Whatever we may think of this as a philosophy, it made popular literature.

(b) *Marxist Evolutionism.* I have just adverted to the possible implications for sociology that a despiritualized Hegelian philosophy might harbor. This suggests that here we have after all more than a phraseological influence [5] of Hegel upon Marx. If, nevertheless, we maintain substantive autonomy of Marx's so-called Materialistic Interpretation of History as against Hegelism, and if we list it as a separate type of evolutionism, we allow ourselves to be guided by two considerations. First, Marx's theory of history developed independently of Marx's Hegelian affiliation. We know [6] that his analysis started from a criticism of the current (and apparently immortal) error that the behavior that produces history is determined by ideas (or the 'progress of the human mind'), and that these in turn are infused into actors by purely intellectual processes. To start with this criticism is a perfectly sound and very positive method but has nothing to do with Hegelian speculation. Second, Marx's theory of history is a working hypothesis *by nature*. It is compatible with any philosophy or creed and should therefore not be linked up with any particular one—neither Hegelianism nor materialism is necessary or sufficient for it.[7] What remains is, again, Marx's preference for Hegelian phrasing—and his own and most, though not all, Marxists' preference for anything that sounds anti-religious.

[5] An example of the purely phraseological influences, of which there are many, will be noticed in passing. The untutored reader of Marx's writings may wonder why Marx speaks so often of 'contradictions' of capitalism when he means nothing but mutually counteracting facts or tendencies: these *are* contradictions from the standpoint of Hegelian logic. This has had an amusing consequence. To this day, the average Marxist, accepting the word Contradiction in the sense it carries in ordinary logic and parlance, infers that Marx wished to charge the capitalist system with *logical* incompatibilities in this ordinary sense every time he spoke of 'contradictions'—which, of course, is not the case.

[6] See e.g. Marx's introduction to his *Contribution to the Critique of Political Economy* (publ. by Kerr, Chicago, 1904). The original German edition (*Zur Kritik der politischen Oekonomie*) was published in 1859, the *Einleitung* (introduction) in the *Neue Zeit*, 1902-3; the English translation by N. I. Stone includes the 'recently published' introduction in an appendix.

[7] I have found that this statement is likely to cause surprise. But proof is easy. For we may fully accept the doctrine of freedom of individual will in the sense in which it is taught, e.g., by St. Thomas Aquinas, and still go on to argue that the exercise of this free will, being limited by physical and social data, will in general produce a course of events in conformity with these data. The economic interpretation is nothing but a hypothesis about what, in turn, determines these data, and per se implies neither absence of the individual's moral responsibility for his acts nor refusal to admit the possibility of supermundane influence upon these data themselves and the ways in which they work out. Marxists, it is true, will not admit this. But they will not admit this for reasons—beliefs, philosophies—that are extraneous to the logically essential content of the economic interpretation of history: *philosophical* determinism is, as a matter of fact, mostly associated with sponsorship of the latter, but in logic it has nothing to do with the *methodological* determinism that is implied in it.

Both the achievement embodied in that hypothesis and the limitations of this achievement may be best conveyed by means of a brief and bald statement of the essential points. (1) All the cultural manifestations of 'civil society'—to use the eighteenth-century term—are ultimately functions of its class structure.[8] (2) A society's class structure is, ultimately and chiefly, governed by the structure of production (*Produktionsverhältnisse*), that is, a man's or a group's position in the social class structure is determined chiefly by his or its position in the productive process. (3) The social process of production displays an immanent evolution (tendency to change its own economic, hence also social, data). To this we add the essential points of Marx's theory of social classes, which is logically separable from points (1) to (3) that define the economic interpretations of history but forms part of it within the Marxian scheme. (1') The class structure of capitalist society may be reduced to two classes: the bourgeois class that owns, and the proletarian class that does not own, the physical means of production, which are 'capital' if owned by employers but would not be 'capital' if owned by the workers who use them. (2') By virtue of the position of these classes in the productive process, their interests are necessarily antagonistic. (3') The resulting class struggle or class war (*Klassenkampf*) provides the mechanisms—economic and political—that implement the economic evolution's tendency to change (revolutionize) every social organization and all the forms of a society's civilization that exist at any time. All this we may sum up in three slogans: politics, policies, art, science, religious and other beliefs or creations, are all superstructures (*Überbau*) of the economic structure of society;[9] historical evolution is propelled by economic evolution; history is the history of class struggles.[10]

This is as fair a presentation of Marx's social evolutionism as I am able to provide in a nutshell. The achievement is of first-rank importance[11] although the elements that enter into it are of very unequal value or, rather, unequally impaired by obvious ideological bias. Least valuable for any but agitatorial pur-

[8] I repeat that the term 'function' here used does not imply causal determination. In fact, an attempt to insist on such 'absolute' or 'mechanical' determination would not achieve anything except to make the theory very easy to refute. Both Engels and Plekhanov, the chief Marxist authorities on the subject, have seen this and both relaxed considerably on the stringency. Emphasis upon 'ultimately' was one of the means of doing so.

[9] One aspect or application of this theory we have discussed in Part I, viz. the doctrine of the inevitable 'ideological bias' of all thought.

[10] Marx's ideas on social evolution and classes are, of course, basic for everything he ever wrote, and comments on them are strewn all through his works—which does not make it any easier to do justice to them. But of all his publications, the following seem to me the most important sources to be used in any attempt at interpretation: the *Communist Manifesto;* the *Class Struggles in France;* the *Eighteenth Brumaire of Louis Bonaparte,* and the *Critique of Political Economy.* (All available in English translations; for details as to dates and publishers, see Sweezy, op. cit. p. 382.)

[11] This achievement should, I believe, be attributed to Marx alone. For every performance of such scope it is, of course, possible to name forerunners. But there were rather less of them than we are accustomed to find in comparable cases. The only

poses is the theory of social classes that Marx associated with his economic interpretation of history: the two-class schema is all but useless for serious analysis; exclusive emphasis upon class antagonism is as patently wrong—and as patently ideological—as is exclusive emphasis upon class harmony of the Carey-Bastiat type (see below, ch. 4); and the proposition that the evolution of forms of social organization is brought about by a mechanism that can be described exclusively in terms of the struggle between those two classes is a simplification that eliminates the essentials of the mechanisms actually at work. A qualification must, however, be added: if we get from Marx an ideologically warped definition of classes and of class antagonisms, and if in consequence we get an unsatisfactory description of political mechanisms, we nevertheless get something very worth having, namely, a perfectly adequate idea of the importance of the class phenomenon. If in this field there existed anything like unbiased research, Marx's suggestions would have led long ago to a satisfactory theory of it.

But the economic interpretation of history is a different matter. If we reduce it to the role of a working hypothesis and if we carefully formulate it, discarding all philosophical ambitions that are suggested by the phrases Historical Materialism or Historical Determinism, we behold a powerful analytic achievement. Points (1) and (3) may then be defended against objections, most of which turn out to rest upon misunderstandings.[12] Point (2) is less reliable: it

claimant for whom it is possible to argue at all is Lorenz von Stein (1815-90), whose *Socialismus und Communismus des heutigen Frankreichs* (1842, later ed., entitled *Geschichte der socialen Bewegung in Frankreich,* 1850, newly edited, 1921) is in fact an important piece of analysis that links up the development of socialist ideas with the realities of social movements and economic changes. This, however, is not the economic interpretation of history; still less is it possible to find the latter in the socialist writers themselves, whom Stein discussed, or in the French historians of the revolution, the restoration, and the Orléans regime. So far as my knowledge of them entitles me to judge, they all emphasize more or less the economic element in the historical processes they describe which they could hardly have helped doing. But obviously this is not enough. I suspect that those who find in this literature anything suggestive of the economic interpretation of the historical process as a whole entertain a different conception of the latter than I thought it proper to adopt. Mere recognition of the importance of the economic factor is a triviality and neither distinctive nor meritorious in itself. The case of Saint-Simon, which may be an exception, will be stated below.

[12] By simple experiment, the reader may easily satisfy himself how well point (1) works. Take e.g. so modest a 'cultural manifestation' as the modern murder story. Observe its chief characteristics—not forgetting its English—and correlate them with the salient facts about the social structure of our time. You will not fail to enjoy an enlightening experience.

I take this opportunity to advert to one of those misunderstandings of which, on one occasion, Engels himself was guilty. Taking 'materialism' mistakenly in its ethical sense, some writers have taken what they called 'historical materialism' to mean that men are actuated by material, i.e. economic, interests as motives in the psychological sense. Marx's theory does not mean this and has room for all kinds of motives.

works well with some historical patterns and not at all with others.[13] This problem Marx does not seem to have taken very seriously. But there was another, to the solution of which he devoted the bulk of his giant powers for the rest of his life. Obviously, the vast fabric, of which the economic interpretation of history was the base, would have had to remain incomplete without a full analysis of that immanent evolution of the economic sector on which the evolution of human civilization as a whole was made to rest. For him the economic interpretation of history was, therefore, still more a program than it was an achievement to be valued for itself.

We have reached a point of vital importance for a proper understanding of Marx's work. On the one hand, we can now visualize his unitary Social Science, the only significant all-comprehensive system that dates from this side of utilitarianism: we see the manner and the sense in which he welded into a single homogeneous whole all branches of sociology *and* economics—a venture that might well dazzle the modern disciple even more than it dazzled Engels, who stood too near the workshop. On the other hand, we now see Marxist economics in its true light. Its individual features, or some of them, will come in for notice and appraisal in their places. Here I wish only to insist on the greatness of the conception and on the fact that Marxist analysis is the only genuinely evolutionary economic theory that the period produced.[14] Neither its assumptions nor its techniques are above serious objections—though, partly, because it has been left unfinished. But the grand vision of an immanent evolution of the economic process—that, working somehow through accumulation, somehow destroys the economy as well as the society of competitive capitalism and somehow produces an untenable social situation that will somehow give birth to another type of social organization—remains after the most vigorous criticism has done its worst. It is this fact, and this fact alone, that constitutes Marx's claim to greatness as an economic analyst. That he was more than an *economic* analyst we have seen in this section. That he was more than an *analyst* need not be explained again.

[13] The Marxist principle can be illustrated by such processes as the elimination of the artisan class by large-scale manufacturing industry. But as Dühring pointed out, other instances can be adduced to show that this 'causality' is often reversed—the truth being of course that there is interdependence between the conditions of production and the social structure. The situation of the Marxist principle can be somewhat improved by recognizing the fact that social structures may outlive the conditions of production that created them—which will account for a certain number of discrepancies without destroying the theory. Another device is more dangerous: we might define, e.g., the activity of a tribe of warlike conquerors as 'productive' and then say that the social organization that results in conquered countries still comes within the range of the Marxist interpretation. But this is very near to making a tautology of it.

[14] We deal elsewhere with the Smith-Ricardo-Millian contribution to the theory of economic change. Even those readers who see merit in it, granting even the possibility that it may have given Marx a basis from which to start, will have to admit that it looks embryonic beside his.

[For a discussion of the views of Marx and Schumpeter on the topics covered in this section, see O. H. Taylor, 'Schumpeter and Marx: Imperialism and Social Classes in the Schumpeterian System,' *Quarterly Journal of Economics,* November 1951. This is a review article of Schumpeter's *Imperialism and Social Classes* (English trans., ed. with an introduction by Paul M. Sweezy, 1951).]

(c) *Historians' Evolutionism.* Mere preoccupation with the problems of describing the events of an ever-changing world does not spell evolutionism in the sense of this section. Professional historians, therefore, are not evolutionists by profession. They become evolutionists—of a distinct type—only when they try to arrange states of society—economic, political, cultural, or general ones—into sequences that are supposed to be necessary in the sense that each such state is the necessary and sufficient condition for the emergence of the one that follows it. The oldest and most primitive way of doing this is by constructing typical stages through which an economy must pass. This method was represented in that period by Friedrich List, whose scheme—hunting, agriculture, agriculture plus manufacture, agriculture and manufacture plus commerce—met with deserved criticism from Karl Knies:[15] we should indeed have put down this scheme as completely worthless were it not for the fact that it may be used (and was used by List) as a simple expository device for impressing upon beginners (or the public) the lesson that economic policy has to do with changing economic structures and therefore cannot consist of a set of unchanging recipes. Another example is Bruno Hildebrand's scheme: exchange economy, money economy, credit economy. Beyond this there is not much to report in this category—the better a historian, the more averse he is to such constructions—except that a vague belief in evolutionary sequences, such as historical sequences that were supposed to bear analogy with the youth, manhood, and old age of individuals, are not infrequently met with in historical writings of that period. An economist and economic historian who indulged in this belief without however being misled by it, as far as I can see, was W. Roscher.[16] It is worth noting that this belief in 'laws of economic history' constitutes one of the main differences between his methodology and Schmoller's, who nevertheless had a type-series of his own: village economy, town economy, territorial economy, and national economy.

(d) *The Intellectualist Evolutionism of Condorcet and Comte.* Condorcet,[17] more than any other writer, elaborated the theory of social evolution that is specifically associated with the thought of the Enlightenment and is present, implicitly or explicitly, in the writings of all the votaries of *la raison:* let us call it Intellectualist Evolutionism. It is the last word in simplicity. Reduced to its essential content, it comes to this: human reason, a given force, wages an incessant war of conquest on man's physical environment and, at any given

[15] See his *Politische Ökonomie vom Standpunkte der geschichtlichen Methode* (1853, enlarged ed., 1883).

[16] The work of List, Hildebrand, and Roscher will be discussed below in ch. 4, sec. 5.

[17] Marquis de Condorcet (1743-94), *Esquisse d'un tableau historique des progrès de l'esprit humain* (1795; see above, Part II, ch. 2, sec. 7d).

stage, on the beliefs or habits of thought that mankind has acquired at previous stages of its history. From this incessant struggle results, on the one hand, an indefinitely increasing insight into the true laws of nature and, in consequence, an even more perfect technological control over the forces of nature and, on the other hand, an indefinitely increasing freedom from erroneous and antisocial beliefs and propensities: human intellect, perfecting itself, perfects the whole of human nature, hence also human institutions, without assignable limit. Since many readers' minds are presumably imbued with this theory—perhaps to the point of accepting this 'progress of the human mind' as a matter of course—we had better make sure that we understand the objection to it: it fails because it postulates what it is to explain. Changes—adaptive and, possibly, also autonomous—in beliefs, in stocks of knowledge and techniques, and in habits of thought are no doubt historically associated with other manifestations of social evolution. But they are conditioned, to say the least, by the facts of a changing social structure, and so are their *modi operandi*. If we attribute, say, modern positivism or the modern airplane to the progress of the human mind, we have evidently not done much toward their explanation. In fact, we have done nothing: we have only renamed the problem. If, in order to remedy this, we appeal to the perfectibility of the human mind, we have still done nothing: we have only postulated the solution. And if, recognizing this, we introduce additional factors of explanation, for example, biological ones, we have left the moorings of intellectualist evolutionism.

But in spite of its patent inadequacy, this theory survived in the liberal or progressive circles that continued the tradition of the Enlightenment. Lecky and Buckle, however much their arguments may differ, can be mentioned again in illustration of this. For us, however, Comte's position is of particular interest. His schema or 'law' of three stages, according to which civilization evolves from a religious or magical stage to a metaphysical and then to a scientific one, clearly hails from the thought of the Enlightenment: it does not differ essentially from Condorcet's. Moreover, it is not only unbelievably narrow but also, in Comte's own sense, speculative and unscientific: research on the lines of his 'positive' program would have immediately revealed the presence of factors and mechanisms that cannot be reduced to the one factor embodied in that 'law.' Observe, however, that, superficially, the law seems easy to verify: rational scientific procedure (though not in politics) is in fact one of the features that are characteristic of our own time; and magic is in fact characteristic of the primitive mind—the question is only how much this means and how far the correlation admits of causal interpretation.

There is one more point to be noticed. The religious, metaphysical, and scientific attitudes are evidently social and not simply individual phenomena. Therefore, Comte's stages may be said to be stages in the development of a collective or group mind. Much more definitely than Condorcet, Comte in fact adopted this concept and he did something toward elaborating it. There is, of course, a world of difference between his collective mind and the national soul of the romanticists. Viewed as tools of analysis, however, both come to much the same thing and both have influenced the work of later sociologists and social psychologists.

(e) *Darwinian Evolutionism.* This is the only kind of biological evolutionism to be noticed here. Lamarck's influence was largely, though not wholly, superseded by Darwin's (who, however, was generous in his references to Lamarck); and Mendel, though he published his three laws in 1866, did not exert any direct influence at all.[18] The 'Historical Sketch' added by Darwin to the third and later editions of the *Origin of Species* will tell the reader the fascinating story of the gradual emergence of the decisive ideas, so that nothing needs to be said about it here.[19] It is, however, necessary to offer the following comments on the social significance of the book and on its significance for the social sciences.[20]

[18] G. J. Mendel (1822-84), an Augustinian monk, not only did excellent experimental work—this is professional opinion; I have, of course, none of my own—but also offered the theoretical interpretation of it that proved acceptable to biologists when his results were independently rediscovered (about 1900). He refrained from any application to social processes. Since we are interested in the sociology of science, the question arises: what can we learn from this case of neglect of a most important performance? Examination of the case seems to show, however, that it teaches us nothing. Robert Mayer personally communicated his discovery (mechanical equivalent of heat) to men (one man at least) of indubitable professional standing, who could and should have understood and promulgated it. Cournot published his *Recherches* (see below, Part IV, ch. 7) in the broad daylight of one of the great intellectual centers. But Mendel lived in a convent, situated in a provincial town, and published his results in an obscure local periodical, that is, in a manner that amounted to hiding them. Thus, this case of neglect is self-explanatory.

[19] The reader is urgently advised to peruse it carefully. It is one of the most important pieces of scientific history ever written, and presents a case study about one of the objects of our interest—the ways of the human mind and the mechanisms of scientific advance. In addition, it elucidates a concept that plays some role in our own story, the concept of Inadequate Acknowledgment of Priorities. Darwin illustrates the meaning of this concept by presenting an ideal instance of what is Adequate Acknowledgment. In everything he did, that man was a living and walking compliment to himself and also to the economic and cultural system that produced him—a point recommended to the reader whenever he feels like ruminating on the civilization of capitalism (and, incidentally, about more modern forms of organization of research).

Charles Darwin (1809-82) took long in evolving, still longer in publishing, the fruits of his labor. *The Origin of Species* . . . was published in 1859. *The Descent of Man and Selection in Relation to Sex* was published in 1871, after Vogt and Haeckel (also others) had already pronounced in favor of its main theses. Chapters 3, 4, 5, and 19 treat matters directly relevant to general and economic sociology.

Herbert Spencer's essay, which Darwin commends so generously, appeared first in the *Leader*, 1852, and his *Psychology* in 1855, whereas Mill's *Principles*, the restatement of 'classic' economic thought, appeared in 1848.

[20] The reader will observe that in what follows I do not of course presume to judge the book as a professional performance in its own field. The delicate question of a research worker's proper behavior in matters that involve the results and procedures in fields other than his own, therefore, does not arise at the moment, though it does arise in connection with 'Darwinist' social theories.

In the first place, the *Origin of Species* and the *Descent of Man* make one of the biggest patches of color in our picture of that period's *Zeitgeist*. Their secular importance for mankind's cosmic conceptions is comparable with that of the heliocentric system. They were very widely read by the general public, passionately discussed, and effective in refurnishing the bourgeoisie's mental house, though it seems that, in most cases, this new furniture did not oust metaphysical furniture that still existed but only occupied empty space. Our fundamental beliefs and attitudes are beyond the power of any book to make or shake; in particular, I do not think that any cultivated person will find his faith destroyed through reading Darwin, provided that person has any faith to destroy.[21]

In the second place, however much or little we may think of the causal role of Darwinism, its symptomatic importance is beyond question. It came, and rode to success, exactly when it should have done so according to the Marxist theory of intellectual superstructures. And it was one current only in a broader river as the independent but analogous developments in geology suffice to show.[22] This was the same river that also carried along the other evolutionisms that we have been discussing above. But in all other respects these were logically independent of either Darwinism or any other biological theory: it is quite important to realize this in order to avoid confusions that threaten our understanding of the intellectual history of the period. Marx may have experienced satisfaction at the emergence of Darwinist evolutionism. But his own had nothing whatever to do with it, and neither lends any support to the other.

In the third place, Darwinism or Darwinist talk did intrude into sociology and economics later on. This will be touched upon in our survey of the intellectual scenery of the next period (Part IV, ch. 3). For the period under discussion, I can find no significant influence upon the social sciences apart from what we may conceive Darwinist influence to have done to people's general habits of thought.[23] Both Darwin and Spencer contributed to psychology, and the latter displayed a propensity for sociological applications from the first. But this is all. In concluding, I wish to comment on Darwin's remark to the effect that he derived inspiration from Malthus' theory of population. It seems very hazardous, to be sure, to dissent from a man's statement about his own

[21] I say *cultivated* person because the case is different for the untrained mind that lacks resources for interpretative and critical defense. But, then, the untrained mind takes shelter behind authority.

[22] These are associated with the name of Sir Charles Lyell (1797-1875) *almost* as much as biological evolution is associated with the name of Darwin. His *Principles of Geology* (1830-33) does not quite 'let the murder out' but, by implication, it says as much as does his *Geological Evidences of the Antiquity of Man* (1863).

[23] In 1872, Walter Bagehot published his *Physics and Politics* (more appropriate titles would have been *Biology and Sociology* or *Biological Interpretation of History*), which uses, among other things, Darwinian social psychology. In itself no more than a piece of brilliant dilettantism, the book contains many suggestions that came to fruition later on. It is still worth reading.

mental processes. But quite insignificant events or suggestions may release a given current of thought; Darwin himself did not include Malthus' work in the Historical Sketch mentioned above, though he did refer to it in his introduction; and the mere statement that 'more individuals of each species are born than can possibly survive' (which, moreover, is doubtful Malthusianism) is, in itself, not more than a platitude. I am afraid, therefore, that the service rendered by economics to the evolution of the Darwinian doctrine bears some analogy to the service rendered to Rome by the celebrated geese.

5. Psychology and Logic

The most interesting products of that period's work in the field of psychology are those that anticipate, or at least herald, the developments of the subsequent period. I am referring to the cerebral anatomy of P. J. Cabanis, F. J. Gall (whose work also includes the first theory of reflex action), Sir Charles Bell, and P. P. Broca; to the physiological or experimental psychology of Tetens and Bonnet, later on continued with much greater success by Johannes P. Müller, E. H. Weber, R. H. Lotze, G. T. Fechner; to the related line taken by Claude Bernard; [1] and, if we insist on including *Völkerpsychologie* in psychology at all, to the work of F. T. Waitz, who was mentioned above in the section concerned with Environmentalism. Furthermore, if we also include philosophies about the collective mind—and if we choose to call them the harbingers of modern social psychology—we have to add, on the one hand, Comte and, on the other hand, Herder and many other 'romantics.'

[(a) *Associationist and Evolutionist Psychology.*] But more directly relevant for the possibility of a psychological foundation of technical economics—if indeed we have any use for such a foundation—are the psychologies of Herbart (1776-1841) and Beneke (1798-1854).[2] The former worked out a simple con-

[1] These names are mentioned merely as pointers for readers who, if they should wish to go further, will meet them in any history of psychology—which is why I refrain from giving titles and dates. The names of Cabanis, Broca, Weber, and Fechner are associated with performances of particular interest to us. Some will be mentioned again in the corresponding chapter and section of Part IV so that we do not lose our thread. The reader will understand, of course, that I am not competent to judge the value of such work as Gall's or Lotze's in its technical aspects and that in consequence my choice of names may be misleading: the list is the list of an economist whose impressions are in part due to chance reading (guided, however, to some extent, by professional advice) and chance contacts. The name of Broca, e.g., stands where it does because this author combined to an unusual degree research in brain anatomy and in cultural anthropology, but also because his work impressed me greatly in my formative years.

[2] See e.g. J. F. Herbart's *Lehrbuch zur Psychologie* (1816) and his *Psychologie als Wissenschaft. . .* (1824-5). Herbart's very influential philosophy and pedagogics do not interest us here. F. E. Beneke's *Grundlegung zur Physik der Sitten* (1822; the opposite pole to Kant's *Grundlegung zur Metaphysik der Sitten*) and *Lehrbuch der Psychologie als Naturwissenschaft* (1833) make psychology the only basis of logic, ethics, and aesthetics and afford an excellent illustration for what is meant in the present book by Psychologism.

ceptual apparatus for the analysis of psychic phenomena as they are given by introspective observation without recourse to physiology. Economists might have learned something from him, though more from his methods than from his results. Barring a few quotations that do not mean anything, I have not however been able to find any instances to prove that either his psychology or his general philosophy exerted any influence upon the professional work of economists. I wonder whether the same should be averred for the element in that period's psychological work that is by far the most *important* one from the standpoint of a history of economics—Hartleyan associationism. This associationism should have been obsolete by then but was revived by a new edition of Hartley's work (1791) and re-expounded with brilliant efficiency by our own colleague James Mill: [3] the mind, a Lockian blank; psychic life, a mechanical system of associations. Even J. S. Mill felt unable to rest content with this, and A. Bain was to combine it with Darwinian elements and elements derived from the German physiological psychologists into something that was pretty far removed from associationist orthodoxy. But for us the question arises: since this associationist orthodoxy was part of Benthamite orthodoxy, shall we not expect that it influenced the economics of the group that was another part of it? Of course, we shall—but we shall be disappointed. The case illustrates very well the nature of the relation of a comprehensive system to its parts. Psychological associationism agrees all right with the utilitarian philosophy or the utilitarian theory of ethics or of behavior in general and in this sense does implement the rest. But if, on the strength of this, we proceed to examine James Mill's little treatise on economic theory, we find that its propositions are completely independent of associationist psychology and are just as compatible with any other: though a province of the Benthamite empire, the economics of the utilitarians was a self-governing province that could have lived equally well if severed from the empire. This verifies a result already arrived at in other connections.[4]

The only thing that needs to be added is evolutionist psychology. As has been mentioned, both Darwin and Spencer faced the problem of the manner in which the human mind acquired each 'mental power': they attempted to construct genetic theories of 'instincts,' emotions, curiosity, memory, attention, beliefs, moral sense, social virtues, and the like. It should be observed that such endeavors are not psychology in the ordinary sense: for example, analysis of the faculty of 'memory' is one thing, and a hypothesis on how we came to have this faculty is another thing. However, genesis may suggest truly psychological theories, and it is understandable that Darwinian influence began to assert itself in professional psychology before long. Economists, however, did

[3] *Analysis of the Phenomena of the Human Mind* (1829).

[4] Observe, in particular, that the same thing also holds for Hume: his economics has nothing whatever to do with either his psychology or his philosophy. And so for Locke. On the other hand, the relation of associationism to utilitarian economics is complicated by the fact that Bentham's own economics differed from the economics of the other utilitarians who were his followers in everything else.

not take to this line of research, though it has obvious bearings upon problems of economic behavior and of its malleability, say, in a socialist organization of society—something worth pondering!

[(b) *Logic, Epistemology, and Cognate Fields.*] In these fields [5] substantial advance would have to be reported both as to philosophical foundations (Kant; Hegel's *Logic* is not logic in any technical sense though relevant to it in several points) and as to formal and practical developments (Lotze, De Morgan). From our standpoint, it is important to mention the work of a man who holds a key position in the history of the fields within our range of vision, Richard Whately [6] (Anglican archbishop of Dublin). And of great significance for the picture of that period's *Zeitgeist* is the effort made by another key man to realize a desideratum that has been formulated again and again—in our own day, by J. Dewey—to bring logic nearer to the actual procedures of science: Whewell's *History of the Inductive Sciences* (1837).[7] The program of *modern*

[5] If we may call mathematics a cognate field, it was the one that made the biggest strides. About these nothing can be said here except that this period—following as it did upon the 'heroic age of mathematics' in which the excitement of pioneer discovery had all but crushed the interest in logical foundations and in critical analysis of concepts and methods—laid the groundwork of modern (rigorous) mathematical reasoning. But a few data on probability must be mentioned, owing to the importance of the subject for statistics and for economic theory. Laplace's *Théorie analytique des probabilités* was first published in 1812; his *Essai philosophique* (which is quite eighteenth century, however) in 1814; Poisson's famous *Recherches* in 1837; Cournot's *Exposition de la théorie des chances et des probabilités* in 1843; P. L. de Tchebycheff's paper ('Des Valeurs moyennes' in Liouville's *Journal de mathématique, pure et appliquée*), 1867; Venn's *Logic of Chance* (often invoked by Edgeworth) in 1866. Fechner's *Kollektivmasslehre* (1897) belongs in this period though not chronologically. The same applies to J. von Kries's *Principien der Wahrscheinlichkeitsrechnung* (1886). The Cournot of probability is the great economic theorist (see below, Part IV, ch. 7, sec. 2). My high opinion of his theory of random events is a layman's opinion. But it was shared by the late Professor Czuber of Vienna.

[6] *Elements of Logic*, which appeared originally as an article in the *Encyclopaedia Metropolitana* (1826). For his work in economics, see ch. 4 below.

[7] William Whewell's (1794-1866) powerful and masterful personality belongs to, and illustrates at its best, that class of scientific men whom we have called Academic Leaders: he was a peerless influence in Trinity College and in Cambridge generally, one of those environment-creating individuals who belong in the history of science even if they never wrote a line. Such was not Whewell's case, however. The *History* is not only a work of erudition but a live source of inspiration (so it was to J. S. Mill), though his *Philosophy of the Inductive Sciences* (1840) is disappointing (at least, so it is to me) and though his *Elements of Morality including Polity* (1845) has been deservedly forgotten. He was also something of an economist. His *Lectures* (1852 and 1862) do not, it is true, amount to much, though he was far too able ever to be quite uninteresting. But he displayed sense for quality by editing the works of Richard Jones (see below, chs. 5, 6) and a touch of originality by making an attempt that no commonplace mind would have made in his day, viz. to express mathematically a few propositions of the economic theory of his time (3rd vol. of the *Cambridge Philosophical Transactions*). This effort does not go beyond stating in symbols what had already been stated in

empiricist logic—as taught by the Vienna positivists such as Carnap, Frank, Richard von Mises, Schlick—is to analyze scientific procedure and to do away with, as not only irrelevant but meaningless, everything else, especially all 'metaphysics.' Whewell was, of course, far removed, subjectively, from either this program or the conceptual constructs with which it is being implemented. But, objectively speaking, his book, owing to the influence it exerted on Mill's *Logic*, is a landmark on the long road that leads toward logical positivism.

[(c) *J. S. Mill's* Logic.] These scanty remarks have prepared us for a discussion of the work in which we are primarily interested. From our standpoint, J. S. Mill's *Logic* must hold a place of honor, not only because we claim the author for our own, not only because we economists are much more likely to turn to it than to any other methodological treatise of that time, but also because it was one of the great books of the century, representative of one of the leading components of its *Zeitgeist*, influential with the general reading public as no other Logic has ever been. A less striking patch of color in our picture than is the *Origin of Species*, it is hardly a less indispensable one—although it does not stand out, as does the *Origin of Species*, when we look back on the historical sequence of performances and ideas that produced the situation of today in the respective fields, and although Mill's [8] book is dead in a sense in which Darwin's is not.

The best way of explaining, to economists, the nature of Mill's performance is to point out the family likeness that exists between his *Logic* and his *Principles of Political Economy*, which will be fully discussed in the appropriate place below (ch. 5). With admirable modesty, Mill disclaimed, in both cases, any pretense 'of giving the world a new theory of intellectual operations' or of economic processes (see the prefaces to the first editions of both books). In both cases, his aim was

words and therefore does not really constitute mathematical economics (there is no mathematical *reasoning*). But his rudimentary demand analysis, considering its date, does not quite deserve Jevons' contemptuous verdict that has since been repeated many times. All this is mentioned here because the brevity of our sketch will not permit notice of performances such as Whewell's in their appropriate places.

[8] J. S. Mill, *A System of Logic, Ratiocinative and Inductive, being a Connected View of the Principles of Evidence and the Methods of Scientific Investigation* (1843). One has in mind the success of this book, as much as or more than the success of its author's *Political Economy*, when one speaks of Mill's sway over the generation of English intellectuals that entered upon their careers in the 1850's and 1860's. Abroad, part of the reading public was impervious to such influence. But the rest embraced Mill's message with even greater enthusiasm. The book was found in the house of a peasant in Ireland. It was called the 'book of books' by an accomplished Viennese woman (a Fabian and suffragist) who felt herself to be progress incarnate. It occupied a place of honor not much below Plato's in the mind of at least one *philological* philosopher I knew as a boy—all of which I say in order to convey, first, that the book was a living force in bourgeois civilization and, second, that the correlation between individuals' enthusiasm for it and their competence to judge it was not quite satisfactory.

to co-ordinate existing elements of knowledge, to develop them, and, as he liked to put it, 'to untie knots' (*scilicet* in *existing* strings). In neither case did he succeed completely; but in both he did eminently useful work, work that was perhaps all the more pregnant with suggestions because it contained stimulating discrepancies of doctrine.

Both works, besides being of the same class of performance, reveal in a similar manner the mental stature and the—shall I say 'moral'?—propensities of their author. Within the range of his comprehension, he was eminently fair and fully resolved to open the doors of his mind to ideas of widely different origin—in the *Logic* he went so far as to pay (via a quotation from Condorcet) a well-deserved compliment to scholastic performance. He was 'matter of fact': though his mind was not 'practical' in every sense of the word, he was always 'practical' and even pragmatist in intention, the practically useful result attracting him before everything else. In the case of the *Logic*, his practical purpose was to analyze scientific procedures with a view, first, to establishing their validity ('to appraise evidence') and, second, to developing rules that might inspire or guide research. This makes it very difficult to describe his fundamental standpoint or standpoints in terms of *modern* 'empiricist' and 'positivist' logic, for the problems and methods that are characteristic of the latter and divide its staff of workers (especially in the *Grundlagenforschung* of mathematics) were largely beyond his ranges of vision and interest. (Wherefore it is unjust, by the way, to criticize from a modern standpoint occasional utterances of his that *seem* to be relevant to modern controversies.) But this essentially practical purpose of the *Logic* also renders it difficult to describe Mill's fundamental views in terms of *older* philosophies. The significance of the Kantian revolution he hardly grasped. In a general way, it may be said that his philosophy had its roots in the English empiricism of the Locke-Hume tradition and, in particular, that it had an associationist psychological background. But I believe, though I cannot prove here, that neither statement is entirely correct. In any case, Mill was not narrowly empiricist or narrowly associationist: Hartleyan associationism comes in for criticism in the *Logic*, especially at a strategic point in Book VI.

The purpose of the book almost makes it a complement of Whewell's, to which in fact it owes much. Let us put it like this: Mill's *Logic* is primarily a theory of scientific knowledge (inference), essentially theoretical as compared with Whewell's book and still more so as compared with any treatise on any individual science; but it is primarily practical as compared with any treatise on pure logic or pure epistemology (which were, however, pretty much one and the same thing for Mill). As regards logical fundamentals, Mill leaned heavily on R. Whately even where he dissented from him.[9]

[9] Another revealing reference in the *Logic* (and in the *Examination of Hamilton*) is to Dr. Thomas Brown's *Lectures on the Philosophy of the Human Mind*, which, edited after Brown's death (1820), had a most successful career. The interesting point is that

Cautious and noncommittal as Mill was with reference to certain points of philosophical fundaments, modest as he was with reference to his personal contribution, in one respect he was neither cautious nor modest: exactly as in his *Political Economy*, in a manner that strikes us as curiously naïve, he cheerfully claimed an entirely impossible degree of finality for the results he expounded. He seems to say to us: why, I have collected and systematized the best ideas of this enlightened age, the principles either promulgated or conformed to by its ablest thinkers—what more can there possibly be left to do? His confident teaching fared in logic much as it did in economics.

Book I, 'Of Names and Propositions' (including Classification and Definition), in which there are passages almost suggestive of modern 'semantics,' and Book II, 'Of Reasoning' (Syllogisms; Deductive Sciences, which Mill holds are really inductive in so far as their premisses are derived by a process of induction from experience), cover ground on which Mill felt that the going was easy: for him who hardly ever looked below the surface, no serious problem arose to bar the way. He felt differently about the ground covered in Book III, 'Of Induction' (or generalization from experience, the core of scientific procedure and the core of Mill's performance). It contains the axiom of the uniformity of the course of nature, his theory of valid induction that is derived from it, his philosophy of causation, his famous 'four methods' (of Agreement, of Difference, of Residues, of Concomitant Variations), all of which is partly marred by faults of thought or exposition that can be explained on only one hypothesis: that even there, though writing on subjects that gripped him intensely, he wrote as he always did—in haste. But precisely because of this, substantial improvement can be effected in several cases without injury to his main positions. On the whole, there cannot be any doubt that Book III constitutes one of the great contributions to the theory of scientific knowledge. The many points of interest in the essentially subsidiary Books IV and V must be passed by, but Book VI, 'On the Logic of the Moral [Social] Sciences' is of first-rank importance to us. It should be perused together with Mill's older (pre-Comtist) essay on the method of economics (1836) that has been included in the volume on *Some Unsettled Questions*.

In order to do justice to this methodology of the social sciences, two things must be borne in mind. First, as an inevitable consequence of more fundamental shortcomings of Mill's general epistemology, there are many things in Book VI to which objections may be raised. But they do not impair its argument very much. Thus, his extension of the methods of the physical to the social sciences, including the concepts of scientific

this Scottish physician and philosopher, though he accepted sensationalism to a large extent, never abandoned 'intuitive' knowledge and had no empiricist theory of causation. The significance of Mill's strong recommendation of the book is not entirely destroyed by his qualifying objections to its argument.

law and of causation, are not nearly as objectionable as one might think because he watered down physical causation so radically as to make its extension to the social sciences practically harmless: his 'naturalism' was naturalism with its teeth pulled. Second, we must not forget that the fame and influence of Mill's work gave wide currency to his views so that much that reads trite and stale—like quotations from Hamlet—does so by virtue of his own achievement.

When all this is borne in mind, nothing remains but admiration. In a running battle with Comte, Mill triumphantly vindicated the actual procedure of economists while conceding—in fact, absorbing—all that should be conceded or absorbed. The standard method of economics was what he called the Concrete Deductive Method supplemented by the Inverse Deductive or Historical Method for research into historical changes of the social set-up as a whole. Had this been properly appreciated, the pointless later squabble of economists over induction versus deduction would have been avoided. The 'purely theoretical' set of problems was taken account of by his 'abstract or geometrical' method, the misuse of which for direct application to practical problems he made the target of scathing [10] criticism. The 'empirical laws,' nicely divided into uniformities of coexistence and uniformities of change, are assigned a place with which we can find but little fault. The impossibility of universally applicable, practical maxims was fully recognized as was *the necessity of studying actual human behavior in all its local and temporal varieties*—which should have taken off the curse from the economic man for all times. The *axiomata media* of his Ethology offered suggestions that are not fully exploited even now. The distinction that had to be fought for, sixty years later, between the problems of the effects that follow from a given cause under given social conditions and the problems of the 'laws' that determine those social conditions themselves is there. In fact, Mill unfolded a program that harnessed the purest of pure theory and the most concrete of institutional research into peaceful co-operation *and this without emasculating either*. Of course, Jevons reads fresh and stimulating even where he utters a platitude; Mill never reads fresh and stimulating even where he speaks valuable wisdom. That was the fault of his early training. But as regards this Book VI, though it contains nothing that was not said better later on—for example, by the elder Keynes—I conclude with advice to the reader to go back to it.

6. Pre-Marxian Socialism

In Chapter 2 above, we have said almost nothing about the socialism and the socialist groups or movements of the period. Painting in the large, we

[10] This adjective is I think justified, though Mill's invariable courtesy, in some cases reinforced by filial respect, made him tone down his wording. It will read surprisingly but can be strictly proved that the methodological doctrine that Mill preached does not differ at all from the position eventually (though not at first) adopted by Schmoller.

had hardly an opportunity for doing so. The omission can be repaired in a few words.[1] The second half of the eighteenth century produced a number of isolated socialist (or semi-socialist) writings but, before the French Revolution, nothing that can be called a movement. The French Revolution itself was bourgeois in origin, character, and ideology. The disintegration after 1791 of both its political set-up and its political thought was, however, associated with a literature that, though of very little importance in itself, was both indicative of a more than momentary socialist humor in a sector of the intellectual world of France, and instrumental in keeping it subterraneously alive during the Napoleonic regime. This provided a basis for the burst of propagandist activity, literary and other, of a socialist (or semi-socialist) nature that we observe in France until the advent of the second empire.[2] The revolution of 1848, though also bourgeois in origin, was quickly to show the existence of a sort of general staff of a revolutionary socialist army and even the existence of more or less definite plans for running a socialist state. Frightened to death, bourgeois groups did what Louis XVI could never be prevailed upon to do, that is, they suppressed the revolution by military force before it was too late. Thus, France holds priority in time as regards modern socialist literature; and among the business classes of all countries, the French business class was during that period the only one to face socialist revolution as a serious possibility. English Chartism, both in 1836-9 and 1840-48,[3] never amounted to anything like that, although it had a basis in early trade union organization that made it *more* serious in another and more fundamental sense. The only other socialist labor movement of importance was the German one that produced two organized parties: Lassalle's Allgemeiner Deutscher Arbeiterverein (1863) and Bebel's and Liebknecht's Socialdemokratische Arbeiterpartei (1869), which amalgamated in 1875.[4] The foundation and career of the First Inter-

[1] The interested reader has at his command plenty of sources of further information from which to supplement the jejune remarks that follow. He must remember that, from the standpoint of the aims of this book, we are not directly interested in social movements and their ideologies per se. In this particular case, brevity is excused in addition by the fact that our statements in this paragraph are not controversial. For general reference, Professor Alexander Gray's *Socialist Tradition* (1946) is recommended.

[2] The literary component of the movement supplied, however, part of the ideas of the *socialisme autoritaire* of Napoleon III, as has been mentioned already, just as socialist and semi-socialist workmen supplied part of the political support that raised him to power.

[3] The People's Charter itself, it should be remembered, was drawn up by William Lovett and Francis Place, the Bentham disciple, and was Benthamite and not at all socialist. In fact, its 'six points' embody nothing but radical parliamentary reform.

[4] Neither A. Bebel's nor W. Liebknecht's achievements come within the scope of this book. But the exploits of Ferdinand Lassalle (1825-64; the reader's attention is called to the biography by George Brandes, there are also several others) in sociological and economic analysis cannot go unmentioned though there will be no occasion to refer to them again. A highly cultivated man of brilliant abilities and indomitable energy, he was first and last a man of action whose intellectual, let alone scientific pursuits—though always attended to with zest—were always secondary to the excitements of a

national (1864) is mentioned here only because of Marx's famous Inaugural Address.[5]

[(a) *Associationist Socialism.*] Now, the one thing that is important for us to keep in mind is that the Marxist phase of socialist thought did not dawn before the beginning of the subsequent period.[6] The socialism of the period under discussion was non-Marxist and associationist.[7] This term is to denote all the varieties of socialist planning that adopt the principle of running production by workmen's associations—of social reconstruction through producers' co-operatives. Associationist socialism is, therefore, extra-scientific, because it does not concern itself primarily with (critical) analysis—as does Marxism—but with definite plans and the means of carrying them into effect. In addition, associationist socialism is unscientific because these plans involve assumptions about human behavior and administrative and technological possibilities that cannot stand scientific analysis for a moment. On both counts, Marx was quite justified in including associationist writers in his category of

fascinating life. An exception should be made, perhaps, for his most finished performance, *Das System der erworbenen Rechte* (1861), a brilliant piece of legal sociology that dazzled many a professional jurist. However, if we do make this work an exception and if we do assume that it was the product of genuine concentration, then we must also recognize that, along with very considerable philosophical and legal learning and strong critical ability, it displays lack of originality. His other writings display the same lack of originality, but unrelieved by learning, though still coupled with ability far and away above the common run of writers, socialist or other. The three most important economic publications, the *Arbeiterprogramm* (1863), the *Offenes Antwortschreiben* (1863), and *Herr Bastiat-Schulze von Delitzsch, der ökonomische Julian* (1864), are all of them brilliant pamphlets that embody, so far as analysis is concerned, a somewhat superficial but ably exploited Ricardianism—which accords with Lassalle's own view inasmuch as he described the only economics that seemed worth while to him as an 'immanent development' of Ricardo's teaching. This, by the way, is all his theory has in common with Marx's. To describe Lassalle either as a popularizer or as a disciple of Marx is quite erroneous. As regards agitatorial tactics and practical proposals, he was the very antipode of Marx—which is what caused the schism that impeded the progress of German political socialism until 1875 (Gotha Congress), when to Marx's infinite disgust, fusion was accomplished on a program that made large concessions to Lassalle's views.

[5] But no Marxist will take pride in this particular performance. Its contents reveal the effects of compromises that were perhaps inevitable but were of the sort that roused Marx's wrath when indulged in by other people. In fact, it was—as Marx himself pointed out with a mixture of humor and bitterness—thoroughly un-Marxist.

[6] Let me point out at once that, *so far as analysis is concerned,* the Marxist phase not only began but also ended with the subsequent period. This statement may seem surprising because we attach quite naturally high importance to the further revivals of Marxism in Russia and New York. But it will be substantiated below (Part IV, ch. 5, sec. 8).

[7] The term is convenient and I beg leave to use it, although I am aware of the awkwardness involved in using the same phrase in the same book in two entirely distinct meanings (psychological associationism—socialist associationism).

Utopian Socialists [8] and in fighting them bitterly. For he realized that they were discrediting serious socialism. By 1840, they had in fact succeeded in imparting to the very word Socialism a connotation of freakishness that helps to explain the attitude toward it that was specific to French economists: [9] to them, and not without reason, socialism came to mean two things, violence and nonsense. Some of the 'utopist' ideas were in fact unalloyed nonsense—in several cases, definitely pathological nonsense—and hardly any of them can be taken quite seriously, though an exception should perhaps be made in favor of L. Blanc (1811-82).[10] For us this is indeed not quite enough to warrant our neglecting them: freaks and dreams may yet enshrine sound pieces of analysis. Search undertaken in this spirit, however, yields but meager results. Not that we do not find sound reasoning and sound observation here and there; but most of what there is of it is trivial. Hence I shall mention only the outstanding examples of Robert Owen (1771-1858) and Charles Fourier (1772-1837),[11] who with Saint-Simon shared in a huge wave of American enthusiasm.

[8] Marx described as utopian any form of socialist thought but his own, which he called 'scientific.' The defining characteristic of *his* scientific socialism is, however, the scientific proof of the inevitability of socialism, so that with him the phrase 'utopian' should not have meant the same as 'not serious,' though it did. By a 'bourgeois economist,' Marx denoted an economist who fails to see this inevitability or, much more restrictively, an economist who believes in indefinite survival of the capitalist order. If the reader observe that these definitions do not coincide with the meanings usually attached to the terms, he will save himself many misunderstandings.

[9] Engels attributed the fact that Marx chose Communist instead of Socialist for use in the title of the Marx-Engels manifesto to Marx's dislike of a term that had acquired a flavor of 'respectability.' It is more likely, however, that Marx disliked it because it had acquired a flavor of oddity.

[10] Louis Blanc (*Organisation du travail*, collected articles first published in 1839) was no doubt also an associationist of humanitarian and rhetorical propensities that earned him semi-benevolent contempt from later critics, bourgeois and socialist. But his proposals differed from, say, Owen's by an element of practicability that shows especially in the more than supervisory role assigned to the bureaucracy (state). This element suggests possible influence upon Lassalle. Blanc once made the proposal that emerged again with some socialists, in and after 1930, to hand over to workmen factories that had closed down. Distribution according to the principle 'to everyone according to his needs' was a pet idea of his (though not adhered to), and he may be responsible for its currency among the socialists of his and a later time.

[11] The interested rearder will find bibliographies of (and on) both in any work of reference. As regards Owen, there was good reason for the emergence of a large literature about him for, quite independently of his plans and experiments of the New Harmony type, his ideas as well as his practice were of seminal importance in very many different ways that had little to do with one another. Thus, his fundamentally paternalistic measures at New Lanark created a model for the labor policy of the modern large-scale concern and, more important than this, initiated a new attitude toward wage questions. His emphasis on the value of strikes and trade unions versus political action makes him a classic in the history and theory of trade unions. His ideas on artisans' co-operatives have made him the patron saint of one of the significant movements of that and a later time. Not only was 'moral grandeur' (Torrens) his but

This is our opportunity for a glance at the American (and not only U.S.) Social-Science Movement.[12] The word Science, when used in connection with this movement, must be taken in a sense akin to the one it carries in the phrase Christian Science rather than in the usual one, for there was little genuinely scientific effort. A society that produces a comparatively prosperous stratum more quickly than it produces a cultural tradition is open to unbalancing infiltrations of ideas, even apart from the influence of physical immigration. A small number of people enjoyed leisure—'lettered ease' it was with some—and had open minds, which compensated shrewdness in business by enthusiasms and radicalisms, as generous as they were uncritical, in everything else. One of the most characteristic of these enthusiasms was the layman's enthusiasm for 'science'—and especially for social alchemy because, to the untrained mind that vibrates with unemployable energies, the real thing is not half so exciting as is the fake. This is the sociology of the movement. Its real importance for the impulse it gave to American economics and sociology is as difficult to appraise as is the real importance for serious research of the romanticist movement in Europe, of which, in fact, the social-science movement may be interpreted as the specifically American counterpart. I can see no relation between it and the performances that eventually established both economics and sociology in the United States, and am inclined to think that its petering out around the epoch of the Civil War was more favorable to social research than was its emergence. But the reader will easily see all that can be adduced for the opposite view.

But how can we account for the presence of sponsors of associationism whose claims to being taken seriously are not open to doubt? Well, for one thing, there is the influence of the literary fashion that the French associationists certainly succeeded in creating. For another thing, there is the support that associationist socialism as a plan for comprehensive social reconstruction derived—quite illogically, of course—from the actual co-operative movement and its literature. Both these elements will, I think, account for the asso-

also, within the sphere of thought and action defined by our examples, sound and even shrewd common sense (as his own business success suffices to prove). But as soon as he stepped out of this sphere, which was truly his own, his complete lack of analytic ability of the more subtle kind showed up immediately. Neither his ideas of the Labor Note that was to replace 'money' nor his ideas of an Equitable Labor Exchange are nonsense in themselves, but he just did not know how to protect his case against the most obvious criticisms.

As regards Fourier, the reader is referred to the one really enlightening item I have come across in the large literature about him: E. S. Mason's 'Fourier and Anarchism,' *Quarterly Journal of Economics* (February 1928). Two points must be made: first, Fourier did base his plan (of which the Brook Farm colony was the most famous embodiment) upon an elaborate analysis of human nature, in general, and of the nature of society, in particular, but it was all conceived in the worst style of eighteenth-century speculation; second, his *phalanstère* organization has but a qualified claim to being called socialist, and it is amusing to note that with the ignorance of actual conditions that characterizes so many of those prophets, he actually reserved for interest and profits a larger relative share than goes to them, on the long-run average, in capitalist reality.

[12] The U.S. branch of it has been described in L. L. and J. Bernard, *Origins of American Sociology: The Social Science Movement in the United States* (1943).

ciationism of Lassalle—his scheme of productive associations that were to be subsidized by the state and, by virtue of this advantage, to compete private industry out of existence.[13] But there is something else: to Marx and to many of us, associationism may be nonsense; but it was not nonsense to the Benthamite mind. In fact, a glance at the utilitarian views on the human mind and on the nature of social relations suffices to show that, once these assumptions concerning the quality—and substantive *equality*—of individuals are granted, associationist hopes cease to be absurd. And this accounts for the cautious associationism of J. S. Mill.[14]

[(b) *Anarchism.*] If we extend the principle of associationism to the political sphere and visualize the dissolution not only of industrial concerns into workmen's co-operatives but also of national states into voluntary 'communes,' we have Anarchism—of which by far the most articulate, but not the most orthodox or most consistent, exponent was P. J. Proudhon.[15] Here we are interested neither in his political anarchism nor in his philosophy, which he himself described as Hegelian, though I find it more easy to link it up with Fichte's. And we are interested in his economics only because it affords an excellent example of a type of reasoning that is distressingly frequent in a science without prestige: the type of reasoning that arrives, through complete inability to analyze, that is, to handle the tools of economic theory, at results that are no doubt absurd and fully recognized as such by the author. But the author, instead of inferring from this that there is something wrong with his methods, infers that there must be something wrong with the object of his research, so that his mistakes are, with the utmost confidence, promulgated as results. Proudhon's *Système des contradictions économiques ou philosophie de la misère* (1846) is the outstanding monument to this frame of mind. He was, among other things, unable to produce a workable theory of market value. But he did not infer: 'I am a fool,' but: 'Value is mad' (*la valeur est folle*). Marx's scathing criticism (*Misère de la philosophie*, 1847) was fully deserved,

[13] Moreover, though the man is to be taken seriously, it is fairly open to question how far his scheme is. Nobody can study that life of high endeavor and tragic failure without becoming aware of the fact that he is studying an important aspect of the German tragedy. In other words: Lasalle was a born political leader, conscious of superlative powers, and there is as little point in proffering the all-too-easy objections to his plan as there is in pointing out logical weaknesses in Disraeli's early thought. The real counterargument would have been to appoint him to cabinet office. But this is precisely what Prussia was congenitally unable to do.

[14] On the extent to which J. S. Mill should be considered a socialist, see below, ch. 5, sec. 1. Mill may have influenced Lassalle.

[15] Of the Proudhon literature, I mention only a work of indubitable scholarly quality, though there are several others that come within this category: Karl Diehl's *P. J. Proudhon, seine Lehre und sein Leben* (1888-96). In Joseph Proudhon (1809-65) we behold a phenomenon that is as rare among socialist thinkers as are horse-drawn vehicles in New York: a real, live proletarian. He was self-taught and this lack of training shows on every one of his many pages. Some of his ideas had been previously published by English socialists. But it is practically certain that he did not know of them.

though not well aimed in every respect. It should be observed, however, that Proudhon's claim to be called an anarchist in his own sense is questionable. For though, repeating an eighteenth-century phrase, he described property as theft in the pamphlet that founded his fame (*Qu'est ce que la propriété?*, 1840), his big idea was gratuitous credit rather than abolition of private property: loans free of interest to be issued in the notes of a public bank so that everyone might have access to means of production and become a proprietor—an idea that was to be revived by some latter-day projects of Social Credit.

Mikhail Bakunin (1814-76), Marx's pet aversion, has no place in a history of analysis, as he himself would have been the first to admit.[16] But there was another anarchistic communist or communistic anarchist who did present a piece of analysis: Weitling, the founder of 'Communia' in Wisconsin.[17] His particular plan does not concern us, but his theory of poverty does because it seems to enjoy a kind of immortality: it always turns up again. It is of the type of social criticism that, like Henry George's or F. Oppenheimer's, traces poverty to private property in land.[18] According to Weitling, there is no objection whatever to private property in other means of production and to private-business management of industry as long as there is free land accessible to everyone—all the trouble arises and *any* kind of property becomes a curse only when land becomes scarce, hence an object of property rights. The lessons I want the reader to learn from this are two. The first is one in the sociology of economic thought. Even so critical a thinker as Locke had no compunctions about the analytic value of the proposition: God gave the earth in common to all men. And this idea asserted itself in all ages, though in very different forms, even in writings that purport to present results of strictly empiricist thinking. The other lesson is one in faulty analysis. In many cases, actual and possible, the institutional structure of the agrarian sector may indeed be responsible for misery of the masses in the sense that their standard of life is lower than it would be with a different structure. In order to prove this possibility, we need only imagine a state of things in which land is so plentiful as to be capable of being a free good but is monopolized, in the technical sense of the term, by a single land-holding corporation that sets a monopoly price on its use. Cases somewhat more realistic than this then become verifications for the quite different proposition that the mere fact of

[16] The best-known communist thinker of the subsequent period, P. A. Kropotkin (1842-1921), is a different case. He made non-negligible efforts at analysis and his sociology of law is not without interest, though sufficiently so to warrant his exclusion from our report. Of course, for a history of economic and political thought (as contrasted with analysis), both he and Bakunin are of immense importance. And still more so for a sociology of economic and political thought. How tsarist society came to produce—in its higher and highest circles—revolutionary communism is in itself a fascinating problem: a crack cavalry regiment was not the worst of nurseries for communist impulses.

[17] Wilhelm Weitling (1808-71), *Die Menschheit wie sie ist und wie sie sein sollte* (1838); *Garantien der Harmonie und Freiheit* (1842).

[18] Not all agrarian socialists do this, of course.

private property in land reduces, of necessity, total real wages. This general proposition can be refuted by a rather elementary argument, which anyone is bound to encounter if he takes a few minutes to consider the question why private property should have that effect. But nobody who has this bee in his bonnet ever takes these few minutes, and if he did he would—like Rousseau in the matter of miracles—go mad rather than give up the idea that feeds his emotional life. And some such 'bee,' though not necessarily this one, is the most cherished possession of a distressingly large number of the people who write on economic subjects.[19]

If we leave the national state untouched and organize economic activity not into small free groups that on principle are self-sufficing but into vocational groups that are more like (though not necessarily quite like) the artisans' and merchants' guilds of the Middle Ages, we get the idea of the Corporative State. Such an idea was developed by Fichte and by many Catholic writers such as Baader. The main point is that these plans do not assume that the state should manage the corporations but rather the other way round: [20] they should hence not be identified with modern fascism; unlike the latter, they are anti-*étatiste* in conception. None of these writers bothered much about economic aspects. It is their cultural vision that is interesting. From our standpoint, there is no comment to be made.

In this connection, we may notice in passing the work of Karl Marlo,[21] an author who has been much commended by nonsocialists such as Roscher and Schäffle. Not a thorough-going socialist, he planned to sail between the Scylla of liberalism and the Charybdis of communism, to insure true equality and true liberty and so on by means of a large amount of nationalization of industry and of corporative organization for the part of economic activity that is not to be nationalized. A strong sense of responsibility that accounts for the bourgeois praise and is quite surprising in a man who was primarily a planner shows in Marlo's concern about the productivity of his system, about population, and about insurance. But the only point that interests us here is his analysis of competitive capitalism. On the one hand, he drew a picture of the condition of the working class that was as gloomy as was Engels'.[22] On the other hand, he attributed this condition not to the historically unique conditions that prevail frequently, though not necessarily, in the earlier stages of capitalist evolution but to the inherent logic of the capitalist system that, if allowed to operate, will always and increasingly depress labor's lot. We observe, first, that the factual picture is biased even *ex visu* of about 1850. For even

[19] Some readers may wonder why, speaking of communism, I do not mention Cabet. But there is nothing to be said about him from our standpoint.

[20] At least, if certain co-ordinating or supervisory functions are left to government, the corporations are to retain a large measure of autonomy.

[21] *Nom de plume* of Karl G. Winkelblech (1810-65): *Untersuchungen über die Organisation der Arbeit* . . . (1848-59).

[22] This is our opportunity to mention again a book that influenced social thought, in Germany at least, far beyond the circle of socialist orthodoxy: Friedrich Engels, *Die Lage der arbeitenden Klasse in England* (1845; English trans. 1887).

then statistics were available that any layman could have read to prove that talk about enslavement and starvation, and still more talk about *increasing* misery of the masses, lacked foundation in fact except so far as sporadic instances were concerned. We observe, second, that the analytic effort is biased in the same direction. For Marlo's analysis of competitive capitalism entirely failed to consider the obvious alternative to the proposition about enslavement and systematically omits to take account of those mechanisms in the capitalist process that tend to work the other way. But this systematic bias is evidently not like the bias of an index number or the bias in a particular source of information. It is typically the bias of ideological delusion, the kind of bias that springs from a writer's extra-analytic convictions and is impervious to either fact or argument. Refuting fact and argument would be met by moral indignation.

This is the point that made it worth our while to mention Marlo at all. Though individually of no great importance or influence, he was one of the many writers who helped, around the middle of the nineteenth century, to crystallize the ideology of the capitalist process. The main traits of this ideology had all emerged by 1776. They gained in definiteness through the efforts of writers such as the Ricardian socialists, Engels, Marlo, and many others in the next three-quarters of a century or so. Then the picture had become fixed. That is to say, it had, for considerable sectors of both the economic literature and the public, reached the status of 'as-everybody-knows' and was no longer questioned but was taken for granted by an increasing number of people. It was, in the thought of these people, substituted for the capitalist reality that increasingly diverged from it. It was the picture that Marx analyzed. It is the picture on which sophomoric radicalism feeds to this day.[23]

[(c) *Saint-Simonist Socialism.*] We could go on indefinitely but, having learned from three examples all that is to be learned for our purpose from this literature, we should not gain sufficiently by doing so.[24] One name, how-

[23] There should really be little difficulty in realizing that Crystallization of Ideologies is the only explanation for the existence of honest belief in the misery, helplessness, and frustration of the working class at a time of the political and economic dominance of the labor interest. Examination of the rationalized arguments only serves to strengthen this diagnosis. But crystallized ideologies that satisfy deep-seated urges defend themselves with desperate energy.

[24] A man who might have served us just as well as did Weitling, though less so than the more serious Marlo, is Charles Hall, *The Effects of Civilization* [i.e. Technological Progress], 1805. The problem to be discussed with respect to him, similar though it is in all other respects, would display another, though cognate, aspect that is not without importance to the social psychology of the social sciences. It may be put by means of the following question: since by all accounts this man was an able physician, how was it possible for him to use, in the field of social criticism, modes of thought that would have prevented him from passing his M.D. exams? I do not mean his recommendations, but the formal properties of his reasoning and his handling of facts. Another such man is J. F. Bray, *Labour's Wrongs and Labour's Remedy* (1839; London School Reprint, 1931). All I wish to say about him is that Marx should not be insulted by its being said that Bray anticipated him in any point:

ever, must be added, that of Saint-Simon.[25] In the main, this pathological genius—Émile Faguet's *fou très intelligent*—affords only another example that illustrates the difference between a man's importance for a history of economic thought and his importance for a history of economic analysis. Saint-Simon's name stands in the history of economic thought because of a message of a semi-religious character and because disciples turned this message—not without altering it—into the creed of a sect. Much has been written about Saint-Simon's posthumous success: not only in France but also in England, Germany, and especially in the United States and in Latin America, Saint-Simonist groups emerged and even a Saint-Simonist intellectual fashion of much wider range. But the groups consisted of small nuclei that quickly repelled serious members and brought discredit upon themselves by freakish developments of the creed. Around these nuclei there were more numerous adherents whose allegiance was not very close and was chiefly phraseological. As to the question how much importance should be attached to the intellectual fashion, men will, as in all similar cases, differ till doomsday. The fashion itself is explained as soon as we visualize the two salient features of the message that combined to produce something that was not to be had from any other creed: on the one hand, its glowing humanitarian optimism; on the other hand, its glorification of 'science' (technology) and of industrialism. Where other humanitarians were sour and doubtful about what sort of a future capitalist industry

---

any argument that works with exploitation must bear misleading witness to some affinity with Marx. The work of F. Huet (*Le Règne social du Christianisme*, 1853), whose proposal of division among the young generation of *biens patrimoniaux*, land especially, as they are released by death, suggests that Saint-Simonist ideas found favor also in Catholic centers. The 'Ricardian' socialists will be briefly considered later. On Engish Christian socialists, see C. E. Raven, *Christian Socialism*, 1848-54 (1920), and L. Brentano, *Die christlichsoziale Bewegung in England* (1883). See also, J. O. Hertzler, *History of Utopian Thought* (1923).

[25] Claude-Henri de Rouvroy, Comte de Saint-Simon (1760-1825) was a Rouvroy and therefore of the—genealogically speaking—best but also most degenerate blood of France; *Oeuvres choisies* (1859); biography by M. Leroy (1925); many works on the Saint-Simonist 'system' of thought and the Saint-Simonist sects, e.g. S. Charléty, *Histoire du Saint-Simonisme*, 1825-64 (1896). On an aspect of special importance for us, see E. S. Mason, 'Saint-Simonism and the Rationalisation of Industry,' *Quarterly Journal of Economics* (August 1931). The question which of his writings I should recommend to the reader embarrasses me greatly: it must be answered quite differently for men of different interests and tastes. As for myself, I know only those contained in the *Oeuvres choisies*. In a general way, I believe that economists will profit from a perusal of *Du Système industriel* (1821) more than from a perusal of his last and most famous work, *Nouveau Christianisme* (1825), which falls somewhat out of line with the rest and contains chiefly preachings of an utilitarian character—increase of the welfare of the most numerous and poorest class and so on—that are more Benthamite than Saint-Simonian. Perhaps I should also mention Bazard's *Exposition de la doctrine de St. Simon* (1830), which is remarkable for clearness. Nothing need be said, for our purposes, of his followers (Enfantin and Bazard were the most important) beyond the general comment on them in the text.

would provide for humanity at large, Saint-Simon gave comfort. Where otheı enthusiasts of industrial progress were harsh and unsympathetic, he preached the golden age for all. It was this combination of features that made Saint-Simonism so popular, for a time, with financiers of the promoter type such as the brothers Pereire of Crédit-Mobilier fame. But can the reader be so thoroughly imbued with intellectualist misconceptions as to believe that, without Saint-Simon's teaching, the Crédit Mobilier would not have been founded and managed exactly as it actually was, and would not have crashed exactly as it actually did?

There is something else, however. Saint-Simon's vision was not implemented by analytic work but nevertheless it is relevant for us in two respects. First, there is a conception of social change that may be said to adumbrate an economic interpretation of history. Saint-Simon felt the breakdown of the *ancien régime* and the advent of a new epoch with a pungent sense of reality—to use William James's phrase—that could not have come so naturally to anyone who was not a Rouvroy. Simplifying this into a breakdown of the feudal world and the advent of the epoch of industrialism *under pressure from economic* (*technological*) *developments*, he grasped some essentials of the eternal flux of social organizations and, within it, of the struggle of economic classes, his idea being that he was to lead humanity out of this struggle by means of the wonderful achievements of 'science'—rant, partly, but rant interspersed with flashes of profound understanding.[26] Second, there is a perception or a glimpse of the true nature of the capitalist process that acquires particular importance from the fact that neither Marx nor his bourgeois peers had it: Saint-Simon saw the pivotal importance of industrial leadership. He confused, it is true, the entrepreneur with the 'scientist' who devises new technologies. And he used his vision in the construction of a new form of social organization and not, as Marx would have done in his place, in any attempt to explain social processes as they are. Still, he did introduce a new factor that might have revolutionized 'classic' economics and might have put an end to analytic—as disguished from normative—equalitarianism. However, nothing resulted from his vision except that his socialism—if indeed his 'system' can be called socialist at all—was hierarchic[27] and not equalitarian. And economists completely failed to exploit this mine.

[26] I do not think, however, that this impairs materially the case for Marx's originality as regards the economic interpretation of history. For I find it difficult to conceive that anyone who had not had the idea himself could have been inspired to construct it from the suggestions proffered by Saint-Simon's writings. At worst, Saint-Simon was in this respect a forerunner in the same sense as Buffon and Erasmus Darwin were forerunners of Charles Darwin.

[27] This comes out very nicely in a letter addressed by Enfantin and Bazard to the President of the *Chambre des deputés* in 1830, a reprint of which the reader will find in Professor Gray's *Socialist Tradition*, p. 168. Let me add one more point: Saint-Simon, too, spoke of 'association' but this has nothing to do with the associationism discussed previously.

CHAPTER 4

Review of the Troops

ACCORDING TO PLAN, we shall survey the general layout of this period's analytic economics in Chapter 5, taking up headquarters in J. S. Mill's *Principles*. The review of the more important men and groups in the present chapter is for the benefit of readers who are unfamiliar with any but the greatest figures. It will not contain more names than are necessary for a general orientation. Others will be introduced as we proceed.

1. THE MEN WHO WROTE ABOVE THEIR TIME

We have emphasized the relative maturity that economics gained during the period under survey. Its relative immaturity might be measured by the number of important performances, the powerful originality of which was recognized later but which the profession completely, or almost completely, failed to recognize at the time. This happened in the cases of Cournot and of the various writers, especially Dupuit, Gossen, and Lloyd, who discovered the marginal utility principle. We shall transfer them to Part IV, merely observing for the moment the melancholy implications of this neglect: it shows a lack of alertness and of purely scientific interest among the economists of the period that goes far toward explaining why economics did not advance more quickly.[1]

[1] We may adduce mitigating circumstances, but substantially the indictment stands. Cournot was not unfavorably placed for getting a hearing. If he failed to get it, this was wholly due to the mathematics in the book. But precisely—what sort of a profession was this that laid aside a work because it was a little difficult of access? Dupuit elicited at least some criticism. Gossen was unfavorably placed and, if he did nothing to circulate his book among professors, the latter's sin may have been venial. But

In addition, there were other performances that fared a little better but also proved to be above their time in the sense that they failed to receive the attention and exert the influence which, enlightened by hindsight, we should deem appropriate. Of these, the most noteworthy are the writings that developed the marginal productivity principle. Since some leaders of the day occasionally did move within its orbit,[2] we shall at once make our bow to two early exponents of that principle who are particularly important, Longfield and Thünen. And I shall append a notice of still another man who wrote above his time, John Rae.

Mountifort Longfield (1802-84) was a lawyer by training and the first incumbent of the chair of political economy—a foundation of Archbishop Whately's—at Trinity College, Dublin. He also wrote on the Poor Law and other subjects, but the only publication of his we need notice is *Lectures on Political Economy* (delivered 1833, publ. 1834, London School Reprint 1931). Anyone who cares to glance at this book will readily understand why, in spite of its merits of exposition and matter, he failed to make a mark, so that he had to be unearthed, along with others, by Professor Seligman in the justly famous article 'On Some Neglected British Economists,' *Economic Journal*, 1903,[3] for which all students of the history of economics have every reason to feel lasting gratitude. But this neglect is readily understandable only if we realize what it is that will impress professional opinion and what it is historians of economics usually look for, namely, on the one hand, a man's views on the practical issues of his day and, on the other hand, the way in which he handles the theoretical tools that are common currency in his day. New ideas, unless carefully elaborated, painstakingly defended, and 'pushed' *simply will not tell*. Longfield's case illustrates so well the important question 'what takes effect and how and why,' because Longfield did not fail to keep contact with Ricardian teaching—he gave Ricardians every opportunity to be led to a more perfect analysis gently and without any violent break—and because he did find successors: he really founded a local 'school' (on this, see R. D. Black, 'Trinity College, Dublin, and the Theory of Value, 1832-1863,' *Economica*, 1945). His successor in the Whately chair, Isaac Butt (*Rent, Profits, and Labour*, 1838),

W. F. Lloyd was 'Student of Christ Church and Professor of Political Economy' at Oxford. His argument on marginal utility was quite straightforward and there was nothing deterrent about it. Several writers brushed against it, e.g. Senior. It must have become known to a number of people. The only construction that it is possible to put upon the fact that Lloyd's argument exerted no influence is that the economists who read it were blind to the analytic possibilities enshrined in it.

[2] Later on, it will become clear to the reader that it would have been quite impossible for them not to do so. Also, it will be explained later why I do not think that they, Ricardo especially, should be credited with more than is implied by the phrase in the text.

[3] Reprinted in E. R. A. Seligman, *Essays in Economics* (1925), ch. 3.

was his professed disciple and—correctly as I believe, if we consider pure theory only—put him on the same level as A. Smith.

Longfield's merits may be summed up by saying that he overhauled the whole of economic theory and produced a system that would have stood up well in 1890. Among other things, his argument against the labor theory of value is one of the best ever penned. However, we must confine ourselves to his two original contributions. He was one of those who anticipated the essentials of Böhm-Bawerk's theory (by making the 'roundabout' process of production the pivot of his analysis of capital). And he presented a reasonably complete and reasonably correct theory of distribution based upon the marginal productivity principle, not only the marginal cost principle. That is to say, he explained both 'profits' (return upon physical capital) and wages in terms of the contributions to total product that result from the addition to the productive set-up of the last element of capital (tools) or labor. Thus at least it seems fair to interpret him, though in details his argument is open to many criticisms (among other things he failed, as did many writers even after 1900, to distinguish clearly between the last laborer added and the least efficient laborer). The argument is still worth reading because it shows nicely the operations by which economists' minds paved their way toward the use of the general marginal principle. But we cannot stay to work this out.

Johann Heinrich von Thünen (1783-1850), the man whom A. Marshall professed to have 'loved above all my other masters' (*Memorials of Alfred Marshall*, 1925, p. 360), meant, of course, much less to his age than did Ricardo. But this is due to the latter's brilliant advocacy of policies. If we judge both men exclusively *by the amount of ability of the purely theoretical kind* that went into their work, then, I think, Thünen should be placed above Ricardo or indeed above any economist of the period, with the possible exception of Cournot. He was a North German Junker and followed the typical profession of the North German *Junkertum* (the correct translation is 'gentry'): for most of his life (after having completed his education at an agricultural college supplemented by two semesters at the University of Göttingen), he farmed the indifferent soil of his medium-sized estate, just about managing to make both ends meet and, sacrificing everything else, to keep up his intellectual interests in wintertime. This practical farmer was a born thinker, however, and quite unable to supervise the teams that ploughed his land without working out the pure theory of the process. His thoughts roamed toward wide generalizations from an early age but, first of all, he was an agriculturist, schooled in the ideas of Thaer, and an agricultural economist. As such he did enjoy recognition in his own country. Later on, he was also recognized more generally but in a peculiar way. Roscher, for example, considered Thünen's work to be one of the most important that had been written in Germany in the field of exact economics. Yet he entirely failed to grasp its true meaning. Reviewers were complimentary. Yet none of them understood the work except the part of it that is listed below under (III). For the rest Thünen, unlike Cournot, *never* came into his own. For though he continued to be quoted, the marginal productivity theory of distribution was independently rediscovered later, and his message was fully understood only at a time when all that would strike the reader was its shortcomings. The first volume of his *Der isolierte Staat in Beziehung auf Landwirthschaft und Nationalökonomie* was published in 1826 (2nd ed., 1842); the first part of the second volume, in 1850. The rest of the second volume and a third were published, from unfinished but well-advanced manuscripts, by H. Schumacher in 1863. There is a new edition with an introduction by Heinrich Waentig in *Sammlung sozialwissenschaftlicher Meister* (vol. XIII, 1910). The third volume contains 'Principles for the Determination of the Rent of Land, the Optimal Period of Rotation, and the Value of Timber of Different Ages for Firs' [This is a literal translation by J. A. S.]. The standard biography is also by Schumacher (1868), but the reader finds the relevant data in Professor E. Schneider's article 'Johann Heinrich von Thünen' in *Econometrica*, January 1934.

Thünen's contributions may be summed up as follows. (I) He was the first to use the calculus as a form of economic reasoning. (II) He derived his generalizations, or some of them, from numerical data, spending ten laborious years (1810-20) in carrying out in detail a comprehensive scheme of accounting for his farm in order to let the facts themselves suggest the answers to his questions. This unique piece of work, undertaken in the spirit of the theorist, makes him one of the patron saints of econometrics. Nobody, before or after, ever understood so profoundly the true relation between 'theory' and 'facts.' (III) Nevertheless, this man who was so fact-minded knew at the same time how to frame ingenious and fertile hypothetical schemata. His peak achievement in this art is his conception of an isolated domain of circular form and uniform fertility, free from all obstacles to or special facilities for transport, with a 'town' (the only source of demand for agricultural products) in the center. Given techniques, cost of transportation, and relative prices of products and factors, he deduced from this the optimal locations (which under those assumptions would be ring-shaped zones) for the various kinds of agrarian activities—dairying, forestry, and hunting included. A theory of rent, in some points superior to that of Ricardo, results as a by-product. Though many people objected to such bold abstraction, this was the part of his work that was understood and recognized in his time. For us, it is important to realize its brilliant originality. Ricardo or Marx (or whoever it is among the theorists of that period who holds the place of honor in the reader's scale) worked on problems that presented themselves from outside by means of analytic tools that had been forged before. Thünen alone worked from the unformed clay of facts and visions. He did not rebuild. He built—and the *economic* literature of his and earlier times might just as well not have existed at all so far as his work is concerned. (IV) In quite the same spirit, he was the second (the first was Cournot, by date of publication at least) to visualize the general interdependence of all economic quantities and the necessity of representing this cosmos by a system of equations. (V) He introduced explicitly the tool of analysis, actually used of course by Ricardo, that may be termed the 'steady state' of the economic process—Marshall's long-run normal—that was akin to statics rather than to the stationary state of 'classical' theory. (VI) As fully as Longfield, and somewhat more correctly, he developed a marginal productivity theory of distribution, at least for the relation between capital and labor, interest and wages. But the fundamental idea itself (which he correctly puts, in words, in terms of partial differential coefficients, Waentig edition, p. 584) is almost a secondary element in the wealth of problems he grouped around it. No idea of these can be conveyed. Instead we must touch on another point, not because it is worth our while in itself, but because it has attracted attention beyond its deserts: Thünen's famous formula for the 'natural wage.' He must have thought a lot of it, because he had it engraved upon his tombstone.

For simplicity, consider a one-year productive process, the only expense of production being wages. Call the dollar value of the national net product p, the total pay roll w, so that total profits (which Thünen, like others, identified with interest) are $p - w$, and the rate of profits (interest) is $\frac{p-w}{w}$. Suppose that the wage receivers spend a fixed amount, a, per year, investing the rest, $w - a$, at the current rate of interest, $\frac{p-w}{w}$. On this investment, they will evidently earn $\frac{p-w}{w}(w-a) = p - w - \frac{ap}{w} + a$. If this expression is to be a maximum, we must have[4] (p and a being treated as constants),

$$\frac{d(p - w - \frac{ap}{w} + a)}{dw} = -1 + \frac{ap}{w^2} = 0$$

from which follows Thünen's formula, $w^2 = ap$, or $w = \sqrt{ap}$. This wage would maximize workers' income from investment. The idea is not without interesting suggestions and might be used among other things in certain schemes of profit sharing. But, of course, this wage is not 'natural' in the sense that the free-market mechanism tends to produce it. The formula does not embody Thünen's theory of wages. Nor is it an essential part of it. The wildly unrealistic assumptions should not, however,

[4] In order to have a maximum and not a minimum, it is further necessary that the second derivative be negative. But this is all right, since it equals $\left(-\frac{2ap}{w^3}\right)$, a, p, and w being essentially positive.

prompt us to declare the argument wrong. Under its assumptions it is quite right.

John Rae (1796-1872; not to be confused with the other John Rae mentioned in this book, the biographer of A. Smith), a Scotsman whose intellectual refinement—he had emerged from the Universities of Aberdeen and Edinburgh as a good classical scholar and mathematician and as a biologist and physician who was at least half trained—and nervous sensibility made him a failure at everything he touched. From 1821 on, he roamed about in Canada, the United States, and other countries, the Hawaiian Islands included, where he had to rough it (two spells of schoolmastership being by far the most congenial of all the employments he tried) until, shortly before his death, he drifted with broken masts into the haven of a friendly house in Clifton, Staten Island. Yet, all the time, he also struggled with what under the circumstances was the greatest misfortune of all, an unmanageable wealth of ideas on the subjects of biology, philology, ethnology, aeronautics, and what-not—all, or most of them, parts of a grandiose plan, conceived in his youth, of a 'philosophical history' of humanity. Up to this point the reader will feel that he is recognizing a well-known type. He is wrong. For one achievement, complete and workmanlike, yet of striking power, refutes the idea the reader may have conceived. This achievement happened to be in our field. In vision and originality, Rae far surpassed the economists who were successful.

The *Statement of Some New Principles on the Subject of Political Economy Exposing the Fallacies of the System of Free Trade and of Some other Doctrines Maintained in the 'Wealth of Nations'* was published in Boston in 1834. In this note we shall try only to appreciate the nature and importance of the performance and record its fate.

Rae had not more than a saving knowledge of economics. It is evident that he owed such training as he had mainly to the work he attacked. But this he had mastered in all its ramifications, premisses, and implications as only a kindred spirit can, and after having developed his own ideas in constant reference to it, he proceeded to erect a structure similarly conceived. For it is this that we must see in his work: another *Wealth of Nations* or, more correctly, something that with ten additional years of quiet work, graced by an adequate income, could have grown into another—and more profound—*Wealth of Nations.* It follows that it would be quite inappropriate to dwell on the many minor good things the work contains—a few will be mentioned in the proper places. The essential thing is the conception of the economic process, which soars above the pedestrian view that it is the accumulation of capital per se that propels the capitalist engine. The conceptual apparatus developed in the First Book is glorified by the new vision but not otherwise remarkable and need not detain us any more than needs the Third Book, which deals with 'the operations' of that imaginary entity, the 'legislator.' Naturally, Rae's dissent from Smith's anti-*étatiste* views will primarily interest the student of economic thought. The Second Book, however, has attracted most of the attention that later economists devoted to the work. It may be called a theory of capital, conceived in unprecedented depth and breadth. To say that it presents the whole of Böhm-Bawerk's theory is to display inability to understand Böhm-Bawerk. But two cornerstones of the latter's structure—one of them also a cornerstone of Senior's—are in fact there: the proposition that 'lengthening' the process of production (postponement) will usually increase the physical amount of final product (ch. v), and the proposition that 'the actual presence of the immediate object of desire' will give to it, in our valuation, a decisive advantage over an exactly similar object that is expected to become available at some future date, even if this expectation be perfectly certain.

As a rule, a work presenting novel ideas will not elicit response if it lacks the support which comes from being written by a well known author. We ought, therefore, to be surprised at the response it met with rather than at the fact that it did not meet with more. J. S. Mill noticed it, and—perhaps in consequence of this—there was an Italian translation in 1856. How, then, can it have been necessary to 'discover' Rae, as Professor Mixter rightly claimed it was? (Cf. C. W. Mixter, 'A Forerunner of Böhm-Bawerk,' *Quarterly Journal of Economics*, January 1897 and 'Böhm-Bawerk on Rae,' ibid. May 1902, and the same author's (rearranged) edition of Rae's work under the title *Sociological Theory of Capital*, 1905, prefaced by the biography from which the data above about Rae's life have been taken.) The answer might serve as a motto for a chapter of the sociology of science. J. S. Mill was invariably fair and even generous. Sensing the quality of the work, he was glad to mention it in a friendly spirit, not only to accept from it a phrase that happened to fit into his line of thought ('effective desire of accumulation') but also to quote it copiously (Book I, ch. 11). He even went so far as to compare Rae's performance on accumulation with Malthus' performance on population. And all this, written in what was to be for forty years the most influential textbook of economics, was insufficient to introduce Rae to the profession or to rouse any curiosity concerning the rest of his book! Or, alternatively, if this impression is wrong and any considerable number of Mill's readers did take it up, there was not one among them to realize its true importance. However, it may be of some significance to note that Senior knew the book (see 'John Rae and John Stuart Mill: a correspondence,' *Economica*, August 1943, p. 255).

2. The Ricardians

Of all the groups that formed and dissolved during the period under survey, the Ricardian circle alone deserves separate treatment. The brilliance of its central figure, the international prestige it enjoyed for a time, its prominence in public debate, its achievements and failures—all this and more can be adduced in justification of the attempt to make readers visualize it as clearly as possible. Moreover, the group was a genuine school in our sense: there was one master, one doctrine, personal coherence; there was a core; there were zones of influence; there were fringe ends. Let us first look at the core. It really consisted only of Ricardo himself, James Mill, and McCulloch. But we add West and De Quincey. For reasons to be explained later, we do not add J. S. Mill. A fortiori, we do not add Fawcett or Cairnes.

David Ricardo (1772-1823) entered upon a business career at the age of fourteen (he was first a broker, then a jobber and operator on the stock exchange, always a man of the money market) and made a considerable fortune. This is relevant for us because it means (1) that, though he came from a cultured home, he was all but uneducated in the scholastic sense; (2) that, since such a career is absorbing, only the dregs of his intellect and energy were available for analytic work until 1814 when he retired at forty-two. Nevertheless, he had done the bulk of his analytic work by then, as far as the workshop of his mind (not publication) is concerned. This is a striking proof of his splendid powers, but also the reason why his work, lacking as it did the benefit of full concentration during the third decade of life, which is of decisive importance in a thinker's career, never penetrated down to the deepest depths, besides remaining badly finished in a formal and technical sense: we have before us the record of a wrestler who fought his matches with his right hand tied behind his back. After this, the reader will not suspect me of inadequate admiration for the man when he reads some of my comments upon the work. I shall go further. There is point in defending a figure of which we are justly proud against certain aspersions that are completely unfounded. Some writers have not been ashamed to suggest that his pecuniary interest—as a 'bear'—determined the part he took in the controversies of his time on currency policy. I reply that Ricardo was able enough to make money on rising as well as on falling markets; and I repeat, in addition, that such writers do not seem to realize what it is they are really saying when resorting to such 'explanations,' since the only schemes of motivation that are open to their direct observation are their own. With less indecency, others have interpreted Ricardo as a representative of the 'moneyed interest' and as inspired by a 'hatred' of the landowning class. This, besides being irrelevant for the scientific contents of his writings, is of course sheer nonsense and only proves, if anything, the inability of these interpreters to understand a piece of analytic work. If I cared to waste space, I could prove this inability in each individual case.[1]

[1] There is more excuse for the indictment that Ricardo was indifferent to the interests of labor. For though nothing can be farther from the truth, in his almost unbelievable carelessness of formulation he used, on two or three occasions, turns of phrase that seem to support this indictment. Ricardo was constantly complaining of being misunderstood (in this respect in a letter to J. B. Say) and not without justice. In part, however, he had only himself to blame. But, in this so-called indifference, there was

Some day, perhaps, we may see completion of Professor Sraffa's comprehensive edition of Ricardo's works, which we have been eagerly awaiting these twenty years [the first five vols. had appeared by April 1952. Ed.]. Meanwhile, there is McCulloch's edition of the *Collected Works* (1st ed., 1846) prefaced by a memoir of Ricardo. At the moment, since we reserve publications on money for the last chapter of this Part, we are concerned only with Ricardo's *Essay on the Influence of a Low Price of Corn on the Profits of Stock* (1815) and his *Principles of Political Economy and Taxation* (1817; 3rd ed., the one to use, 1821; the reader will presumably resort to E. C. K. Gonner's edition, 1882, last printing, 1929). Any thorough study should be supplemented by perusal of his letters to Say, Malthus, Hutches Trower, and McCulloch (for editions, see article on Ricardo by J. H. Hollander in the *Encyclopaedia of the Social Sciences*, which gives a brief but correct sketch and appraisal of Ricardo's work) and by his *Notes on Malthus' Principles* (ed. J. H. Hollander and T. E. Gregory, 1928; see review by E. S. Mason, 'Ricardo's Notes on Malthus,' *Quarterly Journal of Economics*, August 1928). Of all general interpretations, the most important are: K. Marx in *Theorien über den Mehrwert;* J. H. Hollander, *David Ricardo* (1910); and K. Diehl, *Sozialwissenschaftliche Erläuterungen zu David Ricardos Grundgesetzen* (2nd ed., 1905). Still more instructive for our purposes are E. Cannan's comments in his *Theories of Production and Distribution* (3rd ed., 1917). The literature on Ricardo is immense, especially if we count in, as we should, all the references to him in theoretical works such as Böhm-Bawerk's or Taussig's. I wish, however, to single out two relatively recent studies by excellent theorists that illustrate the extent of the range within which critics of the highest competence may differ as regards the nature and value of Ricardo's performance: Professor F. H. Knight's article on the 'Ricardian Theory of Production and Distribution' in the *Canadian Journal of Economics and Political Science*, vol. I (February 1935), and Dr. V. Edelberg's article, 'The Ricardian Theory of Profits' in *Economica*, vol. XIII (1933).

The discussion above goes some way toward explaining the character of Ricardo's work. In utmost brevity, I shall add the following comments, if only to give the reader some points to reflect upon. Ricardo is usually described as a utilitarian, but he was not one. This is not because of his having had another philosophy but because that busy and positive mind had no philosophy at all. He was on good terms, mainly through James Mill, with the philosophical radicals. Presumably, he often expressed assent to utilitarian tenets. Historians are apt to exaggerate the importance of such things. But they do not mean much. Similarly, he had not an inadequate sociology, but none at all: there were certain economic problems that fascinated his powerful intellect but the socio-

also an element of virtue: he was above the unctuous phrases that cost so little and yield such ample returns.

logical framework he took for granted—no matter of reproach this, but simply a matter of division of labor. Given its nature, his theory would not have been improved by being caparisoned sociologically; the critic who misses institutional disquisitions has simply called at the wrong address. But of course this applies only to his theory as theory, it does not apply to his recommendations. In these we do miss insight into the motive powers of the social process and, in addition, historical sense.[2]

Two other points, however, bear directly upon Ricardo's theory as theory. First, Marx's contrary view notwithstanding, Ricardo's was not the mind that, like Thünen's, works from the clay. His method of work was essentially to take hold of the problems that the day presented to him, and to attack them by means of tools that he derived by criticism. The one is obvious at first sight from all his writings except the *Principles* (where it is only less obvious). The other is obvious from the *Principles*. Even if we did not know that Ricardo's thought was inspired by the *Wealth of Nations*, which he took up in 1799 when boring himself at a health resort, we could not help seeing that the argument of the *Principles* starts with a criticism of A. Smith, which really runs through the whole book. With a high degree of confidence, we may reconstruct the development of his thought so far as it was not determined by his interest—analytic and practical—in current events: he studied the *Wealth;* he was shocked at what seemed to him to be a logical muddle; he set about straightening out this muddle; and the *Principles* was the ultimate result of this work of creative criticism. Let us make a note of this: Ricardo's theoretical structure represents a particular way of recoining the *Wealth;* Malthus' theoretical structure represents another way of doing this. As a corollary, I venture to state that Ricardo owed very little to any other writer, though his later study of Say and Malthus and his discussions with both and with James Mill no doubt served to clarify his ideas—of this more in a moment. Second, Ricardo's was not the mind that is primarily interested in either fundamentals or wide generalizations. The comprehensive vision of the universal interdependence of all the elements of the economic system that haunted Thünen probably never cost Ricardo as much as an hour's sleep. His interest was in the clear-cut result of direct, practical significance. In order to get this he cut that general system to pieces, bundled up as large parts of it as possible, and put them in cold storage—so that as many things as possible should be frozen and 'given.' He then piled one simplifying assumption upon another until, having really settled everything by these assumptions, he was left with only a few aggregative variables between which, given these assumptions, he set up simple one-way relations so that, in

[2] I do not think that Ricardo ever did much historical reading. But this is not what I mean. The trouble with him is akin to the trouble I have, in this respect, with my American students, who have plenty of historical material pushed down their throats. But it is to no purpose. They lack the historical *sense* that no amount of factual study can give. This is why it is so much easier to make theorists of them than economists.

the end, the desired results emerged almost as tautologies. For example, a famous Ricardian theory is that profits 'depend upon' the price of wheat. And under his implicit assumptions and in the particular sense in which the terms of the proposition are to be understood, this is not only true, but undeniably, in fact trivially, so. Profits could not possibly depend upon anything else, since everything else is 'given,' that is, frozen. It is an excellent theory that can never be refuted and lacks nothing save sense.[3] The habit of applying results of this character to the solution of practical problems we shall call the Ricardian Vice.

Presently, we shall try to size up the success of the school. Now we want to define the personal success of Ricardo and to see how he succeeded in forming that school. The first step is easy: no doubt it is possible that, with the public as well as with his fellow economists, his reputation was made by his writings on the great economic issues of his time—in the first instance, by his writings on monetary policy, in the second instance, by his writings on free trade. In all the questions he touched, he was on the side that would have won out anyhow, but to the victory of which he contributed usable argument, earning corresponding applause. Though others did the same, his advocacy was more brilliant, more arresting, than was theirs: there is no superfluous sentence in his pages; no qualification, *however necessary,* weakens his argument; and there is just enough genuine analysis about it to convince practically and, at the same time, *to satisfy high intellectual standards* but not enough to deter. His polemical talent, which combined to an altogether unusual degree readiness, force, and genuine politeness, did the rest. People took to his theory because they agreed with his recommendations. He became the center of a circle that looked to him for guidance and in turn defended his opinions. It is neither his advocacy of winning policies per se, nor his theory per se, that, to this day, makes of him, in the eyes of some, the first economist of all times, but a felicitous combination of both.[4]

But what about his contribution to scientific economics? By far the most important one was, I think, the priceless gift of leadership. He refreshed and irritated. In either case, he shook up. The fruits of his reasoning intrigued all the people who did not see the mechanics I have tried to characterize above. His teaching, in its middle and higher layers, established itself as the new thing, compared with which everything else was inferior, obsolete, stale. Very

[3] Speaking of Lord Keynes's theory, Professor Leontief has called this procedure Implicit Reasoning. The similarity between the aims and methods of those two eminent men, Keynes and Ricardo, is indeed striking, though it will not impress those who look primarily for the advice a writer tenders. Of course, there is a world between Keynes and Ricardo in this respect, and Keynes's views on economic policy bear much more resemblance to Malthus'. But I am speaking of Ricardo's and Keynes's methods of securing the clear-cut result. On this point they were brothers in the spirit.

[4] The reader is invited to observe this additional affinity between him and Lord Keynes. Every word in the paragraph above might be written with reference to the latter.

quickly his circle developed the attitude—so amusing but also, alas!, so melancholy to behold—of children who have been presented with a new toy. They thought the world of it. To them it was of incalculable value that only he could fail to appreciate who was too stupid to rise to Ricardian heights. And all this meant controversy, impulse, new zest, new life, and these constitute valuable contributions in themselves.[5] But there was something else. Economic theory is not a stock of political recipes but, to use Mrs. Joan Robinson's felicitous phrase, a box of analytic tools. And these tools are not a heap of disconnected elements but form an engine. This engine grinds out results, within wide limits, no matter what the concrete problem is that is fed into it. It works the same way, formally, whether the problem is the effect of a tax or of a wage policy, or of a piece of regulation, or of protection and what not. Hence the engine, within those limits, may be constructed once for all to stand ready for use whenever needed for an indefinite variety of purposes. This has always been felt instinctively. Cantillon and the physiocrats brought the idea out into the open. But nobody before Ricardo grasped it as vigorously as he did. In the first two chapters of the *Principles*, he undertook to build such a general-purpose engine. This spelled decisive advance. But, of course, if a defective engine meets with success, that advance may easily prove to be a detour. And let me state at once: *a detour Ricardian analysis was.*

Construction of such an engine of analysis entailed the consequence that the individual elements that make up general economics were welded together into a systematic unit as they never had been before. However unsystematic Ricardo's *Principles* is in form, it is a systematic performance of the first order in substance. Among those elements themselves there is none for which priority of publication could be ascribed to Ricardo with certainty. Above I have expressed myself to the effect that Ricardo, though he owed much to A. Smith, owed very little to other authors.[6] I believe, in fact, that his subjective originality was of a high order. Moreover he was frank and generous in acknowledgments: though I have criticized A. Smith and shall criticize A. Marshall for inadequate acknowledgment, I do not think that any such criticism should be made with reference to Ricardo.[7] But objectively, all the ideas of the *Principles*

[5] See preceding footnote.

[6] Barton may be an exception (see below, ch. 6, sec. 6h). Ricardo's preface mentions Turgot, Steuart, Smith, Say, Sismondi 'and others' (besides Malthus and West's essay, see next footnote). But only Smith's influence is of first importance. Say influenced Ricardian teaching only in one point (Law of Markets). I find no trace of any influence of Turgot, Steuart, or Sismondi.

[7] Claims were raised against him, however, especially in three instances. West complained with some bitterness that Ricardo failed to recognize his priority as regards the theory of the falling rate of profits. Ricardo said in the original preface to the *Principles* that 'in 1815, Mr. Malthus . . . and a Fellow of University College, Oxford [West] presented to the world . . . the true doctrine of rent. . .' It is true that he failed to make a similar acknowledgment about profits. But it may be replied that this matter is covered by the acknowledgment of West's priority as to the theory of rent. Torrens was inclined, though mildly, to vindicate a title to priority as regards the theorem of comparative costs. He may have been right. But even if he was, there is a difference

are individually met with before, and we cannot attribute more than effective synthesis to Ricardo, unless (1) we decide to say that, after having gone out with A. Smith to hunt beaver and deer, Ricardo did twist Smith's suggestion into a labor theory of value that was his own, and (2) we decide to disallow Torrens' claim, mentioned in footnote 7.

A Reader's Guide is easy to give but, owing to Ricardo's lack of system (in the formal sense), much less easy to follow. The analytic engine is displayed in the first two chapters of the *Principles*. Every line is important, and sections 4 and 5 of the first chapter are as difficult to absorb as is anything the reader may run up against in economic literature. Chapter 31, 'On Machinery' added in the third edition, to which alone this guide refers, complements those fundamentals in one important point. All the rest is really only development (chs. 3-6), application (chs. 8-18 and 29, all on taxation), defense and criticism (chs. 20, 21, 24, 26, 30, 32), but, unfortunately, contains so many *obiter dicta* on fundamentals as to make it very hazardous to skip. For example, Chapter 27, 'On Currency and Banks,' which together with Chapter 28 deals with matters that the student of Ricardo's general theory might feel inclined to neglect, contains passages that shed much-needed light on Ricardo's handling of the theorem that marginal cost equals price, and on the sense in which he was in full possession of it. Foreign trade is dealt with in the famous Chapter 7, which is also really a supplement to the fundamental ones (and is itself supplemented by chs. 22, 23, and 25). Chapter 19 (and, in a sense, also 21) pledged Ricardo's allegiance to Say's law.

So brilliant a light will attract moths—there are a certain number of obscure Ricardian writers. Moreover many people, noneconomists included, will profess themselves votaries of the light even though they have but a dim perception of it—just as today there are many Keynesians and Marxians who have never read a line of Keynes or Marx. In addition, *some* of the independents, even a few dissenters such as Torrens, will still profess decent respect for the eminent fellow economist from whom they dissent, and be quite ready to use phrases and propositions of his wherever they feel they can. Finally, economists of later generations—conspicuous instances were J. S. Mill and A. Marshall—may pay homage to a great name of the past in such a way as to hide from themselves and others the full extent of the gulf that separates them from him. All this is apt to mislead the retrospective glance and to make the influence of Ricardo and his school look greater than it actually was. In the interest of a true picture of the history of economic analysis, it is necessary to reduce this influence to its proper proportions.[8]

---

between an author's behavior in such matters in a hasty sketch such as the *Principles*—no contradiction to the statement about the systematic nature of Ricardo's performance!—and an author's behavior in such matters in fully matured works that had been elaborated with infinite care such as A. Smith's *Wealth* and A. Marshall's *Principles*. The third claimant was J. Rooke, *Claim to the Original Publication of certain new Principles* . . . (1825), unearthed by Professor Seligman. So far as I can see, he has no case at all.

[8] It cannot be repeated too often that for any purpose other than that of a history of *analysis* there would be no need for any such operation, and that the influence we mean to appraise is influence upon scientific economics only.

We have already seen that the core of the school consisted of only four men besides Ricardo himself. By this I mean that James Mill, McCulloch, and De Quincey were the only unconditional adherents and militant supporters of Ricardo's teaching who gained sufficient reputation for their names to survive. West [9]—partly because he went to India—stood apart. He was, and felt himself to be, no member of any school but the peer of Ricardo and the independent discoverer of the essentials of Ricardian doctrine. His evident resentment against Ricardo was probably unjustified. But his regret at being ousted from what he conceived to be his place, by the latter's superior force and brilliance, was not. For the *Essay* contains in fact not only a formulation of the 'Ricardian' theory of rent but also the application of the law of diminishing returns to a theory of profit, hence the pivot of the Ricardian system. Therefore, though we have no choice but to include him in the 'Ricardian' school, we shall temper this injustice by speaking occasionally of West-Ricardian doctrines.

James Mill must certainly be recognized as a man of light and leading, irrespective of what we may think of the value of the light he shed and of the leads he gave.[10] McCulloch [11] has been so roughly handled by Marx and others,

[9] Sir Edward West (1782-1828), one of the foremost scientific economists of the age, has never received his due. His *Essay on the Application of Capital to Land . . .* (1815, reprinted in Professor Hollander's series of economic tracts, 1903) is much more than a mere statement of the law of diminishing returns, which is how it is usually described in the history of economics. His second book, *Price of Corn and Wages of Labour . . .* (1826), is marked by the same independence of thought.

[10] We have met James Mill (1773-1836) twice already, both times in strategic positions: as the author of the *Analysis of the Phenomena of the Human Mind* (1829) and as the exponent of the official Benthamite doctrine on government. We have to add his monumental, and indeed path-breaking, *History of British India* (1817), which posthumously grew into ten volumes and was the cornerstone of his reputation with the general public, and his two economics books (a third, the earliest one, I do not know), viz. *Commerce Defended* (1808) and *Elements of Political Economy* (1821; 3rd ed., the one to be used, 1826). The author in the preface described the latter as a 'schoolbook' and as devoid of originality (not quite true, though the original points were not all improvements. As has been recognized, e.g. by Marx, the book represents an effort that was by no means contemptible). The standard biography by A. Bain (1882) fails to do justice to the economics of James Mill and also to solve the enigma of the man —that intellectual machine that did not know how not to work.

[11] John Ramsay McCulloch (1789-1864) was a journalist, academic teacher, and civil servant and, though the most unphilosophical of men, may be counted in with the philosophical radicals. Neglecting for the moment his factual work, I shall mention only his *Principles of Political Economy* (1825; 5th ed., 1864); his *Literature of Political Economy* (1845), a fairly comprehensive annotated catalogue and immensely useful as such (the comments on each author, written from the standpoint of a naïve and unquestioning faith in Ricardian doctrine, are a revelation for anyone who wishes to grasp the spirit of the Ricardian school); and the *Essay on the Circumstances which Determine the Rate of Wages* (1826), his most ambitious effort in economic theory. Both his letters to Ricardo and Ricardo's letters to him have been published, in 1931

Böhm-Bawerk among them, that it seems right to emphasize his merits rather than the fact that his ability, though of a most useful kind, was not of a high order. His factual work, an important achievement, will be mentioned later. His zest for social reform—into which entered an element that spells some analytic merit: he was a leading exponent of the 'wage-fund theory' but realized that this theory does not prove the futility of trade-union wage policy—should recommend him to modern critics. Moreover, he rose to be one of the best-known figures of the profession in his day, and succeeded in keeping the flag of Ricardianism flying when practically all other economists had deserted it: and this is something. Finally, he wrote the textbook that was the most successful general treatise England produced in the first four decades of the nineteenth century, and this, all the shortcomings notwithstanding, is not negligible either; [12] the book was more directly influential with the public than was Ricardo's and really created what we might call lower-level Ricardianism. De Quincey, of Opium Eater fame, is a different case. His delight in refined logic makes him the very antipode of the rough and ready McCulloch. But he touched economics peripherically only. And his contribution, though interesting, was sterile.[13]

None of the three added anything substantial, and the touches they did

---

and 1895 respectively, by Professor J. H. Hollander. They are one of the most important sources for the study of that time's methods of theoretical reasoning.

[12] Speaking of texts, we should not pass by Mrs. Jane Marcet's *Conversations on Political Economy* (1816), which enjoyed a great success (7th ed., 1839). James Mill's was an elementary, but not an easy, text on pure theory. McCulloch's was the saleable stuff for the college course in general economics. Mrs. Marcet's was economics for what we should call high-school girls. The reader should really look at it and note two interesting points about it. The first is the date: the book appeared *before* Ricardo's *Principles* and, though not orthodox Ricardianism in every particular and though lacking Ricardian rigor, yet presents many of the most important tenets of the Ricardian school. This is significant, and greatly enhances the interest of the performance, at which it is quite out of place to sneer. Second, if nevertheless so many later economists did sneer at it, this was due not only to male prejudice but also to the nature of the publication: not for a moment did Mrs. Marcet doubt not only that the definitive truth about economics and economic policy had been discovered at last but also that this truth was so delightfully simple as to be capable of being taught to every school girl. This frame of mind was then common and is highly characteristic of that age—exactly as a similar frame of mind is common among modern Keynesians and not less characteristic of our own age.

[13] 'Dialogues of Three Templars on Political Economy,' *London Magazine*, April 1824—let us bow to the editor who published such material and to the reading public that did not thereupon discontinue subscription—and *Logic of Political Economy* (1844). The book survives, I think, only through J. S. Mill's generous quotations from it. I cannot see in it anything original. The concept of Difficulty of Attainment is Ricardo's, and had already been formulated by the latter in a much more suggestive way ('the real value of a commodity is regulated . . . by the real difficulties encountered by that producer who is least favoured,' *Principles*, ch. 27).

add—James Mill and McCulloch especially—were mostly of doubtful value.[14] They did not even succeed in summing up Ricardo correctly or in conveying an idea of the wealth of suggestions to be found in the latter's *Principles*. What they did convey was a superficialized message that wilted in their hands and became stale and unproductive practically at once. It was not their fault that Ricardo's system failed from the first to gain the assent of a majority of English economists—and not only, as the Ricardians tried hard to believe, of the dunces and laggards. This was owing to its inherent weaknesses. Nor was it their fault that the system was not made for a long career. But it was their fault that defeat came so quickly. Ricardo died in 1823. In 1825, Bailey launched his attack that should have been decisive on the merits of the case. Actually it was not, for schools are not destroyed so easily. But the decay of the Ricardian school must have become patent shortly after, for in a pamphlet published in 1831 we read that 'there are some Ricardians still remaining.'[15] In any case, it is clear that Ricardianism was then no longer a living force. The prevailing impression to the contrary can be easily accounted for. There were the henchmen who continued to stand by their guns and to teach exploded doctrine as if nothing had happened. There was the lag of public opinion, which is as slow to realize the passing of an obsolete doctrine as it is to realize the birth of a new one. And there was something else that is still more important and will explain why few if any historians will agree with me: there was Ricardo's *personal* prestige, the great name that survived the work. As has been pointed out already, Ricardo, though not particularly fortunate as regards his immediate followers, has been all the more fortunate in another respect. J. S. Mill emphasized his early Ricardianism throughout and neither realized himself nor made it clear to his readers how far he had actually drifted away from it by the time he wrote his *Principles*. And, to a lesser extent, even Marshall and Edgeworth did the same thing. Moreover, Ricardo's fame does not rest on his theoretical structure alone. On the one hand, there were his contributions to the theory of money and monetary policy and his theory of international trade. On the other hand, certain individual elements of that structure proved more durable than did the whole. The most important instance is his theory of rent, in spite of the fact that logically it should have been scrapped with the rest.

Foreign zones of influence present, in part, a different picture.[16] Marx and Rodbertus did much to keep Ricardian thought alive. Partly by virtue of their influence, partly because of the weakness of domestic competition—and, later on, also because of the prevalent dislike for the Austrian theory—Ricardo remained to the end of the century *the* great theorist for most of those German economists who had any theoretical ambitions at all: the names of Wagner,

[14] Ricardo is, e.g., not chargeable with either James Mill's or McCulloch's theories of interest or with the whole of the latter's wage-fund theory.

[15] This phrase from C. F. Cotterill, *Examination of the Doctrine of Value . . .* (1831), is quoted by Professor Seligman (op. cit. sec. 3), to whom I owe this reference.

[16] For influence of Marx and Rodbertus, see below, sec. 5.

Dietzel, and Diehl are illustrative examples. For the period under discussion, but not beyond it, an analogous statement holds—or almost holds—for Italian economics. There are strong traces of Ricardo's influence in the writings of Ferrara and in the textbooks. Rossi affords another instance if we count him as an Italian, but almost the only one of importance if we call him a French economist. France, following her own tradition, resisted Ricardian influence more than did any other country. In the United States, McCulloch's textbook conquered a large amount of ground—tying with Say's for first place in teaching. And there was also Ricardian influence on a higher level far into the next period—of front-rank names, Taussig's is an illustration.

What I meant by 'fringe ends' of the Ricardian school may be best illustrated by indicating the most important group that comes within the meaning of this term, the so-called Ricardian socialists. Of course, Marx was the greatest of Ricardian socialists, but the group is usually defined more narrowly; namely, so as to comprise a number of writers who, mainly in the 1820's and 1830's, argued the case of the working class on the proposition that labor is the only factor of production. Though this proposition harks back to Locke and Smith and not to Ricardo, it is likely that the Ricardian theory of value did encourage these socialist writers and also offered suggestions to them. Since the writings of this group, which of course is entitled to a great place in the history of socialist thought, offer but little that is relevant to a history of economic analysis, we shall confine ourselves to mentioning the two names that seem to be, for us, more important than others. William Thompson's *Inquiry into the Principles of the Distribution of Wealth . . .* (1824) is a fair example, on its higher level, of the group's argument, of its tempered equalitarianism, and of its habit of considering ideals of distribution, irrespective of the repercussions that realization of these ideals might have on production. Benthamite influence is strongly marked. Thomas Hodgskin's *Labour Defended against the Claims of Capital . . .* (1825) and *Popular Political Economy* (1827) display at least traces of genuinely analytic intention.[17] It should be observed that as soon as an author combines the idea that labor is the only source of wealth and that the values of all commodities can be represented in terms of labor hours with the idea that labor itself is a commodity, he is inevitably drawn to the conclusion that the market mechanism robs the workman of the difference between the labor value of 'his' product and the labor value of the amount of work invested in that product. This, barring details, is the Marxist theory of exploitation. Accordingly, several Ricardian

[17] J. F. Bray's *Labour's Wrongs and Labour's Remedy* (1839) has been reprinted by the London School (1931) and has thereby been transformed from the least into the most accessible of these writings. This is my only reason for mentioning it. See M. F Jolliffe, 'Fresh Light on John Francis Bray,' in *Economic History, A Supplement of the Economic Journal*, February 1939.

socialists have been called forerunners of Marx. The phrase 'forerunners' may mean much or little, and if it is not made to mean too much, that statement may be allowed to pass muster, though I cannot find any instance (not even in Thompson and Hodgskin) that would amount to full anticipation of all that Marx's theory of exploitation means within his system. But the charge of plagiarism is unfounded, if for no other reason, because that combination of ideas is bound to occur to any student of Ricardo who develops his teaching in the direction in which Marx wished to develop it. It is significant that this charge, though often repeated by economists, was in the first instance raised by a writer who was not an economist himself, Anton Menger (1841-1906; brother of the economist), to whose *Recht auf den vollen Arbeitsertrag* (1886; the English trans., *Right to the Whole Produce of Labour*, 1899, has an important introduction by H. S. Foxwell) the reader is for the rest referred. The theory of the more important writers of the group stands out better in Esther Lowenthal, *The Ricardian Socialists*, 1911.

3. Malthus, Senior, and Some of Those Who Also Ran

In spite of our objections to speaking of national schools, we shall review by countries the rest of the men still to be mentioned. For England, since we have noticed Longfield already and since we reserve J. S. Mill and Cairnes for the next chapter—and Jevons, of course to the next period—we are left primarily with Malthus and Senior. But we must not confine ourselves to the performances that are known to history and leave all others in the shade. This would create a wrong picture. For historical performances are rarely like erratic blocks in a plain. They are more like peaks that rise from clusters of smaller eminences. In other words, a science develops by small accretions that create a common fund of ideas from which, by chance as well as by merit, emerge the works that enter the hall of fame. Therefore we must add at least a few of those writers who, though they failed to achieve historic fame, yet did important work and exerted an influence upon developments in analysis that are anonymous but not negligible. In taking some account of them, we shall also establish our proposition that the West-Ricardo school was never dominant in English economics.[1]

(a) *Malthus*.[2] Marx poured on him vitriolic wrath. Keynes glorified him.

[1] Let me repeat that writers whose performance was wholly in the fields of money, banking, and cycles will be dealt with separately.

[2] Thomas Robert Malthus (1766-1834) was a clergyman and a professor of history and political economy at the East India College at Haileybury. As we already know he leapt into fame, from complete obscurity, in 1798 when he published his *Essay on the Principle of Population* (2nd ed. 1803; 3rd 1806; 6th 1826). Of his numerous other writings (neglecting those on money), the following are, for us, the most important: (1) . . . *High Price of Provisions* . . . (1800); (2) *Letter to Samuel Whitbread on . . . the Poor Laws* (1807); (3) *Observations on the Corn Laws* (1814); (4) *Inquiry into the Nature and Progress of Rent* (1815); (5) *Grounds of an Opinion on the Policy of Re-*

Both the vituperation and the eulogy are readily seen to be due to prejudice. Marx—or the laicist bourgeois radical in him—hated nothing so much as the clerical cloth. Moreover, though he never gave any credit to the men who stood for free trade in food, he had nothing but withering scorn for those who did not. These were just hirelings of the landed interest for Marx and, of course, for his obedient followers. This way of disposing of Malthus' contribution is no better than other people's method of disposing of Ricardo's on the grounds that he was a Jew and 'for the money interest.' But Keynes's partiality for Malthus, though morally admirable—for those are few who extol a forerunner and Keynes believed Malthus to have been a forerunner of his—went to lengths that are not much less unreasonable than was Marx's hatred.[3] And right from the publication of the *Essay on Population* to this day, Malthus has had the good fortune—for this *is* good fortune—to be the subject of equally unreasonable, contradictory appraisals. He was a benefactor of humanity. He was a fiend. He was a profound thinker. He was a dunce.

The man whose work stirred people's minds so as to elicit such passionate appraisals was *ipso facto* no mediocrity. The man who realized that some economic problems are like the problems 'de maximis et minimis in fluxions' [calculus] was no dunce. His case illustrates the difference between ability and brilliance. Soundness would be the word for him if it were not for a failing that he shared with many—most?—economists. He had a few pet ideas, which he was bent on applying to practical problems. And when he did so, his usual common sense was apt to turn out nonsense.[4] Moreover he was not a good controversialist.

---

stricting the Importation of Foreign Corn (1815); (6) *Principles of Political Economy* (1820; i.e. one year after Sismondi's *Principles*); (7) *Measure of Value* (1823); and (8) *Definitions in Political Economy* . . . (1827)—(4) and (6) being in turn the most important of these. See especially J. Bonar, *Malthus and His Work* (1885, 2nd ed., 1924; the standard work on Malthus, a *little* unsatisfactory with respect to pure theory), and Lord Keynes's charming essay on Malthus in *Essays in Biography* (1933), which the reader is sure to enjoy and which makes it superfluous for me to say anything concerning the subject of 'backgrounds and formative influences.' Let me notice briefly the three accusations of plagiarism that have been leveled at Malthus by Marx. The first we know already: it refers to Malthus' forerunners, Townsend especially, in the theory of population. The second concerns his theory of rent (diminishing returns). Marx was quite sure that Malthus had plagiarized Anderson but failed to produce any substantial reasons why: the type of argument that makes Malthus a plagiarist in this case would, if admissible, also make a plagiarist of Marx. The third concerns the theory of gluts: Malthus is supposed to have plagiarized Sismondi. Apart from the considerable differences between the theories of the two, there is no reason why Malthus could not have arrived at the position he took in the *Principles* from ideas that were present in his mind *at least* as far back as 1814 (see Keynes, op. cit. p. 141).

[3] A passage in the essay referred to above actually reads as if Lord Keynes attributed to Malthus the 'beginning of systematic economic thinking' (p. 125).

[4] The outstanding instance of this is his *Letter to Samuel Whitbread* (see last footnote but one). In this piece he argued against a housing program of Whitbread's (cottages to be built by the parish authorities) on the ground that this would encourage

For the public and also for a majority of the profession, Malthus was and is primarily the Malthus of the *Essay on Population*. His second title to fame, his contribution to monetary analysis, has almost escaped the attention of historians. His third title, the one that has brought his name to the fore in our own time, is his theory of saving and investment or his theory of 'general gluts.' [5] For the moment, we are concerned with a fourth title to fame only, namely, as the author of a system of economic theory that recoined the theory of the *Wealth of Nations* in a manner that was the alternative to Ricardo's recoinage. Deferring consideration of his theory of rent and of other points of comparative detail, we must now make sure of this point.

We have seen that Ricardo's work, so far as general theory is concerned, started from the *Wealth of Nations* and recoined the latter's theoretical contents by a method that centered in the concept of value. Exactly the same thing is evidently true of the work of Malthus as presented in his *Principles*. Except for his theory of saving and investment, which on the face of it seems to be Malthus' own,[6] all the elements that enter into the analytic apparatus of that work, and even its terminological arrangements, point to the First Book of the *Wealth of Nations*. Only, whereas Ricardo recoined the doctrine of the *Wealth* by means of the labor-quantity theory of value, Malthus recoined it by means of the theory of value that A. Smith actually used, namely, the theory of supply and demand,[7] also following A. Smith's example in choosing labor as a unit of value (*numéraire*). Therefore, Malthus adopted the line that won out ultimately and pointed much more directly to the Marshallian system than did Ricardo's, notwithstanding the fact that it was with the latter and not with the former that Marshall endeavored to keep in contact.[8]

---

improvident marriages. Even Keynes had nothing to say for this. He treated this just as an incident and condoned it good-humoredly. This means, however, that he failed to see its implications concerning the recommendations that emanate even from front-rank economists. Is the public really to be blamed for not taking them seriously?

[5] For the discussion of these three phases of Malthus, see above, ch. 1 and below, chs. 6 and 7.

[6] Unless we choose to hunt for forerunners far back in the eighteenth century, the only author that might qualify as a forerunner in this respect is Lauderdale. Sismondi is not a forerunner but a competitor though, so far as his teaching coincides with Malthus', he holds priority as to publication. [J. A. S. had penciled a note—'Quesnay?']

[7] We shall see later that the labor-quantity and the supply-and-demand theories should not, in logic, be put into opposition. But both Ricardo and Malthus took them mistakenly for alternatives. I adopt this view for the moment, because they do serve nevertheless to characterize the two different apparatus of analysis.

[8] This tendency of Marshall's, which runs throughout his *Principles*, has done much to obscure the actual situation. Here I shall only state by anticipation that, in spite of all that Marshall said, it is the supply-and-demand apparatus which dominates the analysis of his Fifth Book. There is, however, another confusion to which I want to draw attention at once. Analysis that works by means of supply and demand has no difficulty in covering short-run phenomena as well as long-run phenomena. It has been repeated over and over again that Malthus, unlike Ricardo, was primarily interested in short-run phenomena. To some extent this is true. But it has been assumed too readily

This also holds with respect to another difference between the two. We have seen that Ricardo's analytic apparatus is geared to the problem of distribution—to the explanation of relative shares. Malthus, again returning to A. Smith and again anticipating A. Marshall, geared his apparatus to the analysis of the whole economic process. Hence he treated total output (Marshall's 'national dividend'), not, like Ricardo, as a datum, but as the chief variable to be explained.[9] Therefore, Malthus should indeed, though for a reason that does not coincide with that which induced Lord Keynes to arrive at a similar result,[10] stand in the history of analysis not only as the author of a valid alternative to Ricardo's theory but as the sponsor (or rather as one of the sponsors) of the victorious one. This is much. At the same time, it is all. It is perfectly compatible with recognition of these facts that much less ingenuity went into Malthus' than into Ricardo's analytic schema, and that the former was throughout in the most unenviable position an economist can be in, namely, in the position of having to defend plain sense against another man's futile but clever pirouettes.

(b) *Archbishop Whately and Professor Senior.* Next, we look at Senior and the man who had been his tutor, Whately. The latter's [11] importance for us is as great as it is elusive. He was not profound or very learned. He was not orig-

---

that it was *because* of this interest in short-run phenomena that he selected supply and demand as the pivot of price analysis. This is not true. As should be clear from the text, his difference with Ricardo on the subject of value was much more fundamental than that—which Ricardo failed to realize. [It is possible that J. A. S. intended to eliminate this footnote. There was a faint line through it.]

[9] Incidentally, this different point of view involved a different conceptualization and naturally led him to find fault with Ricardo's. This he made particularly clear in his *Definitions.* Once more he expressed himself inadequately. He reproached Ricardo with a use of terms that was both unusual and inconsistent, as if this were all. But, just as before, there was something more fundamental at stake than terminology. What he should have objected to this time was Ricardo's analytic intention of which the terminology was but the consequence. This intention was open to objection on the ground that it neglected the really relevant problems for the sake of propositions that were partly less relevant to the purposes of economic analysis and partly sterile.

[10] For Keynes, the decisive point was Malthus' attitude toward saving. For us, it is his sponsorship of the Smith-Marshall output analysis, which, as these two names suffice to show, is not necessarily bound up with that attitude.

[11] Richard Whately, D.D. (1787-1863), was an Oxford don who became (Anglican) Archbishop of Dublin, where he founded the chair of political economy and rendered innumerable services of the same type. But they do not sum him up or characterize him. Primarily, he was a theologian and a leader of Anglican Church policy and opinion. But this does not sum him up either. Nor does, finally, his extensive activity in the *Sozialpolitik* of his age and country. His *Introductory Lectures on Political Economy* (1831; enlarged ed., only one known to me, 1855) and his *Easy Lessons on Money Matters* (1833) would not suffice to place him high as an economist. More interesting is an appendix to his *Logic,* 'On certain Terms which are peculiarly liable to be used ambiguously in Political Economy' (republished in the Library of Economics Reprint of Senior's *Outline*). There is an instructive life by Miss E. J. Whately (1866) that pictures not only a man but also an environment and an epoch.

inal or even brilliant. But his clear and strong intellect grasped calmly and firmly whatever it did grasp within an unusually wide range of interests. And in his age, country, and world, he was a leader of the formative type, an ideal illustration of what is meant by a key man. He led quietly, without seeming to do so, by the weight of his personality and of his advice which was never more valuable than when it was obvious. For in ecclesiastical politics, as in economics, the obvious is sometimes precisely what people are most reluctant to see. His most important service to economics was, however, that he formed Senior, whose whole approach betrays Whately's influence.

Senior [12] has been treated with comparative neglect by many economists and with uncalled-for scorn by some. In reaction to this, others have made a 'genius' of him, which he assuredly was not, if I understand what this word means. In our picture he will enter a triumvirate with Malthus and Ricardo: he was one of the three Englishmen whose works are the main stepping stones between A. Smith and J. S. Mill. But J. S. Mill had, logician though he was, no eye for Senior's great performance. To the latter's eternal honor—which he may have to share with Whately—it must be recorded, in the first place, that he attempted to unify and present economic theory according to the requirements of the postulational method, that is, as a series of deductions from four induced or empirical postulates, which we shall discuss in Chapter 6. This, even if the result fell considerably short of perfection, makes him indeed the first 'pure' theorist of that period—always excepting Cournot and Thünen, perhaps also Longfield—and suffices by itself to condemn those who refuse to pay their respects to him. In the second place, he adumbrated a much improved theory of value and a much improved theory of capital and interest. In the third place stand various smaller merits, some of which will be mentioned in their proper connection (population, decreasing returns, rent). In the fourth place, his brilliant contributions to the theory of money, to be mentioned in the last chapter of this Part, are, considered as purely intellectual performances, not inferior to Ricardo's. I should put his subjective originality quite as high as Ricardo's. Objectively, he had been anticipated, like Ricardo,

[12] Nassau William Senior (1790-1864) was a highly educated Oxford man of whose uneventful life, financed mainly by modest independent means, two facts only need be recorded here: he held the Drummond Professorship at Oxford twice (1825-30 and 1847-52); and he worked on several important royal commissions. His work with these commissions amounted to a respectable quantity of factual research and should also clear him from any suspicion of having been a doctrinaire laissez-faire man. Besides his lectures on money, now available in the London School Reprints (1931), only his *Outline of the Science of Political Economy* (1836; Library of Economics Reprint, 1938) is essential for us. We owe to Dr. Marian Bowley an excellent interpretation of Senior's work and of its place in the history of economics (*Nassau Senior and Classical Economics*, 1937), to which I wish to call my readers' attention and which enables me to cut short this note. Differences between her interpretation and mine are few and not important. Her tendency to distance Senior from the 'classic' economists—to whom he belongs according to the terminology adopted in this book—creates, however, some differences that are more apparent than real.

on most of the individual points he made. Why, then, will so few economists agree with an estimate that puts Senior on a par with Ricardo, and why has his influence been restricted, substantially, to what J. S. Mill took over from him? [13]

There are three excellent reasons for this that illustrate the difficulty of even as much comparative appraisal of economists as is inevitable, if we are to get a picture of a scientific situation at all. First, even if we are firmly resolved to estimate analytic merit only, we are apt to forget that Ricardo speaks to us from a pedestal, the pedestal of a reputation made in public discussion of political issues. There is no such pedestal under the figure of Senior. He counts as an analytic economist only. His work on problems of policy is buried in bluebooks that hardly anyone reads. His public utterances made no mark and he was a nobody, or almost so, to the general public. Second—and this was entirely the fault of his mental make-up—he was, what is the word? Lazy? By this I do not mean to suggest that he did not do a lot of work, but rather that he lacked the kind of energy that will run purposefully to definite conclusions. Ricardo was the horse that will take hold of the bit, put out its nose, and gallop for what it is worth. Senior was the horse that drops the bit, puts its nose down, and refuses to stretch. His *Outline*, still worse in arrangement than Ricardo's *Principles*, discusses, criticizes, hesitates, swerves. It fails to impress, as the latter does, by ardor. Worse still, Senior's reader gets the impression, nay, he is told in so many words, that all economic analysis amounts to is the search for, and consistent use of, a convenient terminology. Was this Whately's fault? [14] In any case, nothing could be further from the truth and nothing could have been more uninspiring. Other economists—in fact most of them throughout the nineteenth century—used and defended the hunt for the meaning of words as a method of research. But nobody went as far as Senior, who seemed inclined to *solve* all problems of his 'science of political economy' by laying down definitions. We shall have no difficulty in understanding how such a 'method' must have impressed hostile critics. And, third, Senior had a curious talent for 'putting his foot in it.' Even good Homer dozes off occasionally, as an old slogan avers. But Senior dozed off, that is, uttered ineptitudes, rather too frequently. He was careless. And though *able* he was not *clever*. Thus, to quote only the most famous instance, he actually wrote (*Letters on the Factory Act . . .* 1837) a statement to the effect that

[13] J. S. Mill's opinion of Senior was even higher than we might infer from his references to him: Mill had his copy of the *Outline* interleaved with sheets on which to note his own comments. These comments, published by Professor von Hayek in *Economica*, vol. XII, August 1945, are of the utmost interest.

[14] With his usual common sense, Whately pointed out (in his *Elements of Logic*) that many of the issues economists quarreled about were purely verbal and that loose use of terms, both a cause and a consequence of loose thinking, was a fertile source of misunderstandings. But he overshot the mark, when he seemed to consider the possession of 'a vocabulary of general terms as precisely defined as the mathematical,' not only as an important desideratum but practically as the only thing needful.

the profits of cotton mills, assumed to be 10 per cent, would be completely wiped out by a reduction of the working day by one-eleventh because the whole of those profits was produced in the last hour. This could not have happened with Ricardo, though we might put Senior above him in other respects.[15]

(c) *Some of Those Who Also Ran.* For the reason explained at the beginning of this section, I shall now add a few more names. Other writers would no doubt mention other names, in part at least, but my selection is this: Bailey, Chalmers, Lauderdale, Ramsay, Read, Scrope, and Torrens.[16] Their performances differ widely in nature and are difficult to co-ordinate, though they do round off our picture. However much I wish to avoid cataloguing, I nevertheless present them in alphabetical order.

Bailey,[17] as already mentioned, attacked the Ricardo-Mill-McCulloch analysis on a broad front and with complete success. His *Dissertation,* which said, as far as fundamentals are concerned, practically all that can be said, must rank among the masterpieces of criticism in our field, and it should suffice to secure to its author a place in or near front rank in the history of scientific economics. Nor did his work pass unnoticed. Several writers, Read among them, acknowl-

[15] That Senior arrived at this absurd result after a careful examination of facts, only makes matters worse, as far as his competence in applied theory is concerned. On the other hand, Marx's scathing attack upon Senior's argument in the first volume of *Das Kapital* does not enhance our idea of Marx's competence either. In all the pages of vituperation that he bestowed upon it, he failed to adduce the decisive criticism, which he does not seem to have perceived. He overlooked also another thing, namely, that Senior's argument would have been correct (at least in principle), if Marx's own theory had been. The reasoning of both Senior and Marx may, however, give pause to those who refuse to recognize the advance in analytic technique that has occurred since. And the case also serves to illustrate another point that cannot be impressed upon the reader's mind too often. The essential thing is that both Senior and Marx committed mistakes, revelatory of inadequate technique. These mistakes were mistakes quite irrespective of the cause for which they argued. To note that Senior was 'for' and that Marx was 'against' the mill owners is entirely irrelevant. And to blame the one and to praise the other, according to the side we take ourselves, is childish.

[16] It was Professor Seligman's paper 'On Some Neglected British Economists' (mentioned above), which drew my attention to Read; Dr. R. Opie's paper (in the *Quarterly Journal of Economics,* November 1929) which drew my attention to Scrope, who until then had impressed me only by his contributions to monetary theory and policy; and Marx's *Theorien über den Mehrwert* which drew my attention to Ramsay. Two important names, those of Jenkin and of Jennings, are being transferred to Part IV. Of course, West was quite typically one of those who 'also ran.' But it seemed better to couple him with Ricardo.

[17] Samuel Bailey (1791-1870). The only publication of his that need be mentioned is *A Critical Dissertation on the Nature, Measures and Causes of Value; chiefly in Reference to the Writings of Mr. Ricardo and His Followers* (1825; London School Reprint, 1931). Perhaps I should add his reply to a grossly unfair criticism in the *Westminster Review,* 'Letter to a Political Economist,' 1826. Both in unfairness and lack of understanding of Bailey's points, the Westminster reviewer was however outdone by Marx (*Theorien über den Mehrwert*).

edged indebtedness to him and followed his lead, and it is safe to assume that his influence extended beyond the range of explicit recognition. Nevertheless, historians who to this day fail to give Bailey his due are only accepting the facts of the case as it presented itself at the time. Writing in 1845, McCulloch did not risk provoking laughter when he wrote in his *Literature of Political Economy* that Bailey had not properly appreciated the Ricardian theory and had not 'succeeded in any degree in shaking its foundations,' in the face of the fact that a poll of writers on value from 1826 to 1845 would produce a considerable majority for Bailey. These are the explanations I have to offer. First, in science as in art and especially in politics, there is such a thing as coming too soon; and failure, much more complete than was Bailey's, is the usual result of premature action. Second, Bailey's criticism was indeed constructive and did suggest by implication how the system he attacked could have been replaced by a more satisfactory one; but he did not try to do so, and those who followed in his wake and tried were no match for the shadow of Ricardo. They no doubt undermined his system and thus helped toward J. S. Mill's transformation of it, but they did so by a slow process of attrition rather than by spectacular victory.

In this process of attrition, Chalmers' [18] influence counted for a good deal, at least in Scotland. As a theorist, he was thoroughly un-Ricardian and followed the line of what we have called Malthus' recoinage of the *Wealth of Nations*. He also followed Malthus in matters of general gluts and oversupply of capital. If it were possible to speak of a Malthusian school *in general theory* (which I doubt), Chalmers would have to figure as its McCulloch—which is, after all, not so left-handed a compliment as it may seem to the reader.

Lord Lauderdale [19] stands somewhat out of line and holds only a secondary position in the history of economics, but one that is fully deserved and independent of the additional recognition that should now be extended to him on account of his argument against debt redemption (*Three Letters to the Duke*

[18] The Rev. Thomas Chalmers (1780-1847), whose activities included teaching of moral philosophy and political economy (at St. Andrews) and divinity (at Edinburgh), was a man of many merits. We cannot claim more than a fraction of him for analytic economics. Only two of his works need be mentioned: his *Enquiry into the Extent and Stability of National Resources* (1808), partly incorporated in his *On Political Economy* (1832). The latter is a book of considerable importance, but not easy to appraise. It presents a curious mixture of sound insights and technical shortcomings. And these shortcomings sometimes account for patently untenable results such as the proposition that a loss of foreign markets is almost a matter of indifference to a country—which overlooks the whole of the division-of-labor argument—though it may be interpreted as an overstatement of the true proposition that (after adaptation) the loss of foreign markets need not affect *employment*. We shall have to mention the book again. Chalmers seems to have coined the phrase, though of course not the concept, 'margin of cultivation,' and is the author of the argument, much appreciated by J. S. Mill, that explains why ravages of wars are in general quickly repaired.

[19] James Maitland, eighth Earl of Lauderdale (1759-1839), *Inquiry into the Nature and Origin of Public Wealth . . .* (1804). This is the only publication of his that counts as an analytic performance.

of Wellington . . . 1829), which was based upon an argument against excess saving and for excess expenditure.[20] The topics of value, capital, and interest owe something to him, as we shall see, but more important than are these contributions in themselves is the invigorating impulse he gave: he was a man who thought for himself and was not prepared to accept fundamentals as handed to him by the Smithian tradition. Though a dilettante and, from the standpoint of the nascent profession, something of an outsider, he was a writer of force and, in most cases, of sense.[21]

The only author who ever did justice to Ramsay is Marx, who dealt fully with him in the *Theorien über den Mehrwert*.[22] Even Professor Seligman, who revived his memory (op. cit.) emphasized his dependence upon French writers more than I think justified. It is true that, especially in his theory of enterprise and profits, he had been anticipated by Say. It is also true that he was not the first to introduce those ideas to English economics, and that he might even have 'borrowed' at second hand. But he synthesized better than did others and, more important, many suggestive details were his own. It is easy enough to see that he made no mark. But it should be added that he came near to doing so and that his lack of success has perhaps more to do with his unpopular opposition to the repeal of protection to agriculture than with his most serious shortcomings. There is thus no reason to think little of him.[23]

Read [24] impaired his chances of success by certain oddities, especially by his doubtful speculations about the 'Right to Wealth.' His attacks upon the Ricardian socialists are of little interest to us. Nevertheless his work is of some importance for us, first, because it bears witness to the influence of Bailey, whom Read followed in his Ricardo criticism, and to the anti-Ricardian current that was running strong around 1830; second, it has some merit and in turn exerted some influence of its own, particularly in the analysis of profit

[20] On this, see F. A. Fetter, 'Lauderdale's Oversaving Theory,' *American Economic Review*, June 1945.

[21] Of late, an attempt has been made to 'explain' both his analysis and his recommendations in terms of his interests as a landlord. We know what to think of the explanatory value of this.

[22] Marx's recognition of Ramsay must, of course, be appraised with reference to his habits of criticism. If these are taken into account, this recognition means a lot. Also it speaks highly of Marx's scholarship, for when he wrote Ramsay was practically forgotten. Sir George Ramsay's (1800-1871) only relevant work is his *Essay on the Distribution of Wealth* (1836).

[23] Ramsay's case is food for thought, particularly in one respect: when a writer has failed to make the right contact with his contemporaries—excepting those rare cases in which a valiant champion arises to laud him to the skies posthumously—historians assume a strange attitude of hostility toward him and set up standards that would dwarf A. Smith, whereas, in more fortunate cases, they quite commonly sponsor absurd claims to originality or other merits that are never revised.

[24] Samuel Read (no personal data that I know of); the only work that needs to be mentioned here is his *Political Economy. An Inquiry into the Natural Grounds of Right to Vendible Property or Wealth* (1829). E. R. A. Seligman (op. cit. sec. 4) has noticed all the points about it that matter to us.

and interest. Among the writers it influenced directly, the most eminent one is Scrope,[25] the monetary reformer of index-number fame, who was not only the author of numerous pamphlets on money and banking, poor laws, agricultural labor, and other topics but also an economic theorist of some importance. His *Principles of Political Economy* (1833) was, however, written for popular consumption and did not develop his analysis at all satisfactorily. It is easy to notice his original ideas on population and the 'tabular standard.' But these are not what I mean just now. Much more important for us is the insight into the nature of economic equilibrium: he saw how the mechanism of demand and supply, turning on everybody's tendency to maximize returns, solves both the problem of allocation of resources (production) and the problem of income formation (distribution), thus disposing, incidentally, of the whole West-Ricardian construction. In the analysis of interest and profits, too, he made headway: it is there that he seems to have owed something to Read.

All the performances so far mentioned in this section—and our list is very incomplete—were un-Ricardian or anti-Ricardian; and it would be quite impossible to draw up a parallel list of Ricardian writings. Moreover, the antagonism to the West-Ricardian schema that all of them display was primarily scientific and not political: Read's hostility to the Ricardian socialists may have set him against the Ricardian theory of value, but for the rest I cannot find *motivating* political antagonisms between these writers and the Ricardians.[26] The theory that resolves all differences between economists into differences of their politics and always looks to 'what a man stands for' fails in this case as it does in the case of the victory of the marginal utility theory in the next period. Finally, the writings of which we have noticed examples put later developments in a new light: a continuity of effort reveals itself to anyone who pays attention to these writings that is completely lost in the usual story of a prevalent Ricardianism—J. S. Mill figures as a Ricardian in this story—spectacularly shattered by 'revolution' around 1870.

The last author I am going to mention, Torrens,[27] cannot be described as

[25] George Poulett Scrope (1797-1876) was one of those delightful Englishmen of laborious leisure to whom our science, like others, owes so much. Among other things, he was an authority on volcanoes and a M.P. His reputation as an economist rests mainly on his work on central-bank policy and on stabilization of the price level. But there is also *analytic* merit—and striking independence and originality—in some of his pamphlets on other practical questions. Though accepting the fundamental slogans or principles about the 'system of natural liberty' current in his time, he bravely swam against the stream in such matters as his unemployment-insurance scheme and his advocacy of public works. When dates are considered, the insight—I repeat: the *analytic* insight—implied in this places him high above the common run of the economists of his time.

[26] Ramsay's qualified support of the corn laws, e.g., can be defended also on a Ricardian basis. This is why I italicized the word *motivating*.

[27] Another strong, interesting, and sympathetic type! Colonel Robert Torrens (1780-1864), a professional soldier who had seen service, finding himself on half-pay after the Napoleonic Wars, proceeded forthwith to make for himself a fresh career in politics and finance and a name as an economist as well. He is chiefly known for his advocacy of Peel's Act: excepting Lord Overstone, he was the only economist of standing who

anti-Ricardian. But neither can he be described as a Ricardian. Professor Seligman has argued the case for Torrens' independent discovery of the 'Ricardian' theory of rent, with priority over Malthus and West, and of the principle of comparative cost, with priority over Ricardo. On the one hand, this is enough to secure him a place in the history of analysis; on the other hand, this seems to include him in the Ricardian group. His exploits in general theory, however, are distinctly un-, if not anti-, Ricardian. But they are difficult to appraise because Torrens was careless in formulation and not a good technician and offers his wheat much mixed with chaff. He did not accept the central Ricardian doctrine that issues in the proposition that profits depend exclusively on wages. But his argument against it strongly suggests that he failed to grasp the sense in which Ricardo held it. What he put into its place may have been substantially valid as he meant it. But as it stands, it is not particularly enlightening. He needs an interpreter to do for him what the Ricardo admirers of around 1890 did for Ricardo. Until such an interpreter appears and succeeds it is premature, to say the least, to rank him, as has been done in one instance—presumably in reaction to the contemptuous treatment he received on other occasions—with Ricardo and Malthus as one of the 'founders of the classic school.'

4. France

If French economics of that period is to be seen in its true proportions, two facts must be borne in mind. First, as we know, the Parisian scene was colored until 1848 by the activities, literary and other, of socialist groups to an extent for which there is no contemporaneous parallel anywhere else. Not so spectacular but equally important in the long run were the activities, also literary and other, of Catholic critics of economic and political liberalism ('the principle of 1789'), which went, however, beyond criticism toward the goals of Catholic social reform.[1] Laicist bourgeois of ultraliberal persuasion formed a third group. All this makes fascinating material for the sociology of political and social ideas. But it makes poor material for the history of scientific eco-

identified himself with it. Like Scrope, he wrote a great many pamphlets and 'letters' on topics of the day. The marvel is that he also ascended into the rarified air of pure theory. The writings that are important in this respect are: *An Essay on the External Corn Trade* (1815); *An Essay on the Production of Wealth* (1821); *On Wages and Combinations* (1834). See Seligman and Hollander, 'Ricardo and Torrens,' *Economic Journal*, September 1911.

[1] I am going to use this opportunity to mention Alban de Villeneuve-Bargemont (1784-1850; especially: *Économie politique chrétienne*, 1834), a central figure in a broad movement. It is extremely difficult to do justice to his work. Those—laicist liberals in particular—who look at his social philosophy and his politics, decide whether they like it or not, and appraise him accordingly have indeed an easy task. But ours is not so easy. We have to realize, first, the depth and social significance of his convictions; the wisdom of many of his practical recommendations; the scientific value of much of his sociology; and, at the same time, the defects of his technical economics, which was in fact rudimentary. These defects should not decrease in the least our respect for the man *or his thought;* only, they happen to be relevant from the standpoint of this book.

nomics. Second, excellent factual work was done during the period, the great performance of Le Play topping a highly creditable record. For the rest, however, there are only two first-rank men to mention (besides Cournot of course), namely, J. B. Say and Sismondi.

Jean-Baptiste Say (1767-1832) was one of those men who illustrate two important though slightly paradoxical truths: first, that, in order to appraise a man properly and to put him into the right place, it is sometimes necessary to defend him not only against his enemies but also against his friends and even against himself; second that there is a fundamental difference between superficiality of exposition and superficiality of thought.[2] Superficiality is in fact what strikes Say's reader first. His argument flows along with such easy limpidity that the reader hardly ever stops to think and hardly ever experiences a suspicion that there might be deeper things below this smooth surface. This brought him sweeping success with the many; it cost him the good will of the few. He sometimes did see important and deep-seated truths; but when he had seen them, he pointed them out in sentences that read like trivialities. He never bent—as even Ricardo did—to the task of hammering them out so that they might be recognized by everyone for what they were and stand criticism and wear and tear. Also he invariably mismanaged his case in controversy by replying to criticism in a desultory manner, without bestowing the requisite amount of work on it. Hence, the historian must restate his argument for him and, in doing so, must often neglect infelicitous wording or even discard downright silly bits of reasoning that only carelessness will account for. Everyone realizes that this must also be done for Ricardo and Marx because, in their cases, the roughness of the surface invites digging. But the economists were few indeed who were able and willing to render this service to Say.

Thus he never got his due. The huge textbook success of his *Traité*—nowhere greater than in the United States—only confirmed contemporaneous and later critics in their diagnosis that he was just a popularizer of A. Smith. In fact, the book got so popular precisely because it seemed to save hasty or ill-prepared readers the trouble of wading through the *Wealth of Nations*. This was substantially the opinion of the Ricardians, who treated him with some respect because of the Law of Markets, which they accepted from him,[3] but for the rest put him down as a writer—see McCulloch's comments upon him in the *Literature of Political Economy*—who had been just able to rise to Smithian, but had failed to rise to Ricardian, wisdom. For Marx he is simply the 'insipid' Say (*der fade Say*). For later critics he was merely one of the

[2] Let me illustrate this: nobody will call Hegel's exposition superficial, but some (misguided) individuals may think that his elaborate show of profundity covers many shallows. J. B. Say, as will be argued in the text, presents an instance of the opposite kind.

[3] Even as regards this law, they displayed some inclination to assert claims of their own (on behalf of James Mill), although Say's priority is beyond the possibility of doubt.

exponents of economic liberalism to be disregarded on this count alone. Where he did live on, in the theory of cycles, his law was voted either wrong or else a valueless tautology. In our own time he experienced a curious kind of renaissance. His Law of Markets was declared—mistakenly as we shall see—to be the basis of the whole structure of classic economics in the Keynesian sense of this term (see above, ch. 1, sec. 1). This gave him sinister importance—but at least it gave him importance.

But even his friends were taken in by that deceptive semblance of superficiality. Even for those French historians who were ready enough to protect his memory, he was primarily the exponent—one of them said 'vulgarizer'—of A. Smith's teaching. To this merit, it is true, they added various others, of which we may take notice by anticipation: Say cast the subject matter of economics into the schema—production, distribution, and consumption; its methodology owes something to him; he pointed toward a utility theory of value; he helped to establish the triad of factors—land, labor, and capital; he emphasized the figure of the entrepreneur, using the term (which occurs in Cantillon); and, of course, he was Say of Say's Law of Markets. All of this, as usually put, makes only a modest case since some of these merits are per se of minor importance or even of doubtful value. We shall comment on all of them in due course. At present, we are concerned with the fundamental error that vitiates appraisal of Say's position in the history of economics, namely, with the usual interpretation of his relation to A. Smith.

Say's work grew from purely French sources, if we consider Cantillon a French economist. It is the Cantillon-Turgot tradition, which he carried on and from which he *could* have developed—whatever it was he actually did—all the main features of his analysis including, by the way, his systematic schema and his entrepreneur.[4] The most important of these features, and his really great contribution to analytic economics, is his conception of economic equilibrium, hazy and imperfectly formulated though it was:[5] Say's work is the most important of the links in the chain that leads from Cantillon and Turgot to Walras.

Only two facts about his life are relevant to our purpose. Barring some unimportant cases during the French Revolution, he was the first French academic teacher of economics, first at the Conservatoire National des Arts et Métiers (1819), later at the Collège de France (1830). And, for a considerable part of his life, he was a practical businessman and thus enjoyed the advantage of having first-hand knowledge of what he was writing about. Intellectuals who know business only from newspapers are in the habit of congratulating themselves on their detachment. But obviously there is

[4] Although I am pleading for justice to him, I must emphasize that, to some extent, this reduces his claims to originality. The Cantillon tradition had never died out in France.

[5] In part, the imperfections alluded to are due to the fact that the task is an essentially mathematical one, which he was not equipped to handle. This adds to the difficulties of doing justice to him also in other respects: his Law of Markets is expressed in loose words that may be made to carry different exact meanings.

also another side to the matter. The principal items in his list of publications for us are his *Traité d'économie politique* (1803; Prinsep's trans., 1821, is from the 4th edition which, however, it is dangerous to use without also referring to the 1st, for Say had a way of forgetting what he really meant) and his letters. The *Cours complet d'économie politique pratique* (1828-9) does not add a great deal. His works (*Oeuvres*) form vols. IX-XII of the Guillaumin *Collection des principaux économistes* (1840-48). The *Traité* needs no reader's guide. But I wish to reiterate the warning that profitable perusal is much more of a job than it looks.

J. C. L. Simonde, who called himself 'de Sismondi' (1773-1842), was something of a practical farmer and an amateur politician—excellent exercises in realism—but primarily a laicist intellectual, who enjoyed living on the fringe end of *le monde*, and a historian. His main achievement is, I think, his *Histoire des républiques italiennes du moyen âge* (1807-18). Of these 16 volumes, I have a skipping knowledge, which is, however, more than I can say with reference to the 31 volumes of his *Histoire des Français* (1821-44). Of the rest of his historical work, which also covers literary history, I know only his *Histoire de la chute de l'empire romain . . .* (1835), the scholarly shortcomings of which are partly compensated for, to an economist, by interesting sociological vistas and analyses. His economics are much more English than French. His *Richesse commerciale* (1803), is indeed not quite the Smithian brew it has been made out to be, even if we disregard the un-Smithian recommendations in the second volume. The real Sismondi, the Sismondi of later years, shows occasionally. On the whole, however, the traditional opinion is sufficiently near the truth. Sismondi's reputation as an economist rests on his *Nouveaux Principes d'économie politique . . .* which appeared in 1819.[6] But we know that the essentials of this work had actually been written by 1815 for an article that Sismondi contributed to Brewster's *Edinburgh Encyclopaedia*, though this article was not published until after the *Nouveaux Principes*. By then—at the latest—he was in possession of all the elements of doctrine that are associated with his name. His later works, such as his *Études sur l'économie politique* (1837-8), emphasized and developed the main points—and his claims—but do not add anything essentially new.[7]

Sismondi's work received critical notice immediately, especially from the Ricardians. As the tide went against the latter, Sismondi's fame increased steadily until, with social reformers and opponents of laissez-faire in general, he was eventually raised to one of those positions to which it becomes etiquette to pay respect. In part, this was owing to attitudes that have little to do with analytic achievement; he preached the gospel that the true object of economics is man and not wealth. He attacked Ricardianism as mere 'chrematistics' and as unrealistic chrematistics to boot.[8] He advocated once more the intervention of the state in eco-

[6] The 2nd edition of the *Nouveaux Principes* came out in 1827 with not insignificant changes.

[7] Selections of Sismondi's works have been published in German with an introduction and comments by Professor Amonn (1945-9). See also A. Aftalion, *L'Oeuvre économique de Simonde de Sismondi* (1899); and H. Grossman, *Simonde de Sismondi et ses théories économiques* (1924).

[8] Sismondi never lost an opportunity to extol A. Smith at the expense of the 'new school' (the Ricardians). In matters of method, he diagnosed A. Smith's as truly scientific and 'experimental' (meaning empirical), whereas he condemned Ricardo's as abstract

nomic affairs. And he was thoroughly pro-labor. Whoever did any or all of these things was as sure of applause from some quarters as he was of adverse criticism from others. But it must be added that he was in fact one of the most important forerunners of later *Sozialpolitik* and that some of his recommendations—for example, the recommendation that employers should be made to guarantee their workmen security against unemployment, sickness, and destitution in old age—are among his most genuinely original contributions.[9] As regards analytic economics, his reputation rests primarily upon his argument against Say's law and his underconsumption theory of crises (if indeed his theory should be thus labeled; see below, ch. 7, sec. 6). But even if the uncritical recognition that was extended to him on this score—mainly by economists whose strength was not in economic theory—were more justified than it is, these points would not express his true importance in the history of analysis.

The distinctive feature of Sismondi's analysis is that it is geared to an *explicit dynamic model in the modern sense of this phrase*. The terms, Static and Dynamic, we have met already. We shall use this opportunity to take a first step toward a closer acquaintance with their meaning. For this purpose, let us start with a famous statement of Ricardo's, made in a letter to Malthus: [10] 'You always have in mind the immediate and temporary effects . . . [I] fix my whole attention on the permanent state of things which will result from them.' This is not quite true, but if it were, it would mean this: suppose we have before us an economic process that is perfectly balanced and ideally adapted to its data; then let us impose arbitrarily some change in some element or elements of it, say, in some prices or quantities; this disturbance will produce immediate adaptations, some of which will in turn produce further disturbances; but in the end, when everything has had time to straighten itself out, a new perfectly balanced state of the economic organism will result that is again ideally adapted to its data.[11] Ricardo was evidently of the opinion that the important thing is to investigate the properties of this new 'normal' state *in comparison with the properties* of that 'normal' state from which we started: the new 'permanent' incomes, prices, and quantities are compared with the old incomes, prices, and quantities. For this procedure, the term Comparative Statics came into use later on (see below, Part

---

speculation that had lost contact with reality. It should be observed, however, that his arguments, so far as they are valid against Ricardo, are just as valid against Smith.

[9] The more limited modern idea of the 'guaranteed wage' may with justice be said to have been visualized by him. The originality of his suggestions stands out in one point especially: his idea was to turn the social costs of labor-saving improvements into business costs of employers.

[10] Professor Hollander quoted this letter in his Introduction to Ricardo's *Notes on Malthus' Principles* (ed. 1928, p. lxxxviii).

[11] This is by no means always so and, even if it is, requires proof that raises a number of delicate questions. Just now we neglect this, just as Ricardo himself neglected it

IV, ch. 7, sec. 3). It implies, of course, both that the sequence of intermediate or 'transitional' states through which the system has to pass on its way to the new 'normal' state does not affect the latter—that is to say, that the new 'normal' state depends only on the old 'normal' state and on the nature of the disturbance but *not* on that sequence of transitional states—and also that the transitional states are relatively unimportant, at least in the sense that they do not present any very interesting problems to the analyst.

Sismondi admitted, just as uncritically as had A. Smith and Ricardo, that such a new equilibrium state—he used the term equilibrium—will eventually emerge. But he urged that the road toward it may be so long and lead through such severe upheavals—he said: 'terrible sufferings'—as to make it practically impossible for the analyst to deal cavalierly with the incidental phenomena. So far, so good. Malthus did (independently) the same thing. But Sismondi took a further step, credit for which he does not have to share with Malthus or anyone else except, possibly, with Quesnay. He realized that the most important of the reasons why transitional phenomena are of the essence of the economic process—and hence not only relevant to its practical problems but also to its fundamental theory—is that the economic process is chained to certain sequences that will exclude certain forms of adaptation and enforce others. An example will help. If the money income generated by a given process of production were always to be spent on the output of this same process of production, we should have a reason to believe [12] that the public's 'purchasing power' and the output of goods and services would, barring individual errors, always correspond to one another so that, *at least as a possibility,* the latter could always be sold at cost-covering prices. But suppose that the economic process is chopped up into periods in the following way: the money income of any period t is generated by processes of production, the output of which becomes available in period $t + 1$; and this same income is spent in period t on the output of the period $t - 1$. In this case, we lose one of the reasons we have for believing that income and output will correspond to each other in the sense mentioned above: the money income of period t is the result of decisions taken in period t, whereas the output offered in period t is the result of decisions taken in period $t - 1$, hence taken in possibly different circumstances—a fact that evidently may be a source of difficulties in adaptation and of new phenomena incident thereto. The example is oversimplified and otherwise unrealistic. But it suffices to show that the economic process is a system of periodicities and lags and, by virtue of this alone, harbors a world of problems that simply do not exist for Ricardian economics or any other economics of the same type. Analysis that takes account of this fact and attempts to deal with these problems is called dynamic

[12] This condition would not be sufficient. However, in order to make my point as simple as possible, I neglect this fact here.

analysis. We shall have to attend to it later on (Part IV, ch. 7 and Part V). Now we shall break off an argument that has, for the moment, no other purpose but to define the distinctive feature of Sismondi's analysis.

Nobody can ever have been unaware of the facts at which we have just glanced. A long list of pieces of analysis could be compiled, from mercantilist times on, that contain, unsystematically and rudimentarily, some dynamic elements. Even Ricardo would be represented in this list. But Sismondi's great merit is that he used, systematically and explicitly, a schema of periods, that is, that he was the first to practice the particular method of dynamics that is called period analysis. Moreover, he saw clearly the difference this makes and in particular the disturbances, discrepancies, and hitches that result from the fact that economic life is bound to sequences of which every unit is determined by the past and in turn determines the future. At the same time, this great analytic merit is his only one. He handled his own tool—like other ideas of his—so clumsily as seriously to impair its usefulness. And all the other arguments he adduced against the Ricardian system, and for the propositions that he tried to put in place of it, were technically so faulty as to make it easy for the Ricardians to dispose of them and even to take him not quite seriously. Thus, we have before us, once more, one of those situations where a man was *rightly* defeated and, on another level of discourse, was nevertheless right. The Ricardian judgment about him prevailed also with the non-Ricardians of the second half of the nineteenth century. And the applause of those who appreciated his fervent social sympathies or the mere fact that he found hitches in the capitalist process was, so far as scientific economics is concerned, no compensation for this—for the competent theorist this applause was rather in the nature of a verification of his own adverse opinion.[13]

In the chair at the Collège de France,[14] Say was succeeded by the Italian Rossi, Rossi by Chevalier,[15] whose tenure extended to 1879, and Chevalier, in

[13] As an illustration of Sismondi's technical incompetence, I refer the reader to his numerical argument on pp. 374-84 of the first volume of the *Nouveaux Principes*. Sismondi correctly perceived that his period analysis greatly weakened the 'classic' argument about free competition. But then he tried to show by a numerical example how the competitive struggle leads to deadlock; and what his figures actually show is exactly the contrary—they display the mechanism by which the hitch will in general be avoided.

[14] The Collège de France is neither a college nor a graduate school in the American sense, though somewhat more like the latter than like the former. Appointment to a chair is an honor that spells recognition of the appointee's leading position rather than an opportunity for inspiring and directing research. Lectures are addressed to a wide public and sometimes are (or were) frequented by *le monde*.

[15] Michel Chevalier (1806-79) was undoubtedly one of the most eminent economists of that period—known to fame as the Chevalier of the Cobden-Chevalier commercial treaty between England and France (1860), which was followed by quasi-free-trade treaties between France and a number of other countries. His various activities, often

turn, by his son-in-law, Paul Leroy-Beaulieu, whose career covers practically the whole of the next period. This academic succession should be noticed because it was also a succession in spirit and doctrine. In the high heavens, Say's true successor was indeed the great Walras. But on a less exalted level and as to 'applied' economics, attitudes in economic policy, systematic arrangement, and also as to the lower ranges of economic theory, these men (Rossi less than the other two) may be considered as followers of Say and as the core of a school which, if we date it from 1803, the year of the publication of Say's *Traité*, boasts of a history of about a century. We shall consider it in the next Part. For the present, besides noting that interesting fact itself, we confine ourselves to the following comments. First, so far as nonsocialist economics is concerned, this group was not to meet significant opposition until the next period. During the period under discussion and a little beyond, it ruled supreme, controlling in particular the professional journals and institutions, and also the Société d'Économie Politique which was founded, like the *Journal des économistes*, in 1842. Second, the school and all its members were —partly, as has been mentioned before, owing to the presence until 1848 of a strong socialist menace to bourgeois society—strongly liberal in the laissez-faire sense and anti-*étatistes*.[16] This naturally accounts for the hostility of modern critics that also reflects upon Say himself, but it should be unnecessary to point out that their derogatory judgments are unhistorical. Third, the school had many members of admirable character, strong intelligence, and great experience in practical affairs. But, fourth, owing partly to the practical turn of their minds and their too exclusive concentration upon economic policy, they lacked interest in purely scientific questions and were in consequence almost wholly sterile as regards analytic achievement. Their very existence as a

in the service of, but never in subservience to, the French government produced a respectable quantity of valuable work of a factual nature and, occasionally, singularly infelicitous predictions such as that gold would fall in value (in 1859!) and that universal free trade would be realized before the century was out. That factual work may be illustrated by his *Lettres sur l'Amérique du Nord* (1836) and his *Intérêts matériels en France* (1836), models of their type. It is, however, to be expected that, for sheer lack of time, such a man cannot have contributed to the efficiency of the apparatus of analytic economics, and that a history of analytic economics has to mention him mainly for the purpose of explaining why that apparatus showed so little improvement for decades together. It was not that economists were incapable. Chevalier, e.g., was beyond doubt a very intelligent man whose work of factual analysis, were comparison admissible, many of us would place above that of the mere analyst. But all the energies of many of the able men who took to economics were absorbed by the immediately practical—invested in a process of production that may be likened to primitive hunting. Chevalier's systematic work (*Cours d'économie politique*, 1st ed., 1842-4; a volume *La Monnaie* was added in 1850), the harvest of his lectures at the Collège de France that kept strictly on the surface of things, bears saddening witness to this—though, for the kind of performance it was, it merits admiration rather than contempt.

[16] Some of its members, Chevalier included, experienced however a Saint-Simonist spell in their youth.

group will appear to the modern radical as a bar to 'progress.' From a quite different standpoint and in a different sense, it likewise appears so to us.

But a few more names must be mentioned in further illustration. First, I shall mention two who stand out from the rest and illustrate the virtues of the school at its best, though they also illustrate its weaknesses, Dunoyer (1786-1863) and Courcelle-Seneuil.[17] Next we notice J. A. Blanqui and Joseph Garnier, meritorious workers [18] who met with success in their own day as well

[17] Admirable men both of them, who always stood uncompromisingly for what they considered the right course for their nation to take! But in spite of all the genuine brilliance—coupled with strong sense—that we find in Charles Dunoyer's *De la Liberté du travail* (1845), we cannot rank it as a scientific performance. Socialists will agree with us on the ground that his every sentence was ideologically conditioned and served some 'apologetic' purpose. But it is not this which motivates our own judgment. If it were, we should have to exclude practically all socialist writings that are not less ideologically conditioned. The book adds nothing either to our knowedge or to our control over facts. The case of J. G. Courcelle-Seneuil (1813-92) is different. His *Traité théorique et pratique d'économie politique* (1858); *Traité . . . des entreprises industrielles, commerciales, et agricoles* (1855); *Traité . . . des opérations de banque* (1853), to mention only a few of the literary fruits of a busy life, were models of their kind and have served as such. Even if one does not attach much importance either to his rudimentary graphs or to certain unsuccessful terminological innovations of his (theory—plutology; applied economics—ergonomy), there is in his works that clear grasp of economic affairs that comes from firsthand experience and that one misses so much in the modern literature. At the same time, I do not think that it is possible to say more for him than this. His work illustrates our old truth that it is one thing to be a good economist and quite another to be a theorist.

[18] J. A. Blanqui (1798-1854), the brother of the revolutionist of the 'putschist' type, L. A. Blanqui, was also an academic successor of Say, viz. at the Conservatoire National des Arts et Métiers. He is chiefly known for his *Histoire de l'économie politique en Europe* (1837), an interesting compilation that enjoyed international success because of its indubitable usefulness. Much more important was his *Résumé de l'histoire du commerce et de l'industrie* (1826), a judicious abstract that seems to me to be very well done (considering its date and the resources on which such an undertaking could then draw) and his researches into labor economics. Joseph Garnier, 1813-81 (not the Comte Germain Garnier, who is chiefly known as the translator of the *Wealth of Nations*, 1802, and as a late physiocrat and need not detain us further), was a pupil and close associate of Blanqui and an indefatigable teacher, scholastic administrator, and writer. His highly successful *Éléments de l'économie politique* (1845; entitled *Traité* from 1860 on; we may add his *Éléments des finances*, 1858, which also grew into a *Traité*) is chiefly interesting as a sample of French pre-Millian economics. His *Éléments de statistique* commands the same kind of interest. His annotated French edition of Malthus' *Essay on Population* (1845) is more significant. He had to be mentioned because it has been said—and, to judge by quotations, not without reason—that he enjoyed international reputation. It may be proper to add here the name of Charles Ganilh (1758-1836), who also continued to be quoted in that type of theoretical literature whose authors thought it necessary to preface whatever it was they had to say by a complete survey of the older writers who had pronounced upon their subject. His *Systèmes d'économie politique* (1809), an early history of economic thought, deserves to be noticed on account of its date as well as because it did not fall in, uncritically,

as later: both, but especially Garnier, kept on being quoted. Third, Destutt de Tracy, also, has been too often quoted, though mainly in the literature of his own time, to be passed by completely.[19] A few others will be mentioned as occasions arise. But no occasion will arise to mention Canard and Bastiat. So their names may as well stand here.

Canard's performance (N. F. Canard, *Principes d'économie politique*, 1801, a curious revival of Cantillon's *Trois rentes*) is sometimes listed among early contributions to mathematical economics (on the strength of a few algebraic formulae that mean nothing) but would otherwise partake of the blessings of deserved oblivion, had not a misfortune befallen it. This misfortune consisted in its being 'crowned' by the same French Academy that later on failed to extend any recognition to Cournot and Walras. And those Olympians who felt their neglect the more bitterly on account of the honor done to Canard visited him with a scathing contempt that bestowed upon him an unenviable immortality: in the history of scientific bodies, Canard is forever sure of a place. The book is, however, far from being the worst that was ever written. It had some influence on Sismondi.

with the prevailing current of Smith-Say free trade. His *Théorie de l'économie politique* . . . (1815) is redeemed from complete insignificance by its 'realistic' or 'factual' quality.

[19] A. L. C. Destutt, Comte de Tracy (1754-1836) was a figure of some importance in the intellectual scenery of the Napoleonic Empire (and a little before and a little after)—a thinker by the grace of nature, though the latter had failed to add the gift of originality. He had, moreover, been formed in the eighteenth-century world; and while such attention as his thought received is an interesting symptom of the survival of eighteenth-century attitudes, his thought itself is a not less interesting example of partially successful adaptation. Philosophically, he belongs in the Condillac tradition, politically—in spite of a number of critical reservations—among the many heirs to Montesquieu. His broadly conceived *Élémens d'idéologie* (the best translation I can think of is one into Scottish: *System of Moral Philosophy*) began to appear in 1801, a *Traité de la volonté* being one of the installments. Another installment of what was to remain a torso, was a treatise on economics, republished under this title (*Traité d'économie politique*) in 1823. With due respect for the spacious whole of which this treatise—which belongs to the Say group—was a component part, I have to confess that I cannot find in it anything to distinguish it except one feature: Destutt de Tracy was not a philosopher for nothing. He had an eye for logical rigor. Hence he insisted on neat conceptualization. One of his definitions—that production means change of form or place; Ramsay added time—was taken up by some English economists. But, by stressing what may be termed the physical aspect of production, it obscures the economic one. He also insisted that value must be measured in a value unit, it being the essence of measurement to compare the thing to be measured with a given quantity of the same thing chosen as a unit (as, e.g., length is measured in meters). Ricardo quoted this statement approvingly, but it is misleading. Other examples could be quoted in order to show that his preoccupation with logical foundations, which might have produced useful results, remained sterile.

Frédéric Bastiat's (1801-50) case has been given undue prominence by remorseless critics. But it is simply the case of the bather who enjoys himself in the shallows and then goes beyond his depth and drowns. A strong free trader and laissez-faire enthusiast, he rose into prominence by a brilliantly written article, 'De l'influence des tarifs français et anglais sur l'avenir des deux peuples' (*Journal des économistes*, 1844), which was grist to the mill of the small group of Paris free traders who then tried to parallel Cobden's agitation in England. A series of *Sophismes économiques* followed, whose pleasant wit—petition of candlemakers and associated industries for protection against the unfair competition of the sun and that sort of thing—that played merrily on the surface of the free-trade argument has ever since been the delight of many. Bastiat ran the French free-trade association, displaying a prodigious activity, and presently turned his light artillery against his socialist compatriots. So far, so good—or at any rate, no concern of ours. Admired by sympathizers, reviled by opponents, his name might have gone down to posterity as the most brilliant economic journalist who ever lived. But in the last two years of his life (his hectic career only covers the years 1844-50) he embarked upon work of a different kind, a first volume of which, the *Harmonies économiques*, was published in 1850. The reader will please understand that Bastiat's confidence in unconditional laissez faire (his famous 'optimism')—or any other aspect of his social philosophy—has nothing whatever to do with the adverse appraisal that seems to me to impose itself, although it motivated most of the criticism he got. Personally, I even think that Bastiat's exclusive emphasis on the harmony of class interests is, if anything, rather less silly than is exclusive emphasis on the antagonism of class interests. Nor should it be averred that there are no good ideas at all in the book. Nevertheless, its deficiency in reasoning power or, at all events, in power to handle the analytic apparatus of economics, puts it out of court here. I do not hold that Bastiat was a bad theorist. I hold that he was no theorist. This fact was bound to tell in what was essentially a venture in theory, but does not affect any other merits of his. I have said nothing of the charge that he plagiarized Carey that was urged by Carey himself, and then by Ferrara and Dühring. Since I cannot see scientific merit in the *Harmonies* in any case, this question is of no importance for this book. But readers who do take interest in it are referred to Professor E. Teilhac's balanced and scholarly treatment of it in *Pioneers of American Economic Thought* (English trans. by Professor E. A. J. Johnson, 1936). His argument establishes, with considerable success, that much that seems at first sight unrelieved plagiarism is accounted for by the French sources that Bastiat and Carey had in common. Bastiat's *Oeuvres complètes* with a biography were published in a second edition (1862-4).

For the rest, we must be content to notice what I believe to be one of the best textbooks of 'classic' economics, Cherbuliez' *Précis*.[20]

5. Germany

In the German section of our picture we see first of all the old 'cameralist' tradition—the tradition of the German Consultant Administrators—in a process of partial transformation under the influence of A. Smith. Though translated for the first time immediately after publication (1776-8), the *Wealth of Nations* took time to become effective. The profession of the *Staatswissenschaft* did not at first like it much, and, as has been mentioned before, some were inclined to put Steuart's *Principles* above it. But they experienced a very thorough change of heart around 1800, when first a few and before long a majority turned enthusiastically Smithian. This was in fact more natural for them than had been the initial resistance because, as has also been mentioned, their own ideas had been moving on similar lines for many years before that.

The works of Hufeland, von Jakob, Kraus, and von Soden suffice to exemplify this Smithian cameralism: Gottlieb Hufeland (1760-1817), *Neue Grundlegung der Staatswirthschaftskunst* . . . (1807-13; the second volume, on money, is rather interesting); L. H. von Jakob (1759-1827), *Grundsätze der National-ökonomie* (1805, enlarged and improved later on); C. J. Kraus (1753-1807), *Staatswirthschaft* (1808-11); Count F. J. H. von Soden (1754-1831), *Die Nationalökonomie* (1805-24). Jakob and Kraus were also philosophers (Kantians). All four were Smithians in the sense that almost all their thought and work in economics fed and turned upon the *Wealth of Nations*. Kraus, an influential teacher, who instilled his opinion into many future public servants,[1] embraced it with uncritical enthusiasm: he spoke of it as the only 'true, great, noble, and beneficent system' and was one of those who compared it to the *New Testament* in importance. Hufeland and Jakob, though Smithian enough, did not go quite so far as this; von Soden was still more independent. His criticisms of A. Smith were not well taken but he occasionally followed lines of his own. In particular, he adumbrated the idea, later on developed by List, that the true aim of foreign trade or any other policy was not so much immediate gain in welfare but rather the development of the nation's productive resources, a 'mercantilist' point of view, which is of importance not only for recommendation but also for analysis. All four were men of

[20] A. E. Cherbuliez (1797-1869), a Swiss lawyer by training and for part of his life by vocation, later a politician and professor of economics, was at first a political scientist rather than an economist. He was past forty when he seriously turned to economics, and he never produced anything original. But he excelled at exposition and his *Précis de la science économique* . . . (1862), deserves notice as one of the high points of the textbook literature of that period. Its success was considerable, but rather below its merit.

[1] Some of those public servants co-operated in the Stein-Hardenberg legislation. There is thus a not uninteresting relation between the *Wealth of Nations* and that Prussian reformer, von Jakob, who taught at the University of Kharkov as well as at the University of Halle, acted as a consultant to official commissions in St. Petersburg, and did much toward spreading Smithian doctrine in Russia.

some eminence, and I am prepared to defend my choice. But the reader should understand that several other names might have served equally well.

Two men should be added who are not usually listed as German economists. The one, Count G. F. Buquoy-Longueval (1781-1851) was a very interesting man: a great Austrian nobleman, very wealthy, very radical (as an old man he took part in the revolution of 1848), a gifted dilettante in many fields, more than a dilettante in at least two (theoretical mechanics and economics). He wrote, among older things, a *Theorie der Nationalwirthschaft* . . . (1815; supplements 1816-19) and a tract on money and monetary policy, . . . *Ein auf echten Nationalcredit fundiertes Geld* . . . (1819), both of which are Smithian in their bases but contain several interesting and original suggestions, that of a managed paper currency among others. Man and writings are forgotten unjustly, so I think.

The other man to be added fared better and, having been discussed in his day in England and France, has kept a place in the history of our subject: H. F. von Storch (1766-1835), who, though a German by race and training, is usually treated as Russian because of his career in the Russian service. His historical and statistical studies on Russia should be mentioned first (especially: *Historisch-statistisches Gemälde* [picture] *des Russischen Reiches am Ende des achtzehnten Jahrhunderts*, 1797-1803). I have 'skipped' through the 9 volumes but am not competent to judge how far Storch succeeded in exhausting the possibilities offered by his materials. As regards his systematic work (*Cours d'économie politique* . . . 1815) and his venture in income analysis (*Considérations sur la nature du revenu national*, 1824) it should be pointed out that the factual bent of the former and the ethical commonplaces contained in it do not justify the habit of historians of doctrine of placing him—as a member or as a forerunner—with the later historico-ethical school. He was not more 'factual' than A. Smith, and to separate him methodologically from his English contemporaries only serves to blur contour lines: Senior's factual work is in the reports of royal commissions instead of in his *Political Economy* but this is no reason for speaking of irreconcilable methodological differences between the two. If Storch doubted the possibility of formulating universal laws about economic phenomena, he did so in a sense that Senior and J. S. Mill would have heartily approved, that is, in the sense that the concrete economic phenomena, as historically given, do not obey simple and universally valid rules. For the rest, his analysis may be best described by the term 'critical Smithianism': his bases and conceptual apparatus are substantially Smithian but Storch disagreed with both Smith and Say on a number of important points. Particularly as regards income analysis. Storch has some claim to being listed, along with Lauderdale, Malthus, and Sismondi, as a forerunner of Keynesianism and of similar tendencies that asserted themselves, on and off, later on. However, if I understand his argument in the *Considérations*, there is not much in it: like all the authors in that line, he neglected, as much as other people overstress, the equilibrating mechanisms in the capitalist process. But we shall return to this. For the present, I want to make sure that the reader does not forget this man: though he does not rank high as a theorist, he is a significant figure.

Smithianism, increasingly leavened with a little (often misunderstood) Ricardo and relieved of some of the older stuff about eighteenth-century administrative policy—this is the formula that characterizes the common run of German economics until and even a little beyond the end of the period under survey. This material took the textbook shape that proved satisfactory for decades in the work of Rau.[2] But from this level and far above it rose the performances of two men of remarkable talent and force, Hermann and Mangoldt. In deference to a curious habit of the German historians of economics, I add Bernhardi.

Considering that Thünen and Marx followed paths of their own that were not within sight of that common run, we might feel inclined to discount the reputation of F. B. W. von Hermann (1795-1868) on the ground that he stands out for lack of competition. There is something in this. Nevertheless, his *Staatswirthschaftliche Untersuchungen* (1832; enlarged ed. 1870; reprint 1924), though it has not made scientific history, largely merits the many compliments that have been paid to it, even by A. Marshall. Hermann's good sense saved him all the energies that others spent on their doubts about 'abstract methods' and that sort of thing, and his acute and balanced mind played unimpeded about the fundamentals of economic theory. His method was as simple as it was meritorious, considering the date of his book: he started from 'supply and demand' and proceeded to investigate the factors behind it. His neat conceptualization did the rest and the success was considerable: it is not generally realized that his work spelled a long stride beyond Ricardo. This suffices to characterize his merits as a theorist in a general way. But it does not do justice to his factual work (statistical and other), and it does not do justice to the man, who as politician, civil servant, and teacher has left his mark upon the formative years of Germany.

Hans von Mangoldt (1824-68) is much less well known. Nevertheless, this civil servant and professor (at Göttingen and Freiburg) was among the century's most significant figures in our field. Apart from his historical work on the industry of Saxony, there are two important con-

[2] K. H. Rau (1792-1870), professor first in Erlangen and then in Heidelberg, certainly had sound common sense, learning, and mediocrity. But if any other qualities are needed for the production of a successful textbook, he must have had them also. The many editions of his *Lehrbuch der politischen Ökonomie* (1826-37: 1st vol., theory [the 'laws']; 2nd vol., applied economics or economic policy, or *Polizeiwissenschaft;* 3rd vol.—the best—public finance) are less indicative of its sweeping success than is the fact that Adolf Wagner thought it worthy of being remodeled instead of being replaced by an entirely new one. As a teacher, Rau must stand high in the history of economics, although little can be said in favor of the book except that it marshalled a rich supply of facts very neatly—and that it was just what the future lawyer or civil servant was able and willing to absorb.

tributions which we have to notice: his *Die Lehre vom Unternehmergewinn* (1855; substantially a rent-of-ability theory of entrepreneurial gain) and his *Grundriss der Volkswirtschaftslehre* (1863; the 2nd ed., published posthumously in 1871, leaves out the most original element in it, namely, the geometrical apparatus that Mangoldt devised for the theory of international values; but Edgeworth brought it to light again).

Theodor von Bernhardi (1802-87) owes his reputation to Roscher's history of German economics. I have called the habit of listing his name indefinitely a curious one because there is really no reason for it that will stand examination. The title of the work in question I had better give in translation: *Critical Essay on the Arguments that are being adduced for Large and Small Properties in Land* (1849). Bernhardi, an extremely intelligent layman of wide culture and experience, discussed those arguments no doubt very sensibly. But it was not this which aroused Roscher's enthusiasm. Bernhardi put his topic into a spacious—and specious—framework of general considerations about the social and economic backgrounds from which English 'classic' doctrines arose, showing their historical and sociological relativity and their limited validity—quite successfully of course—but also showing inability to realize the difference between views or recommendations on practical questions and theorems.

Since Thünen and Marx (if the latter should indeed be called a German economist at all) are noticed elsewhere, we are, for the rest, left with List and Rodbertus, on the one hand—it is slightly disconcerting to observe that Thünen, Marx, List, and Rodbertus were all of them nonprofessorial economists—and with Roscher, Hildebrand, and Knies, the members of what has been termed the Older Historical School, on the other.

Friedrich List (1789-1846) holds a great place both in the opinion and in the affections of his countrymen. This is owing to his successful championship of the customs union of the German States (*Zollverein*), the embryo of German national unity. What this association means to Germans cannot be understood by members of those fortunate nations for which the right to national existence and national ambitions is a matter of course. It means that List, like all those whose names are associated with that long and painful struggle, is a national hero. Far be it for me to criticize this attitude or to withhold admiration from List in any other respect except the one that unfortunately happens to be the only one that counts in this book. Even as a scientific economist, however, List had one of the elements of greatness, namely, the grand vision of a national situation, which, though not in itself a scientific achievement, is a prerequisite for a certain type of scientific achievement—that type of which, in our own day, Keynes is an outstanding example. Nor was List deficient in the specifically scientific requisites that must come in to implement vision if it is to bear scientific fruits: his analytic apparatus was in fact ideally adequate for his practical purpose. But the individual pieces of this analytic apparatus were not particularly novel.

List saw a nation that struggled in the fetters imposed by a miserable immediate past, but he also saw all its economic potentialities. The national future, therefore, was the real object of his thought, the present was nothing but a state of transition. He realized that, in an essentially transitional state of this kind, policies lose their meaning when they are geared to the task of administering an existing set of conditions that is visualized as substantially permanent. This he expressed by his doctrine of 'stages'—a felicitous device, so far as his educational purpose was concerned, but in itself not more than an old eighteenth-century idea. Furthermore, he realized (like Soden) that emphasis upon the national future modifies welfare considerations *ex visu* of the present. This he expressed by his doctrine of 'productive forces' (*Produktionskräfte*) that in his system hold place of honor as compared with the consumers' goods that can be made available at a given level of the productive forces—not unfelicitous, this, as an educational device but not much more than a label for an unsolved problem. Finally, as regards his best-known contribution to the education of German public opinion on economic policy, the infant-industry argument, this is clearly Hamiltonian and part of the economic wisdom that List imbibed during his stay in the United States. So fully Americanized had List become then that he actually advocated financing railroad construction by the issue of banknotes, for which practice there were only—and hardly wholly creditable—American precedents. It should be remarked, in passing, that List's argument about protection issues into the free-trade argument: if this is not obvious, we can convince ourselves of it by noticing the fact that J. S. Mill accepted the infant-industry theory, evidently realizing that it ran within the free-trade logic.[3]

This, I think, does justice to, and at the same time reduces to its proper proportions, List's analytic gifts and performance. Those who insist on making their hero the possessor of merits of all conceivable types have put his thought into spurious relations of the kind that create spurious history. He was an heir to eighteenth-century thought. He was an offshoot of romanticism. He was a forerunner of the historical school of economics. There is not more in all this than that everyone is heir to everything that went before him and a forerunner of everything that comes after him. He was a great patriot, a brilliant journalist with definite purpose, and an able economist who co-ordinated well whatever seemed useful for implementing his vision. Is this not enough? Of all his writings the *Outlines of American Political Economy* (1827) is the most interesting for us because it displays his system in its earliest stage of development. His mature work that grew out of this, *Das nationale System der politischen Ökonomie* (1841; English trans. 1885), remains a classic in the eulogistic sense of the word, all the comments above notwithstanding. A new and comprehensive edition of his works (*Schrif-*

[3] Incidentally, it may be remarked that to call List's plans 'nationalist' or 'imperialist' is to play upon double meanings in both cases.

ten, Reden, Briefe) has been published (1927-32) by the German List Society (List-Gesellschaft), which also publishes *List-Studien*.

Johann Karl Rodbertus' (1805-75) name also owes something to circumstances: on the one hand, he did not meet either the competition or the criticism he would have met in England; on the other hand, though he spurned class struggle and revolution and was fundamentally a conservative monarchist, he was also a votary of a certain type of state socialism that was acceptable to a large sector of the public. For the rest, his social and political philosophies, including the manual workers' natural right to the whole product of industry (on the time-honored ground that all commodities are products of, or cost, manual labor only), are no concern of ours. But certain recommendations must be mentioned because they shed light on the analysis from which they proceed. The proposition that it is the institutional pattern alone that deprives labor of part of 'its' product was reflected in his recommendation to change this institutional pattern by state action such as taxation (one of the first proposals, in the liberalist world of that age, to use taxation for purposes other than revenue) and to fix not only prices and wages but also property incomes. His theory of rent of land was reflected in, but is not essential to, an extremely sensible proposal that has had some practical effect in Germany, namely the proposal to substitute for the mortgage that embodies a capital claim a mortgage that embodies only the right to an annual payment. His theory of poverty and of cycles was reflected in the proposal, which sounds so modern, to eliminate both by a redistribution of incomes.

Rodbertus' analytic schema can be most briefly and at the same time most tellingly described in this way. Fundamentally, and in the same sense as Marx, he was a Ricardian. His analytic effort was an effort to develop Ricardian doctrine in a certain direction and was in essentials parallel to, though different from, Marx's effort. According to dates of publication, Marx could have derived inspiration from Rodbertus, particularly as regards the unitary conception of all non-wage incomes—Marx's surplus value and Rodbertus' 'rent'—which is a feature of both schemata. In the main, however, Rodbertus' example can at best have taught Marx how not to go about his task and how to avoid the grossest errors. Therefore, and also because Marx's theoretical developments seem to me to follow naturally from Ricardo's formulations—given the direction in which those developments were to aim—I do not think that there is any cogent reason for challenging Engels' repudiation of the idea that Marx had 'borrowed' from Rodbertus.

To call Rodbertus a Ricardian is, of course, to limit the range of his originality. In addition, there is W. Thompson's priority—such as it is—for any sort of exploitation theory, and Owen's for Rodbertus' labor notes (currency).[4] But neither amounts to

[4] With both Owen and Rodbertus, and in essentially the same manner, units of labor are not merely what units of gold are in a gold currency, but the mechanism of this labor money also serves to 'correct' values.

much. For his own convenience, the reader should keep in mind the following three points that I mention here by anticipation as specifically characteristic of the caliber of Rodbertus' theorizing (all of which have found admirers, however): (I) his thoroughly untenable theory of rent;[5] (II) his factually and theoretically equally indefensible theory that the relative share of labor in the national dividend tends to fall in the course of capitalist development; and (III) his underconsumption theory of crises that is based upon the proposition that overproduction must periodically result from labor's inability to buy back a sufficient amount of its product owing to (II)—a type of underconsumption theory that should be, but unfortunately is not, beneath discussion. Sismondi, who has some passages that seem to point in the same direction, actually did much better than that. Rodbertus' most important works are: *Zur Erkenntniss unsrer staatswirthschaftlichen Zustände* (1842); *Sociale Briefe an von Kirchmann* (1850-51; English trans. as *Overproduction and Crises*, 1898; 2nd ed., 1908); *Zur Erklärung und Abhülfe der heutigen Creditnoth des Grundbesitzes* (1868-9). Other writings that are of interest to us, including letters that contain some important clarification, have been posthumously published from time to time. There is a considerable Rodbertus literature, mostly German. I mention only H. Dietzel's *Karl Rodbertus* (1886-8), which makes up by analytic competence what, owing to its date, it lacks in information. It was A. Wagner's championship that brought Rodbertus to the fore in the last two decades of the nineteenth century.

Reasons will be offered, as we go along, for believing that it is in the interest of a realistic picture of developments in our field to confine the concept, Historical School of Economics, to the age and to the group of Gustav von Schmoller (see below, Part IV, ch. 4). This implies that it is not good practice to speak of an Older Historical School, a term that has been introduced, chiefly for use in the polemic against Schmoller's 'historism,' to denote a group of writers who, while appreciating the importance of historical research, displayed no hostility toward 'theory.' I maintain that such a position does not constitute a distinctive characteristic and that the economists who are usually mentioned in this connection do not, in any useful sense, form a group, let alone a school. But we must notice these economists themselves: Hildebrand, Knies, and Roscher. The first,[6] a man of restless activity

[5] Meaning now rent of land in the usual sense and not in Rodbertus' sense, in which rent means profits plus interest plus rent of land.

[6] Bruno Hildebrand's (1812-78) chief work, *Die Nationalökonomie der Gegenwart und Zukunft* (1848; new ed. by Gehrig, 1922), displays hostility to the concept of natural law (in the sense that makes economic laws epistemologically analogous to physical laws); it places emphasis upon the moral-science character of economics (his term was *Kulturwissenschaft* as opposed to physics, *Naturwissenschaft*) and on other features that recur in the programmatic pronouncements of the Schmoller school and also in Windelband's and Rickert's methodologies of the social sciences. In addition, he did historical research. But his own programmatic pronouncement at the head of the first number of the *Jahrbücher für Nationalökonomie und Statistik*, which he founded in 1862, was remarkable for catholicity and obviously not intended to start or to espouse a distinct methodological party. In any case, if we do wish to label him a historical economist, he should be called a forerunner of the Schmoller school rather than a member of that triumvirate that does not form any real unit at all.

and considerable influence, comes nearest to having been a historical economist in the later and genuine acceptance of the term. Knies, one of the most significant figures of German economics, will be mentioned in our survey of the next period, to which his main work belongs. This work was in the field of economic theory, however, and his only title to a place in the older historical school rests upon a methodological *professio fidei*, which is very interesting as such but, considering his own practice, does not mean very much. It belongs in the period under discussion and will be noticed below (ch. 5, sec. 2b). Roscher,[7] who taught at the University of Leipzig for forty-six years, added to the influence which this implies the influence of many works that never fell below a highly respectable level: honest scholarship and sound common sense is written all over them, and the sympathetic understanding that his gentle and highly cultivated mind extended to all types of scientific effort helped to make them perhaps more useful to many generations of students than would have been more original productions. Marx poked insipid fun at him. There were those to whom he looked like an obstacle to advance. On the whole, however, there is hardly another economist of that period who enjoyed so nearly universal respect inside and outside of Germany. With complimentary intention, writers who found it difficult to credit him with original results have tried to find something original in his method or approach. This is how he got into the position of being considered either one of the 'founders' of a historical school in general or a leader of the so-called 'older' historical school. He invited this by speaking frequently of his historical method or standpoint. But we shall see later that there is not much in this and that he should be classified, so far as his analytic apparatus is concerned, as a very meritorious follower of the English 'classics,' though a follower who happened to have a particularly strong taste for historical illustration

I think the discussion above blocks out all the salient features of the scenery that it is necessary to keep in mind for our purpose. Incompleteness is essential in a venture of this kind and should need no excuse. But all the same it seems desirable to atone for the absence of three names that some readers may miss. I have already mentioned Lorenz von Stein, in connection with the economic interpretation of history, and

[7] W. G. F. Roscher's (1817-94) indefatigable industry turned out a large number of publications, of which we have already mentioned *Zur Geschichte der englischen Volkswirthschaftslehre im sechzehnten und siebzehnten Jahrhundert* (1851-2) and *Geschichte der Nationalökonomik in Deutschland* (1874), monuments of scholarship. Neglecting all other items of an impressive list, among them two additional contributions of his to the history of economics and several studies in economic history, I shall mention only his extremely successful *System der Volkswirthschaft* published in five volumes: *Grundlagen der Nationalökonomie* (1854; a 26th ed. appeared as late as 1922; English trans. 1878); *Nationalökonomik des Ackerbaues . . .* (1859; 14th ed., 1912); *Nationalökonomik des Handels und Gewerbfleisses* (1881; 8th ed., 1913-17); *System der Finanzwissenschaft* (1886; 5th ed., 1901); and *System der Armenpflege und Armenpolitik* (1894; 3rd ed., 1906).

should perhaps have included him in this sketch because his most important works were all first published within the period. I have transferred him to the next, however, since his influence was to increase considerably in the 1870's and 1880's. A similar reason motivated my transferring Albert Schäffle. But I am going to use this opportunity to comment briefly on Dühring who does not fit in anywhere else.

Eugen K. Dühring (1833-1921) had to abandon a lawyer's career owing to failure of eyesight quickly followed by complete blindness, and thereupon embarked, on the one hand, upon an academic career and, on the other hand, upon an intellectual effort that resulted in the conquest of a vast domain extending from mathematics, mechanics, and theoretical physics in general, to ethnology, economics, and philosophy. The truly admirable—in fact almost unbelievable—feat was, however, that in several stretches of that vast domain he attained the mastery requisite for original achievement. In particular, he published a brilliant history of mechanics (*Kritische Geschichte der allgemeinen Principien der Mechanik*, 1873), which, when awarded an academic prize, drew from the judges the curious comment that the level of the work was far above what would have been necessary to win the prize; and, more important, it was appreciatively noticed by Ernst Mach (see preface to first edition of the latter's *Mechanics*). In the history of the anti-metaphysical and positivist currents of thought, moreover, he cannot fail to retain a prominent place. In another sphere of thought—that philosophy of life which corresponds to the earliest meaning of the term philosophy—he developed an attitude or system which we may like or not, but which is both interesting and original (he called it 'personalism'). And there is his social philosophy—or system of social reform—that is entitled to the same comment (he called it 'societary'; it has some affinity with that of Rodbertus). The reasons why this significant thinker should have met with little except rebuffs are to be found mainly in a temperament that was at the same time generous and aggressive and that, by ferocious attacks, made enemies of practically all the individuals and groups he noticed at all. He experienced a revival, however, in the 1920's. All this had to be said to make it quite clear that any disrespectful attitude toward him is entirely out of place, and also to protect what follows from misunderstanding.

In the field of economic sociology he has indeed a considerable performance to his credit, namely, the anti-Marxist theory—which is partly tenable—that many of the property relations of the capitalist era have resulted not from the economic logic of capitalism, but from an extra-economic sequence of political causation. But in no other respect, since we exclude political thought and policy recommendations, is there, for us, positive contribution to report. He was—strange to say, considering his achievement in mechanics—a bad technician. He had no awareness of the analytic weaknesses of such an argument as that capitalist property (for institutional reasons) keeps the working class at a level of minimum of existence and deprives it of the fruits of technological improvement (wherefore the state must step in to assure labor of its appropriate share—again an affinity with Rodbertus). He had an unbounded enthusiasm for Carey and went into paroxysms of rage about Bastiat's plagiarism; but he displayed no grasp of either the strong or the weak points in Carey's system. And since this is what matters to us, we shall have no occasion to mention him again. Of Dühring's works the following are in our field: *Carey's Umwälzung der Volkswirtschaftslehre und Socialwissenschaft* (1865); *Capital und Arbeit . . .* (1865); *Kritische Grundlegung der Volkswirtschaftslehre* (1866); *Kritische Geschichte der Nationalökonomie und des Socialismus* (1871); *Cursus . . .* (1873). See E. Laskine, 'Les Doctrines économiques et sociales d'Eugène Dühring,' *Revue d'histoire des doctrines économiques et sociales* (1912) and G. Albrecht, *Eugen Dühring . . .* (1927).

6. Italy

The political and administrative structure of every nation reflects itself in the organization of its scientific work. Thus, like everything else, scientific work was highly centralized in France. In England, quite different conditions produced a similar result: we find in every field, including economics, a relatively small and closely knit group within which severe selection operated to reduce to a few the names of real significance. Such structures are easy to describe. German economics, being much more decentralized, presented greater difficulties. Italian economics was still more decentralized. And I confess my inability to draw, in the available space, any satisfactory picture at all. All that can be said in general about the economic research, which was done during this period in the various centers of national life, is that it was not on the same level with the achievements of either the earlier times of Beccaria and Verri or the later times of Pantaleoni and Pareto. This shows in many ways, particularly in the dominating strength of foreign influence. The leads given by A. Smith, Malthus, Ricardo, and Say, whether accepted or subject to adverse criticism, were the starting points and material for work that was often able but primarily derivative. Hence also the characteristic interest both in Italian works of the past (the fifty volumes of Custodi's collection of the *Scrittori classici italiani di economia politica* appeared 1803-16) [1] and in the translation of foreign works (the 1st and 2nd series of the *Biblioteca dell'Economista* appeared, 1850-68). This is all the more remarkable because examination of available facts reveals plenty of ability in the personnel of Italian economics. By way of illustration, I mention two men of conspicuous brilliance, Rossi and Scialoja, whose careers also point to the cause—we know it already and it is always the same story—of the relative weakness of the scientific performances of strong men.[2] Two examples of

[1] In Spain we find the same phenomenon; Juan Sempere y Guarinos' *Biblioteca española economico-politica* was published 1801-21.

[2] I wish I could draw a picture of Pellegrino Rossi (1787-1848), whose failures in his many political activities reveal more ability than do the successes of other people. This Italian, who became a Swiss constitutional reformer and professor of Roman history, then a professor of economics and constitutional law in Paris and a Peer of France, then French ambassador to Rome, and then again Papal prime minister, produced among other things a *Cours d'économie politique* (1840-54; the 3rd and 4th vols.

relative weakness of performance in economics that were simply due to width of range are Valeriani and Romagnosi.[3]

More concentrated effort produced significant performance in the cases of Gioja and Fuoco in the earlier and of Messedaglia in the later part of the period. Gioja's [4] work may be described best as an attempt to rewrite the *Wealth of Nations* from the standpoint of the united Italy he visualized. Pearls are hidden in an unprofitable heap of rubbish—that is partly redeemed, however, by the statistical work it contains. It is easier to do justice to Fuoco.[5] He was a theorist of note who does not merit oblivion. In some pieces, for example the one on the use of the concept of limits in economics, he displayed considerable originality. His conception of economic equilibrium in some respects marked progress beyond Say's. He is regularly mentioned in Italian histories—mainly, however, in connection with his preoccupation with the theory of rent—but seems to have exerted no influence at all. This was different with Messedaglia.[6] I have chosen him for mention because of the

were published posthumously) that merited its success but does not merit any further mention in a history of analysis. All the vast cultural horizons, all the practical insights that show throughout, do not alter the fact that, analytically, it was diluted Ricardianism plus a little Say. Antonio Scialoja (1817-77) wrote a nondescript *I principii della economia sociale* (1840)—that was, however, very well written and correspondingly successful—and not much else. But he was 23 when this text came out! What could a man have done who was able to accomplish such a feat in the absence of politics, public service, and so on, all interspersed with imprisonment, exile, cabinet office.

[3] L. M. Valeriani (1758-1828) was something of a polyhistor and much admired in his time and country. The little steam he reserved for economics was put to good use, however, in his theory of prices (*Del prezzo delle cose tutte mercantili,* 1806), which could have taught Senior and Mill how to handle supply and demand functions. Italian historiography credits him (and Scialoja) with having used mathematics. But his (and Scialoja's) merit in this respect hardly goes much beyond the perception of a great possibility. Other Italians perceived this possibility, e.g. Fuoco. G. D. Romagnosi's (1761-1835) name survives in the history of law and criminology. He was also a philosopher and something of a mathematician and physicist. But his economic philosophies, which were of an anti-*étatiste* but equalitarian nature, are not worth our while—they may be described as the foothills of Italian utilitarianism.

[4] Melchiorre Gioja (1767-1829). *Opere principali* (all I know) were posthumously edited, 1838-40.

[5] Francesco Fuoco (1777-1841), *Saggi economici* (1825-7) and *Introduzione . . . dell'economia industriale* (1829). Another interesting piece of work that holds a position in the long controversy on the productivity of credit, *Magia del credito svelata,* was published in 1824, in pursuance of a curious business transaction by Welz, who posed as the author.

[6] Angelo Messedaglia (1820-1901) was professor of law and later on of economics and statistics in Padua and Rome. His quiet professorial life, which suffered interruption by political activity for a brief period only, had its share in his achievement as had his bent for patient research. But the divine spark was not lacking. He affords an excellent example for the study of the particular combination of gifts, tastes, and circumstances that make for solid scientific success and are adequate for reaching any ranks but the

strategic position he holds in the history of Italian economics and statistics. Maffeo Pantaleoni expressed, I believe, the opinion of a large majority of the Italian profession when he wrote that Messedaglia was one of the three men—the other two being Cossa and Ferrara—whose teaching formed 'all' (?) Italian economists of the subsequent period in which Italian economics was again to shine so brightly. This solid achievement rests on no one of his individual performances taken by itself, though most of them are of a high order of scholarship, for example, his monographs on public loans, population —only those two belong to the period—statistical theory, and money. More than by their individual contributions to their subjects, they influenced as messages of the spirit of scholarship and as examples of research that refuses to serve the day. We add Nazzani for the same reason that justifies inclusion of Cairnes with the English economists of the period—he was perhaps the most eminent Italian exponent of 'classic' theory and his chief contributions belong here in spite of their dates.[7]

Besides being woefully incomplete,[8] this sketch suffers also from the impossibility of giving due weight to the factual work done by Italian economists, particularly on agricultural problems including problems of ownership and tenancy, which would affect our impression considerably. But little can be done about this. Of texts, I shall mention, besides Scialoja's, also Boccardo's and the one I personally like best, de Cesare's.[9] The most conspicuous figure of Italian economics of that period and perhaps for twenty years beyond it, Ferrara, I left to the last. He was a great leader. He formed a school of his own. But affection and admiration for him has crystallized so as to lend to his figure enlarged dimensions.

Francesco Ferrara (1810-1900) was primarily a scholar and teacher. But he was also a politician who played his role in the formation of a united Italy and in the task of organizing the new national state. I mention those activities and also his passionate interest in the issues of economic policy for two reasons. First, they explain why, like Ricardo, he speaks to us from a pedestal that did not consist of scientific achievement

highest. Any work of reference will supply the reader with a list of his publications, a few of which will be mentioned later on.

[7] Emilio Nazzani (1832-1904), *Sulla rendita fondiaria* (1872), republished with three other essays (wages, profit, English 'classics') in one volume, 1881.

[8] One of the many lacunae may be filled by mentioning the history of Italian economics, *Storia della economia pubblica in Italia* (1829), by Conte Pecchio, whom McCulloch—of all men—reproached for national bias!

[9] G. Boccardo (1829-1904), *Trattato teorico-pratico di economia politica* (1853), the answer to the student's prayer before exams. Another Millian treatise. Carlo de Cesare's (1824-82) *Manuale di economia pubblica* (1862), though also 'classic' fundamentally, was something more than that, much broader and deeper than Boccardo's. It was the work of an eminent man whose bibliography includes many an excellent report on many a thorny question—of one of those men who are invaluable servants to their nations, indeed so entirely given to this service that knowledge would never advance by a yard if there were not other mental types.

alone: Italians may well revere the great economist as one of the founding fathers of their state. Second, those activities and his attitudes in discussion of practical issues are very revelatory of his character: we behold a man of the most punctilious honor and conscience, impervious to any temptation—in environments that offered many—a single-minded lover of his nation, uncompromising to a fault; but we also behold a doctrinaire of almost unbelievable inflexibility. Economically and politically he was an ultra-liberal in the sense defined in the second chapter of this Part. And the slightest deviation from this ultra-liberalism was anathema to him. In this respect, like many liberals, he was tyrannically intolerant —a godsend for the opponent who knows how to make use of this trait. He never seems to have so much as tried to understand any standpoint but his own. *Sozialpolitik* simply roused his wrath. This is relevant for us because as he was in politics, so he was in science. He entertained an uncritical confidence in the powers of economic theory: hence the historical school, also, simply roused his wrath. Such leadership evidently has its dangers. But we must not forget its merits. Strength of conviction convinces. And it can hardly avoid one-sidedness and narrowness. Ferrara carried the flag of economic theory over an arid stretch of ground, keeping it alive, inculcating interest in it as only ardor can, stimulating his audiences, preparing the ground for better things to come. This was his achievement and it was great indeed. But his own exploits in the realm of theoretical analysis were, all the compliments of later writers and all efforts at favorable interpretation notwithstanding, distinctly unsuccessful. He saw clearly enough that economic phenomena and problems form a coherent set and that it is the theory of value which unifies them. But as the principle of this theory of value he adopted Cost of Reproduction in terms of labor, a principle that can be made general only by the most desperate twists of logic and, in any case, tells us little more than the old cost-of-production principle does if properly stated. There would be no point in singling out for criticism examples of impossible pieces of reasoning. Let us rather admire the strategist who won victories with such defective equipment and add that both his learned discussions of older authors and his pieces on banks, government fiat money, and other subjects contain many valuable things. His most important work, the *Esame storico-critico di economisti e dottrine economiche del secolo XVIII e prima metà del XIX* (1889-90) has been mentioned above. For a much more favorable appraisal, see Professor G. H. Bousquet's brilliant sketch, 'Un grand économiste Italien, Francesco Ferrara,' *Revue d'histoire économique et sociale*, vol. XIV, 1926, and also the introduction and notes to Ferrara's *Oeuvres économiques choisies* (ed. by G. H. Bousquet and J. Crisafulli, 1938).

7. United States

For the preceding period, we found that the small economic literature of the United States did not quite deserve the low opinion that a majority of American economists seem to entertain about it. For the period under survey, however, the opinion that Dunbar expressed in 1876, namely, that American literature had contributed 'nothing towards developing the theory of political economy'[1] has not been invalidated by the information made available by more recent research. It is indeed not true if we take account of problems raised, suggestions made, and factual work done, but it is true if we emphasize the word theory. Since this is the opinion prevailing in the profession, our account can be brief. Before presenting it, I wish to ask the question why that should have been so.

Minds that are unfamiliar with the sociology of scientific effort take it for granted that analysis follows the practical problem or, to put it differently, that it is induced by the needs of life. But in this case there were plenty of practical problems and they were eagerly discussed, sometimes with a degree of passion that was quite out of proportion to their importance. Nevertheless, we find hardly more than traces of an impulse to develop analytic tools for dealing with them. Moreover, there was plenty of demand for economic teaching—the quantity demanded was much greater than was the supply of competent teachers—which called forth courses and textbooks in response. One would think that giving a course or writing a textbook would induce a man to do at least a little thinking for himself, and that it would be difficult for a man to do either without asking himself when reviewing his derivative material: 'Could I not do better than this?' But evidently this is not so: the demand for courses and textbooks produced courses and textbooks and not much else. Does this not show that there is something to one of the theses of this book, namely, that need is not the necessary and sufficient condition

[1] C. F. Dunbar (1830-1900), 'Economic Science in America, 1776-1876,' *North American Review*, 1876, reprinted in his *Economic Essays* (1904). For more information that I am going to present, the reader is referred to E. R. A. Seligman, 'Economics in the United States,' two articles that are combined into a chapter of his *Essays in Economics* (1925); F. A. Fetter, 'The Early History of Political Economy in the United States,' *Proceedings of the American Philosophical Society*, 1943. Among other American publications on the subject, I wish to mention particularly J. R. Turner, *The Ricardian Rent Theory in Early American Economics* (1921); and the useful bibliographies in M. J. L. O'Connor, *Origins of Academic Economics in the United States* (1944). The most important non-American contribution seems to me to be E. Teilhac, *Pioneers of American Economic Thought in the Nineteenth Century* (trans. from the French by E. A. J. Johnson, 1936), a scholarly book that I feel all the more bound to recommend because its approach so completely differs from mine. [Had J. A. S. completed his History, he would have added Joseph H. Dorfman's *Economic Mind in American Civilization*, of which the first two vols. (1946) cover the period 1606-1865, and the third vol. (1949) the period 1865-1918.]

of analytic advance and that demand for teaching produces teaching and not necessarily scientific achievement? The solution of the riddle seems simple, however. We have it as soon as we observe that absence of creative research was not peculiar to American economics of that period. We find the same state of things elsewhere, for example, in the fields of mathematics and theoretical physics where there is nothing to record until we reach the lonely peak that was Willard Gibbs—although there was no lack of technological problems, some of which, moreover, were solved with striking success. This suggests a common cause, and I do not see how we can avoid finding it in the conditions of the country and the aptitudes of her men: the task of exploiting the possibilities of the natural environment—which, given the social structure, presented itself in the form of unparalleled opportunities for business enterprise—both *absorbed* the creative talent of the country and *drew* to it talent of this type. Circles that did cultivate intellect and scholarship were quantitatively unimportant and sterile in scientific initiative. This, I believe, agrees with what Dunbar meant to convey, although he expressed himself in a manner that invites objection.[2]

But I have emphasized the word theory, and what I meant by it was analytic apparatus. No such emphasis is needed in the cases of any of the textbooks I know, for they were commonplace, and worse, in any and every respect. Teaching fed mainly on McCulloch and Say, and where home-grown texts were used, it was McCulloch and Say again, except for some contributions of the Carey school.[3] But as regards the most significant figure in that period's

[2] Professor F. A. Fetter (op. cit., preceding footnote) has in fact objected to an explanation by 'environment' (rightly, of course, because the word itself explains nothing) and replaced 'environment' by two other factors: 'false authority' (of the English 'classics') and interested partisanship 'which blocks the path to disinterested scientific effort.' But the first of these factors needs to be explained in turn: for the hold of authority, false or not, is not a matter of course; the creative mind does not submit to authority; and, following this line, we are led back to the environment that either does not contain scientific talent or else absorbs it into other pursuits. As regards the partisan spirit, it was surely not absent in England, where economic analysis did flourish all the same. Nor does it in itself interfere with scientific effort. Finally, with great respect for Professor Fetter's high authority, I beg leave to remark that professors are not exempt from bias and that I sense some in the attitude of many excellent men to the nationalist school: surely, another interpretation may be put on the protectionist views of American economists of that and later times than subservience to either pecuniary interests or prejudice.

[3] On Say's success in the United States and also on his influence upon Carey, see Teilhac, op. cit.; the Prinsep translation of Say's *Traité* was first published in 1821. An American edition of McCulloch was published by J. McVickar, the first incumbent of the chair of political economy at Columbia. Destutt de Tracy was introduced to the American public, by no less a personage than Jefferson, in 1817. Of the home-grown products, the Rev. Francis Wayland's *Elements of Political Economy* (1837) was, I believe, the most successful. Having heard and read a number of scathing comments about it, I experienced something like agreeable surprise when I read it.

American economics, Carey,[4] that restrictive emphasis upon theory is very much needed. For he lacked creativeness only in that respect. And his case points an interesting moral about what technical deficiency may do to a man's reputation in the long run: [5] Carey's name has no doubt suffered much more from political animosity than from that deficiency; but nobody could have treated him with contempt had he stated his case with tolerable competence.

Carey's idea of the fundamental unity of all science—a sort of generalized Comtism—was not the idea of a man whose intellectual life is enclosed by tariff walls. The man who propounded once more the fundamental sameness of scientific law in all departments of knowledge was no doubt wrong; but there was an element of greatness in his errors. And the man who could conceive of the United States as a world unto itself, with all this implies economically, morally, culturally, had no doubt the gift of grand vision in the same sense as had List. In the light of this vision, his protectionism and his 'harmony' of agricultural, manufacturing, and commercial interests—his conception of a 'balanced' economy—acquire a new significance and one that is completely overlooked by all those who saw nothing in him but a mouthpiece of the business class. We need not like that protectionism and we need not like Carey's whole vision. In particular, we may feel that the United States would be a happier place and would have attained a higher cultural level by now if a larger part of the country's energies had gone into other than business pursuits and if, in consequence, her industrial development had been slower. This, however, is a matter of personal evaluation and does not excuse us from recognizing that Carey's was a great vision and that, in most respects, this vision expressed adequately both the situation and the spirit of the country. Moreover, we cannot excuse ourselves from recognizing that this vision

[4] For a list of his more important followers, see F. A. Fetter, op. cit. p. 56n. They—and presumably others—formed a school in our sense and also had personal contact with the Master, which was how they referred to him. The school was called and also called itself 'nationalist,' but it should be observed that this term entirely lacked the connotation of aggressiveness it has today.

[5] Henry C. Carey's (1793-1879) economic opinions were in part conditioned by those of his father, Mathew, who already felt himself to be the leader of a 'nationalist school.' Of the son's works, those that are most important for us are: *Essay on the Rate of Wages . . .* (1835; this first economic piece of his already displays his characteristic weakness on the side of analysis); *Principles of Political Economy* (1837-40); *The Past, the Present, and the Future* (1848); *The Harmony of Interests, Agricultural, Manufacturing, and Commercial* (1851); *Principles of Social Science* (1858-9); and *Unity of Law* (1872). This list neglects his writings on money and credit and several other things. The next to the last item is the one read and suffices for those who do not wish to make a thorough-going study of Carey. We need not go into the Carey literature beyond mentioning again his German admirer, Dühring. J. S. Mill described his *Principles of Social Science* as the 'worst book on political economy I ever toiled through' (G. O'Brien, 'J. S. Mill and J. E. Cairnes,' *Economica*, November 1943, p. 274) and said that he never met with 'such an apparatus of facts and reasonings in which the facts were so untrustworthy and the interpretations of facts so perverse and absurd' (ibid. p. 280).

was independent of its deplorable analytic implementation and capable of being implemented more satisfactorily. This, however, is precisely what Carey's critics refused to recognize. Most of them were more or less well-trained economists. They had no difficulty in showing that Carey's theory was no good at all. And, on the strength of this, they condemned his message without making it clear—and presumably without being aware of the fact—that the essentials of this message were beyond the range of theoretical analysis.

A comparison of Carey with the English free traders, on the one hand, and with List, on the other, will bring this out still more clearly. The English free traders and List also argued from a comprehensive social and political vision that we may or may not accept; both, moreover, argued from their respective national standpoints; both, finally, advocated policies that suited some group interests better than others. In all these respects there is no difference whatever between the cases of Carey and of either the English free traders or List except, of course, so far as our own preferences are concerned. But the English free traders implemented their visions and their politics analytically and with success—the theorem of comparative costs was a major contribution to our analytic apparatus. *This* is the reason why they may claim a place in the history of scientific analysis—not because of the advocacy of free trade per se. List made no original contribution to the analytic apparatus of economics. But he used pieces of the existing analytic apparatus judiciously and correctly. And this, too, spells *scientific* merit. Carey's case differs from both in that he made negative contributions to analysis. And my point is that this was entirely unnecessary either for the analytic implementation of the manner in which he saw American reality and problems or for the formulation of his policies, including protection, balanced economy, and all. If he lacked the gifts of the creative analyst, he could have used existing analytic tools as did List and, taking up his stand on United States data, could have argued that English views on many economic problems did not apply to American conditions and had to be modified by introducing other factual assumptions. Had he done so with a modicum of competence, his detractors would still have retained all the ammunition in the arsenal of politics, but he would have been all right on the scientific front.

He was, however, unable to distinguish the theoretical from the factual element in English free-trade teaching and distinguished neither from the element of political volition. He saw only the practical recommendations and naïvely thought that they followed from theoretical premisses which it was therefore incumbent upon him to demolish, root and branch.[6] Instead of saying simply that 'pressure of population' was, for the calculable future, evidently of no importance in the United States, he entered upon an infelicitous attempt to refute the Malthusian theory. Instead of saying simply that the most important practical—social and political—implications of the 'Ricardian' theory of rent did not apply in a new country, he argued ineptly (in the *Principles*

[6] It will be seen that he thus committed the same mistake that was committed by his free-trade critics.

of *Social Science*, 1858-9, not before) that this theory was totally invalid because cultivation did not typically proceed from richer to poorer soils, but from poorer to richer.[7] Instead of simply emphasizing the fact that under conditions of rapid development, rising cost curves are incessantly shifting downward so that the Ricardian theorem that equates prices to the cost of the 'least favored' producer loses much of its practical importance, he discussed decreasing and increasing costs as if they embodied conflicting propositions about the same phenomenon. And in his highest flight, his theory of value, he blundered so catastrophically as to crush its one good point. This theory is a labor-quantity theory that contains the improvement that it is not the labor quantity actually invested in a commodity but the labor quantity necessary for reproducing it that determines its value.[8] He observed that this quantity falls rapidly in the course of technological progress. And from this he inferred that labor's relative share must increase in the course of technological progress—which, besides being actually false, does not follow from the logic of his argument. In this case, it is particularly clear that what he strove to express was by no means wholly wrong: a competent theorist could have worked it up into a valuable contribution; but he made it read wholly wrong because he was unable to find for it the correct expression. There is no need to go on. But one interesting question remains. Plenty of people admired Carey's diagnosis of American reality and shared his views on economic policy and his enthusiasms. A prize, in terms of success and reputation, awaited the man who could have weeded the errors from his volumes and put his system into a defensible shape. Moreover, this prize was not hidden—and there were followers for whom it would have been the most natural thing in the world to pick it up. Why did nobody try? Well, opportunity is only a necessary and not a sufficient condition for a great performance. It does not of itself produce the man capable of using it. And the brains that could have done the job were producing boots.

However, though nobody undertook the task in all its wide dimensions and though nobody undertook it effectively even in any of its parts, a number of writers did attempt it within a narrower compass and with inadequate force. These writers were not all of them forerunners or followers of Carey. Nor did they form any school in our sense of the term. But, reasoning as they did on the same data and problems and, to some extent, in the same spirit, they produced publications that have some affinity with Carey's as well as a certain family likeness between one another. Some of them described their economics as American Political Economy, and this phrase may be fittingly applied to all of them. They were all more or less protectionist. But the family likeness

[7] The reader will realize, of course, that it is not his assertion about historical fact that condemns Carey as a thinker—for it is possible to put up a case for his theory that, historically, poorer soils are cultivated before richer ones: this may occur for more reasons than one—but his belief that this assertion, true or false, is relevant to the Ricardian theory.

[8] This theory, which Carey elaborated in his *Principles of Political Economy* (1837-40), differs essentially from Ferrara's theory of cost of reproduction.

extends beyond this feature to others that are more relevant to us, namely, to the features of their modest analytic apparatus that was for the most part derived, by either acceptance or criticism, from A. Smith. There was, however, no first-rate man among them, and they made next to nothing of the great opportunity before them. Nor did they attain any dominant position. Accordingly, they do not dominate the following list, which offers, I believe, a fairly representative sample of that period's United States economists: Raymond, Everett, Tucker, Bowen, and Amasa Walker.[9] If we like, we can include in American performances also List's early book, which was a typical product of the American environment, and possibly also John Rae's great work, which was discussed in the first section of this chapter. Of course, this excludes writings on money and banking and the still more important factual work that was done by United States economists.

8. Factual Work

In the course of the review above, we have repeatedly had occasion to commend the admirable factual work done by men who are usually classed as 'general economists' or even as theorists only but who are not fully understood unless the proportion of their time and energy that went into the hunt for, and the presentation of, facts is taken into account. Let us glance once more at a selection of relevant names, great and small: Blanqui, Chalmers, Chevalier, Garnier, Gioja, Malthus, Messedaglia, McCulloch, Mangoldt, James Mill (*History of India*), Roscher, Senior, Storch, and Thünen. This list, which could easily be lengthened, suffices to show that the economics of the period under survey, taken as a whole, was anything but the speculative thing it is sometimes made out to be and that the opinion—the source of much pointless controversy—that the economics profession then neglected factual research is utterly unfounded. The opposite opinion would in fact be nearer to the truth:

[9] For a more favorable appraisal than is implied in my way of mentioning Daniel Raymond (1786-1849), who wrote *Thoughts on Political Economy* (1820; 2nd ed., entitled *Elements of Political Economy*, 1823) see Teilhac, op. cit. The difference is largely accounted for by Professor Teilhac's emphasis upon the economic-thought aspect of Raymond's work, which is indeed more interesting than is his analysis. The presence of analytic effort must, however, be recognized. He produced a theory of capital (in the intermediate-goods sense) that, considering its date, is not without merit. On A. H. Everett's chief performance, see below, ch. 6. George Tucker (1775-1861) wrote, among other things, *Laws of Wages, Profits, and Rent Investigated* (1837); for other contributions of this not insignificant economist, see below, sec. 8b and ch. 7, sec. 3. Francis Bowen's *American Political Economy* (1870; first publ. as *Principles of Political Economy applied to the Condition, the Resources, and the Institutions of the American People*, 1856) stands here only because of its title. Amasa Walker's (1799-1875; father of Francis A. Walker) *Science of Wealth* (1866) must be mentioned as a representative performance of the 'non-American' line of United States economics. Perusal of the book will give the reader a good idea of what this economics then had to offer. For the rest, the reader finds all he needs for further study in Seligman, op. cit.

many of the shortcomings of the 'classic' analytic apparatus find their most natural explanation on the hypothesis that the amount of work bestowed upon it was inadequate, whereas it is not possible for us to level the analogous criticism at the period's factual work, especially if we include, as we must, the work of economic historians and of the students of legal institutions that we have sampled already in the preceding chapter. This section will present additional examples of important types of factual work and thus help to round off our picture and to establish our thesis that the 'classic' period fully maintained the tradition of factual research that, as we know, harks back to the sixteenth century.

[(a) *Tooke's* History of Prices.] Of particular interest to us is the type of analysis that combines presentation and explanation of facts in such a way that the two cease to be distinct tasks and mutually condition one another at every step: the type of analysis that arrives at its results by means of discussing individual situations. We must be content to notice the peak achievement of this genus, the *History of Prices and of the State of the Circulation from* 1792 *to* 1856 by Tooke and Newmarch.[1] A better title would have been: Analysis of England's Economic Processes from 1792 to 1856, with Special Reference to the Condition of the Currency and of Credit. Jevons called it 'unique,' and so it is. Never before or after has that method been used on an equally large scale, or, so far as influence upon purely theoretical research is concerned, with similar effect. Whether the authors handled it as well as they might have done is another question. I am not alluding to the fact that, of course, they argued for one policy and, still more obviously, against another: this does not impair the value of either their facts or their reasoning, both of which may be appreciated by any opponent of their views concerning desirabilities. Nor am I alluding to the discursiveness and repetitiveness of their work: in 'realistic' theory of this type neither is without its function—the

[1] Thomas Tooke (1774-1858) was the author of all six volumes, if the term 'author' is taken in the sense of the Latin *auctor*. But only the first four volumes (1st and 2nd, 1838; 3rd, 1840; 4th, 1848) were substantially his work, the collaborators playing the role of research assistants. The last two volumes (1857) were mainly the work of William Newmarch (1820-82), who, though greatly influenced by Tooke, holds his place in his own right. Newmarch, besides being one of the more important critics of Peel's Act and the doctrines of the 'currency school,' was a leading member of the Royal Statistical Society, and the originator of the *Economist* index number and the same journal's 'Annual Commercial History.' As regards index numbers (which, by the way, were not used in the *History of Prices*, a striking example of economists' resistance to new methods), he was not particularly original, but the 'Commercial History' is an interesting model for an interesting type of work. Economists are even today not fully alive to its scientific importance and to the methodological questions it raises, and have hardly succeeded in bringing modern theory to bear upon it or in otherwise improving upon Newmarch's performance. The *History of Prices* has been republished (1928), ed. by Sir T. E. Gregory with an introduction that fully discusses its nature and origin, and should be carefully perused by the reader. This reference is to replace a survey of the various writings of Tooke's that paved the way toward the *History*.

method is essentially one of 'thrashing out' things, and this cannot be done with Ricardian brevity. I am alluding to more fundamental defects of which no trained reader of these volumes can fail to become aware very quickly. Both authors were no doubt deficient in command of economic theory. Tooke was in addition a somewhat 'woolly' thinker—who often impaired his case by missing the opponent's point. And this told. Not only did his arguments sometimes call forth derogatory comment, that was quite justified as far as it went; but also, his authority, great as it was in his day and as it remained for the rest of the century, was never what it might have been had there been more theoretical edge to his thought. The work is nevertheless a classic and an example to follow. But it seems to cry out for rewriting by a better-trained or else a more adroit hand.

[(b) *Collection and Interpretation of Statistical Materials.*] Though anything but a novelty, work of the kind of which Tooke's and Newmarch's is an outstanding instance was in that period powerfully propelled by the opening up of new sources of statistical figures. Those were the times when governments began to establish statistical bureaus and commissions; when the first attempts were made at international co-operation (the first international statistical congress met in 1853); when statistical societies emerged almost everywhere—in England, for instance, several were founded in the 1830's, of which the Statistical Society of London (1834) was presently chartered as the Royal Statistical Society.[2] To a great extent the compilation, from the raw material provided by the official bureaus, of presentable statistical records remained the task of individual investigators, as it had been in the preceding period, especially but not exclusively of the men who by virtue of their official position were able to command the requisite assistance. But these investigators were no mere diggers. They did not confine themselves to marshalling data and to developing estimates: many of them also offered interpretations. And so we find, flowing from this source, another stream of work that differed indeed from Tooke's and Newmarch's in that it started from the statistical material instead of from the economic problem and, in consequence, emphasized the statistical information per se more than had Tooke and Newmarch. But, though sometimes only as a by-product, they turned out analytic work as well.

Attention has been called, in our survey of pre-Smithian times, to what may be described as analyses of the economic state of a country. In the period under discussion, this line of research produced a number of performances for which Colquhoun's, Porter's, and Tucker's will serve as examples.[3] They—

[2] The American Statistical Association was organized in 1838.

[3] Of Patrick Colquhoun's (1745-1820) many writings, only two need be mentioned, his *Treatise on the Population, Wealth, Power, and Resources of the British Empire* . . . (1814), unintelligently sneered at by McCulloch, and the anonymously published *Considerations on the Means of affording Profitable Employment to the Redundant Population of Great Britain and Ireland* (1818). The first is particularly important, not so much because of its estimates of national wealth, but because of the economic reasoning, however primitive, which is offered in explanation of the facts presented, and of the

and others of the same type—no doubt suffer from the fact that their authors did not know how to use economic theory as a tool of factual analysis; but as far as this goes they are in the same boat with modern publications of this kind. Other types of that period's statistical economics will be represented by the names of McCulloch, Baxter, Dieterici, Villermé, Le Play, and Wells.

McCulloch's (see sec. 2 above) most significant statistical work, his *Dictionary, Practical, Theoretical, and Historical of Commerce and Commercial Navigation*, 1832 —a heroic labor—is in spite of its dictionary form, a treatise in which facts and analysis intertwine very effectively. This was the kind of thing at which he was really good —the man should in fact not be judged by his *Principles* alone.

Robert D. Baxter (1827-75) was an economist of major importance. His careful and competent handling of his figures, and his much quoted estimates (of national income and wealth), admirable though they are, constitute the least important of his services to economic analysis. Of much greater interest for us are his bold ventures into the statistical theory of the benefits that accrue to the public from railroads and of the pressure and incidence of taxation (for which purpose he also collected family budgets). These studies are not faultless, mainly because he was weak on the pure-theory side, but the mere fact that he made a serious attempt to answer numerically such questions as how the burden of rates divides itself between landlord and tenant should secure for him a place in the history of econometrics. I want to refer especially to: *The Budget and the Income Tax* (1860); *Results of Railway Extension* (1866); *National Income: the United Kingdom* (1868); *The Taxation of the United Kingdom* (1869). *In Memoriam* by his widow is well worth reading.

Karl F. W. Dieterici (1790-1859) was a professor of Political Economy (*Staatswissenschaft*) and director of the Prussian Statistical Bureau in Berlin. *Statistische Übersicht der wichtigsten Gegenstände des Verkehrs und Verbrauchs im preussischen Staate und im deutschen Zollverbande . . .* (1838-57). Also important: *Der Volkswohlstand im preussischen Staate . . .* (1846) and *Über preussische Zustände, über*

---

attempt to state and to solve problems—to paraphrase factually, as it were, the more popular doctrines of the times.

On a larger scale, and with greater success, this was also done by George R. Porter, a civil servant and for some time chief of the statistical department of the Board of Trade. His *Progress of the Nation in its Various Social and Economical Relations, from the beginning of the Nineteenth Century to the Present Time* (1836-43) has received deserved credit as the standard record of English economic development during the first half of the nineteenth century, i.e. as a source book of economic facts and figures. As such it has been remodeled—very freely indeed—and continued by Mr. F. W. Hirst and his associates (1912). But this is not what matters for us. The relevant point is that the work, as originally planned and executed, is really a treatise of general economics, dealing successively with population, production, interchange, public finance, consumption, accumulation, moral progress, and colonies in a manner not entirely dissimilar to Mill's *Principles*, of which, in a sense, it ought to be considered as the companion volume: in particular neither Mill's free trade nor Porter's free trade is complete without the other.

George Tucker has been mentioned already and will have to be mentioned again. The work of his that is relevant here is: *Progress of the United States in Population and Wealth in Fifty Years* (1843; 2nd ed., 1855). It is mainly a study in U.S. demography. For us, however, more important is the fact that it is also a study in economic analysis.

Arbeit und Kapital (1848). His delightful serenity in matters of 'method' deserves to be recorded. His lecture *De via et ratione oeconomiam politicam docendi* (1835), though stressing quite reasonably the fundamental importance of the historical aspects of the economic process, arrives at the result which might be said to sum up, by anticipation, all that ever came of the methodological squabble of a century: *et mere philosophando et mere experiendo erratur.* And he showed his good sense by extolling Ricardo's attention to facts. Though he never embarked upon a venture as comprehensive as Porter's, his neat and trustworthy publications of the results of the statistical bureau he directed are glorified by his grasp of the needs of scientific economics that enabled him to pick out fertile projects. Thus, his statistics of consumption continue to this day to render assistance to analysis.[4]

The work that justifies the inclusion in our sketch of the name of Louis R. Villermé (1782-1863), who was not exclusively, or even primarily an economist, is his investigation, undertaken as a research project (quite as such things are done today) under the Académie des Sciences Morales et Politiques, into the conditions of labor in several French manufacturing industries: *Tableau de l'état physique et moral des ouvriers employés dans les manufactures de coton, de laine, et de soie* (1840). His recommendations (protection to children) do not interest us here. The work is important as an outstanding instance of a large class, in which method of procedure has hardly made any progress at all since that time.

P. G. Frédéric Le Play (1806-82), mathematician and mining engineer by training and professor of metallurgy by vocation, figures here and not in the next period although some of the publications and activities that made his international fame belong to the latter. The Société Internationale des Études Pratiques d'Économie Sociale, which was founded by Le Play in 1856, started the publication of a fortnightly review, *Réforme sociale*, in 1881. The work that is relevant to our purpose was done during the period under discussion: *Les Ouvriers européens* (1st ed., 1855; 2nd ed., 1877-9). He was not a technical economist and heartily despised the misunderstood bits of economics he knew. Nevertheless, he deserves a place in the history of economic analysis because of his method of studying family budgets that may some day help to bring into existence a theory of consumption worthy of the name. It consists in an immensely painstaking investigation of a limited number of individual cases, each considered as intensively as possible, in the whole setting of its social, moral, and cultural conditions. We cannot go into the program of social betterment that is associated with the name of that great man. But he formed a school that is associated with that program and continues work along that line.

As has been mentioned already, statistical economics flourished in the United States, and from the famous Hamilton *Report on Manufactures* (1791) to the end of the period we observe an ever-broadening stream of such publications. However, we shall be content to add another illustrative instance, namely, the earlier work of D. A. Wells—his later and much better-known work belongs to the next period.[5] He turned to eco-

[4] Among other things, they established the fundamental fact that the consumption of the masses may fall in *cyclical* upswings (that it may fall in prolonged spells of inflation is of course common knowledge).

[5] David A. Wells (1828-98) was a geologist and chemist who had published a successful textbook in each of these subjects before he took to economics and the civil service during the Civil War. The two publications that should be mentioned here

nomics in his early middle age, attracted by his interest in the practical questions of his day and country, and our analytic apparatus owes nothing to him. Yet he was a significant economist whose works repay study even today. He was a master of the art of making the most of imperfect material.[6] Moreover, his sound and conscientious mind enabled him to represent the elements of a situation in their right perspective without precisely knowing why: his was that sound practical judgment in which many of the best theorists are woefully deficient and which was to show up to still greater effect in some of his later publications.

Of course, all that I have been able to present in this section is a scatter of instances that in addition may not have been the best to choose. Thus, barring what is implied in mentioning Tooke and Newmarch and also Senior, I have entirely neglected all the *scientific* economics to be found in English official reports. It is hoped, however, that even these bits of information will help the reader to form a correct idea of the scientific situation of that period. But the question must, I suppose, arise in his mind how, under the circumstances described, it was *possible* for even the most unfair of critics to speak of undue preponderance of 'theoretical speculation.' The only answer I have to offer is this. Criticism of scientific economics comes to a great extent from ignorant outsiders, and these ignorant outsiders include many individuals who call themselves economists. This fact alone makes it understandable that criticism mistook the significance of a feature of that period's economic work that we have noticed before. Economics then gained the status of an established field. This meant, among other things, greater specialization not only of individuals but also of publications and the emergence of purely theoretical treatises. It is hardly possible to overlook the factual complement in the *Wealth of Nations*—though some critics seem to have accomplished even this feat—and it is still less possible to overlook the factual work in Vauban's *Dixme royale*. But if an economist, such as Senior, chooses to deal with the analytic apparatus of economics separately, then it is much easier to overlook his factual work—especially if it be hidden in commission reports—and thus, comparing the *Outline* with the *Wealth* (which is of course absurd), to arrive at the discovery that there is a methodological gulf between the two and that Senior was indulging in pure speculation whereas A. Smith was keeping his eyes upon historical fact.

[(c) *Development of Statistical Methods.*] The groups of workers in any department of scientific knowledge should not perhaps be compared to the corps of an army. For the latter, at least in principle, move according to some plan, whereas the scientific groups are essentially unco-ordinated: one group

are: the famous *Our Burden and our Strength* (1864) and his *Reports of the Special Commissioner of the Revenue* (1866-9).

[6] Professor Kuznets has told me that Wells's estimates of national income are deserving of confidence which, considering the data at his disposal, represents an even greater feat than Baxter's, who had at least income-tax data to go on.

rushes on, the others lag behind, and each fails to give support to the others or to avail itself of the possible support it could derive from them. The progress in statistical method illustrates this. We have already noticed that there was considerable advance on the probability front. We should add to this the Gaussian law of error and the method of least squares, achievements that meant an important addition to the economist's box of tools. However, nothing to speak of came of this opportunity during this period in which, on the contrary, the statistician's pure theory and the economist's pure theory were almost completely divorced—to remain divorced until our own day. I wonder if I can create in my reader's mind the proper feeling of surprise at this. Let us for this purpose transfer ourselves into a better world and, from this better world, look at the situation of economics. We then behold a field in a large part of which reasoning is essentially and inevitably quantitative—surely all economists would have acquired a saving knowledge of mathematics. But even if they failed to see the necessity of doing this in order to improve their pure theory, would they not surely do so in order to improve their handling of statistical figures, to the importance of which, as we have just seen, they were fully alive? They would be on the lookout for new tools of statistical research and, of course, rush to use them if they were proffered, as they were being proffered, from outside. And we should expect the author of the period's leading treatise, J. S. Mill, laboring in the sweat of his brow, to acquire and to teach command of those tools. Observe that, with a profession intellectually alive and moderately conscious of the scientist's duties, there would have been nothing impossible in all this. But as a matter of fact, if we let our glance shift back to the real world, we see nothing of all this until about a century later, and even then all we see is a painful struggle to realize it. What we do see, for the period under discussion, is ignorance born of intellectual inertness or else, which comes to much the same thing, preoccupation with the practical problems of the day that life itself solved without needing any assistance. It was not quite so in demography or what is usually understood by social statistics. This is our only opportunity to mention the name of Quetelet.

Adolph Quetelet's (1796-1874) importance for our subject is small—I know of no economist of that period whose *economics* shows any traces of his influence. He was a mathematician and astronomer, and entered the field of social statistics by the door of probability. Here, so far as I can see, his merit is confined to meritorious propaganda: there is nothing original in his *Lettres à S. A. R. le duc régnant de Saxe Coburg-Gotha sur la théorie des probabilités, appliquée aux sciences morales et politiques* (1846). But he joined the brilliant band of statistical administrators who during that period led and inspired the new statistical bureaus and, with indefatigable energy, did much to improve methods and projects and especially to promote international cooperation.

He was much more than that implies, however. His vigorous and original investigations into the distribution of human characteristics mark a step in advance that had never to be retraced and, as an example to follow, had eventually also some importance for economics. But he took another step that, after a brief success, had to be retraced: he plunged into a philosophy of a sort of statistical determinism by conceiving the theory that those investigations were revealing a stable type of average man whose properties linked up with simple general 'causes,' deviations being of the nature of errors of observation in the Gaussian sense. He thus hoped to reduce, on a statistical basis, the methodology of the social to that of the physical sciences. The development of thought in this matter went wholly against this theory, and many serious workers came to consider it, perhaps more than is justified, as a mere freak. His merits concerning anthropometry are of course not affected thereby. See especially his *Sur l'homme* . . . (1835; English trans., 1842), later expanded into his *Physique sociale* . . . (1869) and, for criticisms, G. F. Knapp, 'Quetelet als Theoretiker,' and several other notes, *Jahrbücher für Nationalökonomie und Statistik* (1871-2) and Maurice Halbwachs, *La théorie de l'homme moyen* (1912).

Economists even failed to avail themselves of the most primitive devices for presenting figures. All the more necessary is it to notice the fact that at least simple charting—line, bar, circle, and pie graphs—had been introduced into economics right at the beginning of the period by Playfair.[7] Moreover, there is no excuse for the hesitation with which fact-presenting economists took to the use of price index numbers or theoretical economists to the task of providing a theory for them. We have seen that the idea had emerged before A. Smith. A great step toward full realization of the importance of the method was made in 1798, when Sir George Shuckburgh Evelyn presented a paper to the Royal Society in which, with apologies for treating a subject so much below the dignity of that august body, he used an index number—of a primitive kind no doubt but which was superior to Carli's—for measuring the 'depreciation of money.'[8] Lowe[9] added nothing to the idea of a 'tabular standard' beyond Evelyn's, but he improved the technique and recommended the use of index numbers for the purpose of 'lessening the injury from fluctuations and giving a uniform value [over time] to money income,' that is, of creating a stable unit of deferred payments—the idea that was to become so popular in the next period and still more so in the 1920's and 1930's. G. Poulett Scrope seems to have been the first to introduce the subject into a general treatise (1833).

[7] William Playfair, brother of the physicist, John Playfair, to whom he gave credit for having suggested his graphical methods, was a man of varied experience in business and economic journalism. He first introduced those methods in his *Commercial and Political Atlas* (1786), which contained 44 charts and was translated into French. His most telling graph, however, was used to illustrate his argument in *A Letter on our Agricultural Distresses;* it displays the course of the price of wheat and of wages over 250 years. See Funkhouser and Walker, 'Playfair and his Charts,' *Economic History*, February 1935, with illustrations. I owe my acquaintance with Playfair's work to this article, and know only the two publications mentioned. For others, see the bibliographical note appended to the article.

[8] *Philosophical Transactions*, 1798, Part I. Arthur Young (*Enquiry into the Progressive Value of Money in England*, 1812) was the next to follow him and the first to attack him.

[9] Joseph Lowe, *The Present State of England in regard to Agriculture, Trade and Finance* (1822), a book that seems to have met with some success and contains many interesting discussions, e.g. on population. The author is, however, very unfair to Evelyn's pioneering attempt.

CHAPTER 5

General Economics: A Cross Section

1. J. S. Mill and his *Principles*. Fawcett and Cairnes

Mill's *Principles* was not only the most successful treatise of the period under survey but also qualifies well for the role of the period's classic work *in our sense*. Having decided to choose it as headquarters from which to survey the general economics of that period, we had better begin by a preliminary glance at the man and the book.

John Stuart Mill (1806-73) was—John Stuart Mill. That is to say, he was one of the chief intellectual figures of the nineteenth century and is so familiar to every educated person that it might seem superfluous to add anything to what can be read in dozens of books. Moreover, most of what economists need to know about him has been admirably said by Sir W. J. Ashley in the introduction to his edition (1909) of the *Principles*, which I hope is in the hands of every student.[1] A few points must be touched upon all the same. Most of us have heard or read of the severe intellectual training to which James Mill, the father, subjected his son from early childhood and which,

[1] Attention is called particularly to the appendix of this edition, which puts, with substantive success, many items of Millian doctrine into their relation to contemporaneous, earlier, and even later thought, and should be carefully studied. For the rest, competent analyses of Mill's economic work are rarer than are competent appraisals of his work in philosophy and logic. But there is one that has been written by a master: Edgeworth's article—'Mill, John Stuart,' in *Palgrave's Dictionary*—on no account to be omitted. Moreover, E. Cannan's *Theories of Production and Distribution* (3rd ed., 1917), the most important individual reference for this and the next chapter, discusses Mill's economics very fully.

much more cruel and injurious than daily whippings would have been, accounts for that impression of stunted growth and lack of vital strength that comes to us from many passages in the imposing work of his life. Most of us, I suppose, also know that it was first a salary and then—after 1858—a pension from the East India Company which financed his needs (fairly comfortably), and that his duties, though not on the average very arduous, meant further injury to his thought: as has been pointed out already, not only interruption but also mere anticipation of possible interruption paralyzes creative research. Then, too, his unflagging interest in current issues caused additional interruption and loss of energy. This interest and the office combined account for the incessant hurry that all his writings display, even the one that is the most finished of all in a literary sense, the essay *On Liberty*. Finally, being all intellect and having been taught to despise any but intellectual interests—and of these all that do not come within the pale of utilitarianism, though he outgrew this part of his father's teaching as he did others—he never knew what life really is. He did create an intimate *foyer* for himself by his friendship and, later, marriage with Mrs. Taylor. But he intellectualized that too, and anyone who has an ear for the note of hysteria in the Preface to the essay *On Liberty* will need no other indications—to be gleaned, for example, from his *Autobiography*—in order to feel that he lacked many of the requisites, not indeed of the theorist but of the philosopher of social life.

We behold the picture of the purebred laicist radical. But, unlike other laicist radicals, this one never allowed indoctrination to stifle criticism. With an honesty and internal freedom that cannot be too much admired, he took the critical axe to the foundations of his laicist and utilitarian religion—for this is what it was—and, still more important, he opened the doors of his mind to any message he was able to comprehend. He tried to get on terms with the ideas of Carlyle and Coleridge; [2] he studied Saint-Simonism and Comtism profoundly; by his critique he proved how seriously he took the question raised by the Hamiltonian philosophy; and, honestly wrestling with all this and much besides, he actually allowed himself to be drawn away from his early moorings. He was the opposite of a zealot. Not only the range of his interests but also, in a sense, the range of his comprehension was quite abnormally wide.

[2] In two articles contributed to the *London and Westminster Review* (1838 and 1840, reprinted in *Dissertations and Discussions*, vol. I) J. S. Mill formulated his mature opinion on the contribution of Coleridge and his group to sociology and, by implication, on their influence upon himself. Perusal of these articles must, I think, enhance our respect for their author. Mill goes a long way toward accepting their criticism of eighteenth-century rationalism—and the 'interest philosophy of the Bentham School'—and shows himself quite open to their romanticist conception of history: in fact, I do not think that the man who wrote these articles—and the passages on James Mill's theory of government in the *Logic* (see above, ch. 3, sec. 5c)—can properly be called a utilitarian at all. But he understood technical economics too well to throw it overboard on that account. To critics who did not understand it equally well, this looked like hesitation and like endless shifting of standpoints. Actually, however, his views were, *in this respect*, perfectly consistent and, in addition, far ahead of his time.

But now I have to add a point that is extremely difficult to make and very liable to be misunderstood. You can travel far and wide and yet wear blinkers wherever you go. Mill's comprehension never went below certain layers—we have noticed this already when discussing his *Logic*—and his intellect never got over certain barriers. What was below these layers and beyond those barriers he put down as nonsense by means of the well-known trick of our subconscious apparatus of self-defense.

Of his three great works, the *Logic* (1843), the *Examination of Sir William Hamilton's Philosophy* (1865),[3] and the *Principles of Political Economy with Some of their Applications to Social Philosophy* (1848), only one is in our field. The list of his other writings [4] strengthens an impression that interests other than economics were dominant with him, since the list contains only one item that deals with questions of technical economics: *Essays on Some Unsettled Questions of Political Economy,* containing his freshest and most original contributions to economics. And in fact, if we claim him for our own, nevertheless, we must always remember in justice to the man that, after his late twenties, he never was a full-time (or even 'full leisure-time') economist except in 1845-7, when he wrote the *Principles.* As regards the influences that helped to shape his economics, those of his father and of Ricardo himself come first, of course. But I have said already, and have emphasized by my refusal to include J. S. Mill in Ricardo's school, that the economics of the *Principles* are no longer Ricardian. This is obscured by filial respect [5] and also, independently of this, by J. S. Mill's own belief that he was only qualifying Ricardian doctrine. But this belief was erroneous. His qualifications affect essentials of theory and, still more, of course, of social outlook. Ricardianism meant no doubt more to him than it did to Marshall. But Mill's and Marshall's cases are similar in that for reasons of their own, commendable or not, they stressed Ricardian influences unduly at the expense of others. From Marshall's *Principles,* Ricardianism can be removed without being missed at all. From Mill's *Principles,* it could be dropped without being missed very greatly. The influence that J. S. Mill failed to stress adequately was Say's. He did stress it in one point only, the Law of Markets. But it is present in Mill's theory of value

[3] The *Logic* and *Hamilton's Philosophy* have been discussed above in ch. 3.

[4] Any work of reference will give this list. For us, the most important items, in addition to the three above, are: the *Autobiography* (1873; two new editions by J. J. Coss, 1924, and H. Laski, 1924); *Some Unsettled Questions* (publ. 1844; written about 1829 and 1830); *On Liberty* (1859); *Considerations on Representative Government* (1861); *Utilitarianism* (1863); and *Auguste Comte and Positivism* (1865).

[5] This no doubt commendable attitude of the son also obscures the nature of the influence of the father in other respects, e.g. in respect to associationist psychology. This influence may indeed be called dominant if we mean by influence the total effect of a man's teaching upon another man. But it is not dominant at all if we count as influence only effects that show in conformity of views. In many if not in most departments of thought, the son, though still reacting to his father's opinions, arrived at different, often opposite, standpoints. On one point noticed above, it is an enemy of James Mill's teaching that speaks to us from the pages of the son.

and cost—which is essentially a compromise between Ricardo's and Say's, with all the emphasis put upon the Ricardian elements—that is to say, in the very heart of his theoretical structure. The other influence to which Mill submitted, semiconsciously and rather reluctantly, was that of Senior, who also receives explicit recognition in one point only—abstinence. There are many others, Malthus' and Rae's, for example, which Mill accepted consciously and hence recognized frankly—for he was scrupulously fair to others, always ready to give credit to them, and quite indifferent to any claims of his own. This fairness and this indifference are among the strongest and most lovable traits of his character and the remarks above on the influence of Say and Senior must not be interpreted to imply any aspersion or any doubt on this score.

Mill's declared purpose in writing the *Principles* and the performance actually embodied in it fit like hand and glove. The original preface is worth reading. He might with little change have reprinted the preface to the *Logic*. Once more, the program was to untie knots and build bridges. There is no claim to novelty or originality—though several would have been justified. Mill simply explained that there had been no equally comprehensive treatise, especially none that paid so much attention to practical applications, since the publication of the *Wealth of Nations*. This, however, was obsolete, both as regards facts and as regards theory. So he would aim at the 'sufficiently useful achievement' of writing 'a work similar in its object and general conception to that of Adam Smith, but adapted to the more extended knowledge and improved ideas of the present age' which is 'the kind of contribution which Political Economy at present requires'—and exactly the kind of book he wrote. For a man of Mill's powers and standing, modesty could not have gone further. Two comments should be added.

First, there is a side to this admirable modesty that may perhaps be held responsible for a less admirable consequence. Had Mill conceived a less modest idea of his task, he might have produced an even better book. As it was, he took his task altogether too lightly: not Hercules himself could write a *Wealth of Nations* in eighteen months, which seems to have been the actual time invested. But, as we have had occasion to remark with respect to the *Logic*, Mill, however modest on his own behalf, was not at all modest on behalf of his time. 'This enlightened age' had solved all problems. And if you knew what its 'best thinkers' thought, you were in a position to answer all questions. I do not mean to repeat what I have previously said on Mill's attitude of speaking from the vantage ground of definitively established truth. But I mean to add that this attitude, besides being ridiculous, made for sterility and—yes—superficiality. There is too little attention to groundwork. There is too little thinking-things-through and much too much confidence that most of the necessary thinking had been done already. The Smith-Mill-Marshall line is clear enough. But the middle term is not on a par with the other two, owing to relative insufficiency of labor applied. What looks like so many tergiversations or what gives the impression, energetically voiced by Marx, that Mill never says a thing without also saying its opposite is in part due to this cause. But to a greater part it is due to Mill's judicial habit of mind that forced him to consider all aspects of each question. Also, it is due to something that is still more creditable. He was a man of strong preferences. But he also was incorruptibly honest. He would not twist either facts or arguments if he could help it. When the preferences—his social sympathies—did assert themselves all the same, he was not slow to apply the pruning knife. Hence many an inconclusive result, or even many a contradiction.

Second, Mill emphasized repeatedly, though not in his preface, that his *Principles* differed from other treatises in something he ascribed to his wife's influence, namely, in moral tone or atmosphere. There is, in fact, plenty of warm-hearted humanitarianism about the book and plenty of solicitude for the welfare of the laboring class. More important, however, is a cognate aspect: he restricted the domain of inexorable law to the physical necessities to which production is subject and emphasized for all the rest, all institutions in particular, that they are man-made, changeable, malleable, and 'progressive.' There was for him no invariable natural order of things social, and economic necessity meant to him largely necessity in regard to a given state of the changing institutional frame. However much he glorified his age in other respects, the actual state of society he beheld he did not consider as either ideal or permanent. Book IV, Chapter 7 of the *Principles* and many other passages, even some of those that criticize the utopian socialism of his time, are conclusive on this point and also as regards the direction that he expected social development to take. Though repeatedly changing his position in details, he was, from about his middle twenties on, an evolutionary socialist of associationist complexion. For a history of analysis, this fact is important only in as much as it refutes the absurd indictment that 'classic' economists believed in the capitalist order as the last and highest wisdom that was bound to persist in *secula seculorum*. If it be replied that Mill was a solitary exception, the answer is that this is not true, but that, even if it were true, this exception was responsible for the most successful and most influential treatise of that age. For the sociologist of capitalism, this fact is still more interesting: nothing can be more revealing of the character of bourgeois civilization—more indicative, that is, of its genuine freedom and also of its political weakness—than that the book to which the bourgeoisie accorded such a reception carried a socialist message and was written by a man palpably out of sympathy with the scheme of values of the industrial bourgeoisie.

J. S. Mill was exactly what is meant by an evolutionary socialist. His attitude toward socialism went through a steady development, the traces of which are but imperfectly discernible in the successive editions of the *Principles*. Moreover, the three articles on socialism which Miss Helen Taylor published in the *Fortnightly Review* (1879) after Mill's death are perhaps more misleading than helpful: they were written in or about 1869 as exploratory sketches for a book on socialism which Mill then intended to write, and contain little more than critical appraisals of the French and English socialist literature prior to 1869 and of current socialist slogans; the book presumably would have contained a positive complement that might have reversed the impression the reader of these sketches is likely to get. However, neglecting all minor points, we may with some confidence describe Mill's attitude to socialism as follows. Emotionally, socialism always appealed to him. He had little taste for the society he lived in and plenty of sympathy with the laboring masses. As soon as he had gained intellectual independence, he readily opened his mind to the socialist—mainly French—ideas of his time. But, being a trained economist and thoroughly practical-minded, he could hardly fail to perceive the weaknesses of what a little later was labeled Utopian Socialism by Marx. Reluctantly and with a partial exception in favor of Saint-Simonism, he therefore arrived at the conclusion that those plans were but beautiful dreams. This was the first stage. On the face of it, a completely negative attitude to socialism—coupled with thoroughgoing radicalism in some respects, for example, with respect to property in land —might be considered compatible with what he wrote in the first edition of his *Principles*. But there is no reason to doubt his statement in the preface to the third edition (1852) which was to the effect that he never intended to 'condemn' socialism 'regarded as an ultimate result of human progress,' and that his objections merely rested on 'the unprepared state of mankind.' The alterations and emendations in the text went, however, further than this suggests (see in particular the new second paragraph of ch. 7 of Book IV) and really amount to *explicit* recognition of socialism as the Ultimate Goal. This marks a second stage. And there was a third: on the one hand, he came to believe that 'progress' was accelerating wonderfully and that this 'ultimate end' was coming rapidly within view; on the other hand, he came to believe that capitalism was near to having done its work so that purely economic objections were losing part of their force. At the same time he always stoutly denied the presence of any tendency in the capitalist system to deteriorate the condition of the working class or to reduce its relative or absolute share in the social product; and not less stoutly he refused to entertain the idea of transition by revolution, basing his argument against it mainly on what seemed to him the insuperable difficulties of management that would arise in this case. But such views *define* Evolutionary Socialism. They do not substantially differ from those which the leader of German Revisionism, E. Bernstein (see below, Part IV, ch. 5, sec. 8b), was to defend thirty years later. Naturally, they were gall and wormwood not only to Marxists but to all socialists who base their argument on the thesis of inevitably increasing misery and for whom the revolution is an essential article of faith. And Mill's teaching on the subject, precisely because it was so perfectly honest and because it expounded unpalatable truth in evident sympathy with the Ultimate End, grew much more distasteful to them than would have been straight hostility. All this is very important for understanding Mill's *Weltanschauung*—particularly for those of us who hold that a man's class interest or philosophy will determine his economic theory and his views on economic policy, and who have been taught to look upon the *Principles* as a verbalization of bourgeois ideology.

The success of J. S. Mill's *Principles* was sweeping and much more general, also much more evenly distributed over all countries in which economics received attention, than was that of Ricardo's. This was primarily due to a happy combination of scientific level and accessibility: Mill did present analysis that satisfied competent judges, yet, barring very few points that proved stumbling blocks, every economist could understand him. The book's many editions measure only its direct influence. To this must be added, so far as teaching is concerned, the litter of other textbooks it produced. Both students and general readers seem to have experienced a need for a still simpler presentation, even in England. And this demand was provided for by Fawcett.[6] On a higher level, even people who accepted Mill's claim of finality in substance could not fail to discover that many individual stones in his structure were loose. The most eminent of the English economists *of this period* who undertook to mend the structure—with debatable success—was Cairnes.[7] He

[6] Henry Fawcett's (1833-84) *Manual of Political Economy* (1863) ran through six editions in his lifetime. The heroic energy of this eminent man, who lost his eyesight at twenty-five and nevertheless taught, wrote, practiced sports, was an active and independent Member of Parliament, and even a successful cabinet minister (Postmaster-General), cannot be sufficiently admired: he rightfully commanded the highest respect of his fellow economists. He was Marshall's predecessor in the Cambridge chair. In a history of economic analysis, however, he must rank below many far lesser men and no attempt can be made to do justice to him.

[7] John E. Cairnes's (1823-75) career—if career is indeed the word to be used—as a research worker, writer, academic teacher, and, though behind the scenes, politician was marred by ill health, the obvious reason why he failed to fill to the full the measure of his great ability. Even so he attained front rank: everyone would have mentioned him when asked, after Mill's death in 1873 (Jevons not being as yet appreciated according to merit), who was England's first scientific economist. The work of his that is for us the most important, *Some Leading Principles of Political Economy Newly Expounded*, appeared in 1874. Nevertheless, we allocate its author (unlike Jevons, whose *Theory* was published earlier, i.e. 1871) to the period under survey, because he expounded the old analytic economics and explicitly distanced himself from the new, which had just emerged into the light of day—showing, in doing so, that he entirely failed to appreciate its significance and possibilities. We range him, therefore, with the 'classics' (in quotes) but not with the Ricardian school. He belongs in Mill's group and there is the same reason as in the case of Mill for not calling him Ricardian. Of course, we might have deferred notice of him until the next period and made him, with Sidgwick, Nicholson, and others, a member of the group of 'survivals.' The other work of his that matters to us is his *Character and Logical Method of Political Economy* (1857), a landmark in the history of methodology.

may be called Mill's pupil, for he always reasoned with reference to the latter's teaching—even where he did not mention the fact explicitly—and he entertained toward Mill, as his correspondence shows, feelings that can be rendered only by the term 'reverence.' [8] Nevertheless, he sometimes criticized Mill sharply and, by virtue of this criticism, constructed something that, though entirely within the Millian groundwork, was in some measure his own. He was a born, but not a very original, theorist. Though most of his contributions have been sterile, his work, both analytical and methodological, marks an important stage. In calling him a born theorist, we must not forget however—as has been forgotten by some critics, particularly of the German historical school—that the bulk of his working hours went into practical problems and that it was his 'factual' contribution (in particular his *Slave Power*, 1862), which accounts for his reputation with the English public of his time.

2. Scope and Method: What Economists Thought They Were Doing

The preceding chapter has given us some idea of what the economists of that period actually did. We shall see presently how far their work reflected itself in J. S. Mill's *Principles*. But it is one of the characteristic features of the period that economists began to interpret themselves, that is to say, to theorize on (or to 'rationalize') their own aims and procedures. In research as elsewhere we first act and then think. It is only when a field has grown into an established science that its votaries will develop an interest, not untinged with anxiety, in problems of scope and method and in logical fundaments generally. This is perfectly natural, although excessive activity of this type may be a pathological symptom—there is such a thing as methodological hypochondria. The emergence of that interest—almost, though not quite, absent before—is indicative of the relative maturity that economics then gained. The results that this interest produced are, in themselves, of no great importance for us. We are all of us bad interpreters of ourselves and untrustworthy witnesses to the meaning of our practice. But precisely because of this, we cannot afford to neglect the period's methodology entirely. For critics have taken it literally, and hence it has become a source of misunderstandings concerning the scope and meaning of 'classic' economics.

(a) *Definitions of the Science*. We know that economists had experienced a need for defining their field even before A. Smith. During the period under discussion, their sense of responsibility for a distinct field having grown much stronger, practically all the writers of treatises tried their hands at defining it. Here are a few samples. J. B. Say defined Political Economy, by way of subtitle, as *exposition de la manière dont se forment, se distribuent et se consomment les richesses*. McCulloch defined Political Economy as the 'science

[8] A few of Mill's letters to Cairnes have been published by Mr. Hugh S. R. Elliot (ed. *Letters of John Stuart Mill*, 2 vols., 1910). The correspondence I mean, however, has been published by G. O'Brien in 'J. S. Mill and J. E. Cairnes,' *Economica*, November 1943. It whets one's appetite for more.

of the laws which regulate the production, accumulation, distribution, and consumption of those articles or products that are necessary, useful, or agreeable to man and which at the same time possess exchangeable value' or the 'Science of Values' (*sic!*). According to Storch, Political Economy is the science 'of the natural laws which determine the prosperity of nations.' Senior's Political Economy is 'the Science which treats of the Nature, the Production, and the Distribution of Wealth.' J. S. Mill contented himself in the *Principles* with 'the nature of Wealth, and the laws of its production and distribution, including: directly or remotely, the operation of all the causes by which the condition of mankind . . . is made prosperous or the reverse.' Roscher said: 'Our aim is simply to describe man's economic nature and economic wants, to investigate the laws and the character of the institutions which refer to the satisfaction of these wants, and the greater or smaller measure of success they have had.' These examples will suffice to give an idea. If we realize that it is hopeless and, moreover, pointless to try to frame a definition that will fit all the activities of the economics profession, we shall not feel inclined to judge harshly any of the obvious inadequacies of these and other definitions. Certain features are worth noting, however.

All the definitions of the period emphasize the autonomy of economics as against the other social or moral sciences—which is, of course, perfectly compatible with the recognition of close relations. Most of them emphasize its analytic (scientific) character.[1] Both these facts, though they may not be to the taste of every critic, should be registered as landmarks on the road of analytic economics. A third fact must also be noted, however, because it gave rise to one of the most important, as well as irritating, of those misunderstandings to which I alluded above. The reader will observe that the definitions quoted are none too specific as regards the facts and problems that are to come within the scope of economics: J. S. Mill's, for example, reads like a comprehensive catchall, and even Senior's, taken by itself, leaves the reader in doubt as to what it is that Production and Distribution of Wealth imply, since the whole of a society's institutional pattern is obviously relevant to production and distribution. Now, the 'science' to be defined was, of course, called Political Economy.[2] Most continental writers used this term in a very wide sense. But

[1] This seems to indicate a break with the past, if we go, e.g., by Sir James Steuart's definition or by the one A. Smith offered at the beginning of the Fourth Book of the *Wealth*. But the break is more apparent than real. On the one hand, some authors, Sismondi for instance, kept to the old practice of defining economics by a practical aim. On the other hand, most of A. Smith's work is genuinely analytic in nature in spite of that definition; and the economists of the period continued to proffer value judgments and to recommend policies in spite of their definitions. This will be discussed below in subsec. c.

[2] With the exception of *Staatswirtschaft*, which was used by some German writers, the terms used on the Continent, even *Nationalökonomie*, were equivalents of Political Economy. The term Economics came into use in the subsequent period and then only in England and the United States. The German equivalent of this, *Sozialökonomie* or *Sozialökonomik*, never caught on.

most of the leading Englishmen, and especially James Mill and Senior, confined it to what is perhaps more properly called economic theory, and it is to this that their methodological pronouncements referred.[3] To critics, this looked like a tremendous difference in attitude and outlook. They felt that the English 'classics' had no eye for anything but 'wealth,' that their political economy was nothing but speculative 'chrematistics' (Sismondi) and so on. But we have already seen that this was not so. Their practice proves that they did not mean to restrict either their activities or their interests. What they did restrict was the use of a word. Thus, Senior would indeed have excluded from his political economy any factual analysis and any treatment of welfare problems. But what did that matter if at the same time he welcomed both to what he called the Great Science of Legislation? [4]

(b) *Methodology*. From the standpoint thus gained we have no difficulty in absolving, once more, the 'classics' of any major errors of procedure. Their procedures were crude and often clumsy. Many of their controversies arose from nothing but an inability to see the opponent's point and some were purely verbal (as are many of ours).[5] The ridiculous 'method' of trying to analyze a *phenomenon* by hunting for the meaning of a *word* was rampant. But such as they were, the procedures actually used were not open to any serious objection of principle. They were thoroughly sensible and exactly what the nature of each type of problem would suggest to minds that were armed with little more than simple common sense. The 'classics' theorized in order to straighten out points that involved some logical complications; they assembled facts whenever they thought it useful to do so. The same cannot, however, be said about their methodological pronouncements, even apart from the fact that these—at least the English ones [6]—referred to economic theory alone.

[3] Realizing the danger that lurked in this terminology, Archbishop Whately made the unsuccessful suggestion: to replace the term Political Economy *in this sense* by the term Catallactics—from καταλλάτειγ, to exchange. In this he showed his usual good sense. But having failed to make his meaning clear, he himself was misunderstood and thus really made matters worse. The reader will not have to tax his imagination very heavily in order to visualize how this must have struck critics: What!—Political Economy, the science of the economic fate of humanity, entirely reduced to a miserable theory of bargaining!

[4] J. S. Mill adopted instead the term Social Philosophy.

[5] One of the points at issue between Ricardo and Malthus was, e.g., whether the rent of land owed its existence to the 'bounty' or to the 'niggardliness' of nature. Nothing shows so clearly the primitivity of the analytic apparatus of the time as does the fact that two able men could actually discuss whether the return to a factor is due to its productivity *or* its scarcity!

[6] The most important methodological treatises of the period are: Senior's *Four Introductory Lectures on Political Economy* (1852); Cairnes's *Logical Method;* and J. S. Mill's fifth essay in *Some Unsettled Questions* (this essay was first published in the *Westminster Review*, 1836) and the relevant passages in his *Logic*. Several critics have held that Mill's position in the latter differed from that he had taken in the essay. This is a misunderstanding. The essay deals with the methodological aspects of 'political

But in most cases it is possible to put matters right by means of small corrections. Thus, most economists, J. B. Say and J. S. Mill in particular, thought altogether too much of the analogy with the physical sciences, which the latter declared to be the 'proper models' for economic theory (*Autobiography*, p. 165)—a point for critics to fasten on but actually irrelevant, since no practical use was made of it.[7] J. B. Say, while correctly emphasizing that economics is an observational science, nevertheless called it 'experimental.' But this can be easily corrected into 'empirical.' Furthermore, practically all economists used the term Law or even Natural Law, the avoidance of which would have saved them much obloquy from philosophy-minded critics. But this habit was quite harmless, since what they really meant was nothing but Montesquieu's 'necessary relations' between economic phenomena or Marshall's 'statements of tendencies.' In view of J. S. Mill's insistence on 'the very limited and temporary value of the old political economy,' there is no excuse for later critics who harped on those words. In fact, all the really valid points in the latter's methodological credo could have been copied out from Mill. Again, Mill used the term *a priori* in a misleading sense [8] and also placed unnecessary emphasis upon 'deduction.' This was perhaps responsible for the absurd argument of later times about 'induction vs. deduction,' but, always remembering that he thought of the theoretical apparatus of economics when speaking of methods of political economy, we readily see that it never caused any errors in practice.[9] Finally, as regards the method of 'isolating' economic phenomena or motives, or of abstracting from noneconomic ones, not only the practice of the 'classics' but even their methodological rationalization of it was free from serious error. It is difficult to believe that any critic who raises objections on this score can

economy' in the sense of economic theory. The passages in the *Logic* deal with the methodology of a much wider sector of the social sciences, mainly with what is called economic sociology in this book. The epistemological situations of the two fields differ substantially, and there is no contradiction between prescribing 'deductive' methods for the one and 'inductive' (or 'inverse deductive') methods for the other. The chief reason for this is that economic theory, owing to its quantitative character, admits of systematic elaboration to a much greater extent than does the analytic apparatus of any other social science.

7 We have already observed that the introduction of the terms Statics and Dynamics does not involve any such use, i.e. any borrowing of a method from any physical science. Nor do economists borrow from mechanics when they employ the term equilibrium any more than does a bookkeeper who 'balances' an account.

8 This is all the more surprising, because in his *Logic* he even made geometry an empirical science and because, though not an empiricist to 100 per cent, he certainly was more of an empiricist than was Kant.

9 This, to repeat, is the real test. The literal meaning of a methodological profession of faith is of little interest except for the philosopher. Alternatively, our test may be formulated by saying that any objectionable piece of methodology is immaterial whenever it can be dropped without forcing us to drop any result of the analysis that is associated with it.

have studied J. S. Mill.[10] Of course, this statement must be understood to refer to the principles of isolation and abstraction per se as the 'classics' applied them for *the purpose of carving out the domain of purely economic research.* Only, so far as this goes, I maintain that, in principle as well as in practice, their procedure did not differ either from that of A. Smith [11] or from that of later economists as formulated by the later methodologists, Carl Menger and John Neville Keynes (see below, Part IV, ch. 4), and as accepted, around 1900, by a large majority of non-German economists. But I do not maintain that individual 'classic' writers, when reasoning within that domain, always 'isolated' relevant factors and 'abstracted' from others faultlessly. This would be absurd on the face of it, because it would imply that practically all their propositions were faultless: any criticism that does not charge either logical error or misstatement of facts can be formulated as an objection to the manner in which the criticized author 'isolates' or 'abstracts.'

The distinction that I have just tried to convey will help us greatly in understanding the methodological situation of the period, that is to say, the nature and extent of differences about 'method' that then existed among economists. At first sight, we have the impression that the *scientific* controversies of the times turned largely upon method. Thus, the two most famous and most prolonged controversies, the one on value and the one on general gluts, speedily led to the familiar situation in which, no progress being made with more concrete arguments, the parties fall back upon objections to one another's methods. In itself, this means little beyond admission of inability to convince

[10] As a matter of fact, men like Roscher, who had mastered J. S. Mill, did not raise any such objection. But then, as will be shown presently, he was really no critic of the 'classics' in the sense in which this implies a methodological creed, incompatible with theirs. The majority of later German critics, however—those of the genuine historical school—cannot have had much first-hand knowledge of Mill or of the 'classics' in general, for it is hard to believe that if they had they could have misunderstood Millian methodology as completely as they did: they argued rather against a wrong picture of it that had become fixed by the time they wrote. And, considering their absorption in a research program of their own, this is after all not so difficult to understand. But what about Ingram (see below, Part IV, ch. 4)? How was it possible for him to preach the gospel of a 'new economics' that took its methodology from Comte? The only answer I am able to offer—and which must suggest itself to any professional who makes a study of Ingram's *History of Political Economy*—is that both his knowledge of economics and his interest in it did not go beyond general 'philosophies' that were inspired by generous enthusiasm for the great slogans of his day but never came to grips with real problems. His other objections to 'classic' economics point to this conclusion still more clearly than does his Comtist objection to an autonomous economics.

[11] This is so important as to justify repetition: A. Smith's work *looks* less 'abstract' because it includes so much factual information that the *specialized* later works on economic theory did not include—but left for other specialized works to provide. But where he does move within the orbit of economic theory, his reasoning is not less abstract than is, say, Ricardo's. With the latter, 'abstractness' shows more because he confines himself to topics of an 'abstract' nature, and does not provide illustrative foliage, but this is all.

the other man, coupled with a declaration of being unconvinced by him—or, in a word, deadlock. For instance, when in the controversy on gluts, Malthus (and Sismondi) objected to Ricardo's procedure as too abstract and Ricardo himself emphasized the abstract nature of the argument,[12] they simply verbalized a sigh of despair. It would be quite wrong to infer that Malthus and Sismondi really objected to Ricardo's 'method' in the sense in which this word came to be used in the later Battle of Methods (see Part IV, ch. 4). That this was not the case can be established by analysis of their own modes of reasoning: these were 'theoretical' in the same sense as was Ricardo's—just as Lord Keynes's theory is theory in the same (logical) sense as is Marshall's. In other words, Malthus and Sismondi theorized in a different way and partly with an eye to different sets of facts, but their practice proves that they had no objection to theorizing per se, such as had, for a time, the later Schmoller school or the American institutionalists.

But was not *this* objection (against theory per se) raised by other people? It was, but only in isolated instances that had no significant influence upon the work of a large majority of economists.[13] One such root-and-branch objector was Comte. But as we have seen, he exerted no perceptible influence *within the period* and on *economists:* J. S. Mill, so far as technical economics is concerned, yielded not an inch. Another was Le Play. He initiated an important program of research but, for the rest, he was hardly known among the economists of the period. I doubt whether R. Jones and B. Hildebrand can be called root-and-branch objectors. But even if they can, they were no more than forerunners. Cliffe Leslie did not declare for a distinctive historical method in economics until 1876. Ingram did not raise the flag of his New Economics until 1878. Knies,[14] it cannot be too often repeated, was primarily an economic theorist and, for the rest, an able general economist without any

[12] For, though 'abstractness' is usually urged *against* an argument, it may also serve in its defense. Marxists, in particular, frequently—and in some cases with justice—save a perilous situation by yielding the doctrine (in controversy) on one level of abstraction with the reservation that the same doctrine is quite right on a higher level of abstraction.

[13] I am not speaking now of extra-scientific objectors such as Carlyle. Nor am I speaking of those objections that arise from the general public's dislike of anything that looks like a complicated argument, nor, finally, of those objections that simply express everyone's natural preference for his own chosen type of work.

[14] As already stated, Knies's chief work and also the better part of his activity as a teacher belong to the next period. But the only one of his writings that connects him with the historical school appeared during the period under survey: *Die politische Ökonomie vom Standpunkte der geschichtlichen Methode* (1853; greatly enlarged, 1883). This book presents an interesting problem. It expresses not only a sense of the general flux of social institutions and of the impossibility of framing universally valid 'policies'—and other things that the author could have just as well taken from J. S. Mill—but actually outlines essential parts of the Schmoller program. But the modes of procedure actually employed in all his subsequent publications are so many disavowals of these principles. As a teacher, too, Knies was very far from inculcating economic historicism.

distinctive bent as to method. As for Roscher, who described Ricardo and Malthus as 'political economists and discoverers of the first rank' and who went out of his way to express agreement with J. S. Mill's methodology,[15] a comparison of his *Grundlagen* with J. S. Mill's *Principles* fails to reveal any fundamental difference in procedure—he even speaks of natural laws. It is true, nevertheless, that he laid claim to having used a historical or 'physiological' method. But, as is evident from Chapter 3 of the Introduction to that work, all he meant by this was to dissociate himself from what he called the 'idealistic' method that prescribes norms for an ideal state of society, whereas he wished to describe things as they are 'after the manner of the investigator of nature' [16] (op. cit. vol. I, p. 111). We therefore emerge with the result that, barring isolated rumbles, the Battle of Methods had not been engaged as yet and that—taking the word method in the sense that is relevant here—methodological peace substantially prevailed. This was also Cairnes's opinion.

(c) *The Science and the Art.* Most of the writers of standing who paid serious attention to the fundamental questions of methodology clearly saw, and strongly emphasized, the distinction between arguments about what is and arguments about what ought to be: the distinction between the 'science' of economics and the 'art' of policy.[17] But it would be a great mistake to read into their statements the meaning which this distinction acquired later, when the question of 'value judgments' was raised. Senior, who was more explicit on the point than was anyone else, said indeed that the economist's conclusions 'do not authorize him in adding a single syllable of advice.' But by this he did not mean that the economist as a scientific worker is debarred from presenting practical advice because such advice presupposes ultimate valuations that are extra-scientific by nature—preferences that are beyond the range of scientific proof. This is the point of view that was taken by Cairnes (who did not, however, adhere to it in practice) and later on, more explicitly, by Sidgwick and by M. Weber. Senior and Mill and their contemporaries did not mean this at all. They merely meant that questions of economic policy always involve so many noneconomic elements that they should not be dealt with on the basis of purely economic considerations—which, by the way, in itself suffices to show how little there is in the common indictment that the

[15] W. Roscher, *Grundlagen* (English trans., *Principles of Political Economy*, 1878, vol. I, p. 106n.).

[16] This does not apply, without qualification, to L. Wolowski's 'Preliminary Essay' that Roscher's translator, J. J. Lalor, prefixed to the English translation (1878). In 1878 things looked different and, by a not unnatural confusion, Lalor spoke of Roscher as the 'founder' of what was *then* the Historical School. This gives a completely wrong picture.

[17] Confusions between the two and even denials of the validity of the distinction were of course frequent; but not more so than they have been at any later time, including the present. In the large majority of cases the distinction was firmly kept in view. For France, Charles Coquelin's article on political economy in the *Dictionnaire de l'économie politique* is typical in this as it is in other respects. Roscher's emphasis upon the distinction between what is and what ought to be deserves particular notice.

English 'classics' never saw anything but the economic aspects or, still worse, the wealth or even the profit aspects of things. But none of them really questioned the validity of value judgments that were based on 'philosophical' grounds and took proper account of the noneconomic as well as the economic elements of a given case—the value judgments of 'the writer or statesman who has considered all the causes which may promote or impede the general welfare' as distinguished from 'the theorist who has considered only one, though among the most important of those causes' (Senior, *Outline of Political Economy*, p. 3). This, as we have seen, was also J. S. Mill's opinion and in fact practically everyone's. There is, of course, sound sense in it: one could only wish that the economists of that (or any) period had never forgotten this piece of wisdom—had never been guilty of the Ricardian Vice.[18] However, it still remains true that the real problem of value judgments never occurred to them. *To the end of the period, economists considered their recommendations concerning policy as scientific results which followed from scientific, though not purely economic, analysis.* In this sense they were after all, as later critics sneeringly remarked, purveyors of recipes. Fortunately they also were more than that.

3. What Mill's Readers Actually Got

Mill's readers got, in the first place, factual information to the extent of about one-sixth of the book. On the face of it, this is a smaller proportion of space than either A. Smith or Roscher allotted to the presentation of facts, and what there is of this factual presentation is extremely ill-balanced, facts about 'peasant proprietors,' for example, taking a share more commensurate with Mill's own interest in the subject than with its probable interest for his readers. But this may be a wrong view to take. As Mill's preface emphasized, his treatise abounds in practical 'applications.' And these have reference to factual material that Mill often failed to present, perhaps because he assumed that his readers could easily supply the deficiency from universally accessible sources—such as the work of Babbage.[1] If we count as 'factual' all discussions

[18] See above, ch. 4, sec. 2.

[1] Charles Babbage, *On the Economy of Machinery and Manufactures* (1832). This work, which was widely used (also by Marx), is a remarkable performance of a remarkable man. Babbage (1792-1871), who was one of Newton's successors in the Lucasian chair of mathematics (Cambridge), one of the founders of the British Association for the Advancement of Science (1831) and of the Statistical Society, and a versatile writer on many subjects, was also an economist of note. His chief merit was that he combined a command of simple but sound economic theory with a thorough first-hand knowledge of industrial technology and of the business processes relevant thereto. This almost unique combination of acquirements enabled him to provide not only a large quantity of well-known facts but also, unlike other writers who did the same thing, interpretations. He excelled, among other things, in conceptualization: his definitions of a machine and his conception of invention are deservedly famous. It is interesting to note that in some points he recognized the priority of Gioja, whose name should in

in the book that in this sense presuppose factual information, although the information is not actually presented, then, if I have estimated with anything like accuracy, the 'factual' portion of the book increases to a little more than two-thirds of the whole, a little less than one-third being left for exposition of the analytic apparatus. In the second place, his readers got a fairly thorough—but none too thorough—grounding in 'theory.' However, as has been pointed out already, no contact whatever is made with any statistical *method*.

From another standpoint, we can illustrate Mill's range of topics by means of the following list of headings that, as the reader can easily satisfy himself, could be lengthened both by including further minor items and by dividing up some of the major ones: prices, price fixing, competition, custom, monopoly; wages and employment, wage policy, trade unions, poor laws, and other items of the *Sozialpolitik* of that age; socialism, with special attention to Saint-Simonism and Fourierism; producers' and consumers' co-operatives; future of the working class; education; population; enterprise and forms of enterprise, capital, profit, interest; saving and investment; technological advance; money and banking, central banking, foreign exchanges, government paper money; crises; foreign trade; colonies; private property, inheritance; partnerships, companies, bankruptcy legislation; rent, ownership of land, primogeniture, peasant proprietorship, metayage, cotter tenancy, slavery; 'progress,' 'maturity' (stationary state); government policy and government control; grounds for and limits of laissez-faire; public finance, especially taxation and public debts. I do not think that this list is conspicuous for either narrowness of range or remoteness from the practical issues of the day. It should be observed particularly that all that interested later generations could have been hung on hooks presented by Mill without upsetting his system. For instance, later institutionalists could have inserted into Mill's niches all the additional material of a specifically institutional nature that they might have wished to insert, *without thereby destroying the general character of the treatise:* there was room for everything within its spacious folds; and everything could have come to it as a development of existing points, nothing need have come to it as a revolution.

J. S. Mill arranged his material in five books: 'Production,' 'Distribution,' 'Exchange,' 'Influence of the Progress of Society on Production and Distribution,' and 'On the Influence of Government.' The last also contains things other than public finance but nevertheless mainly corresponds to A. Smith's Fifth Book. In Book IV, the shortest, Mill concentrated what he had to say on the subject of economic evolution—a happy innovation in exposition. The titles of the first three books suggest the influence of Say's arrangement or, rather, a not very felicitous attempt to improve upon it. The central theory of value, which should come first on logical grounds (and does come first with Ricardo and Marx), is presented in Book III as if it had to do only with the

---

fact be coupled with his. By way of contrast to his sound well-balanced treatment, I mention A. Ure's (*Philosophy of Manufacture*, 1835), who also presented interesting facts, but was not Babbage's equal as an analyst.

'circulation' of goods and as if production and distribution could be understood without it. This is worth mentioning because it points to a fundamental weakness of the 'classic' construction. I do not accuse the 'classics' of having failed to sense the pivotal importance of the analysis of value (choice) which is, if I may say so, the specifically economic element about the economic process. But there is some truth in Professor Knight's indictment that the 'classics' had 'no clear or definite conception of the meaning of *economy* as a process of maximizing a value return' and that 'the problem of *distribution* . . . was not approached as a problem of valuation at all.' [2] To this extent, we must qualify our recognition of Ricardo's chief merit. He and all the 'classics,' including Mill, did indeed make progress toward the acquisition of an analytic apparatus that would unify all purely economic problems; but, partly owing to the shortcomings of their groundwork, they never realized its possibilities to the full. They still divorced production from distribution—J. S. Mill even took credit for doing so—as if they were governed by different 'laws.' The first to point this out was Ferrara.[3] But Say's and Mill's combined authorities kept this plan of exposition alive for many decades to come. It is not worth our while to discuss its variants. Roscher, for example, has: Production, Circulation, Distribution, Consumption, Population—including Credit with Production.

The five books are preceded by 'Preliminary Remarks,' which, among less interesting things, contain a short sketch of what we should call the evolution of economic society—a universal economic history in a nutshell. This, of course, is not in itself surprising in a work that aimed at doing again what A. Smith had done. But much beyond what tradition leads us to expect from Mill is his handling of the factors to which he attributes causal roles in the shaping of the fortunes of a society or country. Environment, race (*racially* differentiated quality of human material), class structure, habits or propensities, combine to make a colorful and, what is more, a very realistic picture. There are no intellectualist and in particular no utilitarian errors about it: 'knowledge' is considered as a consequence as well as a cause 'of the state of the production and distribution of wealth,' and objective conditions receive more emphasis than ideas or principles. Such prefatory sketches of economic history—though of course not always of this quality—became more and more popular as the century wore on: Marshall's is the peak performance of this type.

[2] F. H. Knight, 'Ricardian Theory . . .' op. cit. p. 6. The second part of that statement goes perhaps too far. But Professor Knight supports it by a highly significant passage from a letter of Ricardo to McCulloch, where the former avers in so many words that the relative distributive shares 'are not essentially connected with the doctrine of value.' Though this cannot be taken literally—for it could be refuted from Ricardo's own argument—it does show that the full implications of the fact that capitalist distribution is a value phenomenon were not clearly seen even by Ricardo. They were seen by Marx.

[3] In his *Prefazione* to Say.

4. The Institutional Frame of the Economic Process

(a) *The Institutions of Capitalist Society.* Economic sociology covers, first, the facts of economic behavior from which economists forge certain assumptions and, second, the institutions that characterize the economic organization of the societies to be studied. 'Classic' practice as regards the former will be more conveniently discussed in the next chapter. As regards the latter we must distinguish three questions. Many writers, primarily the English theorists—such as Ricardo, James Mill, and Senior—did not bother to specify the details of the institutional frame they visualized, but took them for granted. Is it true, as has been averred so often, that they believed in the permanence of the capitalist order of things or even that laissez-faire capitalism is the only possible form of civilized society? What were the institutions they took for granted? When they did discuss them, what methods did they use?

The first question must, I think, be answered in the negative. It is true that Ricardo, for example, by virtue of the very fact that he failed to specify his institutional assumptions, creates an impression to the effect that the problems of social change were beyond his range of vision. But this does not follow. All that follows from his practice is that they were beyond his chosen field of inquiry. There is no reason to believe that, had he offered a description of the institutional frame, this description would have differed significantly (though his value judgments might have) from that of J. S. Mill, who, aiming as he did at systematic completeness, was more explicit. But as we know already (see sec. 1, above) there cannot be any doubt whatever about the latter's awareness of the historical relativity of social institutions and also of some at least of his 'economic laws.' To this extent, the current belief that this awareness was confined to isolated forerunners of later historicism, such as R. Jones and Sismondi, is certainly erroneous. It would be nearer to the truth to say that explicit belief in the permanence or in the unsurpassable excellencies, for all times, of capitalism occurred only in isolated instances.

The reader should observe, however, that this does not amount to crediting the 'classic' theorists with the idea that the capitalist order is only a historical phase and bound to develop, by virtue of its own inherent logic, into something else. This idea belongs to Marx alone. Even J. S. Mill held only that men could, should, and would change capitalist institutions through a rational perception of what he considered to be their defects. He did not hold that institutions would change of themselves or even that they would have to be changed because they would become *objectively* untenable. He saw that 'opinions . . . are not a matter of chance' [1] but the product of social conditions, and we might feel tempted to develop this in the Marxist direction. But this would hardly be justified: we must, I think, leave him in the citadel of eighteenth-century faith in intellectual progress, from which he occasionally sallied forth, no doubt, but to which he always returned. Practically, this matters but little. Scientifically, it makes a great deal of difference.

[1] Last but one paragraph of Book II, ch. 1, § 1.

The second question is an easy one. Economists, wishing to serve their time and countries, took for granted—and reasoned in terms of—the institutions of their time and countries. Since conditions differed as between different countries, this accounts for certain differences in outlook that, at the time and later, were erroneously construed as differences of analytic principle. The traits of the picture that were selected by the English 'classics' stand out very clearly. They envisaged the legal institutions (if we disregard the historical survivals that suggest another type of society) of a private-property economy that left so much room for free contracting as almost to justify the practice of economists to leave limitations out of consideration. This only means, of course, that no account was taken of limitations explicitly and consciously. As a matter of fact, English economists always reasoned with reference to the actual extent of the sphere that English law and administrative practice left for private decision and to the actual use that was being made of this freedom within that sphere—subject to the prevailing moral habits. Failure to be specific about all this exposed the English 'classics' to much mistaken criticism concerning their apparent neglect of ethical aspects.

The unit of that private-property economy was the firm of medium size. Its typical legal form was the private partnership. Barring the 'sleeping' partner, it was typically managed by the owner or owners, a fact that it is important to keep in mind in any effort to understand 'classic' economics. The facts and problems of large-scale production and, in connection with them, those of joint stock companies were recognized by economists after everybody else had recognized them. They received textbook status at the hands of J. S. Mill, who duly blamed A. Smith for his narrow views on corporate business—forgetting only the detail that there was little merit in realizing its importance in 1848 and that actually he was doing no more than what A. Smith had done, namely, describing with sober and somewhat platitudinous common sense that which stood before his eyes. Two further points deserve notice.

In the normal case, these firms were supposed to work under what the 'classics' called Free Competition. With them, this competition was an institutional assumption rather than the result of certain market conditions. And so firmly were they convinced that the competitive case was the obvious thing, familiar to all, that they did not bother to analyze its logical content. In fact, the concept was usually not even defined.[2] It just meant the absence of mo-

[2] It is interesting to note that J. S. Mill in Book II, ch. 4, of his *Principles*, which deals with 'Competition and Custom,' while expressing a conviction to the effect 'that only through the principle of competition has political economy any pretension to the character of a science'—which presumably means that there is more of determinateness about prices and quantities of commodities in the case of competition than there is in other cases—he does not think it necessary to state what competition is. The only author to handle perfect or pure competition correctly was Cournot, who also indicated, though he did not formulate in so many words, a correct definition (see below, Part IV, ch. 7, sec. 4).

nopoly—which was considered as abnormal and was vigorously condemned,[3] but was not properly defined either—and of public price fixing. J. S. Mill took credit, not without justification, for two important steps. First, he emphasized the importance of customary prices, mainly for earlier civilizations and for the Continent, but in certain cases, such as rent and professional fees, also for England. And, second, he emphasized the fact, though custom was the only reason he gave for its existence, that competition often 'falls short of the maximum' and that in this case a general correction must be applied, 'whether expressly mentioned or not,' to all conclusions arrived at on the hypothesis of perfect competition (Book II, ch. 4, § 3). Into such a picture co-operative price setting could enter only, if at all, as another deviation from normal practice like straight monopoly and as a conspiracy against public welfare exactly as it does now. There was, however, an exception to this: in J. S. Mill's scheme of things, trade unions were a normal element of the institutional pattern and laws against them 'exhibit the infernal spirit of the slave master' (Book V, ch. 10, § 5).

The other point to remember is this. Many English economists were severely critical of the English land system.[4] But when not engaged in criticizing it or in discussing alternatives, they also took it for granted in the sense that they reasoned with reference to it and to the English type of landlords who owned but did not operate large estates. In this particular case, however, reasoning in terms of existing institutions carried an advantage that may be made to stand out by contrast with the reasoning in terms of the owner-managed firm: landlords and farmers being different persons, it was easy for the theorist to keep their economic 'functions' distinct; owners of firms—'capitalists'—being then mostly the same people who also operated these firms, it proved less easy for the theorist to recognize this distinction of 'functions.' This teaches us an interesting lesson: it *may* happen, though we have no right to see in this occurrence more than a stroke of luck, that a *particular* historical pattern, which taken as a whole has nothing permanent about it, reveals facts and relations that are of general analytic importance. Usually, of course, it is the other way round, and we must always look out, on the one hand, for limitations that their particular institutional assumptions may impose upon the results of the 'classics' and, on the other hand, for possible justifications of these same results that may be found occasionally in the peculiarities of the social pattern they envisaged.

[3] For Roscher's unconditional eulogy of competition and his uncritical condemnation of monopoly, see op. cit., Book II, ch. 1, § 97.

[4] So much so as to be unable to see at all its strong points. I am not referring now to the political society and the cultural values it produced: a bourgeois radical cannot in fairness be expected to see these. But many economists also had no eye for the advantages of a system that separated the *administration* of land from the *operation* of it and thus e.g. eliminated the most serious of the problems of agricultural credit. Rational socialism could do worse than copy the system, replacing, of course, the landlords by a public agency.

Our third question—concerning the method used by the 'classics' in discussing social institutions—will be addressed, for brevity's sake, to J. S. Mill alone.[5] As an example, consider his views on inheritance.[6] The discussion culminates in the recommendations (a) that freedom of bequest be the general rule, except for a modest compulsory provision for descendants and for a provision to the effect that no person should 'be permitted to acquire by inheritance more than the amount of a moderate independence'; and (b) that 'in the case of intestacy, the whole property escheat to the State,' also with a proviso in favor of 'just and reasonable' provision for descendants. In themselves these recommendations and also the particular ideas of 'justice' that enter into them are only interesting from standpoints other than ours: to the historian of civilization they reveal part of the schema of cultural values that was harbored by a leading intellectual who belonged to the middle class and lived in the mid-Victorian era.[7] But there is, besides much pure ideology, also something behind those recommendations that is analytic in nature and admits of the application of a scientific method. Only, this scientific method is not the one we might expect. Mill's problem is not to explain, historically and sociologically, the origin and the various forms of the institution of inheritance. This, as he said in so many words in the case of the institution of property (§ 2 of Book II, ch. 1), is no concern of 'social philosophy.' What does concern the latter is the problem of social expediency, though not the expediency of any institution as it actually is, but as a community that is unhampered by any tradition or 'prejudice' might introduce it—under advice, I suppose, of the social philosopher. This is perhaps not the most scientific way of putting the matter but it

[5] This carries the disadvantage that our answer will be lopsided. Let me therefore state explicitly that more history-minded economists and, *a fortiori*, contemporaneous students who specialized in the history of institutions are not as a rule oblivious to the indictment I am going to level at Mill. His case is, however, important for general economics because he set a textbook fashion that prevailed far beyond the period under survey. The discussion of property and inheritance, e.g., that we find in the deservedly successful textbook of von Philippovich is exactly on Millian lines as far as its methodology is concerned.

[6] *Principles*, Book II, ch. 2 and Book V, ch. 9. This treatment of the same subject in two different parts of the treatise, which is highly inconvenient for the reader and a bar to any well-rounded exposition, is one of the many symptoms of the haste with which the work was produced.

[7] From Mill's essay on *Utilitarianism* it is clear that he was not blind to the doubtful standing of the concept of 'justice.' Yet he was no more able to do without it than were (or are) other economists. Even Ricardo occasionally finds some things 'just' and others 'unjust.' In Mill's case we cannot help discovering—perhaps with a wry smile—a marked association between what he thought right and proper and the modest privileges that he enjoyed himself. Socrates—an intellectual—should really have a moderately larger allowance than should a fool, he argued (as had his father), and if anything is certain, it is that J. S. Mill did not identify himself with the latter. The emphasis above upon 'moderate independence' points in the same direction. For only to the middle-class bourgeois is the desirability of anyone's 'moderate independence' as evident as it was to him.

indicates Mill's method of analyzing social institutions clearly enough: expediency of an institution turns upon its effect on, or role in, the economic organism—in practice upon the effects to be expected from given changes of a given pattern—and these effects Mill then proceeded to analyze. In doing so this fighter against prejudice proves himself indeed the most defenseless victim of prejudice against anything that is very far removed from his own mode of life or thought—displaying in this a deplorable narrowness of outlook [8]—but in themselves both the task and the method are scientific (analytic) in nature.

(b) *The State in 'Classic' Economics.* In Chapter 2 of this Part we learned a number of facts about the 'politics' of the period's economists and about the meaning and limitations of what has been called the System of Natural Liberty. In Chapter 3, we made the acquaintance of several types of political sociology, among them the Marxist Theory of the State. In Chapter 4, we had the opportunity to notice, here and there, the positions taken by individual economists with respect to the role of the state in economic affairs. In this section, we shall disregard all this, and all philosophies, ideologies, and political preferences—which were in part simply the philosophies, ideologies, and preferences of the business class that, standing on its own feet economically, did not want anything from the state except legal protection and low taxes—including the political recommendations associated with them. Instead we shall concentrate on one question only: how did all this affect economic analysis? Or, since all this enters or influences economic analysis by way of the *assumptions* economists make about the nature of the state (governments, parliaments, bureaucracies) and its normal functions and efficiency: how far were the assumptions made by economists realistic, considering the historical conditions to which their analytic propositions were to apply?

My answer is that these assumptions reproduced tolerably well the actualities of the time in those economists' *countries*. Practically all economists *believed*—no matter what they *desired*—that, as J. S. Mill put it, laissez-faire was the general rule for the administration of a nation's economic affairs and that what was significantly called state 'interference' was the exception. And, though for different reasons in different countries, this was so in actual practice not only as a matter of fact but also as a matter of practical necessity: no responsible administrator could have held then, and no responsible historian should hold now, that, social and economic conditions and the organs of public administration being what they were, any ambitious ventures in regulation and control could have issued in anything but failure. For the rest, wide differences existed between the economists of different countries with regard to what public administration could and 'should' do. But, as has been pointed out in Chapter 2, they are largely accounted for by differences, not in economic principles, but in the actual conditions of different countries.[9] And

[8] If the reader refer to Mill's text, he will presumably not agree with me. But this is only because he shares Mill's prejudices. However, our own prejudices are still prejudices.

[9] Of course this was not all of it, and one of the reasons why it was not is that different historical developments had, in different countries, induced different political doc-

practically all of them—so far as professional economists are concerned—come within the range covered by the phrase, 'differences of opinion as to the extent of the exceptions—necessary or only desirable, approved or disapproved—to the laissez-faire rule.'

The special case of England will illustrate this.[10] There, no revolution had occurred to sweep away the top-heavy structure of eighteenth-century bureaucracy, which was inefficient, wasteful, littered with sinecures, associated with unpopular mercantilist policy and even with political corruption. Before a new and more efficient structure could be erected, the old one had in any case—I mean, irrespective of what, if anything, one wished to put in its place—to be pulled down bit by bit in order to clear the ground. And until this had been done, the existing machinery of public administration was simply not up to any of those complicated tasks that modern regulation or *Sozialpolitik* involves. It is to the credit of J. S. Mill's judgment that he was aware of this. He was not on principle averse to a large amount of government activity. He had no illusions about any philosophically determined 'necessary minimum' of state functions. But he realized the superiority, which was in the circumstances simply not open to doubt, of the businessman's administration of the productive resources over what could possibly have been expected from the public official of his day. He realized more than that. No careful reader of his treatise can fail to notice the number of times he, after arriving at the result that something or other (for example, restriction of the income tax to consumers' expenditure) is 'desirable,' refuses to turn this value judgment into a recommendation because of insuperable administrative difficulties: they actually were insuperable *then.* It is true that the other English 'classics'—not to mention the anti-*étatiste* monomaniacs, whom that social situation produced, especially in France—not only failed to see that those conditions were essentially transitional but also advocated, as a matter of course, that the red tape that was being eliminated should never be replaced by anything: that government and bureaucracy should 'naturally' be confined to a certain minimum of functions. But even this, representing as it did a real tendency, does not *so far as it was an assumption about part of the institutional frame of the economic process* impair the value of their economic analysis.

But we can go a step further. From our argument it might seem to follow that, if 'classic' analysis, in the respect under discussion, was valid because its assumptions about the role of the state were realistic though time-bound, it must be invalid for any other period because those assumptions were time-bound though realistic. This is in fact true for a large number of propositions

trines about state and bureaucracy that led economists to 'absolutize' their nationally conditioned opinions, i.e. to exalt them into eternal truths. The situation was complicated by migration of ideas, such as the migration of 'Smithianism' to Germany, where it conquered not only many economists but also most leading bureaucrats. We cannot stay to analyze the consequences.

[10] It will be seen that what I am going to say applies to no other country. But it is not possible, in the available space, to do more than indicate the point of view from which such problems should be seen.

in applied economics—still more so for recommendations. But it is not so for the 'classic' analysis itself. We always need to understand whatever it is we wish to regulate or control. This means that, however comprehensive the economic tasks of government may be at any time, we always need theory of the 'classic' type as long as it is a question of regulation and control only—in socialism we need of course a different type of theory. We do not go to 'classic' economics for information about, say, the factors that account for unemployment because of its *analytic* defects. But the fact that its assumptions about the role of legislation and public administration do not fit the conditions of our time does not in itself constitute a valid reason for our refusing to do so. Of course, the reader will understand how difficult it must have been to accept this for later historians of economic thought, who were interested in little else but ideas, social doctrines or philosophies, and political recommendations, and who were in no position to decide which 'classic' propositions must, and which need not, be dropped when we drop any given element of their institutional frame.

(c) *The Nation and the Classes.* In concluding this section, I wish to advert to two of the many lacunae in our survey of the institutional aspects of 'classic' economics: we have not dealt with the manner in which the economists of that period handled the social phenomenon that we call Nation or Country; and we have not dealt with their conception of the class structure of society. The former is relevant for economic analysis in three ways. First of all, it is a factor—some would say the dominant factor—in the general sociology or social philosophy of many economists: of this all that needs to be said for the purposes of this book, has been said in Chapter 3 (especially under the heading Romanticism). From this we distinguish, second, the national viewpoint in economic policy, about which we have learned something in Chapter 4 (Carey, List), but which will be touched upon again in the section below that deals with foreign trade (ch. 6, sec. 3). Third, it is a question of considerable interest to ask how far the economists of that period took account of national differences of economic behavior and of consciousness of nationality as a motive of economic behavior: this question will be treated below (ch. 6, sec. 1). The subject of Social Classes offers a convenient transition from this to the next section.

In economics, as in all the social sciences, the term Class denotes two different things that, in strict logic, have nothing to do with one another. When we speak of Social Classes or of the Class Structure of Society, we mean to denote a real phenomenon that exists independently of the activity of research workers: actually or metaphorically, we may hold that a social class is an entity that thinks and feels and acts. But we also speak of classes when we mean nothing but categories that owe their existence to the classifying activity of research workers. Thus, when we speak of working-class movements, we are indeed referring to masses of individuals but of individuals that rally around a group standard and form, as it were, a psychological corporation, a social class. When we consider the group of all the people who derive their incomes from selling services (personal efforts), we find that we are combining social types that have very little in common and hardly ever feel and act in unison—such as street sweepers and movie stars, manual workers and executives, charwomen and generals: in short, we are considering a category that we have formed ourselves. If this were all, we should have merely to advert to the existence of another source of confusion in economic discussion and to make sure in each individual case what it is we mean or a given writer means when using the term Class—social classes that are red-blooded realities, or categories of participants in the economic process that are pale abstractions.[11] But associated with this simple distinction is an important issue that may as well be noticed at once.

Marx's two 'classes of participants in the economic process,'[12] capitalists and proletarians, are not mere categories but social classes. This feature is essential to the Marxist system. It unifies his sociology and his economics by making the same class concept fundamental for both. On the one hand, the social classes of sociology are *ipso facto* the categories of economic theory; on the other hand, the categories of economic theory are *ipso facto* the social classes. The importance of this feature becomes particularly clear when we observe its bearing upon class antagonism, which in this system is at the same time an exclusively economic phenomenon *and* the all important fact about all presocialist human history. We shall understand that from this standpoint any attempt to form economic categories other than social classes is bound to appear as an attempt to leave out or obscure the very essence of the capitalist process or, to use a phrase current among Marxists, to 'rob economic theory of its social content.' Such an attempt is not only tainted with 'apologetics': it is futile and cannot produce solutions of the real problems of economics.

But non-Marxist economics was not less bound to take, with increasing emphasis, the opposite view, and to look upon the very feature Marxists took (and take) pride in, as a blemish due to the survival of prescientific patterns of thought. This was the inevitable consequence of analytic advance that made more and more for a clear distinction of the purely economic relations from others with which they are associated in reality. In analyzing economic phenomena, categories other than those suggested by the class structure of society have proved more useful, as well as more satisfactory, logically. This does not involve overlooking any relevant class-struggle aspects, or simply class aspects, of the relations investigated.[13] All it does involve is greater freedom for all the various aspects of reality to assert their rights.

[11] Some modern economists call these abstractions Functional Classes. We ourselves shall, for greater clearness, use the term Categories, however objectionable it may be in some respects.

[12] Unfortunately, there is no good English equivalent for the German *Wirtschaftssubjekt*.

[13] The proof of this pudding is, of course, in the eating. No general professions of faith or general arguments about the impossibility of analyzing, e.g., distribution of income in terms other than the terms of social classes can settle the matter. Of course, the question is complicated by another, viz., the question of the validity of the Marxist theory of classes. But, in this connection, this is a side issue. Even if it were valid, the

As we shall presently see, the economists of the period under survey did take a great stride toward an economic analysis in terms of categories of economic types and away from economic analysis in terms of social classes. But they did not proceed in the logical way; that is, they did not work out a theory of social classes, insert it into their economic sociology, and then construct economic categories for use in economic analysis: this procedure would have required an awareness of the problems involved from which they were far removed. Instead, they took a short cut: they simply turned, with little modification, the social groupings that are known to the popular mind into categories of economic analysis. With the exception of Marx, whose analysis of social classes, however defective, is still analysis, they made no analytic effort. And the need for such an effort never occurred to them because, as a matter of fact, the social groupings of the man in the street were sufficiently drenched with economic meanings to make them adequate for the rough purposes of 'classic' economic analysis. The man in the street always had been greatly impressed by the landed aristocracy that towered over the rest of society. Hardly less distinctive and impossible to overlook was the position, on the other end of the scale, of the agricultural and industrial 'poor.' For the rest, the man in the street saw farmers, artisans, manufacturers, moneyed men, bankers, merchants and so on, rather than a single business class, and he would certainly have reserved other special positions for the professions. In the latter respect, 'classic' economists agreed with him more or less.[14] But for the rest of those groups, they (the 'classic' economists) did perform the modest service to analysis that consists in throwing them together, for some though not all purposes, into a single economic category, for which the label 'capitalists' soon came to be generally used in economic literature.[15]

Thus Marx, alone of all leading analysts, retained the class connotation of the categories of economic types, consciously and as a matter of principle. The prevailing tendency to get away from it, which he did

methodological necessity of a conceptualization adapted to the special tasks of economic analysis would still remain. Most modern socialists, by using modern theory, testify to their agreement with the view taken in this book. Much more important is it that Marx himself, in his analytic practice, agrees with us. For he uses his classes only for the purpose of interpreting the results that the capitalist economy produces; as will be seen presently, he does not introduce his classes as *actors* in his basic analytic work. He emphasizes indeed the social-class aspect whenever he can. But, except in the political sphere, his classes do not struggle with each other *as classes*.

[14] The analytic difficulty which the 'classic' wage analysis opposed to the inclusion of the professions in the labor category was in part avoided by those authors who described the professions as unproductive and thus excluded them from the economic society to which their propositions primarily applied. Those who counted skills as capital could also include them with capitalists.

[15] The public did not adopt it to any great extent until after 1900. But while the term Capitalist gained citizenship in the economist's lingo, the term Capitalism was, throughout the nineteenth century, hardly used except by Marxists and writers directly influenced by Marxism. There is no article under this heading in *Palgrave's Dictionary*.

not fail to notice, he simply put down as one of the symptoms of the degeneration of bourgeois economics that, so he held, had no longer the courage and honesty to face the real issues. By the same token, he noticed with approval those vestiges of the popular confusion of the two aspects that may be found in the earlier 'classics,' especially in Ricardo. The existence of such vestiges is what we should expect in a process of analytic development that was not only slow but also subconscious. But how important were they? It is true that Ricardo spoke of distribution of the 'produce of the earth' as a process of distribution between 'three classes of the community' (Preface). This does seem to imply class connotation. If, however, we wish to take this phrase literally, we must take the whole sentence literally—and this would make a physiocrat of Ricardo. Further, it is true that his theory of wages, so far as it fits any part of reality at all, fits only the wages of manual labor—of the proletarian *class*. And finally Ricardo, according to traditional interpretation, emphasized antagonism of class interests—the interests of the landlords, in particular, being held to be 'always opposed' to those of the rest of society. This, of course, is what Marx liked best and what other economists who also took it for an essential feature of Ricardo's economics, such as Carey and Bastiat, liked least. But as regards the old wage theory that Ricardo adopted, it is very obvious that he did not impart to it any class-struggle twist. And it seems much more realistic to see in its very partial validity the inevitable result of a defective analytic apparatus than of any intention to emphasize class aspects. As regards his general handling of class interests, two things must be carefully distinguished. Like most 'classics' Ricardo was much alive to political implications. Being one of the champions of free trade in corn, he thought of it as a political measure that was to be carried against the *economic* interest of a *social* class—which in this case would understandably merge in his mind. And this happened, of course, every time there was a political issue on the anvil. But this is all right—the political viewpoint brings in party strife and party brings the social-class element: nothing is further from my thought than any wish to argue for a treatment of *political* questions that neglects this class element and reasons in terms of an imaginary common good. But quite another question is the significance of the opposition of class interests in Ricardo's economic analysis per se. This reduces to propositions about the long-run tendencies of relative distributive shares (see below, ch. 6, sec. 6). He held, for example, that the landlord's share tends to increase at the expense, primarily, of the capitalist's share. This, however, does not constitute class antagonism either in the Marxist or in the usual sense. Marx, recognizing two classes only, saw class 'struggle,' economic *and* political, only between these two and thereby testified to his belief that opposition of interests *in the Ricardian sense* does not constitute class antagonism. In the usual sense, class antagonism means antagonism between social classes—a reality that manifests itself, for example, in the political arena. For this phenomenon to arise, the Ricardian antagonistic tendency in distributive shares is neither a necessary nor a sufficient condition. This seems to establish our thesis, namely, that the class connotations of Ricardo's categories are in fact no more than survivals and nonessential to his system; and that, in particular, Carey and Bastiat and all the writers who took similar lines were in error when, believing that the Ricardian tendencies in distributive shares spelled social warfare, they set about disproving them.

5. The 'Classic' Schema of the Economic Process

Into the sociological frame just sketched, the 'classics' fitted a schema of the economic process, the general features of which it is our next task to describe. In itself this task is simple enough. But it is rendered more difficult by the facts that the form the schema took in the classic (in our sense) work of the period, J. S. Mill's *Principles*, is of course not more than 'representative' of a large number of schemata that more or less differed from it; that even so it was the outcome of long discussions that were in part pointless, sometimes merely verbal, but which loom large to the backward glance; and that the state of analytic work looked very different at different stages. The very proposition that there was anything like progress toward clarification of the issues and improvement of the results of analysis will be voted a misrepresentation by readers who either forget, or on principle disapprove of, the aim and viewpoint of a history of *analysis*.

(a) *The Actors*. Any schema of the economic process must first of all settle the question of the *dramatis personae* to be admitted to the scene and thereby prejudge many of its features. These actors were, of course, firms and households and not social classes, or else there could not have been competition: this also applies to Marx's *theory*. As we know, these actors were classified by means of turning the social groups known to common experience into the three categories of economic types (or 'functional' classes): landowners, laborers, and capitalists.[1] Of course, this merely continued an old practice that had been sanctioned by A. Smith. Since the three were mere categories, each defined by an economic trait, it was recognized without difficulty that an individual was capable of belonging to two (for example, if he was an artisan) or to all three of them (for example, if he was a peasant, tilling his own soil). Marx, as we also know, substituted his two-*class* schema for this tripartite division of types.[2]

In one respect, however, there was significant, if halting, advance. A fourth category or type eventually received explicit recognition, the entrepreneur. Not that economists had ever accomplished the impossible feat of overlooking the most colorful figure in the capitalist process. The scholastic doctors, at least

[1] Subgroups were, of course, introduced when desirable. But in dealing with the general pattern of economic theory, we may neglect this fact.

[2] Sismondi was the only other economist of major importance to do the same thing. But he did so only for purposes of simplification, not as a matter of principle.

since the times of St. Antonine of Florence, had distinguished the businessman's *industria* from the workman's *labor*. Seventeenth-century economists had displayed an unmistakable, if inarticulate, understanding of the type. Cantillon was, so far as I know, the first to use the term entrepreneur. But these suggestions petered out without coming to fruition. A. Smith glanced at the type occasionally—he speaks occasionally of the undertaker, the master, the merchant—and, if pressed, would not have denied that no business runs by itself. Nevertheless this is exactly the over-all impression his readers get. The merchant or master accumulates 'capital'—this is really his essential function—and with this 'capital' he hires 'industrious people,' that is, workmen, who do the rest. In doing so he exposes these means of production to risk of loss; but beyond this, all he does is to supervise his concern in order to make sure that the profits find their way to his pocket. J. B. Say, moving along in the French (Cantillon) tradition, was the first to assign to the entrepreneur—per se and as distinct from the capitalist—a definite position in the schema of the economic process. His contribution is summed up in the pithy statement that the entrepreneur's function is to *combine* the factors of production into a producing organism. Such a statement [3] may indeed mean much or little. He certainly failed to make full use of it and presumaby did not see all its analytic possibilities. He did realize, to some extent, that a greatly improved theory of the economic process might be derived by making the entrepreneur in the analytic schema what he is in capitalist reality, the pivot on which everything turns. But he failed to realize that the phrase 'combining factors,' when applied to a going concern, denotes little more than routine management; and that the task of combining factors becomes a distinctive one only when applied not to the current administration of a going concern but to the organization of a new one. In any case, however, he turned a popular notion into a scientific tool.

In Germany, the concept of the entrepreneur was a familiar element of the 'cameralist' tradition. And so was the corresponding term, *Unternehmer*, which

[3] Lest the reader feel inclined to read this either into Cantillon or into A. Smith, let me further explain my reasons for believing that Say's formulation should be considered a distinct step in analysis. Cantillon said indeed that the entrepreneur acquires means of production at certain prices with a view to selling at uncertain (expected) prices. This describes one of the aspects of the businessman's activity very well; but it does not describe (or, at any rate, emphasize) its essence. A. Smith considers indeed the case of the capitalist who lends his capital to other people and thus seems to recognize the distinct function of those people who take the trouble and risk of employing it. But the businessman who borrows from the capitalist still remains a vicarious capitalist, i.e. an intermediary between the owner of capital and the labor force; and to provide the latter with tools, means of subsistence, and raw materials is still all he does. It might be said that the distinctive function that Say made explicit is implied both by Cantillon and Smith. But analytic progress—not only in economics—hinges in great part on making things explicit that have been implied or implicitly recognized for ages. A. Smith also knew that we pay for goods because we want them, but this does not make him a marginal utility theorist.

the economists of the period continued to use—it occurs, for example, in Rau's textbook. The analysis of the entrepreneurial function developed steadily if slowly, culminating in the work of Mangoldt.[4] How much of it, if anything, is due to influence from Say, I feel unable to tell. But in England this influence shows more clearly. Ricardo, the Ricardians, and also Senior took indeed no notice of Say's suggestion and in fact almost accomplished what I have described as an impossible feat, namely, the exclusion of the figure of the entrepreneur completely. For them—as well as for Marx [5]—the business process runs substantially by itself, the one thing needful to make it run being an adequate supply of capital. But some of the non-Ricardian and anti-Ricardian writers of the late 1820's and the 1830's did take it up, Read and Ramsay—the latter used the term 'master' rather than entrepreneur, though he spoke of enterprise—deserving special mention. The decisive step was taken by J. S. Mill, who brought the term entrepreneur into general use among English economists and, in analyzing the entrepreneurial function, went from 'superintendence' to 'control' and even to 'direction,' which, he admitted, required 'often no ordinary skill.' But this defines the function of management and not anything distinct from mere administration. If this were all, he might as well have been content with the good English term, manager—which was in fact adopted later on by A. Marshall—and have spared himself all regrets about there being no good English word for entrepreneur. A reason why he did not do so was possibly that managers are frequently salaried employees and they do not necessarily share in business risks, whereas J. S. Mill, like all the authors of that period and most authors of the next one, wished to make risk-bearing an entrepreneurial function alongside of 'direction.' But this only served to push the car still further on the wrong track.[6] And there

[4] See above, ch. 4, sec. 5 and below, ch. 6, sec. 6a. The work marks in this respect the most important advance since Say.

[5] In his case this stands out particularly because he went into so much detail about the process of accumulation. Accumulated capital, with him, invests itself in a wholly automatic manner. All the phenomena and mechanisms in the emergence of mechanized large-scale enterprise that hinge upon the personal element are completely shut out from his range of vision. A famous passage in the *Communist Manifesto* (concerning the 'wonders' that the 'bourgeoisie' has accomplished) seems to contradict this, since mere investment of accumulated capital could hardly be said to be productive of 'wonders.' But this conception of entrepreneurial achievement—for what else could be responsible for the bourgeois miracles?—entirely failed to influence his basic analysis.

[6] Since many modern economists also include risk-bearing among entrepreneurial functions, it may be well to point out at once the objection to the idea. It should be obvious, so soon as we have realized that the entrepreneur's function is distinct from the capitalist's function, that an entrepreneur, when he employs his own capital in an unsuccessful enterprise, loses as a capitalist and not as an entrepreneur. It has been said that if he borrows at a fixed rate of interest, the capitalist being entitled to repayment plus interest irrespective of results, it is the entrepreneur who bears the risk. But this is a typical instance of a very common confusion of economic and legal aspects. If the borrowing entrepreneur has no means of his own, it is obviously the lending capitalist who stands to lose, his legal rights notwithstanding. If the borrowing entre-

it stuck. There were various attempts at improvement and development during that period and the subsequent one. Substantially, however, J. S. Mill's conception of the entrepreneurial function prevailed throughout the century, which means that, after all, Say's suggestion came to very little. We shall presently return to the subject.

(b) *The Agents.* The reader is requested to observe how very short, simple, and natural the step is from the recognition of the three categories of participants in the economic process—landowners, workmen, and 'capitalists'—to a general schema of this process. The categories are characterized by a purely economic trait: they are respectively the suppliers of services of land, of labor, and of a stock of goods that is labeled 'capital.' This seems to settle their role in production and, quite unbidden, the famous triad presents itself, the triad of agents, or factors, or requisites—or instruments (Senior)—of production. And, not less easily, a triad of incomes emerges to correspond to the triad of factors—rents, wages, and 'profits.' Surely nothing could seem more useful and more simple or more obviously in accord with fact to any person not influenced by previous acquaintance with economic controversy. This is the first point about the triad of factors that I want the reader to realize.

The second point to be borne in mind is that the triad is, nevertheless, not popular with modern economists. It established itself, more or less, around the middle of the nineteenth century and took a new lease of life through A. Marshall's sponsorship of it.[7] And it still survives, owing to its handiness in elementary teaching. Beyond this, however, modern economists do not like it particularly: some look upon it as a relic of bygone stages of analysis, a clumsy tool, an encumbrance rather than a help. But for the moment, we are not concerned with this, but with a third point. For reasons quite different from those that motivate the attitude of modern theorists, economists of the period under survey were reluctant to accept the triad, which accordingly conquered but slowly and incompletely—a fact that, considering the obviousness of the schema, calls for explanation. Moreover, examination of these reasons will teach us an interesting lesson about the 'ways of the human mind' in our field.

In Chapter 6 of the First Book of the *Wealth of Nations*, A. Smith decomposed the price of products into three components: wages, rent, and profit. In Chapter 7, these prices are built up again from these same components.[8] In itself, this points strongly enough toward the triad of factors.

preneur has means by which to effect discharge of his debt, he too is a capitalist and, in case of failure, the loss again falls upon him as a capitalist and not as an entrepreneur.

[7] Marshall had indeed a fourth factor or agent of production, Organization. But this is only a label for a compound of topics—such as division of labor and machinery—of which business management is only one. It is not an agent in the same sense as are land, labor, and capital.

[8] These are equilibrium prices. As we know, the arrangement referred to embodies A. Smith's manner of recognizing the fact of general interdependence between the elements of the economic system and constitutes one of his greatest merits in the field of pure analysis. But we also know that it was much misunderstood—some critics even saw circular reasoning in it.

But the pointer is completely lost in the argument of Chapter 6. There, laborers, landlords, and capitalists are indeed introduced as participants in the process of distribution, but their shares are not construed as returns from the productive employment of their factors: if not wholly denied, and even if occasionally 'recognized,' [9] this factor-value aspect of distributive shares is brushed aside in favor of quite another aspect. A. Smith, it will be remembered, tries to show how the landlord's and the capitalist's shares are 'deducted' from the total product that 'naturally' is, in its entirety, the product of labor. And this seems to point toward a different conceptual arrangement, which reserves the role of factor of production for labor alone and bars the outlook on the triad of factors in spite of the fact that A. Smith's language on the first page of Chapter 7 is clearly suggestive of it.

A. Smith's exposition has been restated, in the first place, because it anticipates instructively the situation that prevailed in this corner of economic theory throughout the period. Whether under A. Smith's influence or independently, some economists took the line indicated by the one of A. Smith's pointers, and some took the line indicated by the other. But the majority hesitated and compromised, though the tendency was all along in favor of the triad of factors. In the second place, we have started from A. Smith because his exposition illustrates very well the nature of the main obstacle that stood in the way of smooth acceptance of the three-factor schema. In order to see it, we must recall once more that the proposition that labor alone produces the whole product has no empirical content that could be relevant in an analysis of the facts of the economic process: clearly, nobody can maintain that labor is all that is needed in order to produce something, except in a class of cases without importance. But the proposition may have 'meta-economic' meaning of an ethical color and it agrees well with the emotional propensities and the political doctrines of sponsors of the interests of labor who, like A. Smith, loved to declaim about the laborer who produces everything for everybody and himself 'goes in rags.' They thought that they were gaining a point for labor by clinging to that doctrine, and they were confirmed in this childish belief by the no less childish belief of many sponsors of the triad that setting up land or capital as factors of production was gaining a point for landlords or capitalists.[10] They failed to see that their ethical philosophies and political doctrines were logically irrelevant for the explanation of economic reality as it is. In other words, they failed to see that all that matters for this purpose is

[9] Thus, A. Smith described the gross revenue of society as 'the whole produce of their land and labour' (beginning of ch. 2, Book II).

[10] I do not deny, of course, that slogans for popular consumption may be derived from either analytic set-up. To that extent—that is, if meant for the sole purpose of taking in slow-witted people—neither was childish. Only the honest belief was childish that any analytic arrangement about factors of production could *in good logic* strengthen the political use either for or against the claims of their owners. That this is not so has been pointed out repeatedly in this book: even if there were any sense in maintaining that, e.g., land produces everything, this would not constitute any reason why the returns from it should go to its owners.

the simple fact that, in order to produce, a firm needs not only labor but all the things that are included in land and capital as well, and that this is all that is implied in setting up the three factors. In still other words, they had not yet a clear conception of the distinctive purposes of analysis—have we?—and *of what is and what is not relevant to the analytic purpose.* It will be realized therefore that to see this distinctive purpose and to perceive that the three-factor schema served it in a simple way was, under the circumstances, not quite so easy as one might infer from its obviousness and that hence its adoption spelled considerable analytic merit after all.

There is, however, another aspect to the matter. If one accepts a labor-quantity theory of value, either in Ricardo's or in Marx's manner (see below, ch. 6, sec. 2a), the three-factor schema, which we have been commending for its simplicity, meets with *analytic* difficulties that are quite independent of any philosophies. For the distributive shares must be paid from prices of products that, owing to the presence of claimants other than labor, cannot in general be proportional to the quantities of labor embodied in those products. A new problem therefore arises concerning the manner in which those other claims are satisfied. And in attempting to solve *this* problem, we find the triad of factors that puts these factors all in fundamentally the same logical position very inconvenient to handle: [11] from *this* standpoint the mere fact that all agents are equally 'requisite' cannot any longer be regarded as decisive. Note this interesting fact: from the standpoint of any theory of value other than the labor-quantity theory, this problem appears as a choice example of a spurious problem, that is, a problem that owes its very existence to defective analysis and disappears, without any trouble, if the defective element, in this case the labor-quantity theory of value, be removed; but from the standpoint of the labor-quantity theory of value, the problem in question becomes the most important of all, the problem the solution of which must reveal the innermost secret of capitalist society. Marx had therefore plenty of reason to rise in wrath against the triad of factors and to condemn it as a piece of vile apologetics that, reducing colorful struggles of social classes to colorless allocations of returns to co-operating factors, emasculated capitalist reality.[12] Sometimes,

[11] James Mill and McCulloch tried to do this with very indifferent success.

[12] Conceiving of economic analysis as an element in social evolution—and theories other than his as the fog that rises from it—Marx, as stated above, was of the opinion that, after Ricardo, 'bourgeois economics' had entered a stage of decay along with the society that produced it. It is not without interest to ask what the facts were he took for manifestations of this decay. The first we know already: it was the refusal of 'bourgeois' economics to couch its analysis in terms of social classes. The second, related to the first, was precisely the increasing tendency to adopt the three-factor schema. The third was the tendency to assert that the economic process, however much given to stalling under the impact of 'disturbances,' was yet free, in its pure logic, from inherent hitches. Marx took this for another piece of 'whitewashing' though, from another standpoint, it was the natural consequence of improved analysis. The fourth was the tendency to replace what Marx considered to be profoundest truth by a description of the surface phenomena of business practice as they appear to the business-

the task of analysis is rendered difficult by the nature of its problems—wave mechanics is a good example. Sometimes the difficulties are not in the things but in our own minds.

As soon as this is understood, we can deal very briefly with the facts of the case. The aversion to the triad schema that was due to philosophical or political or emotional causes gave way eventually and in the end asserted itself merely in verbal concessions. The obstacle of the labor-quantity theory was, of course, next to insuperable for Ricardo himself and for the Ricardian socialists, including Marx. But it was overcome by the non-Ricardian and anti-Ricardian theory of the 1830's—which shows again that the Ricardian teaching was really in the nature of a detour. On the Continent, Say—possibly following Turgot's lead—established the triad schema [13] and the practice of dealing, both in the theory of production and in the theory of distribution, with the 'services' of the three factors on the same footing. In England, Lauderdale was the first major writer to set up capital as a distinct factor. Malthus placed no emphasis upon the triad but his theoretical set-up implies it. Torrens, Read, and Senior, especially the last, are the most important of the economists who helped it toward anchorage in English economics.[14] J. S. Mill, finally, adopted it in substance but hesitatingly and without going through with it—in a way that mirrors the actual doctrinal situation very well. He started like Petty with two 'requisites' of production, a felicitous term that disarms unintelligent criticism by avoiding any suggestion to the effect that 'agents' might be morally entitled to 'rewards.' [15] Then he noticed the fact that the economic process of every period also depends on the stock of goods that is available at the beginning of the period *which is all that is implied in setting up 'capital' as a distinct factor.* And so he recognized capital as a factor but distinguished it from the other two, the two 'original' ones.[16] Senior had spoken of capital as a 'secondary' agent in contrast to the two 'primary' ones. There is in fact point in maintaining that capital is a 'factor with a difference.' For, if capital is goods, it raises problems of depreciation and renewal that the other two factors do not raise. And if capital is so defined as to include wage goods, it is not quite on a par with land and labor but stands to them, so far as the wage goods are concerned, in a relation that is peculiar to it. But J. S. Mill did not go much further than this. Though he did recognize occasionally that in this schema the rent of land enters or does not enter into price and cost exactly as do wages, he yet refused to put land quite on a par with labor. He

---

man. It is for the reader—and an excellent exercise it would be—to make up his mind on these points *now.*

[13] He also generalized 'land' into 'natural agents.'

[14] And in spite of Say's priority and in spite of the fact that we moderns do not think very highly of it, there was considerable merit in this around 1830.

[15] The term Requisite is, so far as I know, due to James Mill, who has labor and capital, however, instead of labor and land. J. S. Mill uses also the term Agents.

[16] If we wished to be nasty, we could quote him to the effect that he started with two factors and, after prolonged discussion, 'reduced' these two factors to three (Book I, ch. 1, § 1 and ch. 7, § 1).

therefore clung, officially as it were, to the Ricardian theory of rent, although it was quite superfluous for him.[17] And capital remained stored-up labor for him, as it had been for James Mill, although from the standpoint of his schema and if he wished to 'resolve' capital into something else, he should have 'resolved' it into stored-up services of labor *and land*.[18]

To sum up: the question what is and what is not to be 'recognized,' by the analyst, as an agent of production is a mere question of analytic convenience and efficiency. As such, however, it is very important, for the way in which a writer answers it will, to a considerable extent, determine his schema of the economic process and the formulation of the problems to be solved. At an early stage of analysis, the triad of *agents* suggests itself primarily because it links up nicely with the three categories of participants in the economic process that are derived from the layman's picture of society. But it so happens that the triad also makes economic sense because it presents a complete list of the requisites of physical production, the items of which are both nonoverlapping and distinguished by economically relevant characteristics. Therefore, it makes a useful basis to start from. J. B. Say seems to have been the first to realize this fully. But most of the economists of the period did not look at the matter in this light. They believed that when they were deciding what to 'recognize' as an agent, they were dealing with momentous real problems of analysis and, still more important, of social justice. Hence we find widespread reluctance to adopt the triad, which was reinforced, in some cases, by a theory of value that did not work well with it and by the fact that the role of capital in the productive process does display certain traits that are not shared by the two 'original' or 'primary' agents. And so one-factor schemata and two-factor schemata survived throughout. Moreover, even writers who in fact adopted the three-factor scheme displayed a tendency to make verbal concessions to the other two[19]—which further obscures the situation.

(c) *The Model.* In every scientific venture, the thing that comes first is Vision. That is to say, before embarking upon analytic work of any kind we

[17] The specifically Ricardian element in the theory of rent was logically superfluous for him because mere 'requisiteness' of land plus its scarcity is all that is needed to explain the price of its services. Yet he commits himself to the Ricardian view of rent, e.g., in the last sentence of § 2, ch. 2, of Book III.

[18] Let us notice at once that this 'resolution' of capital goods, e.g., a machine, involves *two* problems: first, the 'resolution' of the machine into the factors that enter into it and include services of other capital goods; second, the 'resolution' into land and labor only (or, with Marx, into labor only). In the next period it was especially Böhm-Bawerk and, following him, Wicksell who used and propagated the 'resolution' into land and labor.

[19] Such a verbal concession that veils a man's acceptance of the triad is instanced by the turn of phrase that capital increases the productivity of labor (or that its function consists in making labor more effective). This *seems* to point toward a one-factor theory by confining the honorific quality of productivity to labor alone but actually does, so far as explanation of facts is concerned, exactly what 'recognition' of capital as an agent of production is meant to do.

must first single out the set of phenomena we wish to investigate, and acquire 'intuitively' a preliminary notion of how they hang together or, in other words, of what appear from our standpoint to be their fundamental properties. This should be obvious. If it is not, this is only owing to the fact that in practice we mostly do not start from a vision of our own but from the work of our predecessors or from ideas that float in the public mind. We then proceed to conceptualize our vision and to develop or correct it by closer examination of facts, two tasks that of necessity go together—the concepts we possess at any time and the logical relation between them suggesting further factual investigation and further factual investigation suggesting new concepts and relations. The total or 'system' of our concepts and of the relations that we establish between them is what we call a theory or a model. We have had ample opportunity to observe how difficult a task conceptualization is in the early stages of analytic effort, chiefly because the scientific fraternity takes time to learn, by a process of trial and error, what is and what is not important in an 'explanation' of the phenomena envisaged. In economics, particularly, there are many inhibitions to overcome before the nature of the analyst's task can be clearly understood. But model building, that is, conscious attempts at systematization of concepts and relations, is more difficult still and characterizes a later stage of scientific endeavor. In economics, efforts of this kind date, substantially, from Cantillon and Quesnay. In the period under discussion, a model evolved from the Cantillon-Quesnay pattern that, since we already know the actors and the agents that figure in it, may be briefly described as follows. Consideration of details will be deferred to the next chapter.[20] Moreover, comments on the 'classic' schema of economic evolution will be deferred to the next section. In this section I shall present the 'classic' schema of a stationary process only—a schema which, in this respect, was much like that of Quesnay.

From A. Smith on, most of the English 'classics' used the term Stationary State. But this stationary state was an actual condition of the economic process which they expected to materialize sometime in the future. Taken in this sense, the subject of the stationary state belongs in the next section. Here we are concerned with a different kind of stationary state, namely, with a stationary state that is not a future reality but only a conceptual construct or tool of analysis that serves to isolate, for the purposes of a preliminary study, the group of economic phenomena that would be observable in an unchanging economic process. The first to recognize explicitly the methodological importance of doing this was J. S. Mill. But Marx, whose schema of Simple Reproduction (*Capital*, vol. I, ch. 23) is the schema of an economic process that merely reproduces itself in time, went much more deeply than Mill. All other writers, however, including A. Smith and Ricardo, actually used that tool but, not being aware of the fact that they were using any particular device of this kind, they used it in a haphazard and unsatisfactory manner. This point be-

[20] This procedure entails the disadvantage that certain concepts will have to be used before they have been fully explained. No serious inconvenience will, however, arise from this.

ing both important and somewhat difficult to understand calls for additional comment.

We have repeatedly had the opportunity to advert to the slow development, not completed within the period under discussion or even within the next one, of the notions of economic (or social) statics and dynamics. J. S. Mill, who as we have seen probably took them from Comte and used them in his logic, defined statics as the theory of 'the economical phenomena of society considered as existing simultaneously' (*Principles*, Book IV, ch. 1, § 1). This definition, by itself, might pass muster as an anticipation of the modern definition (Frisch). Statics as thus defined pivots on the concept of (stable or unstable) equilibrium that appears in Mill and in the 'classic' literature generally, for example, in the garb of such constructs as the 'natural' or 'necessary' prices. But a little later, we learn that in the passage quoted he did not really think of the statics that is defined by his wording or, rather, that he confused it with 'the economical laws of a stationary and unchanging society.' As we shall see more clearly later on, these are different things: we can study a changing process by means of a static method (comparative statics, see below, Part IV, ch. 7, sec. 3a) and an unchanging process by means of a sequence analysis of the kind which Sismondi occasionally used, and which relates economic quantities that belong to different points of time—i.e., by means of a dynamic theory in the sense of Frisch. Mill, following Comte, understood by dynamics something altogether different, namely, the analysis of those forces that produce fundamental change in the long run—the kind of thing we shall discuss in the next section. All this is confusing enough. But we must add a final element to the confusion. In addition to speaking of a static *theory* and of a stationary *state*, which is an analytic tool, Mill also, like Ricardo, expected the economic process to settle down, at some future time, into a stationary state of a special kind that will not be an analytic device for facilitating the study of a nonstationary reality but will be itself a reality. I repeat that, in all this, Mill did no more than to make explicit what everybody fumbled for.

Some of the fundamental features of the 'classic' model or models of the stationary process may be thus described in Ricardo's words (*Principles*, ch. 31). Suppose that a capitalist 'employs a capital of the value of £20,000' and 'that profits are 10 per cent.' Of this capital, £7000 are 'invested in fixed capital, viz. in buildings, implements, etc. etc.' and 'the remaining £13,000 is employed' as wage capital [21] 'in the support of labour.' 'Each year the capitalist begins his operations by having food and necessaries in his possession to the value of £13,000 [plus another quantity of the value of £2000 destined for his own consumption, J. A. S.], all of which he sells in the course of the year to his own workmen for that sum of money, and, during the same period, he pays them the like amount of money for wages: at the end of the year, they

[21] Ricardo wrote 'circulating capital,' but see below, ch. 6, sec. 5b.

replace in his possession food and necessaries of the value of £15,000, £2000 of which' he then consumes himself in the following year[22]—a piece of sequence analysis that is certainly the last word in simplicity—which is why I refrain from elucidating it either by a system of equation or by a *tableau* of the Quesnay type.[23]

Now, first, one feature of this model was generally accepted throughout the period, by Marx not less than by Say. This was the physiocrat notion, which it embodied, that the fundamental flows of goods (and money) that constitute the economic process consist of a flux and an (augmented) reflux of 'advances.' Yet, unlike the physiocrats, the 'classics' made the capitalists the sole source of these advances, and the value of the *goods* advanced swelled in the industrial process instead of in agriculture only. Nevertheless, it was substantially the old idea of Quesnay as it had already been transformed by Turgot. I cannot emphasize too strongly that this was a particular way of *interpreting* the economic process and not at all directly suggested by the practice of life: in practice, the employer 'hires' the workman—or he may be said to 'buy' the latter's services—but he does not advance anything to him. Moreover, this interpretation means more than recognition of the trivial facts that whatever is being consumed must have been produced before; or that society at any moment always lives on the past and works for the future; or, finally, that initial stocks are always among the data we must start from. J. B. Clark's theory of the synchronized process or, for that matter, Walras' system (both discussed below, Part IV, ch. 7) proves sufficiently that these facts do not force us to make them the pivots of our analysis. But if we do make them the pivots, then a number of consequences suggest themselves that are not avoided simply by refusing to recognize them. If 'capitalists' actually advance labor's real income and if this is to mean more than a monetary arrangement, discounts and 'abstinence' will have to be admitted among the essentials of the economic process whether we like them or not;[24] that is, no analysis of pro-

[22] Ricardo neglects, of course, the wear and tear of the machines, etc. This could be easily avoided, but we shall do the same thing. The £2000 must be consumed each year or else the process would not be stationary.

[23] But, in spite of its gauntness, the model we took from Ricardo will still serve two purposes that may be of some help to the reader. First it will illustrate what dynamic analysis in the modern sense is and in what it differs from the kind of investigation that J. S. Mill denoted by Dynamics. Second, it will explain what sounds like a paradox even to some economists of today, viz., how it is possible to treat a stationary process dynamically. This consists simply in describing such a process in terms of quantities that belong to a sequence in time or in terms of relations that link quantities that belong to different points of time. The particular form of dynamic analysis which this model displays is, for obvious reasons, often called Period Analysis.

[24] Talk about exploitation may cover up this state of things but cannot alter it. If I were asked what I consider the easiest method for upsetting Marx's theoretical structure, I should certainly answer: start from Marx's admission that capitalists advance wages and develop the logical consequences of this admission. I should add, of course, that this is the answer to the question what is the easiest, not to the question what is the most profound, set of moves for the anti-Marxist to make.

duction and consumption will be complete that does not take account of them in one way or another. This is important enough to justify a distinctive label for all analytic patterns that do work with the notion under discussion. We may call them *advance economics* and distinguish them from *synchronization economics,* that is, all analytic patterns that do not in a stationary process assign any fundamental role to the fact that what society lives on at any given moment is the result of past production, on the ground that, once a stationary process has been established, the flow of consumers' goods and the flow of productive service are synchronized so that the process works *as if* society did live on current production.

Second, we may as well introduce another classification of analytic patterns ('theories'), though its practical usefulness is in the analysis of growth rather than in the analysis of stationary states. No economist has ever denied, of course, that, like every other engine, the economic engine is given to stalling, besides being sensitive to disturbance by factors external to itself. But economic models differ according to whether they are or are not built on the assumption that the economic engine has or has not an *inherent* tendency to develop hitches (merely by working normally and according to design), which then make it stall or stop working normally and according to design. The various forms of underconsumption theories of crises that we shall discuss later on may serve as examples: they all of them hold that, because of oversaving or other reasons, the economic system, as it goes on functioning, develops strains and stresses by virtue of its own design or logic, for example, the strain or stress that—really or supposedly—shows in the impossibility of selling the products it is capable of producing at prices that will cover costs. With apologies, I introduce the term *hitchbound* for models that do recognize the existence in the economic system of such inherent tendencies to stall, and the term *hitchless* for models that do not. For the moment, all we get from an application of this distinction is the statement: all the models of stationary processes that were ever constructed are hitchless. Marx, for example, makes this very clear—hitches do not occur in his schema of Simple Reproduction; they enter his picture only with Accumulation.

A few comments may be useful. To begin with, though all economists do recognize the propensity of the economic engine to stall on any number of provocations and its sensitiveness to the impact of external disturbance, there is still room for disagreement as regards the importance of this propensity to stall and sensitiveness to disturbance, in particular as to the importance of both, relatively to the importance they would have in a planned economy. These questions may well make all the difference in an appraisal of the relative efficiency of different forms of economic organization. Next, let us notice that, precisely because of this, there is no question of apologetics or 'whitewashing' involved in constructing a hitchless model. For the economist who constructs such a model may still have so high an opinion about the sensitivity of the economic system he wishes to describe that he may, because of this sensitivity, rate its efficiency lower than does another economist who prefers a hitchbound model but has no such high opinion about the importance of the hitch. Malthus' model of economic growth was hitchbound. But this did not make him a 'planner.' Finally, observe that the analyst's choice between constructing a hitchbound and constructing a hitchless model is to some extent a question of mere analytic convenience. Two economists may entertain exactly the same opinion about something that both of them recognize as a stress. Nevertheless, the one may think it more useful to build a hitchless model first and then superimpose the stress, and the other may think it more useful to introduce the stress, as it were, on the groundfloor, and include it in his model from the first so that he gets a hitchbound model. The same man may do the one for some purposes and the other for other purposes. It is only our inability to divorce research from politics, or our suspicion, all too often justified, that the other fellow cannot analyze with single-minded devotion to truth, which makes problems and party issues out of decisions that do not excite anyone in more fortunate fields of research.

Third, the model from which we started may be complicated in various ways without losing its fundamental simplicity. Thus, we can easily introduce current production of producers' goods and investigate the simple conditions for equilibrium that exist between the various departments of production.[25] Also, we can easily introduce servants, physicians, teachers, and so on. More important, the reader may wonder what has become, in that model, of the third class of actors, the landowners. Why they do not figure in Ricardo's text will become clear presently. Marx treated them as a sort of appendage to the 'capitalists.' The 'capitalists' employ labor and extort from it Surplus Value. But this surplus value is not all Ricardian profits. The 'capitalist' must share his loot, the surplus value, with the landlords. Thus, in a second act of the drama of distribution, the surplus value is split into profits and rent, both of which are therefore simply parts of a unitary exploitation gain. Everybody not completely blinded by indoctrination will, however, realize immediately that, so far as description of fact and not agitatorial phraseology is concerned, this comes to the same thing as saying that the capitalist hires services of land exactly in the same sense in which he hires services of labor. In fact, all we

[25] Marx, more directly inspired by Quesnay than was any other economist of his time and perceiving more clearly the importance of such research, tried to construct tableaus or reproduction schemata of his own, starting from Quesnay's *tableau*. Technical handicaps prevented him from getting very far either in this or in the attempt to replace it by arithmetical or algebraic equations. However, *in magnis voluisse sat est* and he saw more intuitively than he was able to express. His efforts naturally centered on the case of 'extended' rather than of 'simple' reproduction. But he developed the condition of stationarity all right, and also the condition of equilibrium between the two departments of consumers' goods and producers' goods production. The interested reader finds all he needs in P. M. Sweezy's *Theory of Capitalist Development* and in its Appendix by Shigeto Tsuru.

need to do in order to arrive at this result is to ask the question why landlords are in a position to prey upon the 'capitalist's' loot. The only answer is that the services of land, also, are requisites of production. As soon as we realize this not very recondite truth, we arrive at what, to any unbiased mind, must seem to be the most natural view to take: the landowners should enter the model of the stationary process, along with labor, as another class of owners of productive services, which, at the beginning of (or during) each period, they stand ready to exchange for the income goods that the 'capitalists' were supposed to possess.[26] This should be extended, of course, to the 'capitalists' (or whoever the people are) who own the nonwage capital.

Fourth, as our discussion of Agents must have led readers to expect, the frame provided by the model under study was filled in, not by one but by two theories (or types of theories) of production and distribution, which were but very imperfectly welded in J. S. Mill's mongrel performance. This was because the triad of agents and returns was gaining ground so slowly—we know the reasons why—that types of analysis that were distinctly more primitive not only survived but also prospered.

On the one hand, then, we have the analysis that is associated, primarily, with the names of Turgot and Say; partially, hesitatingly, and mixed with incompatible elements, it was also outlined by A. Smith. It accepted the triad of agents and returns in its fullest and deepest meaning. Let me restate this meaning. Production in the economic sense of the term[27] is nothing but a combination, by purchase, of requisite and scarce services. In this process, each of the requisite and scarce services secures a price, and the determination of these prices is all that distribution or income formation fundamentally consists in. Thus the process effects, in one and the same series of steps, production in the economic sense and, through the evaluation of productive services incident to production, also distribution or the formation of incomes. Thus, in this schema, capitalist production and distribution cease to be what they would be in a socialist community, namely, two distinct processes: we behold but one

[26] This curious idea, according to which capitalist employers are supposed to hold cabbages and shoes, which they sell to their workmen, must be viewed as a measure of simplification designed to bring out essentials and meanings that underlie the treacherous mass of surface phenomena in a monetary economy. 'Capitalists' who are not themselves producers of food and necessaries are supposed to acquire these from the 'capitalists' who are. Even if it should be granted that this schema brings out the essentials correctly, we have still to observe that it neglects so many intermediate steps and draws together the essentials so closely—another example of this is the 'classic' theory of saving and investment—that the possibility of deriving practical conclusions from such a theory becomes questionable.

[27] It is highly characteristic of the difficulties most authors experienced in the task of conceptualization that the large majority kept on defining production technologically. They philosophized about man's inability to 'create matter' and his ability to displace it and to change its forms in useful ways and other completely irrelevant things. Say's phrase to the effect that production produces utilities pointed in the right direction, but much more important was his emphasis upon the combination of services in connection with his definition of entrepreneurial activity.

process of choices and evaluations of which production and distribution are merely two different aspects. And all types of incomes are by this schema explained on one and the same principle, the principle of pricing the services of co-operating factors. The analytic task of showing how this principle, so obvious in the case of consumers' goods or their services, may be made to apply also to the case of producers' goods or their services, was not clearly discerned, let alone accomplished before the rise of the theory of imputation in the next period (see Part IV, ch. 5, sec. 4a), except perhaps by a few forerunners, such as Longfield and Thünen. But the fundamental thesis, that the production-distribution process of capitalist society is in the last analysis a web of exchanges, for one another, of productive (or directly consumable) services—the employing entrepreneur acting as an intermediary—stands out with unmistakable clearness in Say's *Traité*. Among leading English authors, Lauderdale, Malthus, and Senior came more or less near to grasping this idea. But only Say made something like a success of it. It is nothing short of pathetic that, owing to a complete lack of understanding on the part of opponents and owing to complete ignorance of even the most elementary mathematical tools on the part of exponents, this promising start not only was left to hibernate for decades but also acquired a reputation for superficiality and sterility.

On the other hand, we have the type of analysis of which the Ricardian detour is the outstanding example. It would of course be an exaggeration to say that Ricardo was entirely blind to the aspect of the economic process described above. He had glimpses of it now and then, and Professor Knight went perhaps too far if he accused Ricardo of not having seen the problem of distribution as a problem of valuation *at all*.[28] But it is true that Ricardo failed to see the explanatory principle offered by the valuation aspect. This failure is intimately related to a peculiarity of the Ricardian work that is essential for understanding him and proves better than does anything else that this work constitutes in fact a detour and falls out of the historical line of economists' endeavors.

For A. Smith, A. Marshall, and ourselves, the factors that explain the size and rate of change of the Social Product or National Dividend or Total Net Output are of primary significance. This was not Ricardo's view. On the contrary, in his preface to the first edition of the *Principles*, he tells us: 'To determine the laws which regulate this distribution [of total product between landowners, capitalists, and laborers, J. A. S.] is the principal problem in Political Economy.' That is to say, he all but identifies economics with the

[28] See F. H. Knight, 'The Ricardian Theory of Production and Distribution,' *Canadian Journal of Economics and Political Science*, vol. I, February 1935. But Knight supported his indictment effectively by a quotation from a letter of Ricardo's to McCulloch to the effect that 'the proportions in which the whole produce is divided between landlords, capitalists and labourers . . . are not essentially connected with the doctrine of value' (ibid. p. 6n.). This is not true even from Ricardo's own standpoint. [Substantially this same footnote appears above, sec. 3. J. A. S. had taken out this section (5) for revision (his notes indicated dissatisfaction with the looseness of the argument) just before his death.]

theory of distribution, implying that he had little or nothing to say about—to use his language—'the laws which regulate total output.' This is a strange view to take, though it must be added at once that he did not always adhere to it, as his chapters on foreign trade and on machinery show. It enables us, however, to state the fundamental problem Ricardo wanted to solve in terms of an equation between four variables: net output equals rent plus profits plus wages (everything measured in Ricardian values, see below, ch. 6, sec. 2a). And it does still more for us. It rids us of one of these four variables. For, since we have nothing to say about total net output, we can accept its amount, whatever it is, as a datum. So we really start with an equation that contains only three variables. But one equation in three variables is still a hopeless business. Therefore, Ricardo (ch. 2) places himself on a margin of agricultural production where rent is zero. Observe carefully what this means for Ricardo's analytic set-up. By numberless writers the West-Ricardo theory of rent has been discussed in isolation, and with nothing but the question in mind whether it was 'right' or 'wrong.' This question is completely pointless. The West-Ricardo theory of rent cannot be discussed in isolation, that is, without reference to the whole of the West-Ricardo system. It is within this system only that it acquires analytic meaning and, in fact, owing to Ricardo's inability to deal with systems of simultaneous equations, imposes itself. Outside of the West-Ricardo system considered as a whole, it has very little meaning and is hardly worth bothering about.

Let us go on. That theory of rent having fulfilled its only purpose, which is to get rid of another variable in our equation, we are left, on the margin of production, with one equation and two variables—still a hopeless business. But, so it occurred to Ricardo, wages are not really a variable either, at least not within that equation. He thought he knew, from external considerations, what they will be in the long run: here the old Quesnay theory comes in, reinforced by Malthus' law of population—the wages will be roughly equal to what is necessary to enable 'the labourers, one with another, to subsist and to perpetuate their race without either increase or diminution.' And so we reach the blessed goal at last: profit, the only variable left, is determined too. Call this patchwork ingenious, if you so please, but do not deny that it is patchwork—and rather primitive patchwork at that.

Marx's schema is open to a similar objection.[29] He also eliminated rent from the fundamental problem, though in a different way. His equation of distribution, in terms of Marxist values, then reads: net output equals wages plus surplus. Again we can take the net output as a datum. And again the surplus is a residual, the determination of which depends upon the external considerations that determine wages.

J. S. Mill's system, on the contrary, absorbed enough of the Say conception—and in addition was sufficiently helped by Senior's notion of abstinence—to be free from any such objection, and it offered all the elements of the

[29] On Marx's elimination of rent from the final problem, see above, ch. 1, sec. 4; on his equation of distribution in terms of Marxist values, see below, ch. 6, sec. 6g.

complete model that Marshall was to build. But he retained so many Ricardian relics that there is some excuse for Jevons' and the Austrians' not seeing that they were developing his analysis and for believing instead that they had to destroy it.

6. The 'Classic' Conception of Economic Development

I have tried to explain above (Part I, ch. 4, sec. 1d) the meaning and role of what I have called Vision—that first perception or impression of the phenomena to be investigated which factual and 'theoretical' analysis, in an endless relation of give and take, then work up into scientific propositions. But when we are concerned with nothing more ambitious than to formulate the way in which—on the plane of pure logic—economic quantities 'hang together,' that is, when we are concerned with the logic of static equilibrium or even with the essential features of a stationary process, the role of Vision is but a modest one—for we are really working up a few pretty obvious facts, perception of which comes easily to us. Things are very different when we turn to the task of analyzing economic life in its secular process of change. It is then much more difficult to visualize the really important factors and features of this process than it is to formulate their modi operandi once we have (or think we have) got hold of them. Vision (and all the errors that go with it) therefore plays a greater role in this type of venture than it does in the other. This may be illustrated by the Stagnationist Thesis of our own time, that is, the notion that the capitalist system has spent its powers; that the opportunities of private enterprise are giving out; that our economy is, amid convulsions, settling down to a state of Secular Stagnation or, as some prefer to call it, Maturity. No doubt facts and arguments have been collected in order to establish this notion, which has also been embodied in theoretical models. But it should be obvious that these facts and arguments rationalized a pre-existing vision or impression which they would have been powerless to create, if for no other reason, because the relevant observations extend over a period that is much too short and was much too much under the influence of clearly abnormal events to warrant any conclusions or predictions of that kind. Economists' visions were in no better case a century or so ago. We shall consider three types of vision of the economic future of humanity that the writers of the period under survey tried to formulate and to establish. In other words, we shall consider three types of theories of economic development.

The first type, associated primarily with the names of Malthus, West, Ricardo, and James Mill, fully justifies their being labeled 'pessimists.' Its well-known features were: pressure of population, present already but still more to be expected; nature's decreasing response to human effort to increase the supply of food; hence falling net returns to industry, more or less constant real wages, and ever-increasing (absolutely and relatively) rents of land. We are now not concerned with the manner in which these 'classics' gave analytic effect to this vision of theirs, that is, with the manner in which they formulated their 'laws' of population, decreasing returns in agriculture, and so on, and with the analytic use they made of them. To this we shall attend in the next chapter. Here we are concerned only with what they thought they *saw*, that is, with the vision that was at the back of their analysis—or, if you prefer, with their preconceptions.

The most interesting thing to observe is the complete lack of imagination which that vision reveals. Those writers lived at the threshold of the most spectacular economic developments ever witnessed. Vast possibilities matured into realities under their very eyes. Nevertheless, they saw nothing but cramped economies, struggling with ever-decreasing success for their daily bread. They were convinced that technological improvement and increase in capital would in the end fail to counteract the fateful law of decreasing returns. James Mill, in his *Elements*, even offered a 'proof' for this. In other words, they were all stagnationists. Or, to use their own term, they all expected, for the future, the advent of a stationary state, which here no longer means an analytic tool but a future reality.

Apparently, J. S. Mill was in better case. He dropped all 'pessimism,' and he was even intelligent enough to realize that there was no reason to look upon the future of the masses 'as otherwise than hopeful.' However, this was only because he believed—as other Malthusians such as Chalmers had believed before him—that mankind was learning the Malthusian lesson and was about to restrict propagation voluntarily so that the race between capital and population would be won by the former. In this he proved himself a better prophet than did others. But he had no idea what the capitalist engine of production was going to achieve. On the contrary, toward the end of his life (around 1870) he really became a stagnationist in the modern sense, believing that the private-enterprise economy had pretty much done what it was able to do and that a stationary state of the economic process was near at hand. But there is this difference between him and our own stagnationists. He did not, as A. Smith and Ricardo had done, view the stationary state with misgivings (*Principles*, Book IV, ch. 6), because he had eliminated the bogey of overpopulation. But neither did he share the modern stagnationist's misgivings, because he did not fear the bogey of underconsumption. To him the stationary state looked rather comfortable—like a world without 'bustle' (his term) in which a philosopher like himself would not mind living and in which there would be moderate prosperity (or better) all round.[1] The question, whether the social structure of capitalism could persist in circumstances in which the main function of the capitalist entrepreneur was being lost, we may answer for him by saying that he visualized the advent of the stationary state as a very gradual process so that institutions and minds would have no difficulty in making the currently necessary adjustments.

In agreement with all the English 'classics'—perhaps we might say, with the spirit of his age—he greatly underrated the importance in economic de-

[1] This stationary state was a state of a peculiar kind and did not conform to the definition given above. It did not quite exclude technological progress or increase in capital. It was really stationary with respect to population only, it being assumed that this would cause everything to go on more quietly.

velopment of the element of personal initiative and, correspondingly, he greatly overemphasized the importance of mere increase in physical producers' goods. And in this again, he overemphasized the importance of saving.[2] Accepting the Turgot-Smith theory of the investment process, he took it for granted that the important thing was to have something to invest: the invesment itself did not present additional problems either as to promptness—it was *normally* sure to be immediate—or as to direction—it was sure to be guided by investment opportunities that were equally obvious to all and existed independently of the investing man.[3] Saving, then, was the powerful lever of economic development. And it never created obstructions; the saving act itself did not, since the sum saved was immediately spent on productive labor; the resulting expansion of productive capacity did not, since products of correctly planned production were always capable of being sold at cost-covering prices.[4] To use our own term, J. S. Mill's schema of economic development, like Say's, was essentially hitchless. Malthus' and Sismondi's schemata are examples of hitchbound ones, the hitches arising in both cases not so much from saving per se, but from the resulting increase in productive capacity. Ricardo's also was hitchbound, but for another reason, namely, the reason enshrined in his interpretation of the law of diminishing returns.

The second type of vision of the economic future—the 'optimistic' type—can be best illustrated by such names as Carey and List. Whatever we may think of the virtues of their technical analysis, at least they did not lack imagination. They felt intuitively that the dominant fact about capitalism was its power to create productive capacity, and they *saw* vast potentialities looming in the near future. With less imagination but with plenty of sound judgment, the majority of economists on the Continent refused to share the 'pessimism' of the Ricardians and of Malthus. At least, most of them watered it down. But beyond this, it was natural for those who more or less followed Say's lead so far as technical theory was concerned to realize that neither facts nor analysis were bearing out the Ricardian vision. These were called 'optimists' and, partly but not wholly under Marxist influence, there grew up a tradition to despise them as shallow. This view is in fact historically associated with

[2] Of course we may define saving in such a way as to make that statement meaningless. But I mean by saving (or thrift) the distinctive phenomenon we all know (unless we are too familiar with the economic theory of the 1930's) and therefore consider it as a factor in the process of the accumulation of physical capital goods. My statement then means that J. S. Mill, like all the authors that followed the Turgot-Smith line, was at fault in believing that thrift was the all-important (causal) factor in that process.

[3] This mechanistic view, too, was an important element in the economic *Weltbild* of the 'classics.' They were entirely unaware of how great a part of capitalist reality they thereby suppressed in silence.

[4] The latter proposition is more delicate to handle than J. S. Mill and the economists of his time and line realized. But its opponents were below and not above the limited truth it asserts. Also, though in a particularly narrow way—through saving alone—Mill thus did recognize the most obvious of all truths about capitalist development, viz., that, by virtue of its logic, it tends to raise the standard of life of the masses.

many writers—the Bastiat type—who fully deserve to be so called. But in itself this 'optimism' was the result of both a vision and a theory that were more correct than those of the 'pessimists': the degree of truth of a doctrine is by no means always positively correlated with the ability of its exponents.[5]

The third type of vision of the economic future and of corresponding theories of economic development will be represented by Marx alone. Based upon a diagnosis of the social situation of the 1840's and 1850's that was ideologically vitiated in its roots,[6] hopelessly wrong in its prophecy of ever-increasing mass misery, inadequately substantiated both factually and analytically, Marx's performance is yet the most powerful of all. In his general schema of thought, development was not what it was with all other economists of that period, an appendix to economic statics, but the central theme. And he concentrated his analytic powers on the task of showing how the economic process, changing itself by virtue of its own inherent logic, incessantly changes the social framework—the whole of society in fact. We have already dwelt on the grandeur of this conception; we shall briefly discuss its analytic aspects below.

Only two points can be mentioned here. First, nobody—not even the most ardent of optimists with whom Marx had this point in common—had *then* a fuller conception of the size and power of the capitalist engine of the future. With a quaint touch of teleology, Marx said repeatedly that it is the 'historical task' or 'privilege' of capitalist society to create a productive apparatus that will be adequate for the requirements of a higher form of human civilization. However much our modern positivism may resent this way of putting it, the essential truth of what he meant to convey, in this respect, stands out clearly enough.

Second, the motor of Marx's economic development was indeed not quite the colorless Saving of J. S. Mill: he linked it—or investment—to technological change in a manner that is not to be found in the latter's *Principles*. But all the same the motor is Saving, which with him is as promptly turned into investment as it is with Mill. This fact is hidden but not abolished by Marx's use of the term Accumulation and by his violent diatribes against the 'nursery tale' (*Kinderfibel*) that physical capital is created by saving. There are good reasons as well as bad ones for Marx's dislike of the latter term. In particular, capitalist fortunes do not typically arise from saving income dollars and piling

[5] In this and other respects, the case is similar to that of the doctrine of the essential harmony of class interests. On investigation, this doctrine turns out to be only partly tenable—but rather more so than does the doctrine of the essential antagonism of classes. But the latter has been preached with unsurpassable force and, moreover, renders the radical intellectual's ideology. The former has never been put forcefully or even convincingly. And it does not suit the book of the radical intellectual. So he who holds it is likely to be sneered at as a sort of Caspar Milquetoast, and this is quite as effective as, or more so than, serious argument would be. In the present case, there is something else however. No matter what the reason is, it is a fact that pessimistic views about a thing always seem to the public mind to be more 'profound' than optimistic ones.

[6] It was pointed out above that Marx took his picture of social reality from the radical ideology of his formative period.

them up neatly, but by the creation of sources of returns, the capitalized value of which then constitutes a 'fortune.' However, the implications of this he would not have liked any better than he did the picture of good and frugal boys who save till they find themselves rich. So it had to be Exploitation forever, so exclusively in fact as to endanger the explanatory value of his schema: for the social process as a whole, the essential point is in any case the capacity-creating use made of capitalists' gains—no matter whether or not they arise from exploitation and are invested again for the purpose of further exploitation—and this essential point, so a history of analysis has to notice, is fundamentally the same with Marx and Mill, however different the phraseologies were in which they conveyed it.

CHAPTER 6

[General Economics: Pure Theory] [1]

[1. AXIOMATICS. SENIOR'S FOUR POSTULATES]

TO SENIOR belongs the signal honor of having been the first to make the attempt to state, consciously and explicitly, the postulates that are necessary and sufficient in order to build up—it is misleading to say to 'deduce'—that little analytic apparatus commonly known as economic theory, or, to put it differently, to provide for it an axiomatic basis. The merit of the attempt is but little decreased by the fact that his list of postulates was incomplete and otherwise defective and by the further fact that he invited attack by defining that ap-

[1] [Section 1 of this chapter was written much earlier than the remainder of the chapter. The typescript was dated December 1943. It was obvious that J. A. S. intended to revise these pages on Senior and to make them the introductory section to this chapter. There were many notes clipped to the early typescript. There was no title for this section and no title for the chapter, but the remaining sections were relatively complete with titles for sections and subsections. This section is presented as written, although it lacks the proper introductory remarks and the revisions J. A. S. would have made.]

paratus so narrowly or else by equating this theory to 'political economy.' It is increased by the fact that the attempt occurs in the course of a general theoretical house cleaning and is part of a wider attempt at rigorous conceptualization. First he polished Wealth and (exchange) Value; then he stated his four Elementary Propositions—the postulates; finally he presented, under the inadequate heading of Distribution (Exchange or Value and Distribution would be more adequate), a set of additional concepts and of relations that together with the immediate development of the postulates, which settle most matters usually dealt with under the heading Production, are supposed to make up the theoretical organon. As a venture in pure theory, his performance is clearly superior to that of Ricardo. We shall now consider the postulates, using in doing so every opportunity that may arise of looking further afield.

[(a) *The First Postulate.*] The first reads as follows: 'That every man desires to obtain additional Wealth with as little sacrifice as possible.' [2] Implicitly at least, some such proposition underlies all theoretical reasoning and it would just as well fit into Ricardo's or Malthus' texts. Adam Smith and J. S. Mill took it for granted, Lauderdale came near to stating it explicitly. In the language of the next period—in Marshall's for instance—it can be expressed by saying that every man desires to maximize the difference between the sum total of his satisfactions and the sum total of his sacrifices, both discounted to the present moment. But what is its nature and standing?

Senior calls it 'a matter of consciousness' and distinguishes it from the three other propositions, which are 'matters of observation.' But it would not affect his meaning if we called it a matter of introspective observation. Moreover, there are, in his 'development' of this proposition (e.g. pp. 27-8) [3] various comments on the behavior of Dutchmen and Englishmen and Indians of Mexico that are obviously based upon an external observation of sorts. We may therefore provisionally speak of observation even in this case and proceed forthwith to state the following generalization about all four of them or any other proposition an economist may see fit to postulate. In so doing we exemplify—and in part justify—Say's opinion on economics being an observational science (though he said experimental), which will thus be seen, appearances notwithstanding, to involve no disagreement with Senior.

Nobody ever denied—or, by his practice, belied—the truth that economic theory, like any other theory, is founded upon observation. Senior, by taking little trouble with observations and concentrating upon inference from them, may have created a wrong impression and he may himself have held erroneous views about the relative importance of observing and inferring, but he did not *in fact*—though he did *in phrase*—treat economics as *toto cælo* 'deductive.' Now, the facts observed enter theory as hypotheses or assumptions or 'restrictions,' that is to say, as generalized statements induced or suggested

[2] [The postulates are discussed in Nassau William Senior, *An Outline of the Science of Political Economy* (1st ed. 1836; 6th ed. 1872; publ. in the Library of Economics, 1938).]

[3] [Page references are to the edition published by the Library of Economics.]

by observation.[4] When we wish to stress our confidence in their validity, we often call them Laws—compare for instance Keynes's 'psychological law' of the propensity to save. When we simply wish to stress our resolve not to challenge them in the course of a particular argument, we call them Principles. But all these words really mean one and the same thing, and there is no point in philosophizing about them. This applies to frontier facts as well as to facts that belong to our field proper. The difference, as pointed out above, is only that in the first case we do not, in the second we do, feel fully responsible for the validity of our statements about them.

Quite another question is whether or not we are to be satisfied with an observation of the Seniorian or, for that matter, the Ricardian or Millian kind. Three aspects of this question must be carefully distinguished if we are to understand 'classic' or any other theoretical procedure. There are first the two problems of observation by introspection and by common or everyday experience. Many economists of later times, especially the founders of the so-called Austrian School, have stoutly stood for both. Wieser in particular seems quite in accord with J. S. Mill in accepting common experience as a valid basis for theory to start from. Critics have sometimes gone so far as to rule both out entirely on the ground that introspection and common experience are nothing but cloaks for purely speculative assertions. This extreme form of the criticism is indeed open to the reply that some postulates—such as that businessmen on the whole prefer making money to losing it—are evidently not miles from the truth and that it is vexatious to insist upon elaborate research for the purpose of establishing them. But a less extreme form of the same criticism is not invalidated by such cases. There are others—savings habits for instance—in which introspection and common experience cannot be convincingly invoked; and even where they can, the relative importance and the *modus operandi* of the facts that enter a postulate may still have to be ascertained by more substantial methods.

This opens up the second aspect of our question. Senior's postulate embodies observation, but possibly inadequate observation. Does this justify us in rejecting everything that is between the covers of his book? Evidently not. The postulate divested of unnecessary utilitarian associations is plausible. All that could be objected to it on grounds such as that he overemphasized selfishness, overestimated the rational element in our behavior, and neglected historical differences in the intensity of the desire for 'wealth' at different times and in different places, is amply taken into account in his comments upon his proposition. If we feel misgivings nevertheless, all we have to do is to start appropriate research. Anything else is pure filibustering. So long as the strong *prima facie* plausibility of the postulate is not destroyed by the results of such research, and so long as particular problems are not specified for which plausibility is not enough and which were nevertheless attacked by those critic-economists, we may indeed feel that Senior's analysis was primitive—we know

[4] It should be noticed that this is only one of several meanings of the word Hypothesis. We have met others. The same remark applies to Laws and Principles.

that the whole of Senior's, Ricardo's, and Mill's work is primitive, in inference no less than in observation—but we cannot deny its scientific character or call it wrong on principle.

The third aspect of our question comes into view when we ask ourselves whether Senior's first postulate could not be reformulated in a way that would get round the objections that have been or might be raised. But since the economists of that period, if guilty of Psychologism, were certainly much less guilty of it than were the economists of the next period, we had better defer discussion of this point until later.

[(b) *The Second Postulate: the Principle of Population.*] Senior's second postulate states the principle of population: 'That the Population of the world, or, in other words, the number of persons inhabiting it, is limited only by moral or physical evil, or by fear of a deficiency of those articles of wealth which the habits of the individuals of each class of its inhabitants lead them to require' (op. cit. p. 26). We take this opportunity to touch briefly upon the contribution of Malthus and the discussion that developed about it. Moreover, it will be convenient to add a few remarks about the history of the theory of population in the subsequent period so that we may drop it from our picture in Part IV. This decision is suggested by the fact that its interest for *analytic* economics greatly declined during the second half of the nineteenth century and that it then grew into a semi-independent science, which it is impossible to deal with in this book. [J. A. S. note: 'but came back in our time.']

We have seen already that all the facts and arguments that Malthus presented in the first edition of his *Essay* (1798), down to the details of the analysis as well as of the applications, had been worked out before by so large a number of writers that we may speak of them as widely accepted at the beginning of the nineties. The case therefore differs essentially from the bulk of all those cases, still more frequent in economics than in other sciences, in which a proposition that we associate with an individual name has been anticipated by 'forerunners.' This does not amount to a charge of plagiarism or even to a denial of 'subjective' originality. But it does reduce Malthus' contribution to effective co-ordination and restatement. The significance of its tremendous success at the time—with the profession and with political society—is underlined by the fact that, for about a century to come, theory of population was to mean arguments pro and con the Malthusian theory.

Also, I have already alluded to the attempts that have been made to account for this success, and for Malthus' performance itself, by the ideological mechanism. While giving my reason for refusing to accept this explanation, I have, however, admitted that there are two facts that do lend some support to it. The one of them is that the theory was immediately used as an argument against measures of social betterment. William Pitt availed himself of it. Malthus himself published a pamphlet, which is judged mildly if described by no worse term than silly, in which he argued, as Townsend had before him, that the proposal to encourage parishes to build cottages must on no account be entertained because building cottages would encourage early marriages (*Letter to Samuel Whitbread* . . . 1807). In the public mind this sort of thing then assumed the form that the masses had themselves to thank for their economic situation and that nothing much could be done about it. The second fact is this: Malthus himself related that the argument developed in his mind in the course of discussions with his 'social-minded' father; and in the subtitle of the first edition of the *Essay*, he pointed significantly to the 'speculations of Mr. Godwin [5] [the author of the radical bible of the day], M. Condorcet, and other writers.' I still think that these facts do not prove more than that every idea can and will be made to *serve* some ideological purpose as soon as it emerges into the limelight.

We are not, however, concerned with the application of this theory to practical questions—or any applications except the one to the theory of wages, which will be noticed later—but only with the theory itself. As presented in the first edition, it clearly was intended to mean that population was actually and inevitably increasing faster than subsistence and that this was the reason for the misery observed. The geometrical and arithmetical ratios of these increases, to which Malthus like earlier writers seems to have attached considerable importance, as well as his other attempts at mathematical precision, are nothing but faulty expressions of this view which can be passed by here with the remark that there is of course no point whatever in trying to formulate independent 'laws' for the behavior of two interdependent quantities. The performance as a whole is deplorable in technique and little short of foolish in substance. But it is at least not open to the criticism that Malthus merely asserted the horrible triviality that, *if* increase in population should go on in a geometric ratio (with a common ratio greater than unity), it must at some time in the future produce a state of things in which people will be crowding this earth as herrings crowd a barrel.

The second edition of the *Essay on the Principle of Population* (1803) is a completely new work which, besides copious statistics, contains an entirely

[5] William Godwin's (1756-1836) principal work (*Enquiry concerning Political Justice*, 1793, 2nd [amended] ed. 1796) and his essays published in 1797 under the title *The Enquirer* are highly interesting documents of the time and would have to hold a place of honor in any history of political thought, as a monument, in particular, of that bourgeois type of anarchism which condemns not only violence but also any sort of compulsion. It is essentially anti-*étatiste*—and posits equality as an end in itself. But his attempts at economic analysis, as he would have himself admitted, remained too rudimentary (though less so than those made by other members of the group which I have chosen Godwin to represent) to require report, except in so far as his book *Of Population* (1820) is concerned. It is curious to write—and should be mentioned to the credit of Malthus—that when the *Essay on the Principles of Population* appeared, Godwin considered its argument not only convincing but *new*. He changed his mind about the former point however, and in his own book undertook to annihilate Malthus' argument. In doing this he showed considerable analytic power. In spite of Bonar's adverse judgment (*Malthus and His Work*, pp. 369 et seq.), it should I think be admitted that Godwin succeeded in making several points which can be considered real contributions.

different theory.[6] For the introduction of the prudential check ('moral restraint'), though it was no more a new discovery than was anything else in Malthus' theory, makes all the difference. Only it does not (1) raise the intellectual level of the performance or (2) make its results any more tenable or (3) add to its explanatory value. As regards the first point, it is sufficient to note that it did not occur to Malthus to discuss any effects of his moral restraint other than the effect on numbers—for example, effects on the quality of the population or on schemes of motivation. As regards the second point, the new formulation made it indeed possible for adherents to this day to take the ground that Malthus had foreseen, and accounted for, practically everything opponents might say; but this does not alter the fact that all the theory gains thereby is orderly retreat with the artillery lost. As regards the third point, the various 'if's' that were then introduced leave—of all the claims to universal validity—only the triviality mentioned above and, beyond this, the possibility of explaining individual historical situations by the possible failure of other elements of the environment to develop along with population which does not require any general principle. Professor Cannan (op. cit. p. 144) did not exaggerate when he wrote that the *Essay* 'falls to the ground as an argument, and remains only a chaos of facts collected to illustrate the effect of laws which do not exist.'

Malthus himself was reluctant to admit all the consequences that lurked in his qualifications of 1803. On the contrary, he clung to his original conclusions as much as possible, particularly to the relevance of his theory for his own time. It was therefore by no means superfluous, as some admirers kept on assuring their readers, that Senior and Everett[7] (also others), either facing honestly those consequences or else arriving at their conclusions independently of a study of Malthus' qualifications, pointed out from different stand-

[6] [There is some repetition in this section of material already presented in Chapter 4 and elsewhere which J. A. S. would undoubtedly have taken care of in his revision.]

[7] Senior in his *Two lectures on Population, to which is added a Correspondence between the author and the Rev. T. R. Malthus* (1829) developed the views which were expounded again in his *Outline*. He always treated Malthus with infinite respect—he even called him a benefactor of humanity (sic!)—and did all in his power to minimize his deviation from what he evidently considered to be established doctrine. All the less justification is there for the practice of some later writers who, with nauseating pontificality, treated Senior as a none too intelligent pupil who needed to be set right by Malthus. As a matter of fact, it is perfectly clear that Senior realized the extent to which Malthus' qualifications ought to have spelled recantation and to what degree his adherence to some of his former opinions spelled contradiction.

A. H. Everett, an American diplomatist and newspaper editor, was perfectly right to call his book *New Ideas on Population* (1823). For his main point, viz., that increase in population means increased production of food and is likely to induce improvements in the methods of its production, *was* new in his day, much more so at any rate than anything Malthus ever said. It introduced one of the two relations that are lacking in Malthus between the increase of population and the increase of subsistence, and in general presented, quite independently of the specifically American elements of its argument, a useful approach to the population problem as a whole.

points and by different arguments how little there was really left. This is pathetically obvious in Senior's formulation of the principle in his *Outline*—'that the population of the world . . . is limited only by moral or physical evil, or by fear of the deficiency of those articles of wealth which the habits of individuals of each class of its inhabitants lead them to require.' Nevertheless Senior, unlike Everett, continued to consider it as a fundamental postulate of economics, and still more was it so considered by Ricardo, James Mill, McCulloch, and others. J. S. Mill dealt very briefly with population in his chapter 'Of the Law of Increase of Labour' (*Principles*, Book I, ch. 10). It is true that he explained this by declaring that the subject had been fully dealt with by Malthus to whom he refers his readers. But one might be tempted to infer that he was disposed to discount the importance of the principle. He might have been because, following a trend that had become established by the time he wrote his *Principles*, J. S. Mill put the law of population into a relation to the 'law' of diminishing returns from land—which, it is worth while noting, was entirely absent from Malthus' *Essay*—and because he was prepared, as we shall see, to admit plenty of exceptions and qualifications of that law. Nevertheless, it is certain that he entertained a strong belief in the validity and immediate importance of the Malthusian theory. In the *Principles* he showed this by his interest in the problems of a stationary population (Book IV, ch. 6) and in particular by his blunt assertion, which is as categorical as it is unsupported, that 'the density of population necessary to enable mankind to obtain, in the greatest degree, all the advantages both of co-operation and of social intercourse has, in all the most populous countries, been attained'—thereby suggesting that any further increase of (European) population would be productive of nothing but 'pressure.' Still more convincingly, however, this belief shows in his indubitable sympathy with birth control.[8]

Thus—interesting phenomenon—the teaching of Malthus' *Essay* became firmly entrenched in the system of the economic orthodoxy of the time in spite of the fact that it should have been, and in a sense was, recognized as fundamentally untenable or worthless by 1803 and that further reasons for so considering it were speedily forthcoming.[9] It became the 'right' view on

[8] See N. E. Himes, 'John Stuart Mill's Attitude towards Neo-Malthusianism,' *Economic History: A Supplement of the Economic Journal*, January 1929. Malthus, most predecessors, and some of his successors, such as Senior, seem to have included birth control with 'vice' or 'moral evil' along with prostitution. But all the leading philosophical radicals seem to have looked to it as the true solution of the problem. So did Bentham himself and, of course, Francis Place. James Mill gave a lead in the same direction in his *Elements* (1821, p. 34). Grote held the same opinion. In such matters, it is not safe to trust to logic. Attitudes to these questions link up with intimate elements of our psycho-physical organism that may exert influences of which we are entirely unaware: individual ideologies arise not only from social location. I think, nevertheless, that in the case of J. S. Mill the pressure of a purely economic diagnosis of the Malthusian kind may be reasonably asserted, at least as a rationalization.

[9] It should be observed that this survival was of course greatly facilitated by a surface observation: clearly, the most obvious reason for misery and squalor in the individual

population, just as free trade had become the 'right' policy, which only ignorance or obliquity could possibly fail to accept—part and parcel of the set of eternal truth that had been observed once for all. Objectors might be lectured, if they were worthy of the effort, but they could not be taken seriously. No wonder that some people, utterly disgusted at this intolerable presumption which had so little to back it, began to loathe this 'science of economics,' quite independently of class or party considerations—a feeling that has been an important factor in that science's fate ever after.

The majority of the profession, however, especially in England, submitted. After 1850 the interest of economists in the population question declined, but they rarely failed to pay their respects to the shibboleth. So did Marshall, though he stripped it of practically all its salient features, and so did Böhm-Bawerk and Walras, who in their theoretical work never used it at all. At the end of the century the one leading man to take it seriously and to emphasize it again and again was Wicksell, who also resuscitated the doctrine of optimal population which, however, had commanded support throughout. One might have expected these rumbles to die out but on the contrary, after the First World War, they actually revived again in a cannonade: Mr. Keynes stepped forth to hold that the Malthusian issue was as vital as it had ever been; and that in fact it had entered on a new lease of life since—he put the date somewhere in the first decade of the century—nature had begun to yield a decreasing response to human effort. The profession was startled, as presumably it was intended to be. Sir William Beveridge espoused the opposite view. But the controversy subsided for the unscientific reason that people had more pressing concerns in a world in which a spectacular fall in the birth rate and a no less spectacular torrent of unsaleable foodstuffs and raw materials were about to set in. Mr. Keynes said somewhere that economics is a 'dangerous science.' It is indeed.[10]

The decline of the Malthusian *theory* or, at all events, of its role within the system of general economic theory, was not however due to its opponents. We can pass quickly over their contributions, which—with the possible exceptions of those of Godwin and Everett which have been mentioned already—hardly ever met the theoretical issue. One point they made which, as we have seen, was not of minor importance where immediate applicability of the

---

proletarian family was size. The inference that all would have been better off and happier if all had restricted the number of their children follows by means of the same fallacy that led people to infer from everyone's tendency to make the best of his situation that, if all are left to their own devices, a maximum of 'happiness' must result for all.

[10] Keynes's first pronouncement on the matter occurs in his famous *Economic Consequences of the Peace* (1919). Sir William Beveridge presented his view in an address to Section F of the British Association, published in the *Economic Journal*, 1923, and in an article, 'Mr. Keynes' Evidence for Overpopulation' in *Economica*, 1924. Keynes replied and the newspapers did their best to confuse issues. See on postwar discussions in general: A. B. Wolfe, "The Population Problem Since the World War,' three articles in the *Journal of Political Economy*, 1928 and 1929.

theory is in question: they showed more or less effectively that, at best, the Malthusian theory might apply at some distant future but that it was no good as an explanation of present poverty. This ground was taken by Oppenheimer,[11] but had been taken before—in a sense by Senior and much more strongly by William Hazlitt (*A Reply to the Essay on Population*, 1807). Under this heading we may mention the 'Ricardian socialists' of the twenties of the nineteenth century such as W. Thompson,[12] who emphasized that the Malthusian theory would work out quite differently in different forms of social organization and that, for example, the economic independence of women and a higher standard of life would alone suffice to put a different complexion upon the matter; and Karl Marx, who developed this 'institutional relativity' [13] into the sweeping proposition that 'overpopulation,' as observed in capitalist society, has nothing to do with any immutable laws but is specific to this form of organization and simply an incident to its mechanism of accumulation.

Other objectors tried to replace the Malthusian geometric progression by other laws of increase (e.g., Sadler, 1830, Doubleday, 1846), which do not soar toward infinity but display maxima or plateaus that might be reached before the point of Malthusian pressure. The difficulty was to motivate these forms without using moral restraint or other Malthusian factors. On this rock all those ships foundered—nothing was proposed beyond more or less dilettantic hints. These laws induced others that do not carry causal implications—not necessarily, at least—but merely aim at describing actual and, by risky extrapolation, future developments. Verhulst's (1845) was one of the earliest of these attempts, and many statisticians have tried their hand at this task ever since (for example, Knibbs, Pearl, Hotelling). Laws of this type are of course neutral to the Malthusian issue. Still other objectors pleaded what might be termed attenuating and compensating circumstances—Carey was one of the most eminent of these and Chalmers was another—or the undesired (anti-eugenic) effects of birth control. For our purposes it does not seem necessary to go into this [14] or into the opinions proffered by biologists. But it is necessary to mention a theory which, whether or not it can be stated so as to

[11] Franz Oppenheimer, *Das Bevölkerungsgesetz des T. R. Malthus* (1900).

[12] *Inquiry into the Principles of the Distribution of Wealth* (1824).

[13] This term was suggested by Professor A. B. Wolfe's article on 'Population' in the *Encyclopaedia of the Social Sciences*, to which I take the opportunity of calling the reader's attention.

[14] A few general references should, however, be added: J. Garnier, *Du Principe de population* (1857), a good symptom of Malthus' conquest in France; A. Messedaglia, *Della teoria della popolazione* . . . (1858), an able criticism of Malthus' workmanship; L. Brentano, 'Die Malthussche Lehre und die Bevölkerungsbewegung der letzten Dezennien' (*Abhandlungen der historischen Klasse der Königlich Bayerischen Akademie der Wissenschaften*, vol. XXIV), interesting because it reflects an opinion that foreshadowed the important development to be mentioned in the text, if for no other reason. Comparison is instructive of this and the earlier book by Travers Twiss, *On certain Tests of a Thriving Population* (1845). K. Kautsky, the official head of Marxian orthodoxy, contributed: *Der Einfluss der Volksvermehrung auf den Fortschritt der Gesellschaft*

become compatible with Malthus' text, yields the exact opposite of Malthus' conclusion: Mombert's 'prosperity theory' (*Wohlstandstheorie*) of population, according to which we are to expect a fall in the birth rate from the rationalizing influence on behavior of a higher standard of life.[15] In a sense, Malthusians might claim this as an elaboration of 'restraint,' moral or otherwise. But, so far as it goes, it turns effectively the tables on any prediction that increase of subsistence (in a wide sense of the word) will always or normally induce an increase in the rate of propagation.

An ordinary mortal might have thought that the fall in birth rate, first in the upper then also in the lower strata, first in urban then also in agrarian areas, and the rapidly approaching goal of a stationary population, should have set worrying economists at rest. But that mortal would thereby have proved that he knew nothing about economists. While some of them were still fondling the Malthusian toy, others zestfully embraced a new one. Deprived of the pleasure of worrying themselves and of sending cold shivers down the spines of other people on account of the prospective (or present) horrors of overpopulation, they started worrying themselves and others on account of a prospectively empty world.

[As has been pointed out, in note 1 at the beginning, this section was written much earlier than the other five sections and had not been integrated with the rest of the chapter. There were numerous notes to be used in revision and rewriting.

There is no discussion here of Senior's third postulate: 'That the Powers of Labour, and of the other Instruments which Produce Wealth, may be indefinitely increased by using their Products as the means of further Production.' This third postulate is, however, discussed below in Section 5 (Capital), under the subheading *Senior's Contributions*.]

[(c) *The Fourth Postulate: Diminishing Returns*.] We shall take up the fourth postulate next: 'That, agricultural skill remaining the same, additional Labour employed on the land within a given district produces in general a less proportionate return, or, in other words, that though, with every increase of the labour bestowed, the aggregate return is increased, the increase of the return is not in proportion to the increase of the labour.' It is the fact or hypothesis or principle or law or tendency of Diminishing Returns. There is nothing remarkable about Senior's formulation of it except that he stressed more than did other authors, especially more than did Ricardo, the importance of the necessary condition of its validity—a given and constant techno-

(1880). Finally, I may quote a later Malthusian: F. Virgilii *Problema della popolazione* (1924) and again, R. Gonnard's *Histoire des doctrines de la population* (1923), and especially J. J. Spengler's scholarly and exhaustive study on 'French Population Theory since 1800' (*Journal of Political Economy*, two articles, October and December 1936).

[15] Paul Mombert; see, e.g., his contribution on population ('Bevölkerungslehre') to M. Weber's *Grundriss der Sozialökonomik* (1914) or his *Bevölkerungsentwicklung und Wirtschaftsgestaltung* (1932). Among 'forerunners' were Brentano (see preceding footnote) and, at a stretch, Sir Archibald Alison, *The Principles of Population* (1840). On Mombert see below, Part IV, ch. 6, sec. 1b.

logical horizon, or the proviso, 'agricultural skill remaining the same'—and also the importance of true exceptions, which makes a lot of difference to the tones of the picture.[16] There is, however, a point about his management of diminishing returns that does merit particular attention. All the leading economists of that period confined diminishing returns to land and many had asserted an opposite 'law' for manufactures, especially West and McCulloch.[17] But nobody that I know of has been so emphatic about this 'law' of increasing returns in manufactures as was Senior, who asserted with little qualification that 'additional labour when employed in manufactures is *more*, when employed in agriculture is *less*, efficient in proportion' (*Outline*, pp. 81 et seq.), without explaining fully to his readers, perhaps without fully perceiving himself, that this law of increasing returns, if it exists, is of an entirely different nature and should never be put as an alternative, with equal rights, alongside the law of decreasing returns. Thus Senior—or West and Senior—must be held responsible for the tradition, which took such time in dying, that agriculture was the domain of the latter and 'industry' the domain of the former. This quite misleading arrangement was not set right until the next period. Edgeworth took the first steps toward breaking it up. Marshall grew out of it, of course, but he did not expressly renounce it. To the last he linked decreasing returns primarily with the production of raw materials in a way suggestive of Senior's teaching.

For the rest, we shall avail ourselves of this opportunity to survey the development of the principle of decreasing returns during the period. We have seen that the principle is not found in the *Wealth of Nations*. In fact, all that A. Smith says is that 'progress of improvement' increases the 'quantity of work' that can be done by the same number of hands 'comparatively less rapidly in agriculture than in manufactures.' This clumsy sentence expresses a statement of fact that may be true at some times and not at others and has nothing to do with diminishing returns. But it is the germ of an opinion that greatly influenced the later argument about diminishing returns. As stated above, Ricardo and others recognized, and Senior emphasized, the fact that the operation of diminishing returns is interrupted by technological progress. On the face of it this fact might suffice to break the connection—so fundamental for the West-Ricardo-Malthusian picture of economic evolution—of diminishing returns with the pressure of population. This consequence was

16 It will facilitate matters if we list at the outset the possible meanings of Diminishing Returns. The phrase may mean (1) that if we add equal increments to the quantity of one of the factors employed, keeping the others constant, total product will from a certain point on increase only at a decreasing rate; we call this Decreasing Marginal Productivity; (2) that if we add equal increments to the quantity of one of the factors employed, total product divided by the quantity of the factor will, from a certain point on, decrease; we call this Decreasing Average Productivity; (3) that if we add equal 'doses' of all other factors to land, the resulting increments of product or (4) the resulting average products will decline; these last two propositions, which we call Millian Diminishing Returns, reduce to the first two.

17 See West's *Essay* (1815), § 25 and McCulloch's *Principles* (1825), p. 277.

however avoided—in the end also by Senior—by minimizing the possibilities of technological progress in agriculture. The Smithian proposition was sharpened into what really was an additional postulate to the effect that in agriculture technological progress would not in the long run be strong enough to get the better of diminishing returns: marginal labor costs of foodstuffs would actually rise in the calculable future [18] and not merely 'tend to rise.' And this prophecy—there is no other word for it—was, for the Ricardian group and the public, the really important thing, without which decreasing returns would have been what it should be: an analytic tool that per se commands but moderate practical interest.

The chief merit of having forged this analytic tool we have assigned, in spite of the existence of forerunners, to Sir Edward West (see above, ch. 4, sec. 2) because so far as I know he was the first to create the form it retained throughout the period and beyond, including the 'prophecy' or additional postulate just discussed.[19] He distinguishes the two cases that have become classical: decreasing returns owing to the necessity of resorting to inferior land and decreasing returns owing to the 'fact' that additional labor 'cannot be bestowed [West does not add: after a certain point] with the same advantage as before on the old land' (§ 10). The first case, which we can generalize so as to include inferior location—as West meritoriously does (§ 9)—is logically plain sailing, resting securely on the observation that pieces of land definitely differ in fertility with reference to any given product or method.

However, this does not get us far, since decreasing returns in this sense are neither necessary nor sufficient for the uses West himself or anyone else ever made of the 'law.' [20] The second case of decreasing returns is the one that

[18] It is necessary to stress that the rise would occur in the *calculable* future, for this is what made the proposition practically relevant. Ricardo and Malthus meant *more* than that it is possible to assign, for *any* rates of technological progress, a series of finite production figures that cannot be reached at all or cannot be reached without returns decreasing so sharply as to raise marginal costs above what they had been at the preceding step, whatever the rate of improvement.

[19] There is, of course, no reason to question his claim to independent discovery of the fundamental idea and no doubt whatever about his having been the first to see it in all its bearings upon questions of economic theory. West's *Essay on the Application of Capital to Land* (1815), though far from faultless, must therefore be ranked among the most original as well as important performances in that field.

[20] Throughout the period and even later, it was this sense, however, that held the place of honor as it had been the one to occur to Steuart and Ortes. In consequence, many authors thought they were refuting the West-Ricardo theory of rent by pointing out that there need not be, in the economic domain, any land so poor as to pay no rent at all, and by holding that if all land were of uniform quality, there would be no Ricardian rent. Even Menger used this argument. Ricardo's text, however, excuses this to some extent. For he inadvertently makes differential fertility a condition of the emergence of rent.

Though diminishing returns in this sense do not seem to be very problematical, they nevertheless came in for adverse criticism. H. Carey's main objection deserves notice if only as an example . . . [note unfinished].

really matters and ought to be formulated (if we confine ourselves to land) as follows: suppose that to a given plot of land equal increments of labor (or of a fixed combination of factors) are successively applied in order to raise a given crop, then, if other things are kept strictly equal, a point will be reached after which the consequent increments of that product will monotonically decrease to zero (and, if further application were persisted in, to absolutely increasing negative figures). It is Ricardo's merit to have—though less rigorously—expressed just this. West also must have had this meaning in mind, for it is the one which is relevant in the *Essay on the Application of Capital to Land*. But his wording is not clear and points, if taken literally, to a 'law' of decreasing average returns rather than to a 'law' of decreasing marginal returns. And it is the former that was subsequently formulated by a majority of authors, who must either have confused it with the latter or have erroneously considered it the more important of the two.[21] This is true even of Marshall (*Principles*, Book IV, ch. 3, § 1) who worded 'the law of or statement of tendency to diminishing returns' almost exactly as did Senior. That they are not equivalent and that it is the marginal concept which is needed in all maximum problems, was not expressly stated until 1911 when Edgeworth pointed it out. Sound instinct, however, prevented the confusion from producing mistakes. But it was the main reason I can see why the definitive conquest of the idea of diminishing physical returns did not *ipso facto* and immediately lead to a marginal-productivity theory and why the latter had a separate history at all.

[21] Senior, e.g., says 'that agricultural skill remaining the same, additional labour employed on the land within a given district produces in general a less proportionate return, or, in other words, that though, with every increase of the labour bestowed, the aggregate return is increased [indefinitely?], the increase of the return is not in proportion to the increase of the labour.' Now, the significance of literary statements of essentially quantitative propositions is always doubtful. But *I think* that both parts of the sentence are intended to mean this: denoting total return by y and total labor applied by x, additional labor Δx, will produce an additional product Δy such that $\frac{y + \Delta y}{x + \Delta x} < \frac{y}{x}$, which is a proposition about average returns. So late and so eminent an author as Böhm-Bawerk clearly confused average and marginal returns in an unguarded moment (but not in his actual work) and has been accordingly taken to task by Professor Karl Menger (son of the economist). This was done in an article that—amounting to reading us the logician's riot act—is immensely useful for any economist who wishes to take his logical responsibilities seriously, and is strongly recommended for study ('Bemerkungen zu den Ertragsgesetzen' and sequel, *Zeitschrift für Nationalökonomie*, March and August 1936) although, as Professor Menger himself took care to point out, some of the logical severities displayed are there only for illustration's sake and not because of their importance for the practical handling of those two concepts. It is a curious fact that in spite of Edgeworth's decisive contribution mentioned in our text, these matters were not fully settled until this article appeared—hence, that it took from 1815 to 1936 to clear them up and that it might have taken still longer but for the lucky chance that the problem happened to attract the interest of an eminent mathematician. This fact will illustrate how much justification there is for the complaint of some economists that the profession bestows too much attention on theory.

The 'law' of diminishing returns is of course an empirical statement—a generalization from observed facts that only further observation can either verify or refute. It is interesting to report that theorists have almost unanimously displayed an aversion to admitting this. One after another has tried to 'prove' it from logically anterior and, as they thought, more obvious assumptions. This can in fact be done for the 'law' of diminishing average returns, which has been shown [22] to follow from assumptions that may be held to be simpler than is the 'law' itself. Moreover, this 'law' also follows, if we add assumptions nobody will care to challenge, from the 'law' of decreasing marginal returns. But the latter cannot be so derived unless we introduce further assumptions that reduce the proof to a triviality.[23]

2. Value

As we have seen at various turns of our way, the problem of Value must always hold the pivotal position, as the chief tool of analysis in any pure theory that works with a rational schema.[1] More or less, this was recognized by all the economists of that period—by Marx not less than by Say—although some haze continued to linger on this point. Any impression to the contrary

[22] This has been done by Karl Menger (op. cit. pp. 48 et seq.) in his discussion of the similar though not identical proofs offered by Böhm-Bawerk and Wicksell. These proofs did not accomplish what their authors evidently wished to accomplish, namely proof that *the* law of diminishing returns is a 'theorem of mathematical necessity,' but they did prove that, in the sense stated above, the law of average diminishing returns is. Thus these proofs are much superior to some that had been offered before, of which the most primitive one—and, at first sight, most plausible one—was founded on the erroneous belief that the mere fact of the cultivation of any but the best land was all that was needed—for, unless returns to additional investment in the best land were decreasing, why should people resort to inferior land? Some of these arguments have also been analyzed by Menger, who, moreover, supplied exact proof (p. 43) of the theorem stated in the next sentence of our text. Though space forbids us to go into details, it should be mentioned that both Böhm-Bawerk's and Wicksell's proofs require that doubling *both* the land and the 'capital' or labor applied should at most double the product (i.e. the absence of 'economies of scale').

[23] Factual investigations are therefore called for not only to find particular forms of marginal-return functions but also to make sure of their fundamental property. A number of such investigations have been summarized by E. H. Phelps Brown, in a report, 'The Marginal Efficiency of a Productive Factor,' published in *Econometrica*, April 1936. Special forms have also been derived from hypotheses drawn from the physiology of plants, see E. A. Mitscherlich, 'Das Gesetz des Minimums und das Gesetz des abnehmenden Bodenertrages,' *Landwirtschaftliche Jahrbücher* (1909).

In any case, Wicksell was definitely wrong in holding that the validity of the 'law of the soil' did not stand in need of 'experimental' proof. For even in the case of average returns, there is still the homogeneity assumption to be tested that was mentioned in the preceding footnote. But he was right in his counter-criticism of Waterstradt (two articles published in *Thünen Archiv*, 1906 and 1909), who had attacked the 'law' by methods so faulty as to put him in the wrong.

[1] We have also learned that not every theory does this.

is mainly due to economists' preoccupation with things other than pure theory —especially with the institutional aspects of economic life. The value on which analytic effort converged was exchange value. J. S. Mill only clinched prevailing practice when he emphasized that the term Value was, in economic theory, essentially relative and that it meant nothing but the exchange ratio between any two commodities or services. Similarly, the term price meant nothing but the exchange ratio between the (arbitrary) unit of any commodity or service and the good selected for money. We may also take J. S. Mill's teaching as typical of an attitude that has been much discussed of late: the problem that really mattered throughout was the explanation of these exchange ratios or price *relations* (relative prices). Money prices (absolute prices) were treated as an affair of secondary importance, to be dealt with apart in the chapter on money. Since, then, value was a ratio, it followed as a matter of course that all values were incapable of increasing or decreasing simultaneously. It also followed that there was no such thing as the total value of all the services of wealth (or of all wealth) taken as a whole, although Ricardo and Marx took a different view on this point.

Nobody raised the theoretical question whether it is really possible or admissible to carry out the fundamental analysis of the price system in terms of exchange ratios or relative prices alone. This implies, of course, that the intervention of real money (that is, of money which not only supplies a unit of account but also actually circulates and in addition functions as a 'store of value') does not affect the determination of the exchange ratios themselves or anything else that is essential to the understanding of the economic process. Or, to put the same thing in the usual way, this implies that money is in fact a mere technical device that may be disregarded whenever fundamentals are on the program, or a veil that must be removed in order to discover the features behind it. Or, in still other words, this implies that there is no essential *theoretical* [2] difference between a barter economy and a money economy. Nobody tried seriously to prove this or even realized the necessity of doing so in order to establish the validity of that procedure.[3] This was to come in our own time. For the moment let us merely notice that this exclusive emphasis upon 'real' analysis may have had its advantages, even if it should have proved inadequate when confronted at a later stage of analytic development with higher standards of scientific rigor. It served to counteract lingering primitive errors. It helped to clarify concepts and relations. It asserted the rights of a point of view that stood in need of being asserted then and perhaps may do so again.

But the economists of that period did not even make a serious effort to prove the determinateness of an economy without a circulating medium. Systematic efforts of this kind—since Cournot's example remained without in-

[2] Practically, of course, nobody ever denied that, since the technical device may get out of order, a society's system of money and credit always does make a lot of difference to its economic process.

[3] See, however, J. S. Mill, *Principles*, Book III, ch. 26.

fluence—cannot be said to antedate Walras (see below, Part IV, ch. 7). However, in this as in other instances, in economics as in other sciences, we find that intuitive perception of the inherent logic of things led beyond what was actually proved. Like the leading theorists of the preceding period, the 'classics' sensed the existence of what we now call economic equilibrium and, if they did not try to prove its existence, they made it, as it were, plausible, embodying their intuition in certain empirical rules, such as the tendency of 'profits' to be roughly equal in different but similarly conditioned lines of business.[4] We derive a similar proposition from the principle of maximizing net returns and associate it with the principle of substitution. The 'classics,' it has been held,[5] were not in possession of the latter principle.[6] This is true and so it is that this constitutes one of the most serious shortcomings of their analytic apparatus. But if they did not formulate it explicitly and did not apply it systematically, neither were they entirely unaware of it. They used it in individual cases. And it is implied in some of their propositions.

(a) *Ricardo and Marx.* By theories of value we mean attempts at indicating the factors that account for a thing's having exchange value or—though this is not strictly the same—the factors that 'regulate' or 'govern' value. Let us begin with Ricardo. A. Smith, we remember, may be credited with three different theories of value: the labor-quantity theory illustrated by his beaver and deer example; the labor-disutility theory conveyed by his reference to 'toil and trouble'; the cost theory he actually used in the central part of his analysis. We also know that in addition he recommended labor (along with 'corn') as a relatively stable unit by which to express commodity values (*numéraire*).[7] Ricardo, starting his theoretical work by a study of the *Wealth of Nations,* was displeased with what he rightly felt to be a logical muddle and came to the conclusion that the labor-quantity[8] theory of value as conveyed by the beaver and deer example was the one to adopt, not only for 'primitive' conditions in which there was no scarce factor other than labor,

[4] Their concern with differences in the rates of return earned, at the same time and place, in different occupations—discussion of which was, since A. Smith, part of the stock in trade of every textbook—was chiefly motivated by a desire to protect the fundamental assumption of equality.

[5] See, e.g., G. J. Stigler, 'Stuart Wood and the Marginal Productivity Theory,' *Quarterly Journal of Economics,* August 1947, p. 647.

[6] As has been noted above, Senior made the maximum principle explicit. But it has also been noted that neither he nor anyone else knew how to make full use of it.

[7] It cannot be repeated too often that choosing labor for this role—for instance on the ground that the significance of a man-hour is less subject to change than is the significance of an ounce of gold, no matter whether this is so or not—has nothing whatever to do with adopting a labor theory of value. Malthus, for instance, was an opponent of the latter. But he recommended labor days for the purpose of expressing values (for 'measure of value'). Though this should be quite clear, it is worth emphasizing again because these two things have so often been confused even by first-flight theorists such as Ricardo.

[8] Meaning the quantity of labor that a commodity 'embodies.'

but generally for all cases, even where there were also other scarce factors. His first chapter is an attempt to carry out this idea. A. Smith's cost theory he evidently thought logically unsatisfactory (perhaps circular). The labor-disutility theory he neglected, probably because it did not occur to him that it was different from the labor-quantity theory. And throughout, he mixed up his argument against A. Smith's lapse from the labor-quantity theory of value with an argument against A. Smith's (and Malthus') choice of labor as a measure of value.[9] Before going on, I shall first try to remove this difficulty from our path.

Two things must be distinguished. On the one hand, Ricardo, like everybody else, was of course aware of the fact that there can be no commodity (labor no more than any other), the *exchange value* of whose unit could serve as an invariant standard by which to measure the variations in the exchange values of other commodities (*Principles*, ch. 1, § 6). On the other hand, his labor-quantity theory of value seemed, subject to qualifications that will be discussed presently and are neglected for the moment, to provide a method by which to measure these variations all the same: where the exchange value of a unit of labor was bound to be unsatisfactory, the unit of labor itself—since according to this theory the amount of labor embodied in a commodity 'governs' its value—really was what was needed in order to have a measure of exchange values after all. Subject to the qualifications we are now neglecting, all that was necessary in order to have a commodity of at least theoretically invariant value was to imagine one that always embodied the same quantity of labor. Such a commodity would then provide a stable yardstick with which to measure the variations in the relative prices of all the others. The pounds and shillings of his numerical examples must be understood to stand for such a commodity.[10]

It is very important to grasp the implications of this logical *tour de force*. By virtue of it, commodities acquired absolute values, which were capable of being compared, added up, and of increasing and decreasing simultaneously, the very thing that was impossible so long as exchange *value* was defined simply as exchange *ratio*. This is what pleased Marx so much about Ricardo's theory of value. But the latter failed to work out the idea completely. Moreover, he created much unnecessary confusion by adopting for his concept the term Real Value. Our own meaning of this term, which refers to the value of a monetary quantity in terms of the goods it will buy, was gaining currency at that time, and people were puzzled by Ricardo's use of it according to which, for example, 'real' wages might be falling (if the quantity of labor em-

[9] Meaning the quantity of labor a commodity 'commands' in the market, which differs in general from 'labor embodied.'

[10] Ricardo derived some satisfaction from thus fulfilling Destutt de Tracy's precept that values should be expressed in units of values as lengths are expressed in units of length. In this, however, he erred. For, whatever we may think of Destutt de Tracy's precept, a little reflection will show that Ricardo did not satisfy it or rather that he satisfied it only by means of a verbal trick: the values he measured in terms of physical labor hours were not themselves (though they were for Marx) just labor hours.

bodied in the goods that constitute real wages in our sense was decreasing, owing, for instance, to technological improvement) when everybody else would say that they were rising (if the quantities of those goods themselves were increasing).

Another point must be mentioned which is of considerable importance for understanding Ricardo's theory of distribution—which was primarily concerned with relative shares—and in particular his famous theorem that 'there can be no rise in the value of labour [real wages in his sense] without a fall of profits' (see, e.g. § 4, *Principles*, ch. 1). The true significance of this theorem will be discussed later. But, in the place referred to, Ricardo reduced it to a triviality by explaining that, if the product be divided between capital and labor, 'the larger the proportion that is given to the latter the less will remain for the former'—which is in fact how James Mill and many later interpreters (e.g., A. Wagner) understood the theorem. How was this possible? Evidently Ricardo, when he penned this passage, thought that relative shares are always rendered by the relation between the labor hours embodied in the absolute shares. This, however, is not true generally but only if the total quantity of labor applied is kept constant. (On this tangle, see Cannan, op. cit. pp. 341 et seq.)

Ricardo, then, tells us on the first page of his work that utility is a necessary condition for the emergence of exchangeable value and that 'possessing utility, commodities derive their exchangeable value from two sources: from their scarcity, and from the quantity of labour required to obtain them.' Illogically identifying scarce commodities with commodities, the quantity of which cannot be increased by labor, and setting them down as rare exceptions, he turns to the category of those that may be increased by human industry. I cannot stay—but the reader should—to point out all the shortcomings of this start and shall proceed at once to state the central theorem of the Ricardian theory of value: in conditions of perfect competition (which Ricardo failed to specify) the exchange values of commodities will be *proportional* to the quantities of labor contained or embodied in them.

The first thing to be observed about this proposition, which hails from the *Wealth of Nations* (Ricardo referred specifically to Book I, ch. 5), is that it is not in itself a theory of value in the sense defined above. Such a theory is contained in Ricardo's next sentence, 'that this [i.e. labor applied or embodied, J. A. S.] is really the foundation of the exchangeable value of all things.' The proposition in question is a theorem on values intended to be valid in perfect equilibrium only. Of this Ricardo was perfectly aware. In Chapters 4 and 30, he therefore dealt with the Cantillon-A. Smith concept of market price, which he made dependent, like the price of monopolized commodities, on supply and demand *as if determination of price by supply and demand were entirely different from, and incompatible with, determination of price by quantity of labor embodied*. But, not being in full possession of an explicit perfect-equilibrium concept, he expresses this by saying that his labor-quantity law applies to natural prices, that is, to the relative prices that will ultimately prevail when fluctuations due to temporary disturbances shall in each case have subsided. This is the reason why interpreters and indeed Ricardo himself spoke of his law—and of his reasoning in general—as 'abstract' and as envisaging fundamental or long-run tendencies only. He did not use the Marshallian term Long-Run Normal but he had got the idea.

The second thing to be observed is that our theorem would be true (for perfect equilibrium in perfect competition) if labor—and labor of one kind and quality—were the only requisite of production. In fact, it would then follow as a special case from the more general marginal-utility theory of a later time.[11]

The third thing, then, to be observed about Ricardo's labor-quantity law is the manner in which he tried to overcome the difficulties that stand in the way of generalizing a result that holds—though he never proved it—in a special case. The rest of his first chapter (§§ 2-7) is devoted to an attempt to show that his labor-quantity law of equilibrium values, though not generally true, yet constitutes an acceptable approximation throughout the range of perfect competition. But this chapter does not deal with the fundamental difficulty that arises from the existence of scarce natural factors: their elimination from the problem is left for the second chapter. Following suit, we also neglect them for the moment.

Ricardo saw, of course—what Marx was to elaborate—that the labor whose quantity is to 'govern' or 'regulate' values must be of the quality a laborer normally does in any given time and place, not more or less efficient than that, and that it must be applied according to the prevailing standards of technological rationality: to use Marx's term, it must be *socially necessary* labor. The time employed in acquiring skills, including the labor of the teacher, must be counted in[12] and so must be 'the labour also which is bestowed on the implements, tools, and buildings with which such labour [the directly applied labor, J. A. S.] is assisted' (sec. 3). But what about natural skills or those elements in skills that are not themselves acquired by labor? Following the eighteenth-century tradition noticed above, Ricardo did not think much of their importance. For the rest, he relied, as had A. Smith, on the market mechanism to determine a scale for the evaluation of different (natural) qualities of labor by means of which an hour of superior labor may be expressed as a multiple of the normal labor hour: if a 'working jeweller'

[11] In order to show this, it is sufficient to refer to a theorem that is rationally deduced within the marginal utility theory, though it has been frequently implied in 'classical' pieces of reasoning, especially where the 'classics' made use of the 'law' of the uniform rate of profit. This theorem reads that, in equilibrium, all factors will be allocated to all their possible uses in such a way that the last increments of each factor employed in all these uses produce increments of products that are of equal value. If the products are beavers and deer, and if labor is all that is needed in order to kill them, beavers killed per hour of hunting must be worth as much as deer killed per hour of hunting and beavers will hence exchange for deer in inverse proportion to the time it normally takes to kill them. But this is the Ricardian theorem, which, by the same token, cannot be true if there are also other scarce factors.

[12] This Ricardo did not say explicitly. But it is only fair to interpret him in this sense.

is being paid twice as much per hour as is a 'common labourer,' one hour worked by the former will simply be counted as two hours worked by the latter. Since such relations do not vary greatly from year to year, they have 'little effect, for short periods, on the relative value of commodities.'[13] This may or may not be so. But it should be noticed that this appeal to market values—that are evidently not determined by any quantity of labor—in the course of an argument that is to expound the labor-quantity law spells in strict logic the surrender of the latter, no matter whether this be acknowledged or not.

But acknowledgment of failure of the labor-quantity principle came in Sections 4 and 5. There, Ricardo faced the facts that relative values of commodities are not 'governed' exclusively by the quantities of labor embodied in them but also by 'the length of time which must elapse before' they 'can be brought to market.' For this is what his argument amounts to: unequal proportion between that part of capital which 'is to support labour' and that part which 'is invested in tools, machinery and buildings,' and unequal durability of the latter or unequal rate of turnover of the former—which are the facts discussed—are relevant to the relative values of the products only because of that time element which they bring into the picture of the productive process.[14] They simply mean different periods of investment of the (possibly) equal quantities of labor embodied in the capital goods or (to put quite bluntly the common-sense business fact of which Ricardo was thinking) different amounts of carrying charges that, logically, are on a par with quantity of labor in influencing 'natural,' that is, equilibrium, values.

So the murder is out. To be sure, Ricardo tried to minimize the damage to his fundamental construction by pointing out that quantity of labor still remains the most important determinant of relative value, which is why above we have described his theorem as an approximation. This seems to do more justice to his thought than does the interpretation that appeals to other historians: these, following a lead of Marshall's, prefer to say that Ricardo had 'really' a cost theory of value. It is true that *in effect* Ricardo ended up by co-ordinating the element of accrued profits with the element of quantity of labor. It is also true that sometimes (see ch. 30, first sentence) he did make Cost of Production (evidently including the former element) the 'ultimate regulator' of values. But if this were all, his exposition would reduce simply to a roundabout way of stating a view that was current in his time: it would be difficult to see what it was he fought for with so much insistence and what the ensuing controversies were about.

Only if we recognize that he believed, wrongly of course, that labor applied is something more fundamental or important than are accrued profits, shall we understand why he first introduced his theory of values under the

[13] It is of some interest to note that Ricardo, while professedly arguing about long-run phenomena, displayed in this case no compunction at using a short-run argument—another instance of his extreme carelessness.

[14] Let us notice once more that this constitutes an important link between Ricardo and Böhm-Bawerk.

assumption that capital structures were exactly similar in all industries. The comfort is of course quite illusory that he drew from the fact that *then* (if we accept his elimination of the influence of natural agents) the relations of quantities of labor applied would 'regulate' relative values. Logically it would be just as admissible to say that, with equal quantities of labor applied, it is capital structure or 'time' which regulates relative values. Therefore, he must have thought that the former proposition is true in some sense in which the latter is not. And our interpretation—the interpretation that is characterized by the word approximation—seems to me the most obvious one in the case of a writer who was quite free from either emotionalism or philosophical preconceptions.

Another point must be mentioned, however. What Ricardo did in Chapter 1, Sections 4 and 5 was to recognize the *fact* that carrying charges do influence relative values. He also formulated some of the consequences of this fact. But he did so, as it were, with a shrug of his shoulders and did not make the slightest attempt to *explain* it unless we accept the phrase 'just compensation for the time that the profits were withheld' as a token of such an explanation. Here as elsewhere he was content to remain on the surface of things. But he did worry about what his admission would do to his pet proposition that 'no alteration in the wages of labour could produce any alteration in the relative value of . . . commodities,' which is, throughout the book, the practical spearhead of his theory of value. On principle, it must also be given up, of course (see § 5, last paragraph). *But actually it is retained,* again, as I like to say in order to be as fair as possible to him, as an approximate truth. The effect of the admission is confined to a particular theorem: if wages, say, rise, the relative prices of goods into the production of which 'fixed capital' or 'fixed capital' of high durability enter largely will fall, and the relative prices of goods 'which are produced chiefly by labour with less fixed capital or with fixed capital of a less durable character than the medium in which price is estimated[15] will rise,' a proposition that has been dubbed in our time, the Ricardo Effect—and a curiously devious way of admitting something of which one does not wish to admit the implications.

It is not worth our while to stay to describe the way in which the inner-circle Ricardians, James Mill, De Quincey, and McCulloch, handled Ricardo's theory of value and the spurious problems it created.[16] But it will be con-

[15] This is correct. Marx slipped when he replaced this by the *average* composition of total capital.

[16] However, we may note in passing a device that McCulloch used to generalize Ricardo's labor-quantity theorem. Recognizing that, looking at the matter from Ricardo's standpoint, the main trouble was connected with the element of time, he simply took the view that the labor quantity embodied in durable capital goods goes on to do further labor during their lifetime. A harsh critic might call this a purely verbal expedient and an inept one at that. But it is also possible to see in it a particular way toward renunciation of the labor-quantity theory and toward recognition of a multiplicity of 'factors' or services of production, all of which help to create product value. If we look at his reasoning in this light, it amounts to generalizing the concept of labor. In itself

venient, before we take up the contributions of Ricardo's opponents and then the half-way house position of J. S. Mill, to consider with the utmost brevity some essentials of the doctrine of Ricardo's only great follower, Karl Marx.

Marx's theory of exchange value is also a labor-quantity theory, perhaps, if we neglect such stepping-stones between Ricardo and Marx as W. Thompson, the only quite thoroughgoing one ever written. At first we are, indeed, struck by the similarity of Marx's argument to Ricardo's. Marx asked himself what it is that makes commodities, so heterogeneous as to value-in-use, comparable at all, and emerges with the conclusion that is the fact that they are all the products of labor. Having established to his own satisfaction this highly debatable proposition—for the fact that all commodities have value-in-use is not only as true but more general—Marx proceeded to deal with the difficulties that beset this approach at the threshold almost exactly as Ricardo had dealt with them. He added precision and elaboration here and there—I have already mentioned the 'socially necessary labor'—but failed, like Ricardo, to notice the danger that lurks behind the assumption that the market prices of labor of different nonacquired qualities may be used in order to reduce labor hours of superior quality to multiples of standard ones.

I take this opportunity to mention a point of technique that Marx considered one of his most important contributions to economic theory: his distinction between labor, the *quantity* of which is measured in hours, and 'labor power' (*Arbeitskraft*), the *value* of which is given by the quantity of labor that enters into the goods the workman consumes (including the goods and services used up in bringing him up and training him) and in a sense 'produces' his labor power. These goods and their real value are, of course, essential elements also of Ricardo's analysis. But he did not identify explicitly this real value with the real value of the commodity *labor power*. Senior, as we know, took a step toward doing so. Marx, however, not only completed this step but also, in his exploitation theory (see below, sec. 6b), put the labor-power concept to a use of which neither Ricardo nor Senior had thought or would have approved.

But even non-Marxist historians should have realized—though, mostly, they have not—that there is a much more fundamental difference between the labor-quantity theory of Marx and the labor-quantity theory of Ricardo. Ricardo, the most unmetaphysical of theorists, introduced the labor-quantity theory of value simply as a hypothesis that was to explain the actual relative prices—or rather the actual long-run normals of relative prices—that we observe in real life. But for Marx, the most metaphysical of theorists, the labor-quantity theory was no mere hypothesis about relative prices. The quantity of labor embodied in products did not merely 'regulate' their value. It *was* (the 'essence' or 'substance' of) their value. They *were* congealed labor. Lest non-metaphysically disposed readers should refuse to be very much impressed by

---

this does not do much for us. But it points in the direction of a more fruitful theory all the same.

this, let me at once point out the practical difference that this made for our two authors' analytic structures.

When Ricardo recognized that the element of time—or of the carrying charges that accrue in the course of the productive process—entered into the determination of values or relative prices, this meant for him the necessity of admitting that his hypothesis was contradicted by the facts and that, in the manner described above, it had to be reduced to a mere approximation. But Marx had recognized from an early stage of his thought—certainly before he published the first volume of *Das Kapital* (1867) [17]—that exchange ratios do not, not even as a tendency, conform to Ricardo's equilibrium theorem on values, *which accordingly forms no part of Marx's teaching*. This, however, was no reason for him to modify his value theory: value was always, for every commodity as well as for output as a whole, identical with labor embodied, however relative prices might behave, and his problem was precisely to show how, in consequence of the mechanism of perfect competition, these absolute values *without being altered* came to be shifted about in such ways that in the end commodities, while still retaining their values, were *not* sold at relative prices proportional to these values. For Ricardo, deviations—other than temporary—of relative prices from his proportionality theorem spelled alterations of values; for Marx, such deviations did not alter values but only redistributed them as between the commodities. This is why we may say that Marx actually went through with the idea of an absolute value of things,[18] whereas Ricardo, although his argument implies this idea in spots, never made it the pivot of his analytical structure. Or, to put it differently: whereas for Ricardo relative prices and values were essentially the same thing and whereas hence the economic calculus in terms of values was the same thing as the calculus in terms of relative prices, values and prices were not the same thing for Marx, so that he created for himself an additional problem that *apparently* does not exist for Ricardo, namely, the problem of the relation between the two calculi or the problem of *Wertrechnung und Preisrechnung*.[19]

[17] This fact is evident from the material published in the *Theorien über den Mehrwert* (1905-10) and hence was not evident at all before the publication of these volumes. In consequence, even the greatest of nineteenth-century Marx critics, Böhm-Bawerk, took the view that Marx expounded a labor-quantity theory in the first volume of *Das Kapital* which Marx's *later* thought convinced him to be hopelessly at variance with facts, so that he was driven to shifting his ground in those writings that were, after his death, published by Engels (1894) as the third volume of *Das Kapital*—Marx's aversion to continuing publication of his work was interpreted as a confession of failure. In other words, the value theory of the first volume was interpreted too much in Ricardo's sense. This was an error, and one that spelled missing the essential point of Marx's value theory. This is not to deny, of course, that some of the criticisms proffered retain validity in spite of this error. Nor do I wish to assert that Marx carried out the program appropriate to his point successfully. This is sufficiently obvious from our text, although it is impossible to clear up the matter fully within the space at our command.

[18] He was the only author who ever did.

[19] See on this Ladislaus von Bortkiewicz (1868-1931), 'Wertrechnung und Preisrechnung im Marxschen System,' three articles in the *Archiv für Sozialwissenschaft*

Some of the implications and applications of this value theory will be discussed later on. But three points about it should be made before we temporarily leave the subject. First, for us it is nothing but a construction devised for purposes of analysis and to be judged in the light of considerations of analytic usefulness and convenience. For orthodox Marxists it may indeed be sacred truth in some extra-empirical realm of Platonic ideas, where the 'essences' of things are exhibited. And it may have been something of the kind for Marx himself. Actually, however, there is nothing mystic or metaphysical about the Marxist theory of value. Its central concept in particular, absolute value, has nothing to do with the meanings we attach to this word in some parts of philosophy. It is nothing but Ricardo's real value fully worked out and fully made use of. Second, if readers have followed the argument, they will realize that the objections that may be made against Ricardo's use of the concept of real value do not apply to Marx's theory. Even if we do not admit that labor embodied is the 'cause' of exchange value in the ordinary sense, there is no logical rule to prevent us from *defining* labor embodied as exchange value, though this gives another and perhaps misleading sense to the latter term. For, on principle, we may call things what we please.[20] Third, whereas Ricardo simply recognized the actual existence of carrying charges and then stopped, Marx made at least an attempt, successful or not, to absorb them into his schema. For him, the carrying charges were also part of the labor embodied in total output. Ricardo had to add them to labor cost and ought to have explained them. For Marx there was no problem of explaining why these elements of product value exist. His only problem was to explain how they come to be clipped off from a total of value that exists independently of them. At this we must let the matter rest for the moment. At a later stage of our argument we shall see that it was after all the same difficulty, namely, the influence of time, which, owing to their different approaches, presented itself to them in the guise of different problems. To use a Marshallian phrase, for Ricardo time was the great disturber of his analytic pattern. But it was also, though less overtly, the great disturber of Marx's.

(b) *The Opponents of the Labor-Quantity Theory of Value.* Remember: the Ricardians were always in the minority, even in England, and it is only Ricardo's personal force which, as we look back, creates the impression that his teaching—his coinage of Smithian metal—dominated the thought of the time and that the other economists were just opponents of what was then called the New School—opponents, too, that were not quite up to the latter's doctrines. The opposite is nearer the truth, in the matter of value as in others,

(1906 and 1907) and the same author's 'Zur Berichtigung der grundlegenden theoretischen Konstruktion von Marx im dritten Band des "Kapital,"' *Jahrbücher für Nationalökonomie und Statistik* (1907).

[20] But Marx would no doubt have avoided much confusion and futile controversy had he named his absolute-value concept differently. The word 'value' was not at all well chosen to express its actual analytic significance. But much agitatorial glamour would have been lost by choosing a different one. Also, he may have wished to join up with Ricardo's real value, which was not less misleading.

although our impression is no doubt reinforced by the fact that nearly all those opponents, whatever else they may have been, were with but few exceptions inferior to Ricardo as controversialists.

Discussion of the problems of value on non-Ricardian lines that carried over from the eighteenth century collided with the Ricardian forces and blazed into controversy about 1820, the year in which Malthus' *Principles* appeared. The active phase of this controversy lasted little more than ten years and notwithstanding the testimony of a very few stalwart defenders—McCulloch and Marx stood arm in arm at this point—and of some historians ended in the defeat of Ricardianism. It had its full complement of mutual misunderstanding and of logical errors, but on the whole it moved on a creditable level. The peak performance was Bailey's [21] (see above, ch. 4, sec. 3c), the influence of whose criticism was much greater than appears on the surface. He showed up the weaknesses of Ricardo's analytic structure forcefully, in particular, the futility of Ricardo's method of eliminating natural agents from the value problem, the arbitrariness involved in calling quantity of labor 'the sole determining principle of value,' the defects of the concept of real value and of the Ricardian theory of profit, and so on. The discourteous reply from some Ricardian in the *Westminster Review* (1826) was pathetically inadequate, and though but few contemporaries did justice to him, it became clear in time that he had in fact turned the tide and dealt a fatal blow. Considerations of space forbid the describing of the controversy in detail.[22] Instead, we shall confine ourselves to what was, for the time being, the main point at issue between Say, Malthus, and Ricardo, noticing other names and aspects only so far as this purpose requires.[23]

To get at that main point, we must first recall that the pioneer performances of the marginal utility theory, which the period produced, failed indeed to exert any perceptible influence, but that many writers perceived that

[21] Samuel Bailey, *A Critical Dissertation on the Nature, Measures, and Causes of Value; Chiefly in Reference to the Writings of Mr. Ricardo and His Followers* (1825).

[22] Three other main contributions, however, should not go unmentioned: first, a tract entitled *Observations on Certain Verbal Disputes on Political Economy . . .* (1821), which displays sound sense for the spurious or fictitious nature of part of the issues involved; second, another tract, entitled *An Essay on Political Economy . . .* (1822), notable for an early recognition of the logical weakness of any explanation of value by cost and of the fact that cost affects value only through affecting supply; and a third, already mentioned, C. F. Cotterill's *Examination of the Doctrines of Value* (1831), which, though inferior in vigor of thought to the one just mentioned, should not be forgotten because of his defense of (most of) Bailey's tenets. [The two anonymous tracts are mentioned by Seligman, *Essays in Economics*, pp. 81-2.]

[23] Say and Malthus were, so far as value is concerned, as much on one side as they were on opposite sides in the question of saving and general gluts. But there was no perfect agreement between the two in the first case, and no perfect agreement between Say and Ricardo in the second. Ricardo's position in the controversy on value may be pretty completely understood from his *Letters to Thomas Robert Malthus*, 1810-1823 (ed. J. Bonar, 1887), his *Notes on Malthus' 'Principles,'* and chs. 20 and 30 of his own *Principles*.

utility was more than a mere *condition* of exchange value, in the sense in which Ricardo meant this phrase, and that in fact it was the 'source' or 'cause' of exchange value. Only they were no more able to do anything with this idea than were the Ricardians, who, precisely for this reason, refused to accept it. And so this approach came to nothing. J. B. Say, for instance, following the French tradition (Condillac, in particular), made exchange value dependent upon utility but, failing (like Condillac) to add scarcity, stumbled over the fact, so often explained before him, that such 'useful' things as air or water normally have no exchange value at all. He said that actually they do have value; only this value is so great, infinite in fact, that nobody could pay for them and hence they go for nothing.[24] It is true that he did not stop at this ineptitude. He did rise to the imperfect (yet so significant) statement that price is the measure of the value of things and value the measure of their utility, a statement that heralds Walras': *les valeurs d'échange sont proportionnelles aux raretés* [marginal utility, J. A. S.]. Mostly, however, he merely used a rather primitive supply-and-demand analysis. The same applies to Hermann (see above, ch. 4, sec 5). As in France, perhaps in part under French influence, a utility-theory tradition had developed in Germany. But it was equally inoperative: it stopped at recognitions of the utility element that are difficult to distinguish from the Ricardian way of assigning to utility the role of a condition of value. Hermann went further than others but he also confined himself substantially to working with supply and demand. Some English economists, such as Craig[25] and Senior, did better. As regards the latter, there is truth in the common view, shared by Walras, that credits him with the notion of marginal utility. But I can only repeat: he did not go through with it and, after a glimpse, it practically vanished behind mere supply and demand. Lord Lauderdale and, more elaborately, Malthus went straight to the supply-and-demand apparatus and concentrated entirely upon it.

Thus, for Ricardo, the main point at issue was from the first labor quantity versus supply and demand. The utility theory of value, which he had glanced at and rejected (as the 'source' or 'cause' of exchange value), was not really in the picture, though he criticized it in his chapter on 'Value and Riches.' The cost theory of value was not wholly an enemy. For he looked upon his own theory as a reformulation of it and frequently himself invoked cost in terms of labor *and* capital. The true enemy was the supply-and-demand theory, which 'has become almost an axiom in political economy, and has been the source of much error' (ch. 30, third paragraph). The reader should observe

[24] Condillac, on the contrary, states that such things have a price—which consists in the effort to appropriate them, for instance, by breathing, drinking, and so on.

[25] John Craig's *Remarks on Some Fundamental Doctrines in Political Economy* . . . (1821) is a performance of considerable merit. Among other things, he understood the mechanism by which variation in any price will, through setting free or absorbing money income, influence other prices. He also understood, like Say, that (marginal) value in use must be 'accurately measured' by (must, in equilibrium, be proportional to) value in exchange. If we may indulge in what is no doubt a mistake and read into his statement all that our bracketed reformulations convey, we find a whole Marshall *in nuce*.

how very interesting this is and how revelatory of 'the ways of the human mind.' It implies, of course, that Ricardo was completely blind to the nature, and the logical place in economic theory, of the supply-and-demand apparatus and that he took it to represent a theory of value distinct from and opposed to his own. This reflects little credit on him as a theorist.[26] For it should be clear that his own theorem on equilibrium values is only tenable, so far as it is tenable at all, by virtue of the interplay of supply and demand. Ricardo could not have failed to discover this, had he tried to deduce that theorem rationally instead of merely positing it intuitively. That is to say, had he but stopped to ask *why* exchange values of commodities should be proportional to the quantities of standard labor embodied in them, he would, in answering this question, have found himself using the supply-and-demand apparatus by which alone (under appropriate assumptions) that 'law' of value can be established. Then he could never have denied the validity of the 'law' of demand and supply for the long-run normal prices of the goods the quantities of which can be indefinitely increased by human industry, while admitting its validity for short-run market prices and for the prices of monopolized or 'scarce' goods. For, as Malthus pointed out painstakingly (*Principles*, 1st ed., ch. 2, §§ 2 and 3), supply and demand come in quite generally [27] to determine prices in both the long-run and the short-run cases, and the difference between them consists only in the level at which supply and demand fix them, which has certain properties in the one case that are absent in the other. In other words, the concepts of supply and demand apply to a mechanism that is compatible with any theory of value and indeed is required by all. But so great was Ricardo's personal authority with some later writers that traces of this mistake of his may be found not only in J. S. Mill's but even in A. Marshall's *Principles*.

However illogically, the supply-and-demand mechanism actually drifted into the place of a theory of value,[28] the exponents of which may even be said to have held the fort against the labor-quantity theory throughout the period. This was not only due to Ricardo's carelessness but also to their own. We have seen that they failed in their analysis of the element of utility, though they brushed against it time and again. No more than Ricardo did they trouble to work out a theory of exchange which, in their case as in his, among other things, accounts for faulty handling of the concept of scarcity—the basic importance of which for the whole field of value theory was, however,

[26] The same applies to Marx, who took the same view without observing that his exploitation theory presupposes that supply and demand do their work.

[27] This is not strictly true except in pure competition in Professor Chamberlin's sense. In the case of monopoly there is no supply function; in the case of monopolistic competition, also in Professor Chamberlin's sense, there is neither a demand nor a supply function of the kind that exists in the case of pure competition. To be true, the statement above must be confined to the latter case.

[28] Malthus (*Principles*, 1st ed., p. 495) went so far as to call 'the principle of supply and demand' the 'first, greatest, and most universal principle' of Political Economy. [All future references are to the first edition of the *Principles*.]

asserted by Lauderdale, Malthus, and Senior—and for failure to understand monopolistic pricing.[29] But the sponsors of supply and demand, again with the unnoticed exception of Cournot (and very few others, such as C. Ellet and D. Lardner), even experienced difficulty in setting on its feet the very supply-and-demand apparatus, the claims of which to a place in economic theory they tried to assert. They talked of desires or desires backed by purchasing power, of 'extent' of demand and 'intensity' of demand, of quantities and prices, and did not quite know how to relate these things to one another. The concepts, so familiar to every beginner of our own days, of demand *schedules* or curves of willingness to buy (under certain general conditions) specified quantities of a commodity at specified prices, and of supply *schedules* or curves of willingness to sell (under certain general conditions) specified quantities of a commodity at specified prices, proved unbelievably hard to discover and to distinguish from the concepts—quantity demanded and quantity supplied. Malthus made indeed some progress toward clarification. But the reader needs only to look up Senior (*Outline*, pp. 14 et seq.) to satisfy himself of the blundering way in which he tried to explain these simple matters. Or were they so simple after all? Is it not a fact, which stares at us from the histories of all sciences, that it is much more difficult for the human mind to forge the most elementary conceptual schemes than it is to elaborate the most complicated superstructures when those elements are well in hand?

Lauderdale, Say, Malthus, and others all asked themselves the question how cost of production fits with supply and demand. Say's contribution is enshrined in the proposition that cost of production is nothing else than the value of the productive services that are consumed in production; and that the value of the productive services is nothing else than the value of the commodity which is the result—another of those sayings of his that indicate possible insights without making them explicit enough for contemporaries and later critics to understand. Malthus, however, though he probed less deeply, explained things much better so far as he saw them. In particular, he nicely indicates the locus of cost of production, which 'only determines the prices of commodities, as the payment of it is the necessary condition of their supply' (*Principles*, ch. 2, § 3)—a turn of phrase that points far ahead toward Jevonian teaching. Another lesson to conclude with. Many circumstances combined to keep the theory of those writers in a state that cannot be described as anything but primitive; but one of them was obviously the lack of the

[29] This is the more remarkable because Cournot produced within the period (1838) his classic theory of monopoly, which, however, passed unnoticed. One of the consequences of this state of things was the prevalence of very loose ideas on what monopoly really is. Even Senior spoke of a 'monopoly in land.' But in his case nothing more was involved than misleading terminology: he did not mean more than scarcity of land and did not actually try to explain rent by a nonexistent monopoly in it. Others did, however, and it is not always easy to tell whether a given author only used current phraseology in order to denote operation of scarcity in the case of a 'costless' factor of production or actually meant to assert what would be true only if landowners acted like a single seller.

appropriate technique: essentially quantitative relations cannot be stated satisfactorily without mathematics. It is the same defect that also marred J. S. Mill's attempt at summing up.

(c) *J. S. Mill's Half-Way House.* 'Happily, there is nothing in the laws of Value which remains for the present or any future writer to clear up; the theory of the subject is complete.' So J. S. Mill wrote in 1848 (*Principles*, Book III, ch. 1, § 1)—evidently well pleased with the analytic structure he was about to erect from existing material. Actually, the structure is not an attractive residence. Its main merit consists in the fact that it showed up its defects so clearly as to make even casual visitors desirous of remodeling it.

On the one hand, there is no doubt that Mill himself sincerely wished to restate Ricardian doctrine in an improved form. And so his work in this field has been and is being interpreted to this day. Leaning heavily on De Quincey's exposition of that doctrine, Mill accepted Utility and Difficulty of Attainment as conditions of exchange value. But the energy with which he insisted on the relative character of the latter completely annihilated Ricardo's Real Value and reduced other Ricardianisms to insipid innocuousness. Also, abstinence takes its place along with quantity of labor as an element in 'cost.' In other points, shifts of emphasis do the rest to destroy what it was Mill's intention to rebuild.

But on the other hand, Mill's own main contribution was to develop the supply-and-demand analysis so fully that, as Marshall himself was to indicate, there remained not so very much to do beyond removing loose ends and adding rigor in order to arrive at something not far distant from Marshallian analysis. He did not achieve perfect clarity [30] or in fact a complete and correct statement of the theory of supply and demand. But he went much further than the majority of economists before him—always excepting Cournot—and may be said to have been the first to teach its essentials. In particular, he wrote out, in words, the Equation of Demand and Supply, and he made full use of it in his chapter on international values, which is discussed below.

It is quite true that he paid token tribute to Ricardo's shadow by introducing supply and demand in the modest role of determinants of value in the case of commodities that are 'absolutely limited in quantity' (Book III, ch. 2)—with which he classed, erroneously of course, monopolized commodities, whereas he let the commodities 'which are susceptible of indefinite multiplication without increase of cost' be determined by this cost (ibid. ch. 3) and commodities 'which are susceptible of indefinite multiplication, but not without increase of cost' by 'cost of production in the most unfavourable

30 See, e.g., his comments upon Senior's statement that limitation of supply is essential to the value of labor itself ('Notes on N. W. Senior's Political Economy; by John Stuart Mill,' publ. by Professor F. A. von Hayek in *Economica*, August 1945). Mill replied that 'labour being painful, would not be incurred without some sort of equivalent pleasure and advantage even if labourers could be multiplied indefinitely by a volition or if every man could work a hundred thousand hours in the four and twenty.' But disutility of labor is only relevant because it operates to limit the supply of labor.

existing circumstances' (ibid. ch. 5). But he was concerned not so much with supply and demand per se as with the level at which supply and demand [31] will fix equilibrium price in each of those cases. And he was truer to his thought when he formulated the 'law of supply and demand' quite generally as he did in his 'Notes on Senior,' defining supply and demand as quantity supplied and quantity demanded: 'the value of a commodity in any market will always [32] be such that the demand shall be exactly equal to the supply.' And I maintain that this, in fact if not in intention, replaces Ricardo's law of equilibrium values and, incidentally, completes the scrapping of Ricardo's central concept of real value.

This interpretation is reinforced by a passage in the chapter on international values: whenever the 'law of cost of production is not applicable,' we must 'fall back upon an antecedent law, that of supply and demand' (Book III, ch. 18, § 1). Should this *not* mean that Mill embraced—without being fully aware of it—the very same analysis that was anathema to Ricardo, then the sense of this passage escapes me. Nor is there anything to oppose this interpretation in the heap of blundering propositions that Mill called 'Summary of the Theory of Value' (Book III, ch. 6). Quite unimportant concessions are made to the labor-quantity theory [33] (see especially propositions XIII and XV). On the other hand, definitely anti-Ricardian doctrine is repeatedly asserted (see especially propositions I, V, VIII). And the Ricardian theorem that rent is not an element in the cost of production is upheld with qualifications which, if correctly stated and developed (which Mill did not do), amount to renouncing it (see proposition IX) and point toward the opportunity cost theory.[34] A muddle, all this, no doubt. But it was not a hopeless muddle. Let us rather call it a fertile one—for this muddle contained all the elements that

[31] [Throughout this book J. A. S. refers to 'supply and demand' whereas Mill and Marshall usually wrote of 'demand and supply.']

[32] The proposition is true only for competitive *equilibrium*, which is all he meant by 'natural' or 'necessary' price. Yet Mill, while perfectly aware of this, used the word 'always.' I mention this because we shall meet, in sec. 4 on Say's Law, a similar difficulty of interpretation. Let me therefore point out at once that 'always' or 'necessarily,' when they occur in those old writers who were so delightfully lacking in precision, *do not necessarily mean assertions of identities*. Mill obviously meant an equation and not an identity. He meant 'always in equilibrium.' And so may have Say.

[33] But a disutility-plus-abstinence theory fits better into his general system of thought. It would be almost though not quite correct to say that Mill (and Cairnes) transformed the Ricardian labor-quantity theory into the Marshallian 'real-cost' theory.

[34] See also Book III, ch. 16, 'Of Some Peculiar Cases of Value,' which, another proof of how hastily the work was put together, strays far from the matters to which it is germane and in which we read (§ 1): 'Since cost of production here fails us, we must revert to a law of value anterior to cost of production, and *more fundamental*, the law of demand and supply' [my italics, J. A. S.], and this after a statement, made only three paragraphs before, which seems to *exclude* cases of free competition from the operation of the law of supply and demand, precisely the only ones to which it applies strictly. Indeed, for Mill Malthus had written in vain.

were necessary to straighten it out.[35] Cairnes was the first to try to do this, though without any great success. Marshall did succeed in doing this, though not without invoking ideas from outside Mill's range of vision (see Part IV, chs. 5 and 6).

3. The Theory of International Values

Some of the aspects of that period's policy of international trade have already been dealt with (chs. 2 and 5). Its monetary aspects will be surveyed in the next chapter. Here we shall consider, with the utmost brevity,[1] the purely theoretical core of the 'classic' teaching in international trade for which J. S. Mill introduced the phrase Theory of International Values. We are primarily interested in two things: in the contributions this theory made during that period to the analysis of international trade; and in the relations of these contributions to the theory of 'domestic' value sketched out above. The 'classic' writers, being most of them ardent free traders, were no doubt much concerned with pointing out the advantages or 'gains' that accrue to a country from international trade. Therefore, much of what they had to say on the subject pertains to the field of welfare economics and constitutes in fact their most important exploit in this field. But this is of secondary importance from the standpoint of this section.

As regards contributions to the analysis of international economic relations —remember, we now neglect the monetary angle [2]—we have three novelties to record: (1) a distinct theory of international values; (2) the theorem of Comparative Cost; and (3) the theory of Reciprocal Demand. The first was that a distinct theory of international values emerged at all. This was, in a sense, in conformity with old tradition, since already the mercantilist writers had looked upon foreign trade as something that differed essentially, in nature and effects, from domestic trade. But for the 'classics,' who did not accept the rationale of the mercantilist distinction, it was by no means evident that there was any theoretically—or even practically—relevant difference or, if

[35] As regards methods that had been new in his youth, he was surprisingly backward: for instance, ch. 15, 'Of a Measure of Value' does not contain a single reference to price index numbers—an indication of narrowness of outlook that might be illustrated also by other examples.

[1] The resulting inadequacy is more tolerable than it would be otherwise because readers may be referred confidently to an excellent study of the subject in Professor J. Viner's *Studies in the Theory of International Trade*, chs. VIII and IX.

[2] The fact that it is possible to neglect the monetary angle and to consider the barter angle separately is of course due to a property of the 'classic' pattern of economic analysis that has been discussed above. It would not be possible within every system of economic theory. We may add that in the conditions of that epoch it was somewhat less unrealistic than it would be now to identify international economic relations with trade in commodities and services and to consider this trade as a barter of commodities against commodities—though, on principle, it was just as inadmissible as it would be now.

there was, what it consisted in. In fact, economists have never quite agreed on this.[3] The group in which Ricardo was the brightest light selected immobility of factors of production as a criterion. That is to say, they defined domestic trade as the trade relations of industries or firms between which capital and labor move without hindrance, thus assuring, in equilibrium, equal rates of return to investment and work of the same difficulty, riskiness, and so on—which was quite essential to their 'domestic' theory; and they defined foreign trade as the trade relations of industries or firms between which—for reasons such as distance,[4] difference in language, difference in legal institutions, unfamiliarity with conditions of life and habits of business—capital and labor do not move freely. This has often been misunderstood. The 'classics' were, of course, not unaware of the facts of international migration of both labor and capital, just as they were not unaware of the fact that neither is completely 'mobile' within a country. All they did was to set up, for purposes of analytic convenience, the two limiting cases as 'ideal types' that, though neither actually occurs in real life, represent important constituents of what does occur in real life. It is another question how the lack of realism involved affects the practical applicability of this schema. It could be shown, however, that, so long as there is any difference at all between domestic and international mobility, a theory based upon this schema will retain relevance. It can also be shown, moreover, that what the 'classic' theory of international value thereby loses in applicability in the field of international relations it gains in the field of domestic relations, where imperfect mobility prevails. Cairnes (*Leading Principles*, Part I, ch. 3) conceptualized this by introducing the terms Industrial and Commercial Competition. The former term denotes trade relations with mobility and the latter, trade relations without mobility. He also introduced the concept Non-competing Groups to denote groups of workmen (local and occupational) or of firms, the members of each of which will not or can not normally move into any of the others. Using this terminology, we may say that the 'classics' really developed, in addition to what purported to be a general theory of value, a theory of value for the case of non-competing groups or of commercial competition. They did this, no doubt, because they thought primarily of the application to the analysis of international trade; but

[3] Perhaps the most obvious difference between foreign and domestic trade follows from the fact that most people take different attitudes toward the advantage of their own and the advantage of a foreign country. The common habit of expressing oneself as if it were nations as such that trade (and not individuals) is in part due to this difference in attitude. But some authors have stressed the importance of national monetary and credit systems. Others have looked upon problems of location as the core of the theory of international economic relations.

[4] The element of distance thus did enter the picture. But it entered the picture only in this and in no other way. The 'classic' writers did not make distance per se, i.e. cost of transportation, the center of their picture. This was done by some of their later followers or critics, Sidgwick in particular, but must not be confused with the quite different and much more modest role that was assigned to distance by Ricardo and Mill.

the theoretical characteristic of their new doctrine is, all the same, not confined to this practical purpose.

The second contribution, as everybody knows, was the theorem of Comparative Costs. As Professor Viner (op. cit. p. 440) has pointed out, A. Smith never went beyond stating that under free trade everything would be produced in the place where costs (taking account of transportation costs) were lowest. He also has pointed out that some earlier writers had formulated the more general proposition that, under free trade, commodities would be imported whenever they can be obtained most cheaply in this way. This includes the case of exports that cost less than it would cost to produce the corresponding imports at home, and thus implies the theorem of Comparative Costs.[5] I also follow Viner, however, in believing that there was distinctive merit in stating explicitly that imports can be profitable, even though the *commodities imported* can be produced at less cost at home than abroad. This merit belongs to Torrens (*The Economists Refuted,* 1808) and to Ricardo. The former baptized the theorem, the latter elaborated it and fought for it victoriously.[6] The simplest way of conveying it is to let Ricardo's famous example do duty once more. Take two countries, England and Portugal, and two commodities, wine and cloth. Portugal, being more efficient than England in both lines of production, can produce a certain quantity of wine by the labor of 80 men and a certain quantity of cloth by the labor of 90 men, whereas in England the production of the same quantities of wine and cloth takes, respectively, the labor of 120 and of 100 men. Under these circumstances, Portugal will advantageously 'specialize' in wine and import cloth, while England will 'specialize' in cloth and import wine provided, of course, that wine and cloth exchange on any terms between the limits of one unit of English cloth for $9/8$ of a unit of Portuguese wine and one unit of English cloth for $5/6$ units of Portuguese wine. In the former case, all the advantage goes to England, and Portugal is no better off than she would be without trade; in the latter case all advantage goes to Portugal, and England is no better off than she would be without trade. So far as this goes, any intermediate exchange ratio is possible with advantage to both countries, and if traders in both countries acted as monopolists, the exchange ratio would be indeterminate between those limits. Ricardo and his immediate followers did

5 To the instance mentioned by Viner may perhaps be added M. Delfico's argument in his memorandum *Sulla liberta del commercio* (1797).

6 In spite of weak resistance that was in part supported by incompetent argument, the theorem may be said to have conquered in England. In the United States it did not catch on so well and still less did it do so on the continent of Europe, where it was widely misunderstood even among free traders. But Cherbuliez gave a good account of it. And von Mangoldt improved it, or carried it further, in one very important point (see Viner, op. cit. pp. 458 et seq.; but if the reader refers to the original text, he should turn to the first edition of Mangoldt's *Grundriss*, which appeared in 1863 and contains the relevant appendix that the editor of the posthumous second edition of 1871 thought fit to omit; see above, ch. 4, sec. 5).

not worry about this but glibly assumed that the advantage would be halved—which may have spelled error but also may have been merely carelessness.

Other writers, among them Torrens, realized however that the indeterminateness of the terms of trade or exchange ratios would be in general removed, at least under conditions of perfect competition (or of one-sided monopoly), by the mechanism of what Torrens was, I think, the first to call Reciprocal Demand (in print). J. S. Mill, surpassing himself in generosity, not only defended Ricardo against any charge of having committed a mistake but also disclaimed credit for the original conception of this idea, although he had developed it in all essentials in an essay written as early as 1829-30 but not published before 1844 (in his *Some Unsettled Questions*). From it, he took the substance of Sections 1-5 of the famous Chapter 18 of his *Principles* (Book III) [7] that to all intents and purposes set the theory of reciprocal demand on its feet—the third novelty that was contributed during that period to the general analysis of international economic relations.

The problem being complex and quite beyond his command of technique, J. S. Mill dealt with it by means of a number of simplifying assumptions some of which he tried to remove in Sections 6-9 of the chapter. In particular, he confined his argument at first to the case of only two commodities and of two countries—the latter, it should be added, of similar size and productive capacity—and it is in fact in this case that the principle involved can be best displayed. In order to determine the point at which, within the limits set by comparative costs, the exchange ratio or the terms of trade between the two countries and commodities will tend to be fixed, Mill fell back once more upon the 'antecedent' (logically fundamental) law of supply and demand. He perceived that (under fairly comprehensive assumptions) the equilibrium exchange ratio would be determined by the condition that the quantity of each of the two products that the importing country is willing to take at this ratio be equal to the quantity that the exporting country is willing to give at this ratio (Equation of International Demand).[8] It is assumed that, if the one country is willing to take more or less at this ratio than the other is willing to give, competition of 'buyers' or 'sellers' will adjust the exchange ratio until

[7] It is only these five sections of that chapter that have attained such fame. The rest of the chapter, added in the third edition, in deference to the 'intelligent criticisms' of friends, has had no share in the applause and has been voted 'laborious and confusing' even by good Millians such as Bastable and Edgeworth. I cannot quite share either opinion. There are valuable contributions in the rest. For instance, Mill never came so close to a grasp of the nature and use of the concept of elasticity of demand (which he called 'extensibility') as he did in § 8 of that chapter. Some of the criticisms that were leveled at it rest on nothing but the clumsiness and ambiguity of expression that are unavoidable in a verbal presentation of this topic reinforced by nothing except numerical examples.

[8] The equivalent formula that the ratio is such as to equalize the values of exports and imports is simpler but brings out less well than does ours that the proposition is an equilibrium condition and not an identity

it fulfils this condition.[9] It should be recorded to Mill's credit that he saw that this will not exclude multiple equilibria,[10] and there are more delicate questions that cannot be touched upon here. Also it should be recorded that he put the apparatus he created to good use. His treatment in Section 5 of the effects of technological improvement in an export industry that are not necessarily favorable to the exporting country deserves to be mentioned in particular. For further light on the matter the reader is primarily referred to Professor von Haberler's well-known treatise.[11]

Let us note at once that in this field Marshall did not do more than to polish and develop Mill's meaning. He cast it into an elegant geometrical model (*The Pure Theory of Foreign Trade*, 1879) that greatly clarified the theory.[12] But he was well aware (see *Memorials of Alfred Marshall*, ed. by A. C. Pigou, 1925, p. 451) that his curves 'were set to a definite tune, that called by Mill.' This applies even to the geometrical apparatus: Mill's reads almost like a somewhat clumsy instruction for choosing these curves rather than any others. Edgeworth's famous restatement ('The Pure Theory of International Values,' *Economic Journal*, 1894, reprinted in *Papers Relating to Political Economy*, vol. II) added many interesting details but also did not go beyond Mill in fundamentals. Serious attacks do not antedate the 1920's, and even then leading masters in the field substantially adhered to his teaching.

Since advocacy of free-trade policy was the main practical purpose the 'classical' writers had in mind when they developed their theory of international values, they were naturally much interested in displaying the 'gains' that accrue to a nation from foreign trade. We have noticed elsewhere the

[9] This implicit assumption of Mill's really constitutes an additional condition, the so-called secondary or stability condition.

[10] The matter is a little complicated. On the one hand, as Professor Viner has pointed out (op. cit. p. 537), Mill had the correct idea of the nature of his equation of supply and demand, i.e., he saw and asserted against objectors that it was an equilibrium condition and not an 'identical proposition,' which would, of course, be incapable of determining an equilibrium point. This passage from a letter of his to Cairnes (*Letters*, ed. by Hugh S. R. Elliot, 1910) should be borne in mind precisely because it proves that he understood this difference perfectly. But, on the other hand, he stated (§ 6 of the chapter on international values) that 'it is conceivable that the conditions [of the equation of international demand] might be equally satisfied by every numerical rate which could be supposed,' and this *would* make an identity of that 'equation.' If, however, we read this passage in its context, we readily realize that it does not really mean more than the perception of the possibility of the existence of more equilibrium positions than one, and then a distinct merit emerges to claim recognition instead of the demerit to which critics—including Edgeworth—have called attention.

[11] G. von Haberler, *The Theory of International Trade* (1936, chs. 9-12). The reference also covers the subject of comparative costs and is intended to help all those readers who will find my brief account unsatisfactory or even ununderstandable.

[12] On this model, see Haberler, op. cit. pp. 153 et seq.; also Appendix J of Marshall's *Money, Credit and Commerce*. There is a London School Reprint (1930) of the papers of 1879 under the title, *Pure Theory (Foreign Trade—Domestic Values)*.

bias which this imparted to their argument and their tendency to underestimate the possibilities of unilateral gain from protection. Here we are more interested in finding out how they defined these gains and how they tried to quantify them. Of course, in the early stages of the discussion it was quite sufficient to say that foreign trade will supply a nation with commodities which it could not produce at all or could produce only at higher cost. The latter element having been reinforced by the introduction of the comparative-cost principle, it was not less natural for Ricardo to stress the resulting saving in cost per unit of product. There are two aspects to this. On the one hand, this comes to the same thing as stressing the gain in quantity of product per unit of costs.[13] Ricardo recognized, of course, that foreign trade cannot increase the sum total of real value (in his sense) in a country, but 'it will very powerfully contribute to increase the mass of commodities, and therefore the sum of enjoyments' (*Principles*, ch. 7). There he stops because he strongly believed that utility (value in use) cannot be *measured*.[14] But still we might express Ricardo's meaning by saying that foreign trade increases enjoyment per unit of his real value. In any case, this is as far as he went into the welfare economics of foreign trade—further, however, than is commonly believed. On the other hand, foreign trade does bear upon the structure of Ricardian real value in this way: if, as was the case with England, imports consist to a considerable extent of foodstuffs and other necessities—such as cotton—that enter largely into the consumption of the working class, then the share of the latter in total value will fall and the real value of profits and the rate of profit will rise. Needless to say, this is an essential part of Ricardo's free-trade argument: foreign trade increases indeed the 'happiness of mankind' by improving the allocation of resources and by giving 'incentives to saving and to the accumulation of capital'—'by the abundance and cheapness of commodities' which it brings about—but does not, except temporarily, raise profits unless it is instrumental in reducing the Ricardian real value of wage goods just as would a technological improvement in their production.

So far as there is anything at all in Malthus' argument on the subject, it does not contradict Ricardo's. Of course, as Professor Viner has pointed out (op. cit. p. 531), he might have said that the 'sum of enjoyments' is a treach-

[13] Referring to the example by which Ricardo explained the operation of the comparative-cost principle, we observe that *if* England and Portugal each produced one unit quantity of cloth and one unit quantity of wine without trade, this would take 390 labor units in all whereas, after specialization through free trade, these same four unit quantities would take only 360 labor units.

[14] But since he said that foreign trade will *increase* the sum of enjoyments (the word 'sum' is out of place, of course, if utility is not measurable), he should not have said that utilities cannot be *compared*. The latter is in fact implied by the comparative-cost principle, which is relevant only because comparison of utilities is possible. At a stretch, we might credit Ricardo with the modern idea that there is such a thing as 'ordinal utility,' although there is no such thing as 'cardinal utility'—that a utility is capable of being greater or smaller than another, although it is not capable of being a multiple of another.

erous concept to use because foreign trade will influence the distribution of incomes, conceivably in a direction that may be unfavorable to small incomes. But he did not say this. Nobody did at the time excepting some politicians who argued on this line, in the English corn law controversy, on behalf of farmers. I do not maintain, of course, that either Ricardo or Mill handled the welfare aspects of foreign trade satisfactorily. Objectively, Mill's theory of reciprocal demand was a step in advance because it pointed more directly toward welfare (utility) aspects. But Mill himself did not exploit the possibilities, such as they were, that his approach suggests. This was reserved for Marshall and Edgeworth, who developed methods which, though they have become obsolete by now, gave satisfaction to many in the 1890's (see below, Part IV, ch. 7, Appendix). They, Edgeworth especially, criticized Mill for estimating benefit from foreign trade exclusively by the criterion of exchange value (terms of trade).[15] In view of Ricardo's emphasis on increase of means of enjoyment, this criticism hardly applies to him. In the case of Mill there is more to it, but not much more. Both saw the nature of the 'social gains of trade' correctly. It is truer to say that they did not attempt to measure them at all—and there is something to be said for stopping at what Cairnes regretfully called an 'indefinite and vague result' (*Leading Principles*, p. 506 of English ed.; the pagination differs in the American ed.)—than it is to say that they attempted to estimate them from the terms of trade.

Let us now ask the question how were the theories of comparative cost and of reciprocal demand related to Ricardo's and Mill's general theories of value or, to put it in the usual way, what was the relation between their theories of foreign and domestic value?

First of all, what was the relation of the theories of comparative cost and of reciprocal demand to one another? Mill's generosity has obscured the obvious answer. As we have seen, in his *Essays on Some Unsettled Questions*, 1844 (Essay I, 'Of the Laws of Interchange between Nations'), he presented his equation of reciprocal demand as a modest supplement to Ricardo's comparative-cost principle that the great pioneer had had no time to add himself. Most historians and critics have taken the same view. But it should be clear that this view is entirely wrong. The demand-supply schedules, whose intersection gives the geometrical picture of the equation of reciprocal demand, represent an approach that Ricardo always rejected except for temporary fluctuations and for monopolized commodities. They introduce a new and more general principle just as, in the monetary department, the general theory of the rates of foreign exchange does not supplement the proposition that, under international gold monometallism, exchange rates fall within the gold points—and are, *in this sense*, 'determined' by them—but ousts it from the key position it used to hold. Just as a general theory has reduced the gold-point theorem

[15] That is to say, Edgeworth and others accused Mill of believing that a country's *total* gain from trade always increased or decreased as its gain *per unit of exports* (the quantity of German linen that England received for a unit of her cloth) increased and decreased, just as writers on wages sometimes assume that the national pay roll always increases or decreases when wage rates do.

to the status of one of many propositions about a special case, so the theory of reciprocal demand has reduced the comparative-cost principle to the status of a proposition about a particular aspect of trade under commercial competition, that indeed retains some importance—because it is particularly useful in destroying a prevalent error—but is no longer fundamental to the theory of international values.[16] Thus the two are not complements of one another, any more than they are alternative theories of international values, but their relation is that of a particular theorem and a comprehensive theory.

Now for the relation of comparative cost and reciprocal demand to the general value theories of their authors. As regards Ricardo, we may look upon the comparative-cost principle as an exception from the labor-quantity law, for it describes a case where commodities no longer exchange according to this law. This exception is the more serious because it covers not only international values but also, in all cases of less than perfect mobility of labor, domestic values. In fact, together with all the other exceptions and qualifications that Ricardo was forced to make, it really rips up the entire fabric of Ricardo's theory of value. But we can also, with almost equal justification, interpret the comparative-cost principle as an outgrowth of the labor-quantity theory from the standpoint of which the problem of international value did present itself to Ricardo and which does supply the technique of his argument. Accordingly, it has been held by high authorities (Ohlin, Mason) that Ricardo's analysis of international trade is vitiated by its dependence on an obsolete theory of value. But it must not be forgotten that, as Haberler has shown, the principle of comparative cost admits of restatement in terms of opportunity costs.

Quite different is the relation between Mill's reciprocal demand and his general theory of value. Reciprocal demand—notwithstanding an impression to the contrary that might be created by Mill's wording, which was as we know at times misleadingly Ricardian—is completely independent of any labor-quantity or even real-cost theory of value. On the contrary, it blends perfectly with his general supply and demand theory, which, by virtue of reciprocal demand, is successfully extended to the case of international values.[17] This

[16] I quite agree with Professor von Haberler's phrase that the comparative-cost principle 'merges' into a general theory of international value of which the equation of reciprocal demand is the central theorem (op. cit. p. 123). But precisely because I approve of *this* phrase, I cannot approve of the other phrase Haberler uses in the same place, viz., that the theory of reciprocal demand is 'an essential supplement to the theory of comparative costs.'

[17] We may thus consider Mill's theory of international values (or of commercial competition) as a particular case of his general supply and demand analysis, defined by the assumption that there be no mobility of factors. But there is nothing to stop us from putting it the other way round and from saying that the general case is represented by his theory of international value and that domestic value constitutes the particular case, which is defined by perfect mobility of factors. This is worth our while to observe because a similar situation has emerged of late with respect to Keynesian doctrine: most economists would describe the difference between the Walrasian and the Keynesian models by saying that the latter is, as it were, cut out of the former by means of several restrictive ('particularizing') assumptions; but Lord Keynes himself regarded

case, joining the list of all the other cases in which analysis by 'cost of production' also fails, thus helps to strengthen and to unify Mill's theory of value, whereas it weakened that of Ricardo. Now, supply and demand, considered as a theory of value (which it is not really, as we know), is a half-way house between real-cost and marginal-utility theories. Therefore, Mill's equation of reciprocal demand constitutes another step away from the former and toward the latter. *And this is the reason why the theory of international values, as formed by Mill, stood up under the fire of criticism so much better than did the rest of the 'classical' system and why it remained dominant doctrine right into the* 1920's.

A discussion of the criticisms—both justified and unjustified—that were leveled, then and later, at both the comparative-cost principle and the equation of reciprocal demand would be interesting in itself and highly revelatory of the amount of ability and analytic power that went into economic controversies at various times. More important still, such a discussion would greatly improve the reader's understanding of the theory of international values and of what it can and cannot do. But it is quite out of the question to embark upon such a discussion here. Fortunately, however, reference to the works of Viner and Haberler will amply fill this lacuna.[18] Recommending careful study of both, I can therefore conclude with the following two remarks.

First, the student of the 'classical' literature on international values must bear in mind that he is dealing with very rough groundwork rather than with a complete structure. For instance, neither Ricardo nor Mill can have looked upon a theory that deals only with two commodities and two countries as more than an illustration of principles—Mill did in fact treat briefly the cases of three commodities and three countries (Book III, ch. 18, § 4)—though they certainly believed the task of generalizing it to n commodities and n countries to be easier than it was.[19] The same goes for the 'classical' practice of confining analysis to the case of constant costs: variable costs, increasing and decreasing, must no doubt be introduced into the 'classic' theory, but the critic who cannot do this should blame himself rather than the pioneers. Also, the 'classics' did not ask themselves what the dropping of their assumptions of

his theory as the general case from which the writers whom *he* described as classics (Marshall and his immediate followers) cut out the special case which yields full-employment equilibrium by assuming away certain facts. The reader will observe that this, though in strict logic a distinction without a difference, matters a great deal in the psychology of scientific warfare.

[18] This must not be interpreted to mean that I agree with those eminent authors in every detail of their analysis.

[19] Mill held that trade among any number of countries and in any number of commodities 'must' take place on the same essential principles as trade between two countries and in two commodities. This is not quite so. The generalization to more than two countries presents indeed no great difficulties. It was undertaken within the period by several writers, who also realized how far this extension affects the validity of results. But extension to n commodities raises more difficulties. So far as I know, it was first tackled by M. Longfield (*Three Lectures on Commerce,* 1835).

'free' competition and of full employment of resources might do to their theories. It can be shown, however, that monopolistic competition and permanent unemployment do not destroy the validity of either the comparative-cost principle or the equation of reciprocal demand, although both do make considerable difference to the practical inferences to be drawn.[20]

Second, when we indict the many slips and inadequacies that no doubt disfigure the 'classical' analysis, we should never fail to notice that many of them may be removed without much injury to essentials and that they are fairly matched by slips and inadequacies on the part of their critics. An example is the manner in which the 'classics' treated the question of the 'ratios . . . in which the advantage of the trade may be divided between the two nations.' Mill had explained already in the *Essay* of 1829 (published 1844) that these ratios may vary all the way between the limits set by comparative costs and even considered the 'extreme case' in which 'the whole of the advantage . . . would be reaped by one party.' He may have underrated the likelihood of such cases—for example, he hardly thought of the case of a large and a much smaller country—and there are other criticisms to make of his treatment of this question. In substance, however, he was all right, and the corrections that might be applied leave his argument substantially intact. But even, if that were not so, the case would be of serious importance only with two commodities, two countries, and constant costs—conditions that would be automatically eliminated in any more realistic presentation of the theory. Another though related example is the manner in which the 'classics' treated the question of the extent to which countries would specialize in the line of production in which they have a comparative advantage. Ricardo's carelessness, assisted by the carelessness of his critics, has created the impression that he considered nothing but complete specialization and that he considered such complete specialization to be the theoretically and practically ideal case. But even if these allegations were wholly true—which is debatable—they would not amount to much. As regards the first, complete specialization of the trading countries, *if physically possible*—that is to say, if both countries are big enough—would indeed be the rule under the Ricardian assumption of constant costs. If we drop this assumption, as we must do in any case, we also get rid of the offending proposition. As regards the advantages of complete specialization in comparison with partial specialization or with no trade at all, Ricardo and Mill certainly did not think the matter through properly. And critics found it easy to show that complete specialization is necessary in order to reap the full advantages of international trade only in a limiting case whereas, in general, partial specialization may be more 'advantageous' and, in other limiting cases, complete specialization may not be better than no trade at all. Since, however, trade that is not 'advantageous' in the Ricardo-Mill sense will also not be profitable, the requisite corrections again do not

[20] The simplest way of convincing oneself of this as regards persistent underemployment of resources is to consider the argument for protection that gains in force—though it may be debatable how much it gains—in this case.

greatly matter. Their effect may indeed be to obscure fundamental truth rather than to reassert it.

Not all weaknesses of the 'classical' analysis of international values are venial. Even Mill had a very imperfect conception of all the repercussions of international trade upon the structure of domestic values, which he also, though not so much as Ricardo, took as given or, which is not much better, as adjusting themselves appropriately. Primitive technique and bias for free trade, moreover, account for the nearly complete neglect of all those cases in which well devised tariffs might greatly benefit at least one and conceivably all of the trading countries.[21] But on the whole it is more misleading than it is true to say that the 'classic' theory of international values has ever been refuted,[22] though, as has been said already in another connection, some of the practical inferences that the 'classic' writers drew from it have been refuted. And the 'classic' theory was altogether unequal to the burden they put upon it in making it a 'guide to policy.' Above all, it does not 'prove free trade.'

4. Say's Law of Markets

In a famous chapter of his treatise (*Traité d'économie politique*), J. B. Say expounded a doctrine that has come to the fore again during the last decade: his *loi des débouchés* or *Law of Markets*.[1] The fact that it has become the target of adverse criticism from Keynes and the Keynesians has invested it with an importance not naturally its own. Because of this, we shall have to return to it in our discussion of the Walras-Marshall system, of which, ac-

21 That this neglect should not be attributed to bias only is shown by the case of Edgeworth, who did much to remedy that state of things and still remained a strong free trader. At the time, it was Torrens especially who in his tracts on *The Budget* (1841-4) pointed out the possibilities enshrined in the 'classic' theory, for an analysis of protective measures that does not quite bear out the 100 per cent argument of the more ardent free traders (which must in fact be explained by England's position and interests rather than by any theory), who, for tactical reasons, were very reluctant to admit the real extent of the possibility of unilateral advantage from protection. Cournot's contribution to the theory of international values lies in this field. Only it does not lie in the argument of Chapter 12 of his *Recherches*, which has come in for derogatory criticism time and again and part of which he disavowed himself, but in the argument of Chapter 10 which, though not faultless either, shows successfully that, under international trade without barriers, the total quantity produced of a commodity may conceivably be smaller than it would be if the two markets were completely isolated from each other. But he does not seem to have realized the limitations of this argument.

22 See O. von Mering, 'Ist die Theorie der internationalen Werte widerlegt?' *Archiv für Sozialwissenschaft*, April 1931.

1 Book I, ch. xv, pp. 76-83 of the Prinsep translation (1821). It occupied four pages only in the first edition of the *Traité* (1803) but in response to criticism continued to expand, in successive editions, growing more woolly all the time. Law of Markets is the usual English version of the French *loi des débouchés*. The term Outlets would render Say's meaning better. Prinsep used the term Vent.

cording to some Keynesian critics, it is a basic proposition. For the same reason, we must now discuss its original meaning and its earlier fortunes with greater care than would otherwise be called for.

Our first task is to find out what Say's original meaning really was. With so inexact a writer this is not always easy. But in this instance his meaning is clear enough, illustrated as it is by his examples and conclusions. Let us start with one of these examples, which he added by way of comment upon the plight of the English export industries around 1810, that was a standard example of Sismondi's for the deadlocks that unrestrained production might cause. Say's argument was that the trouble did not lie with the superabundance of the English products but with the poverty of the nations that were expected to buy them. Take the case of Brazil. If English producers were unable to dispose of the wares they tried to export to that country, there could be only two reasons for it: either English exporters were making mistakes as regards the commodities the Brazilians wanted—as, in the then state of information about distant countries, they actually did—or else the Brazilians had nothing to offer in return or to export to third countries in order to procure the money with which to pay the English producers. In other words, the trouble was not that England produced too much but that Brazil produced too little. Also, as Say did not fail to emphasize, it would not have remedied the situation if the Brazilians had produced acceptable equivalents but had been prevented from exporting them by import restrictions in England or in third countries. So far as this goes, Say's reasoning amounts simply to part of the ordinary free-trade argument, which was gaining currency at the time and was to be formulated later by Sir Robert Peel in the adage: 'in order to be able to export, we must open our ports to foreign commodities'—an oversimplification no doubt, but one that contained a good deal of fundamental truth and of practical wisdom. This stands out particularly when we remember that, in the picture of the 'classics,' international economic relations reduced wholly, or almost wholly, to commodity trade: if we exclude movements of short- and long-term capital and disregard the vagaries of gold production, then exports and imports must 'ultimately' pay for one another.

More clearly than did others, Say perceived however that this argument derives from a more general principle that applies also to domestic trade. Under division of labor, the only means normally available to everyone for acquiring the commodities and services he wishes to have is to produce—or to take part in the production of—some equivalent for them. It follows that production increases not only the supply of goods in the markets but normally also the demand for them. *In this sense*, it is production itself ('supply') which creates the 'fund' from which flows the demand for its products: products are 'ultimately' paid for by products in domestic as well as in foreign trade. In consequence, a (balanced) expansion in all lines of production is a very different thing from a one-sided increase in the output of an individual industry or group of industries. To have seen the theoretical implications of this is one of Say's chief performances. We have now to make them clear to ourselves.

Consider an individual industry that is too small to exert perceptible influence upon the rest of the economy and upon the social aggregates such as national income. Therefore, the conditions in the rest of the economy may be considered as data for the purposes of an investigation into the operations of this industry, a procedure that we shall discuss in Part IV, Chapter 7, under the heading of Partial Analysis.[2] In particular, the demand schedule for the product of the industry in question is derived from the income generated by all the others: its own contribution to total income being negligible, that schedule may be considered as given independently of its own supply and so may (in general) the prices of the factors it uses. We then have given independent demand and cost schedules that summarize the whole of the economic conditions of society to which the industry in question has to respond and which may be said to determine the output it will produce at each price (supply schedule). The 'right' or equilibrium amount thus being, in general, well defined by this demand and this supply schedule, there is no difficulty or ambiguity in saying that, in any particular case, the industry has produced 'too little' or 'too much' and in describing the mechanisms that will be set in motion by such under- or overproduction. But it stands to reason that the particular industry's equilibrium output, the output that is neither too great nor too small, is the right output only with reference to the outputs of all the other industries. There can be no point in calling it right irrespective of them. In other words, demand, supply, and equilibrium are concepts with which to describe quantitative relations *within* the universe of commodities and services. They do not carry meaning with respect to this universe itself. Strictly speaking, there is no more sense in speaking of an economic system's total or aggregate demand and supply and, incidentally, of overproduction than there is in speaking of the exchange value of all vendible things taken together or of the weight of the solar system taken as a whole. But if we do insist on applying the *terms* demand and supply to social totals, we must be careful to bear in mind that they then mean something that is entirely different from what they mean in their usual acceptance. In particular, this aggregate demand and aggregate supply are not independent of each other, because the component demands 'for the output of any industry (or firm or individual) comes from the supplies of all the other industries (or firms or individuals)' [3] and therefore will in most cases increase (in real terms) if these supplies increase and decrease if these supplies decrease. This is the proposition which (like Lerner) I call Say's Law and which I believe renders Say's fundamental meaning.

As stated, Say's law is obviously true. Nevertheless, it is neither trivial nor unimportant. In order to convince ourselves of this, we need only notice the errors that arise to this day from the mistaken application to social aggre-

[2] The argument above is unnecessarily restricted. The essential point is actually independent of the particular assumptions of partial analysis. But our exposition is not materially impaired and gains much in simplicity by the use of the restrictions involved. For the same reason, also, we confine ourselves to the case of perfect competition.

[3] A. P. Lerner, 'The Relation of Wage Policies and Price Policies,' *American Economic Review*, Supplement, March 1939, p. 158.

gates of propositions derived by means of the demand-supply apparatus. Thus, observing that 'depression in a particular industry may be cured by a restriction of output,' the man in the street sometimes believes that 'to cure depression in the economy as a whole all that is necessary is that there should be a general restriction of output,' [4] and less crude reasoning of this kind occurs too often, even in writings of scientific standing, to permit us to brush aside Say's law as a stale truism. Moreover, Professor Lerner's example may be reformulated, I think, in a manner that will bring out the considerable, if negative, importance of Say's law for the theory of crises or 'gluts.' It avers correctly that crises can never be *causally explained* solely by everybody's having produced too much. Finally, the law, at least by implication, amounts to a recognition of the general interdependence of economic quantities and of the equilibrating mechanism by which they determine one another, and therefore has a place—as have other contributions of Say's—in the history of the emergence of the concept of general equilibrium.

But Say himself was little interested in the analytic proposition per se which for us constitutes the merit of his chapter on *débouchés*. Like many other economists of all times, he was much more anxious to exploit it for practical purposes than to formulate it with care. He was an addict to the Ricardian Vice (see above, ch. 4, sec. 2). The chapter, being mainly an argument for laissez-faire and against restrictions upon production, abounds in reckless statements, which were precisely the ones to attract attention. His readers were treated to a picture of the capitalist process that showed only a triumphant onward march of industry with nothing to disturb permanent advance at full employment except sectional maladjustments and restrictive government policies. All the other ills under which people groaned vanished before the battle cry, Supply creates its own Demand, which was made to mean much more than it can possibly mean when properly interpreted. It is not worth our while to stay in order to collect the grains of truth that even this picture contains and to point out, for example, that the difficulties experienced by French industry in 1811, 1812, and 1813 were in fact largely caused by the policy of the Napoleonic regime (Milan Decree and the rest) and that it was the lack of complements to what it produced, rather than the quantities of what it did produce, that accounts for the economic vicissitudes of those years. But it is worth our while to note that Say's careless statements, whatever else of merit or demerit impartial criticism may find in them, gave ample scope to the propensity of hostile critics to speak of capitalistic apologetics—'whitewashing,' reckless denials of real difficulties, shallow optimism, 'dwelling in a dreamland of equilibrium,' and the like. Still more is it worth our while to scrutinize some of the analytic consequences of his carelessness.

The first point to be made is that, though Say's law is not an identity, his blundering exposition has led a long series of writers to believe that it is one —and this in no less than four different senses.

[4] Lerner, ibid.

I. Some writers have *defended* Say's law on the ground that it asserts not more than that 'whatever is sold is bought' or that the sum the seller receives is the same sum that the buyer pays. This interpretation is obviously wrong. But a sentence in Say's chapter actually reads as if he had intended to mean precisely that. It may be remarked that, as has been shown by Richard Goodwin in an unpublished paper, the truism just stated is by no means useless. Only it is not Say's law.

II. Other writers, who are disposed to allow Say's law to stand for the case of a barter economy and who base their objection to it entirely on the neglect of the role of money which it seems to them to imply, point to the fact that in a barter economy every 'seller' is inevitably also a 'buyer.' In this sense, there is indeed identity of selling and buying and again it is true that Say himself may be quoted in support. But *this* identity is quite irrelevant for Say's purposes. To make it relevant, it would be necessary to prove that, in barter, everyone's offer is *at all exchange ratios* equal to what other people wish to take at the same ratios. This is obvious nonsense, of course, for disequilibrium is as possible in a barter economy as it is in a money economy, though the latter may display additional sources of disturbance. This mistake had already been made by Malthus and has been often repeated.

III. Still another interpretation of Say's law as an identity has been adopted by Lord Keynes and will be presented in the more exact form that O. Lange has given to it ('Say's Law . . .' in *Studies in Mathematical Economics and Econometrics;* Lange, McIntyre, Yntema eds., 1942). Denoting by p_i the going price of a representative commodity or service i, by D_i the quantity demanded, and by S_i the quantity supplied at that price, he makes Say's law mean, if there are $n - 1$ commodities (exclusive of money):

$$\sum_{i=1}^{n-1} p_i D_i \equiv \sum_{i=1}^{n-1} p_i S_i$$

which, if money be considered as the nth commodity, is equivalent to $D_n \equiv S_n$. It is perhaps not superfluous to state explicitly that my interpretation of Say's law amounts to replacing the identity signs ($\equiv$) by equality signs ($=$), valid only in a state of perfect equilibrium of the system. Of course, there is nothing to stop us from developing, as a useful exercise in pure theory, the consequences of the hypothesis, $D_n \equiv S_n$. But it should not be called Say's law, because Say, though he did not consider the problem of hoarding, did consider the problem of increasing the effective quantity of money in case increase in transactions should require it. Once more, however, Say himself is to blame for this interpretation. In his excessive zeal for establishing the practical importance of his theorem, he expresses himself in several places as if indeed the total monetary value of all commodities and services supplied (exclusive of money) would have to equal the monetary value of all commodities and services demanded (exclusive of money), not only in equilibrium but 'always and necessarily.' This is, of course, logically wrong if he actually meant it, but is practically wrong even if he meant only 'always and necessarily in equilibrium' but at the same time believed—as perhaps he did—that reality actually conformed, or would conform in the absence of government interference, to equilibrium conditions most of the time: the reader will realize how easily these two meanings can be confused.

IV. The last type of identity or tautology was ludicrously created by Say for the express purpose of making his law unassailable. Driven to something very like despair by the attacks upon his law, he simply reformulated his concept of production so as to confine it to the production of things, the price of which will cover cost. What could not be sold except at a loss does not constitute production in the economic sense any more so that overproduction is excluded by definition![5] The professional world has laughed at him ever since. Space does not permit us to analyze the psychology of this miscarriage or to make the attempt to discover a defensible kernel in it.

The second and only other point that needs to be made here about Say's carelessnesses concerns his treatment of the element of money, which must prove a vicious hurdle for anyone who relies on the model of a barter economy. Say's few and fragmentary pronouncements on the subject may be divided into two groups: pronouncements of a theoretical nature and pronouncements concerning the practical doubts his readers might harbor about the realism of his rosy picture. The former may be reduced to a single theorem: the intervention of money does not make any difference of *principle* to his law. With or without money, products exchange, in the last analysis, for products, since money is nothing but a medium of exchange that, owing to the losses of satisfaction or business gain that are incurred by keeping it idle, everybody will try to spend as promptly as the given habits of income and business payments permit. Now we are being taught a different doctrine so generally that it is necessary to emphasize that there is nothing wrong with this theory per se if it is stated and used with due regard to its abstract character and to the assumptions it involves.[6] The main criticism that may be leveled at it and the main reason why we prefer another theoretical pattern is that Say, like practically all the theorists of that age, neglected the store-of-value function of money and therefore the fact that there is an element in the 'demand' for it that is not accounted for by his theory. Whatever the *theoretical* consequences for the whole organon of economic theory that may follow from this, they do not justify wholesale rejection of this theory or refusal to recognize that as an early step in analysis it had its value. Much pointless controversy might have been spared us, and much confusion among beginners might have been avoided, if we had been content to *insert* the 'demand for cash to hold' into the theoretical pattern that Say adopted and to speak of supplementing rather than of refuting it or of adding a second to his first approximation.

The 'practical' group of Say's pronouncements on the monetary questions raised by his law may be rendered as follows. Unlike his interpreter J. S. Mill, he evidently did not think much of the practical importance of the phenomena that might be produced by widespread refusal to spend receipts promptly either on consumption or on 'real' investment (that is, investment involving demand for goods and services). Had he been asked whether he admitted that such refusal, if it occurred, would create disturbances and, if so, why he

[5] This new concept of production was first presented in a letter to Malthus (1820); see *Mélanges et correspondance* . . . , p. 202) and then in two articles in vols. 23 and 32 of the *Revue encyclopédique* (see especially the earlier one entitled 'Sur la balance des consommations avec les productions') and is embodied in the 5th ed. of the *Traité* (1826) and in the *Cours complet* (1828-9).

[6] Inasmuch as loss of satisfaction or interest is made the reason why people should spend promptly, it might even be claimed that in this passage Say pointed beyond his sketch toward a more complete theory.

had not pointed this out, he might with justice have replied that he was writing for readers of normal intelligence. But he did advert, in a perfunctory note (*Traité*, op. cit. p. 77), to the fall in price level that would be induced by expansion of output if the circulating medium failed to expand correspondingly. He answered, however, that if the increase in traffic requires more money, this want will be 'easily supplied' by the creation of substitutes such as trade bills, bank notes and demand deposits and that in addition money will 'pour in' from abroad. This was taking the matter a great deal too lightly and shows that his opponents had at least that much of a case: Say's argument was practical in intention, and he understated unjustifiably the gulf that separates his theorems from the realities of the economic process to which he applied them uncritically.[7]

We turn to the controversy that developed around Say's law. Critics being mainly interested in its practical implications, this controversy turned chiefly on the question of 'general gluts.' Therefore, a few remarks are sufficient for the moment.

Say's teaching—wheat and chaff—was accepted by Ricardo (*Principles*, ch. 21) and the Ricardians. James Mill, as his son claimed, may even have discovered the law independently.[8] It was attacked almost simultaneously by Sismondi and by Malthus,[9] who were followed by Chalmers and others. Some of their arguments were wrong to the point of ineptness (though Say's replies were not much better), and J. S. Mill, in summing up in favor of Say (*Principles*, Book III, ch. 14), had little difficulty in disposing of them. In doing so, and in pointing out that difference of opinion in this matter involves 'radically different conceptions of Political Economy, especially in its practical aspect,' he applied an important improvement to Say's exposition, though it is

[7] Moreover, we are here giving him the full benefit of the implications of his footnote. His text, where he tried to dispose of the whole problem by asserting that the true fund of purchasing power is goods and that any amount of money will do for any amount of physical transactions—statements that are also not simply wrong but hold only in the sphere of abstract logical principles—is still more objectionable. It is interesting to note, however, that part of his argument—that which attacks the view of the businessman, who blames scarcity of money for his troubles—had been expounded already by Sir Josiah Child.

[8] It appeared first in James Mill's *Commerce Defended* (1808), so that Say's priority is beyond question. Let me add that he, and especially Ricardo, went beyond Say on one point (see Ricardo's *Principles*, ch. 21, note 2). Say admitted that abundance of disposable capitals relative 'to the extent of employment for them' or, as we say, to the available investment opportunity, will reduce the rate of interest, although he held that *at falling rates of interest* this investment opportunity will indefinitely expand. This—with appropriate qualifications with regard to the conditions that prevail in depressions—is quite correct and evidently involves no contradiction. But Ricardo thought that it does and held—which is also correct but only within his own theoretical model and not without it—that, *except for a rise in* (*the real value of*) *wages*, investment is possible to an indefinite extent without depressing the rate of 'profits.'

[9] The first edition of Sismondi's *Nouveaux Principes* was published in 1819; the first edition of Malthus' *Principles* in 1820.

quite clear that he did not look upon it as a correction of Say's thought. He fully admitted that there are times of crisis at which 'there is really an excess of all commodities above the money demand; in other words there is an under-supply of money. . . Almost everybody is therefore a seller and there are scarcely any buyers: so that there may really be . . . an extreme depression of general prices, from what may be indiscriminately called a glut of commodities or a dearth of money.' This passage is very interesting in various respects. First, it shows that, Say's wording notwithstanding, an eminently competent follower of Say did not interpret his doctrine as implying denial of the actual occurrence of 'general gluts.' Second and *a fortiori,* the passage disposes of all those interpretations of Say that turn his law into an identity of some kind or another and reinforces ours.[10] Third, there is a curiously modern ring about this passage, which should not go unnoticed. Notice, in particular, the phrase 'under-supply of money,' which evidently does not mean that mines or printing presses have not produced a sufficient quantity of money but is the exact equivalent of the modern phrase 'excess demand of firms and households for cash to hold.' This goes some way toward reducing to their proper proportions the objections that may be raised against Say's cavalier treatment of the monetary factor—besides setting an example for the manner in which such deficiencies in their predecessors should be treated by serious and fair-minded workers.

So far as this point is concerned, there seems to be no difference at all between Mill and Marshall. Both recognized the importance that the desire to hold money, rather than to spend it on goods and services, may acquire in certain situations—crises and depressions in particular. And the only difference there is on this point between Mill and Keynes is this: the former confined this excess demand for money to situations of this kind, of which it is one of the consequences and which therefore cannot be explained by it; whereas the latter considered the excess demand for money in depressions only as the most spectacular form of a phenomenon that, in less spectacular forms, is well-nigh ubiquitous or is well-nigh ubiquitous at least in certain phases of capitalist evolution, so that it may become the cause of either cyclical downturns or 'secular stagnation.' Malthus seems to have taken the latter view.[11]

A much more important reason for Malthus' dissent from Say and much more basic to his principle of effectual or effective demand was, however, his opinion that saving, even if promptly invested, may lead to deadlock if carried beyond a certain optimal point (op. cit., ch. 7, § 3). He did not go as

[10] It might be objected that J. S. Mill himself asserted the identity that has been discussed under (II) above in a passage of his ch. 14, § 2, where he stated that every buyer is a seller *ex vi termini.* But the later argument of Mill's chapter proves sufficiently that sellers may refuse to become buyers and therefore that, if they do buy, they do so from choice and not by virtue of the meaning of the term Sellers.

[11] This is how I interpret, as did Lange (op. cit. p. 61), the passage in Malthus, *Principles* (footnote on pp. 361-2 of the 1st ed.).

far as Lauderdale,[12] who was the real anti-saver of the age. He granted to the pro-savers even more than he should have done, namely, that increase in capital cannot be effected *in any other way* than by saving. But he maintained that, carried beyond an optimum point, saving would create an untenable situation: the effectual demand for consumers' goods from capitalists and landlords would not increase enough to take care of the increased supply of products that results from an ever-increasing conversion of revenue into capital; and the effectual demand for consumers' goods from laborers, though it would increase indeed, cannot constitute a motive for further accumulating and employment of capital. It is this which constitutes Malthus' fundamental objection to Say's law. The mistake involved will be analyzed below. But it cannot be charged to Keynes. Though many passages in Malthus and also in Lauderdale undoubtedly are suggestive of part of today's (or yesterday's) anti-saving argument, I cannot help thinking that Lord Keynes should not have approved of Malthus' every word so sweepingly.[13] However, the idea of a schedule of aggregate demand for consumers' goods taken as a whole, though without any awareness of the problems this concept raises,[14] is in fact present in Malthus' analytic set-up, and it may be therefore claimed with justice that he anticipated Wicksell, who was the next first-flight economist to adopt it.

Since the question of general gluts will come up again in the next chapter, I leave the matter at this point. And since neither Say, nor Malthus, nor Mill was aware of the problems of determinateness of equilibrium that the monetary factor may raise, we shall leave this aspect for the next Part. But some readers may welcome a summary with further reference to Keynes's analysis, which accordingly I shall present now.

Keynes, of course, never meant to contradict the proposition that has been called Say's law above. This shows in his warning that his Aggregate Supply Function and Aggregate Demand Function[15] must not be confused with

[12] Malthus, in referring (op. cit. p. 352 n.) to Chapter 4 on Parsimony in Lauderdale's *Inquiry* and in expressing the opinion that Lauderdale went 'as much too far in deprecating accumulation as some other writers [Smith included] in recommending it,' wrote a sentence that is worth quoting both because of its wisdom and because it is so characteristic of the man: 'This tendency to extremes is exactly what I consider as the great source of error in political economy.'

[13] See *General Theory*, pp. 362-4 and especially the essay on Malthus in Keynes's *Essays in Biography* (1933, pp. 139-47) on the controversy between Malthus and Ricardo on our subject, where generous enthusiasm carried Keynes beyond all bounds of reason. There he punctuated his report with applause for Malthus and derogatory comments on Ricardo's 'blindness' and became blind himself to obvious weaknesses in the former's and to all the strong points in the latter's argument. But the collection of extracts he presented is nevertheless interesting, especially because it contains some pieces that have not as yet been published elsewhere.

[14] Therefore, the principal comment to make upon Malthus' dissent from Say is *not* that he may not have done justice to possible elements of truth in Say's practical conclusions, but that he did not understand the *theory* at the back of them.

[15] For the meaning of these terms, see *General Theory of Employment, Interest and Money*, p. 25. The warning, with respect to the concept of aggregate supply price occurs on p. 24, n. 1. This does not alter the fact that this terminology is misleading.

supply and demand functions 'in the ordinary sense.' But he believed that Say's law asserts 'that the aggregate demand price of output as a whole is equal to its aggregate supply price for all volumes of output' (op. cit. p. 26); that is, he interpreted Say's law as Lange did later on. Our own interpretation may be restated as follows if, in order to facilitate comparison, we waive our objection to the concepts of aggregate demand price and aggregate supply price: the law asserts that aggregate demand price of output as a whole is *capable of being equal* to its aggregate supply price for all volumes of total output; or, alternatively, that equilibrium *within* total output is possible for all volumes *of* output whereas equilibrium is not possible for all outputs of shoes; or, still differently, that there is no such thing as equilibrium or disequilibrium of total output irrespective of the relations of its components to one another.[16] If correct, this interpretation seems to remove Keynes's objection. Actually this is not so, however. For the weaker proposition which asserts only the possibility of equilibria at all levels of total output and no identity of 'demand for and supply of total output' still yields the further proposition—which is, however, not equivalent to it—that competition between firms always *tends* to lead to an expansion of output up to the point of full utilization of resources or maximum output.[17] And *this* is the proposition to which Keynes really meant to object. Since, however, the only reason he had for objecting was that people do not spend their whole income on consumption and do not necessarily invest the rest [18]—thus barring, according to Keynes, the way toward 'full employment'—it would have been more natural not to object to this proposition either, just as we do not object to the law of gravitation on the ground that the earth does not fall into the sun, but to say simply that the operation of Say's law, though it states a tendency correctly, is impeded by certain facts which Keynes believed important enough to be inserted into a theoretical model of his own.[19]

So it gets down to this. A man of the name of J. B. Say had discovered a theorem of considerable interest from a theoretical point of view that, though

[16] From this it is no great step to a more usual formulation, which will be familiar to many readers, viz., that total output is always in neutral equilibrium. In itself it is meaningless, since there is no equilibrium of output as a whole. But I believe that some at least of the writers who expressed themselves in that way meant just this. If so, they stated a true proposition although in a very misleading way.

[17] If readers refer to the second paragraph on p. 26 of the *General Theory*, they will find that Keynes formulates this proposition much more strongly as the drift of his argument requires. But there is no justification, from any standpoint, for going beyond the formulation of the text—unless it be that Say was just as much given to overstatement.

[18] This statement is crude. Possibly rigidity of wages constitutes another reason. But we cannot go into this here. See below, Part v, ch. 5.

[19] This would have made Keynesian theory a special case of a more general theory. But Keynes preferred to start from a pattern that contained the obstructions to full employment, which he believed he saw, and then to look upon what he called the classical theory as the theory of the special or limiting case in which those obstructions assume the particular value of zero.

rooted in the tradition of Cantillon and Turgot, was novel in the sense that it had never been stated in so many words. He hardly understood his discovery himself and not only expressed it faultily but also misused it for the things that really mattered to him. Another man of the name of Ricardo understood it because it tallied with considerations that had occurred to him in his analysis of international trade, but he also put it to illegitimate use. Most people misunderstood it, some of them liking, others disliking what it was they made of it. And a discussion that reflects little credit on all parties concerned dragged on to this day when people, armed with superior technique, still keep chewing the same old cud, each of them opposing his own misunderstanding of the 'law' to the misunderstanding of the other fellow, all of them contributing to make a bogey of it.

5. Capital

Under this heading we shall carry on our discussion about the 'classic' analysis of the structure of the productive process beyond the point reached in Chapter 5. But first we must attend to some matters of terminology.

(a) *Terminological Squabbles about Wealth and Income*. No better illustrations than these squabbles can be found for what has been said above on the futility of the 'method' of hunting for the meaning of words, which nevertheless we cannot afford to neglect entirely (1) because the manner in which writers conceptualize may serve as a measure of their analytic maturity or experience; (2) because it is interesting to see how they fitted recalcitrant facts into the conceptual arrangements they adopted; and (3) because in many cases terminological discussion is only the garb of more significant things and in particular reveals parts of a writer's analytic set-up or model.[1]

The chief divisions of 'classic' economics being production and distribution, the first question seems to be what it is that is being produced and consumed. The answer was Wealth.[2] But this only served to raise discussions on what this wealth is or, since it is obviously identical with the goods produced and distributed (or, possibly, their value), what ought to be included in these. These discussions display a surprising degree of analytic immaturity. Authors wavered between wealth considered as a fund or stock and wealth considered

[1] Of this the reader can best convince himself by a perusal of Malthus' *Definitions in Political Economy* (1827), which may be called the standard work of the genus and, to repeat, merits much more attention than it has received. Among other things it contains one of the best criticisms of Ricardo's theoretical set-up ever written (ch. 5). Also one cannot fail to admire the wisdom of the Rules for the Definition of Terms (ch. 1).

[2] Many authors, Senior in particular, in making Wealth the fundamental concept of economic theory, emphatically disclaimed any idea of implying that Wealth was more important than Happiness, Welfare, Virtue, and the like. As for Ricardo, it suffices to point out that the argument for free trade that is so important a part of his work was entirely a welfare argument.

as a flow of goods;[3] they sometimes even failed to make it clear whether they meant a social total or wealth per head; they gravely discussed the 'problem' of the relation between wealth ('riches') and value or the 'problem' of the relation between social (national) wealth and private wealth; in defining goods some were insensitive to redundance or irrelevance of criteria; and even some of those who did not hold either a social philosophy according to which labor alone produces the whole product or a labor theory of value insisted on the element of human exertion as a *definiens* of wealth or economic goods. To adduce instances of blemishes of this kind would serve no useful purpose. It is sufficient to state that that discussion substantially centered on A. Smith's definition—material objects that are useful and transferable and cost labor to acquire or produce—and that Senior partly improved and partly condensed this into 'all things that have exchange value.' The improvement consisted in the replacement of the labor-cost requirement by the requirement of 'limitation of supply': Senior at least realized clearly the logical relation between the two, that is, the fact that limitation of supply is the logically decisive criterion and that difficulty of attainment comes in only as one of the factors that limit supply. But J. S. Mill did not see this clearly although he also defined wealth by choosing 'all useful and agreeable things' for *genus proximum* and exchange value for *differentia specifica*.

The way in which economists dealt with recalcitrant cases may be illustrated by the case of human services not embodied in any physical commodity. No difficulty arose for those who, like Lauderdale and J. B. Say, did not restrict the concept of economic goods to material objects.[4] But those who did were faced by a spurious problem, that is, a problem that owed its existence solely to their own conceptualization. We have already noticed, first, an egregious instance of a verbal solution of a verbal difficulty (Ferrara's handling of a 'material' goods concept). Second, we may notice a device adopted by Senior. He counted human beings and their 'health, strength, and knowledge, and all the other natural and acquired powers of body and mind' as articles of wealth, a thing which was done, then and later, by a great many economists.[5] And then he declared that, for example, a lawyer does not sell services

[3] The latter meaning prevailed as the popularity of the phrase, Distribution of Wealth, suffices to show. It was the meaning adopted in the *Wealth of Nations*.

[4] The question of nonmaterial wealth is, of course, wider than that, for such wealth also comprises claims (which cancel out in a closed domain) and such things as patents and good will. The question of what to do with them continued to attract undeserved attention throughout the century and even beyond. Böhm-Bawerk's first publication was on *Rechte und Verhältnisse* . . . (1881). There is no need for us to go into this, however.

[5] E.g. by Walras. There is a slight advantage in doing this: the three agents of production, land, labor, and capital, then receive more symmetrical treatment. I take the opportunity to advert in passing to the attempts that recur from time to time at evaluating statistically the economic value of man. One of the best performances of this kind that belongs, however, to the next period is Ernst Engel's *Der Wert des Menschen* (1883).

but sells himself—the difference between him and a slave being that he does so by his own will and for his own benefit and only for a definite time and purpose, whereas the slave is sold by his owner and for good. The objections to this, however, should *not* be that, legally, Senior's construction is nonsense and that there is no such thing as a 'sale' for a limited time and purpose: for the construction might still be analytically convenient. The true objection is that this conceptual arrangement offers no advantage and is completely unnecessary. But it acquires a certain interest from the fact that Marx—and later on Walras—adopted it also.[6]

It was only toward the end of the period under survey—and then not so much in England as on the continent of Europe—that economists started the discussion on what 'should be' called income, individual or national, that produced another not exactly fascinating literature later on.[7] But we must not infer from this that the economists of that period overlooked income aspects: elements of what we now call Income Analysis were, on the contrary, much in evidence in their writings. The reason why the *word* Income does not occur in them more often[8] is simply that they used other words. Wealth was one of them. We have seen that the 'classics' were not very clear concerning the differences between funds and flows, and between wealth and the services of

[6] In Marx's schema workmen do not sell labor (i.e. services) but their labor force or power (*Arbeitskraft*). It might be urged that, in this case, this arrangement is not otiose but serves a definite analytic purpose. We shall, in fact, see that it comes in handily for his exploitation theory. But, quite independently of other objections to this theory, a little reflection will show that his argument could also have been couched in terms of the labor services themselves. Moreover, the reason why Marx liked his arrangement so much—he considered it as one of his main contributions to economic theory—derives from a factual assumption that is patently false: he conceives that the 'capitalist,' having bought the laborer's 'force,' then decides arbitrarily how many hours the workman is to work. This is not so even where the labor contract does not specify hours: for these as well as other conditions are always implied. An instructor in economics may be simply 'appointed,' but he knows well enough how many hours of teaching that means at the institution he contracts with; and this applies to all kinds of employments. The reader should make sure that he understands *why* it is no objection to say that workmen, having no other sources of income but their labor power, have no choice but to accept 'any' conditions—even in cases where as a matter of fact this is or was true. With Senior, however, this construction served no such purpose and in fact none except to remove an entirely imaginary difficulty. At the bottom of this difficulty was a disability that Senior shared with most economists of his and even a later time: they found it surprisingly difficult to grasp the distinction between wealth and service of wealth—so much so, in fact, that there was some novelty about it even in 1906 when Irving Fisher, in *Nature of Capital and Income,* insisted upon it.

[7] Toward the end of the period under survey two factors helped to start that discussion: first, the growing interest in income statistics (Robert D. Baxter's *National Income* appeared in 1868), and, second, the growing interest, on the Continent especially, in the problems of the income tax (A. Held's *Die Einkommensteuer* appeared in 1872).

[8] This applies to the English 'classics.' Continental writers of the period did use it more. We have already noticed in ch. 4 above the works of Storch and Sismondi.

wealth. Mostly, however, they actually *meant* flows of income goods (or even services) when they spoke of wealth, so that at least in part we have already been commenting on their concept of income when dealing with wealth. This applies in particular to A. Smith, whose wealth is simply the 'whole annual produce of a country's land and labour,' which, alternatively, he also called Gross Revenue (Book II, ch. 2, Modern Library ed., p. 271). Barring technicalities, this is substantially what we mean by Gross National Product. This quantity minus 'the expence of maintaining . . . capital' is his Neat Revenue or (again: substantially) our Department of Commerce National Income. Most economists of the period discussed these definitions—some, like Say, accepting them with minor amendments; [9] others, like Ricardo,[10] finding fault with them.

A. Smith then gave what he evidently thought was only another way of formulating the same thing: 'neat revenue' or, as we should say, *income* was what people, individually and collectively, 'without encroaching upon their capital . . . can . . . spend upon their subsistence, conveniences, and amusements' (ibid., p. 271). This is the basis of what became known in Germany as the Hermann-Schmoller income definition.[11] The modern discussion on what it means to keep capital intact or to maintain capital—another spurious problem—grew from that root.

On Productive and Unproductive Labor. We digress for a while in order to touch briefly upon the famous controversy on productive and unproductive labor. The only reason why this dusty museum piece interests us at all is that it affords an excellent example of the manner in which *the discussion of meaningful ideas may lose sight of their meanings and slip off into futility.* In the case before us, two meaningful distinctions may be discerned. The one

[9] I do not think that Marx was right in charging Say with the ridiculous mistake of overlooking depreciation. All Say intended was to emphasize the basic importance of the 'gross' concept. See *Theorien über den Mehrwert.*

[10] *Principles,* ch. 26. This chapter read so strangely even to Ricardo himself that he felt it desirable to insert qualifying footnotes. But on referring to this chapter, the reader will find that on the last page of it (including footnote) Ricardo successfully corrected an error committed by A. Smith and another error committed by Say. The first four paragraphs of the chapter seem to restrict the net income of a country to profits and rent, and to treat wages like depreciation charges. The reason given for this misleading arrangement is that only profits and rent constitute the national surplus from which taxes and savings can come. But profits are, according to Ricardo himself, not or not wholly a disposable surplus, and wages, according to his own admission, do contain, in general, some disposable surplus—another example of Ricardo's exasperating way of first insisting on a proposition with tremendous energy and then blowing it up himself. But the argument points to a unitary concept of profits plus rent—wholly foreign to Ricardo's usual reasoning—from which Marx may have learned something. The argument also points toward a conception of income that may have some uses and certainly has a great hold on the popular mind, namely, the conception of income as a surplus over necessities.

[11] Hermann, see above, ch. 4. Gustav Schmoller, 'Die Lehre von Einkommen . . . ,' *Zeitschrift für die gesamte Staatswissenschaft,* 1863.

springs from the fact that a private-enterprise system generates incomes that provide for consumption in two ways: directly for the consumption of those who 'earn' them, and indirectly for the consumption of those who are 'supported' by them, for example, children and the retired aged. It stands to reason that the relation between the two, in our example determined (in part) by the age distribution of the population, is no matter of indifference but on the contrary one of the most important characteristics of a society's economic life. Controversies about the question whether or not there are also types of employment that, for some purposes or for all, should be treated as 'supported' out of the incomes earned in the business process, for example, whether public officers should be so treated on the ground that their incomes derive from the taxation of other incomes, may be entirely meaningful.[12] The other meaningful distinction springs from the fact that services of labor (or of natural agents) that are directly bought and consumed by households, such as the services of servants, teachers, and physicians, occupy a position in the economic process that is different from the position of services of labor that are bought and 'consumed' by firms and have, economically speaking, still to go through a business process. That this is not a distinction without a difference—although, of course, these services, in the form of products, also reach the consumers' sphere eventually—is readily seen from the fact sufficiently expressed by the common slogan that these services are paid from some firm's capital, whereas the former are paid from some household's income or revenue.[13] So soon as the servant has received his wages or their equivalent in goods, there is no further problem. When the factory worker has received his wages, further problems arise of selling the product he has helped to produce, of lags, risks, discounts, and so on, all of which are pertinent to the determination of those wages themselves. Thus the distinction is indeed relevant to the structure of the economic process and imposes itself upon the analyst at many turns of his way (e.g. in matters of the wage-fund doctrine, see below, subsec. 6f).

It will be seen that these two distinctions are entirely independent of one another: each has meaning without reference to the other. But both—and a lot of confusion in addition—were bequeathed to the writers of that period by A. Smith. On the first page of his Introduction, he placed great emphasis upon 'the proportion between the number of those who are employed in useful labour, and that of those who are not so employed.' For lack of space, I must leave it to the reader to satisfy himself that, with an admixture of extraneous matter, this passage really adumbrates the meaning of our first

[12] Compare the controversies that have arisen in our own time in connection with the statistics of national income on the question whether or not public administration should be considered as an industry like any other so that there would be no analytically relevant difference between the salary of a government official and the wages of, say, a workman in a motor-car factory.

[13] As will be pointed out presently, this must not be confused with the case of people who live on derived income in the sense intended under the first distinction, e.g. the case of the retired aged.

distinction. Only it does so hazily and, by employing the vague term 'useful,' gives the clue to all the confusion that disfigured the subsequent controversy on productive and unproductive labor, though this phrase does not figure in Book I of the *Wealth of Nations*. This phrase does emerge in Chapter 3 of Book II, where A. Smith, having experienced physiocratic influence, developed his theory of Accumulation. He had no use, of course, for the physiocratic proposition that only labor employed in agriculture is productive any more than he had use for the 'mercantilist' proposition that only labor employed in export industries is. But pouring away the physiocrat wine, he retained the bottles and filled them with wine of his own: he defined labor as productive that 'adds to the value of the subject upon which it is bestowed' (op. cit. p. 314) and exemplified this by the case of factory workers who, as he adds by way of explanation (ibid. p. 316), live on 'that part of the annual produce of the land and labour which replaces capital' (with a profit); and he defined labor as unproductive that does not add (exchange) value to anything and exemplified this by the labor of the menial servant and that 'of some of the most respectable orders in the society' such as the sovereign 'with all the officers both of justice and war who serve under him' and 'are maintained by part of the annual produce of the industry of other people.' Two things are clear: he had got hold of our second distinction; and he had confused it with the first.

The first man to see this quite clearly was Marx, who adopted our second distinction, giving A. Smith ample credit for having uncovered so important an element of the structure of capitalist society, and pointing out that this piece of insight was, in the work of A. Smith, wrapped in considerations that Marx thought superficial and in any case quite unconnected with it.[14] Of course, nobody missed the point entirely—most writers made, tacitly or explicitly, use of it when analyzing the demand for labor. But when they discussed the distinction as such, they lost sight of it and always thought of the first distinction. Nor is this all. We have seen that this distinction also may be made meaningful. But giving themselves up to the associations evoked by the terms 'useful' and 'productive,' economists concentrated on such 'issues' as which activities were worthy of these honorific epithets. Teachers and civil servants did not like to be called 'unproductive,' feeling—sometimes rightly and sometimes wrongly—that this phrase was intended to carry a derogatory meaning.[15] And so a meaningless discussion became a standard item of nine-

[14] Marx elaborated this at length in his discussion of Smithian doctrine in the *Theorien über den Mehrwert*. From his standpoint the decisive distinction was between labor that does 'produce surplus value' and labor that does not. But the distinction between labor that is paid from business capital and labor that is paid from 'revenue' is preferable: a servant might work more hours than are embodied in the 'value' of his labor and hence might be 'exploited' just as may a factory worker. The former's employer may also derive a surplus. The point is, to continue in Marxist language, that this surplus need not be 'realized' in any market.

[15] Some such feelings assert themselves again each time modern economists discuss, for the purposes of national-income statistics, the conceptual treatment to be accorded to government salaries.

teenth-century textbooks in spite of the increasing awareness of its futility, which eventually killed it. An account of all the ramifications and of all the mis-spent ingenuity that sometimes went into it would fill a volume. But it could serve one purpose only, namely, to display the word-mindedness of economists and their inability to tell a real problem from a spurious one.[16] [J. A. S. intended to have this digression On Productive and Unproductive Labor printed in small type so that the average reader could skip it easily.]

(b) *The Structure of Physical Capital.*[17] On its most abstract level, the analysis of economic choice, which is really all that is involved in what we are accustomed to learn in the particular form of a theory of value, can be carried out in terms of unspecified things called 'goods' that have no other properties than those of being desired and of being scarce. It stands to reason, however, that in order to make headway beyond the most arid generalizations we must pick, from our vision of reality, further restrictions upon economic choice such as are implied in our 'know-how' or, less colloquially, in the limitations of a given technological horizon, which will permit some, and exclude other, transformations of our initial stock of goods. In any case, we must postulate given wants, a given technological horizon, given environmental factors such as land and personnel of given kinds and qualities, *and a given stock of produced goods with which to start*. But this is not enough. This initial stock of goods is neither homogeneous nor an amorphous heap. Its various parts complement each other in a way that we readily understand as soon as we hear of buildings, equipment, raw materials, and consumers' goods. Some of these parts must be available before we can operate others; and various sequences or lags between economic actions impose themselves and further restrict our choices; and they do this in ways that differ greatly according to the composition of the stock we have to work on.[18] We express this by saying that the stock of

[16] This discussion induced a related one on the concepts of productive and unproductive consumption that may be illustrated by a statement of Senior's (op. cit. p. 57): 'if a judge . . . required by his station to support an establishment costing £2,000 a year, should spend £4,000, half of his consumption would be productive and the other half unproductive.' Productive consumption, then, was 'that use of a product which occasions another product.' The idea that commodities and services do not leave the economic process for good as soon as they enter the sphere of the households that consume them, but that they 'produce' there the productive services of the members of these households, turns up again and again. In our day it has been adopted by Leontief, in whose system households are treated as an industry that consumes productively like any other.

[17] Some readers will find this subsection difficult reading. It attempts to explain an unconventional view of the role of physical 'capital' within the logic of the economic process that might be pressed into this phrase: from the standpoint of analysis, *capital means a set of restrictions*. This will become quite clear before long, and I believe that the reader will derive some benefit from taking the trouble involved in mastering this subsection.

[18] The stock of wealth of all kinds that exists at an instant of time has been called Capital by Irving Fisher (*Nature of Capital and Income,* 1906, p. 52), who has successfully shown that, properly thought out, the capital definitions of most, if not all, of

goods existing at any instant of time is a *structured quantity or a quantity that displays structural relations within itself* that shape, in part, the subsequent course of the economic process. Naturally we wish, for the purposes of pure theory, to reduce these structural characteristics to as few and as general ones as possible, steering as best we can between the Scylla of unmanageable lifelikeness and the Charybdis of sterile simplicity. Ever since the time of Cantillon and Quesnay, when scientific model-building began, economists have, of course, been aware of all this. In the preceding chapter we have already had a glimpse of the manner in which the writers of the 'classic' period took—haltingly—the first two steps in the analysis of the structural properties of the economic process: the one was to recognize capital as a 'requisite' of production and the other was to adopt the physiocrat (Cantillon-Quesnay) idea of 'advances.' We have now to fill in the more important of the remaining elements of this analysis, which constitutes what is commonly known as theory of capital.

The reader need not be afraid that we shall have to wade through another morass of verbal controversy. The theory of capital does indeed enjoy a reputation for this kind of thing that is rivaled by few other fields. People kept on asking the meaningless question: What is Capital? And some have tried to answer it by speculations about the original meanings of the words *caput*, *capitale*, κεφάλαιον, and the like. Senior even held that 'the term Capital has been so variously defined that it may be doubtful whether it have any generally received meaning' (*Outline*, p. 59). In a sense, this is true.[19] But it is true only: first, owing to relatively minor faults of conceptualization committed by the individual authors, and these we can disregard if their analytic intention is clear enough; second, owing to the wish, the father of so many futile controversies, to have a unitary or all-purpose concept of capital, and this wish I do not share; third, owing to the not less unwarranted wish of many authors to approximate the 'capital' that is useful in their analysis to either the asset or the liability side of a business concern's balance sheet; fourth, owing to occasional waverings between physical capital concepts, on the one hand, and monetary concepts, on the other, which will be noticed in the next footnote. For the rest, the matter is much simpler than it looks because there really is only one dominant analytic purpose to describe that practically all the leading economists tried to serve.

Since it was a requisite of production, capital consisted of goods.[20] More-

---

the writers of the period under survey come precisely to this. We shall not adopt Fisher's concept here but instead we shall simply use the excellent Smithian term Stock. This will make it easier to distinguish it from various other meanings of the term Capital without adding each time: 'in our sense.'

[19] Readers interested in the history of economists' use of the term are referred to Irving Fisher (op. cit. ch. 4, § 2) or to the chapter on the concept of capital in the second volume of Böhm-Bawerk's great work.

[20] But even those authors who expressed themselves most strongly in favor of a physical capital concept sometimes drifted into the preserves of a monetary one. Ricardo and J. S. Mill, among others, occasionally penned sentences which carry meaning only if

over, like our initial stock, it was a *stock* of goods. But, unlike *our* initial stock, it did not include all goods existing at an instant of time. From these the 'classics' separated out their capital by excluding from it, first, natural agents (though not 'improvements' such as drains, fences, and the like) and, second, all consumers' goods other than the means of subsistence of productive labor. Let us stop for a moment in order to make this clear.

First of all, it should be understood that the division of the stock of wealth existing at an instant of time into a mass of things that are capital and another mass of things that are not is a device for describing what we have called above the structure of, or the structural relations within, the universe of goods. The second thing to observe is that the effect of excluding natural agents was to set up, in addition to labor, another 'original' factor of production, though many, especially the Ricardians, failed to realize the implications of it. This, then, would have left us with the stock of produced goods. But, third, the structure of the mass of these produced goods was further analyzed by means of a distinction that warred between two of an indefinite number of possibilities.

On the one hand, if we want to separate out that part which is a requisite of production in the technological sense, we arrive at the concept of produced means of production or, as it was to be called by the Böhm-Bawerkians, of intermediate products. It is, however, one of the salient characteristics of the theoretical schema of the English 'classics' and their continental followers that they understood the term 'requisite of production' in a wider sense which included the consumers' goods that support labor during the process of production. There is no logical reason for not including also the consumers' goods that support landowners—Senior even included those that support capitalists—during that process but, actually, these were mostly excluded by the Ricardians because their schema prevented them from considering rent as an element of cost.

On the other hand, if we want to separate out that part of the mass of wealth existing at an instant of time which is in the business process or serves business purposes—or, as A. Smith put it, from which 'profit is ex-

---

they refer to monetary capital. This has been critically noticed, for the first time I think, by Tchernychevsky, in *L'économie politique jugée par la science* (1874), an elaborate analysis of Mill's *Principles*. It is still more obvious in the *Manual* of Mill's follower, Fawcett. With Mill, capital is 'expended' on raw materials, goes from hand to hand, migrates from industry to industry and from country to country in a manner that suggests that he was thinking of balances and not of goods. It may be replied, of course, that sums of money may be thought of as representing goods and also that, especially within the theoretical organon of that time, monetary processes may be reduced to 'real' processes in the last analysis. But such reductions are dangerous short cuts at best and involve neglecting monetary mechanisms that give rise to many essential problems. Thus, even if the fundamentals of the economic process could in fact be satisfactorily described in real terms, we should still have to observe that, in capital theory as elsewhere, the 'classic' attempt to carry out fundamental analysis in real terms only was seriously at fault.

pected'—we are led to include besides plant, equipment, raw materials, and the 'means of subsistence of productive labor,' also other items, in particular the following two. One is another mass of consumers' goods—which in part overlaps with the one included among requisites of production—namely, the mass of consumers' goods that is still in the hands of manufacturers, wholesalers, and retailers irrespective of who (laborer or capitalist) is going to buy them. The other is cash in hand. The implications of this, though not uninteresting, cannot be considered here. All that can be said is that this distinction is not more right or wrong than is the other. Both serve relevant analytic purposes; that is, both are useful in describing relevant aspects of reality. But we shall keep to the first one ('requisite of production' in the wider sense) because it is more germane to what I have called above the dominant analytic purpose of the epoch, especially of the work that was summed up by J. S. Mill. Marx would have approved of our choice. He was all for the first distinction. The second he considered to be incapable of serving any purpose other than that of copying the surface of reality as it appears to the capitalist.

What has been said above, barring details, reproduces the actual way in which A. Smith 'structured' what he called the 'general stock of any country or society' by separating out capital (*Wealth*, Book II, ch. 1) and by enumerating its chief components. It matters little that he (and Malthus) did not specifically include wage goods or the means of subsistence of labor. For he always argued as if he had included them.[21] Also, the capital concept described represents fairly well the wording of most of the leaders. Thus, Ricardo defined the concept: 'Capital is that *part of the wealth* [my italics] of a country which is employed in production, and consists of food, clothing, tools, raw materials, machinery, etc., necessary to give effect to labour' (*Principles*, ch. 5). This does not differ in essence from Senior's definition: 'an article of wealth, the result of human exertion [meaning, as he explained a few lines further on, 'of labour, abstinence, and the agency of nature,' or simply, a produced article of wealth] employed in the production or distribution of wealth.' Nor does it differ from J. S. Mill's influential passage: 'What capital does for production, is to afford the shelter, protection, tools, and materials which the work requires, and to feed and otherwise maintain the labourers during the process. . . Whatever things are destined for this use . . . are Capital' (Book I, ch. 4, § 1).[22] Marx added nothing to this except that, in obedience to his principle of amalgamating economics and sociology, he confined the term capital to those things of this class that are owned by capitalists—the same things in the hand of the workman who uses them are not capital.

[21] See, e.g., *Wealth*, p. 316 [Modern Library ed.]. No additional comments are needed on A. Smith's inclusion of 'the acquired and useful abilities of all the . . . members of the society,' a precedent that was widely followed: Roscher even included 'virtue.' For this remained entirely inoperative. Note, however, the parallelism with 'the improvements of land' that may have suggested the Marshallian concept of quasi-rent.

[22] The merely verbal concession to the labor theory of value (pointed out above) that is contained in this formulation could be easily rectified.

'What capital does for production,' however, means two very different things, and the distinction between wage capital and the rest—we shall call it technological capital—readily suggests itself and so does a coefficient, descriptive of the quantitative relation between the two, which must obviously constitute one of the most important characteristics of the structure of capital. Nevertheless, it was left to Marx to point this out in so many words and introduce such a coefficient explicitly. Denoting by the term constant capital (c) what has just been called technological capital, and by the term variable capital (v)[23] what has just been called wage capital, he chose for structural coefficient the ratio: $\frac{c}{c+v}$, which he called the Organic Composition of Capital.[24] The merit there is in introducing such a concept explicitly must not be underrated. But, of course, the writers from A. Smith to J. S. Mill had not failed to recognize the peculiar role of wage capital within total capital. This is abundantly indicated by the fact that wage capital is identical not only with Marx's variable capital, but also with the 'classic' wage fund. Moreover, both Ricardo and Mill sometimes used the Marxist concept inadvertently: they sometimes meant variable capital when they actually wrote Circulating Capital.[25]

Not less obvious is the necessity of analyzing the internal structure of technological capital. It was quite clear to the physiocrats, whose various *avances* A. Smith replaced by the distinction between Fixed and Circulating Capital. The former he defined as capital from which the owner derives profit by keeping (using) it, such as factory buildings and machines; the latter he defined as capital from which the owner derives profit by 'parting with it' (turning it over), such as raw materials. Ricardo saw that there was something of deeper significance behind A. Smith's common-sense and commonplace distinction, which accordingly he brushed aside.[26] Let us make an attempt to reconstruct his thought.

[23] He expressed both in terms of labor embodied. But inasmuch as his coefficient always refers to a given point of time, expression in money values does just as well. It should be observed that both measures carry full meaning and in particular allow of intertemporal comparison only for states of perfect equilibrium. The reason why Marx chose those terms (and why we cannot accept them here) is that, in his theory, technological capital transmits to the product only its own value—or that, in the productive process, its value in terms of labor embodied remains constant—whereas wage capital, as it were, swells in the process by virtue of the labor hours that workers add to the labor embodied in it.

[24] Thus, since the labor-hour dimension is present in both numerator and denominator and therefore cancels out, this coefficient is a pure number. Still it is worth while to remember that the components of the coefficient are values and not physical quantities.

[25] Thus, Ricardo wrote in § 4 of ch. 1 of the *Principles*: 'In one trade very little capital may be employed as circulating capital, *that is to say* [my italics], in the support of labour. . .' Other instances are found in ch. 31.

[26] See *Principles*, ch. 1, sec. 4, first footnote. This footnote—saying as it does that the distinction between fixed and circulating capital is not essential—reads strangely in

Evidently, Ricardo's attention was drawn to the problems of fixed capital by the fact that its presence causes exchange values of products to diverge from the labor-quantity law unless, of course, all the branches of industry employ 'the same proportion of fixed and circulating capital.' He also perceived, apparently without difficulty, the further fact that, in order not to disturb this labor-quantity law, this fixed capital would in addition have to be of the same durability everywhere. Finally, however, he perceived something else, namely, the analogy that exists between different durabilities of the fixed capital used in different lines of production and the different rates of turnover of different kinds of circulating capital, such as the farmer's seed and the baker's flour. This, then, makes three apparently different facts that have, at first sight, nothing in common except that they all interfere with the operation of the labor-quantity law of value. Now, by what almost amounted to a flash of genius, he saw that all three of them did so for the same reason or, to put it differently, he saw the same fundamental element in all of them, namely, the time distance between investment and the emergence of the corresponding consumers' good.[27]

This was very easy to see in the case of differences in periods of turnover: wheat that is being used as seed and wheat that is being worked up into flour directly differ (from Ricardo's standpoint) by the time distances between each of them and the emergence of flour *and by nothing else*. But it was not so easy to see that the difference which the presence of fixed capital goods and of fixed capital goods of different durability makes to the process of production, and hence to values, is of the same kind in that it also may be looked upon as a matter of differences in these time distances or rates of turnover. Consider, for example, a machine that, in the Ricardian manner, has been produced by labor alone, say, in a single day. Suppose it is to last ten years. During these ten years, the machine or the labor embodied in it matures into consumers' goods exactly as will raw materials or semifinished products. Each of the days of service 'contained' in it—becoming available in a definite sequence—behaves like the seed in the ground until its turn comes. This definite sequence is a restriction upon economic decision or action, analogous to the restriction placed upon the farmer's decision by the circumstance that he must wait until his seed matures into a crop. There is thus in fact, at least on the most abstract level, no essential difference and no clear line of demarcation between fixed and circulating capital, as Ricardo pointed out in

---

view of the fact that the whole argument of Section 4 turns upon problems of fixed capital. But our reconstruction of his thought will make it clear that he meant not more than that A. Smith's distinction failed to bring out the essential point involved.

[27] I call this a flash of genius without necessarily committing myself to the theory of capital that developed from this flash. In order to clarify a very important piece of doctrinal history, I refrain entirely from criticism at this point. Professor Knight himself, who rejects the theory in question, could therefore accept my exposition just as could have F. W. Taussig, who made it his own. The essential thing, for the moment, is to see the relation between Ricardo's analysis and Böhm-Bawerk's, which has been emphasized by both Knight and Taussig.

the footnote referred to above. Both are nothing but immature (elements of) consumers' goods—intermediate products or 'inchoate wealth' as Taussig was to call them about eighty years later. Or both may be 'resolved' into hoarded labor—James Mill's term, which expresses Ricardo's meaning very well and was to be used again by Wicksell, also about eighty years later [28]—though we must not forget that the various agglomerations of hoarded labor embodied in the various goods carry different indices of time distance or indices of places in the time sequences to which they belong.

Thus, Ricardo's rudimentary capital analysis issues in a time concept of technological capital,[29] time being the element that unifies all its specific forms. Those who entertain sympathies for the labor-quantity theory of value might claim with some justice that he thereby saved the latter by making it valid (to some extent at least) for labor quantities that carry different time indices. Those who accept Böhm-Bawerk's theory of capital might claim, also with some justice, that Ricardo worked up a bad theory of value into a good theory of capital. In any case, Ricardo was clearly Böhm-Bawerk's forerunner so far as this set of problems is concerned. This is not to say that Ricardo's theory of capital was complete or that he saw all the implications of his flash of genius. In particular, he neglected all its short-run implications.[30] Also, though he did study cases of conversion of circulating into fixed capital—the most important case is to be found in his chapter On Machinery—and occasionally brushed against the manifold relations of substitution that exist within the universe of technological capital—the 'Ricardo effect' if thought through would afford an instance—he was, as were most of the 'classics,' too much given to accepting time sequences as technological data and to neglecting the fact that durabilities, and, in general, the relations between the quantities of capital goods of different types, also the relation between wage capital and non-wage capital, are economic variables that depend, and in turn react, upon wage rates, efficiency of labor, rate of interest, and other factors. But this is only another way of restating the fact that his theory was no more than a preliminary sketch—a fact that must always be borne in mind, just as much when we are criticizing as when we are defending his performance.

(c) *Senior's Contributions*. Two most curious facts now call for our attention. On the one hand, Senior realized that Ricardo used the terms fixed and circulating capital in a sense that differed from A. Smith's use (*Outline*, pp. 62-3). But the true meaning of Ricardo's capital analysis escaped him so completely that he saw nothing in that difference except a reprehensibly unusual

[28] More precisely Wicksell said saved-up services of labor and land, and should have added the services of previous accumulations.

[29] If the line of thought, for which he offered but fragments, were carried on to its logical consequences, we might even say that his analysis comprised technological plus wage capital, resolving *all* physical capital into wage capital or rather into a general subsistence fund. This idea is still more clearly indicated in James Mill's *Elements*. Nevertheless, its explicit recognition belongs to Jevons and Böhm-Bawerk, though implicitly it is also present in one of the various aspects of the wage-fund theory.

[30] Such as that fixed capital, in the short run, behaves like 'land.'

use of terms. On the other hand, in spite of this failure to understand the Ricardian analysis, he actually carried it further in two directions—an excellent example of the way in which we blunder along.

First, there is Senior's third postulate or elementary proposition, which reads: 'That the powers of Labour, and of the other instruments which produce wealth, may be indefinitely increased by using their Products as the means of further Production.' This proposition, which might have been derived from Rae, improves Ricardo's theory by adding the powers 'of the other instruments which produce wealth' to those of labor. But it adds also something else that lies entirely beyond Ricardo's analysis. With Ricardo, the time element comes in to cause deviations of values from the labor-quantity law by putting a brake on the supply of the products of the capitals that turn over more slowly than others: the man whose products take relatively long spans of time to reach their markets simply 'must' be compensated for this disadvantage. According to Senior, however, there is more to this higher value of such products than the mere fact, if it is a fact, that a profit of £100 accruing every second year is not economically equivalent to a profit of £50 accruing every year. The profit from the two-year investment will be more than twice the profit from two successive one-year investments of the same quantity of (say) labor, because the productive 'power' of this labor, hence its product, is increased if the product of the first year be used 'as the means of further production' in the second year. Now, Ricardo's real value of a product cannot increase simply because the same quantity of labor produces a greater quantity of product in the two-year process than it would in two successive one-year processes. But Senior's value may.[31] This puts an entirely new face upon the matter and points straight ahead toward Böhm-Bawerk—who, by the way, did not understand Senior any better than Senior did Ricardo, but who nevertheless carried on Senior's capital analysis exactly as Senior carried on Ricardo's. The relation that exists on this point between Senior and Böhm-Bawerk will stand out particularly if we observe that using a product as the means of further production might well be called using it in a 'roundabout' way. The only difference is that Senior confined himself to stating that the productive power of labor is increased 'indefinitely' by using it in that way; whereas Böhm-Bawerk added the hypothesis that the rate of this increase decreases as the 'length' of the productive process increases.

Second, there is Senior's abstinence theory of capital. Though his name is chiefly remembered because of this contribution, it (abstinence) is actually much less important, as an analytic performance, than is the contribution just discussed (using a product as the means of further production). It will be as well to distinguish two different aspects of Senior's abstinence. On the one hand, if for reasons good or bad, we choose to analyze the structure of technological capital in terms of what we have called the time indices of its com-

[31] No difficulty arises from the fact that the value of the greater quantity of product that results from the two-year process *need* not have a greater value than the smaller quantity that results from two successive one-year processes. For in this case the two-year process will not be used.

ponent elements, the fact we wish to emphasize is that these component elements (that is, the various capital goods) have different rates of turnover or that their products become available or 'mature' after lapses of time of different lengths, which somehow or other intrude into the list of costs of production. Whenever we mean this, we had better use the term Waiting that was to be suggested later on by McVane and to be adopted by Marshall. On the other hand, if we adopt the theory that technological capital is the result of a 'conversion of revenue' into something that is expected to *yield* revenue in the future, but, in order to do so, has to be withdrawn from the sphere of revenue *for good*, then we had better use the term Abstinence. In this case we reserve the term for the psychic cost of saving or, *if we keep saving sufficiently close to investment, of the capital goods in which past saving has been invested.* This element of psychic cost then becomes analogous to the 'psychic cost' of labor, later on called Disutility. Going a step further, we can constitute abstinence itself—instead of the saving or the capital goods that result from it—as a factor of production.[32] This is the sense in which Senior's abstinence has been commonly understood and in which the phrase will be used in this book, although his own definition shows that he meant to comprise in his concept also what above has been called Waiting.[33]

Recognition of what the term abstinence—in the strict sense—is intended to denote is, of course, as old as is the recognition of the role of saving. A. Smith's parsimony or frugality means nothing else. Practically all the economists who wrote after 1776 deal with it in one way or another, though not all were prepared to accord to it everything that A. Smith claimed for it. It also entered the theoretical schemata of anti-savers like Lauderdale and Malthus. Ricardo's schema considers waiting rather than abstinence but in any case this schema requires, as our exposition amply shows, a conceptual complement of this kind. Actually, however, the concept was formally established by Read and especially by Scrope. The latter stands to Senior in this respect in the same position as did Rae in respect to the postulate about increasing the productive powers of factors by using their product for further production. No reflection on Senior's subjective originality is intended, but it is important to note that objectively Senior did no more than is implied in bringing an existing doctrinal tendency to a head. Propelled by the sponsorship of J. S. Mill, Cairnes, and, to some extent, Marshall, abstinence analysis became firmly established in English economics, though it was never so popular elsewhere. It is not difficult to guess the reason why the spearheads of the attack

[32] It does not greatly matter whether we call this factor a 'primary' or a 'secondary' one. Senior did the latter but later tendencies favored the former.

[33] Senior defined abstinence as 'the conduct of a person who either abstains from the unproductive use of what he can command, or designedly prefers the production of remote to that of immediate results' (*Outline*, p. 58). The first alone denotes saving or conversion of revenue into capital and is abstinence *stricto sensu;* the second means only rearrangement within the capital structure and is what we mean by waiting. Senior was evidently aware of the distinction, the validity of which is not impaired by the possibility of reducing one to the other by appropriate wording.

upon it are to be found in the writings of Marx and Lassalle, who saw nothing but the apologetic possibilities that the word Abstinence suggests. But this will be more conveniently dealt with below under the heading of profits.

(d) *J. S. Mill's Fundamental Propositions Respecting Capital.* Some additional points about the 'classic' theory of capital may be conveniently made, and others may be restated by way of comment on the four connected 'propositions respecting capital' that J. S. Mill presented in Chapter 5 of Book I of his *Principles*.[34]

'The first of these propositions is, That industry is limited by capital,' though of course industry does not always work up to this limit. Total employment of labor is not so limited, however, since it also proceeds from 'revenue.' J. S. Mill believed erroneously that 'industry's' being limited by capital[35] *implies* that 'every increase of capital . . . is capable of giving additional employment to industry; and this without any assignable limit' (§ 3). Carefully stated (and the 'capable' properly emphasized), this can be shown to be true, and the use of this proposition against the opinions of Malthus, Chalmers, and Sismondi[36]—who asserted that 'wealth' is at any time limited not only by productive power but also by the system's capacity to consume—is perfectly legitimate. Only it should have been stated as an additional proposition—we might call it the Theorem of Hitchlessness—for it does not *follow* from industry's being limited by capital and, though Mill's argument against those three authors was successful as far as it went, it falls far short of proving this theorem. Moreover, the theorem is interesting only if it be made to hold for the total of technological plus wage capital. But Mill restricted it to the latter so that the proposition he meant to defend amounts only to this: 'the portion which is destined to their [the laborers'] maintenance, may (supposing no alteration in anything else) be indefinitely increased, without creating an impossibility of finding them employment'[37]—which is either trivial or

[34] This chapter, though disfigured by slips, inadequacies, and clumsinesses, is not without logical beauty. The reader who knows how to mend these shortcomings will be impressed by its symphonic qualities.

[35] At the end of this chapter's section 1, Mill uses this proposition to combat what he considered a popular fallacy about the effects of a protective tariff. The reader's attention is called to this curious mixture of truth and error, which exemplifies excellently a situation that occurs so frequently in economic arguments: an incontestable truism is used in an inadmissible manner so as to produce a result that should be false and nevertheless is not (wholly) so, because elements of truth extraneous to the logic of the argument may be invoked in order to peg it. Unfortunately, considerations of space forbid us to explain this fully. Mill was no trickster. But the passage nevertheless exemplifies a well-known trick, namely, the trick of making some politically relevant result follow *apparently* from an obvious truth so that the political opponent is subtly put into a position which it is implied only an absolute fool could take.

[36] Mill failed to add Barton.

[37] In the same paragraph Mill inadvertently used a nonphysical capital concept when he spoke of the other 'portion' of capital that is *fixed* in machinery, buildings, and the like. Capital that is *fixed* in machines instead of *consisting* in machines cannot be capital in the sense of his own definition.

false. It is a very interesting question to ask why he should have thus maimed a theorem that was certainly not beyond his range of vision.[38] The answer cannot be that in the short run technological capital is an assemblage of specific goods, the kinds and quantities of which constitute data. For Mill evidently did not intend to write a treatise on short-run analysis. Rather, the answer seems to be that, while of course he was not unaware of the fact that the relation between technological and wage capital is variable, he was inclined on principle—that is, when arguing matters of fundamental principle—to take it for granted, perhaps as technologically fixed, and to neglect the substitutability between the two, the nature and importance of which, though emphasized by Barton and Longfield, were hardly clear to him. This is why he found it so easy (as had Ricardo) to follow the example set by A. Smith and to speak of a 'portion of capital' or of a fund that is 'destined for the maintenance of labour,' that is, to speak of a wage fund. Let us observe at once that one of the most characteristic features of the so-called wage-fund theory, namely, the implied assumption or at least suggestion that this fund is a sort of datum, thus rests on nothing but primitive technique.[39]

We take another step toward understanding the wage-fund theory when we consider Mill's 'second fundamental theorem respecting Capital [which] relates to the source from which it is derived' and which makes capital 'the result of saving' (§ 4): capital increases by revenue's being converted into it. We know already (see above, ch. 5, sec. 6) that the 'classic' schema of economic evolution was at fault both through overrating the importance of mere increase in the items that constitute capital and through overrating the role that (voluntary) saving plays in this increase. Also, the 'classics,' in their anxiety to emphasize the fundamental meanings of economic mechanisms, were given to drawing together much too closely decisions to save and decisions to invest. These decisions, though never quite identified,[40] tended to shade off into each other to the exclusion of all that may intervene between them,[41]

[38] This theorem should read that on the long-run trend (that is to say, neglecting the effect of temporary disturbances) there are no assignable limits to investment opportunity at appropriately falling rates of interest, except possibly, institutional ones. Lauderdale, Malthus, Storch, and others denied this, but Mill, of course, accepted it, and there was no good reason for him not to put it in so many words, especially since it had already been stated by James Mill.

[39] It is not true, however, that Mill's refutation of Malthus' argument depends upon this or on any other part of the wage-fund doctrine, as Lord Keynes seems to have believed (*General Theory*, p. 364).

[40] What they may indeed be said to have identified is (the schedule of) savings and (the schedule of) loanable funds: what was saved was *ipso facto* made available for real investment either in the saver's business or in someone else's except in times of deep depression; and for them there was no other source of loanable funds except saving—the money created by bank credit never being taken into account when fundamental principles were under discussion.

[41] Malthus, on this point, fully shared the prevailing view. See, e.g., his turn of phrase: 'parsimony *or* [my italics] the conversion of revenue into capital . . .' (*Principles*, p. 369n.).

so that saving unconditionally enriches and spending unconditionally impoverishes both individuals and nations. Like Say, Mill reasserted all this; in other words, he reasserted—with added emphasis even—the Turgot-Smith theory of capital formation.[42]

But then how was it that he was able to hold (as he evidently did)—also in conformity with dominant tradition—that saving, and saving alone, invariably increases not total capital only but also wage capital, the wage fund, 'without assignable limit'? No difficulty arises immediately, because the fixed capital, to the production of which the labor is assigned that is compensated from the new addition to savings, must be first produced. Provided that acts of investment follow sufficiently closely upon the decision to save, it is indeed true, at that first turn of the wheel, that demand for productive services —and let us grant their reduction to labor services only—is immediately increased to the full amount of the new addition to savings. That is, the wage fund is increased so as to give, to this amount, 'to labour either additional employment, or [an increase in wage rates, amounting to] additional remuneration,'[43] which means either a larger aggregate produce, if the laborers in question have been unemployed before, or a larger share of labor in the same 'aggregate produce,' if they have to be drawn from other employments. But, so far as new technological capital results from this employment, things may obviously look very different when all the adjustments have taken place. We may be faced by a different 'organic composition of capital,' possibly even an absolute decrease in the variable capital or wage fund. Again, neglecting the possibility that Mill was thinking of short-run effects only, we once more fall back upon the explanation offered before: like all the 'classical' leaders, he took the relation between technological and wage capital as a datum, so that in the final result saving would increase both of them in the same proportion. If this were so,[44] then and only then could we speak of a wage fund in any sense other than that the sum total of wage incomes is uniquely determined under the same conditions as is any other economic quantity, for example, the sum total 'destined' for the purchase of motor cars. Replacement of workers by machinery was, of course, not overlooked. But it was treated, except

[42] This must, however, be taken *cum grano salis*. Mill admits freely (§ 2) that many persons are maintained from capital (*not* from the return to capital) who produce nothing and that there is such a thing as unproductive consumption by productive workers. If saving provides capital that goes into unproductive consumption, it cannot be held, without qualification, that it 'enriches' society or, for that matter, that it is all but synonymous with expenditure on maintaining and aiding productive labor.

[43] Which on Mill's own showing would in general mean unproductive employment of part of the new savings; see preceding footnote.

[44] Strictly it can never be so. For savings, other things being equal, must affect the rate of interest and the rate of interest must affect the rate of turnover of capital, i.e., the relation of technological capital and wage fund, as well as the structure of the former, rare cases excepted in which rates of turnover are actually uniquely determined by technological necessity such as that of the period that must elapse between sowing and harvesting.

by Marx, as a special case that belonged in a separate compartment and was never organically assimilated by the body of theory. And then and only then—that is, by virtue of a hypothesis forced upon the 'classics' by the primitivity of their technique—it does become true that 'demand for labor,' meaning demand for 'productive' labor as distinguished from labor paid out of revenue, or the means destined for the maintenance of such labor, given a certain level of social productivity, can increase and decrease only through saving and dissaving,[45] which in fact become synonymous with 'destining' more or less means for this purpose. Or, to put it differently, the wage fund is a fund or aggregate *sui generis* because its size and variations are determined by a proximate cause *sui generis*, namely, past and present savings; everything else acts upon it only through the rate of saving.

Of course, the 'classics' would not have denied that the rate of savings itself and therefore total wage payments are determined by many factors, some of which are in turn reacted upon by the rate of savings. In addition, they would not have denied that the kinds and quantities of wage goods the workmen actually get depend upon many other circumstances that are not uniquely determined by the rate of savings. But they would have replied that those factors, such as the rate of profit, act upon the wage fund only at one remove, so that their doctrine was formally still valid; and that the circumstances that do directly affect what goods the workmen get, such as the level of social productivity, were simply taken as given. The reader will observe, however, that this means little more than teasing the opponent. It is, of course, always possible to say: 'given *A*, *B*, *C* . . . , then *Y* depends upon *X*'—the practice revived by Keynesian economics and dubbed 'implicit reasoning' by Professor Leontief. Simplification may amount to caricature. Caricature may be ideologically biased, though there is no reason to suspect this in Mill's case.

Mill's third proposition need not detain us. It is to the effect that saving does not decrease consumption. Here again Mill upholds the Turgot-Smith tradition; in fact he does so with increased emphasis: the saver saves and hands over what he would have consumed or its equivalent to some productive worker so that what is saved is spent on consumers' goods '*quite* as rapidly' [my italics; Smith went slightly less far. J. A. S.] as what is not saved.[46] But Mill's 'fourth fundamental theorem respecting Capital' does call for comment. It runs: 'Demand for commodities is not demand for labour' (§ 9). Let us first discard a surface meaning that might be attributed to this proposition. Of course, the derived demand for labor that may be said to be implied in the demand for a commodity is never demand for labor alone, whereas the demand for personal services is. But this is not what Mill meant. What he did mean is enshrined in a confused and embarrassed discussion that has puzzled

[45] I do not again repeat the other assumptions that have to be made which have been indicated already.

[46] It cannot be emphasized too often that unrealistic neglect of intermediate steps is all that can be charged against this theory. At worst, it may be wrong. But it does not involve any logical mistake as some Böhm-Bawerkians seem to have believed. Of course, not every act of saving needs to issue in a net increase of technological capital.

followers not less than opponents. For brevity I shall simply state what I conceive to be the core of the matter.

The industrial employer's demand for labor no doubt derives from the expected demand of consumers for the commodities that are being produced. On a high level of abstraction, on which only fundamental meanings count, it is perfectly proper to emphasize this nexus before any other. This conforms not only to the view that was naturally taken by the theorists of the last decades of the nineteenth century—particularly by those who emphasized 'imputation'—but also to the view of the economists of that period, such as Say, who taught the doctrine that, ultimately, production and distribution reduce to an exchange of services. There is no great harm, from this standpoint, in using such turns of phrase as that demand for commodities *is* demand for labor (and other productive services) or, as Hermann put it, that the true wage fund or source of wage payments is consumers' income. But the reasoning should never have been used—as it has been—for an attack upon Mill's position.

For on a lower level of abstraction, the fact should be taken into account that the consumer's payment for a commodity does not in general pay for the labor that entered into the latter's production. At most, the consumer's payment *enables* the manufacturer to replenish his capital, normally with an addition. For this actually to come about, a distinct decision must intervene in the process, namely, the manufacturer's decision to save or at least not to dissave. It is *this* decision—and it should not be taken for granted—which may be said to 'benefit' labor at the next turn of the wheel and not simply the consumer's decision to buy. So far, then, we have before us a piece of sequence analysis, that is, an analysis of successive steps in a process that is kept continuously running, at an increasing, decreasing, or constant rate, only by a sequence of appropriate decisions.

There is something else, however. If we do assume that consumers' savings are being turned into labor-employing capital promptly, it follows, as we know, that the labor interest would be further benefited, and demand for labor increased, if income receivers also saved, instead of buying consumers' goods. For, barring the disturbances that result from the necessity of industry's changing over from the production of goods consumed by capitalists and landlords to the production of wage goods, this would, on the one hand, increase the amount 'destined' for the maintenance of productive labor and, on the other hand, cause no deficiency of demand for products. We may, then, imagine the saving to take place by the income receiver's handing over to productive workers goods instead of money: the goods will then be produced and find purchasers as before, and the working class would, in addition, receive part of the saver's income goods. If instead of saving, the income receiver had merely shifted his consumer's demand from commodities to personal services, this addition would last so long as he continues this practice. But if the income receiver saves, this addition will last until he decides to dissave to a corresponding amount. There is nothing ununderstandable or illogical in all this. The usefulness or realism of this model is, of course, another question, but it should not be forgotten that, even if we vote that the argument of this paragraph is inadmissible, the argument of the preceding paragraph still stands.

6. The Distributive Shares

From Section 5, Chapter 5, we know that there was indeed a large group of writers who, partly anticipating the dominant tendency of the next period, conceived the problems of income formation as problems in the evaluation or pricing of productive services—thus unifying the phenomena of value, cost (production), and distribution. But we also know that this view, though to some extent sponsored by A. Smith and reasserted by J. S. Mill, was not generally accepted and that even those French, German, and Italian economists who did more or less accept it—and even Say himself or Ferrara—did not go through with the program that this view implied. For the rest, Professor Cannan [1] was right in stating that distribution remained a semi-independent department of economic analysis; and that what people meant by Theory of Distribution, especially in England, was a compound of separate theories of profits, rent, and wages, each of which was based on a distinct principle of its own.[2] We adopt the same schema for the following survey.

(a) *Profits*. By this term, the 'classics' simply meant the sum total of the gains of the business class, the theoretical type of which, with the Ricardians, was the farmer.[3] The analytic work on these profits during the stretch of time that was bounded by the books of A. Smith and J. S. Mill did much to clarify issues and to lay the bases of later analysis, though it can hardly be described as either brilliant or profound. We shall look at it from two points of view, which we respectively denote as the entrepreneurial and the interest point of view.

We have seen in the preceding chapter both that some progress was made in the analysis of the entrepreneur's function in the capitalist process—progress chiefly due to Say—and that, for the time being, this progress did not go very far. One thing, however, did come of it: economic theory acquired at least a fourth agent, the agent that hires or 'combines' the others and this could have led—more than it actually did lead—to a clearer perception of the role of the 'capitalist,' who might have been ousted from his position in the center of capitalist industry and put into a more appropriate place among the

[1] *Theories of Production and Distribution*, 3rd ed., p. 188. Cannan's detailed discussion of the leading English writers' analyses of distribution is again recommended, both for study on its own account and for comparison with the argument of this book.

[2] Such statements are never quite true and must be taken *cum grano salis*. Nevertheless, in this statement, truth greatly prevails over error, so far as England is concerned.

[3] This may seem surprising. But it is really natural enough since the farmer's case displays the three divisions of national income and the 'rentless margin' better than does any other. Also it must be borne in mind that for West and Ricardo the farm held a key position, owing to the relation of marginal cost of food to wages and hence to profit.

owners of factors that are being hired.[4] Though neither Ricardo nor Senior followed suit, we have in J. S. Mill's *Principles* a fair presentation of the point of view that the profession at large actually reached in the period. His analysis of business incomes in particular became the standard, in all countries, for more than half a century to come. The businessman received, first, what Marshall was to call Wages of Management, the importance of which was underlined by von Mangoldt's notion of Rent of Ability, the germ of which is already to be found in Mill. He further received a premium for risk-bearing; nobody that I know of took the trouble to investigate why this item should be necessarily positive. Cantillon's 'buying productive services at certain prices in order to produce a product whose price is not certain' did not, however, come quite into its own until the publication of Professor Knight's work,[5] that is, not within the period. Third, the businessman received interest on the owned part of the capital he employed. But it should be observed that, occasionally, both Ricardo and Marx recognized a fourth type of return, of an essentially temporary nature, that accrues to the businessman, namely, the return he derives for a time from the first introduction into the economic process of a novel improvement such as a new machine.[6] They thus discovered a special case of what is really the most typical of all entrepreneurial gains.

Mill made nothing of the latter item. His analysis strongly suggests that, like everybody else and in spite of his emphasis upon the wages of management, he looked upon interest as the most important element in the total net receipts of the business class. Now, this interest was not a monetary phenomenon. So far as the 'classics,' within the precincts of fundamental analysis, spoke of monetary interest at all, they did not mean a return on money loans per se, as did the scholastic writers and as do some of us, but only a monetary expression for a return on physical capital that, moreover, was expressed in terms of money solely for the sake of convenience.[7] Actually, as we

[4] I must, however, not be understood to mean that I consider this place as the ideally correct one.

[5] F. H. Knight, *Risk, Uncertainty and Profit* (1921). But von Thünen was in full possession of the principle involved.

[6] See, e.g., Ricardo's Chapter 31 On Machinery (first page). Both he and Marx not only recognized the existence of this gain but made it an essential part of their analytic structure. With Marx it is particularly clear that it was indispensable for him because it motivated the process of mechanization which, as he saw, does not benefit the 'capitalist' class permanently.

[7] I use this opportunity to clarify a point that has given rise to a criticism of 'classic' theory that is only in part justified. Many writers of that and even a later time spoke glibly of wages *per hour*, rent *per acre*, and profit *per cent* as if these were comparable magnitudes. It is quite true that, in very many cases, this practice indicates haziness of thinking, to say the least. But it is not always true. Ricardo in particular expressed his real (or absolute labor-quantity) values in terms of a money that also embodied a constant quantity of labor and was invariant in this Ricardian value. Capital goods embodying 100 labor days were therefore capable of yielding, say, '5 per cent'—since this only means that they were capable of yielding a *net* product embodying 5 labor days—without reference to any discounting process. That is to say, this phrase was really quite

know, their capital was goods. The businessman's profits were, in substance, 'profits of stock,' net returns on a stock of capital goods, all of them or some of them. And interest, being simply that part of a business's net receipts which its owner-manager hands over to a lender whom he saves the trouble and risk of doing business, also remained a (pure) 'profit of stock.' This is so with all the economists of that period—Marx not less than Say—and with nearly all of the next period. The point of view is important. A great part of our picture of the capitalist process hinges upon it. Let us therefore make sure of its implications.

In the first place, since pure interest, if we neglect the interest on consumers' loans, was nothing but the bulk of business profits, the fundamental problem was the explanation of those business profits: there was no *separate* problem of interest at all. With the possible exception of Senior's abstinence theory—to be discussed presently—all the theories of interest throughout the nineteenth century are based upon acceptance of this view, including Ricardo's, Marx's, and later on, Böhm-Bawerk's. This was one of the results of the habit of identifying the roles of the industrialist and the capitalist, which subtly influenced the thought even of those who occasionally recognized the essential difference between them, and is the cornerstone of that period's theory of distribution.

In the second place, since business profit itself was conceived as being, essentially, a return on capital goods, it followed that interest was *identical* with (not determined by) the net yield of capital goods. The first to state this theory explicitly, so far as I know, was Nicholas Barbon. Sanctioned by A. Smith, it prevailed throughout the nineteenth century. Of course, it was particularly agreeable to the adherents of the triad schema—though, in a particular form, we also find it in Marx. Barbon had already attempted to explain interest by analogy with the rent of land.[8] Adherents of the triad schema would have had no difficulty in going a step farther and in extending the analogy to wages, thus rounding off their triad of factors by a triad of incomes. The first to show definitively that the yield of capital goods, whatever else it may be, is not interest was Irving Fisher.[9]

(b) *Marx's Exploitation Theory of Interest.* Having removed any danger of confusion, we shall henceforth use the term interest for (the bulk of) what Smith, Ricardo, Senior, and Marx called profit. And having put the problem

---

analogous to the wages per hour or the rent per acre and no circular reasoning was involved in it: the 100 labor days were an 'objective' quantity like the land; and it is only because 'interest per cent' with us refers to a capital value of a different kind—namely, to a capital value that is derived from the returns—that critics objected to Ricardo's language.

[8] This line of thought, later on, bore interesting fruit in Marshall's quasi-rent. But the latter concept really points in the opposite direction: its emergence was one of the earliest signs of dawning recognition of the fact that yield of capital goods per se is *not* interest and should be distinguished from it.

[9] *Rate of Interest* (1907); see below, Part IV, chs. 5 and 6, where this argument will be taken up again. For the moment the pointer above must suffice.

of interest in its proper setting within the analytic thought of that period, we can now make short work of the solutions offered and of the related 'proofs' of the secular tendency of the rate of interest to fall.

The reader will realize, of course, that the doctrinal tendency we have traced to Barbon—that is, the tendency to identify interest with the net yield of capital goods—does not in itself furnish a solution of the problem of the nature of interest or a definite answer to the question what it is that interest is paid for. For that net yield itself needs explanation. But the economists of the period under survey were slow to realize this. Having lost contact with the thought of the scholastic doctors, they were at first inclined to take the solution of this problem for granted and to be content with the vaguest ideas about it. Thus, A. Smith may be credited with two different 'theories' of interest, and Ricardo, as we shall see, with three or even four. But it is more realistic to say that they had no definite theory at all. They simply did not worry about the matter. After all, one of the methods of dealing with a problem—and not always the worst one—is to ignore it. The first to recognize its existence—if we except Turgot—was Lauderdale; and the second was James Mill. The elements of a genuine theory of interest—true or false—were then contributed by Longfield, Rae, Scrope, and Thünen, none of whom made much of a hit at the time. The man who did was Senior. But before following up developments on the Barbon line, we shall deal with the Exploitation Theory.

The essential thing to understand about the exploitation theory of interest is that it is a rationalization of the age-old slogan that expresses the feeling of manual laborers and philosophers about the upper strata's living on the fruits of manual labor. The social psychology of this and the question when and why this became synonymous with *exploiting* manual labor cannot be analyzed here: it must be enough for us to realize the presence of this problem and to recall that this idea entered the *Wealth of Nations* through the philosophy of natural law. There it took the form of the proposition that rent and interest are deductions from a total produce that, in its entirety, should be considered as the produce of manual labor. In this sense, A. Smith gave a lead for the numerous writers who were to work out exploitation theories of one kind or another. More important for us, however, is the fact that turns of phrase, suggestive of the idea that the relation between industrial employers and their workmen *necessarily* involved [10] exploitation, occur quite frequently in the literature of that time even outside of its specifically laborist or socialist branch. These turns of phrase derived quite naturally from the view

[10] It is essential to keep this notion strictly separate from the general observation or impression that labor very often got a raw deal that shocked moral feelings, or from the still more obvious observation that the masses lived in misery whereas other people rolled in wealth that shocked humanitarian sentiment. All this, of course, created an atmosphere favorable to the reception of exploitation theories but forms no part of these theories: for these it is essential that the wage contract *implies* exploitation; it is not enough that it is—often or always—*associated* with exploitation or, simply, with a low standard of living of the wage earner.

of the function of the industrial employer as described by A. Smith. The industrial employer, being simply a capitalist who furnished the workers with tools, materials, and means of subsistence and for the rest did very little, received these 'advances' back with a profit that was evidently part of the result of the workers' 'industry.' This highly unrealistic picture of the role of labor we find, for example, in Mrs. Jane Marcet's *Conversations on Political Economy* (1816), and it is conveyed by Ricardo's naïve sentence: '. . . the capitalist begins his operations by having food and necessaries in his possession of the value of £13,000 . . . : at the end of the year' the workmen 'replace in his possession food and necessaries of the value of £15,000' (ch. 31). Not more than this was necessary for the Ricardian socialists to take the hint; and not more than this is necessary for us to trace Marx's exploitation theory—the particular form, that is, which Marx gave to the exploitation idea—to his study of Ricardo.[11] This is not to deny the possibility that he may also have derived inspiration from the Ricardian socialists, especially from W. Thompson. Besides, there were plenty of other forerunners, for example, Sismondi. But Ricardo's suggestion, together with his theory of value, would have sufficed.

Marx's exploitation theory may be put like this. Labor (the 'labor power' of the workman, not his services) is in capitalist society a commodity. Therefore, its value[12] is equal to the number of labor hours which are embodied in it. How many labor hours are embodied in the laborer? Well, the 'socially necessary' amount of labor hours it takes to rear, train, feed, house him, and so on. Suppose that this labor quantity, referred to the labor days of his active span of life, figures out at four hours per day. But the 'capitalist' who bought his 'labor power'—Marx did not go quite so far as to say that the 'capitalist' buys laborers as he could buy shares, though this is the implication—makes him work six hours a day. Four of these six being enough to replace the value of all the goods that went to the laborer, or the variable capital advanced to him (v), the two additional hours produce Surplus Value (s), the *Mehrwert*. For these two hours the 'capitalist' has not given any compensation. They constitute 'unpaid labor.' To the extent that the laborer works hours that are unpaid in this sense, he is exploited at the rate s/v. This rate of surplus value is not, of course, the rate of interest. The latter equals the ratio between surplus value and total (constant plus variable) capital, that is, $\frac{s}{c+v}$. If we suppose that s/v is equal for all sectors of the economy and all firms—that is to say,

[11] This defines the sense in which an exploitation theory of interest may be attributed to Ricardo. Let me recall the three other interest theories that may be attributed to him, which have been mentioned already and will be mentioned again (subsec. c. below); the abstinence theory; the residual theory; and, possibly, even a productivity theory; V. Edelberg ('The Ricardian Theory of Profits,' *Economica*, 1933), makes Ricardo a productivity theorist, who would have had nothing to learn from Wicksell. Perhaps he is right. In a sense, Newton had nothing to learn from Einstein. But to say so would not make for a realistic history of mechanics.

[12] Strictly *we* ought to say: its equilibrium value under perfect competition.

that all workmen are equally exploited—and further suppose that the rate of interest, $\frac{s}{c+v}$, must also be equal for all concerns, we run up against the difficulty that has been mentioned already, namely, the necessity of redistributing the total surplus among firms in such a way as to make $\frac{s}{c+v}$ equal for all. But in order to avoid going over this ground again, we merely note here that this difficulty constitutes a possible objection to the Marxist type of exploitation theory.[13] For the rest we assume that this difficulty does not prevent us from accepting the ratio $\frac{s}{c+v}$ as the expression of the Marxist rate of interest when we interpret s, c, and v simply as national aggregates, the values of which are proportional to their 'prices,' though we know that this does not hold for the individual commodities.

We may then interpret Marx's exploitation theory as an application of his theory of value to labor: according to it, labor receives not less than its full value and consumers do not pay more for the products than their full value.[14] Therefore, it is exposed not only to all the general objections that may be raised against Marx's labor-quantity theory of value but also to the special objection that may be raised to its application to 'labor power.' For so far as the labor-quantity theory of value is valid at all, it is valid only by virtue of rational cost calculation: only economically applied (socially necessary) labor quantities create value. But evidently human beings are not produced, according to the rules of capitalist rationality, with a view to cost-covering returns. The situation of the exploitation theory could be improved somewhat by inserting into it the Malthusian law in a very strict form or by some other contrivance that would keep wages on a level of the cost of bare subsistence. This was done by Lassalle (iron law of wages, *loi d'airain, ehernes Lohngesetz*). But Marx, wisely perhaps, refused to do this. Malthus' law of population was anathema to him; moreover he recognized both cyclical increases of wage rates beyond the value of labor and a tendency, of longer span, for the degree of exploitation to fall through reduction in daily hours brought about by trade-union action, legislation, and so on. Thus he reduced his exploitation to the rank of an 'absolute law'—an abstract tendency—that need

[13] The nature of this objection will become clear when we consider Marx's relation to the abstinence theory.

[14] This feature constitutes a claim to superiority of Marxist exploitation as against all other attempts to rationalize this meaningless phrase. All the others (this does not apply to the meanings attached to that phrase in our own time by Professor Pigou and Mrs. Robinson) must rely on laborers' being somehow cheated or robbed, either as participants in production or as consumers, and then they have a hard time trying to prove why this should be so always and necessarily. But there is no cheating or robbing involved in Marx's theory. The exploitation there results, irrespective of anyone's misbehavior, from the very logic of the capitalist law of value, and therefore is ingrained in the system much more irradicably than any other exploitation theory can show it to be.

not prevail in real life. Another objection, however, is less serious than it seems. According to Marx, surplus value is a costless gain of the capitalist. Moreover it is not defined as an intramarginal gain, like Ricardian rent. It might be thought that such a gain would induce individual capitalists—whose individual contributions to the total output of their industries is too small to influence prices—to expand output until the surplus falls to zero. This conclusion is indeed inescapable so long as we keep to the schema of a stationary process; such a process could not be in equilibrium until the surplus is eliminated. But we may save the situation by taking account of the fact that Marx thought primarily of an evolutionary process in which the surplus, though it has a tendency to vanish at any given time, is being incessantly recreated.[15] Or else we might drop the assumption of perfect competition though the surplus we may salvage in this way will be quite different from Marx's. Without going further into the matter,[16] we turn to Marx's explanation of the Tendency of the Rate of Profit to Fall, in which both Marx himself and some of his followers took great pride.

If we do grant, first, that there is such a tendency and, second, that Marx's theory of surplus value is all right, then this pride was not unjustified. Few, if any, experiences of an analyst are more gratifying than is the discovery that a theory (say, gravitation) will explain a fact (say, the tides) which the author of the theory had *not* had in mind in constructing this theory.

(c) *Marx, West, and Ricardo on the Falling Rate of Profit.* The first remark to be made applies not only to Marx, West, and Ricardo but to all the economists who busied themselves in finding an explanation for the secular fall in the rate of interest: it never occurred to any of them to ask whether there was such a secular fall. They simply took it for granted and, in doing so, displayed an almost unbelievable degree of scientific carelessness. For the only thing that is so obvious is that medieval princes promised their creditors 80 per cent and more, whereas in 1800 governments were thought to be paying a high rate if they paid about 5 per cent and in 1900 when they paid 3 per cent—and similarly, of course, businessmen. But this was due, obviously, to the very high premium of risk that attached to loans to princes who, mostly, did not even repay the capital; to the primitive organization of money markets; and to the anticipation of inflation. Where none of these factors was present—for example, in the Netherlands in the second half of the seventeenth century—interest was not obviously higher than it was under similar conditions two hundred years later. Since it was the rate of *pure* interest, the

[15] An analogous argument from the incessant displacement of labor in the process of accumulation may serve, instead of the Malthusian law of population, to motivate a tendency in wages to seek the level indicated by the Marxist 'value of labor.' This, too, would not work in the process of simple reproduction, but it could be inserted on the consideration mentioned above.

[16] Marx's economic theory did not attract attention and come in for professional criticism before the next period, when a critical Marx literature developed. The most important performances, especially Böhm-Bawerk's criticism, are mentioned by P. M. Sweezy, op. cit.

fall of which was to be explained, and not the conditions that produced greater or smaller premia of risk or other costs of borrowing, those economists would have been better advised if they had bestowed some trouble on finding out what there really was to explain.

Second, Marx's explanation rested on two propositions. The one was that, in the course of economic development, the Marxist value of constant capital increases faster than does the Marxist value of variable capital because production becomes increasingly mechanized. The other was that only variable capital (wage capital) produces surplus value whereas constant capital, as we have said before, only transmits its own value[17] to the product. Accepting, for the sake of argument, both these propositions and further assuming that the rate of surplus value remains constant and that the Marxist value of capital goods does not fall, we have no difficulty in reaching the conclusion that $\frac{s}{c+v}$ must fall (*Das Kapital*, vol. III, ch. 13). Objections that were raised against this conclusion by Marxists either arose from failure to take account of all these restrictions or else from unwillingness to admit their realism. In fact, we have here another 'absolute law' and, if we look at all that these restrictions exclude,[18] we may well sympathize with those disciples of Marx who feel that, even from the standpoint of the Marxist theories of value and exploitation, no great confidence can be placed in this abstract tendency. But, within the general framework of Marx's theoretical system and the additional assumptions indicated above, it is not logically wrong.

Third, though emphasizing the abstractness of his law, Marx trusted it sufficiently to make it the 'barrier,' inherent in capitalist production, that will eventually prevent the capitalist process from going on beyond a certain limit—which is not indeed the whole of the Breakdown Theory but an important element of it.

By way of contrast I shall now present the West-Ricardian explanation of the historical fall in the rate of interest that, like everyone else, they took to be an indisputable fact. It links up with what may be described as Ricardo's second theory of interest. We have seen above that Ricardo's theoretical set-up really makes 'profit' a residual and simply equates it to what remains to the farmer on rentless land when he has paid his laborers. The origin of this way of viewing 'profit' is obviously in the practical businessman's mode of think-

17 It should not be forgotten, however, that the value of constant capital includes surplus value.

18 Marx spoke of 'counteracting forces' that 'inhibit and annul' the operation of his absolute law. The list of these could have been copied from J. S. Mill (counteracting circumstances, Book IV, ch. 4, § 5), whose 'tendency of profits to a minimum' was in similar case. It should be observed, however, that the latter phrase permits an interpretation that brings the falling rate of profits more definitely within the range of the theorist than, in the nature of things, it is possible to bring any *historical* tendency: within a given setting (including a given technological horizon), it can in fact be proved that the rate of interest tends to the minimum—and the wage rate to the maximum—that is compatible with that setting and its given investment opportunities.

ing as reflected in his profit-and-loss account (income statement): his profit is 'what is left'—the item that balances his account. Since, on the rentless margin of production, the whole of the net product, measured in 'labor embodied,' is divided between labor and capital, both shares also measured in 'labor embodied,' [19] and since labor's share is explained separately, we easily get the two propositions which are, when this point has been reached, really not more than trivial.[20] The one is that 'profits depend upon wages'—what else could they depend upon in this schema? The other is that, under the influence of increase in population and of the law of decreasing returns on land, more and more labor has to be embodied in each additional unit of food and that the value of labor's share must rise—though the per capita amount of wage goods need not rise or may even decrease somewhat—leaving less and less *value* for capital. This and nothing else, as West and after him Ricardo laboriously explained, accounts for the phenomenon that we are supposed to observe in the guise of the falling rate of interest. But there was no need for elaboration. For according to this wonderful theory, it is *logically*

[19] Observe how neatly this fits the Marxist schema: all that we need to obtain the latter is to measure, in addition to labor's *share*, also labor itself (the labor power, that is) in 'labor embodied.' There is in fact no incompatibility between what we call Ricardo's first and second theories of interest: in both, the amount and rate of profit are determined by (the 'real' value of) wages. This follows from the set-up discussed above, after elimination of total output and of rent. The notion of exploitation (no matter whether we call it so or not) simply adds a particular interpretation. But this seems no longer to be so if we attribute to Ricardo an abstinence theory (the same would hold for a productivity theory, which we do not attribute to him, however). In order not to have to return to this point, which is not without theoretical interest, I shall settle the matter in this footnote. We have then 'profit' determined by 'wages' (in general, uniquely). If thereupon we declare, as Ricardo did, that the same profits are a 'just compensation' (i.e., obviously, a price) of waiting, his system seems to become overdetermined: a quantity that is determined already is being subject to an additional condition. This, however, is so only in this system and need not be so in a wider system that may be behind the former. The reader should always be careful to scrutinize arguments from overdeterminateness of a system (which are today so popular) before he accepts them. Suppose 'wages' have determined 'profit' at a certain figure. Further suppose that this figure does not 'justly compensate' the 'capitalists' for their waiting. If this state of things is not expected to mend, the 'capitalists' will reduce their investment (within that schema, they have no opportunity of doing anything else). Capital or at least variable capital, the wage fund, will accordingly be reduced. And, through a series of rearrangements throughout the system that play 'at one remove' or 'behind the scenes'—I leave it to the reader to carry this out—we arrive eventually at a situation in which wages still 'determine' profit but at a level that will satisfy the 'capitalist.' From this, the reader may also learn an important lesson as regards the meaning of the phrase 'determined by'—a lesson which it is indispensable to learn if he is ever to understand economic theory and its tricks and some of its critics and *their* tricks.

[20] And an excellent example they are of that Art of Triviality that, intimately connected with the Ricardian Vice, leads the victim, step by step, into a situation where he has got either to surrender or allow himself to be laughed at for denying what, by the time that situation is reached, is *really* a triviality.

impossible that the rate of interest (excepting short-run 'market' fluctuations) should ever fall for any other reason. In fact, Ricardo (ch. 21) asserted that unless wages rise (in his sense) no amount of accumulation can possibly reduce the rate of profit; and he not only took to task A. Smith for explaining the falling rate of profit by accumulation but also boldly charged J. B. Say with having forgotten his own Law of Markets when he stated that 'the more disposable capitals are abundant' in relation to the extent of investment opportunity, the more will the rate of interest fall.[21] Two things are clear: first that, in the sense meant and within Say's conceptual arrangement, Say's proposition is correct, also that it does not conflict in the least with his Law of Markets; but second that, in the sense meant and within Ricardo's conceptual arrangement, Ricardo's proposition is not wrong either.

J. S. Mill's position is nothing short of pathetic to behold. He had a wide understanding of all the phenomena relevant to interest. In particular, he understood the theoretical problems of monetary interest and of the capitalization of returns more deeply than any other *theorist* of his time: in Chapter 23 of Book III (*Principles*) he anticipated some of the developments in this field that were forty or fifty years ahead. In addition, he had learned from Say, Rae, and Senior. He was fairly in possession of a value theory that was greatly superior to Ricardo's. Thus he was, as he proved himself to be in Chapter 4 of Book IV, in a position to build up an analysis that would have fitted all known facts. But, God knows why, he had to uphold Ricardian doctrine. And so, from Chapter 15 of Book II on, he dealt with these matters in an unnatural and cramped manner so as to force them in a surface conformity with Ricardian doctrine. It would be extremely interesting to analyze this and, by so doing, to arrive at a fuller understanding of how economic analysis moves along, over self-built barriers. But I am afraid that, even as it is, readers will not share my regret at my inability to do so in the available space.[22]

21 On A. Smith's argument, see below, subsec. e. He went exactly as far in stating the antagonistic tendency of wages and rate of profit as facts and common sense (but not the Ricardian conceptualization) will warrant: accumulation, so far as it means additional demand for labor (and services of land), will *ceteris paribus* depress the rate of interest and raise wages (and rents). But Ricardo, entirely neglecting the inapplicability of his conceptual apparatus to this mechanism, would not hear of it.

22 Nevertheless, I shall in this footnote give an example of the methods by which conformity was in part secured and offer a comment that applies to many theories, some of today or yesterday included. The example: even if rent be excluded, the capitalists' advances, for an adherent of the abstinence theory like Mill, cannot possibly consist of wages alone; yet this is precisely what Mill averred in § 6 (Book II, ch. 15). How was this possible? Nothing simpler: 'profits' too are being advanced, of course, but these advances are no advances but a sort of payment on account of the profits that are expected to be earned.

The comment: under appropriate assumptions, in particular if frictions, rigidities, *and sequences* be neglected, all economic quantities, and especially the usual social aggregates, hang together in a definite way; and any process of change that runs through them will affect them all. No proposition to the effect that one of them has

(d) *The Productivity Theories of Interest.* For the votaries of the triad schema and of the theory that incomes are essentially prices (times quantities) of productive services, the natural thing to do was to interpret the yield of capital goods—which they, like all the writers of that period, identified with the rate of interest—as a price for the productive services of those capital goods.[23] This again may be done in several ways, though, unfortunately, all of them meet with this fatal objection: nothing is easier than to show that capital goods or their services, being both requisite and scarce, will have value and fetch prices; nor is it difficult to show that their ownership will often yield temporary net returns; but all the more difficult is it to show that—and, if so, why—these values and prices are *normally* higher than is necessary in order to enable their owners to replace them, in other words, why there should be a *permanent net* return attached to their ownership. This point was not fully brought home to the profession at large until the publication of Böhm-Bawerk's history of interest theories in the first volume of his *Kapital und Kapitalzins* (1884). Until that time (perhaps in some cases even now)

---

particular causal importance and that others depend upon it, however absurd it may be, is ever likely to be contradicted by facts. Thus, in Book IV, ch. 4 of the *Principles*, Mill discussed the tendency of profits to a minimum and the 'counter-agencies' such as capital export, technological improvement, and so on in a perfectly reasonable manner on the lines of Say. But home investment, foreign investment, and technological change all have their effects—though in different degree and direction—on the national wage bill. And so there was no difficulty in making that theory conform to the Ricardian schema. All Mill had to do was to single out the wage link in the chain and to allocate to it the role of ultimate cause: the misuse of the word 'cause' (or of equivalents) is really the only exception we have a *logical* right to take. Yet a theory that has no other logical fault than this may still be a rotten theory, which is good for nothing except for lending sham support to some pet tenet of its author. For instance, what if high rates of profit and high cost of labor go together, as they undoubtedly did in the United States? Mill worried about this, as we know from his letters to Cairnes that have been published by G. O'Brien ('J. S. Mill and J. E. Cairnes,' *Economica*, November 1943, pp. 279-82). Either the fact had to be challenged or else it had to be explained away. To be sure, *this can always be done:* for *any* theory can be made to fit *any* facts by means of appropriate additional assumptions. But it would have been much more simple and straightforward to adopt another analytic schema that recognizes the important fact that high rates of profit and high wages normally go together, without making a difficult problem of it, the more so because such a simple schema had been clearly outlined by A. Smith.

[23] This applies to technological capital only, though the exponents of the productivity theory of interest did not in general restrict their capital concept correspondingly. In fact, as we know, there was a tendency to resolve the stock of technological capital goods into the subsistence fund. But this spells a move away from what we call pure productivity theories, i.e. theories that invoke nothing but the productive service of plant and equipment. Since the total non-wage capital, which according to these theories is the source of interest, is Marx's constant capital that does not generate any surplus at all, we may consider the pure productivity theories as the antipodes of the exploitation theories.

people thought (or think) that the easy proof of the proposition that capital goods must yield a return establishes *ipso facto* that they must yield an income to their owners. This confusion of two different things vitiates all the pure productivity theories of interest (as Böhm-Bawerk called them), both the primitive ones (Böhm-Bawerk's naïve productivity theories) and the more elaborate ones (Böhm-Bawerk's motivated productivity theories). The same confusion vitiates also what Böhm-Bawerk called the use theories, which do not essentially differ from the productivity theories.[24]

Lauderdale, the first exponent of an explicit productivity theory, was also the first to set the example of explicit commission of the logical error pointed out above. But this error was veiled if not mended by his peculiar definition of the productive role of capital, which according to him consists not in 'assisting' but in 'supplanting' labor. The owner of capital receives what the supplanted labor would have received (*Inquiry into the Nature and Origin of Public Wealth*, 1804, p. 165). This is interesting as a pointer toward the relation of substitutability that exists between technological capital and labor, and as a first step in the analysis of the true relation between wages and interest. But it would solve the problem of the net yield of capital goods, as Böhm-Bawerk was to observe, only if machines did not wear out: if they do, Lauderdale's theory explains why they earn their depreciation quota, but it does not explain why they earn more—if indeed they do[25]—which is not so certain after all.

This example suffices. We should not get more light by discussing, for example, Malthus' version, which issues into the statement that 'profits' are 'a fair remuneration for that part of the production contributed by the capitalist' (*Principles*, 1st ed., p. 81). The reader finds in Böhm-Bawerk's pages a list of writers who adhered to the productivity theory of interest throughout

[24] The self-explanatory term Use Theory is not without suggestiveness. The return on durable goods, monetary or imputed, has certainly something to do with the prevailing rate of interest, and it is, in some respects, an improvement if this notion be extended to durable consumers' goods. But 'use' evidently reduces to 'service.' The use theory is usually associated with the name of Hermann (1832) and continued to enjoy for a long time considerable popularity in Germany. Knies and Menger were among its adherents.

[25] Longfield and von Thünen had indeed the great merit of introducing marginal analysis into the productivity theory of interest and of carrying on the investigation into the relations between interest and wages. But on the fundamental point, they are in no better case than other productivity theorists. Longfield, however, improved his situation by calling to his aid the proposition that capital formation requires saving, hence the willingness of savers to 'sacrifice the present to the future'—that is, abstinence. But von Thünen, who was immeasurably superior to him in technique, did not get beyond the formula that interest is determined by the use (or productive effect) of the 'last element of capital applied.' This must not, of course, be understood in the West-Ricardo sense. It must be understood in the sense in which, in our own day, Professor D. H. Robertson seems to wish to uphold it (see his article in the *Economic Journal*, September 1937, one of three rejoinders to an article by Keynes entitled 'Alternative Theories of the Rate of Interest').

the nineteenth century. They were much more numerous on the Continent than in England. Since they made no serious effort to establish the existence of a permanent positive yield of physical capital goods, they *a fortiori* never asked the question whether this yield was interest.

Another type of interest theory will be mentioned here, though our right to range it under the heading of productivity theories may perhaps seem doubtful. It is associated with the names of James Mill and McCulloch and was, to some extent, their joint product [26] and may be rendered by the latter's statement that 'the profits of stock are only another name for the wages of accumulated labour': capital goods themselves are accumulated or hoarded labor; the labor they embody simply goes on to earn wages; if wine, as deposited in the cellar, embodies a certain amount of labor, then, this labor or else 'nature' goes on working while this wine matures; payment for this additional work is interest. The obvious interpretation is that James Mill and McCulloch were grimly resolved to extend their master's theory of value to the cases, which Ricardo himself recognized as being beyond the range of his labor-quantity law, in order to make the latter perfectly general—as Marx tried to do by means of another construction. Critic after critic has held that they achieved this generality by what was nothing but a verbal trick and a very silly one to boot.[27] Also, it may be urged against this theory of interest, that in addition to being a failure as an attempt to peg the labor-quantity theory of value, it is exposed to the same objection that is fatal to pure productivity theories: even if we grant that capital goods are hoarded labor and that the 'capitalist' reimburses himself for the wages of this hoarded labor from his receipts, the theory is, without an appeal to other circumstances, powerless to show why he should get something for that imaginary labor. But precisely this consideration, though it certainly prevents us from accepting this theory of permanent net yield, permits us to put a slightly more favorable construction on it, especially in the version of the unfortunate McCulloch. That is, it permits us to see, in his version, at least a clumsy and roundabout

26 We must confine ourselves to the essential point. But there are several things of interest in the details that we have no choice but to neglect. Among them is the role played by Torrens (*Essay on the Production of Wealth*, 1821) in the discussion that issued in the theory to be mentioned. Torrens held what we shall later describe as a mark-up theory of interest, according to which 'profits' do not enter into what *he* called the natural price of commodities. This natural price he equated to costs. Profits enter only into a market price that therefore means something quite different from A. Smith's and Ricardo's market price. In the first edition of his *Elements* (1821), James Mill argued mainly against this, and betrayed hardly any sign of wishing to adopt the theory, which he did adopt in the second edition (1824) after McCulloch's *Encyclopaedia Britannica* article (Supplement, 1823) had been published. This article contains the statement quoted in the text that he elaborated in his *Principles* (1825).

27 Many critics, including Cannan (op. cit. p. 206), charged in addition that the trick was perpetrated in the service of apologetics. What a lovely justification of 'profits'—to call them wages! Ideology no doubt entered into McCulloch's argument as much as it did into Marx's; and McCulloch may have wished to defend profits as much as Marx may have wished to attack them. But this is beside the point.

way of recognizing, from the standpoint of the labor-quantity theory of value, the requisiteness of physical capital. His verbal trick, thus interpreted, amounts to using 'labor' as a term for what is more properly called 'productive service' and wages as a term for what is more properly called price of productive service. Or, to put it differently, his trick amounts to recognizing that hoarded labor is a peculiar kind of labor that may render services that are also of a peculiar kind as compared with the services of 'live' or 'liquid' labor. This is why—certainly not in the intention to defend it—I have subsumed this theory with the pure productivity theories: it is the pure productivity theory of the labor-quantity men.

The pure productivity theories have an easy explanation to offer for the secular fall of the rate of interest. They need only postulate that technological capital increases more rapidly than does the population available for industrial employment, and a fall of its yield per unit—not necessarily its relative, let alone, absolute share—would in general follow *ceteris paribus*. Since these *cetera* include a given technological horizon (production function), the reader may think that this explanation is not much good. Certainly it is not. Yet there is an advantage in this: whenever correctly formulated,[28] this explanation should have brought out automatically the most important qualifications that are inherent in any proposition about the secular behavior of the rate of *pure* interest and, in doing so, should have raised doubt about the validity of the 'law' of secular fall.

A. Smith had no productivity theory of 'profit.' But all the same he offered an explanation of what he, like everybody else, took to be the indubitable tendency of interest to fall that most naturally follows from a productivity theory, namely, that the rate of profits tends to fall as increasing capitals enter into competition with one another. From the standpoint of West and Ricardo, this was bound to appear as a logical error, for the relative values from which they derived the rate of interest could not possibly be affected by an increase per se of the quantities of goods that form capital.[29]

[28] It can be formulated in different ways. Longfield, e.g., made 'profits' fall because the most profitable investment opportunities are operated first so that, as time goes on, only less and less profitable ones remain available. This meets with the objection that investment opportunity is incessantly widened by technological progress and that there is no reason why opportunities that turn up later should be less profitable than those that turned up before (see last but one sentence in the text). Longfield's formulation is simply a consequence of his marginal-productivity theory of interest: the rate of profit, which 'is equal to the assistance which is given to labour by that portion of capital which is employed with the least efficiency, which I shall call the last portion of capital brought into operation' (*Lectures on Political Economy*, p. 194), will in general decrease when capital increases more than does labor, but *this* decrease must be distinguished from the *secular* decrease to be explained, of which the former is only a component.

[29] Sir Edward West's ingenious argument to that effect merits perusal. It affords an excellent instance of the way in which a theoretical structure, once accepted, may hide from the analyst the most obvious truths. This argument is mainly responsible for Ricardo's view that no increase in capital, unless accompanied by an increase in (the

(e) *The Abstinence Theory of Interest.* So long as physical capital is recognized as a requisite of production *or even of exploitation only,* it must be a service, within the meaning this term carries in economic analysis, to provide it, though, if we do accept the exploitation theory, this service is rendered only to the exploiter and not to society at large. Instead of emphasizing the productive or exploitative service of capital itself, we may therefore just as well emphasize the service of providing it. And so long as we keep to tne Smithian theory that capital goods are the result of saving—as J. S. Mill put it —we may further say that any net yield of these capital goods is in the nature of a payment for the service rendered by saving either to the producing organism or to the exploiter alone. If we do say this, we are adopting the Scrope-Senior Abstinence Theory of Interest. I have introduced the subject in this way to bring into relief the following historically important facts.

First, it will be seen that there is no essential difference, let alone incompatibility, between the productivity and the abstinence theories. Senior, witness his Third Postulate (see above, subsec. 5c) was evidently aware of this. But he did not clearly explain—this was to be done later by A. Marshall and T. N. Carver—precisely what it is that the abstinence theory adds to the productivity theory and what its relation is to the latter. This something is the brake that will prevent the process of creating additional capital goods right up to the limit at which their *net* yield would fall to zero.[30] But because he failed to make this sufficiently clear, both adherents (such as J. S. Mill, who was content with the formula that interest is the price of saving) and opponents (Böhm-Bawerk in particular) consider it in the light of an explanation of the interest phenomenon that is alternative to the productivity explanation and has to stand on the element of sacrifice alone, which is or may be associated with saving.

Second, it will be seen that attacks upon the abstinence theory should not be directed against its logic. For instance, Böhm-Bawerk's attack was based upon a charge of double counting. The saver who lends chooses between the fund he is to give away [31] and the stream of returns he is to receive. There is no room for counting in addition any sacrifice he may be making. Even

Ricardian value of) wages, can ever decrease the rate of profit or cause any hitches in the economic process.

[30] As perhaps some readers know, I am not an exponent of the abstinence theory myself. I am merely trying to expound its rationale, as it appears from the standpoint of abstinence theorists, in a manner which I hope will make the reader understand its emergence as well as the fact that it proved so hardy a plant.

[31] Even if lent for short periods only and periodically reinvested, the fund is normally withdrawn from the saver's consumption for good. There is normally no question of putting off the enjoyment of the fund: normally *this* enjoyment is surrendered definitively in consideration of the quite different enjoyments expected from the flow of the interest payments. This is why the term Abstinence should be retained and why the term Waiting should not, indeed, be discarded but reserved for a different phenomenon or, at least, for a different aspect of the same phenomenon, which it is worth while to distinguish from the one denoted by abstinence as has been explained above.

granting that there would be something in this argument if the phrase 'compensation for sacrifice' exhausted the contents of the abstinence theory,[32] this would not imply that this theory is inconsistent when properly developed and put into its proper setting. There is no paradox at all in holding that a theory is logically unimpeachable and at the same time that it is wrong or at least inadequate. For a cause that may be invoked without logical error for the purpose of explaining a phenomenon need not be the one that actually produces this phenomenon.

Third, in addition to its sound logic, it was its common-sense appeal which recommended the abstinence theory to a long line of authorities, mainly English, headed by J. S. Mill. He handed to Marshall ready-made the doctrine of the two factors of 'real cost'—the disutility (irksomeness) experienced by the laborer and abstinence experienced by the saver.[33] But we have little choice but to attribute a less explicit form of the same doctrine to both A. Smith and Ricardo. However ready the former was to offer pointers toward an exploitation theory, parsimony is what remains if we look in the *Wealth of Nations* for an attempt at a real explanation of pure interest. And however lightly the latter took the problem, the observation that turnover periods of different lengths cannot coexist unless there is a rate of interest to equalize the yields of capitals that turn over in periods of different length, points clearly toward recognition of an element of abstinence or rather of 'waiting.' This interpretation is, on the one hand, reinforced by Ricardo's turn of phrase that interest is a 'just compensation' [34] for this waiting; but it is, on the other hand, weakened by Ricardo's refusal to adopt the explanation of the falling rate of interest which would logically follow from it.

Fourth, with competent economists the case for the abstinence theory was only strengthened by the weakness, both logical and factual, of the attacks upon it, which contrasted so strangely with their vehemence. Here was a piece of apologetics which sent socialists ranting. In their wrath they entirely neglected to work out serious arguments against it, which are indeed not lacking, but instead resorted to insipid gibes about the millionaires who are being paid for their abstemiousness (Lassalle) or about the capitalists who are being paid for abstaining from devouring manure (Marx). Even the 'classics' had enough inkling of marginal analysis to remain unimpressed by the former and it would hardly have occurred to them to take the trouble of rebutting the latter.

[32] The chief difficulty in admitting this is that Jevons and Böhm-Bawerk in introducing their 'psychological discount of future satisfactions' went pretty far toward offering a substitute for abstinence. Böhm-Bawerk's argument against the latter was, however, reinforced by Irving Fisher (*Theory of Interest*, 1930, ch. 20, § 7, especially pp. 486-7, and appendix thereto), who made an effective case against considering waiting or abstinence as independent items of real cost.

[33] I have difficulty in understanding how Cairnes could have claimed this merit for himself. But he did.

[34] This phrase can, of course, be easily divested of the value judgment it conveys, and then reads simply: price of waiting.

However, since Marx's ineptitude was repeated not long ago by an eminent economist of our time, and also because many economists of that epoch have in fact used phrases that lend themselves to misinterpretation (see, e.g., Marx's quotation from de Molinari and Courcelle-Seneuil in *Das Kapital*, vol. I, ch. 24, sec. 3), explanation may be indicated. The capitalist, as we have said above, exchanges a fund against a flow. The 'abstinence' for which, according to the theory under discussion, he is being paid enters into the accumulation of the fund. There is no additional payment for refraining from consuming it even in the cases in which this would be physically possible. But since he receives his compensation in the form of a flow of payments, it may seem as if he were being paid over and over again for abstaining from 'devouring' the capital goods that are emerging and being used up in the course of the employment of his capital. This impression is strengthened by the fact that the promised or, in the case of the employment of capital by its owner, the expected compensation must be actually delivered, in the normal case, if people are to enter into such bargains at all. If the lender or employing owner of the capital be disappointed in this expectation, he will indeed try to recover his loan or to go out of business—which then looks as if he had to be paid again and again in order to leave his capital where it is. But the sophomore who is unable to interpret these facts correctly or, let us add, to understand what these authors meant when they spoke of capitalists who 'lend their instruments of production to laborers,' must indeed be a very unpromising sophomore. This sort of thing in part accounts for, and to some extent excuses, the inability of many good economists to see the deeper things in Marx: they see at first sight so many pieces of nonsense that they cannot get themselves to believe that the man responsible for them could occasionally rise far above the level of his judges.

But the student who is prepared to salute Marx at his best will inevitably ask himself: how is it possible for a man to fall to a level so low as that of Section 3—a man who was capable of rising to heights that are trodden by few and who, occasionally, proved himself an extremely competent analyst also in many minor matters? The needs of the agitator will not suffice by themselves to account for this, especially as most of the rhetoric could have been wound around a sounder support. Hence the suspicion suggests itself that this rhetoric covers something. And it is in fact not difficult to see what it is: it is the presence in the logic of his structure both of the element of abstinence in the strict sense and of the element of waiting. We have already seen that Marx's theory belongs to the family we have called Advance Economics and this implies the recognition of a distinct element—no matter whether you call it a distinct service or a distinct crime—in the economic process which may be the vehicle of exploitation but in itself *is* not exploitation. We have also seen that the dangerous iceberg of abstinence may be seen in uncomfortable proximity to his argument on accumulation, which may just as well be called an argument on saving.[35] We now add that waiting is no

[35] Compare the famous, if slightly vulgar, passage that also occurs in the unfortunate sec. 3 of ch. 24: 'Accumulate, accumulate! That is Moses and the prophets . . . save,

more absent from Marx's structure than is abstinence in the strict sense. This may be shown in the following way. Marx's constant capital merely *transmits* its value to the products without adding anything beyond its own value. But, being itself the product of exploited labor, it *embodies* not only the value of the wage goods consumed by the labor that produced it but in addition surplus value at the prevailing rate. Now, there should be no difficulty in adding this surplus value that is embodied in constant capital to the surplus value that results from the employment of the labor in producing the final product with the help of constant capital. If this could be done, there would be no reason why actual prices should not be proportional to the total labor embodied in them, that is, the labor embodied in the constant capital plus the labor added until the final product emerges, and there would be no problem of turning values into prices. Nevertheless, Marx did not do this but preferred to struggle through hundreds of pages with this very problem. Why? Obviously because he thought that time distance was *not* a matter of indifference. But this amounts to recognizing—though not to admitting—that waiting is after all an element of Marx's structure (value theory), which is what we wished to show.

The abstinence theory of interest is in a particularly favorable position for dealing with any secular decline of the rate of interest. If we look upon abstinence as one of several requisites of production, we have no difficulty at all in stating the conditions under which its relative increase will produce that phenomenon. Tools that were unknown to the period under survey are necessary to do this satisfactorily. But the main propositions could have been derived, semi-intuitively as it were, even on the level of that period's technique. It is but an additional advantage that the historical interpretation and, especially, any prediction of a falling interest rate would follow from this analysis only conditionally and not absolutely. Of course, the same conditions that will cause a fall in the relative price of abstinence will (in general) cause a rise in the relative price of labor. Thus, there is no paradox in saying that J. S. Mill should in good logic have adopted this explanation of the 'tendency of profit to a minimum' or even that he actually did adopt it (Book IV, ch. 3, § 2) but that he easily reconciled it with his lingering Ricardianism, though the 'effective desire of accumulation' which he analyzed so carefully has much more title to being considered as a 'cause' than has the rise in wages.

(f) *The Wage-Fund Doctrine, Precursor of Modern Aggregative Analysis.* Our report on the wage analysis of the period is presented under this heading because everything else that pertains to the subject has been noticed already on various turns of our way.[36] In particular, we know that A. Smith—under the influence of natural-law philosophy—gave a lead toward a residual theory

---

save, i.e., reconvert the greatest possible portion of surplus-value . . . into capital!' We need not trouble either Moses or the prophets in order to see that capitalists 'abstain' with Marx quite as much as they do with Senior.

[36] Among other things, I have adverted to the misunderstandings that were caused by the special meanings which the phrases 'rising' and 'falling' wages carry within Ricardo's theory of value.

of wages: laborers produce the whole produce; the wage problem is to show why they do not get the whole produce but have to submit to certain 'deductions'; hence the wage problem is automatically solved as soon as these deductions have found their explanations. But even for A. Smith himself, and also for James Mill, Sismondi, and Marx, who went further in the direction of Smith's lead than did any other leading economist, analysis of the upper and lower limits of what 'can' or 'must' go to labor is so much more important for their treatment of wage problems than is their general philosophy that it is more instructive to deal with them without further reference to the latter. This agrees with what I believe to be the common opinion of a majority of historians. But I cannot agree with the classification of wage theories, which many of them have adopted, into minimum-of-existence theories, supply and demand theories, and productivity theories. For these are not distinct, let alone incompatible, explanations of wage incomes.

The first is no *theory* of wages at all but simply a *theorem* on the long-run equilibrium level of wages.[37] The supply and demand apparatus is necessary for any wage theory whatsoever and does not identify any particular one.[38] Ricardians (including Marx) failed indeed to recognize this, in the case of wages as in all other cases, for the determination of long-run normals, but even they allowed wages like other prices to be determined by supply and demand in a short run. But with wages, this meant something very different from what it meant with other prices. For if the long-run normal be made dependent upon adjustments of the population, the short run extends over at least fifteen years.[39] For short runs of this and even greater length—indeed for spells of 'indefinite' length—the Ricardians relied on the particular form that the supply and demand apparatus takes in the wage-fund doctrine. But in a different (the normal) form, the supply and demand apparatus was also used, for long-run *and* short-run problems, by all the other leaders, Say and Malthus in particular. Here the demand for labor may be represented by a

[37] On the concept of average rate of wages and the objection that has been raised against it, see below, this subsection. As regards the difference between a *theory* of wages in the sense of fundamental analysis of the phenomenon and an equilibrium *theorem* about it, note the analogies with the so-called quantity theory of money and with Ricardo's law of value.

[38] There was indeed some opposition to applying the supply and demand apparatus to labor on the ground that it involved treating human beings like commodities—on the Continent, especially, the English 'classics' were sometimes indicted for this outrage to human dignity. Nothing of the sort is, of course, involved in this application of the concepts of supply and demand. It should be observed, however, that there was occasionally more in this than a rather cheap emotionalism: the 'commodity labor' does present peculiarities that are relevant even for the most matter-of-fact analysis.

[39] This was pointed out by Barton (see below, subsec. h). Since an increase in real (in our sense) per capita wage incomes does not increase the birth rate immediately; since it takes a prolonged spell of high per capita wage income to produce a quantitatively significant effect; and, finally, since during so long a time new standards of life develop, the case for the 'classic' long-run theory of wages is really much worse than indicated in the text.

schedule that simply describes the quantity of labor taken by employers at varying wage rates. Say's notion of demand for and supply of services of labor *implies* this. But a demand schedule of this kind was made explicit and was actually drawn by Fleeming Jenkin.[40] And such a demand schedule, in turn, *implies* an embryonic marginal productivity theory. The latter, though worked out by Longfield and von Thünen within the period, remained in abeyance, however, so far as the profession at large is concerned. Hence no more need be said about these beginnings of later wage analysis except that the element of productivity, also, must enter into any complete wage theory (in some shape or other) and therefore should not, per se, be identified with any particular one.

We have, then, this situation before us: in some form, practically all the economists of the period attacked the wage problem by means of a more or less well-understood supply and demand analysis.[41] The element of productivity, not adequately worked out by those who got a hearing, is visible in the picture but only dimly. The foreground is dominated by two particular results that may be derived from a supply and demand analysis on the insertion of certain additional factual hypotheses ('restrictions'): the minimum-of-existence theorem as regards longest-run normals and the wage-fund doctrine as regards shorter-run deviations.

The minimum-of-existence theorem, as we know, was an essential part of the teaching of Quesnay and of Turgot. It was, as we also know, handled with care by A. Smith—with so much care in fact that there was not a great deal left of it. Malthus' *Essay* in its original form put, however, a different face upon the matter, though in the later editions of the *Essay* and in the *Principles* we find qualifications that should have produced, but did not produce, recantation. But for Ricardo a strict formulation of the tendency of wages toward 'that price which is necessary to enable the labourers . . . to subsist and to perpetuate their race, without either increase or diminution' (*Principles*, ch. 5), enforced by an equally strict acceptance of Malthus' law of population, is really required or else the long-run level of wages becomes indeterminate. The quotation shows that, at least by 1817,[42] Ricardo was

[40] Fleeming Jenkin's papers on 'Trade Unions' and 'The Graphic Representation of the Laws of Supply and Demand and their Application to Labour' appeared in 1868 and 1870, London School Reprint, 1931. His demand function (x being price, D the quantity bought at that price, and A a constant, takes the form: $D = f(A + \frac{1}{x})$.

[41] This also holds for Marx, for the proposition that wages tend to equal the value of labor power, which in turn is identical with the labor embodied in it, implies the play of supply and demand. Of course, Marx's theory of wages does not consist in this proposition only. On the contrary, it forms an extremely complex whole which covers practically all the aspects of the wage phenomenon and includes careful investigations into the deviation of wages from the level determined by the 'value' of labor, especially into the cyclical deviations. This whole must be pieced together from many parts of his writings and cannot be reconstructed here.

[42] There is nothing to correspond to the sentence quoted in the *Essay on the Influence of a Low Price of Corn on the Profits of Stock* (1815).

aware of this, but the subsequent argument of his chapter on wages also shows that he knew the necessary theorem to be untenable. Following Torrens,[43] he substituted for the 'physical minimum' what it became usual, later on, to call the 'social minimum of existence,' which in Torrens' words means 'such a quantity of the necessaries and comforts of life, as, from the nature of the climate and the habits of the country, are necessary to support the labourer. . .' A little reflection will show that this amounts to accepting customary wages as an institutional datum. This is always possible: anything can be labeled as a datum, which simply means that we give up the hunt for a purely economic explanation of whatever it is we so describe.[44] And it seems more realistic to look upon the 'classic' long-run wage 'theory' in this light rather than in the light of the physical-minimum theorem, which they disavowed themselves and which is of little importance anyhow, owing to the fact that in the matter of wages a huge 'short run' practically replaced the long run.

As stated, the supply and demand apparatus actually used by the English 'classics' for the treatment of wage problems was of a peculiar kind, traditionally described as the wage-fund doctrine.[45] For the sake of simplicity, we shall neglect the supply of and the demand for labor that play in the income sphere —the supply of and demand for directly consumed services of servants, teachers, and so on—and confine ourselves to the supply of and demand for industrial labor (this, of course, in the widest sense: all labor from the employment of which 'profit is expected' as A. Smith put it) as if there were no other employments. Further, we follow 'classic' practice in assuming that, at any given point of time, there is always the given supply of labor represented by a given number of laborers: there is no shifting between laborers and self-employed, no variation in the age at which laborers enter or leave the labor market, no change in hours per day or week, and, except for a qualification to be inserted later, no reserve price below which laborers refuse to accept employment. Without doubt, these simplifications, even though not always strictly adhered to, helped to discredit the wage-fund doctrine. But all that matters to us is that they are not more than simplifications that could be dropped without great difficulty. We then have not a supply *schedule* of labor, but only a given quantity supplied and, so we have assumed, supplied unconditionally for a 'short run' of at least fifteen years. Demand is represented in the wage-fund theory in a somewhat unusual manner, namely, by in-

43 *Essay on the External Corn Trade* . . . (1815; pp. 58-63).

44 There are limitations to this, of course: if we have an economically determined system and then decide to make a datum of some of its variables, we must drop an equal number of equilibrium conditions or else the system becomes overdetermined.

45 Note, however, (1) that, as we have seen in our discussion of Say's law, the supply and demand apparatus does not admit of unqualified application to a commodity as important as labor, whose variations in price influence all social aggregates; and (2) that the wage-fund doctrine may be considered as a clumsy attempt to take account of this.

dicating a 'sum in real terms' [46]—wage goods, means of subsistence, variable capital [47]—that capitalists have decided to spend on labor. This 'demand,' also, is no schedule, at any given moment, *but a given quantity*. And again—as with workers on the supply side who have no reserve price *below* which they refuse to go—there is no price of labor *beyond* which 'capitalists' will refuse to go: having decided what to reserve for their own consumption, they cannot, *given this decision*, spend more than that sum (the wage fund); and, *never allowing capital to be idle*, they (normally) will not spend less.[48]

Since the quantity of labor supplied is given at each moment, since the 'sum' to be spent on it is also given—from considerations that are, as it were, behind the scene—at each moment, and since in equilibrium the quantity of labor demanded must be equal to quantity of labor supplied, we have an equation that will uniquely determine a magnitude that is called the average wage rate.[49] If actual wages are fixed above this rate, there is unemployment; if below it, unsatisfied demand for labor. We shall refer to this as the short-run wage-fund theory. But nobody held, of course, that the supply of labor and the wage fund were actually given constants. On the contrary, propositions about their variation over time were not only a part, but the most important part, of the doctrine. The factor that governed the labor supply was either the Malthusian law or else simply the 'habits' of the working class. The factor that governed the variation of the wage fund, hence of demand, was

[46] This may be understood either in our own sense, namely in the sense of a monetary magnitude corrected by a cost of living index, or in the Ricardian sense of labor embodied in the wage goods. The 'classics' meant sometimes the one and sometimes the other. This has given rise to misunderstandings. Stuart Wood ('A Critique of Wages Theories,' *Annals of the American Academy of Political and Social Science*, 1890) accused the 'classics' of having held that 'no assiduity on the part of the laborers, no improvement in production could raise wages,' i.e. increase the wage fund. Sometimes they did hold this (except that improvements in the production of wage goods will raise profits, hence increase savings and in consequence also the wage fund) but only in the Ricardian sense and not in any sense in which it would be wrong to do so.

[47] Always keep in mind that Marx's variable capital is exactly the same as the 'bourgeois' wage fund.

[48] Observe: this is an equilibrium proposition, for 'capitalists' *could* spend more or less; only if they did they would not be satisfied with the result, hence not be in equilibrium. But it is easy to understand that, with the 'classics' ' sloppiness of both thought and exposition, this did not stand out as it should have, even to themselves, let alone to opponents. Note the analogy of this situation with the situation of the quantity theory of money, the more imperfect formulations of which also read as if it were assumed that people *must* spend, on consumers' goods or investment, every penny they get hold of.

[49] The 'classics' were not blind to the problems involved in speaking of an average wage rate; witness their concern with the differences of wage rates in different employments. Nevertheless, in fundamental wage theory they used the concept of average wage rate quite uncritically. In order not to increase our difficulties, we shall do the same, assuming that there is one kind and quality of labor only, equally remunerated in all occupations. It is important to note in defense of this 'classic' practice that it does not involve anything that could be called an error.

saving. Therefore, given the productive efficiency of the economic process, the course over time of real wage rates (in our sense) and of the per capita real income of the working class depends upon the latter's rate of propagation and upon the community's rate of saving.[50] We shall refer to this as the long-run wage-fund theory.

We may now combine the argument above with what we have found out in previous sections about the notion of the wage fund. In doing so we shall add or recall the necessary minimum of historical references. The basis of the wage-fund doctrine is the proposition that (industrial) wages are 'advanced' from capital. This fundamental proposition goes far back, at least to Cantillon and Quesnay. He who accepts it cannot oppose the wage-fund doctrine, root and branch, however much fault he may find with details, simplifications, or applications. For the long-run wage-fund theory it is equally important that these advances should depend upon saving as their source: this point was driven home by Turgot and A. Smith.[51] We still naturally credit Malthus with contributing to the long-run wage-fund theory 'his' law of population, but it is only haziness about what this theory really says that has induced some historians to list him as a wage-fund theorist in any other respect.[52]

[50] The short-run wage-fund theory, so we have seen, is really no supply and demand theory at all in the usual sense in which this means operating with supply and demand *schedules*. But the long-run analysis above might be couched in terms of such schedules. I shall only indicate how this could be done: labor supply, by virtue of the Malthusian law, could be represented as a function of real (in our sense) wage rates; the problem is to represent the quantities of labor that 'capitalists' demand, also as a function of real wage rates. Since, at any moment, these wage rates depend on the size of the wage fund, since this wage fund's variations are governed by the rate of saving, since, given everybody's propensity to save (Mill's 'effectual desire of accumulation'), savings depend (mainly) on 'capitalists'' incomes, hence on 'profits'; and since according to Ricardo, profits depend upon wages . . . and so on. Not that I think much of this construction. But it has two virtues. First, it brings out an aspect of the wage-fund theory—the dependence of future wages on present profits—which is as important as it is apt to be unpopular and which was no doubt very much in the minds of the wage-fund theorists. Second, it clears up a matter that might bother the careful student. The wage-fund theory has sometimes been rendered by saying that, according to it, the elasticity of expenditure on labor with respect to wage rates is zero (elasticity of demand for labor equal to one). This statement is not felicitous. In the long run it is not true, and in the short run it is misleading.

[51] A. Smith was the first, I think, to speak of 'funds destined for the maintenance of labour.' This phrase was copied by many sponsors of the wage-fund doctrine and gave much offense to its opponents, since it seems to beg the question. J. S. Mill's recantation (described below) issued in the statement that there is no such fund that is 'destined' once for all for the maintenance of labor. But if the objection was that the 'classics' simply postulated the existence of this fund without investigating how it was determined, then there was no point to the objection. For funds are, in the 'classic' theory, 'destined' for the maintenance of productive labor by the decision of the saver and thus are determined if annual savings are.

[52] Thus, Malthus' statement in the *Essay on Population*, that a poor man, if he receive an additional sum of money, while total output of the country remains the

Ricardo, in his chapter on wages, emphasized strongly enough that it is increase in capital that carries the market rate of wages above the natural rate 'for an indefinite period.' In as much as in this chapter he defined capital so as to include 'food, clothing, raw materials, etc.' he may be credited with having introduced another element that is, according to our interpretation, characteristic of both the short-run and the long-run wage-fund doctrine, namely, the assumption that we can treat the ratio between wage and non-wage capital as constant on the understanding that its variation is to be treated apart.[53]

Thus, though adding *edge* here and there, he did not in this respect really go beyond A. Smith. But he did something else. He infected his followers with the Ricardian Vice, that is, with the habit of establishing simple relations between aggregates that then acquire a spurious halo of causal importance, whereas all the really important (and, unfortunately, complicated) things are being bundled away in or behind these aggregates. Thus, James Mill declared, as Mrs. Marcet had done before both him and Ricardo: 'Universally, then, we may affirm, other things remaining the same, that if the ratio which capital and population bear to one another remains the same, wages will remain the same' (*Elements*, ch. 2, § 2).[54] Had somebody objected that the quantity of labor demanded, hence the wage, may obviously vary even if the sum *available* for paying wages remain constant—or something of the kind—he would have replied: 'Oh yes, but we have settled all that behind the scenes just as we have determined that sum previously. As we have shaped our model, there are no other Proximate Causes of the wage rate but that ratio. Everything else acts through them only. For instance, fertility of the soil has nothing to do with the real wages at which labor can be employed. *Of course*, it affords the means of rapidly accumulating capital and this will

same, cannot acquire a larger share in this output without diminishing the share of others, has been held to imply the wage-fund doctrine! That, from first to last, he used the Smithian phrase—funds specifically destined for the maintenance of labor—evidently proves nothing.

[53] Of course, we may also interpret him to the effect that he resolved *all* advances into advances to labor or, which is the same thing, that he resolved the whole of capital into wage capital. J. S. Mill (*Principles*, Book II, ch. 15, § 6) elaborated this explicitly. According to this interpretation, Ricardo would be still more definitely a forerunner of Jevons, Böhm-Bawerk, Taussig, and Wicksell than he is according to our own. But I feel unable to reconcile this with the text of his chapter on wages. In any case, we should have to say—and this is in fact an acceptable compromise—that the larger conception involved in a resolution of non-wage capital into wage capital, while present at the back of his mind, did not influence his analysis of wages but that, even so, Böhm-Bawerk's aversion to having the 'classic' wage-fund theory confused with his own was justified. That Ricardo never co-ordinated the capital theory of his first chapter, Section 4, with the wage-fund theory of his chapter on wages is abundantly clear from the fact that neither he nor his followers ever referred their wage fund to a variable period of time.

[54] And this though he had defined capital so as to *exclude* the 'subsistence or consumption of the labourer.'

of course raise wages in the future. But, *formally*, this does not constitute any objection to my theory—going a step further and keeping population constant, we even can say that wages depend upon capital.'

McCulloch then established himself as the leading exponent of the wage-fund doctrine.[55] But he added nothing. Torrens[56] did add something, though this should have been obvious from the first, namely, that the wage-fund theories offer no reason for denying that a combination of the whole working force can raise wages so as to swallow up not only profits but also depreciation allowances.[57] J. S. Mill's case is quite different. By emphasizing the sequence-analysis aspect of the wage-fund doctrine, he in fact made a point for it and, considering the general level of his technique, there is little to object to in his use of this aggregate that stands, as a sort of intermediate datum, for processes that his technique did not enable him to analyze more satisfactorily. For we must never forget: not only was the wage-fund doctrine, properly stated, not 'wrong' logically; not only did it emphasize, though too narrowly, certain important aspects of the wage problem; but, in addition to this, it was an analytic tool that, within the analytic structure of its time, was distinctly useful, and there is no sense in criticizing it *in abstracto*, that is, without reference to the general-value theory of its time. Nor was there any need for fighting it except in one way: by proffering better tools and letting this one peacefully rust away.

All the more surprising must seem J. S. Mill's 'recantation.' He paid no attention to the attacks, if he knew of them, by Jones and Longe.[58] But in response to the elaborate restatement of the latter's arguments by William Thornton, he wrote a review article that did not indeed spell complete surrender[59] and, in particular, did not induce him to change any of those pas-

[55] His first statement of it, never substantially altered, occurs in his *Encyclopaedia Britannica* article 'Political Economy' (1823), his second in the *Principles* (1825). His *Essay on . . . Wages* was published in 1826, and an enlarged edition under the title of *Treatise on Wages* in 1854.

[56] *On Wages and Combinations* (1834). I do not stay to notice Senior's insignificant contribution.

[57] Observe, however, that James Mill could have replied: 'Oh no. It is not the combination that effects this but the temporary increase it enforces in the funds destined for the maintenance of labor: it is only by influencing these that the combination has any effect at all.' It is perhaps unnecessary to point to modern argument of the same nature.

[58] Richard Jones (*Literary Remains*, publ. 1859) accepted the wage-fund doctrine fully for wages that are being paid out by modern business, but he denied, even then, that this was the only important case. This 'historical' objection received little credit at the time but all the more later on when opposition to the English 'classics' came to be in itself a title to praise. F. D. Longe, *A Refutation of the Wage-Fund Theory . . .* (1866; reprint in Professor Hollander's series, 1904). Other contemporaneous attacks do not present any additional points of interest.

[59] William T. Thornton, *On Labour . . .* (1869). The word Restatement is to denote a fact but is not to insinuate a charge of plagiarism, though Longe did complain that neither Thornton nor Mill mentioned him—inferring (the optimist!) from his

sages—for example, the Fourth Proposition on Capital—that ought to go out if the wage fund does. But it surrendered a phrase, which was all the public took in. The Longe-Thornton argument, as accepted by J. S. Mill, did not amount to more [60] than denying that there exists any definite quantity of wage goods [61] that 'must' under any circumstances go to labor. If, after all that has been explained above, we are not to dismiss this argument as a childish misunderstanding—which is how it appeared to Cairnes [62]—we must interpret it to mean that there is little point in inserting aggregate wages as a 'proximate cause' that, as such, plays a role of its own. But if that was all, why all the fuss about this point of theoretical detail and all the excitement about Mill's alleged recantation?

Well, it was not all so far as the public—even the professional public—was concerned. A thing had happened that happens so frequently in our field. The public had caught hold of the surface meaning of a word and this was all it was interested in. Fund—how definite that sounds! Labor must get it and cannot ever get more! Popular writers, if of a certain color, made this mean that raising wages is 'scientifically impossible.' Popular writers, if of another color, foamed with indignation at so vile an attempt to thwart labor's hopes. How absurd all this was should be obvious.[63] No less obvious should it be

---

having sent his pamphlet to Mill that the latter had read it. Moreover, though Longe anticipated the substance of Thornton's criticism of the wage-fund theory, the latter's book contained several points that were new. Outstanding among them is his emphasis on *expected* consumers' demand as the true guide of the producers. In view of the importance the element of expectations has gained of late, Thornton's book must be allocated a place in the history of analysis that is quite independent of the particular wage-fund issue. J. S. Mill's review article appeared in the *Fortnightly Review*, May 1869, and was, besides being a remarkable display of good feeling in the face of what other men would have taken as a provocation, a gentle correction of superficial misunderstandings rather than a retraction.

[60] Longe and Thornton brought forth also other criticisms than the one we are going to notice. They criticized, e.g., the concept of an average rate of wages and the way in which the wage-fund theory handled the supply and demand apparatus. There is something in these other criticisms but they could all be met without giving up the theory itself and do not go to the bottom of the issue.

[61] Both Longe and Thornton blur the issue—and incidentally betray inadequate grasp of the 'classic' analysis—by speaking of 'money' without making sure that this money stands for physical goods. This is even more true of H. D. Macleod's argument in *Elements of Political Economy* (1858; 3rd ed., *Elements of Economics*, 2 vols., 1881-6).

[62] Cairnes, *Leading Principles*, Part II, ch. 1, especially pp. 214 et seq. But (p. 186) he interpreted the wage fund in a way that left little to defend. This does not apply, however, to his views on Thornton's attack upon Supply and Demand.

[63] But let me repeat: first, that the wage-fund theory implies nothing of the sort; second, that, if it did imply it, it would still be irrelevant to 99 per cent of all wage struggles, in which claims to higher wages are rationalized by arguments that have nothing to do with any equilibrium rate of wages, but contend that, for reasons such as friction or weak bargaining power, workers do not get these equilibrium wages.

that the 'practical' diagnosis behind most of the wage-fund theorizing, even if coarsened for the benefit of the public, is not more than common sense: it makes (real) wage rates and (real) wage income dependent upon the efficiency of the productive process, 'habits' (high or low customary standard of living and, in connection with this, rate of propagation), free trade in food and other necessaries, and the rate of saving—all of which was no doubt tailored to the prevailing English situation but on the whole quite reasonable.[64] If the importance of changes in money wage rates was discounted—as it is being discounted in Keynesian economics—this was but an additional merit. And so were such warnings as may be found in it against irresponsible 'wage policies.' J. S. Mill did not renounce any warnings he had uttered himself. Still there it was—the first English economist of the age had disavowed the hateful scarecrow.

But that emotionalism and the not less absurd belief that 'theories' guide policy [65] lent zest and glamour to what on its merits should have been a dry-as-dust discussion on a technical point. This had its repercussions on scientific literature. In England and the United States, killing the wage-fund 'theory' became a favorite sport: the names of F. A. Walker and H. Sidgwick suffice to illustrate this. On the Continent, especially in Germany, Hermann's opinion—quite all right in itself, but a mistake if framed as an objection—prevailed on the whole: though Rau's textbook (in its 8th ed., 1868) upheld the wage-fund doctrine as it did other heirlooms, Roscher (1854) followed Hermann as did Roesler in his fairly influential history of wage theories and L. Brentano.[66]

(g) *Rent.* Whereas the so-called wage theories that were then current did not invoke different explanatory principles but were nothing but more or less valuable parts of a more comprehensive theory of 'wages and capital' that failed to mature, the period's explanations of the rent of land (generalized into the rent of natural agents) really were different theories based upon different principles. We shall refer to them as the monopoly theory, the productivity theory, and the diminishing-return theory. This is not to deny the presence of a unifying principle. Ricardo himself began his discussion of the subject by defining rent as 'that portion of the produce of the earth which is paid to the landlord for the use of the original and indestructible powers of the soil' [67] (*Principles,* ch. 2), and J. S. Mill started his by recalling the triad

[64] The only element in this that is really inacceptable to the modern radical is the relation between wages and saving.

[65] In the pages of the *American Economic Review* there has been an interesting discussion concerning the actual influence of the wage-fund theory on popular thought and political action.

[66] C. F. H. Roesler, *Zur Kritik der Lehre vom Arbeitslohn* (1861). Lujo Brentano, 'Die Lehre von den Lohnsteigerungen,' *Jahrbücher für Nationalökonomie* (1871).

[67] Let us briefly note that the writers of the period still struggled with the problem of identifying the phenomenon to be explained. A. Smith, as Ricardo noticed, had been vague on the subject and had not always clearly distinguished between pure rent and the total income from the ownership of land, which also includes the return from

of the requisites of production, which comes to the same thing (*Principles*, Book II, ch. 16). This points toward supply and demand—the principle that not only unifies those three theories but also assimilates rent with all other kinds of incomes generated by a stationary business process. But the great majority of economists did not take this route so that it is historically more realistic to speak of three distinct theories after all.

The monopoly theory, espoused by A. Smith,[68] counted adherents, then as always, among politicians and pamphleteers. But its role in the scientific literature was not nearly so important as it seems to be, at first sight, owing to the frequent occurrences of the term monopoly in this connection. The examples of Senior and J. S. Mill will suffice to show this: when we analyze their use of the term, we discover immediately that they did not mean to assert that landowners formed cartels and that the services of land were priced—as a general rule; there is of course the unique mine or vineyard—according to the rules of monopoly theory. All they meant was that rent constitutes a case of pricing 'costless' things that exist in definitely limited quantities, which their defective theory of price led them to identify with the genuine monopoly case. J. S. Mill even wrote of a 'monopolized' thing among the holders of which there is 'competition' (Book II, ch. 16, § 2); and both Mill and Senior really adopted, though quite illogically, the diminishing-return theory to be discussed presently. The reader may well ask whether anyone actually held a monopoly theory of rent that was more than an agitatorial phrase, in view of the fact that monopoly that may be present in any case of pricing is constitutionally incapable of explaining the nature of a return. The writer who, so far as I have been able to make out, came nearest to doing so was T. P. Thompson.[69]

---

improvements, such as drainage, fencing, and the like—what Marshall was to call quasi-rent. The distinction, clearly indicated by A. Smith, established itself quickly however. (Thünen called the total income from land *Gutsrente* and the pure rent *Grundrente*.) Another question arose concerning exhaustible natural agents such as mines, return from which Ricardo's definition excludes. But the similarity of the two cases being easily recognized, no trouble arose about that (*Principles*, ch. 3). The short-run similarity between rent in this sense and returns from any appliance, the quantity of which cannot be changed within the time span that constitutes the short run was, however, not clearly seen before Marshall, and this did entail some consequences of importance: whoever sees this similarity and, hence, that in the short run there is no difference between rent and quasi-rent, is bound, sooner or later, to ask himself whether the yield of physical capital goods is really the same thing as interest.

[68] But after having interpreted the rent of land as a monopoly gain, A. Smith declared that rent 'enters into the composition of the price of commodities in a different way from wages and profits. High or low wages and profit are the cause of high or low price; high or low rent is the effect of it' (*Wealth*, Book I, ch. 11). He does not seem to have observed that this contradicts his monopoly theory of rent for, if rent were a monopoly gain, it would enter into price. However, this blundering sentence may have given a clue to Ricardo, with whose analysis it agrees much better than with Smith's.

[69] Thomas Perronet Thompson, *The True Theory of Rent* (1826), an anti-corn-law pamphlet. I wish I had space to say something on this vital and most interesting man—

The diminishing-return theory (or as we could also call it, the differential-cost theory), as everybody knows, is associated with the name of Ricardo, who made such a success of it that it survived into the twentieth century. It was part of the great Ricardian detour [70] for it was essential to Ricardo's analytic pattern as a device for eliminating the land factor from the value problem (see above, sec. 2).[71] Actually, of course, rent enters or else does not 'enter into prices' in exactly the same sense in which the one proposition or the other is true of wages.[72] Nevertheless, Ricardo achieved his purpose of excluding rent from the price (value) problem in this way. In practice, firms operate under different cost conditions—an observation which then as now was part of the economics of the man in the street—there are 'low-cost' and 'high-cost' firms. We may, of course, array them in ascending order of costs, and we further observe without difficulty that, in a state of perfect equilibrium and perfect competition, price cannot be lower and is not likely to be much higher than the average costs of the highest-cost firm. This is what Ricardo meant when he said sometimes, for example, in Chapter 27 of the *Principles*, that the 'real value of a commodity is regulated . . . by the real difficulties encountered by that producer who is least favoured.' [73] Referring to this, espe-

---

a type who could not be left out of any sociology of nineteenth-century England. The memoir by C. W. Thompson (1869), though not a great performance, is worth reading.

[70] The detour character of Ricardo's work shows in this instance with particular clarity. For he actually did begin with the price 'which is paid . . . for the use of the . . . powers of the soil,' a definition that contains all that is needed for a satisfactory theory of rent, and then, before our eyes, turns away from the open road and embarks upon his detour.

[71] J. S. Mill and Marx also wished to eliminate the land factor from the value problem. But while this was entirely unnecessary for Mill's set-up—as he would have been bound to see had he but stopped to think out the implication of his own ideas, it was as necessary for Marx's as it was for Ricardo's. What Marx actually did was to merge rent with profit into the homogeneous pool of surplus value, and then, at one remove from the fundamentals of distribution, let landlords and 'capitalists' fight it out. This enabled him—as mere decision to do so enabled J. S. Mill—to neglect the existence of rent in his basic analysis of value. On Rodbertus' attempt to rationalize the way in which rent is determined, see above, ch. 4, sec. 5.

[72] J. S. Mill's attempt to get round this (Book II, ch. 16, § 6) is a most instructive example of a type of specious reasoning by which we often delude ourselves when defending a proposition that, from habit, we have come to believe needs no defense at all. The case is so instructive, first, because J. S. Mill erroneously thought that he needed the proposition that rent does not enter into prices and, second, because his argument is ingenious and, at first sight, convincing. He actually arrived at the conclusion that 'rent does not really form any part of the *expenses* [my italics] of production, or of the advances of the capitalist.' And this patent absurdity is coolly upheld on the ground that 'whoever cultivates land, paying a rent for it, gets in return for his rent an instrument of superior power to other instruments of the same kind,' i.e. he enjoys a differential advantage which the payment of rent does not more than compensate!

[73] There is no contradiction between this and A. Smith's apparently opposite opinion that it is the lowest-cost firm that tends to regulate price. For A. Smith thought of the

cially in Chapter 2, he recognized that different portions of the output of a single firm may also be produced at different costs, for example, if produced on plots of different fertility; that these portions too may be arrayed in ascending order of their costs; [74] and that in a state of perfect equilibrium and perfect competition, the highest of these costs will tend to equal price. Finally, he generalized this to include the logically heterogeneous case where it is not possible to speak of different costs of the different portions of any given total output, and where every part of this output costs just as much as every other part, but where it is still possible to *allocate* to each successive increment of output the increase in the cost of total output which must be incurred in order to produce it.[75] Whenever we have decreasing returns in any or all of these senses, there is always [76] an element of product that is being produced without any differential advantages and for which it is therefore tautologically true that its producer does not pay for differential advantages and that payments for *intramarginal* advantages do not enter into *marginal* expenses of production.[77] Now, most of these advantages are essentially temporary—a superior type of machine tends to displace inferior types—and others are linked to persons. There are no permanent differential advantages that are linked to

process by which more progressive firms crowd out less efficient ones and for a time force them to sell at losses. Ricardo described an equilibrium state.

[74] The resulting 'curve' has been called Particular Expenses Curve by A. Marshall (*Principles*, p. 521).

[75] This is as far as Ricardo got. That is to say, we may attribute to him—as we may to other writers of the period such as Rooke—a conception of marginal cost that differs from the modern conception only in technique. But we should not, as some interpreters do, attribute to him—or to any other writers of the period except Longfield and Thünen—an understanding of the principles of marginal productivity analysis: his theory of rent, far from amounting to a recognition of these principles in a particular case, really amounts to a denial of them. This has been obscured by the fact that some later marginal productivity theorists, in particular J. B. Clark, represented their theory as an outgrowth of Ricardo's theory of rent and may have reached their view from a critical elaboration of the latter. Some spoke of a Law of Three Rents without making it clear, perhaps without realizing, that they were not generalizing Ricardo's schema but upsetting it. It cannot be objected that marginal cost and marginal product are logically related and that, therefore, he who understands the one also understands the other. But this is not so: understanding a concept that implies another does not imply understanding the latter, and, to a great part, advance in theoretical analysis precisely consists in elaborating implications of older thought that had not been seen or not clearly seen before. Any doubt or confusion that may exist in the reader's mind on the subject could best be cleared up by perusal of Longfield's *Lectures*.

[76] This presupposes the ordinary assumptions that every pure theory makes, continuity of schedules and absence of institutional inhibitions among others. Many objections that were raised against the West-Ricardo theory of rent did and do rest on nothing but a failure of the critic to understand what pure theory is.

[77] Since these marginal expenses—under usual assumptions—equal price, it is therefore quite true that payments for intramarginal advantages do not enter into price, which is the sense in which A. Marshall upheld the Ricardian proposition—i.e. as an empty truism.

material factors except the differential advantages of location and fertility of land[78] (and other natural agents). And it must have occurred to Ricardo that here was his opportunity to get rid of the element of rent that disturbed his labor-quantity theory of value. From the structure of his argument in Chapter 2 of the *Principles*,[79] it is perfectly clear that it was location and differential fertility of different plots of which Ricardo thought primarily, and that the case of decreasing effects of successive applications of equal 'doses' of labor to the same plot was, for him, a matter of secondary importance and was never fully absorbed into his system, though it not only came in usefully for the purpose of meeting objections but also was necessary in order to make his argument complete.

There is nothing logically wrong with this device. If we do insist on a labor-quantity conception of value, or even on a theory of value that rests on real cost in the sense of disutility and abstinence, and accordingly wish to eliminate requisites of production that are costless in this sense, the device does its duty.[80] But it is not an explanation of the rent of natural agents, but only a substitute for one, which carries meaning only within that theoretical set-up and is nothing but an obstacle to the recognition of important symmetries within any other. However, instead of realizing this and forgetting about it, most economists throughout the nineteenth century treated what soon became known as the Ricardian Theory of Rent as if it had content

[78] Elaborating suggestions of Ricardo (see especially *Principles*, ch. 14), J. S. Mill wrote a sketchy but suggestive paragraph on urban rent (*Principles*, Book III, ch. 5, § 3) that was to be developed by Edgeworth.

[79] Chs. 18 ('Poor Rates') and 32 ('Mr. Malthus's Opinions on Rent'), also his *Letters to Malthus* and *Notes on Malthus' Principles*, are essential complements to ch. 2, and Ricardo's views on rent cannot be fully understood without this additional material. Perusal of it, however, strengthens the impression that emphasis upon the case in which payment of rent is associated with the different effects of equal 'doses' of other factors successively applied to the same plot of land was the result of discussion and his own further thought rather than a ground-floor idea. Even in ch. 2 the passages on this case read like an insertion into an argument that did not originally contain them. This is why superficial readers so often raised the objection that Ricardo's theory postulates the existence of rentless land.

[80] It should not be added, however, that the diminishing-returns theory of rent has the additional advantage of bringing out certain properties of the incomes from the ownership of natural agents that are important for many purposes such as taxation. For these properties can be stated just as well from the standpoint of any other theory of these incomes, such as the marginal productivity theory. It cannot be too often repeated, in particular, that the marginal productivity of an agent that exists independently of any activity of its owner proves nothing for the income of this owner and is, therefore, in itself of no value for purposes of apologetics, though the theory has often been misunderstood in this sense. *Vice versa*, the Ricardian theory of rent is neither necessary nor sufficient for an attack upon the landed interest and it is nonsense to maintain, as A. Held has averred, that we must explain it by the hatred that Ricardo was supposed to harbor for the landowning class.

irrespective of that set-up.[81] Thus, a pointless discussion of its truth or falsity grew to be a standard topic of the economic periodicals of the time. Admirers not only were in a majority but in general also had the better of the argument. For the objections that were raised rested mostly on misunderstandings, which J. S. Mill's standard exposition [82] disposed of with ease. Some of them —such as those of Carey or R. Jones [83]—are interesting examples of typical errors that are again and again committed by would-be theorists who have disdained to learn the art of theorizing. The reader will find what he may need in J. S. Mill and in Cannan.[84]

Requisiteness and scarcity [85] of natural agents being all that is necessary in order to explain the phenomenon of rent, we might expect to find, at least among votaries of the triad of factors of production, vigorous assertion of a

[81] It might be objected that Anderson (see above, Part II, ch. 5, sec. 2) had taught that theory without at the same time anticipating any other part of the Ricardian system. But his teaching on rent is best conveyed by the phrases that rent is a premium paid for the privilege of using superior land and that its payment equalizes the profits of farmers tilling land of different quality. But they point toward a productivity explanation: one pays more for good than for bad land exactly as one pays more for a good than for a bad workman; and competition of capitals enforces that equalization exactly in the same way in both cases. Let us note in passing that J. S. Mill, while denying the allegation that Ricardo made the *cultivation* of inferior land the cause of the payment of rent on the superior, tried to mend the case by asserting instead that it was the necessity of cultivating the inferior land that causes rent to be paid (Book II, ch. 16, § 5). But this is not true either; at least it is not more true than to say that it is the necessity of employing inferior workmen that is the cause of the higher wages of the superior ones.

[82] As a consequence of his immature systematization that was due to the hurry in which his *Principles* was written, Mill impaired his treatment of the subject by dealing with it twice in two far distant chapters: Book II, ch. 16 and Book III, ch. 5. These two chapters are entirely on Ricardian lines, more so than are any others. This is another instance of Mill's failure to see the implications of his own theoretical insight. However, he did glance in passing at cases in which rent constitutes an element of cost of the opportunity-cost type and even admitted that rent is an element of cost when it results from a scarcity value (*Principles*, Book III, ch. 6, prop. IX), without realizing the damaging nature of these concessions that give the whole case away.

[83] R. Jones, *An Essay on the Distribution of Wealth* (1831), of which only Part I, 'On Rent,' was completed.

[84] Did space permit, I should, however, advert to a class of objections that arose from Ricardo's and his followers' carelessness. They spoke of 'doses' of capital and labor that were being applied to land—the term was introduced by James Mill—without making any attempt at dealing with the problems incident to the composition of these doses. Nor did they take account of the difficulty that land cannot be satisfactorily graded as to fertility without reference to given uses. And they committed many other peccadillos. Objections of this kind are not decisive. But neither are they mistaken. We cannot stay, however.

[85] Scarcity, it should be observed, does not imply decreasing returns. Rent would be paid if successive 'doses' of capital yielded increasing quantities of product up to the *n*th dose and nothing at all from the *n*th on.

productivity theory of rent. But, as we have seen on other occasions, mere recognition of the element of productivity does not help us much unless it is streamlined by the notion of *marginal* productivity, exactly as the element of utility will not produce any serviceable theory of price unless streamlined by the notion of marginal utility. A marginal productivity theory was, in fact, presented by Longfield, who not only anticipated the theory that was to win out in the last decades of the nineteenth century, but in addition said practically all that needs to be said from this standpoint on the West-Ricardo theory. Nobody paid much attention, however, and J. B. Say's conception of incomes as prices of productive services—which he himself spoiled by attributing the price of the services of land to the institution of private property in land—also remained sterile for the time being. So great was Ricardo's success that even some writers, who adopted Say's schema in other respects, inserted into it a Ricardian treatment of rent without betraying any symptom of logical discomfort: J. S. Mill himself is the outstanding example and Roscher is another. But application of the supply and demand apparatus, which was being slowly perfected, should have been sufficient to straighten the matter out and to end all doubts as regards such points as whether improvements in agricultural methods of production benefit or injure the landowner's interest. It would be, therefore, a useful exercise for us to analyze the position of Malthus, since he was as prominent among the builders of the Ricardian theory of rent as he was among the builders of the supply and demand apparatus. We cannot, however, go beyond the following comments.[86]

In his *Inquiry* of 1815, Malthus developed a view that looks much like West's and Ricardo's. The latter evidently was of this opinion since he stated in the preface to his *Principles* that Malthus and West 'presented to the world . . . the true doctrine of rent.' But even there we may observe the seeds of the controversy that was to follow.[87] Among other things, Malthus insisted on the proposition that rent is a surplus that we owe to the bounty of nature. Now this clumsy phrase, which has been much misunderstood,[88] adumbrates a productivity explanation of rent. The reason why it was inacceptable for Ricardo was not that it complimented the landlord: his not less clumsy phrases about the 'niggardliness of nature' mean not more than that land is not a free good, a fact that is just as necessary for a productivity explanation as is the bounty. The reason was that this idea was incompatible

[86] Malthus' chief contributions to the pure theory of rent are his *Inquiry into the Nature and Progress of Rent* (1815), ch. 3 of his *Principles*, and his answer to question 3341 in the *Third Report on Emigration* (1827).

[87] For Ricardo's side, see especially ch. 32 of his *Principles* and *Notes on Malthus' 'Principles of Political Economy'* (Hollander and Gregory, ed., 1928). We shall neglect the disagreement between Ricardo and Malthus concerning the relation of the landowners' interests to those of society, which produced nothing worthy of attention.

[88] Some critics saw nothing in it but an attempt at 'justifying' the landlord's income. I cannot see, however, that it improves the case for the landlord if he be represented as intercepting nature's bounty, which is the obvious conclusion for enemies of private property in land to draw.

with his value theory.[89] And so we have after all, in spite of the acknowledgment in Ricardo's preface, a fundamental theoretical difference between the two from the start. Actually, Malthus did not need diminishing returns to account for the emergence of rent. But he did not grasp this clearly and, as was his wont, looked for concrete facts associated with the phenomenon to be described, whether they were essential to it or not. Eventually he produced a mongrel, which was much more vulnerable to Ricardo's rapier than a correct statement need have been, of what he ineffectually strove to express. He even had trouble with rentless land and could not quite assimilate the notion of the rentless last dose of capital. He attached explanatory significance—we sense amusement in Ricardo's comment in the chapter on Malthus' opinions on rent—to the fact that land can produce more than is necessary for the maintenance of the labor employed on it.[90] He was not less sure of the importance of the further fact, already stressed by A. Smith, that agrarian production was peculiar in that it created, as it expanded, additional demand for its products, not in the sense of Say's law, but because increase in food spelled increase in population—which is not true even according to his own (later) views. And so he got the worst of it, although there was a strong case behind all his irrelevancies.[91]

Finally, another range of topics must be touched upon. West and Ricardo looked upon their theory of rent as an explanation of a particular branch of income that goes to a particular class. They did notice in passing, but did not make much of the fact, that the income of this class comprises not only payments 'for the use of the original and indestructible powers of the soil' but also payments for the improvements the landlords have made on it. They might have noticed that, in a short-run that may extend over many decades, payments for these improvements do not display any economically significant differences from those elements of the 'rent' which the farmer pays that may be interpreted as being paid for those 'original' powers. In other words, they might have discovered the phenomenon of quasi-rent. This would not have materially affected their theoretical structure in general or the nature of their rent concept in particular. But other generalizations of this concept did affect

[89] Recall: from the standpoint of a value theory that rests upon 'labor embodied,' neither bounty nor niggardliness of nature can have anything to do with the value of the product; but the idea of an *addition* to product value by something that is not labor would seem from this standpoint particularly objectionable.

[90] It is not without melancholy interest to note how often both in the theory of rent and in the theory of profits this 'argument' recurs in nineteenth-century literature: dozens of authors thought that they were saying something when they gravely pointed to the fact that the productive process produced more than is necessary in order to maintain the labor employed.

[91] Occasionally, however, Malthus made a good point. His view that improvements in agricultural technique affect rent favorably is indeed not truer than is Ricardo's opposite view. But he was right in pointing out in his *Principles* that, this time, Ricardo argued the short-run case (as he did more often than either he or his followers realized), and Ricardo seems to have admitted as much.

its meaning—and were indeed nothing but steps in the inevitable process of disintegration of the original West-Ricardo 'theory' of the rent of land.

We have noticed above the analogy that exists between payments for the services of superior land and payments for the services of superior work. Samuel Bailey was the first to turn this fact into an objection to the West-Ricardo theoretical pattern. He was right, though many later authors, Senior in particular and also J. S. Mill (*Principles*, Book III, ch. 5, § 4), generalized the West-Ricardo concept of rent without polemical intention.[92] There are generalizations that spell additional success for a theory: they enrich and extend, but do not endanger, its original interval of application. But there are others that spell or foreshadow the break-up of the theory: by showing that properties which the theory holds to be peculiar to a given phenomenon are also to be found in others, they destroy its original significance and substitute a new for its old meaning. Generalization of the rent concept was a case of the second kind. By virtue of it, rent, the specific return on unimproved soil, merged into the logically distinct category of Costless Surplus,[93] of which the Rent of Ability, recognized by Mill and put to good use by von Mangoldt, is the most important instance.

(h) *Distributive Shares and Technological Advance.* The study of the nineteenth-century literature on this topic is a tedious task. But it may bring solace to the hearts of those who despair of the value of the technique that developed in the last decades of that century,[94] for the superiority of that tech-

[92] J. S. Mill was no more aware of the implications of this generalization than he was of the dangers that lurked behind his admissions of the opportunity-cost type.

[93] During the period under survey, this meant, primarily, returns that are earned above other people's return without an increase in 'sacrifice' ('real' cost in this sense). But later on it was realized that such a surplus may also be defined in terms of the opportunity-cost analysis. It then means a surplus above what would be necessary in order to draw a service to any particular employment (transference cost). At the moment, we are only concerned with those generalizations that emerged during the period. Reference should, however, be made at once to F. A. Fetter: 'The Passing of the Old Rent Concept,' *Quarterly Journal of Economics*, May 1901.

[94] Some familiarity with the elements of modern technique is in part necessary in order to appreciate the argument of this subsection. The reader finds all he needs for this purpose in J. R. Hicks, *Theory of Wages*, 1932; see especially ch. 6. I wish to point out, however, that in analyzing the effects of factor-saving machinery (no matter whether the factor saved is 'labor,' 'land,' or 'technological capital' itself), we must be careful to distinguish two cases. Technological improvement may impinge upon the productive process from outside, that is to say, through some innovation that revolutionizes the technological horizon of producers (changes their 'production functions'). The 'classic' writers thought exclusively or almost exclusively of this case and hardly every realized—an exception was Barton—that there is another case the effects of which differ substantially from the first: machines may also be introduced that are no novelties to producers and, so far as technological knowledge is concerned, could have been introduced but were not introduced before, because it would not have been profitable to do so. Owing to a change in the relative prices of factors (e.g. an increase in wage rates), their introduction may, however, become profitable. Here we have no change of technological horizons but a change in the combination of factors within

nique—so often called into question—in the solution of practical problems nowhere stands out better than it does in this field. So do, by the same token, the shortcomings of 'classical' analysis. The economists of that period were unable to see the general problem at all: they tried to forge different doctrines for the effects of technological advance on the rent of land and on wages. They had to consider the problem separately, as a semi-independent side issue of the theory of distribution or as something to build onto the latter's main structure instead of solving it on the ground floor of the main structure. We have seen, in fact, that in their analysis of fundamentals they made, and had to make, the assumption that the ratio between wage capital and technological capital is constant and that new savings—this does not apply to Marx, however—are invested in the same ratio. Finally, they were unable to follow the effects of technological advance through the economic system as a whole but picked out bits of them here and there, so that frequently such disjointed elements of what should be a comprehensive theory were marshalled against each other as if they involved different theories.[95] In order to bring this out clearly, we shall confine ourselves to the problem of how technological advance affects the interests of labor [96] and in addition posit this restricted problem in the form in which it posited itself to Ricardo in the famous Chapter 31, 'On Machinery,' which he added to the third edition of his *Principles*, that is, in the form that occurs naturally from the wage-fund standpoint and indeed is an excellent illustration of the wage-fund doctrine, *considered as a method of analysis*. We shall ask: how does the introduction of a newly invented machine [97] affect the size of the wage fund?

Long before the industrial revolution, people realized the obvious fact that machinery often displaces labor. As we have seen above, governments and writers worried about this and labor groups and citizens' guilds fought against machinery, the more so because immediate effects of this kind are concentrated in time and place, whereas the long-run effects on general wealth are much less visible in the short run and much less easy to trace to the machine. The public, too, did not in general look with favor upon machine production because, in addition to being associated with unemployment and child labor, it was then also associated with inferior quality of product. The growing laborist literature [98] voiced those observations and feelings not more strongly than

unchanging production functions. A third case was recognized by A. Smith, namely the case where the introduction of a machine that had been known before becomes profitable as soon as output expands beyond a certain figure.

[95] These shortcomings were not so much due to faulty handling of the 'classic' apparatus of analysis but to deep-seated faults of this apparatus itself. These faults were many. But if we were called upon to name one as more important than others, we should have to name once more the failure of the 'classics' to understand substitution (both of factors and of products) in its full importance.

[96] On the 'classic' theory of the effects of technological advance on the interests of landowners, see above, ch. 6, sec. 6h.

[97] See first footnote of this subsection.

[98] As a typical example, see *Observations on the Use of Machinery in the Manufactures of Great Britain* . . . By a Mechanic, 1817.

did some writers of scientific standing, such as Sismondi,[99] who, mostly, derived from them another argument against saving. Most English economists saw deeper than that and did in this matter exactly the same kind of thing that they did in others, as, for example, in the matter of international trade: preoccupied with what they considered to be fundamental truth and fighting the public's propensity to attend too exclusively to temporary phenomena, they attended too little to temporary phenomena themselves. With the engaging frankness that was justly commended by Marx, Ricardo explained on the first page of his chapter on machinery that he had shared the prevailing view that, barring temporary difficulties of transition,[100] labor-saving machinery had no effect other than to benefit all classes as consumers. Like increase in foreign trade, therefore, the process of mechanization was a matter of welfare—which it was sure to increase—rather than a matter of that value (Ricardian value), with which he was chiefly concerned, except of course that mechanization would reduce the real and the relative values of the products affected by it, a fact to which Ricardo points again and again.[101] The reason why he thought that no (permanent) reduction in wages (total real wages in *our* sense of the word) would be induced by it, was that mechanization would not decrease the wage fund.[102] But then he went on to confess that he had discovered reasons for believing that it would.

Before presenting Ricardo's argument, I shall introduce a book that evidently had more to do with Ricardo's change of mind on the subject of machinery than his reference to it suggests: John Barton's *Observations on the Circumstances which influence the Condition of the Labouring Classes of Society* (1817). It is a remarkable performance and far above the rest of the literature that currently criticized the 'classic' leaders for their lack of realism, actual or supposed. There is even a small element of

[99] French economists of the 'conservative' type, such as de Villeneuve-Bargemont (see above, ch. 4, sec. 4) and L. G. A., Vicomte de Bonald (see *Oeuvres complètes*, ed. J. P. Migne, 1859, vol. II) went still further than Sismondi. But even Sismondi's argument is, so far as its analytic aspects are concerned, nothing short of deplorable in places. See, e.g., his reasoning in *Nouveaux Principes*, vol. I, pp. 375-80, and in 'Du revenu social' in the 1st vol. of the *Études sur l'économie politique* (1837-8).

[100] Marx, with glowing rhetoric, was to point out the terrors that may be and sometimes were covered by that cool phrase. It would have been more to the point, however, if he had pointed out, even though at some sacrifice of rhetoric, that displacement of labor by machines may be temporary so far as the effects of each distinct act of mechanization is concerned, and yet explain permanent presence of unemployment on the assumption that such distinct acts occur often enough. This point should not be overstressed, but a little overstressing of it would have supplied Marx with a theory of permanent unemployment that would have been much less untenable than was his own, besides saving all the trouble and bile he wasted upon the effort to refute what he called the theory of compensation.

[101] It may be noted in passing that the long-run prediction about the course of relative values, which follows from Ricardo's theory of value, constitutes its main factual justification: clearly products that embody less and less labor per unit as time goes on have historically fallen in price, at least relatively to the others.

[102] We see here, clearly and instructively, the effects of Ricardo's general set-up which hid from his eyes any analogy between rent and wages.

truth in the note that Professor Foxwell put on the copy that is in the Kress Library: 'a very able tract. . . Its solid and weighty character contrasts in a marked way with Ricardo's flimsy and unreal speculations' [sic!]. Barton knew better than to object to abstract reasoning per se or to point to facts that seemed to contradict Smith's or Ricardo's *conclusion:* he knew how to reason and to indicate the cause of those discrepancies between theory and facts. Thus his 'reconciliation' of the views of Ricardo and Smith on the subject of the fall in the rate of profits (op. cit. p. 23n.) is as simple as it is ingenious. But we must confine ourselves to the only proposition that is relevant to the point in hand. He denied that demand for labor always and necessarily increases proportionately to the increase in total wealth (capital plus revenue, according to A. Smith) and that it cannot increase for any other reason (as asserted in the Poor-Law Report of the House of Commons, which appeared shortly before the publication of Barton's book).[103] And the reason why he denied it was that annual savings do not necessarily issue in proportional increases in fixed and circulating capital (meaning technological and wage capital) but may increase the one more than the other, according to which of the two is more profitable. He explains correctly that if wage rates rise relatively to commodity prices, 'masters' will try to use as much machinery as possible, whereas in the opposite case they will be induced to hire more hands: here, then, we have a clear perception of the relation of substitutability between capital and labor that improved upon Lauderdale's and anticipated Longfield's but was also ignored by the more influential writers. But though Ricardo did not realize the importance of this principle, he at least accepted the idea that the introduction of machinery into the productive process may injure the interests of manual labor (irrespective of the temporary disturbances that do so in any case) by reducing the total demand for it; and he illustrated this by a numerical example that differs but little from Barton's (op. cit. p. 15).

Ricardo argued like this. A 'capitalist,' who so far has employed a certain number of laborers with a certain amount of 'fixed' capital, decides to introduce a newly invented labor-saving machine and lets part of these laborers produce this machine, which in his balance sheet now stands for part of the wage capital that he used to reproduce, with a profit,[104] year after year before. His motive for doing so is that, since not all firms adopt a new machine simultaneously, a temporary profit is attached to the introduction of the machine. In Ricardo's example, the 'capitalist's' capital remains intact—it neither increases nor decreases in value. *But it has changed its organic composition.* Wage capital has been converted into technological capital—there is now more of the latter and less of the former. When the temporary gain has been eliminated by the competition of other firms who do the same thing, then it is possible that the amount and rate of profit on the total capital will be what they were before the insertion of the machine. Prices of commodities will fall, however, and the manufacturers' wage fund will be permanently

[103] He also denied that 'liberal reward of labour, as it is the effect of increasing wealth, so it is the cause of increasing population.' But into his argument against this we cannot enter here.

[104] In this chapter, Ricardo comes nearer than he does anywhere else to the profit analysis that Marx was to make his own. Nowhere else is their relation so clearly the relation of Professor Ricardo and tutee Marx—though, as may be the case sometimes, neither would have been completely pleased with the other's performance.

decreased and population will have become 'redundant,' which is what Ricardo set out to prove.

Ricardo concluded from this that the opinion prevailing in 'the labouring class, that the employment of machinery is frequently detrimental to their interests, is not founded on prejudice and error, but is conformable to the correct principles of political economy.' It was this sharp-edged pronouncement that monopolized professional attention, reinforced as it was by another passage in the same chapter which affirmed that in cases like the one discussed 'there will necessarily be a diminution in the demand for labour, population will become redundant, and the situation of the labouring classes will be that of distress and poverty.' Friends and foes seem to have seen nothing else and, ever since, Ricardo has stood in doctrinal history as the chief exponent of the view that those statements in fact do seem to express. But, if we take account of the rest of the chapter and bear in mind that it professedly deals with what Ricardo used to call permanent effects, it is clear, first, that they do not follow from the numerical example alluded to and, second, that Ricardo was aware of this and did not mean at all what these statements say. As regards the first point, Ricardo's example covers only part of the course of events that the introduction of the machine sets into motion: his analysis of the case is indeed an example of the method of Comparative Statics, but the second of the two states compared is not a definitive state of equilibrium, for we are not told what happens to the workmen who have lost their jobs, yet they cannot remain unemployed unless we are prepared to violate the assumption that perfect competition and unlimited flexibility of wages prevail. As regards the second point, Ricardo, though in a particularly narrow and inconclusive way, fully recognized that mechanization may increase productive efficiency so greatly 'as not to diminish the gross produce' (gross produce in *his* sense, that is, the *net* national product including wages) in terms of commodities. This amounts to saying that real wage income (in *our* sense) need not fall 'permanently'; and that in any case, the purchasing power of profits and rents being increased by the fall in prices resulting from mechanization, 'it could not fail to follow' that, with constant propensity to save, capitalists and owners of natural agents would fill up the depleted wage fund again by means of increased savings. These admissions (for brevity's sake I neglect others) are not exceptions to his argument but result logically from it, if it be continued beyond the point reached by the numerical example. Thus they make Ricardo the father of what Marx called the Theory of Compensation—the theory that the working class is being compensated for initial sufferings, incident to the introduction of a labor-saving machine, by favorable ulterior effects—which Marx attributed to James Mill, McCulloch, Torrens, Senior, and J. S. Mill, thereby constructing an entirely unrealistic contrast between these men and Ricardo. More or less, most economists have done the same thing, even those who did not wish, as did Marx, to single out this so-called theory of compensation for vituperative comment (see *Das Kapital*, vol. 1, ch. 15, sec. 6).

The controversy that went on throughout the nineteenth century and beyond, mainly in the form of argument pro and con 'compensation,' is dead and buried: as stated above, it vanished from the scene as a better technique filtered into general use which left nothing to disagree about (see reference to Hicks's *Theory of Wages*, first footnote of this subsection). Nevertheless, in order to understand an important phase of past doctrinal history, a few clarifications will be useful. In the first place, the reader must not think that Ricardo was wrong in the result that he formulated in the two statements quoted above. On the contrary, if we interpret him to have meant that mechanization may permanently decrease labor's relative and possibly even absolute share in national income (no matter whether this be real income in our sense or in Ricardo's), he was correct. Only, his argument taken as a whole does not prove it. In the second place, so far as Ricardo meant to convey not only an abstract theorem but a picture of practically relevant processes and likelihood, he obviously underrated the effects of the increase in productive power that mechanized capitalism would display and of the expansion of output that would result therefrom—so that long-run 'distress and poverty' looms larger in his text than it should in a realistic picture. On the one hand, this was due to something that is much worse than defective technique, namely, to lack of imagination: he never clearly realized that the *essential* fact about capitalist 'machinery' is that it does what, quantitatively and qualitatively, could not be done at all without it or, to put it differently, that it 'replaces' workmen who have never been born. But, on the other hand, this was due also to the shortcomings of his analytic apparatus, which did not lend itself readily to the description of quantitative expansion. In particular, in the Ricardian system prices can fall to cost level directly, that is, in a way other than by increase of output (*Principles*, ch. 30): hence he failed to see that total output *in terms of goods* must increase, under conditions of perfect competition, which he assumed, in consequence of mechanization. He further failed to see clearly that, if we express the wage fund also in terms of commodities, it can increase without any increase in saving, though it is then much more natural to say simply that real wage incomes (in our sense) increase than it is to say that the wage fund increases and that real wages increase in consequence of this.

In the third place, the reader who, on perusal of Ricardo's chapter on machinery, sets it down as a mess is perfectly right; and he may well ask for the reason. It seems to me that the reason is that Ricardo, while retaining his own approach in terms of real value ('labor embodied'), at the same time repeatedly crossed the frontier that separates this approach from analysis in terms of goods. Why he did this is clear: his exact reasoning is always in terms of the labor-embodied approach; but this approach does not lead to any results about anyone's distress or welfare, which were what interested him in this chapter. And so he mixed up the two, sometimes speaking of 'distress of labor' when summing up an argument that was in terms of labor embodied and hence irrelevant to real incomes in our sense, that is real income in terms of goods, sometimes speaking in terms of *his* real value in the course of an argument that makes sense only in terms of absolute quantities of goods.

Finally, in the fourth place, additional clarification may be desirable as regards that increase in saving by capitalists to which Ricardo attributed effects that would or may remedy the injury the machine does to workmen. Since this injury, within Ricardo's wage-fund *method*, is described as a reduction in the *Ricardian value of the wage fund*, additional saving will in fact tend to repair the damage. Now this additional saving comes from profits for two alternative reasons. First, even if the rate of profit be not increased permanently (if, in Ricardo's language, the 'value' of profits be not increased), a fall in prices of the goods they consume makes it easier for capitalists to save, which (if propensity to consume remains constant as it always is with both Ricardo and Keynes) they will accordingly do. But, second, if the cheapened goods are, wholly or primarily, consumed by workmen, then, according to Ricardo's theory, the *rate* of profits will increase. And increased saving will follow from this. Let me add that J. S. Mill did accept Ricardo's methods, but did not follow them closely. The main comfort *he* had to offer to the working class was that mechanization occurs in a process that produces ample savings that easily replace reductions in the wage fund caused by mechanization (they would otherwise spill over into colonies and so on) so that these reductions are likely to be potential rather than real. Marx ought to have liked this—for it offers a nice suggestion for the socialist theory of imperialism (see below)—but he did not display gratitude when he used it.

Marx (op. cit. ch. 15) accepted Ricardo's analysis, adding nothing essential but minimizing the Ricardian qualifications, beating out the slender result to its thinnest leaf, making the most of the unemployment that has been historically associated with the process of mechanization, and allowing himself to be carried on by his glowing rhetoric to a pitch of excitement such that he even overlooked some points he might have made for his own theory or against the hated theory of compensation. Perhaps this shows, as do in his case other excesses of this kind, that he was not quite sure of his ground. Certainly it shows that he was aware of the decisive importance of the mechanization problem for his ultimate conclusions concerning the future of the capitalist system. Machines had to throw the laborers 'on the pavement'—still better, because of English machines the bones of Indian weavers had to 'bleach in the sun.' Marxist unemployment is essentially technological unemployment. This technological unemployment had to create a permanent 'industrial reserve army'—Ricardo's redundant population. And the presence of this permanent industrial reserve army—only temporarily absorbed in spells of high prosperity—had to depress real wages (in our sense) to levels of ever-increasing misery, degradation, and so on (*Verelendung*) that would eventually goad the proletariat into the final revolution. Of course, this was only an 'absolute law.' [105] Of course, Marx's effective display of severely selected his-

[105] The reader should remember what this phrase means in the Marxist lingo, namely, the same thing as an abstract tendency that is not necessarily verified in any given stretch of economic history.

torical facts, which fill out his analysis in that chapter, contains a considerable number of qualifications of his own as do some passages in the third volume. But since abstract tendencies drive nobody into misery and despair and since Marx took little heed of his qualifications when it came to ultimate conclusions and purposes (see, e.g., ch. 32, 'Historical Tendency of Capitalistic Accumulation'), no Marx apologetics can be successful that proceed on either of those lines. We have no choice but to take statements like that above seriously. If we do, the failure of Marx's attempt to turn the possibility that Ricardo envisaged into inexorable necessity endangers the logical structure of his system as much as the actual history of the working class endangers any claim it might have to realism.[106]

But it is only the thesis about increasing misery that needs to be dropped from Marx's analysis of the process of technological development, although, from the standpoint of Marxist orthodoxy, it may be all-important. Other results remain. In order to see them in their proper light, let us remember that, in Marx's general schema, social evolution is propelled by a force that is immanent or necessarily inherent in the profit economy. This force is Accumulation: under pressure of competition, the individual concern is compelled to invest as much of its profits as possible in its own productive apparatus;[107] *and it is compelled to invest them primarily in technological capital,* naturally looking always for machines of ever-new types. This does not permanently benefit 'capitalists' as a class[108] for, as Ricardo had already pointed out, any supernormal gain is quickly eliminated by competitors' adopting each technological improvement. But the temporary advantage gained by the one who is first to move gives him a lead in the race: rushing down on declining average-cost curves and annihilating ('expropriating') the weaker ones in the process, capitalist concerns, individually growing in size, build up vast powers of production that eventually burst the framework of

[106] There are Marxists who actually do not mind taking up the ridiculous position that a tendency for the working class's standard of life to fall is in fact observable. Others have confined themselves to the less absurd proposition that Marx's abstract law has been put out of operation, owing to uniquely favorable conditions that have prevailed in the nineteenth century (such as the opening up of new sources of foodstuffs and raw materials through the spectacular cheapening of transportation), but will assert itself eventually if it has not done so already in the 1930's. Still other interpreters have made efforts to make Marx's law mean relative misery only, i.e. a fall in the relative share of labor, which, besides being equally untenable, clearly violates Marx's meaning.

[107] Of course, this is saying the same thing as that the individual concern is compelled to save, a phrase the highly undesirable implications of which Marx fought like a lion to avoid. In pointing out the existence of this compulsion he did, however, betray a much deeper understanding of the capitalist mechanism than can be attributed to the 'bourgeois' economists of his age. But in common with them, he saw nothing but the mechanical aspect of accumulation, hence not the reality of capitalist evolution but only its reflection in growing heaps of inanimate things: besides accumulating these, 'capitalists' did nothing but exploit.

[108] On the 'law of the falling rate of profit,' see above subsec. 6c.

capitalist society. Not all this has stood up. Particularly vulnerable is the last point: Marx never made it clear precisely how the economy of giant concerns is to break down, and his break-down theory (*Zusammenbruchstheorie*) has in fact been renounced by some of his most eminent followers. On the whole, however, one cannot but be impressed by both the analytic and realistic virtues of this conception of capitalist evolution, especially if one compares it to the modest elements of it that Marx found in Ricardo's chapter on machinery.

CHAPTER 7

Money, Credit, and Cycles

1. England's Problems

It is the common opinion that the foundations of the monetary science of today (or yesterday) were laid by the writers who discussed the issues of English monetary and banking policy from the Restriction Act (1797) to the gold inflation of the 1850's. This neglects indeed the French and Italian work of the eighteenth century but nevertheless comes nearer to the truth than such sweeping statements usually do. Many of those writers moved on an unusually high level. They soared with ease into the sphere of abstract generalization and were possessed of a genuine will to analyze. This is the more remarkable because most of them were men of practical affairs and primarily interested in practical measures. We are accustomed to a different state of things: few modern economists would look to men of practical affairs and especially to bankers for help in their analytic task or even consider them as authorities on the principles of their own business. But this situation developed in the next period. In the one under survey, it was the practitioners who were in the van of *analytic* advance, and research workers of different types were in most cases content to take their clues from them.

With most of the leading performers we are already acquainted, especially with Ricardo, Malthus, Senior, Tooke, Torrens, and J. S. Mill.[1] A small num-

[1] Some of the relevant publications of these and others have also been mentioned already. Others will be mentioned in the appropriate places. Ricardo's main contributions will, however, be listed at once. As the reader knows, it was as a writer on monetary policy, in the discussion on war inflation, that Ricardo first made his reputation. His three letters to the *Morning Chronicle* (1809, Hollander reprint as *Three Letters on the Price of Gold,* 1903) were followed by a fuller statement of his views in pamphlet form: *The High Price of Bullion, a Proof of the Depreciation of Bank Notes* (1810). The *Reply to Mr. Bosanquet's Practical Observations on the Report of the Bullion Committee,* Ricardo's only exploit in 'factual' work—but very interesting as

ber of others will be introduced as we go along. But Henry Thornton (1760-1815) must be saluted at once. He was a banker, M.P., philanthropist, and—which he himself and many who knew him would presumably have put first—a leading figure in the influential group of Evangelicals that was known as the Clapham Sect. His *Enquiry into the Nature and Effects of the Paper Credit of Great Britain* (1802) [2] is an amazing performance. The product, according to Professor von Hayek's estimate, of work that extended over about six years during which the author's energy was largely absorbed by business and political pursuits, not faultless in detail and not fully matured, it anticipated in some points the analytic developments of a century to come. No other performance of the period will bear comparison with it, though several, among them Ricardo's, met with much greater success at the time as well as later. In part this was because the author put no emphasis at all upon his novel results—the book reads as if he himself had not been aware of their novelty. Perhaps he was not, though he paid an almost academic amount of attention to such predecessors as he knew. He was one of those men who see things clearly and who express with unassuming simplicity what they see.

We shall confine ourselves almost exclusively to English work—a decision which, for the epoch and the topic, may be justified even apart from the considerations of space that impose it. With qualifications to be mentioned, this work was successfully summed up by J. S. Mill. The relevant chapters of the *Principles* contain some of Mill's best work. It displays indeed some contradictions, hesitations, and unassimilated compromises—as does his work on value—but even these were not unmixed evils since they brought out, in strange contrast to Mill's own belief in the finality of his teaching, the unfinished state of the analysis of that time and thus indicated lines for further research to follow. In any case, it was primarily in Mill's formulation that

such—appeared in 1811; the *Proposals for an Economical and Secure Currency* in 1816. Chapter 27 of the *Principles* (1817), 'On Currency and Banks' retains independent importance in spite of the long quotation from the *Proposals*. The *Plan for the Establishment of a National Bank* (1823) has been reprinted by Professor Hollander in *Minor Papers on the Currency Question, 1809-23, by David Ricardo* (1932; see the discussion of this plan in Professor Rist's, *History of Monetary and Credit Theory*, pp. 177-9), which contains also other pieces that are quite essential to a full understanding of Ricardo's views. Other items might be added. Ricardo's theory of money, credit, and banking gains on acquaintance, and in perusing his letters as well as his evidence before the Committees on the Usury Laws and on Resumption, one discovers more and more fragments that might be combined into a spacious structure. No attempt will be made, however, to do so. We shall have to be content with a few features of Ricardo's analysis that are of major importance to doctrinal history. The reader is warned that this may involve some injustice to his performance as a whole. But the impression the reader is bound to get, that Ricardo did not contribute much that was both true and original, agrees with Viner's judgment (op. cit. p. 122), and so does, I believe, my opinion that as an analyst of money and credit Ricardo was inferior to Thornton.

[2] The Library of Economics reprint (1939) is prefaced by an essay by Professor von Hayek, the scholarship of which is surpassed only by its charm. The reader who misses it deprives himself not only of much valuable information but of an exquisite pleasure.

the work of the first half of the nineteenth century reached the writers of the second half, and we shall therefore keep this formulation in view, as a point of reference, throughout this chapter.

I have commended the taste and ability for theoretical analysis of the writers of that period. Nevertheless, their analysis was too closely bound up with the conditions and problems of their time and country to admit of exposition without reference to these conditions. Accordingly we shall now cast a perfunctory glance at them—neglecting entirely, for the reason stated, the much more exciting experiences of the United States and of some continental countries. Sources of more adequate information are presented below.

To the student who wishes to have a single reference on which to concentrate I recommend Professor Viner's presentation in *Studies in the Theory of International Trade*, Chapters III, IV, and V. This masterly piece of research—admiration for which does not, however, imply agreement in every particular—will serve both for the history of the most important facts and controversies, and as a guide to further historical literature. For statistical figures, see N. J. Silberling, 'Financial and Monetary Policy of Great Britain during the Napoleonic Wars,' *Quarterly Journal of Economics*, May 1924, and 'British Prices and Business Cycles, 1779-1850,' *Review of Economic Statistics*, Preliminary vol. V, 1923, and E. V. Morgan, 'Some Aspects of the Bank Restriction Period, 1797-1821,' in *Economic History, A Supplement to the Economic Journal*, February 1939.

By far the greatest contemporaneous *histoire raisonnée* is Tooke and Newmarch, *History of Prices* (discussed above ch. 4, sec. 8a). Perusal of Sir T. E. Gregory's introduction to the 1928 edition of this work is the second recommendation I have to make. Mr. R. G. Hawtrey's *Currency and Credit* (3rd ed., 1928, ch. 18) and *Art of Central Banking* (1932, ch. 4), usefully supplemented by Mr. W. T. C. King's *History of the London Discount Market* (1936), come next. Further help will be derived from J. W. Angell, *The Theory of International Prices* (1926); E. Cannan, *The Paper Pound of* 1797-1821 (1919), which contains a reprint of the Bullion Report; A. E. Feavearyear, *The Pound Sterling* (1931, ch. 9); A. W. Acworth, *Financial Reconstruction in England*, 1815-22 (1925); R. S. Sayers, 'The Question of the Standard in the 1850's,' *Economic History, A Supplement to the Economic Journal*, January 1933, and 'The Question of the Standard, 1815-44' (ibid. February 1935); R. H. I. Palgrave, *Bank Rate and the Money Market* (1903); and Elmer Wood, *English Theories of Central Banking Control*, 1819-1858 (1936), with a valuable bibliography which in particular presents a list of reports of committees on monetary subjects and of other official papers to which, as usual, no justice can be done here.

(a) *War Inflation*, 1793-1815. In spite of the suspension of the Bank of England's obligation to redeem its notes in gold, 1797,[3] war finance did not produce any great effects upon prices and foreign-exchange rates until about 1800. To the modern student who is inured to stronger stuff, the most striking feature of the subsequent inflation is its mildness: at no time was the public's normal behavior with respect to money seriously disturbed; at no time did the impact of the government's war expenditure blot out those fluctuations that might have been expected to occur in the usual course of things;

[3] This Restriction Act was not passed as a war measure but in order to stop a run upon the bank.

at no time was the government driven to anything more unorthodox than abnormally heavy borrowing from the Bank, and even this borrowing never surpassed the limits beyond which the term 'borrowing' becomes an euphemism for printing government fiat; at no time, finally, was the national wage bill—the chief conductor of inflationary effects—so seriously expanded as to endanger the currency. It was in fact this very mildness of the inflationary process that made diagnosis so difficult. In particular, it made it more difficult to recognize the inflationary element in the situation and to distinguish it from the effects upon foreign exchange of the two circumstances that a great part of war expenditure was for financing allied and English armies on the Continent, and that English exports and imports were for years together seriously interfered with.

Government spent lavishly. But it also did its best, by the introduction of an income tax and in other ways, to keep the inflationary advances from the Bank down to a minimum, and its finance never ceased to remain competent and responsible. But the reticence of the government about the extent of its borrowings from the Bank, quite understandable until Waterloo, was a contributory factor in people's propensity to blame the Bank for whatever consequences they did not like. This propensity, strong at all times, which was fully shared by the majority of writers, must be borne in mind throughout: from Ricardo to the most unsophisticated man in the street, everybody loved to make a whipping boy of the central bank, a habit economists have retained to this day. In public at least, the Bank was unable to defend itself, because no effective defense was possible without giving the government away—and politicians in power are in a position to make their resentment felt. This may conceivably explain much that strikes historians as lack of insight in the official pronouncements. As a matter of fact, the Bank was obviously not free to refuse the government's 'requests' for advances. If there can be any question at all of its 'responsibility for inflation,' it must be understood to refer to its loans to (discounts for) the public, which were inevitably increased as a consequence of the government's deficit spending. But they were rationed and kept down whenever government borrowed heavily, and cannot be said, everything considered, to have been obviously excessive—though it is, of course, always possible to argue that they could have been less had the Bank been willing to take the responsibility for disturbing production in wartime. Moreover, punitive rates [4] above 5 per cent were rendered impossible by the usury laws until 1832. There is no doubt that such inflation as there was

[4] I shall take this opportunity to clear up a point that played a role in the discussion of the Bank's responsibility and arises in every war inflation. Government expenditure financed in any way that does not reduce the public's expenditure by the same amount will raise prices, if it impinges on a well-employed business organism, which in the case before us was so at times but not at others. When prices *have* risen, then, the money cost of producing being increased thereby, nongovernmental borrowing will be increased also: the government inflation produces in this case a secondary wave of credit inflation and also reinforces itself currently. Now it is evidently possible to say, since such government inflation by definition implies increase in the means of payment and since

was strong enough to *accentuate* speculative excesses and breakdowns, a boom in agriculture, and conditions of general prosperity in most of the years to 1815, none of which could, however, have been entirely prevented by the Bank.

On the surface, then, the controversy that contributed so much to monetary analysis was simply a controversy between writers who sought to prove and to indict inflation and to locate the responsibility for it with the Bank, and other writers who sought to deny the presence of inflation or to justify it and to locate the responsibility for rising prices and unfavorable exchanges with circumstances other than the behavior of the Bank. So far as this goes, it is possible to speak of two fairly well defined and opposing groups or parties. Also, the first one may be said to have prevailed in the sense that it succeeded better than did the other in impressing its views upon the famous Bullion Report of 1810.[5] In consequence, it has become usual to affix to the members of this group the meaningless label Bullionists and to the opponents of the report the label Anti-Bullionists, although the report itself really represents various compromises. However, the practical issues and the recommendations as to 'what should be done about it' are of no great importance for us. Important is the analytic quality of the arguments and diagnoses produced. And from this standpoint the party lines lose much of their definiteness and almost all their interest. The differences between the supporters of the Bullion Report are actually much more interesting than is the common bond between them. But before taking leave of this historic document, let us note the significant fact that the Report of the Cunliffe Committee that recommended England's return to gold at prewar parity in 1918 (final report, 1919) displayed little, if any, knowledge of monetary problems that was not possessed by the men who drafted the Bullion Report.

(b) *The Question of the Standard.* About twenty years of irredeemable paper and all the economic changes that had occurred during that time made the problem of deciding on a monetary policy much more difficult than it would have been after a shorter disturbance. *De facto,* though not legally,

the secondary inflation does the same, that the whole trouble is 'increase in the quantity of money.' But since this increase in the quantity of money is an incident in a process that involves many more fundamentally 'causal' elements (the policy that led to the war, among others), and since the secondary inflation is in fact induced by a preceding rise in prices, it is equally possible to say that the bank or banks which finance the increase in both governmental and business expenditure are playing a 'passive' role and in particular, so far as business borrowing is concerned, are but 'responding to needs' that have arisen in consequence of high prices and high money wages—or else that the 'quantity of money' (notes and deposits) increases *because* prices have risen. Neither of these two statements is necessarily erroneous. But each of them becomes erroneous as soon as it is interpreted to deny the element that the other one emphasizes. This, however, is what happened in the English controversy of 1800-1810, as it happens in any discussion of any inflation. But the fundamental futility of any such discussion does not exclude the possibility that participants learn and produce valuable results thereby.

[5] See Cannan's edition mentioned above (*The Paper Pound of* 1797-1821).

England had been on a gold standard when restriction was decreed in 1797. Within a few years a strong political current set in that was to carry her toward the legal adoption of it (1816) and eventually toward the resumption of specie payments at the prewar par (Peel's Resumption Act of 1819, actual resumption 1821).[6] The possibilities of continuing the paper regime of the war (the course recommended by Lord Keynes in 1923) or of adopting bimetallism—or the silver standard—were advocated but not seriously considered. It should be mentioned, however, that Ricardo's Plan, according to which the monetary metal should not enter into hand-to-hand circulation but be held by the Bank for the purpose of redeeming notes, not in coin but in ingots of bullion, was actually embodied in the Resumption Act of 1819, though, meeting with complete indifference on the part of the public and with little favor on the part of the Bank, the relevant permissive clauses did not become operative.

Resumption impinged upon a depressive situation. Postwar readjustments were in any case bound to cause difficulties, particularly in the agrarian sector. Not only the inevitable fall of prices from the war peak—though the exact dates and figures given by Silberling have been criticized, there is little doubt that the price level, by 1819, had fallen by something like 30 per cent in about five years—but also the adaptation of production to entirely new situations presented problems of the kind which it always takes a depression to straighten out. In addition, there was the fact, realized by many but not all the experts, that the prospects of gold production were distinctly unfavorable. Finally, however, there was something else which these experts—just as the experts of 1918—entirely failed to see: quite independently of the preceding war inflation, the English economy was then entering upon one of those prolonged periods of falling prices, interest rates, and profits, of unemployment and instability, that always follow upon 'industrial revolutions.' The last decades of the eighteenth century had witnessed such a revolution—the new cotton machinery, the steam engine, and canal building are but the most conspicuous instances of the events that transformed the very bases of manufacturing and trade. Results began to pour forth from 1815 on, upsetting the pre-existing industrial structure and exerting primarily depressive effect, until the economic process was steadied again, weakly in the 1830's, more strongly in the 1840's, by the beginnings of investment in railroad construction. In a situation such as this, even a slightly restrictive monetary policy is not the matter of indifference which it would be in a situation that is located on an upward trend of prices. And a slightly restrictive effect resumption undoubtedly had.

[6] The outstanding symptom of the increasing momentum of that current was Lord Liverpool's *Treatise on the Coins of the Realm* . . . (1805), which, its complete valuelessness notwithstanding, has retained its place in the history of the subject owing to the political position of its author. Symptomatic of small middle-class feelings and a powerful influence in shaping them into a political force was William Cobbett's agitation against paper (see his *Paper against Gold*, 1810-11, reprinted 1817). It is said that Sir Robert Peel was quite frightened of Cobbett's 'thunder.'

The surviving sponsors of the policy of resumption recommended in the Bullion Report had therefore little reason for celebrating its ultimate success. They had in fact become silent or apologetic a few years before the event. They shared with their opponents the erroneous diagnosis according to which the responsibility for the further fall in the price level throughout the 1820's rested exclusively with resumption. Also, they were glad to join these opponents in entirely irrational accusations against the universal scapegoat, the Bank, which was supposed to have mismanaged resumption and in particular to have caused international depression by raising the value of gold. We cannot go beyond pointing out that Tooke was almost the only writer of note to realize the absurdity of this and to come near to a more reasonable diagnosis in terms of non-monetary factors. For the rest, discussion went against the advocates of the unfettered gold standard until the upswing of 1830-35 and the emergence of another issue deflected attention, and until Russian, Australian, and Californian gold changed the monetary situation and the humors of economists: after 1850, Peel's Act of 1819 became in fact quite popular with them; toward the end of the century irrational admiration for the measure had largely replaced irrational condemnation.

(c) *Bank Reform.* Largely, though not exclusively, the literature on banking in which we are interested centers upon advocacy and criticism of another Peel act, the Bank Charter Act of 1844, which tried to give effect to 'the theory that banking ought to be separated from the control of the currency' [7] and actually enforced what may be described as a '100 per cent reserve plan' for bank notes. Again—like resumption—the measure grew out of a strong current of public opinion that crystallized in the vicissitudes of the years 1836-9 and was thereafter impervious to argument: both public and politicians saw no causes of those vicissitudes other than misconduct or irresponsibility on the part of note-issuing banks. Notes and any troubles that arose about them were clearly visible. Whereas deposits, the use of which was as yet confined to a much smaller sector of the public, passed practically unnoticed, notes circulated widely and their issue was to the man in the street the typical form of the Iniquity of Banking.[8] What the average M.P. presumably thought he was doing, when he cast his vote for Sir Robert Peel's bill, was that he was stopping a flagrant abuse and protecting the people's money.

By 1800, England's banking system had reached an advanced stage of development. In the metropolis there were, besides the Bank of England, a

[7] See P. Barrett Whale, 'A Retrospective View of the Bank Charter Act of 1844,' *Economica,* August 1944. In view of the facts that we are not primarily interested in the Act itself and in its sociological and economic interpretation and that, in addition, it would be quite impossible to do justice to this topic even if we were, perusal of this admirable three-page article is strongly recommended. As regards the history of English banking, we are in a similar position: for facts and figures the reader is referred primarily to the work of E. Wood (mentioned at the beginning of this chapter); our own text cannot aim at more than focusing the reader's attention on a few points necessary to understand the setting in which analysis and controversy ran their courses.

[8] This is the title of an anonymous pamphlet published in 1797.

number of private banking houses (partnerships; the joint stock banks put in appearance after 1826, giving a decisive impulse to deposit banking because they did not have the right to issue notes) and bill brokers. Outside the metropolis, and so far as merchants did not directly bank with London (or, after 1826, with one of the branches of the Bank of England), industry and trade were served by the country banks, whose number declined in the 1820's after having greatly increased during the Napoleonic Wars, and also by bill brokers. Two features must be particularly noticed. First, these country banks, though they had some deposit business, chiefly financed their customers by the issue of bank notes (promissory notes payable on demand in coin or Bank of England notes) in discounting commercial bills. Against these notes they held reserves in varying proportions that were not fixed by law. This practice was obsolescent even before it was killed by Peel's Act of 1844.[9] But for many English writers on banking—and still more so for their continental brethren—the bank note that originates in the discount of a trade bill remained the backbone of the theory of banking throughout the period and beyond.[10] Second, there was another practice which was very common all over England outside of London and especially in Lancashire and which is so interesting for us because it teaches us better than anything else what money really is: traders used bills of exchange for making payments. That is to say, a firm that had sold some commodity would draw a bill on the buyer who accepted it, and then endorse it and hand it on to another firm in discharge of some obligation to the latter. Thus bills of exchange, accumulating endorsements, actually went from hand to hand, often without interest, and were, for the time being, no longer elements in the total demand for money but elements in its supply.[11]

[9] The issue of notes of banks other than the Bank of England was only limited at a fixed amount and not stopped by Peel's legislation of 1844 and 1845. But the intention and the effect were to induce country banks to abandon their note issue voluntarily.

[10] This fact is important to keep in mind, not only because it invited the interpretation of the banking process which we shall presently discuss under the label of Commercial Theory of Banking, but also because it is essential in order to understand fully the point at issue in the controversy around Peel's Act: the advocates of this measure (the so-called Currency School) looked upon the notes of the Bank of England not as instruments of credit, means of payment that originate in commodity trade, but rather as what they actually were by that time, a kind of reserve money; whereas the opponents of the measure (the so-called Banking School), and especially most of its continental adherents who were influenced by the partly different banking practice before their eyes, still clung to the trade-bill bank-note schema. In part, therefore, the whole controversy rested upon a question of fact or, so far as this was being overlooked, on a misunderstanding. The theory of central banking that linked the bank note to the trade bill proved an extremely hardy plant: its influence dominated banking legislation on the Continent beyond the nineteenth century; it asserted itself strongly in the Federal Reserve Act of 1913. For an excellent exposition of this theory, see Vera Smith, *The Rationale of Central Banking* (1936).

[11] This practice received much attention. There were businessmen who went so far as to put bona-fide trade bills 'in the first class of our currency' (see J. W. Bosanquet, *Metallic, Paper, and Credit Currency*, 1842).

The London bankers acted as agents or correspondents for the country banks and stood in a relatively close relation to one another—the London Clearing House was, by the end of the eighteenth century, already a well-established institution. Thus we behold an organic system rather than a number of individual billiard balls. Moreover, the system either had already found, or was rapidly finding, its central organ in the Bank of England, as the lender of *dernier resort* as Sir Francis Baring put it.[12] But even if we had space, it would be extremely difficult to describe the process by which the Bank came to realize this responsibility, to accept it, and to develop routine principles by which to implement it; and it would be still more difficult to appraise, in the light of the conditions of that time, the success which attended its action or inaction at each of the stages of that process.

One of the difficulties we experience in finding out what it was the Bank meant to do at any given time, or even what its practice actually was, is the reticence of its official spokesmen who, even when they were forced to say something, did their best to confine themselves to innocuous trivialities that would give as little scope to hostile criticism as possible. Practitioners of business are rarely able to formulate their own behavior correctly. But in this case there were particular reasons for reticence. The reader will readily understand them if we view the position of the Bank realistically. As I have already stated, the Bank had few friends. Control is now a popular word. It was the reverse of popular in the epoch of intact capitalism. To say openly that the Bank was trying to control the banking system, let alone to manage the general business situation, would have evoked laughter if not indignation: the thing to say was that the Bank was modestly looking after its own business; that it simply followed the market; and that it harbored no pretensions at controlling anything or anybody. Moreover, in the formative stage of its policy, it would have been madness to assume in so many words the responsibilities that we now attribute to a central bank as a matter of course. This would have meant commitments which the Bank could not have been sure of being able to fulfil. Moreover, any spectacular announcement of policy would have brought down upon directors hosts of unbidden advisers, every one of them convinced that he knew much better what the Bank ought to do—and there would have been the danger of public outcries for legislation to force the Bank to take, or to refrain from taking, particular courses of action. Moreover, cool

[12] *Observations on the Establishment of the Bank of England* (1797). In the same year, H. Thornton, in his Evidence before the committees of both the House of Lords and the House of Commons, gave a preview of his ideas on central-bank policy that he was to present more fully in his famous book of 1802. There are two things to be distinguished, which are both covered by the last-resort slogan. On the one hand, the Bank of England was the last source of *cash* and, in this sense, the guardian of the currency. On the other hand, it was the banking system's (the money market's) last source of *credit* and, in this sense, by virtue of its situation if not from choice, the guardian of the credit structure which entailed the consequence, as Thornton saw or foresaw, that its policy had to be essentially different from that of any other individual bank.

refusal to take responsibility in crises did not necessarily mean what it seems to mean. In 1782, 1792, 1811, 1825 the result of such refusals was that the government was forced into action: it issued exchequer bills to merchants in difficulty and thus provided them with material which the Bank was ready enough to discount—and the motive of the refusals may have been precisely to open up this delightfully safe way of coming to the market's aid. There is thus less reason for the indignant surprise some critics of the Bank seem to feel at the reluctance the Bank displayed 'to recognize its responsibilities' and at such sentiments as those of Thomson Hankey (Governor, 1851-2) who, as late as 1867 (in his *Principles of Banking*), came near to denying any responsibility of the Bank for the money market—though what he really denied was only that 'good Bills of Exchange . . . ought at all times to be discounted at the Bank of England' (p. 33 of 2nd ed., 1873). If we add that fine steering looks like no steering, we cannot exclude the possibility that both the insight and the practice of the directors were above—and especially ahead of—what they have been credited with.

Actually, owing to the mere size of the Bank, nothing that happened in England or indeed in the world can, from the first, ever have been irrelevant to its decisions. A little reflection will convince the reader that directors, even if they had been guided exclusively by the Bank's long-run profit interest and even if they had recognized no responsibility to anyone except the Proprietors (stockholders), would have had to do most of the things which, in the historical conditions of every stage of the Bank's career, constituted the functions of a central bank. There is more to the old theory that a central bank serves the economy best if it attends to its own profit interest than we are at present willing to admit. Precisely when directors, clearly and consciously, began to attend to larger considerations is not known. Symptoms that admit of such an interpretation are certainly observable in the Bank's behavior during the Napoleonic Wars, when some methods of credit control developed, such as rationing, *irrespective* of the standing of borrowers, and possibly also attempts at influencing, through the London market, the behavior of country banks.[13] After 1815, the Bank began to shape its permanent peace-time policy by an eminently healthy method of trial and error, much as the Federal Reserve System evolved what was believed to be its permanent policy from 1918 to 1923. We get two interesting glimpses of some milestones on this road from statements made by the Governor, J. Horsley Palmer, in his evidence before the Parliamentary Committee of 1832 on the Bank of England Charter. The one refers to an empirical rule ('Palmer's rule') that had been adopted in 1827, namely, the rule to keep the Bank's 'securities' (discounts, loans, investments) approximately constant so that changes in circulation would occur only as gold flowed into or out of the country and circulation would behave as if it were wholly metallic. This rule—not meant to be obeyed strictly—

[13] On incipient open market operations through the management of government deposits, special deposits, and special advances, see the work of E. Wood (*English Theories of Central Banking Control,* 1819-1858) mentioned above.

anticipated the principle of Peel's Act to some extent and may in fact have been adopted in expectation of some such regulation. More important is the other statement that actually embodied a piece of analysis. Slightly reformulating Palmer's answer to Question 678, we may put it like this. Accepting an unfavorable turn of foreign exchanges as a sign of an 'unduly' great expansion of credit, he averred that the Bank could prevent or stop an outflow of gold by raising its rate: the increased rate would reduce borrowing; reduced borrowing would mean a smaller volume of transactions and employment, and lower prices; reduced prices would increase exports and decrease imports; and this would turn the balance of payments, hence exchange rates. It is gratifying to note that this proposition does not stand in the name of some professor of economics. But it sounded too academic for professors to miss it. And it became the basis of the 'classic' theory of central-bank policy as taught in nineteenth century textbooks. The much more important short-run effect of an increase in bank rate—that it will attract short balances from abroad—was also discovered as we shall see (Thornton, 1802; Tooke, 1838).

We cannot go any further into the evolution of central-bank policy during the period—the increasing importance, within the Bank's deposits, of bankers' balances, its varying policies with respect to its own discount business, its changing attitudes to the money market, and so on. One point cannot be passed by, however. Some critics have averred that the Bank, when it had realized its responsibilities at long last, allowed itself to be guided exclusively by the state of the foreign exchanges, that is, by actual or expected gold movements. Available information does not lend support to this view. Directors seem to have been guided by their diagnoses and prognoses of the general business and political conditions at home and abroad. There was indeed strong correlation between the bank rate and foreign-exchange rates. But this correlation is easily accounted for by the fact that, under the unfettered international gold standard, gold movements were a sensitive index of general business conditions.

2. FUNDAMENTALS [1]

We shall not expect that writers of the type that created the literature we are about to survey would be greatly interested in the logical fundaments of the theory of money and credit—the kind of thing that the German term *Grundlagenforschung* denotes. There is indeed a flavor of primitivity, not to say crudity, about the conceptualization of those economists, which at the time and later led to various misunderstandings and futile controversies. This is no mere matter of terminology. In the case before us, hazy terminology was the result of haziness of thought about what money is and what money does. From the first (Thornton, 'Evidence before the Committees of Secrecy,' 1797), a comprehensive category was formed of all means of payment—also called the circulating medium and sometimes 'currency'—that included full-value

[1] The chief authority on the purely theoretical part of that period's work is Arthur W. Marget (*Theory of Prices*, 1938-42, *passim*).

and token coins, bank notes, deposits subject to check or, alternatively, the checks themselves, and, under certain conditions, bills of exchange. This was all right: obviously, the total of All We Pay With is a meaningful notion; its chief analytic value consists in the recognition it implies of the fact that there is no *essential* difference between bank notes and deposits. And that this fact was not self-evident but had to be 'discovered' is proved by the further fact that some writers refused to recognize it. Lord Overstone and the advocates of Peel's Act of 1844 generally drew a sharp dividing line between bank notes and deposits which was clearly not merely terminological and the precise significance of which is not easy to ascertain, because none of those authors was sufficiently explicit about logical fundaments.[2] Tooke was at first one of those who fought against the conceptual merger of bank notes and deposits, until 1840, when the third volume of his *History* appeared. By 1844 (*Inquiry*), he had changed his mind and adopted it, perhaps—as it is hardly too uncharitable to suspect—because this merger offered a convenient argument against Overstone and Peel's bill.

But even most of those who used that comprehensive concept of Means of Payment[3] did not, as do most of us, identify it with the concept of Money.[4] The great majority of leading authors, among them Thornton, Ricardo, Senior, Fullarton, J. S. Mill, and Marx, defined money, as it had been defined by Galiani, Beccaria, and Smith, as a commodity that has been chosen for means of exchange, measure of value, et cetera. Roscher expressed dominant opinion when he said that the false theories of money may be divided into two groups: those that hold that money is more, and those that hold that money is less, than the most salable commodity. This, on the face of it, makes them Theoretical Metallists (see above, Part II, ch. 6, sec. 2).

[2] The nature of the resulting difficulty of interpretation will be realized if we consider separately the case of English bank notes, Bank of England notes, and Bank of England notes in wartime. As regards the first, as has been pointed out already, there are technical and practical reasons why a man who puts bank notes and deposits on a par *on logical principle* might still refuse to do so for purposes of policy. As regards the second, as we have also seen, the notes of the Bank of England, being 'reserve money' for the other banks, had in fact a distinctive place in England's monetary system, recognition of which was again compatible with treating them like deposits *on principle*. As regards the third, it *may* be held—and this is important to remember in order to understand Ricardo's attitude—that the notes of the Bank of England changed character in wartime and turned into something not essentially different from government fiat. Which of these possible standpoints an author takes makes a lot of difference to his fundamental construction. Yet, unless he is very explicit about it, it is difficult to say which of these standpoints he actually did take—and, in addition, whether he adhered to it consistently.

[3] This was not always done explicitly. Thus this concept must, as we shall see, be attributed to J. S. Mill, whose theoretical construction nevertheless avoids its explicit use.

[4] An example of such identification has been pointed out by Viner (op. cit. p. 247): E. Hill, *Principles of Currency* (1856). Currency, however, did not always, though it did often, mean the same thing as money, but was also used as a synonym for means of payment in the widest sense.

To establish this proposition we must take account of several facts that apparently contradict it. First, not all writers accepted the metallist doctrine as explicitly as did Fullarton (who included in money only full-value coin) and, above all, Marx. Others, notably Thornton (see the first page of *Paper Credit*) implied it rather than stated it. Second, all or most included irredeemable government paper or would have included it if pressed. But this does not contradict our proposition, because paper money may be construed in such a manner as to come within a metallist definition of money. Thus Ricardo, not inelegantly, construed paper money as money, the whole cost of which 'may be considered as seigniorage' (*Principles*, ch. 27). Nor should it be urged that Ricardo cannot have been a metallist because he advocated a monetary system (*Proposals for an Economical and Secure Currency*, 1816) in which gold would be completely eliminated from circulation and because he held that 'a currency is in its most perfect state when it consists wholly of paper money' (*Principles*, ch. 27), for the sentence goes on like this: 'but of paper money of an equal value with the gold which it professes to represent.' Such a gold-certificate currency would function exactly like a gold-coin currency and differs from it not by any basic principle but merely by certain economies. The very idea was to make sure that the value of the monetary unit should fluctuate according to the value of gold: such a system is still metallist.

Third, however, we must take into account the tendency to assimilate bank notes with paper money. Sir Robert Peel, in introducing his bill, defined money to cover coin of the realm and bank notes, the latter being 'paper currency,' and this manner of speaking was very common. But it does not signify that credit means of payment were to be considered as money but merely that, in the opinion of Ricardo and Overstone, bank notes were not credit means of payment but *de facto* money *though they should not be*. Or to put it differently, using a phrase of Roscher's: they were money paper that had illegitimately usurped the role of paper money and were now to be forced to behave as if they were legitimate gold money. This is the whole philosophy of Peel's Act. Therefore, the inclusion in money of bank notes *that are viewed in this light* does not contradict our proposition. J. S. Mill excluded bank notes precisely because, having departed from the Ricardo-Overstone teaching, he did not view them in this light.[5]

But if we claim the majority of writers for theoretical metallism—since most of them also held that it was practical wisdom to base the currency upon gold (or silver), they were also practical metallists—we must be careful to make sure precisely how much this means. It does mean that they—and with unmistakable clearness Ricardo, Senior, Mill, and Marx—construed the phenomena of money from the case of full-value metallic money, as we shall presently see. It also means that this impaired their analysis of the subject of Money and Credit, as will be explained in Section 4. But it does not mean

[5] Hence he was in error when he believed that inclusion or exclusion of bank notes from money was a terminological issue, a mere 'question of nomenclature' (*Principles*, Book III, ch. 12, § 7).

that this metallist basis of their analysis hampered them at every step. Sometimes it was happily forgotten. And at other times apposite constructive devices prevented it from doing harm. One such device we have observed already. Some later German writers have held that the metallist starting point makes it impossible to do analytic justice to the facts of irredeemable paper money. Yet Ricardo and J. S. Mill experienced no difficulty at all in fitting these facts into a metallist theory.

As in the subsequent period, the central problem of monetary theory was the value of money. More definitely than in the preceding period, this value was identified with the exchange ratios between money and goods or the former's Purchasing Power.[6] But the fact that all money prices do not normally change in the same direction, let alone proportion, that is, the fact that gives rise to the problem of the *general* purchasing power or its reciprocal, the general price level, caused difficulties that were very obvious in the discussion on war inflation and were never really overcome. Most of us—uncritically perhaps—believe that we may solve them by the method of index numbers, and this method, as we know, was already available. But few theorists took kindly to it. Wheatley was the first one to do so as far as I know. Most of the rest, up to and including J. S. Mill, distrusted it or even did not grasp its possibilities, the efforts of Lowe and Scrope notwithstanding. Neither did they develop any articulate theory of the price level. They talked loosely about prices in general or general prices or, more precisely, about the scale of prices (Cairnes), but they cannot be said to have done more than adumbrate the idea, and some, among them Ricardo, definitely rejected it.[7] This is the reason why his proof that bank notes were depreciated during the Napoleonic Wars relied primarily on the premium on bullion and why, in dealing with the monetary aspects of foreign trade, he compared prices of individual commodities at home and abroad, though he and others may have believed that these were representative of more general variations.

The leading 'classics' solved the problem of this rather dubious value of money simply by extending to it their general theory of value. Accordingly,

[6] Confusion occasionally arose from the usance of businessmen that identifies value of money with the monetary rate of interest. Economists' anxiety to avoid this confusion may be responsible for the aversion of some of them to recognize the relations between purchasing power and interest. The former term was, however, also used in a different sense, e.g. by J. S. Mill, namely in the sense of the maximum of purchases an individual can effect.

[7] See, e.g., his categorical statement in the *Proposals*. Professor Viner (op. cit. p. 313, where the reader also finds that statement) points out, however, that Ricardo used the term price level in his correspondence. The refusal to recognize the price level as a meaningful, or measurable, concept is, however, a point against Ricardo only from the standpoint of modern economists, who handle it as a matter of course. From the standpoint of the small but distinguished group who believe neither in price index numbers nor in the price-level concept itself (like Professor von Mises, von Hayek, and, with some qualifications, also von Haberler) it is, of course, a point in his favor and proof of sound insight.

they distinguished a natural or long-run normal value of money and a short-run equilibrium value. The former or, as they also said—misleadingly—the 'permanent' value was determined by the cost of producing (or obtaining) the precious metals,[8] the latter by supply and demand.

Observe three things. In the first place, this procedure ratifies our calling them theoretical metallists. In the second place, *both* propositions are obviously equilibrium propositions, though they refer to different types of equilibrium. In the third place, the words 'determined by' are misleading and should be replaced by 'determined at.' For there is no particularly strong causal connotation to this determination. The reader can easily satisfy himself of this by considering the following case: suppose that the public changes its habits of payment permanently so that henceforth everybody holds less cash (in gold coins) than he did before; less gold will then be 'required' at a given level of prices; gold production will, within the assumptions of this analysis, certainly so adjust itself that (marginal) costs equal the new and lower value of the monetary unit; but it should be clear that in this case costs are being adapted to value at least as much as the new value is adapted to the new costs. In other words, our long-run equilibrium proposition is one of many long-run equilibrium conditions and can acquire causal connotation only by the grace of the theorist, that is, by the latter's decision to freeze all other factors in the situation. Even then, a change in the marginal costs of gold will affect the value of money only through affecting the supply of money, as Senior and J. S. Mill recognized.[9] Of course, it must be borne in mind that, owing to the extreme durability of gold, the total stock of it varies but slowly in response to the annual rate of production and that, hence, the pattern of short-run equilibrium will in the case of gold be of greater importance relatively to the pattern of long-run equilibrium than it is in the case of other commodities. Even Ricardo, in spite of his bent for long-run analysis, reasoned about money chiefly in terms of the former, that is, in terms of supply and demand.

We are now prepared to consider the vexed and vexing questions how far the 'classics' accepted the quantity theorem and whether or not it acquired illegitimate authority with them. For three of the leading writers, Thornton, Senior, and Marx, the negative answer is so clear as not to require proof.[10]

[8] This is how it was put by J. S. Mill (*Principles*, Book III, ch. 12, § 1; but the *sedes materiae* is ch. 9), who emphasized the fact that gold is an imported commodity. But, less elaborately, Ricardo and, much more elaborately, Senior and Marx were of the same opinion. Senior was the only one, however, who worked up that theorem into a comprehensive theory: he saw the cost of production of money not only in its relation to the demand for gold in the arts but also in its relation to the public's demand for cash to hold (*Three Lectures on the Value of Money*, delivered 1829, printed 1840, London School Reprint, 1931).

[9] Ricardo should not have admitted it because, in his general theory of value, the price of a commodity can fall without an increase in its supply.

[10] Something will have to be said about Thornton's position, however. The only one of the three to repudiate the quantity theorem altogether was Marx, who called it an

Let us then look at the positions of Ricardo and J. S. Mill. First, recall that mere recognition of the relevance to value of the supply or quantity of gold does not imply acceptance of what we have called the 'strict' quantity theorem (Part II, ch. 6, sec. 4). That is to say, the mere statement that the purchasing power of a monetary unit 'depends upon' supply and demand does not identify any particular theory of money. The first of the troubles with which the reader has to cope in this matter is that Ricardo and James Mill (and a long list of later writers on money, including Pigou and Cannan) did not realize this but, in striking analogy with their procedure in the case of the wage fund, tried to *deduce* the quantity theorem from the 'law' of supply and demand. As a result, in every individual instance, one has to ask himself whether they meant something that does follow from the 'law' of supply and demand—for example, that *ceteris paribus* an increase in the quantity of money will tend to decrease the purchasing power of the unit—or whether they meant more—for example, that *ceteris paribus* (*strictissime*) an increase in the quantity of money will decrease the purchasing power of the unit *proportionately*. The second of the troubles with which the reader has to cope arises from the fact that the term 'quantity theory' covers several meanings, so that if he finds that two writers disagree on whether or not 'the' quantity theory should be attributed to a given author, he must keep in mind the possibility that the two writers simply mean different things by that term. For our present purpose we shall define it to mean: first, that the quantity of money is an independent variable—in particular, that it varies independently of prices and of physical volume of transactions; [11] second, that velocity of circulation is an institutional datum that varies slowly or not at all, but in any case is independent of prices and volume of transactions; [12] third, that transactions—or let us say, output—are unrelated to quantity of money, and it is only owing to chance that the two may move together; fourth, that variations in the quantity of money, unless they be absorbed by variations in output in the same direction, act mechanically on all prices, irrespective of how an increase in the quantity of money is used and on what sector of the economy it first impinges (who gets it)—and analogously for a decrease.

I maintain that Ricardo, before him Wheatley, after him James Mill and McCulloch, held the quantity theory in this strict sense and that no other major writers did. It is true that Ricardo—and the same goes for McCulloch but not for James Mill—introduced qualifications occasionally and that, here and there, he made statements that were logically incompatible with his strict

---

'insipid hypothesis' (*abgeschmackte Hypothese*). It seems that he took this position under the impression that the quantity theory of the value of money and the cost of production theory of money are alternatives between which the analyst has to choose. This is not so: the value of money as 'determined' by quantity and the value of money as determined by cost of production must, in the long run, necessarily coincide, as Mill elaborately showed.

[11] As we shall presently see, this again carries different meaning according to the definition of Quantity of Money an author adopts.

[12] This may be relaxed by inserting the word 'normally.'

quantity theory, exactly as he did in matters of his labor-quantity law of value. In both cases, however, he mentioned them only in order to minimize their importance. In the same sense in which we are within our rights in averring that he held the latter, even though only as an approximation, we are also justified in attributing to him the strict quantity theory, as an approximation.[13]

The case of J. S. Mill is quite different.[14] At the start, he committed himself indeed to a strict quantity theory in the sense defined, even asserting in so many words that variations in the quantity of money will affect its value 'in a ratio exactly equivalent' and that this property is 'peculiar to money' (Book III, ch. 8, § 2). But he closed the chapter by saying that this strict quantity theory is nevertheless under modern conditions 'an extremely incorrect expression of the fact.' The apparent contradiction is easy to resolve. First, he confined the range of application of the quantity theorem to societies that know of no other means of payment except coin and irredeemable paper. The emergence of 'credit,' according to him, changes the situation radically: with a developed system of 'credit,' prices no longer depend, in any simple manner, on the quantity of money in that sense.[15] Second, he emasculated the quantity theorem still further, even for the case of a purely metallic circulation, by restricting its validity to the quantity of money that actually circulates. But the *circulating* quantity of money is certainly not independent of the business situation—output, employment, and so on—as J. S. Mill indicated by his turn

[13] It only serves to blur the lines of historical development if some historians, exactly as in the field of the theory of value, insist that if all of Ricardo's asides be collected and worked out, practically everything might be attributed to him that we find in any later writings. But he is fairly entitled to defense on another score. Writing at a time when 'bank directors and ministers gravely contended . . . that the issues of notes by the Bank of England, unchecked by any power in the holders of such notes to demand in exchange either specie or bullion, had not, nor could have, any effect on the prices of commodities, bullion, or foreign exchanges' (*Principles*, ch. 27), he was quite right to put the case against such foolishness more strongly than Thornton, with a more refined theory, was able to do. His famous analogy between the Bank's power under the Restriction Act and the discovery of a gold mine in the Bank's courtyard was not only telling but, so far as it went, also correct. This does not alter the fact, however, that, in matters of monetary as of general theory, Ricardian teaching is a detour and that it slowed up the advance of analysis, which could have been much quicker and smoother had Thornton's lead been followed—had Ricardo's force not prevailed over Thornton's insight.

[14] Mill's exposition of the theory of money, or the bulk of it, is to be found in *Principles*, Book III, chs. 7-14 and 19-24.

[15] The question arises whether the quantity theorem now applies to quantity of 'money' that includes notes and deposits. In its more modern versions, the quantity theorem is usually understood in this sense. But J. S. Mill did not take this line. Still less did he adopt the proposition that the quantity theorem retains validity for coins plus irredeemable paper, even in a developed credit system, because deposits bear a constant proportion to the reserves that consist of legal-tender money. This proposition, which was to be sponsored at the end of the subsequent period by Irving Fisher, was at the time held explicitly by Torrens and implicitly by Lord Overstone.

of phrase about the quantity of money 'which people are wanting to lay out; that is, all the money they have in their possession except what they are hoarding, or at least keeping by them as a reserve for future contingencies' (Book III, ch. 8, § 2). Moreover, he was quite aware of the implications of this as we have seen in our discussion of his interpretation of Say's law. And if we co-ordinate this with his recognition of the fact that purchases 'on credit' —that is, by means of credit instruments of one kind or another—influence prices as much as do purchases for money (ibid. ch. 12), we discover that in his analytic schema it is not at all the quantity of money per se which acts upon 'general prices' but simply expenditure, and that this expenditure is not closely, let alone uniquely, related to the quantity of coin or paper money. Thus, there is hardly any difference left between Mill's version of the quantity theory and the views of its opponents, contemporaneous or later. J. S. Mill's conceptual arrangement achieved the same end that others achieved by making velocity an economic variable. For to make the relevant quantity of money a variable in the purchasing-power problem by defining it as the quantity that is actually being spent evidently comes to the same thing as to start from a given quantity of money (however defined) and to make average velocity an economic, and in particular a cyclical, variable. The former procedure takes the curse off constant velocity and has in addition this advantage, that it enables us to separate the two constituents of what is usually labeled as velocity: the rate of spending, which is certainly variable, and velocity in a narrower sense, which, being determined by habits of payment, the degree of concentration of industry, and the like, may in fact, normally at least, be treated as an institutional constant. There is no need to show how near this comes to very modern views.

Before going on, I shall hastily mention two points about velocity that were of no great importance at the time though they gained some during the next period. First, then as later, some writers expressed themselves to the effect that the use of credit 'economizes' money or 'makes money more efficient.' This obviously invites the idea that credit increases the velocity of the legal-tender reserve money which, even though at rest in the vaults of banks, may then be said, metaphorically, to 'circulate' with a velocity much greater than it would have, if it actually did circulate. This idea was developed by Rodbertus (*Die preussische Geldkrisis*, 1845; see M. W. Holtrop, 'Theories of the Velocity of Circulation of Money in Earlier Economic Literature,' *Economic History, A Supplement to the Economic Journal*, January 1929, p. 520). Second, attempts at formulating an equation of exchange algebraically—which does not necessarily involve acceptance of the quantity theory—go far back (John Briscoe, H. Lloyd, see above, Part II, ch. 6, sec. 2c), but the most elaborate one of all belongs in the period under survey: J. W. Lubbock's *On Currency* (1840)—an interesting book by a still more interesting man. His equation has been reproduced in Viner (op. cit. p. 249n.) and Marget (op. cit. vol. 1, p. 11, and p. 12, n. 8).

3. Gleanings from the Discussions on Inflation and Resumption

To be sure, no element of Mill's performance originated with him. Yet there is historical merit in it. Both facts will stand out if we now survey a few of the landmarks on the road that led to his position.[1]

The Englishmen who started writing on monetary policy around 1800 knew very little about the English work of the seventeenth and even eighteenth centuries and still less, almost nothing in fact, of the non-English work of those centuries—an interesting example of how the advance of economics has been and is being impaired by these recurrent losses of previous accumulations of knowledge. In particular, they knew nothing about Cantillon and Galiani and not much about Steuart. Even the relatively learned Thornton knew the works of Locke, Hume, Montesquieu, and, of course, A. Smith,[2] but not much else. Substantially they started afresh, which goes far to explain the frequent occurrence of quite primitive arguments, even with the best of them. Since we are not primarily interested in the practical issues at stake but in the methods of analysis that were used in their discussion and in only those methods that bear upon the fundamentals of monetary theory, there is not much to report.

As we have seen, the Order in Council that suspended redemption of the notes of the Bank of England (1797) was a precautionary measure that was taken in response to a crisis and a run. Government borrowing from the Bank did not produce particularly visible effects for several years. When, however, prices began to rise and exchanges to fall, a torrent of articles and pamphlets poured forth whose *thema probandum* was that 'excessive' issue of irredeemable bank notes was responsible for those 'evils.' From his evidence before the two Committees of Secrecy (1797) to his two speeches on the Bullion Report (1811),[3] Thornton's contributions outdistanced all others so far as width of comprehension and analytic power are concerned. Three of them are of the first order of importance for the history of monetary analysis. The first is the treatment of the 'rapidity of circulation' as a variable quantity that fluctuates with the state of 'confidence,' that is, substantially with general business conditions: [4] this rediscovery of a fundamental truth that stands historically in the name of Cantillon was never again lost, but it was so little attended to that it had to be rediscovered once more by Keynes.[5] The second is

[1] Reference is again made to the extensive literature on that development (see above, sec. 1) and especially to the works of Viner and Marget. I now add J. H. Hollander, 'The Development of the Theory of Money from Adam Smith to David Ricardo,' *Quarterly Journal of Economics*, May 1911.

[2] Familiarity with the *Wealth of Nations* implies, of course, some knowledge of the literature that influenced A. Smith. But I do not think that even such English works as Joseph Harris' *Essay* (1757-8) were known in any other sense.

[3] See Appendices I and III to the Library of Economics reprint of *Paper Credit*.

[4] *Paper Credit*, ch. 3, especially p. 97.

[5] *Tract on Monetary Reform*, 1923, pp. 87 et seq. The variability of Keynes's k and k' is in fact the main *theoretical* contribution of the *Tract*.

the introduction of interest into the theory of the monetary process or, more precisely, the casting into a scientific mold of ideas on the relation between money, prices, and interest (see below, sec. 4a) that are intuitively familiar to every banker.[6] The third, which concerns the monetary aspects of international trade, will be discussed below in Section 5.

But there is something else. In bringing his analytic apparatus to bear upon the facts and practical problems of his day and country, Thornton proved himself a past master of the art of economic diagnosis. He was the only one of the leading writers to see the effects of the Bank's note issue and at the same time to keep it in its proper place in the total pattern of factors that shaped the English monetary situation during the first decade of the nineteenth century. Such merits as the Bullion Report of 1810 undoubtedly does possess—especially that honest, if somewhat uninspired, listing of all relevant facts whether causes, consequences, or symptoms—must be ascribed primarily to him.[7]

The other 'bullionists' or supporters of the policy that is embodied in the Bullion Report—resumption of specie payments by the Bank of England at the earliest possible date—are not, either by virtue of equal quality of work or by virtue of close similarity of views, entitled to be classed with Thornton. In addition to Wheatley and Ricardo, who represent a distinctly different school of thought, we merely notice Boyd and Lord King, whose arguments belong to the Wheatley-Ricardo line rather than to Thornton's, and Malthus for whom the opposite would be nearer to the truth.[8] Basically, their case was very simple. That the premium on bullion was proof of a 'depreciation' of bank notes was little more than a definition. That this premium was greater,

[6] It might be said that the 'inflationists' of the seventeenth and eighteenth centuries, the French and Italian as well as the English, had already explored the matter. But they had done so unsystematically and without facing the theoretical issues involved. The only economist who may claim to be Thornton's forerunner in any more significant sense was Hume, and even he was not in possession of the propositions that are characteristic of Thornton's teaching, except the one to be mentioned below. Verri is in the same case.

[7] According to a letter of Francis Horner, quoted in Hayek's Introduction to Thornton's *Paper Credit*, p. 54, the report was 'a motley composition by Huskisson, Thornton and myself.' My impression is that Horner may be, to some extent, considered a pupil of Thornton. Huskisson cannot. But he was an experienced and intelligent man who was not in the habit of running away with one-factor explanations. It is I think fair to say that much of the adverse criticism of the Report was directed against its recommendations of policy rather than against its analysis. But as is usual in such cases, critics who took exception to the recommendations (and this was very understandable) thought themselves in duty bound to attack the analysis from which the recommendations were supposed to follow. Malthus (*Principles*, p. 7), however, paid a judicious compliment to the report's analysis.

[8] Walter Boyd, *A Letter to . . . William Pitt* (1801); Peter King, *Thoughts on the Effects of the Bank Restriction* (1803). King exerted considerable influence upon Ricardo. Malthus' two papers on the 'Depreciation of Paper Currency' and 'Review of the Controversy respecting the High Price of Bullion,' both appeared in the *Edinburgh Review*, 1811 (vols. 17 and 18).

exchanges more unfavorable, and prices higher *than they would have been*, other things being equal, with a note circulation such as would have been possible had the notes been redeemable—that is, simply with a smaller note issue—only unreasonable stubbornness could deny. It was the not much less unreasonable stubbornness, with which they minimized all other factors in the situation, that laid them open to replies which were successful on several points.[9] Disapproval of a note issue greater than the amount possible under redemption of notes on demand presupposes, of course, that the latter is taken for the normal or ideal condition of the currency. This makes theoretical and practical metallists of all these 'bullionists.' But it does not necessarily mean that they held any strict quantity theory—Thornton, for example, certainly did not. There are much more interesting questions which emerge behind these basic ones as soon as it comes to analyzing the mechanism of inflation in detail, particularly the relations between the issue of the Bank of England and the country banks. But we cannot go into these.

The considerable success of the Wheatley-Ricardo line was due not only to Ricardo's force and brilliance but also to the lack of these qualities in his opponents. We shall confine ourselves to the outstanding authority among them, Thomas Tooke,[10] whose writings, though the first of them appeared only in 1826, represent better than do any others the strong as well as the weak points in the case against Ricardo's analysis.

The most obviously strong point—we continue to neglect the issue of policy—was of course that, in an inflation as mild as was the one of the English restriction period, the influence of non-monetary factors and even of factors that affect directly individual commodities or groups of commodities only (such as the cereals) must necessarily account for a much greater part of observed phenomena than would be so in cases of advanced, let alone wild, inflation. A good or bad harvest, a boom or a crisis, will then sometimes dominate a given price situation so as to reduce, for the moment, the inflationary influence to insignificance. The thing for the analyst to do in such cases is to assemble and to discuss the data carefully, year by year or even month by month, in order to make them speak for themselves. Tooke did this very well

[9] On the concessions which the bullionists did make and those which they ought to have made, see Viner, op. cit. pp. 127-38. The 'anti-bullionists' relied, for the explanation of the persistently unfavorable exchanges, mainly on the balance-of-payment argument. See below, sec. 5. In retrospect, it seems as though they would have been wiser had they admitted the basic contention of their opponents and confined themselves to asking what of it and to attacking the recommendation of speedy return to gold at prewar par.

[10] All the reader needs—and more—is contained in the monumental *History of Prices* (6 vols., 1838-57) which we have characterized already. But the work that was the first to present his views in something approaching a systematic form (*Considerations on the State of the Currency*, 1826), a second work (*On the Currency in Connection with the Corn Trade* . . . 1829), and the work in which polemical ardor got the better of him and led him to abandon some of his best results (*An Inquiry into the Currency Principle*, 1844) have some independent importance.

and with a considerable measure of success, and this would have been quite enough to invalidate Ricardo's theory *in its application to the situation then prevailing*. But Tooke aimed at more than this and attacked Ricardo's theory as theory. This, also, could have been done successfully—on lines that could have been derived from Thornton's work—but Tooke was quite unequal to this task. He had no notion of the logical relation between observation and analysis and never understood what facts may, and what facts may not, be adduced in verification or refutation of a theory.[11] And the moment he lost contact with individual situations, which he knew how to analyze, he seemed to lose the ability to think—the most eminent of that large class of economists who are in the same predicament. He then even lost that healthy sense for the absurd, which stood him in good stead in his factual analysis, and had no hesitation in committing himself to obviously untenable propositions such as some of the conclusions in the *Inquiry* of 1844 by which he tried to sum up his views on the fundamentals of monetary theory. The twelfth of these conclusions declares in so many words that prices of commodities do not depend—he failed to add 'uniquely,' which would have saved the situation—'upon the amount of the circulating medium' but that, on the contrary, the amount of the circulating medium 'is the consequence' of prices. However, before we put this down as downright silly, it is as well to recall that he was facing economists who denied entirely the existence of the relation which his twelfth conclusion asserted and that Tooke may be in part justified on this ground—and also be given the benefit of the mitigating circumstance that he was unsurpassable in clumsiness of formulation. The thirteenth conclusion then gives, though in a form that is not less clumsy, Tooke's theory of general prices, which has been much admired, especially in Germany,[12] where, partly improved, it experienced a revival in the first two decades of the twentieth century. Essentially, it comes to this. Since, on the one hand, commodities may be purchased without the use of 'money' and since, on the other hand, 'money' need not all become active (in which case it really is, as far as action upon prices is concerned, nonexistent), the quantity of money on which Ricardo reasoned is not a useful datum. What acts upon prices is expenditure, however financed. Within total expenditure of all kinds and for all purposes, the expenditure for consumption or investment by house-

[11] The best example of this curious failing, which Tooke shared with so many economists of his day and of our own, is his later attempt (in the *Inquiry* of 1844) to refute the theory that a money rate of interest which is lower than the prevailing (marginal) rate of profit tends to raise prices. In 1826, he had upheld and even elaborated this proposition of Thornton's: to have done so is in fact one of his chief services to monetary analysis. In 1844, he tried, however, to refute it, and even to uphold the opposite thesis by 'factual proof.' The reader will realize that this is quite easy to do and about as intelligent as it would be to hold that taking aspirin does not alleviate, in fact even causes, headaches on the ground that the consumption of aspirin is undoubtedly associated with people's having headaches.

[12] The German enthusiasm for Tooke *as a theorist* was I think in great part due to the influence of Adolf Wagner.

holds enjoys a particularly important position. 'And here we come to the ultimate regulating principle of money prices' (*History*, vol. III, p. 276): the fundamentally determining factor consists in 'the revenues of the different orders of the state, under the head of rents, profits, salaries, and wages. . .' In other words, we come out with the 'income approach' to the problem of the value of money.[13] It should be said at once that Tooke himself offers several clues for restating this Income Theory of Money more correctly and for developing it in various ways, one of which ends at Keynes's *General Theory*. But as left by Tooke, it is open to a criticism that greatly reduces its importance: [14] those revenues are obviously not ultimate data; prices determine them as much as they determine prices; and in the complex of factors that generate them, quantity of money has its place. It is not difficult to imagine the gusto with which Ricardo would have taken his hatchet and so trimmed down Tooke's disorderly argument as to be able to show triumphantly that those revenues were nothing but quantity of money times velocity. Still, though we shall have to notice more important contributions of Tooke, the importance of this one should not, if its suggestive power be duly taken into account, be evaluated at zero.

Let us now return for a moment to J. S. Mill and his performance. In the light of what we have learned since we left him, we might describe his teaching as a blend between Ricardo's and Tooke's. He saw the shortcomings of the Wheatley-Ricardo analysis and filed off its rough edges or some of them; he saw the shortcomings of Tooke's analysis and quickly corrected their most glaring faults; but he did much to salvage the truths they contained. To some extent, especially in his treatment of the monetary mechanism of international trade, he rediscovered Thornton's line, and here and there he improved upon it. There are but two qualifications to be added to this appraisal of a considerable achievement that, had it been better understood, might have been instrumental in bringing about a new epoch of monetary analysis.[15] First,

[13] For a history and discussion of this income approach, see primarily Marget, op. cit. vol. I, ch. 12.

[14] In fact, Wicksell, in the preface to his *Geldzins und Güterpreise* (1898), was able to say that 'a closer study of the writings of Tooke and his followers' had convinced him 'that there really was no theory of money other than the quantity theory and that, if the latter was wrong, we actually have no theory of money at all.' This means that one of the men who were most competent to judge refused to consider Tooke's approach as an acceptable alternative to Ricardo's. I confess that I cannot understand such overstatement in a writer of Wicksell's competence and fairness. But he did no more than overstate a truth.

[15] So far as the general theory of money and monetary policy are concerned, the non-English work of the period was little more than the reflex of the English work, though a fuller exposition would have to note a few minor contributions. J. B. Say's theory of money is not one of his strong points. But he was one of the first authors to identify—or, if the reader prefers, to confuse—the velocity of circulation of money and of goods. If, as was natural for a Frenchman—the debacle of the *assignats* having occurred only a decade before—he noticed the phenomenon characteristic of wild inflation, namely, that everyone attempts to get rid of money, which in consequence acquires an abnormal

though his retention of the theorem that an increase in money will, *ceteris paribus,* raise prices *in the same proportion* (the property peculiar to money) is all right when hedged in as he hedged it in, he also retained the erroneous Ricardian doctrine that variations in quantity of money and variations in physical volume of output have nothing to do with one another and will never coincide except by chance. Second, this denial of the possibility of 'monetary stimulation' is but the most important instance of the narrow views on the ideas of monetary management that emerged in the twenties and thirties of the nineteenth century. These must now be briefly noticed.[16]

Even before the passing of Peel's Resumption Bill (1819) or the actual resumptions of specie payments by the Bank of England (1821), many people voiced misgivings about the possible consequences of this step, which was bound to mean a jolt and might mean more than a jolt. When people began to realize that they were in for a serious depression—which actually prevailed, with the exception of the spurts of 1817 and 1824, from 1815 to 1830 and (after the upswing that set in about 1830) resumed from 1836 on—they put, as we have seen, all the blame on the factor that was most obvious on the surface, resumption, and the way in which it was carried into effect by the Bank of England. Politicians were relatively reasonable—the spokesmen of the agrarian interest being the only group that, as a group, went to any unreasonable lengths in this respect.[17] But bankers, financiers, and economists

'velocity,' this would seem small merit had not the same phenomenon been 'discovered' again, with much complacency, by writers in the inflations during and after the First World War. Nevertheless, Say's analysis of money is of interest to us because it shows that he was perfectly aware of people's variable attitudes toward holding cash and thus *may be adduced in support of our interpretation of* Say's law. Also, let us note in passing that Say was to be a strongly hostile critic of England's return to gold at prewar parity which shows that he cannot have considered price level as a matter of indifference. The reader who wishes to know more about French monetary theory is referred to M. Chevalier's volume, *La Monnaie* (1850), and to the relevant articles in the *Dictionnaire d'économie politique* (1853-4, ed. by Coquelin and Garnier). From the Italian literature on money, we shall notice only Ferrara's piece on *Corso forzato,* 1868 (irredeemable legal-tender paper), though his *Prefazioni* and *Lezioni* also contain other contributions to the subject. The German literature was stronger on the theory of credit and banking than on the general theory of money. But there are some original points on paper money in Buquoy's treatise. For the United States, it will suffice to mention E. Lord's *Principles of Currency and Banking* (1829); George Tucker's *The Theory of Money and Banks Investigated* (1839); and W. M. Gouge's well-known *Short History of Paper Money and Banking* (1833)—none of which is particularly strong but all of which were typical performances so far as their theoretical sketches are concerned.

16 Only very few issues and names can be mentioned. For a fuller exposition, see, besides Viner, op. cit., R. S. Sayers, 'The Question of the Standard, 1815-44,' *Economic History, A Supplement to the Economic Journal,* February 1935, and 'The Question of the Standard in the Eighteen-Fifties,' ibid., January 1933, and authorities there referred to.

17 There is not space, nor is there any need in a history of analysis, to tell the story of 'Squire' Western—how he foamed, how he was ridiculed, how he became something

inspired by the viewpoint of bankers and financiers, especially those who felt on the defensive owing to their previous sponsorship of the Bullion Report, had most of them no doubt whatever that the root of all evil was money and nothing else, in most cases not even troubling to establish what seemed so indubitable a diagnosis. Accordingly, they criticized resumption, or at least resumption at prewar parity, as untimely or altogether pointless, and they produced remedies and schemes of reform that ranged all the way from excluding gold from actual circulation and the insertion of silver into monetary reserves, through anticipations of the 'commodity dollar' to a managed paper currency that was to stabilize prices and employment. We know, of course, that history incessantly repeats itself. But it is amazing and perhaps a little sad to observe that economists, swayed by the prevailing humors of the hour, also repeat themselves and that, blissfully ignorant of their predecessors, they believe in each case that they are making unheard-of discoveries and building up a brand-new monetary science. However, there are some things to be gleaned from a history of analysis.[18]

In the first place, the question of diagnosis was indeed neglected, but not entirely. As we should expect, Tooke shone in the discussion. He had the great merit of not being a monetary monomaniac, and his common sense and command of facts enabled him to analyze the decline of prices from 1814 to 1837 in a thoroughly sensible manner. His 'six causes' [19]—good har-

---

of a tragi-comical figure. I cannot help feeling that some injustice has been done to that worthy. His argument would, if anything, have shown up favorably in the U.S. discussion on money, 1930-34. See, e.g., his *Letter to the Earl of Liverpool* (1826).

[18] Ricardo was one of those who smarted under responsibility—real or imagined—for the recommendation of the Bullion Report and for resumption. The main justification for his refusal to share the responsibility for the latter in the form in which it was actually carried out is his Ingot Plan, which he first recommended as early as 1811 (*High Price of Bullion . . .* , 4th ed., Appendix). Essentially, the plan proposed is the same as the system that England adopted on her return to the gold standard in 1925: the Bank was to be 'obliged to purchase any quantity of gold that was offered them, not less than twenty ounces at 3*l.* 17*s.* per ounce, and to sell any quantity that might be demanded at 3*l.* 17*s.* 10½*d.*,' export and import of bullion to be entirely free (*Proposals for an Economical and Secure Currency*, 1816). As has been pointed out already, this means a full and free gold system, except that no gold coins are used in internal hand-to-hand circulation. From the standpoint of the problem of how to mitigate the impact of resumption upon prices, the plan is relevant only by virtue of the fact that the Bank, if it did not have to provide gold for internal circulation, would have needed a smaller gold stock than if part of its notes were to be replaced by coins. Since the writers who blamed the depression on resumption were soon driven back to asserting that the cause of all the trouble was that the Bank, by its purchases of gold, had caused an international deflation—'raised the value of gold'—policy according to Ricardo's plan would in fact have met the chief objection to resumption. The argument itself about the Bank's having 'raised the value of gold' cannot be discussed here. For details of Ricardo's plan and its history, the reader is referred to James Bonar's article, 'Ricardo's Ingot Plan, a Centenary Tribute,' *Economic Journal*, September 1923.

[19] *History of Prices*, vol. II, pp. 348-9.

vests, favorable foreign exchange, removal of obstructions to foreign supplies and the emergence of new sources of raw materials, falling rates of freight and insurance, technological progress, increasing supply of capital, hence lower rates of interest—do not indeed reveal ideal analysis and there is much in them to find fault with from a theoretical standpoint. But at least they contain the most important factor—the tremendous increase in productive efficiency in consequence of the Industrial Revolution—and in addition most of the salient characteristics of that epoch, though Tooke failed at the analytic task of bringing them into their proper relations.

In the second place, the variations in the purchasing power of money brought up the question of 'justice' as between creditors and debtors (or else, so far as the public debt was concerned, taxpayers). As always, 'justice' was what benefited the interest with which each writer sympathized. But more substantial arguments, sometimes crude, sometimes more refined, reinforced or even supplanted considerations of justice. 'Squire' Western made the point that there are situations in which, higher prices being the only alternative to widespread bankruptcy, a falling value of money might be deemed to be in the interest of creditors. Others emphasized that, on the whole, debtors represent the active elements in the economy so that a benefit to them in the end benefits everybody. Still others learned to qualify their dirges about the discouragement of industry through falling prices by stating 'unless this fall is caused by a fall in costs' [20]—though some were for price maintenance even in the face of falling costs. Like Hume (and Wicksell) most writers on currency preferred slowly rising to stable prices. Needless to say, the usual confusion between the prices a writer was interested in and the price level impaired arguments throughout; most writers, as we have seen above, were having a hard time in defining what they meant by 'general prices.'

In the third place, definite ideas of monetary management were taking shape and some of them were more than mere repetitions of seventeenth-century argument. There was the idea of a stable price level; the idea of monetary stimulation of production (what we call pump priming); the idea of stabilizing interest rates; and the idea of stabilizing employment.

Our few illustrative examples will be taken primarily from the economists of 'scientific' reputation. Thornton offered several suggestions for monetary management in times of crisis. Ricardo's plan we have noticed already. Joseph Lowe's tabular standard,[21] intended for voluntary use for the stabilization of long-run contracts, marks a distinct advance in monetary analysis. Inconvertible paper currency was sponsored by T. P. Thompson.[22] Poulett Scrope did not

[20] Some writers, though not the better ones, mentioned fall in costs *besides* increase in supply.

[21] *The Present State of England* (1822). In his *Essay* of 1807, Wheatley had already made a similar proposal. The idea itself, of course, goes back at least as far as Fleetwood.

[22] He presented his ideas on monetary policy first in his *Westminster Review* article 'On the Instrument of Exchange' (1824; reprint 1830). They grew naturally out of a situation in which irredeemable paper had been actually circulating without blotting out sun and moon, whereas resumption proved a painful operation. Many people

go so far as this but adhered to the metallic standard (gold or silver).[23] However, besides sponsoring and elaborating Lowe's tabular-standard idea he tackled the whole complex of problems that arose from variations in the purchasing power of money, including their effects upon labor. He wrongly held that labor's relative or absolute share in 'gross produce' *must* be reduced as the share of creditors (at fixed interest) increases, but he had the merit of emphasizing the influence of falling prices upon employment. This was also done by Bollmann.[24] The only other name I am going to mention, the name of the two heroes of the Birmingham Currency School, is Attwood.[25] The Birmingham Currency School is correctly described by the label it accepted itself:

---

besides 'Squire' Western must have felt that it would be much better to carry the war system into peace practice, i.e. to retain it for good. Thomas Perronet Thompson, like Keynes in 1923—the basic recommendation of the *Tract on Monetary Reform* was precisely this, although Keynes retained a gold reserve—must therefore have voiced the feelings of many more people than were prepared to speak up. The ideas as well as the situations of 1824 and 1923 present in fact striking similarities, and both Thomas Perronet Thompson and Poulett Scrope, but most of all Thomas Attwood (see below) deserve to be known better than they are. So does Glocester Wilson, who, in his remarkable *Defence of Abstract Currencies in Reply to the Bullion Report* (1811), makes the statement that was often sneered at in the second half of the nineteenth century and yet contains a profound truth (which very naturally was commonplace among Austrian writers) that gold is no more essential to the guinea than is brass to the ruler that is made of it.

[23] *On Credit Currency* . . . (1830) and *Examination of the Bank Charter Question* . . . (1833). The whole of the discussion now under survey, of course, bears in many points on questions of bank credit which we shall take up in the next section. In some points, the two discussions merge into one another and our attempt to separate them—which in any case has no other justification than expository convenience—breaks down occasionally.

[24] Justus E. Bollmann, a physician who after some adventures in Europe settled in the United States, occupies a considerable position in the history of the theory of banking in America. The works that are relevant in the present connection are A *Letter to Thomas Brand Esq. . . . on . . . a Resumption of Specie Payments* (1819), and A *Second Letter . . . on the Practicability of the New System of Bullion Payments* (1819). As do his earlier works, *Paragraphs on Banks* (1810) and his *Plan for an Improved System of the Money Concerns of the Union* (1816), those Letters display a grasp of the problems involved that was far above average.

[25] The brothers, Thomas and Mathias Attwood, were both bankers—Mathias also an extremely successful company promoter—and anything but cranks or visionaries. Mathias was simply a bimetallist who stated his case ably and soberly. But Thomas liked pamphleteering, agitation, mass meetings, and phraseological overstatement, and he had to pay the price: professionals did not take him quite seriously. They were wrong, however. A very considerable analytic performance might be distilled from his writings and evidences. See his *Letter to Nicholas Vansittart, on the Creation of Money, and on its Action upon National Prosperity* (1817); *Observations on Currency, Population, and Pauperism* (1818); *A Letter to the Earl of Liverpool* (1819); also his articles in the *Globe*, reprinted under the title *The Scotch Banker* in 1828. It is from these writings that any study of modern ideas on monetary management ought to start.

Anti-Gold Law League. As we might expect, many of its members were just inflationists. But Thomas Attwood was much more than that. If I have caught the meaning of his message, he was an anti-deflationist in the modern sense. He had an almost hysterical horror of what we call deflation and attributed to it every economic difficulty of his age. And in deflation itself he saw nothing but the vagaries of an essentially irrational system of money and credit. But whatever we may think of this diagnosis—many of us are bound to sympathize with it—it had the merit of serving as a magnifying glass that enabled him to see what the leading economists of the period refused to see, namely, that an ideally managed paper money could avoid some consequences of the gold automatism that are in fact functionless. So far as I know, he did not work out his principle fully and systematically. But, barring exaggerations, his advocacy of the principle itself is free from anything that deserves to be called freakish. His claim to being considered as a serious specialist on money is further strengthened by his recommendation to resume gold payments, if indeed they had to be resumed, at a reduced gold value of the pound —a remarkable anticipation of an idea of 1919.

None of these ideas entered Mill's authoritative text except as so many errors that need to be exposed. In his chapter 'Of an Inconvertible Paper Currency' (*Principles,* Book III, ch. 13), besides asserting that a power 'to depreciate the currency without limit' is an 'intolerable evil,' he encountered with a flat negative not only Attwood's but also Hume's and Thornton's arguments about the possibility of monetary stimulation. From our standpoint, we have no right to object to Mill's evident dislike of the idea. Nobody is in duty bound to approve of monetary management, and there were and are perfectly good reasons for distrusting the ability, independence, and what-not of the agencies that would have to undertake it. There are also reasons, good or bad, for wishing to put up with all the vagaries of automatic money rather than with the vagaries of politics. But we do have a right to object to Mill's refusal to consider the theory of managed money and to face squarely the facts and problems that gave rise to the idea. By doing so, he impoverished monetary analysis and left it, in this respect, in a state that explains, though it does not justify, the impression so prevalent in our day that there is an immense *scientific* gulf between him and us.

Nor is his chapter 'Of a Double Standard' (Book III, ch. 10) any more distinguished. What he had to say on bimetallism rests on the suspicion—in general well-founded, of course—that the sponsors of bimetallist schemes simply want to depress the purchasing power of money. Since he disapproved of this, he brushed the whole subject aside without entering seriously into the analytic problems involved, though a considerable literature on silver and on bimetallism developed during the period under survey—Henri Cernuschi's *Mécanique de l'échange* appeared in 1865—and though it was clearly the duty of the writer of a treatise such as Mill's to deal adequately with it irrespective of his sympathies.[26] The little that can be said in this book about

[26] For a time, Ricardo had advocated silver as a standard metal.

those problems will be deferred to Part IV (ch. 8). Gold production moved on a low level until the 1840's. When Russian and then Australian and Californian gold came in to change the situation, facts and effects were zestfully debated throughout the 1850's and 1860's. There could be no reasonable doubt that the new gold was exerting *some* influence upon prices but there was all the more doubt whether this influence, counteracted as it was by the flow of gold to India, China, and other countries and by the concomitant increase in the output of goods, was strong enough to raise English prices by any appreciable amount.[27] This implied investigation of the *modus operandi* of the new gold upon monetary systems, credit, interest, output, and so on all over the world. Nobody doubted that first effects were upon interest; that the easy reserve situation prevented what might have been a financial crisis in 1853; but that high profits and speculation, engendered by the monetary stimulation of the economic process, would lead to stringencies and accentuate cyclical ups and downs.[28] With due respect to many a sensible piece of analysis that a more complete report would have to mention, I cannot but conclude that the gains for economic analysis were slender and that the economists of that time missed an opportunity to build the lessons of those experiences into their general theory of money. This shows also in the way in which the plethora of gold affected opinion on bimetallism.

On the whole, people enjoyed the prosperity that the gold discoveries seemed to have brought: Providence was, for the time being, popular with the stock exchange. Dissent was not lacking, however, and some of the dissenters began to think of the adoption of a silver standard as a remedy for the gold inflation, that is, for reasons exactly opposite to those that had recommended the silver standard to some writers around 1820 [29] and were again to recommend it from the 1870's on. In addition, however, history was putting economists under obligation by performing an interesting experiment in bimetallism under their very eyes. France had then a *de facto* bimetallist system at the rate of 1:15½. As gold fell it began to flow into French circulation and reserves and to drive out the silver. This was the famous parachute effect, as Chevalier called it, that is to say, the effect of bimetallism to absorb

[27] On samples from this literature and on the level of this discussion, see Sayers (op. cit. 1935, secs. II and V). M. Chevalier's *On the Probable Fall in the Value of Gold* (1857; English trans. by Richard Cobden, with a preface, 1859) should be particularly noticed, as should Cairnes's contribution, three articles, 'Essays on the Gold Question' (1859-60), republ. in *Essays in Political Economy* . . . (1873). The discussion gave, of course, a powerful impulse to the development of price-index numbers. It produced Jevons' *A Serious Fall in the Value of Gold* . . . (1863) and the *Depreciation of Gold* (1869), both reprinted in *Investigations in Currency and Finance* (ed. by Professor Foxwell, 1884).

[28] Mill's views on the *modus operandi* of the new gold are concisely formulated in a letter of his to Cairnes (see the Mill-Cairnes correspondence publ. by G. O'Brien, *Economica*, November 1943, p. 279).

[29] On the most important English sponsor of the silver standard, James Maclaren, see Sayers, op. cit., 1933, *passim*.

the depreciating and to set free the appreciating monetary metal and so to stabilize the value of the monetary unit, at least so long as the latter was not entirely displaced. It does not reflect much credit upon economists that this effect had not occurred to them before.[30] But it reflects still less credit on them that they did not understand it fully when they had it before their eyes. The first economist to work out the complete theory of the bimetallist standard at a fixed ratio was Walras.

4. The Theory of Credit

Even today, textbooks on Money, Currency, and Banking are more likely than not to begin with an analysis of a state of things in which legal-tender 'money' is the only means of paying and lending. The huge system of credits and debits, of claims and debts, by which capitalist society carries on its daily business of production and consumption is then built up step by step by introducing claims to money or credit instruments that act as substitutes for legal tender and are allowed indeed to affect its functioning in many ways but not to oust it from its fundamental role in the theoretical picture of the financial structure. Even when there is very little left of this fundamental role in practice, everything that happens in the sphere of currency, credit, and banking is construed from it, just as the case of money itself is construed from barter.

Historically, this method of building up the analysis of money, currency, and banking is readily understandable: from the fourteenth and fifteenth centuries on (and even in the Graeco-Roman world) the gold or silver or copper coin was the familiar thing. The credit structure—which moreover was incessantly developing—was the thing to be explored and to be analyzed. The legal constructions, too—remember that most economists who were not businessmen were jurists—were geared to a sharp distinction between money as the only genuine and ultimate means of payment and the credit instrument that embodied a claim to money. But logically, it is by no means clear that the most useful method is to start from the coin—even if, making a concession to realism, we add inconvertible government paper—in order to proceed to the credit transactions of reality. It may be more useful to start from these in the first place, to look upon capitalist finance as a clearing system that cancels claims and debts and carries forward the differences—so that 'money' payments come in only as a special case without any particularly fundamental importance. In other words: practically and analytically, a credit theory of money is possibly preferable to a monetary theory of credit.[1]

The situation of this period's theory of credit and banking may now be

[30] Ricardo, e.g., did notice this mechanism (*Principles*, ch. 27) by which the standard would be sometimes gold and sometimes silver. But he saw nothing in it but 'an inconvenience which it was highly desirable should be remedied.'

[1] I hope that this sentence is self-explanatory. It will, however, be illustrated in the money chapter (8) of Part IV by a discussion of one of the consequences of economists' failure to go through with the idea adumbrated above.

characterized like this. The English leaders from Thornton to Mill did explore the credit structure, and in doing so made discoveries that constitute their chief contributions to monetary analysis but could not be adequately stated in terms of the monetary theory of credit. But they failed to go through with the theoretical implications of these discoveries, that is, to build up a systematic credit theory of money,[2] and on principle clung to the monetary theory of credit. So they produced in the end something that was neither the one nor the other. An eminent critic of our day who is a strong adherent of the monetary theory of credit, Professor Rist, was therefore, formally, within his rights when he accused some of the authors of that period of having 'confused' money and credit. Their waverings in the use of terms certainly suggest this.[3]

Keeping this in mind, we shall in this section discuss cursorily (a) the most interesting of the period's conquests in the theory of credit, and then (b) a few more points about banking and central banking that are most conveniently presented with reference to the quarrels between the 'currency' and 'banking' schools over the principles embodied or supposed to be embodied in Peel's Act of 1844—though those quarrels, unlike the ones over war inflation and resumption, produced more heat than light.[4]

(a) *Credit,[5] Prices, Interest, and Forced Savings.* As soon as we realize that there is no essential difference between those forms of 'paper credit' that are

[2] We might see the outlines of such a theory in the works of Macleod. But they remained so completely outside of the pale of recognized economics that we transfer them and their author to Part IV. Compare also Wicksell's dictum, mentioned above.

[3] Yet, as we know, facts and ideas that were familiar to the projectors of the seventeenth century and, in a purified form, to the scientific economists of the first half of the eighteenth, such as Boisguillebert, Cantillon, and Verri, might have set the writers of 1800-1850 on the track of what I believe to be a more adequate analysis. But these facts and ideas were practically forgotten by 1800—or a shudder at John Law's practices was all that was left of them—and they had to be rediscovered by men who worked in the strait-jacket of the monetary theory of credit.

[4] The reader is again referred to the works of Viner, Marget, and Rist. And also to V. F. Wagner, *Geschichte der Kredittheorien* (1937); Harry E. Miller, *Banking Theories in the United States before* 1860 (1927; a book the reader will find particularly useful since it is impossible in this sketch to do justice to the important American literature on banking); and L. W. Mints, *A History of Banking Theory* (1945), a work that reports on over 600 items but, as a consequence of its wholesale and uncritical condemnation of the commercial-bill theory of banking, pours away the baby with the bath water.

[5] Writers had difficulty in defining 'credit.' Accordingly, the term was very loosely used all along. Thornton defined it as 'confidence,' which is an obvious logical misfit. We come nearer to what these writers wanted to express and what that difficulty was when we learn that Mill (Book III, ch. 12, § 1) averred that it was Credit which acts on prices and not 'banknotes, bills, and cheques.' He meant that an individual's power to purchase, which is the objective element behind demand in terms of *numéraire,* is not fully represented by the amount of the credit instruments that are actually used in 'payment' or even, so we should add, by the deposits, overdrafts, etc. against which checks are drawn, but by the total amount that an individual could command if he

used for paying and lending,[6] and that demand, supported by 'credit,' acts upon prices in essentially the same manner as does demand supported by legal tender, we are on the way toward a serviceable theory of the credit structure and, in particular, toward the discovery of the relations between prices and interest. Before turning to the period's theory of these relations we must, however, consider the obstacles that prevented many authors from accepting the two propositions just alluded to. We have already seen that the monetary theory of credit in itself constitutes such an obstacle because, developing the theory of the network of credit 'payments' from the case of payment in specie, it assigns to legal-tender money a *logically* privileged position. But we still have to consider some *practical* reasons that seem to militate against an analysis that puts, say, 'money' and 'deposits' on *essentially* the same footing.

In the first place, the law treats different types of means of payment differently. In the case of legal-tender money, it insists on acceptance; in the case of an accepted and endorsed bill of exchange, it does not. For the legal mind, the two are anything but 'essentially the same thing,' since the credit instrument is on the face of it a claim to money. In the second place, and in connection with this, 'money' and 'paper credit,' and again the various forms of 'paper credit,' are not in practice equally well qualified for every purpose. They are not perfect substitutes for one another: legal-tender money is a universal means of payment; bank notes and deposits are less widely acceptable; the accepted and endorsed bill of exchange can circulate only in a relatively small circle of business concerns. And only legal-tender money is recognized, in most historical cases, as the ultimate reserve money of the banking system. These differences are of course quite important, and nobody would think of trying to explain the way in which a given monetary system functions without taking account of them. *And this is why Thornton's perception of the fact that the different means of payments may, on a certain level of abstraction, be treated as essentially alike was a major analytic performance*, for the mere practitioner will in general be impressed by the technical differences rather than by the fundamental sameness.[7] But precisely for the same reason, it is quite understandable that, though Thornton's view eventually prevailed with J. S. Mill, the opposite view found sponsors all along. And this was one of the reasons, though not the only one, why some writers

---

wanted to, i.e. the amount that is actually at his disposal in some measurable form plus something that might be called *potential* credit, which defies measurement, yet is a factor in any given situation. And we may assume, I think, that it is this total that people meant when they used the term Credit.

[6] For jurists, I repeat that the word 'paying' is not used in the legal sense, and is meant to comprise, besides what constitutes legally definitive payment (*solutio*), also much of what legally is a mere substitute for definitive payment (*datio in solutionem*).

[7] We might, therefore, speak of a genuine discovery of Thornton's, were it not for the fact that it had been made long before. See, e.g., the *Discourse* of 1697, attributed to Pollexfen, mentioned above, Part II, chs. 3 and 7.

stoutly denied that 'credit' acts upon prices.[8] Now we turn to the subject of Prices and Interest or, as we may also call it, of the Real and the Money Rate of Interest.

Within the scholastic system, interest being simply the price for the use of money, the phrase Real and Money Rate of Interest is a label on an empty box—there was no problem of any *direct* relation of this kind, any more than there is in the Keynesian system.[9] But when, under A. Smith's influence, Barbon's analysis began to prevail, according to which interest was that part of business gains that accrued to the purveyor of physical capital, the question was bound to arise how *this* interest was related to the interest in the market of money loans, which after all is a distinct phenomenon. A. Smith answered[10] in effect that the loan rate of the money market was simply the shadow of the 'rate of profit' on real capital—the latter being 'lent in the form of money' as the later slogan has it—and that quantity of money, however defined, had nothing at all to do with it. I cannot emphasize sufficiently that this remained the dominant opinion throughout the nineteenth century, at any rate until Wicksell; that it was, as will be presently explained, also Ricardo's; and that even Thornton's contributions to the problem of the relation between 'money,' prices, and the 'real' rate of interest (important though they were), which point to a different conclusion, were largely forgotten.

Thornton related the volume and the velocity of money and other circulating media to interest in the four following ways. (1) He was the first to point out that a high rate of discount will attract gold from abroad. (2) He also pointed out the relevance of the prevailing money rate of interest for the public's willingness to hold cash.[11] (3) Further, he pointed out the effect upon the loan rate of expectations about the future course of prices.[12] (4)

8 Tooke must be classed with them, even after he had recognized the fundamental sameness of notes and deposits, if we take some of his utterances literally. But the denial in turn admits of different interpretations. We shall return to the argument below.

9 Of course, if we dig more deeply, the problem does reappear in both systems.

10 The key performance was D. Hume's essay 'Of Interest' (*Political Discourses*, 1752). A. Smith quoted approvingly its argument against the view of Locke, Law, and Montesquieu that the American gold and silver had been the cause of the fall of the rate of interest that occurred in Europe (*Wealth*, p. 337), but neglected to make full use of the rest of Hume's theory that, anticipating much later work, went some way toward giving the monetary factor its due. Thornton improved upon Hume's position, but neither he nor J. S. Mill was quite fair in their criticism of him. Hume, as we know, was anticipated, in several essential points, by Cantillon.

11 While it should be admitted that the loss involved in holding idle cash varies with the rate of interest and that this fact does make some difference, the empirical correlation between large cash holdings and low rates of interest must not be considered as causally explained by this fact: large cash items and low rates are primarily consequences of decisions to restrict operations in depressive situations, and there would be correlation between them even if there were no functional relation at all.

12 This piece of analysis, succinctly presented in the first of the two 'Speeches'

Finally, soaring high above the commonplace controversy on the question whether or not banks have the power 'to inflate the currency,' he presented (all the essentials of) a complete analysis of the market for loanable funds that pivots on the fundamental equilibrium theorem, that the loan rate (money interest) tends to equal expected marginal profits of investment (marginal efficiency of capital).[13] This requires some elaboration.

First, Thornton's theorem occurs in the course of an argument to the effect that there does not exist, within the logic of the credit mechanism itself and apart from convertibility, any restriction that will prevent bank credit from exceeding the limit beyond which it will cause an inflationary increase in prices; [14] and that, in particular, 'sound banking practice,' that is, the practice of lending on good security only or even discounting bona fide commer-

---

appended to the Library of Economics reprint of *Paper Credit*, pp. 335-6, is nothing short of admirable. It is easy to see that in a period of falling (rising) prices the creditor gets more (less), in terms of goods, than he bargained for. It is less easy, but still easy, to realize that this fact, if foreseen, will influence the terms of the loan contract, a lower (higher) rate in terms of money being stipulated for than would be the case otherwise. But Thornton saw that this is inconclusive, at least if expected price changes are moderate, unless the mechanism be uncovered by which that result is brought about even in the absence of what we may call conscious expectations. So he pointed out that if prices rise (fall), the debtor will make gains beyond (below) expectations, that this will induce him to borrow more (less)—so long as this lasts, the case merges into (4)—and that this will tend to adjust the rate of interest to rising (falling) price levels. It should be observed that, as a short-run qualification, this fits perfectly into what has been called in the text the 'recognized opinion' about the relation between the rate of profit on real capital and the money loan rate. Thornton's idea was taken up again, independently, by Irving Fisher in 1896 (see below, Part IV, ch. 5, sec. 7b) and before that by Marshall.

[13] It is for the reader to decide whether or not this formulation, clad in modern terminology, renders Thornton's meaning faithfully: while it rests on many other passages, it is meant to convey particularly the paragraph on pp. 253-4 of *Paper Credit*. No essential discrepancy, considering the banking practice of the time, is involved in Thornton's speaking of the rate of the Bank of England. Nor should qualms be caused by Thornton's speaking simply of 'the current rate of mercantile profit.' Apart from the fact that my rendering of this phrase might be considered fair, even if there were nothing further to support it, the element of expectation enters into many other arguments of Thornton's (see p. 158) and was perfectly familiar in the literature of the period (J. S. Mill used it in *Principles*, Book III, ch. 12, § 3). But the addition of the adjective 'marginal' to 'profits,' at least in the form of the profits of the least favored firm, is an improvement that was added by Ricardo. If my reading be unobjectionable, it must also be unobjectionable to say that Thornton propounded a theorem that is fundamental to the Marshall-Wicksell-Hawtrey analysis. This is also Professor von Hayek's opinion.

[14] Thornton was primarily concerned with the lending of the Bank of England and with its note issue. He was, however, fully aware of the complications that arise from the influence of this issue upon the country-bank issue and upon the behavior of London bankers and 'other discountants.' This seems to justify the generalizing statement of our text.

cial bills only, does not constitute such a restriction. The reasons for this are, of course, that an expansion of loans, unless accompanied by a compensating reduction of expenditure by people other than the borrowers, will increase money incomes, hence raise demand schedules for goods and services (not necessarily their prices), so that every wave of additional borrowing tends to justify itself *ex post;* and that such an expansion of loans can—at least in favorable situations—be induced by the offer to lend at a rate that is below expected marginal profits. In other words, the equilibrium of Thornton's theorem is unstable: an increase in loans beyond the equilibrium amount will eventually (though not necessarily at first) result in an increase in prices and, if the rate of interest continues to be kept at its old level (the level that induced the first expansion), further borrowing will continue to be profitable at the new level of prices; further expansion of credit will follow, and so on, without any assignable limit, and we shall have the Wicksellian Cumulative Process (for restatement and criticism, see below, Part IV, ch. 8, sec. 2). To enforce stability, other conditions, such as convertibility—direct or indirect—of notes and deposits in gold, are therefore necessary. This practical conclusion, if not the whole of Thornton's analysis, was widely accepted, among others by King, Ricardo, Joplin, and Senior. J. S. Mill also accepted it though, presumably under the influence of Tooke, he toned it down.

Lord King was, so far as I know, the first to follow Thornton in his *Thoughts on the Effects of the Bank Restriction* (1803). Ricardo accepted the doctrine resolutely, at least in the faulty form that, if banks 'charge less than the market rate of interest, there is no amount of money which they might not lend' (*Principles,* ch. 27, but see *High Price of Bullion,* 1810). Senior expressed himself similarly (see *Industrial Efficiency and Social Economy,* S. L. Levy ed., 1928, vol. II; the essay is a review of Lord King's pamphlet), using the term 'usual' rate. Since the market or usual rate itself may be below *that* equilibrium level which would prevent credit inflation, Ricardo and Senior must be interpreted to have meant something akin to Wicksell's 'real rate.' Ricardo seems to indicate this by another faulty phrase that occurs in the paragraph from which I have quoted and lets interest be 'regulated' by 'the rate of profits which can be made by the employment of capital and is totally independent of the quantity or of the value of money.' Clearly two different sets of considerations fight each other in this paragraph. On the one hand, Ricardo meant to uphold what has been described above as the Smithian view of the relation between the 'real' and the money rate of interest. On the other hand, no practical financier could deny that any increase of the circulating medium, no matter whether of gold or notes or anything else, will tend to depress the rate of interest at least temporarily. So he reconciled Thornton's theory, which does not fit at all well into his quantity theory, first, by underlining the 'temporarily' and, second, by emphasizing, to the exclusion of everything else, the inflationary effect of such an increase, as we shall presently see. Tooke might have pointed out, and to some extent did point out, that there are many qualifications to the proposition that low interest raises prices. As it was, probably carried away by his controversial ardors, he in the end denied the existence of any such nexus as unreasonably as he denied the existence of any nexus between quantity of money and prices. J. S. Mill, on this point as elsewhere, 'rationalized' Tooke. This he did by the formula that the lending by banks *qua* lending does act on the interest rate and not on prices; but that, since the 'currency in common use, being a currency provided by bankers, is all issued in the way of loans' (*Principles*, Book III, ch. 23, § 4), the lending by banks *qua* creation of currency acts upon prices and not on the interest rate. The recognition of the currency-creating power of banks (which Tooke denied in the *Inquiry*) is as interesting as the recognition of the relation, so strongly emphasized in the United States, between lending and repaying, on the one hand, and expansion and contraction of the circulating medium, on the other—in which relation some of the more naïve American currency doctors saw (perhaps see) the source of all sorts of evil. J. S. Mill made nothing of all this, as will presently be pointed out again. Still, nothing of it escaped his attention—or should have escaped the attention of his readers.

Second, Thornton knew of course perfectly well that the inflationary process he described presupposes an *uncompensated* expansion of lending. If the increase in loans is compensated, for example, by saving, it will not start that process. But, preoccupied as he was with the operation of 'paper credit' in wartime, he did not bother about this and so he failed to state explicitly the condition for *stable* equilibrium in the market for loanable funds which reads, in Wicksell's formulation of 1898, that loans should equal people's voluntary savings. To some extent, at least, this lacuna was filled by Joplin,[15] though he got still less credit for it than he got for having anticipated the principles of banking policy that, so far as the notes of the Bank of England are concerned, were carried into effect by Peel's Act. Like Ricardo he strongly disapproved of the power of banks to create, by their lending, net additions to the total stock of means of payments, but he did not deny its existence—this was done by others—and pointed out that, if it were done away with and if banks were accordingly prevented from increasing the total of their loans beyond the amount of the public's current savings, then a stable equilibrium in the money market might exist. It will be observed that in this case the equilibrium theorem is nothing but a particular way of stating the Turgot-Smith theory of saving and investment.

Third, Thornton realized not only that bank loans which add to the means of payment may stimulate output rather than raise prices if they impinge upon an underemployed economy,[16] but also that, even after full employment

[15] Thomas Joplin, *Outlines of a System of Political Economy . . . together with the Fourth Edition of an Essay on the Principles of Banking* (1823) and *Analysis and History of the Currency Question* (1832). Joplin was the first to propose a 100 per cent reserve system of banking, the idea being to make money interest behave as it would behave with a purely metallic currency, and to render the creation of bank currency—the creation of means of payment by lending—impossible. In his elaborate statement, the difficulty that all such schemes meet stands out very clearly: preventing banks from creating near-money (this American term owes its origin I believe to near-beer) will not prevent the trade from doing so. Also, in his schema, gold inflows would still be allowed to disturb equilibrium in the money market.

[16] The practical importance of this truth is not great because underemployment of resources will in general occur in depression when there is no demand for additional credit. But its theoretical importance is nevertheless considerable because it forces us to recognize the existence of relations between the circulating medium and output, which the Ricardian or strict type of quantity theory so steadfastly denied.

has been reached, credit expansion may still have some effect upon output, though he immediately proceeded to show that this effect will be smaller than the inflationary one (*Paper Credit*, pp. 236, 239 et seq.). If some money incomes *do not* increase in step with prices, their recipients *may* be forced to curtail their purchases of goods and services, that is, to perform a kind of involuntary saving which *may* increase real capital as does saving in the ordinary sense. Thus he anticipated Wicksell's doctrine of Forced Saving. But Bentham, who coined the phrase Forced Frugality, went much more deeply into the matter and so did Malthus.[17] Ricardo turned a deaf ear to Thornton's suggestion and kept on repeating again and again [18]—almost unintelligently—that 'fictitious' capital cannot stimulate industry, that capital can only be created by saving and not by banking operations, and so on, without ever facing the issue squarely. There was, of course, a reason for this. Here as elsewhere Ricardo was a prisoner to once-for-all conceived ideas. In this case, he had pinned his colors to the mast of a rigid quantity theory. The quantity theory implies that there is no relation between the quantity of 'money' and output. And he just would not admit that there might be one after all.

J. S. Mill was torn between the two opposing views. Almost certainly, under Bentham's influence he had given full scope to the view that expansion of bank credit may result in revenue's being 'converted into capital'—that period's standard formula for the effect of saving—and even used the phrase 'forced accumulation,' [19] which reads like an attempt to improve upon Bentham's 'forced frugality.' In the *Principles*, as we have seen, the fact that banks create means of payment by lending is freely recognized, and this implies the recognition of forced saving. Yet we read of a 'disposable capital' that is 'deposited

[17] This piece of doctrinal history has been brilliantly elucidated by Professor von Hayek in 'A Note on the Development of the Doctrine of "Forced Saving,"' *Quarterly Journal of Economics*, November 1932, to which the reader is referred for further details. Bentham's analysis of Forced Saving was a later addition to the *Manual*—part of which was first published in 1798 by Dumont and something less than the whole of which is included in the *Works*, published 1838-43—and Hayek holds that the passage in question 'received its final form in 1804' and was probably sketched much earlier. According to the rules I follow in matters of priority, I have, however, no choice but to date this theory 1843, although Professor von Hayek is presumably correct in thinking that Bentham made its contents known to his economist friends. Malthus' contribution is in his review of Ricardo's *High Price of Bullion*, *Edinburgh Review*, February 1811. Ricardo's reply, appended to the 4th ed. of the *High Price of Bullion*, was that the recipients of fixed incomes might reduce their savings instead of their expenditure on consumers' goods. But Malthus, since he had nothing to go by except the halting and inconclusive, though suggestive, remarks made by Thornton, and since there is no reason to believe that he was aware of Bentham's analysis, must be accorded a high degree of subjective originality. Joplin, in his *Views on the Currency* (1828), used the terms 'forced' and 'voluntary economy.'

[18] For some samples, see Viner, op. cit. p. 196. Similar sentiments are expressed in the *Principles*. The term 'fictitious' (with reference to finance bills) occurs in Thornton.

[19] Essay on 'Profits and Interest,' publ. in *Some Unsettled Questions* (1844). The date of writing is not quite certain but 1830 is a common guess.

in banks, or represented by bank notes,' which together with the funds of those who 'live upon the interest of their property, constitute the general loan fund of the country' (Book III, ch. 23, § 2). In all this and in the whole tenor of that chapter, Ricardian influence prevails. But in the sixth edition [20] a footnote crept in that reasserted his earlier view. After that, leading economists practically forgot all about 'creation of additional deposits' and 'forced saving,' so much so that they looked askance at Wicksell's rediscovery of them: to borrow a phrase used by Lord Keynes in another connection, these notions, so obviously important and realistic, lived from about 1850 to 1898 a dubious life in the economic underworld—another lesson about the ways of the human mind!

(b) *Gains from the Controversy about Peel's Act of* 1844. For our purpose, it is not necessary to go much further. Most of the (none too numerous) important things that were said in that controversy had been said before. The two groups that opposed one another on the legislative issue involved became known as the Banking and the Currency Schools. Only Tooke, Fullarton, and Gilbart of the former, and Torrens and Overstone of the latter, school are of major interest for us.

Tooke and Torrens we know already, but the latter's writings on money and banking have not been mentioned as yet. From a long list I take his earliest work in the field, *An Essay on Money and Paper Currency* (1812); *The Principles and Practical Operation of Sir Robert Peel's Act of* 1844 . . . (1st ed., 1848); and his *Tracts on Finance and Trade* (1852), all of them even now worth reading. Of course, we shall mention in passing also a few other names, but nevertheless the reader must be warned that our selection is inadequate for any purposes but our own limited one and excludes several writers of importance. Continental and American literature we do not even attempt to cover. As regards the latter, reference is once more made to H. E. Miller, *Banking Theories in the United States Before* 1860 (1927).

John Fullarton (died 1849) made his fortune as a surgeon and banker in India and took to writing on the theory and policy of banking, after having retired from business and having settled down in England. His main work (*On the Regulation of Currencies* . . . , 1st ed., 1844) enjoyed, in England and on the Continent, a persistent success such as few contributions to an ephemeral controversy have ever enjoyed—a success that was greater than were its no doubt considerable merits: but it was the kind of sensible performance that, while meeting higher standards also, is a boon to large classes of not-quite-professional readers. Also, it was appreciated by Marx and popular in Marxist circles right into the twentieth century. R. Hilferding's *Finanzkapital* (1910) drew on it largely and uncritically. J. W. Gilbart (1794-1863) was a banker all his life; the first manager of the London and Westminster Bank, which he helped to found; an able and eminently respectable member of his profession, which looked upon him as a leader; the exponent and in part creator of what was to be, for the rest of the century, orthodox banking doctrine. No student of banking can even now afford to miss his highly successful *Practical Treatise on Banking* (1st ed., 1827); his *History and Principles of Banking* (1834); and, at least, *The London Bankers*

[20] This is the edition of 1865 in the preface of which Mill acknowledged, *especially with reference to that chapter*, his debt to the suggestions and criticisms of 'my friend Professor Cairnes, one of the most scientific of living political economists.'

(1845). His *History of Banking in America* (1837) may be associated, so it seems to me, with a distinct American school of thought on banking, whose chief authority he was. Samuel Jones Loyd, commonly known as Lord Overstone (1796-1883), also a banker but of inherited wealth and position, was a much more brilliant personality and much more influential with politicians. He was the currency school's strong man, and his perspicacity (on the one hand) and his sketchiness (on the other) have led generations of economists to moderate the range and depth of his thought. He has left no systematic work, and the best I feel able to do for the reader is to refer to his *Tracts and other Publications on Metallic and Paper Currency* (ed. by McCulloch in 1857) and his *Evidence* before the House of Commons Select Committee of 1857 (also ed. by McCulloch in 1858).

Neither group was a school in our sense of the word. Within both, there were considerable differences of opinion and especially of level. In fact, it is necessary to distinguish in both cases a popular argument from what was, or may pass muster as, serious analysis—a distinction that is not always easy to carry out because few participants in the controversy presented their cases systematically[21] and in a manner that would have met with the unqualified approval of their own parties. Most participants attacked not the real views but a popularized or even distorted picture of their opponents' positions. And most scientific economists, foremost among them Mill, ranged themselves with the banking school—on the Continent, still more decidedly than in England.[22] But among practitioners and especially among the directors of the Bank of England, Peel's Act counted many adherents.[23]

[21] Torrens and Fullarton came nearest to doing so. But we may add G. W. Norman (*Remarks upon Some Prevalent Errors with respect to Currency and Banking*, 1833) and McCulloch, both of the currency school. McCulloch (see especially his *Treatise on Metallic and Paper Money and Banks* written for the *Encyclopaedia Britannica*, 1858; and also his comments on money and on Peel's Act in his edition of the *Wealth of Nations* of 1850) supported the currency principle in a manner that overemphasized the links that exists between it and Ricardo, the Bullion Report, and the quantity theory as such. It is quite possible to approve of Peel's Act without upholding the latter in its strict sense. I take this opportunity to mention James Wilson, a severe and able critic of the lower ranges of the currency school, founder of the London *Economist*, and Minister of Finance of India, one of those excellent men who fare badly in a history of analysis. See his articles, collected in *Capital, Currency, and Banking . . .* (1847).

[22] See, e.g., Adolf Wagner, *Beiträge zur Lehre von den Banken* (1857), and *Die Geld- und Credittheorie der Peel'schen Bankacte* (1862). We have already noticed his boundless enthusiasm for Tooke. Both in his interpretation and in his criticism, he completely failed to do justice to Overstone. In France, the only question that excited real interest was whether or not the Banque de France should have a monopoly of issue. Those who stood for it sometimes invoked Lord Overstone's authority, those who were opposed (Chevalier, Courcelle-Seneuil, and others) sometimes invoked Tooke's authority.

[23] It must not be forgotten that the directors had every reason to greet an act which left them absolutely free from regulatory interference, except with respect to the note issue, with a sigh of relief.

The first thing that strikes the modern observer when he looks back upon that controversy is the extent of fundamental agreement between the two 'schools.'[24] Neither contained any radical monetary reformers. Both were equally averse to monetary management or any thoroughgoing control of banking and credit. This is obvious for the banking school that fought Peel's Act without offering any other method of control, but it also holds for the currency school that wished to regulate the note issue precisely in order to make the currency 'automatic' and to leave banking business—even central banking—entirely free. That is to say, both groups consisted of laissez-faire men. Moreover, both groups were staunch supporters of the gold standard and, in particular, of the regulation of foreign exchanges by free gold movements. If we neglect those of the banking group's objections to Peel's Act and those of the currency group's arguments for it that were of a purely technical nature,[25] it seems that there cannot have been much left to disagree about. Briefly and not quite adequately, we may say that the 'banking principle' asserted (1) that, given English conditions and banking practice, and in particular proper leadership on the part of the Bank of England,[26] convertibility of notes was enough to secure all the monetary stability of which a capitalist system is capable; and (2) that in any case, even if this were not so, there would be no point in regulating notes alone, since deposits would raise the same problem. Equally briefly and inadequately we may say that the 'currency principle' asserted (1) that convertibility of notes cannot be assured without special restrictions upon their issue; and (2) that the notes of the Bank of England were actually, or should be treated as, mere gold certificates—not as credit instruments like deposits or commercial bills but as ultimate (reserve) money just like the coin or bullion which they *represented*.[27]

[24] The *scientific* affinity between Overstone and Tooke—overshadowed though it is by what seems to have been strong personal aversion—will stand out more clearly in the last section of this chapter. Now I am speaking of their points of agreement on monetary and banking policy and on the kind of economy they meant to serve.

[25] An example is the objection that the strict division of the Bank into two departments would make the gold in the issue department inaccessible to the management of the banking department, except so far as the latter held a reserve of notes. Thus, the banking department might have to refuse help to the market when the coffers of the issue department were replete with gold, as in fact happened in 1847. Let us note in passing, however, that the currency group was right in minimizing, and that the banking school was wrong in exaggerating, the importance of the recurring suspensions of Peel's Act: the necessity of these had been foreseen by Overstone and they were really, though not officially, part and parcel of his scheme.

[26] This proviso, even where not stated explicitly, is a natural one to make in the case of so severe a critic of the Bank of England as Tooke. But it should be made quite generally. The banking school, in particular, never challenged the regulatory function of a central bank.

[27] It is important to note that the words 'certificates' and 'represent' are Lord Overstone's. I believe that Lord Overstone handed out the key to the understanding of his position by using them. That is to say, he meant to deny that the notes of the Bank of England were bank notes at all, as usually understood, especially on the Continent

Only Torrens, in reply to the objection that restriction of the note issue alone is futile, explicitly went beyond this narrow purpose: [28] believing, as we know he did, that the amount of deposits banks are able to create by lending is closely tied to the existing amount of coin plus notes, he asserted that regulation of the note issue would also do something toward regulating the creation of deposits.[29] But if we neglect this, then the agreement between the banking and the currency schools about the basic importance of convertibility of notes is immediately seen to be the fundamental thing, compared with which their disagreement on the question whether or not there was need for special guarantees of this convertibility was a secondary matter. For since the banking school did *not* hold that the circulating medium would regulate itself in the process of competitive banking—why should they have insisted on convertibility at all if they believed this?—and since it recognized the ever-present danger of 'overbanking,' all they can have meant by saying that overissue of notes was 'impossible' is that, with convertibility, it will in the end be severely punished. And this is obviously true.[30] All the currency school can have meant by insisting on the possibility of an overissue of Bank of England notes is *not* denial of this obvious truth *nor* assertion of the not less obvious untruth that with convertibility overissue can go on forever, but merely that, without special restriction upon the issue of the Bank of England, overissue might go far enough to be beyond any remedy other than catastrophe. Thus interpreted, the difference between the two positions remains no doubt of *practical* importance. But it involves none but minor [31] disagreements as regards *analysis*.

(see next footnote). It is only on this hypothesis that the idea of making gold plus notes behave as gold alone would behave—which is how the 'currency principle' is usually expressed—becomes meaningful, i.e. that (1) the quantity of the notes should exactly correspond to the actual gold 'represented' by them except that (2) there should be added a *constant* amount of notes, which was an inheritance from the past and which it would have been highly inconvenient to eliminate.

[28] *Reply to the Objections of the Westminster Review* (1844).

[29] It stands to reason that this idea is capable of being defended, provided one does not put a greater burden upon it than it can bear. It is interesting to note that Torrens anticipated an argument that was in our time brought forth by Edwin Cannan ('Limitation of Currency or Limitation of Credit?' *Economic Journal*, 1924). Professor von Hayek in *Prices and Production*, p. 2, has pointed out that Dugald Stewart had already formulated the issue involved in 1811 in a Memorandum on the Bullion Report (*Works*, ed. by Sir W. Hamilton, 1855, vol. VIII): 'The one opinion suggests the propriety of limiting credit through the median of a restricted currency; the other of limiting the currency through the medium of a well regulated and discriminating credit.'

[30] Fullarton (op. cit. ch. 5) did, however, go too far when he expected convertibility to operate 'with the precision of clockwork.'

[31] Some of these minor disagreements, such as the one on the *modus operandi* upon credit and prices of the outflow and inflow of gold, on internal and external 'drains,' on how far Peel's Act interfered (indirectly and unintentionally) with the effective management of the Banking Department of the Bank, are of considerable scientific interest. Unfortunately, we cannot go into them.

The evolution of English central-bank practice was not substantially interfered with by Peel's Act. The changes that occurred in the attitudes of the Bank of England toward its own customers and toward the loan market, the growing importance of bankers' balances within the total of its deposits, and other features of England's financial history after the passing of Peel's Act were more important than were the effects on policy brought about *by* that Act. Most of these changes were slow to penetrate into the theory of central banking that had become stereotyped by 1850 into what almost amounted to a cult of the bank rate, the *modus operandi* of which was analyzed with little regard to observable facts. All the more important is it to point out that a central-bank policy of much wider scope had been, on a much higher plane, blocked out by Thornton at the beginning of the period. His sound insight into the nature of banking credit and his keen yet balanced sense of the intimate logic of things qualified him well for dealing with this subject. He did this in a manner that anticipated practically everything that was discovered about central-bank policy for a century to come. On page 259 of *Paper Credit*, he summed up his analysis in a set of rules that constitute the Magna Charta of credit management in an intact private-enterprise economy. In order to establish this, I should have to copy out that page. To save space I merely refer to it.

In concluding the argument of this section, we must attend to one more topic. So far we have dealt mainly with the topmost stratum of that period's analytic work. We have noticed several important achievements and we shall notice some more in the next two sections of this chapter. But we have also noticed the failure of those achievements to come to full fruition and in particular the fact that they were not co-ordinated in such a way as to provide a good spring board for the work of the next period. In fact, we find, instead of an effective presentation of the best results, the emergence of a fairly general opinion about the nature and practice of banks that preserved many of the weak spots of the period's analysis, rather than the strong ones, but gained wide currency among both bankers and economists and thus proved an obstacle to further advance. For brevity's sake, no names will be mentioned except those of a few authorities who might, with more or less justification, be invoked in support of some of the propositions to be discussed.[32] These propositions are associated with what has been called the Commercial Theory of Banking and also with part of the argument of the banking school, but in using these labels we must keep in mind that neither the one nor the other is indissolubly wedded to them. Perhaps we had better dub the doctrine in question the Commercial-Bill Theory of Banking.

(1) According to the commercial-bill theory of banking, the essential business of banks—the business that *defines* banks—is the financing of current commodity trade, national and international. It is not essential that this should be done only in the form of discounting bona-fide commercial bills,

[32] The reader will find plenty of names in the work of L. W. Mints referred to at the beginning of this section.

each drawn in connection with a particular sale, but we retain our label nevertheless, because this was considered to be the typical case. Even so, this conception of the business of banks, though still too narrow, does not individuate any particular theory. We get the commercial-bill theory if either or both of the following propositions are added to that definition of the banker's business: (a) banks derive or should derive the funds with which they discount from deposits entrusted to them by the public; and (b) they satisfy the needs of commodity trade without influencing prices thereby and without having the power—in justice we should always add 'normally'—to influence the amount of credit outstanding.

(2) It should be obvious without further explanation how these propositions link up with definite errors which, as we have seen, were fully exploded by the work of the better writers of the period, and especially by Thornton It should also be obvious that this view of banking—the helpmate of commodity trade, who offers his money to satisfy the needs of business but does not force it upon business, who has nothing to do with price fluctuations and overtrading (to put it strongly)—expresses very well the professional ideology of bankers who like to see themselves in this light. But finally it should be observed that there are elements of practical truth and wisdom in this doctrine. If reformulated to the effect that bankers had better be careful about their cash position and maturities and that they had better look with equal care at the soft spots in the applications for credit before them, it becomes quite unobjectionable. In other words, a faulty theory, in this as it does in other cases, covers wise advice. The proposition that sound business principles of discounting are all that is needed to keep the economic ship on an even keel should indeed have been recognized as erroneous ever since Thornton; but action in conformity with it would, nevertheless, have avoided all the worst breakdowns in financial history.

(3) However, we should notice a few arguments about this needs-of-trade attitude that aimed at more than inculcating responsible lending practice. First we mention one that is perfectly true so long as we confine ourselves to considering the individual banking business in a competitive system of many banks. Credit expansion for the individual bank is, in fact, severely limited by the drain on reserves that it will eventually entail. Of course, this is no longer true for all banks taken together; [33] but even for all of them, if the system be really competitive, that penalty on stepping out of line is a more effective brake upon expansion in line than critics of banking practice are usually prepared to recognize. Second, there is less but still something in Fullarton's unjustly famous Law of Reflux, which simply recalls to the minds of reformers the commonplace fact that normally loans are repaid and that their repayment annihilates purchasing power, so that, though by itself

[33] Professor Viner (op. cit. pp. 239 et seq.) has pointed out that this distinction, which we are in the habit of claiming for our own epoch, when in fact it penetrated into teaching, was widely understood ever since the 1820's.

this does not prevent inflationary expansion of credit, there is a very material difference between the case of bank credit which does, and the case of government paper money which does not, 'flow back' automatically. Finally, third, we mention the central needs-of-trade argument that has been so uncritically vaunted by some and so uncritically rejected by others—the argument that the discounting of bona-fide bills carries its 'proper' limitation with it and that in addition it makes the circulating medium expand and contract 'elastically' as production and trade expand and contract. For this view, it is possible to invoke the authority of A. Smith and Tooke. It is, however, hardly necessary to point out its inadequacies. All the more necessary is it to point out its true core. Consider the most normal of all normal cases: a commodity has been produced *and sold;* the producer *A* draws on the trader *B* for the amount; *A* discounts the accepted bill at his bank and expends the money on his current production, while *B*, selling the commodity to ultimate consumers, collects from them the money with which to redeem the bill at maturity, the date being so chosen as to make this normally possible. Note that this is a piece of observable practice and no theoretical construct; that a bank that confines itself to *this* sort of business can, in fact, not increase its lending on its own, because commodities must be first produced *and sold;*[34] and that there is an obvious sense—though one only out of several—in which it might be averred that bank money of this kind would vary in a manner roughly corresponding to the flow of commodities, does not raise prices, and is endowed with 'elasticity.' We may indeed doubt whether this case has the importance attributed to it by sponsors of the doctrine. And we may not like this kind of elasticity but there is no warrant for denying its existence. I repeat that none of the errors alluded to is inseparable from either the position of the banking school or of the commercial theory of banking.

5. Foreign Exchange and International Gold Movements

The period's analysis of the monetary aspects of international economic relations, in the form that J. S. Mill imparted to it, proved an extremely durable achievement and, though now under critical fire, still underlies much of the

[34] This version *does not* involve the error commonly implied in the statement that banks cannot give credit beyond the 'requirements' of their customers; and it is likely that Tooke did not mean more than this. The typical attitude of the respectable English banker may have confirmed him in this opinion as well as in the opinion that such credit does not act upon prices. On the other hand, it must not be forgotten (this has been very instructively shown by Kepper, see below, sec. 6) that Tooke did not strictly adhere to the commercial-bill theory of bankers' money. In places, he apparently committed himself to a much wider definition of customers' requirements, holding that *no* kind of short-run credit can ever be inflationary that serves a serious business purpose (he seems to have made an exception for purely speculative transactions in times of 'overtrading'). This of course is not only difficult to defend but even difficult to understand, unless we interpret it as a corollary of his opinion that banks cannot lend more than the public saves. But in the *Inquiry* he admitted that they can.

best work of our own time.[1] In order to appreciate it, we must bear in mind the following two facts.

In the first place, the 'classic' writers, without neglecting other cases, reasoned primarily in terms of an unfettered international gold standard. There were several reasons for this but one of them merits our attention in particular. An unfettered international gold standard will keep (normally) foreign-exchange rates within specie points and impose an 'automatic' link between national price levels and interest rates. The modern mind dislikes this automatism, as much for political as for economic reasons: it dislikes the fetters this automatism clasps on government management of the economic process—dislikes gold, the naughty boy who blurts out unpleasant truths. But most of the economists of the period under survey liked it for precisely the same reasons. Though they compromised in practice as in theory and though they admitted central-bank management, the automatism—a phrase beloved by Lord Overstone—was for them, who were neither nationalists nor *étatistes*, a moral as well as an economic ideal. It stands to reason that this alone will make a lot of difference between their problems and ours and that this difference in practical outlook is bound to assert itself—though perhaps it should not—in purely analytic work.

In the second place, the 'classic' writers were primarily concerned with commodity trade. Although they did not fail to consider international lending, subsidies, and tributes, the monetary problems of commodity trade (payment for imports and receipts from exports, the gold movements and variations in price levels incident to these, and the effects of gold movements on domestic credit structures and interest rates) were their central problems, so much so that *they treated everything else from the angle of commodity trade.* In consequence, international finance did not get its due in their analysis—the credit transaction that did was the transaction embodied in the commercial bill (including, it is true, the finance bill), which, directly or more distantly, corresponded to commodity transactions. But the South American loans and mining stocks, for instance, that were being issued in 1824 and that for the time being dominated the London money market left no footprints in basic theory. For us, the exactly opposite approach seems more natural: we are likely to look upon international capital transactions as the basic phenomenon to which commodity trade is subsidiary, by which it is controlled, from which it must be understood. And this point, too, would suffice in itself to divorce modern analysis from what may be described as the

[1] I believe this to be true of the work not only of Taussig but also of Viner and Haberler, who no doubt developed the 'classic' analysis and also accepted various new tools and propositions of others, but did not challenge the 'classic' fundaments. These were, indeed, challenged by Ohlin and other front-rank economists but their contributions too may be formulated as improvements rather than reconstructions. Professor Viner's survey of the situation (op. cit. ch. 6) may be referred to in support of this view. An impression to the contrary rests primarily upon the fact that modern analysis envisages other practical problems and conditions.

Commodity-Trade Theory of international finance (or of international payments or of international gold movements).

The commodity-trade theory of international finance is thus open to the criticism—as is the theory of international values—that its conception of the phenomena with which it undertakes to deal is much too narrow.[2] Also, it must be pointed out that its particular assumptions disqualify it for direct practical application. But there is another criticism that strikes at it within its own precincts and should be mentioned at once because it has received undue prominence during the last twenty years or so. A theory of international finance that pivots on commodity trade will naturally emphasize the equilibrating role of variations in relative prices. It has been pointed out, first by Wicksell, that adjustments to disturbances of trade relations may and often do take place without actual changes in prices and also without actual gold movements. This is true, of course, and no classic writer, least of all Ricardo, would have denied it. But if the 'classic' theory be nevertheless criticized on the ground that it put an altogether unjustifiable burden upon the price mechanism and in doing so failed to notice other equilibrating factors, then the critic is wrong because price variations of the kind the 'classic' theory visualizes imply shifts of demand curves which in turn imply variations in income, as we shall see presently. Moreover, in the pattern which the 'classics' chose for analysis, price variations in fact do hold the key position. All the critic can rightfully say is that this is no longer so in patterns in which prices are rigid and capital movements dominant. Finally, several writers of the period under survey explicitly introduced the factors that critics miss in the classical picture.[3]

In the third place, the 'classic' theory of international finance was not fundamentally new. Thornton, who blocked it out, referred—approvingly and critically—to Locke, Hume, and A. Smith, and Hume's analysis undoubtedly was the starting point of the period's work. But Hume himself did no more than formulate effectively the result of a long development in the course of which 'mercantilist' work had been slowly moving toward the doctrine of the 'classics.' Thornton's teaching prevailed, more or less, with most of the leading writers of that and the subsequent period, from Malthus[4] through Tooke to J. S. Mill and Cairnes and eventually to Taussig. But Wheatley dissented from it and was followed by Ricardo.[5] We proceed to consider the point at issue.

[2] On this, see J. H. Williams, 'The Theory of International Trade Reconsidered,' *Economic Journal*, 1929, reprinted in *Postwar Monetary Plans and Other Essays* (1944), Part IV.

[3] This has been shown by Viner (op. cit. pp. 293 et seq.), who in particular mentions Longfield, Torrens, and Joplin.

[4] *Edinburgh Review*, 1811, the review articles referred to already on another occasion (above, sec. 3).

[5] To some extent, as McCulloch has pointed out, they were anticipated by Barbon. See above, Part II, chs. 6 and 7.

For this purpose, we start from a state of monetary equilibrium between two countries.[6] Being in possession of the theory of international values and of the equilibrium condition given by the equation of reciprocal demand (which, as we know, comprises the principle of comparative cost), we readily see that the condition of monetary equilibrium which we must now add is simply that, claims from commodity transactions canceling one another, there should be, under our assumptions, no movement of gold from one country to the other. We proceed to investigate the properties of this equilibrium by assuming it to be disturbed and by analyzing the adjustments that will follow. First, we assume a disturbance occurring in the sphere of money: we assume, like Hume, that in one of the two countries everybody's holding of monetary gold is suddenly doubled. Without committing ourselves to any strict quantity theory, we may aver that in this country incomes and business funds in terms of gold, hence expenditure, will increase; that demand schedules for all commodities will shift upwards; that gold prices will rise in consequence; that exports will decrease; and that gold will flow out until equilibrium is re-established. Nobody ever challenged this, though the highly artificial process assumed might have given plenty of scope for quibbling.[7] Second, instead of assuming that gold has increased in one of the two countries, assume that commodities have decreased, for example, because of a bad harvest. The reader will be tempted to argue that, the 'need' for food imports having increased, an unfavorable balance of trade will ensue and produce an export of gold through which adjustment will, for the time being,[8] be achieved. But on reflection, he will realize that this is not strictly correct and does not constitute a generalization of Hume's argument but a deviation from it. For the bad harvest per se does not produce an unfavorable balance. Needs are not incompressible. So far as the need for food imports is imperative, other imports can be curtailed: in other words, all that has happened is that the people in the country that experienced the bad harvest are, for the time being, poorer than they were before and have to readjust their consumption and investment to a lower level of real income; but on this lower level the balance of trade can be, and in the absence of money and credit would have to be, just as much in equilibrium as before. Actually, however, we do get

[6] We make the following assumption partly in order to reproduce the 'classic' pattern and partly in order to simplify exposition: no international economic relations except commodity trade with perfectly flexible (and competitive) prices, hence incomes; no credit whatsoever; perfectly free international gold standard; two countries only, differing not too much in size, for neither of which foreign trade is of negligible importance; no gold mining; gold, though considered as a commodity, all absorbed in the monetary function; no cost, risk, or loss of time involved in its transportation or in the transportation of commodities. Evidently a fairly complete theory can be derived by dropping these assumptions one by one.

[7] I have reduced the scope for quibbling by reasoning in terms of income and expenditure rather than of mere quantity of money. But there still remains some.

[8] The next step would be an increase of incomes and prices in the other country, which will counteract the process even before normal harvests, re-establishing previous conditions, reverse it entirely.

the unfavorable balance also if we reason correctly *per analogiam* of Hume's argument, only we get it as the effect rather than as the cause of the export of gold. Since gold has not been decreased by the failure of the harvest and since we may assume that money incomes and money expenditures have not decreased either, but since there is now less of commodities to buy, prices will rise or gold in terms of commodities will get *cheaper* or, as we may also say, from the standpoint of the previous price level, gold has become *redundant*. This curtails exports and fosters imports of commodities other than gold exactly as if gold and incomes and expenditures had increased, output having remained unchanged.[9] We have thus reduced the disturbance that arose in the commodity sphere to a disturbance in the monetary sphere.

Thornton, who began his investigation into the nature of monetary equilibrium in international trade by presenting the example of the crop failure (*Paper Credit*, p. 143), *seemed* to argue in the way that has just been shown to be open to objection. It is true that in other places (e.g., ibid. pp. 244, 247), his argument indicates that he understood the point I have been trying to make. But he was so hazy and so hesitant about it that Wheatley and later on Ricardo were right in asserting that the factors that operate *on* the value or purchasing power of gold are one thing and that the operation *of* the value or purchasing power of gold is another thing. But they so mismanaged their case as to leave contemporary as well as later writers to wonder whether they had any case at all.[10]

[9] It should be superfluous to point out that the sequence of events described is only to express the logic of the process and need not always be actually observable. But this does not constitute an objection any more than it constitutes an objection to the usual theory of the effects of a specific tax imposed upon a commodity—that its price need not, as the explanatory schema seems to postulate, first rise by the whole amount of the tax, then fall again owing to the consequent reduction of quantity demanded, and so on until it settles at the new equilibrium level, and that in practice some steps may be omitted. Similarly the gold may start to flow at once in payment of the additional grain import, and the influence of the crop failure on the price level in the affected country may never show fully: this need not effect the role of price variations in the explanatory schema.

[10] On this controversy, see Viner, *Canada's Balance of International Indebtedness, 1900-1913* (1924), ch. 9. Wheatley and Ricardo introduced not only irrelevant or nonessential but also erroneous arguments. For instance, both Wheatley and Ricardo denied that a crop failure will create 'redundancy' of currency, though Ricardo admitted this in a letter to Malthus (*Letters*, p. 13). But Wheatley, perhaps because he had a clearer conception of the price level, came much closer than did Ricardo to grasping the principle involved. Thus, he said boldly that, in spite of all the subsidies and other sums sent abroad during the Napoleonic Wars, it would have been possible to enforce 'influx of money to any extent' (*Essay on the Theory of Money . . .*, 1st vol., p. 194). Barring the obvious exaggeration, this clearly implies, though it does not state, the principle that it is a monetary mechanism which is *immediately* behind exchanges and gold flows and that these are never determined uniquely by the factors—such as political payments or *conditions that determine the demands for individual commodities*—that operate at one remove.

But had they? Is it really more than hairsplitting when we insist that gold flows out because it is the 'cheapest exportable commodity' and not because of a bad harvest when the bad harvest makes gold the 'cheapest exportable commodity'? Instead of any other answer, I shall merely point to a fact of considerable importance both for the history of economic analysis and the history of economic thought. It is natural for bankers or writers who place themselves in the position of the individual banker to say that banks cannot expand credit beyond limits that are given to them irrespective of their own behavior. It is not less natural for bankers and students of the problems of the individual bank to start from the obvious fact that outflows or inflows of gold result from unfavorable or favorable exchanges which in turn result from the demand for and supply of claims on foreign places. Excepting the quality of the individual paper, the factors behind demand and supply seem to be all that the banker has to analyze for purposes of diagnosis and forecasting: political factors, business situations, state of the crops, and so on; and this is in fact the standpoint on which Goschen placed himself in writing his famous *Theory of Foreign Exchanges* (1861).[11] Since demand for and supply of foreign paper reflect a country's current (and prospective) balance of payments, we may call this the Balance-of-Payments Theory of foreign exchanges. Decades of quiet conditions may pass without anyone's becoming aware of the fact that there is anything missing in this theory. But if people keep on applying it in conditions of violent disturbance, the presence of another factor becomes obvious that cannot be resolved into those which we may unearth by analyzing the individual items of the balance of payments, namely, the value (purchasing power) of the monetary units in which balances of payments are expressed. We may label as Relative Inflation the variations in the value of a country's monetary unit, in relation to the value of other countries' monetary units, and speak accordingly of an Inflation Theory of Foreign Exchanges. We shall return to this subject in Part IV, Chapter 8. Now I wish merely to point out that the first rumble of the prolonged battle between these two theories—though it should be clear that they do not amount to alternative explanations—is audible in the controversy between Thornton and Wheatley-Ricardo: when, in the latter's phraseology, gold becomes 'redundant' in a country or 'the cheapest exportable commodity,' then this country experiences 'relative gold inflation.' So Wheatley and Ricardo did have a case and one that was more than chopping-logic, though, so far as

[11] George J. (afterwards Lord) Goschen (1831-1907), Chancellor of the Exchequer in the second Salisbury administration (1886-92) and of historical importance as the last of the ministers of finance in the pure tradition of classic liberalism (it is highly significant though that this liberalism had taken shelter in a conservative cabinet), was a banker of German extraction. His book describes extremely well what a highly educated and intelligent dealer in foreign exchange would know about foreign exchanges. As a piece of analysis, the performance, which nowhere goes below a well-observed surface, does not rank highly. But it explained things about which politicians and academic economists are likely to know but little and hence was a boon for both. The success of the book was sweeping and it is still worth reading.

their attack upon Thornton is concerned, they may have been unjust because Thornton's fine mind paid but little tribute to the fallacy in the balance-of-payments argument.

When countries are in monetary equilibrium with reference to one another, then, so it has been stated above, gold is distributed between them in such a way that there is no profit in transferring any part of a country's holding to any other country. We may express this by saying that the purchasing power of gold is internationally at par and also, from the standpoint of the inflation theory of foreign exchange, that this parity and its variations are the (immediately) determining factors in the foreign-exchange market. This Purchasing-Power Parity theory, or some rudimentary form of it, goes far back and can, as we have seen above, certainly be attributed to Malynes. During the First World War, a particular coinage of it became associated with the name of Cassel. But the principle involved must also be attributed to Wheatley and Ricardo [12] in whose work it appears, as it was to appear in Cassel, in characteristic association with a strict (and crude) quantity theory.[13]

The 'classic' reasoning about gold movements and exchange rates can be generalized without much difficulty to irredeemable paper.[14] Its application to the cases of loans, subsidies, and absenteeism [15]—a standard topic of the economics of the period—presents more difficulties. Of course, the divergence of views just described carries over into the discussion of these cases. But this is not the only problem. All of these cases, but especially international loans,

[12] This is not the opinion of Professor Viner (op. cit. pp. 126 and 382 et seq.). But this is only because he reserves the term for the Casselian form of the principle. This, of course, cannot be attributed to Ricardo, who always fought shy of the price level concept that is essential to the Casselian form of the principle though not to the principle itself. The struggles of economists with the emerging price-level concept have been discussed above.

[13] On a certain level of monetary theory, quantity theory and purchasing-power parity theory are simply complements or even two different aspects of the same thing. It is, however, possible to show that, on other levels, they may be so formulated as to constitute logically independent, though still related, propositions.

[14] Wheatley (*Essay on the Theory of Money*, 1807) saw more clearly than did others that even in this case it was 'redundancy'—i.e. pressure upon the price level—and not any occurrence in the world of commodities per se that would cause an unfavorable turn of exchange rates. There is an echo of this in J. S. Mill's rather inadequate treatment of the subject (*Principles*, Book III, ch. 22, § 3).

[15] Irish landlords, living in England on the rents of their Irish estates, naturally were being increasingly discussed, the main purely economic question being whether or not their living and spending in England and not Ireland made any difference to the Irish people. McCulloch returned a negative answer on the ground that it does not matter where a man consumes what he consumes ('Essay Showing the Erroneousness of the Prevailing Opinions in regard to Absenteeism,' *Edinburgh Review*, 1825, reprinted in *Treatises and Essays on Money, Exchange, Interest*, 1859); Senior a weakly affirmative one (*Edinburgh Review*, 1825; see also Senior's *Outline*, p. 156).

M. Longfield's performance (*Three Lectures on Commerce and One on Absenteeism*, 1835, London-School Reprint, 1937) is of some analytic interest.

raise questions that cannot be satisfactorily treated by a schema derived from the miraculous increase in the gold stock of a country or from the failure of a harvest: among other things, income effects begin to play a qualitatively different role and interest a decisive one. Results were correspondingly unsatisfactory. Nevertheless modern criticism—*qua* criticism—often errs by not paying sufficient attention to the particular conditions of the transactions that individual authors envisaged and the sequence of events that were imposed by these conditions. Take J. S. Mill's famous treatment of unilateral political payments—say, an annual tribute—that served as a starting point and evoked much criticism in the discussion on German reparations after 1920 (*Principles*, Book III, ch. 21, § 4). The treatment is short and oversimplified, but substantially correct so far as the one case considered is concerned, namely the case where the recipient *insists* on receiving annual sums of money, the first of which the debtor country has no choice but to collect from the pockets of its citizens. Here the gold movement is not a question of automatic mechanisms at all but is simply imposed by the initial conditions of the problem. Under these conditions, a fall in prices in the paying country can hardly fail to come about. This will increase exports and decrease imports and would bring back the gold but, as Mill constructed the case, the paying country's claims to this gold will be absorbed by the receiving country's claim to the next instalment of the tribute, so that gold stock, incomes, expenditures, and prices in the paying country are kept down and its excess exports are kept up. Another case might no doubt be constructed that would produce a different sequence of events and contain no gold movements and no price changes at all but only income changes and commodity movements. But either case serves to illustrate what from the 'classic' standpoint is the essential thing, namely, that the true equilibrating factor is the commodity transfer. And neither is very realistic.

6. 'The' Business Cycle

One of the most important achievements of the period under survey, and one of the few that were truly original, was the discovery and preliminary analysis of business cycles. It is true that the crises of 1815, 1825, 1836-9, 1847-8, 1857, and 1866 pressed the phenomenon upon the attention of even the most academic of economists. But similar breakdowns had occurred, with similar regularity in the eighteenth century, and nevertheless nobody had gone deeply into the matter: nobody had distinguished them clearly from the effects of war and other external disturbances or seen in them anything but chance misfortunes or the results of manias or errors or misconduct. The first suggestion that there might be deeper causes to these breakdowns, causes which are inherent in the economic process, are indeed to be found in the 'mercantilist' literature, mainly in connection with the ideas that were later on worked up into the various underconsumption theories. But these ideas were not made explicit before the controversy on gluts, during and after the Napoleonic Wars, which we know already and which ended, for the time being, in their defeat. After some additional comments on this controversy, we shall consider the analyses of business cycles that are primarily due to Tooke and Lord Overstone and then end up with the contribution of Marx. For an extensive treatment of the subject, the reader is referred to the work by von Bergmann.[1]

The facts about crises that the press and the public primarily notice and to which they naturally attribute such effects as bankruptcies and unemployment are the collapse of credit and the unsalability of commodities: press and public are inveterate adherents of monetary and overproduction 'theories.'[2] It was against the popular ideas of the latter kind that J. B. Say argued in his chapter on the 'Law of Markets.' As has been stated already, so far as the subject of crises is concerned, the main merit of that law was a negative one. Say showed successfully that, however large the phenomenon of overproduction may loom in the historical picture of individual crises, no causal explanation can be derived from it: there is no sense in saying that there is a crisis *because* 'too much' has been produced all round. Though negative, this contribution was very important. It may be said to stand at the fountainhead of the scientific analysis of cycles and to mark the point at which the latter broke away from pre-analytic thought. But the positive application that Say attempted to make of his law was much less valuable. He inferred from it erroneously, though with apparent logic, that, if general overproduction was no explanation, then partial overproduction must be at the root of the trouble —that some commodities are unsalable because their complements are lacking, or that the apparent overproduction of some was really underproduction of others. This is the Disproportionality Theory of Crises,[3] as it was called

[1] Eugen von Bergmann, *Die Wirtschaftskrisen: Geschichte der nationalökonomischen Krisentheorieen* (1895). Most authors of systematic works on business cycles present some information on the history of business-cycle analysis, and there are also a few other histories. Analytically, Professor Friedrich Lutz's *Das Konjunkturproblem in der Nationalökonomie* (1932) moves on a much higher level than does von Bergmann's work. Nevertheless the latter is the only one I know who presents the results of extensive research in the literature of the period—a fact which is surprising in the case of a subject that looms so large in modern work. Scholarly effort has been directed toward the work of individual authors or groups of authors or toward individual issues or theories rather than toward a comprehensive survey. On Tooke and Overstone, e.g., there is the excellent book by Georg Kepper, *Die Konjunkturlehren der Banking- und der Currency-schule* (1933). On American work, see H. E. Miller, *Banking Theories in the United States before* 1860 (1927, ch. 16).

[2] Today, the 'theory' of business cycles means very much more than explanatory hypotheses: it means a whole apparatus of the theoretical and statistical tools of analysis. For the nineteenth century, however, it is approximately correct to say that hypotheses as regards the 'causes' of crises or cycles were the main, if not the only, contents of what was meant by theories of crises.

[3] The disproportionality that Say envisaged was primarily a disequilibrium within the same stage of the productive process: overproduction of shoes with reference to the production of coats. We had better confine the term to this meaning—there is, of course, no objection to forming larger categories than shoes and coats—and distinguish

later on, which died from lack of vitality in the course of the nineteenth century, though individual adherents might be named throughout. One of them was Ricardo. Slightly improving the idea in Chapter 19 of his *Principles*, he made a reasonable though, of course, inadequate case for Sudden Changes in the Channels of Trade as the most important single cause of disturbance.

As we know, Sismondi and Malthus (followed by Chalmers) were the leaders in the campaign against Say's law—some of their arguments having been anticipated by earlier writers, especially Lauderdale. It is very difficult to label their theories, which neither of them systematized completely and which with both of them, but especially with Malthus, were theories of stagnation and prolonged unemployment rather than theories of 'crises.' Malthus, however, came much nearer to definiteness and may I think be credited—or debited—with an underconsumption theory of the oversaving type: [4] stagnation ensues when people save and invest to such an extent as 'to leave no motive to a further increase of production' owing to the incident fall in prices and profits.[5] It cannot be emphasized too often that this argument, whatever its incidental merits—and one of them is that it locates the source of stagnation in the saving-investment process—is, as it stands, definitely erroneous if intended to explain 'crises,' though not if merely intended to show the possibility of production's becoming stationary. But Sismondi offers such a multi-

it from theories which attribute cycles or crises to disproportionality between stages taken as a whole, e.g. between investment goods production and consumers' goods production. For disproportionalities of the latter kind are always linked to other factors, e.g., monetary ones or oversaving, and therefore are symptoms or consequences rather than 'causes.'

[4] In a sense, of course, underconsumption can always be described as overproduction. Accordingly, von Bergmann labeled Malthus' theory a 'motivated overproduction theory.' It seems more conducive to clear distinctions to avoid the latter phrase whenever an author locates the seat of the trouble with the behavior of consumers, even if the result is also some sort of overproduction—just as, for the same reason, we have adopted a strict definition of the phrase Disproportionality. We shall distinguish three types of underconsumption theories, all of which put in an appearance during that period. There is, first, the oversaving type just mentioned, of which Malthus was the chief exponent. There is, second, the nonspending type that emphasizes disturbances which arise from saving decisions that are *not* offset by decisions to invest. Malthus, as we have seen, glanced at this idea, which is an old one—to be attributed, e.g., to Quesnay and several of his French predecessors—but which did not play any great role in modern economics until our own time. And there is, third, the mass-poverty type that attributes gluts to the inability of labor, owing to low wages, to 'buy its own product.' The most important sponsors of this theory were Sismondi and, much more definitely, Rodbertus. This theory, as Marx well knew, is beneath discussion since it involves neglect of the elementary fact that inadequacy or even increasing inadequacy of the wage income to buy the whole product at cost-covering prices would not prevent hitchless production in response to the demand of non-wage earners either for 'luxury' goods or for investment.

[5] See Malthus' letter in J. M. Keynes, *Essays in Biography*, p. 143; also the contemporary German discussion of the controversy between Malthus and Say by K. H. Rau, *Malthus und Say über die Ursachen der jetzigen Handelsstockung* (1821).

plicity of responsible factors that he cannot be classified satisfactorily. The oversaving argument is no doubt present and forms the core of his analysis of disequilibria of production and consumption.[6] But underconsumption owing to low wages is still more prominent, both because of the 'vicious' distribution of incomes per se and because of the unemployment created by labor-saving machinery. Then there is, incident to his sequence analysis, the idea that increasing outputs meet totals of purchasing power that have been earned some time before by participation in the production of a smaller output. Further, Sismondi made much, and rightly, of all the random vicissitudes through which the road leads to the theorists' smooth ultimate long-run normals. Thus he became the patron saint of all those 'explanations' that are content to talk about the anarchy of capitalist production, the lack of knowledge of what the other fellow does and of what buyers want, and so on, though all the crudities that are to be found in the literature of this kind must not be attributed to him. The phenomena of the post-Napoleonic depressions suggested to him a rich array of sources of trouble of all sorts that was easier to shape into an indictment than into an analytic organon.

Thus, he stands also in the current of ideas that produced a 'theory' which was to command much support by very able economists from, roughly, 1850 to the end of the nineteenth century, and will have to be mentioned again. In a nutshell, it may be expressed by saying that crises will occur when anything of sufficient importance goes wrong. One of the chief representatives of this view was Roscher.[7] But in addition to this common-sense, if somewhat commonplace, theory Roscher presented what can only be described as a fricassee of most of the ideas that were current at the time he wrote. Emasculating all of them, he accepted Say's law but reduced it to an identity;[8] he accepted and amplified Ricardo's sudden changes in the channels of trade; he cautiously accepted Malthus' oversaving factor though he said that Malthus

[6] See, especially, besides Sismondi's article in Brewster's *Edinburgh Encyclopaedia* and the *Nouveaux Principes*, his article on 'Balance des consommations avec les productions' in the *Revue encyclopédique*, May 1824. In this same periodical (June and July 1827) he also crossed swords on the subject with Dunoyer.

[7] *Principles* (*Grundlagen*, 1st ed. 1854; English trans., 1878), Book IV, §§ 216-17 on 'Commercial Crises,' and § 220, entitled 'When Saving is Injurious.' The theory that every circumstance that suddenly and largely increases production or decreases consumption or 'disturbs the ordinary course of industry, must bring with it a commercial crisis' is still more fully explained in *Ansichten der Volkswirtschaft* (1861). This view of the matter, sometimes glorified by a shrewd and instructive analysis of individual situations, was very common in France. Courcelle-Seneuil, Chevalier, and many other authors who differ only in the relative emphasis they put on the circumstances that are particularly apt to play a role—credit expansion, e.g.—could be quoted to this effect. A very typical example will suffice, however: Joseph Garnier's *Éléments* (1845; later *Traité*) and especially his article on 'Crises commerciales' in the *Dictionnaire universel théorique et pratique du commerce et de la navigation* (1859).

[8] In doing so, however, he hit upon a formulation that is not inelegant and will ring familiarly to modern ears though, as we know, it misses Say's meaning completely: he said that Say's law is true for *all* commodities *including money*.

had overstressed his point; he admitted that saving is 'injurious' if savings are not invested (*Principles*, § 220); he accepted several points that had been made by Sismondi; finally, perhaps under the influence of J. S. Mill, he recognized the role of absorption of funds in fixed investments [9]—all this without any effort at rigorous formulation or co-ordination. The situation that produced performances like this invited factual investigation and there were several good monographs on individual crises, but I shall only mention the comprehensive and very successful history of crises by Wirth.[10]

Of much greater interest than the work we have been surveying so far was the cycle analysis of Tooke and Lord Overstone. Though 'crises' commanded the scene throughout the century, it occurred to many observers from the 1820's on—among whom, not much to their credit, the scientific leaders of the profession were not conspicuous—that crises are but phases in a more fundamental wavelike movement and cannot be really understood except within this broader setting. From the first, writers used the term 'cycle' or 'commercial cycle' in order to denote the units of this movement [11] and spoke of a 'periodicity' of these cycles, by which most of them meant not more, however, than a definite sequence of phases irrespective of duration.[12] Some, however, did suggest approximate, if not exact, equality of duration and among these the 'ten-year cycle' eventually gained a certain popularity—even Marx experimented with it in a noncommittal manner. This pioneer work produced within the period the seminal performances of Jevons and Juglar, which will however be more conveniently considered in Part IV. In the footnote below, I mention a few others that have been almost forgotten. Observe that there is no relation between this work and the earlier discussions on gluts. It grew up independently and owes little if anything to the general

[9] This theory was elaborated at that time by several authors, among others by V. Bonnet, *Questions économiques et financières à propos des crises* (1859).

[10] Max Wirth, *Geschichte der Handelskrisen* (1858). His contributions to analysis are insignificant. But he was one of the first to attempt descriptive classification of crises (credit crises, capital crises, crises of speculation, etc.), an approach to the problem that appealed to many students in Germany. Also he emphasized the international aspects of crises.

[11] The idea was new but the word was not. Sir William Petty used it with reference to the sequence of good and bad harvests ('dearths and plenties') in his *Treatise of Taxes and Contributions* (1662), in the course of an attempt to evaluate the normal rent of land. There is no evidence that he had any notion of a general economic cycle or that he wished to explain it by the variations in crops.

[12] Some confusion about this has arisen from the fact that some modern writers who use the phrase 'periodicity' in the strict sense—recurrence in constant periods—attribute the same sense to all writers who use the word and then speak of assertion or denial of periodicity when they should speak of assertion or denial of periods of constant duration. This must be borne in mind throughout. Lord Overstone spoke of 'conditions which are periodically returning' but did not assert that they were recurring in *equal* periods. Juglar (see below, Part IV, ch. 8, sec. 9a) spoke of the *retour périodique* of crises, but his dating displays very unequal time distances between them. Moreover, he expressly denied that the material suggests the presence of anv definite period.

economics of the epoch. Its authors stood to the professed economists on a footing of cool and reciprocated indifference. Yet one should think that each group might have derived help from the other.[13]

But Tooke and Overstone did influence opinion within the fold—and were in turn influenced by it—and their work succeeded in setting on foot what may be described as a new analysis of 'the' business cycle.[14] Also, they influenced one another more than they realized or, at any rate, were prepared to admit, and the affinity between their methods and results is more important than are the differences. The prevailing impression to the contrary is due, in the first place, to their antagonism in matters of central-bank policy, especially to their controversy over Peel's Act. In the second place, they were very different types and would express the same fact or result so differently that it would look like two different facts or results. In the third place, they did differ in several points of theory and factual diagnosis, which both of them stressed unduly but which, so far as business-cycle analysis is concerned, amount to less than they seem to.

In the state of research in the 1830's, the mere fact that they saw and

[13] I mention, first, John Wade, who was a complete outsider and whose politeness toward 'political economy' barely veils feelings akin to contempt. In his *History of the Middle and Working Classes* . . . (1833), he developed a pretty comprehensive theory of 'the commercial cycle of depression and prosperity,' to which he attributed an average length of between five and seven years, in terms, chiefly, of prices and employment. Faulty and inconclusive though his reasoning is, it is of some interest as a primitive instance of an endogenous dynamic model that reproduces alternation of depression and prosperity by virtue of a lagged relation between prices and consumption. The second work to be mentioned, Hyde Clarke's 'Physical Economy' . . . (*Railway Register*, 1847) I know only from Jevons' report (*Investigations in Currency and Finance*, pp. 222-3). He had a ten-year cycle (1796, 1806, 1817, 1827, 1837, and 1847 being the crisis dates, which suggest a little manhandling) *and in addition a longer period of about* 54 *years*, a striking anticipation of the major cycles or spans of later days, especially of Kondratieff's long waves (see below, Part IV, ch. 8). But his attempts at explanation in terms of meteorological facts came to nothing. Next, I want to advert to interesting work published in the *Transactions of the Manchester Statistical Society*, notably the papers by W. Langton (1857-8) and John Mills (1867-8). Both present some evidence of a decennial cycle which both associate rather vaguely with psychological ('moral') factors. The former, in addition, anticipated Jevons' analysis of the 'autumnal drain' and noticed the fact that the third quarter of the year is particularly favorable to the outbreak of crises; the latter specifically labeled his cycles as credit cycles. In the United States, periodicity in the sense of recurrence was recognized quite early. For the rest, the question whether or not bank credit was the cause of cycles was zealously debated (see, e.g., the discussion in C. Raguet's *Treatise on Currency and Banking*, 1839; this writer produced also an interesting but inadequately motivated overconsumption theory of cycles). R. Hare ('Do Banks Increase Loanable Capital?', *Hunt's Merchants' Magazine*, 1852) was one of the earliest of the few writers who attributed to cycles the function of speeding up economic advance.

[14] Some contemporaneous writers, Hyde Clarke and Langton especially, recognized a multiplicity of cycles that run their courses simultaneously. Tooke and Overstone, however, knew just one type of cyclical fluctuations.

understood—intuitively at least—the phenomenon of cyclical variations in business situations constitutes in itself fundamental affinity. But the manner in which they gave expression to their vision illustrates very well the difference in their mental set-up that induced so many historians to overlook all they had in common. With Tooke's method of arriving at results from discussion of individual situations, the perception of the phenomenon was merged so completely into the ocean of his details that it nowhere stands out clearly, and the very fact that he saw it needs to be established against high authority.[15] Lord Overstone, who theorized—though no doubt also from facts, especially the facts of his experience as a banker—boldly and purposively set forth that the 'state of trade' (his quotes) 'revolves apparently in an established cycle' that he divides into states of quiescence, improvement, growing confidence, prosperity, excitement, overtrading, convulsion, pressure, stagnation, and distress, 'ending again in quiescence.' [16] No importance attaches to these ten phases any more than to Tooke's two or three. But the sequence makes sense all the same.

Neither author made any conscious attempt to associate with his phases *general* characteristics that would have produced a standard picture of the cycle. But it could be shown that they saw all those that experienced practitioners of business would see and practically all that our wealth of statistics has taught us to see. Prices, interest, credit, gold movements, speculation, and investment, in their relation to business activity and overtrading, naturally were foremost in their minds. There is this difference though: preoccupied as he was with the historical facts of successive situations, Tooke presented a rich assortment of relevant elements that is entirely absent from Overstone's publications and presumably was not fully present in his thought. In that assortment, two things merit particular attention. First, Tooke emphasized throughout the importance of the 'corn trade' and, in connection with this, of harvests. We cannot credit him with a harvest-theory of the cycle—any such one-factor theory was quite alien to his way of thinking. But we should, I think, credit him with having kept this element before the eyes of students

[15] That authority is Sir T. E. Gregory. But Tooke's description (as has been pointed out by Kepper) in chs. 9 and 10 of the *History* (2nd vol., particularly the last paragraph of sec. 2, ch. 9) of the developments from 1828 to 1837 shows conclusively his awareness of a definite cyclical mechanism which, in this place, he describes in terms of a lag of supply behind consumption during 'a state of rising markets' and of the reverse in the subsequent phase of 'stagnation.' 'Phases, within which the changes and alternations between periods of confidence and discredit, of the spirit of enterprise and despondency' revolve, are noticed on p. 175 of vol. I. There is even a suggestion of a ten-year cycle.

[16] This famous passage, that has been often quoted, occurs in his 'Reflections suggested by a Perusal of Mr. J. Horsley Palmer's Pamphlet on the Causes and Consequences of the Pressure on the Money Market,' 1837 (republ. *Tracts*, p. 31). But it is only from unsystematic comments dispersed over the whole of his collected tracts, letters, evidences (see above, sec. 4b) that a conspectus of his opinions can be gained. There remain many loose ends and also some contradictions that cannot be resolved—it is fair to assume that he never completely thought out his ideas.

and with having given an impulse to this theory which commanded some support even before Jevons wrote.[17] Second, he emphasized that periods of prosperity are associated with investment in fixed capital—this particularly in connection with the boom in railroad construction during the 1840's—and technological change.

Emphasis on these two elements constitutes, of course, an important step in causal analysis. The cycle theory of both Tooke and Overstone is primarily an 'endogenous' theory, that is to say, both authors tried to show how each phase of the cyclical process is induced by the conditions prevailing in the preceding one. But neither was content with this. Though Tooke's method produced a much larger array of explanatory, auxiliary, and random factors, Lord Overstone also recognized the more important categories, especially technological improvement, which he came near to considering as the most important of the causes of upswings. It is, therefore, quite wrong to attribute to him personally that purely monetary theory of the cycle which saw nothing in the latter but the vagaries of an ill-regulated currency and credit system and which no doubt counted adherents among his English companions-in-arms and still more in the United States.[18] Overstone himself explicitly stated that it is not the policy of banks which produces upswings.[19] The sense in which this explanation is, nevertheless, possible for modern exponents of monetary theories of the cycle—Hawtrey and von Mises in particular—may be defined in terms of two propositions.

First, no matter what he thought about the problem of ultimate causation, Lord Overstone certainly believed that expansion of bank loans, by means of bank notes and 'created' deposits, beyond the boundary of 'real' capital [20]

[17] Von Bergmann (op. cit. p. 239) mentioned a French author, Briaune (*Des Crises commerciales . . .* , 1840; *Du Prix des grains, du libre échange et des réserves,* 1857), who presented a clearcut harvest theory in the sense that the cycle is fundamentally nothing but the effect of spells of good and bad harvests upon society's total income.

[18] Even G. W. Norman (*Remarks upon some Prevalent Errors with respect to Currency and Banking*), who, of writers of some reputation, came nearest to holding a purely monetary theory of cycles in the sense above, qualifies it drastically by admitting many other causal factors. For American examples, see H. E. Miller, op. cit. p. 193 et seq.

[19] See, especially, his A *Letter to J. B. Smith* (1840). No doubt he sometimes expressed himself rather carelessly on the subject, but I do not think it correct to say that the statements alluded to are *contradicted* by others, or that they are no more than the sort of illogical concessions which people engaged in political controversy are frequently compelled to make.

[20] This is the phrase he used in his *Evidence before the House of Commons Committee on Bank Acts,* 1857, and the appendix thereto (republ. 1858). I think it safe to identify this real capital with the stock of purchasing power that the banks absorb from the savings of the public or gain through imports of gold, so that his argument aimed at Ricardo's 'fictitious' capital. Possibly, this distinction linked up, in his banker's mind, with the different but related distinction between funds that are available for long-period investment and funds which, though available for short periods only, are nevertheless used for the financing of long-period investment.

is responsible for a course of events that differs qualitatively from what would happen if lending always remained within these boundaries. Miscarriages, so he argued, would also happen in the latter case; but, however frequent, they would be each of them individual occurrences, not necessarily connected with one another, hence capable of being currently absorbed. But if credit has been substantially expanded beyond that boundary, then the whole structure of the economic process is distorted. Investment by firms is *generally* increased to an extent that the underlying conditions of the economy do not warrant and which, therefore, justifies itself only so long as this inflation goes on. This is more than is implied in the statement, which Tooke never denied, that excessive easy money will facilitate 'overtrading' and accentuate its consequences.

Second, Lord Overstone explained the turn of affairs from 'overtrading' to 'convulsion, pressure, stagnation' by a purely or predominantly monetary mechanism: recession was the reaction to the preceding boom, but it was primarily a reaction to the credit expansion of the boom. This credit expansion raised prices, thereby causing drains of cash (into circulation as well as to foreign countries) and threatening convertibility of bank notes. This was bound to raise interest rates and this again to shake confidence and to contract bank deposits and the amount of commercial bills outstanding (*Tracts*, 1857, p. 264 et seq.). Nothing of all this was worked out with the care and thoroughness to which later analysis, aided by hostile criticism, has accustomed us. But the general import is clear enough: it is money and credit which, themselves unstable, unstabilize economic progress, and it was bank reform which was needed in order to stabilize it, not indeed completely—Overstone repeatedly disclaimed this—but so far as it is capable of being stabilized at all. Tooke criticized all this adversely: he did not believe in the existence or, at all events, in the importance of 'fictitious' capital; he minimized the role of interest in the cycle; he did not think that the contraction of credit was the most important factor in *causing* the downturn. This was indeed enough for him to arrive at different conclusions as to policy. But when we take account, on the one hand, of the qualifications that Overstone applied to his argument, and, on the other hand, of all the qualifications that Tooke applied to his denials, we find the range of their disagreements considerably narrowed.

Thus, a rich crop of ideas and of analytic performances may be garnered and put to the credit of that period's account. We have noticed the overproduction theories and at the same time the elimination of their most naïve types; we have noticed several underconsumption theories and, in their case also, critical work that exposed their errors; we have noticed the random-disturbance theories in the most varied editions; we have noticed the discovery of the business cycle and the emergence of both monetary and investment theories of it; even an overconsumption and the harvest theory were not absent; above all, we have noticed the beginnings of statistical work on the problem. But, strange to say, nobody seems to have known all these bricks or to have understood that they were bricks awaiting the hand that would combine them in a comprehensive structure—comprehensive though provisional—

before the period was out. J. S. Mill failed at the task though he offered more of a synthesis than appears at first sight.[21] He described the cyclical mechanism in terms of expectations of profit—induced by favorable or unfavorable occurrences—that act upon dealers' stocks, hence upon prices which eventually go on rising for no better reason than that they have risen and, when it is realized that the rise has gone beyond the extent warranted by the initiating occurrence, begin to fall until they go on falling because they have fallen. Carefully pointing out that this could happen even 'in a community to which credit was unknown,' he then emphasized the fact that readily extensible credit will greatly increase the violence of such fluctuations. But commercial crises—defined as situations in which 'a great number of merchants and traders at once either have, or apprehend that they shall have, a difficulty in meeting their engagements'—may also arise without 'particular extension of credit' when a large proportion of the capital which usually supplies the loan market is absorbed by unusual demands for foreign payments, fixed investments, and the like. He argued against naïve overproduction and underconsumption theories, especially the oversaving theory, yet found, within the events of depression, place for both excess supply and underspending. Interest also gets its modest place, and so does the purely monetary mechanism of internal and external drains. Nor is periodicity (in the wide sense of the word) absent. I think this is enough to impart to readers the sense of flatness I experienced myself in trying to reconstruct Mill's analysis of the cycle. But though commonplace, all this is also common sense and not a bad foundation for further work. In perusing what A. Marshall said on the subject,[22] we find indeed much more material and do not have the same sense of flatness; but substantially his treatment does not amount to more than an elaboration of J. S. Mill's suggestions. Many other students were influenced or even initiated by Mill. Even Marx may have learned something from him.

Marx's analysis of business cycles is an 'unwritten chapter' and no coherent picture of it has emerged, or is likely to emerge, that would command the approval of all, or even of all orthodox, Marxologists.[23] Several methodolog-

[21] This is in part because Mill nowhere concentrated all he had to say about crises or cycles. He dealt perfunctorily with the subject in Book III, ch. 12, § 3 of the *Principles*. But pertinent material is found in many other places, especially in chs. 14 and 23 of Book III and in ch. 4 of Book IV.

[22] The *sedes materiae* is Book IV on 'Fluctuations of Industry, Trade, and Credit' in *Money, Credit, and Commerce*, published in 1923 but consisting chiefly of results of much earlier work (some of which dated from the 1880's). In addition, there are several relevant passages in Marshall's *Principles*. The phrase above that 'prices rise or fall because they have risen or fallen' is Marshall's.

[23] On the Marxist literature on the subject, see P. M. Sweezy *Theory of Capitalist Development*, Part III. More nearly correct than Dr. Sweezy's own interpretation seems to me to be the one by H. Smith, 'Marx and the Trade Cycle,' *Review of Economic Studies*, June 1937, to which readers are particularly referred—a reference that is to excuse in part the brevity of the comments which follow. The only other excuse I have is the impossibility of presenting, from the vast mass of relevant material, a tolerable account within the available space. Most of this material is to be found (the

ical features call first for our attention. As always, Marx was conscious of reasoning—sometimes on the same page—on widely different levels of abstraction. In the matter of cycles, this is particularly important to note because, each cycle being a historical individual and in part conditioned by circumstances for which there is no exact analogue in other cycles, we have always to deal with—and even to construct *ad hoc* theories for—facts the relevance of which varies according to the level of abstraction on which we wish to move: a cycle theory may still aim at being general or fairly general, and yet contain elements that are nonessential from the standpoint of a pure model. This greatly increases the difficulties of interpretation. Moreover, Marx attended carefully to the vital distinction between general institutional conditions that permit cyclical movements and 'causes' or factors that actually produce them. For instance, the famous 'anarchy' of capitalist society, the intervention of money between 'real' transactions, and the vagaries of bank credit were for him facts to be taken account of, but as permissive—though necessary—conditions only, and not as 'causes': he perfectly realized the emptiness of any 'theory' that contents itself with pointing to these and similar facts.

Finally, he distinguished, from both conditions and causes, another set of facts, the symptoms.[24] It stands to reason that neglect of these distinctions must be a fertile source of errors in analysis and of futile controversy and that this methodological contribution is in itself sufficient to give to Marx high rank among the workers in this field.

Next, we must try to appraise the apparent relation, which a passage in the *Communist Manifesto* seems to suggest, between cycles and the ultimate breakdown of capitalist society. Marx used the notion of a (perhaps decennial) cycle as a matter of course. Crises were never more for him than a phase in the cyclical process. Yet if he did believe, as he seems to have done, that crises tend to become more destructive as the capitalist epoch wears on, it is natural to assume that he associated this supposed fact[25] with the ultimate

---

famous but inadequate passages in the *Communist Manifesto* and in volume I of *Das Kapital* are really of minor importance) in volumes II and III of *Das Kapital* and especially in the *Theorien über den Mehrwert*. Several letters are also essential, e.g. Marx's correspondence with Engels on the renewal period of durable capital in the English textile industry.

[24] On p. 695 of *Das Kapital* (vol. I, English trans. publ. by Kerr, 1906) occurs the sentence: 'The superficiality of Political Economy shows itself in the fact that it looks upon the expansion and contraction of credit, which is a mere symptom of the periodic changes of the industrial cycle, as their cause.' Of course, Political Economy as a whole does not do this. Yet there is a lot of truth in what Marx meant to express.

[25] There is a lot to be said both about this 'fact' itself and about Marx's belief in it. That he held such belief can be 'proved' in the same way that we can 'prove' that Marx believed in a violent and spectacular breakdown of the capitalist order of things. It may be that he held, and toward the end of his life abandoned, both these beliefs. For us it is more important to note (a) that the thesis that crises increase in intensity is not logically inherent in his general theory, and (b) that some later Marxists, and especially Hilferding, repudiated it until the events of 1929-32 provided the semblance of a verification.

breakdown or even that he expected that capitalism would break down *in* a final crisis that would be so disastrous as to set fire to the framework of capitalist society. It is more fair to Marx's fundamental conception, however, to neglect such evidence as there is for his having taken this view and to emphasize that, in his analysis, the cyclical process per se and the trend that points toward breakdown—especially if the breakdown amounts to not more than stagnation—are *as a matter of fact* two distinct phenomena, each of which might exist without the other. There was nothing in this to have prevented him from looking upon recurrent crises as 'contributory causes' to an ultimately untenable social situation.

Finally, we must try to collect Marx's contributions to a fundamental or 'causal' explanation of the cycle, trying to find out, as so many others have tried before us, whether any definite theory of it can be attributed to Marx even though he never penned one explicitly. The first step is easy. Marx clearly visualized that the 'decennial cycle' that ('interrupted by smaller oscillations') runs along in a sequence of phases (or 'periods,' as he said) of average activity, prosperity, overproduction, crisis, and stagnation[26] is 'characteristic of modern industry' and not merely the result of a series of incidents or accidents. And he definitely located its source in the process of accumulation. But beyond this, one thing only is certain, namely, that he treated this process, including the increase in productive capacity it brings about and the 'industrial reserve army it creates,' as a movement away from equilibrium, and crises as the catastrophes which periodically re-establish equilibrium and, by means of radical destruction of capital values, recreate the conditions for profitability of business. This is a promising approach that avoids many possible errors and irrelevancies and purposively leads up to the question that remains: why should the process of accumulation be *essentially*[27] disequilibrating?

Since Marx considered the cycle as an essential form of capitalist life, we cannot accept a random-disturbance theory as an answer. Since he passed a contemptuous judgment on credit-theories of the cycle, we can exclude these, however much he made of speculation and other excesses that are facilitated by an expansible credit system. He certainly was not an adherent of any naïve overproduction theory of crises in the sense of Fourier's *crises pléthoriques*.[28] Nor should he be saddled, as he frequently has been, both by

26 *Das Kapital*, vol. I, ch. 25, sec. 3 (p. 694 of English trans., 1906).

27 There is no difficulty in understanding why, in real life, it is exposed to disequilibrating factors, such as speculative manias, errors, miscarriages of all sorts. But these factors do not solve the ultimate theoretical problem why cyclical fluctuations should be *inherent* in the logic of capitalism—as Marx well knew.

28 The reader must not allow himself to be misled by the frequency with which the phrase overproduction occurs in Marx's writings—as we have seen, it occurs even in his sequence of phases. It has with him no meaning other than a descriptive one. In his phenomenology of cycles all-round unsalability of goods, of course, does play a role. But he was above allocating any causal importance to it. Some followers (e.g. K. Kautsky in *Das Erfurter Programm*, 1891) were not.

friends and foes, with that underconsumption theory which associates crises with inadequacy of labor's purchasing power and which, to the layman, seems so closely connected with exploitation.[29] But this theory belongs to Rodbertus and not to Marx, who, like the good economist he was, was quite aware of its weakness and repudiated it in so many words.[30] Thus, finally, we seem to be left with the falling rate of profit—the consequence, with Marx, not of accumulation per se but of the relative increase in constant as against variable capital—and several possibilities do in fact come into view of harnessing this 'law' to serve the purpose in hand. To begin with, this 'law' can live on the highest level of abstraction. Further, there is no question but that prosperity periods are periods of supernormal investment and that the resulting increase in productive capacity has an effect upon prices and profits that need not be of causative, but must always be of considerable, importance.[31] Finally, Marxist accumulation leads to unemployment and tends to undermine the industrial structure that exists at any time (destruction of smaller and less efficient firms and so on). Marx seems to have realized, however, that none of these elements will readily explain the cyclical form of the process of accumulation and still less the occurrence of *crises*. In any case, perhaps wisely, he did not commit himself to an explanatory hypothesis clearly based upon any or all of them.[32]

[29] See above, this sec., note 4. Since nobody has ever attributed to Marx an underconsumption theory of what in the passage referred to we have called the nonspending (Keynesian) type, it should be superfluous to insist on the fact that Marxist capitalists are always in a hurry to invest and that hence this element of the case has no place in his system. Since these capitalists invest because they have got to—owing to the pressure of competition—the same reasoning applies to Malthusian underconsumption.

[30] See on this H. Smith, op. cit. pp. 193-5. Underconsumption of workers does come in but only in an indirect and secondary manner, not as the fundamental cause: if wages were higher, i.e. the degree of exploitation smaller, the rate of accumulation would also be smaller; since accumulation is responsible for the cycles, we might therefore expect that these would be less pronounced in that case.

[31] This fact can, of course, be expressed by the phrase Overproduction of Capital. But this does not make Marx a sponsor of either an overproduction or a disproportionality theory.

[32] We have had to omit many features of Marx's speculations on cycles, e.g. his brief and superficial references to the existence of a self-generating mechanism that works by virtue of its momentum; we have, however, mentioned his interest in the replacement cycle of durable capital. This search for additional facts seems to support the guess that the ultimate problem remained unsolved in his mind.

Part IV

From 1870 to 1914

(And Later)

CHAPTER 1

Introduction and Plan

1. Coverage

This Part is to cover the history of analytic work from about 1870 to 1914. For justification of the first date I invoke a fact that few economists will deny, namely, that it was around 1870 that a new interest in social reform, a new spirit of 'historicism,' and a new activity in the field of economic 'theory' began to assert themselves; or, that there occurred breaks with tradition as distinct as we can ever expect to observe in what must always be fundamentally a continuous process. The justification for the second date is the thesis that the First World War was an 'external factor' powerful enough for its outbreak to be made a terminal point, though the influences that were to put an end to that epoch of economic analysis and to usher in another were all clearly visible before and though they did not conquer until another decade or so had elapsed.

All this must be taken with the same qualifications that apply to any attempt to periodize anything, and in particular with qualifications similar to those with which we found it necessary to safeguard our conception of the preceding period. A number of men and of works ride astride both periods and cannot be assigned to either without much arbitrariness; and there were many overlaps in views, attitudes, and methods. Partly because of this, some men and works that belong chronologically to either the preceding or the following periods have been allocated to this Part. There is, however, also another reason for referring, sometimes rather fully, to developments of our own period and for carrying our story, in some matters, down to date (1949): modern developments will be but cursorily treated in Part v, and it seems desirable to use opportunities as they arise for indicating, at least in a number of important points, how modern work harks back to the work of 1870-1914—how far it is on the foundation laid by the latter that we ourselves are building.

But all the qualifications that are necessary in order to prevent periodization from becoming misleading—or downright nonsense—should not blind us to the fact that the period we are about to discuss actually forms a real unit, which would have to be recognized quite irrespective of the claims of expository convenience. The breaks with tradition around 1870 were meant to be breaks by the men whose names are associated with them: they may have looked to those men more abrupt and more important than they do to the historian, but this does not mean that they were wholly imaginary. Upon these 'revolutions' followed two decades of struggle and more or less heated discussions. And from these again emerged, in the nineties, a typical classical situation in our sense, the leading works of which exhibited a large expanse of common ground and suggest a feeling of repose, both of which created, in the superficial observer, an impression of finality—the finality of a Greek temple that spreads its perfect lines against a cloudless sky. But in the last decade or so before the outbreak of the First World War, even the superficial observer should have been able to discern signs of decay, of new breaks in the offing, of revolutions that have not as yet issued into another classical situation.

2. Paraphernalia

Through 'revolution' and consolidation, that period witnessed substantial advance. I suggest that we are likely to underrate its achievements as much as we are to overrate the achievements of the period from A. Smith to J. S. Mill. In part, this is due to a fact that is the main cause of the difficulties some readers will encounter in perusing this Part: economists began to develop more complex techniques, which increasingly took the place of the simple ones of old that every educated person had been able to master without special training. As a natural and inevitable result, economics became both more specialized and less accessible to the reading public, and because of this economists earned plenty of—entirely unreasonable—reproach not only from spokesmen of this public but also from the less technique-minded in their own midst. This process was slow, however, and leaders who, like Marshall, harbored the ambition to be 'read by businessmen' and who wrote accordingly, still secured full-dress reviews in the daily press. It hardly needs pointing out that any such success was bought at a price, and that against such advantage to the science and the public as we may see in it, we must set a loss of analytic efficiency.

The science grew still more in bulk than in wisdom. This was in part the consequence of its rapid 'progress' in professionalization and professorialization. We have noticed that even in the preceding periods economists recognized each other as people possessed of a special competence and that there had developed something like professional standards of performance. These became much more definite in the period under discussion during which economics—or even each of the recognized branches of the economic trunk—developed into a full-time job. This induced increasing professionalization as much as it was in turn furthered by it. In the preceding period, most of the leading economists were not academic teachers. In the period under discussion, practically all were. In England, the change shows still more strikingly than it does anywhere else, because there professors of economics (or academic teachers with different titles), having been very few before, increased but little in absolute number during that period but nevertheless conquered the field.[1] In the United States, the increase in the number of academic teachers was spec-

[1] On conditions in the department of money and banking, see ch. 8 below.

tacular after Harvard had acquired her first regular professorship in political economy in 1871 (Columbia's oldest chair in moral philosophy and political economy dates from 1818) and Yale in 1872. Germany, Italy, Spain, and the northern countries developed their economic professions on old-established lines, but France took a big step by establishing in 1878 professorships of economics at all the faculties of law in the country, whereas up to that year there had not been any regular and recognized teaching in economics at all except in Paris.

Measured by modern standards, research facilities—beyond library facilities that were greatly extended, especially in the United States—remained extremely modest. In many places, they were entirely absent.[2] Teaching methods improved in different ways in different countries. We must remember that both in England and in the United States the professional study of economics was still something new that had to fight its way and to establish its methods by a process of trial and error,[3] and that in some other countries economics remained throughout the period a very minor adjunct of the study of law. Even in Prussia and some other German states, where economics had a much more independent position in the faculties of arts and sciences ('philosophical' faculties) that provided a curriculum and granted the Ph.D. in economics, there were usually only two full professors in economics[4] and perhaps one or two lecturers (*Privatdozenten*). American students will throw up their hands in holy horror when they read that one and the same man was expected to teach general economics, public finance, labor, money and banking, 'agrarian policy,' international trade, and industrial organization and control (*Industriepolitik*), all in three courses. But the seminar (every professor gave a general seminar, covering indiscriminately all these subjects, as students' papers became available), and later on the specialized seminar, developed to complement the lecture courses (not all of which were exactly fascinating, I am afraid) and to secure individual attention at least for students working on their Ph.D. theses. Progress took different lines elsewhere, though the seminar method was widely copied. Enough has been said, however, to convey an idea of a state of things that explains many of the difficulties that hampered the advance of economic analysis and reduced the level of the average economist's competence below what it might have been—this level of competence in turn accounts for the frequency of pointless controversies that arose from nothing but a failure to understand, and for a fact that still further complicates the historian's task. A lifelike picture is difficult to draw and an average is difficult to strike when

[2] This is, however, likely to give too unfavorable an impression. In Germany, for instance, very adequate (real) incomes and long vacations supplied professors, especially at the big universities, with plenty of facilities for research.

[3] In this respect, it is highly significant that in Cambridge (England) a Tripos in Economics and associated branches of political science was not organized until 1903. Before that economics was indeed taught but not recognized as a full-time professional study. After that, teaching expanded but throughout the period there was nothing like the 'economic faculty' of today.

[4] A number of English and Scottish universities had just one teacher of economics.

there is so wide a gulf between the performance of a small number of leaders and the rest of the profession.

The growing professions organized themselves and provided outlets for their current production. Again, it is neither necessary nor possible to go beyond a few important and familiar facts. The Verein für Sozialpolitik was founded in 1872, the American Economic Association in 1885 (the Historical Association in 1884), and the Royal Economic Society—to use the name it eventually adopted—in 1890: three significant dates. The Royal Economic Society provided for the profession a central body and a journal; the American Economic Association provided, in addition, the yearly meetings we know with their large programs of papers and discussions. The Verein took its name from a special purpose, which was not 'scientific' in itself (see below, ch. 4) [5] and involved a definite pledge, which in the first decades of its career determined both the topics and the spirit of the annual discussions. Eventually, however, it tended to become what the other two organizations were from the first—an association of substantially 'scientific' character for the whole field of economics. Still more important is another feature of the Verein that was absent from the program, as well as from the practice, of the American and English associations: from its beginnings it organized team-work research. Every member of its central committee had the right to suggest projects. Those that were accepted by the executive committee were entrusted to subcommittees, and these in turn assembled groups of interested members and presented the results of their investigations for discussion in the annual meetings. The original papers together with the discussions are published in the 188 volumes of the Verein's *Schriften*.[6] There is a case against, as well as a case for, such large-scale team work. But it is important for the reader to keep in mind this earliest instance of it.

New outlets for scientific work were provided in the shape of new journals. To mention but a few of outstanding importance, the *Revue d'économie politique*, the *Giornale degli Economisti*, the *Economic Journal*, the *Quarterly Journal of Economics*, the *Journal of Political Economy*, the *American Economic Review*, the *Ekonomisk Tidskrift*, *Schmoller's Jahrbuch*, the *Archiv für Sozialwissenschaft und Sozialpolitik*, the *Zeitschrift für Volkswirtschaft, Sozialpolitik, und Verwaltung* (predecessor of the *Zeitschrift für Nationalökonomie*) all date from that period. Comprehensive dictionaries of economics were, of course, no more of a novelty than were professional journals. Nevertheless, such

[5] The original statutes of the American Economic Association to some extent followed suit by virtue of Article III, which read: 'We regard the State as an agency whose positive assistance is one of the indispensable conditions of human progress'—a sentence that was intended to convey a principle of policy. But it was soon felt that this did not fit the actual nature of the Association, and the article was accordingly dropped as early as 1888.

[6] The way this system worked and the results it turned out have been described by Franz Boese—who acted as secretary for many years—in his *Geschichte des Vereins für Sozialpolitik*, 1872-1932 (1939; last volume of the *Schriften*). The unassuming simplicity of this report serves only to make it all the more impressive.

co-operative enterprises as *Palgrave's Dictionary of Political Economy*, the new *Dictionnaire d'économie politique*, the *Handwörterbuch der Staatswissenschaften*, all reflect the vigorous growth of a—for the time being—new age and of 'its achievements, its undiminished controversies, its many fruits, its escape from "orthodoxy" [really? J. A. S.], which seems to have weighed so heavily on the previous generation.' [7] Finally new institutions were established in which economics, in one way or another, held the place of honor. Let us salute the one that is by far the most important: the London School of Economics (1895).[8]

One more point: those who are wont to emphasize the importance for scientific achievement of professorial chairs, research funds, organizations, and the like would have to infer that English achievement was at or near the bottom of the international scale. As a matter of fact, it was at the top. The supremacy in economic research that England had held during the preceding period was indeed no longer unchallenged. Many of the decisive contributions and especially of the original ones were non-English to a much greater extent than before. England retained supremacy only in the same sense that she retained supremacy in industry and finance. But she did retain it, especially so far as prestige was concerned. And again, this was not only due to the performance of her leaders; it was also and perhaps primarily due to the quality of the 'second line': it was not only due to the supreme competence (or more) of Marshall and Edgeworth; it was also due to the nearly complete absence of downright incompetence among the rest. Hence the lesson: funds and chairs are not everything; there are things that cannot be hired or bought; and if these things do not develop in step with funds and chairs, the latter may prove to have been provided in vain.

3. Plan of the Part

On the whole, the plan of this Part is on the same lines as that of Part III. No sacrifice has been made, however, on the altar of symmetry. Many things seemed to deserve emphasis that were of no or less importance before and vice versa; and many rearrangements seemed indicated for other reasons.

As before, we shall prepare ourselves for our main task by casting a glance at social backgrounds—the *Zeitgeist*—(Chapter 2) and at such developments in neighboring fields as did exert or might have been expected to exert some influence upon economics (Chapter 3). The reader who finds these surveys superficial is once more reminded that the facts to be mentioned in these two chapters are not mentioned for their own sake. This is a history of economic *analysis*, a history of the attempts of men to apply their reason to the task of understanding things, not a history of the attempts of men to apply their

7 This is how Lord Keynes expressed himself on the occasion of the Royal Economic Society's Jubilee in 1940 (*Economic Journal*, December 1940, p. 409). Of course, we must make allowance for the occasion.

8 See Professor von Hayek's most instructive sketch of its career during its first fifty years: *Economica*, February 1946.

reason—and volition—to the task of changing them. Then follow comments on two allied groups of men and ideas that lend themselves to separate treatment, the group whose work centered in the contemporaneous interest in social reform and whose leaders were with singular infelicity dubbed 'socialists of the chair' (*Kathedersozialisten*); and the group that was called, and called itself, the historical school (Chapter 4).[1] The much-debated question of economists' value-judgments will be touched upon in connection with the former, and the famous 'battle of methods' (and its American counterpart, the institutionalist controversy) in connection with the latter. To some extent, this arrangement impairs our picture, because when we go on to a brief survey of the men, groups, and developments in 'general economics' (Chapters 5 and 6), we shall have already eliminated two of the most important influences upon this 'general economics.' Let me hence entreat the reader to peruse these chapters in their order. The last two chapters of the Part deal with sets of topics that it has seemed best to reserve for separate treatment. Chapter 7 (Equilibrium Analysis) corresponds [2] to Chapter 6 of Part III and assigns the same piloting function to Walras that was assigned to Senior in Part III. It aims at presenting the emergence of the elements of modern pure theory in a manner that will, I am afraid, prove as unsatisfactory to the modern theorist as it will seem overloaded to the non-theorist. The latter may be right in contenting himself with what he will have read on these matters in Chapters 5 and 6. The Appendix to Chapter 7, on the fortunes of utility theory and its successors to the present day, stands by itself, or almost so, and should only be read by those who take special interest in the matter.[3] Segregation of the topics of money, credit, saving and investment, and business cycles in the last chapter (8) calls but for this remark: segregation imposed itself for reasons of exposition as it did in Part III; but in submitting to this necessity, I do not wish to convey the impression that I accept the current views about the monetary theory of this period. This will be made abundantly clear as we proceed.

[1] [Originally, J. A. S. intended to treat these subjects in two separate chapters, but later combined them. The consolidated chapter was left unfinished but is presented below (ch. 4) in the condition in which it was found.]

[2] [J. A. S. had some doubts about this statement. He left a note in pencil: 'Can this stay?']

[3] [At the time of writing this Note on Utility, J. A. S. intended to make it a separate chapter but later made it an appendix to Chapter 7. The original plan called for 10 chapters, subsequently reduced to 8.]

CHAPTER 2

Background and Patterns

The nearer an epoch is to us, the less we understand it: our own we understand least of all. For this reason alone, the sketch of the cultural pattern of the period to be surveyed must be drawn with greater care than was required in the case of the preceding period. Moreover, the cultural pattern actually grew everywhere more complex as the bourgeois era wore on. The reader will please recall what has been said in Part iii (ch. 3) on the subject of the lack of uniformity in the cultural pattern or *Zeitgeist* of any epoch: to speak of a single dominant *Zeitgeist* at all spells distortion of the facts—in most cases ideological distortion. But this fundamental truth of cultural sociology applies to the period under discussion with a vengeance. However severely we must simplify things, the following comments will make this abundantly clear.

1. Economic Development

The period we are about to survey was again one of rapid economic development. It was then that Germany and the United States acquired the status of front-rank industrial powers. But elsewhere, for instance in Austria, Italy, Japan, and Russia, industrialization proceeded at a *rate* (though not of course in terms of absolute figures) that was not less remarkable. After 1900, England failed to keep in step, but up to about that year she experienced an increase in wealth that may be characterized by the fact that, from 1880 to 1900, English *real* wages per earner increased by nearly 50 per cent.[1] This created an entirely new standard of life for the masses.

But until almost the end of the century expansion in physical output was accompanied by falling prices, widespread unemployment of labor, and business losses. The spells of 'prosperity' were shorter and weaker than were the

[1] A. L. Bowley, *Wages and Income in the U. K. since* 1860 (1937), Table xiv, p. 94. Of course, this means only that the total wage bill kept its percentage position in total national income.

'depressions.' In fact, the whole span between 1873 and 1898 has been dubbed the Great Depression.[2] This particular edition of the 'paradox of poverty in plenty' is not difficult to explain. All the observable phenomena can be satisfactorily accounted for by the impact of the products pouring forth from a productive apparatus that the two previous decades had greatly expanded. In a socialist society, such periods might be hailed as periods of harvest. In capitalist society, they do not cease to be that. But this aspect is entirely lost in the fears, sufferings, and resentments generated by the dislocation of existing industrial structures that is the first consequence of technological or commercial progress. An example will illustrate this. In the seventies and eighties, improved land and sea transportation brought greatly increased quantities of cheap American wheat to Europe, which meant severe depression to European agriculture. Of course, this was an essential element in the 50 per cent increase in the real wages of English labor that we have noticed above. But European farmers and their spokesmen did not look at it in this light. And if they had, they would have derived very little comfort from it. Agrarian sectors were everywhere important enough to spread their depression to others. But, though this would take more space to show, the industrial sectors had analogous troubles of their own. In a sense, these were surface troubles incident to a process of adaptation that led from one long-run spell of prosperity to another. But for many individuals and groups the only available method of adaptation was bankruptcy. For labor it meant unemployment or the ever-present threat of it.

The reader will find it easy to visualize the practical problems that resulted from this and the reactions to them of groups, classes, parties, and governments. It is on this background that we shall have to paint for the rest of this chapter. So obvious is this that there is less danger of forgetting it than there is of exaggerating the extent to which the facts alluded to—*both* the 'progress' and its vicissitudes—determined political and cultural history. For instance, those facts do explain much of the radicalization of the masses we observe: the rising standard of life and a novel sense of power contributed to that result not less than did the threat of unemployment. They also explain much of the general zest for social reform, of the tendencies toward industrial organization (especially of the cartel type), of the increasing government activities, of the dissatisfaction with the results produced by free trade, even of renascent militarism. But the further fact that none of these tendencies showed any signs of weakening during the fifteen years before the war, years that were of quite different economic complexion—most of them in fact gathered further momentum—should warn us not to trust such explanations too much. There are deeper things. . . [J. A. S. intended to expand this section.]

[2] For a historian's protest against this phrase, see H. L. Beales's article, 'The Great Depression in Industry and Trade,' *Economic History Review*, October 1934. The author makes it last only to 1886. But all the symptoms that this phrase is to indicate persisted for about another decade.

2. The Defeat of Liberalism

On the whole, the business class still had its way throughout the period, at least up to the beginning of this century, though much more so in the United States than in Europe. But its serene confidence in the virtues of laissez-faire was gone and its good conscience was going. Hostile forces were slowly gathering with which it had to compromise. Still more significant, it grew increasingly willing to compromise and to adopt its enemies' views.[1] Economic liberalism[2] thus became riddled with qualifications that sometimes implied surrender of its principles. Political liberalism, from the eighties on, lost its hold upon electorates much more rapidly than appears on the surface: only in a few countries, such as Germany and Austria, did genuinely liberal parties—in the sense in which this term is used in this book—meet with open defeat at the polls; in others, especially in England, the strength of existing political organizations and their leadership was so great as to make it possible for them to win victories on radicalized programs.[3] The reasons why, and the extent to which, all this was different in the United States need not, it is hoped, be explained. What would have to be a lengthy analysis may be summed up by saying that, barring a number of groups and movements, none of which was strong enough to influence national politics perceptibly, all the average American's radicalism amounted to—and this also goes for economists—was hostility to Big Business ('curbing monopoly').

Before trying to see how all this mirrored itself in those departments of public policy in which we are primarily interested (section 3) we must briefly

[1] This statement involves a distinction between enforced and voluntary retreat that a popular theory of political behavior refuses to accept. According to this theory, no class ever retreats voluntarily. Any facts that I might adduce in support of my distinction would by the sponsors of this theory be interpreted as 'strategical' retreat. But if the occurrence of such strategical retreats be admitted, the theory in question ceases to be meaningful—any 'concession' that is not directly enforced is then strategical by definition—unless the strategical purpose of each 'concession' is established. I maintain, though I cannot prove here, that this is possible in some cases but not in others—e.g. not in the cases of 'paternalistic' employers or in the cases of groups that are covered by the label of bourgeois radicalism.

[2] On the meaning that this term and the term Political Liberalism carry in this book, see Part III, ch. 2.

[3] This resolves an apparent paradox that might puzzle the reader. It does seem paradoxical to speak of decline of English liberalism in a period that covers the sweeping victories of Gladstone in 1880 and of Sir Henry Campbell-Bannerman in 1906. The paradox disappears, however, when it is remembered that we are not concerned with party labels even where the continuity of a political organization is reinforced by (substantial) continuity of personal leadership, as was the case with the Gladstonian party. In the latter case, the point I wish to make is illustrated by the split of the liberal party that occurred in the eighties. Viewed superficially, it occurred on the question of Irish Home Rule; but most of those who renounced allegiance on this issue had also other reasons for doing so: they did not wish any longer to be towed along by the radical wing.

glance at what we have described above as political forces hostile to bourgeois laissez-faire that were gathering momentum during that period. Orthodox socialism is the most obvious one. But it was not, during that period, the most important one. In any case, its career may be assumed to be so familiar to the reader that very few comments will suffice for our purpose.[4] First, the period saw the rise of Marxist parties in almost all countries. But even the most successful of these, the German Social Democratic Party, which by weight of talent and numbers was an important factor in politics, kept on principle aloof from political responsibility[5] and thus reduced its practical influence, even on matters of social legislation, far below what it might have been. None of the other Marxist parties was numerically significant except the Austrian one. The non-Marxist socialist parties, which shaded off into non-socialist labor groups and which felt no qualms about political co-operation with bourgeois parties, did get near or into political office here and there. These events—which raised the much-debated issue of Millerandism[6]—and the appearance, in 1906, of a Labour party in the English Parliament are, of course, tremendously important. But for the time being their importance was symptomatic only. For those who had their ear to the ground another symptom was still more significant—and much more so than were the most flamboyant revolutionary speeches. To be sure, there were many bourgeois who habitually exploded at the mere sound of the word Socialism. But there were others who were in sympathy with socialist ideas and, to an extent much greater than is commonly realized, lent practical support to them in one way or another, though not always openly. Of course, the non-socialist vote of the socialist parties was in many cases nothing but the manifestation of temporary resentments. But the number was on the increase of those who approved of the ultimate ends of socialism or who approved of the immediate aims of socialist parties—or who did both and still professed that they were not socialists.

The growth of bourgeois radical groups and parties was immediately of greater practical importance. They varied greatly in type and program—from liberal groups of the old type that had taken aboard more or less important items of social reform, to groups of intellectuals that descended from the

[4] Readers who feel this assumption to be unwarranted will do well to compare, e.g., the relevant parts of H. W. Laidler's *Social-Economic Movements* (1944).

[5] We cannot go into the reasons for this attitude. But it was not altogether a matter of sour grapes.

[6] Alexandre Millerand, later on President of the French Republic, rose into notoriety as a labor lawyer and entered the Chambre as a *radical-socialiste*. The *radicaux-socialistes* were not socialists as a party but formed the left wing of bourgeois radicalism: the party label expresses very well the social situation of latter-day capitalism that I am trying to describe. However, Millerand made his position more definitely socialist later on; and he had become the leader of a group of 60 deputies of more or less socialist persuasion when, in 1899, he accepted office in the Waldeck-Rousseau administration. He thus was the first and for some time the only socialist to take office in a bourgeois cabinet in one of the great nations. Hence his name came to denote this practice which, however, caused no difficulties in the northern countries.

philosophical radicals of old and differed little, if at all, from 'reformist' socialists such as Eduard Bernstein (ch. 5, sec. 8, below). The reason why radicals of the more advanced type carried political weight out of all proportion to their voting power—or, like the English Fabians,[7] without having any voting power at all—was that their support was often needed by governments in precarious positions, both where radicals formed parties of their own and where they formed the left wing of a bigger party of different complexion. This very situation characterizes the epoch.

Bourgeois radicalism *might* be considered as a mere by-product of the growth of socialism. And the latter was without doubt the product of laissez-faire society: one need not be a Marxist in order to realize that the private enterprise system tends to develop toward a socialist form of organization. The facts we have been discussing so far, however ominous they may have been for the bourgeois order of things, were therefore part and parcel of this very order and in this sense perfectly 'natural.' But there were others that did not fit into the schema or logic of capitalist evolution. Some of these do not present any difficulties of analysis either, but some others do.

As regards the first category, we shall in fact have no difficulty in understanding that rapid capitalist evolution will evoke resistance from strata that are threatened by it and cannot adapt themselves to a new form of existence. This was the case with the European peasantry—also with English and especially Irish farmers—and, on the continent of Europe, with the independent artisans. Landlords were, of course, in the same boat. Very naturally, they clamored for protective legislation—that was bound to violate the creed of economic liberalism—and lent support to groups and parties that were anti-capitalist though not socialist.[8] Even within the range of these phenomena, however, we cannot be sure that this was all. Many of the spokesmen of these groups did not feel that they were concerned with a particularly difficult economic situation—they felt, unlike the bourgeois radicals, that the whole liberalistic schema, including its legal and moral aspects, was fundamentally wrong.

The second category consists of cases where the same attitude stands out better and presents much more of a problem because it does not link up so obviously with a definite economic plight. In countries where the bureaucracy was a powerful factor and where, as in Germany, it had sponsored *economic* liberalism in the preceding period, a significant change occurred: without as yet becoming definitely hostile, the bureaucracy began to look upon the business class in a different way—to consider it as something to be controlled and managed rather than to be left alone, much as the American bureaucracy does today. The white collar class that increased rapidly in numbers and the other groups that were beginning to be called the 'new middle class'—the 'old' consisting of farmers, artisans, and small traders—displayed a remarkably

[7] On the Fabians, see below. [J. A. S. intended to discuss the Fabians in ch. 4, sec. 1, but this chapter and section were not completed.]

[8] In England, things did not work out in this way or at least did so much less markedly. The reasons for this, extremely interesting though they are, must not detain us.

strong resistance to socialist propaganda. But the minority that embraced economic or political liberalism in our sense was not much greater, if at all, than the minority that went socialist. The rest evolved attitudes and reform programs of their own. Finally, individuals and subgroups of all classes broke loose from economic and political liberalism—though often retaining the label—to do likewise. And they had one thing in common in spite of all the differences in interests and cultural preconceptions that no doubt existed between them: the central or controlling position that they allocated to the State and the Nation—the National State. Accordingly, these tendencies are commonly referred to as 'nationalistic' or 'neo-mercantilist' or 'imperialist,' but though these and other phrases do express individual aspects of an attitude that is as difficult to define as it is to explain, they do not express the whole of it. Marxists have simple formulae to offer that will fit these phenomena into their scheme—the simplest being perhaps that 'imperialism' is the last stage (or 'last card') of capitalism. Popular social psychology has other simple formulae to offer. I have none and must content myself with pointing out that we have been looking at the roots of modern totalitarianism.

Quite different from this in nature, but equally hostile to economic and political liberalism in our sense, was another movement that is much easier to define because it defined itself. We adopt, for brevity's sake, the usual but misleading name for it: Christian Socialism. Also for brevity's sake, we confine ourselves to the Roman Catholic branch of it, which was the only one to form great independent parties (like the German Center party) that present a unique feature: they are held together exclusively by the religious allegiance of their members, who for the rest differ in economic interests and political attitudes as much as it is possible to differ—through the whole range from extreme conservatism to extreme radicalism—and yet co-operate effectively.

Throughout the period, the Catholic Church was on the continent of Europe the object of legislative and administrative attacks from hostile governments and parliaments—in England hostility did not go beyond violent talk about 'Vaticanism'—which is what might have been expected in a predominantly 'liberalistic' world. What could not have been expected is that these attacks everywhere ended in retreat and that they left the Catholic Church stronger than it had been for centuries. Political Catholicism arose from a renascence of religious Catholicism. Looking back, we see not merely reassertion of the Catholic standpoint by people who had never abandoned it; we see also a change of attitudes among people who had: around 1900 it was a common observation to make that in a Catholic family the old and elderly were laicist and liberal and the youngsters believers and 'clerical.' This is one of the most significant patches of color in our picture. But for the purposes of this book another fact is of still greater importance. Political Catholicism from the first stood for social reform. I cannot do more than mention the names of de Mun, von Ketteler, von Vogelsang.[9] This concern of the Catholic Church with

[9] The reader will find a survey in F. S. Nitti, *Catholic Socialism* (English trans., 1895).

the conditions of labor was nothing new and only adapted an old tradition to the problems of the epoch.[10] But something that was new developed toward the end of the century, namely, a definite scheme of social organization that, making use of the existing elements of groupwise co-operation, visualized a society—and a state—operating by means of self-governing vocational associations within a framework of ethical precepts. This is the 'corporative' state adumbrated in the encyclical *Quadragesimo Anno* (1931). Since it is a normative program and not a piece of analysis, no more will be said about it in this book. I merely add the name of the man who has done more than any other for this conception of society, Heinrich Pesch, S.J.[11]

Finally, what was the attitude of economists? This question is difficult to answer because the republic of economists was torn by the same dissensions that agitated the political bodies. Individuals were still fairly numerous who clung to the liberalist faith in its integrity—particularly numerous in the United States. And there were also strictly liberalist groups—in Europe, the Paris group (see below, ch. 5, sec. 3) being the outstanding instance. But Marshall professed himself in sympathy with the aims of socialism and spoke without explanation and qualification of the 'evils of inequality'; also he was the first theorist to prove *theoretically* that laissez-faire, even with perfect competition and independently of those evils of inequality, did not assure a maximum of welfare to society as a whole; and he favored high taxation more than is compatible with simon-pure liberalism. This goes for most of the English economists. If we class them as 'liberals,' it is owing to the strong stand they made for free trade and also, perhaps, to the fact that we do not sufficiently attend to the metamorphosis of the creed of the English liberal party discussed above. Most German economists were pillars of *Sozialpolitik* and thoroughly averse to 'Smithianism' or 'Manchesterism.'[12] On the whole, the economic professions of all countries were politically supporters of the counter-

[10] Official recognition was extended to the Catholic sponsors of the cause of labor by several encyclicals, especially *Rerum Novarum* (1891).

[11] That great man (1854-1926) was not particularly proficient in analytic economics, which is why his treatise, *Lehrbuch der Nationalökonomie* (1905-23) will not be mentioned again though, so far as scholarship is concerned, it has few equals. Other works of his bring out his doctrine still better, e.g. *Liberalismus, Sozialismus, und christliche Gesellschaftsordnung* (1896-9). The reader is referred to the work of a man who may, I believe, be considered his pupil: O. von Nell-Breuning, *The Reorganization of the Social Economy* (English trans., 1936). The understanding of Pesch's doctrine is rendered more difficult by both Marxist and liberalist misinterpretations, and also by a tendency—common to friends and foes alike—to link it too closely with scholastic views. There is, of course, the same background of social and moral philosophy, but there is little affinity between the problems visualized by, say, Molina and Pesch.

[12] There were always some thoroughgoing liberals in the Gladstonian sense, even in Germany. But they were few and distinctly unpopular among their brethren. Schmoller once asserted publicly that a 'Smithian' was unfit to occupy a professorial chair. Even American 'New Dealers' did not go quite so far as this. The career of a more than competent economist of that type, Julius Wolf, illustrates the point. He was strongly pro-capitalist—and was 'cold-shouldered' in consequence.

tendencies to liberalism rather than of the still dominating liberal ones. In this sense, we can say that the alliance between economics and liberalism—and, with exceptions, between economics and utilitarianism—was broken.

3. Policies

In all departments of public policy, events reflected both the still dominant current of laissez-faire liberalism and the counter-currents that were indicative of the redistribution of political weights and of the new attitudes adumbrated in the preceding section.

(a) *Free Trade and Foreign Policy.* Around 1870, many observers—M. Chevalier among them—predicted confidently that universal and perfect free trade would prevail before the century was out. Implicitly and explicitly they also expected the victory of those principles and practices of foreign policy that are associated with free trade, such as the settlement of disputes by mutual concessions or arbitration, reduction of armaments, international gold monometallism, and the like. Such expectations were not so absurd as they seem to us now. For all those things are, in fact, among the essentials of economic and political liberalism in our sense, and expectations cannot be called absurd that follow from the logic of a dominant system. Moreover, until the turn of the century, there was more than logical deduction to support them. England upheld free trade, and other powers [1] kept their deviations from it within reasonable bounds. There were several major wars. But allowance must be made for survivals and for inherited situations. Moreover, peace was concluded in each case by consent and without display of vindictiveness. The International Court at The Hague and several cases of settlement of disputes by arbitration seemed to promise further advance toward a pacific if not pacifist state of affairs. Until (roughly) 1900, military expenditure remained comparatively moderate everywhere [2] and was not unsuccessfully fought by min-

[1] France returned to her protectionist tradition—but in a mild form—as soon as she was free to do so after the fall of Napoleon III. Germany at first continued her nearly free-trade policy. Bismarck's tariff reforms were in the protectionist direction but, compared with modern standards, very moderately so. The treaty policy of his successor, Caprivi, was an attempt to return to a regime not substantially differing from free trade. The pressure of the agrarian interests and those of the heavy industries account for a more purposeful but still moderate protectionist policy later on. The United States re-emphasized protectionist tradition in the nineties. Russia and Spain continued their protectionist policy. But all in all and compared with what was to happen in and since the First World War, it is approximately correct to say that, in principle and actual practice, the world was 'substantially free trade.' It is only in comparison to the principles professed by extreme free traders that it can be called aggressively protectionist, at least, if we exclude the United States, Russia, and Spain. This applies also to the use of tools of foreign-trade policy other than tariffs. The most important exception, the continental sugar subsidies, was abolished within the period.

[2] Comparison is with national incomes as well as with budgetary totals.

isters of finance.[3] England and France greatly expanded their colonial empires, and Germany and Italy made a beginning in colonial enterprise, by means of the unblushing use of force. But even here the contemporaneous 'liberal' observer might have taken comfort from certain facts. The significance of so strong a display of the 'imperialist' attitude as was England's treatment of the Boer republics, for instance, is materially reduced by the facts that this policy was strongly opposed throughout by part of the Liberal party and that the leader of this party (Sir Henry Campbell-Bannerman) scored a resounding victory at the polls very shortly after (1906).

It is only our knowledge of the outcome that induces us to place a different interpretation upon those 'exceptions' and 'backslidings' and also upon such things as the increase of the German fleet, the military preparations of the Balfour government, Germany's blustering, and England's efficient *entente* policy. All the same, it is true that all of this, these 'exceptions' included, heralded a new attitude that developed *against* the resistance of Gladstonian liberalism and got the better of it [4] toward the end of the period, witness the armament race and other unmistakable symptoms. This 'imperialist' or 'neo-mercantilist' attitude was general. But it stood out in classic purity in the protectionist ('Tariff Reform') campaign in England that was associated with the brilliant leadership of Joseph Chamberlain, though it ended, for the time being, in failure. The essential element in the program was Imperial Preference, not protection per se: economists' arguments about the economic merits or demerits of protective duties thus failed entirely to meet the real—the imperialist—issue.

(b) *Domestic Policy and Sozialpolitik.* Toward the end of the preceding period, extension to new strata of the right to vote had ceased to be a patent in which liberal parties had a proprietary interest. The period under discussion brought further extensions which clearly presaged, though they did not reach, universal suffrage. This was, of course, in keeping with the liberal current; but it was a potent factor in producing the counter-currents. The rest of domestic policy was in keeping with this—on the whole and with exceptions that must not detain us. In the field of industrial policy, the first measures of regulation or control put in an appearance—the Interstate Commerce Act,

[3] When the atmosphere changed, most of these ministers gave in. A notable exception was Böhm-Bawerk (see below, ch. 5, sec. 4a), who resigned on army estimates in 1904.

[4] Once more, let me advert to the fact that this attitude is open to two different interpretations: the one that may be summed up in the proposition that 'imperialism is the last stage of capitalism' and amounts to holding that capitalist interests *turned* 'imperialist' under the new conditions of large-scale production—dumping, rising wage costs, and so on; and the other that may be summed up in the proposition that the bourgeoisie, losing hold, accepted 'imperialist' policies as it accepted other things—making, of course, the best of them—that were not in its own line. But for our present purpose it does not greatly matter which of these theories we accept. The fact of the emergence of a new attitude, at variance with the liberal creed, is beyond doubt and this suffices.

regulation subject to judicial revision of the prices charged by utilities, and the Sherman Anti-Trust Act are American examples.[5] But public regulation or control still remained 'interference,' a term that does not necessarily imply disapproval but seems to indicate an opinion to the effect that legislative or administrative activity in the field of industry requires special justification in every individual case or class of cases. Much more important, however, was the new attitude toward social reforms in the interest of labor—*Sozialpolitik*.

The reforms actually carried out consisted chiefly in (a) legislation enabling governments to take a different attitude toward organized labor and strikes (in England the decisive steps were taken in the late seventies, by the Disraeli government); (b) legislation about hours and other conditions of work (an English instance is the introduction of the 8-hour day for miners, 1908); (c) social insurance (accident, sickness, old age, and eventually unemployment). Here Germany led (the acts of 1884 and 1887, expanded by legislation in the nineties) but the English non-contributory old-age pensions of the Campbell-Bannerman government and the further steps taken under the Asquith government marked important advances beyond the German example. Barring some enactments in individual states, there was practically nothing of the kind in the United States. In Europe, however, all countries advanced on these lines though at different rates of speed.

For us, however, the important thing is not what was actually done. Nor are we primarily interested in the questions how far the measures actually carried may be fitted into the liberalist schema and how far they mean only continuation of older policies—older policies of the liberalist or else the paternalistic state. To some extent both questions may certainly be answered in the affirmative; there was less of a new departure than either friends or foes of *Sozialpolitik* were inclined to believe. It is the new spirit in which they were taken that is important to us, the new attitude toward them by a large part of the bourgeois public, and the fact that they were understood—again: by friends as well as foes—to be the first installments of a much wider scheme of reconstruction. It is this relation to future fundamental reconstruction which places *Sozialpolitik* in the counter-current, even where it enjoyed the support of the new species of reforming liberals as distinct from the support of radicals on the one hand and conservatives on the other. Finally, it is important to notice the relation in which *Sozialpolitik* stood to imperialism or nationalism or neo-mercantilism. This relation was not universal, that is to say, it was not present in the scheme of one type of supporters, the bourgeois radicals. Where these furnished the principal contingent of supporters, as they did in England, the relation fails to show on the surface. But with men of the type of Joseph Chamberlain, social reform and imperialism were complements even there. In Germany, this shows much more clearly. The age is not understood

[5] Interpretation often presents difficulties. Thus, the Sherman Anti-Trust Act may be interpreted as a measure in defense of competition, one of the essential elements of the liberalist schema of things. This was indeed its ideology. But it will also bear interpretation in a sense that puts it in the counter-current, viz. as an expression of a novel attitude toward business interests.

so long as account is not taken of those to whom national self-assertion and *Sozialpolitik* were but two sides of the same medal.

(c) *Fiscal Policy.* Since nothing shows so clearly the character of a society and of a civilization as does the fiscal policy that its political sector adopts, we shall expect current and counter-current to show particularly clearly in this field. They do.

On the one hand, the balanced budget—in fact the budget that shows some surplus to be applied to the reduction of debt—remained a fundamental article of financial faith, although practice often failed to conform to it; further, taxation was for raising revenue only and was not to exert any other effects beyond what was inevitable; and in order to keep taxes as low as possible, expenditure was to be confined to 'necessary' purposes. Gladstone (and his chancellors of the exchequer) kept to these principles throughout. So did Goschen, the Chancellor of the Exchequer of the second Salisbury administration (1886-92), and, so far as they were able to do so, all the continental ministers of finance whose names are likely to go down in history, such as Raymond Poincaré, Witte, Pierson, Böhm-Bawerk,[6] and Miquel. The three last names may be used to exemplify an advance beyond Gladstonian finance—an advance partly paralleled in England by the introduction of the super-tax in 1909 —that may yet be said to fit the scheme of laissez-faire liberalism: the introduction of the progressive income tax on the total income of individuals as ascertained from their declarations, which was, of course, something quite different from the income tax in the English acceptance of the term. We are so familiar with it that we have lost the sense for the boldness of this innovation. But if the reader reflects that at the time (early nineties) no great country had introduced anything like it and that the English system then carried well-earned prestige owing to its economic and administrative success, he will realize the greatness of the achievement that is primarily associated with the names of the Prussian minister of finance, Johannes von Miquel (1891-3), and of the Austrian minister of finance, Eugen von Böhm-Bawerk.[7]

On the other hand, the counter-current asserted itself victoriously: all the three principles mentioned were violated. The first, the balanced-budget, or rather the budget-in-surplus, principle was never, so far as I know, violated intentionally, unless we so interpret the Freycinet program of reconstruction after the Franco-German War and the Japanese program of development after the Sino-Japanese War.[8] Deficit financing, on the whole, remained stigmatized as frivolous and unworthy of respectable governments. But the other two princi-

[6] With reference to Pierson, see below, ch. 5, sec. 6.

[7] Böhm-Bawerk was minister of finance three times, but not when the great Austrian reform of direct taxation was actually carried (1896). The political credit goes to other men. But he had resigned his professorship and entered the ministry of finance as a senior permanent officer in 1889 in order to prepare that reform, which was mainly his work. Another famous theorist shared in it, however, viz., R. Auspitz (see below, ch. 5, sec. 4a), who was then in parliament.

[8] For the purpose of alleviating depressions, public works were repeatedly resorted to, e.g. in Austria in the eighties.

ples gradually lost their hold upon political consciences: Sir William Harcourt's progressive estate duty (1894) and Lloyd George's 'people's budget' (1909), for instance, aimed at other goals than mere revenue raising; and the third principle broke down on the side of expenditure for social purposes, desire for which put an end, toward the close of the period, to the popularity of low taxation of the higher incomes and of 'retrenchment.'

(d) *Money*. Substantially the credo of economic and political liberalism prevailed in the field of monetary policy throughout the period. In fact, it prevailed longer than that, as the English Cunliffe report of 1918 (final report, 1919) and the English Gold Standard Act of 1925 suffice to prove: of all the articles of that credo, the gold standard was the last to go.

Silver remained the monetary metal of the greater part of mankind and, as we shall see more fully in Chapter 8, enjoyed support of one kind or another everywhere.[9] But all 'advanced' nations stayed on, or established, the gold standard, in some instances at considerable sacrifice. Most modern economists will feel that even England could have done with a little monetary stimulation during the eighties. Also they may wonder why the German Empire was so keen on adopting the gold standard after 1871. But they will be quite unable to understand why countries such as Austria-Hungary, Italy, and Russia, which had entered the period with paper currencies that were depreciated in terms of silver, should have retarded their growth and imposed hardships upon themselves in order to raise their monetary units to a largely arbitrary gold parity. These countries could just as well have stayed 'off gold' or, if they had to have it, could have introduced the gold standard at the gold value (of their currencies) that happened to prevail when it occurred to them to take this action. The riddle becomes still more baffling when we reflect that there was no political pressure to enforce that policy: for all the interests that really count politically—farmers, landowners, manufacturers, workmen—all suffered by it and even the benefit to creditors was by no means beyond doubt; only government employees were clear gainers. We cannot go into the question how far, in the conditions of the times and particularly from the standpoint of each individual country, an economic case may be made out for it all the same. It must suffice to point to certain extra-economic and extra-national considerations that were without doubt decisive: past experience with depreciated currencies had invested the gold standard with a prestige that was for the time being unchallengeable; the unfettered or 'automatic' gold currency had become the symbol of sound practice and the badge of honor and decency; and there was the admired example of England, whose creditor position, moreover, added further weight to it. Perhaps this explanation raises more problems than it solves. That it is true is certain.

But the counter-currents asserted themselves also in monetary policy. We observe a growing awareness of the necessity to control money markets by central bank action other than the 'classic' discount policy. As the period wore

[9] It is not without interest to note that A. J. Balfour was in favor of bimetallism, though his cabinet colleagues would not hear of the slightest concession to it.

on, we also observe a growing reluctance in all countries to play the gold standard game, as witnessed by resort to the gold exchange standard and, even in England and Germany, to 'gold devices.' Perhaps the gold standard was never 'automatic'; by the end of the period, it certainly had ceased to be so if it ever was (see below, ch. 8). The reasons for this were more political than purely economic: they link up with neo-mercantilist attitudes and with the increasing strain in international relations that began to be felt around 1900, also with increasing public expenditure. Arguments against the unfettered gold standard multiplied. It was losing its popularity like a naughty child that tells embarrassing truths.

4. Art and Thought

So far, whenever we probed below the surface of routine activities, which almost everywhere ran on bourgeois lines, we have discovered new patterns in process of formation, counter-currents indicative of impending fundamental change. We get the same impression when we cast a glance on the manifestations of that period's *Zeitgeist* in the Arts and in Philosophy.

(a) *Bourgeois Civilization and Its Recalcitrant Offspring.* According to a common saying, that period had no style. There is some truth in this: no doubt, the business and professional classes lived, as a rule, uninspired lives in ugly homes that dishonored the elements of past styles they combined; bought ugly furniture of similar type and nondescript pictures; supported a theatrical and a musical tradition of which the glories were inherited from the past; and read a literature that was largely commonplace in all varieties except the professionally scientific one. This style of life in all its manifestations—in England it came to be called Victorian—is now a byword of stodginess or dreariness and in fact testifies to the bourgeoisie's lack of capacity for cultural leadership, which is as pronounced as is its lack of capacity for political leadership.

Nevertheless, diagnosticians who leave it at that are wrong, and it is easy to indicate the point at which they go wrong: they fail to credit the bourgeois civilization of that period with all its great creations; and they fail to see that parents' lack of ability to lead may turn their children against them but does not alter the fact that they are their children. The period saw the emergence, through a succession of stages, of a new music; of a new style of painting; of a new novel, a new drama, and a new poetry; and, in the midst of Victorian horror, of a new architecture. To be sure, the bourgeois public looked with amazement on most of these creations and did its best to smother them. Equally sure is it that many of the creations were by nature hostile to the social structure from which they sprang; and that many of the creative individuals were enemies of the social world they beheld, and felt themselves to be the demiurgos of another. But this does not alter the facts that both the works and the men did spring from that structure; that most of the men were bourgeois by birth and upbringing; and that their works were as much the products of the bourgeois mind as were the railroads and the power plants.

Thus, capitalist society was on its way toward a new civilization all its own when it was overtaken by the meaningless catastrophe of 1914-18 that put its world out of gear.

(b) *Bourgeois Civilization and Its Philosophy.* We have had glimpses of that period's religious and political schemes of thought—and of certain changes that occurred in both—that should suffice to convince us that the *Weltanschauung* of laicist liberalism did not prevail unchallenged. However, so far as it did prevail, we have as little difficulty in describing the bourgeois public's mental furniture as we have in visualizing the physical furniture of its homes. If we discard various sublimations and evasions we find utilitarian ethics—centering upon social service in the utilitarian sense—and, as a 'philosophy,' an evolutionary rather than mechanistic materialism.[1] Religion, in most cases dropped tacitly rather than renounced explicitly, was replaced by an 'attitude'—a word that we have all the more reason to record because it was used by one of the leading economists of the period, A. Marshall [2]—that preserved the ethical inheritance of Christianity and was in general not actively hostile to the abandoned beliefs and to the churches that taught them though, as we know, there also was militant laicism.

This made for historical reading: for some it was the means of completing a work of destruction; for others it was the means of satisfying cultural and ethical sympathies that survived dogmatic allegiance. This seems to be the secret of the huge success with the general public of such works as Ernest Renan's *Life of Jesus,* which was laicist in import yet completely free from any explicit hostility to Christianity. But the preference for historical reading extended beyond the sphere of theology and for a similar reason: uncritical liberalism was meeting with many disappointments (as we have seen) and hence was losing its superficial optimism; outside of the strongholds of Catholicism and Marxist socialism, the period was one of faltering beliefs all round, particularly as regards political democracy; and history and historical criticism appeal to such a frame of mind. Nowhere was this so much the case as it was in France. The success with the public of Hippolyte Taine's *Origins of Modern France* (English trans., 1876-94) will therefore be our only

[1] These terms, I trust, are self-explanatory. But it should be emphasized that evolutionary materialism took two distinct forms: the prevailing tendency was Darwinian but the evolutionism of the Condorcet-Comte type (see above, Part III, ch. 3, sec. 4d) was widely adopted by people who had never heard of either Condorcet or Comte.

[2] See J. M. Keynes, *Essays in Biography,* p. 162. The masterly pages of the Marshall biography that center in that passage are by far the most instructive ever written about the process, as observed in the Cambridge milieu, by which Christian belief, gently and without any acerbities, was dropped by the English intelligentsia. This development is paralleled by similar ones elsewhere. The cases of Marshall and of other Cambridge men such as Sidgwick differ from those of similarly conditioned men on the Continent, so far as I can make out, only by the fact that the former, having started their intellectual travels with a thorough grounding in Anglican theology (and, owing to the constitutions of Cambridge and Oxford colleges, with definite obligations toward it), arrived at their final positions by way of conscious wrestling rather than by growing agnostic through indifference, as did many of the latter.

illustrative example.[3] *History* of art, *history* of literature, *history* of philosophy all appealed for the same reason. Classical education, which was as yet almost intact, fostered these habits.

Of course, this was not all. Equally in accord with the spirit of the age was the widespread interest in the physical sciences, which in response produced a large popularizing literature: there was not as yet 'science for the millions' but there was what might be termed 'science for the tens of thousands.' All that it is necessary to mention for our purposes, however, is the prominence, within the total demand for this literature, of demand for books and periodical articles on biological evolution, mainly of the Darwinian type. After what has been said above, we shall understand this and in consequence the popular success of even the professional writings of such men as Haeckel.[4] Where a writer combined evolutionism with sponsorship of naïve laissez-faire, we shall understand still better. This combination accounts for the vogue of the writings of Herbert Spencer.[5] At this point we might stop were it not

[3] But the success of literary criticism of a similar pessimistic type would illustrate our point still better. It must suffice to mention a man and a book that were much in fashion: Émile Faguet (professor of poetry), *Le Culte de l'incompétence* (English trans., 1911)—a highly characteristic performance.

[4] Ernst Haeckel (1834-1919), see, e.g., his *Anthropogenie* (1874; English trans., 1879). He invited lay interest by his highly militant attitude (see his *Kampf um den Entwicklungsgedanken,* 1905; English trans., 1906) and by his attempt to expand the theory of evolution into a general philosophical scheme (see his *Welträtsel,* 1899; English trans., *Riddles of the Universe,* 1900). The reader will understand that I am mentioning Haeckel as a representative instance. I might mention just as well a dozen of other more definitely 'popular' writers.

[5] Herbert Spencer (1820-1903)—trained in physics and mathematics, railroad engineer, inventor, writer on current economic topics, sometimes on the staff of newspapers (which included subeditorship for five years of the London *Economist*)—was a genuine philosopher in the particular sense of being by nature made for a life of thought, to which in fact he settled down in 1860 in order to produce, from 1862 to 1896, his *Synthetic Philosophy* that comprised, besides the introductory *First Principles,* the *Principles of Biology, Psychology, Sociology, Ethics.* His eight volumes of *Descriptive Sociology*—an impressive collection of facts compiled by the sweat of the brows of his research assistants—is the only other work that need be mentioned here (though some of his most characteristic utterances occur in parerga, such as *The Man versus the State,* 1884). Spencer was a man of representative eminence who, to an amazing degree, was at the same time profound, clever, and silly. The man who rediscovered Buffon's idea of the evolution of higher (complex) organisms from lower (simpler) *before* Darwin's paper had thrilled the scientific world may justly be called profound. And the man who invented the velocimeter (for locomotives) and a dozen of other gadgets was all that the phrase 'clever' conveys. But no other word but 'silly' will fit the man who failed to see that, by carrying laissez-faire liberalism to the extent of disapproving of sanitary regulations, public education, public postal service, and the like, he made his ideal ridiculous and that in fact he wrote what would have served very well as a satire on the policy he advocated. Neither his economics nor his ethics (normative as well as analytic) are worth our while. What is worth our while to note is the argument that any policy aiming at social betterment stands condemned on the

necessary to advert to the surprisingly favorable reception accorded by the bourgeois reading public to the first products of a spirit contemptuously hostile to its civilization.

I do not mean the revival of Thomistic thought, which cannot be described as contemptuously hostile to bourgeois civilization as a whole—but only to its specifically laicist edition—and which was, in any case, not yet a live power in the general public's thought.[6] Nor do I mean the increasing popularity, among non-socialist readers, of Marxist writings, for these, though hostile enough to the economic arrangements of the capitalist world, cannot be described as hostile to the bourgeoisie's cult of utilitarian rationality or to its laicism or even (so far as Marxist orthodoxy is concerned) to its democratic humanitarianism.[7] What I do mean is a current of thought that turned precisely against this liberal cult of rationality and 'progress' and this liberal and democratic humanitarianism. On the political plane, it may be called anti-democratic, on the philosophical plane, anti-intellectualist. Nietzsche would make a bad example both because his teaching does not constitute a sufficiently pure form of this line of thought and because its influence was —and is to this day—smaller than we are sometimes invited to believe. Bergson's name had better be reserved for our list of the currents in the professional philosophy of that age. But there was one man who represented ideally what we are trying to visualize: that man was Georges Sorel.[8]

---

ground that it interferes with natural selection and therefore with the progress of humanity. The reader should observe, however, that the almost pathetic nonsense could have been avoided and that the sound element in his argument could have been partly salvaged by adding 'unless methods more humane and more scientific than natural selection can be found in order to achieve what survival of the fittest is supposed to achieve.'

[6] It was in this period that the teaching of St. Thomas Aquinas was declared to be official teaching of the Roman Catholic Church (encyclical *Aeterni Patris*, 1879). But this only sanctioned an existing state of things and did not exert influence beyond the Catholic clergy. The vogue of Thomism among the laymen of all countries—many Protestants and Jews among them—that was to make him one of the most influential of 'modern' authors dates from the twenties only. The vogue in the United States came a little later still.

[7] Marx was often read vicariously in as much as the ideas of many a bourgeois intellectual hailed from him. But he was also read directly, outside of the camp of orthodox socialists, particularly by intellectuals without training in economics. There is a curious explanation for this. Marx is, for the economist, one of the most difficult authors. But it is a fact that the layman who reads him never discovers that he does not understand him.

[8] Georges Sorel (1847-1922) was the author of a great many works that are held together by his antagonism toward bourgeois intellectualism: although in every other respect they present a curious assortment of topics and (sometimes irreconcilable) views that are extremely difficult to interpret, they all assert both the negative and positive implications of the anti-intellectualist principle and display in all its extent the range of economic, political, and cultural problems that this principle puts into new light. His (temporary) sympathies with revolutionary syndicalism, Italian fascism, and Leninist bolshevism exemplify but one aspect of his thought and are of secondary impor-

On the theory that the work of professional philosophers stands in a closer relation to a period's *Zeitgeist* than does the scientists' work in the various 'sciences,' I shall now append a desperately brief survey of some —to be precise ten, to be numbered I-X—of the many currents in the period's philosophical thought. Philosophy is to be defined strictly, though the philosophers' concern with questions of epistemology and logic will be included. Our selection must not be understood to imply evaluation: we are interested in currents that are characteristic for the period whatever our opinion of their merits. This is why I do not touch upon Thomism again. The purely philosophical aspects of Marxism—Engels carried on Marx's philosophical interests and the German party had, as it were, an official party philosopher, Dietzgen—are in line with the German classic philosophy of the preceding period and therefore implicitly noticed with it. Our keynote is: we are about to glance at the philosophy of an essentially unphilosophic and anti-metaphysical age in which the proposal to strike out the word Philosophy from university catalogues was actually made.

Accordingly, we shall expect professional (and professorial) philosophers to interest themselves intensively in the history of philosophy. This is what we find (I). Excellent histories of the philosophies of all ages and nations appeared in numbers. I shall name but one name, that of the man whose work seems to me to have been the peak achievement of the 'historical philosophy' of that or any other age: Wilhelm Windelband.[9]

Similarly, we shall understand that declining fervor of philosophical creation should have facilitated the survival or renascence of philosophical creations of the past. This we also find. Provided we call utilitarianism a philosophy at all, it affords an instance, for it certainly was taught throughout the period, especially, under the influence of J. S. Mill, in England (II). Elsewhere we find, for example, Neo-Kantians and Neo-Hegelians and other 'Neo's'; and there were always some adherents of Herbart and Schopenhauer (III).

Next, we notice another body of thought, the emergence of which conforms not less to expectation. Whoever believes that experimental science has effectively destroyed the bases not only of religious belief but also of metaphysical speculation may, in case he experiences a void or,

---

tance in the whole of it. His most characteristic utterances are perhaps his *Procès de Socrate* (1889) and his *Illusions du progrès* (1908), but of all his works the *Réflexions sur la violence* (1908; English trans., 1914) is the best known by far. The bourgeois found in them, among other things, feelings of admiration for industrial leadership and of contempt for parliamentary democracy. From our standpoint, it is relevant to note the affinity of some of Sorel's ideas with some of one of the greatest economists of the period, Pareto. Other affinities do not interest us here.

[9] To save space, no references to individual books are given in this survey except in cases in which there is a special reason for drawing attention to a particular work—the interested reader can supply them without trouble.

being a philosopher, wishes for employment, conceive the idea—or take it from Comte—that a picture of the universe (*Weltbild*) might be pieced together from the most general results of the individual sciences. The substitute for philosophy may take many forms and does not necessarily constitute philosophy as the universal science, *scientia scientiarum*, though the idea sometimes has been expressed in ways that suggest analogy with a holding company.

Philosophy in this sense will look very different according to the individual philosopher's training. One type emerged from the hands of philosophers grounded in the physical sciences—a type of positivism or monism that does not differ in any matter of principle from the 'empirio-criticism' of Avenarius and Mach (IV).[10] Another type which emerged from the hands of philosophers who were psychologists or sociologists by training later on came to be called Philosophical Anthropology (V) and is not always easy to distinguish from parts of Social Philosophy or straight Sociology.[11]

Both types invited misunderstandings of the specialist's theories[12] and trespassed upon his preserves, and they were not unnaturally resented.[13] The resulting atmosphere impaired the success of enterprises such as the Unity-of-Science movement of later days or, at any rate, the philosopher's influence on them. It also impaired the authority of yet another type of research, which will be mentioned here, though it does not belong to the domain of philosophy in the strict sense—the type of research that continued the efforts of Whewell and Mill and of the German *Wissenschaftslehre* or general methodology of scientific procedure in the preceding period. For examples, I choose the works of

[10] Let us note the strong affinity of Mach's views with those of W. K. Clifford, K. Pearson, and J. H. Poincaré. Pearson's *Grammar of Science* (1892) and J. H. Poincaré's *La Valeur de la science* (1904) are the two books I should recommend to readers desiring an easy guide to empirio-criticism.

[11] Georg Simmel's *Soziologie* (1908) illustrates the latter point.

[12] An amusing—or sad?—example of the occurrence of such misunderstandings even in the domain of physical sciences is the following: philosophers use the term Relativism frequently and in several different senses. It so happened that one of the most important novelties in the physics of the period was dubbed relativity theory, a term that has, of course, nothing whatever to do with historical or philosophical relativism in any sense. Nevertheless, a number of instances can be adduced of writers who made themselves ridiculous by interpreting the Einstein theory as a manifestation of the latter. I owe this fact (which at first I refused to believe) to Professor Philipp Frank.

[13] Economics, not sheltered like physics by age-old prestige, was frequently victimized. As an example, I mention G. Simmel's *Philosophie des Geldes* (1900), which treats of topics nearly all of which belong to the economist's sphere. Matters were not improved by Simmel's declaration that no proposition of the book was intended to be understood in the specialist's sense (*ist einzelwissenschaftlich gemeint*)—which was, of course, interpreted to mean that he would not accept criticism from the only people who understand, or should understand, the subject.

Jevons, Sigwart, and Wundt.[14] The methodologies of the social sciences and particularly of economics by Carl Menger, (J. N.) Keynes, and Simiand will be mentioned in another connection (see below, ch. 4, sec. 2). But the contributions by Dilthey, Windelband, and Rickert must be mentioned here, both because of the influence they exerted (though, so far as I know, only in Germany) and because of a typical shortcoming that illustrates what has been said above.[15] We return to the high road. As we walk along it, we shall shut our eyes to everything except the following pieces of the scenery.

A historian who insists on forcing thought into unique correlation with the structural changes in the social organism would assuredly hold

[14] The three works differ widely from one another. Jevons' *Principles of Science* (1874) is of course of particular importance to us since the author was one of the leading economists of that period. It is not concerned with the practice of any or all of the individual sciences but is what may be called a theory of scientific thinking. Two strikingly original features stand out that anticipate later tendencies: (1) the central position assigned to the idea that all analysis (whether 'deductive' or 'inductive') reduces ultimately to statements of identities; (2) the basic position assigned to probability—to the idea that scientific truth is basically stochastic. Christoph von Sigwart's *Logik* (1st ed., 1873-8), less original, more comprehensive than Jevons' *Principles*, is also an analysis of fundamentals. Wilhelm Wundt's (see below, ch. 3, sec. 3) *Logik . . .* (1st ed., 1880-83) is the only one of the three to analyze, and to start from, the actual practice of individual sciences. Here, therefore, the difficulty arose that, in the present state of individual sciences or even in their state as it was in 1880, no man can have that intimate knowledge of actual procedure that comes only from personal experience of detailed research. Wundt realized his limitations and tried to solve the problem by calling in the aid of specialists, but this course, obviously, had disadvantages of its own and results were distinctly indifferent.

[15] Wilhelm Windelband (1848-1915), *Geschichte und Naturwissenschaft* (History and Physics; a rectorial address that attracted great attention, 1894; 3rd ed., 1904); Heinrich Rickert (1863-1936), *Kulturwissenschaft und Naturwissenschaft; ein Vortrag* (Cultural and Natural Science; 1899; see also *Grenzen der naturwissenschaftlichen Begriffsbildung*, 1902; 2nd ed., 1913); Wilhelm Dilthey (1833-1911), *Einleitung in die Geisteswissenschaften* (the term is best rendered by 'sciences of mind and society excluding physiological psychology'; 1883). I mean no disrespect to those eminent men, who were sovereign masters of wide domains. But their minds had been formed by the tasks and the training of the philosopher, historian, and philologist. So when they proceeded, with enviable confidence, to lay down the law for us, they drew an entirely unrealistic dividing line between the 'laws of nature' and 'the laws of cultural development' or the 'formulation of laws' (nomothesis) and 'historical description' (idiography), forgetting that great parts of the social sciences ride astride this dividing line, which fact seriously impairs its usefulness (though, for the truly philologico-historical disciplines it does retain validity). They were simply strangers to the problems and the epistemological nature of those parts of the social sciences, yet failed to add the proper qualifications to their arguments. That this was apt to mislead the many economists who listened to them—Max Weber, e.g., was strongly influenced by Rickert—was as inevitable as it was regrettable. But let us note the striking saying of Dilthey that reads like a motto of Max Weber's methodology: 'We *explain* the phenomena of nature, we *understand* the phenomena of the mind (or of culture).'

that his theory is admirably verified by the emergence at that time of a philosophy that found the criterion—or even the definition—of truth in the value for our individual and social life of the beliefs that are to be accepted as true—Pragmatism (VI). But the elements of this philosophy are as old as is philosophy itself, and the manner in which it was formulated by William James amounts to little more than systematic elaboration of ideas that have never quite been absent from any kind of human action or thought and were bound to assert themselves sooner or later through the mechanism of filiation of philosophic thought alone.

Whereas pragmatism at least did not clash with the main currents in the *Zeitgeist* of the period, Henri Bergson's *L'Évolution créatrice* (1907) did (VII). His anti-rationalist and anti-intellectual philosophy is something entirely different from the anti-rationalism of pragmatism, which merely meant the negative of the existence of 'pure' truth, the product of a pure reason that is unconnected with the purposes and values of life: Bergson meant that the new truth or, more generally, the new creation is not worked out by logical processes at all. This involves indeed —which James's philosophy did not—an entirely new *Weltanschauung* wholly at variance, among other things, with the views then current (the Marxist one included) about cultural development. Not equally novel, but still more influential owing to the personal force of its great teacher, was the philosophy of Benedetto Croce (VIII), which is of particular interest for us because Croce himself is something of an economist and because he is associated, more than is the case with any other philosopher, with some aspects of the professional work of Italian economists. Though it is impossible to convey in a few sentences an idea of his work as a whole—and, unfortunately, precisely of the most original elements in it—it is possible to reduce to a single sentence the basic philosophical principle involved: a Hegelian spirit embodies itself in the actual course of universal history so that the subject of philosophy becomes identical with the metaphysics of the historical process.[16]

No survey of the philosophical currents of that time can afford to omit the name of Edmund Husserl and the beginnings of Phenomenology (IX), though no attempt at brief characterization seems to me to promise anything but confusion. Therefore, I prefer to resort to a reference.[17] But I may say that of all the philosophies of our time, Husserl's is the most autonomous with respect to social or socio-psychological facts: nothing but the filiation of philosophical ideas can account for it and, apart from what it owes to preceding philosophies beyond which it tries to advance, it could have been written just as well in scholastic times. This also holds for a body of philosophic thought that in other respects

[16] Disciples of Croce sometimes resent the imputation of Hegelianism and declare it to rest upon misunderstanding. The 'emanatistic' nature of the principle above is, however, undeniable.

[17] Marvin Farber, *The Foundation of Phenomenology* (1943). Of course, this book discusses mainly the fullfledged phenomenology of the subsequent period.

seems to—though 'seems' more than 'does'—involve a wholly different approach to problems that are not problems of any 'other' science. I am referring to Cambridge philosophy of the pre-Wittgenstein days which in the last years of that period may be said to have been dominated by Bertrand Russell and G. E. Moore (x). As the last sentence but one suggests, this conception makes philosophy a non-speculative special science that like any other science has its special task, the task in this case being to analyze the meanings of terms (such as number) or propositions that are used with confidence, but uncritically, in those other sciences or in everyday life. But, treated in this spirit, even topics such as the analysis of mind and the analysis of matter seem to me to pass from the domain of philosophy into the domain of epistemology or logic. And this is the fundamental reason why there is a path from the philosophy to the new logic and, in particular, to Bertrand Russell's and A. N. Whitehead's *Principia Mathematica* (1911-13). But here we must stop. No history of any kind of analysis, economic or other, should ever be published that does not take account of the developments for which the term New Logic is intended to stand. But this is precisely what this history cannot do.

Finally, we must ask the question: what did any of this mean to the period's leading economists? With the utmost confidence I answer: very little indeed—still less than it meant in the two preceding epochs and that, we know, was not much. But, in view of the fact that a different opinion is frequently expressed, we must go into the matter a little more deeply. In doing so, we must divide our question into two parts. First: what influence did philosophy—or any particular philosophy—exert upon the analytic work of economists or, more precisely, did they arrive at any results that may be shown to depend upon philosophic influences? Second: what did philosophy, or a particular philosophy, mean to them as men and citizens; how far did it influence their general attitudes and horizons? This distinction, as we have had occasion to observe, is important for all times and places. But it acquires additional importance for a period in which economics grew more specialized and more technical.

As regards the first question, it has been answered elsewhere for Marx and the Marxists. That answer will not, however, greatly differ from the one I am about to return for the rest of the economists: no philosophy can be proved to have influenced the economists of the period in the sense that they arrived at or failed to arrive at any analytic conclusions which they would not have arrived at or failed to arrive at without guidance from any philosopher—except in their methodological investigations and squabbles. It is natural that, when trying to clarify their ideas about their own methods of procedure or when engaged in controversy about them, economists should invoke not indeed philosophical teaching in the strict sense but the teaching of methodologies written by philosophers—Max Weber affords a conspicuous instance. But it would be nothing short of ridiculous to aver that economists allowed philosophers to teach them their business when they were investigating the conditions in domestic industry, or railroad rates or trust problems of their time, or merchants' guilds in the twelfth century, or, for that matter, the validity or otherwise of Böhm-Bawerk's theory of interest. Edgeworth professed utilitarianism in season and out of season. Yet analysis shows that these professions may be struck out from his economic propositions without being missed.[18]

As regards the second question, the answer is different. Practically all the economists of the period sprang from bourgeois families and were the beneficiaries or victims of an elaborate education that in most countries included philosophy even in its secondary (that is, pre-university) stage. As youngsters they could not have avoided some grounding in philosophy, even if they had hated philosophy like poison. The presumption is, however, that they did not hate it. The kinds of philosophy they got were mostly of the types that have been numbered I, II, III, V, and, in Italy and toward the end of the period, perhaps VIII. And this means overwhelming emphasis, direct or indirect, upon the German classics, particularly Kant. It is interesting to note that Marshall, in the preface to his *Principles*, mentioned Hegel's *Philosophy of History*—and the writings of Herbert Spencer (!)—as among the chief influences that affected the 'substance' of his views.[19] And many economists of that time might have expressed themselves similarly; their study of philosophy certainly made more civilized beings of them. Many readers will, no doubt, disagree with me if I go on to say that this was all, and that ethical and cultural attitudes are influenced but little by philosophies, and a man's social sympathies and political preferences not at all. Since in this book we are concerned only with methods and results of analysis, this difference does not greatly signify.

[18] They could not, of course, be struck out from his speculations on ethics.

[19] If this were to be taken seriously, then our answer to the first question asked above would, of course, be wrong. But it is not to be taken seriously. No Hegelian or Spencerian influences can be traced in Marshallian analysis. If he really thought that his preoccupation with *das Werden* as against *das Sein* (he used these German words) had anything to do with Hegelianism, the only possible inference would have to be that he had never understood Hegel. Marshall was still more enthusiastic about Kant, whom he described as his guide and the only man he ever worshipped (J. M. Keynes, *Essays in Biography*, p. 167). But the fact remains well established that he made a serious study of both.

CHAPTER 3

Some Developments in Neighboring Fields

The facts about developments in neighboring fields that will be assembled in this chapter are of necessity fragmentary. They are, to repeat it once more, impressionist patches of color which any other writer—according to his ideas about what has been or could have been relevant to the development of economic analysis—would have chosen in a different way. In fact, had I been writing histories of these fields for their own sake, I should have chosen differently myself. This inevitable arbitrariness—reinforced by the inevitable arbitrariness that comes from my personal limitations—is much more serious for this period than it was before, for it is in this period that the wealth of specialized work became unmanageable and that any attempt at neat logical tectonics becomes futile. Another point of view that influenced selection must also be kept in mind, namely, the ease or difficulty with which the reader can himself supply the necessary information. For economics, sociology is a most important neighbor. But at the same time, owing to its immature state, its historical development is the most difficult to get at. Psychology and, still more, historiography, however important they are for us, need less comment because their developments have been more satisfactorily described. And though statistics is for us the closest of all neighbors, its development during that period is so well known to the student of economics that we can pass it by entirely in this chapter, on the understanding that a few facts that must be recalled will be mentioned in the section on Econometrics below.[1]

1. History

As regards historiography, the great event, from our standpoint, was the close alliance with economics implied in the program of the Historical School

[1] [Part iv, ch. 7, sec. 2. J. A. S. intended to write more at length on econometrics in the recent period in Part v but completed only a few preliminary pages.]

of Economics. But precisely because this event will have to be discussed in some detail in Chapter 4, little needs to be said about historiography in general. The historian's partial conquest of the economic field was of course not his only one—all social sciences, including jurisprudence (where the conquest had taken place in the preceding period) and sociology, came partially under his sway. This, in turn, made him a student of social states and processes to an extent to which he had not been one before: the impersonal facts of social history (leavened, sometimes, by biological and psychological theories of less than unquestionable standing[1]) gained ground at the expense of the romance of battles and intrigues. And even within social historiography, work geared to problems—such as the emergence of the feudal domains in the sixth and seventh centuries, the origin and function of towns, the organization of medieval trade, the rise of capitalism, and the like—gained ground at the expense of work defined by country and period. Of course, historians of legal institutions—who were mostly lawyers by training—had always done work of the former kind and, so far as they are concerned, all we have to note is the greatly enlarged scope and the greatly improved methods of their work. But the important thing is that the tendency became general.[2] Another tendency that is much in evidence in modern economic historiography, the tendency to emphasize quantitative aspects, was of course not entirely absent—it never had been—but it was not yet a universally recognized item of the economic historian's program. Some topics that are statistical in nature did, however, attract interest.[3] And the important question—How much?—

[1] This may be illustrated by the imposing work of Karl Lamprecht (1856-1915), who was, in the first instance, an original and indefatigable research worker in economic history (see, especially, his *Deutsches Wirtschaftsleben im Mittelalter*, 1885-6), but who adopted an evolutionary schema (with stages, like Comte's) for which he claimed all but universal validity and which he cast into terms of a social psychology of his own (see his monumental *Deutsche Geschichte*, 1891-1909). This social psychology was a curious mixture of original ideas—one was, e.g., the study of an extensive collection of children's drawings—and something very like irresponsible dilettantism. But he valiantly stood by his guns in the face of not unnatural criticism (see his *Moderne Geschichtswissenschaft*, 1905; English trans., 1905).

[2] Representative figures in the host of legal historians were, e.g., Brunner, Gierke, Maitland, Maine, Vinogradoff. In order to illustrate the type of work to which I meant to refer when speaking of a general tendency toward problem-history writing, I shall mention but two names; one, which has been mentioned already, is Hippolyte Taine (1828-93). The work that matters in the present connection is: *Les Origines de la France contemporaine* (1876-93; English trans., 1876-94). The other is Georg von Below (1858-1927, especially: *Territorium und Stadt*, 1st ed., 1900-1902). These two names have probably never before been put into juxtaposition.

[3] See, e.g., the inevitably imperfect exploratory work in the history of prices that was done by Thorold Rogers (*History of Agriculture and Prices in England*, 1259-1793; 7 vols., 1866-1902) and G. d'Avenel (*Histoire . . . de tous les prix* . . . 7 vols., 1894-1926), neither of whom seems to me to receive today all the credit he deserves. In addition, d'Avenel had an eye for the wider implications for social and political history of prolonged and pronounced price changes.

turns up where we should hardly have expected it.[4] Finally, 'general' history grew increasingly institutionalized and increasingly inclined to emphasize economic conditioning of historical process. Economists are apt to attribute this to Marxist influence. This influence did assert itself toward the end of the century. But the tendency in question was in full swing before, and to hold that Marx influenced historians, other than professional economists or professed socialists, in the seventies and eighties is to exaggerate greatly the specialist's speed of reaction to factors external to his field. As an outstanding example, I mention Karl W. Nitzsch (1818-80),[5] a man who is particularly important for us owing to his close relations to some historical economists, especially Schmoller.

Remark. The reader will please remember the warning at the head of this chapter about disconnected patches of color. Even so, I cannot leave the subject without having pointed out the importance for the progress of historiography during that period of entirely new sources of material. The most important single instance is afforded by the Egyptian papyri: papyrology revolutionized the science of Roman Law. J. A. S.

2. Sociology

During the period under survey, Sociology more or less struggled into academic recognition, not as a universal science of man in society—as Comte had conceived it—but as one of the social sciences, though one that was not too sure of what its subject matter really was. All social sciences run up against certain fundamental problems of society, and none of them can afford to surrender its claims to some competence in matters of motors and mechanisms of social life—witness the necessity under which we have found ourselves of recognizing an Economic Sociology. But room and need for the study of society and social processes per se are bound to emerge as soon as the growth of materials and the development of techniques enforce increasing specialization. The social science of Aristotle and the scholastic doctors formed a single unit—and one that was no full-time job, even as a whole. The philosophy of natural law was in the same case. Hume or A. Smith or Turgot or Beccaria had no difficulty in embracing sociology as well as economics and much besides. But this changed in the course of the nineteenth century: width of scope then became increasingly inimical to quality of work. More and more, writers who inquired into the nature of society as such or who asked such questions as what it is that determines the social structure or produces revolutions and the like ceased to be writers on such topics as money or interest or employment. This defines one type of sociology by subject though not by method. In addi-

[4] I have been much struck by the quantitative spirit, as it were, that pervades the works of one of the greatest economic historians of that period, Alfons Dopsch, whose material was certainly not propitious. See his *Wirtschaftsentwicklung der Karolingerzeit* (1912-13) and also his later work, *Wirtschaftliche und soziale Grundlagen der Europäischen Kulturentwicklung . . . von Cäsar bis auf Karl den Grossen* (1918-20).

[5] See, in particular, his posthumous work, *Geschichte des deutschen Volkes bis zum Augsburger Religionsfrieden* (1883-5).

tion, ethics, religious law, and many other topics that, as we have seen, had been made the subject of positive—non-metaphysical—analysis before, then naturally fell into the province of the student of society as such. Finally, there were groups of social problems, such as sex relations, that all but lacked accredited specialists, and others, such as education, that presented aspects in which the accredited specialists were not primarily interested.

Thus an imperfectly autonomous sociology grew and expanded in spite of a reception that was not conspicuous for cordiality. Of course, there were good as well as bad reasons for this grudging welcome. It was not all a matter of trade unionism. The serious workers in the field that came to be known as sociology were flanked by swarms of *littérateurs* whose presence discredited a fundamentally good cause and this is the reason for a fact that greatly increases our difficulties of exposition: many of the best sociologists preferred to call themselves something else, for example, lawyers, geographers, ethnologists, anthropologists, historians, economists, if they were in a position to do so, in order to stress the element of professional competence in the face of the indictment of dilettantism. The case for the two last categories was particularly strong. Historiography was raising itself to a new level of technical efficiency: historians who were justly proud of this achievement cannot have viewed with pleasure the activities of writers who used their results in ways that habitually violated their new standard of scholarship. Similarly, economics was also climbing a long, steep, stony path toward a new level of technical efficiency: economists had enough to do in defending their work against the laggards in their own ranks and against a public that always misunderstood; they did not relish being teased by semi-philosophical and semi-literary irregulars. That some of these irregulars, who were at one time justly condemned for professional incompetence, proved to have been fundamentally right at another time is neither paradoxical nor *in itself* proof of the incompetence of those who were responsible for the condemnatory sentence.[1]

The surface was troubled still further by the internecine warfare between the various groups of sociologists who, like psychologists and economists, always claimed too much for their own methods or materials. But below the surface, there was both healthy achievement and promise for the future. The reader can easily satisfy himself from what has been said in the last but one paragraph that a science of society was in the making that included indeed many semi-independent or wholly independent provinces, yet was much more definite than was then believed. There was a sort of headquarters—headquarters without power to command, to be sure—in a region held by the problems of society, social relations, social processes as such.[2] And there were, steadily

[1] Incompetence of professional leaders *may* of course be the cause of the phenomenon alluded to. The history of thermodynamics presents a well-known case (Robert Mayer). But each case must be judged on its merits.

[2] Society may be defined so as to mean an entity. But it may just as well be defined as a term that is to stand for the total of relations between groups or individuals or the total of a set of processes—just as the soul may be defined as a 'thing' as well as a term that denotes all 'psychic phenomena.' The relational concept of society was

expanding, the 'applied' or 'special' fields such as the sociology of religion (hierology), of ethics, of all the arts—more recently also of knowledge, *Wissenssoziologie*—politics, economic institutions, and many others. Most of these served two kinds of masters: the practical lawyer or the practical educator, for instance, would be but ill served by treatises on the sociology of law or the sociology of education and both need another type of work. This division does not, however, depend entirely upon the needs of practical life but extends to purely scientific pursuits: the scientific economist, quite independently of any practical applications of his work, needs complete autonomy in part of his field—no sociological considerations would improve Professor Hicks's *Value and Capital*. But between the sociologies of law, education, and economic behavior, as well as of all those other subjects, and that headquarters sociology, there is lively give and take, which in a sense unifies the whole of them. Headquarters cannot stay purely speculative—at the very least they need exemplifying and verifying materials—and thus are forced to draw upon all those 'applied' or 'special' fields; and these in turn use concepts and imply propositions that are drawn from, or else contributed to, headquarters. And to some extent all this was done, though with much ungraciousness and in the midst of many unnecessary quarrels. All this, however, tells us but little about methods and approaches which are largely determined by the materials used.[3] We turn to a brief and highly selective examination of this aspect.

[(a) *Historical Sociology*.] Remembering both the vigorous advance of historiography and also its salient features, we shall not be surprised to learn that much of the best work done during that period in sociology was historical in nature. First, much of the work done by historians *was* sociological: a

---

expounded with particular energy by Georg Simmel (1858-1918), *Soziologie* (1908) and earlier in *Die Probleme der Geschichtsphilosophie* (1892)—mark the highly significant implications of the title. This makes of sociology the theory of human relations (*Beziehungslehre* is the word used, in our own time, by Professor Leopold von Wiese). The opposite view that postulates existence for society per se is the one taken by 'universalists' (Othmar Spann and his school) although it is found also in non-universalist writings: in the former case society is a frankly metaphysical entity; in the latter, a methodological construct.

[3] That the nature of a worker's material is the chief element in determining the approach, method, and *methodological creed, including the militant attitudes this creed may imply*, is a fact of great importance for understanding the history of the social sciences, though it grew less important in the last quarter of a century or so. It will stand out in its full importance when we consider the further fact that the choice of material was not in all cases free—perhaps not even in the majority of cases. For during that period a man was often—perhaps as a rule—*first* a philosopher, historian, ethnologist, lawyer, etc., and *then* turned this equipment to sociological use. But whenever this was the case, the man was prisoner of his material and methods and could not change over to others at a moment's notice: the materials and methods that he had learned to master in his formative years were the materials and methods that he really understood. These facts must never be forgotten if we are to diagnose correctly the group antagonisms in sociology (and elsewhere) and their influence upon its history.

historian who writes what for a lack of a better term we have called 'problem history' is hard to distinguish from a sociologist. Second, many of the best sociologists drew primarily on historical material and understood this material better than any other. Third, going beyond this, some sociologists defined sociology as the analysis of the historical process.[4] I hope I have made it sufficiently clear that the important thing is not the general 'theories of history,' that is, the comprehensive hypotheses about the prime movers, if any, of the historical process of which the so-called materialistic interpretation of history discussed above is by far the most successful. Much more important in the long run were the contributions toward the solution of those more restricted problems of which examples have been given in the preceding section.[5] The attempts to schematize economic history by defining successive stages (e.g., village economy, town economy, territorial economy, national and international economy—Schmoller's schema) present but little interest and need not detain us.

[(b) *Prehistorical-Ethnological Sociology*.] But the term Historical Method in Sociology should really be extended to cover the use of logically contiguous material such as prehistoric archaeology—of which only beginnings had existed before the period under discussion—and of ethnology—which then experienced its decisive development. For however much the fact-finding methods of historical, prehistorical, and ethnological research differ, the method by which the sociologist draws inferences from these different materials is fundamentally the same. We may therefore speak of a historical-prehistorical-ethnological sociology that definitely established itself during that period.

Within my very limited range of knowledge, the most impressive example of prehistoric sociology is Oswald Menghin's *Weltgeschichte der Steinzeit* (1931). The term ethnology I use in the sense which is perhaps more often expressed by the term cultural anthropology. The term anthropology is reserved for physical anthropology. I hope I am not misled by affection for a teacher of mine, if I call the two great works of the Finnish sociologist, Edward Westermarck (1862-1939), who taught sociology at the London School of Economics, 1906-30, the peak achievements of ethnological sociology during that period (*History of Human Marriage*, 1889, and *Origin and Development of Moral Ideas*, 1906), though in details neither has stood the test of time. But the formation of the period's most important 'school' of ethnology (to which, in a sense, Westermarck belonged) is associated with the research and teaching of Sir Edward B. Tylor (1832-1917); see especially: *Primitive Culture* (1st ed., 1871, many

[4] This was the case, e.g., with Marx and Croce; only the latter said 'philosophy' rather than 'sociology.' A history of sociology written from this standpoint is Paul Barth's *Philosophie der Geschichte als Soziologie* (1897), a very successful book, a fourth edition of which appeared as late as 1922. In spite of its misleading title, it is essentially a (still useful) history of sociology, written from the standpoint above, except that it exaggerated the role of general theories about historical causation. Let us note a saying of von Wieser's to the effect that 'sociology is history without names'—one of those exaggerations that are the means of inculcating important truths.

[5] I shall mention a masterpiece to illustrate the kind of work I mean: René Maunier, *L'Origine et la fonction économique des villes* (1910), which must stand for a large literature.

later ones). This school, though not averse to bold construction (Tylor himself, e.g., sponsored the idea that animistic beliefs were the embryos of religion) always retained a firm foundation in actual ethnographic work: by this it may perhaps be distinguished from the ethnological branch of social psychology (see below, sec. 3e) into which it otherwise tends to shade off. Methodologically, it presents several points of interest, for example, the application of statistical procedure (see Tylor: 'On a Method of Investigating the Development of Institutions,' *Journal of the Anthropological Institute,* 1888-9). Methodological superiority and extensive ethnographic research are also its distinctive traits as against the continental body of work in which J. J. Bachofen (1815-87; *Mutterrecht* [matriarchate], 1861) was perhaps the best-known figure. We cannot go much further—though it seems incongruous not to mention Frazer's *Golden Bough* (1890) and many other equally famous works, such as L. H. Morgan's *Ancient Society* (1877)—but we have a special motive for adverting particularly to a school which followed and follows Fritz Graebner's teaching (*Methode der Ethnologie,* 1911). Among other things, a prominent member of it, M. G. Schmidt, wrote the only treatise on ethnological economics we possess (*Grundriss der ethnologischen Volkswirtschaftslehre,* 1920-21); see also Wilhelm Koppers, 'Die ethnologische Wirtschaftsforschung,' *Anthropos,* 1915-16. But still more important for us is the theory of cultural areas (*Kulturkreistheorie*) that is characteristic of this school. The salient point is briefly this. Any investigation into primitive forms of civilization, of course, runs up against the problem of 'origins'—for example, of observed types of tools or articles of adornment and the like; or of observed types of behavior, such as the domestication of animals—and also against the problem of the factors responsible for observed changes in time ('progress'). Ethnologists or cultural anthropologists proffered widely different explanations in individual cases.[6] But the great majority of them agreed—or rather took it as a matter of course—that observed behavior or the observed types of physical things that reflect behavior must, on principle at least, be explained in terms of the conditions of the group or tribe to which each finding is to be attributed: that is to say, most ethnologists adhered to what may be called a theory of 'independent origins' and 'autonomous development.' Now, Graebner and his followers challenged this theory. On the strength of the fact that primitive cultural patterns are very stable over long periods, they denied the independent origins and the autonomous development of such things as similar tools but took the occurrence of similarities as an indication—if not proof—of a common source from which the use of, say, a particular type of button would spread by diffusion instead of being autonomously invented. Hence the existence of areas of culture—*Kulturkreise.* Whether or not we accept this theory to its full extent—its very logic makes it difficult to do so—its fundamental importance for the whole of sociology is evident. Even limited acceptance imparts a serious shock to the evolutionary views of that period and makes quite a difference to what we have called headquarters sociology.

[6] On 'theories' about the Origins of Invention, see, e.g., the book of this title by Otis T. Mason (1895), which it is interesting to compare with modern work on the subject, such as Usher's or Gilfillan's. But the most fascinating work of the period in the field of origins is to be found in the books and articles of Eduard Hahn. See especially *Die Haustiere . . .* (1896) and *Die Entstehung der wirtschaftlichen Arbeit* (1908). I am in no position to appraise the validity of the criticisms leveled at Hahn's work. But there is no doubt that in perusing it an economist must, for the time being, turn into an institutionalist whatever his views on the scope and method of economics may be at other times: for surely these things are infinitely more important and enlightening than anything a mere economist can say.

We conclude this part of our survey with a reference to Friedrich Ratzel's *Anthropogeographie* (1882-91; 4th ed. 1921-2), a performance of formative influence and especially the forerunner, if not the basis, of increased work on human geography. Perhaps it means stretching a point if we include this type of research among the bases of *historical* sociology.[7] It is certainly more related to that specialty which has come to be denoted by the term Ecology, the study of spatial relations of groups and institutions, which is now being intensively cultivated in the United States. But, potentially at least, human geography complements the material of historical sociology—as Ibn Khaldun had realized—and the outstanding contribution of that period had therefore to be mentioned.

[(c) *Biological Schools.*] Application to social phenomena of the results of biological research loomed too large in the thought of that period to be passed by entirely. We might wish to do so because the field is infested by ideological bias and by dilettantism to an extent that surpasses anything that even we economists are accustomed to. But we cannot do so, among other reasons, because biological considerations, though they touched the work actually done by economists only peripherically, hovered around it all the time. No attempt will be made to describe the development of professional biological work: [8] it must suffice to state that none of it exerted any influence upon sociological or economic thought except the work done on the lines of Darwinism and the work done by its Mendelian and other critics. Of these, the most important for us is August Weismann (1834-1914).[9] And the points at issue that are most important for us were the importance of innate and the inheritance of acquired characteristics.

There is, of course, no such thing as a biological sociology in the sense in which there is a historical sociology. Biological considerations may come in to furnish more or less important explanatory hypotheses—just as may economic considerations or any others—but the sociology they enter remains what it is by virtue of its own methods and materials. Emphasis upon biological factors or aspects is therefore all that can be meant by the loose phrase Biological Schools. We shall deal with them under four headings.

In the first place, we notice the idea that society, being an 'organic' system and not a 'mechanical' one, can be fruitfully analyzed in terms of an analogy with biological organisms such as the human body. As an example that stands in the name of an economist I mention a work by Schäffle.[10] But the obvious puerility of this idea must not blind us to the fact that emphasis upon the 'organic nature' of the economic process may be but the means of conveying an eminently sound methodological principle—as it was, for instance, with Marshall. Theorists—especially of the 'planning' type—often indulge in the

[7] Readers familiar with Professor A. P. Usher's teaching will not think so, however.

[8] There are many sources from which this lacuna may be filled, e.g. the *History of Biology* (English trans., 1928), by Erik Nordenskiöld.

[9] All of his writings that matter for us are available in English translations.

[10] Albert E. F. Schäffle (see below, ch. 5, sec. 4), *Bau und Leben des sozialen Körpers* (1st ed., 1875-8). Fortunately, the work is not entirely spoilt by its author's attempts to discover in the social body nerves and digestive organs.

deplorable practice of deriving 'practical' results from a few functional relations between a few economic aggregates in utter disregard of the fact that such analytic set-ups are congenitally incapable of taking account of deeper things, the more subtle relations that cannot be weighed and measured but may be more important to a nation's cultural life than the things that can.[11] 'Organic' considerations are perhaps the most obvious antidote—though in themselves hardly an adequate one—against such uncivilized procedure.

In the second place, we notice the attempts that were made to apply the Darwinian concepts of Struggle for Existence and Survival of the Fittest to the facts of industrial and professional life in capitalist society. Two things must be carefully distinguished. On the one hand, it may be—we cannot argue the case here—that certain aspects of the individual-enterprise system are correctly described as a struggle for existence, and that a concept of survival of the fittest in this struggle can be defined in a non-tautological manner.[12] But if this be so, then these aspects would have to be analyzed with reference to economic facts alone and no appeal to biology would be of the slightest use; vice versa, any opinions that biologists may entertain on the subject would be ruled out as laymen's talk. On the other hand, there may be genuine appeal to biological facts and theories; this is the case whenever the question of inheritance of physical or mental qualities of the human material is brought in. The relevance of this question for an appraisal of the effects of certain institutions and policies is manifest, or should be.

Then, as later, these two things were but imperfectly distinguished.[13] Here we are concerned with the second question only and in particular with its relation to the period's discussion on social reform. The argument that measures in favor of the lowest strata of the population may have the effect of deteriorating the average quality of the human stock is, of course, much older than Darwinism.[14] During the period under discussion, it found many supporters, the most important being Herbert Spencer, who added, however, nothing but

[11] An example will illustrate this. We have already referred to the fact that Russia, in the last decades of the nineteenth century, pursued a policy of monetary restriction that may have retarded her economic development. At the same time, I hinted at the possibility of making out an *economic* case for this policy. This was no contradiction. The opinion that that policy was simply foolish rests on nothing but rather obvious mechanics of the monetary and credit system and fails entirely to take account of the fact that a given monetary policy is the result of all the factors that constitute the economic, political, and moral pattern of a nation and influences them all in some obvious, and in other not so obvious, ways. Appraisal of the effects of a policy that neglects this is, from a practical standpoint, simply valueless. And it is precisely this which may be meant by him who urges 'organic considerations.'

[12] To *define* those who survive as the 'fit,' that is to say, to *define* fitness by survival, would, of course, be tautological (meaningless).

[13] Correct practice in this respect is one of the many merits of an author who was never recognized by the economic profession and seems to be entirely forgotten now, perhaps because he had the courage to tell unpopular truth: William H. Mallock (1849-1923). See his *Social Equality* (1882) and *Aristocracy and Evolution* (1898).

[14] For an example, see above, Part II, ch. 5, sec. 1c.

an elaboration, based upon research into biological selection, of the old idea. Critics objected not so much to the biology involved—in most cases they were in no position to do so—as to the application of the concept of natural selection to the facts of social selection, to the practice of identifying the 'fitness' that makes for survival with 'socially desirable' characteristics, and so on in what is by now a well-worn and familiar way. Two points about this discussion must be regretfully reported. Economists entirely failed to bestow on these problems the amount of attention they deserve: flippant phrases pro or con form the bulk of their contribution; the only one of the leading men to take more trouble was Pigou; and to him I refer the reader who wishes more information.[15] Worse still, in taking sides, economists revealed to a deplorable degree the influence of ideological bias.[16] And this is as true, if not more so, of those who pooh-poohed the idea of possible danger to the quality of the human stock as it is of those who uncritically affirmed it. Thus the question of Nature versus Nurture has remained in a most unsatisfactory state to this day.

In the third place, we notice work that belongs under the second heading but which will be segregated for the sake of emphasis, namely, the work in statistical biology, biometrics, to which we also owe important methodological help. Two great names will suffice: Karl Pearson and Sir Francis Galton.

Karl Pearson (1857-1936) surely does not need an introduction, any more than he needs a monument other than *Biometrika*. Therefore, let us merely recall his two famous adages that are so pregnant with significance: 'ability runs in stocks' and 'the nation is being recruited from its failures.' Sir Francis Galton (1822-1911) is the man whom I should choose as an illustrative example if I were asked to define the specifically English type of great man of science and the specifically English type of scientific creation. His training was medical, but apart from this he roamed in utmost freedom and informality over all parts of the world of thought that happened to attract him. Unconnected with universities and teaching, positing his own problems and going about treating them with an untutored originality that is perfectly fascinating —he was the most genuine yet the most unacademic of scientists, much like his kinsman Darwin. Of his many exploits, the following are relevant for us: he was the man who may be said to have independently discovered correlation as an effective tool of analysis; the man who set eugenics on its feet (in 1905 he founded the Eugenics Laboratory); the man who realized the importance of, and initiated, a new branch of psychology, the psychology of individual differences; and the man who tackled, although by an entirely inadequate

[15] This was in 1912. I refer, however, to *Economics of Welfare*, 3rd rev. ed., 1929, Part I, ch. 10. The happy as well as famous phrase—'environments, as well as people, have children'—occurs on p. 115.

[16] It is interesting to note that the ideology involved is not necessarily class ideology. It often is, of course. But a man may be quite unable to see the element of truth in the selective argument simply because it does not go well with some cherished scheme or ideal of his. And these schemes or ideals are not uniquely correlated with location in the class structure.

method, the problems of Nature and Nurture (*Hereditary Genius*, 1869; *Inquiries into Human Faculty and Its Development*, 1883; *Natural Inheritance*, 1889)—all of which makes him in my humble opinion one of the three greatest sociologists, the other two being Vico and Marx.

In the fourth place, we notice the racial theories. As here understood,[17] they are a subgroup of the biological theories. It is, of course, perfectly possible to believe that the range of individual variation is very great—think for instance of the immense differences we observe in mathematical or musical talent—and even that an individual's position in the statistical distribution is primarily a matter of inheritance without believing that the sociologically relevant characteristics differ racewise. To believe the latter constitutes, then, the special feature of the racial theories. Extra-scientifically, this 'racialist' belief is as old as humanity and its towering monument is the Old Testament. Attempts to establish it by scientific methods do not, however, antedate the period under discussion to a significant extent. This is why I refrained from mentioning the strongest performance in this field (that of Gobineau) in Part III, where it chronologically belongs. The only other name that will be mentioned is Ammon's. The other side is represented, at its highest, by Boas.[18] This extreme

[17] Symbiosis in a territory, especially if its effects be reinforced by political union, will in general suffice to produce a certain number of common interests and habits and also consciousness of them. These facts have, of course, never been called into question. Nor has the importance for sociology been questioned of the further fact that they are apt to create relatively durable—e.g. 'national'—types of behavior. By racial theories, we mean only theories that associate these types of behavior with physical characteristics that are common to groups. It should be observed that, since those 'psychological' or 'cultural' types possess some degree of durability and since the physical types are not absolutely stable, these two types of differentiation tend to shade off into one another. Just now, however, it is important to emphasize their conceptual distinctness.

[18] Joseph Arthur Comte de Gobineau (1816-82) earned immortality by the superlative power of his novels and historical sketches (e.g. *Renaissance*, 1877), which should rank high as *sociological* performances. Here we are interested in his *Essai sur l'inégalité des races humaines* (1853-5), a work, like his novels, of impressive personal power, which is why our text emphasizes the element of 'strength,' using the word in a sense different from that in which we speak, e.g. of a strong, that is, convincing, piece of criticism. A great vision is all but spoiled by faulty—in fact dilettantic—methods and obvious absurdities, although he who condemns Gobineau on these grounds could never, if he were fair and logical, admire Marx. As to material and method, Alfred O. Ammon (1842-1916) is vastly superior, although still open to a formidable number of objections (see his *Gesellschaftsordnung* . . . 1895). Scientific conscientiousness and high competence have induced Professor Franz Boas, 1858-1942 (see especially, *The Mind of Primitive Man*, 1911; the German original uses the word *kulturarm* instead of primitive) to make, especially between the lines, concessions that cut more deeply than he seems to realize: not all of his—sweepingly adverse—conclusions follow from the facts presented. I am afraid I have to conclude this note with a piece of advice that unfortunately imposes itself often in sociological and economic matters: read the enemies of the racial theory in order to see its strong points; read the exponents of the racial theory in order to see its weak ones.

brevity is justified by the fact that economists, who are or should be vitally interested in the range of variation of individual 'abilities' and in the question of their inheritance, are but mildly interested in the specifically racialist aspect of the latter. In fact, so far as I know, Werner Sombart is the only economist of note that ever made significant use of the element of race.[19] The only comment I feel it necessary to make is that here we have a case in which research into a real problem has been made all but impossible by what can only be described as warring infantilisms—infantilism of both parties to the controversy. For the problem is a real one and not merely an excrescence of overheated imaginations. It is important for sociology in many respects, of which the theory of social classes is but one instance.[20]

[(d) *Autonomous Sociology*.] Seeing how widely we have defined Historical Sociology, the reader might well wonder whether there can be any nonhistorical sociology. For every sociologist or economist, however speculative his bent of mind, must use some facts, most of which are bound to be of a historical nature in our sense of the term. But this is not what I meant. We define a man as a historical sociologist only if he does serious historical or ethnological work himself or if at least he arrives at his results by analysis based upon such work done by others. Desultory use of historical facts for purposes of illustration or even verification of a theory does not make a man a historical sociologist. By the same token, the reader who wonders whether there can be any non-psychological sociology, because it is indeed difficult to imagine any piece of sociological analysis that does not use 'psychic' facts of one kind or another, has missed the essential point. It is the use of the methods and results of professional psychology that will, in this book, define psychological sociology or Social Psychology (see below, sec. 3e) and not the use of the facts of common experience observed and conceptualized by the sociologist himself, however psychological these facts may be by nature. In Chapter 7 below, we shall study in some detail an economic example of this distinction which will teach us that this is not merely a matter of words but a point of considerable methodological importance and a source of many misunderstand-

[19] In his book, *Die Juden und das Wirtschaftsleben* (1911; English trans. 1951), which can hardly be described as a model of analysis. But incidental references to race are all the more frequent in economic writings. We have noticed an instance in Mill's *Principles*.

[20] The teaching of the Cambridge ethnologist, A. C. Haddon, was a shining example of a scientific attitude toward the problem and of effective use of ethnological material in dealing with it. But this was in lectures; I cannot find it in his published work. Another author (once famous, now almost forgotten) should be mentioned, whose treatment of the matter is free from the particular element that causes all the trouble now and shows how the explanatory value of racial differences may be exploited without implying anything about unique correlation between racial and cultural characteristics and, above all, without implying anything about all-round 'superiority' or 'inferiority' of one racial type as compared with others. This is Ludwik Gumplowicz, 1838-1909 (professor of public law at the University of Graz), *Rassenkampf* (1883), and *Grundriss der Soziologie* (1885)—though his (physical) anthropology left something to desire.

ings. The latter were fostered by the fact that sociologists and economists who never seriously applied professional psychology and never did any work that called for any of its methods, nevertheless, described their own procedure as psychological, thus exposing quite needlessly their pseudo-psychological constructs to professional criticism.

We shall therefore recognize the growth during that period of an autonomous sociology, which groped for its own problems and methods, even though the products of this sociology were full of pseudo-psychological and pseudo-historical concepts and propositions. Society, class, group, structure, domination and subordination, leadership, assimilation, and adjustment are examples of the items which entered that part of this autonomous sociology that we have above described as 'headquarters' or 'pure sociology.' Cooley,[21] Giddings, Hobhouse, Ross, Simmel, Spann, Steffen,[22] Tarde, Tönnies are names that represent widely different approaches to it though we could, had we space, reduce many of these differences to far less than those authors themselves—all of whom still repay perusal—would have thought possible or desirable.[23] The efforts of these and other men did not indeed produce any 'general sociology' that was at all as widely accepted as was the 'general economics' of the preceding period. Such a general sociology was adumbrated rather than created. Perhaps that was only natural in a science that then struggled into existence. But the fact that the subsequent period did not complete this task requires explanation. Evidently, this was or is because sufficiently important sociologists did not bestow sufficient work on it. And this in turn was due not only to the fact that in postwar times sociologists grew increasingly absorbed in

[21] Charles H. Cooley (1864-1929); let us mention a characteristic work of this author: *Social Organization* (1909) and add one by John Dewey: *Human Nature and Conduct* (1922).

[22] G. F. Steffen (1864-1929), the Swedish socialist leader; his *Sociologi* (1910-11) must not go unmentioned.

[23] The names mentioned—selected with much injustice to others—have been written down to indicate the types of sociological literature to which I meant to refer and also to provide suggestions for the reader that will automatically lead him further. It is not without regret that I omit the comments by which I might have tried to characterize the work of each of these men. One comment, however, cannot be omitted: to throw together such antipodes as, e.g., Simmel and Spann will seem to the critic to be explainable by nothing less than complete ignorance or lack of understanding on my part; and no other explanation may occur to him of my listing with non-psychological sociologists an author (E. A. Ross) who wrote a *Social Psychology* (1908) and another (Gabriel Tarde) who wrote *La Psychologie économique* (1901). I shall, therefore, indicate the two lines on which that attempt to reduce differences would proceed: on the one hand, I could show that these differences, to a surprising degree, result from philosophies and methodological creeds that affected language more than substance; on the other hand, I could show that the differences of the latter type produced propositions that are complementary rather than antagonistic. An author who traces cannibalism to certain spiritual ambitions will in general think that he has said something that is quite incompatible with the theory that bases explanation of cannibalism on the fact that human flesh tastes like pork and is, in the circumstances in which cannibalism occurs, a *recherché* delicacy. But that is not so.

special and very 'factual' problems but also to another: pure theory really thrives only in quantitative fields; where problems are of necessity non-mathematical, its scope is fatally limited and it soon fails to attract. We proceed to mention a few examples of the period's performances in special fields that, however, belonged to autonomous sociology—to sociology that did not borrow methods and results from outside. We choose Durkheim to represent hierology, Ehrlich to represent the sociology of law, Le Bon to represent the sociology of politics.

Durkheim's name must not be omitted from these pages for reasons other than that he was one of the leading sociologists of religion. Besides contributing to several other special fields, he formed a school of sociology that followed a method based upon a principle that was anything but new but assumed a particular form in his hand. He realized that individual behavior can never be explained exclusively from the facts that pertain to the individual himself and that it is necessary to fall back upon the influences of his social environment. This can be done in many ways. Durkheim's way was to construct a group mind—or, since his method was to explain things by means of material about primitive civilizations, a tribal mind—that feels and thinks and acts as such: since this idea itself is of romantic origin, we may describe Durkheim's position as a sort of positivist romanticism. The fundamental explanation of the phenomenon of religion, for example, that was derived from this principle may be conveyed by the phrase: religion is the group's worship of itself. No attempt was made to buttress this theory by anything that resembles professional psychology, social or other. This is why Durkheim's [24] methods should not be confused with Lévy-Bruhl's.

The time-honored 'philosophy' of law, of course, always contained genuinely sociological elements. It survived during the period—in part, thanks to required courses on 'history of philosophy of law'—but independently of this, there evolved a strictly scientific research into legal phenomena. One of the most important lines of advance consisted in studying the actual legal ideas and habits of the people ('live law,' *lebendes Recht*) and in making generalizations from these, rather than the abstractions of jurisprudence, the basis of the theory of legal practice. This was Ehrlich's idea which, produced in a small Austrian university under the most unfavorable circumstances imaginable, attracted world-wide, if sporadic, attention by its sheer weight.[25]

No other department of social life stood more sorely in need of research guided by scientific interest than did politics, where the dreams of the philosopher had produced ideological issues in utter disregard of the most ob-

[24] See, especially, Émile Durkheim (1858-1917), *Les Formes élémentaires de la vie religieuse* (1912; English trans., 1915); but also *De la Division du travail social* (1893), and *Les Règles de la méthode sociologique* (1895). There is quite a Durkheim literature. Professor Pitirim Sorokin deals with him in *Contemporary Sociological Theories* (1928), a work which I take this opportunity to recommend.

Lévy-Bruhl is discussed below, sec. 3e.

[25] Eugen Ehrlich (1862-1922), *Grundlegung der Soziologie des Rechts* (1913); see Roscoe Pound, 'Scope and Purpose of Sociological Jurisprudence,' *Harvard Law Review* (1911-2).

vious facts. Political scientists and economists alike, when talking about public policy, kept on constructing pleasant vistas of a public good, which it was the high destiny of 'statesmen' to pursue, and of a state that floated in the clouds very much like a beneficent deity.[26] The facts of group warfare, machines, bosses, pressure-group propaganda, mass psychosis, and corruption were looked upon as aberrations—'party politics' was looked upon as something that really should not exist—instead of as essentials. But during that period there began something like an awakening of the scientific conscience, and political sociology—the study of political institutions as they actually work—put in an appearance. As a symptom we might choose the delightful book of a delightful man that everyone will read with pleasure as well as profit.[27] But instead I choose the books—successful at the time but smothered by hostile criticism by now—of a man whose merit it was to drive home, with unsurpassable energy, one point that is of fundamental importance in the analysis not only of political, but of any, groupwise action. Le Bon's performance is one of a large class: the class of performances that make stand out before our eyes, and thus 'discover' for analysis, what everyone always knew to be true in everyday life. Everyone knows from experience that in a crowd, no matter whether this crowd is a raging mob in the streets of a non-English town (for English mobs do not 'rage') or a faculty committee of elderly professors, we immediately drop to a level of intelligence, morality, and responsibility that is lower than the one we habitually move on when thinking and acting by ourselves. And the merit of having presented this phenomenon with all its implications is great indeed, in spite of everything that might be urged against Le Bon's material and method.[28]

Finally, we must mention three works of considerable importance which had economists as authors—Veblen, Wieser, and Pareto. Appraisal or even characterization is, however, impossible in the space at our command. Max Weber's sociological work will be noticed in Chapter 4 below.[29]

[26] We have noticed that A. Smith was remarkably free from that sort of thing. But James Mill was not. He was no 'statist' of course, but the 'grand principles' of his ideal of a democracy were all the more free from analytic scruple.

[27] *Human Nature in Politics* (1908; 3rd ed., 1914) by Graham Wallas.

[28] Gustave Le Bon (1841-1931), *La Psychologie des foules* (1895; English trans., *The Crowd; A Study of the Popular Mind*, 1896, 16th impression, 1926). From this book stems a considerable literature that has largely succeeded in removing technical objections. But an unpopular idea or fact will never be rescued by rational argument in its defense.

[29] Thorstein Veblen's work was practically all in economic sociology, but I refer specifically to his *Theory of the Leisure Class* (1899). Friedrich von Wieser's *Gesetz der Macht* (best rendered by Sociology of Power) appeared *in extenso* in 1926 but the fundamental idea was already presented in *Recht und Macht* (1910). Vilfredo Pareto's *Trattato di sociologia generale* (1916), in its English translation under the title *Mind and Society* (1935), enjoyed considerable success in the United States during the thirties: I have never been able to make out whether this was on account of its interesting analytic schema or on account of the profusion of home truths that Pareto expressed about the mortality of decadent liberalism.

3. Psychology

The wealth of the period's developments in *professional* psychology—as distinguished from work of more or less psychological nature that was done in other fields—defies description, though most of them grew from older roots and few only spelled new departures. For our purpose, however, we can reduce this wealth to five items: (a) experimental psychology, (b) behaviorism, (c) gestalt psychology, (d) Freudian psychology, (e) social psychology. None of these exerted during that period any real, as distinguished from phraseological, influence upon economic research. But they must be mentioned because of the light their development sheds upon that period's *Zeitgeist* and because of their potential importance, which will be indicated in each case.

(a) *Experimental Psychology.* The quest for measurable facts or at least for facts observable by methods other than introspection was, of course, nothing new. Psychology had always been observational in this sense, and many of its votaries had always professed allegiance to the method of physics. But the 'empiricism' of Hobbes, Locke, Hume, and Mill had been, so far as psychology is concerned, merely programmatic and did not induce actual experiment and measurement. These developed in the preceding period and gathered momentum in the one under survey. The most telling symptom was the advent of the psychological laboratory. Wundt's Leipzig laboratory may serve as a landmark.[1] Its methods and its spirit exerted formative influence far and wide, even on men like William James and G. Stanley Hall, who quickly outgrew both the narrow scope of experimental psychology in this sense and Wundt's personal message. The statistical complement of this type of work was much improved later on in the United States (Edward L. Thorndike). One of the many offshoots of it that should, but does not, interest economists intensely is noticed in the footnote below.[2]

[1] Wilhelm Wundt (1832-1920) was one of the outstanding and most influential men of science of that age. Not of first-rank originality, but a worker, leader, teacher, writer of almost unbelievable energy and fertility, he left his mark also on other lines of advance (see, e.g., above, ch. 2, sec. 4b). The Leipzig laboratory has a long history and was the ripe fruit of a long line of previous efforts. Wundt was a medical man by training and approached psychology from physiology in a way that makes him a direct descendant of R. H. Lotze (*Medicinische Psychologie,* 1852). Other names that may serve as stepping stones for readers who wish to follow up the origins of what on occasion has looked in the past, and possibly may look again at some future time, like an important ally of economic theory are these: Johannes Peter Müller, E. H. Weber, G. T. Fechner, Ewald Hering, H. von Helmholtz—physiological psychologists all of them, whose work centers in the problem of Measurement of Sensation (psychophysics). It is very interesting to note that it has not so far occurred to economists to explore the opportunities this line of research might conceivably offer (see on this ch. 7 below).

[2] This is the study of differences among individuals of characteristics and especially of abilities. Many roots and lines should be distinguished, but I mention only one that links up with Wundt's teaching and is represented by William Stern's *Differen-*

Wundt's laboratory work found a curious complement in his ten volumes of *Völkerpsychologie* (1900-1920). This is a study of language, myths, and mores that seems to have more to do with the ideas of Hobbes and Vico than with the Leipzig laboratory. It is mentioned here, instead of under ethnological sociology to which it really belongs,[3] because from Wundt's own standpoint and within his scheme of thought this type of research in fact complements the material that the laboratory produced, though it does so over a wide gap and will not do so at all from any other standpoint than his. It was only much later that genuine psychometrics displayed any tendency to enter the field of social phenomena.

(b) *Behaviorism*. In a sense Comparative Psychology (mainly animal psychology)[4] and, through comparative psychology, Behaviorism,[5] though new departures both of them, may be said to stem from Wundt's experimental psychology. Since some American economists have shown more interest in the programmatic pronouncements of behaviorists than they have in any other of the developments in psychology,[6] it is important for the reader to realize the severe limitations to which the application of behaviorist principles is subject in the social sciences. Fundamentally, the behaviorist method amounts to a resolution of behavior into objectively observable responses—that is, reactions that we can observe without resorting to introspection or any other psychological interpretation of 'meanings'—to objectively controllable stimuli: the method accepts the reacting organism as a perfect blank without any propensities of its own (much as Locke had done with the 'mind') and (going beyond Locke) avoids the whole complex of concepts and interpretations that is indicated by words like consciousness, sensation, perception, will, urge, or instinct. This is why the behavior of the lower animals and the simplest reactions of man in early childhood are the stronghold of the behaviorist method. Any step beyond the precincts of this stronghold is an achievement that helps us to do without certain tools, the validity of which it is possible to challenge.

tielle Psychologie (1911), and another that hails rather from Galton—inasmuch as it implements an idea of his—and will be represented by Charles Spearman's theory of the Central Factor (see the latter's *Abilities of Man*, 1927, with general survey of the field). Both books should be required reading for all economists. Of course, this particular aspect of child psychology and pedagogics is also of obvious importance to us (see, e.g., E. L. Thorndike, *Educational Psychology*, 1913-14, vol. III).

[3] This is also why I mention here the names of Lazarus and Steinthal (to whom is due the phrase *Völkerpsychologie*, usually translated as 'folk psychology' though tribal psychology would express the meaning better), who may be considered as Wundt's immediate predecessors in this field.

[4] See C. L. Morgan, *Introduction to Comparative Psychology* (1894).

[5] The word and the most radical formulation of the program are John Broadus Watson's; see his *Behavior: an Introduction to Comparative Psychology* (1914); also *Behaviorism* (1925).

[6] The frequent occurrence of the word Behavior in modern economic literature may be due to this.

But beyond the range within which it is operational, that is to say, beyond the range within which it is actually possible to produce uniquely determined responses by controllable conditioning, the method itself becomes invalid. A generalization to the effect that man's behavior is uniquely determined by his environment that cannot be established experimentally is not so much wrong as meaningless. But precisely this generalization is the goal of some behaviorists' argument: it marks the frontier that separates a fundamentally sound method of research from an ideology, the popularity of which is not difficult to understand. The support it lends to extreme environmentalism is obvious.

(c) *Gestalt Psychology* (Ehrenfels, Köhler, Koffka, Wertheimer, Riezler) develops from a single basic fact: no individual element of any set of elements is perceived or appraised or interpreted individually—a sound in a song, a color in a carpet, or even a glass of wine that is part of a dinner is never 'experienced' in isolation and, if it were, it would mean to us something quite different from what it does mean actually, that is, as part of the definite set in which it occurs. All we need to say about this evidently highly important discovery—for it was nothing less, though my formulations sound trivial enough—is, first, that its development belongs mainly to the subsequent period and only the beginnings of it to the one under discussion; and, second, that among the many possible uses to which gestalt psychology may be put in the social sciences, there is at least one of considerable importance. Gestalt psychology may be used in order to arrive at a sensible and non-metaphysical concept of psycho-sociological collectives—such as society itself.

(d) *Freudian Psychology*. Before the end of the century psychoanalysis was a therapeutic method—to be traced to the teaching of J. M. Charcot in Paris—that had scored remarkable successes, especially in cases of 'hysterical' inhibition of motion, in the hands of Josef Breuer and Sigmund Freud. But about 1900, though it always remained a therapeutic method, it began to reveal a very much wider aspect—it began to develop into a general theory of the working of the human mind. The old idea of a subconscious personality and its struggles with the conscious ego was elaborated and made operational with unsurpassable effectiveness by Freud.[7] Again I cannot—and perhaps need not—do more than point to the vast possibilities of application to sociology—political sociology especially—and economics that seem to me to loom in the future: a Freudian sociology of politics (including economic policies) may some day surpass in importance any other application of Freudism, though so far only a small beginning has been made (W. H. R. Rivers). Nor can I go into certain other currents of thought that display important parallelisms with

[7] Freud's writings are now available in a cheap American edition to which the reader is referred. It occurs to me that my few sentences on Freud might be interpreted in a derogatory sense. Nothing could be further from my intention. All great achievements are but final acts of birth that are preceded by long prenatal histories. Freud had a large number of pupils who split up, however, into different groups, some of which cannot be called Freudian any more. But potential fertility for the social sciences is a feature of all of them (all of them I know, that is).

Freud's, however different in method and aim they may be in other respects. But I will mention T. Ribot.[8]

(e) *Social Psychology*. This branch of psychology is usually defined very widely so as to include all types of research that have anything at all to do with psychic facts relevant to social phenomena and, in particular, all types of research that are based on the concept of a group or national mind or other collectives of this kind. This practice may be useful for the purpose of co-ordinating all conceivable sources of conceivably relevant facts or suggestions. But we cannot adopt it because it makes social psychology useless as a pigeon-hole (the only use we have for the term here): for our purposes there is no point at all in throwing together men and methods that differ as widely as Herder and romanticist philosophy and history, Westermarck or Tylor and cultural anthropology, Ross and 'autonomous' sociology, and so on. Thus we are left with a very restricted field in which, during that period, McDougall was the most important figure.[9] He was a professional psychologist and tried to block out a special psychology that would account for phenomena of interaction between individuals or groups and for the shaping influence a group mind, once formed, exerts upon the individuals that are born into it. The fact that he emphasized the creative element and reasoned in terms of instincts and emotion explains why his teaching, after a strong initial success, lost favor in a time that was rapidly becoming behaviorist and environmentalist. Less of a professional psychologist was Lévy-Bruhl.[10] But he was still primarily interested in mind and only secondarily in society. Not many names would have to be added in order to draw up a fairly complete list. Psychological investigations (mostly of a statistical nature) were carried out in the service of several practical specialties—child psychology, I think, coming nearest to relevance for problems of general sociology—that cannot be noticed here.

[8] See, especially, Théodule Ribot (1839-1916), *Maladies de la personnalité* (1885; English trans., 1895), another book that I should make required reading for economists if I could. The parallelism above mentioned is evident not so much from comparison with Freud's own writings as it is from comparison with the writings of some men who began as followers of Freud, notably, of Alfred Adler. One more book of Ribot's should be mentioned: *Evolution of General Ideas* (English trans., 1899).

[9] See, especially, William McDougall, *Introduction to Social Psychology* (1908).

[10] Of Lucien Lévy-Bruhl's (1857-1939) many works it will suffice to mention *Les Fonctions mentales dans les sociétés inférieures* (1910; English trans., 1926).

CHAPTER 4

[Sozialpolitik and the Historical Method[1]]

[1. SOZIALPOLITIK]

ECONOMISTS EXPERIENCED the influence of the new atmosphere as they had experienced that of early liberalism and as they were to experience, in our day, that of socialism. In all these cases this meant not only or even primarily

[1] [EDITOR'S NOTE. This chapter was in an unfinished and unsatisfactory state. It had no titles and no sub-titles; these were inserted by the editor. My knowledge about it is gleaned from what J. A. S. said in the introduction to Part IV and from a folder which I found containing two sections of typescript clipped to their respective manuscripts. This folder also contained a great many notes and pamphlets and reprints which J. A. S. apparently intended to use in his work of revision. On the outside of the folder was written 'Part IV/4.' Originally, it had been 'Part IV/4, 5' but the 5 had been erased when the author decided to incorporate the material in a single chapter instead of in two separate chapters.

In Part IV, Chapter 1, Section 3, *Plan of the Part,* J. A. S. has this to say: 'Then follow comments on two allied groups of men and ideas that lend themselves to separate treatment, the group whose work centered in the contemporaneous interest in social reform and whose leaders were with singular infelicity dubbed "socialists of the chair" (*Kathedersozialisten*): and the group that was called, and called itself, the historical school (Chapters 4 and 5). The much-debated question of economists' value-judgments will be touched upon in connection with the former and the famous "battle of methods" (and its American counterpart, the institutionalist controversy) in connection with the latter.'

The treatment of the socialists of the chair is very incomplete. In fact, it looks as though a whole section on these people in Germany had been omitted. It is obvious that the treatment of people of this type in France has been omitted. The carbon of this particular section is dated December 17, 1943. The carbon of the section on the historical school is dated January 10, 1943. These were undoubtedly preliminary studies and would have been completely rewritten. The section on the socialists of the chair and value judgments is especially unsatisfactory, but it is published here because Schumpeter felt so keenly that the work of many economists has been and is im-new facts and problems but also new attitudes and (extra-scientific) creeds [2] and hence, for a time at least, revolt against those restraints which in each epoch, as it wears on and as initial enthusiasms cool, the men who are engaged in the work of analysis find it necessary to impose upon themselves. The 'mercantilist' writers had not discovered that there was anything for an economist to do except to propose measures and fight for them; the economists of the 'liberal' age were at first in no better state, though they eventually did discover the difference between a theorem and a recommendation; and the economists of the period under discussion, yielding to what the reader may call either temptation or the call of duty, similarly deviated from the stony path that leads to scientific conquest.

[(a) *Influence upon Analytic Work.*] The manner in which and the degree to which the economists of that time allowed their analytic work to be influenced by the new spirit of economic policy differed greatly, however, as between countries and groups. In England, continuity in research and teaching was never in serious danger. The small body of English economists moved with the times, of course—which was not difficult for pupils of J. S. Mill—but did not jettison pieces of scientific apparatus along with old value judgments. In part this was due to the fact that the average member of that body understood economic theory much better than did the average economist in any other country, and hence he was in a position to realize the full extent of the latitude it left for any social creed he might choose to embrace. For the rest, that singularly happy state of things was simply an instance of the genuine freedom guaranteed by the English environment that removed many sources of irritation. Opposition to what many people believed to be an alliance between economics and laissez-faire policy existed both within and without the small group of orthodox socialists. But it did not amount to much. In particular it did not amount to a new 'School of Thought.' [A note indicated that J. A. S. intended to write a paragraph on the Fabians at this point.]

In the United States scientific tradition was not anything like as strong. But the 'radicalism' of the typical member of the economic profession did not go beyond the points covered by old doctrine: antagonism to protection and to 'monopolistic' big business, which then developed into the typical American economist's pet aversion. The processes of competitive capitalism were also under fire—some economists were sympathetic with the 'popula-

paired by their value judgments, and also that this need not be so with respect to their analysis. This belief of his is obvious in all his writings.

The treatment of the historical school is also incomplete. After some discussion of the older and younger historical schools and the *Methodenstreit,* there follows a discussion of historical economics outside Germany, especially in France and England. But there is nothing at all about the United States and American institutionalism, which had been promised in the Plan of the Part.]

2 [At top of this page a great many shorthand notes and the following statement in the hand of J. A. S.: 'I do not see what more I could say in order to protect from misunderstanding the following piece of plain speaking.']

tionist' movement, others lent qualified support to the ideas of Henry George,[3] and views indicative of hostility to the capitalist order as such were not absent though very few voiced them as candidly as did Thorstein Veblen. But that fire was weak. The large majority of economists conformed to the bluff convictions of businessmen who did not as yet share the misgivings of their European peers. No economist whom anyone would care to call 'leading,' in any sense whatsoever, identified himself with any radical scheme of social reform.

[Not completed: J. A. S. evidently intended to sketch the development of social reform in France and Germany before going on to the paragraphs which follow.]

I do not hesitate to say that this achievement was one of the most important in the records of the economic *profession*. Having made this quite clear I hope that what follows will not be misunderstood. That achievement, great as it was, evidently did not belong to the sphere of scientific analysis. And since this is a history of scientific analysis, it does not in itself concern us here. What does concern us is another aspect of it—which I readily concede is a less important one—namely its influences on teaching and research. Appraisal of this influence will then offer an opportunity to touch upon, so far as it is necessary to do so, the problem of the economist's value judgments.

The efficiency of teaching indubitably suffered. I have emphasized above the share that the academic lecture hall had in spreading the spirit of social reform. The German 'socialists of the chair' certainly fulfilled the ideal of progressive politicians and laymen—the ideal of the professor who preaches reform and denounces obstructing interests. Lujo Brentano addressed his classes as he would have political meetings, and they responded with cheers and countercheers. Adolf Wagner[4] shouted and stamped and shook his fists at imaginary opponents, at least before the lethargy of old age quieted him down. Others were less spirited and effective but not less hortatory in intent.[5] Such lectures need not necessarily be weak in the technical instruction they impart, but as a rule they are. He who thinks this a cheap price to pay for ethics and ardor will please consider for a moment where, say, internal medicine would be if its teachers, instead of developing the analytic powers of their pupils, indulged in rhetoric about the glories of healing. An increasing number of students left the universities and entered the practical vocations

[3] [The note on Henry George intended at this point was not written. For a discussion of this writer, see below, ch. 5, sec. 7.]

[4] On A. Wagner, see below, ch. 5, sec. 4 and ch. 8, sec. 2.

[5] I do not mean to assert that German lectures or seminars were exactly fascinating. The two examples adduced were exceptional. As a rule, the professor read from a manuscript that was often yellow with age, or presided languidly over seminar meetings at which candidates for the Ph.D. read preliminary drafts of their theses. This is the scene American visitors beheld and their experience may be one of the causes of irreconcilable—and I think, exaggerated—hostility to the lecture method of teaching which we observe in many American universities.

open to economists with an equipment that was nothing short of lamentable, and some of the best of them left thoroughly disgusted.[6]

[(b) *Verein für Sozialpolitik.*] As regards research, a credit item first claims recognition. It has been pointed out above that the German economists' zeal for reform concentrated upon individual problems or measures much as did that of the Fabians in England: fundamental reconstruction of society was to come about in time, as a by-product rather than as the result of efforts directly aimed at it. This procedure involves accumulation of facts on a large scale, and the impressive series of the *Schriften des Vereins für Sozialpolitik*—188 'volumes' most of which actually consisted of several volumes—testifies to a relentless will to dig, to which we are indebted for an invaluable extension of our factual knowledge. Much additional work of the same type was done by individuals and groups either in connection with or outside that corporate effort of the profession.[7] If, because of considerations of space, the *Schriften* are allowed to stand as the only example of this kind of analysis, it must be understood that this instance is to illustrate what constituted the greater part of the work done by the economists of all countries—in England, as before, it was done partly for Royal Commissions.[8]

[6] However repugnant to scientific etiquette jokes and anecdotes may be, there are cases in which they illustrate a situation better than could anything else. So I will risk offering two such illustrations. The one is a definition of economics that obtained some currency at the time: 'economics, what is that? Oh, yes, I know . . . you are an economist if you measure workmen's dwellings and say that they are too small.' The other is a *dictum* I once heard from a very intelligent and accomplished German woman: 'I have taken courses and examinations in economics, but I know nothing and care less about it. You see, I felt I had to comply with the fashion of "studying" at a university, but I did not mean serious work. So I chose economics because all that is required there in order to satisfy examiners is the ability to chat a little about ethics, reform, control, and that sort of thing.' Of course, I do not mean to say that these were the standards of most or even many teachers. The significance of the anecdote should not be overrated. But neither should it be equated to zero, not at least for the last three decades of the nineteenth century.

[7] The importance of that effort, which as an effort of a national group of professional economists has no equal, makes it desirable to say a few words about its organization. It was essentially a team-work arrangement. Every member, especially every member of the large council, was free to suggest a project of research. The Verein decided which were to be taken up and then entrusted individuals or small committees with the direction of the research involved. These in turn parceled out the work among a number of collaborators and integrated the results that were to be published in the *Schriften*. Moreover, they arranged for discussions of those results at the meetings of the Verein, appointing 'reporters' (usually two) and other participants. Success at these meetings was of some importance in a man's academic career. [Some of this information has already been presented in Chapter 1 of this Part.]

[8] To mention a few of those Commissions whose reports are particularly interesting from the standpoint of economic analysis: *Shipping Dues* (1853), *Coal Supply* (1866), *Agriculture* (1881), *Housing* (1885), *Depression of Trade* (1886, particularly the 3rd report), *Gold and Silver* (1887), *Poor Laws* (1909—especially the famous minority report).

Many of the volumes presented work of a high grade that was not only exemplary in its minute attention to detail but also analytically significant and inspired by considerations of scientific as well as practical urgency. The Verein's comprehensive price studies (begun in 1910) may serve as an example. Most of them, however, were no better and no worse than such investigations were and are at all times and in all countries. But an investigation into the influence of gold production, directed by Arthur Spiethoff (*Der Einfluss der Golderzeugung auf die Preisbildung*, 1890-1913, vol. 149 of the *Schriften*), that was a part of them, rose far above the general level. On the whole, however, the economists responsible for the reports that fill those volumes of the *Schriften*, cared little for analytic refinement. They took no end of trouble with their facts, but most of them went straight from their impressions of the factual pattern to recommendations, just as would have any nonprofessional worker. They neither used nor contributed to theoretical or statistical technique, in spite of their obvious opportunities for doing so. And the analytic apparatus of economics did not improve but even deteriorated in their hands.

Moreover, if abilities adequate to describing the trade practices of distributors of milk plus a fervent allegiance to the ideals of the Verein—glorified no doubt by a little philosophy and other elements of German culture—were all a man needed in order to establish himself as an economist and, in due course, to receive academic preferment, we cannot be surprised that supply adapted itself to the character of demand. Otherwise excellent men ceased to care for the higher spheres of scientific invention and rigor. Men who cannot be described as otherwise excellent threw them overboard with a sigh of relief and prided themselves on doing so. And though there always were a few who tried to keep the flag flying,[9] economic theory as understood in England was in many places almost completely in abeyance for several decades, not only as a field of research but also as a means of training students in scientific habits of mind. When, in the first decade of this century, a reaction began to set in, under Austrian and foreign influence, against 'economics without thinking,' the full extent of the damage done revealed itself in the fact that people hardly knew what economic theory meant: many thought that it was a sort of philosophy of economic life or else simply methodology. Many foreign observers laid all the blame for this state of things at the door of the historical school. But the historical school, though cultivating *another* purely scientific interest, still cultivated a *scientific* interest; it should not be held responsible for that substitution of convictions for performance.

[(c) *The Problem of 'Value Judgments.'*] Concern about the future of economics may have been one of the reasons why an increasing number of men felt it desirable to shape the Verein into something more like a scientific society and, when this had to some extent been attained, to bring forward the question whether economists were within their rights when they took it upon themselves to deliver judgment—moral or other—on the phenomena they analyzed. During the first decade of the century, this problem of the *Werturteil*

[9] [Note intended here on Diehl, Dietzel, Oppenheimer, and Lexis.]

(value judgment) caused heated discussions which culminated in what almost amounted to a row at the Vienna meeting of 1909. To many people it will seem obvious a priori that this attack upon the principle of the Verein's historic practice must have come from economists who were out of sympathy with the policies sponsored by it. This however was not so. The enemies of the Verein had of course always protested against its lack of scientific 'objectivity.' But within the Verein the most prominent leaders in that campaign for freedom from evaluation (*Wertfreiheit*) were M. Weber and Sombart,[10] both of whom belonged to the radical wing of the Verein and were anything but exponents of capitalist interests.

Nevertheless it is abundantly clear from what has been said so far that it was not the epistemological problem involved which accounts for the bitterness of that controversy, but considerations of a different order. One may feel no qualms at all about the logical status of value judgments within a science and yet hold (a) that the substitution of a creed for analytic ability as a criterion of selection of the personnel of a science will impede advance; (b) that those who profess to be engaged in the task of widening, deepening, and 'tooling' humanity's stock of knowledge and who claim the privileges that civilized societies are in the habit of granting to the votaries of this particular pursuit, fail to fulfil their contract if, in the sheltering garb of the scientist, they devote themselves to what really is a particular kind of political propaganda. And it is easy to see that those who thought differently were bound to realize that what was at stake was not a point of scientific logic but their professional standing and all that was dearest to them in their professional activity.

The epistemological problem in itself is neither very difficult nor very interesting and can be disposed of in a few words. It will be convenient to do so with reference to the English environment in which the problem arose in the natural course of things—as a science comes of age, the critical searchlights are turned on all its habitual attitudes and practices—and in which those political acerbities that elsewhere affected the handling of the question were much less important. We have seen how awareness of the problem came about and how it was dealt with by the succession of economists between Senior and Cairnes. The distinction between reasoning about 'what is' and about 'what ought to be' having been well established before, the correct interpretation of this distinction was formulated by Sidgwick[11] in a manner

10 [J. A. S. wrote: Leave page for note on Sombart.]

11 In the introduction to his *Principles of Political Economy*, 1883 (3rd ed., 1901, pp. 7-8): 'I have been generally careful to avoid any dogmatic statements on practical points. It is very rarely, if ever, that the practical economic questions which are presented to the statesman can be unhesitatingly decided by abstract reasoning from elementary principles. For the right solution of them full and exact knowledge of the facts of the particular case is commonly required; and the difficulty of ascertaining these facts is often such as to prevent the attainment of positive conclusions by any strictly scientific procedure.

'At the same time the function of economic theory in relation to such problems is none the less important and indispensable; since the practical conclusions of the most

which left little, if anything, to be desired and which seems to have been accepted—in principle at least—by Marshall and his immediate followers.

An 'ought,' that is to say, a precept or advice, can for our purpose be reduced to a statement about preference or 'desirability.' The relevant difference between a statement of this nature—for example, 'it is desirable to bring about greater economic equality'—and a statement of a relation—for example, 'the amount people will attempt to save out of a given national income depends, among other things, on the way in which the income is distributed'—reveals itself in the fact that acceptance of the latter depends exclusively on the logical rules of observation and inference, whereas the acceptance of the former (the 'value judgments') always requires, in addition, the acceptance of other value judgments. This difference is of little moment when the 'ultimate' value judgments, to which we are led up as we go on asking why an individual evaluates as he does, are common to all normal men in a given cultural environment. Thus, there is no harm in the physician's contention that the advice he gives follows from scientific premisses, because the—strictly speaking extra-scientific—value judgment involved is common to all normal men in our cultural environment: we all mean pretty much the same thing when we speak of health and find it desirable to enjoy health. But we do not mean the same thing when we speak of the Common Good, simply because we hopelessly differ in those cultural visions with reference to which the common good has to be defined in any particular case.

Sidgwick had his full share of the typically English confidence in the 'ultimate values' that happen to prevail in one's own country at one's own time. Therefore he recognized, beyond the frontiers of the 'science' of economics, the existence of a corresponding 'art,' whose propositions were precepts but precepts not much less enforceable than are propositions of the logico-factual kind. He saw, however, the real problem as he showed by an excellent illustration which, slightly amplified, will serve to sum up the central point in that controversy.

An indefinite number of impulses and considerations enter into the making of a protectionist or free trader. Among them are some which link up with a man's tastes in national styles or ideals. Therefore no scientific argument can compel him to embrace or abandon protectionism.[12] But his motivation

untheoretical expert are always reached implicitly or explicitly by some kind of reasoning from some economic principles; and if the principles or reasoning be unsound the conclusions can only be right by accident.'

[12] It should be observed that this does not mean either that an economist's convictions in the matter cannot be made the subject of scientific analysis or that they are uninteresting. As regards the first, we may wish to explain why a given individual or group entertains a given conviction about given economic policies. Such an analysis is perfectly scientific. As regards the latter, an economist's views may reflect the attitude of the stratum he hails from and thus assist us in the diagnosis of a political pattern; besides, the economist in question may be sufficiently interesting as an individual to make it worth while to notice his political preferences. But none of these things has anything to do with the problem in hand.

may, and as a rule does, imply also propositions about causes and effects, some or all of which may come within the province of the economic analyst. If it should be the case, for instance, that our man is a protectionist because he believes protection to be a remedy for unemployment, then the economist is within his rights if he points out that this is so in some cases but not in others and that, in this sense, the man 'ought' not to be protectionist unconditionally. The reader will realize that considerations of this order greatly reduce the practical importance of the issue so far as its purely epistemological aspect is concerned. In particular, if an economist is inspired by the typically historical sense for environment, he may be able to proffer—from a knowledge of which value judgments are associated with a given environment—historically relative advice without leaving the precincts of his professional competence. This goes some way, though not the whole way, toward justifying economists' value judgments. It also explains, in part at least, why the controversy on value judgments did not produce any very important results. But it does not alter the fact that the progress of economics—including progress in its practical usefulness—has been and is being severely impeded by economists' quasi-political activities.

[2. Historism]

It is one of the major aims of this book to destroy the myth that there ever has been a time when economists as a body scorned research into historical or contemporaneous fact or when economics as a whole was purely speculative or lacked its factual complement. What, then, is the distinctive characteristic of the group that called itself the Historical School and how was it possible for its members to look upon its program as a new departure? Evidently, it would not do to include everyone who recognized that economic history is an important source of economic truth. Nor can we draw the line around all those who displayed an extensive command of historical facts or a sense of the historical flux of policies and of the historical relativity of propositions: for this would still include List and Marx and Marshall. Not even the actual performance of historical work is enough: there would be no point in a definition that includes James Mill.

These considerations, however, point directly to what we are looking for. The basic and distinctive article of the historical school's methodological faith was that the organon of scientific economics should mainly—at first it was held that it should exclusively—consist in the results of, and in generalizations from, historical monographs. So far as the scientific part of his vocation is concerned, the economist should first of all master historical technique. By means of this technique, which was all the scientific equipment he needed, he should dive into the ocean of economic history in order to investigate particular patterns or processes in all their live details, local and temporal, the flavor of which he should learn to relish. And the only kind of general knowledge that is attainable in the social sciences would then slowly grow out of this work. This was the original core of what became known as the Historical

Method in economics.[1] The resulting attitude and program is what economists of a different persuasion meant by Historism.

Of course, the term History must be interpreted broadly so as to include both prehistoric and contemporaneous fact and the contributions of ethnology. Our way of defining the historical school no doubt tends to obliterate the frontier line between the historical economist and the economic historian. But this is no disadvantage. For the methodological creed of the historical school may be summed up precisely in the proposition that the economist, considered as a research worker, should be primarily an economic historian. The work of economists of the historical school in fact supplemented, and was supplemented by, the work of economic historians proper, a species of the historical genus that was by then well established and did not always welcome what it was sometimes inclined to look upon as unfair competition.[2]

As thus defined, the historical school cannot be said to have ever been dominant in any country. But in German economics it was, during the last two or three decades of the nineteenth century, by far the most important factor of a purely scientific nature. This is why we are going to acquaint ourselves somewhat more fully with the performance of the German historical school before dealing briefly with the parallel movements in other countries.

[(a) *The 'Older' Historical School.*] In deference to established tradition we shall first notice the work of three writers, Bruno Hildebrand, Wilhelm Roscher, and Karl Knies, who are usually mentioned together under the heading of Older Historical School. As a matter of fact, however, they did not form a school in our sense—the reader should remember that in this book the term School means a definite sociological phenomenon and hence cannot be used at will for any group of writers we may choose to select—and their relation to economic history was neither uniform nor very different from that of a host of other economists of all ages. Hildebrand was an active man of many merits who, by program and performance, emphasized the evolutionary

[1] It will be seen that this meaning of historical method outlined above has nothing to do with other meanings of the same term, such as the sum total of the historian's techniques or a genetic method of presentation.

[2] Nobody can fail to notice the trade-union aspect of that antagonism. But there was also a more presentable reason for the hostility of some economic and—because historical economists occasionally went beyond anything that can be called economic history—other historians. Economists, Schmoller's pupils in particular, did not always take much trouble about acquiring the historian's equipment, and their work in fact failed sometimes to meet the historian's professional standards. Indictments of this kind were even leveled at Schmoller himself.

However that may be, for us the fact, which our definition took into account, viz., that there is really no dividing line, spells a considerable difficulty. We cannot include the historical literature of the period, yet we really ought to do so. Any history of economics in the wide sense sponsored by the historical school would be woefully incomplete if it did not mention such men as Georg von Below, Alphons Dopsch, or Sir Henry Maine and many others, who contributed to our knowledge of the economic and social institutions and processes of the Middle Ages more than economists ever did, but I must draw the line somewhere.

character of economic civilization—without renouncing belief in 'natural laws' however—and the basic importance of historical material more than did the majority of his contemporaries. Roscher was the incarnation of professorial learning, mainly of a philosophico-historical nature, and must indeed be mentioned both on account of his scholarly labors in the field of the history of economic thought and as a leading figure on the stage of academic economics. On that stage he conscientiously retailed, in ponderous tomes and in lifeless lectures, the orthodox—mainly English—doctrine of his time, simply illustrated by historical fact. However, this does not make a historical economist in the term's distinctive sense. Nor does talk about 'historical laws' or approval of Mangoldt's epigram that economics is 'the philosophy of economic history' —especially if, for the rest, one theorizes exactly as do other people. Knies was the most eminent of the three. But his main performance was in the field of money and credit, where he made his mark as a theorist. His only connection with the historical school consists in a programmatic book, in which he stressed the historical relativity not only of policies but also of doctrines and which owes to commendation, by genuinely historical economists, a prominence it does not quite deserve.[3]

[(b) *The 'Younger' Historical School.*] The new departure, the distinctive research program, and the emergence of a genuine school must in fairness be associated with the name of Gustav von Schmoller[4] (1838-1917). In a sketch as short as this, we must concentrate on his work and leadership. The second-line leaders—whom the same fairness demands we must resolutely label as such—Brentano, Bücher, Held, and Knapp, we can only mention below.[5] And the work of less prominent men must be passed by entirely.

Schmoller led the school—the Younger Historical School as it came to be called—by example as well as by word. In his early days he produced a monograph on the clothiers' and weavers' craft of Strassburg, which, not otherwise particularly distinguished, acquired importance in its programmatic setting and

[3] [*Die politische Ökonomie vom Standpunkte der geschichtlichen Methode* (1853; enlarged ed. 1883). Knies is discussed in chs. 5 and 8 below.]

[4] Of his writings on method, it will suffice to mention the collections: *Zur Literaturgeschichte der Staats- und Sozialwissenschaften* (1888), and *Grundfragen der Sozialpolitik und Volkswirtschaftslehre* (1897; in the latter, especially the important address on 'Changing Theories and Established Truths in the Field of the Social Sciences'); and the last edition of his article 'Volkswirtschaft und Volkswirtschaftslehre' in the German Encyclopaedia (*Handwörterbuch der Staatswissenschaften*), which renders his ripest thought on the subject. I take this opportunity to add that Schmoller brought to bear on his task of leadership not only energy, fighting spirit, and a tremendous capacity for work, but also considerable strategic and organizing ability. Among other things, he founded a periodical—which became known as *Schmoller's Jahrbuch*—and edited a series of monographs—the *Forschungen*—which served the cause and provided facilities for the publication of the school's work. He was a typical 'scholarch.'

[See also long article by J. A. S., 'Gustav v. Schmoller und die Probleme von heute,' *Schmoller's Jahrbuch*, vol. L, 1926, pp. 337-88.]

[5] [The note planned on these men was not written but Brentano, Held, and Knapp are mentioned elsewhere.]

became the model of the work of a host of pupils and of followers who were not pupils. His concern with historic work, however, went much further than that instance would suggest. He also did work not usually done by anyone who is not a professed historian; for instance, he took a leading part in the great edition of documents relating to the history of the public administration of Prussia, and always spoke of this achievement with loving pride. Thus, though historical work done by economists was not in itself a novelty, it was then undertaken on an unprecedented scale and in a new spirit. To those critics who felt that the thing was being overdone—and who spoke of Historism in a derogatory sense—it can fairly be replied, first, that all human achievement is of necessity one-sided, and, second, that in spite of all that was accomplished it is impossible to indicate a single field—at least I cannot indicate one—in which the work of the period went as far as we could wish.

Much of this work was no doubt rather pedestrian.[6] But the sum total of it meant a tremendous advance in accuracy of knowledge about the social process. It must suffice to list the main headings: economic (especially fiscal) policy and administration; the class structure of society; medieval and later forms of industry, especially of craft guilds and merchant guilds; the growth, functions, and structures of cities; the evolution of individual industries; of bank credit; and (one of the finest pieces of Schmoller's work) of government and private enterprise.

Schmoller's own circle did not do much in the field of agriculture. But it was sedulously cultivated by others and produced some of the best work of historical economics; the outstanding names are Hanssen, Meitzen, and Knapp.[7]

[6] The following fact will be appreciated by admirers of Henrik Ibsen's stupendous ability to delineate his characters by a few traits pregnant with significance. In his *Hedda Gabler*, Ibsen wishes to create, as quickly as possible, the impression that one of the two male characters, Hedda's husband, is a thoroughly mediocre academic drudge, not to say a dunce. And what is the first thing about him that Ibsen conveys to readers or audiences? That Dr. Tessman has just completed a work on the linen industry of Brabant in the sixteenth century! This no doubt was done by a layman for laymen. But still . . .

[7] Georg Hanssen's (1809-94) work—it will be enough to mention his *Agrarhistorische Abhandlungen* (1880-84)—and teaching (in Göttingen) were methodologically original in two respects: on the one hand, he taught his many pupils to start, in reconstructing agrarian history, from the conditions they had before their eyes, and thus brought out the analytic or explanatory value of past conditions with a liveliness and force all his own; on the other hand, he opened up a new source of material—maps and other topographical documents, reflecting the earlier forms of peasant holdings and casting new light on the structure of the manorial economy.

This material was fully exploited by August Meitzen (1822-1910), who brought the experience of the statistician to bear upon the task. His *Siedelung und Agrarwesen der Westgermanen und Ostgermanen, der Kelten, Römer, Finnen und Slawen* (1895) is, in the first instance, an attempt to depict and compare the ways in which those peoples settled on their land, built their villages, and planned their economy. But for our purpose still more important are the analytic uses made of the results of this monumental

Before we glance at some attempts at synthesis, it is necessary to insist on certain features of this work that have not always received the attention they deserve.

First, we have noticed that Schmoller himself and most of his pupils threw themselves into the fight for social reform, asserting their personal value judgments with the utmost vigor.[8] This has obliterated the fact that their *scientific credo* was extremely critical of value judgments and of the practice of economists to identify themselves with political parties and to recommend measures. One of Schmoller's objections to what he called 'Smithianism' was precisely that these Smithians were so bent on producing political 'recipes.' In part, no doubt, he took this stand because he did not like the particular recipes that were proffered by economic liberalism. But this was not all of it. Beyond his allegiance to different principles of economic policy there was the respect for the economic fact and the will to let it speak for itself.

Second, the same truly scientific spirit of criticism made the school look askance at the broad generalizations that are in the nature of philosophies of history. Schmoller realized, of course, the inevitability of theories in the sense of explanatory hypotheses, and he was less cautious in framing them than it is usual for professional historians to be. But he stopped far short of any attempt at reducing the whole historical process to the action of one or two factors. A single hypothesis of the Comte-Buckle-Marx kind he did not even visualize as an ultimate goal—the very idea of a simple theory of historical evolution seemed to him a mistaken one, in fact unscientific.

This point is essential in order to understand his scheme of thought and in particular in order to distinguish it from all those schemes that have nothing

---

piece of research. Meitzen tried to infer from them the early geographical distributions of those peoples, their agricultural technique, their customs, and their racial descent; and ventured into bold theories, that did not remain unchallenged, about the factors that shaped their social organization.

Georg Friedrich Knapp (1842-1926) stayed in this field—which has nothing to do with the two others in which he also left his mark—for about fifteen years, during which he produced two masterpieces—'classics' in the eulogistic sense of the word—*Die Bauernbefreiung und der Ursprung der Landarbeiter* (1887) and *Grundherrschaft und Rittergut* (1897), which describe the metamorphosis of the German agrarian world that occurred at the threshold of the capitalist era and was both the consequence of, and a potent factor in shaping, the social evolution of Germany. Knapp's analysis has not only created the standard pattern for quite a literature, but its main results have passed into the common stream of economic teaching. It is a pity that it is impossible to convey in a sketch like this what might be termed the general message of a performance of this kind. Knapp's marvelous equilibrium of comprehensive vision and detailed research, for instance, is something that can be felt and, by being felt, even learned from him, but it cannot be described in a few sentences. It stands to reason that a man, so long as he is engaged in work of this kind, would rarely if ever feel the need of theoretical training, lack of which was bound to prove a serious handicap in the field of money.

[8] [J. A. S. apparently intended to go into this subject at greater length in the early pages of section 1 of this chapter but did not do so.]

in common with his except the reference to history, which, as has been stated above, is too general to be of use. For instance, the view that history is our source of facts might be called Comtist. But Comte turned to this source (or told us to do so) in order to discover—by a procedure which he believed to be the same as that used in the physical sciences—'historical laws.' Schmoller's scientific intent was quite different. For him, Comte's suggestion was the very incarnation of the 'naturalist error' and Comtist historical laws were shams. In fact there is no trace whatever of Comtist influence in his work. This should be clear from our sketch of it and of the program behind it. And it should also be clear that the roots of both the work done and of the program are to be found exclusively in the German past: the high level of historiography; the widespread respect for the historical fact; the low level of theoretical economics; the lack of respect for its values; the supreme importance attributed to the state; the small importance attributed to everything else—these points individualize the school and they were all of them typically German, in their strengths as well as in their weaknesses.

Third, Schmoller always protested against an 'isolating' analysis of economic phenomena—he and his followers spoke of a 'method of isolation'—and held that we lose their essence as soon as we isolate them. This view, of course, was simply the consequence of his resolve to feed economics exclusively on historical monographs. For their materials as well as their results are obviously refractory to any attempt at isolating—in most cases, in fact, they become meaningless if isolated. Though perfectly understandable—and, for all economists who have no bent for 'theory,' perfectly acceptable—this consequence indicates a limitation of the scope of economic analysis of the Schmollerian type to which corresponds an almost illimited extension of its subject matter. Nothing in the social cosmos or chaos is really outside of Schmollerian economics. In principle, if not quite in practice, the Schmollerian economist was in fact a historically minded sociologist in the latter term's widest meaning. On this level, specialization would indeed impose itself again if decent work is to be turned out. But the divisions would be enforced by the material and would be of the same kind as those that must exist between medievalists and, say, Romanists.

This is the scientific meaning of the label that Schmoller affixed to his school. He did not call it historical simply, but historico-ethical. The label also carried a different meaning—it was to express protest against the wholly imaginary advocacy of the hunt for private profit of which the English 'classics' were supposed to have been guilty. But below this surface meaning, which no doubt served well enough with the public, there was one that was less suggestive of salesmanship: the school professed to study *all* the facets of an economic phenomenon; hence *all* the facets of economic behavior and not merely the economic logic of it; hence the *whole* of human motivations as historically displayed, the specifically economic ones not more than the rest for which the term 'ethical' was made to serve, presumably because it seems to stress hyperindividual components.

Fourth, it is of course a delusion to hope that the results of monographic historical research will weld into 'general economics' merely by being co-ordinated and without the aid of mental operations other than those that produced the monographs. But we must not overlook that, though such research plus a co-ordinating study of its results will never produce articulate theorems, they may produce, in a mind appropriately conditioned, something else that is much more valuable. They may exude a subtle message, convey an intimate understanding of social or of specifically economic processes, a sense of historical perspective or, if you prefer, of the organic coherence of things, which is extremely difficult, perhaps impossible, to formulate. Perhaps the analogy with a physician's clinical experience—or part of it—will prove more helpful than misleading.

These considerations will go a long way toward clarifying the possibilities of synthesis that were within the reach of the Schmoller school. The most obvious one is of course a comprehensive economic history; and the outstanding example, for the German Middle Ages, is Inama-Sternegg's *Deutsche Wirtschaftsgeschichte* (1879-1901).[9] But Schmoller himself visualized a different possibility. When the shadows lengthened, he endeavored to take stock of what he and his groups had achieved or intended and to show the world what a systematic treatise of the historical school would look like. An 'Outline' (*Grundriss*)[10] of two volumes was the result. But by that time he had silently unlearned the lessons of extreme 'historism.' Into a framework that did not depart fundamentally from oldest tradition, he fitted the rich materials of social history, giving for every type or institution a sketch (in some cases, a masterly sketch) of its historical evolution on the lines of his personal theory of it—in the chapter on social classes, for instance, historical and ethnological material is arranged around a division-of-labor theory of the phenomenon. Of course he had to use a conceptual apparatus, and occasionally to reason in the same way as do economic theorists, traditionally so-called. He theorized weakly—so weakly in fact that his theory (in this sense) is not even thoroughly bad—but he displayed no reluctance to do so. In matters of value and price Schmoller in fact adopted, or meant to adopt, the teaching of Carl Menger. I am tempted to sum up by saying: think of J. S. Mill's treatise; imagine another that bestows as much emphasis and competence on the institutional aspects as

[9] Karl Theodor von Inama-Sternegg (1843-1908) was an economist and statistician who, in the later part of his career, acquired international reputation by his work at the head of the Austrian statistical service (we should say Statistical Board) and by his simultaneous activity as a teacher who powerfully influenced a generation of statisticians and economists. But the illustrative value of the scientific career of this eminent man is in the fact that his own personal research was purely historical. He edited historical documents. He published two purely historical monographs in which he expounded the so-called Manorial Theory, i.e. the theory that the organization of the manor was the primary factor in shaping markets, towns, and industrial life in the dawn of capitalism. The history mentioned in our text was the result of his way of synthesizing, and it is this synthesis *by an economist* which is significant here: it did not differ in principle from a professional historian's idea of a synthesis.

[10] *Grundriss der allgemeinen Volkswirtschaftslehre* (1900-1904).

Mill bestowed upon theory in the traditional sense, and reduce correspondingly the space and thought allotted to the latter; and you have Schmoller's *Grundriss*, barring of course politico-philosophical backgrounds, which do not concern us here.

[(c) *The Methodenstreit.*] Thus, the leader had sheathed the sword. More important still, the flood of 'historism' had begun to ebb and a feeling of neighborly tolerance had begun to prevail all round. Comfortably assured of the survival of both parties, we may therefore turn back for a moment to consider the famous clash between theoretical and historical economists that has come down to posterity as the Battle of Methods (*Methodenstreit*). The main facts were these. When 'historism' was nearing high tide, Carl Menger, in 1883, published a book on methodology [11] that dealt on a broad front with the fundamental problems of procedure in the social sciences but was very obviously intended to vindicate the rights of theoretical analysis and to put the Schmoller school in its place—and a very secondary place it was! [12] Schmoller reviewed the book unfavorably in his *Jahrbuch*, and Menger replied in a pamphlet entitled the *Errors of Historism*,[13] which fairly steamed with wrath and of course elicited rebuttal. This not only created a lot of bad feeling but also set running a stream of literature, both of which took decades to subside. In spite of some contributions toward clarification of logical backgrounds, the history of this literature is substantially a history of wasted energies, which could have been put to better use.

Since there cannot be any serious question either about the basic importance of historical research in a science that deals with a historical process or about the necessity of developing a set of analytic tools by which to handle the material, the controversy, like all such controversies, might well seem to us to have been wholly pointless. This impression is strengthened by the surprising fact, which stands out clearly enough if one cares to look below the ruffled surface of polemical arguments and slogans, that neither party really did question its opponent's position *outright*. The quarrel was about precedence and relative importance and might have been settled by allowing every type of work to find the place to which its weight entitled it. The reasons why, for a time, neither party felt able to adopt this standpoint are important

[11] *Untersuchungen über die Methode der Socialwissenschaften und der Politischen Ökonomie insbesondere.* Since our interest in methodology per se is but a limited one, justice cannot be done here to this book, which is no doubt one of the significant performances in its field although, so far as logical fundaments are concerned, it hardly goes beyond Mill's *Logic*. I take the opportunity to refer readers interested in methodology to Professor Felix Kaufmann's excellent treatise, *Methodenlehre der Sozialwissenschaften* (1936); [English trans., *Methodology of the Social Sciences*, 1944].

[12] A little later, substantially the same ground was taken by Menger's followers headed by Böhm-Bawerk ('The Historical vs. the Deductive Method in Political Economy,' *Annals of the American Academy of Political and Social Science*, 1890) and by German theorists who were not followers but opponents of Menger's theoretical teaching, especially H. Dietzel ('Beiträge zur Methodik der Wirtschaftswissenschaften,' *Jahrbücher für Nationalökonomie*, 1884, and other publications).

[13] *Die Irrthümer des Historismus in der deutschen Nationalökonomie* (1884).

enough for the sociology and history of science—of any science—to require explicit statement.

The first thing to be observed about all controversies between scientific parties is the large amount of mutual misunderstanding that enters into them. This element is not absent even in the most advanced sciences where homogeneous training, habits of exact statement, and a high level of general competence could be expected to exclude it. But where, as in economics, conditions in all these respects are immensely less favorable than they are in mathematics or physics, men frequently have but an inadequate notion of what the other fellow really worries about. Hence a great part of the fighting is directed against positions which are indeed hostile fortresses in the imagination of the warrior but which on inspection turn out to be harmless windmills.

Secondly, this situation is made worse by the fact that methodological clashes often are clashes of temperaments and of intellectual bents. This was so in our case. There are such things as historical and theoretical temperaments. That is to say, there are types of mind that take delight in all the colors of historical processes and of individual cultural patterns. There are other types that prefer a neat theorem to everything else. We have use for both. But they are not made to appreciate one another. There is a parallel for this in the physical sciences: experimenters and theorists are not always the best of friends. But again, things will be more difficult where neither party can boast of spectacular successes that conciliate and impress. Moreover, every decent workman loves his work. And this alone, for some of us, implies dislike for other 'methods' in a perfectly irrational and impulsive way.

Third, we must never forget that genuine schools are sociological realities—living beings. They have their structures—relations between leaders and followers—their flags, their battle cries, their moods, their all-too-human interests. Their antagonisms come within the general sociology of group antagonisms and of party warfare. Victory and conquest, defeat and loss of ground, are in themselves values for such schools and part of their very existence. They will try to appropriate labels that are considered honorific—in our case, *both* parties laid claim to such epithets as 'empiric,' 'realistic,' 'modern,' 'exact'—and to affix derogatory labels—'speculative,' 'futile,' 'subordinate'—to the work of the enemy. These labels may mean little or nothing in themselves, but they acquire a life of their own and in turn keep controversy alive. All this gives scope to personal vanities, interests, and propensities to fight that may, as they do in national and international politics, count for more than any real issues—in fact to the point of obliterating the real issues.

[(d) *The 'Youngest' Historical School: Spiethoff, Sombart, and M. Weber.*] The controversy petered out as all controversies of this type do and the zeal for the historical monograph returned to normal. But the work of the Schmoller school was carried on under the leadership of new men who hailed from Schmoller; had experienced the influence of his message in their formative years; and, though they differed from him and from one another in aims, methods of research, and performance, remained faithful to the fundamental principles he had been foremost in asserting. We might almost speak of a 'youngest' historical school. By far the most eminent members of it are Spiethoff, Sombart, and M. Weber.[14]

So far as technical training is concerned, Spiethoff is no historian at all. But Schmoller's fundamental precepts came into his approach to a problem in this way: at the beginning of each of his great research projects mentioned above stood a simple conceptual apparatus, constructed with care but with a view to adequacy for the particular investigation rather than with a view to refinement per se; with this apparatus and a provisional analytic idea or hypothesis, he attacked in detail selected sets of facts that the apparatus and the idea indicated as relevant, sometimes going so far as to analyze the economics of an individual apartment house or of a particular firm; finally, he described the general features of the pattern that emerged without the help of any elaborate method, and these general features, properly adapted to the questions to be answered, were his 'theoretical' results. I daresay that the reader is not

[14] For the sake of convenience I mention them here, although their work, and still more their influence, belongs in part to the next period.

The international reputation of Arthur Spiethoff—for a long time assistant to Schmoller (and also for a long time *de facto* editor of the latter's quarterly journal, the *Jahrbuch*, before Spiethoff edited it under his own name), later on professor in Bonn—rests upon his outstanding performance in the field of business cycle research. Neglecting earlier papers of a purely theoretical nature on this and cognate subjects, capital theory in particular, we shall content ourselves with mentioning the article 'Krisen' in the 4th ed. of the *Handwörterbuch der Staatswissenschaften* (vol. VI, 1925), which presents in a compressed form what really amounts to an extensive treatise. His highly interesting scientific *credo*—recognition of a large number of historical 'styles' of economic life, each requiring its own theory in addition to a common fund of concepts and propositions belonging to 'timeless theory'—is contained in his paper 'Die Allgemeine Volkswirtschaftslehre als geschichtliche Theorie: die Wirtschaftsstile' in *Schmollers Jahrbuch*, 1932. Far removed from Schmoller's position, Spiethoff's will nevertheless bear interpretation as a development of it in a particular direction. His method of approach characterized in the text is illustrated in his book *Boden und Wohnung* . . . (1934), an inquiry into the pricing of dwelling room and the rent of urban land, and by two series of publications by his pupils which he edited and the preparation of which he supervised with the minutest care: the *Bonner Städteuntersuchungen* and the *Beiträge zur Erforschung der wirtschaftlichen Wechsellagen* (Contributions to the Study of Business Cycles).

[While J. A. S. taught at Bonn (1925-32), he came to know Spiethoff both as a valued colleague and as a firm friend. After the death of J. A. S., Spiethoff together with Erich Schneider arranged for the publication in Germany (and edited) a collection of many of the earlier articles and essays of J. A. S. The first of three volumes will appear in 1952.]

As a man and as a scholar, Werner Sombart (1863-1941) was in every respect the opposite of Spiethoff. The difference between the fame of the two men—not only with the public at large—provides food for thought on the subject of the sociology of science. The only work of his that need be mentioned here, his *Modern Capitalism* (*Der Moderne Kapitalismus*, 1902, 2nd ed., much enlarged, 1916-27) shocked professional historians by its often unsubstantial brilliance. They failed to see in it anything that they would call real research—the material of the book is in fact wholly second-hand—

much impressed with the novelty of this procedure, which may seem to him nothing but obvious common sense. But it was new in its neatness, the crystal-clear distinction of the steps, and the equal attention bestowed on all of them—in the success with which Spiethoff did not clamor for, but actually developed, 'realistic theories' of a certain type. It should be observed that, though a man of wide cultural interests, he remained a research worker strictly within the traditional boundaries of economics. He did not care to merge economics into an all-embracing sociology. In this respect he did not follow Schmoller's example.

But Sombart did; and, throwing aside all qualms about the limits of professional competence, even out-Schmollered Schmoller. His *Modern Capitalism*—which title really covers a much wider area—represents a third type of historical-school synthesis, to be distinguished alike from the general economic

---

and they entered protests against its many carelessnesses. Yet it was in a sense a peak achievement of the historical school, and highly stimulating even in its errors.

Max Weber (1864-1920) was one of the most powerful personalities that ever entered the scene of academic science. The profound influence of his leadership—in large measure due to a chivalrous ardor for doing the right thing that sometimes verged upon the quixotic—upon colleagues and students was something quite outside of his performance as a scholar, yet was a vitalizing force (milieu-creating rather than school-creating) which it was impossible not to mention. Some earlier researches of his, such as his *Römische Agrargeschichte* (1891) can be passed by with the comment that, unlike Sombart, he did some historical research in the professional's sense. The few sentences of the text to which I must unfortunately confine myself in dealing with the purely analytic aspects of a monumental achievement will be adequately substantiated by reference to the following works: (1) *The Protestant Ethic and the Spirit of Capitalism* (appeared in German as 'Die protestantische Ethik und der "Geist" des Kapitalismus' in *Archiv für Sozialwissenschaft und Sozialpolitik*, 1904-5; republ. in *Gesammelte Aufsätze zur Religionssoziologie*; English trans. by T. Parsons, 1930). This is the work that advanced the famous theory, so full of far-reaching implications, that the religious revolution from which Protestantism emerged was the dominant factor in the molding of the capitalist mind and thus of capitalism itself. It attracted much more attention than the studies in the sociology of the great religions that followed (in later volumes of the *Archiv*) and gave rise to a controversy in which sociologists of all countries took part. (2) 'Roscher und Knies und die logischen Probleme der historischen Nationalökonomie,' *Schmollers Jahrbuch*, 1903-5, the most important of his many 'methodological' studies. (3) *General Economic History*, the report of a course given at the University of Munich a year before his death, and compiled mainly from students' notebooks; English translation by no less an authority than Frank H. Knight. (4) *Economy and Society* (*Wirtschaft und Gesellschaft*), a part of the *Grundriss der Sozialökonomik* (a work of many volumes by many authors which began to appear in 1914) which Weber initiated and edited and which, though it can only be mentioned in passing, is an important landmark on the road of German economics. (5) *Adaptation and Selection in the Labor Force* (an investigation of the Verein für Sozialpolitik suggested and led by him; only fragments have appeared in the Verein's *Schriften*), which I mention merely as an example of the freshness and originality of his ideas and as an illustration of a type of problem that readily occurred to him. This example also will come in usefully when we discuss American Institutionalism.

history type and from the type of Schmoller's *Grundriss*. It is a vision of the historical process that has an artistic quality and is drawn into the sphere of science by being nourished with historical fact and expressed by means of a primitive analytic scheme. It is *histoire raisonnée*, with the accent on the reasoning, and systematized history with the accent on system in the sense of a succession of frescoes of social states. The kind of historical theory that emerges is best illustrated by Sombart's theory—though it is traceable to Marx and though he abandoned it in the second edition—of the early accumulation of industrial capital from the rent of land: they are explanatory hypotheses suggested by facts. However, his theories are not exclusively or even primarily economic. An attempt such as his defies departmentalization. *All* factors operative in the totality of the historical process do come in and must come in: wars and Jews enter *pari passu* with saving or gold discoveries. *And this is quite all right* so long as we remember (a) that such comprehensiveness is the privilege of just that one type of scientific endeavor; (b) that this type cannot live except on the food provided by other types of work if it is not to degenerate into irresponsible dilettantism; and (c) that Sombartian success depends on a combination of personal qualities not usually found together in the requisite intensity and cannot be had by wishing for it—which it is just as well to emphasize in view of the wide international appeal of Sombart's work.

Sombart's 'methodological' pronouncements followed fashions too closely to be interesting. At first he was duly contemptuous of those who 'drilled Robinson Crusoe' (see below, ch. 6, sec. 1, n. 2). When the wind changed he was anxious to be recognized as a theorist and took credit for having used, in spots, the 'deductive method.' Considering the relation of his work to American institutionalism this change of front is important to remember. Much more important is it, however, to note the same absence of hostility to economic theory (in the narrow sense of the term) in M. Weber, whose views on the nature of the logical processes in the social sciences were much more significant.[15]

Weber did not confine himself to mere professions of methodological faith couched in general phrases. He really went into the matter and analyzed the forms of thought actually used within his range of comprehension, that is mainly those used by historical economists and sociologists. And he emerged from gigantic labors with a definite and positive doctrine. This doctrine turns on two concepts: the Ideal Type and the Meant Meaning. In the social sciences, he held, we perform operations of a kind entirely foreign to the physical sciences. In the physical sciences explanation never means more than description. In the social sciences explanation involves the understanding of 'cultural contents,' the interpretation of Meanings: hence the term Interpretative Sociology (*Verstehende Soziologie*). There is no sense in asking what the fall-

[15] In working his way toward his methodology, M. Weber availed himself (not always to advantage) of such help as he thought he could derive from contemporaneous philosophic work. In particular, the influence of Rickert's and also of Windelband's teaching is occasionally very noticeable.

ing stone is about beyond stating the law of its fall. But there is sense in asking what a consuming household is about. In order to make headway with the analysis of the latter—and of all social phenomena—the observer must understand his subject of research in a sense in which he cannot and need not understand the falling stone. For this purpose he must create types which, though not necessarily pure like the economic man, are abstractions in that they possess only essential and lack non-essential properties: they are *logical* ideals. And we try to get at an understanding of what such a type does, feels, says, by asking not what his actions, feelings, utterances mean to us, the observers, but what they mean to the type under research or, to put the same thing into different words, we try to unearth the meanings that the types intend to attach to themselves and their behavior. If this conveys something to the reader, then he will realize that this theory of the logic of the social sciences—whatever its merits or limitations and its sources in professional philosophy—is quite neutral as between the various kinds of analytic activity. In particular, economic theory in the traditional sense is not ruled out. And it makes precious little difference to the practical work of a theorist whether Mr. Methodologist tells him that in investigating the conditions of a profit maximum he is investigating 'meant meanings' of an 'ideal type' or that he is hunting for 'laws' or 'theorems.' As a matter of fact, in the epoch of his ripest thought, M. Weber was not unwilling to declare that, so far as his almost complete ignorance of it enabled him to judge, he saw no objection of principle to what economic theorists actually did, though he disagreed with them on what they thought they were doing, that is, on the epistemological interpretation of their procedure.[16]

Indeed, he was not really an economist at all. In an atmosphere not disturbed by professional cross-currents, it would be the obvious thing to label him a sociologist. His work and teaching had much to do with the emergence of Economic Sociology in the sense of an analysis of economic institutions, the recognition of which as a distinct field clarifies so many 'methodological' issues.

So far we have been dealing with a specifically German phenomenon that grew out of specifically German roots and displayed typically German strengths and weaknesses. Of course, some of the factors that account for the rise of the German historical school were ubiquitous. Moreover, in every country there were other factors that favored parallel movements—Comtism was one of the most important of these. Finally, the work of the German school was far too important to remain without influence on the course of things in other countries. Nevertheless, it is important to realize that these parallel movements, though similar, were yet essentially different; that they owed less to

[16] It was with this motivation that he invited two strong partisans of economic theory, in the Marshallian sense, to write the 'theory' and the sketch of the history of doctrines and methods for his *Grundriss der Sozialökonomik*. Again, this is relevant in view of the fact that he is sometimes invoked as a champion of institutional economics. [The two strong partisans of 'theory' were Joseph A. Schumpeter and Friedrich von Wieser. The sketch of the history of doctrines and methods was the *Epochen der Dogmen- und Methodengeschichte* of which this *History* is, in a sense, an outgrowth.]

the German example than one might be tempted to suppose; and that, with the possible exception of American Institutionalism, none of them was strong enough to cause a break in traditions and to redirect research, partly because that tradition was stronger and more ably defended.

In Italy, the German development was sympathetically noticed by some, as was the German *Sozialpolitik*. But neither influence availed to upset the existing patterns. Italian economics had always been strong on the 'factual' side and continued to be so. Nobody seems to have thought of fighting over it. Although some leaders—such as Einaudi—did some or most of their work in the field of economic history, it would hardly occur to anyone to speak of an Italian historical school in the sense of a distinct scientific party.

The same holds true for France. The great tradition of French historiography continued, of course, and, following the interests of the times, economic history received additional attention. Some economists did historical work. I shall mention only Levasseur.[17] Later on some work was done on lines suggestive of those of Sombart, for example, by Henry Sée. And those brilliant historians or historical sociologists, like Hippolyte Taine or Alexis de Tocqueville before him, whose works have become 'required reading' for any cultivated person, painted to a considerable extent in economic colors. Nothing of this spelled any new departure for professional economics.[18] But Simiand's work and methodological creed did. Though he owed nothing to German influence—if his work had any source in the past, that source was Comte—his views of traditional theory, which his *théorie expérimentale* was to replace, and his arguments against it (speculative castles in the air and so on) were pretty much those of Schmoller. Only, no group has as yet rallied to his standard.[19]

[17] Pierre Émile Levasseur's (1828-1911) most important work was: *Histoire des classes ouvrières en France depuis la conquête de Jules César jusqu'à la Révolution* (1859) and *Histoire des classes ouvrières en France depuis* 1789 *jusqu'à nos jours* (1867; the second editions of both works add the words *et de l'industrie*). But it did not occur to him to secede—on methodological or any other grounds—from the group mentioned below in Chapter 5, as is abundantly clear from his textbook.

[18] Some readers might miss the name of the Belgian economist Émile de Laveleye (1822-92), who was a man of many merits and in his time enjoyed a well-deserved international popularity that has kept his name alive. But the only reason for making him a member either of the German or of a non-existent French historical school is that he wrote a book *De la Propriété et de ses formes primitives* (1873), a historico-ethnological analysis of private property. His elementary textbook (*Éléments d'économie politique,* 1882) is neither distinguished nor distinctive and shows that so far as analytic technique is concerned he did not stray far from the beaten path (there is an English translation with an introduction by F. W. Taussig, 1884).

[19] François Simiand (1873-1935) formulated his methodological creed in *La Méthode positive en science économique* (1912), which seems to me to come nearest of all that has been written in Europe on questions of procedure to represent the institutionalist view. Criticism, made less effective than it could be by the large element of misunderstanding that enters into it, and methodological considerations, which in their positive suggestions are often very valuable, also claim a large space in the only other work of

[(e) *Economic History and Historical Economics in England.*] Turning to England, we first notice the quality and quantity of the work done by economic historians that rose to new levels during the period and laid the foundations for the still greater achievements in our own time. The performance of Cunningham may serve as an example.[20] He did, and felt himself to be doing work that was and always had been essential to 'economic science' which is 'primarily analytic' as he put it (*Growth of English Industry and Commerce*, vol. I, p. 18). He wished to see it used by theorists and he asserted its claim to a place in the economist's curriculum. But beyond expressing the belief that the conceptual apparatus of analytic economics is not readily applicable to conditions anterior to the capitalist epoch, he nowhere indicated a desire to see it replaced by generalizations proceeding from historical research.

That claim on behalf of economic history did not meet any appreciable resistance. Several economists, such as Rogers,[21] were primarily economic his-

---

his I am going to mention: *Le Salaire, l'évolution sociale et la monnaie* (3 vols., 1932). This work shows his methods in action and is unique in the infinite care bestowed on working out, before the reader's eye, every step of his analysis. Though the results are not, perhaps, wholly encouraging and could, such as they are, have been arrived at in a less laborious manner, it is precisely to that care that the work owes its very considerable significance—it should really be more widely known. Is it unfair to add, to so short a notice, a point which may thereby acquire undue importance? Professor Simiand (op. cit., vol. II, pp. 544 et seq.) very properly holds up to scorn the minimum-of-existence theory of wages, which is in fact an excellent example of bad workmanship (though really it should not be invoked in a criticism of modern theory). But he overlooks the fact that the faultiness of this theory proves nothing against any kind of method except that it is not foolproof. And he further overlooks that this particular miscarriage occurred precisely because the economists of the eighteenth and the beginning of the nineteenth century followed the method that Professor Simiand advocates: they ascertained what then was a broad fact—viz. that workmen as a rule did not earn more than a bare subsistence—fitted a hypothesis to it, found it verified, and there they were. Had they been better theorists, they could not possibly have put such implicit faith in that fact.

[20] William Cunningham (1849-1919) was a very prolific writer. For our purposes, it suffices to mention his great work, *The Growth of English Industry and Commerce During the Early and Middle Ages* (1st ed. 1882, greatly improved 5th ed. 1910-12), *An Essay on Western Civilization in its Economic Aspects* (1898-1900), and his *Progress of Capitalism in England* (1916).

It seems unjustifiable to pass by such meritorious work as Leone Levi's *History of British Commerce . . .* (1872, 2nd ed. 1880) or Arnold Toynbee's (1852-83) famous *Lectures on the Industrial Revolution in England* (posthumously published in 1884), which remained the standard work on the subject until they were replaced by Mantoux's book (*La Révolution industrielle au XVIIIe siècle*, 1905). But it is impossible within the compass of this sketch to do justice to historical work as such, and listing names and titles would serve no useful purpose. This is also the reason why the reader will find no reference to the leading economic historians of the last thirty years.

[21] J. E. Thorold Rogers (1823-90), twice professor of economics in Oxford. His main performance was his *History of Agriculture and Prices in England*, 1259-1793, seven

torians so far as their research was concerned. Alfred Marshall was a better historian than most of those who later attacked his economics as unhistorical, speculative, and so on. His *Industry and Trade* alone suffices to prove that, though the whole extent of his historical acquirements was not known outside of his circle until the publication of Keynes's biographical essay.

Under these circumstances there was evidently no room for a historical school in the sense of a scientific party committed to fighting for a distinctive program. As a matter of fact there were but the merest fragments of one. There had been a 'forerunner,' Jones.[22] And later on, at the time of the ascendancy of the Schmoller school in Germany, some English economists professed allegiance to more or less similar principles. The most important men to remember are Ashley, Ingram, and Cliffe Leslie.[23]

But though all three of these men attracted attention and made their marks, none of them succeeded in forming a group, let alone a militant one. This

volumes, of which the first appeared in 1866. His more popular *Six Centuries of Work and Wages* (1884) is more widely known, however. He also prepared an edition of the *Wealth of Nations,* wrote a not very brilliant *Manual of Political Economy for Schools* (1868), and other things. He devoted much energy to the propagation of Cobden-Bright ideas. His reputation as a scholar, however, rests wholly on the *History.*

[22] Richard Jones (1790-1855), who, among other things, was Malthus' successor as professor in Haileybury, was a vital personality of strong convictions. His dislike of Ricardian economics took the form of vigorous protests against hasty generalization and of an advocacy of patient factual research, *the results of which were eventually to replace the provisional structures of existing 'systems.'* And he gave an example of what was in his mind in the first and only part completed—on Rent—of his *Essay on the Distribution of Wealth and the Sources of Taxation* (1831). Thus he does not badly fit the role that historians of economics assigned to him, although it is not easy to be sure what either his programmatic pronouncement or his example amounted to. Some of the objections leveled at Ricardo were not well taken; but it is more important that many of them were such as any theorist might level at any other theorist, e.g. the objection, anticipated and refuted by Ricardo himself, that the latter's law of diminishing returns in agriculture was invalidated by the fact of technological progress. Moreover, in his discussion of 'Primitive Political Economy' (mentioned above, Part II, ch. 7, sec. 3), he argues from the standpoint of the opinions of his time without displaying any sense of the historical relativity of doctrine. Still, both the pronouncements and the example do suggest historical school ideas. His lectures and essays, stimulating reading, have been edited by W. Whewell under the title *Literary Remains* (1859).

[23] William James Ashley (1860-1927), unquestionably the strongest personality of the three, professor at the University of Birmingham and the academic leader in Joseph Chamberlain's protectionist movement, conformed more than any other English economist to the German professional type of that time. Having in his early years experienced the influence of economic and legal historians (Toynbee and Maine, in particular, and later on the influence of the Germans), he ran true to that type in his works—such as his excellent industrial monographs and his very successful *Introduction to English Economic History and Theory* . . . (2 vols., 1888 and 1893)—as well as in his methodological pronouncements and in his sympathies with *Sozialpolitik* and economic nationalism. But he had absorbed enough from his English environment to be proof against the crudenesses of his prototype: nobody who lived in England could possibly

was so even in the seventies. Later on, when Marshall's leadership asserted itself, the majority of economists (and practically all the talent) flocked to his standard. Some opposition there was, but it was only in part methodological in nature. We may mention Hobson and the Webbs.[24] The modest trickle of

misunderstand economic theory so completely as Schmoller had done in the early part of his career.

John Kells Ingram (1823-1907) was a quite different sort of man. He commanded a much wider cultural background (he was a philosopher and poet, and was in 1866 appointed Regius professor of Greek in Dublin, and also wrote on Shakespeare and Tennyson) but he can hardly be said to have done any economic research at all. His *History of Political Economy* (first in the *Encyclopaedia Britannica*, 1885, independently published, 1888; latest edition, with a supplementary chapter by W. A. Scott, 1915) is conclusive proof both of his wide philosophical (especially Comtist) and historical erudition and his inadequate command of technical economics. The latter fact made it easier of course for him than it would otherwise have been to talk glibly about the New Economics to which the future belonged (compare, e.g., his address at the Dublin meeting of the British Association for the Advancement of Science, 1878, on 'The Present Position and Prospects of Political Economy') and with which his name was associated on the strength of programmatic pronouncements. High sentiment and moral tone—in which Marshall was soon to compete—protest against isolating economics from the work of other social sciences, emphasis upon (Comtist) evolution and historical relativity, induction *vs.* deduction, were the main points that appealed to the public.

Thomas E. Cliffe Leslie's (1826-82) name survives not because of his scholarly work of the 'descriptive' kind—though some of it is of high grade, such as, e.g., his work on Irish, English, and European land systems—or because of his papers, some of them forceful and brilliant, on current questions of policy, but because of his advocacy of the historical method, which was both judicious and effective and did not fail to impress. The two papers that present his methodology or, as he preferred to call it, philosophy of the social sciences (reprinted in his *Essays in Political and Moral Philosophy*, 1879; a 2nd ed., that left out some but added others, appeared posthumously) read much like a reformulation of the Schmollerian program; in view of the dates of their first publication (1876 and 1879) this should not induce us to deny them originality. And if we consider certain unguarded statements made by theorists, such as Senior, we may even discover some merit in the otherwise none too startling assertion that economists must always start from and verify deductions by facts.

[24] John A. Hobson's (1858-1940) feud with Marshallian economics was not primarily methodological. However opposed to the theories of his contemporaries, he always fought them by theories without challenging their methodological credentials. All the same, there was a methodological aspect to that antagonism. For instance, Hobson's insistence upon what he considered to be irrational behavior of consumers and upon the institutional factors that, rather than 'rational choice,' determine this behavior really implies a research program of the historico-sociological sort. This is important to realize because it supplies one of the links between Hobson and American institutionalism.

Beatrice (1858-1943) and Sidney Webb (1859-1947) have to be mentioned in this connection, first, on account of the nature of their research, which contributed substantially to the achievement of English economic historians (see especially, *History of Trade Unionism*, 1894, and the *Manor and the Borough*, 1908); and second, on

controversial literature need not detain us further. But we must record the excellent performance of J. N. Keynes that settled most of these methodological issues in a spirit of judicial reasonableness and to the satisfaction of the profession. For two decades this book held a well-earned position of authority. Its perusal may be recommended even at this distance of time because of its merits as well as of its success.[25]

[The manuscript of this chapter stops at this point. The section on American Institutionalism was apparently never written.]

---

account of the fact that they lent the support of their great influence on a large section of opinion to methodological views akin to those of the German historical school. This at least was the impression I gathered from lectures on method delivered by S. Webb at the London School of Economics.

[25] John Neville Keynes (1852-1949; father of Lord Keynes), *Scope and Method of Political Economy* (1st ed. 1891). Of those minor yet notable contributions that were overshadowed by his success, we may however mention those of Bagehot and Cairnes. Walter Bagehot's vigorous pen repeatedly touched methodological subjects. Without questioning the validity of Ricardian procedure, he was inclined to limit its application to the cultural pattern of capitalist business and to look upon historical research as its natural complement. See in particular his essay on 'The Postulates of English Political Economy,' republished in *Economic Studies* (1880).

John E. Cairnes's *Character and Logical Method of Political Economy* (lectures delivered 1856, publ. 1857) was never appreciated according to its merit, either at the time or later, because, like Senior before him, he used the term Political Economy to designate what most people always considered as a small part of either Political Economy or Economics, viz. the logical scheme of economic rationality commonly known as 'pure theory.' His own works simply prove that he was far from believing that this logical schema (which, as will be remembered, does not even constitute the whole of economic theory in our sense) comprises all our knowledge about economic affairs. But by virtue of a misunderstanding, for which the blame rests with him in part, he was later on, e.g., by Ingram and Schmoller, represented as an uncompromising advocate of 'deduction' who had no use for any factual research. However, his analysis of the nature of that schema was a real contribution. Its purely hypothetical character, its unrealistic assumptions, the width of the gulf that separates it from the observable economic phenomenon, the difficulty of verifying its component propositions by statistical or other observational evidence (he even spoke of the *impossibility* of establishing or refuting 'economic laws' by such evidence), all this was exhibited more clearly than ever before, though he stopped short of the obvious conclusion that such a schema can never yield any 'laws' but only serve in an instrumental capacity.

CHAPTER 5

The General Economics of the Period: Men and Groups

1. Jevons, Menger, Walras

The call of social reform created a new focal point for the practical interests of the economics profession; but though it influenced tone and direction, it did not affect the technique of analytic work. The historical school meant indeed to revolutionize the methods of the science; but this revolution ended in compromise even in Germany. So far as these influences went, General Economics remained, in scope and method, substantially what it had been before. But its analytic core, for which the term Value and Distribution became increasingly popular, experienced a revolution of its own which was to subside into a typical Classical Situation around 1900 and constitutes, in our field, the third great event of that period. According to a familiar tradition from which it is convenient to start, this revolution centered in the rise of the marginal utility theory of value that is associated with the names of three leaders: Jevons, Menger, and Walras. We pause to salute them.[1]

Throughout his modest career as a civil servant and teacher, William Stanley Jevons (1835-82) never made a mark that was at all commensurate to the importance of his achievement. During his life he was better known for his writings on money and finance and on other practical questions of current

[1] Forerunners will be mentioned in ch. 6, sec. 3, below.

interest—even for his sunspot or harvest theory of business cycles (see below, ch. 8)—than for the performance that was to make him immortal. In England, moreover, his memory was overshadowed by the strong leadership of Marshall, who consistently discounted the 'Jevonian revolution.' There are many reasons for this. Jevons left hardly any personal pupils, a fact that was in turn due not only to lack of opportunity (he never taught in a strategic position) but also to his amiable modesty or lack of assertiveness (which was quite compatible with the 'compensatory' habit of making large claims of revolutionary novelty for his ideas). But it is also true that his work in economic theory lacks finish. His performance was not up to his vision. Brilliant conceptions and profound insights (particularly his championship of mathematical modes of thought, his theory of value, his theory of capital and interest) were never properly worked out; they were stated as *aperçus* and so intermingled with old stuff as to look almost superficial. Marshall's definitely ungenerous attitude toward him did the rest. In England, therefore, he never got his due. In particular his originality was never recognized as it should have been. For he was without any doubt one of the most genuinely original economists who ever lived. In very few other cases (John Rae is another) is it so difficult to speak of 'roots' as it is in the case of Jevons. He heard of his forerunners only after the event, which, in his particular case, was quite excusable, especially since he gave generous credit to those whom he did discover later on. Perhaps he owed more to Mill than he knew: he harbored a strong aversion to Mill's *Principles*, which he had to use in his teaching; but Mill's tergiversations, which are such excellent targets for rifle practice, may nevertheless have taught him many things. Barring this, however, he seems to have built the essentials of his teaching from bricks of his own manufacture. The bulk of his work in pure theory is contained in his *Theory of Political Economy* (1st ed. 1871; the date that fixes his priority as regards the concept of the 'final degree of utility' is however 1862, when he read a paper, 'Notice of a General Mathematical Theory of Political Economy,' at the Cambridge meeting [section F] of the British Association for the Advancement of Science); the bulk of his work in the fields of money and cycles has been assembled by Professor Foxwell in a volume entitled *Investigations in Currency and Finance* (1884), study of which no economist should neglect. In addition, Jevons was as much a logician as he was an economist. I mention his *Principles of Science* (1874), a work of truly Jevonian force and originality which has not, so it seems to me, received the recognition it deserves. A bibliography is appended to his *Letters and Journal*, edited by Mrs. W. S. Jevons in 1886. Mrs. and Professor H. S. Jevons contributed a brief article on his life and work to *Econometrica*, July 1934.[2]

[2] This is perhaps my best opportunity to mention the work of a man that is forgotten now but drew praise from both Jevons and Marshall: the *Plutology* (Melbourne, 1863; London, 1864) by W. E. Hearn, who taught in the University of Melbourne. The book has failed to impress me greatly. But in parts it does read curiously Jevonian. The date of its publication proves, however, Jevons' independence as regards the utility aspect.

Carl Menger (1840-1921) was, after a brief career in the civil service, appointed to one of the two chairs of Political Economy at the faculty of law of the University of Vienna, which he held for the rest of his official career (1873-1903). This location was by no means ideal, both because there was no local tradition in the subject, let alone one that commanded the attention of the world, and because the future lawyers and civil servants who formed his audience were but mildly interested in what he had to say—if you were well up in civil and public law, you could afford to flunk the economics examination. But nothing daunted, this hickory of a man asserted himself eventually, found personal pupils of his own intellectual caliber, and—though not without an embittering period of strife—founded a school, which displayed vitality and coherence and, though lacking all the means and advantages that usually condition such achievement, exerted international influence until it was (temporarily?) dispersed in the 1930's. His fundamental principle of marginal utility was his own—subjectively—though Jevons holds, of course, priority of rediscovery. And so were, both subjectively and objectively, many of the theorems that occur in the course of its elaboration. He was a careful thinker who rarely slipped, if ever, and his genius stands out only the more impressively because he lacked the appropriate mathematical tools. The ultimate roots of his teaching were in that German theoretical tradition which had reached peaks in Hermann and Thünen. But the influence of Smith, Ricardo, and especially J. S. Mill is also unmistakable. With Menger, as with Jevons, it was their teaching which he meant to revolutionize. Precisely because of this they were, in a sense, his teachers. His *Grundsätze der Volkswirtschaftslehre* (1st ed. 1871; the 2nd ed. 1923, the work of his old age, adds nothing essential) as well as his other writings, some of which will be mentioned later, were republished (1933-6) in four volumes by the London School of Economics. The Introduction by F. A. von Hayek to these *Collected Works* (vol. 1) is the best source of information on the man and the thinker. See also H. S. Bloch, 'Carl Menger,' *Journal of Political Economy*, June 1940. [An English translation of the *Grundsätze*, *Principles of Economics*, with introduction by F. H. Knight was published in 1950.]

As has been emphasized before, economics is a big omnibus which contains many passengers of incommensurable interests and abilities. However, so far as pure theory is concerned, Walras is in my opinion the greatest of all economists. His system of economic equilibrium, uniting, as it does, the quality of 'revolutionary' creativeness with the quality of classic synthesis, is the only work by an economist that will stand comparison with the achievements of theoretical physics. Compared with it, most of the theoretical writings of that period—and beyond—however valuable in themselves and however original subjectively, look like boats beside a liner, like inadequate attempts to catch some particular aspect of Walrasian truth. It is the outstanding landmark on the road that economics travels toward the status of a rigorous or exact science and, though outmoded by now, still stands at the back of much of the best theoretical work of our time. Unfortunately, Walras himself attached as much importance to his questionable philosophies about social justice, his land-nationalization scheme, his projects of monetary management, and other things that have nothing to do with his superb achievement in pure theory. They have cost him the goodwill of many a competent critic, and must, I imagine, try the patience of many of his readers. In any case, the tribute above must be understood to refer to his pure theory alone.

Marie Esprit Léon Walras (1834-1910) was a Frenchman and not only by virtue of his birthplace. The style of his reasoning and the nature of his achievement are characteristically French in the same sense in which Racine's plays and J. H. Poincaré's mathematics are characteristically French. So are all the roots of his achievement. He emphasized himself the influence of his father Auguste Walras and of Cournot. But, as has been pointed out before, we must add that of Say, his true predecessor. And behind the figure of Say there looms the whole French tradition—Condillac, Turgot, Quesnay, Boisguillebert—however much or little he may have consciously absorbed from it. He paid conventional respect to A. Smith. The rest of the great Englishmen meant little to him.

His career displays the typical inability of the born thinker to master the practical problems of personal life. He was much too original to be a success at his schools. His training as a mining engineer, to which he owed his mathematics, failed to gain him a living. He turned to free-lance journalism, developing his various ideas about social reform—the ideas typical of the French middle-class radical of his time—but he made no mark.[3] A lucky chance, however, rescued his genius from the danger of going to waste. In 1860, he attended an international congress on taxation in Lausanne, where he read a paper that was well received. In the audience was M. Louis Ruchonnet, who later became chief of the department of education of the Canton de Vaud and, in 1870, founded a chair of political economy at the faculty of law of the University of Lausanne which he offered to Walras. Having found the anchorage he needed, Walras went to work and remained at work until the end. But his creative period roughly coincides with his tenure of professorial office (1870-92). All of his work that counts (and some material that does not), most of it previously published in memoirs and articles (beginning in 1873), was eventually consolidated into three volumes: *Éléments d'économie politique pure* (1st ed. 1874-7; 5th definitive ed. 1926); *Études d'économie politique appliquée* (1st ed. 1898; 2nd ed. edited by Professor Leduc, 1936); *Études d'économie sociale* (1st ed. 1896; 2nd ed. edited by Leduc, 1936). The first volume (*leçons* 5-34) contains the great achievement. The second volume contains supplements, some of which are of the first order of importance, especially those on money and credit. The third volume is, from our standpoint, of little interest. See his 'Autobiography' in *Giornale degli Economisti*, December 1908; his 'Bibliography' in *Revue du droit public et de la science politique*, May and June 1897; his correspondence with Jevons in *Journal des économistes*, June 1874; William Jaffé, 'Unpublished Papers and Letters of

[3] He acted, however (1866-8), as editor of *Le Travail*, an organ of the co-operative movement, to which he contributed currently.

Léon Walras,' *Journal of Political Economy*, April 1935; and J. R. Hicks, 'Léon Walras,' *Econometrica*, October 1934.

At the present time, when it would be hard to find a theorist who does not acknowledge Walras' influence, the statement will read strange that he formed no personal school. But the students of law who had the opportunity of listening to him at Lausanne were hardly accessible to his scientific message: his professorship brought him peace and security but very little influence. And his professional contemporaries were mostly indifferent or hostile. In France, practically no recognition was extended to him during his lifetime, though he found a few followers, such as Aupetit. In Italy, Barone was an early convert. Pantaleoni too was among the first to understand the importance of his work. It was through Pantaleoni, I believe, that he found his brilliant pupil and successor, Pareto,[4] who was the man to found what under the circumstances became a Paretian rather than a Walrasian 'school of Lausanne.' As a coherent school, this was, however, confined to Italy or almost so. In England, the parallel and much more powerful teaching of Marshall excluded any direct influence until Professor Bowley presented the gist of the Walras-Pareto system in textbook form (*Mathematical Groundwork*, 1924). The Germans (including the Austrians) saw nothing in Walras' work but the Austrian doctrines dressed up in the particularly repellent garb of mathematics. In the United States, Walras acquired two first-rank followers, Fisher and Moore, but was practically ignored by the rest of the profession. All along he had had stray admirers, of course. But it was only in the 1920's, that is to say, long after his ideas had won out and a decade or so after his death, that he got his due. 'If one wants to harvest quickly, one must plant carrots and salads; if one has the ambition to plant oaks, one must have the sense to tell oneself: my grandchildren will owe me this shade' [5]—so he once wrote to a friend.[6]

Without going for the moment into the question what the Jevons-Menger-Walras 'revolution' amounted to or whether or not it succeeded in creating a new engine of analysis, we shall now proceed with our survey of men and groups in order to get a provisional idea of the lay of the land in the general economics of that period. As in Chapter 4 of Part III, this survey will be carried out by countries.

2. England: [The Marshallian Age]

Before 1885, the year of grace in which A. Marshall delivered his Inaugural Lecture in Cambridge, the English situation may be characterized like this. There was plenty of good current work, factual in particular, such as New-

[4] Concerning Walras' influence on Aupetit, Barone, Pantaleoni, and Pareto, see below, secs. 3 and 5.

[5] Quotation from the Preface to Professor Étienne Antonelli's *L'Économie pure du capitalisme*, 1939. [Translation by J. A. S.]

[6] [The reader is reminded that J. A. S. intended to have all the biographical sketches (with their many references) printed in small type so that they could be treated virtually as footnotes.]

march's; there was no lack of occasional sparks such as are to be found in the writings of Bagehot or Cliffe Leslie; there was competent teaching, deriving from J. S. Mill, Cairnes, and Fawcett, worthily upholding the flag. But there was nothing out of the common except the message of Jevons, and this, so far as theory was concerned, was as yet not more than a voice crying in a wilderness of dead wood. An after-dinner speaker of 1876 admirably expressed a very general feeling [1] when he said that, though much remained for economists to do in the way of development and application of existing doctrine, *the great work had been done.* It was Marshall who changed all that and led out of the valley on to a sunlit height. In England, the period is emphatically the Marshallian Age. His success was as great as A. Smith's, if account be taken of the facts that a science must inevitably grow less accessible to the general public as its techniques develop and that Marshall had no winning political horse to back, such as free trade had been in its prime.

[(a) *Edgeworth, Wicksteed, Bowley, Cannan, and Hobson.*] Marshall's figure overshadowed not only those English economists who continued to dwell in the post-Millian stratum of analysis, such as Sidgwick and Nicholson, though neither was without merit; [2] but it also overshadowed Edgeworth and Wicksteed, who indeed lacked Marshall's range of comprehension, both of historical and contemporaneous fact and also his personal force but who were his intellectual equals within the compass of the theorist's craft.

Francis Ysidro Edgeworth (1845-1926), one of the successors of Senior in the political economy chair at Oxford (1891-1922) and editor or co-editor of the *Economic Journal* (1891-1926), descended from a family of the Anglo-Irish gentry and was, in everything except sports, a typical product of a classical Oxford education. Two masters have drawn pictures of the man and the thinker—Keynes in the *Economic Journal* (March 1926; the piece is reprinted in *Essays in Biography*, pp. 267 et seq.) and Bowley in *Econometrica* (April 1934)—to which I must be content to refer. But a few points must nevertheless be mentioned here in order to place him for us. First, I mention his utilitarianism, which strongly asserted itself from the beginning (*New and Old Methods of Ethics*, 1877) and looked so incongruous in a man whose mind was nothing if not 'cultured'; it did much to keep alive—quite unnecessarily—

[1] See W. S. Jevons, 'The Future of Political Economy,' *Fortnightly Review*, November 1876.

[2] The only work by Henry Sidgwick (1838-1900) that has to be mentioned here, is his *Principles of Political Economy* (1883, 3rd ed., 1901). Substantially in the Millian tradition, it improves upon it by the neatness of its conceptualization and offers many valuable suggestions even where, as in the theory of international values, it fails to follow them up or to follow them up correctly. The treatment of money and interest deserves particular notice. His old-fashioned method of hunting for the meaning of words has been mentioned already.

Joseph Shield Nicholson (1850-1927), who held the Edinburgh chair from 1880 to 1925, did excellent work on money but at the moment we are concerned only with his *Principles of Political Economy* (1893, 1897, 1901). Entirely unoriginal and dwarfed by Marshall's performance, the work was yet a creditable achievement.

the unholy alliance between economics and Benthamite philosophy on which I have commented repeatedly. But let me also repeat that in his case, as in that of Jevons, we can leave out the utilitarianism from any of his economic writings without affecting their scientific contents. Second, Edgeworth's name will stand forever in the history of statistics: I do not mean primarily his work on Index Numbers (see below, ch. 8, sec. 4) but his work on statistical methods and their foundations that centered in his Generalized Law of Error. Third, there is the long series of his papers on economic topics, the powerful originality of some of which, hidden as it was by quaint peculiarities of presentation (that not everyone will find as delightful as I do myself), has never except by a few been adequately appreciated. In actually novel contributions (indifference curve, contract curve, decreasing returns, general equilibrium, and so on) to the analytic apparatus of economics, they amount to as much as, *or more than*, do Marshall's *Principles*. Then, fourth, why was this great figure so entirely overshadowed by Marshall? The answer—which is interesting from the standpoint of the sociology of science and in particular of the question: what succeeds, and how and why?—seems to be this: Edgeworth lacked the force that produces impressive treatises and assembles adherents; amiable and generous,[3] he never asserted himself in any claims of his own; he was oversensitive on the one hand, overmodest on the other; he was content to take a backseat behind Marshall whom he exalted into Achilles; hesitating in conversation, absent-minded to a pathological degree, the worst speaker and lecturer imaginable, he was personally ineffective—unleaderly is, I think, the word. His *Papers Relating to Political Economy* (3 vols., 1925) together with *Mathematical Psychics* (1881, London School Reprint, 1932) contain practically all his work in economic theory. *Edgeworth's Contributions to Mathematical Statistics* have been summarized by Professor Bowley in a pamphlet published under the auspices of the Royal Statistical Society in 1928.

I wish that space permitted me to do justice to the personality of Philip Henry Wicksteed (1844-1927) as it radiated upon me, in 1906, during an hour's chat on the lawn in front of his house at Wantage—his repose that owed nothing to callousness, his benevolence that was not weakness, his simplicity that went so well with his refinement, his unassuming modesty that did not lack dignity. As it is, I can merely record that this theologian, who was a lecturer on Dante, stood somewhat outside of the economic profession —one of the reasons why his work, particularly excellent on the pedagogical side, did not leave a more discernible mark. Is it believable that his most original piece of work *An Essay on the Co-ordination of the Laws of Distribution* (1894, London School Reprint, 1932) went almost unnoticed, that two copies only were sold, and that even today Professor Stigler is the only economist I know to rate it at its true value? His *Common Sense of Political Econ-*

[3] I think that everyone who knew Edgeworth will approve of the epithet 'generous.' But his generosity was of a peculiar kind. It all went in the direction of Marshall and of the Ricardo-Mill inheritance. Alas for human nature! He was distinctly ungenerous to the Austrians, to Walras, to Wicksteed, and, for reasons I have not been able to understand, to H. L. Moore.

omy . . . (1910; new ed. together with *Selected Papers and Reviews*, introduction by Professor Lionel Robbins, 2 vols., 1933) contains several original points and is far more than a popularization of then established doctrines. Particularly in matters of foundations and of critical elucidation of concepts (for example, in connection with the theory of dimensions which he did much to advance in an article, 'On Certain Passages in Jevons' *Theory of Political Economy*' in the *Quarterly Journal of Economics*, April 1889), his ideas were much ahead of his time. The general complexion of his system is Jevonian—he was in fact the only Jevonian theorist of note—but he shook off so many old things that still stuck to Jevons' exposition and added so many corrections and developments—partly under Austrian influence—that he may be said to have worked out something that, though of course a revision of the marginal utility system, was his own.

Wicksteed was independent of Marshall rather than an opponent. Equally independent and still less of an opponent was Professor Bowley at the London School of Economics, the first part of whose career falls within the period under survey and who then developed what may be termed his scientific style, which anticipated the statement of scope in the constitution (section I) of the later Econometric Society: 'The advancement of economic theory in its relation to statistics and mathematics.' This program that Bowley was to carry out in a long series of publications was then novel and defined a distinctive position. But it attracted little notice at the time, the less so because Bowley did nothing to promote it by way of methodological declarations of policy. Another 'independent,' this one more of an opponent, was a vital teacher, also at the London School, and at that time better known both to the profession and to students, Cannan.[4] There were others whom we ought to, but cannot afford to, mention. Also, there was opposition, and not only from those who kept to older forms of thought. There were, of course, 'heretics' like Hobson.[5] More important, there were anti-theorists, like Sidney Webb,

[4] The readers of this book know Edwin Cannan (1861-1935) already from his *History of the Theories of Production and Distribution . . . from* 1776 *to* 1848 (1893) to which reference has been made repeatedly in Part III. This work, his editions of Adam Smith, his *History of Local Rates in England* (1896) constitute his main scholarly achievements. But nobody can peruse his lively short tracts on money and monetary policy without pleasure and profit. This of course entirely fails to do justice to the teacher and the man, his common sense, his lovable outspokenness, the strength of his convictions—virtues that, from standpoints other than our own, more than compensate for lack of analytic refinement.

[5] John A. Hobson (1858-1940), who had the good fortune to establish himself as an archheretic in the heyday of Marshallian supremacy and to survive into a time in which this had become a badge of honor, was in many respects a very interesting man—vital, versatile, and aggressive. He was an educated man—in the sense of having had a classical education—and an emotional radical, a combination that is responsible for much of the English social-science literature of that time. In economics he was self-taught in a wilful way that made him both able to see aspects that trained economists refused to see and unable to see others that trained economists took for granted. He could never understand why the professionals did not take to his message and, like

whom anything like analytic refinement moved to scorn.[6] But there was no opposition from anyone of comparable stature as an analyst: much more than Ricardo had ever done, Marshall actually commanded the scene. The great master who was also a masterful man—to some he looked pontifical—made almost the whole of the rising generation of English economists his pupils and followers.

[(b) *Marshall and His School.*] Marshall created a genuine school, the members of which thought in terms of a well-defined scientific organon and supplemented this bond by strong personal cohesion. Professor Pigou, his successor in the Cambridge chair; Professor Robertson, who succeeded Pigou; and Lord Keynes—to mention only a few of the most familiar names—were formed by his teaching and started from his teaching, however far they may have traveled beyond it. After 1930, Keynes himself and most of what may be termed the third generation did indeed renounce allegiance. But so far as purely scientific analysis is concerned, this means less than it seems to mean. And though some of them grew to dislike Marshall, not only his modes of thought but also his personal aura, his stamp is still upon them all.[7]

That school was—in a sense still is—a national one and very alive to its specifically English character. I have compared Marshall's success with A. Smith's. In fact, the former was still more spontaneous and immediate than was the latter: the *Principles* were received with a universal clapping of hands, and the newspapers, which at first were rather cold to the *Wealth*, vied with one another in complimentary full-dress reviews of the *Principles*. But one qualification imposes itself: abroad, Marshall's work never succeeded as had

---

so many of his type, was by no means averse to the comfortable explanation that his Marshallian opponents were actuated by an inquisitional propensity to crush dissent, if not by class interest: the possibility that, owing to his inadequate training, many of his propositions, especially his criticisms, might be provably wrong and due to nothing but failure to understand never entered his head, however often it was pointed out to him. Belated recognition came in Keynesian times mainly on account of his doctrine of underconsumption, which will be noticed below in ch. 8. From the long list of his books and pamphlets, it will suffice to mention: *The Physiology of Industry* (with A. F. Mummery; 1889); *The Evolution of Modern Capitalism* (1894; perhaps his best performance); *The Industrial System* (1909); *Gold, Prices, and Wages . . .* (1913); *The Economics of Unemployment* (1922). But nobody who wishes to understand the man and, incidentally, the economist's comedy—or tragedy—of errors should miss his delightful *Confessions of an Economic Heretic* (1938).

[6] In 1906 or 1907 Sidney Webb gave a course of lectures on method at the London School, one of which I attended. If it be safe to generalize from this lecture and its tone, he must have presented in that course just about what a German *Kathedersozialist* would have done. The lecturer said nothing about Marshall and his teaching. The implications were, however, strongly anti-Marshallian. The difference was not primarily political: Marshall was largely in sympathy with the aims of the Fabians (as they were at that time); the difference was primarily one of scientific method.

[7] This is not true of Professor Hicks, whose basis is much more Walrasian than Marshallian. This fact is more significant than is the spectacular breaking away of the Keynesians.

A. Smith's. The reason is not far to seek. Marshall's message—however much he liked the idea of being 'read by businessmen'—was after all a message to the economics profession. And the economists of all countries who were open to economic theory at all had by 1890 evolved or accepted systems that, however inferior in technique, were substantially like Marshall's in fundamental ideas. First and last, Marshall was, and felt himself to be, the great *English* economist of the period. But this does not alter the fact that Marshall's great work is the classical achievement of the period, that is, the work that embodies, more perfectly than any other, the classical situation that emerged around 1900. I believe that Lord Keynes meant to express a similar evaluation when he listed the publication of the *Principles* as the first of the three events in 1890 from which the 'modern age of British economics' is to be dated.[8] Although we shall have to move within its orbit throughout this Part, it will be convenient to assemble here the main points about Marshall's work as a whole.

The portrait of Alfred Marshall (1842-1924), the man, the academic man, the teacher, the thinker, has been painted with unsurpassable brilliance by Lord Keynes ('Alfred Marshall,' *Economic Journal*, September 1924, reprinted in *Essays in Biography*, 1933) and so has been the portrait of the tutelary deity of his life, Mrs. Marshall, whose memory can never be separated from his ('Mary Paley Marshall (1850-1944),' *Economic Journal*, June 1944). Two other references are strongly recommended to the reader's attention: the *Memorials of Alfred Marshall* (ed. by A. C. Pigou, 1925), and the article on 'The Place of Marshall's *Principles* in Economic Theory' by another leading Marshallian, Mr. G. F. Shove (*Economic Journal*, December 1942). An extensive and presumably complete list of Marshall's writings was published by Keynes in the *Economic Journal*, December 1924; it is reprinted in the *Memorials*. But the bulk of Marshall's published work is in the *Principles of Economics* (1st ed., 1890, described as Volume I until the 6th ed., 1910; in what follows, references are to the 4th, 1898); in *Industry and Trade* (1919); and *Money Credit and Commerce* (1923). The three volumes are all essential: nobody knows Marshall who knows only the *Principles*. They are supplemented by a posthumous volume of *Official Papers* (1926). For the rest, it must suffice to mention his *Pure Theory of Foreign Trade* and his *Pure Theory of Domestic Values* (privately printed, 1879, London School Reprint, 1st ed., 1930); his and Mrs. Marshall's *Economics of Industry* (1879), a most important stepping stone to the *Principles*; and, finally, the highly revealing address on 'The Old Generation of Economists and the New' (1896) published in the *Quarterly Journal of Economics*, January 1897.

Marshall and A. Smith have more in common than similarity of success and of position in the history of economics. Neglecting a number of time-

[8] *Economic Journal*, December 1940, p. 409. The other two events were the foundation of the Royal Economic Society (British Economic Association) and the completion of Palgrave's *Dictionary of Political Economy*. [Keynes was mistaken as to the date of the last event. Palgrave's *Dictionary* was completed in 1893 and published in 1894. The introduction by Palgrave is dated Christmas, 1893.]

bound differences, we find strong similarity in the visions or general conceptions of the process and, in particular, with respect to economic evolution. Also we find an approximately equal distribution of weights as between 'theory' and 'facts,' although Marshall's superior art succeeded in banishing mere narration from the pages of the *Principles*—so that to readers who neglect *Industry and Trade,* his treatment looks more 'purely theoretical' than it is and much more so than does A. Smith's. But the similarity extends still further to the aim, plan (I am not referring to non-essentials such as sequence of topics), and nature of the performance. Marshall was aware of this. He is reported to have said: 'It's all in A. Smith.' There is more in this remark than mere recognition of the fact that today's work necessarily grows out of yesterday's—there is recognition of kinship. And there is a final similarity: both the *Wealth* and the *Principles* are what they are, partly at least, because they are the result of the work of decades and fully matured, the products of minds that took infinite care, were patient of labor, and indifferent to the lapse of years. This is all the more remarkable because both Smith and Marshall were extremely anxious to preach their wisdom and to influence political practice—yet neither of them allowed himself to be hurried into print before his manuscripts were as perfect as he felt able to make them.[9]

A reader's guide through the *Principles* is superfluous, I trust. Suffice it, then, to say that Book v (Theory of the Equilibrium of Demand and Supply) contains the core of the analytic performance. Book vi on Distribution is an extensive application of the analysis of Book v. Book i presents first 'an economic history in one lecture,' so severely scaled down that what remains reads like a series of trivialities and almost entirely fails to convey the breadth and depth of the research that actually went into it; and second an almost unbelievably insular sketch of the history of economics. Book ii, Some Fundamental Notions (concepts), could have been written by any nineteenth-century hewer of wood and drawer of water. Books iii (Wants) and iv (Agents of Production) contain several novelties and, occasionally, deep insights (e.g. in ch. 12, §§ 11 and 12), all smothered by a mass of things that might have been improved by pruning.

The reader who pierces the highly polished surface, on which everything seems to be reduced to commonplace, is first of all struck by the tremendous wealth of analytic and factual detail, drilled into order by a stupendously skilled taskmaster to whom it never seems to have occurred that nothing will make a book more difficult than will the attempt to make it too easy. Everything finds its appointed niche in a vast structure and everything is, before being displayed in its niche, analytically chiseled into shape by an artist in neat and economical conceptualization. In the second place, that reader will

[9] To my mind this was wholly a virtue. Reason for a different opinion will be found in Keynes's essay. But Lord Keynes's arguments read like an *oratio pro domo*. And though Marshall did indeed lose some of the claims to priority he might have had in the matter of money, it is not true that delay of publication robbed him of any as regards the topics treated in the *Principles*. The position of the *Principles* would, in this respect, be no different if it had appeared in 1880.

discover a quality that comes near to constituting Marshall's chief claim to immortality: in Marshall he beholds not only a high-powered technician, a profoundly learned historian, a sure-footed framer of explanatory hypotheses, but above all a great economist. Unlike the technicians of today who, so far as the technique of theory is concerned, are as superior to him as he was to A. Smith, he understood the working of the capitalist process. In particular, he understood business, business problems, and businessmen better than did most other scientific economists, not excluding those who were businessmen themselves. He sensed the intimate organic necessities of economic life even more intensively than he formulated them, and he spoke therefore as one who has power and not like the scribes—or like the theorists who are nothing but theorists. I am afraid that this achievement—so remarkable in one who moved primarily within academic circles and largely shared their prejudices—together with the Olympian repose, which his attitudes to hotly debated practical problems display, accounts in part for the unpopularity that surrounds his name today.

In the third place, the reader who gets still further and knows how to see the analytic skeleton under the smooth skin and all the flesh will behold the apparatus of what we now call Partial Analysis, that is, the set of tools that have been forged for the purpose of analyzing the phenomena in relatively small sectors of the economy—individual 'industries' that are too small to call forth, through variations in their own outputs, prices, and demands for factors, repercussions in the social aggregates (especially in real and monetary national income), so that everything that happens outside of such sectors may be treated as given (see below, ch. 7, sec. 6). Book v is the classic masterpiece of this partial analysis that has been so much admired by some and so severely criticized by others. The questions involved will be discussed later on. At the moment another matter calls for our attention. The partial-analysis viewpoint is so much in evidence throughout Marshall's text, and the handy concepts of partial analysis that he forged or refurbished have been so generally received into current teaching that there is some excuse for those who see in Marshall the master of partial analysis and nothing more. All the same, this fails to do justice to the depth and range of Marshall's thought. It is not only that the wider conception of the general interdependence of all economic quantities receives intermittent attention in the *Principles:* Marshall actually formulated this wider conception—embryonically but still explicitly—in the notes XIV and XXI of the Appendix. And the *Memorials* contain a passage (p. 417), rightly emphasized by Mr. Shove in the article referred to above, that reads: 'My whole life has been given and will be given to presenting in realistic form as much as I can of my note XXI.' It seems fair, therefore, to list Marshall also among the builders of the general-equilibrium system as well as of the marginal utility analysis per se.

There is more to another opinion that restricts Marshall's achievement. His theoretical apparatus is strictly static. This does not prevent him from dealing with evolutionary phenomena or indeed any phenomena of economic life that are refractory to the application of the methods of statics. As Keynes pointed out in his *Treatise on Money* (II, p. 406), Marshall 'was a little disposed sometimes to camouflage the essentially static character of his equilibrium theory with many wise and penetrating *obiter dicta* on dynamical problems.' But in order to do so he had to get off the driver's seat of his analytic engine, the arms of which do not reach these problems: the range of the *Principles* is much wider than that of the theory which the work expounds, and the theory itself is impaired by the strain to which it is subject, especially in the neighborhood of the phenomena of decreasing average cost.

In the fourth place, no unbiased reader can fail to perceive the twin *facts* that will be fully discussed later on, namely, that Marshall's theoretical structure, barring its technical superiority and various developments of detail, is fundamentally the same as that of Jevons, Menger, and especially Walras, but that the rooms in this new house are unnecessarily cluttered up with Ricardian heirlooms, which receive emphasis quite out of proportion to their operational importance. It is therefore understandable that a few English writers and the majority of non-English ones have put Marshall down as an eclectic, who tried to reconcile and to combine (or to compromise between) the analytic principles of the English 'classical school' (meaning Ricardianism) and the analytic principles of the 'marginal utility school' (meaning, mainly, Jevons and the Austrians). It is not less understandable that both Marshall himself and the Marshallians refused to accept this interpretation, not without irritation. They are right. Marshall's powerful engine of analysis—though it may look antiquated by now—was the result of a creative effort and not of a synthetic one: especially those will have to admit this who, like myself, discount the importance of the Ricardianism in it. This leads, however, to the questions of the roots of Marshall's work and of its originality. These questions are no mere matters of dusty records. They must be answered in order to light up an important phase in the history of economics.

The roots of Marshall's work are easy to lay bare. As an economist, he was trained, or rather trained himself, in the tradition of A. Smith, Ricardo, and J. S. Mill. In particular, his acquaintance with economics commenced with reading Mill in 1867-8 (*Memorials*, p. 10), and he retained what might be called a filial respect for J. S. Mill throughout his life though he was under no delusion concerning the latter's intellectual stature. In addition, the preface to the first edition of the *Principles* extends guarded recognition to the influence of Cournot and Thünen, which is indeed unmistakable. No economist other than these five, not even Jevons, Dupuit, or Jenkin,[10] is credited with

[10] H. C. Fleeming Jenkin (1833-85) was an economist of major importance, whose main papers belong chronologically to the previous period but who has been reserved for discussion here because these papers form an obvious stepping stone between J. S. Mill and Marshall in four important respects: he was the first *Englishman* to discuss, with nearly the same clearness as had Verri and Cournot, demand functions; he both developed and applied to problems of taxation the concept of consumers' rent; he used diagrammatic representation, in principle, much as Marshall did later on; and he greatly improved the theory of wages, particularly in the matter of the influence of trade unions upon wage rates. In addition, like Sismondi but much more neatly, he

any influence on fundamentals, though many are recognized on individual points of minor importance. But the resulting picture is entirely possible. We have noticed the peculiar character of J. S. Mill's treatise, which hovers between Ricardo and Say and invites corrective reformulation. A man such as Marshall, who was trained in mathematics and physics and to whom the concept of limits and hence the formal part of the marginal principle would be as familiar as would be his breakfast bacon, need only have allowed his mind to play on Mill's loose statements and to work out their exact model (system of equations) in order to arrive at a point where the purely theoretical parts of the *Principles* came in sight. The incidental innovations would then naturally appear to him as mere developments from Mill instead of as 'revolutionary.' Moreover, strong leaders who are sure of a disciplined majority do not make revolutions—either in science or in politics—but lead on smoothly, leaving fuss and revolution to minority groups that have to shout in order to be heard at all. I think that this agrees pretty well with the opinion espoused by the Marshallians.[11] In any case it is my justification for attributing to Marshall (within pure theory, remember) *creative* achievement.

By this admission we have already prejudged the question of originality. Though Marshall never left any doubt that he felt under no obligation to Jevons, let alone to the Austrians and Walras, the full extent of his claim to *subjective* originality was not known to the world before the publication of the *Memorials*, Keynes's biographical essay, and Shove's paper. This claim is accepted here without question. Of course, this does not touch *objective* originality or priority. A 'marginalist' treatise published in 1890—or, for that matter, in 1880—could have improved and developed existing doctrine (which Marshall certainly did) but it could not have revealed fundamentally new truth. According to what I believe to be the ordinary standards of scientific historiography, such merit as there was in the rediscovery of the marginal utility principle is Jevons'; the system of general equilibrium (including the

suggested a time-labor system, essentially the 'guaranteed wage.' He was an engineer, first a practical, later an academic one, and his contributions to economics passed all but unnoticed. But Marshall referred to him. See Colvin and Ewing eds., *Papers, Literary and Scientific* (1887), with a life by no lesser celebrity than R. L. Stevenson. However, there is now a London School Reprint of Jenkin's economic essays with the title, *The Graphic Representation of the Laws of Supply and Demand, and other Essays on Political Economy*, 1868-1884 (1931).

[11] If I take, as I think I may, Mr. Shove's article as the official pronouncement of the Marshallian group, there remains, so far, only one point of difference. Mr. Shove holds, supporting his statement by quotation, that the basis of Marshall's work is to be found in Ricardo rather than in Mill. With Mr. Shove's interpretation of Ricardo and Mill, which minimizes the difference between them, this does not matter a great deal. With my interpretation of the relation between the two, it makes more difference—which roughly coincides with the admission of, or refusal to admit, the importance of the role of J. B. Say in the emergence of Marshallian economics. There is no really practicable bridge between Ricardo and Marshall, though one can, no doubt, be built. There is a bridge, already in existence, between Mill (or even Smith) and Marshall.

theory of barter) is Walras'; the principle of substitution and the marginal productivity theory are Thünen's; the demand and supply curves and the static theory of monopoly are Cournot's (as is the concept, though not the word, price elasticity); the consumers' rent is Dupuit's; the 'diagrammatic method' of presentation is also Dupuit's or else Jenkin's. If this had been always clearly understood, there would be no more to be said.[12] But it has not been generally understood—perhaps it is not even understood now by *all* economists[13]—with the result that the reputation of others has suffered and that there exists, in many minds, a picture of the scientific situation of that time that it is the duty of the historian to correct. This duty is painful because the reason for this state of opinion is largely Marshall's own fault. The case of the Austrians versus Marshall (and Edgeworth) will be considered later and therefore need not be touched upon here. In striking contrast to the generosity he lavished on Ricardo and Mill, Marshall was less than generous to all those whose contributions were closely related to his own. The one exception is Thünen, whose work was properly recognized not only in a general way in the Preface to the first edition of the *Principles* but also in the passage (p. 704 of the 1st ed.) that speaks of 'von Thünen's great Law of Substitution.' But Cournot received only general recognition and is not referred to where we should have expected specific reference, primarily in the theory of monopoly. However, we are not concerned with leveling any indictment against Marshall on the score of inadequate acknowledgment of *indebtedness*—of this charge Keynes and Shove have largely cleared him—but with his inadequate acknowledgment of *priority*. The case of Jevons is the most obvious one. But the case of Walras is worse. Marshall, of all men, mathematically trained as he was, entertaining as he did the highest opinion of the central importance of his own note XXI, cannot have been blind to the greatness as well as to the priority of Walras' achievement. Yet Walras' great name occurs in the *Principles* only on three unimportant occasions that have nothing to do with that achievement.[14] And exactly the same holds for the

12 The question of the propriety of making, even by implication only, claims to independent discovery of results that to the knowledge of the claimant have appeared in print before is one that everyone of us must settle for himself. Some have scorned to do so.

13 Time and again, I have been impressed by the fact that competent and even eminent economists have an uncritical habit of attributing to Marshall what should, in the 'objective' sense, be attributed to others (even the 'Marshallian' demand curve!). But we need not go beyond the Cambridge circle. On pp. 222 et seq. of the *Essays in Biography*, Keynes attempted to list, 'with the help of notes supplied by Professor Edgeworth,' some of the 'more striking contributions to knowledge' contained in the *Principles*. There are six of them (excepting the comment on the historical introduction), all evidently meant to be taken as objective novelties. Not one of them can be accepted without qualifying reference to the work of others, though in conjunction and as elements of a general treatise for a wider circle of readers, they were of course new enough.

14 Edgeworth, too, was sadly ungenerous to Walras as well as to the Austrians. But his lack of generosity was somewhat like the lovable ungenerosity of devoted mothers

less important cases of Dupuit and Fleeming Jenkin, who received but footnote recognition and this not in the right places. I hasten to emphasize extenuating circumstances. One of them has been formulated by Lord Keynes: Marshall perceived in the work of Jevons and the Austrians technical faults and other inadequacies that might have impaired the success of the new organon unless the offending authors were kept at arm's length. There are other such circumstances. Continuity of analytic work is an asset, and the originators of the new theoretical system, or at least Jevons and the Austrians, had needlessly broadened the gulf that separated them from their predecessors. Also Marshall was very conscious of his role as a *national* leader. He may have felt it his duty to uphold the national tradition.

Fortunately, however, I can conclude on a more pleasant note. The greatest thing about Marshall's great work still remains to be said. Behind the great achievement there is a still greater message. More than any other economist —with the exception, perhaps, of Pareto—Marshall pointed beyond himself. He had no theory of monopolistic competition. But he pointed toward it by considering a firm's Special Market. It has been stated above that his pure theory was strictly static but also that he pointed toward economic dynamics. He did no econometric work. But he always reasoned with an eye to the statistical complement of economic theory and did his best to frame concepts that would be statistically operational; and in his address on 'The Old Generation of Economists and the New' he outlined important parts of the program of modern econometrics. Naturally, his work is out of date. But there is in it a living spring that prevents it from becoming stale.

3. France

The French situation from 1870 to 1914 was curious indeed. Walras was at work (to 1892 or thereabouts) and Cournot was emerging from oblivion. In the factual branch of analysis, there were LePlay and his school, Simiand, Levasseur, Mantoux, Martin, and many others.[1] Counting peak performances only, we might feel inclined to put French economics at the head of all countries. But, excepting those of the factual branch, the peak achievements almost entirely failed to percolate, and there were hardly any symptoms of that wider activity that makes up lost ground so rapidly in our own day.[2] The indifferent

---

and wives who cannot see any merit in competitors of their wholly admirable sons or husbands. He was never, so far as I know, ungenerous on his own behalf.

[1] Concerning LePlay, see above, Part III, ch. 4; Simiand and Levasseur are discussed in ch. 4 of this Part.

[2] But mention must be made of the Walrasian work of Aupetit and the textbook presentations of Walrasian or Paretian doctrine by Laurent and Antonelli. Albert Aupetit's *Essai sur la théorie générale de la monnaie* (1901), a youthful work of striking quality that still deserves perusal, marks a not unimportant step in the theory of money but is mentioned here because of the still greater significance of the relatively early reformulation of Walrasian equilibrium theory it presents. Hermann Laurent (1841-1908) wrote a brief but very good abstract of the Walras-Pareto theory (*Petit*

reputation of academic French economics in that period is, however, not due to its deficiencies in the field of 'pure theory'—and there is no reason to think little of it so far as applied fields are concerned—but to something else that will preclude recognition by modern radicals *a limine*, namely, to liberalism in the Gladstonian sense. So obvious were the political affiliations of the leading group of French economists and so completely did their politics dominate every line they wrote that we have no choice but to adopt political criteria for the rest of this sketch.

Accordingly, we consider first the laissez-faire ultras who are known as the Paris group because they controlled the *Journal des économistes*, the new dictionary, the central professional organization in Paris, the Collège de France, and other institutions as well as most of the publicity—so much so that their political or scientific opponents began to suffer from a persecution complex. It is extremely difficult, even at this distance of time, to do justice to this group that was also a school in our sense. I shall mention only a few names that will guide any interested reader to its works and, instead of characterizing individuals, attempt to characterize, in a few lines, the group as a whole. The most distinguished names, then, were Paul Leroy-Beaulieu, Courcelle-Seneuil once more, Levasseur, the indefatigable Gustave de Molinari, Yves Guyot, Maurice Block,[3] and Léon Say. They were anti-*étatistes*, that is to say they indulged in a belief to the effect that the main business of economists is to refute socialist doctrines and to combat the atrocious fallacies implied in all plans of social reform and of state interference of any kind. In particular, they stood staunchly by the drooping flag of unconditional free trade and laissez-faire. This accounts easily for their unpopularity with socialists, radicals, Catholic reformers, solidarists, and so on, though it should not count for us. But what does count for us is the fact that their analysis was methodologically as 'reactionary' as was their politics. They simply did not care for the purely scientific aspects of our subject. J. B. Say and Bastiat, and later on a little diluted marginal utility theory, satisfied their scientific appetite. Some who sympathized with the politics of the group—though they were no members of its inner circle and are hence, very significantly, mentioned but rarely—took a higher flight and did notable work. This holds particularly for two men who should always be listed among economists of eminence, Colson and Cheysson. It is not without importance to note that both were engineers by training and in this respect continued a French tradition that is adorned by

Traité d'économie politique mathématique, 1902) and Professor Étienne Antonelli actually risked a Walrasian course of lectures at the Collège Libre des Sciences Sociales that he published in 1914 under the title *Principes d'économie pure*—a pioneer venture. There were various writings on 'mathematical economics,' some of which will be mentioned later. They had little influence.

[3] Leroy-Beaulieu and Courcelle-Seneuil are discussed above, Part III, ch. 4. Maurice Block's survey work, *Le Progrès de la science économique depuis Adam Smith* (1890; 2nd ed., 2 vols., 1897), will be mentioned as a fair specimen of what the school conceived of as purely analytic work. Neither should Leroy-Beaulieu's *Essai sur la répartition des richesses* (1881) go unnoticed.

the name of Dupuit and is now more alive than ever: if I were willing to use the term School in any other sense than that adopted in this book, I should certainly form a school from those brilliant French engineers in the public service who contributed, and are contributing, so substantially to scientific economics.[4]

But even the others, whose flights cannot be described as high, had one great merit. Their philosophies were deplorable, their theory was weak; but when they wrote on practical questions they, like their predecessors and like Marshall, *knew what they were writing about*. That is to say, they lived and thought in close proximity to business and political practice, which most of them knew from experience and not from newspapers. There is an atmosphere of realism and shrewdness about their works that partly compensates for lack of scientific inspiration.[5]

The politicians can hardly have liked a group that stood for free trade and otherwise indulged in an impracticable liberalism. So, when the government proceeded to establish chairs in economics in all the law faculties of all the universities of France (1878), it saw to it that the new professors should not all of them be of the political complexion of the Paris group. This wrought a change, of course, but—apart from bringing the light of economics to the most unfortunate provinces that had had to dwell in outer darkness until then —this change was at the beginning more political than scientific. However, the new men who felt themselves to be new men in more senses than one drew together, founded the 'heterodox' *Revue d'économie politique* (1887), doubted (most of them) the Natural Law that booms laissez-faire, looked with

[4] Clément Colson (1853-1939) did not follow the vocation for which he was trained but was a public servant in the term's widest and most honorific acceptance. We cannot go into his many activities—which included teaching—and merits. It must suffice to mention his *Transports et tarifs* (1890), which still repays perusal, and his *Cours d'économie politique* (1901-7), a work that is not equally commendable in all its parts but rises to considerable heights in places, especially in transportation.

Émile Cheysson (1836-1910; *Oeuvres choisies*, 1911) was another man of many merits. I shall only refer to a *conférence* of his that was published in 1887 under the title 'Statistique géometrique.' It brims over with suggestions, some of powerful originality, on statistical demand, revenue, and cost curves, location and transportation rates (he has a sort of rate-indifference curve), wages (where he develops a model of the kind that is now known as 'cobweb'), sales as functions of wages, rational choice of sources of raw materials, quality, variation of product, profit maximization. I am indebted to Dr. H. Staehle for having pointed out to me this amazing assemblage of tools and ideas that I should otherwise have overlooked.

[5] The frank contempt with which both higher-powered theorists and anti-liberals treated the group is therefore not justified. Take Yves Guyot (1843-1928) to whom a brilliant theorist has referred as *ce pauvre Guyot*. This theorist was perhaps right if he had, e.g., Pareto in mind as a standard of comparison. But I have to add that, were I a businessman or politician, I should have consulted Guyot—who was a wizard at practical diagnosis—rather than Pareto in order to be enlightened on, say, the prospects of employment or of metal prices in the next six months. We are all of us liable to deserve the epithet *ce pauvre* if we are made to confront a task very much out of our line.

more favor on protection that was carrying the day anyhow, and allowed themselves to be caught in modest programs of social reform. Scientifically, very little came of this at first. But in the course of the thirty-five years, counting from those appointments, by the grace of the spirit of the times, substantial improvement was effected and not only by the new professors themselves; the Paris milieu was livened up, though the little knot of laissez-faire stalwarts, not less remarkable for longevity than for strength of conviction, held out like Leonidas' Spartans at Thermopylae. As for representative names, it will suffice to mention P. L. Cauwès, who, more a jurist than an economist and influenced by German *Sozialpolitik* and German historism, was a man of sense and force even if not much of a scientific economist; Charles Gide and Charles Rist, who rose into prominence later on; [6] and two men whose performances were among the first harbingers of a new epoch in French economics, Landry and Aftalion.[7] So far as I know, none of the groups that expounded systems of social reconstruction, socialists and solidarists included, made any contribution to be noticed in a history of analysis.[8]

4. Germany and Austria

As we know, in Germany *Sozialpolitik* and the work of the historical school asserted their influence upon general economics more than in any other country. These interests did not entirely destroy tradition nor did they entirely crush out the 'theoretical' component in general economics. But in places they came near doing so: although a reaction had set in by 1900 and was running strong by 1914, the men who were then in their twenties were practically untrained in the art of handling analytic tools and some of them actually conceived of 'theory' as consisting of philosophies about socialism or individualism and the like and of quarrels about 'methods'—they had no conception of theory as a 'box of tools.' Broadly speaking, genuinely home-grown theory was insignificant and anaemic and the only live impulses came from the Austrian and the Marxist schools. The situation, thoroughly decentralized as it was—much as in the preceding period—is difficult to describe by means

[6] Charles Gide (1847-1932) cannot occupy any great place in a history of analysis but played a most useful and most creditable role all the same. He was an all-round leader, free from prejudice, in sympathy with all that was going on, and made by nature for imparting this sympathy to others. He wrote one of the most successful textbooks of the period, and, in collaboration with C. Rist, a still more successful *Histoire des doctrines économiques* (1st ed., 1909; 7th ed., 1947; English trans., 1915; with additions from 6th and 7th French eds., 1948) that is widely used still. There were several other performances in this field (Perin, Espinas, Denis, Dubois, Rambaud, Gonnard).

[7] Adolphe Landry, *L'Intérêt du capital* (1904). Aftalion and Juglar will be mentioned in ch. 8 in the fields to which their works belong.

[8] Professor G. H. Bousquet's *Essai sur l'évolution de la pensée économique* (1927), Gaëtan Pirou's *Les Doctrines économiques* (1925), and the well-known *History* by Gide and Rist will usefully complement the sketch above.

of a brief sketch. Simplifying to the utmost, I propose to deal with it as follows: we shall first consider the Austrian school; then we shall glance at a number of representative men who form a group in no sense except that they had laid the foundations of their reputations in the preceding period and exerted considerable influence—as 'elder statesmen'—in the one under survey; finally, reserving the Marxists for separate treatment at the end of the chapter, we shall add additional representative names that will serve to complete the picture, begun in the preceding chapter, of the 'life and work' of German economics so far as impressionist patches of color can be said to complete any picture. In all three subsections *this purpose of painting a picture that must not be overcrowded has been kept in view at considerable 'pain-cost' of injustice to many individuals.*[1]

(a) *The Austrian or Viennese School.* The close cultural relations that existed between the Austro-Hungarian monarchy and Germany did not prevent the emergence in Austria of a scientific situation in our field that differed completely from the German one. This was largely due to two personal facts: to the fact that Carl Menger was a leader of quite unusual force; and to the fact that he found two disciples, Böhm-Bawerk and Wieser, who were his intellectual equals and who completed Menger's success. They cannot really be called second generation but have title to be considered as co-founders of what, considering all circumstances, was to be a school of surprising importance and durability. There were several other followers of some note (such as Sax and Zuckerkandl), and of course a second generation did rise within the period. But I think it to be both right and conducive to a correct impression to confine this subsection to those two [2] leaders and to two other men who, personally rather than doctrinally, stood somewhat apart and never got all the credit they deserve, Auspitz and Lieben.

Eugen von Böhm-Bawerk (1851-1914) was, so far as his career was concerned, primarily a public servant. This must be kept in mind in appraising his scientific work, exactly as Ricardo's business avocations must be kept in mind if we are to do justice to his. *What is before us to read is not the finished work that Böhm-Bawerk had in mind*—parts of the published performance were written in a hurry, the consequences of which Böhm-Bawerk never had the opportunity to remedy. In order to show this, let us cull a few relevant facts from the record of a life conspicuous for single-minded devotion to duty, complete disinterestedness, high intellectual endeavor, wide cultural interests,

[1] In this respect, I am all the more open to criticism because I cannot plead ignorance of the details of what is for me a very familiar scene. But some of the lacunae of my exposition can be filled from many sources, especially from the two following *Festschriften,* which shed light on the period under survey although only one appeared in the period: (1) the Schmoller Festschrift of 1908: *Die Entwicklung der deutschen Volkswirtschaftslehre im neunzehnten Jahrhundert;* (2) the Brentano Festschrift of 1925: *Die Wirtschaftswissenschaft nach dem Kriege,* especially Professor Amonn's contribution, 'Der Stand der reinen Theorie' (vol. II, part 3).

[2] Von Philippovich will be mentioned below. L. von Mises, whose book on money appeared at the end of the period, will be mentioned in our chapter on money.

and genuine simplicity—all of which was entirely free from sanctimoniousness or any propensity to preach. His early scientific development must have been seriously interfered with by his entering the civil service immediately on completing the usual legal studies that, as we know, left but little room for economics. He was thirty when he was appointed to the University of Innsbruck, and the eight years he taught there define the whole of the time that he was able to devote, in the plenitude of his powers, to scientific economics. He was a hard, systematic, and effective worker, and we need not, perhaps, deduct very much from his fund of energy on the score of academic teaching. More of it, however, went into his polemics, by which he established himself as by far the most eminent champion of Menger's teaching.[3] The rest went into the chief work of his life, *Kapital und Kapitalzins* (1st vol., 1884; 4th ed., 1921; English trans., 1890; 2nd vol., 1889; 4th ed., 1921; English trans., 1891). Volume I, *Geschichte und Kritik der Kapitalzinstheorien* appeared in English as *Capital and Interest;* Volume II, *Positive Theorie des Kapitales* as *Positive Theory of Capital.* Work on the second volume that contains his own creative contribution—the first contains a series of criticisms of interest theories—had to be curtailed and the volume had to be hurried through the press in parts as the author wrote it—anticipating his re-entry into the Ministry of Finance for the purpose of preparing the great fiscal reform of 1896. Distinct ideas are but imperfectly welded together; in essential respects the author changed his standpoints while writing; different currents of his own thought run side by side; the decisive later chapters are frankly provisional (see Preface to the unchanged 2nd ed.) and as he was *able* to make them, not as he *wanted* to make them. A brilliant but absorbing career followed from 1889 to 1904, during which he held cabinet office three times and had no more leisure than is implied in scanty leaves of absence and occasional hours that he snatched from official work, especially in the early mornings. Even so he kept up a peripherical relation with academic teaching (he was Honorary Professor at the University of Vienna, occasionally conducting a seminar). Also he was able to do some writing of a polemical or expository nature. Among other things, he produced his famous criticism of the Marxist system.[4] But he was not able to do original work. Leisure came indeed in 1905, when (refusing the most lucrative post in the gift of the Crown) he accepted appointment as 'ordinary' (full) professor at the University of Vienna. This spelled freedom from all but self-imposed duties and also from the petty vexations of modern life, since all 'authorities' of that environment were infinitely respectful to the Privy Councilor full of honors. But he was older in mind and body than in years. Though he conducted his famous seminar to his death (1914), his creative force was spent. He did work at his *Kapital* and added formidable appendices, but no *real* progress was possible any more. The revised and en-

[3] These and later parerga of his have been republished as *Gesammelte Schriften* (2 vols., 1924-6) by Professor Franz X. Weiss, one of the ablest of Böhm-Bawerk's pupils.

[4] *Zum Abschluss des Marxschen Systems* (1896) translated as *Karl Marx and the Close of His System* (1898). [New edition (with Hilferding's reply), ed. with introduction by P. M. Sweezy, 1949.]

larged third edition of *Kapital und Kapitalzins* was published in three volumes, 1909-14 [volume II was expanded into two volumes, II, 1 and II, 2]; an unchanged fourth edition with an introduction by von Wieser appeared in 1921.

Let us neglect Böhm-Bawerk's championship of the marginal utility principle, his critique of Marx, and a few other things that might be mentioned, and ask what was the nature and significance of his main contribution. The answer that most people are likely to return is: a theory of interest and, in connection with it, the 'period of production.' This answer is wholly inadequate. The Böhm-Bawerkian theory of interest and, incidentally, the Böhm-Bawerkian period of production are only two elements in a comprehensive model of the economic process, the roots of which may be discerned in Ricardo and which parallels that of Marx. Part of it is, naturally, a complete theory of distribution—not of interest alone—that culminates in 'The Capital Market fully Developed' (see Part 2 of *Positive Theorie*, Book IV, 3rd and 4th eds.), where the stock of goods, the period of turnover, wages, and interest are simultaneously determined. If we wish to label his place in the history of economics, we had better call him the bourgeois Marx.[5]

There is thus a Ricardian root to Böhm-Bawerk's achievement[6] though he was entirely unaware of it. Equally unaware was he of the fact that he had been anticipated, in one essential point by Rae.[7] Finally, much more definitely, he was anticipated by Jevons—his relation to the latter is not unlike that of Marshall. Occasional anticipations on this point or that occur fairly frequently, one of them, as we have seen, in Senior and another in Newcomb's *Principles*. Subjectively, however, he was so completely the enthusiastic disciple of Menger that it is hardly necessary to look for other *influences*. It is not only that he followed Menger in matters of value and price: even the two propositions that the productivity of a given 'quantity' of capital can be increased by extending the period of production and that we habitually undervalue future pleasures as compared with present ones—two cornerstones as we shall see of the specifically Böhm-Bawerkian theory of capital and interest—had been indicated by

[5] There is a good reason as well as a bad one for the surprise the reader is likely to feel as he reads this statement. The good reason is that Marx was much more than an economist. Of course, the statement refers only to Marx's *economic* theory of the capitalist process. The bad reason is that when thinking of Marx, we have habitually in mind what are non-essentials from the standpoint of this book—the agitatorial gesture, the prophetic wrath. Leaving these out and looking at the cold analytic steel frame below, the reader will not find my statement so surprising. Böhm-Bawerk's marginalism makes but a technical difference; being a more efficient tool, it clears from his path the spurious problems that Marx encountered on his.

[6] This has been pointed out repeatedly by Professor Knight and also by Dr. Edelberg (see above, Part III, ch. 4, sec. 2).

[7] When he wrote the original work, Böhm-Bawerk did not know more of Rae than the quotations in Mill that do not reveal the core of Rae's analysis. He used Rae in the 3rd ed. See on this C. W. Mixter ('Böhm-Bawerk on Rae,' *Quarterly Journal of Economics*, May 1902), who, however, greatly overstates the case for Rae.

Menger.[8] It is this rather than Jevons' priority that raises the question of Böhm-Bawerk's originality. It could be argued that a man who had it in him to develop such embryonic suggestions into an imposing organic whole hardly needed any suggestions at all. But it is not necessary to do so. It is Böhm-Bawerk's model or schema of the economic process adumbrated above which makes him one of the great architects of economic science, and this schema was quite outside Menger's as well as Jevons' range of vision.

A few of the best minds in our field, Wicksell and Taussig [9] in particular, have in fact considered him as such. But much more numerous, from the first, were critics and detractors. This is due, in the first place, to Böhm-Bawerk's reserve, which, though he had very many pupils, prevented him from turning them, as did Marshall, into disciples: hence he never acquired a scientific bodyguard that would stand ready to sally forth in his defense. In the second place, the famous controversialist had accumulated many accounts that some people were not slow in settling.[10] In the third place, as explained above, Böhm-Bawerk's work had not been permitted to mature: it is essentially (not formally) a first draft whose growth into something much more perfect was arrested and never resumed. Moreover, it is doubtful whether Böhm-Bawerk's primitive technique and in particular his lack of mathematical training would ever have allowed him to attain perfection. Thus, the work, besides being very difficult to understand, bristles with inadequacies that invite criticism—for instance, as he put it, the 'production period' is next to being nonsense—and impedes his reader's progress to the core of his thought. In consequence, criticism of individual points was often successful, and such piecemeal defeats injured the reputation of the whole. He even got criticism from such eminently fair-minded men as Irving Fisher, who seems never to have realized how much his *Theory of Interest* owes to Böhm-Bawerk, though he, of all men, was certainly anxious and even over-anxious to do justice to any predecessors he could find. By the time Keynes wrote his *Treatise*, it was

[8] This is the more noteworthy because Menger, far from welcoming that theory as a development of suggestions of his, severely condemned it from the first. In his somewhat grandiloquent style he told me once: 'The time will come when people will realize that Böhm-Bawerk's theory is one of the greatest errors ever committed.' He deleted those hints in his 2nd edition.

[9] That eminent man (Taussig) told me once (I *think* it was in the spring of 1914) that he considered Böhm-Bawerk the greatest economist of all times, excepting Ricardo alone (or even that he considered Ricardo and Böhm-Bawerk, on a par, the two greatest economists: I do not remember which).

[10] Let us note in passing the indictment of unfairness in criticism that has been so often leveled at Böhm-Bawerk, e.g. by Marshall. As raised, I believe this indictment to be without foundation. But Böhm-Bawerk's was an advocate's mind. He was unable to see anything but the letter of the opponent's argument and never seems to have asked himself whether the offending letter did not cover some element of truth. This often impaired his critical argument, though his criticism nevertheless remains the best existing series of exercises in theoretical thinking of that type. It is thus understandable that unsympathetic readers of his sometimes derived an impression that is voiced by that indictment.

an almost general opinion that Böhm-Bawerk's theory was just a curious error —and not to be discussed seriously any more. And yet his ideas keep on turning up and *teaching people, critics and detractors included, their business.* This, in fact, his ideas had done from the first: though Böhm-Bawerk got few compliments, and acquired few disciples, he was and still is one of the profession's great teachers.[11]

Friedrich von Wieser (1851-1926) was a very different man. He was a born thinker, and a brief spell of civil service in his youth and a still briefer spell of cabinet office in his middle sixties were the only interruptions in a pacific and uneventful academic career in Prague and Vienna. This thinker is, however, difficult to characterize. The great thing about him was a spacious vision that went deep below the surface. But he implemented this vision very imperfectly, for he not only lacked, like Böhm-Bawerk, the necessary technical training, but in addition, the natural aptitude for turning out an effective argument. His sociology, which merits more attention than it has received (*Recht und Macht*, 1910; *Gesetz der Macht*, 1926), has been already mentioned; his significant contribution to the theory of money will be mentioned in the appropriate place. Of his three great works in general theory, the first, *Über den Ursprung und die Hauptgesetze des wirthschaftlichen Werthes* (1884) has the merit of re-emphasizing and developing the Mengerian argument on value (he coined the term *Grenznutzen*, marginality) and no other, though even that meant a great deal at the time; the second, *Der Natürliche Werth* (1889; English trans., 1893) worked out the Austrian theories of cost and distribution (he coined the phrase *Zurechnung*, imputation), which Menger had not more than sketched, and this work must in spite of the latter fact and also in spite of glaring faults of technique, rank high as an original achievement; the third, *Theorie der gesellschaftlichen Wirtschaft* (in M. Weber's *Grundriss der Sozialökonomik*, I, 1914; English trans. *Social Economics*, 1927), while adding nothing essentially new, is an impressive summary of a lifetime's economic thought. History knows him—the extent to which it knows him, however, varies greatly from historian to historian—chiefly as the man who rounded out the Austrian structure, though some of his ideas were more akin to those of Walras than to those of Menger. The best appreciation of his significance as a theorist is to be found in Professor Stigler's book, to which reference is here made

[11] This holds true independently of the Böhm-Bawerkian revival incident to the great success, in the early 1930's, of Professor von Hayek's theory of business cycles. Professor Knight was not tilting at windmills when he opened his vigorous attack upon Böhm-Bawerk's teaching in 1933 ('Capitalist Production, Time, and the Rate of Return,' *Economic Essays in Honour of Gustav Cassel*) and 1934 ('Capital, Time, and the Interest Rate,' *Economica*, August) that evoked a lively controversy (for main items see N. Kaldor, 'The Recent Controversy on the Theory of Capital,' *Econometrica*, July 1937). Unfortunately, the essential point about Böhm-Bawerk's message has been only occasionally noticed or brushed against in this literature.

once for all.[12] His *Gesammelte Abhandlungen* have been edited, with a biographical introduction, by Professor von Hayek (1929).

Space does not permit more than a brief reference to the work of two remarkable men: Rudolf Auspitz (1837-1906), an industrialist who fought the cartel that increased his profits (which increase he handed over to his employees), a politician who was co-author of the bill that introduced the progressive income tax, and Richard Lieben (1842-1919), his relation and scientific collaborator, a private banker of artistic tastes. They produced one of the outstanding theoretical performances of the age, the *Untersuchungen über die Theorie des Preises* (1889; the first part was published separately in 1887; French trans., 1914). Technically, they were immensely superior to their compatriots and both because of this and because they put partial-analysis problems into the foreground, their work looks less 'Austrian' than it is. It received some recognition from Edgeworth and more from Irving Fisher, but was without honor at home. Their total and marginal supply and demand curve apparatus (they did not use average curves) was an original contribution at the time, as was the general theory of the appendix that was not noticed at all.

I have described the Austrian school as the one of the two live influences in German general economics. But this influence did not assert itself perceptibly until after 1900, and even later the German attitude toward it was not wholly friendly.[13] There were several reasons for this. First it was but natural that men primarily interested in the practical problems of their day and in historical work should not welcome the renascence of a type of research that they considered fundamentally wrong or at least uninteresting. Second, many men but especially Schmoller—who frankly admitted his error later on—associated theory with 'Manchesterism,' that is, with unconditional laissez-faire. They therefore thought that they beheld not only a renascence of a type of analysis they did not like but also a renascence of a type of economic thought—or of a political economy—they abhorred. Third, most of the existing theorists were either under Marxist influence—and the Marxists naturally were incapable of seeing in a new theory anything but a new piece of bourgeois apologetics—or else were the faithful followers of the English 'classics': some of them out-Marshalled Marshall in their admiration for Ricardo and J. S. Mill but, unlike Marshall, refused steadfastly to advance beyond them.[14] Nor were the various *guerrilleros*, who tried new starts for them-

[12] George J. Stigler, *Production and Distribution Theories* [of Jevons, Wicksteed, Marshall, Edgeworth, Menger, Wieser, Böhm-Bawerk, Walras, Wicksell, J. B. Clark], 1941. This excellent work by a competent theorist is perhaps the best survey in existence of the theoretical work of that period's leaders and is strongly recommended. This recommendation does not imply agreement in every point of fact or evaluation.

[13] Even as late as 1918, the great success of G. Cassel's *Theoretische Sozialökonomie* was due as much to its usefulness as a textbook as to the fact that, on the surface, it was hostile to both the Austrians and to Walras.

[14] H. Dietzel (discussed below) went further than anyone else: he actually thought that it was possible to preserve the whole of the 'classic' structure, and this in 1921! (*Vom Lehrwert der Wertlehre . . .*, 1921.)

selves, any more disposed to accept an analytic schema which, however simple it was, could not be appreciated without some theoretical training. In England, an initial advance soon ran up against the Marshallian castle that 'frowned in awful state' upon the Austrian cottage. In the United States recognition was freely extended by a number of economists. But since the country developed a 'marginalist' school of its own and since some of the most eminent American economists, Irving Fisher in particular, followed Walras rather than the Austrian triumvirate, the situation did not differ very much from the English one. In France, the Austrian teaching fell in with a national tradition and, being more acceptable than the mathematical one of Walras, made considerable headway, Leroy-Beaulieu, Gide, Landry, Colson (who however was more Walrasian) and many others extending more or less hospitality to it. In Italy success was substantial at first. But the Austrian impulse soon petered out or was submerged by the teaching of Pareto. The earliest as well as the most lasting of the Austrian successes were in the Netherlands and in the Scandinavian countries.

(b) *The Elder Statesmen.* Science progresses, so Böhm-Bawerk once told a restless and recalcitrant young man, through the old professors' dying off. However, before promoting the progress of science by doing so, these old professors are in the picture and some of them must be mentioned. I choose Roscher, who lasted until 1894, Knies, Schäffle, Stein, all of whom we have met already and all of whom exerted significant influence.

No more need be said of Roscher. Karl Knies (1821-98) was above all a great teacher who made Heidelberg a center of study and research in which the most diverse types were welcomed and made to work together. Of his many works, I shall mention only his chief performance *Geld und Credit* (1873-9). Albert Schäffle (1831-1903), the Swabian radical—if he lived today and in the United States, we should characterize him as a New Dealer or even as a Parlor Pink—Austrian cabinet minister (1871), and then a student enjoying lettered ease in his little home town for over thirty years, had less opportunity for teaching but exerted formative influence as a writer. But unless there is more to his ambitiously conceived *Bau und Leben des sozialen Körpers* (1875-8) than I am able to find in it, economic *analysis* cannot be said to owe much to him. His works in taxation will be mentioned in their place. [The section on taxation in ch. 6 was not completed, Ed.] Lorenz von Stein (1815-90), the student of French socialism, professor in Vienna, 1855-88, established himself as an authority on public administration and public finance. His textbook of economics is insignificant and I mention him merely because it seems incongruous to leave out of the picture a no doubt brilliant figure.

(c) *The Representatives.* The names of academic leaders that first arise in one's mind, when one thinks of German economists of the period under survey, are of course those that have been mentioned in the preceding chapter, and in particular Brentano, Bücher, Knapp, Schmoller, Sombart, Wagner, and M. Weber. I select in order to illustrate various aspects of the situation, Bortkiewicz, Diehl, Dietzel, Launhardt, Lexis, Philippovich, and Schulze-Gaevernitz. But there I must stop. Many successful teachers, such as Johannes

Conrad, the kindly mentor of many American visitors, or Gustav Cohn or Pohle or Held or the excellent Nasse or Herkner must be passed by.

Of the first group only Adolf Wagner (1835-1917) needs additional comment. We know him already as a leader in the fight for *Sozialpolitik* and a—politically—conservative reformer. Besides he has to his credit substantial performance in the field of money that will be noticed in Chapter 8. Also, we shall have to notice his work in public finance (*Finanzwissenschaft*, 4 vols., 1877-1901). It is on these achievements that his historical reputation must be expected to rest. Now we have to consider him as an analytic economist in general. He felt himself to be a 'theorist' in the sense that he was opposed to historism. But though by no means friendly to the Schmoller school, he emphasized historical relativity by his famous, if not exactly novel, distinction between the 'historico-legal' and the 'economic' categories (of institutions, forms of behavior, and processes) which it is perhaps unnecessary to explain. He used to say that Rodbertus and Schäffle were the two economists from whom he had learned most and he always displayed a critical interest in Ricardo, who for him remained 'the' theorist to the end. Of the work of his age he absorbed but surface meanings, though he extended recognition to many foreign economists, Marshall and Taussig in particular—in that formal way that means so little—and received similar recognition, especially from Marshall, in return. Always excepting the field of money, his originality or even his competence in analytic economics cannot be rated high. Yet his name will live much longer than will that of many an expert analyst. Of his voluminous works that are, to an almost intolerable degree, affected by *rabies systematica*, only his *Principles* (*Grundlegung der politischen Oekonomie*, 1st ed., 1876) superseded by his co-operative enterprise, the *Handbook* (*Lehr- und Handbuch der politischen Oekonomie*), need be mentioned here.

Our second group consists of very heterogeneous material. Ladislaus von Bortkiewicz (1868-1931) was a trained mathematician and physicist [15] and ranks high as a statistician of the Lexis school. As a theorist he is known chiefly as one of the most competent critics of Marx [16] and Böhm-Bawerk. His essentially critical bent prevented him from producing, so far as economic theory is concerned, any creative work. Nor is this all. His criticism was at its best when directed toward details—in a sense he was a comma hunter—and he had no eye for the wider aspects and deeper meanings of a theoretical model. Bortkiewicz described himself as a Marshallian. But this meant no

15 This characteristic he shared with Wilhelm Launhardt (1832-1918), professor at the Technological School of Hanover, whose *Mathematische Begründung der Volkswirthschaftslehre* (1885), though substantially Walrasian and disfigured by many inadequacies, must yet be listed as a notable and, in some points, original performance (especially as to transportation and location). Thus, Germany was not entirely without 'mathematical economics.' It is curious to observe—and characteristic of the conditions in our field—that a type of research may be present and in full view and yet pass unnoticed.

16 On this, see P. M. Sweezy, op. cit., who entirely accepts Bortkiewicz' revision of Marx's theory of prices.

more than that he liked some of the least admirable and least progressive features of Marshall's *Principles*. He could have exerted beneficial influence in Berlin, however, if he had not stood on a side track—quite overshadowed by Schmoller and Wagner—and if he had been less ineffective as a teacher.

Karl Diehl (1864-1943), on the contrary, stood on no side track: he occupied in Freiburg what was—partly before him and partly owing to him—one of the most prominent German chairs of economics. And he was a most effective teacher, not so much in the lecture hall as in his seminar, which formed and stimulated a large number of pupils. He was of a strongly institutionalist bent—all for historical relativity in particular. But this did not prevent him from being a genuine 'theorist,' that is, an economist who does not drop theory when he has done with some philosophies and quarrels about concepts, but who uses theory as an instrument with which to solve problems. His theory was neither original, nor very modern, nor very refined—its roots were in the English 'classics' [17]—but it was serviceable theory all the same, and in the existing situation meant a good deal.

Heinrich Dietzel (1857-1935), the incumbent of another leading professorship (in Bonn), was a man of a different stamp. He, too, was primarily a theorist and the superior of Diehl in rigorous logic. But he was less effective as a teacher, both by temperament and by the singular sterility of his scientific message. He just 'dug his toes in' and stayed, intellectually, in the position, the 'classic' position, he had reached in his early manhood. Though he did some respectable work on 'classic' lines and contributed an interesting volume on theory (*Theoretische Socialökonomik;* method mainly) to Wagner's *Lehr- und Handbuch*, he is not likely to be remembered except for his controversy with Böhm-Bawerk.

Wagner's and Dietzel's cases show that it was the nature of the 'theory' taught, rather than either *Sozialpolitik* or historism, which accounts for what at first sight looks like an eclipse of analytic work of this kind that may not amount to a great deal in itself but seems to be necessary to vitalize the rest. The case of Wilhelm Lexis (1837-1914), the great statistician, displays the same thing from a slightly different angle. Lexis did work of a high grade in many fields, especially on questions of monetary policy and foreign trade. He was also prominent among the critics who attacked the Marxist system when the third volume came out. But all these writings show weaknesses on the theoretical side that are surprising in a man of no doubt remarkably keen intellect. His textbook solves the riddle, however: it shows conclusively that he took no interest whatever in the work of improving the apparatus of analysis; having grown to maturity in an anti-theoretic atmosphere, he entirely failed to perceive the scientific possibilities of the new ideas that were cropping up in his middle age. Since his purely intellectual interests were in any case

[17] His *Sozialwissenschaftliche Erläuterungen zu David Ricardos Grundgesetzen* (see above, Part III, ch. 4) was his main scholarly achievement in this field. But his monumental *Principles* (*Theoretische Nationalökonomie,* 4 vols., 1916-33) is also a considerable work that still repays perusal. His work on Proudhon has been mentioned before.

in the theory of statistics, he did not even bother to use mathematics—which he would not have had to acquire laboriously—in the service of his economics.

We must on no account omit to mention Eugen von Philippovich (1858-1917), although we shall have to mention him again in order to use his famous textbook as a representative sample of what it was 'the student got.' He was one of the greatest teachers of the period, a man of intellectual stature, passionately interested in the social and economic issues of his time, yet a careful thinker and open to all the currents in scientific economics that were within his range. These virtues and in particular this catholicity of scientific taste made him an ideal mediator when mediation was sorely needed. He gave their due both to Schmoller and to Menger and all they stood for; he was wholeheartedly in sympathy with *Sozialpolitik* of a New-Deal type, and though not a man of 'theory' himself—his own research was wholly of a 'practical' nature—he saw to it that analytic culture should not, within the sphere of his influence, drop to zero level. Much earlier than the other Austrians, he got on terms with the spirit of German economics—he was professor in Vienna—and it was due to his influence, exerted mainly through his textbook, that marginal utility theory filtered through to German students at all.

Gerhart von Schulze-Gaevernitz (1864-1943) illustrates—at its best—still another type. So far as technical economics is concerned, this Freiburg professor can hardly be called an economist at all. But he was more—a genuine social philosopher, almost what I should like to call a social theologian, and at the same time a political observer who did not lack realism. He thus produced works [18] of wide scope that, whatever our opinion may be about their epistemological standing, have their place, besides being masterpieces of their genus. They were written with a purpose—they preached a social message. But though this is much, it is not enough unless a good technician teaches in the next room. He never seems to have realized that, if we are to apply our reason to social and international affairs, we need not only social visions, ideals, and facts, but also, since we are not Laplacian demons, certain techniques, and he unwittingly injured his pupils, some of whom were to rise to eminence, by failing to impart to them the saving minimum of technical economics (and, for this purpose, to learn it himself).

Even in Marshallian England, there were Hobsons. But in Germany and Austria in a situation such as I have been trying to describe by 'patches of color,' where the all-round competence of *all* professional economists, hence the level of criticism, cannot be high, Hobsons must thrive and free-lance economists must be numerous. Trained men also, the training being what it was, would often indulge in misplaced originality that arises simply from failure to understand or master the existing apparatus of the science. Even able

[18] They remind one of Adolf Held's *Zwei Bücher zur sozialen Geschichte Englands* (ed. by G. F. Knapp, 1881), another man of this type whom I hate to omit. Schulze-Gaevernitz's two most important and also, I think, most characteristic works are: *Zum socialen Frieden* (1890; the translation of the subtitle is: 'a description of England's education to *Sozialpolitik* in the nineteenth century'), and *Britischer Imperialismus und englischer Freihandel* (1906).

men may then blunder atrociously, misconceive problems, take their errors for discoveries. In consequence, we have a long list of men who even attained success with the profession and filled considerable positions but are difficult to characterize from a professional standpoint. I shall mention some of the most eminent writers of this type but I shall not return to some of them: Effertz, Gottl, Liefmann, Oppenheimer, and Spann. Treating such men in this manner involves the duty of saying why.

This duty cannot be fulfilled properly: it would take a volume. I can only state my reasons, not establish them. Otto Effertz, who was the only man in our list who failed to attain a professorship and was something of a tragic figure, produced a work, *Arbeit und Boden* (1890-91), which in its final form, which differs considerably from the original one, was published in French under the title *Les Antagonismes économiques* (1906). It is typically the work of an able man who does not know how to go about his task. My reason for excluding Effertz from my subsequent report is that removal of provable mistakes reduces his argument to commonplace. For a different opinion, see the introduction to the French volume. I fear that the only way of appreciating Professor F. von Gottl-Ottlilienfeld, who held a conspicuous place and found many adherents—or else my reason for excluding him—is to read him.[19] Robert Liefmann (1874-1941) was an economist of merit, especially on cartels. Our trouble is with his theory (summed up, for example, in *Grundsätze der Volkswirtschaftslehre*, new ed., 1922), which presents an interesting feature. His fundamental principle of equalization of marginal returns in money (and the whole of his 'subjective' theory of prices) is (barring slips) nothing but a particularly inconvenient expression of the main content of the Austrian theory. But having discovered it independently, he stoutly denied any affinity, wasted powers that were well above average on conducting controversies, and asserted claims that nobody would or could take seriously. Meaningless talk about imaginary issues such as 'subjectivism' and 'objectivism' (or 'materialism' and 'naturalism') in price theory did the rest. His net contribution to topics *relevant to the purposes of this book*, and excepting his work on cartels, is zero. Franz Oppenheimer (1864-1943) was a man of mark, a leading Zionist, a 'positivist' sociologist who is not likely to lose his place in the history of that line of thought, a powerful teacher who shaped many growing minds and did much to keep the flag of economic theory flying by spirited controversy. His Henry-George attitude toward private property in land [20] in itself would not suffice for my refusal to go at length into his doctrines. The reason

[19] The psychic cost of doing so may, however, be substantially reduced by reading instead Professor von Haberler's review of the methodological writings of Gottl that were republished in 1925 under the title *Wirtschaft als Leben.* (The review is in the *Zeitschrift für Nationalökonomie*, May 1929, entitled 'Kritische Bemerkungen zu Gottls methodologischen Schriften.') But no such helper is available for the rest of Gottl's writings.

[20] Oppenheimer was one of the many writers, among whom are A. Smith and Senior, who spoke of a monopoly in land. This, however, is not what I mean by the phrase in the text. He was also one of those less numerous writers who, like Henry George (and some who have been noticed in Part III), ascribed all phenomena that looked to them like deviations from proper functioning of the capitalist engine to landed property or to the exclusion of workmen from free access to land (*Bodensperre*), which, of course, involves the thesis that private property is the reason why land is a scarce factor at all. The abolition of this *Bodensperre* is (substantially) what his Liberal socialism that made a hit with many minds amounts to.

for this refusal is that the case of his analytic apparatus (his 'objective' theory of price) is beyond remedy or, rather, because there is only one remedy for its defects, namely, training in theory. But he was not devoid of insight and threw out many good ideas. Among other things, he saw the use of the concept, and coined the word, Comparative Statics (see below, ch. 7, sec. 3).[21] Professor Othmar Spann,[22] whose teaching at the University of Vienna (from 1916 on) was a great success and who formed a genuine school in our sense, has been mentioned already on previous occasions. Neither his social philosophy nor his epistemology nor his sociology is in question here. We are concerned with his theory only. And this was completely barren of results. It is only the use of certain phrases that distinguishes the works on public finance or cycles or any others that profess to apply that theory.[23]

5. Italy

The most benevolent observer could not have paid any compliments to Italian economics in the early 1870's; the most malevolent observer could not have denied that it was second to none by 1914. The most conspicuous component in this truly astounding achievement was no doubt the work of Pareto and his school. But once more it must be emphasized that dominant schools do not dominate. The Pareto school with its allies and sympathizers never dominated Italian economics any more than the Ricardo school dominated English, or the Schmoller school German, economics. The really remarkable thing is on the contrary that, even independently of Pareto, Italian economics attained a high level in a variety of lines and in all applied fields. Some of the excellent work done especially in money and banking, public finance, socialism, and agricultural economics will be noticed later, but it cannot be made to stand out as it should. Not even the various currents in general economics can get their due, least of all those that originated in historical or other factual work which in Italy really fertilized general economics and did not, as in Germany, conflict with 'theory'—the kind of general economics that may be represented by the work of Luigi Einaudi, although it was only after 1914

21 Of Oppenheimer's many works we need, for our purposes, notice only: *Theorie der reinen und politischen Ökonomie* (vol. III of his comprehensive *System der Soziologie;* 5th rev. ed., 1924) and *Wert und Kapitalprofit* (2nd ed., 1922). Professor Alfred Amonn's elaborate critical analysis of Oppenheimer's theoretical structure may prove helpful (*Zeitschrift für Volkswirtschaft und Sozialpolitik,* 1924). There is quite an Oppenheimer literature, of which I mention only E. Heimann's 'Franz Oppenheimer's Economic Ideas' in *Social Research,* February 1944. If the reader refers to this article, he will find that, although Professor Heimann extols Oppenheimer as a social philosopher and political thinker and makes the most—as is proper in a memorial article—of the strong points of Oppenheimer's teaching, the implied appraisal of his purely analytic work does not differ substantially from that above.

22 See, e.g., his *Fundament der Volkswirtschaftslehre* (3rd ed., 1923).

23 The doctrine, or the influence, of Gottl, Oppenheimer, and Spann did not mature until the 1920's. But I wished to use this opportunity in order to relieve Part v. At least the formative stage of the thought of these authors comes within the period under survey.

that he rose to a leading position. We shall divide our sketch into three parts, which we respectively inscribe to the elder statesmen, Pantaleoni, and Pareto. An interesting figure that falls out of our inevitably oversimplified picture, Achille Loria, is noticed in the note below.[1]

(a) *The Elder Statesmen.* As already mentioned, the vigorous renaissance of Italian economics is often associated with the teaching of Ferrara, Messedaglia,[2] and Cossa.[3] Sociological conscience compels us to emphasize the facts that Italy was sure to revive her brilliant tradition in the field as soon as circumstances became more favorable; that national unity brought about such circumstances and produced in addition new national problems and opportunities; and that, though the worldly means at the disposal of Italian economics were modest, there was a large number of ill-paid professorships. These facts do not, however, detract from the merit of these great teachers and those who were to follow them. The personal element looms large in the explanation of the achievement: an unusual number of unusually able men certainly made the most of these objective opportunities. It was the particular merit of Cossa

[1] Achille Loria's (1857-1943) work is a curious cross product of genius and bad training in analysis. But this bad training was itself of a curious kind that, however, occurs not infrequently in economics. He was not ignorant but on the contrary even unusually learned. The English 'classics' he knew almost by heart and Marx only slightly less completely. Also he was well read in history and philosophy. But he either had not learned the art of economic analysis or else he had no bent for it. Moreover, he lacked self-criticism completely where pet ideas were concerned. Thus, he was led—like many older writers—to attach quite unwarranted importance to the explanatory value of the presence or absence of free land that became the keynote in his economic and sociological thought. He combined this idea with a wholly untenable development of Ricardo's theory of value and with the Marxist unitary conception of non-wage income—which then, at one remove, splits into interest (profit) and rent—and from these elements he constructed a 'land-property system of economics' that, in conception and intent, parallels—Marxists will say, caricatures—the Marxist system in a way that is not unlike Oppenheimer's. He believed himself to have founded a school. But all that I could undertake to establish from the literature is that he interested and stimulated many of his contemporaries and that, from some of them, he drew the kind of recognition in which it is difficult to distinguish politeness from acknowledgment and acknowledgment from allegiance.

[2] On Ferrara and Messedaglia see above, Part III, ch. 4, sec. 6.

[3] Luigi Cossa (1831-96), professor in Pavia, was first of all a great teacher, one of those men who do not need the opportunities of the modern American teacher but will, as if by magic, extract from large classes of very mildly interested students the minority that is ready to open its mind to the vivifying influences of the personal interview. Second, he was a very learned man. His *Guida allo studio dell'economia politica* (1876, English trans., 1880) is indeed a guide, but one that guides by means of introducing the neophyte to the authors of the past. The title of the French translation (the book was translated into several languages and very widely read) is really more characteristic of its content: *Histoire des doctrines économiques* (1899). Being based on original research, it ranks high as a history of economics. [The French trans. and a new English trans. (1893) were based on the third (revised and enlarged) Italian ed., entitled *Introduzione . . . dell'economia politica* (1892).]

and Messedaglia to teach *science* and to propagate the spirit of scholarship, to lead away from the eternal squabbles about politics—laissez-faire versus *Sozialpolitik* in particular—and to let the rising generations discover that there was serious work to be done. Though they succeeded only in part—who could have done more?—and though the old controversy went on not only undisguised but also in the guise of apparently scientific squabbles on 'natural laws,' they not only instigated research but also helped to create the atmosphere of research. This research, so far as general economics is concerned, no doubt started from foreign examples, notably the examples of the historical and the Austrian schools. But, by way of criticism as well as of original work, it became rapidly 'nationalized.' A great many men responded successfully to the stimulus and a great many should be mentioned—such as Supino or Ricca-Salerno, the pupil of Cossa and teacher of Loria, Conigliani, Graziani. But we must refrain.

(b) *Pantaleoni.*[4] The *Principi di economia pura* (1889) will serve as a landmark. Austrian or 'Austro-Walrasian' in fundamentals, enriched by Marshall's apparatus of foreign and domestic trade (from his privately printed pamphlets of 1879), it gave an important lead away from old and toward new things. In this consists its importance, for though it is brilliantly written—Edgeworth was not wrong when he called it a 'gem'—and is still worth reading, there is nothing entirely original in it. Pantaleoni's original ideas are scattered in his papers and addresses. To mention but a few, he was one of the first *theorists* to try his hand at the subject of price fixing (*prezzi politici*); he contributed to the theory of industrial combinations (*sindacati*); he toyed, not without success, with the tricky concept of collective maxima of satisfaction; he wrote suggestively on the problem of evaluation of assets in the absence of prices; above all, as Moore was to recognize, he was the first theorist to adumbrate a theory of endogenous fluctuations. Nothing of this he carried very far. But

[4] Maffeo Pantaleoni (1857-1924) was a man of many activities and this remains true even if we discard all the non-scientific ones. His prominence in Italian economics dates from the book mentioned in the text above, but his prominence in the Italian profession dates from 1900, when he was appointed to the chair of Pavia, or rather from 1902, when he succeeded Messedaglia at the University of Rome. Before the *Principi* (English trans., 1898; this trans. is from the 2nd ed., 1894), he wrote another book of importance on incidence of taxation (*Teoria della traslazione dei tributi,* his master's thesis, 1882). But the full extent of his influence and his originality cannot be appreciated from either. His suggestions were thrown out in papers out of number, the most important of which are republished in *Scritti vari di economia* (1904-10) and in *Erotemi di economia* (1925). His 'La crisi del 1905-07,' published in *Annali di economia,* 1925, though a report occasioned by a government inquiry, is a substantial contribution to the theory of cyclical fluctuations. This and other factual work—some of which is not without importance for statistical theory—must be taken into account in any appraisal of the man and scholar: he was anything but a 'pure theorist,' although he understood 'pure theory' as few people ever did. After his death a number of eminent Italian economists wrote tributes to him that are published in the *Giornale degli Economisti,* 1925 (a bibliography is added). See also G. Pirou, 'Pantaleoni et la théorie économique,' *Revue d'économie politique,* 1926.

he disseminated suggestions and helped to get things going. And he introduced Pareto to the work of Walras.

Again, many names ought to be mentioned here. I shall confine myself to three, however. The first is Barone [5] who began to publish in the early 1890's. He was the man who showed Walras how to dispense with constant coefficients of production; who formulated the limits of the validity of Marshall's partial analysis; who went in some points beyond Marshall and in others (in the theory of public finance) beyond Edgeworth; and—no doubt on the basis proffered by Pareto—blocked out the theory of a socialist economy in a manner on which the work of our own time has not substantially improved. Only the last performance, and his excellent textbook, have received adequate recognition. But he did better than the second man I am going to name, G. B. Antonelli, whose remarkable performance has received no attention at all.[6] The third name to be mentioned is that of Marco Fanno,[7] whose early work belongs to this period.

(c) *Pareto*. At long last we approach the eminence that was Pareto. If we follow his disciples in speaking of a Paretian epoch, we should date it from about 1900, when he began to define a position and to form a school of his own, as we noted above. Like all genuine schools, this one had a core, allies or sympathizers, and a foreign sphere of influence. Many writers come under each of these headings. But if we sample the Italian economists who, then or later, attained international reputation, we find that followers of strict observance—those who formed the 'core'—were in a small minority. I think that the names of Amoroso, Bresciani-Turroni, Del Vecchio, Einaudi, Fanno, Gini, de Pietri-Tonelli, Ricci will arise in the mind of everyone who knows the scientific situation of 1910-40. Of these only Amoroso and de Pietri-Tonelli belong to the core of the Paretian school.[8] Einaudi and his pupils stood entirely aloof and on ground of their own. And all the others were at most 'allies or sympathizers' in the sense that they recognized Pareto's eminence, allowed themselves to be influenced by him in individual points though substantially they went their own way—perhaps the word 'ally' is altogether too strong. In order to appraise Pareto's international sphere of influence, the

[5] Enrico Barone (1859-1924) was a soldier, politician, and teacher, who had a good mathematical training. Most of his publications appeared in the *Giornale degli Economisti*. A few will be referred to later on. His *Principi di economia politica* first appeared in 1908. I have never been able to understand why the services of this brilliant economist were not more recognized in his own country.

[6] G. B. Antonelli, *Sulla teoria matematica della economia politica* (1886). This little treatise seems to me to anticipate later work in some important points.

[7] See especially Fanno's *Contributo alla teoria dell'offerta a costi congiunti*, supplement to the *Giornale degli Economisti*, October 1914.

[8] The contributions of Luigi Amoroso, professor in Rome, are contained in a large number of papers, but we mention for the moment only his *Lezioni di economia matematica* (1921). Similarly, the original work of Alfonso de Pietri-Tonelli, professor in Venice, must be looked for in his papers. We mention, however, his treatise, the 3rd ed. of which is available in French: *Traité d'économie rationnelle* (1927). Note that the French term *rationnelle* simply means the same thing as *pure*.

reader must distinguish four different things. First Pareto's sociology was a success internationally and, for a short time within the 1930's, created the limited Pareto vogue that we have noticed already in the United States. Second, the famous Pareto Law of the (statistical) distribution of incomes evoked much interest and criticism, mostly hostile, all over the world.[9] Third, Pareto as a 'pure' economist became a familiar figure in England and the United States when Allen and Hicks developed his theory of value (indifference-curve approach, see below, Appendix to ch. 7), giving generous credit to him. This was, however, only in the 1930's. Fourth, the rest of Pareto's economics remained practically unknown in the Germanic countries, except for some adverse criticism of his theory of monopoly especially in Germany. Things were more favorable to Pareto in France (but not before the late 1920's), where Bousquet sponsored his doctrines, and Divisia and Pirou noticed them.[10]

The Marchese Vilfredo Pareto (1848-1923), the son of a Genoese father and a French mother, was trained (and throughout his prime practiced) as an engineer. This means more than that he had a good training in mathematics. His powerful mind roamed far beyond the precincts of applied science into the realm of the pure concepts that are perfectly general: few people can ever have realized with such intensity as did he that, ultimately, all exact sciences or parts of sciences are fundamentally one. Early interest in economic theory is indicated by an address in 1877 to the *Reale Accademia dei Giorgofili*[11] on the *logic* of the 'new economic schools.' But still more obvious is an early interest in economic policy. This calls for comment, because Pareto's legiti-

[9] Pareto published his statistical law of the distribution of incomes by size in his *Cours* (1896-7) and in the *Recueil*, published by the faculty of law of the University of Lausanne on the occasion of the national Swiss exposition of 1896, under the title: 'La courbe de la répartition de la richesse.' The large literature evoked by this publication (which still runs on) testifies conclusively to its importance and to its stimulating influence. The discussion has been unpleasantly warped by the political preconceptions of both critics and sponsors. But two contributions may be recommended to the reader (as introductions) from the long list of the serious and competent ones: D. H. Macgregor, 'Pareto's Law,' *Economic Journal*, March 1936, and C. Bresciani-Turroni, 'On Some Methods of Measuring the Inequality of Incomes,' in the Egyptian periodical *Al Quanoun Wal Iqtisad*, 1938. E. C. Rhodes' 'The Pareto Distribution of Incomes,' *Economica*, February 1944, while excellent, presents some difficulties for non-mathematicians. The implications—real or supposed—of the law for our outlook on the income structure of capitalist society were, so far as I know, first seriously discussed in English by Professor Pigou in *Wealth and Welfare* (1912). Though serious, his discussion displays symptoms of emotional bias.

[10] See, especially, G. H. Bousquet, *Cours d'économie pure* (1928), also the same author's *Essai sur l'évolution de la pensée économique* (1927) and *Instituts de science économique* (1930-36). François Divisia, *Économique rationnelle* (1928); G. Pirou, *Les théories de l'équilibre économique: L. Walras et V. Pareto* (1934).

[11] To this extent, what has been said about Pantaleoni's influence must be qualified. The reference is due to Professor de Pietri-Tonelli's memorial address on Pareto to the Italian Society for the Progress of the Sciences, published in three parts in the *Rivista di Politica Economica*, 1934-5, which is herewith recommended to the reader.

mate influence has been reduced by the aversion to his politics of so many of his readers: he looked to them (at all events until his general sociology, *Trattato di sociologia generale*, appeared in 1916) like an uncritical ultra-liberal in the laissez-faire sense. But his liberalism, economic and political, was of a peculiar kind and had a peculiar root. He was a man of strong passions, passions of the kind that effectively preclude a man from seeing more than one side of a political issue or, for that matter, of a civilization. This disposition was reinforced rather than mitigated by his solid classical education that made the ancient world as familiar to him as were his own Italy and France—the rest of the world just existed for him. And, watching with passionate wrath the doings of the politicians in the Italian and French liberal democracies, he was, by indignation and despair, driven into an anti-*étatiste* attitude which, as events were to show, was not really his own. Add to this the fact that at the same time he was (like Marx) a product of the civilization he hated, and therefore (also like Marx) a positivist and laicist, and you will understand the liberalist surface of his earlier writings.

He was 45 when he left Italy and business practice, having accepted the chair of Lausanne vacated by the retirement of Walras. Indifferent health and the acquisition by inheritance of adequate means motivated his own retirement, at a comparatively early age, to Céligny on the Lake of Geneva, where, in the almost twenty years of thought and assiduous writing that were still before him, he was at leisure to fill to the full the measure of his genius and of his intellectual ambitions. There he grew to be the 'lone thinker of Céligny,' who was looked upon, with something akin to awe, somewhat as an ancient sage. The interesting fact deserves to be noticed that so great an influence could have been exerted by a man who lived in resolute though hospitable seclusion in a shabby house full of cats (hence Villa Angora) that was then not convenient to visit.[12]

If we now discard his sociology and also Pareto's Law, the indubitable greatness of his performance is as difficult to define as its roots are easy to indicate. Ferrara and others, Cournot among them, may have provided suggestions, but his work, as it shaped in Lausanne where he first put his mind fully to analytic economics, is so completely rooted in Walras' system that to mention other influences can only mislead. To the non-theorist this shows less than it should, because Pareto's theory floats in a sociology, philosophy, and methodology that are not merely different but diametrically opposed to Walras' ideas. But as pure theory, Pareto's *is* Walrasian—in groundwork as well as in most details. Nobody will deny this, of course, as regards Pareto's work until 1900 that centers in the *Cours d'économie politique* (1896-7). This is simply a brilliant Walrasian treatise. Later on Pareto discarded the Walrasian theory of value and based his own on the indifference-curve apparatus invented by Edgeworth and perfected by Fisher. He also overhauled Walras' theory of produc-

[12] A charming picture of the man and thinker has been drawn by Professor G. H. Bousquet in his *Vilfredo Pareto, sa vie et son oeuvre* (1928; English trans., same year). I use this opportunity to refer to the same author's *Introduction à l'étude du Manuel de Vilfredo Pareto* (1927).

tion and capitalization and he departed from the latter's teaching in matters of money and others, adding various developments of his own. The new system was presented in the *Manuale di economia politica* (1906), the mathematical appendix of which was greatly improved in the French version (*Manuel*, 1909).[13] But even the *Manuel*—always disregarding the sociology—is not more than Walras' work done over, as can be established by drawing up the exact models of both authors. It was, however, done over with so much force and brilliance as to grow into something that deserves to be called a new creation, though various deductions from the achievement are in order: there are not unimportant points in which Walras' system remained superior. Recognition of the quality of his creation does not excuse Pareto's less than generous attitude toward the teaching of Walras from which he put himself at a greater distance than was really necessary.[14]

6. The Netherlands and the Scandinavian Countries

Two facts describe the scientific situation in the Netherlands that prevailed at the beginning of the period: a high level of competence and culture in our field, based upon an old tradition that was being worthily kept up by such men as Mees; and the absence of a domestic impulse toward scientific revolution. Dutch economists were quite above any 'battle of methods' and but mildly affected by either historism or any other of the new tendencies of the age. They carried on the usual discussions about socialism, *Sozialpolitik*, money, free trade, but on the whole things were quiet. Thus they were both able and willing to accept the 'new theories'—in the Austrian edition rather than in the Walrasian or Marshallian ones simply because Menger's teaching was available, in a usable form, before the others. The leading Dutch economist of the period, Pierson, inserted this teaching in his own and founded[1] a

[13] Having already mentioned the *Trattato di sociologia generale* (1916), we need, for the purposes of this book, add only the following publications to the *Cours* and the *Manuel: Les Systèmes socialistes* (1902-3) and 'Économie mathématique' in the French edition of the *Encyclopaedia of the Mathematical Sciences*, 1911 (the corresponding article in the earlier German edition is insignificant). The articles that appeared in the 1890's in the *Giornale degli Economisti*, though not uninteresting—they should be republished—were, from Pareto's own standpoint, obsolete by 1900; later articles in the field of pure theory were merely chips of the *Manuel* or the *Encyclopaedia* article.

[14] Personally, the aristocratic Pareto and the middle-class radical Walras did not like one another.

[1] Nicolas Gerard Pierson (1839-1909) was primarily a public servant—a director of the Dutch Central Bank at an early age; later on its president, Minister of Finance, Prime Minister, and a parliamentarian to the last. Such a career will not prevent a strong intellect like his, when coupled with a giant's capacity for work, from achieving eminence as a scientific economist—he was in fact a prolific writer, who published about a hundred books and papers—but it will absorb those sources of energy that produce original creations. His chief work, the *Leerboek der Staatshuishoudkunde* (1884-90), is available in English (*Principles of Economics*, 1902-12, from

school that, supported by leaders such as Verrijn Stuart and de Vries, lasted well into the 1920's, when it assimilated newer tendencies without any violent break.[2]

We might repeat all this, with very little change, for the Scandinavian countries, which may for our purposes be taken as a unit. But I shall merely mention the names of Birck (Copenhagen), Davidson (Uppsala), and Cassel[3] (Stockholm), and then hurry on to the Nordic Marshall, Wicksell, whose work was one of the most important factors in the emergence of the economics of our own time, and not only in Sweden.

No finer intellect and no higher character have ever graced our field. If the depth and originality of his thought do not stand out more clearly than they do, this is only owing to his lovable modesty, which led him to present novelty—semi-hesitatingly—as little suggestions for the improvement of existing pieces of apparatus, and to his admirable honesty, which pointed incessantly to his predecessors, Walras, Menger, and Böhm-Bawerk, although, with much more justification than did others, he might have presented his system of analysis as substantially his own creation.

Knut Wicksell (1851-1926), like Marshall, was a trained mathematician. He was also, for his time, a radical who knew how to get himself into trouble, but

---

the 2nd ed. of the original)—a performance that, in the doctrinal development of that time, filled a function similar to that of Pantaleoni's work.

[2] See, e.g., C. A. Verrijn Stuart's *Grondslagen* . . . [Fundaments . . .], 1920.

[3] Professor L. V. Birck's (1871-1933) position may, so far as economic theory is concerned, be compared with Pierson's. See his *Theory of Marginal Value* (1922). Professor David Davidson is chiefly known as the author of a history of Sweden's central bank, for his contributions to the theory of money, and as a friendly critic of Wicksell. But he was also a theorist of note—so I infer from his work on capital formation (owing to my scanty reading knowledge of Swedish, I cannot say, however, that I really know it). See the excellent work by Mr. Brinley Thomas that interprets Swedish doctrine for the English-reading public (*Monetary Policy and Crises: a Study of Swedish Experience*, 1936). Professor Gustav Cassel's (1866-1945) international fame rests upon his contributions to, and role in, the discussion on monetary policy during and after the First World War (see below, ch. 8) and upon his textbook, *Theoretische Sozialökonomie* (1st ed., 1918; English trans., *The Theory of Social Economy*, 1923). But he started as a theorist with a paper, 'Grundriss einer elementaren Preislehre' (*Zeitschrift für die gesamte Staatswissenschaft*, 1899) that made the attempt, important considering the date, to reformulate the Walrasian equations without using utility concepts. His fresh—fresh in more than one sense—book on *The Nature and Necessity of Interest* (1903), in spite of some unfounded criticisms and still more unfounded claims to originality, is a considerable performance that deserves perusal as an antidote to the theories of interest that became current in the 1930's. Cassel, as a theorist, belongs in this context because he too was one of those second-generation writers who rounded off the Jevons-Menger-Walras structure. Only he followed Walras rather than Menger. His textbook, in its fundamental conception, is mainly a version—or popularization—of Walras' doctrine (minus utility) in spite of the fact that Walras' name does not occur in it. Cassel was an effective and inspiring lecturer and some of the opinions, in matters of pure theory, of modern Wicksellians may still be traced to his teaching.

who never learned to sacrifice to his emotions what he believed to be scientific truth. In this respect, he was not unlike J. S. Mill, who must be listed among the formative influences that acted upon Wicksell's work and with whom in particular he shared an almost passionate neo-Malthusianism.[4] Barring this qualification, his life may be described as that of a quiet and retired scholar. He attained a professorial chair (Lund) only late in life and occupied it for a comparatively short span of years. Nevertheless, his influence spread—by virtue of its own momentum—particularly after his retirement, when he took part in current discussions more actively than before. He had many pupils of very high quality. Practically all the well-known Swedish and Norwegian economists of today are, more or less, his pupils. His international reputation, however, was not commensurate with his achievement until, in the late 1920's and the early 1930's, it began to dawn upon the professional world that he had anticipated, to a very large extent, all that was most valuable in the modern work on money and interest. This part of his work will be considered later on, as will his work on taxation. In this and the following two chapters we are chiefly concerned with his performance in 'general theory.' Attention is drawn to the standard biography, which carefully analyzes Wicksell's work, by Professor Emil Sommarin, unfortunately not available in English ('Das Lebenswerk von Knut Wicksell,' *Zeitschrift für Nationalökonomie*, October 1930).

His first publication on economic theory, *Über Wert, Kapital und Rente* (1893, London School Reprint, 1933) is the work of a mature man of 42 and contains the skeleton of the first volume of his *Lectures* (1901; German ed., 1913; English ed., with excellent introduction by Professor Robbins, and two important appendices, 1934). Volume I of the *Lectures* embodies the bulk of his contributions in that field, though several papers (e.g., his last piece of work, the paper on the theory of interest ('Zur Zinstheorie') in *Die Wirtschaftstheorie der Gegenwart*, ed. H. Mayer, III, 1928) ought to be added. No reader's guide will be offered: no student of economics has completed his training who has not read the whole of this volume, although the first part is elementary and, for us, valuable mainly for the purpose of dispelling erroneous ideas, old and new, about the utility theory and 'marginalism' in general. The main original contributions are pointed out in Professor Robbins' introduction.

7. The United States

The background of individual performance in the United States from about 1870 to 1914 is adequately described by the following familiar facts. During

[4] Wicksell himself would have attached great weight to his work on population problems. But in this Part of the present book we are only peripherically interested in these and cannot therefore do justice to that work. It must suffice to state that Wicksell always considered limitation of the birth rate as an essential factor in the future of the working class and that the tendency of the birth rate to fall that began to assert itself in his time was unconditionally welcomed by him as it would have been by J. S. Mill.

that period the American economic profession established itself both nationally and internationally. It acquired definite standing at the universities and in the country, an organization, and all the paraphernalia of an established department of scientific knowledge; and it came to be increasingly recognized by the other national professions. Also American economics increasingly professorialized itself. But, starting from near zero at 1870, these developments went on at such a rate of acceleration that the growth of fully competent personnel lagged behind the opportunities that were opened up. Many of the men who entered the new profession were practically untrained; and they approached their professional activities with their minds full of preconceived ideas that they were not prepared to put through any analytic mill—even the spirit of the old social-science movement kept on reasserting itself and had much to do with the success of institutionalism. So had sympathies with Populism that many economists entertained. Others, not finding in the country what they wanted, continued to rely on European ideas and methods though no longer exclusively English ones—the pilgrimage to Germany, in particular, became for those who could afford it almost a regular incident of their career, something like the cavalier's tour of old. When they met, after having found their individual bearings, they had difficulty in understanding one another, and of locating, let alone appreciating, one another's standpoints. Disagreement was hence largely disagreement owing to misunderstanding. Surprisingly different intellectual levels—not only as regards scientific apparatus—were found side by side, for there was no uniformity either in professional training or in general education. For a considerable stretch of time, there were no recognized professional standards, and competent teaching was not always guaranteed. Most were at their best when working on some factual problem of national interest, which they learned to master thoroughly, and it was in this type of endeavor that the first successes occurred. But from the first, 'theory' was unpopular with the majority and likely to evoke opposition quite independently of the reinforcing German influence, and long before this opposition was rationalized and made vocal. All this had its obvious advantages as well as disadvantages. Moreover, it all straightened itself out in time—through a long, arduous, wasteful, but not inglorious struggle.

The best way to recall to the reader's mind a number of figures that, with one or two exceptions, should be familiar to him, will be to adopt a schema similar to the one that has served us before. First (a) we shall glance at a few of those men who helped to prepare the ground for the developments from the 1890's on. They do not exactly correspond to what we have called the 'elder statesmen' before. They were simply good economists and good teachers who, both before and after those developments began, stood for straight thinking and were instrumental in raising standards all round. We shall then (b) form a group of Clark, Fisher, and Taussig. And we shall (c) combine into a final group some representative men whose names, in one way or another, we need for the purpose of general orientation.

But we cannot afford to pass by the economist whose individual success with the public was greater than that of all the others on our list, Henry

George.[1] The points about him that are relevant for a history of analysis are these. He was a self-taught economist, but he *was* an economist. In the course of his life, he acquired most of the knowledge and of the ability to handle an economic argument that he could have acquired by academic training as it then was. In this he differed to his advantage from most men who proffered panaceas. Barring his panacea (the Single Tax) and the phraseology connected with it, he was a very orthodox economist and extremely conservative as to methods. They were those of the English 'classics,' A. Smith being his particular favorite. Marshall and Böhm-Bawerk he failed to understand. But up to and including Mill's treatise, he was thoroughly at home in scientific economics; and he shared none of the current misunderstandings or prejudices concerning it. Even the panacea—nationalization not of land but of the rent of land by a confiscatory tax—benefited by his competence as an economist, for he was careful to frame his 'remedy' in such a manner as to cause the minimum injury to the efficiency of the private-enterprise economy. Professional economists who focused attention on the single-tax proposal and condemned Henry George's teaching, root and branch, were hardly just to him. The proposal itself, one of the many descendants of Quesnay's *impôt unique*, though vitiated by association with the untenable theory that the phenomenon of poverty is entirely due to the absorption of all surpluses [2] by the rent of land, is not *economically* unsound, except in that it involves an unwarranted optimism concerning the yield of such a tax. In any case, it should not be put down as nonsense. If Ricardo's vision of economic evolution had been correct, it would even have been obvious wisdom. And obvious wisdom is in fact what George said in *Progress and Poverty* (ch. 1, Book IX) about the economic effects to be expected from a removal of fiscal burdens—if such a removal were feasible.

[(a) *The Men Who Prepared the Ground.*] The work and services of the men in the first of our groups will be illustrated by the names of Dunbar, Hadley, Newcomb, Sumner, Walker, and Wells.

Charles F. Dunbar (1830-1900) was no product of the academic hothouse. His very American career—American in a sense that is now but a reminiscence—led through business, farming, law, journalism, and newspaper management to the first (regular) professorship of economics in Harvard plus vigorous participation in university administration plus highly successful activity in the editorial chair of the *Quarterly Journal of Economics*, which he founded in 1886. We shall not expect that he did creative research. How is it then that no history of American economics could be complete without mentioning him

[1] Henry George (1839-97) is too familiar a figure to need introduction. Besides *Progress and Poverty* (1879) only the posthumously published *Science of Political Economy* (1897) need be mentioned here. His *Complete Works*, with a *Life*, were edited by his son (1906-11). A scholarly appreciation of all the backgrounds and affinities of the Georgian doctrine may be found in E. Teilhac's *Pioneers of American Economic Thought* (1936), ch. III.

[2] Business profits he analyzed into a premium of risk, wages, and interest, exactly like Mill; therefore he did not consider them to be disposable surpluses.

and what can students have got from him? Both questions can be answered simultaneously: he knew the subject matter of economics from first-hand experience; his mind was clear and penetrating; his writings may not have been 'scholarly' in the strictest sense, but any scholar could have learned from them (and still can);[3] his administrative ability enabled him to organize the studies in our field in a way that made the most of the opportunities then existing; and, after all, the essentials of the scientific apparatus of that time were not so complicated that an able man—a mind that intuitively knew what is what—could not have mastered them in a very short time. And so, though not a great economist in the sense appropriate to this book, he was a great economist in the sight of God.

Arthur T. Hadley (1856-1930) was more of a purely academic man, though he was also more of an administrator than a teacher or scholar. The work for the sake of which he is mentioned here is his *Economics . . .* (1896). The reader should really look at it. He will find a core of not very refined, but eminently serviceable and realistic, theory embedded in a forceful presentation of the institutional framework (plenty of policies and politics)—the ideal thing for all-round introduction on a respectable level, and glorified, as seems to have been his teaching in general, by a gift for felicitous formulation. Who can beat—on that level—his definition of increasing and decreasing cost? You have increasing cost if a producer sets a price at which he is willing to sell a given quantity or less, and decreasing costs if he be willing to sell at that price a given quantity *or more.*

Simon Newcomb (1835-1909) was an eminent astronomer who also taught, and wrote on, economics but not enough to acquire the influence he deserved. He is chiefly remembered as a sound-money man and a laissez-faire ultra, but his name stands here because of his *Principles of Political Economy* (1885), the outstanding performance of American general economics in the pre-Clark-Fisher-Taussig epoch. He had not 'got on' to the Jevons-Menger-Walras level and his analysis was substantially 'classic.' But his presentation was masterly and highly suggestive, also original in several points. But among these points is *not* the Equation of Exchange that Fisher credited to him; this was but a formulation of what was then an old story.

William G. Sumner (1840-1910), wholly an academic man and also a sound-money, laissez-faire ultra,[4] was for the rest a different kind of person. He was

[3] His best work has been collected in his *Economic Essays* (ed. by O. M. W. Sprague with introduction by F. W. Taussig, 1904). But his *Chapters on Banking* (privately printed 1885; 1st ed. 1891; 5th ed. by O. M. W. Sprague as *Theory and History of Banking,* 1929) is still worth reading.

[4] Though the 'politics' of our men are none of our business, it might be argued, in the cases of Newcomb and Sumner, that their ultra-liberalism went so far as to imply arguments, theoretical and factual, that reflect upon their judgment as *scientific* economists. This would be true for any contemporaneous European. But it must not be forgotten that in the United States environment of that epoch, the attitude of Newcomb and Sumner might have been supported by facts that would have impressed Marx himself, when in his historical mood, but do not lend any support to the economic liberalism of, say, M. de Molinari.

a sociologist of eminence (his analysis of 'folkways' was an extremely fertile contribution) and his historical work on money and finance ranks with the best performances of American economics.[5] But this is not why he is mentioned here. In addition to all that, he was a powerful and stimulating teacher of wide horizons—he, the historian and sociologist, drew Irving Fisher's attention to the possibilities of *mathematical* theory!—who, from his chair in Yale, spread the message of high standards of scholarship.

Francis Amasa Walker (1840-1897), the son of Amasa, was, like Dunbar and Hadley, primarily an administrator (Massachusetts Institute of Technology). He was also, for a time, a genuine soldier and a civil servant of distinction (revenue, census). But his indefatigable industry enabled him to earn a great reputation as a scholar. This reputation rests primarily upon his work in money and currency policy (see below ch. 8), but he performed creditably also in the field of general economics.[6] He was the kind of man who cannot touch anything without improving it, and his many activities brought him very much to the fore—among other things, he was the first president of the American Economic Association, a president of the American Statistical Association, co-president (or 'assistant' president) of the Institut International de Statistique. As a scientific economist, he therefore got rather more than his due both in his day and in the historical record. In particular, his own contributions to economic theory (residual-claimant theory of wages, emphasis upon the role of the entrepreneur, criticism of the wage-fund theory) received perhaps more attention than they would have if made by a less prominent man. But I am saying this to protect the memory of others—and the historical standing of American economics of that time—and not to discount the services of a man whose name certainly deserves to live forever in the history of our subject.

David A. Wells (1828-98) we have met already. He is mentioned again to impress upon the reader's mind how important in the total of American research was the factual component—also in the makings of American general economics. His famous *Recent Economic Changes* (1889), which every modern student of economics should study, illustrates admirably what I mean. Wells stands here as the representative of a large class. Carroll D. Wright (1840-1909) would have made an almost equally good one. But this sketch must not degenerate into a catalogue.

[(b) *Clark, Fisher, and Taussig.*] There cannot be much difference of opinion, among either adherents or opponents, about the actual positions in American economics held by Clark and Taussig in the first decade of this century, though there may be about Fisher's position at that time. The difficulty is to appraise their positions in the *history* of that economics. The three men were cast in very different molds. All they have in common is eminence and

[5] His main achievement was the *History of American Currency* (1874), followed by the *History of Banking in the United States* (1896).

[6] See especially *The Wages Question* (1876) and his textbook *Political Economy* (1883). A bibliography that gives an idea of the range of his activities has been compiled in the *Publications of the American Statistical Association*, June 1897.

the fact that they were all purebred academic economists. Perhaps, however, there is also something else. All three of them stood out as economists in the technical sense; for the rest they accepted unquestioningly the grand commonplaces of their time and country: they were all three of them typically *animae candidae Americanae*. But not even their detractors will deny that, however much helped by the times, they were for the world at large 'the' great American economists of that period.

John Bates Clark (1847-1938), last of the claimants to independent discovery of the principle of marginal analysis and architect of one of its most significant theoretical structures, did not conquer an adequate pulpit until 1895, when he was called to Columbia. There he remained until his retirement (1923), and there he witnessed the vogue of his teaching that may be said to have lasted from 1895 to 1910. But the fundamental elements of his theoretical system were all worked out before, mainly, I think, during the 1880's, though some seem to have emerged in his mind in the early 1870's before his visit to Europe. In part, this shows in the papers he published in the 1880's, which, if space permitted, could be shown to display stages of the development of his thought in a very interesting manner. They also corroborate the claim alluded to because they reveal his own individual route to marginal productivity distribution: what he did was to turn the 'Ricardian' theory of rent, which with Ricardo had no other function than to eliminate rent from the price problem by making it an intramarginal surplus, into a principle that was of general application to all kinds of competitive returns ('law of three rents') *without becoming tautological in the process*—marginal utility (and disutility) coming in quite naturally on this route. In spite of the priority of Thünen, on the one hand, and Jevons, Menger, and Walras, on the other, this was an achievement of the first order of importance and, so we may add now, of subjective originality. Nor was it his only one. Apart from his theory of capital (see below, ch. 6, sec. 2c), he made a great stride toward a satisfactory theory of the entrepreneur's function and the entrepreneur's gain and, in connection with this, another great stride toward that clarification of all economic problems that must result from a clear distinction between stationary and evolutionary states. He identified this indeed with the distinction between statics and dynamics. But this did not greatly matter. He saw the essential points involved in constructing the model of a stationary state and he created, for the purpose of describing its properties, the concept of Synchronization. To call him simply the master of American marginalism, therefore, spells failure to grasp the whole of his analytic message. If his achievement fell short of that of Böhm-Bawerk, Marshall, and Walras in some respects, it rose above theirs in others.[7]

[7] Clark's first book, highly characteristic of the man and of his outlook on the world—perhaps also of the spirit of an environment—is not relevant to our purposes except as regards one point I am about to mention in the text: *The Philosophy of Wealth* (1885). It contributed greatly to establishing his reputation, however. His famous *Distribution of Wealth* appeared in 1899, and is a theory of a stationary process, all the essential elements of which he had published before. So far as per-

But it is as the master of American marginalism that he was and is chiefly known to the American profession and to the world.[8] The reader has presumably heard so often of the Clark school or the Marginalist school that he may be surprised at the difficulty I experience in adopting this phrase. All American and many foreign economists who were interested in economic theory at all were of course greatly influenced by Clark and they learned from him. There is no question about this. The circle of 'allies and sympathizers' was extremely large, and there certainly was a 'foreign sphere of influence.' But the precise extent of his influence is difficult to determine because, so far as his theory of distribution goes, this influence is inextricably mixed with the influences of all the other builders of similar systems. Even in the United States, one has to look very closely at an author—at his theoretical mannerisms, for instance—in order to make sure whether he got his marginal productivity theory from Clark or from Marshall or from the Austrians. More important, there was no clearly discernible 'core' in the sense in which there was a nucleus consisting of sworn disciples such as Ricardo or Marshall had. Strictly Clarkian treatises are as rare as treatises displaying Clarkian influence are numerous. Among theoretical writings of importance, the one that comes nearest to developing *Clarkian* doctrine is Carver's,[9] but, textbooks excepted, I do not know of any other.

Nevertheless, Marginalism came quickly to be considered the badge of a distinct school. And not only that: it even acquired a political connotation, growing, in the eyes of some, into a reactionary monster that stood ready to defend capitalism and to sabotage social reform. In logic, there is no sense whatever in this. The marginal principle per se is a tool of analysis, the use of which imposes itself as soon as analysis comes of age. Marx would have used it as a matter of course if he had been born fifty years later. It can no more serve to characterize a school of economics than the use of the calculus can serve to characterize a scientific school or group in mathematics or physics. To this day, the very use of the term Marginalism is indicative of erroneous

sonal aspects are concerned, the date is as misleading as is 1890 in the case of Marshall. Of almost equal importance is his *Essentials of Economic Theory* (1907). Of his other works only *The Control of Trusts* (1901; rewritten in collaboration with his son, 1912) and *The Problem of Monopoly* (1904) need be mentioned here. But we should not forget his factual work, mainly with the Division of Economics and History of the Carnegie Foundation. Let me draw the reader's attention to the charming *Memorial* to that great and lovable man, prepared by his children and privately printed in 1938.

8 See on this the chapter on Clark in Paul T. Homan, *Contemporary Economic Thought* (1928).

9 Thomas N. Carver, *Distribution of Wealth* (1904). I take this opportunity to mention the name of an American theorist who developed marginalist theory independently of Clark—Stuart Wood, another case of striking 'subjective originality.' By 1889 Wood had in fact discovered for himself a whole Walrasian system with variable coefficients of production (substitution) added. So far as theoretical groundwork goes, he could have written the Marshallian treatise. See G. J. Stigler, 'Stuart Wood and the Marginal Productivity Theory,' *Quarterly Journal of Economics*, August 1947, especially p. 644.

conceptions of the nature of the principle. A fortiori, it cannot have any bearing upon policy or social philosophy: this is perfectly understood in England, where no radical or socialist takes offense at it. It is only the political or ethical interpretation that is put upon the results of marginal analysis which can have such a bearing. And, as has been pointed out before, Clark was not free from blame. He was, of course, within his right when, in a book on the *Philosophy of Wealth*, he expounded his ethical evaluations, though they were of a type that is apt to get on radical nerves. But he went further and asserted that distribution according to the 'law' of marginal productivity is 'fair.' And this, in the eyes of a profession, the large majority of which did not take kindly to theory in any case, created an association between 'Clarkian marginalism' and capitalist apologetics in the face of the refuting fact that this 'marginalism,' barring differences in technique, plays exactly the same role it played with Clark in the reasoning of scientific economists of socialist persuasion, such as Professors Lange and Lerner.[10]

Frank William Taussig (1859-1940), whom we are to consider next, must suffer still more than either Clark or Fisher from my inability to draw, within the available space, well-rounded pictures of individuals as such. He rose to prominence later than Clark, and his influence was still increasing when, in 1917, he accepted the chairmanship of the newly created Tariff Commission and, during the war, various other public duties from which he returned with enhanced reputation and authority. Barring this interruption he was a teacher at Harvard throughout his adult life—and certainly one of the greatest teachers of economics who ever lived. His teaching in the classroom, his guiding advice, and, last but not least, his example formed innumerable young minds and no man had more to do with the steady rise of standards throughout the period than had he. However, except in the field of international trade, he did not form a school in our sense. Measuring by hours of work, his research was primarily factual: in particular, he was the country's great authority on international trade and especially the tariff. Even in this field, facts came first—earlier publications on the subject developing into his classic *Tariff History of the United States* (1888)—and theory came afterwards (*International Trade*, 1927), though he was a master of the art of welding factual and theoretical analysis. Also he developed an interest in economic sociology that produced important results. His *Inventors and Money Makers* (1915) and his *American Business Leaders* (in collaboration with C. S. Joslyn, 1932) are

[10] In order not to have to return to this subject, let us use the opportunity to notice another factor that keeps that association alive. Reformers, like other people, are not above making mistakes. It is the duty of the professional economist to point them out. Now, if the economist in doing so uses 'marginal' methods, the criticized person's humanly understandable resentment will often take the form of complaints that he has been attacked by the reactionary monster called Marginalism. If there be in fact logical error on his part, he could in general be convicted of it without the use of this modest piece of apparatus. But not understanding theory, he is not aware of this and he naturally turns against these parts of the critic's argument which he understands least of all.

the chief examples. The roots of his theory are to be found in Ricardo and in Böhm-Bawerk, whose influences show clearly in his most ambitious theoretical venture, *Wages and Capital* (1896; London School Reprint, 1932). Formed by an older tradition, he displayed a curious resistance to the newer doctrines—Böhm-Bawerk's capital theory excepted—which is perhaps why, of all their exponents, Marshall appealed to him most. But this resistance wore away, and in the end nothing was left of it except certain formal reservations that are not entirely unlike Marshall's. A turning point is indicated by his 'Outlines of a Theory of Wages' (*Proceedings of the American Economic Association*, April 1910) that frankly embraced marginal analysis. Criticisms may no doubt be raised, from a technical standpoint, against the general economics he taught, and some of them are valid even ex visu of 1900. But he was more than a theorist, historian, and economic sociologist. Above all, he was a great economist. The first edition of his *Principles of Economics* (1911) will help us to appraise 'what students got' at that time.[11]

Irving Fisher (1867-1947) was a Yale man from first to last—one of the two stars of the first magnitude that glorify Yale's scientific record, the other being Willard Gibbs, the great physicist. He was a mathematician by training and even taught astronomy for a year. We neglect all those of his scientific or propagandist activities (temperance, eugenics, hygiene, and others) that have nothing to do with economic analysis and, for the moment, also his writings on money and cycles, which will be noticed in the last chapter of this Part. Also we cannot go into his considerable contributions to the theory of statistics (index numbers, distributed lags,[12] and others) beyond emphasizing that with him statistical method was a part of economic *theory* and no longer a mere adjunct to it—in other words that he was essentially an econometrician standing in line with Petty and Quesnay. The following remarks must be confined to his three main works in general theory. The first, his thesis—*Mathematical Investigations in the Theory of Value and Prices* (1892, reprint 1926)

[11] Since it is impossible to do full justice to that great figure within this book, the reader's attention is drawn to a memorial that was published in the *Quarterly Journal of Economics*, May 1941, by some of his colleagues. [This was written by J. A. Schumpeter with the assistance of Arthur H. Cole and Edward S. Mason.]

[12] It should be observed, however, that the idea of distributing the effect of a disturbance upon several subsequent values of the variable affected is of the utmost importance for economic theory. Clearly, it is unrealistic—and in fact a counsel of despair—to say that a disturbance in some variable x that occurs at the time t will just affect the value of x (or of any other variable that depends upon x) at the time $t + n$ and at no other. We all know that a violent change in, say, a price or a set of prices will affect subsequent values of this and other prices over a more or less prolonged period and with an intensity that varies within that period. Economic reasoning that fails to take account of this cannot be said to have outgrown childhood. Yet Fisher was the first to face this problem and to try to develop a method that will take care of it statistically. This method (improved by Franz L. Alt) was very imperfect. But it constitutes a pioneer venture that will bear fruit through the ages. The reader will find all references in Alt's paper, 'Distributed Lags,' *Econometrica*, April 1942.

—is a masterly presentation of the Walrasian groundwork. To this, however, Fisher added (at least[13]) two contributions of first-class importance and originality: he indicated a method for measuring the marginal utility of income (which he developed later in his paper published in *Economic Essays Contributed in Honor of John Bates Clark*, 1927) and in the second Part of the *Mathematical Investigations*, where he treated (as Edgeworth had done) the utility of every commodity as a function of the quantities of *all* commodities, he developed the fundaments of indifference-curve analysis. The second, his *Nature of Capital and Income* (1906), which was much admired by Pareto, besides presenting the first economic theory of accounting, is (or should be) the basis of modern income analysis.[14] In the third, *The Rate of Interest* (1907, done over and republished in new form in 1930 as *The Theory of Interest*),[15] his generous acknowledgment of the priorities of Rae and Böhm-Bawerk did not allow the powerful originality of his own performance to stand out as it should. The 'impatience' theory of interest is but an element of it. Much better would its nature have been rendered by some such title as: Another Theory of the Capitalist Process. Among the many novelties of detail, the introduction of the concept of marginal efficiency of capital (he called it marginal rate of return over cost) deserves particular notice.[16]

This, together with Fisher's work in the fields of money and cycles, will substantiate the statement that some future historian may well consider Fisher as the greatest of America's scientific economists up to our own day. But this was not the opinion of his contemporaries. In the profession and the world at large, Fisher was, so far as the period under survey is concerned, not widely recognized until he became the Fisher of the 'compensated dollar,' which most people did not like. Even later on it was 'stable money' and '100 per cent

[13] There are others. But I wish to confine myself to the two that are generally recognized by now.

[14] Again, this is the main thing about it. The appendices contain a wealth of suggestions that are stimulating even to him who does not agree with all of Fisher's results.

[15] The volume includes much, but not enough, of *Capital and Income*, and the gist of Fisher's monograph on 'Appreciation and Interest,' *Publications of the American Economic Association*, August 1896.

[16] Two remarks should be made in passing. First, the identity of the Fisherian concept with the Keynesian marginal efficiency of capital has been recognized by Keynes (and Kahn) but denied by some of the followers of Keynes, notably by Professor Lerner. Second, when emphasizing Fisher's generous acknowledgment of Böhm-Bawerk's work, I did not contradict my statement in sec. 4a above. Fisher did not fully realize the extent of Böhm-Bawerk's achievement and was unduly influenced by the surface defects of the latter's exposition. This is quite compatible with saying what is indeed obvious, that Fisher did generously recognize all he saw in Böhm-Bawerk: Fisher, Keynes, and Wicksell are the three authors whom I should name if I were asked to illustrate by examples what it is I mean by 'adequate acknowledgment.' In fact, these three exemplify more than I mean: all three must be defended against the consequences of their readiness to unearth predecessors that, in some points, goes so far as to obscure the true state of things.

reserve against deposits,' and so on which diverted attention from his genuinely scientific work. In these and other matters, Fisher, a reformer of the highest and the purest type, never counted costs—even those most intensive pain costs which consist in being looked upon as something of a crank—and his fame as a scientist suffered correspondingly. In addition, the very nature of his achievement did not make for quick success. The *Mathematical Investigations* passed practically unnoticed, of course, and came into its own only when the contents were no longer of any except historical interest. The contents of *Capital and Income* were considered by most people as elaborate trivialities. The *Rate of Interest* fared better, nationally and internationally, but it is doubtful whether it conveyed its message fully before the reformulation published in 1930.

[(c) *A Few More Leading Figures*.] The economics profession reminds the outsider of nothing so much as of the Tower of Babel. However, to some extent we have seen already, and to a greater extent we shall see in the next chapter, that this impression is, on closer inspection of the scenery, not only easier to explain but also less justified than it might seem. In this subsection we shall carry our work of description a little further by mentioning a few more leading figures that stand out, here and there, from the divisions of the ever-growing army of United States economists that was then, as it is now, surging on in apparent disorder. The reader is asked once more to bear in mind that we have noticed the men in the institutionalist movement [17] in the preceding chapter (Veblen and Commons in particular) and that a few more men will be mentioned in our survey of the period's work in applied fields.[18] But he is also asked to remember that the point of view appropriate to our purpose excludes or pushes into the background men whose services were invaluable to the profession and to their students if they did not do the kind of work that matters here, which means chiefly, if they neither contributed to the development of our apparatus of analysis nor proved themselves masters in its use. I exemplify by the honored names of Henry C. Adams, Ely, Hollander, Laughlin, Seager, and Seligman.[19]

[17] [It will be recalled that J. A. S. intended to write on American institutionalism in Chapter 4, which was not completed.]

[18] No doubt this procedure has its disadvantages even apart from the impossibility of doing full justice to the work in the applied fields. In order to illustrate these disadvantages let us select a man like William Z. Ripley (1867-1944). The man who wrote on the races of Europe, and wrote and lectured on railroads and labor—and this is far from describing his activities exhaustively—is certainly not adequately characterized by his work in any or all of these fields. Some who were students of his at Harvard told me that they received more inspiration from him than from anyone else, and the department then included Taussig, Carver, and Young. He therefore certainly ought to figure among 'general economists,' whatever his deficiencies in technical analysis may have been. And this goes for many men of his type.

[The survey of the period's work in the applied fields (ch. 6, sec. 6) was unfortunately not completed.]

[19] The reader who desires to do so can easily follow up the suggestion implied in mentioning these names. Particular reference should be made to the very instructive

In one of those divisions which in fact he did much to create, Professor Frank A. Fetter (1863-1949) rose to a leading position in the first decade of this century. He was primarily, though not exclusively, a theorist, a man of scientific progress and no friend to theoretical survivals. He has sometimes been classed as an 'Austrian,' but this is not quite correct. It is true that at that time all serious theoretical endeavor had to start from the bases laid by Jevons, Menger, and Walras and that non-mathematicians would prefer the Menger version to the other two. It is also true that he did not like Marshall —precisely because of the latter's attempts to preserve outmoded heirlooms— a feeling that was perhaps reciprocated. But all this does not suffice to make a man a *follower* of Menger. On that basis, Fetter erected a building that was his own, both as a whole and in many points of detail, such as the theory of 'psychic income.' The vivifying influence upon the American profession's interest in theory of his critical exploits cannot be evaluated too highly.[20]

Fred M. Taylor (1855-1932) is another name that comes to mind whenever we feel able to muster sufficient complacency to congratulate ourselves on the present level of economic analysis in the country. He was eminently a teacher of economic theory—down to the minutiae of theoretical reasoning— and formed very many minds, among them those of some of the most prominent economists of today: there is a Taylor school though not in the one-master one-doctrine sense. His own work developed from, and went into, his teaching and he was very hesitant about publication. But when it eventually did appear, his *Principles of Economics* (1911; 9th ed., 1925) was a great success. Though technically it is open to many objections, I wonder whether modern students would not do well to refresh themselves by a dive into Taylor's world of problems, which of course—like the problems of most of the theorists of that age—seem now very remote. Taylor's highly significant contribution to the theory of the socialist economy will be noticed elsewhere.

As the period drew toward its end, the non-mathematical theorist found himself confronted by an increasingly difficult task. This was Taylor's predicament and the main source of his inadequacies. The same applies to Herbert

---

obituaries of Ely, that excellent German professor in an American skin (by H. C. Taylor in the *Economic Journal*, April 1944), and of Seligman, that kindly leader and indefatigable worker (by G. F. Shirras, ibid. September 1939). Hollander's work on Ricardo has been mentioned, however, and some of Laughlin's on money and of Adams' and Seligman's on public finance will be mentioned in the appropriate places. Carver has been mentioned above.

[20] Perusal of Fetter's *Principles of Economics* (1904) is not quite enough to substantiate the statements above. But the book gives all the essentials of what may be called the Fetter system. Some of his papers we shall meet later. The one on the relation between rent and interest illustrates a fact that blurs the frontier line of Fetter's influence, viz. the fact that there are parallelisms between his teaching and Fisher's. The one on 'The Passing of the Old [Ricardian] Rent Concept' is Fetter's most directly anti-Marshallian performance. I do not know how Marshall took the— wholly justified—stricture. But I do know that Edgeworth resented it on the not quite convincing ground that he did not like papers with titles like that.

J. Davenport (1861-1931). If we want to appraise the historical position and services of these men and others like them, we must not apply modern standards of rigor, because at that time there was as yet valid excuse for those who had no conception of things that seem elementary now—such as continuity, incremental quantities, determinacy, stability, and so on. In consequence, they on the one hand struggled with difficulties that seem imaginary now, and on the other hand failed to see problems that bother us.[21] H. J. Davenport was an excellent theorist and a great teacher in his day, and the profession is under considerable obligation to him for the infinite pains he took to straighten out the fundamental problems of the theory of his time.[22] There is another interesting point about him. He was an enthusiastic Veblenite and a strong radical of the Middle Western type who saw the evil spirits of reaction stalk both the professional and the national scene without making any effort—obviously unnecessary—to verify their existence. Davenport thus affords one of the examples that show that preoccupation with the theory of that epoch was perfectly compatible with institutionalist sympathies.

The work of these and other men shades off without violent break into that part of the work of our own period that may be identified with such men as J. M. Clark, F. H. Knight, J. Viner, and A. A. Young. This pointer must suffice.[23] We must be content to glance at one of the brightest 'patches

[21] This illustrates well the sense in which, even in economics, it is possible to speak of 'progress' and to evaluate a given state of development meaningfully as one that is 'lower' than our own. This cannot be done with 'economic thought' in general. The economists of that time had opinions on social and economic policy that differ from those that prevail now. But *this* difference is due to social conditions and to *Zeitgeist,* and there would in fact be no sense at all in our feeling superior to them or in speaking of progress accomplished. But in matters of analysis, so far as we are trying to do the same kind of thing that the theorists of that time tried to do, it is possible to speak of progress from an inferior to a superior technique, just as there is definite sense in saying that dentistry or transportation of our time is superior to that of 1900.

[22] See especially his *Value and Distribution* (1908), one of those books that are bound both to bore and to benefit their readers. It contains several points that are, subjectively at least, original. His *Economics of Enterprise* (1913), although devoted not to criticism but to construction, is really less original. I have heard of, but do not know, his manuscript on the Marshallian system, *The Economics of Alfred Marshall* (1935). His textbooks made no mark. But several articles of his would have to be gone into if space permitted.

[23] Though there is no need to 'introduce' such well-known figures as the first three, I take the opportunity of saying a few words on Allyn A. Young (1876-1929). This great economist and brilliant theorist is in danger of being forgotten. A volume of essays, *Economic Problems, New and Old* (1927), and *An Analysis of Bank Statistics for the United States* (1928; first publ. in the *Review of Economic Statistics,* 1924-7) constitute the bulk of his published work and do not convey any idea of the width and depth of his thought and still less of what he meant to American economics and to his numerous pupils. But *ex ungue leonem*—that is to say, the reader may form some idea of that lion from a single claw, namely, his paper 'Increasing Returns and Economic Progress,' *Economic Journal,* December 1928. He was among the first to

of color' in the picture of that epoch, Patten, and then at a lonely peak, Moore.

If vision were everything, Simon Patten (1852-1922)—who taught at the University of Pennsylvania from 1888 to 1917—would, historically, have to be put down as one who had few equals if any. If technique were everything, he would be nowhere. As it is he is somewhere between, standing apart on ground largely his own. He is chiefly remembered for his advocacy of protectionism—this alone was a barrier between him and the large majority of the profession—for his conception of an 'economy of plenty,' in which neither diminishing returns nor thrift would be of primary importance any more. This savors, on the one hand, of dilettantism, but, on the other hand, of later currents of thought, successfully anticipated. Neither impression is quite correct, but at the time the profession was inclined to take the former view of the matter, though it never failed to recognize what may be called the seminal importance of Patten's ideas, and still less to appreciate the vigorous teacher and delightful conversationalist—breakfast with whom was apt to shade off into lunch.

Henry Ludwell Moore's (born 1869) position in the history of economics is as assured as Patten's was among his contemporaries. To forget him in any future historical record of our science would be as easy as it would be to forget Sir William Petty. And this is as true of future economists who admire, as it is of future economists who disapprove of, every line he ever wrote. For his name is indissolubly associated with the rise of modern econometrics, which must inevitably, whether we like it or not, become more and more synonymous with technical economics. The least of his titles to lasting fame is that his work is the scientific fountainhead of the torrent of statistical demand curves that was to pour forth in the early 1930's. The great thing was his bold attempt to create, by a number of ingenious devices, *a statistically operative comparative statics* (see below, ch. 7). This venture, embodied in a series of papers that he worked up into his *Synthetic Economics*, published in 1929, is one of those landmark achievements that are bound to stand out irrespective of whether or not we make use of them. It is therefore necessary, both in the interest of our picture of that epoch's scientific situation and of the sociology of science, to stay for a moment in order to explain why a man of such stature did not acquire a greater reputation. For, though he got some credit for his statistical demand curves—mostly through his follower Henry Schultz —and caused some raising of eyebrows by his crop theory of cycles—an im-

understand the stage of transition that economic analysis entered upon after 1900 and to shape his teaching accordingly—which, so far as I have been able to make out, may be described as a cross between Marshall's and Walras', with many suggestions of his own inserted. One of the reasons why his name lives only in the memory of those who knew him personally was a habit of hiding rather than of emphasizing his own points: one must, for example, be not only a specialist but also a very careful reader to realize that in his concise and unassuming analysis of national bank statistics, there is enshrined the better part of a whole theory of money and credit.

proved version of the Jevonian theory—his reputation has not been what it should be to this day.

The first reason is, of course, the nature of his work. To try to make the Walrasian system statistically operative is something that was altogether beyond that epoch's scientific horizon.[24] The second reason was that he was a very modest and at the same time very sensitive man. His research program could have been understood, and it might even have attracted institutional support, if it had been pushed by vigorous propaganda and if it had been represented as a program of revolt against existing—'orthodox'—theory (which, in a sense, it was). But Moore was not the man for such tactics: when he did not meet with response, he retired into himself; he was the very opposite of a high-pressure salesman.[25] But there is a third reason. Moore published indeed a series of papers that should have familiarized the profession with his thought. His first books, however, deterred rather than attracted even competent judges. In order to rate at its true value his ingenious *Laws of Wages* (1911), or his *Economic Cycles: Their Law and Cause* (1914), or his *Generating Economic Cycles* (1923), it is necessary to make a lot of allowances for the peculiar merit of pioneering effort. In some points, this also applies to *Synthetic Economics*, which was, however, internationally noticed. The route this book chalks out is, however, not only difficult but, in the age of developing alternatives, also unpopular. Nevertheless, all modern analysts should study this book with care, though it is quite possible that by so doing they will become admirers of Moore rather than followers.

8. The Marxists

We have occasionally observed that many economists of that period were radicals in the sense in which we use the term today. Socialism has been called an intellectual Proteus, and it is difficult to say how many of those radicals should be called—at least potential—socialists. But neither their radicalism nor their socialism is any business of ours so long as it does not involve differences in analytic approach or, to put it perhaps more tellingly, so long as it involved only different aims, sympathies, and evaluations of the capitalist economy and civilization but not a different 'theory' of the economic process: if we have mentioned radical or socialist convictions at all, this has been done only in order to destroy widely held prejudices against the scientific work of that time. For example, the Fabians are for us just a group that did economic research and there is no reason to separate them from other people who did the same thing on the ground that they were planners or, according to some definitions, socialists. In this section we are interested

[24] His *Forecasting the Yield and the Price of Cotton* (1917) was not. But theorists had not yet discovered that this was economic theory.

[25] I am indebted to Professor F. C. Mills for a picture of Moore's character and ways. It is similar to the impression I received myself when meeting Moore at Columbia in 1913. [At the end of 1951, Moore was still alive and living in complete seclusion.]

in those socialists only who professed a different and specifically socialist *scientific* economics. Of these, the Marxists were so much more important than were any others that we may, for our purposes, consider them as the only ones. But we shall naturally touch also upon their *socialist* critics whose work acquires meaning only with reference to the system criticized.

The Marxists were a group or sect in more senses than one. But among other things they were also a scientific school, for, as has been explained before, dependence upon a creed, though it may affect, does not destroy the scientific character of the work of a group. It is only as a scientific school in our sense—as a group whose members did analytic work, accepted One Master and One Doctrine, and worked in close, if not always harmonious, contact—that Marxists come in here. All other aspects of Marxism—perhaps the essential ones—must be neglected. Now, scientific work done on Marxist lines, and even full mastery of the scientific contents of Marx's work, was until about 1930 so largely confined to German and Russian writers that, for the purposes of general orientation, no others need be mentioned at all.[1] Also, as pointed out already, it was in Germany and Russia only that Marxism exerted a strong influence upon the work of non-socialist economists: for a time, theory-minded economists had in these countries hardly any choice but to turn to Marx (or, in Germany, to Rodbertus).

The conquest by Marxism of the socialist part of the Russian intelligentsia was not due wholly to the strong cultural influence of Germany; it was partly due also to the fact that Marxist speculation was congenial to the Russian mind. But it was largely due to the German influence, and the relation between Russian and German Marxists remained very close (though not always amicable) in a personal sense, until Lenin's death or even until Trotsky's defeat. From the standpoint of analytic work done, it is only necessary to mention, among the strictly orthodox writers, Plekhanov and Bukharin.[2] But

[1] This is obvious for England: nobody has as yet credited to H. M. Hyndman and his group any contribution to economic analysis. This statement does not involve denial of some influence upon the English intellectuals, though this influence was then notoriously small. Nor is it denied that Marxism became an influence in English *economics* later on. But an analogous statement for the Latin countries requires qualification principally because of the work done, by socialists and others, on the Marxist theory of history. No qualification is, however, involved in the recognition of the fact that Marxist ideas were more widely known and more carefully interpreted in France, Italy, and Spain than they were in England, for this did not spell any analytic work to speak of in technical economics. Japanese Marxism, also, is of later date. As regards the United States, the same holds true, but an exception should possibly be made for the writings of Daniel De Leon. See, e.g., his *Reform or Revolution?* (1899).

[2] G. V. Plekhanov (1855-1918), the old leader of the small Marxist party of Russia and its leading figure until the beginning of this century, would deserve a very different place in a history of a different kind than we can allocate to him in this one. But in addition he was a scholar and a thinker. Though not much of an economist, he stands very high as a Marxist sociologist and, in particular, as an analyst of the socio-psychical 'superstructure.' This, at least, is the impression I have received from

it must not be forgotten that Marxism was the chief formative influence of practically all the Russian economists of the age. Marx was the author they really tried to master, and the Marxist education is obvious even in the writings of those who criticized Marxism adversely. The most eminent of these semi-Marxist Marx critics was Tugan-Baranowsky who is discussed below.

[(a) *Marxism in Germany*.] At the basis of the success in Germany are two facts: first the tremendous success of the Social Democratic party; and second the official adoption of Marxism by this party (Erfurt Program, 1891). Both these facts raise most interesting problems of political sociology into which we cannot go. But it must be emphasized on the one hand that, from the standpoint of Marxist orthodoxy, these two facts are really one, because any truly socialist party must of—presumably 'dialectical'—necessity be Marxist; and on the other hand that, from any standpoint other than that of Marxist orthodoxy, this adoption by a party that was rapidly growing toward political responsibility of a creed that prescribed abstention from political responsibility, in capitalist society, was obviously not the only possible, but on the contrary a most astounding, course to take—a course that was bound to cause weakening dissensions within the party, as in fact it did before the century was out. Actually, however, the party did go Marxist with a will, and its huge organization offered inspiration, support, and employment—a regular career, in fact —to orthodox Marxists only and, on principle at least, to no other socialists, however devoted or radical. On this basis developed a large and able corps of intellectual adherents that produced a large orthodox literature. Besides the party newspapers, it had as an outlet a 'heavy' magazine, *Die Neue Zeit*—later on there was also the Austrian *Kampf*—study of which is perhaps the best method of acquiring familiarity with the group's work. The non-Marxist socialist was something of an outcast and had a rather uphill fight that the party had plenty of means of turning into defeat. This is one side of the medal.

so much of his work as is, directly or indirectly, accessible to me. See especially his *Fundamental Problems of Marxism* (English trans., 1929). All I know of the writings of N. I. Bukharin (1880-1938), one of the stalwarts who were crushed by Stalin, is *Der Imperialismus und die Akkumulation des Kapitals* (1926), which leans heavily on the German performances to be mentioned (and really is part and parcel of the German discussion), and *The Economic Theory of the Leisure Class* (written 1914; English trans. 1927), a still less original performance. Some readers may miss Lenin's name, the better part of whose voluminous writings belong to the period under survey. But Lenin was a man of action, one of the shrewdest and most clear-sighted tacticians that ever lived. It is a mistake, from the standpoint of his Russian and other admirers, to insist that, being canonized now, he must also have been a great thinker. Perhaps he did contribute something to political thought, though I find in Marx all the points he ever made in the writings that are accessible to me, with one exception: he admitted frankly what Marx never either saw or admitted, viz., that the 'emancipation' of the proletariat can never be achieved by the proletariat itself, a great improvement (considering all implications) of political sociology. See, e.g., *State and Revolution* (English trans., 1919). He did not contribute anything to economic analysis which was not anticipated by either Marx himself or the German Marxists. The same goes for Trotsky.

Before looking at the other we shall see what the results were for economic analysis. It is clear from the outset that, under those circumstances, literature was bound to be apologist and interpretative in nature and that no substantive novelties and no substantive dissent were possible except in the guise of cautious reinterpretation of the Master's meanings.

Until his death (1895) Friedrich Engels, as the grand old man of the party, wielded an authority that was indeed challenged sometimes—by Rosa Luxemburg for instance—but never successfully or in any matter except tactics. Doctrinal leadership (with little say in practical politics) passed to Karl Kautsky (1854-1938), who had known Marx and was cut out for the role of high-priest, not least because he was not absolutely rigid and knew how to make concessions to dissent, within the inner circle of party writers, on individual points.[3] He edited the *Theorien über den Mehrwert* (1905-10), composed what may be called the official reply to Bernstein's criticisms and many other pieces of apologetics and countercriticism, wrote learnedly on the economic interpretation of history, and tackled problems of applied theory, especially the question of socialist agricultural policy, thus contributing here and there even to a development of Marxist doctrine. There was nothing very original in all this. The nature of the position he had taken up from the first would have precluded originality even if he had had any spark of it. But taking Kautsky's work as a whole, we may well speak of a historically significant performance.[4] The writers who, amidst acrimonious controversies, succeeded in working out more or less novel aspects of Marxist doctrine are usually referred to as neo-Marxists. Though the productive years of most of them fall within the period under survey, many of their publications belong to the next. We adopt, however, the same practice that we also follow in some other matters, namely, the carrying of our survey down to the present in

[3] Kautsky's association with Marx and Engels and his unquestionable loyalty were not the only qualities that recommended him for that function. No doubt, nobody can walk on stilts all his life and not look stilted. And both his adherence, in principle, to every letter of the faith, and the reinterpretations which, in actual fact, he permitted himself and others to make, reduced his popularity with ardent followers bent upon having their own innings. Also, though primarily a theorist, he was really not a good theorist, and he was no match for the keenest intellects of the group. But nothing of this should be allowed to obscure either his high character or his ability or the services he rendered to Marxism and, through Marxism, to the social sciences in general.

[4] The book that contains perhaps more of what was specifically his own than does any other is his *Die Agrarfrage* (1899), in which he tried to extend Marx's law of concentration to agriculture. He met criticism in his own camp, and Otto Bauer's *Sozialdemokratische Agrarpolitik* (1926) is far removed from Kautsky's views. But his work created the literature in which Bauer's is the most notable performance. Kautsky's—not unsuccessful—reply to Bernstein, *Bernstein und das Sozialdemokratische Programm* (1899); *Die materialistische Geschichtsauffassung* (2nd ed., 1929); exegetic work on *Das Erfurter Programm* (1891; English trans. under the title *Class Struggle*, 1910); and the article on 'Krisentheorien' (*Die Neue Zeit*, 1901-2) are probably the other publications that should be mentioned.

order to relieve Part v. I select for purposes of illustration Bauer, Cunow, Grossmann, Hilferding, Luxemburg, and Sternberg.

Of those that this choice omits I regret most of all Max Adler.[5] But this brilliant man suffered such loss of energy by his party activities and his practice of law that he was never able to do justice to his gifts, though he was an important element of the Viennese circle of Marxist theorists. Otto Bauer (1881-1938), a man of quite exceptional ability and not less exceptionally high character, was to some extent in the same predicament even before he rose to the position of leadership. But, besides the book on agrarian policy that has been mentioned already, at least his 'Akkumulation des Kapitals,' *Die Neue Zeit*, 1912-3, may be mentioned as a contribution to analysis of force and originality; many other writings are of great interest for the student of Marxist political thought. Rudolf Hilferding (1877-1941), a close friend and ally of Bauer's, wrote a notable reply to Böhm-Bawerk's criticism of Marx (*Böhm-Bawerks Marx-Kritik*, 1904; English trans. with introduction by P. M. Sweezy, 1949) and other things, which a fuller review could not pass by, but must be mentioned principally as the author of the most famous performance of the neo-Marxist group: *Das Finanzkapital* (1910). Whatever may be thought of the rather old-fashioned monetary theory of the first chapter and the monetary theory of crises of the fourth, its central thesis (that banks tend to gain control over industry at large and to organize the latter into monopolistic concerns that will give increasing stability to capitalism), though a hasty generalization from a phase of German developments, is interesting and original (see especially the third chapter) and had some influence upon Lenin. The one publication by H. Cunow (1862-1936) that is relevant in this connection is his series of papers 'Zur Zusammenbruchstheorie,' *Die Neue Zeit* (1898-9). Rosa Luxemburg's (1870-1919) *Gesammelte Werke* were published in 1925-8, but her most important contribution to Marxist theory is *Die Akkumulation des Kapitals* . . . (with the subtitle: Contribution to the Economic Explanation of Imperialism, 1912). [P. M. Sweezy has pointed out to me that there is a second book with the same title (but different subtitle) written in answer to her critics while she was in prison during the war and published in 1921. Ed.] H. Grossmann (*Das Akkumulations- und Zusammenbruchsgesetz des kapitalistischen Systems*, 1929) and Fritz Sternberg (*Der Imperialismus*, 1926) represent a younger generation. The first is chiefly a Marxist scholar. The latter, who recently published a highly successful book (*The Coming Crisis*, 1947), is less concerned with Marxist theory but tries rather to write what he believes Marx would write were he alive today. Their works fall in with the Marxist revival to be noticed presently.

Most of the titles mentioned point toward a goal that, in spite of their violent altercations, the neo-Marxists have in common. Identifying, in the true Marxist spirit, thought and action, theory and politics, they were primarily interested in those parts of the Marxist system that have, or seem to have, direct bearing upon socialist tactics in what they believe to be the last—the 'imperialist'—phase of capitalism.[6] Accordingly, they were but mildly

[5] Not to be confused with Victor Adler, the leader who unified (for a time) the various national sectors of Austrian socialism, and Fritz Adler, the son of Victor, who was to gain notoriety of a different kind in and after the First World War.

[6] This holds for all of them, although to very different degrees. And this is the point of contact with Leninist and Trotskyite doctrine, which turned completely on Imperialism. Comparison of the ideas of say Bauer and Hilferding with the ideas

interested in Hegelian dialectics, the labor theory of value, and such questions as whether or not it is possible to transform Marx's values into 'production prices' without altering the sum total of surplus value. All the more interested were they in 'imperialism' and in the problem of the breakdown of capitalism, hence in the theory of accumulation, of crises, and of increasing misery. It is impossible to do justice to the widely different features of the more or less ingenious systems of the individual writers. Very broadly speaking, the upshot was this. They were relatively successful in elaborating an economic theory of protection and of a, real or alleged, tendency of capitalist society to develop an increasing propensity to wage wars. Neither exposition nor criticism can be attempted here.[7] But critics who feel inclined to be too severe on this theory should remember what sort of arguments it is intended to replace: it may be wrong, but it constitutes the first attempt to look at the phenomenon in something like a scientific spirit. The increasing misery was either discarded silently or deferred to some indefinite future when counteracting factors would have spent their force (compare, for example, Sternberg's theory of the 'closed season' during which that tendency is suspended). The modus operandi of accumulation and the breakdown theory provided the battleground that was most hotly contested. And here the most sensational event was Hilferding's frank renunciation of the breakdown theory: he even contended that capitalist society, if left to itself, would increasingly consolidate its position and petrify into a sort of feudal or 'hierarchic' organization. Naturally, this was high treason to some. But even those or some of those who rejected Hilferding's theory watered down Marx's spectacular breakdown—for, if words mean anything, this is what Marx envisaged—to a mere inability of capitalist society to keep up its traditional rate of accumulation, which means little more than the settling down into a stationary state that was envisaged by Ricardo and hardly corresponds to the ideas evoked by the word Breakdown.[8]

[(b) *Revisionism and the Marxist Revival.*] Before going on, let us glance at the other side of the medal, Revisionism. As has been observed, it was not to be expected that so large a party, with so large a fringe of sympathizers, would indefinitely accept such doctrinal discipline as the strict Marxists insisted on imposing. It was indifference to philosophical and theoretical minutiae rather than acceptance of them that secured the passing of the Erfurt reso-

---

expounded in Lenin's *Imperialism* (English trans., 1933) is instructive, the more so because, in other respects, the neo-Marxists were anti-Bolshevik.

[Two long essays in German by J. A. S. (originally publ. in 1919 and 1927), the first of which attacked these neo-Marxist views, have been translated into English under the title, *Imperialism and Social Classes* (1951).]

[7] The reader will find an extremely orthodox exposition of this line of reasoning in P. M. Sweezy's *Theory of Capitalist Development*, already referred to.

[8] The work of Hilferding and Luxemburg has been briefly but admirably discussed by Eduard Heimann in *History of Economic Doctrines* (1945).

lutions. Retribution came when Bernstein,[9] a man of sufficient importance who was not indifferent to doctrine and who, moreover, believed the Marxist creed to be injurious to the party, made up his mind to risk frontal attack. 'Dialectics,' historical materialism, class struggle, labor theory, increasing misery, concentration, breakdown (including the revolutionary ideology), all came in for wholesale condemnation at his hands. We are not interested in the ensuing row, or in the tactics of August Bebel, the man in supreme command, who, like the good tactician he was, displayed at first the requisite amount of wrath, then accepted formal submission without going to extremes—though minor lights were penalized in various ways—and finally acquiesced in a state of things in which revisionism was allowed in the party on condition of refraining from active hostility. Nor are we interested in the facts that several outstanding party men were or became revisionists, that the wing acquired its own periodical (*Sozialistische Monatshefte*) and its own writers. For though some of these writers did creditable work, especially on individual practical questions—as did, for example, Schippel on foreign-trade policy—this work inevitably lost most of its distinctive color. All we are interested in is the question what net results the revisionist controversy produced for Marxist analysis. It is safe to say that Bernstein's attack had a stimulating effect and produced here and there better and more careful formulations. Perhaps it had also something to do with the increasing readiness of Marxists to jettison prophecies of spectacular misery and breakdown. On the whole, however, results cannot be rated very highly so far as the scientific position of the Marxists is concerned. For on analysis, Bernstein's attack proves to have been much weaker than one would infer from its effects on the party and on the general public. Bernstein was an admirable man but he was no profound thinker and especially no theorist. In some points, especially as regards the economic interpretation of history and the concentration of economic power, his argument was distinctly shallow. In others, he proffered the sort of common sense that any bourgeois radical might have produced. Kautsky was, if anything, more than equal to the task of answering him. And if it had not been for the political implication of the attention he got, Marxists need not have worried greatly about him.

We go on to notice two phenomena that belong to later times. Marxist analysis displayed few, if any, symptoms of decay before 1914. The contrary assertion was often made, of course, but only by writers with whom the wish was father to the thought. But during the 1920's we observe a phenomenon that was scientifically much more important than revisionism had been: we find an increasing number of socialist economists—some of them quite radical in politics and not all revisionist or 'laborist' in the political sense—who, while professing the utmost respect for Marx, nevertheless began to realize

[9] Eduard Bernstein (1850-1932) was a tried socialist, besides being a scholar and a delightful man, and carried weight as one of the old guard. But years of exile did not radicalize him. They fabianized him. Of his writings, only his book of 1899 need be mentioned. It is available in English under the title *Evolutionary Socialism* (1909).

that his pure economics had become obsolete. Marxism remained their creed, and Marxist remained their allegiance, but in purely economic matters they began to argue like non-Marxists. To put it differently, they learned the truth that economic theory is a technique of reasoning; that such a technique is neutral by nature and that it is a mistake to believe that something is to be gained for socialism by fighting for the Marxist or against the marginal utility theory of value; that no technique can be exempt from obsolescence; and that the literary defense of the cause of socialism stands to lose efficiency by clinging to outworn tools. The importance of this for the evolution of a genuinely scientific economics cannot be estimated too highly: here was at last a recognition, by the group most averse to this recognition, of the existence of a piece of ground on which it was possible to build objectively scientific structures. For the 1920's this tendency may be represented by the names of Lederer and Dobb, both of whom also exemplify the fact that political ardors need not suffer by that recognition in the least: [10] with neither of them was it a matter of watering down practical issues; with both of them it was a matter of logic. This gain was not quite lost in the turmoil of the 1930's. It may still be averred that, in spite of the Marxist revival we observe, the scientifically trained socialist is no longer a Marxist except in matters of economic sociology. The names of O. Lange and A. P. Lerner may be invoked as illustration.[11]

The other phenomenon we have to notice is precisely that Marxist revival. The sociology of it is too obvious to detain us. But there are three aspects of it that deserve attention from our own standpoint. First, though the gain for analysis of the tendency just referred to has not been *quite* lost of late—as our illustrative examples show—it has been lost in part: economists of high standing have turned Marxists, not in the sense of accepting Marx's social or political message—this would be their affair—nor in the sense that they (like Lange) accept much or all of Marx's economic sociology—this would be capable of defense—nor finally in the sense that they pay respect to Marx's historical greatness—few people would quarrel with them about this—but in the sense that they actually try to revitalize Marx's pure economics, thus joining forces with the surviving neo-Marxists. The outstanding examples are P. M.

[10] Emil Lederer (1882-1939) who, during the last years of his life, was a member of the Graduate Faculty of Political and Social Science of the New School for Social Research in New York, may be described as the leading academic socialist of Germany in the 1920's and was an influential teacher in the Universities of Heidelberg and Berlin. His little textbook (*Grundzüge der ökonomischen Theorie*, 1922) displays the tendency in question very well. Maurice Dobb was never impregnated with Marxism; allowance must be made for the English environment. But his sympathies, intellectual and other, are obviously with Marx rather than with Marshall or with the Fabians. Nevertheless, he cannot be described as a Marxist so far as economic analysis is concerned. See his *Capitalist Enterprise and Social Progress* (1925).

[11] O. Lange made the position in question very clear in his paper on 'Marxian Economics and Modern Economic Theory,' *Review of Economic Studies*, June 1935, to which I refer the reader.

Sweezy and J. Robinson.[12] Second, there are the attempts to Keynesify Marx or to Marxify Keynes. These attempts are very revelatory of prevailing ideologies but also indicate awareness of a purely analytic task. It is in fact possible to enrich the meanings of both these authors by points culled from the other, though they are at opposite poles in matters that are of decisive importance analytically. But these attempts have never, so far as I am aware, gone to the length of trying to revive Marx's theoretical apparatus.[13] Third, though the Marx vogue in England and in the United States is in part simply the natural consequence of immigration, it is also something more. On the English or American student of economics, Marx's doctrine impinges as something new and fresh, something that differs from the current stuff and widens his horizon.[14] This impact may indeed spend itself in scientifically worthless emotions, but it also may prove productive. In any case, Marx's influence must be listed among the factors of the scientific situation of today.

[12] I have strongly recommended Sweezy's *Theory of Capitalist Development* (1942) as an admirable presentation of Marx's (and most of the neo-Marxists') economic thought. The thing that calls for notice now is that Dr. Sweezy believes that the economic theory there presented is actually usable theory ex visu of today and that it is not only equal but superior to the technique used, for example, by Lange. Still more remarkable, and something of a psychological riddle, is Mrs. Robinson's *Essay on Marxian Economics* (1942). On this, see Mr. Shove's article, 'Mrs. Robinson on Marxian Economics,' in the *Economic Journal*, April 1944.

[13] One of the most interesting of these attempts has been made by S. Alexander in his paper, 'Mr. Keynes and Mr. Marx,' *Review of Economic Studies*, February 1940.

[14] One reason for this is that Marx has not been and is not being currently taught, especially not in theory courses. And one reason for this in turn is that he is so difficult to fit in. Because both of his virtues and of his faults (e.g. because of his diffuseness and repetitiveness that make 'assignments' difficult), he either is crowded out or else crowds out the rest of the material teachers feel they should convey.

CHAPTER 6

General Economics: Its Character and Contents

1. Outposts

(a) *The Sociological Framework of General Economics.*[1] As we have seen, economic sociology and in particular historical and ethnological knowledge of social institutions progressed most satisfactorily during the period under survey. But the general economics on which I am going to report now was but little affected by these developments. Its institutional framework was left practically untouched, that is to say, it was left in the shape in which it had been thrown by the English 'classics' and in particular by J. S. Mill. Nations remained amorphous agglomerations of individuals. Social classes were not living and fighting entities but were mere labels affixed to economic functions (or functional categories). Nor were the individuals themselves living and fighting beings: they continued to be mere clotheslines on which to hang propositions

[1] I refer again to P. T. Homan, *Contemporary Economic Thought* (1928). The book deals with the thought of the period we are discussing rather than with the thought that was 'contemporary' in 1928. Another general reference that should be repeated is to G. J. Stigler, *Production and Distribution Theories* (1941).

of economic logic. And, with improving rigor of presentation, these clotheslines stood out even more visibly than they had in the works of the preceding period.[2] Critics sneered. They saw that all this was poor sociology and even poorer psychology. Like their predecessors in the first half of the nineteenth century, they failed to see that, for a limited range of problems, this was at the same time sound methodology. Owing to the importance of the problems of interpretation involved, I shall digress for a moment in order to make, once more, an attempt at clarification.

The Marxists especially but also others accused the marginal utility theorists of psychologism, that is to say, of entirely missing the true problem of economics, which is to analyze the objective facts of the social process of production, and of substituting the completely secondary problems of the psychological reactions or subjective attitudes of individuals to those objective facts (see, e.g., K. Kautsky's remark on the Austrian school, p. xix of his preface to the first volume of Marx's *Theorien über den Mehrwert*, 1905-10). The Austrians and other groups, with all their misplaced emphasis upon 'psychological' magnitudes, had only themselves to blame for this mistaken objection, which can be disposed of, so far as the objectors were Marxists, by pointing out that the 'new' theories were hardly more psychological than was that of Marx, who never hesitated to appeal to capitalists' psychology (e.g., in the matter of accumulation) whenever he felt it convenient to do so. In addition, however, an increasing number of critics objected not indeed to psychology per se, but to the hedonistic or otherwise unsound psychology from which economic theorists were supposed to derive their

[2] This accounts for the survival and even the increased use of two conceptions that were particularly effective in provoking the critic's mirth or wrath. First, in order to display certain aspects of the pure logic of choice, some theorists employed the old concept of an isolated individual whom they called Robinson Crusoe. The less the critic understood what the theorist was about, the more he was amused by the picture of economists' attempting to solve social problems by 'drilling Crusoe.' Second, in order to display other aspects of the pure logic of economic behavior, some theorists, Pareto for instance, employed the concept of the economic man, *homo oeconomicus*. Nothing that was wrong was implied in the actual use they made of it. But critics did not look at this actual use, but only at the ridiculous caricature itself, which they believed was the economist's idea of human nature. Inept defense sometimes made matters worse, though some of the leaders, Menger and Marshall in particular, said all that should have been necessary to prevent misunderstanding. The latter's felicitous phrase, that the economist is studying man in the ordinary pursuits of business life, went some way in the right direction. Two points should be noted in addition: first, the fact that the German word, *Wirtschaftssubjekt*, is not synonymous with economic man though it has been often thus translated; second, the ease with which the use of the latter term can be avoided without altering the meaning of the statements in which it occurs—instead of saying that economic man will do this or that, we can always say that this or that course of action *would*, e.g., maximize satisfaction or profit.

propositions. These objections will be briefly noticed in another place (see below, ch. 7). Here, we are concerned with three other sources of criticism or misunderstanding which, for purposes of identification, we shall label Political, Sociological, and Methodological Individualism.

By Political Individualism we mean simply a laissez-faire attitude in matters of economic policy, the attitude that was dubbed Smithianism or Manchesterism in Germany. Economists who built their theoretical structures from assumptions about the behavior of individual households and firms were under suspicion of *recommending* the results of the free interplay of individual self-interests which they *described*. In the eyes of the critics, this suspicion seemed verified by the facts that many of those theorists actually were economic liberals in that sense and that some, for example, Pareto in the first stage of his career, did harness their theory into the service of an ultra-liberal policy. But this meant no more than that, like everyone else, the laissez-faire men among the theorists of the period indulged in the bad habit of giving vent to their political preferences whenever practical applications were under discussion. As has been pointed out, however, the majority no longer adhered to unqualified laissez-faire. It moved with the times. The English and the Austrians accepted *Sozialpolitik* and progressive taxation. Marshall professed to be in sympathy with the ultimate aims of socialism, though he expressed himself in so patronizing a way as to evoke nothing but irritation. Walras is best described as a semi-socialist, Wicksell as a bourgeois radical. More important, however, is it to realize that the political liberalism, so far as actually espoused by the theorists of the period, had nothing to do with their marginal utility theories. Marxists no doubt believed that these had been excogitated for purposes of social apologetics. But the 'new' theories emerged as a purely analytic affair without reference to practical questions. And there was nothing in them to serve apologetics any better than had the older theories. In fact, the contrary would be easier to maintain (compare, e.g., the equalitarian implications of the 'law' of decreasing marginal utility); and it was 'bourgeois' economists who developed, during that period, the rational theory of the socialist economy (see below, ch. 7, sec. 5); it was Marshall, Edgeworth, and Wicksell who reduced the doctrine that free and perfect competition maximizes satisfaction for all to the level of an innocuous tautology.[3]

By Sociological Individualism we mean the view, widely held in the seventeenth and eighteenth centuries, that the self-governing individual constitutes the ultimate unit of the social sciences; and that all social phenomena resolve themselves into decisions and actions of individuals that need not or cannot be further analyzed in terms of superindividual factors. This view is, of course, untenable so far as it implies a theory of

[3] How independent of political preference the new theory of value really was is nicely shown by the cases of Walras and Pareto: in matters of theory, Pareto, who was nothing but a follower of Walras, improved the latter's system in a number of technical points; politically there was a wide gulf between them.

the social process. From this, however, it does not follow that, for the special purposes of a particular set of investigations, it is never admissible to start from the given behavior of individuals without going into the factors that formed this behavior. A housewife's behavior on the market may be analyzed without going into the factors that formed it. An attempt to do so may be suggested by considerations of division of labor between different social disciplines and need not imply any theory about the theme of Society and Individual. In this case we speak of Methodological Individualism. How does this concept apply to the actual procedure of the general economics of that time?

On the one hand, it is true that the formative influences of environments, group attitudes, group valuations, and so on were not taken into account in any other way than they had been by J. S. Mill,[4] and that this was one of the reasons why, in conscious contrast, the historical school should have emphasized 'ethical' aspects as much as it did. Marshall, who did more in this direction than any other of the leading theorists, still remained within established tradition. It is also true that the failure of theorists to go further than this made itself felt—as it does now—in their treatment of a number of problems that are nevertheless 'purely economic.' On the other hand, however, it may be shown that, within the range of the problems that primarily interested them, that is within the range of the problems that come within the *logic* of economic mechanisms, the procedure of the theorists of that period may be defended as methodological individualism, and that their results, so far as they went, were not substantially impaired by the limitations that are inherent in this approach.

(b) *Population.* As we know, the theory of population, mainly the Malthusian theory, formed an essential part of the general economics of the preceding period. This means more than that economists worried about pressure of population and that apprehensions on this score influenced their vision of the social future and their ideas about economic policy. It means that hypotheses about actual and expected rates of increase in population entered into their theorizing just as did the law of decreasing returns, and that in consequence their theoretical analysis would have been incomplete without those hypotheses. Senior, therefore, had been quite right when he included a diluted Malthusianism among the fundamental postulates of economic theory. The essential point to grasp is that this ceased to be so during the period under survey. No theorist writing in, say, 1890 would have thought of doing what Senior had done. And this was *not* primarily because, very obviously, there was no longer any immediate reason for worrying about pressure of

[4] The reader will find an instructive analysis of this range of problems, with particular reference to Marshall, in two articles by Professor Talcott Parsons in the *Quarterly Journal of Economics,* November 1931 and February 1932 ('Wants and Activities in Marshall' and 'Economics and Sociology: Marshall in Relation to the Thought of His Time').

population: it was because the marginal utility system no longer depended upon a particular hypothesis on birth or death rates and was in a position to take account of whatever hypothesis an author might think fit to make. Hence the population branch of general economics tended to wilt and in its place developed a special field, not necessarily cultivated by economists alone, of population studies. This is why, since we cannot survey this special field properly, we are no longer vitally interested in the subject and why we are going to dismiss it with the following three comments.

First, though no longer essential to general economics, a topic that had been essential for so long was not abandoned quickly. It is of some interest to note that most of the leaders continued to accept, in one form or another, the Malthusian thesis, at least for an indefinite future: Böhm-Bawerk, Marshall, Walras (to some extent), and especially Wicksell,[5] all paid their respects to it, even though they no longer based upon it any part of their analytic structures. For the rest, an inconclusive discussion pro and con the Malthusian Law lingered on in textbooks and monographs.[6]

Second, the fall in the birth rate that began to set in first in the higher income brackets then also in the lower, first in towns then also in the country, first in some nations then in practically all industrialized ones, has in the subsequent period given rise to a sort of Malthusianism in reverse, that is to say, to widespread concern about the economic consequences to be expected if birth and death rates should keep on behaving as they did in the twenties—an extrapolation that, barring details and technique, reproduces Malthusian

[5] Wicksell was particularly emphatic in considering increase of numbers as the main danger to an ever-increasing standard of life of the working class—so much so that he got himself into trouble with the Swedish government. Let us note in passing that he revived the concept of optimum population. On this, see L. Robbins, 'The Optimum Theory of Population' (in Gregory and Dalton eds., *London Essays in Economics in Honour of Edwin Cannan*, 1927). Concerning 'Pareto on Population,' see Professor J. J. Spengler's instructive articles in the *Quarterly Journal of Economics*, August and November 1944.

[6] Perhaps I ought to mention, as standing out from the rest: Professor F. A. Fetter's youthful essay, *Versuch einer Bevölkerungslehre* (1894); F. Oppenheimer's *Das Bevölkerungsgesetz des T. R. Malthus* (*Law of Population*, 1900); and A. Loria's *Malthus* (1909). For general surveys see R. Gonnard, *Histoire des doctrines de la population* (1923) and F. Virgilii, *Il problema della popolazione* (1924). A curious flare-up of the discussion (*Economic Journal*, December 1923) should be noticed if only in order to illustrate the mental processes of economists. At the threshold of a period of unsalable masses of foodstuffs and raw materials, Keynes had contended that from somewhere in the first decade of the century 'nature' had begun to respond less generously to human effort than before—an interesting misinterpretation of the rise of agricultural prices that had then occurred—and even that pressure of population had been one of the causes of the First World War and also of the Russian Revolution (sic!). For this he was attacked, in the name of common sense, by Sir William H. Beveridge. But, nothing daunted, he kept on asserting (for a time) that the Malthusian devil was stalking the scene once more. It must be added, however, that few, if any, economists followed Keynes's lead in this instance. Most of them felt indeed the urge to worry. But they were soon busy worrying in the opposite direction.

methodology in the opposite direction.[7] In the period under discussion, we find only the first beginnings of this. In addition, the falling birth rate itself—or rather the motives responsible for its obvious immediate cause, contraception—presented a problem in explanation that was attacked from various standpoints. I must be content to mention what seems to me the most important performance in this field, though it also belongs to the next period, Mombert's 'prosperity theory' of the falling birth rate.[8]

Third, the really valuable progress accomplished in this field consists in the great improvement of the methods of marshalling and interpreting demographic material. This achievement greatly helped to create the new specialty mentioned above and to remove population problems from the mere economist's sphere of competence.[9] This is not to say, of course, that these problems will not re-enter general economics. The theory of secular stagnation or 'maturity' contains a hypothesis on population in its set of fundamental postulates and thus illustrates the possibility that the tendency noticed in this subsection may be reversed in the future.

2. The Vision, Enterprise, and Capital

The 'revolution' in economic theory we are going to appraise also left other things untouched in general economics besides its sociological framework. This statement must not be understood to mean that there was no advance respecting those parts of general economics that were not affected. There was substantial advance—as we shall see all along and especially in our discussion of that period's theory of money and of cycles. Only this advance was not essentially connected with the 'new' theory of value and distribution and could have come about nearly as well without the latter's help. In this section, we

[7] See, e.g., Enid Charles, *The Twilight of Parenthood* (1934). For the most effective statement of this new worry of economists, see Mr. R. F. Harrod's brilliant paper on 'Modern Population Trends,' *Manchester School*, 1939, and Professor John Jewkes' criticism of it, 'The Population Scare,' ibid. October 1939.

[8] There were many forerunners within the period—L. Brentano, for instance—but we cannot afford to survey them. For Paul Mombert, see his contribution (*Bevölkerungslehre*) to M. Weber's *Grundriss* and his *Bevölkerungsentwicklung und Wirtschaftsgestaltung* (1932).

[9] If we could deal with the literature of the period, we should, in the purely statistical line, have to mention such names as Lexis, Knapp, Knibbs, and Pearson. Not to leave the reader quite without pointers, I shall mention in addition Carr-Saunders' *Population Problem* (1922); H. Wright's textbook on *Population* (1923); R. R. Kuczynski's *Measurement of Population Growth* (1936); and L. I. Dublin's (ed.), *Population Problems in the U.S. and Canada* (1926). This choice is not meant to imply anything beyond a belief that these works open up convenient approaches to the history of the subject. Others would make other choices, I suppose. One of the achievements of the period that has received no mention at all—the work of historians on the population problems of the past—must finally be recognized at least by mentioning the name of what I believe to have been the outstanding performer in the field, Julius Beloch (*Die Bevölkerung der Griechisch-Römischen Welt*, 1886).

shall survey some topics that were left untouched by the 'revolutionaries'—and a fortiori by Marshall, who did not feel himself to be a revolutionary—within the range of the strictest possible definition of economic theory.

(a) *The Vision.* The first item to be mentioned is the economists' Vision of the economic process. We are already familiar with this concept and with the role that Vision plays in any scientific endeavor (see Part I), and nothing more needs to be said about it. Now, it is perfectly obvious that all the leaders of that time, such as Jevons, Walras, Menger, Marshall, Wicksell, Clark, and so on, visualized the economic process much as had J. S. Mill or even A. Smith; that is to say, they added nothing to the ideas of the preceding period concerning what it is that happens in the economic process and how, in a general way, this process works out; or to put the same thing differently, they saw the subject matter of economic analysis, the sum total of things that are to be explained, much as Smith or Mill had seen them, and all these efforts aimed at explaining them more satisfactorily. No conceptual creation of the period points toward a new fact or a new slant. This may be illustrated by their treatment of competition. Their economic world, like that of the 'classics,' was a world of numerous independent firms. To a surprising extent they continued to look upon the competitive case not only as the standard case that, for certain purposes, the theorist might find it useful to construct, but also as the normal case of reality. Even the owner-managed firm survived much better in economic theory than it did in actual life. The great merit that must nevertheless be put to their credit is that they complemented this vision by an analysis that was far superior to that of the 'classics.' As we shall see, they defined competition and analyzed its modus operandi with ever-increasing success; they worked out the theory of other cases such as straight monopoly, oligopoly, and so on; Marshall, moreover, glanced at the case where firms are rushing down descending cost curves, and thus clearly pointed toward the set of phenomena that were to attract theorists' attention in the 1920's and 1930's. But in all essentials, the vision of the analysts of the period remained Mill's. However much more they worried about 'trusts' and cartels, they treated them as exceptions or, at any rate, as deviations from the normal course of things (see below, ch. 7, sec. 4).

We also know that the subject that is most closely related to Vision is economic evolution or, as practically all non-Marxist authors of that period continued to call it, 'progress.' Within the precincts of this conception, there was no change at all. The reader may satisfy himself of this by studying the 36th *leçon* of Walras' *Éléments d'économie politique pure* [1] (1926). Marshall's theory of progress is much richer than are those of either his contemporaries or predecessors but, stripped to bare bones, it comes to the same: population increases, accumulation proceeds; markets widen in consequence; and this induces internal and external economies (cost-reducing improvements in the

[1] The line of argument that interests us now is blurred by the insertion of marginal productivity considerations, especially of variable coefficients of production. But the rest—the distinction between economic and technological progress notwithstanding—could have been written by J. S. Mill. See, in particular, the theorem on p. 383.

organization and technique of production). To these effects we must add those of non-induced or revolutionary inventions that just happen—all of which may, but for the calculable future need not, be interfered with by the action of the law of decreasing returns in the production of food and raw materials. All this does not go *fundamentally* beyond J. S. Mill or even A. Smith. In particular, this progress is thought of as a continuous and almost automatic process that does not harbor any phenomena or problems of its own.

(b) *Enterprise.* In most minds, the idea of economic evolution will call up the associated idea of enterprise. Here again analytic advance, though substantial, proceeded mainly along the old lines. No doubt the entrepreneur was being distinguished from the capitalist, and his profit from interest, with ever-increasing clearness as time went on. But the majority of contributions amounted to little more than elaborations of Mill's three elements of profits or of Mangoldt's rent of ability idea, and differences in explanation were chiefly differences of emphasis or formulation. A brief survey will suffice under these circumstances. Jevons and, excepting Böhm-Bawerk, the Austrians had very little to say about the matter. Böhm-Bawerk's theory was a friction or uncertainty theory, whichever the reader prefers: the source of entrepreneurs' profits was the fact that things do not work out as planned, and persistence of positive profits in a firm was due to better-than-normal judgment. Observe that the obvious common sense of this explanation may easily cover up its inadequacy.[2] Walras' contribution was important though negative. He introduced into his system the figure of the entrepreneur who neither makes nor loses (*entrepreneur ne faisant ni bénéfice ni perte*). And since this system is essentially a static theory—despite some dynamic elements that will be noticed in the next chapter—he thereby indicated a belief to the effect that entrepreneurs' profits can arise only in conditions that fail to fulfil the requirements of static equilibrium and that, with perfect competition prevailing, firms would break even in an equilibrium state—the proposition from which starts all clear thinking on profits.[3] Marshall went further than most, however, in his careful anal-

[2] Let us notice at once that Böhm-Bawerk coupled this theory of profit (in the sense of entrepreneurial gain, *Unternehmergewinn*) with a theory of interest (*Kapitalzins*) that was still a theory of profit in the Ricardo-Marx sense. We shall discuss this point below.

[3] With Walras this means only, of course, that firms ('entrepreneurs') would not reap surpluses beyond the current interest on such capital as they may own, rent at the market rate of such natural agents as they may own, and wages for their managers at the rate usually paid for such managerial services as they employ (including those of the self-employed owner-managers). Moreover, such conditions would be in the nature of a limiting state: if this limiting state should occur in practice, the entrepreneur might still hope for more than that since reality is never stationary. There was thus no justification whatever for Edgeworth's objection to the concept of the *entrepreneur ne faisant ni bénéfice ni perte* on the ground that such an entrepreneur would have no motive to go on. Another criticism, however, does impose itself: Walras postulated zero (surplus) profits (in the sense indicated), but he did not prove as a theorem that profits would converge toward zero. *Under his other assumptions, however,* there is no difficulty in doing so. Thus, this criticism, though logically valid, is purely formal. See below, ch. 7, sec. 7.

ysis of earnings of management that expanded and deepened Mill's wages of superintendence so greatly as to make practically something new out of them. He also offered other helpful suggestions. One was his reception of Mangoldt's idea of rent of ability, though he did not use it for the special purposes of an explanation of profits but more generally in the explanation of all supernormal returns to personal exertion. Another suggestion was enshrined in his concept of quasi-rent.[4] Clark's contribution was the most significant of all: he was the first to strike a novel note by connecting entrepreneurial profits, considered as a surplus over interest (and rent), with the successful introduction into the economic process of technological, commercial, or organizational improvements.

Among the rest, many authors developed Mill's (or A. Smith's) element of risk.[5] This was done most successfully by Hawley and especially by Professor Knight. To the latter we owe, in the first place, a very useful emphasis upon the distinction between insurable risks and non-insurable uncertainty; and, in the second place, a profit theory that linked this non-insurable uncertainty on the one hand to rapid economic change—which, barring extra-economic disturbances, is the main source of this uncertainty—and on the other to differences in business ability—which are much more obviously relevant to the explanation of profits and losses in conditions of rapid economic change than they would be otherwise. He thereby achieved a synthesis that is not open to the main objection against the ordinary type of risk theories. A further step in the same direction was taken by Dobb.[6] No attempt can be made to go further into the large literature of the subject that embodies and indeed characterizes a considerable part of the analytic developments of the period under survey, then produced some of its best performances in the 1920's, and finally petered out so far as its theoretical component is concerned.[7] Factual work,

[4] I do not mean, of course, that quasi-rent is identical with or uniquely related to entrepreneurial profit. But it comes in handily in an analysis of business gains. A third suggestion may perhaps also be attributed to him. The Cambridge economists, in the 1920's and 1930's, came to distinguish normal profits from those windfall profits that result from the operation of the monetary system. We are not ready as yet to consider this schema. But we may note that Marshall's *obiter dicta* on the cyclical behavior of credit and prices contain the germs of a theory of windfall profits of this type, as his treatment of the earnings of management contains the substance of the theory of normal profit.

[5] The objections to this have been pointed out already. The reference in the text is to F. B. Hawley, *Enterprise and the Productive Process* (1907); and to F. H. Knight, *Risk, Uncertainty and Profit* (1921). Though the latter work does not belong chronologically in the period under survey, it is like others mentioned here in order to light up an important line of analytic advance that starts from roots within that period.

[6] M. Dobb, *Capitalist Enterprise and Social Progress* (1925), already quoted in another context.

[7] I shall, however, mention in this footnote a few more contributions that, for one reason or another, may be considered as representative. The American work on the problem may be said to have been started by F. A. Walker (*The Wages Question*, 1876; 'The Source of Business Profits,' *Quarterly Journal of Economics*, April 1887).

which in this field meets with particular difficulties, did not get beyond beginnings. The record of successful research practically begins in the 1920's, especially in the United States where scarcity of material was an almost prohibitive obstacle before.[8]

There is one more point, however, that cannot be left untouched. All the theories of entrepreneurial activity and of entrepreneurial gains that have been mentioned are functional. That is to say, they all started by attributing to entrepreneurs an essential function in the productive process, and they all went on to explain entrepreneurial gains by success in filling that function. No doubt, different authors defined this function in different ways. But Mr. Dobb's later turn of phrase that entrepreneurs ('undertakers') are the people 'who take the ruling decisions' of economic life (op. cit. p. 54) might well serve as a common motto for them all. In describing the period's work on this topic as one of its major contributions to economic analysis, we have placed ourselves on the same standpoint.[9] It is natural, however, in a matter that concerns the central figure of the capitalist economy and, moreover, in a matter on which reliable factual information is, for most economists, so difficult to acquire, that *any* functional theory must be under suspicion of ideological bias and that it must sooner or later be met by equally suspicious opposing theories, the burden of which is to establish that the entrepreneur fills no 'productive' function at all but merely preys upon the productive activity of

---

A late contribution of note was C. A. Tuttle's paper on 'The Function of the Entrepreneur,' *American Economic Review,* March 1927 (also see his survey, 'The Entrepreneur Function in Economic Literature,' *Journal of Political Economy,* August 1927). German work simply continued an old tradition, see, e.g., Victor Mataja, *Der Unternehmergewinn* (1884) and the earlier publication, J. Pierstorff, *Die Lehre vom Unternehmergewinn* (1875). It is a question of some interest why most of this literature should have been either American or German. Perhaps because the figure of the entrepreneur was at that time more prominent in the United States and in Germany than it was in England or France? Or perhaps also because at least the English economists took the entrepreneurial function and entrepreneurial profits so much for granted as to see little need for more analysis of them than they found in Marshall—just as most of them considered the problem of interest as satisfactorily settled? But I take the opportunity to call the reader's attention to an important contribution which, if it does not exactly deal with the problems of the profits of enterprise, yet bears on them and so may be mentioned here: F. Lavington, 'An Approach to the Theory of Business Risks,' *Economic Journal,* June 1925.

[8] One of the reasons for this was that, by and large, American business did not adopt adequate methods of depreciation and cost accounting until the crisis of 1907. Factual investigation into the facts of profits had, therefore, to work on rough indications that might easily mislead.

[9] It should be emphasized at once, however, that, for those theories of entrepreneurial activity—or some of them—to be valid, it is not necessary to go beyond the proposition that this activity fills a function that is essential in *capitalist society.* How, by whom, and with what degree of efficiency analogous functions might be filled in any other organization of society, e.g., a socialist one, is an entirely different question. What the writers of that period thought about this does not affect at all the instrumental value of their theories as applied to the capitalist process.

others. Such theories enjoy wide currency in the popular economics of our time. Our first question is: has any such theory been held by any economist of repute?

The reader might think of Marx and the Marxists. If so, he mistakes the point that is at issue at the moment. Throughout the period there was a considerable number of economists who did not go along with the tendency toward a divorce of the entrepreneur from the capitalist and of the entrepreneurial gain from capital gain. All these economists continued to identify the entrepreneur, on principle, with the capitalist in the same sense as had A. Smith and Ricardo. For them, hence, the principal thing to explain was the return that accrues to capital. Of all the economists who retained this approach, the Marxists were, as a group, the most important. Thus, the Marxist theory of exploitation is a theory of the exploitation of labor by capital; and it is therefore correct, as is and has been the usual practice, to list this theory among theories of *interest*. The entrepreneur is undoubtedly present in the Marxist drama. But he is present behind the scenes and his gain is not a Marxist problem. It can be inserted into the Marxist system only by means of an un-Marxist reinterpretation. Even in Marx's description of the process of concentration, it is big *capitalists* that prey upon—'expropriate'—the smaller ones. So soon as we realize this and accordingly exclude the Marxists as well as the other authors who adopted a similar view,[10] we have difficulty in finding any accredited exponents of what we may call the depredation theory of entrepreneurial gain. Veblen comes nearest to being an instance: though even in his case certain qualifications should be made, we may perhaps consider him as the scientific ancestor of the popular theory alluded to above. But modern scientific socialists do not qualify—as may be seen from the writings of Lange and Dobb.

Under these circumstances, it is hardly worth while to raise the question whether functional explanations of the entrepreneur's role and gain are ideologically vitiated or deserve to be discounted on the ground that their authors' minds may have harbored apologetic intentions.[11] Unfortunately, this does not settle the matter. For in the first place, the functional theories do not cover the whole contents of the profit or loss item as known to business practice. This is so not only because this item also includes returns to owned factors—some of those theories, especially the older ones, following J. S. Mill's example, did include these—but also because the entrepreneur, and even the mere manager, especially the owner-manager of a concern, is so placed as to be the recipient of (positive or negative) 'leftovers': the word residual as applied to his profit, has therefore more definite meaning than it has in the case of the other claimants to shares in total receipts. Moreover, the entrepreneur or owner-manager who stands between the commodity and factor markets has

[10] On the same ground we exclude in particular various bargaining-power theories that were also used primarily for the purpose of explaining *capital* profit.

[11] Of course, this does not exclude the possibility that ideological bias is present in the Vision of the economic process that causes economists to emphasize the functional aspect at the expense of others in an analysis of a historical development.

more opportunity for exploiting favorable situations [12] and is more vulnerable to other people's doing the same thing than is anybody else. Total net profits in the sense of the gain item in an entrepreneur's personal income statement are hence an agglomeration of elements of quite different nature, and they are not anything like as closely related to whatever it is that, adopting some particular theory, we may conceive 'pure' profits to be as other people's total receipts are to their 'functional' incomes. The difference may be very considerable and constitutes a reason, though not the fundamental one, why we should not speak of a tendency of entrepreneurial gains toward equalization.

The fundamental reason is that entrepreneurial gains are not permanent returns at all but emerge each time—to adopt the language of the Knight-Dobb theory—an entrepreneur's decision in conditions of uncertainty proves successful and have no definite relation to the size of the capital employed. In other words, entrepreneurial gains, though always present like technological unemployment, yet arise, also like technological unemployment, from a sequence of events each of which, being unique, would not of itself cause permanent gains or unemployment. There is no mechanism to equalize such 'individually temporary' gains except at zero level. But many theorists of that epoch, explicitly or tacitly, did assume the existence of such a tendency simply because they had not completely got rid of the association of entrepreneurs' gains with capital gains that can indeed, if allowance be made for risk, be shown to display such a tendency. This topic is difficult—though in a sense that differs from that in which the non-mathematical student of today finds modern theory difficult—and cannot be further pursued. But I want to add that, partly for this reason, we also should not speak of 'supply of business ability.' English authors and others did this because they were prone to assimilate what they significantly called earnings of management with wages. This language is capable of defense but should not induce us to draw supply curves for entrepreneurial services even if we believe in supply curves for any other kind of work.

In the second place, it should be observed that, whatever their nature in other respects, entrepreneurs' gains will practically always bear some relation to monopolistic pricing. Whatever it is that produces these gains, it must of necessity be something that, for the moment at least, competitors cannot parallel for, if they did, no surplus over costs (including entrepreneurial 'wages') could emerge. The successful introduction of a new commodity or brand is perhaps the best illustration of this. Moreover, there are means available to the successful entrepreneur—patents, 'strategy,' and so on—for prolonging the

[12] A special case of this is what Professor Robert A. Gordon called the 'gains of position' that members of the executive group in a corporation may be able to make. See his *Business Leadership in the Large Corporation* (1945), p. 272. In the text above I mean, however, a much wider category of gains to which the same term might be applied, viz., gains that are not made in the fulfilment of the entrepreneurial 'function' but can be made by those who fill this function. I think it fair to say that the economists under discussion did recognize this phenomenon. It would indeed have been difficult for them not to do so.

life of his monopolistic or quasi-monopolistic position and for rendering it more difficult for competitors to close up on him. Obviously, this may be linked up with the elements of the case that have been glanced at in the preceding paragraph in such a way as to yield a picture of reality that may, for practical purposes, differ but little from that drawn by a straight depredation theory. Rare birds indeed are the economists who give the proper weight to this set of facts and at the same time do not overstress them. It is here rather than in the fundamental question of theory involved that ideological bias as well as political interest assert themselves. On principle, a sponsor of a functional theory is at liberty to give as much weight to predatory activities as he pleases.[13] But most economists who wrote before 1914 may have underutilized this freedom as much as many of their successors have abused it. It must not be forgotten, however, that the widespread hostility to big business and to 'trusts,' so far as there was any *analytic* meaning to it, does imply equally widespread recognition of the facts referred to.

(c) *Capital*. Once more we have to report advance, but advance almost wholly unconnected with the 'revolution' in value and distribution.[14] Throughout the period, economists of all countries displayed a propensity to adhere to the deplorable 'method' of trying to solve problems by means of hunting for the meaning of words. There was a controversy about the concept of capital, or rather there were several of them, in particular one in which the chief figure was Böhm-Bawerk and another in which the chief figure was Irving Fisher.[15] All this must not blind us to the fact that serious and not fruitless analytic work was actually done, partly even through the instrumentality of that unprepossessing 'method.' We briefly note the main points.

First, as we know, Fisher defined capital as the stock of wealth that exists at any moment. Analysis stands to gain from this in two ways: it always gains when added emphasis is placed on the fundamental distinction between funds and flows; and in this particular instance, as Fisher's argument shows, it gained a stepping stone between the economist's capital concept and the accountant's capital account. Most economists continued, indeed, to define capital as a

[13] This is his advantage over sponsors of depredation theories who must hold, if their theory is to be distinctive, that entrepreneurs had nothing at all to do with the emergence of the modern industrial apparatus except to plunder it and to sabotage its working: this is of course easy to refute both by theoretical and historical analysis.

[14] The period's analysis of capital formation (saving and investment) will be discussed in sec. 5 below and in the next chapter.

[15] Böhm-Bawerk's contribution to this activity is contained in the 2nd vol. of *Kapital und Kapitalzins*, and Fisher's in *Nature of Capital and Income*, and in all the authors cited in both. Parallel to this capital controversy went the controversy on income (which experienced a curious revival in our own day). German contributions were particularly numerous but I shall cite only R. Meyer, *Wesen des Einkommens* (1887) and for the rest refer the reader to Fisher. Since income did not as yet play the role it came to play in the Income Analysis of today, we shall not bother about this concept further. Let me, however, recall Fetter's concept of Psychic Income (*Principles*, ch. 6) and Fisher's development of the same concept (op. cit. ch. 10).

stock of goods but as a particular category of goods rather than as the total stock.[16]

Second, though 'physical' concepts still enjoyed greater popularity, non-physical ones began to intrude. Capital tended to become a fund or a sum of assets consisting of money or evaluated in money. This tendency shows well in the work of Menger, who at first, in his *Grundsätze,* defined capital as 'goods of higher order,' but later on (in his contribution to the theory of capital, 'Zur Theorie des Kapitals,' which he published in *Jahrbücher für Nationalökonomie,* July 1888) as 'productive property . . . [considered] as a sum of money productively used.' This foreshadows later tendencies, but we shall not go on to show how this point of view cropped up here and there because not much came of it at the time except in uninfluential instances.[17] The conception of capital as the discounted value of streams of expected returns put in appearance, in the wake of the works of Böhm-Bawerk and Fisher, in the guise of *value* of capital rather than of capital *sans phrase*. But it should be clear that this makes less difference than some later authors were inclined to think.[18]

Third, the majority of writers kept to the triad of factors—of which 'capital' was one—and to the parallelism between the items of this triad and the items of a corresponding triad of incomes (entrepreneurial income standing apart). This also applies to Marshall despite his formal introduction of a fourth factor, organization.

Now, all the analysts who kept to that triad and to that parallelism had in fact a strong analytic interest—it is ridiculous to speak of a political one—to define capital in a way that would qualify it to stand, in production and distribution, on a par with the labor factor and the land factor. They also had an analytic interest that was indeed weaker but still strong to deal with capital as a homogeneous quantity, the increase and decrease of which would have an unambiguous meaning. Some achieved this, quite illogically, by putting a capital factor expressed in dollars alongside of a labor factor expressed in labor hours and of a land factor expressed in acres—a practice for which instances

16 A number also worried themselves—unnecessarily as I think—about the distinction between social and private capital.

17 We may, however, note in passing that monetary concepts of capital carry the no doubt minor advantage that they bear a relation to Capitalism which physical concepts per se do not. Outside of the circle of Marxists and of economists more or less influenced by Marxist doctrine, the term Capitalism was hardly ever used. Marx, as we know, defined as capitalist an economy in which physical capital is owned by people other than the workmen. One might think that this should have induced non-Marxist economists to find characteristics of their own for the capitalist economy. But this was not the case unless we are content with such labels as private-enterprise economy or private-property economy, which do not differ much from the Marxist one.

18 It is perhaps owing to Böhm-Bawerk's not wholly felicitous way of expressing himself that his critics often failed to notice that this idea—that capital value is the result of a discounting process ('capitalization' in a special sense) is one of the main points in his capital theory.

can be found even in the 1930's.[19] In any case, however, it should be clear that, on principle, any such quantification of capital is quite inadmissible so long as capital means an assemblage of physical goods—factories, machines, lubricants, raw materials, and the like. Such an assemblage of goods can never be considered as a quantity in the ordinary sense of the term but only in the sense in which a matrix may be referred to as a 'complex quantity.' [20] Nor is this all: the same applies to the land and the labor factors that are not homogeneous quantities either. And still this is not all. The elements of these three 'complex quantities' or matrices are not clearly separated from one another but shade off into one another: a railroad track, though made by man, behaves like a natural agent; the skill of a lawyer is—or may be looked upon as—the result of 'investments,' and so on. In our own day all this has been brought home to us, with unsurpassable energy, by Professor Knight, who accordingly described 'the entire notion "of factor of production" ' as 'an incubus on economic analysis' that 'should be eliminated from economic discussion as summarily as possible.' [21] Our agreement with him must, however, be qualified in two directions. In the first place, in asserting his perfectly correct view of the matter, Professor Knight was being seriously unjust to past performance and unnecessarily so. As has been explained above, the triad of factors is one of those things whose introduction constitutes one step in advance though, at a later stage of analysis, its elimination may constitute another.[22] In the second place, it would hardly be easy to eliminate the factor idea entirely. For the condemnation Professor Knight passes upon it may be expressed by saying that he admits an indefinite variety of factors [23] within which there is no economically significant difference. But, disregarding the difficulties of presentation that would arise from the adoption of this view, there are significant differences within the world of requisites of production that are not less real and important because no sharp dividing lines exist between them. Even an attempt to take account of these differences by reasoning on an ideally pure (and homogeneous) labor, an ideally pure (and homogeneous) natural agent, and

[19] J. B. Clark's more sophisticated attempt to quantify capital will be mentioned presently; it is not considered in this place in order not to divert the reader's attention.

[20] In order to understand this, the non-mathematical reader need only look up the first page of ch. 2 and the first page of ch. 6 of Bôcher's *Introduction to Higher Algebra*, without troubling about what follows in either case. The term complex as used in this connection must not be confused with its meaning in the phrase 'complex number.'

[21] The quotation is from *Econometrica*, January 1938, p. 81.

[22] Professor Knight should be the first to recognize this, because the foremost early sponsor of the triad, J. B. Say, used it precisely for asserting the plurality of factors and the very view of distribution that Professor Knight himself adopts, namely, the view that 'distribution' *is* simply the pricing of productive services. The triad may have been a crude tool to use for these purposes but it certainly was an effective one. The other instances of serious injustice, to be mentioned presently, occur in Knight's criticism of Böhm-Bawerk's doctrine that has been closely followed.

[23] In strict logic, the number of these factors would have to be infinite, for conceptually they form a continuum.

an ideally pure (and homogeneous) type of capital good—say shovels, one exactly like the other—would hardly have to be listed among the most heinous of the offenses theorists have ever committed against realism. The reader should carefully observe, however, that this argument is not intended to carry us back to the standpoint of the economists alluded to at the beginning of this paragraph. All I wished to convey is that segregation of physical capital goods from labor and land is not inherently objectionable and that it may serve useful purposes in the analysis of structural relations within the economy. I did not wish to defend the particular purpose that was foremost in the minds of those economists, namely, the purpose of constructing an entity called (physical) capital, the price of whose services would constitute interest just as the price of the services of labor constitutes wages and the price of the services of natural agents constitutes rent. We are not concerned with interest just now.[24] But in order to avoid misunderstandings I want to say at once that I consider that theory of interest completely untenable[25] and the triad arrangement, so far as it serves the purposes of that theory, wholly unfortunate.

However, though a majority of economists adhered to the triad schema, the tendency was away from it even among sponsors of 'physical' capital concepts. Menger's concept of goods of 'higher order' (consumers' goods being goods of the lowest order) has often been mentioned in this connection. But the strongest attack upon the triad came from Böhm-Bawerk. He not only destroyed, by one of the most brilliant of his many efforts in criticism, the theory of interest alluded to above, but he also fought the idea that 'physical' capital is a distinct factor of production, capable of being treated on the same plane with the 'original' factors, labor and natural agents.[26] Both the analytic motive and the wisdom of this reduction of the triad to a dyad are open to doubt but, so far as it exerted any influence at all, it certainly served to discredit the triad. This dyad must, of course, be distinguished from a different one that is more in line with Professor Knight's views and became more and more popular

[24] As has been pointed out by Professor von Hayek (*The Pure Theory of Capital*, p. 5), capital analysis has been crippled all along by too exclusive emphasis on the problem of interest that tended to crowd out all other problems of physical capital. In the work cited, the reader finds plenty of examples of these other problems.

[25] Of course, in the economic system everything is related to everything. Therefore the statement above does not amount to saying that the structure of the set called physical capital is irrelevant to interest.

[26] It is therefore regrettable to find that a theorist of Mr. Kaldor's rank should have expressed the exactly opposite view of Böhm-Bawerk's theory of capital in sentences that clearly violate both the letter and the spirit of Böhm-Bawerk's analysis (*Econometrica*, April 1938, p. 163). And it is surprising that he should have supported this view by the question: 'if this [namely, to show that capital *is* a distinct factor of production and that capital and interest *can* be brought into the framework of production and distribution theory on the same plane as labor and land] is *not* what the theory was aiming at, what was its purpose?' A colleague of Professor von Hayek should not have found it difficult to answer this question. For the rest, I beg to remind Mr. Kaldor of the fact that Böhm-Bawerk was the author of a theory of interest that is most appropriately called a premium (*Agio*) theory.

as that period wore on: an increasing number of economists decided to assimilate natural agents with capital goods on the ground that the former's peculiarities, if any, did not warrant separate treatment.[27]

Finally, we must notice the boldest of all attempts that has ever been made to quantify physical capital, J. B. Clark's. He also included land in his concept of capital goods. But alongside this concept he set up another, Pure Capital, that was to denote a fund of abstract productive power. Had he defined this pure capital in monetary (or any value) terms, the construction would be readily understandable. But he thought of it as a physical thing, the meaning of which he tried to convey by analogies. A waterfall consists, in any given fraction of a second, of individual drops of water, but these individual drops pass on and are replaced by others and yet the waterfall as such remains the same waterfall. Similarly, pure capital consists at any moment of individual capital goods; those individual goods (or most of them) are indeed destroyed and replaced by others, yet pure capital as such remains (or may remain in a steady state) the same pure capital. Of course, it is possible to express in this way any set of elements, such as population, that renews itself [28] so long as one does not delude oneself into believing that such a construction will solve any problems. Clark, however, allowed himself to be so deluded and confidently believed that he had established the existence of a permanent factor of production, capable of yielding a net income.

Fourth, the event in this field that attracted most attention internationally, and has ever since proved a fertile source both of controversy and of positive work, was the publication of Böhm-Bawerk's theory of capital. Since Jevons had anticipated the main ideas, it will be convenient to start from his chapter on the theory of capital (*Theory of Political Economy*, ch. 7). There, Jevons declared that he was going to follow the 'classic' (Ricardian) tradition with which he professed himself in fundamental agreement.[29] Noticing, however—as had Marx—that Ricardo's capital concept embraced such disparate things as wage goods on the one hand and plant, equipment, and raw materials on the other, he suggested that the term capital should be confined to the wage goods only, apparently for the same reason that induced Marx to separate

[27] Such an arrangement, according to purpose, may or may not be convenient. And this is all that should be said about it. Actually there was a prolonged discussion on whether inclusion of land in capital was 'right' or 'wrong,' exactly as if a real issue had been involved. The interest that economists displayed—in this instance as in so many others—in a wholly imaginary 'problem' is, however, the only thing worth noticing about this discussion, and we need not stay in order to examine arguments or counter-arguments.

[28] F. Divisia called such sets *ensembles renouvelés*.

[29] Considering the essentially essayistic or 'sketchy' character of the whole book, I venture to suggest the hypothesis that, when starting to write on the subject of capital, Jevons realized that it had nothing to do with the department of theory that he believed himself to have revolutionized. He therefore actually intended to deal with capital on 'classic' lines. As his ideas developed, he cannot have failed to notice that he was chalking out novel ones. But careless as he was, he allowed the introduction to stand as it had been written before he fully knew what he was going to say.

these wage goods as variable capital from the rest, the constant capital. Asking himself the question how best to define the distinctive function of this wage-good capital, he very naturally hit upon the answer, which was indeed anything but new, that it served to support labor [30]—had he wished he might just as well have said to *exploit* labor—during the time it takes to finish the job on which workers are being actually employed. But at this point another current of ideas sets in that was not explicitly present in the argument of the Ricardians.[31] Capital, so Jevons tells us, 'allows us *to expend labour in advance*.' And command over wage-good capital is therefore a prerequisite for introducing '*whatever improvements in the supply of commodities lengthen the average interval between the moment when labour is exerted and its ultimate result or purpose accomplished*' (p. 248; Jevons' italics), for example, for building a railroad. The time we can 'finance'—which in the Jevonian argument is the same thing as the time for which we have enough wage goods to support the labor that, directly and indirectly, is employed in building the road—is therefore one of the circumstances that restrict our choice between methods of production, hence a determinant of the resulting product. This time, which now enters both the production process and the concept of capital, must, however, be thought of to include not only the time of construction and production but, in case the product consists of durable goods or of a stream of goods, also the time of 'uninvestment.' We are thus led to distinguish between 'amount of capital invested' and 'amount of investment of capital,' the latter being determined 'by multiplying each portion of capital invested at any moment by the length of time for which it remains invested' (p. 249). The well-known explanatory diagrams follow, as well as explanatory examples. This is, or suggests, a novel conception of the time-structure of the productive apparatus. The reader himself would do well to look up Jevons. In addition, I venture to ask him two things: to disregard details and to concentrate on the fundamental idea; and to admit that so far this idea is not obvious and complete nonsense.[32]

Reasons have been offered for believing that Böhm-Bawerk's theory of capital was subjectively original. But it will be convenient to treat this theory as if it were nothing but an elaboration of the Jevonian ideas.[33]

To begin with we have to discard the difficulty that arises from the fact that Böhm-Bawerk, though his subsistence fund plays exactly the same role as

[30] Only labor—it was a strange lapse for the great foe of the labor theory of value to overlook, in this argument, all other requisites of production.

[31] It may, however, have been induced by other writers, such as Hearn, whose *Plutology* (1863) Jevons quoted in this chapter as he did in others.

[32] This request may sound strange but is amply motivated by some arguments proffered in the discussion of the 1930's. I might even add another request, viz. to admit that 'duration,' in the sense that is obvious from our text, is not just a technical detail without economic relevance.

[33] Its affinities with Ricardian and Marxian ideas are, however, obvious (see above, ch. 5, sec. 4).

Jevons' wage-good capital,[34] defined his capital as intermediate products. We accept Jevons' concept but cannot dismiss this point without emphasizing Böhm-Bawerk's conception of intermediate products (such as tools and raw materials) as consumers' goods in the process of maturing (Taussig's 'inchoate wealth'). There is depth in this conception that is not found in Jevons.[35]

Next, recalling the emphasis placed by Jevons on the relation between the stretch of time that his wage-good capital allows us to 'finance' and the use of superior methods of production, we find the same idea embodied with added emphasis in Böhm-Bawerk's concept of the 'roundabout process of production' (*Produktionsumwege*), that is, production of consumers' goods via the production of intermediate goods. The extra productivity (*Mehrergiebigkeit*) of superior technology is linked so closely with the insertion of additional stages of production and this, in turn, with the extension of the time during which a given investment remains locked up that we are set wondering whether, leaving aside relatively unimportant exceptions (which he went out of his way to recognize), Böhm-Bawerk was in a position to admit the occurrence of improvements that shorten that time instead of extending it.[36] He postulated,

[34] Böhm-Bawerk's subsistence fund even suffers from the same defect—that was later on removed by Wicksell—namely, that it is merely a fund for supporting labor (conceived as homogeneous exactly like Ricardo's) and not also for the payment of the services of natural agents (possibly also of capital itself). But the reason for this was merely a desire to simplify a problem that taxed his technical aptitude as it was.

[35] Also, something is to be said for the other side of Böhm-Bawerk's medal. His intermediate products are inchoate consumers' goods. But, looked at from the other side, they are accumulated productive services (as they had been for the 'classics'—hoarded labor). This raises indeed the question of the 'resolution' of capital into the 'services of the two original factors,' of which Böhm-Bawerk made so much and of which his critics have made still more. Owing to the fact that no intermediate product can, since gorilla days, ever have been produced by labor and services of natural agents alone, such a resolution may not be admissible. But neither is it necessary, as will be shown near the end of this section.

[36] In view of the unending stream of criticisms that have been leveled at Böhm-Bawerk on this score, two points should be borne in mind. First, as we shall see presently, Böhm-Bawerk characterized his roundabout process by a figure that does not represent pure time. His 'period of production' may increase when the clock time taken by the productive process does not increase—this is the case of 'broadening' vs. 'lengthening' the capital structure—or even when it decreases. Second, Böhm-Bawerk should have made it clear that his reasoning applies only to 'improvements' that have been from the first within the producers' *technological horizon.* Inventions that widen this horizon should be excluded as they always are in the ordinary theory of production for which the technological horizon ('state of the arts') is a datum. But it is the intrusion of inventions—of methods of production that are new, not in the sense that they had not been operated before but in the sense that they had not been known before—which will be seen, on examination, to provide the cases where the adoption of 'superior' technique is attended by a shortening of the 'period of production' *even in Böhm-Bawerk's sense.* So long as we move within a given and constant technological horizon, Böhm-Bawerk's postulate is far from absurd. In order to show this, let us start from a state in which the economy is in perfect (competitive) equilibrium; and

then, that the product of a given quantity of 'labor' increases with every increase in Jevons' 'amount of investment of capital.' But he also postulated that this increase proceeds at a decreasing rate.[37] This amounts to setting up a law of decreasing (physical) returns that is formally analogous to the law of decreasing marginal productivity of any other factor: in the arithmetical tables by which Böhm-Bawerk illustrated his ideas (see, e.g., *Kapital und Kapitalzins*, II, p. 463 et seq. of the 3rd ed.), he 'applied,' as it were, successive units of time to a given amount of resources (actually: a month's labor). The restriction involved is stronger than necessary but made the going much easier for Böhm-Bawerk than it would have been without it. In appraising the standing of this postulate we must, however, never forget this lesson from the practice of the physicist: a postulate may be justified not only by establishing observationally the facts it asserts but also by its results.

Finally, Jevons' 'amount of investment of capital'—which has a time dimension—divided by his 'amount of capital invested'—which has no time dimension—gives Böhm-Bawerk's famous Period of Production. This quantity is to characterize, by a single figure, the structure of production, if possible of total national production, and to serve as the fundamental variable of capital theory. Formally, it represents a gravitational center. Think of n particles of the masses $m_1, m_2, \cdots m_n$ that lie on a straight line. Choosing this line for axis and denoting the co-ordinates of the particles on this axis by $x_1, x_2, \cdots x_n$, we find that the co-ordinate X of their center of gravity is

$$X = \frac{m_1x_1 + m_2x_2 + \cdots m_nx_n}{m_1 + m_2 + \cdots m_n}$$

let us, *but only in order to simplify the argument*, further assume that productive resources are given, constant, and (this is really a pleonasm) optimally allocated. The only reason why in these conditions there could be methods of production that are known to be 'superior' to those in use, and yet are not being used instead, evidently is that these superior methods cannot be 'financed' in the Jevons-Böhm sense. But, since under the conditions assumed, the wage-good capital is being fully *and optimally* used, the only reason, in turn, for that impossibility is that the superior methods would 'lock up' too much capital for too long a time. Now let the wage-good capital increase, all other requisites being kept constant. Everyone would agree that this will tell primarily in favor of new investment in productions involving a longer 'period.' This is all that is necessary. That part of the increase will be absorbed by wages, hence go toward financing production for immediate consumption, is so far from being an objection as to be even an essential part of Böhm-Bawerk's theory of wages. In extenuation of the sins of the critics it should be admitted, first, that with the printer's devil waiting at his door, in 1888, for new batches of manuscript, he put his argument unsatisfactorily from the start, and, second, that when criticisms poured in upon him, he frequently mismanaged his defense (particularly in the matter of inventions).

[37] Denoting physical product by p, means of production by $a, b, c, \cdots$ and time by t, we have then $p = f(a, b, c \cdots t)$, that is to say, the idea really reduces to the introduction of *some* kind of time factor into the production function (see below, ch. 7, sec. 8). Böhm-Bawerk's postulates were (1) that $\frac{\delta f}{\delta t} > 0$; and (2) that $\frac{\delta^2 f}{\delta t^2} < 0$.

Now let the *m*'s represent, instead of *n* masses of particles, *n* quantities of physical resources that are being successively applied, at *n* points of time, $t_1 \cdots t_n$, to the production of a consumers' good that, after another spell of time of storage,[38] is sold and consumed. This set-up inevitably imposes upon us either the necessity of identifying these physical resources with a single homogeneous agent—Böhm-Bawerk chose, like Jevons, homogeneous units of labor [39]—or else the assumption that these resources consist of doses of invariant composition. For axis we now choose time instead of distance, and for zero point on this axis the point of time at which the consumers' good is sold. Evidently the *t*'s are all to the left of this zero point, hence negative, and *decrease* numerically as we proceed from the first act of investment in t_1 to the right toward the zero point. The expression [40]

$$T = -\frac{m_1t_1 + m_2t_2 + \cdots m_nt_n}{m_1 + m_2 + \cdots m_n}$$

which has only a time dimension (since the resource dimension cancels out), is Böhm-Bawerk's period of production. The phrase is most infelicitous—it is difficult to think of a more infelicitous one—and to a considerable extent responsible for the flood of adverse criticisms. But the meaning of the thing itself is clear: it is the average of the time distances from the sale of the products of all the units of 'invested labor.' [41]

The need for comments on this theory of capital (in addition to those that have been made already) is much reduced by the fact that Professor Knight, by far the most eminent of its critics, has admitted that, under all the assumptions made by Böhm-Bawerk, it is valid.[42] First of all, it must be emphasized

[38] This is a slight deviation from Böhm-Bawerk's set-up.

[39] Strictly, it should be 'subsistence' considered as a homogeneous quantity. Obviously, however, he did not like to go as far as this.

[40] The expression is made positive by prefixing a minus sign, since the *t*'s enter negatively. The reader will see that it is quite reasonable to consider 'investment' as an essentially negative quantity from the standpoint of the 'investor': it is something he gives away. *T* itself should be positive, however.

[41] In his *Rate of Interest*, Irving Fisher asked the question why that weighted average should be considered as the 'correct' method of measuring the period of production. This question evidently embarrassed Böhm-Bawerk greatly (see Exkurs III in the 3rd and 4th eds. of *Kapital und Kapitalzins,* II) but it should have been easy to answer. In fact it should never have been asked: for the formula simply *defines* something that Böhm-Bawerk chose to call the period of production.

[42] This short cut has, of course, its dangers; in addition it deprives the reader of the benefits of exercise in the art of theorizing that he conceivably might reap from a fuller discussion. In order to make up for this, I refer the reader to Mr. Kaldor's survey article, 'The Recent Controversy on the Theory of Capital,' *Econometrica*, July 1937, the first three footnotes to which present a bibliography for the 1930's, including of course the papers of the protagonist, Professor Knight, to which I have only to add (except Knight's 'Reply,' ibid. January 1938, and Kaldor's 'Rejoinder,' ibid. April 1938) F. Burchardt, 'Die Schemata des stationären Kreislaufs

again that here we are not concerned with Böhm-Bawerk's theory of interest or with the bearings upon it of any of the elements of his capital theory. This makes a lot of difference. As an example, consider the argument that in a synchronized process in which production and consumption run along continuously, with all its elements perfectly co-ordinated, the idea of periods of production ceases to have any importance or even meaning and production may safely be treated as timeless. Now, it may be true that in such a process the period of production ceases to have any importance in the explanation of interest.[43] But that is not the same as saying that the concept has *no* use or even meaning in such a process. Even in Clark's waterfall, assuming it to be perfectly steady, we may, for example, try to define the time which a drop of water takes on the average to get from top to bottom, which would be a method, though a very imperfect one, of describing some of its properties. Similarly, Böhm-Bawerk's period of production would, if his assumptions be accepted, express one of the most meaningful characteristics of an economic process, however 'cycleless' it may be. This has been shown, in one of the none too numerous constructive contributions to Böhm-Bawerk's capital theory, by Professor Marschak.[44]

In the second place, we must bear in mind Böhm-Bawerk's technical disabilities, which resulted in his idea's being much more open to formally successful attack than it would have been if presented in a stronger armor. This armor has been strengthened, however, by several writers, especially by Gifford[45] and Marschak. In the third place, and independent of technical blemishes, it must not be forgotten that the concept of period of production, as framed by Böhm-Bawerk, was only a device to express an aspect of the economic process and that it neglected all others, which is what Wicksell meant when he said that Böhm-Bawerk's capital theory was so 'abstract' as hardly to

---

bei Böhm-Bawerk und Marx' (*Weltwirtschaftliches Archiv*, October 1931 and January 1932); W. Eucken, *Kapitaltheoretische Untersuchungen* (1934); and J. M. Thompson, 'Mathematical Theory of Production Stages in Economics,' *Econometrica*, January 1936. F. A. von Hayek's *Pure Theory of Capital* (1941) not only presents Professor Hayek's latest views but also sheds interesting light (in Part I) on the capital controversy. Of earlier criticisms I shall mention only Fisher's in his *Rate of Interest* and von Bortkiewicz' 'Der Kardinalfehler der Böhm-Bawerkschen Zinstheorie' (*Schmoller's Jahrbuch*, 1906). The interesting thing about the latter is its spirit of uncompromising hostility that differs so strikingly from the spirit he displayed in his famous critical pieces on Marx. Böhm-Bawerk's not wholly felicitous reply to both is in the 3rd and 4th editions of *Kapital und Kapitalzins*.

[43] Though I raised this point myself 40 years ago, I do not consider now that it is well taken.

[44] Jacob Marschak, 'A Note on the Period of Production,' *Economic Journal*, March 1934. His reasoning seems to run in value terms, but in the ratio of total value of existing stocks of commodities to the value of the flow of finished consumers' goods the value dimension cancels out.

[45] C. H. P. Gifford, 'The Concept of the Length of the Period of Production,' *Economic Journal*, December 1933. Marschak, op. cit.

constitute even a first approximation to reality. For both reasons the whole construction no doubt looks gaunt, not to say freakish.

Some of the features that account for this impression can be removed without great difficulty. Jevons knew better than to let labor be added to a growing intermediate product until a finished consumers' good emerges that is consumed at once: as stated already, he included the process of 'uninvestment' so that his period was not simply a period of *production*. Böhm-Bawerk himself, inspired by Rae, added the gradual using up of durable consumers' goods. Wicksell showed how services of natural agents might come in along with labor. His pupil, Professor Åkerman, also inspired by Rae, dealt in one of the most important works in this field, with the problems of fixed capital, which is so curiously absent from Böhm-Bawerk's schema.[46] One of those features of Böhm-Bawerk's schema that seemed most ridiculous to critics—that his period of production seems to start from a state in which all production proceeds without any tools or materials at all and people catch fish with their bare hands—can be removed so soon as we realize that all economic theory is a theory of planning and inevitably has to accept the results of the past—plant, equipment, and stocks all included—*as data*. We shall then cease to try to construct an economic process *ab ovo* and, looking forward only, consider instead of the 'amount of investment of capital,' the 'amount of investment to be done.'[47] Incidentally, this would also remove one of the motives for 'resolving' all capital goods into 'labor and land' or labor alone. Similarly, we can get rid of the 'linearity' of Böhm-Bawerk's schema of production—of the idea that all products emerge as the result of processes during which, in each intermediate stage, nothing is added to the result of the previous stage but labor. Nor does it seem impossible to me to derive from the 'periods' of individual firms the social period of production that is needed in Böhm-Bawerk's theory. But no satisfactory answer that I can see exists to another objection.

[46] Gustaf Åkerman, *Realkapital und Kapitalzins* (1923-4). See on this Wicksell's comments, republ. in the 2nd appendix to his *Lectures*, and Åkerman's own partial reformulation in: *Om den industriella rationaliseringen . . .* (1931). Erik Lindahl's contribution (available in English under the title, 'The Place of Capital in the Theory of Price,' as Part III of his *Studies in the Theory of Money and Capital*, 1939) complements this from a different standpoint, located nearer to Walras.

[47] It is a question of some interest why Böhm-Bawerk did not do this. I think that the answer is to be found in a curious attitude that was common to all the Austrians. They were never content with explaining a state of a process by the preceding states of the same process. They suspected circular reasoning in any argument that did this—or at least a begging of the fundamental question. Any truly 'causal' explanation had to be 'genetic.' It had to uncover the (logical) origins of things. Hence the capital concept had to be developed from conditions in which there was no capital. As it was, Böhm-Bawerk relied, for the purpose of getting a reasonably short period, on an ad hoc postulate, namely that, as we go back into the history of a given industrial process, the quantities of resources that have been applied in the past but are still present in it (iron mined in Roman times that may be still present in a modern pocket knife) *decrease with time much more rapidly than the time increases with which they have to be multiplied.*

In order to make Böhm-Bawerk's conception of the structure of capital serve his analytic intention, this structure must be a physical fact; and the different quantities of product that different time-structures turn out must be comparable physically. In order to secure the first requisite, we need indeed a physically homogeneous resource, the elements of which differ in nothing but the time dimension; in order to secure the second requisite, the products that enter Böhm-Bawerk's tables must all be the same in kind and quality, differing in nothing but physical quantity. Neither requirement can be fulfilled except in special cases. And it is this which reduces the analytic value of Böhm-Bawerk's capital theory, so far, to such value as may still attach to the nonoperational illustration of an aspect of reality.[48] But, so the reader might well ask, if we recognize all this and if we introduce all those corrections, what is left of Böhm-Bawerk's capital theory and in particular of his period of production? Well, nothing is left of them except the essential idea. And this keeps on proving its vitality by every piece of criticism and every piece of constructive work it evokes.[49]

3. The Revolution in the Theory of Value[1] and Distribution

In this section, we shall try to formulate, in an entirely elementary manner, what this so-called revolution consisted in and what difference it made to economic analysis. For this purpose, we shall adopt the language of the marginal utility theory in its original and most uncritical form. And we shall use primarily the Austrian edition of it, because the Austrians (Menger, Wieser, Böhm-Bawerk), in spite of their defective technique, succeeded in bringing out certain fundamental aspects more clearly than did either Jevons or Walras. Marshall's teaching will come in, as an instructive contrast, both in this section and in the next chapter, where we shall move on the higher level of Walras.[2]

[48] Situations like this are more frequently met with in economics than one might think. Marx's system offers several examples. Another is Professor Pigou's Pound of Resources, which he first introduced (1st ed. of *Wealth and Welfare*) and then dropped. Still another is Marshall's baskets of goods that he used in his theory of international trade. Perhaps the problem is not insoluble. (See, e.g., W. Leontief's article, 'Composite Commodities and the Problem of Index Numbers,' *Econometrica*, January 1936.) In any case, the examples adduced show that arguments that labor under the difficulty alluded to are not necessarily valueless.

[49] A recent constructive reinterpretation of Böhm-Bawerk that has not been mentioned yet is presented in J. R. Hicks, *Value and Capital* (1939), ch. 17. It is not in Böhm-Bawerk's spirit. But it proves that Böhm-Bawerk's ideas worried Professor Hicks. Professor Douglas unintentionally erected a monument to Böhm-Bawerk's memory in Chart 9 of his *Theory of Wages* (1934), p. 128.

[1] Instead of using this traditional phrase, I might also have used 'exchange ratios' or 'relative prices.' For most of the purposes of that period's theory, these three terms all mean the same thing.

[2] Only a few essentials will be discussed and no systematic attempt will be made to reproduce and criticize the phrasing of individual authors. For more complete analysis

The history of the marginal utility theory itself and of its successors will be treated in Chapter 7. But we need a few elements of it right now. Menger started from what he supposed were the obvious facts of human wants, which he formalized in this way: first, there are different categories of wants or tastes or desires (*Bedürfniskategorien*), such as the desire for food, for shelter, for clothing, and so on, which define the concept of Goods and can be arranged in a definite order of (subjective) importance; second, within each of these categories of wants, there exists, given as a psychic reality, a definite sequence of desires for additional increments of each good (*Bedürfnisregungen*), which we experience as we go on consuming successive increments. Menger illustrated this by a numerical table that has been reproduced by Professor Stigler (op. cit. p. 144), and dealt carefully with the large number of questions that arise in connection with the schema—such as how far wants may be treated as data in spite of their expansibility and malleability. Neglecting these questions, we proceed at once to state the postulate—or 'law'—that was fundamental to the 'new' or 'psychological' theory of value: as we go on acquiring successive increments of each good, the intensity of our desire for one additional 'unit' declines monotonically until it reaches—and then conceivably falls below—zero. Or, replacing Menger's discrete figures by a continuous curve or function, and the phrase 'desire for one more unit' [3] by Marginal Utility: 'The marginal utility of a thing to anyone diminishes with every increase in the amount of it he already has' (Marshall, *Principles*, p. 168). Waiving various objections, we may define from this (as a sum or integral) the concept of Total Utility and then also say that the total utility of a thing to anyone increases, up to the point of satiety, with every increase in the amount of it, but at a decreasing rate.

In either form this is what Marshall called the Law of Satiable Wants and what the Austrians called *Gesetz der Bedürfnissättigung*. In honor of the most important 'forerunner' it is also called Gossen's First Law.[4] We add immediately the proposition which is—or should be—called Gossen's Second Law. Unlike the first it is not a postulate but a theorem: in order to secure a maximum of satisfaction from any good that is capable of satisfying different wants (including labor or money), an individual (or household) must allocate it to these different uses in such a way as to equalize its marginal utilities in all of

the reader is referred to Professor Stigler's book, *Production and Distribution Theories* (1941).

[3] Instead of unit, Menger said *Teilquantität*, by which, as Professor Stigler points out, he meant a small but finite increment. If, for the sake of analytic convenience, we use continuous and analytic functions, we mean infinitesimal increments. The word 'unit' is never strictly correct. The phrase Marginal Utility is Wieser's (*Grenznutzen*). Jevons said Final Degree of Utility, Walras *rareté*. The latter term, which we will surely translate by scarcity, suggests that there is little to the case of objectors who, like Cassel, wished to discard utility but nevertheless to retain scarcity. The turn of phrase 'desire for one more unit' is Fisher's, who also spoke of 'wantability.' Pareto introduced the term *ophélimité élémentaire*; Clark, the term Specific Utility.

[4] See below, Appendix to ch. 7, 'Note on Utility.'

them.[5] At first sight both statements are nothing but somewhat technical renderings of sad trivialities. But we must not forget that the proudest intellectual structures rest on trivialities that are entirely uninteresting in themselves. What could be more trivial than that a body at rest will remain at rest unless something (a 'force') acts to set it in motion (Newton's First Law)? Let us, then, look at the structure that was erected on those trivialities.

(a) *The Theory of Exchange Value.* The first problem that Jevons, Menger, and Walras—Gossen too—tackled by means of the marginal utility apparatus was the problem of barter. Like their 'classic' predecessors, they realized the central position of exchange value although, also like these predecessors, they did not make it sufficiently clear to their readers and perhaps did not sufficiently realize themselves that exchange value is but a special form of a universal coefficient of transformation on the derivation of which pivots the whole logic of economic phenomena.[6] Their barter theories or, to use Whately's term once more, their catallactics, differed greatly as regards technical perfection and correctness: the peak achievement of the period is contained in *leçons* 5-15 of Walras' *Éléments*.[7] But they all—also Gossen's—aimed at the same goal, which was to prove that the principle of marginal utility suffices to deduce the exchange ratios between commodities that will establish themselves in competitive markets and also the conditions under which ranges of possible exchange ratios must be substituted for uniquely determined ones. In other words, they established what A. Smith, Ricardo, and Marx had believed to be impossible, namely, that exchange value can be explained in terms of use

[5] Menger spoke of the different wants that a good is capable of satisfying as being 'satisfied to an equal level of urgency.' This is all right so far as it goes. But it is interesting to note how hesitant many writers were about this Second Law.

[6] In consequence, history-minded or sociology-minded critics understood still less what these economic theorists were about. Taking at face value the simplified schemata by which the latter introduced their subject, and finding, e.g., that these schemata dealt with the bartering of consumers' goods that were present in given quantities, these critics wondered what could be the relevance of such analysis, not only to the great problems of social life but also to the really interesting purely economic problems of production and distribution. Veblen's essay, 'The Limitations of Marginal Utility' (republ. in *Place of Science in Modern Civilization,* 1919) exemplifies this attitude to perfection.

[7] Walras was the only one of the three to deal with the case of three and more commodities—involving indirect exchange—and to state anything approaching satisfactory equilibrium conditions in terms of excess demand. Jevons' chapter on the 'Theory of Exchange' is far inferior. Menger's treatment of the problem is all right so far as it went. But it did not go very far. When Böhm-Bawerk tried to elaborate his theory, defective technique told immediately, and his famous horse market duly came in for easy criticism from Edgeworth: the latter's most important contributions are in the *Mathematical Psychics* and, incidentally, in many of his papers. I mention specially the one in the *Giornale degli Economisti,* March 1891, where the reader also finds an interesting paper by Arthur Berry in the June 1891 number. Marshall's *Principles* contain all that the reader needs to know about the barter theory as it had shaped before the century was out (see mainly pp. 414-16, and Appendix, Notes I, II, and XII).

value.[8] Jevons, Menger, and Walras would all of them have approved of this statement. It is this which they meant when they claimed to have discovered the 'cause' of (exchange) value. However, even if granted, this would not in itself have amounted to a great deal, especially since the 'paradox of value' had been, as we know, resolved a dozen times before.[9] It is more important that the 'new' theory of exchange was more general than had been the old ones [10] and that it proved more fertile in results—many of them due to Edgeworth—even in the cases covered by the old ones. But this is not the essential point either. The essential point is that, in the 'new' theory of exchange, *marginal utility analysis created an analytic tool of general applicability to economic problems*.[11] This will become clearer as we go on.

(b) *Cost, Production, Distribution.* The concepts of marginal and total utility refer to consumers' wants. Hence they carry direct meaning only with reference to goods or services the use of which yields satisfaction of consumers' wants. But Menger went on to say that means of production—or, as he called them, 'goods of higher order'—come within the concept of economic goods

[8] In Marxist terms, this means that fundamentally the 'exchange economy' (*Tauschwertwirtschaft*) is also a 'use economy' (*Gebrauchswertwirtschaft*), which Marxist orthodoxy denied on principle. Nothing, of course, is gained or lost for socialism whichever view we adopt. But both parties, or at all events the Marxists, thought that there was practical significance to this issue. It may not be superfluous to point out that this issue has logically nothing to do with the issue of modern popular economics, production for use vs. production for profit.

[9] See, e.g., above, Part II, ch. 6, sec. 3. But all the same there is point in emphasizing, against one particular form of unfair criticism, that it is not true that A. Smith or Ricardo or J. S. Mill scorned this approach to the economic phenomenon because of its obviousness. The truth is that they did not see how 'value in use' could possibly be made to explain 'value in exchange.' They saw no further than that the former was a condition of the latter.

[10] This can best be realized by comparison with the labor-quantity theory of exchange value. The latter, so we have seen, is not 'wrong' as the revolutionaries, especially the Austrians, were in the habit of saying. It is much more enlightening to say that it covers only a special case. Even where correct, the theorem that 'prices' of commodities tend to be proportional to the labor quantities embodied in them does no more than state a property of equilibrium prices. It does not give a description of the process that establishes these prices and therefore cannot be called a theory of prices at all, any more than the statement that in certain conditions the price level will be proportional to the quantity of money, even where correct, can be called a theory of money; or the statement that in certain conditions real wages will equal minimum-of-existence requirements, even where correct, can be called a theory of wages. So far as this goes, the revolutionaries did not revolutionize an existing theoretical structure, but they erected one where none had stood before.

[11] This was felt but not properly brought out by the revolutionaries themselves. In part this was due to the fact that the tool of general application—the theory of maximizing behavior—appears in the theory of exchange in the guise of a special case. It had never been made to stand out, stripped of all non-essentials (including marginal utility itself), and reduced to its logical fundamentals before the publication of P. A. Samuelson's *Foundations of Economic Analysis* (1947; chs. 1, 2, and 3).

by virtue of the fact that they also yield consumers' satisfaction, though only indirectly, through helping to produce things that do satisfy consumers' wants directly. Let us pause for a moment to consider the meaning of this analytic device that looks so simple or even trite and was nevertheless a genuine stroke of genius.[12] It enables us to treat such things as iron or cement or fertilizers—and also all services of natural agents and labor that are not directly consumed—as incomplete consumable goods, and thereby extends the range of the principle of marginal utility over the whole area of production and 'distribution.' The requisites or factors or agents of production are assigned use values: they acquire their *indices of economic significance* and hence their exchange values from the same marginal utility principle that provides the indices of economic significance and hence explains the exchange values of consumable goods. But those exchange values or relative prices of the factors constitute the costs of production for the producing firms. This means, on the one hand, that the marginal utility principle now covers the cost phenomenon and in consequence also the logic of the allocation of resources (structure of production), hence the 'supply side' of the economic problem *so far as all this is determined by economic considerations*. And it means, on the other hand, that, in as much as costs to firms are incomes to households, the same marginal principle, with the same proviso, automatically covers the phenomena of income formation or of 'distribution,' *which really ceases to be a distinct topic*, though it may, of course, still be treated separately for the sake of convenience of exposition. The whole of the organon of pure economics thus finds itself unified in the light of a single principle—in a sense in which it never had been before.

Most of the problems that arise from this set-up can be discussed only on a level on which Walras rules supreme. But, though I believe that Jevons should be credited with a vision of the facts above and if so holds priority, the credit for having worked out that theory systematically, on the plane on which we are moving now, should go to the Austrians and particularly to Menger, whose *Grundsätze* contain all the essentials. Professor Stigler, indeed, pointed out many a 'hiatus' in Menger's treatment and rightly attributed them to his preoccupation with the threshold problems of the valuation of directly consumable goods. This accounts in fact for the impression that he was neglecting cost aspects. But on Stigler's own showing, Menger had all the essential results. Nor must we forget that the *Grundsätze* was, in a sense quite different from that applicable to Marshall's *Principles*, intended to be but an introduction. Actually, it was left for Wieser to work out the Austrian theory of cost and distribution explicitly. But he was the worst technician of the three great Austrians. And objections to methods that were peculiar to him crowded upon his readers—and especially Wicksell—so as to impair the effect of what was really a great performance. Böhm-Bawerk expounded, developed, and defended the Mengerian theory of value. But in this field he neither had nor asserted claims to originality. The best formulation of the Austrian doctrine was presented later on by Wicksell.

[12] In an embryonic form this device had already been used by Gossen.

If the explanation of the exchange value of means of production is based upon their indirect utility or use value to the consumers of their final products, that is to say, if their economic significance is to be derived from the contribution which they severally make to consumers' satisfactions, the problem naturally arises how the contribution of each of them is to be isolated, seeing that all 'factors' are equally 'requisite' for the final product and that complete withdrawal of any one of them will in most cases result in a zero product. The very fact that some German critics continued to urge that this problem was insoluble and that, because it was, the marginal utility theory was inapplicable to the evaluation of any goods other than consumers' goods present in given quantities, hence inapplicable to production, should suffice to show that here was in fact a real and non-trivial difficulty, removal of which was the prerequisite for the fundamental idea's becoming analytically operative. Menger removed it by applying the analogue of the method that he had used to resolve the value paradox. He accepted the impossibility of separating the contributions of 'factors' to the product that results from their co-operation. But he observed that in order to remove the difficulty it was sufficient to determine their *marginal* contributions (Wieser's *Grenzbeitrag*).[13] And these can be very simply found by withdrawing successively small quantities of each requisite of production, keeping the others constant each time, and ascertaining the loss of satisfaction this will cause to the consumers of the product or products.

Some technical points about this procedure [14] will be discussed in the next

[13] This should, however, have convinced both the marginalists and their critics that the marginal utility theory of income formation was constitutionally incapable of 'defending' the capitalist method of distribution. For it is obvious that the merits—moral or other—of, e.g., the labor factor are not affected if, relatively to the available quantities of other factors, laborers are so numerous that their marginal contribution is small.

[14] It is interesting to note some of the troubles that arose both for the Austrians themselves and for their critics from their lack of experience in handling the relevant concepts. Thus, there was a discussion within the Austrian circle whether or not Menger had been correct in taking as guide the loss of consumers' satisfaction incident to the loss of a small quantity of some factor: some held that we should observe instead the gain that a small increase in any factor might cause. A problem of secondary importance arises indeed in the case of discontinuities. But so long as we are concerned with a first formulation of the fundamental principle, we are within our rights in not bothering about these, and *then* all qualms on that score are simply due to failure to understand the logic of infinitesimals—of which examples could be cited even from the 1920's. Again, the objection turned up fairly early that, if you withdraw a small quantity of some factor from a technically adjusted going concern, you will cause a disturbance that will not be smaller than any that would be caused by further withdrawals but, on the contrary, so upset the plan of production as to render the rest of that factor next to useless and the schedule of *decreasing* productivities of the 'successive units' of a factor imaginary. And a curious situation arose in which this and similar objections remained unanswered because some of the marginal utility theorists did not know how to reply and because others who knew did not think it worth while to do so.

chapter. But we must notice at once that this was the way in which the Austrians rediscovered marginal productivity. Theirs was, however, a marginal productivity with a difference. In order to clarify this point, let us recall the usual distinction between marginal physical productivity and marginal value productivity. Marginal physical productivity of a 'factor' is the increment of product that results from an infinitesimal increment in the quantity of that factor. Marginal value productivity of a 'factor' to a firm [15] is this physical increment multiplied by the corresponding increment in this firm's total revenue or gross receipts. Both these concepts do enter into the Austrian theory. But they do not enter on its ground floor, and they had been developed independently of it.[16] Fundamentally, the Austrian marginal productivity was indeed a value productivity but one that did not presuppose the price of the product: it was not physical marginal productivity multiplied by any price but physical marginal productivity multiplied by some consumers' marginal utility. It was on this basis that they worked out their theory that was at the same time a theory of production and of distribution: the tools of their barter theory, forged beforehand, then came in to implement it and to show how this works out in a private-property economy.

Now, this conception of marginal value or utility productivity makes obvious common sense only in the case of a Crusoe economy. Crusoe may indeed be reasonably supposed to value his various scarce means of production according to the satisfactions he knows to be, on the margin, dependent upon their possession. To use Wieser's term, he may indeed be supposed to *impute* these satisfactions to those means (his own ability to work being just one of them) and so, for his own practical purposes, to perform a subconscious process of imputation. But if we are to maintain that a similar process of imputation constitutes the innermost meaning of the mechanisms of 'acquisitive society' (Tawney's term), it is necessary to construe this imputation as vicariously performed by firms that do not psychologically experience those consumers' satisfactions and in any case want to maximize pecuniary gains instead. To prove this is the real problem. So far as it can be proved at all, it can be proved only by showing that the barter or price mechanisms of free markets will operate in such a way as to insure the results that *would* follow if fac-

[15] Both physical and value productivity are in the first instance defined with reference to individual firms. But the Austrians, especially Wieser, as well as J. B. Clark, being interested in the social process as a whole, attempted to proceed directly to social productivities, social values, social marginal utilities. This created another class of difficulties that are typical of an early stage of analysis, difficulties that Marshall and Wicksell were much better equipped to avoid. Not much came from the discussion on Social Value, however, and we shall not go into it beyond noting that this desire to reason in social terms accounts for the curiously semi-socialist constructions of Wieser and Clark in which society itself plays the role of directing agent.

[16] This is why in this case we find a different set of forerunners: while in matters of marginal utility we have Dupuit, Gossen, and so on, we have here mainly Longfield and Thünen. This is also the reason why Menger, if indeed he was familiar with Thünen's work, failed to discover in it anything bearing directly upon his own.

tors were first evaluated as Crusoe evaluates them and if these utility values were then turned into exchange values or prices in the same manner in which the utility values of consumers' goods are turned into exchange values in a simple consumers' goods market.[17] Even to posit this problem, which is obviously neither trivial nor without interest, would have spelled considerable achievement. But Menger and Wieser, barring technical defects, went almost the whole way toward actually solving it, and thereby also solved the fundamental problems of allocation of resources (production) and of the pricing of these resources (distribution).

However, the construction involved in applying the method of imputation was not only far removed from any actual mental processes that may be credited to any deciding agents—this does not greatly matter considering the 'as if' that enters this as it does so many other scientific constructions—but also unnecessary. In order to determine the prices of factors and their distributive shares we do not need to know their utility values first. All we need to know is consumers' tastes, the technological conditions of production, and the initial distribution of ownership of 'factors'; then the principle of maximum net revenue, implying a principle of minimum cost, will do the rest. But the Austrians insisted on asserting their fundamental idea at every step and, in order to accomplish this, thought it necessary to divide up between the factors the *use value* of the product just as the *receipts* from the sale of the product are actually divided up between factors, the idea being that the former process (a methodological fiction) would yield the explanation of the latter process (a reality). Therefore, their problem of Imputation (*Zurechnung*) took the following form: to find the utility functions of producers' goods from given utility functions of consumers' goods. It was greatly complicated for them by their technical deficiencies and gave rise to a considerable literature—positive and critical—which, starting from the original contributions of Menger, Wieser, and Böhm-Bawerk, explored various blind alleys and produced more heat than light. It is, however, not necessary for us to go into this.[18] But whatever we

17 Some critics bluntly asserted that the Austrian theory of value, being a theory of the evaluation of consumers' goods, was inapplicable to the behavior of people who produce not for the satisfaction of their own wants but for markets. This, of course, indicates complete inability to understand Menger's reasoning. Others found circular reasoning in the proposition above because producers who produce for the market value their products for the sake of the money they hope to get, which presupposes the idea of expected prices, the very thing that is to be explained. The error involved in this argument should be clear. I use this opportunity to mention at once the two other vicious circles that have been charged to the Austrian theorists (often by members of their own group), though both will have to be mentioned again. The second is: we know only from a man's behavior (actual choices) which one of several quantities of goods he prefers; it is therefore circular to *explain* his choice by his preference. The third is: we value money for the sake of the goods that it will buy; hence, in the case of a purchase by means of money it is circular to hold that price is determined by the utility values of the two things to be exchanged.

18 Professor Stigler is emphatic in expressing the same opinion. He gives, however, a small sample of this literature (op. cit. p. 5n.). His judgment to the effect that some of

may think of the technical merits of the theory of imputation, it expresses a profound truth which the simple statement that production and distribution are matters of evaluating productive services does not convey in itself. And it yields a satisfactory theory of costs.

Discussion of the marginal *utilities* of means of production in the spirit of the theory of imputation easily leads to the recognition of the relevance to these marginal utilities of the elements of complementarity and substitutability [19] of factors and of their alternative uses. By this route the Austrian arrived at what has been called the alternative-use or opportunity theory of cost [20]—the philosophy of the cost phenomenon that may be expressed by the adage: What a thing really costs us is the sacrifice of the utility of those other things which we could have had from the resources that went into the one we did produce.

Sporadically, this theory of cost had turned up in the past, especially in J. S. Mill's *Principles*, but only to explain special cases which failed to fit into the older schemata. As a general theory and as an explanation of the fundamental social meaning of cost—both in capitalist and in socialist society—*it was new*. There should be no doubt also that it makes a much better theory of distribution. But I want to advert particularly to the fact that it emphasizes a phenomenon that got all but lost in Marshall's analysis. Consider the allocation of a requisite of production, say, labor, of a given type in a two-commodity economy. As we go on allocating more and more labor to the production of commodity A and less and less of it to the production of commodity B, marginal utilities of the commodity A will fall and marginal utilities of commodity B will rise. We may express this by saying that the utility returns from the A-production are decreasing and that costs in the A-production are increasing: we have derived, from the marginal-utility principle, a new 'law of decreasing returns,' which is independent of any physical law of decrease, and which will assert itself even in face of a physical law of increasing returns.

---

the monographs on the subject have been grossly incompetent is, I am afraid, only too justified.

[19] The idea of substitutability was, of course, familiar to Thünen. But Menger was the first to formulate it explicitly: 'it is . . . certain that not only can fixed quantities of goods of higher order be combined in production in the way in which we observe this in chemical products. . . [But] general experience teaches us that a given quantity of any good of lower order can result from very different combinations of goods of higher order.' (*Grundsätze*, p. 139 [trans. by J. A. S.]). To say the least, this foreshadowed the 'law of variable proportions' and even the concept of 'equal product curves.' Moreover this formulation is superior to Marshall's later 'principle of substitution.'

[20] The latter—very felicitous—term is due to D. I. Green, 'Pain Cost and Opportunity Cost,' *Quarterly Journal of Economics*, January 1894, and has gained wide currency in the United States owing to the vigorous sponsorship of Professor Knight. The most exhaustive treatment of this whole set of problems is to be found in H. J. Davenport's *Value and Distribution* (1908), who preferred the equivalent term Displacement Cost.

(c) *Interdependence and Equilibrium.* If we behold the bustling crowds that work and trade in order to make a living, we shall indeed have little difficulty in linking up their behavior with appetites for gain and appetites for goods. But it will be by no means obvious to us that the process that generates real income can be satisfactorily described, so far as its formal logic is concerned, by any simple principle or that there is any inherent logic to it at all. The history of analytic effort in this field is the history of a growing awareness, partial at first, ever more general later on, of the presence of a logically coherent economic process, an awareness that first attained conscious formulation in the works of such men as Cantillon, Quesnay, A. Smith, Say, and Ricardo. But it was only in the period under discussion that the conception of an economic cosmos that consists of a system of interdependent quantities was fully worked out with all its problems, if not quite satisfactorily solved, at least clearly arrayed and with the idea of a general equilibrium between these quantities clearly established in the center of pure theory.

This was the achievement of Walras. So soon as we realize that it is the general-equilibrium system which is the really important thing, we discover that, in itself, the principle of marginal utility is not so important after all as Jevons, the Austrians, and Walras himself believed. But analysis of Walras' schema at the same time discloses the fact that marginal utility was the ladder by which Walras climbed to the level of his general-equilibrium system. If the marginal utility principle ceased to be all-important after this level had been reached, it was nevertheless all-important heuristically. This observation sheds new light on the achievement of Jevons and the Austrians. They, too, found the ladder. Defective technique only prevented them from climbing to the top of it. But they did climb as high as their technique permitted. In other words: we must see in the Jevons-Menger utility theory an embryonic theory of general equilibrium [21] or, at all events, a particular form of the unifying principle that is at the bottom of any general-equilibrium system. Though they did not make it fully articulate, mainly because they did not understand the meaning of a set of simultaneous equations, and though they saw in marginal utility the essence of their innovation instead of seeing in it a heuristically useful methodological device, they are nonetheless, just like Walras, among the founding fathers of modern theory. This also holds for J. B. Clark. Later critics were so delighted with their own technical improvements and so anxious to renounce communion with Jevons and the Austrians that they entirely failed to perceive this.

In what sense was a revolution effected? And did this revolution produce a new theory of the economic process?

The answer to the first question will depend upon what we mean by that much misused word. If we mean change that is both thoroughgoing and discontinuous, then the claim of these pioneers of modern theory—the claim to having revolutionized the 'pure' part of economics—should be admitted. For though J. S. Mill's shaky structure invited reconstruction on the lines actually adopted by Jevons, Menger, and Walras, and though Marshall may be said

[21] This aspect is particularly in evidence in Wieser's *Natural Value.*

to have done much the same thing by reform rather than by revolution, the controversies of that age testify strongly to the break that had occurred. We are apt to smile at Gossen's boast of having accomplished a Copernican feat. But this boast was less unreasonable than it may seem at first sight. The replacement of the geocentric by the heliocentric system and the replacement of the 'classic' by the marginal utility system were performances of the same kind: they were both essentially simplifying and unifying reconstructions. The comparison strikes us as ridiculous only because of the different intellectual standings of astronomy and economics. Similarly, we smile when we learn that the Negro soldier-statesman Toussaint L'Ouverture (1743-1803) described himself as the Buonaparte of Santo Domingo. But this is because France's importance in the world is so much greater than is Santo Domingo's rather than because there is any obviously ludicrous disproportion between the two men, each taken with reference to his environment.[22]

This bears upon the habit, which has developed especially in the United States, of describing the 'marginalist' theory as neo-classic. Considering how much of the old framework and the old attitudes was taken over by the 'marginalists,' we might feel inclined to approve of it. Marshall's efforts to preserve continuity—and still more a semblance of it—lent additional support to the implied, and somewhat derogatory, appraisal of the revolutionaries' performance. But so far as pure theory is concerned, there is no more sense in calling the Jevons-Menger-Walras theory neo-classic than there would be in calling the Einstein theory neo-Newtonian: as we know already the term Eclectics, as applied to Marshall and his followers, is still more misleading. For this, however, he had only himself to blame.

The second question, as it stands, must of course be answered in the negative. No theory in the sense of pure theory can ever be a theory in the sense of complete analysis of the phenomena to which it refers. Factual assumptions are as important as is the analytic apparatus that distills results from them.[23]

22 I believe, in fact, that it is impossible, after analysis of the two careers which display certain striking similarities from their splendid beginnings to their melancholy ends, to say with confidence that less personal energy and genius went into Toussaint L'Ouverture's achievements than into Napoleon's. But economics is to astronomy, as Santo Domingo is to France.

23 The marginal utility theorists were (like most theorists to this day) only imperfectly aware of the formal character of their analysis. Preoccupied as they were with what they believed to be psychic facts, they thought that they were teaching much more about economic reality than was actually the case. I take this opportunity to comment once more on a meaningless controversy that nevertheless seemed important to many an able man, viz. the controversy about subjectivism and objectivism in pure theory in general and in the theory of price in particular. Actually, the 'subjective' theory must always appeal to 'objective' facts (data) if it is to produce concrete results; and any 'objective' theory must always state or imply postulates or propositions about 'subjective' factors of behavior. In other words, any complete subjective theory must be also objective and vice versa, and differences on this score can only be due to differences of emphasis on different parts of the analyst's task. Yet the 'issue' was accepted as real and gravely discussed by all scientific parties alike.

Moreover, economic life is a unique historical process and our authors had no explanatory schema of economic change other than the one they had inherited from A. Smith; even if they had had one of their own, their marginal utility theory would have been completely neutral to it. Finally, they had no more explicit dynamic schemata than had their 'classic' predecessors and they struggled through the inadequacies thereby created very much in the same manner. It might seem that, if our question were reformulated in the light of these three qualifications, the answer should be Yes: the marginal utility theorists certainly seem to have succeeded in creating a use-value schema of economic statics that was complete in itself. Unfortunately, we must qualify still further. Not all of the problems of pure theory were capable of unique solution within the marginal utility theory. We have had examples already, namely the theories of enterprise and of capital: as regards these, marginal utility theory completely failed—and very naturally—to restrict the range of possible difference of opinion. Another case of failure of the unifying power of the marginal utility principle is the theory of interest. This is the main reason why we shall have to enter into a separate discussion of the distributive shares after all, although the occasion will be used to touch also upon a few other matters (below sec. 5). Before we do this it will be useful to discuss Marshall's attitude to the Jevons-Menger analysis.

4. Marshall's Attitude and Real Cost

The reader is requested to refresh his memory of what has been said in the preceding chapter on the subject of Marshall's attitude to contemporaneous and earlier work closely similar, in fundamentals, to his own. In view of the thoroughly un-Marshallian interpretation of the work of the Austrians and, to a lesser extent, of Jevons, which has been presented in the preceding section,[1] it is necessary to consider Marshall's different appraisal of this work and some of the arguments by which he supported it.[2]

I submit that the impression the reader of Marshall's *Principles* is bound to receive, in spite of qualifications that Marshall inserted occasionally, is this. Marshall maintained (1) that English 'classic' analysis stood in need of corrective reinterpretation here and there but that there was nothing fundamentally wrong with it; (2) that Jevonian and Austrian criticisms had been largely due to failure to understand and to interpret it properly; [3] (3) that the posi-

[1] A point of particular importance should be emphasized once more. We have seen in ch. 5, sec. 2, that the contents of 'note XXI' in the Appendix to the *Principles* constitutes the core of Marshall's theoretical analysis. This note blocks out a system of general equilibrium. In the preceding section it has been maintained that the theoretical analysis of the Austrians also amounts to an embryonic—and highly defective—equilibrium system.

[2] For the sake of brevity, Marshallian criticisms of Jevons will be treated as if they also had been directed against the Austrians and vice versa. The reader will have no difficulty in satisfying himself that this is permissible in the instances discussed.

[3] Nothing illustrates this better than does Edgeworth's famous phrase, the echo of

tive contribution of Jevons and the Austrians consisted in elucidating the demand side of market phenomena, though Ricardo had, of course, not been ignorant of these rather obvious things; and (4) that in overstressing demand aspects Jevons and the Austrians had erred at least as much as Ricardo and Mill had erred in the opposite direction. These positions must be considered from three different angles. First, as regards Jevonian and Austrian criticisms of Ricardo, Marshall's irritation, though unjustified in part,[4] was not unnatural. We may readily grant that Nicolaus Cusanus and Copernicus did not prove the geocentric theory to be 'wrong' but that they simply applied some corrections to it. Second, as regards the performance of Jevons and the Austrians, Marshall, by nature and acquirement, could not help being severe toward their deplorable technique. We are no longer concerned with this. Third, however, as regards the fundamental meaning of that performance, Marshall's interpretation amounts to serious though of course unintentional misstatement. It is on this point that our argument in the preceding sections needs countercritical supplement.

Marshall illustrated his criticism of what he conceived to be overemphasis on demand aspects by a famous simile. 'The "cost of production principle" and the "final utility" principle are undoubtedly component parts of the one all-ruling law of supply and demand; [5] each may be compared to one blade of a pair of scissors. When one blade is held still, and the cutting is effected by moving the other, we may say with careless brevity that the cutting is done by the second; but the statement is not to be made formally and defended deliberately.' [6] Even when we narrow down the Austrian analysis to this particular

---

Marshall's voice, viz. that Marshall had dispersed the mists of 'ephemeral criticism' that for a time had clouded the 'eternal heights.'

[4] This should be evident from our discussions in Part III. But we also know that Marshall's irritation was less unjustified with respect to criticisms of Mill than it was with respect to criticisms of Ricardo. And though Marshall did not admit this in so many words, he may be called as a witness for our view: he *never* espoused the specifically Ricardian elements in the 'classic' structure, such as, e.g., the labor-quantity theory of value, which he quietly modified so that it is no longer what Ricardo had intended it to be.

[5] The reader should observe that this statement, though it may be held to conform to Mill's teaching, is thoroughly un-Ricardian. It is Malthusian.

[6] *Principles*, p. 569. The passage is an almost verbatim repetition of another passage on p. 428 that leads up to the statement 'that, *as a general rule*, the shorter the period which we are considering, the greater must be the share of our attention which is given to the influence of demand [utility] on value; and the longer the period, the more important will be the influence of cost of production on value' (p. 429). Strictly interpreted, this statement is of course as true as it is trite. In its general import, however, it gives a wrong lead. This can best be explained by an analogy: it is wrong to say that foreign exchanges are determined by supply and demand in the case of paper currencies, and by the gold mechanism in the case of gold currencies; what should be said is that *the factors behind* supply and demand determine foreign-exchange rates in any case, but that in the case of gold currencies the gold mechanism will in general

point—doing which implies neglect of all its wider aspects—we have still to recognize that its essential achievement was precisely the new theory of *supply and cost* that it yielded. It is in this sense only that Jevons' saying should be understood: '*Value depends entirely upon utility*' (*Theory*, p. 1). Hence it is meaningless to accuse either Jevons or the Austrians of wishing to minimize the importance of the very theorem which they were the first to deduce rationally and which Wieser called the 'law of cost.' They stood in no need of being told about the two blades of Marshall's pair of scissors. What they aimed at showing was that *both* blades consist of the same material—that both demand and supply (no matter whether the case is one of exchanging existing commodities or one of producing them) may be explained in terms of 'utility.'

In appearance at least, there is more to another form that Marshall gave to what was substantially the same indictment. Both Jevons and the Austrians were in the habit of expressing themselves in terms of causal chains, which ran from the value of consumable goods to the value of resources as if the utility of a quantity of a consumers' good were first determined independently and then, in turn, determined causally the value of the producers' goods that went into its production. It was child's play for a superior technician to point out that this was inadmissible since the utility of the consumers' good depends upon its quantity and the latter upon its cost. Jevons and the Austrians were held up to ridicule as people who, like school children, had to be taught that 'when three balls, A, B, and C, rest against one another in a bowl . . . the position of the three mutually determines one another under the action of gravity,' because they were contending instead 'that A determines B, and B determines C' (*Principles*, p. 567). But Marshall of all men should have realized that this criticism takes advantage of deficiencies in technique, in particular of a glaring inability to understand the logic of interdependence, and entirely fails to do justice to the substance of the position criticized. To keep again to Marshall's simile, what Jevons and the Austrians really did was not the nonsense imputed to them in that passage but something very different; they discovered precisely that the position of the balls is to be accounted for by a single principle, gravitation in the case of mechanics, utility in the case of economics. Half the generosity lavished upon Ricardo might have revealed the great achievement behind the poor technique and reduced criticism to the one point that could have been justifiably made though Mar-

prevent departure from gold parities beyond the gold points. Similarly the marginal utility principle applies to the demand *and* the supply sides of the value problem in any case, both in the long and in the short run. Cost of production is not an independent principle taking charge in the long run. But the marginal utility principle, acting upon the data of the situation, will in the long run (granting a number of assumptions) so operate as to equate exchange value to costs. Accomplished Marshallians will think this note superfluous. But I have heard the misinterpretation in question so often—and so often with reference to Marshall, even from competent economists such as Bortkiewicz—that I cannot myself think it so.

shall never made it: that Jevons knew not enough mathematics and the Austrians none at all.[7]

The only other point that must be attended to in this connection is Marshall's Real Cost. If the Austrians had used this term, they would have meant by it the consumers' goods (as distinguished from the satisfactions afforded by their consumption) that we 'sacrifice' when we decide to produce others. Marshall meant 'The exertions of all the different kinds of labour that are directly or indirectly involved in making it [a commodity]; together with the abstinences or rather the waitings required for saving the capital used in making it' (*Principles*, p. 418). This point turns up here because, at the time, it was discussed within the general controversy on the nature, cause, or 'ultimate standard' of value or cost. The quarrel was exclusively a Mengerian one. For most of the other sponsors of the 'new' theory of value, such as Gossen, Jevons, Auspitz, Lieben, and Clark—not Walras though—experienced no qualms about admitting both disutility of labor (Jevons' term) and abstinence into their analytic structures. Since all these authors were in no mind to rehabilitate the 'classics,' by pegging the independent role of costs or in any other way, this should suffice to show that recognition of disutility and abstinence does not impair the marginal utility position or constitute the adoption of another one. But the Austrians were of a different opinion. Böhm-Bawerk fought hard indeed in order to minimize the importance of both, evidently believing that allegiance to marginal utility theory compelled him to do so. Let us take the measure of the problems involved.

Abstinence is, of course, very important for every economist who holds an abstinence theory of interest. But, though holding an abstinence theory of interest of course involves introducing abstinence into the general theory of value, the question has always been dealt with primarily in connection with the theory of interest and we shall do the same (sec. 5). As regards disutility of labor, we have our choice: either we can take (with a given population) the quantity of labor hours available as a datum, for example, as institutionally fixed; or we can make it a variable to be determined, in which case our system contains one more 'unknown' and one more independent equation (which says that, for every workman, the marginal disutility of labor must in equilibrium equal the marginal utility of his wage income). Which we choose will depend on considerations of realism and considerations of analytic convenience.[8] But the point is that our choice does not make any great difference to our theoretical pattern. For the element of disutility acts upon the value of

[7] Marshall's severity was the more uncalled for because he occasionally fell into the same kind of error himself. On p. 440 of the *Principles* we read: 'In a stationary state then the plain rule would be that cost of production governs value.'

[8] As the reader presumably knows, the disutility equation was thrown out by Lord Keynes on grounds of realism. Böhm-Bawerk also threw it out on a ground of realism though a different one, viz. that the individual worker must accept the regulation working day and cannot vary the quantity of labor he is willing to offer. But whereas Böhm-Bawerk could have inserted the disutility equation if he had wanted to do so, Lord Keynes's analytic set-up made it imperative to throw it out.

products only through its (possible) influence upon the quantity of labor offered, and leaves the principle of opportunity costs untouched for purposes of allocation of the quantity that is being offered. It is always the latter that matters in the first place, whereas disutility matters, if at all, at one remove. Moreover, if we attach enough importance to having our value theory based upon utility only, all we have to do is to replace disutility of labor by the utility of leisure.[9] Hence, Böhm-Bawerk did not gain much by the limited success of his attempt to minimize the importance of disutility. But neither did Marshall gain much by introducing Real Cost: always excepting the special service that abstinence rendered in his theory of interest, it can be left out without being missed—not to speak of the difficulties inherent in the concept of a sum of all disutilities and abstinences 'directly or indirectly involved' in producing a commodity. Thus, we return from this excursion with the same result that we always get when inquiring into the nature and importance of Marshall's deviations, *in what purport to be fundamentals*, from the Jevons-Menger-Walras analysis: they are negligible.[10]

5. Interest, Rent, Wages

Any pure theory needs facts in order to produce concrete results. This platitude must be repeated because economists are in the habit of including certain particular facts in what nevertheless they call a pure theory. Thus they speak of a minimum-of-existence 'theory' of wages although the minimum-of-existence theorem may be deduced from any general theory of wages, provided we introduce the appropriate factual assumption about the behavior of workmen. But the marginal utility theory not only needs to be complemented by a supply of particular facts if it is to apply to concrete cases; it also needs to be complemented by additional material in order to produce general theoretical propositions. As has been stated at the end of Section 3, it does not, of itself, yield any general theory of interest though it does supply, of itself, adequate explanations of rents and wages. Since it is interest that causes the trouble, we shall begin by discussion of the interest theories of the period under survey.

(a) *Interest.* We know already that the economists of that period sharpened the distinction between entrepreneurial gains and interest. But most of them still took the view that we have traced to Nicholas Barbon (Part II, ch. 6, sec. 7b), namely, that interest constitutes the bulk of business gains—the part of business gains that results from the application of physical capital and is a return to physical capital in the same sense in which rent is a return to land and wages are a return to labor. In this respect, it is highly significant that

[9] This is to be recommended in any case. The particular problem in which disutility plays a role, e.g. the problem of explaining why increase in wage rates sometimes results in a decrease in the amount of work done, becomes even easier to solve when we use the concept of leisure (and put leisure on one of the axes of an indifference diagram, the other axis representing wages, monetary or real).

[10] In addition, it is difficult to understand how Marshall can have believed (if he did) that introducing real cost of *this* type would help *Ricardo's* position in any way.

Böhm-Bawerk, in his critical history of interest theories, dealt with Ricardo's and Marx's theories of 'profit' without raising the question whether the returns thus denoted were really the same thing as 'interest.' He would have answered this question much as A. Smith or J. S. Mill had answered it. Monetary interest remained for him simply the shadow of the interest that is earned by supplying physical goods—which really were what, though perhaps 'in the form of money,' the capitalist owned. This is all the more remarkable because Böhm-Bawerk's own work was principally instrumental in dissolving this schema.

To begin with, it is not recognized sufficiently that Böhm-Bawerk's criticisms of existing explanations of interest awoke a new awareness of the problem involved in that view of the matter. It is true, more or less, that all the theories of interest survived that had been inherited from the preceding period. Even a theorist of Pareto's rank felt no compunction in declaring that the fact that (physical) capital bears interest was not more of a problem than is the fact that the cherry tree bears cherries.[1] But the standing of some of the simple theories that used to satisfy a majority of economists rapidly declined. Few writers cared to go on holding that because one can produce more wheat with the help of a harrow than without it, a net return must result from using it: Böhm-Bawerk's admonition that the physical productivity of capital is not enough to prove its value productivity took the wind out of the sails of the productivity theory of interest even though it was not immediately destroyed.[2] Similarly, Böhm-Bawerk showed successfully that, in themselves, 'use theories' of interest (Knies, Menger, Walras) were no good: there is no doubt that the services of durable goods, such as houses or machines, are priced and that their prices times their quantities constitute returns to the owners of these goods; but since these goods have to be insured and amortized, it does not follow, without appeal to some other element in the case, that these returns are net. Disregarding a number of other theories that received their *coups de grâce* at the hands of Böhm-Bawerk, we may say broadly that the only survivors that

[1] Another opinion of Pareto's deserves comment. He thought that to search for the 'cause' of interest was in itself a mistake. The interest rate, being one of the many elements of the general system of equilibrium, was, of course, simultaneously determined with all of them so that there was no point at all in looking for any particular element that 'caused' interest. In order to show the error involved in this view of the matter it is sufficient—as it was in the case of Marshall's objection that is embodied in his simile of the three balls resting against each other in a bowl—to remember that the proposition, 'interest is determined by all the conditions of the system of general equilibrium,' fails to prove the existence of a positive rate of interest. Why the system so works as to produce a positive rate remains a distinct question that calls for a distinct answer. It calls for an explanatory *principle* just as does the position of the balls in Marshall's bowl. And no such principle is supplied by the mere fact of the general interdependence that subsists between all economic magnitudes. Therefore, something might be said for Böhm-Bawerk's distinction between the problem of the existence of interest and the problem of the factors that determine its rate, however ridiculous this distinction might seem to be at first sight.

[2] [J. A. S. intended to write here a long note mentioning the names of Wieser, Clark, and Knight.]

had any strength left were the Marxist exploitation theory, the abstinence theory, and, on a distinctly lower level, several forms of bargaining-power theories. Of newcomers we shall only notice the theories of Böhm-Bawerk and Irving Fisher.

Substantially, Böhm-Bawerk's criticism of Marx's theory was successful. Nevertheless the latter survived in the circle of Marxist orthodoxy until it was silently discarded by later socialist theorists, who were not Marxists any longer. Having commented upon it already (ch. 5, sec. 8) we proceed at once to the abstinence theory. Here Böhm-Bawerk's attack was not successful, not only in the sense that it failed to convince but also in the sense that it was unconvincing.[3] Marshall had no difficulty in formulating an explanation of interest that took account of abstinence[4] without being open to logical objection. In fact, he succeeded in reviving the productivity theory as well by linking it to the element of abstinence. If physical capital is to yield not only returns but also net returns, something must prevent it from being produced up to the point at which its earnings would no more than repay its cost. Abstinence qualifies—logically—for the role of this something. We may, with Senior, call it a cost so that employment of capital yields a return over the *other* cost elements. Or we may say that that abstinence acts as a brake to the production of capital goods so as to prevent it from reaching that point—which renders Carver's version.[5] Böhm-Bawerk attacked both versions, as it seems to me, without success.[6] Most writers whose views on interest display more or less affinity to

[3] Böhm-Bawerk tried to show that any appeal to abstinence involves 'double counting.' He might have held indeed that he who saves makes a choice between present and future enjoyments and that, if the latter be properly discounted for time distance, there is no room for an additional compensation for any abstention involved. But it should not be denied that there is room for it if the future returns upon the sum saved are not discounted. In fact, it may be held that emphasis upon the 'sacrifice' of saving was precisely the method by which abstinence theorists introduced the element of time preference, although Böhm-Bawerk refused to admit this. Actually, however, he found double counting in the practice of abstinence theorists of counting abstinence as cost along with the 'labor' involved in producing a capital good. This argument I have never been able to understand. These considerations do not salvage the abstinence theory nor is it intended that they should. But they absolve it from the charge of *logical* error and again bear witness to what we have called the logical strength of the abstinence theory. But a theory may be wrong for reasons other than logical error.

[4] As we know, he preferred, without good reason as I think, the term 'waiting' that was suggested by S. M. McVane ('Analysis of Cost of Production,' *Quarterly Journal of Economics*, July 1887).

[5] See Carver's *Distribution of Wealth* (1904), and his earlier paper on 'The Place of Abstinence in the Theory of Interest,' *Quarterly Journal of Economics*, October 1893.

[6] Again, this was because he tried to prove them wrong in logic. But this should not induce us to join those critics of Böhm-Bawerk who spoke of misplaced ingenuity, hair-splitting, metaphysics, irrelevant psychology, and what not. Surely if economic theory is to be taken seriously at all, every effort at clarification of this issue should be welcomed. We do not solve problems by tiring of them.

Böhm-Bawerk's—such as Jevons before him and Fetter after him—made no difficulty at all about abstinence, with the exception of Fisher.

I have said that the bargaining-power theories moved on a lower level of theoretical analysis. In fact, no first-class theorist ever held one. There is a very good reason for this. Either the bargaining power that is to explain the surplus called interest consists in the possession of some requisite of production. In this case appeal to the bargaining power of the owners of this requisite is otiose, because the real explanation of the resulting net return has still to be sought in the role of this requisite in the economic process. Thus, neither Marx nor Böhm-Bawerk appealed to the bargaining power of the capitalist, though this element might easily be recognized in both their theories. Instead, both tried elaborately to show *how* the mechanisms of capitalist markets produced the surplus or premium, which the mere term 'bargaining power' does nothing to explain. Or else, the bargaining power is held to consist of something distinct from the possession of a requisite. It could consist, for example, in the power to levy taxes for the benefit of capitalists. But in this case, the existence of such a power and its adequacy to explain the phenomenon of interest would have to be proved, a task no theorist who knows his business would undertake.[7] We confine ourselves to a single example of a theory of this type, the mark-up theory of Lexis. Interest exists because businessmen are in a position to charge prices for whatever they sell that are higher than their costs. If by costs we mean expenses, this is of course so but does not prove the existence of a surplus over expenses plus compensations for the services of owned factors evaluated at equilibrium prices. In order to establish the existence of such a surplus, general enough to account for interest, it is no doubt possible to fall back upon imperfections of competition; but this would imply the thesis that there is no interest in perfect equilibrium and perfect competition which in turn would require adequate proof.[8]

The outstanding performance of the period that dominated discussion and exerted formative influence even on many of its fiercest critics was Böhm-Bawerk's. It has been emphasized already (see above, sec. 2c) that this performance centered in a highly simplified picture of the manner in which, given a certain supply of labor and of subsistence, interest and wage rates are simultaneously determined and in turn determine the organic composition of capital.[9] It has also been emphasized that this central schema is in part independ-

[7] Thus, the political power of the farming interest in the United States certainly explains, among other things, the processing tax introduced for its benefit in the early days of the Roosevelt administration. This tax may be held to have increased the farmers' 'profits' or 'rents.' But it evidently cannot be invoked as a fundamental explanation of either. The same applies to protective duties.

[8] It is perhaps unnecessary to re-enter upon a discussion of theories of net returns (whether of interest or rent) that rest on nothing but a misuse of the concept of monopoly and see monopoly gain in every case of a scarce factor on the ground that such a factor is, in capitalist society, not equally accessible to all.

[9] This Marxist concept is quite appropriate here. The word Capital, also, is used here in the Marxist sense. I think that this conveys Böhm-Bawerk's idea better and

ent of, and in part but imperfectly co-ordinated with, Böhm-Bawerk's causal explanation of interest, a fact that we have ascribed to the unfinished state of his work. Now we are concerned with this causal explanation. It runs in terms of goods: Böhm-Bawerk strongly believed that money does not play any other role in this matter than that of a technical device that occasionally gets out of order.[10] The fundamental proposition is that interest arises from an exchange of present against future consumers' goods and *is* essentially a premium (*Agio*), attaching to the former. Thus defined, the problem consists in indicating the reasons why the market where present consumers' goods are exchanged for (claims to) future consumers' goods so works as to produce normally such a premium or, in other words, why people are normally prepared to promise, for the delivery of present goods, delivery of greater quantities of goods of the same kind and quality at some future time.[11] As the reader presumably knows, Böhm-Bawerk adduced three such reasons. First, a man may be prepared to return to a lender more than he received, because he expects to be better off in the future.[12] Second, a man may be prepared to promise to repay more than he receives because most people do not experience future enjoyments with the

more briefly than would his own terminology. In addition, it defines both the extent to which there is similarity between the two schemata and the extent to which Böhm-Bawerk surpassed the Marxist schema by treating a problem not explicitly treated by Marx. It should be observed however, first, that a system of relations much more complicated than Böhm-Bawerk's would be necessary in order to do justice to this problem; and, second, that if we introduce durable plant and equipment explicitly, we realize immediately that Böhm-Bawerk's schema is essentially a long-run one for, in the short-run, plant and equipment are simply given, as are natural agents, and can be assigned a marginal productivity, not in the Jevons-Böhm-Bawerk sense but in the ordinary sense.

[10] More precisely, he held a crude quantity theory: the whole of the money (taking account of velocity) buys the whole of the goods. There is a striking parallelism between this proposition and another: the whole of the subsistence fund buys the whole of the labor supply. Both propositions are reminiscent of 'classic' theories (quantity theory and wage-fund theory), *not* at their best. But the necessary corrections can be inserted without great difficulty.

[11] To repeat, whatever else may be objected to in this way of positing the interest problem, there is no point in objecting to it because it involves psychology. If we throw out Böhm-Bawerk's argument on this ground, we must consistently also throw out Lord Keynes's and even Marx's (see, e.g., Marx's argument on the motives of accumulation).

[12] There is much more to this reason than critics are in the habit of conceding. It applies not only to the case of the student who has a well-disposed aunt in delicate health: in a progressive society a majority of people may be correctly expecting larger income streams in the future; whereas, for a retrograde society, Böhm-Bawerk is substantially right in assuming that the correct anticipations of dwindling income streams will not make that premium negative for any normally conditioned person so that the positive premia, which some may still be prepared to pay, will take effect even in this case.

same pungent sense of reality as they experience present ones.[13] Individuals, classes, and nations differ greatly in this respect, and the differences in the intensity with which they realize the future is one of the most important of the factors that determine their fate, a truth that cannot be too strongly impressed upon modern economists. But Böhm-Bawerk, like Bentham and Jevons before him, held that *some* undervaluation of the future in this sense is a general characteristic of normal man. Observation of actual behavior, especially in the public sector, goes far toward supporting this contention.[14] Third, a man may be prepared to pay a premium for present goods because command of present goods may enable him to embark upon physically more productive processes of production that require a 'longer' period of production in Böhm-Bawerk's sense (technological superiority of present consumers' goods; see above, sec. 2c), so that a present stock of consumers' goods may mean more consumers' goods in the future. A generation that has witnessed the Russian Five Year Plans should have little hesitation in placing at least limited confidence in this argument. Of course, it is necessary to emphasize the phrase 'to embark' much more than it has been emphasized by Böhm-Bawerk, who in dealing with this 'third reason' committed several errors.[15] For unless we do so

[13] In the first case—the case of favorable expectations—borrowers undervalue future as compared with present goods, because they expect in the future to be further down on the *same curve* of marginal utility of income. In the second case—the case of systematic undervaluation of future enjoyments that are expected to give pleasure of the same intensity when they shall have become present enjoyments—borrowers have a *different curve* of marginal utility of income for the present and for each of the subsequent income periods.

[14] This could be established only by an extensive discussion of historical evidence, which space does not permit us to enter upon. For it is quite true that our common impression to the effect that general undervaluation of the future does exist in modern society may be in part a simple consequence of the existence of interest and that, hence, the task of establishing that there is also independent undervaluation, capable of 'causing' interest, is not so easy, especially since apparently contradictory evidence is not lacking. Such a discussion would also have to take issue with the many objections that have been raised. A particularly interesting one must, however, be mentioned. Some writers seem to believe that, if there existed systematic undervaluation of the future, society would have to plan for economic doom or general liquidation. *But this is precisely what society actually does*, and it is one of the most profound problems of economic analysis to show why capital equipment nevertheless expands instead of dwindling. This problem is obscured by the practice of postulating that the economic engine is being maintained, or is maintaining itself, as a matter of course.

[15] Most of them have been straightened out by Wicksell and his disciples (see especially Wicksell's contribution, 'Zur Zinstheorie (Böhm-Bawerks dritter Grund)' to *Wirtschaftstheorie der Gegenwart*, vol. III, 1927). In general, however, these errors have been allowed to play an unduly great role: unlike the sympathetic critics of Marx or Ricardo or Keynes, the critics of Böhm-Bawerk never took the trouble to distinguish his essential ideas from their ill-tailored garb. I take the opportunity to advert to two difficulties that I experience in trying to present his teaching fairly. The first is lack of space. The second is that I have the strongest reason a theorist can possibly have for disagreeing with Böhm-Bawerk, viz. the reason that I have a different theory of

we are likely to be caught in the gears of the synchronization argument: Böhm-Bawerk's third reason would, in itself, not account for any persistent surplus from the continued repetition of a process of given 'length,' once it has been introduced and the whole economy is adapted to it; it is only the successive 'extensions' of the period which would keep interest alive, even if there were no other reason for its survival.[16]

As it stood, this explanation of interest was not accepted by any economist of note. Even Wicksell added so many qualifications and developments to it that he cannot be listed as a follower in any strict sense. Nevertheless Böhm-Bawerk's theory of interest exerted not only the kind of influence that is implied in stirring up discussion and stimulating thought but also a much more direct one. This was due to the fact that it admits of a simplification that one may accept without committing oneself to the details of Böhm-Bawerk's analytic structure. This simplified version reads like this: interest arises from the interaction of ('psychological') time preference with the physical productivity of investment. And in this diluted form, Böhm-Bawerk's theory became not only one of the interest theories of the period but the most widely accepted one of all, though each author added special features of his own that did not as a rule meet with the approval of any considerable number of other authors.

---

interest of my own. But I wish neither to force my own views upon the reader nor to criticize Böhm-Bawerk from my own standpoint. I therefore accept his 'version' of the problem; and speak of 'error' only in cases where a statement or analytic arrangement of his can be proved to be wrong or inadequate from *his* standpoint. [J. A. S. carried on a famous controversy with Böhm-Bawerk on a dynamic theory of interest in the *Zeitschrift für Volkswirtschaft, Sozialpolitik und Verwaltung*, 1913.]

[16] An analogous consideration also defends the abstinence theory against objection based on synchronization. However, there are also in both cases more delicate questions to consider into which we cannot enter. But I shall briefly notice one of them which bothered Böhm-Bawerk himself as well as his adherents and critics. They all were not quite sure about the relations of the 'three reasons' to one another. At first sight they are all cumulative in the sense that they are all reasons for undervaluing a future loaf of bread as compared with a present one. But this is not all of it. If we formulate the third reason by saying that it leads to undervaluation of the future because command over present consumers' goods enables a man to be better off in the future, we may assimilate this third reason with the first one, taking account however of the circumstance that possession of present goods is a *condition* for being better off in the future in the case of the third reason but not in the case of the first. But in both cases we have furthermore to take account of the fact that, if the second reason be operative, the greater future wealth will be 'psychologically discounted.' And to the extent to which this happens, the first and third motives for paying a premium are weakened by the second. Again, on the face of it, each of the three reasons, provided of course we believe in them, should be capable of producing a premium even if operating in the absence of the two others. Böhm-Bawerk himself tried to show (a) that the two first reasons will not necessarily produce a premium without the third (see his polemic against Fisher, *Exkurs XII* in the 3rd ed.) but (b) that the third reason *is* capable of producing a premium by itself.

Many examples could be cited.[17] But by far the most forceful and brilliant performance of this kind was Irving Fisher's Impatience Theory of Interest.[18] The phrase is self-explanatory. But it points too exclusively toward Böhm-Bawerk's 'second reason.' The third reason is not absent in Fisher: it appears in the garb of Investment Opportunity which, though stripped of certain specifically Böhm-Bawerkian features, expresses, but much more elegantly, essentially the same facts.[19] Also, Fisher brought out more clearly than had Böhm-Bawerk himself an aspect of the latter's interest analysis that is perhaps the most important of all.

We have seen that a majority of the non-Marxist writers of that period continued to look upon interest as an income that stands on the same plane with rent and wages as the payment for the services of a physical requisite of production (plant, equipment, and so on, or else abstinence) that in turn stand, within the sphere of production, on the same plane with the services of natural agents and labor. The 'agio' or premium theory of interest involves an entirely different conception. Being a general time discount that applies to the returns from productive services of all kinds, interest as it were preys upon them all,

[17] For instance, Marshall's cautious reference (*Principles*, p. 142) to the 'productiveness *and prospectiveness*' of capital may be interpreted in this sense. Lord Keynes was therefore quite right when he treated what I have called the simplified version of Böhm-Bawerk's theory as the one that was being commonly accepted even in 1936 (see *General Theory*, p. 165). Still more interesting is the fact that he accepted it himself. He did indeed declare it inadequate but only in the sense that it needed to be supplemented by the element of liquidity preference (ibid. p. 166). But, with Keynes himself, though not with all of his followers, this did not amount to renouncing it but only to amending it.

[18] Fisher elaborated this theory (without as yet substituting the term impatience for the terms 'agio' or time preference) first in the *Rate of Interest* (1907) and then presented another version in *The Theory of Interest* (1930). Not without justification, he wrote in the preface to the latter work that his theory was 'in some degree every one's theory.' Still more justified is the dedication to John Rae and Eugen von Böhm-Bawerk, 'who laid the foundations upon which I have endeavored to build.'

[19] It is, therefore, difficult to understand how, in the same preface, Fisher could have written: 'So far as I know, no other writer on interest has made use of income streams and their differences, or rates of return over cost per annum.' If Böhm-Bawerk's numerical tables are *not* a clumsy method of representing points in income (product) streams and their differences, I for one fail to see what they do represent. I take this opportunity to touch upon a minor point. Both some critics and some adherents (including Wicksell and Pierson) strove hard to interpret Böhm-Bawerk's theory of interest as a productivity theory, and Böhm-Bawerk himself, wearied by their insistence, protested in the end but weakly (*Geschichte und Kritik*, 3rd ed., p. 705n.). But his theory is a productivity theory only in the sense in which all interest theories are, including those of Marx and Keynes. For interest is an element of every price; every price can be represented as the result of a demand and a supply; and however we define capital, productive purposes must always figure among the factors that motivate the demand for it. In any non-trivial sense, however, his theory is not like the productivity theories properly so-called but the very opposite of them as will be shown presently.

upon the returns from the services of physical capital goods not less than upon any others. It is, therefore, something that differs in nature from all productivity returns properly so-called,[20] not only from rents of natural agents and wages of labor but also from the productivity returns of capital goods. Böhm-Bawerk did not bring this out well, though his theory of 'capitalization' (of the manner in which the values of land and capital goods are determined) [21] suffices to prove that this was in fact his view. But Fisher's terminology did. In order to underline the novelty of this view, let us again notice its affinity, in this respect, with the exploitation theory of Marx; given the appropriate ideology—and phraseology—it might have been presented as a novel exploitation theory.

A minor consequence of this was that returns from physical capital goods could no longer be diagnosed as interest in the fashion set by Barbon and sanctioned by A. Smith. Several circumstances combined to suggest their assimilation with the rent of natural agents (see below, subsec. b). A much more important consequence was that interest now entered the theories of rent and wages in an entirely new manner. In fact, this is the most important reason why we have once more to take up these subjects instead of resting content with a simple reference to the theory of imputation or of marginal productivity *sans phrase*.[22]

(b) *Rent.* Disregarding minor issues and various blind alleys, we shall survey developments in this field in three steps. First, we shall consider the theory of rent that was to explain the incomes derived from the ownership of natural agents, no matter whether they are supposed to be 'indestructible' or not. Sec-

[20] I say 'productivity returns properly so-called' because there is an ambiguity in the term 'productivity' as there is in the term 'requisite' that tends to obscure the point I am trying to make. In a sense, time is a requisite of production, hence productive. So, in capitalist society, is money. And for some purposes the concept of marginal productivity may be applied to both. But neither is a requisite and productive in the same sense as is labor or land or a shovel. Böhm-Bawerk averred that his subsistence fund was productive in the first sense but not in the second, exactly as Marx would have done. But both he himself and his followers and critics confused the two meanings.

[21] This theory was developed by Wicksell as well as by Fisher, but it constitutes one of Böhm-Bawerk's most characteristic contributions. Before him the treatment of this problem was dominated by the cost aspect. Of course, business practice had been familiar with the discounting process as applied to a house or machine long before. But it was Böhm-Bawerk who introduced this practice into economic theory and gave it its theoretical interpretation just as Marshall introduced the concepts of prime and supplementary costs that had been familiar to every businessman and yet constituted novelties in economic analysis.

[22] In other words, 'The Relations between Rent and Interest' now became a problem that had not existed for J. S. Mill. See, especially, Professor F. A. Fetter's paper bearing this title in *Publications of the American Economic Association*, 3rd series, vol. v, February 1904. A. Marshall, by a different route, was led to coining the concept of quasi-rent which takes care of part of that problem. In addition, he recognized that the concept of interest is applicable to new (prospective?) investment only; and that capital already invested in plant and equipment yields quasi-rent and not interest (*Principles*, pp. 605-6).

ond, we shall consider certain generalizations of the concept of rent which that theory suggested. Third, we shall notice a tendency to harness the concept of rent into the service of entirely different purposes. Under each of these three headings we shall observe a struggle between old and new ideas that was an important cause, if not the only one, of waverings, hazinesses, and spurious issues.[23]

First, then, as regards the rent of natural agents, it is obvious that the Jevons-Menger-Walras analysis provided a perfectly good explanation of this rent phenomenon and, if adequately complemented by the facts of every concrete case envisaged, also all the 'laws' or propositions about it we need. All that had to be done was to take a clue from Say or Cantillon, that is, to recognize that rent is simply a matter of pricing the services of these requisites of production and to apply the marginal principle to the formation of these prices. Account being taken of Böhm-Bawerkian time preference, the result would read: the rent of natural agents tends to equal the discounted values of their marginal products. This theory allows automatically for differences in quality of natural agents of the same kind. And, as thus explained, rent does and does not enter into the prices of products exactly as do wages. In fact, rent in this sense and wages are parallel phenomena. The main purely economic difference between them is that the *total* supply of any natural agent may, in many cases, be taken as fixed and hence does not react to variations in its price, whereas the total supply of labor is in general less irresponsive. But this difference does not affect the explanatory principle involved, which remains the same for both cases. Moreover, it is irrelevant for the question of allocation of the supply available for any *particular* use of a natural agent that is capable of serving more than one: how much land, at what rent per unit, is available for the production of cane sugar when the same land could also be used for the production of cotton is merely a matter of opportunity cost.[24]

This theory, sponsored by the Austrians and by Walras, was however not as readily or generally accepted as we might expect, considering its simplicity and usefulness. There were two reasons for this and for the consequent survival of the 'Ricardian' theory of rent.[25] On the one hand, many economists

[23] As far as Marshall's teaching is concerned, waverings and hazinesses have been trenchantly analyzed by F. A. Fetter, 'The Passing of the Old Rent Concept,' *Quarterly Journal of Economics*, May 1901. Professor Fetter's argument may be generalized so as to include a large number of economists.

[24] It is perhaps unnecessary to explain the treatment of the case of natural agents that admit of only one use and of the cases (such as the case of the vineyard that might also be used as pasture for goats) that raise similar difficulties.

[25] Marx's and Rodbertus' theories of rent benefited but little by the dislike that many economists displayed for the marginal productivity theory, though the former survived of course in the circle of Marxist orthodoxy. L. von Bortkiewicz' destructive criticism of both was hardly necessary in order to convince economists of their weaknesses: see his papers on 'Die Rodbertus'sche Grundrententheorie und die Marx'sche Lehre von der absoluten Grundrente,' *Archiv für die Geschichte des Sozialismus und der Arbeiterbewegung*, 1910-11. But the two papers are worth mentioning, neverthe-

experienced an emotional resistance to a theory that seemed to treat the landlord's 'unearned incomes' on the same plane with the workman's compensation for the sweat of his brow. These sentiments were completely irrational because there is nothing in that theory to prevent an economist from differentiating as much as he pleases between the two on moral or political grounds.[26] But they were effective nevertheless and they told for the 'Ricardian' theory, because the latter seemed—though it really is not—much better qualified to support an adverse value judgment on the rent of land. On the other hand, as we have seen, 'classic' doctrines kept, throughout the period under survey, a strong hold on the thought of many economists. Of these doctrines none had percolated more widely, or enjoyed a more established fame, than had the 'Ricardian' theory of rent. Moreover, it was easier to defend than were other parts of 'classic' analysis because, *formulated with proper care*, it did not assert anything that was positively wrong. Menger's criticism of it (*Grundsätze*, pp. 144-5) was justified but only amounted to saying that the necessity of having to construct, for so important a class of phenomena, a separate theoretical apparatus was in itself proof of the defects of the 'classic' analysis.[27] Defenders were, therefore, in a relatively favorable position. By far the most eminent of these was A. Marshall, who made the most of this opportunity for fighting a rear-guard action in defense of Ricardo.[28]

In any case, the 'Ricardian' theory remained in the center of discussion and continued to hold the attention even of its opponents. Not all of these came from the marginal productivity camp. The monopoly theory of rent was bound to lose ground in a time when general price analysis was so greatly improved,

---

less, because they are excellent examples of a type of theoretical work that seems to have gone out of fashion completely.

[26] Thus Walras was a strong land reformer in spite of the fact that he sponsored the productivity theory of rent.

[27] In other words, the criticism simply averred that for the Jevons-Menger-Walras analysis Ricardo's theory was superfluous. And so it is (see above, Part III, ch. 6, sec. 6, on the role that the theory of rent played in the Ricardian system). To put it still more bluntly, the 'revolutionaries' were in a position to scrap the whole of Ricardo's second chapter excepting the first sentence of the second paragraph.

[28] Marshallians will perhaps condone the slight irritation that some readers of Marshall may possibly feel at the length to which he went in this respect in spite of the fact that (disregarding everything else) his great summary of his theory of distribution proves beyond reasonable doubt that he accepted the marginal productivity theory of rent. But he refused to recognize the break with Ricardo's general theory which this involved and, e.g., attacked Jevons (who actually was exceptionally gentle on the 'Ricardian' theory of rent) for holding that 'rent does enter into price' (*Principles*, p. 483n.), as if, *as meant by Jevons*, this proposition were definitely false. The reader can easily satisfy himself—this would in fact be a good exercise—that this is not so. Marshall's corrective formulation (presented in quotes) asserts nothing that is wrong but also nothing that invalidates the Jevonian proposition attacked. Besides, the Jevonian proposition had been anticipated—only without awareness of its importance—by J. S. Mill.

but it did not die out entirely.[29] Other approaches were also tried but none of them met with any great success.[30]

Second, extensions of the concept of rent just discussed suggest themselves readily in view of the difficulty of drawing a logically tenable line between what objects are, and what are not, natural agents or, which is only another way of expressing the same thing, of agreeing on the defining characteristics of natural agents. Thus, violating his original definition of rent (income derived from the ownership of land and other free gifts of nature, *Principles*, p. 150) Marshall denied that mining royalties are rents.[31] Other writers were more impressed with the analogy. But he made no difficulty about the extension—if indeed it can be called an extension at all—of the concept of rent from rural to urban land.[32] Much more important, however, was one of his most felicitous creations, the concept of quasi-rent or 'income from an appliance for production already made by man,' that embodies the recognition of two facts that were particularly important in connection with the new theories of interest: the fact that any price paid for the services of capital goods is closely analogous to the price for the services of natural agents; and the fact that this analogy holds particularly for the short run and decreases with the increase in the length of the time to which a proposition is intended to apply.[33]

Another class of extensions sprouted directly from Ricardian roots. A man who still persisted in seeing point in Ricardo's emphasis upon 'differential rent' was likely to discover, as Bailey had done before, that such differentials were not confined to land. We have had occasion [34] to notice Mill's, Mangoldt's, and Walker's interpretations of entrepreneurial gains as rents of differential ability. Marshall presented the general case for the latter concept though, in my

[29] F. Oppenheimer's book on *David Ricardos Grundrententheorie* (1909; 2nd ed., 1927) may be cited as an example.

[30] See, e.g., Achille Loria's work, *Rendita fondiaria . . .* (1880).

[31] Moreover he did so on the untenable ground that royalties do enter into the price of the mineral mined in a sense other than that in which does the rent of agricultural land.

[32] Also see Edgeworth's work on the subject (republished in vol. I of his *Papers*) and Wieser's *Theorie der städtischen Grundrente* (1909). The latter reads like an application of Ricardo's theory of rural ground rent, Ricardo's marginal land being replaced by the 'peripherical' urban land that yields no higher rent when used for building than it would in its optimal agrarian use.

[33] There is, of course, no sharp dividing line between quasi-rent and rent proper. If we assume that the greater part of a landlord's income is also quasi-rent, then we may say that, at any given moment, the bulk of capitalist income (in the Marxist sense) is quasi-rent. Also there is no sharp dividing line between quasi-rent and wages. A physician's income is in part quasi-rent though usually classed with wages. The 'rent' or 'quasi-rent' yielded by a piece of land that has been reclaimed by the owner's labor is, in part, at least, in the nature of wages. A little reflection will show that this is more than an otiose play with concepts.

[34] [On Bailey, see above, Part III, ch. 4, sec. 3c; on the interpretation of entrepreneurial gains as rents of differential ability, see above, sec. 2b.]

opinion, this only served to expose its emptiness.[35] Similarly, a man who has acquired Ricardo's habit of deducing rent from the physical 'law of decreasing returns from land' may easily discover the ubiquity of this phenomenon wherever factors are being applied to a fixed quantity of one of them: [36] this amounts to generalizing Ricardo's rent concept by generalizing Ricardian decreasing returns. If the fixed factor is plant and equipment—which may in fact be taken as fixed in the short run—we shall, after a certain point, observe decreasing physical returns to successive 'doses' of those factors that can be varied in the short run, and the Marshallian quasi-rent then appears as the exact analogue of the 'Ricardian' rent of land.[37]

Third,[38] the aspect of the 'Ricardian' theory of rent that appealed most to policy-minded economists was the aspect suggested by the words Surplus or Residual. Strictly speaking these words, as applied to the rent of natural agents, had lost their meaning in the Jevons-Menger-Walras analysis, which was no longer under the necessity of explaining rent as a 'leftover' sui generis but was

[35] *Principles* VI, ch. 5, § 7 and ch. 8, § 8. The statement in the text requires protection against two misunderstandings. First, it must not be understood to refer to the entire contents of the two paragraphs just cited, which contain many a profound remark. Second, it must not be understood to imply denial of the importance—which on the contrary I think paramount both for economic and for sociological analysis—of the wide range of variation of the 'natural' abilities of men. All I mean is that the theory of rent contributes nothing to our understanding of the role of supernormal abilities and that nothing is gained by calling their earnings rents except that by so doing we are enabled to show—which was indeed Bailey's purpose—that differential fertility of different plots of land is entirely superfluous also in the theory of the income from ownership of natural agents.

[36] Let us repeat that it was in this manner that J. B. Clark found his way toward a marginal productivity theory of distribution. At least this seems to be the natural inference from his 'Distribution as Determined by a Law of Rent,' *Quarterly Journal of Economics*, April 1891. But in order to be able to travel this way, he had to renounce community with Ricardo, for whose teaching it was essential to hold that the rent phenomenon is specific to the land factor.

[37] More precisely, it appears as the exact analogue of the so-called second case of Ricardian rent, which refers not to the application of capital and labor to decreasingly fertile or more distant plots of land but to the application of successive 'doses' of capital and labor to the same plots of land. It should be observed, however, that the true importance of the quasi-rent concept is quite independent of this analogy.

[38] I am not going to include here the 'psychological rents' that result from the 'laws' of decreasing marginal utility or increasing marginal disutility. One of them, consumers' rent, will be considered later (see below, ch. 7, sec. 6 and Appendix). In addition, we may speak of a savers' rent that may be derived, if we wish, from the fact that savers' behavior can be described in terms of a marginal equality between the advantages of saving or consuming an additional dollar's worth of resources, and that there is hence a surplus of advantage on the intramarginal dollars; and of a laborer's rent (Marshall's producers' rent) that may be similarly derived from the balance, at the margin, of the advantages of another hour's leisure or work which implies that there is a surplus of advantage on the intra-marginal hours of work. The validity of these concepts is one question; their value is quite another. In any case, these 'rents' must not be confused with those associated with 'laws' of physical returns.

able to explain it directly and on the same fundamental principle with other types of income. But economists soon found that they might retain the surplus aspect all the same. Rent might be capable of being interpreted as the payment for the services of a requisite of production, but this payment was not necessary in order to call forth the corresponding service, whereas it was in the cases of the services of capital goods and of labor—a fact that seemed important for questions of welfare economics and of taxation. Marshall, shifting emphasis to this surplus aspect of rent, gave a lead toward expressing it by saying that the services of natural agents were 'costless' in the sense that in order to have them, society need not incur 'real cost' (disutilities of labor and saving).[39] But if we elaborate this unearned-surplus aspect of rent, we discover two things.

In the first place, we discover, as we discovered before from another standpoint, that rent defined as a 'surplus' is no more confined to natural agents than is rent defined as a productivity income. Similar surpluses, that is, differentials over and above the payments that would be necessary to call forth the corresponding supplies of goods and services, are scattered all over the economic organism. Many workers, and not only movie stars, receive much more than the amount necessary to induce them to do what they are actually doing, and in many cases they would offer more service if they were paid less per service unit. Even if we carry the hypothesis of perfect competition as far as it is possible without getting ludicrously out of contact with facts, there are plenty of situations of advantage, some short-lived, others more durable, in which such surpluses are earned. Under conditions of monopolistic competition, let alone straight monopoly,[40] such situations must be still more frequent. Finally we may include gains from situations of advantage that are created by 'collusion' (contrived scarcities) or by *specific*[41] institutional pat-

[39] The reader will observe that this is something different from saying that the payment for such services does not 'enter into the price of products.'

[40] Again, the reader will perceive the essential difference between subsuming monopoly gains under surpluses of this kind and explaining the rent of land as a monopoly gain: the two have nothing to do with one another. But any difficulty the reader may have in realizing this bears witness against the advisability of calling these surpluses rent. It constitutes in fact a typical instance of unnecessary confusion being created for no better reason than a preference for terms that, like rent, have acquired derogatory associations. If it were not for this, it would be readily recognized that 'surplus' does all that is needed and that the term 'rent,' in this connection, is redundant.

[41] By emphasizing the word 'specific' I mean to convey that mere reference to the general institutions of capitalist society, such as private property, covers an economist's failure to explain a return more often than it affords explanation. This is why, much to the displeasure of critics of a certain type, competent economists of all times have always looked askance at work that uncritically used the phrase Institutional Rent. The case is different, of course, where the existence and the modi operandi of specific institutional factors can be fully established. Examples are afforded by protective duties (including measures of some of our states that in effect amount to protective duties), certain features of recent labor legislation, and so on.

terns. A tendency has asserted itself in our own time to combine all such surpluses under the heading of rent. Though the incomes from ownership of natural agents are included, they only form a special case of rent in this sense, the theory of which has but little in common with the theory of rent surveyed in the first part of this subsection.

In the second place, however, we also discover that part of the surplus gains under discussion divide up into two classes between which there is an analytically significant difference. Consider a natural agent, perfectly homogeneous in quality, perfectly divisible, and perfectly transferable between the different uses (industries) that it is capable of serving, and let us assume perfect competition all round. Each of these uses will then be governed by what we have called opportunity cost. The users of the factor may therefore have to pay all that its services are worth to them, in which case no surplus attaches to its use.[42] And the owners may receive, from each group of users, no more than they could receive from any other. They derive no surplus over *opportunity* cost, though the whole of their receipts may be, in another sense, a surplus over Marshallian *real* cost.[43] In another class of cases this is not so. It is unnecessary, I hope, to adduce examples in which owners of requisites of production, whether or not they be natural agents, earn surplus gains over *opportunity* costs: technological difficulties of 'transforming savings' into certain types of capital goods suffice to create, for the owners of the latter, gains over opportunity costs that are also gains over real costs which, at least in the short run, even otherwise quite unimpeded competition may be inadequate to remove.[44] The distinction between surplus gains over real costs that are also surplus gains over opportunity costs, and surplus gains over real costs that are not, is sufficiently important to be recommended to the reader's attention, especially because the former do not, and the latter do, play an essential role in the process of allocation of resources.[45]

[42] This does not hold for marginal quantities if the intramarginal 'surplus' is absorbed by payments to other factors. [J. A. S. questioned this note and the sentence to which it applies.]

[43] This proviso should suffice to negative any idea of using opportunity cost for apologetic purposes.

[44] The wording of the sentence above is inspired by a passage in Pareto's *Cours* (2nd vol., § 745 et seq.). Pareto's share in *this* generalization of an aspect of the old rent concept, which was to gain popularity in the Anglo-American literature of our own epoch, deserves to be mentioned in spite of doubts as regards the analytic progress thereby accomplished. Not that the facts envisaged by the Paretian theory of rent are unimportant. But I can see no point in grafting them upon the quite heterogeneous facts that are satisfactorily described by the marginal productivity theory. See, however, the work of one of Pareto's disciples, Professor G. Sensini, *La teoria della 'rendita'* (1912).

[45] See especially Joan Robinson, *The Economics of Imperfect Competition* (1933), ch. 8. Mrs. Robinson may be considered to be the chief authority on the 'new' theory of rent at which we have glanced. Four references on the subject of this subsection are added to enable interested readers to fill the many lacunae of our sketch: A. S. Johnson, 'Rent in Modern Economic Theory,' *Publications of the American Economic*

(c) *Wages*. Longfield's and Thünen's old marginal productivity theory of wages was the new thing in the 1880's and 1890's and, at least among leading theorists, the accepted thing for the rest of the period and beyond it. Böhm-Bawerk's amendment, namely, that the real wage rate, in perfect equilibrium and perfect competition, should be equated to the Discounted Marginal Product of Labor rather than to the Marginal Product of Labor gained some votes after 1910, in the United States mainly because Taussig threw the weight of his authority into the scale.[46] We need not stay long to discuss the types of wage theories that preceded the vogue of the marginal productivity analysis, partly because most of them did not amount to much and partly because we have learned the necessary minimum about them already.[47] Suffice it then to

Association, 3rd series, III, November 1902; B. Samsonoff, *Esquisse d'une théorie générale de la rente* (1912); the contributions on the rent of land, especially that of F. X. Weiss, 'Die Grundrente im System der Nutzwertlehre,' in *Wirtschaftstheorie der Gegenwart* (III, ed. Hans Mayer, 1928-32); and Gerhard Otte, *Das Differentialeinkommen im Lichte der neueren Forschung* (1930), a work that clarifies many hazy points and incidentally establishes the emptiness of the concept of differential rents all the more effectively because the author does not mean to do so.

[46] Böhm-Bawerk's amendment, just like the analogous amendment in the case of rent, is merely a consequence of his theory of interest. How far it is invalidated by the argument from synchronization is therefore not a separate question: it is answered as soon as we have answered it for interest. But another question arises here: how far should Böhm-Bawerk's (and Taussig's) theory of wages be interpreted as a rehabilitation of the wage-fund theory? We may indeed arrange our terminology in such a way as to bring out a strong similarity (which Taussig was inclined to do). And we may interpret so much into Ricardo, McCulloch, and J. S. Mill as to make them 'forerunners.' On the whole, however, I am inclined to think that this blurs the essential lines of doctrinal development instead of bringing them out. In Böhm-Bawerk's structure, 'capital' plays so different a role in relation to wages and joins forces with so many elements which the wage-fund theorists did not see that it seems more confusing than enlightening to stress the tenuous affinity that no doubt exists. In any case, if we are not content with Jevons and Rae as predecessors, it is the affinity with Senior and Marx that should be emphasized rather than the one with the wage-fund theorists properly so called.

[47] The wage-fund controversy has been followed into the period under survey in our description of the issue in Part III (see ch. 6, sec. 6f). For the Marxist theory of wages, see Part III, ch. 6, secs. 2 and 6. The use of the bargaining-power element in the explanation of wages coincides of course with its use in the explanation of 'profit.' Though the wage theorists other than the marginal productivity theorists added points of value here and there (for example they inquired with care into the relation between wages and hours on the one hand and workmen's performance on the other; see L. Brentano's influential contribution under that title, English trans., *Hours and Wages in Relation to Production*, 1894), for the most part they went on discussing the 'classic' problems. Two American works, however, took a higher flight. One was F. A. Walker's *Wages Question* (1876), which expounded the 'residual-claimant' theory. The idea was really not quite new: in substance Senior had already had it (*Outline*, p. 185 et seq.). But Walker worked it out and propagated it in his popular textbooks. It may be best conveyed by contrast with Ricardo. Ricardo, as we know, first eliminated rent from the price problem so as to be left with 'profits' plus wages. Then

recall that most of these wage theorists went on killing the wage-fund theory—some of them in the mistaken belief that they were thereby gaining a point for labor—and that, with practical unanimity, they held that wages were not paid out of capital but out of consumers' income (George, Walker, Sidgwick, Brentano, and many others). Though this argument, as we also know, rests upon a misunderstanding of the wage-fund theory, it should be noticed that it did, in fact even though not in intent, pave the way for the marginal productivity theory.

Let us cast at least a perfunctory glance on the victorious onward march of this analysis as applied to wages, neglecting all minor points. Jevons' statement in the brilliantly original Chapter 5 of his *Theory* must be mentioned first.[48] Menger's presentation is, however, fully equal to it in spite of being still more incomplete. Walras' earlier formulation is somewhat impaired by the fact that his constant production coefficients, like Wieser's, exclude the possibility of taking account of relations of substitution between labor and other requisites of production *within each firm*. Marshall established the marginal productivity analysis of wages in England, succeeding more completely than he seems to have wished. But Edgeworth's various contributions should not be forgotten (see especially his paper on the 'Theory of Distribution,' 1904, republished in *Papers Relating to Political Economy*, vol. 1). Among other things, he exploited the new catallactics for the purpose of treating special cases of wage determination. A particularly felicitous idea of his was to invoke the theory of international values in order to elucidate the relation between employers and employees—treating them by analogy with different nations that trade with one another—or between non-competing groups of workmen. Wicksteed and especially Wicksell then greatly improved the Austrian theory.

The development in the United States was largely independent of the con-

---

he went on to determine wages independently (by equating them to the minimum of existence), and profits remained as a residual (unless indeed we credit him with an abstinence theory, which we now do not do). Similarly, Walker determined the other shares in distribution independently so as to be left with wages as a residual. Opponents (Taussig, e.g.) pointed out that this clashes with the facts of the modern wage contract. But the decisive theoretical objection is in the methodology that such a theory involves, to wit in the very attempt to determine independently any elements of a system of interdependent elements.

The other work was F. W. Taussig's *Wages and Capital* (1896, London School Reprint, 1932). It must be mentioned here and not among American contributions to the marginal productivity theory, because in 1896 its author had not yet accepted the latter. In fact, so far as the book is concerned, he had not even noticed it: there is not even mention of the name of Thünen. Its claim to historic importance rests upon his, in great part original, attempt to graft Böhm-Bawerkian doctrine upon the 'classic' system. But it is recommended to the attention of the reader also for another reason: it is a masterly performance in a style of theoretical reasoning that has completely gone out of fashion. By perusing it, the reader, besides learning a lot, will be able to acquire an idea what this style was like at its best.

[48] It is interesting to note, however, that it does not introduce any time discount on the marginal product of labor.

temporaneous development in Europe. The marginal productivity theory, in a very advanced version that took full account of the relations of substitution among productive factors and came 'close to the modern concept of a marginal rate of substitution,' sprang ready-made from the brain of Stuart Wood, whose two papers on the subject should assure his position in the history of analytic economics: [49] 'A New View of the Theory of Wages' (*Quarterly Journal of Economics,* October 1888 and July 1889) and 'The Theory of Wages' (*Publications of the American Economic Association,* IV, 1889). Simultaneously with the latter (i.e. in the same volume of the *Publications*) J. B. Clark published his marginal productivity theory of wages, 'The Possibility of a Scientific Law of Wages.' In 1892 appeared H. M. Thompson's *Theory of Wages.* Taussig, thereby joining the 'marginalists,' introduced Böhm-Bawerk's amendment into American wage theory ('Outlines of a Theory of Wages,' *Proceedings of the American Economic Association,* April 1910).

For the rest, I shall confine myself to mentioning three standard works of our own epoch which are all based upon the marginal productivity theory of that period. The first is P. H. Douglas' *Theory of Wages* (1934), which will have to be mentioned again as one of the boldest ventures in econometrics ever undertaken. The second—whose great merits are somewhat impaired by not quite adequate handling of the tools of theory—is J. W. F. Rowe's *Wages in Practice and Theory* (1928). The third, so far as theory is concerned, by far the most significant Marshallian performance in the field, is J. R. Hicks's *Theory of Wages* (1932). These stepping stones will carry the reader to the beginning of the Keynesian controversies.

Since consideration of some of the more delicate questions about marginal productivity must be postponed to the next chapter, this is really all that needs to be said for the moment (see, however, the subsection on Labor Economics below). But in view of the fact that misunderstandings persist to this day concerning the nature and value of the marginal productivity analysis in its specific application to wages, the reader will perhaps condone or welcome, as the case may be, the following explanatory comments in spite of the repetitions some of them involve.

First, then, let us recall what has been said above about the difference between Longfield's and Thünen's marginal productivity and that of Jevons and Menger. Longfield's and Thünen's concept is the one revived by Stuart Wood and the one that is commonly used now. The current textbook simply says that, in perfect equilibrium and perfect competition, the money wage rate of every kind of labor equals the physical marginal increment of the product due to the 'last' increment of labor applied (marginal product of labor) multiplied by the equilibrium price of the product. But with Jevons and Menger and also with Marshall, this was not the basic concept. Their basic concept was the increment of satisfaction individual consumers experience from that increment

[49] Justice, but not more than justice, has been done to his performance by Professor Stigler ('Stuart Wood and the Marginal Productivity Theory,' *Quarterly Journal of Economics,* August 1947), to whom the statement above in quotes is due.

of product.[50] Only a theory that uses this concept is a genuine imputation theory of wages and really should be distinguished from simple marginal productivity theories that do not use it. But both yield the same results, of course, and if we do not care for the 'deeper meanings' that Jevons and Menger believed the imputation theory reveals, we may deduce the usual formula for the competitive wage rate without using that concept.[51] In many important cases of applied wage theory we do not even need the usual formula but may treat the determination of the wage rate simply as a matter of supply and demand. *And this is why Fleeming Jenkin must now be added to the list of the builders of modern wage theory* (Part III, ch. 6, sec. 6f). He used nothing but the simple supply and demand apparatus—taking everything for granted that may be behind it—and was nonetheless able to derive important results, for example, about the possibilities of trade-union policy. But an important limitation of his considerable performance should be noticed at once, especially because it carries over to the Marshallian analysis of wages. An analysis that uses the simple demand-supply apparatus is essentially Partial Analysis, that is to say, it takes as independently given the factors that determine the demand and supply schedules. As we shall see, this is inadmissible in the case of so important an element of the economic system as is labor as a whole. To illustrate the point, let us for a moment consider the most obviously practical implication of this. So long as we operate with given demand and supply *schedules* which do not change when wage rates change, then we shall ordinarily have a single equilibrium rate of wages such that any increase of it creates (or increases) unemployment. And practically all economists of this period would have subscribed to the latter proposition, even for a general increase of wage rates.[52]

[50] Denoting by U_i the total satisfaction of consumer i, by x_j quantity of the commodity j he consumes, and by L the labor that goes into this commodity, the concept in question is given by $\frac{\delta U_i}{\delta x_j}\frac{\delta x_j}{\delta L}$. This, barring the partials, is Jevons' expression which recurs in Marshall's *Principles*. It should be re-emphasized that the marginal utilities as well as the marginal physical products involved are individual marginal utilities and marginal products of individual firms. No question of social evaluation comes in to add to our troubles, though Wieser's and Clark's expositions seem to suggest this. Nor need we meet any such thing as a marginal social product. This concept has indeed been introduced by Professor Pigou as a tool of his welfare economics and discussed by Professor Edgeworth (see his paper, 'The Revised Doctrine of Marginal Social Product,' *Economic Journal*, March 1925). But this was a special construction for a special purpose and has no place in the *explanatory* theory of wages now under discussion.

[51] This usual formula (marginal physical product times equilibrium price), of course, does not apply to any cases other than that of pure or perfect competition in all factor and product markets. See below, ch. 7.

[52] The specifically Böhm-Bawerkian version reads like this: if in a state of equilibrium an increase of wage rates is imposed upon the system, then another and longer 'period' of production becomes the most profitable one; if this is adopted, however, the existing subsistence fund suffices only for a smaller number of workmen; hence

Second, recalling what has been said about the formal character of the marginal productivity theory, let us ask ourselves how far this theory provides a 'causal' explanation of wage rates. On the one hand, it is clear that in order to enable it to explain any particular level of wages that we observe in any given place at any given time, it is necessary to feed into it the particular facts of that place and time; and these facts, such as the available amounts of complementary factors, and not the margins of productivity may then be called the true or ultimate causes of that wage rate. On the other hand, it is equally clear that wage rates, being elements in a system of interdependent magnitudes, are simultaneously determined with all its other elements so that even in pure theory—that is, irrespective of the facts of any particular case—they cannot be said to depend upon a margin of productivity as if this were an ultimate datum. However, this is all that Marshall can have meant when he wrote that wage rates are determined *at* the margin and not *by* the margin. But this argument only parallels Marshall's argument about marginal utility—about the three balls resting against one another in a bowl—and admits of a similar reply.[53] In any case, it does not reduce the value of the marginal productivity theory as a tool for solving wage problems.[54]

Third, he who wants to use the marginal productivity of labor as an explanatory principle and as a tool for solving wage problems must, of course, understand it and acquire some experience with it. If he fails to fulfil these conditions, difficulties will crowd upon him which, human nature being what it is, he will turn into so many objections, especially if, suspecting apologetic traps,[55] he dislikes the theory in the first place. But for the period under discussion there was an excuse for this. The theory was not only not developed in a manner that would have shown its usefulness—as it stands out, for example, in Hicks's *Theory of Wages* (1932)—but in many cases it was also faultily formulated. Some economists even had difficulty in seeing the difference between the marginal product of labor and the product of marginal (least efficient) labor. Others seem to have believed that the marginal produc-

---

the rest become unemployed. Observe that this argument far transcends the simple supply and demand argument; and also that it is intended to hold only for an imposed increase of wages and not for one that results from an increase in the subsistence fund.

53 Its formulation is left to the reader as a useful exercise.

54 See, e.g., the treatment of the wage-minimum problem in Pigou's *Wealth and Welfare* (1912).

55 It is hoped that it is unnecessary to go into this again. I should perhaps add, however, that the large majority of economists who defend increases in monetary wage rates or resist reductions have very little to fear from admitting the correctness of the theory. For their arguments will in general be based upon assertions of fact that have nothing to do with it. Few if any will care to espouse arguments that really conflict with it so soon as the common-sense complement of it is brought home to them in each individual case. Moreover, the fact that the use of the marginal productivity theory is a proposition about a rate of wages that would prevail in perfect equilibrium and perfect competition in itself suffices to show the vast expanse of territory the theory leaves uncovered.

tivity theory of wages breaks down if increased wage incomes or reduced hours increase the efficiency of labor.[56]

Fourth, in consequence of this we find that many labor problems continued to be treated by means of the tools that had served the 'classics.' This holds in particular for the machinery problem. It received plenty of attention but analysis rarely rose above the old arguments pro and con the 'compensation theory.' Such as it was, this discussion on technological unemployment provides, however, one of the answers to the Keynesian indictment that the theorists of that period knew of no unemployment other than 'frictional': for technological unemployment, even if essentially temporary so far as the effects of any individual act of mechanization is concerned, may evidently become a permanent phenomenon through being incessantly re-created.[57] The purely theoretical question of full employment in perfect equilibrium and perfect competition will be considered in the next chapter, and nothing need be added to what has been said before on the supply of labor.

6. The Contribution of the Applied Fields *

We have repeatedly noticed that the economists of the period, or most of them, approached questions of economic policy, or many of them, in a new spirit. In this section we shall not dwell on this fact again, but rather hunt for the contributions to analysis that resulted from their preoccupation with practical questions. In all cases, these preoccupations advanced scientific knowledge mainly by increasing our command over facts. Gains for our analytic apparatus, though of course not absent, were much smaller than they might have been. We shall briefly survey the more promising fields (except money and cycles, which are considered in ch. 8).

But we shall not consider developments in the field of business economics (business administration, *Privatwirtschaftslehre*), including accounting and 'actuarial science.' It has been emphasized from the first that there is really no better reason for separating it from general economics than that a large

[56] The theory of substitution, Marshall's exposition of it notwithstanding, was far from being common property even by the end of the period. This is the reason why Charles J. Bullock's paper on 'The Variation of Productive Forces' (*Quarterly Journal of Economics*, August 1902) in spite of various shortcomings deserves to be put on record as a major contribution.

[57] We are free, of course, to define the concept of frictional unemployment so widely as to include technological unemployment and also the other types of unemployment that were recognized—mainly: unemployment from imperfections of competition; unemployment from monetary causes; and unemployment from business fluctuations, whatever their cause—but then the indictment loses its force for, *thus* defined, friction is no longer an *obviously* inadequate explanation of the observed facts of unemployment. In particular, the indictment should not have been directed against Pigou's *Theory of Unemployment* (1933). For the period, see especially W. H. Beveridge, *Unemployment* (1909).

* [The following section was unfinished and untyped at the time of the death of J. A. S.]

majority of economists, believing themselves to be concerned with the affairs of nations, used to consider the details of the economic lives of households and firms to be outside of their sphere and also, perhaps, somewhat below it. Actually, this material is basic to the work of the economist so soon as he goes beyond the most jejune assumptions about individual behavior, and co-operation between business and general economics is a primary necessity for both. But during the period under survey, there was so little of it that all we could do would be to list the results of the explorations of business practice undertaken by business economists, which failed to inspire general economists as completely as the advance of economic theory failed to inspire business economists.[1] Let us note, however, that Marshall, by dealing extensively with the behavior of businessmen, gave an important lead toward a merger of large parts of business and general economics; and that Irving Fisher (in *Capital and Income*) took a first step toward co-ordinating the economist's and the accountant's work.[2]

(a) *International Trade.* [This subsection was planned but not written.]

(b) *Public Finance.* From the comments made on this subject in Chapter 2, we recall that the period was eminently one of what I might term comfortable finance—the result of increasing wealth and relatively peaceful conditions, on the one hand, and of bourgeois influence upon public expenditure and taxation, on the other. Pressure on economic activity was accordingly light—so light as to justify exclusion from the general analysis of the determining factors of the economic process. We have also noticed that toward the end of the period a new spirit began to assert itself in political practice, and this new spirit did not fail to show in the writings of economists. It is not only that leading academic authorities, such as Marshall, began to approve of what was then considered high direct taxation—including inheritance taxes—but also that they began to espouse what was a mortal sin against the spirit of Gladstonian finance, namely, a policy that went beyond taxing for revenue and aimed at taxing in order to change ('correct') income distribution. Adolf Wagner for Germany and A. C. Pigou for England may serve as examples. The counter-argument that points to possible harmful effects of high and progressive taxation on effort and capital formation—which on the popular level took the shape of the goose that laid the golden eggs—was much in evidence, the more so because practically all economists of standing took a view very favorable to saving.

More analytic effort went into two old topics that were bound to benefit from the new theories. The one was 'justice.' Ethical postulates changed with the times, of course, and the 'principle of ability' to pay and a 'social theory of taxation'—including, among other things, special taxation of privilege, a

[1] Nothing characterizes the situation better than does the fact that certain elementary propositions of economic theory (e.g. about increasing and decreasing average costs) were actually 'discovered' by business economists for themselves.

[2] An important, though later, response should be mentioned at once, Professor J. B. Canning's *Economics of Accountancy* (1929).

term whose coverage tended to widen—began to make converts.[3] But I do not mean these and other canons of justice per se, but genuinely analytic performances that were induced by their advocacy. It may or may not be the economist's business to posit imperatives; but it certainly is his business to rationalize given imperatives by analyzing their implications. How much there was to be done in this line, we may infer from the fact that many economists were completely muddled about the very meaning of such ideas as equal, proportionate, and minimum sacrifice. Some thought (the error was originally Mill's, I believe) that equal sacrifice implies minimum sacrifice; others thought that the 'law' of decreasing marginal utility of income suffices in itself to deduce progressive taxation from a postulate of equal sacrifice.[4] These and other matters of this type were cleared up by a number of writers, among whom I mention the outstanding contributions of Edgeworth, Barone, and Pigou.[5]

The other topic was Shifting and Incidence. [This subsection was not completed.]

(c) *Labor Economics*. In Chapter 2, we surveyed the political conditions of that period which were bound to impart a powerful impulse to the study of labor problems. In Chapter 4, we registered some of the effects produced upon the economic profession by *Sozialpolitik* and still more by the spirit of *Sozialpolitik*. In Section 5c of this chapter, we surveyed the contribution that economic theory made to labor economics. It remains to notice briefly the latter's descriptive or 'practical' or institutional part which, owing to the policy-minded economist's aversion to 'theory,' was then no better correlated with analytic economics than, in general, it is now.[6] Broadly speaking, we may

[3] E. R. A. Seligman's *Progressive Taxation in Theory and Practice* (2nd ed., 1908) must stand for a large body of literature in all countries. But both because of the eminence of the author and because of the originality of his idea of making taxation semi-voluntary, I also mention Wicksell's doctor's thesis, *Finanztheoretische Untersuchungen* (1896), the suggestions of which have been partly developed by E. Lindahl, *Gerechtigkeit der Besteuerung* (*Justice in Taxation*), 1919.

[4] It does so if marginal utility of income decreases at a rate greater than that suggested by Daniel Bernoulli's hypothesis (see above, Part II, ch. 6, sec. 3b). If it decreases at a lower rate, then the postulate of equal sacrifice of 'utility' requires that higher incomes pay a lower percentage than smaller ones (though, of course, higher absolute amounts).

[5] F. Y. Edgeworth's papers on problems of taxation, one of them of fundamental importance, are republished in vol. II of the *Papers Relating to Political Economy* (1925). As usual, his exposition proceeds by what I beg leave to describe as picking out currants—such propositions as, e.g., that a tax on one of two related goods may induce a fall in the prices of both; or that a tax on both may confer a net benefit on the producer of one of them—so that we have difficulty in visualizing the spacious whole that is in fact the peak performance of its field and period. E. Barone's 'Studi di economia finanziaria,' *Giornale degli Economisti*, April-May, June, and July-August 1912, is a still more comprehensive treatise, of great power and originality, cast in the form of three separate studies. A. C. Pigou's various contributions were eventually combined in *A Study in Public Finance* (1928).

[6] This should not be interpreted to mean that the faults were all on one side. Labor economists displayed indeed an unreasonable dislike for anything that looked

say that the period under discussion laid, in all essentials, the groundwork of modern labor economics. The subject did not quite attain the status of a recognized special field in the sense of modern American teaching and research practice. But it commanded the services of a rapidly increasing number of specialists. Principally these specialists were out for practical reform of legal institutions and administrative practice, and they had their own ideas about what it means 'to apply reason to human affairs.' But this fact-finding and their recommendations did not fail to benefit general economics. As an example, take the minority report of the English Poor Law Commission (1909). This seminal performance, a belated reaction to the severe unemployment that had prevailed in England between 1873 and 1898, taught many an economist who stood in need of such a lesson that unemployment was at times very little influenced by factors under the workman's control: at all events, it was, or should have been, important raw material on which the general economist could exercise his analytic powers.

In addition, monographs and treatises on labor questions began to appear in increasing quantities. Two famous monographs by Beatrice and Sidney Webb and Herkner's treatise or textbook are familiar samples [7] from a rapidly swelling literature. Statistical research was hampered by the inadequacy of material. But some efforts were nevertheless made in all countries.[8] As every reader of Marshall's *Principles* knows, general treatises allowed more and more space to labor economics, also to its purely institutional aspects. Previous textbook practice in this respect was far surpassed by the textbook of von

---

like analytic refinement, and an unreasonable distrust in the mysterious formulae of the theorists' wage analysis. They did try to make things easier for themselves by putting theoretical arguments out of court *a limine*. But the theorists did not always enter the problems of the labor economist in a proper spirit of co-operation. They were not always anxious to profit from the latter's facts and recommendations in order to enrich their analysis. And some were as obnoxious as were most of the labor economists to the charge of putting the other fellow's argument out of court *a limine*. There were exceptions. Some conspicuous ones will be mentioned in the text. On the whole, however, co-operation and consequent cross-fertilization were less in evidence than were their opposites.

[7] B. and S. Webb, *The Public Organization of the Labour Market* (1909); and *The History of Trade Unionism* (rev. ed., 1920). H. Herkner, *Die Arbeiterfrage* (1894); comparison of the contents and methods of this book with the contents and methods of any modern American textbook on labor economics is strongly recommended.

[8] For England, in addition to Booth's survey of *Life and Labour of the People in London* (2 vols., 1889-91; 17 vols., 1903) see, e.g., Robert Giffen's papers read to the Royal Statistical Society in 1883 and 1886 ('Progress of the Working Classes in the Last Half Century,' and 'Further Notes on the Progress of the Working Classes in the Last Half Century'). In 1895 began A. L. Bowley's unrivaled publications on English wages. The first of many articles, 'Changes in Average Wages in the United Kingdom between 1880 and 1891,' appeared in the *Journal of the Royal Statistical Society*, 1895. For complete list, see bibliography appended to Bowley's *Wages and Income in the United Kingdom since* 1860 (1937). Of the many attempts that were made in the United States to overcome formidable difficulties, I mention only: Scott Nearing, *Wages in the United States*, 1908-1910 (1911).

Philippovich. We might fitly conclude these remarks by pointing again to the greatest venture in labor economics ever undertaken by a man who was primarily a theorist, Professor Pigou's *Wealth and Welfare* [9] (1912).

(d) *Agriculture.* [Planned but not written.]

(e) *Railroads, Public Utilities, 'Trusts,' and Cartels.* The statements with which I introduced the subsection on Labor Economics might almost be repeated for what was done during that period in the fields of these and cognate topics. Again, the historian of economic thought would have to notice not only new problems but also a new spirit of dealing with them. The historian of economic analysis has little to report beyond a rich crop of historical and 'descriptive' work, some of which has retained its interest to this day. For the rest we must confine ourselves to a few bald comments that are necessary in order to round out our sketch.

Any decent theory of cost and price ought to be able to make valuable contributions to railroad economics, and railroad economics ought to be able to repay the service by offering to general theory interesting special patterns and problems. As has been pointed out before, there are great possibilities in a co-operation of economists and engineers; and few fields offer such possibilities as obviously as does the railroad business. We find something of this but not much, though more could be unearthed from technological journals. As an example, I mention the work of Wilhelm Launhardt, who not only investigated the influence upon operating costs of gradients and curves but also produced a theory of railroad rates that, among other things, contained the theorem—his argument for government ownership is based upon it—that the social advantage from railroads will be maximized if charges be not higher than—as we should say—marginal cost. It follows from this that the whole overhead would have to be financed from the government's general revenue—the theorem that has been much discussed in our own day after having been independently discovered by Professor Hotelling.[10] This is very much more interesting than are generalities about the desirability of nationalization or regulation which, of course, were published in shoals.

Most of the work of which Launhardt's is an example was, however, done

[9] This work substantially embodies the main points of its author's previous *Principles and Methods of Industrial Peace* (1905). In *Economics of Welfare,* the successor of *Wealth and Welfare,* Pigou's labor economics are to be found in Part III and in chs. 1, 5, 7, and 13 of Part IV.

[10] W. Launhardt, *Die Betriebskosten der Eisenbahnen . . .* (1877). The theorem above occurs on p. 203 of his *Mathematische Begründung der Volkswirthschaftslehre* (1885), which, for basic theory, adopts the principles of Jevons and of Walras, though we must accept Launhardt's claim to independent discovery 'of a similar approach,' since we have accepted the analogous claim of others. His treatment presents several original points that are all of them to its credit. But his almost ruthless use of particular forms of function—by which he produces results of disconcerting definiteness—should be studied and improved rather than condemned *a limine.* I add his *Kommerzielle Trassierung der Verkehrswege* (1872). The author was professor at the Technological Institute in Hanover. Neither *Palgrave's Dictionary* nor the *Encyclopaedia of the Social Sciences* mentions his name.

in France. It must suffice to mention the performances of Cheysson,[11] Picard, and Colson. English railway economics of the period is, I believe, represented at its best by the descriptive analyses and the little textbook of Acworth. Professor Pigou's treatment of railway rates is, however, more fertile in results relevant to general economics,[12] especially as regards the issue: cost of service principle versus value of service principle ('what the traffic will bear'). The quantity of American railroad publications of the period was, I am afraid, quite out of proportion to its quality. Serious analytical slips may be proved even against works of standing that were in other respects meritorious and most of them are quite forgotten by now. Hadley's [13] textbook is one of the not too numerous exceptions. All aspects of the subject, historical and institutional, there receive adequate treatment. In addition, however, the book moves on a high level of analytic correctness; and nobody will ever surpass the telling example by which he drove home the truth that discrimination may, and often will, benefit all parties concerned, including the one that is being discriminated against (the case of the two oyster-producing villages that cannot supply a given inland market unless one pays a higher freight rate than the other). It is, however, characteristic of a comparatively backward state of analysis that this case was treated like a curious exception instead of being made to follow from a more general set-up in which absence of discrimination would constitute a special (or limiting) case.

Like railroads, public utilities should have proved both an important field of application and an important source of particular patterns for the theorist. Very little was accomplished, however,[14] that will bear comparison with Dupuit's earlier contributions.[15] The European discussions on nationalization and municipalization present but little interest from our standpoint. Nor is there any benefit to the analytic apparatus of economics to report from the American discussion on rate regulation that dealt with the problem of the

[11] Émile Cheysson. The misleading title of an address of his that brimmed over with original ideas is 'Statistique géométrique,' 1887. Railroad costs and tariffs are only one of several subjects there dealt with in the true spirit of econometrics. The *Encyclopaedia of the Social Sciences* says of him that he contributed nothing new to sociology or economics. A. M. Picard, *Traité des chemins de fer* (1887), and C. Colson, *Transports et tarifs* (1890; English trans., 1914).

[12] W. M. Acworth, *Railways of England* (1889), *Railways of Scotland* (1890)—still worth reading even from the standpoint of 'pure' theory, *Elements of Railway Economics* (1st ed., 1905). Professor Pigou's contribution was made within the framework of *Wealth and Welfare* (Part II, ch. 18 in *Economics of Welfare*).

[13] A. T. Hadley, *Railroad Transportation* (1885).

[14] I may illustrate the kind of thing that I should have expected to find by Marshall's Pittsburgh gas case. See A. Smithies, 'Boundaries of the Production Function and Utility Function,' in *Explorations in Economics* (1936), p. 328. Marshall's treatise contains a large number of similar suggestions that have never been appreciated as they should.

[15] See especially: *De la Mesure de l'utilité des travaux publics* (1844) and *De l'Influence des péages sur l'utilité des voies de communication* (1849), which will be noticed again in ch. 7 below.

'reasonable return on the fair value of the property' which the Supreme Court held public utilities should be permitted to earn. The various 'theories' of valuation for indemnity, taxation, and rate-regulation purposes that the legal mind produced offer curious examples of logical muddle. Many economists did useful work in trying to clear it up and seem, for example, after efforts extending over more than half a century, to have convinced lawyers that the attempt to define a 'reasonable' rate of return with reference to the value of a property that is itself derived from expected returns, involves circular reasoning. But this suffices in itself to characterize the level of this branch of economic analysis.

CHAPTER 7 *

Equilibrium Analysis

* [Editor's note to Part IV, ch. 7. Although this chapter on Equilibrium Analysis had been carefully planned from the beginning, it did not exist in any final form at the death of J. A. S. It was found in a fairly large number of small segments, some in typescript and some still in manuscript. Occasionally there were alternative versions

1. Fundamental Unity of the Period's Economic Theory

Even for the preceding period we have been able to discern a considerable amount of agreement as regards the essentials of economic analysis and, in fact, a kind of average or modal system of general economics, deviations from which were the less frequent the greater they were. With much more confidence can we aver for the period under survey that there existed by about 1900, though not a unified science of economics, yet an engine of theoretical analysis whose basic features were the same everywhere. This should be obvious from our survey in the preceding chapter. But it may be helpful, in view of the different impression we get when we behold the troubled surface and in view of the different opinion entertained by many historians, to show this once more.

Nobody denies that, numerous differences in detail notwithstanding, Jevons, Menger, and Walras taught essentially the same doctrine. But Jevons' and Marshall's analytic structures do not, in essence, differ more than the scaffolding differs from the completed and furnished house, and note XXI in the Appendix to Marshall's *Principles* is conclusive proof of the fundamental sameness of his and Walras' models. Wicksell's engaging frankness reveals the two pillars of his arch to the most perfunctory glance: the one is Walrasian, the other Böhm-Bawerkian. J. B. Clark's blueprint, however independently conceived, embodied substantially the same principles as did Marshall's Book VI; Pareto and Fisher developed Walras. And, so far as professional theory is concerned, these names cover practically all of what we may call the period's primary work in 'general theory'; the teaching associated with them, as has been shown in the two preceding chapters, shaped practically all of the secondary or derivative work of the period, except that of the Marxists.

---

of the same subject. There is a brief and very early treatment of the whole chapter, which was not used because I believed it to have been superseded by the later, more elaborate version here published. The first four sections had been written long ago but sections 3 and 4 were in the process of revision. The last two sections and the Note on Utility, which appears as an appendix to the chapter, were written in 1948 and 1949. Most of section 7 (The Walrasian Theory of General Equilibrium) was still untyped. Section 8 (The Production Function) and the Note on Utility had been typed, but J. A. S. had hardly read the former and had no opportunity to revise the latter. In a sense, all the sections were unfinished in that J. A. S. indicated by shorthand notes that he would have made changes in the text and added footnote references.

I am very much indebted to Richard M. Goodwin, who first put the various parts of this chapter together for me. As both a student and valued colleague, he had worked with my husband on these problems and was probably better fitted than anyone else for this task.

I have for the most part followed his suggestions, but I have added one or two things which turned up after Goodwin's departure for Europe and removed some 'alternative versions' and the early version of the whole chapter mentioned in the first paragraph of this note. The interested scholar will find this material, along with the rest of the manuscript, deposited in the Houghton Library at Harvard University.]

Why, then, do the structures of these leaders look so different? And why is it that many even of those of us who do see the fundamental sameness in them nevertheless deny the underlying unity of that period's 'general economics'? The answer to the first question is: because there were plenty of differences in technique, in details, and in views on individual problems, and because in addition leaders and followers alike overemphasized them. The most important differences in technique turned on the use or the refusal to use the calculus and systems of simultaneous equations: the same 'theory' looks quite different in this garb and without it—especially to the man who is not familiar with the former. An example for the differences in details and at the same time for the propensity to overemphasize them is afforded by the controversy on 'real cost' (see above, ch. 6, sec. 4). And examples of differences in views on individual problems are the differences in the theory of capital and the different attitudes as regards Partial Analysis (see below, sec. 6), which Marshall elaborated and Pareto affected to despise.[1] But differences of this kind —and controversies arising out of them—are part and parcel of the very life of every field of knowledge: if we allowed them to obscure the sameness of fundamentals, we could never speak of the scholastic doctors as a group that was united as regards methods and fundamental results; we might not even be able to speak of a Marxist school.

With reference to the second question, it must be remembered that our proposition of fundamental unity does not apply to the first part of the period but only to the Classical Situation that emerged roughly around 1900. Before that there was, of course, not more but less agreement among leading theorists than there had been around 1850. The system that was established by Jevons, Menger, and Walras in the 1870's and 1880's and found its classic form in Marshall's *Principles* (1890) came to most theorists as something new and unfamiliar. Nothing, in fact, proves so convincingly that, forerunners notwithstanding, it actually was something new, as does the resistance it met with. While the fight was on and individual adherents were being won here and there, Mill's economics—to choose Mill once more as representative—was in possession, and one more cause for dissension was being added to those that had divided economists at the end of the preceding period. This also accounts

[1] Marshall and Pareto—the latter not only with respect to the 'literary economists' but also with respect to Walras—are good instances of that overemphasis upon matters of comparative detail that produces, and not in laymen alone, the impression of the presence of fundamentally different 'systems.' But the outstanding instance is Cassel: the fundamental lines of his analytic structure are Walrasian. Yet in the later editions of his *Theoretische Sozialökonomie* (*Theory of Social Economy*, 1st German ed. 1918; 4th ed. rev., 1927; English trans. 1923 and 1932) he did not even mention Walras' name. And in his first paper on general theory ('Grundriss einer elementaren Preislehre,' *Zeitschrift für die gesamte Staatswissenschaft*, 1899) he presented a simplified version of Walras' system for which he claimed fundamental novelty on the ground that it eliminated the marginal utility theory of value though it retained, in a different terminology, all that is essential to it. And the claim was widely accepted!

for the fact that the laggards who clung to the old doctrines, even after victory had been substantially won by the new, were both more numerous and more respectable than would have been the case if the changes had been less 'revolutionary.' A random sample from the economists—or even theorists—taken from the whole period, therefore, might well seem to refute the proposition here advanced. But in addition there was a large number of 'outsiders,' that is, of writers who championed theoretical systems of their own and condemned professional theory without bothering to master it. And, finally, there was something else. Then as always, the majority of economists were absorbed in the task of investigating the facts and practical problems of the various departments of public policy. This majority, which was reinforced by the historical and institutional groups, had little use for 'theory' and did not welcome a new type of it. They never accepted it as an instrument of research but looked upon 'marginalism' as a sort of speculative philosophy or as a new sectarian 'ism' which it was precisely their business to eliminate by what they considered truly scientific and realistic research (see ch. 4 above). Hence they passed, in methodological and programmatic pronouncements, all sorts of sweeping judgments upon it. On the surface, the result was bedlam, especially in Germany and in the United States—a multitude of discordant voices, all of which seemed to testify to the presence of an impasse. The reader must try to understand, on the one hand, how very natural this was and, on the other hand, that it did not mean what it seems to mean.[2] Below the phrase-troubled surface, there was no impasse.

2. Cournot and the 'Mathematical School': Econometrics

It was during the period under survey that the inevitable happened: mathematical methods of reasoning began to play a significant and indeed decisive role *in the pure theory of our science*. Numerical or algebraic formulations and numerical calculations had occurred of course in the earlier stages of economic analysis: there were the political arithmeticians, the physiocrats, and many isolated instances such as Briscoe, Ceva, H. Lloyd, Condillac, whom we have noticed in their places, or the two authors rescued from oblivion by E. R. A. Seligman.[1] But the use of figures—Ricardo made ample use of numerical illustrations—or of formulae—such as we find in Marx—or even the restatement in algebraic form of some result of non-mathematical reasoning does not con-

[2] The truth that economic theory is nothing but an engine of analysis was little understood all along, and the theorists themselves, then as now, obscured it by dilettantic excursions into the realm of practical questions. But it was emphasized by Marshall who, in his inaugural lecture at Cambridge ('The Present Position of Economics,' 1885), coined the famous phrase that economic theory is not universal truth but 'machinery of universal application in the discovery of a certain class of truths.'

[1] *Essays in Economics* (1925), pp. 82-3. One was an anonymous author, 'E. R.,' who in his *Essay on Some General Principles of Political Economy* (1822) used algebra in his treatment of incidence of taxation; the other was Samuel Gale, who wrote *An Essay on the Nature and Principles of Public Credit* (1784-6).

stitute mathematical economics: a distinctive element enters only when the reasoning itself that produces the result is explicitly mathematical.[2] Of this, however, I know only three clear cases that antedate von Thünen and Cournot: D. Bernoulli, Beccaria, and, if we attach enough importance to even a glimpse of an equilibrium system, Isnard.[3] The non-mathematical reader may welcome an attempt at defining more closely the nature of the service that mathematics rendered to the economic theorists of the period under survey.

[(a) *The Service Mathematics Rendered to Economic Theory.*] We shall presently touch upon the services that mathematics rendered in the treatment of statistical material. Here we are concerned with its use in theoretical analysis that is *quantitative* but not *numerical.* Now, the layman when he hears of the application of mathematics to economics thinks primarily of technical operations ('calculations') that involve the use of 'higher' mathematics, that is, the things that first come into view in the more advanced ranges of the college student's algebra and analytic geometry and then soar out of the range of the non-mathematical mortal. It is quite true that during (a little more than) the last quarter of a century really advanced methods have increasingly imposed themselves upon economists, methods that would be recognized as either 'hard' or else very 'special' by professional mathematicians. Prior to 1914, however, this was not so, and very few publications that appeared earlier required of their readers—or even their authors—any proficiency in technical mathematics. What was required, beyond the rudiments of algebra and analytic geometry, was a knowledge of the calculus, and even of this the general ideas or logic rather than the more difficult techniques, for example, of integration. Barone was quite right when he averred in 1908 that though mathematics was becoming indispensable to the theorist, every normal and normally educated person could acquire what was needed of it by the spare-time work of about six months.

The logic of the calculus may be expressed in terms of a small number of concepts such as variables, functions, limits, continuity, derivatives and differentials, maxima and minima. Familiarity with these concepts—and with such notions as systems of equations, determinateness, stability, all of which admit of simple explanations—changes one's whole attitude to the problems that arise from theoretical schemata of quantitative relations between things: problems acquire a new definiteness; the points at which they lose it stand out

[2] This is why N. F. Canard (*Principes d'économie politique,* 1801) and William Whewell ('Mathematical Exposition of Some Doctrines of Political Economy,' *Cambridge Philosophical Transactions,* 1829, 1831, and 1850) do not figure here. Perhaps, however, Whewell should be considered as an intermediate case. He does not quite deserve Jevons' derogatory comment.

[3] On Thünen, see above, Part III, ch. 4, sec. 1; D. Bernoulli, above II, 6, 3; Beccaria, above II, 3, 4d; and Isnard, above II, 6, 3.

The bibliographies drawn up by Jevons (Appendix I to his *Theory*) and by Irving Fisher (Appendix to the English trans. of Cournot's *Recherches*) are not quite complete but, on the other hand, much too inclusive: they list every writing known to their authors that displays as much as a single symbol.

clearly; new methods of proof and disproof emerge; the maximum of return may be distilled from the little we know about the form of the relations between our variables; and the logic of infinitesimals disposes automatically of much controversial matter that, without its help, clogs the wheels of analytic advance.[4] Did space permit, it could be shown instructively that a great part of the controversies of that period consisted simply of controversies between people who lacked a powerful tool of thought and people who possessed it. But some examples have been presented in the last chapter and others will occur in this.

Since this kind of service consists simply in sharpening the edges of our analytic tools and therefore does not necessarily involve elaborate calculations, a man's mathematics does not necessarily show on the surface of an argument: mathematical theory is more than a translation of non-mathematical theory into the language of symbols, but its results can, in general, be translated into non-mathematical language. This is the reason why the non-mathematical majority of economists never realized the full extent of their obligations to the mathematically trained minority: the typical theorist never realized, for instance, that he did not fully understand Marshall, who was careful to banish his mathematics from the surface of his argument. And so this majority found it easy to look upon those mathematical economists who did flaunt their mathematics as a particular sect or 'school' that was of no particular importance to the profession at large. But mathematical economists form no school in any meaningful sense of the term, any more than do those economists who read Italian: all the differences of opinion that can be conceived to exist between economists at all—a certain class of errors alone excepted—may and do exist between the mathematically trained ones. And the latter's contributions to the period's dominant analytic structure were much greater than people realize even now. Let us see. In the preceding section we have associated that structure with nine names: Jevons, Menger, Walras, Marshall, Wicksell, Böhm-Bawerk, Clark, Pareto, and Fisher. This makes six mathematical to three non-mathematical economists. And if we add, as we should, von Thünen, Cournot, Dupuit, and Gossen, we have ten to three. Nor would the situation be changed if we considered a wider circle of economists who wrote or began writing before 1914, for this would have to include F. Jenkin, Edgeworth, Auspitz and Lieben, Pigou, Moore, Bowley, Cassel, also Pantaleoni, and others who are difficult to match, so far as front-rank performance is concerned, by names from the non-mathematical camp: a lesson to ponder on for the non-mathematical reader of these pages, at least if he be young.[5]

[4] So far as technique goes, the 'new' theories of value and distribution really amounted to not less than the discovery of the calculus for economics—which in itself suffices to show the absurdity of any opposition on principle to 'marginalism.'

[5] There is wide variety in the mathematical acquirements of the men who are mentioned above. Confining ourselves to the first six, we find that Jevons knew very little—much less than would have been good for him to know. Walras, Marshall, and Wicksell had had a regular mathematical training, Marshall much more of it than he showed, Walras less than he needed. Pareto and Fisher were accomplished mathe-

But since the essentials of the marginal utility and the marginal productivity theories were worked out also by economists who were complete strangers to 'higher' mathematics, it was natural for these and for the non-mathematical majority of the profession at large to think that, except perhaps for a few otiose refinements, mathematical reasoning in economics did not add anything to what could be found out without it. This view was all the easier for them to take because they were not aware of the shortcomings of their own products: on the contrary, in several cases of some importance they made virtues of these shortcomings.[6] And so we shall understand that the men who, around 1900 or even later, were in positions of leadership or influence—and this means in or past middle age—had no difficulty in excusing themselves from learning what they looked upon as a difficult and uncongenial technique that might after all turn out to be of little value. Not less understandably, they rationalized this attitude and produced in its defense a number of methodological arguments such as that the attempt to apply mathematics, the tool of physics, to the social sciences was a mistake on logical principle, and others of the same kind, into which, at this hour of the day, it is no longer worth while to go.[7] These particular rationalizations have worn away although the attitude itself has not. But the movement gained enough ground during the period to produce that important symptom of success: the emergence of a small crop of derivative—interpretative and introductory—works.[8] Of unfavor-

---

maticians. Differences of similar range persist to this day. And not less important than the differences in training were and are the differences in natural aptitude: Böhm-Bawerk was not a trained mathematician but, like Ricardo, he was a born one.

[6] An amusing case of this kind was a belief prevalent in the Austrian circle to the effect that the non-mathematical Austrian theory offered 'causal' explanations of the phenomenon of price, whereas the merely 'functional' Walrasian theory of prices explained nothing but relations between prices, supposing these to be already understood. The construction of causal chains between utility, cost, and prices which, as we have seen, spelled miscarriage in the eyes of Marshall, spelled for the Austrians simply a different—and superior—theory.

[7] The case for the 'Mathematical Method in Political Economy,' *ex visu* of that period, has been presented under that heading by Edgeworth in *Palgrave's Dictionary*, and by Irving Fisher, in Appendix III to his *Mathematical Investigations in the Theory of Value and Prices*, where the reader also finds a selection of testimonials pro and con, some of which convey prevalent attitudes very well. But the earliest and, in its brevity, perhaps best of all the arguments for the 'mathematical' method—already coupled with the complaint that its use is 'anathema' to economists—is to be found in Dupuit's *De la Mesure de l'utilité des travaux publics* (1844), which has been reprinted with other works by Dupuit in *Jules Dupuit, De l'utilité et de sa mesure* (ed. M. de Bernardi, 1933).

[8] The earliest text, so far as I know, is W. Launhardt's *Mathematische Begründung der Volkswirthschaftslehre* (1885), which taught the doctrines of Jevons and Walras and in addition some original results of the author, especially on transportation (see above, ch. 5, sec. 4). H. Cunynghame's *Geometrical Political Economy* appeared in 1904; A. Osorio's *Théorie mathématique de l'échange*, in 1913; W. Zawadski's *Les Mathématiques appliquées à l'économie politique*, in 1914; J. Moret's *L'Emploi des Mathématiques en économie politique*, in 1915. There were others but nothing that

able symptoms, let us notice the indifference or even hostility displayed by eminent mathematicians [9] and the fact that there were economists who were well versed in mathematics and yet unfriendly to 'mathematical economics'—the outstanding instance being Lexis.

Mention has already been made of some performances in the field of mathematical economics that belong chronologically to the preceding period. But consideration of the greatest of all, Cournot's, has been deferred until now because, quite neglected before, it acquired seminal importance in the period under survey.

[(b) *The Contribution of Cournot.*] Antoine Augustin Cournot (1801-77),[10] after a successful career at the École Normale Supérieure, was not less successful as an academic teacher and administrator: he was appointed professor of analysis and mechanics at Lyons, 1834; Rector of the Academy (University) of Grenoble, 1835; Inspector General of Studies, 1838; Rector of the Academy (University) of Dijon, 1854. I mention these otherwise irrelevant facts because some of his American admirers, greatly mistaking the psychology generated by the French civil service, have displayed a tendency to make a sort of martyr of him on account of the failure of the *Recherches*. Almost certainly

---

will stand comparison with Bowley's *Mathematical Groundwork* (see ch. 5, sec. 1), which appeared early in 1924.

[9] The outstanding instance is J. Bertrand's attack upon this nascent branch of the mathematical sciences in the *Journal des Savants*, September 1883. It was eagerly seized upon, as an authoritative condemnation, by people who understood neither mathematics nor economic theory, and hence received more attention than it deserved. Though some of Bertrand's strictures were quite justified, most of them were much less serious than he believed them to be, partly because he was inadequately familiar with the economics involved.

[10] The economic work of Cournot has been appraised by many writers, among them Edgeworth (art. 'Cournot' in *Palgrave's Dictionary*); and both the man and his work in economics have been often commemorated in more recent times. See especially: H. L. Moore, 'The Personality of Antoine Augustin Cournot,' *Quarterly Journal of Economics*, May 1905; René Roy, 'Cournot et l'école mathématique,' *Econometrica*, January 1933, and 'L'Oeuvre économique d'Augustin Cournot,' ibid. April 1939; A. J. Nichol, 'Tragedies in the Life of Cournot,' and I. Fisher, 'Cournot Forty Years Ago,' both in *Econometrica*, July 1938.

The *Recherches sur les principes mathématiques de la théorie des richesses* was published in 1838; the English translation by N. T. Bacon (1897) is prefaced by a biographical note by Irving Fisher and, in its second edition (1927), also by useful 'Notes on Cournot's Mathematics.' We shall confine ourselves to this work. (The English trans., *Researches into the Mathematical Principles of the Theory of Wealth*, will be referred to hereafter as the *Researches*.) But Cournot re-entered the field of economic theory twice, both times without making any noticeable impression: he published *Principes de la théorie des richesses* in 1863, and a *Revue sommaire des doctrines économiques* in 1877. Neither publication is without interest, but both avoid the use of mathematics. The mathematics in the *Recherches* have (some slips notwithstanding, of which one is serious) the professional touch but are very elementary. Not even determinants occur and, so far as the calculus is concerned, nothing beyond Taylor's theorem.

he thought of this failure as a small disagreeable incident in an otherwise prosperous career. Moreover, he had every reason to congratulate himself on the reception of what he—again, almost certainly—considered his really important works. Of these, I mention his *Exposition de la théorie des chances et des probabilités* (1843), an admirable performance that met with deserved recognition at the time and later;[11] and his three ventures in the type of philosophy or epistemology that grows out of theoretical physics and was to become so popular around 1900: *Essai sur les fondements de nos connaissances* (1851); *Traité de l'enchainement des idées fondamentales dans les sciences et dans l'histoire* (1861); and *Considérations sur la marche des idées et des événements dans les temps modernes* (1872).

Cournot was fairly well read in economics. But whatever the nature of the interest that made him take up Smith or Say or Ricardo, it was certainly a purely scientific interest that made him take up his *pen*. He had no practical object in view and he made haste to assure his readers that '*theory* ought not to be confounded with systems [of, I suppose, rules of policy], although in the infancy of all sciences the instinct of system necessarily attempts to outline theories.' And he proposed to deal with a number of problems that lent themselves particularly well to treatment by 'that branch of analysis which comprises arbitrary functions, which are merely restricted to satisfying certain conditions' (Preface to the *Researches*). Neither systematic completeness nor novelty of principle was aimed at or achieved. A few concepts and propositions that existed already but only in a hazy and confused form were neatly restated in a more rigorous manner. *And all the historical greatness of the performance is in the surprising success that attended the execution of this modest program.*

There are three introductory chapters, of which the second (on 'relative' and 'absolute' changes in value) suggests some influence of Ricardo; and the third presents the algebra of foreign exchanges whose importance (Jevons did not see this, but Walras did and profited by it) consists in the circumstance that it implies the algebra of the price mechanism in general: it is this reason and not any great gain to be derived for the theory of foreign exchange itself which justifies the advice not to miss it. Chapters 4-9 are the famous ones. They are the nucleus of Marshall's *Partial Analysis*, namely: the demand function; the theory of monopoly, including also the familiar theorems on taxation of monopolized commodities; the theory of perfect competition; and, finally, the treatment of oligopoly and of a particular case of bilateral monopoly, both of which have become the whipping boys of a larger literature (see below, sec. 4). Chapter 10, though disfigured by a serious slip, deserves more attention than it has as yet received. Chapters 11 and 12 have been, to some extent rightly, voted out of court by the overwhelming majority of critics. But at least the former is historically interesting because its argument anticipates

[11] This is of course a layman's tribute. But the late Professor E. Czuber of Vienna, an authority on probability, on whose advice I studied the book forty years ago, also expressed admiration for it. Czuber, I believe, had not even heard of the *Recherches*.

the post-Marshallian (Keynesian) idea of supplementing partial analysis by income analysis: Cournot recognized, of course, that 'for a complete and rigorous solution of the problems relative to some parts of the economic system,' it is 'indispensable to take the entire system into consideration' (op. cit. p. 127), which is precisely what Walras was to do. But, exactly like the Keynesian group of post-Marshallians, Cournot believed that 'this would surpass the powers of mathematical analysis and of our practical methods of calculation' and therefore envisaged instead the possibility of treating such problems in terms of a small set of aggregates in which Social Income and its variations were to hold the place of honor. He did not get very far but it seemed worth while to notice this first explicit reformulation of an old practice which we shall have to discuss again.

In order to rate at its full value Cournot's performance in what I have described as the famous chapters and particularly in Chapter 4 (Of the Law of Demand) and in Chapter 5 (Of Monopoly) it is necessary to remind ourselves that at that time 'literary economists' experienced the greatest difficulty in formulating the simple relation that became so familiar as 'Marshall's demand curve'; that, if we neglect Verri's forgotten contribution, Cournot created the theory of it; and that his treatment of monopoly was an even more striking feat of the same type, for nobody had anything useful to say on monopolistic pricing until Marshall published his masterly version of Cournot's theory. If we add Cournot's theory of the competitive mechanism and of costs, we shall indeed see the justice in his posthumous rise from almost complete oblivion to his present place in our hall of fame. But this place is inscribed to the master of partial analysis, who in addition was the first to show what mathematics can do for us. I do not think it historically correct to attribute to him more than a vague and nonoperational idea of *general* equilibrium.

So far we have been considering the aid that mathematics was beginning to render, during the period under survey, to what is best described as pure theory. The specifically econometric program—mathematical theory plus statistical figures—was struggling toward conscious formulation all the time but, with some important exceptions to be noticed presently, did not quite get there all the same. The message of Petty and Davenant was as yet in abeyance; and even most of those theorists who also did statistical work did not contemplate a wedding between the two lines of research. All the more important is it to cast a glance, on the one hand, at the relation between economists and the *theory* of statistics and, on the other hand, at the progress of work that was econometrics without the name.

As regards the first, let us recall a few facts. Higher statistics grew up from the theory of probability. Jacques Bernoulli's theorem, which has every claim, in a sketch like this, to stand at the beginning, induced the work that culminated in the contributions of A. de Moivre, Laplace, and Gauss. The latter's law of error and method of least squares—vigorously propagated in the social sciences by Quetelet—became the pride and at the same time the curse of applied statistics for more than half a century.[12] All this belongs to the preceding period, as does the work of Poisson and Cournot. The period under survey (almost) begins with Lexis' new departure, which at first made but a little dent in the position of Gauss's law of error. Later on, however, before the nineteenth century was out, a boom in statistical theory set in: to put the reader on the track of its achievements it is sufficient to mention the names of Fechner, Thiele, Bruns, Pearson, Edgeworth, and Charlier. Though Lexis and Edgeworth [13] were economists, analytic economics drew very little profit, during that period, from their contributions to statistical methodology—incomparably less than did astronomy or psychology or biology.

As regards the second, an important type of econometric work may be illustrated again by Engel's Law,[14] which, though published originally in 1857, did not attract international attention before the period under survey. Even then neither Engel himself nor anyone else seems to have realized its interest for economic *theory*. It states that (in a set of families in which tastes do not differ significantly and in which all of them face the same prices) percentage expenditure on food is on the average a decreasing function of income. Also, we have already met another example of such statistical 'laws' that might be inserted into economic theory—Pareto's law of the distribution of incomes by size.

The works of Fisher and of Moore, discussed above, were indeed genuinely econometric and the latter may be said to have given the decisive impulse that started the modern torrent of statistical demand curves.

For this there are several bibliographies that will help the interested reader, for example, the one by Louise O. Bercaw, 'Price Analysis,' *Econometrica*, October 1934,

[12] The curse because it induced an incidental belief to the effect that deviations in statistical material from the law of error are simply due to paucity of observations.

[13] Let us use this opportunity to notice in passing Edgeworth's contributions to the subject, Economic Theory and Probability. I am unable to work up any enthusiasm for his manner of introducing a priori probabilities into purely theoretical reasoning. Still, his *Metretike or the Method of Measuring Probability and Utility* (1887) has not perhaps received adequate attention. Also see his papers 'Miscellaneous Applications of the Calculus of Probabilities,' *Journal of the Royal Statistical Society*, 1897 and 1898. Of major interest was his attempt to use probability considerations for the determination of the optimum amount of a banker's cash reserve and then, of course, for index numbers (see below, ch. 8, sec. 4).

[14] Ernst Engel (1821-96), Director of the Prussian Bureau (*Amt*) of Statistics was primarily an administrator and as such highly successful. But his active mind set itself in addition unconventional tasks that led to publications of permanent importance, such as his monographs on the labor contract (in the journal *Arbeiterfreund*, 1867); *Die Industrie der grossen Städte* (1868); *Der Kostenwerth des Menschen* (1883; this was Part 1 of *Der Werth des Menschen*, of which the remaining parts were never published); and others. The paper in which he first published his 'law' is entitled 'Die Produktions- und Consumtionsverhältnisse des Königreichs Sachsen' (*Zeitschrift des statistischen Büreaus des Königlich Sächsischen Ministeriums des Innern*, November 1857). It was republished in 1895 (*Lebenskosten Belgischer Arbeiterfamilien*) and in the same year in the *Bulletin de l'Institut International de Statistique.*

which presents the material that appeared 1927-33 and refers to other bibliographies that go further back. Henry Schultz's treatise on the *Theory and Measurement of Demand* (1938) is, as the reader presumably knows, the standard work on the subject into which we unfortunately cannot go in this book. Several other pioneer works besides Moore's had appeared by 1914, however, among them Lehfeldt's 'The Elasticity of Demand for Wheat,' *Economic Journal*, June 1914. The latter, so far as I can make out, was the first modern follower of Gregory King.

Whatever may be thought of the immediate practical value of the many demand curves that have been obtained, it is certain that trying to meet the problems that arise in their construction and interpretation is one of the best methods of developing our analytic powers. Precisely for theory, therefore, the subject of statistical demand curves is of the utmost importance. The history of this type of work belongs, however, almost entirely in the present period. The same holds for the work in fields other than the theory of demand, especially in the fields of statistical production functions, statistical cost, and statistical supply functions. For a preliminary study, readers are referred to H. Schultz, *Statistical Laws of Demand and Supply* (1928); J. Dean, *Statistical Determination of Costs* (1936); W. A. Tweddle and Richard Stone, 'Study of Costs,' *Econometrica*, July 1936; the reports of a committee of the Econometric Society presided over by Mr. E. H. Phelps Brown, ibid. April and July 1936; and Reinhard Hildebrandt, *Mathematisch-graphische Untersuchungen über die Rentabilitätsverhältnisse des Fabrikbetriebs* (1925). Perusal of these books and papers will put the reader on the track of methods, problems, and results that foreshadow important parts of the economic theory of the future.

But as we have seen, while little progress was made before 1914 on the lines just glanced at, investigations into agricultural technology, particularly into plant and soil nutrition—quite essential to such old topics of economic theory as the law of decreasing returns—and also into cattle feeding had already reached a high degree of development during the period under survey. The first of the reports of the Phelps Brown Committee mentioned above has the particular merit of bringing home to its readers the theoretical importance of such work and of disabusing them of the idea that the marginal productivity theory is just an armchair speculation.

But the theory of the period did not lend itself to the insertion of such results. The majority of theorists, including some of the greatest, were completely unaware of the possibility of a theory that might eventually achieve numerical results. Accordingly it never occurred to them to frame their schemata in a manner that might have made them amenable to statistical treatment: the very idea would have seemed to them fantastic. However, there were exceptions. Both Cournot and Jevons saw that possibility looming in the future. Pareto and Marshall realized its presence. The latter's address 'The Old Generation of Economists and the New' (1896) is the first pronouncement by a leading theorist in favor of an econometric program. More important still, Marshall *theorized* with a view to making his concepts numerically operative, and his occasional appeal to statistical figures [15] has more than illustrative importance. Institutionalist critics have hardly done justice to the implications of this. Individual workers in special fields, as we know (see, e.g., Cheysson's per-

[15] See, e.g., his table of figures about the effects on yield of different amounts of ploughing and harrowing as reported by the Arkansas Experimental Station (*Principles*, p. 232).

formance or that of the writers on railroad transportation, above, ch. 6, sec. 6) did however make some progress.

3. The Concept of Equilibrium *

(a) *Statics, Dynamics; the Stationary State, Evolution.* We now return to a subject which we have left in the shape it had received at the hands of J. S. Mill. In order to make it easier for the reader to follow the exposition of this section, I shall first restate, with a few explanatory comments, the definitions that are adopted in this book. The first two are due to Ragnar Frisch.

By static analysis we mean a *method* of dealing with economic phenomena that tries to establish relations between elements of the economic system—prices and quantities of commodities—all of which have the same time subscript, that is to say, refer to the same point of time. The ordinary theory of demand and supply in the market of an individual commodity as taught in every textbook will illustrate this case: it relates demand, supply, and price as they are supposed to be at any moment of observation—nothing else is taken into consideration.

But the elements of the economic system that interact at a given point of time are evidently the result of preceding configurations; and the way itself in which they interact is not less evidently influenced by what people expect future configurations to be. Thus, to keep to our example, we may conceive of the situation in our market as determined, or at least influenced, by previous decisions of producers which cannot be understood from the conditions of the point of time chosen for observation but only from the conditions that prevailed at the time when those decisions were taken. Hence we are led to take into account past and (expected) future values of our variables, lags, sequences, rates of change, cumulative magnitudes, expectations, and so on. The *methods* that aim at doing this constitute economic dynamics.

The relation between static and dynamic theory may be elucidated from two different if related points of view. On the one hand, static theory involves a higher level of abstraction: dynamic patterns also abstract from a good many things; but the static pattern drops additional features of reality, namely, those enumerated at the end of the preceding paragraph, and is still nearer to a pure logic of economic quantities than is dynamics. On the other hand, static theory may be said to constitute a special case of a more general dynamic theory: this we see from the fact that we may derive static patterns from dynamic ones by the simple process of equating to zero the 'dynamizing factors' that may occur in the latter.[1]

* [J. A. S. left one early version (typed) and three incomplete 'alternative formulations' (in manuscript) of this section. Two of the later versions appear here as subsections a and b. The other two versions have been deposited with the rest of this manuscript in the Houghton Library at Harvard University.]

[1] In our example, the simplest possible set-up consists in making quantity supplied (S_t) at time t depend, not upon the price at the moment considered, but upon the price that prevailed some time before. If this 'production lag' be taken as the unit of

Now, an observer fresh from Mars might excusably think that the human mind, inspired by experience, would start analysis with the relatively concrete and then, as more subtle relations reveal themselves, proceed to the relatively abstract, that is to say, to start from dynamic relations and then proceed to working out the static ones. *But this has not been so in any field of scientific endeavor whatsoever:* [2] always static theory has historically preceded dynamic theory and the reasons for this seem to be as obvious as they are sound—static theory is much simpler to work out; its propositions are easier to prove; and it seems closer to (logical) essentials. The history of economic analysis is no exception.

By a stationary *state,* as the term implies, we mean not a method or mental attitude of the analyst, but a certain state of the object of analysis, namely, an economic process that goes on at even rates or, more precisely, an economic process that merely reproduces itself. Nevertheless, when understood in the sense we are concerned with here, it is nothing but a methodological fiction. Essentially, it is a simplifying device. But it is also something more. When we try to visualize how such a process might look and which of the phenomena of reality might be present in it, we *ipso facto* discover which of them are lacking. And we thus acquire a tool of analysis that helps us to locate the sources of the latter—a service the importance of which it should be (but unfortunately is not) superfluous to emphasize.[3] The term evolution may be used in a wider and in a narrower sense. In the wider sense it comprises all the phenomena that make an economic process non-stationary. In the narrower sense it comprises these phenomena minus those that may be described in terms of continuous variations of rates within an unchanging framework of institutions, tastes, or technological horizons, and will be included in the concept of growth.

The reader will please observe that, in logical principle at least, 'statics' and 'dynamics,' on the one hand, and 'stationary' and 'evolutionary' states, on the other hand, are independent of one another. We may describe a stationary process by a dynamic model: this will be the case whenever we make the conditions for stationarity of a process in any given period depend upon what happened to the process in preceding periods. We may also describe an evolutionary process by a succession of static models: this will be the case when-

---

time and if quantity demanded (D_t) at time t still depends on the price (p_t) prevailing at the same time t, then we may express this set-up by two equations: $D_t = f(p_t)$ and $S_t = F(p_{t-1})$. From this we get the static set-up by putting the lag equal to zero: $D_t = f(p_t)$ and $S_t = F(p_t)$.

[2] In mechanics, for instance, static relations have been worked out first, dynamical ones later, and it was only Lagrange who conceived of statics as a special case of dynamics.

[3] We neglect here a class of problems in which the concept of a stationary state—as of a state of 'secular stagnation'—acquires another meaning, viz. the meaning of a state of economic society that is actually in the offing. This is the meaning that has come into prominence in the line of thought that may be indicated, briefly, by the sequence: A. Smith-Ricardo-Mill-Keynes-Hansen (see Part v, ch. 5).

ever we deal with disturbances of a given state by trying to indicate the static relations obtaining before a given disturbance impinged upon the system and after it had had time to work itself out.[4] The latter method of procedure is known as Comparative Statics. So far as I know, the term has been first used by F. Oppenheimer [5] in *Wert und Kapitalprofit* (1916, 2nd ed., 1922).

Finally, the reader should also observe that the conceptual devices sketched have nothing to do with any similar ones that may be in use in the physical sciences. The widespread impression to the contrary is due to two facts. First, though they embody nothing but habits of the human mind that are as general as is ordinary logic, they—or similar devices—have, precisely for this reason, been adopted wherever the character of the facts under analysis seemed to suggest them. Since the physical sciences and mechanics in particular were so much ahead of economics in matters of technique, these conceptual devices were consciously defined by physicists before they were by economists so that the average educated person knows them from mechanics before he makes their acquaintance in economics, and hence is apt to suspect that they were illegitimately borrowed from mechanics. Second, such devices being unfamiliar in a field where a looser conceptualization prevailed, some economists, I. Fisher in particular, thought it a good idea to convey their meaning to the untutored mind by way of the mechanical analogy. But this is all. We know that actually the concept of economic statics may be traced to zoology rather than mechanics and, what is much more important, primitive and subconscious use has been made of it from the very beginnings of economic analysis.

Having thus cleared the ground, I shall endeavor to show (1) that those improvements in the analytic apparatus of economics were, actually or potentially, slowly worked out during the period under discussion but not quickly enough—or rigorously enough—for them to take full effect upon analysts' practice before 1914; and (2) that the latter fact slowed up advance and explains some of the most serious shortcomings of the actual achievements.

(1) The concept of the stationary state had been, as we know, quite familiar in the preceding period. But it was used to denote an actual state of the economy to be expected at some future time rather than as a methodological fiction: in the latter capacity it had been used to the full only by Marx, who called it

[4] For instance, this is what the old quantity theory of money did, so far as it involved the proposition that an increase in the quantity of money will, *ceteris paribus*, raise price level proportionately. Obviously this assumes that 'transitional' phenomena may be neglected and hence refers to an 'ultimate outcome' of the processes started by this disturbance of the previous state of the economic organism. The example shows well that this procedure must be highly questionable.

[5] It should be pointed out explicitly that, as defined, dynamic theory in itself has nothing to do with historical analysis: its time subscripts do not refer to historical time —the simple model we used as an example tells us nothing about whether that demand-supply configuration obtained in the times of President Washington or of President Roosevelt; and its sequences are theoretical and not historical or, as we may also put it, it uses theoretical and not historical datings.

simple reproduction. However, independently of him it began to be used in the period under discussion for the purpose of singling out, for preliminary analysis, a set of particularly simple problems: as such it was recognized, for example, by Marshall,[6] who spoke of the 'famous fiction of the "Stationary state" '—though, as a methodological fiction the stationary state was not at all 'famous' in 1890—used it repeatedly, and was, so far as I know, the first to point out that we may increase its usefulness for analysis by defining it differently (more or less strictly) for different purposes. Also he gave the lead, followed by many and especially by Cassel,[7] for an extension of the idea to the case of balanced progress, that is, to the case of a society in which population and wealth grow at about the same rate and in which 'methods of production and the conditions of trade change but little; and, above all, where the character of man himself is a constant quantity'—a conception which has acquired additional interest in our own day owing to its bearing upon the problem of full employment in the models not only of a stagnating but also of an expanding economy.[8] This extension of the concept of stationarity should have separated out neatly the phenomena of evolution in the narrow sense of the term, and so it did. But with all the leaders of the period this meant setting these phenomena aside rather than constructing a comprehensive theory of them.

Neither Walras, who used the phrase *point de vue statique*, nor Marshall, who used the phrase *statical method*, failed to distinguish static theory from the theory of the stationary state. But most writers confused them, witness the growing popularity of the phrase 'static state,'[9] which is the hallmark of this confusion. Nevertheless, though more clearly visualized than rigorously defined, the system of economic statics did emerge during the period and in fact constitutes its great achievement. But the nature of economic dynamics was not even clearly visualized—some identified it with a historical theory of change or else with a theory that allows for trends; others with a theory of general interdependence as against partial analysis of sectional phenomena; still others with a theory of a modern as against the tradition-bound economy of the Middle Ages; and a few simply with the theory of small variations of

[6] See *Principles*, pp. 439 et seq. The crowning achievement in this line of analysis is, of course, Professor Pigou's *The Economics of Stationary States* (1935). The first methodologist to analyze this tool was, I think, J. N. Keynes, *Scope and Method of Political Economy*.

[7] Cf. *Theory of Social Economy*, ch. 1, § 6. Marshall's pointer is on p. 441 of the *Principles*.

[8] Because of this, it will be useful to point to three modern pieces of work that reflect the distance we have traveled since: E. Lundberg, *Studies in the Theory of Economic Expansion* (1937); R. F. Harrod, 'An Essay in Dynamic Theory,' *Economic Journal*, March 1939; E. Domar, 'Capital Expansion, Rate of Growth, and Employment,' *Econometrica*, April 1946.

[9] With J. B. Clark, statics was simply the model of a stationary society; dynamics was the model of evolutionary change (see especially *Essentials of Economic Theory*, 1907). Cassel (op. cit.) used static and stationary interchangeably.

economic quantities.[10] Many, among them Böhm-Bawerk, would not hear of statics and dynamics at all—for them there was just one type of theory, which no doubt admitted of varying degrees of abstraction but not of logically distinct 'methods.' And there were those in whose hands the whole discussion degenerated into a quarrel about words. All this goes to show the importance, even for purely practical purposes, of logically rigorous definitions: for had the nature of the statics of the day been subjected to rigorous analysis, the problems of dynamics would have emerged almost of themselves. But all was not mere confusion. We also find suggestions that point toward the dynamics of our time. They were not more than suggestions, sometimes not more than *obiter dicta*. I can only refer to the (relatively) clearest and most important of them, which are all due to Pantaleoni.[11]

(2) Precisely because even the most advanced thinkers of that time had no explicit dynamic schema or method to help them, they failed to realize the severe limitations of their static schema or method. For these reveal themselves only in the light of dynamic considerations. In consequence, they incessantly stepped out of their statics without having a right to do so and without being aware of it. The situation was made worse by the prevalent confusion between static theory and the theory of a stationary—or quasi-stationary—state.

[This version breaks off at this point, obviously unfinished, with three lines of shorthand notes to indicate how the argument was to be carried on.]

(b) *Determinateness, Equilibrium, and Stability*. From the workshop of Walras the static theory of the economic universe emerged in the form of a large number of quantitative relations (equations) between economic elements or variables (prices and quantities of consumable and productive goods

[10] This is, I think, what Walras meant by *phase dynamique de trouble continuel de l'équilibre par des changements dans ces données* (*Éléments*, p. 302). Certainly it is what Barone meant in his important paper 'Sul trattamento di questioni dinamiche,' *Giornale degli Economisti*, November 1894.

[11] In this connection, two papers of his are of fundamental importance: 'Caratteri delle posizioni iniziali e influenza che esercitano sulle terminali,' *Giornale degli Economisti*, October 1901; and 'Di alcuni fenomeni di dinamica economica,' an address before the Italian Association for the Advancement of Science, September 1909. Both are republished in *Erotemi di economia*, vol. II, 1925. The main points are these: (1) Pantaleoni raised the question of the relation of an observed configuration of elements of an economic system to *temporally* (not only logically) anterior initial conditions; so soon as one raises this question one has raised the fundamental problem of dynamics. (2) Though Pantaleoni's definition of dynamics is not quite satisfactory (*Erotemi*, p. 79), he had the decisive idea and in consequence realized that economic statics is nothing but a *caso particolare* of economic dynamics (ibid. p. 76). (3) He realized that there are two types (*generi*) of dynamical patterns: one that issues in a position of equilibrium and another that does not but presents fluctuations that may go on indefinitely (ibid. p. 77). H. L. Moore was much impressed by these ideas, the importance of which for general theory he was perhaps the first to realize. Nevertheless, his method was substantially one of comparative statics.

or services) that were conceived as simultaneously determining one another. As soon as this great feat had been accomplished—as soon as this Magna Charta of exact economics had been written, which we shall presently study in some detail—a type of research began to impose itself that had been unknown in pre-Walrasian economics. Pure theory there had been from the first, or almost. But its technique had been a simple affair. The Walrasian system of simultaneous equations, however, brought in a host of new problems of a specifically logical or mathematical nature that are much more delicate and go much deeper than Walras or anyone else had ever realized. Mainly they turn upon determinateness, equilibrium, and stability.[12] They are much too difficult and especially too technical for us. But a few fundamental points about them must be noticed if we are to understand the nature of that period's achievement and the way in which modern work links up with it.

For this purpose, let us consider a distinction that was very characteristic of the analytic methods of that period, as it presents itself both in the critical and in the constructive part of Böhm-Bawerk's work. He was out to 'explain' or 'understand' the phenomenon of interest. This task seemed to him to involve two different things. First, it seemed obviously necessary to unearth the 'cause' or 'source' or 'nature' of interest. Second, after this had been done and the result had been critically safeguarded against other 'theories,' there arose the problem of what determines the *rate* of interest. Mathematical economists, Pareto especially, poured contempt upon this methodology. But it may be salvaged, to some extent, by reformulating it like this: since the economic system cannot be treated as a set of undefined things, we must in fact first define what its elements (including interest) are to mean before we can formulate the exact problem of their determination in terms of certain properties of the functions (relations) which this meaning involves. Then follows logically the proof that the problem can in fact be solved (proof of the existence of a solution) and, finally, the investigation into the 'laws' that the solution reveals (the properties of the solution). When we have done all this, we say that we have 'explained' or 'understood' whatever the element or elements we wished to 'explain' or 'understand.'

More generally, and at the same time more simply, we say that we have determined a set of quantities (variables) if we can indicate relations to which

[12] The non-mathematical reader may, however, acquire an idea of this type of problem from Professor Hicks's *Value and Capital;* and the mathematical reader from the Mathematical Appendix to *Value and Capital,* and from the papers by Professor A. Wald, 'Über einige Gleichungssysteme der mathematischen Ökonomie,' *Zeitschrift für Nationalökonomie,* December 1936 (summing up the results of two earlier and more technical papers); Professor P. A. Samuelson, 'The Stability of Equilibrium: Comparative Statics and Dynamics,' *Econometrica,* April 1941, and 'The Stability of Equilibrium: Linear and Nonlinear Systems,' ibid. January 1942; and Professor J. von Neumann, 'A Model of General Economic Equilibrium,' *Review of Economic Studies,* 1945-6 (trans. of an earlier German paper). These complement one another nicely. Also see R. Frisch, 'On the Notion of Equilibrium and Disequilibrium,' *Review of Economic Studies,* February 1936.

they must conform and which will restrict the possible range of their values. If the relations determine just a single value or sequence of values, we speak of unique determination—a case that is, of course, particularly satisfactory. The relations may yield, however, more than one possible value or sequence of values—which is less satisfactory but still better than nothing. In particular, the relations may determine only a range.[13] In the light of what has been said in the preceding paragraph, we realize that 'determining' a set of quantities in the sense in which we use this phrase is indeed not all that is involved in the task of 'explaining' a phenomenon. But we also realize that it is an indispensable and important part of—or, more precisely, an indispensable step in—this task. And this answers the question, so often asked with a sneer, why theorists should bother so much about 'mere determinateness.'

If the relations which are derived from our survey of the 'meaning' of a phenomenon are such as to determine a set of values of the variables that will display no tendency to vary *under the sole influence of the facts included in those relations per se*, we speak of equilibrium: we say that those relations define equilibrium conditions or an equilibrium position of the system and that *there exists* a set of values of the variables that *satisfies* equilibrium conditions. This need not be the case, of course—there need not be a set of values of variables that will satisfy a given set of relations, and there may exist several such sets or an infinity of them. Multiple equilibria are not necessarily useless but, from the standpoint of *any* exact science, the existence of a 'uniquely determined equilibrium (set of values)' is, of course, of the utmost importance, even if proof has to be purchased at the price of very restrictive assumptions; without any possibility of proving the existence of uniquely determined equilibrium—or at all events, of a small number of possible equilibria—at however high a level of abstraction, a field of phenomena is really a chaos that is not under analytic control. Again, we derive a simple and convincing answer to the layman's question concerning the good we expect from all our worry about 'determined equilibrium'—and to the more specific question why this concept played such a role in the thought of Walras and Marshall.[14]

[13] Illustrative examples: suppose then we have to do with people who, if they experience an access of income of one dollar, invariably borrow another and promptly spend both (in Keynesian terms this means a marginal propensity to consume equal to 2); if this goes on, the monetary values of the system will be inflated to infinity, but the process is perfectly determined. The reader should bear this in mind because of the frequent confusion we find of determinacy and equilibrium. Again, the reader can easily satisfy himself that a monopolist may make the same maximum amount of profits at two or more different prices of his product. Finally, price is in general indeterminate in cases of bilateral monopoly. But it is indeterminate within limits which are perfectly determinate themselves.

[14] Its role in the thought of the Austrians, in Wieser's particularly, was actually just as fundamental. If it does not show explicitly, this was owing exclusively to their technical disabilities. Historians who shared these disabilities spoke of the 'equilibrists' (*sic*) as a sort of school or sect. In fact, however, the writers thus labeled only brought out more clearly what all the theorists of the period—actually also of the preceding period—groped for.

The relations from which we start, according to whether they link elements that carry the same time subscript or different ones, may define a static or a dynamic equilibrium. The leaders of that period used only the former concept—at least in their mathematical set-ups—and do not seem to have had any precise ideas about the problems that center in the latter. We shall, therefore, confine ourselves to static equilibrium except so far as description and criticism of their analysis forces dynamical aspects upon us. It should be emphasized, as it has been in the first part of this section with respect to the terms 'static' and 'dynamic' themselves, that the concept of equilibrium, whether static or dynamic, has nothing to do with any borrowing, legitimate or not, from those physical sciences in which analogous concepts occur. They are logical categories and as such as general as is logic itself. They occur both in the physical and the social sciences because it is the same human mind that works both.

Whether static or dynamic, equilibrium may be stable, neutral, or unstable. Before we go into this matter it will be well to comment briefly—and very superficially—on the meaning of a system of simultaneous equations and on the conception of simultaneous determination of a set of variables. We start again from the first two of the four steps into which we have split exact analytic procedure and which are, for the first time in the history of economics, clearly discernible in Walras' work, namely, the enquiry into the nature of the phenomena we are to study and the discovery of the relations which, guided by our knowledge of their nature, we conceive to subsist between them. When we have succeeded in expressing these relations by equations, we are ready to take the third step: we put them together into a system (a theoretical 'model') and ask whether there is a unique set of values of the elements that appear in this system as variables (or 'unknowns') that will satisfy all those equations which must all hold simultaneously—hence the phrase simultaneous equations. So far, it is hoped, everything is plain sailing. But the answer to this question—in most cases negative of course—is extremely difficult to provide. Plain common sense can indeed indicate certain conditions that must be fulfilled if such a unique set of values—a 'solution'—is to exist. Thus, the equations must be genuine equations and not mere identities (such as x is x); [15] they must be independent in the sense that none must be implied in one or more or all of the others; [16] they must be sufficient in number; and, of course,

[15] But identities that express the fact that x and y, which occur in the rest of the system, are really identical ($x \equiv y$) permit suppression of either x or y and thus may contribute toward determinateness just as much as does an equation. Confusion between propositions that are identities and propositions that may determine equilibrium values is a frequent source of error and controversy. See J. Marschak, 'Identity and Stability in Economics: A Survey,' *Econometrica*, January 1942.

[16] Independence must, however, be distinguished from autonomy. In the argument above nothing is required but that no equation should *follow* from the others *mathematically*. It does not matter here whether or not, for *economic* reasons, one or more equations could not hold unless others do, though this matters greatly in other respects. The concept of autonomy—which is due to Frisch—is far beyond our range.

they must not contradict one another.[17] But these conditions are adequate and easily verifiable only in a particularly simple class of cases to which the Walrasian system does not belong. Very advanced argument involving some complicated tools of modern mathematics is needed to cope with the problem of which we shall get but a glimpse in section 7. Walras and Marshall were far from solving it—for one thing because some of the mathematical tools required did not exist in their creative time—and cannot even have had a clear conception of its nature and difficulty. But, as we shall also see, Walras did more than 'counting equations.' [18]

[This version too is unfinished. A single paragraph from the early version (see Appendix) follows here, because it very briefly defines stable, neutral, and unstable equilibrium. These concepts will be touched upon again in later sections of this chapter.]

Thus we may consider stationary and evolutionary *processes* and we may analyze both of them by either a static or dynamic *method.* We shall now introduce the concept of equilibrium. The simplest and for most purposes the most important case is that of static equilibrium. Suppose we have settled the question, what elements in an economic universe we wish to determine and what are the data and the relations by which to determine them. Then the question arises whether these relations that are supposed to hold simultaneously (simultaneous equations) are just sufficient to determine sets of values for those elements (variables) that will satisfy the relations. There may be no such set, one such set, or more than one such set, and it does not follow that our system is valueless if there exist several. But the most favorable case and the one every theorist prays for is of course uniqueness of the set. Such a set or such sets we call equilibrium sets and we say that the system is in equilibrium if its variables take on the values thus determined. It goes without saying that these values are very much more useful for us if they are *stable* than if they are *neutral* or *unstable.* A stable equilibrium value is an equilibrium value that, if changed by a small amount, calls into action forces that will tend to reproduce the old value; neutral equilibrium is an equilibrium value that does not know any such forces; an unstable equilibrium is an equilibrium value, change in which calls forth forces which tend to move the system farther and farther away from equilibrium values. A ball that rests at the bottom of a bowl illustrates the first case; a ball that rests on a billiard table, the second; and a ball that is perched on the top of an inverted bowl, the third case. Naturally, the conditions which insure stability and the absence of which produces instability are of particular interest in order to understand the logic of the economic system. In this sense it has been said that it is the stability conditions that yield our theorems.

17 The far-reaching importance of the latter point (which also shows that such purely logical questions may bear directly upon hotly debated practical issues) should be noticed in passing. If a system or model that correctly expresses fundamental features of the capitalist society contains contradictory equations, this would be proof of inherent hitches in the capitalist system—proof of real, instead of imaginary, 'contradictions of capitalism.'

18 See Marshall, *Principles*, Mathematical Appendix, Note XXI *in fine*.

4. The Competitive Hypothesis and the Theory of Monopoly *

It has been stated above that the economists of the period under survey substantially retained the habit of their 'classic' predecessors, which was to consider 'competition' as the normal case from which to build up their general analysis; [1] and that like those predecessors they overrated the range of application of such an analysis. In fact, instances abound of writers who considered competition as the normal case *either* in the sense that it covers most of actual business practice (Walras, the Austrians); *or* in the sense that deviations from the competitive schema, though frequent, may be taken care of by occasional recognition (Marshall, Wicksell); [2] *or* in the sense that competition 'ought' to be the normal case and 'should' and could be enforced by appropriate policies (Clark); *or*, finally, in the sense that the actual system, however noncompetitive in parts, nevertheless works out, on the whole, as if it were competitive (Cassel). Moreover, while not all of them were uncritical eulogists of competition (see below sec. 5), nearly all of them were apt to yield to the specific bias of the economic theorist that has nothing to do with political preference, the bias for easily manageable patterns. And it stands to reason that the theorist's generalized description of economic behavior is greatly simplified by the assumption that the prices of all products and 'factors' cannot be perceptibly influenced by the individual household and the individual firm, and hence may be treated as given (as parameters) within the theory of their behavior.[3] These prices will then be determined, in general, by the mass effect of the actions of all households and all firms in 'markets,' the mechanisms of which are relatively easy to describe so long as the households and firms have no choice but to adapt the quantities of commodities and services they wish to buy or to sell to the prices that rule. We may call this the Principle of Excluded Strategy and accordingly say that the bulk of the period's pure theory was a pure theory of static equilibrium *that excluded*

* [This section was found in four parts, three in typescript (each with pages numbered independently) and one in manuscript with the pages unnumbered. The parts seemed to follow consecutively except the last, which was very short and apparently written quite early. The part in manuscript was the treatment of oligopoly, obviously not completed. Still another shorter treatment entitled 'Monopoly, Oligopoly, Bilateral Monopoly,' probably a preliminary study (not typed), has been deposited with the rest of the manuscript in the Houghton Library at Harvard.]

[1] But compare also what has been said on Mill's qualifications and warnings, which have not always been given due weight. Nor should we forget that Cournot built his analysis from the monopoly case.

[2] But Pareto denied emphatically that competition actually 'rules' in our society; see *Cours*, vol. II, p. 130.

[3] It is interesting to note that in 1939 Professor Hicks was just as convinced that successful theoretical analysis is substantially confined to the competitive case as J. S. Mill had been in 1848: abandonment of the competitive hypothesis threatens 'wreckage . . . of the greater part of economic theory' (*Value and Capital*, 1939, p. 84).

strategy. The all-round rise of the level of scientific rigor eventually produced if not the term yet the substance of what we now call pure or perfect competition.[4]

(a) *The Competitive Hypothesis*. This notion had been made explicit by Cournot at the end of Chapter 7 and the beginning of Chapter 8 of his *Researches:* after having started with the case of straight monopoly (discussed below) he first introduced another seller and then additional ones until, by letting their number increase indefinitely, he finally arrived at the case of 'illimited' (unlimited) competition, where the quantity produced by any one producer is too small to affect price perceptibly or to admit of price strategy.[5] Jevons added his Law of Indifference, which defines the concept of the perfect market in which there cannot exist, at any moment, more than one price for each homogeneous commodity. These two features—excluded price strategy and law of indifference—express, so far as I can see, what Walras meant by *libre concurrence*. Pareto's definition (*Cours* I, p. 20) comes to the same thing. This does not however dispose of all the logical difficulties that lurk behind the concept of a competitive market,[6] and some of these must now be noticed briefly.

The mechanism of pure competition is supposed to function through everybody's wish to maximize his net advantage (satisfaction or monetary gain) by means of attempts at optimal adaptation of the quantities to be bought and sold. But exclude 'strategy' as much as you please, there still remains the fact that this adaptation will produce results that differ according to the range of knowledge, promptness of decision, and 'rationality' of actors, and also according to the expectations they entertain about the future course of prices, not to mention the further fact that their action is subject to additional restrictions that proceed from the situations they have created for themselves by their past decisions. As we shall see below, Walras was very much alive to these difficulties and in places (e.g., in the last paragraph of the 35th *leçon* of the *Éléments*) he clearly saw the necessity looming in the future of constructing dynamic schemata to take account of them. For himself, however, he saw

[4] The term pure competition, which will be used in this book, was introduced by Professor E. H. Chamberlin in his *Theory of Monopolistic Competition* (the preface of the first edition is dated 1932, but the substance of the argument, in all essentials, is contained in an unpublished Ph.D. thesis presented in 1927). See below, Part v, ch. 2.

[5] The advantage of this approach is that it emphasizes the fact that pure competition *results* from certain conditions: this is much better than to posit it as an institutional datum. In addition Cournot emphasized (op. cit. p. 90) that the quantity produced by each producer must be 'inappreciable not only with reference to the total production, $D = F(p)$, but also with reference to the derivative $F'(p)$ so that the partial production [of every single producer] could be subtracted from D without any appreciable variation resulting in the price of the commodity.'

[6] The first author to display logical discomfort at the handling of the concept by others was H. L. Moore ('Paradoxes of Competition,' *Quarterly Journal of Economics*, February 1906, and *Synthetic Economics*, pp. 11-17) but his own treatment of it is not more satisfactory.

not less clearly that, absorbed in the pioneer task of working out the essentials of the mathematical theory of the economic process, he had no choice but to simplify heroically (*Éléments*, p. 479). Thus, he postulated (at first) that the quantities of productive services that enter into the unit of every product (coefficients of production) are constant technological data; that there is no such thing as fixed cost; that all the firms in an industry produce the same kind of product, by the same method, in equal quantities; that the productive process takes *no* time; that problems of location may be neglected. Under such circumstances it was but natural that he used or abused the prerogatives of the pioneer still further by narrowing down all the possible types of reaction to a single standard type.[7] For us the question arises: how much of this did he mean to include in his 'free competition'? It has been held (by Professor Knight among others) that Walras, and the theorists of that epoch generally, intended to make 'omniscience' and ideally rational and prompt reaction attributes of pure competition; deviations from this pattern would then find room in the spacious folds of an entity called 'friction,' which would thus emerge as a helpmate of pure competition with the assignment to pick up whatever the latter proved incapable of carrying. It is submitted, however, that there is no point in overloading pure competition like this, and that it is quite possible to separate, in interpreting the writers of that epoch, their concept of pure competition as defined in the preceding paragraph from any further assumptions that they may have made, in general or for particular purposes, about knowledge, promptness, and rationality of action and all the other things mentioned above, even in those instances in which they did not carry out this separation themselves.[8]

Marshall, however, did not take this line. Just as Walras, more than any other of the leaders, was bent on scraping off everything he did not consider essential to his theoretical schema, so Marshall, following the English tradition, was bent on salvaging every bit of real life he could possibly leave in. As regards the case in hand, we find that he did not attempt to beat out the logic of competition to its thinnest leaf. On the first pages of his *Principles* he emphasized economic freedom rather than competition and refrained from defining the latter rigorously. Moreover, throughout the *Principles*, he paid much attention to the problems of individual firms—the manner in which they conquer their Special Markets within which to maneuver, the manner in

[7] He did, however, here and there, make some use of a none too precisely defined Law of Great Numbers. In this he followed a suggestion of Cournot's.

[8] An example that will illustrate the importance of this point is afforded by the statement that, according to pre-Keynesian theory, there could not be involuntary unemployment in conditions of perfect competition, except unemployment of the 'frictional' type (Keynes, *General Theory*, p. 16). The implied criticism is entirely disposed of so soon as it is remembered that 'full employment' is a property not of pure competition per se but of perfect equilibrium in pure competition. But if pure competition implied ideally prompt adaptation, then both full employment and perfect equilibrium in general would practically always have to be present—'friction' permitting—and it could in fact be argued that such a theory does not fit reality.

which they lose them again, and certain consequences that follow therefrom. It is submitted that there is more in this than mere dislike of naked abstractions. There is awareness of that set of problems that later on developed into the theory of monopolistic (Chamberlin) or imperfect (Robinson) competition, whose patron saint Marshall may indeed be said to have been. But there is also a subtle difference in attitude toward these problems between him and the modern exponents of this theory that is not easy to convey.

If we are of the opinion, on the one hand, that from all the infinite variety of market patterns pure or perfect monopoly and pure or perfect competition stand out by virtue of certain properties—of which the most important is that both cases lend themselves to treatment by means of relatively simple and (in general) uniquely determined rational schemata—and, on the other hand, that the large majority of cases that occur in practice are nothing but mixtures and hybrids of these two, then it seems natural to accept pure monopoly and pure competition as the two genuine or fundamental patterns and to proceed by investigating how their hybrids work out. This renders the attitude of the theorists of monopolistic or imperfect competition. But instead of considering the hybrid cases as deviations from, or adulterations of, the fundamental ones we may also look upon the hybrids as fundamental and on pure monopoly and pure competition as limiting cases in which the content of actual business behavior has been refined away. This is much more like the line that Marshall took. Should the reader feel that I am laboring to convey a distinction without a difference, he is requested to ask himself whether the definition of pure competition that has been given above really fits what we mean when talking about competitive business. Is it not a fact that what we mean is the scheme of motives, decisions, and actions imposed upon a business firm by the necessity of doing things better or at any rate more successfully than the fellow next door; that it is *this* situation to which we trace the technological and commercial efficiency of 'competitive' business; and that this pattern of behavior would be entirely absent *both* in the cases of pure monopoly and pure competition, which therefore seem to have more claim to being called degenerate than to being called fundamental cases? [9] This, if I am not mistaken, is beginning to be widely felt today—hence the search for a 'workable' concept of competition (J. M. Clark) that might well start with an analysis of Marshall's argument. The latter was, however, singularly unfortunate in this part of his teaching. Neither theorists nor institutionalist enemies of theory saw the hints that they could have developed.

(b) *The Theory of Monopoly.* We have already surveyed the work and views of that period's economists concerning the practical problems of monopoly, oligopoly, and monopolistic practice that were thrust upon their attention owing to the developments in the sphere of largest-scale business. Now we must turn to the theoretical tools they provided for use in this field. Several

[9] The moral of this story is, of course, that dissecting a phenomenon into logical components and working out the pure logic of each may cause us to lose the phenomenon in the attempt to understand it: the essence of a chemical compound may be in the compound and not in any or all of its elements.

excellent critical histories permit us to confine ourselves to the most general outlines.[10] The chief performance was Cournot's and the period's work may be described as a series of successful attempts to develop his statics of straight monopoly and as another series of much less successful attempts to develop and to correct his theories of oligopoly and bilateral monopoly. Second honors are divided between Marshall and Edgeworth.[11]

In order to appreciate Cournot's performance it is necessary to recall the fact that, as we have noticed not without surprise, practically no *theory* of monopoly had existed before him, in spite of all the talk about it, and that even his starting point, the 'Marshallian' demand function (*loi du débit*) had not been properly defined before 1838. Let us first observe that the demand function, $D = F(p)$, hence also the total revenue function, $pF(p)$, and the marginal revenue function, $F(p) + pF'(p)$ (*Researches*, p. 53), *are objectively given to the monopolist* who, on the one hand, can exploit a given demand schedule at his pleasure and, on the other hand, is not supposed to be able to alter it to his advantage, for example, by advertising or by teaching his customers new uses of his product. For the first time, we are thus presented, by implication, with a definition of monopoly but with one *that excludes the large majority of all the 'single sellers' we can observe in real life*.[12] The given revenue functions Cournot then proceeded to confront with total and marginal cost curves[13] in

[10] See, e.g., Gaston Leduc, *Théorie des prix de monopole* (1927); the first and third chapters in E. H. Chamberlin's *Monopolistic Competition* (5th ed., 1946), where the reader also finds an almost complete bibliography; F. Zeuthen, *Problems of Monopoly and Economic Warfare* (1930); H. von Stackelberg, *Marktform und Gleichgewicht* (1934, ch. 5); J. R. Hicks, 'The Theory of Monopoly,' *Econometrica*, January 1935.

[11] Walras' contribution is insignificant. Along with Cournot we might, however, have mentioned Dupuit and Ellet. Some of Edgeworth's contributions are in the *Mathematical Psychics* (1881), the rest of them, especially a translation of his important 'Teoria pura del monopolio' (*Giornale degli Economisti*, July 1897) are in his *Papers Relating to Political Economy*. Also see A. C. Pigou, *Wealth and Welfare* (1912) and *Economics of Welfare* (4th ed., 1932, Part II, ch. 15); and despite its date, Bowley's *Mathematical Groundwork* (1924).

[12] Nevertheless, most economists accept this highly restrictive definition to this day and yet persist in applying the term monopoly and the Cournot theory of it to all cases of single sellers. The logical implications of the Cournot theory have been analyzed by P. M. Sweezy, 'On the Definition of Monopoly,' *Quarterly Journal of Economics*, February 1937. This is Chamberlin's Isolated Monopoly; his pure monopoly is . . . [note unfinished].

[13] These cost curves he did not consider, as he did the revenue functions, to be given independently of the monopolist's action: he noticed especially that a monopolist when in control of several plants would operate only those that could be operated most economically, whereas competing firms would tend to operate all plants so long as any profit could be made from operating them (p. 87). Also it should be noticed that he discussed the case of decreasing marginal cost—thus, also by implication, presenting the correct meaning of 'decreasing cost' that Edgeworth was to elaborate about sixty years later. Finally, he emphasized the fact that constant elements in total cost do not influence price, and that in particular no account is taken of cost if the whole of it is constant and hence marginal cost equals zero.

order to derive the theorem, now so familiar to every beginner, that (instantaneous) gain will be maximized if the monopolist sets a price for which marginal revenue equals marginal cost (op. cit. p. 57). This theorem is, of course, strictly static and belongs to the realm of partial analysis (see below, sec. 6). Also it relies exclusively on the maximum criteria afforded by the calculus, that is, the existence and the uniqueness of the maximum are proved, and the manner in which the monopolist's optimum price is affected by a change in cost is determined, for small displacements only.[14] But in spite of these and other criticisms which cannot be presented here,[15] this was a splendid performance, for which, as for the treatment of taxes on commodities produced under a monopoly (ch. 6), we ought to entertain the highest admiration.

In Chapter 13 of Book v, Marshall reproduced this analysis by means of a technique of his own that not everyone will consider superior to Cournot's.[16] But he added something that was truly his own. Cournot had indeed realized that a monopolist's cost structure may be more favorable than that of a competitive industry. But it was left for Marshall to point out the full importance of this possibility and to present it in the full regalia of his practical wisdom: his argument actually amounts to denying the existence of a presumption that the price usually set by a modern industrial monopoly is higher and the quantity produced by it is lower than would be the case if the same commodity were produced 'under free competition.' Again, Cournot had known, of course, but had failed to emphasize that monopoly price is determinate in a sense that differs from the sense in which competitive price is: under pure competi-

[14] The criteria that the calculus offers for finding out whether or not a continuous function of one variable displays a unique maximum are that the first derivative of the function should vanish and that its second derivative should be negative; and these criteria answer the question only for a small interval and say nothing about whether or not the same function displays other maxima beyond that interval. However, Cournot framed his assumptions about the shape of the total revenue and total cost functions in such a way as to make sure of a single maximum. But his proof that a small increase in marginal cost will increase the monopolist's optimum price though, according to the form of the demand curve, sometimes much more and sometimes much less than the amount of the increase, *is* seriously restricted by the assumption that the increments in cost and price are so small that their squares (and higher powers) and products can be neglected. In § 32 of ch. 5 Cournot attempted to free himself from this restriction by the device of splitting up the two increments, if they are *not* small, into small elements and of passing from the old cost figure to the new one by these small steps, to each of which his proof is supposed to apply. It is perhaps clear why this procedure is not admissible.

[15] In particular, Cournot's proof on pp. 87-9 of the proposition that the monopolist's optimum price is *always* higher than the price under pure competition even though, for equal total quantities produced, 'the costs will always be greater for competing producers than they would be under a monopoly' is open to objection.

[16] Marshall reasoned in terms of monopolist's total net revenue rather than in terms of the marginal condition (Monopoly Revenue Schedule, *Principles*, p. 539). This is why the Marginal Revenue Curve that was reasserted by Chamberlin and Robinson struck economists around 1930 as something of a novelty.

tion, firms have to accept the ruling price; monopolists are under no such compulsion and may well set prices that are lower than the instantaneous optimum, either for strategic reasons in their own profit interest or for other reasons in the interest of somebody else, especially of their customers. Marshall realized what this means. An outlook was thus opened up on a wide variety of important phenomena and problems [17] that was soon to be lost again in ideological mists.[18] But, like Cournot, he failed to give adequate attention to one very important aspect of monopolistic strategy, Price Discrimination. The theory of it had been developed in a rudimentary form by Dupuit, Walras,[19] and Edgeworth. Pigou's presentation of this range of problems in *Wealth and Welfare* indicates the extent to which discrimination was understood by the economists of the period. We must not forget, however, that the specialists in applied fields, notably in the field of transportation, had got further than that.[20]

[17] See §§ 6-8 of the monopoly chapter and in particular Marshall's argument on what he called *compromise benefit*, p. 549. Observe once more: Marshall added in this chapter little, if anything, to Cournot's analytic skeleton; but, as in so many other spots, he developed from it, with a broad and deep insight all his own, an *economic analysis* that almost dwarfed both that skeleton and the technically superior performance of a later age. Even the statistical complement of the theory of monopoly is clearly visualized.

[18] However, if Marshall's broad and deep comprehension of the monopolistic and quasi-monopolistic phenomena of his age failed to bear fruit, his historical greatness as an economist stands out all the better because he saw more in them than the results of functionless rapacity or, as a leading theorist of our own day has put it, of producers' desire for an easy life.

[19] *Éléments*, §§ 382-4. Walras believed that discrimination is also possible in 'free competition.' It is, but not in perfect equilibrium of pure competition—an interesting example of the necessity of keeping carefully distinct the properties that define competition, the properties that define equilibrium, and the properties that define competitive equilibrium. Walras committed no mistake, however: he saw that it is only in the presence of elements of monopoly that discrimination does not violate equilibrium conditions.

[20] I can find no proof of the conditions under which discrimination may improve the situation of *all* parties concerned, including the one that is discriminated against. But Hadley's oyster case presents an interesting instance that shows this possibility. Suppose that a quantity of oysters that fills a freight car can be sold in an inland market, A, for $150, and that A is connected with an oyster bed at B by a railroad whose minimum charge for the freight car is $20. The people in B are just willing to supply a quantity of oysters that would fill half a car per day at $62.50. But since they would have to pay for the whole car, the business would net them a loss of $7.50 (62.50 + 20 − 75). There is, however, another oyster village near by, C, whose inhabitants are also willing to sell a quantity of oysters that would fill the other half of the car at $62.50. Road transportation from C to B costs $5. Evidently, the business becomes possible and all parties—consumers at A, producers at C *and* B, and the railroad—are 'benefited' if these $5 are divided up between the producers at C and the producers at B, which can be done by the railroad's charging differential freight rates for the same service to the people in B and the people in C. (Arthur T. Hadley, *Railroad Transportation*, 1885, ch. 6, pp. 116 ff.)

[(c) *Oligopoly and Bilateral Monopoly*.] Cournot left two other legacies, however. The one was a theory of oligopoly [21] or, as it came to be called from the special case that was mostly discussed, of duopoly. As stated above, he met oligopoly on his way when, starting from monopoly, he went on to introduce one, two, three . . . competing firms of comparable size until he landed at 'illimited' (unlimited) competition, for which he derived correctly another of those theorems that are now familiar to every beginner, namely that, in equilibrium of pure competition, price equals marginal cost. At the starting point as well as at the end point, his argument was all right so far as it went. Hence nothing could have been more natural than to apply the same reasoning also to the intermediate situations. Admitting, then, for simplicity's sake, one competitor only and, also for simplicity's sake, neglecting cost of production,[22] he was easily led to argue that this competitor will, on finding a monopolist in possession, offer in the market—assumed to be perfect—that quantity of the (perfectly homogeneous) commodity which will maximize his revenue, the output of the former monopolist being what it is. This former monopolist will thereupon adjust his output to the new situation, the newcomer will then do the same, and so on, price falling all along, as automatically as if, at each step, the resulting total output of both duopolists were put up for auction. And Cournot showed not inelegantly, by means of his apparatus of Reaction Curves,[23] that under his assumptions this step-by-step adaptation of quantities

[21] This term was introduced by Sir Thomas More (see above Part II, ch. 6) and has been reintroduced by Karl Schlesinger (*Theorie der Geld- und Kreditwirtschaft*, 1914), U. Ricci (*Dal protezionismo al sindacalismo*, 1926), and Chamberlin (op. cit.), but was not used in the period because writers dealt only with the case of duopoly. Cournot, since he used 'illimited competition' for what we call pure competition, might be credited with the term 'limited competition.' Pigou used 'monopolistic competition.' The term 'incomplete monopoly' sometimes denoted the case where one of several competitors controls so large a part of an industry's output as to be able to influence price by his own single-handed action, whereas the others have to accept the price he 'sets.' See, e.g., Karl Forchheimer, 'Theoretisches zum unvollständigen Monopole,' *Schmollers Jahrbuch*, 1908. This important case of price leadership does not present the problems of 'genuine' oligopoly and has in fact been tacitly excluded by most writers on the subject.

[22] Cournot's example, two springs that produce mineral water of identical quality, suggests an assumption that has been almost universally adopted in the later discussion of duopoly, namely, the assumption that the cost structures of the duopolists are exactly alike. This seems to bring out the pure logic of the duopolistic situation. Actually it defines a very special case and represents an element of duopolistic situations that is particularly important for the more general case of oligopoly and enables us frequently to narrow down ranges of indeterminateness. Cournot's procedure may be excused by invoking the privileges of the pioneer. But those who dealt with the problem after him should have realized that they did not gain but lost something by making the same assumption. As it was, only Marshall seems to have been fully aware of this.

[23] The outputs of the one duopolist, the former monopolist, being shown on the X-axis of a rectangular system of co-ordinates and the outputs of the other duopolist on the Y-axis, the reaction curves plot the two equations that represent the maxi-

issues into a unique state of stable equilibrium, namely, a state in which the duopolists sell equal quantities at a price that is below the monopoly price and above the competitive price, and which, if departed from, will be re-established 'by a series of reactions, constantly declining in amplitude' (op. cit. p. 81).

Since this result—whether attacked or accepted—became the backbone of all further work on oligopoly and the starting point of a discussion that lasted into the 1930's, we shall, in order to extract the moral of the story,[24] first of all try to make clear to ourselves what we are to think of Cournot's solution and what we might expect, in the absence of historical information, the further development to have been. To begin with, it should be clear that Cournot's solution is not absurd. It is not true that his duopolists are supposed to act on an assumption about one another's behavior that is incessantly belied by the facts, that is, the assumption that each takes the quantity offered by the other as constant when he cannot help observing that the other keeps on adjusting it. No such assumption is implied. All that is required is that each chooses this particular method in order to find out how the other will react, or that he takes the other's output as given *for the moment* and as a guide for his own next step. Equally clear, however, should it be that the behavior selected by Cournot is not the only possible or even the 'normal' one. The duopolists may agree to co-operate. Or, without any agreement, explicit or tacit, they may still both of them set the monopoly price.[25] Or they may fight

---

mum revenue condition of both duopolists (for duopolist I, for instance, if D_1 and D_2 stand for the quantities offered by both and $f(D_1 + D_2)$ for the price, $f(D_1 + D_2) + D_1f'(D_1 + D_2) = 0$). That is, the reaction curve for duopolist II shows the quantity that he will offer, if duopolist I offers any given quantity (op. cit. p. 81 and Figs. 2 and 3). Both reaction curves are concave to the origin and intersect in a single point and in a manner such that this point fulfils the condition of stability. (For full explanation see also note 17 in Fisher's introductory 'Notes on Cournot's Mathematics.')

24 This will be more instructive for us than would be a presentation of its details. For these I refer again to ch. 5 of von Stackelberg's *Marktform und Gleichgewicht* (1934), although I cannot agree entirely with either his history of the work on the duopoly problem or with his own theory of duopoly. See Professor Leontief's review of von Stackelberg's book, 'Stackelberg on Monopolistic Competition,' *Journal of Political Economy*, August 1936.

25 Cournot was, of course, aware of the possibility of coalition, and he was justified when, in order to deal with duopoly, he excluded this possibility. He was also aware of the possibility that duopolists might independently decide to charge the monopoly price, but he ruled it out on the ground that, at any given moment, one of the two is induced to take a further step along Cournot's chain of reactions by the temporary advantage he thereby secures (op. cit. p. 83). This is less easy to justify. For *either* both duopolists are perfectly and equally rational and are facing an ideally perfect market, in which customers shift in response to the slightest difference in price and in which there are no other differences between the duopolists' offerings, not even differences of distance or of pleasantness of service: then neither can hope to conquer, or fear to lose, more than half the market, even temporarily, and it is hardly possible to derive comfort from Cournot's general admonition that 'in the

either with a view to driving or to bribing the competitor out of business or with a view to making him conform to a desired pattern of behavior. In doing so, either or both may try to bluff. Any of these courses of action may eventually lead to a stable situation. But there is no guarantee that it will, and even if it does, it will in most cases do so by destroying the specifically duopolistic pattern. So far, then, the only thing that can be averred about the latter without introducing further assumptions seems to be that there is no general solution.[26] However, we see immediately that, though the course a duopolist or oligopolist will choose depends in part on the kind of man he is—and so far as this is the case, all we can do is to list possible types of behavior—it also depends in part on the general business situation and on a concern's position relative to its competitors, particularly on its own and their cost structures. And this opens up a way that leads out of the impasse and to many results that are specific to particular situations and often do no more than narrow the range of 'indeterminateness,' but are not without interest all the same.

We know already why Cournot neglected all this: in his brief sketch of the theory of pricing he evidently wished, starting from pure monopoly, to follow an unbroken line of reasoning that would lead up to the case of pure ('illimited') competition without having to vary anything except the number of competitors. On this line he met nothing but quantity adaptation, and hence this pattern drifted for him not unnaturally into a key position. The criticism that may be directed at him, therefore, is that he neglected or overlooked the fact that, as we leave the case of pure monopoly, factors assert themselves that are absent in this case and vanish again as we approach pure competition, in other words, that the unbroken line from monopoly to competition is a treacherous guide. The next steps to take in analysis—when from the 1880's on economists discovered Cournot's solution and began to take interest in it—should therefore have been to realize this situation, to recognize those factors that shape price strategy, and to work out the theory of the more important ones—all of which would have opened up the fertile region of the pricing problems of modern industry including, among other things, the problem of 'delivered prices' or of locational price differentiation. This would have wedded pure

moral sphere men cannot be supposed to be free from error' because the error involved would, under his assumptions, be too obvious. *Or* the situation does not fulfil some or all of those conditions: then the whole of Cournot's reasoning becomes inapplicable. The reader should note the interesting fact that we have here the possibility of a unique and stable solution at the monopoly price *precisely so long as there is no agreement between the duopolists*. If they do co-operate, there arises the question how to divide the monopoly gain which they are making jointly, a question for which there is no unique solution or no solution at all. But if they act independently, no such question arises.

[26] This is often expressed by saying that, generally, the problem is indeterminate. But, as Pareto has pointed out, in all cases in which insolubility proceeds from the incompatibility of the duopolists' aims, it is more correct to speak of overdeterminateness (*Manuel*, p. 597).

analysis to 'institutional' fact and would have produced a richer and more useful theory of price.

Actually, with a lag of more than half a century, we have more or less reached this position, although much remains to be done. Professor Chamberlin's work may be mentioned at once as an outstanding landmark on this road.[27] But during the period under survey there is but little to record that foreshadows this development. As examples, I mention Marshall's frequent emphasis on the fact that if the duopolists (oligopolists) operate individually under a 'law of increasing returns,' then the one who can expand with the greatest relative advantage stands a chance 'to drive all his rivals out of the field,' which implies, although Marshall does not say so,[28] the recognition of a particularly important type of price leadership; [29] I mention also the attempt made by Edgeworth [30] to treat duopoly as a limiting case of related demand for monopolized commodities. For the rest, however, most of the work done comes under the heading of sterile criticism or equally sterile defense of the Cournot solution. J. Bertrand was, so far as I know, the first to make an attack upon it that challenged it on principle but so inadequately [31] that I doubt whether it would have made much impression if Marshall, Edgeworth, Irving Fisher, Pareto,[32] and others had not, though wholly or partly for other reasons, repudiated Cournot's solution. By the end of the century, there was,

[27] The chief importance of Chamberlin's *Monopolistic Competition* seems to me to lie beyond the problem of pure oligopoly. But in his ch. 3 he also dealt with this problem according to the adage: 'duopoly is not one problem but several.' That is to say, he recognized the necessity of a systematic analysis of all possible types of behavior. I do not quite see the reason why von Stackelberg described this position as 'eclectic' since his own position, though different, comes ultimately to the same thing so far as this point is concerned.

[28] The passage, which appears in the first edition on p. 485n., underwent a number of changes later on. If this means that Marshall was not quite pleased with it, we can only agree.

[29] Price leadership instead of monopoly may result if the strong firm cannot, or does not wish to, drive out all its rivals. This shows that it is unwise, though it may be logically unobjectionable, to disregard incomplete or partial monopoly entirely in any treatment of oligopoly.

[30] In his paper, 'La teoria pura del monopolio,' *Giornale degli Economisti*, 1897, trans. in *Papers Relating to Political Economy*, vol. I, pp. 111 et seq.

[31] *Journal des Savants*, September 1883. Bertrand imputed to Cournot the hypothesis that each duopolist tries to undercut the other, which involves a misunderstanding of Cournot's argument and points toward a result that is, if anything, worse than Cournot's.

[32] *Cours* I, p. 67, and, differently, in *Manuel*, pp. 595 et seq. The latter treatment is repeated in his Encyclopedia article and simply amounts to the 'proof of the overdeterminateness of the problem' mentioned already. But (*Manuel*, pp. 601 et seq.) Pareto did point toward the multiplicity of possible patterns, some of them determinate, which we recognize now, and has thus some claim to be considered as the precursor of the modern theory of oligopoly.

among leaders, only Wicksell[33] left to defend it, and by 1912, in *Wealth and Welfare*, Pigou was able to write that indeterminateness, or, more precisely, the existence of a range of indeterminateness of the quantity of resources devoted to production in duopolistic situations, was 'now accepted by mathematical economists.' Though this attitude is in fact acceptable when the problem is posited in full generality, that is, without any information whatever except that there are several sellers (or buyers), each of whom may influence price and output significantly, the reader will realize also that this is not more than a first step, which invites further analysis in the light of additional information (hypotheses). He will, therefore, not be surprised to learn that, given the basic weakness and sterility of the criticisms, the Cournot solution experienced a renaissance during the 1920's which merged into the situation adumbrated above.

[The manuscript breaks off at this point. Since J. A. S. at the beginning of this subsection (4c) said that Cournot left two other legacies of which one was a theory of oligopoly, the following three paragraphs, concerned with Cournot's contribution to bilateral monopoly, seem to follow logically. This short treatment had been written much earlier, was already typed, and had many penciled notes in shorthand.]

Cournot left also another legacy. In Chapter 9 of the *Researches* he dealt with a case that differs from duopoly but bears a fundamental similarity to it. Two different commodities, each controlled by a monopolist, are jointly demanded by competing producers of a third commodity and serve no other purpose whatever. This case opens up an outlook on a wide variety of industrial configurations which we are far from having fully explored as yet. Moreover, Cournot's treatment teaches important lessons about how to deal with problems of this kind and about useful simplifications that can be introduced, as temporary expedients, in order to make headway. These two merits are of seminal importance. But for the rest, Cournot's treatment is open to objections similar to those that have been raised against his treatment of the straight duopoly problem. He lets the prices of the two commodities be independently determined by the condition that each monopolist endeavors to maximize his own net revenue, assuming this time that the price of the other's commodity is given; that is to say, he postulates a behavior which is only one of many possible ones and which moreover, even if realized, does not always lead to a position of stable equilibrium. Edgeworth, Bowley, and Wicksell are the most important of the authors who carried the discussion further. But the most valuable materials for the analysis of problems of this type are to be found in Marshall's Book v.

For bilateral monopoly we have a theoretical prototype, namely the theory of isolated exchange. The indeterminateness of the latter case had been well understood by several authors of the eighteenth century; for example, Bec-

[33] See the brief argument in *Lectures* I, pp. 96-7, and the somewhat more elaborate one in his review of Bowley's *Mathematical Groundwork* (*Economisk Tidskrift*, 1925, German trans. in the *Archiv für Sozialwissenschaft und Sozialpolitik*, October 1927 [with an introduction by J. A. S.]).

caria. Carl Menger and, following him, all the Austrians emphasized this result because it was part of their argument that was to establish the determinateness of competitive equilibrium price. The easiest way of satisfying oneself of this is to study Böhm-Bawerk's horse-market case, in which the price of a horse would remain indeterminate within the limits of the buyer's and the seller's utility estimates until increasing numbers of buyers and sellers eventually narrow down the range to a point.[34] What the Austrians strove to express was expressed much more correctly and elegantly by Edgeworth in his *Mathematical Psychics* of 1881,[35] where the apparatus of indifference and contract curves was used precisely for the purpose of analyzing the range of indeterminateness in bilateral monopoly. A. Marshall popularized the result by means of his apple and nut market (*Principles*, p. 416 and Appendix, note xii). There he also added Berry's result,[36] namely, that if the marginal utility of one of the commodities exchanged be constant—a case of some value as an approximation if the commodity in question be money—then the quantity bought of the other commodity will be uniquely determined 'by whatever route the barter may have started.' [37]

This relation between the theory of bilateral monopoly or oligopoly to the case of isolated exchange teaches us to see the main problem in the determination of the factors that limit the range of indeterminateness. About this, however, the theory of isolated exchange has really little to say. In all cases of this kind that arise in modern industry, particularly in modern labor markets, determinateness of the ranges between which exchange rates may be expected to fall—sometimes even unique determinateness of individual exchange rates—will depend on the particular circumstances of the case which must be introduced by special assumption. Success will depend on our ability to find hypotheses which, though not of general application, will yet cover a

[34] In the case of a market that deals in units as big as horses the range is of course never strictly narrowed down to a point. But the reader will readily see that in principle this does not make any serious difference.

[35] See also his article in the *Giornale degli Economisti*, March 1891.

[36] *Giornale degli Economisti*, June 1891.

[37] In general this is not so, however. And in analyzing the markets of reality we must take account of the fact that the deals carried out at the beginning of the market will influence the prices and quantities that are exchanged later on in the same market. This applies to pure competition as much as it does to bilateral monopoly or oligopoly. Though the practical importance of this is in many cases much reduced by the fact that every individual transaction is normally a link in a chain of stable relations that teach each party to understand the conditions under which all the other parties act, it is quite true that in order to arrive at uniquely determined prices and quantities in a competitive market it is necessary to make certain assumptions that look very artificial at first sight. This is the meaning of the Walrasian 'bons' and of the Edgeworthian 'recontract' (see N. Kaldor, 'A Classificatory Note on the Determinateness of Equilibrium,' *Review of Economic Studies*, February 1934). As is perhaps not superfluous to note, bilateral monopoly or oligopoly thus merely brings out with particularly unmistakable distinctness some of the logical difficulties that pervade the whole of the pure theory of markets.

considerable number of cases or describe individual ones of particular importance. But again, as in the case of duopoly and oligopoly, we meet two formidable difficulties: in practice, behavior is shaped, much more than by the observable data of a situation, by expectations that change rapidly in the turmoil of capitalist development; and even if this were not so, behavior could never be fully understood from the objective factors of the given situation without taking account of the kind of people who are in a position to make strategically important decisions and whose numbers are in most cases so small as to make modes unreliable.

5. The Theory of Planning and of the Socialist Economy

We know already that most of the leading theorists of that period were by no means the unquestioning addicts of laissez-faire they have sometimes been made out to be. For the purposes of this chapter, however, it is still more important to emphasize that neither were they all of them unconditional eulogists of pure competition. Walras, though his land-nationalization scheme does constitute a qualification, reproduced indeed the old proposition that a state of pure competitive equilibrium all round guarantees a maximum of satisfaction for all parties concerned. But he did so in a novel and rigorous manner that brought into full daylight all the assumptions involved, though he does not seem to have realized how much he reduced its practical importance thereby. Marshall did realize this. Not only did he point out the trivial truth that the proposition in question assumes 'that all differences in wealth between the different parties concerned may be neglected' (*Principles*, p. 532), but he went on to show that even if we disregard this trivial truth,[1] we cannot assert that the prices and quantities of competitive equilibrium are necessarily the ones that maximize aggregate satisfaction—granting for the sake of argument that there is meaning to this concept—as compared with the ones that other arrangements might produce. This he illustrated by cases in which 'welfare' may be increased by subsidizing the employment of resources in industries where expansion of production is attended by more economies than it is in others.[2] We shall return to this and cognate subjects in the digression

[1] As Marshall well knew, this trivial truth means much less in practice than it seems to mean at first sight. For it takes no account of the possible ulterior effects of inequality upon the Social Dividend, which may be very important if the latter's development is considered over time. As in the special case of the free-trade argument we must distinguish between welfare effects *ex visu* of a given point of time and welfare effects *ex visu* of historical developments that may be impeded by social arrangements that increase 'welfare' at a given level of the Social Dividend. But an analysis whose rigorous core is confined to statics invites neglect of this distinction and overemphasis upon the situation existing at a given moment. (See, below, the discussion on Welfare Economics in the Appendix to this chapter.)

[2] This formulation agrees with Mrs. Joan Robinson's ('Mr. Fraser on Taxation and Returns,' *Review of Economic Studies*, February 1934) and R. F. Kahn's ('Some Notes on Ideal Output,' *Economic Journal*, March 1935). Marshall's own exposition (op. cit. pp. 533-6) is open to objection on several counts (particularly from the

appended to this chapter. Meanwhile I am content to point out that measures of the kind envisaged by Marshall come within the range of any reasonable definition of planning. No doubt he only scratched the surface. But any proposition that avers that a piece of planning can 'improve' upon the working of ideally perfect competition means a breach in an old wall and is therefore of great historical importance. No mere criticism of capitalism on ethical or cultural lines—however important in other respects—could have accomplished precisely this. Others, Edgeworth and Pareto among them, were not slow to widen the breach.[3]

Of far greater importance was another achievement. Three leaders, von Wieser, Pareto, and Barone, who were completely out of sympathy with socialism, created what is to all intents and purposes the pure theory of the socialist economy, and thus rendered a service to socialist doctrine that socialists themselves had never been able to render. As we know, Marx himself had not attempted to describe the modus operandi of the centralist socialism which he envisaged for the future. His theory is an analysis of the capitalist economy that is no doubt geared to the idea that this economy, by means of the inevitable 'breakdown' and of the 'dictatorship of the proletariat' resulting from this breakdown, will give birth to the socialist economy; but there is a full stop after this and no theory of the socialist economy that deserves the name follows.[4] Most of his disciples, as we also know, evaded the problem instead of meeting it, though some, Kautsky in particular, did display awareness of its existence by pointing out that the socialist regime, after the revolution, would be able to use the pre-existing capitalist price system as a provisional guide—an idea that points in the right direction.

Now the Austrians were in the habit of using the model of a Crusoe economy for the purpose of explaining certain fundamental properties of economic

---

standpoint of those who abhor the use of the consumers' surplus concept) but I believe that the statement in the text above renders what he really meant and that the usual criticism is hardly fair to him. The main point of this criticism was first made, not against him but against Pigou's formulation of his doctrine, in a review, 'Pigou's Wealth and Welfare,' by A. A. Young (*Quarterly Journal of Economics*, August 1913). It turns on Marshall's suggestion that subsidies to industries that realize (relatively to others) large economies in expanding might be advantageously raised by taxes on the product of industries that 'obey the law of diminishing returns.' Though valid within static theory, the objection can be met by considerations that lie outside its precincts.

[3] Wicksell also attacked the doctrine of maximum satisfaction. But he held (*Lectures* I, pp. 141 et seq.) 'that free competition is normally a sufficient condition to ensure maximization of *production*' (my italics). This is not correct either, although the extent of the error depends on what we mean by 'normally.' But his position was nevertheless far ahead of that of Walras.

[4] It is indeed possible to assemble from Marx's writings a number of hints that go beyond the phrases of his day, e.g. the hint at the necessity, in the socialist commonwealth, of an elaborate bookkeeping system. But substantially he confined himself to such phrases as that, of course, workmen will be anxious to produce most efficiently so that, we are led to infer, there really will be no scarcity problem (no problem of 'economizing' factors) at all.

behavior. Therefore, it was particularly easy for them to realize that there was nothing specifically capitalist about their basic concept of value and its derivates such as cost and imputed returns: these concepts are really elements of a completely general economic logic, of a theory of economic behavior that may be made to stand out more clearly in a model of a centrally directed socialist economy than it can in the capitalist garb in which it presents itself to the observer whose historical or contemporaneous experience is with a capitalist world. For instance, when we are trying to describe how Crusoe allocates his scarce resources in order to maximize the satisfaction of his wants or, in other words, to formulate the rules he follows in transforming these resources into objects that will satisfy his wants, we discover immediately that his economy may be characterized by certain 'coefficients of transformation' which fill the same function that prices fill in competitive capitalism. If we consider a socialist economy, it is still more obvious that, for instance, maximization of satisfaction requires that the ratio of marginal utilities for each pair of consumers' goods must be identical for all comrades; that in every line production must be so organized as to make the technologically optimum use of all means of production; and that the marginal value productivity of all scarce means must be the same in all their uses or, at all events, must in every use be at least as great as it would be in any other. But all this amounts to saying that any attempt to develop a general logic of economic behavior will automatically yield a theory of the socialist economy as a by-product. The first to realize this explicitly was von Wieser (*Natural Value,* 1st German ed., 1889).

Pareto, in the second volume of his *Cours* (1897),[5] excelled Wieser in clearness and skill of presentation, if not in insight, and has more claim than any other individual to being considered as the originator of the modern pure theory of the socialist economy.[6] Actually, however, his contribution has been overshadowed by that of Barone, who presented the whole of the subject in a famous piece of work that, so far as essentials are concerned, has remained unsurpassed to this day.[7] Many economists of our own day have added details and some further developments. I mention O. Lange and A. P. Lerner and for the rest refer the reader to A. Bergson's paper mentioned in footnote 6.

Barone's performance consists in a nutshell in this: after having presented on Walrasian lines[8] the system of equations that describes economic equilibrium under conditions of pure competition in a private-property economy, he wrote down the analogous system of equations for a socialist economy of a certain type. Whereas in the private-property economy incomes, simultane-

[5] See, e.g., p. 94 of the second volume. He carried his argument considerably further in ch. 6, §§ 52-61, of his *Manuel* (1909).

[6] The development of this theory has been described by Abram Bergson in his contribution 'Socialist Economics' (in the *Survey of Contemporary Economics,* ed. H. S. Ellis, 1948) in a manner that leaves nothing to be desired.

[7] Enrico Barone, 'Il Ministro della produzione nello stato collettivista,' published in the *Giornale degli Economisti,* 1908, trans. in F. A. von Hayek, ed., *Collectivist Economic Planning* (1935) as 'The Ministry of Production in the Collectivist State.'

[8] There are, however, several original points, two of which will be mentioned below.

ously with all the other variables of the system, are determined by the economic process itself—so that, as we have said before, production and distribution are but different aspects of one and the same process—there is of course a separate problem of distribution in the socialist commonwealth. That is to say, society must first of all decide by a separate act, for instance by a clause in its constitution, what the 'incomes' or relative shares in the social product of the individual comrades are to be. Then a central social agency or ministry of production could be created for the management of the economic process, and a unit of account could be introduced. A definite amount of such units could be allocated to every comrade, which he is free to spend according to his tastes on the consumers' goods that the commonwealth produces or to 'save,' that is to say, to hand back to the ministry of production in consideration of a premium that the latter is prepared to pay for deferment of consumption.

We thus derive demand functions for consumers' goods and supply functions of labor and saving, and the reader will have no great difficulty in seeing how, guided by these functions and by its own technological knowledge, the ministry will cause appropriate quantities of consumers' and investment goods to be produced. This arrangement is, of course, not the only possible one and can be varied in many ways. For instance, we may exempt provision for investment from the range within which comrades are permitted free choice, and subject it to the decision of the ministry or of a parliament, just like expenditure for national defense. Also, we may either offer the comrades equal 'incomes,' and then postulate that they must accept the ministry's directions as to the kind and amount of work which they are to do, or else we may devise a system of differential income rates so as to call forth the free offer of the kinds and amounts of work that are to be done in every line, thereby introducing 'wages' and labor markets. Barone blocked out a theory of a socialist commonwealth that assumes freedom of choice all around as to consumption, as to saving (investment), and as to employment. But whether we follow him in this or not, the formal similarity between a socialist order of things and the order of things that would obtain in a perfectly competitive capitalist society stands out strongly. It is not even lost in the case of dictatorial socialism: the perfect dictator would in fact behave according to a pattern of which the prototype is the Crusoe economy. But also the nondictatorial socialist commonwealth can be run on principles other than the principle of consumers' sovereignty. It is quite thinkable, for instance, that comrades should not get what they actually wish to have but what some experts or bureaucrats think that they should have. However, theoretical difficulties do not arise in any of these cases but only in the case of federalist socialism, where there is no central agency and each industry is controlled autonomously by the workmen attached to it: in this case the problem becomes oligopolistically indeterminate.

The essential result of Barone's or any similar investigation is that there exists for any centrally controlled socialism a system of equations that possess a uniquely determined set of solutions, in the same sense and with the same qualifications as does perfectly competitive capitalism,[9] and that this set enjoys similar maximum properties.[10] Less technically, this means that so far as its pure logic is concerned the socialist plan makes sense and cannot be disposed of on the ground that it would necessarily spell chaos, waste, or irrationality. This is no small thing and we are within our rights when we emphasize again the importance of the fact that this service to socialist doctrine has been rendered by writers who, since they were not socialists themselves, thereby victoriously vindicated the independence of economic analysis from political preference or prejudice. But, at the same time, this is all. We must not forget that, just like the pure theory of the competitive economy, the pure theory of socialism moves on a very high level of abstraction and proves much less for the 'workability' of the system than laymen (and sometimes theorists also) think. In particular, the proposition about the maximum properties of the solution that characterizes the equilibrium of a socialist economy is of course relative to its institutional data, and avers nothing concerning the question whether this purely formal maximum is higher or lower than the corresponding maximum of the competitive economy—especially if we refuse to go into the further questions, whether the one or the other institutional set-up is less exposed to deviations from its own ideal or more favorable to 'progress.' These questions are so much more important in practice than is the question of determinateness or 'rationality' per se, that it is sometimes not easy to tell whether the later critics of the socialist plan, especially von Mises,[11] really meant to deny the validity of the Pareto-Barone result. For it is quite possible to accept it and yet to hold that the socialist plan, owing to the administrative difficulties involved or for any other of a long list of reasons, is 'practically unworkable' [12] in the sense that it cannot be expected to work with an efficiency comparable to the efficiency of capitalist society as revealed by the index of total output. But although pure theory contributes little to the solution of

[9] See below sec. 7. In fact, it can be shown that the case for unique determinateness (which, of course, implies consistency) is somewhat easier to establish for centralist socialism than for a private-property economy, even if perfectly competitive.

[10] Of course, so far as the competitive regime fails to achieve a true maximum, the socialist plan would also have to deviate from the competitive pattern.

[11] L. von Mises, 'Die Wirtschaftsrechnung im sozialistischen Gemeinwesen,' *Archiv für Sozialwissenschaft und Sozialpolitik*, 1920; trans. in F. A. von Hayek, ed., *Collectivist Economic Planning* (1935) as 'Economic Calculation in the Socialist Commonwealth.'

[12] See A. Bergson, op. cit. While we cannot go into this set of problems, it is necessary to point out that there is also a purely theoretical anti-socialist argument (sponsored by Professors von Mises, von Hayek, and Robbins), which is definitely wrong, namely the argument that, although there *exists* a determined set of solutions of the equations that describe the statics of a socialist commonwealth, there is, without private property in means of production, no mechanism by which to *realize* them. They can be realized by the method of 'trial and error' described below.

these problems,[13] it helps us to posit them correctly and to narrow the range of justifiable difference of opinion. We thus arrive at the same conclusion as in the case of non-socialist planning; ever since Marshall, the theoretical possibility of improving the purely competitive mechanism by public policy should no longer be a matter of controversy; but it is of course still possible—as Marshall well understood—to criticize either particular measures or even the whole idea of planning on such grounds as lack of confidence in the political or administrative organs that are available for the task. (It seems as if Marshall had been alone in understanding this situation.)

6. Partial Analysis

The unwieldy system of the innumerable quantities that make up the budgets of all the individual households and firms—microanalysis, to use Frisch's phrase again—invites simplification, for instance, by combining them into a few comprehensive social aggregates—macroanalysis. But there is also another method that, for some purposes, achieves simplification just as effectively. When we are interested in those economic phenomena that can be observed in small sectors of the economy, for example in individual 'industries' of moderate size and, in the limiting case, in individual households or firms, we may assume that nothing that happens in these small sectors exerts any appreciable influence on the rest of the economy. This assumption does not necessarily imply that the latter remains unchanged, although this is what we mean when using the ceteris-paribus clause; but it does imply that, if some external influence be exerted upon the small sector under consideration, then this sector adjusts itself without exerting, in turn, more than a negligible effect on the rest of the economy or any element of it (Principle of the Negligibility of Indirect Effects): a change in wage rates, for instance, that occurs in a small sector, whether brought about by the conditions of this sector or imposed from outside on it alone, may be treated as if it did not affect national income or market demand schedules at all. This postulate defines the method of Partial Analysis. Though it has been used since the beginning of time, it acquired a novel definiteness and an apparatus of its own at the hands of Cournot, von Mangoldt, and, in the period under survey, Marshall, who, as we have already noticed, became and remained for many economists primarily the master of partial analysis.[1] The method appeals to our common

[13] It does contribute something, however. First, it removes an objection by virtue of which the critic might excuse himself from entering at all into a discussion of the practical details of the socialist plan. Second, it shows up certain relevant properties of the latter, e.g. that it would be free from the class of wastes that are inherent in imperfectly competitive situations such as the economic warfare between oligopolists.

[1] In addition to developing the appropriate conceptual apparatus, Marshall also developed the general philosophy of the method which turns upon the principle of the negligibility of indirect effects. See especially *Industry and Trade*, 3rd ed., Appendix A, p. 677. There he did not hesitate to invoke the authorities of Newton and Leibniz, with the Nautical Almanack thrown in. With due respect both for Marshall

sense, which tells us that, so long as we are content with an approximation, we need not take account of at least the great majority of effects and counter-effects that, on principle, the slightest alteration in the conditions of, say, the production of pins exerts upon national income and through national income upon the demand for gasoline. But the same common sense should also tell us that the postulate, which is so powerful a simplifier, severely restricts the method's range of application and in fact removes from it all the relations that cannot be observed in small sectors but only in the economy as a whole.[2] Therefore, while it is understandable that partial analysis has been and is being widely used, it is equally understandable that it has been condemned from the first by theorists of the sterner type, especially by Walras and Pareto.[3]

[(a) *The Marshallian Demand Curve.*] The standard tool of partial analysis is Cournot's or Marshall's market demand curve. It represents the quantity of a commodity that buyers are willing to purchase at a given price as a function of this price alone:[4] all the other factors that affect their willingness to purchase, especially their incomes, are taken care of by the shape of the demand curve. Moreover, the marginal significance to them of the income unit ('marginal utility of money') is not supposed to vary as they move along the demand curve *so that the purchases they have made at any price P_0 have no influence upon their willingness to buy additional quantities at any price*

and for his admirable attempt to display, in this case, the intimate relation that no doubt exists between scientific methods in all their fields of application, we cannot deny that the argument for the principle mentioned does not carry the same weight in economics that it carries in astronomy.

[2] The wage-rate problem illustrates how neglect of these restrictions may produce error and futile controversy. The results of partial analysis concerning the effects of variations of wage rates in small sectors are completely inapplicable in the case of variations of wage rates in large sectors or the whole of the economy: propositions that are true for small sectors may be nonsense for the economy as a whole.

[3] Walras attacked the partial analysis of Cournot, von Mangoldt, and Auspitz and Lieben (*Untersuchungen über die Theorie des Preises*, 1889, of which the first chapter had been printed and distributed in 1887 and which contains industrial total cost and expenditure curves plotted together with the curves of their derivatives) in an article reprinted as *Appendice* II to the 4th ed. of the *Éléments*. He showed there that neither a demand nor a supply curve that represents quantity demanded or supplied as a function of the price of that commodity alone can ever be accepted as exact because to change the price of a commodity amounts to disturbing the whole of the existing equilibrium situation, every element of which must be correspondingly readjusted; and that, if we wish to uphold the method as one of approximation, we meet with the difficulty that the assumptions which it is necessary to make for this purpose are, in strict logic, contradictory. Pareto repeated these arguments with added emphasis. And they have been re-emphasized time and again.

[4] Usually we put the independent variable, in this case the price, on the X-axis of a rectangular system of co-ordinates and the dependent variable, in this case the quantity, on the Y-axis. This is in fact usually done in the French literature. But Marshall chose the X-axis for quantity co-ordinate and the Y-axis for price co-ordinate, and this is usually done in the Anglo-American literature.

$P_i < P_o$. If the significance people attach to a unit of their incomes should vary for reasons other than that they spend more or less upon the commodity in question, then the individual and market demands are displaced and/or altered in shape (they 'shift'). In his *Principles* (pp. 171 et seq.) Marshall developed the theory of these demand curves carefully, laying in fact the whole foundation for the demand studies of the future. But he hardly emphasized enough the severity of the restrictions to which their validity, even as approximations, is subject. Actually they can be used only for commodities that are relatively unimportant—absorb but a small part of buyers' total expenditure—or for relatively very small variations in the prices of important ones.[5] It is in such cases only that demand *curves* of individual households may be treated as 'translations' of the law of diminishing utility into terms of price (op. cit. p. 169) without having to be redrawn for every price and that Marshall's development of Dupuit's invention, consumers' rent, acquires its true meaning.

[(b) *Elasticity Concepts.*] The concept of consumers' rent will be discussed below in the Appendix to this chapter. I take this opportunity to introduce Marshall's price elasticity of demand (embryos of which are, as we have seen, contained in Cournot's and Mill's treatises). The behavior at any point of any continuous and differentiable 'curve' is rendered by its slope or differential coefficient at that point: if the ordinate (the price in our case) be denoted by Y and the abscissa (the quantity in our case) by X and if x_0 identify the point in question, the expression is $\left.\frac{dy}{dx}\right]_{x=x_0}$. Fuller information is conveyed by higher derivatives but this does not concern us here. Our expression has, however, the disadvantage that it is not a pure number and that its value is not invariant with respect to the units in which the price y and the quantity x are measured. A simple device for remedying this is to divide the increments dy and dx by the respective price and quantity to which they refer. Thus we get: $dy/y \div dx/x$ or: xdy/ydx, which is called the flexibility of price. If, however, we wish to express the sensitivity of quantity demanded to small variations in price, we had better choose the reciprocal of this, that

[5] Marshall himself was of course aware of the fact that the 'marginal utility of money' is not in general constant with respect to variations of expenditure upon any particular commodity: this awareness is obvious from his mathematical notes II and VI in the Appendix to the *Principles* and from the text of the *Principles* itself (see especially p. 207). But in chs. 3 and 4 of Book III he argued nevertheless on the assumption of constancy (where in these chapters he allows 'marginal utility of money' to vary, it is because people's *money incomes* change). And this involved no great error because he was careful to make tea the standard example on which to reason and by which to illustrate—a commodity of sufficiently small importance to pass muster as an instance in which partial analysis, even in its strictest acceptance, is a tolerable approximation and actually neglects nothing but quantities of the second order of smallness. Both adherents and critics have overlooked this. Incidentally, they also overlooked that the requisite small importance can practically always be enforced by sufficiently narrow definitions of commodities: if meat is not unimportant enough, we may consider the demand for lamb chops.

is, $dx/x \div dy/y = ydx/xdy$, the 'elasticity.' And since this expression is essentially negative because quantity demanded falls when price increases and vice versa, at least with the Marshallian demand curve, we might prefix a minus sign so as to have a positive number: $-ydx/xdy$ is, then, what Marshall called elasticity of demand and what is now called, more precisely, price elasticity of demand. The cases must be rare in which so modest a contribution has met with such applause (see, for example, Lord Keynes's eulogy in *Essays in Biography*, p. 228). We may as well continue this report of the history of 'elasticity' concepts—the word is infelicitous for it raises in the beginner's mind quite unjustified associations—to avoid the necessity of having to return to it in Part v.

First, Marshallian elasticity of demand refers to a point on the demand curve—it is 'point elasticity'—and is therefore applicable, with increasing inaccuracy, only to infinitesimal changes in price and quantity. Hence, the wish to have a measure that will apply to finite stretches of the demand curve. This problem of 'arc elasticity,' first posed by Mr. H. Dalton, has been the subject of a discussion to which Professor A. P. Lerner made the leading contribution, 'The Diagrammatical Representation of Elasticity of Demand,' *Review of Economic Studies*, October 1933 (see also Professor R. G. D. Allen's analytic treatment and Lerner's reply, 'The Concept of Arc Elasticity of Demand,' I and II, *Review of Economic Studies*, June 1934). But it must not be forgotten that point elasticity serves tolerably for variations of a few per cent of price whereas arc elasticity, intended to serve for larger variations, is much more likely to violate the restriction to which partial analysis is subject.

Second, reasoning in terms of elasticities presents the same advantages that it possesses in the case of the Marshallian demand curve in many other cases. Accordingly a rich crop of elasticity concepts has matured—we speak of elasticities of the total, average, and marginal cost functions; of income elasticity of quantity demanded; of elasticity of substitution (Hicks, J. Robinson); and so on. Income elasticity presents a new problem: no difficulty arises when we express the elasticity of an individual's demand for a commodity with respect to his income; but if we express the elasticity of aggregate demand for a commodity with respect to national income, we run up against the fact that given changes in the latter have different effects upon quantity demanded, according to the manner in which the increase or decrease of national income is distributed among buyers or potential buyers. This problem has been treated by Professor Marschak and by Mr. P. de Wolff (see, e.g., the latter's 'Income Elasticity of Demand,' *Economic Journal*, April 1941). Finally we may notice R. Frisch's 'elasticity calculus' (see R. G. D. Allen, *Mathematical Analysis for Economists*, 1938, pp. 252-3).

Third, in introducing the concept of income elasticity we have already stepped out of the domain of the Marshallian demand curve but without leaving the domain of partial analysis. We do the same thing or, at all events, we *practice* partial analysis while recognizing that the sector studied is actually an element of a more comprehensive system, when we use the concept of 'partial elasticity,' for example, of partial price elasticity. In itself, the concession we make in this case consists only in replacing the ordinary differential coefficient that enters into the elasticity expression by a partial differential coefficient in order to indicate that we are not simply 'freezing' the rest of the economy but that we are holding its elements constant *at a certain level*. But once we have gone as far as this we may equally well express the elasticity of demand for a commodity with respect to variations in the price of any other commodity ('cross elasticity') or, successively, with respect to variations in the prices of all commodities, factors as well as products. This has been done systematically by H. L. Moore (see his *Synthetic Economics*, 1929) and, for the elasticity of substitution, by Hicks and Allen (see the latter's exposition, op. cit. pp. 503 et seq.). In those cases elasticity concepts become tools of general analysis, that is, tools that may be used for the purpose of exploring relations in which we are primarily interested because they also assert themselves in the economy as a whole.

[(c) *Concepts Useful for General Analysis.*] It follows that partial analysis is not separated from general analysis by any sharp dividing line but rather shades off into general analysis as we extend the scope of the concepts that have been in the first instance conceived for its purposes. The best illustration of this is Marshall's Book v. Primarily, it is the classic of partial analysis, the theory of the individual industry that is small relative to the economy as a whole.[6] Industrial demand curves are there matched with industrial supply curves from which they are supposed to be independent.[7] The theory of these supply curves is a development of Cournot's theory of costs and is subject to restrictions that are still more severe than those that partial analysis places upon demand curves.[8] But Marshall clothed his schema with such a mass of luxuriant detail as to give it an importance not really its own and to make it the backbone of a study of all non-aggregative industrial processes,

[6] This implies of course the existence of perfect markets—markets in which there is but one price for all buyers—and hence the existence of well-defined and perfectly homogeneous 'commodities,' the production of each of which defines an 'industry' that faces a definite market demand curve. Marshall and all the economists of his age were not fully alive to the difficulties inherent in these concepts that have induced Professor Chamberlin and others to abandon the idea of 'industrial demand curves' altogether. But, neither were they blind to them.

[7] The principle of the negligibility of indirect effects requires that the variations in the quantity produced by any industry must not affect the incomes earned in the same industry so strongly as to shift the demand curve for its product, let alone the aggregate demand for all products.

[8] This is why Barone, who has done more than anyone else to clear up this situation, did not use supply curves of products as freely as did Marshall. Instead he confined himself to speaking of supply curves of individual factors, in order to avoid the assumption that the prices of the latter are given and do not change relatively to one another as we move along supply curves of *products*, an assumption that is admissible in special cases but not in general. See 'Sul trattamento di quistioni dinamiche,' *Giornale degli Economisti*, November 1894. Pigou also, from his own standpoint, realized this restriction more explicitly than did Marshall himself. See in particular his 'Analysis of Supply,' published in the *Economic Journal* as late as June 1928.

a role which it has been made to play right into our own time.[9] And in doing so he developed concepts that are also valuable in general analysis or, as we have put it before, serve the purpose of exploring relations in the economy as a whole. An example is the concept of quasi-rent: the fact that 'appliances made by man' may behave exactly like natural agents for longer or shorter periods of time, though displayed by Marshall in connection with his partial analysis, is of course just as important in a general analysis of the Walras type.[10] But the most important example is the 'principle of substitution' which creeps in quite modestly (op. cit. p. 420) à propos of producers' substituting less expensive for more expensive combinations of factors and eventually rises to the proud position of 'Thünen's great law of substitution,' which pervades and controls the whole economic process and opens one of several possible roads toward the recognition of the universal interdependence of economic quantities.[11] From the standpoint, and within the precincts, of partial analysis,

[9] In developing this schema Marshall no doubt put a greater burden upon it than it is actually able to bear. The most important instance of this practice may well be mentioned here. This schema works best when a monotonically falling market demand curve for the product of a small industry is made to intersect with an industrial supply curve that is monotonically rising in the operative interval. But Marshall was evidently reluctant to confine himself to this construction, which seems to leave out of account the fact that in practice firms and industries operate on falling supply curves most of the time. He therefore admitted such falling supply curves and introduced for their explanation his famous concepts of internal and external economies. But it should be clear that supply curves which do depict these phenomena deal with an irreversible process and are therefore not at all like the ordinary supply curves on which a firm can travel back and forth. They depict historical processes in a generalized form. This led to a well-known difficulty about the equilibrium of an industry under conditions of pure competition: whenever a falling supply curve intersects with a demand curve from below, that is, in such a way that, to the left of the point of intersection, marginal costs are lower and, to the right of the point of intersection, marginal costs are higher than are the demand prices for the respective quantities, Marshall would say that the point of intersection is a point of stable equilibrium, whereas it is quite clear that there is no reason for any individual firm to call a halt at that point unless we admit some element of monopoly. But the difficulty is quite gratuitous. In the case of both internal economies and external economies the industrial supply curve is displaced (shifting downward) and there is no point whatever in calling the curve that depicts this displacement a supply curve.

[10] Marshall's handling of this concept, just as his handling of the rent concept, was somewhat impaired by inconsistencies. But it was, as we have seen, one of the most important tools he produced in his attempts to grapple with the difficulties inherent in the 'element of time.' Similarly, his theory of long and short periods grew out of considerations about small industries, or even individual firms, but is also of general applicability (see *Principles*, p. 519); and still more obviously is this the case with Marshall's theory of expectations (see, e.g., pp. 422 and 446) and risk.

[11] This becomes obvious if we add to the technical or *factor* substitution introduced on p. 420 of the *Principles*, the still more fundamental *product* substitution practiced by consumers. Though Marshall also recognized the latter he never fully co-ordinated the two in the manner that was developed before him by Carl Menger. In consequence, Marshall's principle of substitution never appeared in his work and the

this universal interdependence was demonstrated by numerous investigations into the theory of joint and composite demand and supply and of the values of related commodities in general which produced some of the most illuminating passages of Book v of the *Principles* and which were further developed by Edgeworth. In fact, it stands to reason that the comprehensive but gaunt and colorless idea of the universal interdependence that subsists between all elements of the economic system—and so easily provokes sneers about everything's depending upon everything else—can be brought home and made alive to the many by means of concrete cases about the relations between the values of beef and mutton or again of tea and sugar—the relations between the values of 'competing' or 'completing' commodities (Fisher). And this can be done without violating the restrictions inherent in the methods of partial analysis. We do indeed in such cases, sometimes with a slight disregard of strict logic, go beyond direct effects and take into account also indirect ones; but still we do so only within small sectors that do not produce significant effects upon the whole economy, at least not effects significant enough to affect the quantities, such as national income, that determine the setting of the small sector. In such cases the relations, in the small sector which can be managed by partial analysis, illustrate or exemplify *to a limited extent* the relations in the whole of the economic cosmos.[12]

But they do so only up to a point. Beyond this point the methods and results of partial analysis remain inadequate and may become even misleading. Marshall realized this. It is very instructive to observe how carefully he watched his step wherever his argument rose into the realm of the 'general' theory of distribution.[13] However, it is obvious from his appendix (note XXI) that, had he wished to go further, he would have sought the necessary comple-

---

work of his group in its true light, namely in the light of a special proposition within the theory of marginal utility: however emphasized, it remained, as later on with Cassel, a supplementary principle that was added to, instead of being derived from, the fundamental theory of values and costs.

[12] Of Edgeworth's many contributions in this line—contributions that *treat* partial analysis cases but *illustrate* general relations by doing so—I shall mention only one: his famous taxation paradox which the reader had better study in Professor H. Hotelling's version, 'Edgeworth's Taxation Paradox and the Nature of Demand and Supply Functions,' published in the *Journal of Political Economy*, October 1932. The extent to which partial and general analysis may co-operate in the sense explained in the text, shows up well in Marco Fanno, 'Contributo alla teoria dell' offerta a costi congiunti,' *Giornale degli Economisti*, October 1914, and in a later work of the same author which belongs here, 'Contributo alla teoria economica dei beni succedanei,' *Annali di Economia*, 1926.

[13] See in particular *Principles*, pp. 587 et seq. and the manner in which he arrived at the 'general theorems' on pp. 609 and 611. As regards the former passage it is noteworthy that he did not postulate the existence of social production functions (i.e. production functions that are to apply to the economy as a whole) but, after having carried out his analysis within the individual industry or even firm, confined himself to stating that 'the substance of the problem is the same in every industry' (p. 588). We shall return to this in sec. 8.

ments of partial analysis in the methods of general microanalysis of the Walrasian type rather than in a separate body of aggregate analysis (macroanalysis).

We shall see (Part v, ch. 5) that it is the latter solution which appeals to many economists of our own day, especially to members of the Keynesian group. These divide up economic theory into a theory of the individual firm and a macroeconomic theory that is to take care of the relations between aggregate consumption, investment, employment, and so on. It is therefore worth our while to point out, first, the historical connection that exists in this respect between Marshall and his apparently so rebellious followers of the 1930's and, second, the extent to which this combination of the theory of the individual firm and macroanalysis has been anticipated during the period under survey.

As regards the first point, the fact that Marshall made the small industry his *cheval de bataille* in Book v of his *Principles* should not be allowed to obliterate the not less important fact that much of his analysis of industries was really carried out in terms of the economy of the individual firm,[14] and that even beyond what this implies Marshall assembled practically all the bricks and all the mortar required for the theory of the individual firm, including even a fairly complete assortment of all those circumstances that prevent the sweeping generalizations of pure theory from working out in real life and have been repeatedly adduced as objections against his own generalizations (see in particular *Principles*, Book vi, ch. 8 and the notion of normal profit there developed, especially pp. 696 and 700). Therefore, so soon as the concept of the industry gave way under modern criticism, the one of those divisions of economic theory lay ready at hand while the desirability of the other imposed itself much more obviously on his pupils than it would have imposed itself upon pupils of Walras.

As regards the second point, it cannot be too often repeated that Marshall himself gave no lead toward macroanalysis. But macroanalysis itself and its combination with microanalytic explanations of individual behavior were old. Quesnay's *tableau* is a macroanalytic description of a stationary circuit flow of economic life, and Quesnay supplemented it, as we have seen, by a microanalytic theory of exchange. In the following period, Ricardo did much the same thing: his distributive shares are aggregates but the reason why they behave as they are supposed to do is derived from a fragmentary micro-

[14] The bridge between the theory of the small industry and the theory of the individual firm was his Representative Firm (later on reformulated, by Pigou, into the Equilibrium Firm). This curious construct embodies a most interesting attempt to resolve or to circumvent the difficulties that arise when we try to describe industrial processes by means of concepts developed from the life of individual firms. It is neither an average nor a marginal nor a leading firm but one in the position and structure of which the conditions of the industry are at any given time reflected in such a manner that certain propositions hold with respect to it that do not hold with respect to any actually existing firm or with respect to any industry as a whole. Marshall's authority as a teacher secured mechanical acceptance of the concept. But it received neither the criticism nor the development it deserves.

analysis. During the period under survey Böhm-Bawerk also did much the same thing: he started with a theory of individual behavior and with a theory of exchange that is based upon it; but, on the highest floor of his building there is almost nothing left but aggregates such as (value of) the sum total of wage goods, (value of) total output, and an aggregative 'period of production' to boot. Similarly, Wicksell reasoned on a social production function without displaying any symptoms of critical discomfort. And there is hardly any need for adding that this Quesnay-Ricardo-Böhm-Wicksell method is also that of Lord Keynes.

7. The Walrasian Theory of General Equilibrium *

In this section we shall analyze the logical structure of Walras' system of the conditions or relations (equations) that are to determine the equilibrium values of all the economic variables, to wit: the prices of all products and

* [This section on the Walrasian Theory of General Equilibrium was written in the last year (possibly in the last few months) of the author's life. The material in subsections (a), (b), and (c) was found in typescript (unread by J. A. S.), whereas subsections (d) and (e) were in manuscript. J. A. S. probably intended only 4 subsections; his subsection (b) included what is now (c). The pages were not numbered and there were no titles for the subsections, but the intended order seems perfectly clear and agrees with the order in Walras' table of contents (*Éléments*, pp. 489-91). There was no opportunity for the inevitable minor revisions and corrections usual in any work of this kind, but the final writing shows every sign that the author knew what he wanted to say. He had started and abandoned many other attempts before the final one.

He had not made up his mind, however, concerning the title and the brief introductory paragraphs. There were at least three unfinished introductions, one of which appears below in this note and a second as the first two paragraphs of the text. There were also three different titles suggested: the one actually used above for this section, the one given below, and a third, 'General Analysis: The Walrasian System.'

The following unfinished introduction may have been the last one:

'7. *Walrasian Microanalysis.* In this section I shall sketch the main features of the Walrasian system, reformulating certain points for convenience of exposition and leaving a number of others for closer consideration in section 8 and in the appendix to this chapter. This system that Walras embodied in a system of *equations* will be discussed verbally. Barring a brief remark, we shall assume pure competition all round.

'We consider a closed domain that does not act upon, or experience any influence from, the outside world. In this domain there are households which sell productive services (we neglect for the sake of brevity services that are consumed directly, such as personal services, except those that are consumed by their owners in the form of leisure or pleasure grounds) and purchase products; and firms that purchase productive services and sell products. But whereas the households sell their services only to firms, the firms sell products not only to households but some firms also produce certain products (raw materials and equipment) for sale to other firms. In order to make the essential problems stand out clearly, we shall at first disregard these intermediate products and reason as if firms did nothing but combine labor and services of natural agents into products for sale to households and then introduce . . .']

factors and the quantities of these products and factors that would be bought, in perfect equilibrium and pure competition, by all the households and firms. Let us notice at once that, since the determination of these quantities implies the determination of individual as well as group and social incomes, this theory also includes all that is covered by the concept of Income Analysis and that the conditions or relations to be considered, though they are fundamentally microanalytic in nature (they refer fundamentally to the quantities bought and sold by individual households and firms), also include macroanalytic aspects, for example, as regards total employment in the society. It cannot be too strongly impressed upon the reader that it is not correct to contrast income or macroanalysis of, say, the Keynesian type with the Walrasian microanalysis as if the latter were a theory that neglects, and stands in need of being supplemented by, income and macroanalysis.

Attention should also be drawn at once to three other points. First, I have spoken above of prices of products and factors. But Walras' theory of pricing, primarily and on the ground floor, refers to prices of *services* of products and factors. This amounts to the same thing only as regards products and factors that do not serve more than once. For all the others, the problem of pricing the products and factors themselves is a distinct problem that is solved on a second floor, as we shall see. It would be unnecessarily pedantic, however, to insist on this where no misunderstanding is to be feared. Second, I have spoken of prices 'that would be paid in perfect equilibrium and pure competition.' This manner of speaking is not Walrasian: Walras, much like J. B. Clark, conceived these equilibrium prices to be, normally, the actual level around which prices oscillate in real life,[1] which involves a claim which I do not wish to make. Third, Walras grouped his productive services into services of land, labor, and 'capital proper,'[2] but this does not spell acceptance of the old triad of factors: actually Walras admitted an indefinite number of means of production and services. [This piece of manuscript breaks off here.]

(a) *Walras' Conceptualization*. The description of the economic pattern

[1] Like Clark, he used the analogy with the 'level' of a lake in order to convey his idea—the old idea of A. Smith.

[2] As we know, Walras defined *capitaux*, in a wider sense, as all 'goods' that serve more often than once and, in a narrower sense, as durable goods that are themselves produced (*capitaux proprement dits*). Their services he called *revenus*, no matter whether they are consumed by the owner (e.g. as leisure in the case of 'personal capital': this leisure is still *travail*) or used productively. This conceptual arrangement which Walras derived from his father, Antoine Auguste Walras (1801-66; *Théorie de la richesse sociale*, 1849) and which was (substantially) adopted by Irving Fisher, has its logical advantages but is for us important only in so far as it must be borne in mind if Walras' reasoning is to be correctly understood (*leçon* 17). For the same reason, I repeat that the capitals, in addition to rendering services that are directly consumed or are transformed into products, may also render a *service d'approvisionnement* that may in turn be consumable or productive. *Leçons* 18 and 19 describe minutely Walras' set-up of the process of production and the accounting system of his firms—matters that have not attracted the attention they deserve.

that Walras' equations were to express is contained in *Éléments*,[3] *leçons* 17-19. The functioning of this pattern is further illustrated by the *tableau économique* presented in *leçon* 35, where he also indicated his opinions concerning the oscillations that occur around the equilibrium state.[4] We are introduced to his entrepreneur and, by means of a most useful analysis of a simplified accounting system, to the structure of a typical firm's operations. This analysis dovetails with a list of assets[5] that determines much, if not everything, in Walras' theoretical organon. For our present purpose it will be useful to note, or to note again, some of the salient features of this list of assets. As we know, the Walrasian entrepreneur is the agent (a physical person or a corporation)[6] that buys raw materials from other

[3] [*Éléments d'économie politique pure ou théorie de la richesse sociale* (1st ed. 1874-7; 4th ed. 1900; the *édition définitive*, 1926, is the one quoted throughout unless a different one is mentioned specifically).]

[4] These views do not differ essentially from those of A. Smith. Walras' analogy of market equilibrium with a *lac agité par le vent*, which is so characteristic for his belief in the reality—normality even—of the equilibrium level of values, has been repeated by J. B. Clark. It should be emphasized once more that this uncritical belief, undoubtedly held widely at that time, is untenable; but that this fact does not render analysis of the properties of those equilibrium levels either superfluous or practically useless (see above, sec. 3 on the 'dreamland of equilibrium'). It should also be emphasized that Walras (see, e.g., *Éléments*, p. 370), though he did underestimate the distance between his theory and the facts of capitalist reality, was by no means unaware of its existence. And no indictment at all can be leveled against Pareto on this score.

[5] Every object that enters the range of economic consideration, even 'labor power' (Marx) or the *capitaux personnels* (Walras), may be treated as an asset, if we halt the economic process for a moment and list every element of it. Presently Walras sets the process into motion when the difference between funds and flows asserts itself, and we are told how the assets are kept reproducing themselves. There are thirteen kinds of assets: the 'capitals' (all things that serve more often than once, including land, labor power, and produced capitals) that produce 'services' for direct consumption (including leisure); the 'capitals' (land, labor power, and produced capitals consisting of plant and equipment) that produce productive services; and in addition to these six items, the *produced capitals* (*plant and equipment*) *that are ready for sale in the hands of their producers* and yield no services as yet (the *capitaux neufs*); the stocks of consumers' goods that serve once only in the hands of the consumers; the raw materials and semi-finished goods in the hands of the producers, who are going to use them; the stocks of (transient) consumers' goods and raw materials in the hands of the producers who hold them for sale; and finally three types of money stocks, namely money held by consumers to finance consumers' transactions, money held by producers to finance producers' transactions, and *monnaie d'épargne*. The Keynesian controversy makes the translation of the last item a delicate task. I think that 'money earmarked for the purpose of investment' comes nearest to rendering Walras' meaning.

[6] Although Walras blamed English economists for confusing the entrepreneurial function with that of the capitalist and French economists for confusing it with that of labor (entrepreneurship being a kind of labor), his theory of entrepreneurship does not go much further or deeper than J. S. Mill's or J. B. Say's. All he did was to

entrepreneurs, hires land from landowners, personal aptitudes (*facultés personnelles*) from workmen, capital goods from capitalists, and sells the products that result from the co-operation or combination of their services for his account.[7] Into this and the meaning of the concept of entrepreneurs who, as such, neither make nor lose, we need not go again. Important is it, however, to notice three other things.

First, Walras was careful—much more so than other writers—to construct theoretically, and to identify practically, the various 'markets' through which his economic mechanism works and the interaction of which constitutes his analytic organon. Simplifying and combining as much as we can, we have the two fundamental markets, those of the products and of the productive services, and in addition the market that determines the prices of the capitals, hence also the rate of new revenue and the market of means of payment. The reader may be somewhat surprised at my emphasizing this apparently trivial matter. But the strict association of every part of the argument with an identifiable market, even on the highest level of abstraction, is an essential feature of Walras' procedure that starts in each of these four cases with a theoretical solu-

isolate the 'combining function' more clearly. As is shown by the fact that he admitted corporations into the circle of entrepreneurs, his conception was one belonging to the range of ordinary business routine and is roughly equivalent to Marshall's fourth productive agent, organization.

[7] As a result of Walras' strict distinction between capitals (*capitaux*), i.e. goods (including labor power) that serve more often than once, and services (or *revenus*)—a distinction which lapses in the case of goods that serve but once—the Walrasian theory of pricing runs on two levels: immediately (on the first level) we have to do with the pricing of services only (which includes the pricing of transient goods). On another level we then meet the problem of the pricing of these capitals themselves (from which the pricing of the labor power, unless enslaved, is of course in practice excluded). All incomes uniformly result from the sale of services, a conceptual arrangement that creates no difficulty in the case of 'land' (permanent factors) and labor but, in the manner to be explained, begs the question of the existence of a net income in the case of produced and durable goods that wear out in time. For the moment we note again that Walras really admitted an indefinite number of productive services, although he gave in to tradition by grouping them into services of various kinds of land, labor power, and produced capitals and thus *seems* to accept the old triad of factors. We must also note that, foreshadowing later developments, he stated at once (p. 197) that only land and labor power (plus plant and very few items of equipment) are hired in kind. Most of the durable instruments of production are hired by entrepreneurs not in kind but in money, which is what capitalists save and lend, although at first, before having introduced money into the productive process, Walras allows capital goods to be let in kind. This seems to involve a stricter parallelism between lending money and lending capital goods than, as we shall see, Walras was prepared to admit: actually his capitalists have money and not goods to lend to entrepreneurs; and it is only for perfect equilibrium in pure competition that the process is supposed to go on *as if* capitalists were owners of produced durable goods. This subtle point must be kept in mind—mathematically, it makes all the difference between an identity and an equilibrium condition—particularly if we are to see the affinity between the Walrasian and the Keynesian system.

tion of an equilibrium problem and then investigates the manner in which this theoretical solution works out 'practically' in the corresponding market.[8]

Second, we observe when going over Walras' list of assets that very considerable emphasis is placed upon stocks or inventories: there are inventories of new capital goods, consumers' goods' inventories held by households and by firms, raw-material inventories held by both their producers and their users, and also, as we have seen, stocks of money (cash holdings) of various types. Since the existence of these inventories presupposes a certain past behavior of the people concerned and since their current reproduction presupposes certain expectations, the system—even if perfectly stationary—still depicts a process in time and might therefore be called 'implicitly dynamic.' If Walras did not feel like this and if we agree with him in calling it static, this is only because of a device that was perhaps justified by the purpose of exhibiting the logical skeleton of economic life but is highly artificial all the same: he tried to build up an equilibrium state *ab ovo* in the manner in which it would be built, if smooth and instantaneous adaptation of all existing goods and processes, to the conditions obtaining at the moment, were feasible. His households do not purchase consumers' goods or sell productive services outright. Nor do his firms (entrepreneurs) purchase productive services and offer products outright. They all merely declare what they *would* respectively buy and sell (produce) at prices *criés au hasard*, that is, announced experimentally by some agent in the market, and are free to change their minds if these prices do not turn out to be the equilibrium prices: other prices are thereupon announced, other declarations of willingness to buy or sell (and to produce) are written down on *bons*—pieces of paper that do not carry any obligation—until equilibrium values emerge, namely prices such that no demand willing to pay them and no supply willing to accept them remain unsatisfied. And the only mechanism of reaction to these variations of experimental prices that Walras recognizes is to raise the prices of commodities or services, the demand for which at these prices is greater than the supply, and to reduce the prices of commodities or services, the supply of which at these prices is greater than the demand.[9] I shall not stay in order to proffer the obvious arguments that may be adduced in mitigation of such heroic theorizing.

[8] Each of four problems—pricing of products, pricing of productive services, pricing of capital goods, and 'pricing of money'—is thus solved twice: in each case we have first a proof of the existence of an equilibrium solution and second the proof that this solution is the one which the market mechanism under pure competition tends to establish or, slightly more technically, we have in each of the four cases two distinct proofs (or attempts at proofs), the one of the *existence* of an equilibrium solution, the other of the tendency toward it. Since the latter proof involves the statement that, if the equilibrium solution be once hit upon, it would not be departed from without the intervention of an additional force, we equate the proof of an equilibrium tendency to a proof of the *stability* of the equilibrium solution.

[9] Edgeworth's method of arriving at equilibrium prices and quantities by means of 'recontracting' comes of course to the same thing.

[Apparently there is no discussion of the last of the 'three other things' that it is important to notice.]

[(b) *The Theory of Exchange.*] Since the equilibria in the two basic markets, the consumers' goods and the service markets, and the way in which they interlock—simultaneously determining one another—are of decisive importance for the strength of the Walrasian structure we shall now consider these two basic markets separately. For this purpose we neglect both saving and the production of *capitaux neufs,*[10] a procedure which involves the assumption that the produced capitals are just as permanent and indestructible as is 'land.' Further, in order to emphasize the steps in the procedure, we shall indeed introduce a *numéraire*—the standard commodity in terms of which all exchange relations are to be expressed—but no money that actually circulates or is being held.[11] Several questions that cannot be answered without impeding the progress of our argument will be reserved for section 8.

We know already that Walras based his structure on an elaborate theory of exchange which fills two distinct roles: first it was to describe the fundamental features of economic logic which, with Walras, amounts to the same thing as the fundamental mechanism of competitive markets in general; second, it was to yield the behavior equations (maximizing equations) of the households. As regards the first role, Walras' theory of economic logic issues into a marginal utility explanation of economic value that will be discussed, in its historical setting, in the appendix to this chapter. Here we are not interested in such questions as whether there is any sense in speaking of marginal utility as the 'cause' of value, but immediately proceed to a discussion of the second aspect of the Walrasian theory of exchange. We can do this because, as has been pointed out by Pareto,[12] the concepts of marginal and total utility are redundant so long as we merely wish to formulate equilibrium conditions. On other features of this theory of exchange a few comments are nevertheless desirable.

Making ample use of the concepts that we have just voted superfluous, Walras first developed brilliantly the theory of (competitive) exchange of two

10 For brevity, we also postulate that firms do not purchase raw materials from one another: they all of them simply combine 'services' into products for sale to households. Unfortunately, we cannot similarly throw out the services that are directly consumed by their owners.

11 This simplifying measure must not, however, be interpreted, either with reference to Walras himself or with reference to our own presentation, as the theory that money does not enter into the fundamental process of determining values and is merely a technical device or 'veil.' All that we mean is that we shall posit this question separately, meanwhile reserving the right to scrap or modify the results at which we are aiming just now, if it should turn out that the intervention of money requires us to do so.

12 Implicitly this was already seen by Antonelli, Boninsegni, and others. For Pareto's statement see e.g., *Manuel* p. 542. Equation 9 on that page does not only without marginal utility but also without any 'index function': the first 76 paragraphs of the appendix to the *Manuel* render the Paretian version of Walras' *leçons* 5-16.

commodities. The point to notice is that he fully recognized the possibilities that there may be no solution to the problem or else multiple equilibria which in his set-up reduce to three, two stable and one unstable, whereas in general no such situation will occur and unique equilibrium prices will practically always emerge if there are many commodities in the market.

[This piece of manuscript ends here but the next one seems to follow with no serious break in the argument.]

[(c) *Determinateness and Stability of Simple Exchange.*] Since the theory of exchange, besides providing the theoretical description of the behavior of consumers (households), also serves to display the fundamental properties of economic action in general (the logic of choice), there is point in raising right here the questions of determinateness and of stability of simple exchange in a perfectly competitive market, indirect exchange (arbitrage) being duly taken into account and a standard commodity (*numéraire*) but no money being used.[13] We raise these questions in the same sense as did Walras, except for one point that will appear presently.

People—say n of them—endowed with definite tastes and possessing, to begin with, arbitrary quantities of an arbitrary number of well-defined commodities, say m in all, appear on the market, in order to take advantage of the possibilities this market may offer to them of improving upon the satisfaction of their wants as guaranteed by their original possessions.[14] We thus accept Walras' manner of speaking of a tendency on the part of all participants to maximize their satisfaction.[15] We also accept the usual assumptions about

[13] The arbitrage operations are supposed to be carried out in terms of the *numéraire*. It should be repeated, however, that they are supposed to be organized in such a manner as not to deflect any quantity of the standard commodity from its uses as a commodity. If people *hold* any part of the *numéraire* commodity this would turn it into money.

[14] Those original possessions of every participant in the market are data that are subject to certain conditions such as that the quantities originally possessed should all be non-negative, that at least one of them should be greater than zero, and that the original distribution should not violate the hypothesis of pure competition. For the rest, in *leçon* 14, Walras establishes that, in full equilibrium, prices would not change if the commodities were redistributed between participants so long as the sum of the possessions of each participant remains equivalent in terms of *numéraire* (*théorème des répartitions équivalentes*). I mention this theorem, which space does not permit us to discuss, to give an example of Walras' awareness of the necessity of establishing every point in his schema by formal proof. It is this awareness (whatever the success or shortcomings of his proofs) that made him the teacher of all theorists of the future.

[15] As already stated, this is not necessary. But it was the almost universal practice of Walras' generation, not only of the mathematical economists such as Edgeworth and Marshall but also of the Austrians, most explicitly so of Böhm-Bawerk. The questions that are now before us are not affected by our lapse into primitive utility theory. We do not imply measurability, and maximizing an index of satisfaction would do just as well.

continuity and differentiability, at least of the resulting market 'curves.' Finally we assume for the moment, as did Walras, that the marginal utility functions of every participant, for every commodity, not only exist but are functions of the quantity of this commodity alone, that is, independent of whatever other commodities he might possess. They are all monotonically decreasing. We then have: $n(m-1)$ Behavior Equations expressing for all n participants the quantities (including zero quantities) they will give away or acquire at any given system of exchange relations (or prices in terms of the *numéraire*) by virtue of the condition that they will go on exchanging until no further exchange can increase their individual satisfactions; [16] n equations such that all the quantities the participants acquire and give away, each quantity multiplied by its price in the standard commodity, must add up to zero, if we give minus signs to quantities given away and plus signs to quantities acquired (Individual Balance Equations); finally m equations such that, for every commodity, the total amount of quantity given away must equal the total amount of quantity acquired for the market as a whole (Market Balance Equations).[17] These are $m(n+1)$ conditions or equations. But, as is easily seen, one of them, for example the last one of the set of market balance equations, may be shown to follow from the rest of these and from the household balance equations and must therefore be thrown out as not independent. Thus we are left with $m(n+1)-1$ independent ones by which to determine the variables or 'unknowns,' namely, the m equilibrium prices and the mn quantities exchanged by the households. Now, we may say *either* that, since the price of the *numéraire* commodity in itself is of necessity always equal to unity, there are only $m-1$ prices to determine; *or* that, since the two first sets of equations (the behavior and the household balance equations), considered by themselves, are homogeneous of zero degree in the prices, it is only the exchange ratios and not the absolute prices which we can determine, though we can then translate these ratios into absolute prices by means of the *numéraire*-price identity.[18] The reader should make sure that he understands the perfect equivalence of these two ways of putting the matter and also the

16 This means, as we know, that they will continue to exchange until the marginal utilities to them of the quantities of all commodities that can be had for a unit of *numéraire* (if the *numéraire* is cigarettes and the unit a package, then the marginal utilities of a package's worth of every commodity) are equal.

17 The prices for which the last group of equations is verified are the market equilibrium prices. In the terminology foreshadowed by Walras but definitively established by Professor Hicks (*Value and Capital*, p. 63) we can express this last group of equations also by saying that, for every commodity, excess demand must be zero

18 A function $x_1 = f(x_2, x_3 \cdots x_r)$ is called homogeneous of zero degree if, λ being any positive arbitrary constant, the dependent variable remains the same when the independent ones are all multiplied by λ, so that $x_1 = f(\lambda x_2, \lambda x_3 \cdots \lambda x_r)$. Putting now λ equal to, say $1/x_2$, we get $x_1 = f(1, x_3/x_2 \cdots x_r/x_2)$, that is to say, a relation in which the former independent variables of which there are r, are replaced by ratios of which there are only $r-1$.

special sense in which it is true to say, that in this set-up absolute prices (or the 'price level') are indeterminate.[19]

Now we ask: do these conditions suffice to determine values of these variables? This, to repeat, is the question of the 'existence,' in the mathematical sense, of a set of values that will satisfy the conditions. This question is synonymous with the question *whether the equations embodying the conditions are capable of being simultaneously solved.* But it is neither the question whether there is any tendency in our market to establish these solutions, if they do exist, nor the question whether these solutions or equilibrium values are stable or not.

Of all the unjust or even meaningless objections that have been leveled at Walras, perhaps the most unjust is that he believed that this existence question is answered as soon as we have counted 'equations' and 'unknowns' and have found that they are equal in number. We have already seen that he made sure of one additional prerequisite—independence of equations. But as we analyze his argument we discover further that, though his mathematical equipment was no doubt deficient, his genius saw or sensed all or almost all the other relevant problems and practically always arrived at correct results. If he failed to answer all questions satisfactorily, there was immortal merit in his having posited them. If his work is not the culmination of this type of analysis, it certainly is its foundation.

He saw the possibility that our system of equations may not admit of any solution at all. He also saw, and even proved, that the solution, if it exist, may not be unique. All he claimed was that solutions exist normally and that, *if the commodities in the market are numerous,* there will *in general* be a unique solution (*Éléments,* p. 163). Since in his schema quantities demanded and offered are single-valued functions of the prices and since his marginal utility functions are monotonically decreasing, so much may be readily granted, although Walras did not emphasize, perhaps was not fully aware, that the unique solution, where it 'exists,' need not be economically meaningful in the sense that an actual system might work with it.[20]

[19] This merely means that, although it seems natural to put the 'price' of the *numéraire,* p_n, identically equal to unity, $p_n - 1 \equiv 0$, we could of course just as well put it equal to any other arbitrary figure without altering anything else *in this set-up.* Walras discussed the theory of the *numéraire* very carefully, giving, among other things, the rule for translating the prices expressed in one *numéraire* commodity into prices expressed in another (*Éléments* p. 150). It should be clear that this rule does not apply to *money* or does so only under quite unrealistic assumptions.

[20] The occurrence of such a case, e.g. of the inability of some participants in the market to secure a 'maximum of satisfaction' above starvation point, might be treated as a special form of economic, if not of mathematical, breakdown of the system. In itself, however, it is perfectly natural that a system that only represents the logic of certain relations cannot, in the absence of additional information, tell us anything about the size of the resulting shares in terms of goods. Also it cannot be repeated too often that since so far as Walras treated only a problem in the pure logic of simultaneous determination of variables, and therefore neglected, e.g., all lags of any

We may as well ask the further question: can we not do better than that? This question divides up into two parts. We ask first, can we state more rigorously the conditions on which the existence of solutions, and especially of a unique solution, depends within the Walrasian assumptions themselves? The answer is affirmative. Such a more rigorous statement has in fact been provided by Professor Wald.[21] Without going into several delicate questions that Wald's brilliant work raises (and without subscribing to every sentence of it), we simply note that Walras' analysis emerges substantially unimpaired.[22] But, second, we have to ask whether the existence theorem still stands if, as we must, we make total and marginal utility a function of all the commodities that enter a household's budget. This is of course the real difficulty. But the answer, under restrictions that seem tolerable, is affirmative even in this case. It has been given by Professor Amoroso.[23] For a treatment of the whole subject from the standpoint of the theory of demand the reader is referred to the standard work by Professor Wold.[24]

We turn to the question of stability, with which we shall include the question of the presence of a tendency toward such unique (theoretical) solutions as may exist.[25] It is one of the greatest merits of Walras to have distinguished

kind, the explanatory value of this part of his argument does not go beyond clearing up one of the many aspects that even pure theory must attend to.

21 See Abraham Wald (1902-50) in the periodical *Ergebnisse eines mathematischen Kolloquiums* (vols. 6 and 7, 1935 and 1936), and Wald's non-technical report on his investigation in 'Über einige Gleichungssysteme der mathematischen Ökonomie,' *Zeitschrift für Nationalökonomie*, December 1936. [This article has been translated as a memorial to Wald, 'On Some Systems of Equations of Mathematical Economics,' *Econometrica*, October 1951.]

22 Wald's (justified) attack upon the manner in which Walras tried to establish stability is another matter and will be touched upon presently. I do not think it correct, as Wald does, to mix this up with the question of the 'existence' of solutions in the sense explained. I also think that Walras' reason, given on p. 163 of the *Éléments*, for expecting that the solution will in general be unique, if there are very many commodities in the market, compares favorably with Wald's more rigorous statement that uniqueness will exist if the marginal utility functions are such that the utility value (marginal utility times quantity, the concept is due to von Wieser and Fisher) is an increasing function of the quantity. See also Walras, *Éléments* p. 125.

23 That is, Amoroso proved in a manner with which I cannot find any (serious) fault that, given the prices, the set of the quantities of commodities with which an individual will leave the market is uniquely determined, not indeed always but under acceptable hypotheses. This is only part of the *thema probandum* but, in the case where marginal utilities are partial differentials, a very important one. See 'Discussione del sistema di equazioni che definiscono l'equilibrio del consumatore,' *Annali di Economia*, 1928.

24 Herman Wold, 'A Synthesis of Pure Demand Analysis,' three (English) papers in the *Skandinavisk Aktuarietidskrift*, 1943-4.

25 I wish to re-emphasize that in general it seems to me an error to identify the problem of the 'tendency' with the problem of 'stability': a golf ball that rests on a green has no tendency to get into the appropriate hole unless there is a player to

between the 'existence' and the 'stability' problems and to have paralleled the argument about the former by an elaborate argument about the latter. However, he treated the problem of stability in a peculiar way, because it posed itself to him in connection with what in strict logic is an entirely different problem, namely, the problem of the relation between the mathematical solution of his equations and the processes of any actual market: first and foremost he was anxious to show that the people in the market, though evidently not solving any equations, do by a different method the same thing that the theorist does by solving equations; or, to put it differently, that the 'empirical' method used in perfectly competitive markets and the 'theoretical' or 'scientific' method of the observer tend to produce the same equilibrium configuration. Posing this problem then naturally puts the question of stability into the foreground, that is, the question how the mechanism of competitive markets drives the system toward equilibrium and keeps it there.

Since it is clear from the outset that the markets of real life never do attain equilibrium, this question can only be posed for markets that are still nothing but highly abstract creations of the observer's mind. The people, who appear with initial stocks of commodities and definite marginal utility schedules, are confronted with prices *criés au hasard* by someone. They decide to give away certain quantities of some commodities and to acquire certain quantities of others at these prices. But as we know they do not actually do so but only note on *bons* what they would 'buy' or 'sell' at those prices should they persist or, if they enter into contracts, they reserve the right of recontract. It is easy to see that if no recontract proves necessary and if the *bons* are redeemed, then the conditions embodied in the equations must indeed be fulfilled in practice. Whenever they are not, there will be recontracting at different prices, which are higher or lower than the original ones, according to whether there is positive or negative excess demand in the respective commodities, until demand and offer are equated in all cases (*Éléments*, p. 133). Whatever we might have to say about this on the score of realism,[26] it seems at first sight to be intuitively clear that, *so long as no other mechanism of reaction is admitted than the one exclusively considered by Walras*, equilibrium will be attained under these assumptions; that, in general, this equilibrium will be unique and stable; and that the prices and quantities in this configuration will be those we get from our theoretical solution.[27] Nevertheless, Walras himself

hit it and sometimes not even then. But if somebody puts it into the hole it will stay there in stable equilibrium. This should show the rationale of distinguishing between the two problems. In our case, however, the factors that make for stability of the equilibrium situation are at the same time 'forces' that may account for a tendency of our variables to get into the equilibrium configuration. And so we waive our objection, which is important only for evolutionary processes.

[26] See again Nicholas Kaldor, 'A Classificatory Note on the Determinateness of Equilibrium,' *Review of Economic Studies*, February 1934.

[27] This *prima facie* impression may account for the fact that even today theorists are not greatly exercised about the problem *as thus posed*. We may combine the individual demands and offers in the m commodities into m equations of the form $D_i(p_1 \cdots$

displayed hesitation on a very important point that has been strongly re-emphasized by Professor Wald (*Zeitschrift*, op. cit. p. 653). It is this. Equilibrium values in the perfect market are established by a game of trial and error (*tâtonnement*)—prices being adjusted and quantities being readjusted in response. For clearness, suppose that all prices except one do equate the respective demands and offers. We have a rule by which to adapt the one price that does not equate demand and offer. But if we do adapt it we thereby upset the equilibria in all the other sections of the market, whose prices are no longer equilibrium prices since they equate supply and demand in these other markets only with reference to the one price that failed to do so. Therefore we have in turn to adjust the others, and the only reason Walras gives for expecting that the new configuration is nearer to equilibrium all round than was the original one is that this is 'probable,' because the effects of the adjustment of the price that was originally out of line upon the excess demand of the corresponding commodity are direct, strong, and all *in the same direction*, whereas the effects of the necessary readjustments of the other prices are most of them indirect, weaker, and not all in the same direction: in *part they compensate one another*. As it stands, this attempt at proving both tendency toward, and stability of, the equilibrium of the market evidently lacks rigor. This has been increasingly recognized of late but no entirely satisfactory solution of the problem has been offered as yet.[28] [This subsection is unfinished.]

[(d) *Walras' Theory of Production*.] We turn to the second branch of Walras' pure theory of the economic process, namely, the theory of production, which, as we know, is nothing but a theory of the manner in which the

---

$p_m) = O_i(p_1 \cdots p_m)$. Of these equations we lose one owing to the fact that it follows from the others. Of the m prices we lose one owing to zero homogeneity. Stability is secured by imposing the condition that any price higher than the equilibrium price induces negative, and any price lower than the equilibrium price induces positive, excess demand, a condition carefully safeguarded by Walras. All the doubts that really worry theorists, so far as they do not proceed from their qualms about the assumptions that identify Walras' set-up, enter only on the introduction of genuine money.

[28] Readers who are sufficiently interested in these delicate questions may welcome the following signposts on this road. First we note that Pareto did not improve the Walrasian argument *in this respect* except for recognizing more explicitly that oscillations in the neighborhood of values may lead away from them as well as toward them. Second, from Pareto to Hicks, very little advance was made in this respect, however much headway was made in others. It was Professor Hicks who formulated stability conditions that were then improved by other writers, especially Samuelson and Metzler. Samuelson was, I believe, the first to point out that the problem of stability cannot be posed at all without the use of an explicit dynamic schema, i.e. without specification of the manner in which the system reacts to deviations from equilibrium. Third, our report shows that Walras did present such a dynamic schema: he specified a *sequence* of steps by which the system is supposed to work its way toward stable equilibrium for which he did not receive the credit he deserves. This schema covers not more than a special case but for this special case a more rigorous proof is possible in spite of the fact that he himself failed to give it.

mechanism of pure competition allocates the 'services' of all the different kinds and qualities of natural agents, labor power, and *produced means of production*.[29] This theory of allocation in turn is the same thing as the theory of the pricing of these services, because it is the price mechanism which brings these services into the place they actually hold in the great jig-saw puzzle and keeps them there. Finally, we do not say more than this when we say that the theory of production tells us which quantities of which products each firm will decide to produce, and which quantities of which productive services it is going to buy in view of the given tastes of prospective consumers of its products and the given propensities of these same consumers considered as 'owners' of productive services. Now, the total quantities of these services, that is, the quantities of them that are potentially available during a given period of time, are given because their sources are. But they need not be completely absorbed by production, nor do they necessarily go to waste if they are not. For an essential feature of the Walrasian schema is that they are all of them capable of being consumed by their owners directly.[30] Thus, their total quantities and the propensities of their owners to consume them—possibly even to acquire further quantities of them for the purpose of consumption—or to part with them, constitute the second group of data, and Walras' problem was to show how these data interlock with those of the first set, the consumers' tastes, so as to produce a consistent set of quantities and values.[31]

We perceive immediately that Walras strove for a solution of this problem that was to be entirely symmetrical with the solution he had previously worked

[29] Remember that these produced means of production, on the level on which we are moving now, are being let in kind, and are indefinitely durable, postulates that we are going to remove presently.

[30] With Walras, the services that are used in production therefore have also a use value for their 'owners.' This creates difficulties that are particularly obvious in the case of specific instruments of production, such as machines. To assume that, potentially at least, a machine can, at the will of its owner, be instantaneously turned into an easy chair is indeed heroic theorizing with a vengeance. Only in part is this assumption then relaxed in the theory of the 'new capitals' (*capitaux neufs*). But it has its virtue when it is the logic of the structure of the capital-goods stock which is to be explained *ab ovo*. We may make it more tolerable by saying that a capitalist's former decision as regards the use of the capital good he actually owns has determined what species of capital good he actually does own. It stands to reason that this attempt at saving the situation wrecks completely the *static* framework of the theory. No such assumption was made by either Marshall or the Austrians but this was only because they were less rigorous than was Walras. Let me use this opportunity to emphasize again that, on an infinitely higher level of rigor, Walras really reformulated the theories of production of A. Smith, J. B. Say, and J. S. Mill. The latter's theory of production, of course, must not be looked for exclusively in his Book I.

[31] In his *Manuel*, Pareto refined this set-up into his general theory of tastes and obstacles which, in fact, leads on to a higher level of abstraction and serves especially to bring out more clearly the logical problems that are lurking in this set-up. The practical value of the Paretian generalization shows in the ease with which it embraces the case of the socialized economy. But it does not help us much on the level on which we now find ourselves.

out in his general theory of barter in a multi-commodity consumers' goods market. In fact, his theory of production may be described as an attempt to resolve, in the spirit of J. B. Say, the case of production into the more general case of exchange between services and goods and, in the last analysis, simply between services. He was aware of the costs of this attempt and was willing to pay them. First, though he did introduce into his mechanism an entrepreneur who was not merely a capitalist, he reduced him, as we saw, to the purely formal role of buyer of productive services [32] and seller of consumers' goods without any initiative—or income—of his own.[33] In order to emphasize this, we shall replace the term 'entrepreneur' by the impersonal term 'firm': it is clear that in Walras' thought the households were really the agents that, both as buyers of products and as sellers of services, determine the economic process. Second, though he was, of course, aware of the fact that production and adaptation of production involves delays, he at first *purement et simplement* neglected these delays (*Éléments*, p. 215), deferring partial recognition of their role to the far-off section on circulation and money. We do the same thing and even accept, for the moment, the apparently impossible assumptions of constant coefficients of production,[34] absence of any overhead, and all firms in every industry producing exactly equal amounts of product.[35] And we ask, first of all, as we did before in the case of multi-commodity barter, whether with all these 'simplifications'—some of which were in the end discovered to be complications—there exists a unique set of solutions for a system of equations that covers both consumers' and producers' behavior, or represents, as it were, the chassis of economic life.

[32] We have seen that Walras was fully aware of the importance of the stocks and flows of raw materials and semifinished products that entrepreneurs buy from other entrepreneurs. But where he posed the fundamental problem of production (*leçons* 20 and 21), he dealt with them cavalierly, confining himself to showing—which is indeed easy if we neglect all sequences or lags—that these purchases by entrepreneurs from other entrepreneurs are intermediate steps in a process, the understanding of which does not suffer by leaving them out.

[33] Let me emphasize once more that in the equilibrium of a purely competitive process, where nobody is able to exert any influence upon the prices of either services or products, every entrepreneur would in fact be an *entrepreneur ne faisant ni bénéfice ni perte:* this is neither a paradox nor a tautology (i.e. it is not the result of a definition) but, *under Walras' assumptions*, an equilibrium condition (or, if you prefer, a provable theorem). [This point is further discussed in the next section (8).]

[34] This involves really two distinct assumptions: (1) that these coefficients, namely, the quantities of all services that enter the unit of the product, are technologically given or that there is, for each product, only one technologically possible way of producing it; and (2) that these coefficients do not vary in function of the quantity produced or that there are no economies or diseconomies of scale. This set-up was altered, later on, by Walras himself. But these questions will be taken up in the next section.

[35] Walras does not seem to have observed what was often urged later on, namely, that this makes the number of firms indeterminate though it does not prevent determinateness of the output of each industry. Since this is not important in our present argument, we defer consideration of this point also to the next section.

Intuitively we realize that, with the same qualifications that we had to make in the general case of multi-commodity exchange and with the further qualifications that are imposed upon us by the additional assumptions made by Walras in order to reduce the problem of production to manageability, the answer will be affirmative. We may balk at the assumptions. We may question the value of a theory that holds only under conditions, the mere statement of which seems to amount to refuting it.[36] But if we do accept these qualifications and assumptions, there is little fault to be found with Walras' solution. It comes to this: the households that furnish the services have in *Walras' set-up* definite and single-valued schedules of willingness to part with these services. These schedules are determined, on the one hand, by their appreciation of the satisfaction to be derived from consuming these services directly[37] and, on the other hand, by their knowledge of the satisfaction they might derive from the incomes in terms of *numéraire* that they are able to earn at any set of consumers' goods and service 'prices.' For the 'prices' of consumers' goods are determined simultaneously with the 'prices' of the services and with reference to one another: every workman, for instance, decides how many hours of work per day or week he is going to offer in response to a wage in terms of *numéraire* that is associated with definite prices, in terms of *numéraire*, of all the consumers' goods that would be produced with the total amount of work being offered at that wage rate. Mathematically, we express this by making everybody's offer of every service he 'owns' a function of all prices (both of consumers' goods and the services) and, for the same reason, everybody's demand for every commodity another function of all prices (both of the services and the consumers' goods). Everybody's demand for the *numéraire* commodity follows simply from everybody's

[36] Those who, like myself, do not go so far, must rate the pioneer performance as such very highly and see a merit precisely in the fact that Walras chalked out the work that had (in part still has) to be done in the future.

[37] Cassel's popularization of Walras' system lacks this feature. In consequence, Cassel had to put the (potentially) existing quantity of services equal to the quantity to be employed in production in equilibrium. It has been pointed out by Wicksell and later on by von Stackelberg ('Zwei kritische Bemerkungen zur Preistheorie Gustav Cassels,' *Zeitschrift für Nationalökonomie*, June 1933) that it will in general be impossible to fulfil this equilibrium condition with constant coefficients of production. This is not serious because the difficulty vanishes when we introduce variable coefficients, i.e. substitutability (see sec. 8). But if we accept the constant coefficients and at the same time refuse to accept Walras' theory that part of the services are directly consumed by their 'owners,' then there will be in general unemployment of some services for which the necessary complements do not exist. These unemployable surplus services will then, by seeking employment, depress the wages of the employed services of the same kind, but this lowering of wages may do but little (namely, by cheapening the products which absorb relatively much of the services in which there is a surplus) to reduce the unemployment and thus may unstabilize the whole system, *owing to incompatibility of equilibrium conditions*. The case is of no importance. But some Keynesians may have it in mind when arguing for the possibility of unemployment equilibria.

balance equation, which (since we are as yet abstracting from both genuine money and saving) is exactly analogous to the balance equation in the case of multi-commodity barter, except that in the present case the offers are offers of services and only the demands refer to commodities.[38] From these individual demands and offers we get the aggregate (net) offers of services and the aggregate demands for products in the market, all in function of all service and product prices. But the rest of the set-up is crippled—evidently in order to focus attention upon the great social relation between the ultimate factors that simultaneously shape consumption and production—by the assumption of technologically fixed and constant coefficients of production, which readily yield the remaining restrictions that we need for the determination of prices. To determine prices we need the equations, equal in number to the number of services, which express that the quantities of the services employed in all industries must add up to the total offer of these services, and the equations, equal in number to the number of products, which express that the coefficients of production of the services used in each industry, each multiplied by the price of these services, must equal the unit price of the industry's product or that in all industries average cost, in Walras' case the same as marginal cost, must equal price.

The number of variables to be determined can easily be shown to be equal to the number of equations. As to the mathematical question whether these can be solved for the variables—whether an equilibrium solution 'exists'—we have to say much the same as before: Walras did not present an answer that will satisfy the standards of the modern mathematician, though it could be shown[39] that he saw and either took *or avoided* all the hurdles that stand in the way to an affirmative answer. Of course, we have to repeat that, in the same sense as before, existence of a set of solutions or even of non-negative solutions does not necessarily mean the existence of economically meaningful—that is, practically possible, 'tolerable,' and so on—solutions. But within his assumptions and with qualifications already mentioned, the affirmative answer

[38] Walras has often been berated on the score of the clumsiness or heaviness of his mathematics. It is submitted, however, that the argument in *leçon* 20, where he solves the 'theoretical' problem, is not inelegant, particularly as regards the manner in which the offers of services emerge from marginal equilibrium conditions (op. cit. p. 210). It seems to me that some critics, including some mathematical critics, stand to learn from it. Present practice, born of pedagogical convenience, is to make the individual demands for products functions of *their* prices only and of 'income.' While this practice has its advantages, especially now when it helps the student to grasp the relation of Keynesian to Walrasian economics, it really obscures Walras' fundamental conception and makes things more difficult in the end.

[39] Space to do this is lacking. We must confine ourselves to repeating that his assumption that services have use value for their 'owners,' in fact, avoids the only serious difficulty which in the case now under discussion is added to the difficulties glanced at in the case of simple multi-commodity barter, namely, the difficulty that lurks behind the constant coefficients of production. Of course, the statement in the text must be understood to hold without qualification only where marginal utilities are exclusively functions of the quantity of the corresponding commodity.

stands and objections against it are much more due to the critics' failure to understand Walras than to any mistakes or oversights of his.[40] Also it may be averred that, *so far as this part of the Walrasian analysis is concerned*, our result is, or comes near to being, the common opinion of theorists.[41]

As regards questions of stability and of the presence in the economic process of a tendency to establish that equilibrium set of prices and quantities, the situation is still more seriously affected than we have already found it to be in the case of multi-commodity barter by the difficulty of accepting Walras' assumptions.[42] We have again to rely on the method of *bons*. But in this case, if the prices that are being experimentally fixed (*criés*) at first do not prove to be (miraculously) the equilibrium prices, the rearrangements that are to lead toward equilibrium involve instantaneous rearrangements of all the tentative decisions to produce that are embodied in the *bons*, which is a matter of much more difficulty than would be mere rearrangement of tentative decisions to acquire or to give away existing commodities. And even if all firms and all owners of productive services did succeed at this task, they would still have to carry out this production program which takes time, during which nothing must be allowed to change. Walras himself posed the problem exactly as he posed it for the case of multi-commodity barter, namely, in the guise of the question whether his theoretical problem was the one that is actually solved in the markets of the services; and he arrived, by the same reasoning, at the same conclusion, namely, that a process of trial and error car-

[40] One of these objections, which was of course never raised by mathematical economists, deserves mention in passing. By suitable eliminations we may represent all product prices and quantities as functions of the prices of the services. It should be clear that this formal truth does not constitute the latter as 'causes' of the former, since the service prices themselves are determined in an argument that at every step takes account of the corresponding product prices. Some economists, however, Austrians especially, inferred from this universal and simultaneous interdependence of all prices that the Walrasian system fails to explain *any* prices at all: this was sometimes expressed by calling it 'functional' to distinguish it from the Austrian 'causal' system. I indulge in the hope that it is unnecessary, at this hour of the day, to go into this.

[41] For a rigorous proof, the reader is referred to A. Wald (*Zeitschrift*, op. cit.). The reader may indeed derive a slightly less favorable impression from this paper, but he should observe that Professor Wald deals with Cassel's system rather than with that of Walras. The modification suggested by Zeuthen and K. Schlesinger, which Wald mentions on p. 640, has merits of its own but is not necessary in order to make *Walras'* system tractable.

[42] However, if we do accept them, stability may be proved, if anything, more convincingly than it can in the barter case. This has been done for a pattern that admits substitution by Professor Hicks (*Théorie mathématique de la valeur*, 1937) and others, particularly by L. M. Court ('Invariable Classical Stability of Entrepreneurial Demand and Supply Functions,' *Quarterly Journal of Economics*, November 1941). Both reintroduce the entrepreneur whom we have eliminated and therefore put their proofs into the form indicated by the title of the latter paper. Historically, it is important to note that, however superior in technique, these and other contributions do no more than spell out the suggestions that are already present, although some of them only implicitly, in Walras' analysis.

ried out under conditions of pure competition and with only the one mechanism of reaction allowed—prices being increased where there is positive and reduced where there is negative excess demand—will 'probably' insure that each step in adjustment actually does lead toward, and not away from, equilibrium. I have thought it necessary to put this matter fully before the reader. Lest he should thereupon turn away from Walras' construction on the ground of its hopeless discrepancy from any process of real life, I wish to ask him whether he ever *saw* elastic strings that do not increase in length when pulled, or frictionless movements, or any other of the constructs commonly used in theoretical physics; and whether, on the strength of this, he believes theoretical physics to be useless. In the footnote below, I add one or two other comments that may reduce the reader's discomfort. It remains true, however, that both Walras himself and his followers greatly underestimated what had and has still to be done before Walras' theory can be confronted with the facts of common business experience.[43]

[43] First of all, the reader should observe that his discomfort stems mainly from his familiarity with an economic process that is incessantly disturbed by technological revolutions. In any process that, without being strictly stationary, is at least not too far removed from stationarity, households and firms would have a reliable stock of routine experience that would help them greatly to perform the tasks that look so impossible at first sight: the tentative prices, to which they are to react by formulating tentative programs of production and consumption, are not really *criés au hasard*, as Walras has it, but are rather informed guesses to be corrected, as a rule, by relatively small adjustments. It is only in order to bring out the logic or rationale of the derivation of demand and supply functions that Walras refuses to avail himself of this fact. We can learn from Marshall how to put flesh and skin on Walras' skeleton, although it does remain true that a more realistic theory raises a world of new problems that are beyond Walras' (and also Marshall's) range. Second, the elements of reality that do enter Walras' schema are indeed overgrown by other elements which we must try to conquer in due course. But the former are nevertheless observable or verifiable even where they take such unfamiliar forms as *tâtonnement* by means of *bons*. Third, it should not be said that in Walras' system all the burden of adaptation is put upon prices alone: quantities are adapted to prices as prices are to quantities, and it is only an abbreviated manner of speaking which accounts for the impression alluded to. Fourth, there is realism in some of the items of Walras' set-up in which we should least expect it. Thus, a little reflection will show that workmen's demand for the 'services' of their own labor power (i.e. for leisure) is actually a very important factor in the shaping of the process of production. Though it would be absurd to deny this for the present age, there never was a time in which this demand was completely ineffective, and the surface fact that a laborer accepts a fixed working day which he is powerless to alter ('he must accept it or die' says a contemporary economist) contradicts Walras' analytic arrangement very much less than it seems to. Finally, fifth, classroom experience induces me to add that propositions such as Walras' law of cost or full employment in perfect competition are indeed properties of his system when in perfect equilibrium. But they are unobjectionable when properly understood (on the full-employment proposition see the remark at the end ot this section) and, above all, they are theorems that follow from the postulates that define the system and not postulates that are imposed upon it (so that they could cause overdeterminateness).

[(e) *The Introduction of Capital Formation and of Money*.] The rest of this section may be cast into the form of an answer to the question how the fundamental schema of consumers' and producers' behavior is affected—or possibly upset—by the introduction of capital formation and of money. Though both subjects have been touched upon in the preceding chapter and will again have to be treated in the next, they must also receive attention here to enable the reader to appreciate Walras' structure as a whole and to realize the extent to which he anticipated modern work in these fields in some respects and prepared the ground for it in others.

In the Walrasian system, the theory of capital formation is, on the one hand, the foundation of the theory of interest and, on the other hand, itself rests on the theory of capital-goods prices. At first we consider only the prices of produced capital goods. So far, we have a theory for the prices of their services only and even this was arrived at by means of an assumption which we must now drop, namely, that the quantities of produced capital goods are given once and for all, and they never wear out or perish by accident. Accordingly, we now deduct an allowance for depreciation and also an insurance premium.[44] What remains is the 'net revenue' yielded by the capital goods. We have noticed before that Walras took the existence of such a surplus over depreciation and insurance as an undeniable fact which he made no effort to establish.[45] However, if we accept this for the sake of argument, then we can proceed at once to construct the theoretical market for capital goods which, according to Walras' laudable practice, we need in order to determine their prices.[46] In this market capitalists—and not as entrepreneurs (firms)—demand *new* capital goods which the firms that produce them offer in response to that demand.

The new capital goods that are being demanded and produced may not suffice, just suffice, or more than suffice to make up for the loss the existing capital stock currently suffers from accident or wear and tear. The last of these three cases *defines* saving, which, expressed in terms of the *numéraire*, is therefore the excess of net income, the total net value of the services sold by households, over consumption, the total value of the products bought by households. Hence, exactly as in Keynes's *General Theory*, current saving is *tautologically equal to current 'investment.'* Saving is here merely a word that identifies a particular kind of demand, namely, the demand for capital goods. So far there is no meaning to the phrase 'offer or supply of saving' unless we wish to denote by it that part of the households' services that is of-

[44] Walras considered both as technologically determined constants. This is, of course, unsatisfactory but should be considered as another of the privileges of the pioneer.

[45] Neither did Pareto, Barone, and others in the direct line of succession make such an effort. But Wicksell and Fisher filled this gap with Böhm-Bawerkian material.

[46] The market we are describing now is nothing but a theorist's construction that Walras himself later on abandoned to replace it by the stock market. To criticize this theoretical device on the score of lack of realism would spell misunderstanding.

fered against capital goods [47] instead of being offered against bread or beer, and to say that current saving can get out of step with current investment has no more sense than to say that saving can get out of step with itself. Hence, equality of current saving and current investment is an identity and not an equilibrium condition. The equilibrium condition is that the sum total of saving in a given period should be equal to the costs to the capital-goods-producing firms of the capital goods (produced and) sold in the period, since these firms, like all others, are subject to Walras' law of costs.

Now—and this is not as in the system of Keynes's *General Theory*—the only motive that capitalists can have *in this set-up* for demanding capital goods is in the net revenue expected from them, no matter whether this net revenue consists in the use value to them of the durable objects acquired or in the yield in *numéraire* to be collected from letting them to firms (or to people who wish to consume their services directly). From this follows another equilibrium condition which must be fulfilled by their prices: these prices must, under ideal conditions, be proportional to their net yields or else arbitrage operations would set in to enforce this proportionality. But this may be expressed by saying that our capital-goods market is really a market of streams of perpetual net revenues, from which standpoint all capital goods are on the same footing irrespective of their physical shapes. In order to emphasize this aspect, Walras created an ideal or imaginary commodity that represents 'perpetual net revenue.' This gadget—another purely theoretical construct [48]—enables us to endow each household with a marginal utility and a demand function for 'perpetual net revenue,' [49] and to replace all the (unknown) prices of the capital goods *by a single price*, which then helps to determine them, namely, the price of a unit of 'perpetual net revenue' per unit

[47] Remember that capital goods are goods that serve more than once. It would be more correct to define them as goods which (or parts of which) survive the period of account.

[48] Pareto, Barone, and others accepted this ideal or imaginary commodity and simply called it 'saving' (*risparmio*). Notice that this construct may also be harnessed into the service of theoretical schemata other than Walras'. Even in Walras' schema, it acquired a new—and more realistic—connotation where he introduced money, as we shall see presently. For the moment, the concept does not mean anything but the total heap of all new capital goods, expressed in terms of *numéraire*, and only serves to isolate one aspect of them but has no separate existence: if Walras nevertheless speaks of a market of *capital numéraire*, this market is—unlike the market of *capital monnaie*, which we have not introduced as yet—*not* distinct from the market of the capital goods themselves.

[49] The marginal utility functions are conceived as monotonically decreasing functions of the quantity of this ideal commodity alone, as in the case of all other commodities. But the demand functions for these commodities are, also as in the case of all other commodities, functions of all the prices of all products and services. Note that this implies that they are also functions of the incomes: the difference in this respect between the theories of Walras and of Keynes (*General Theory*) is *not* that Walras neglected the influence of income but that Keynes neglected the influence of the prices of the products.

of time—a profound move on the analytical chessboard. This single price results from the condition of proportionality mentioned above, which may be reformulated by saying that the total demand for new capital goods (identically equal to saving) must be distributed between the industries that produce these new capital goods in such a way as to equalize their net value products (in terms of *numéraire*) per unit of cost (in terms of *numéraire*).[50] Thus the single price in question is simply the reciprocal of the rate of 'perpetual net revenue' (*taux du revenu net perpétual*), which is a factor of proportionality, common to the values of all capital goods and readily identified—so long as there is no money—with the rate of interest.

With infinite care, to which justice cannot be done here, Walras developed this theory for both the cases of produced durable goods such as homes, the services of which are to be directly consumed, and of produced durable goods that are to be used in production, supplying the marginal utility (maximizing) conditions for static equilibrium[51] and arriving, as regards determinateness and stability, at results analogous to those arrived at in the cases of multicommodity exchange and of production. If space permitted comment, it would have to be similar to the comments submitted in those cases. We must be content to state without proof that Walras' system is not—we are still following an analysis that abstracts from genuine money—upset by the facts, as stylized by him, of capital formation and by the excursion that the theory of it involves into 'progressive' or else 'retrograde,' that is, non-stationary, states. But let us summarize what else we have got so far.

First, we have a theory of the prices (values in terms of *numéraire*) of capital goods which we have not had before. In the first instance, this was a theory of the pricing of new capital goods. But this theory is then readily extended to the cases of existing produced capital goods and of non-produced capital goods ('land'; Walras even extends it to labor power) by the simple device of applying to them the same 'rate of perpetual net return' (or of interest)[52] that emerges in the case of new capital goods.[53] Second, as a by-product of the theory of capital-goods prices we have a theory of interest which now enters

[50] Remember that, with Walras, marginal and average costs are of necessity equal. The correction that is necessary, if this is not so, is obvious.

[51] He realized, of course, that, with positive saving, the economy under study was no longer stationary. But he also realized that its theory may still be static, if the propensities to save (*dispositions à l'épargne*) and the propensities to consume (*dispositions à la consommation*) remain unchanged during a certain time (*Éléments*, p. 244; this is perhaps the most convincing passage for showing that Walras fully grasped the distinction between a static *theory* and a stationary *process* (see above, sec. 3).

[52] Let us note that the most important modern sponsor of this identification—which implies the belief that the existence of the 'rate of perpetual net return' is an undeniable fact that does not require either proof or verification—is Professor F. H. Knight.

[53] From this it might be inferred, though not quite conclusively, that Walras associated the fact of interest with a 'progressive' society and was not unaware of the possibility that it might vanish in a retrograde, if not a stationary one. I take this opportunity to refer the reader to the brilliant papers of Professor C. Bresciani-Turroni,

all demand and supply equations. From these, then, a comprehensive theory of its role in the economy may be read off.[54] The prices of the capital goods themselves do not enter any of the final equations of the Walrasian system other than those that describe their own conditions of supply and demand *qua* products. Third, since saving is merely a species of demand, there cannot be any question of equalizing its 'demand and supply' by varying the rate of interest or anything else. What is equalized by virtue of an equilibrium condition—not merely set tautologically equal—is the amount that people have decided to save and invest and the costs of the new capital goods. Now if this equality is not realized, this means that the values of new capital goods will be above or below their costs to the firms that produce them and therefore will have a motive to expand or restrict their production. But there is another aspect to this. Suppose that the values of new capital goods have risen above their costs. If for the sake of argument we assume that the expected net yield of the capital goods has not changed, this implies that the *rate* of perpetual net return has fallen, in other words, that a unit of perpetual net return will be more expensive for the capital-goods purchasing capitalist than it was before: it is this rise in the *numéraire* prices of new capital goods which brings home to the capitalist the implied fall in his rate of net return. In still other words, it is not the fall in the rate of interest which plays any direct causal role, but it is the rise in the values of capital goods which reduces (tautologically) the rate of interest.[55] Of course, the rate of interest thereupon also assumes an active role so far as it enters the demand and supply functions of all products and services. Yet it is important to notice that, *in this analysis*, it plays a passive role in the first instance because this puts a different complexion on its significance in the economic process and serves especially to put the capitalists' reactions in a different light: they are reactions to the increase in the price of a particular type of goods the capitalist demands and not reactions to the decrease in the price of a service he renders.[56] Finally, it follows

on 'The Theory of Saving,' *Economica*, February and May 1936, which shed a lot of light on the theory of saving and its history.

[54] This was a stroke of genius. But its validity, of course, depends on Walras' conception of interest. It is in order for me to observe, neglecting my principle of effacing myself in this book, that the admiration I keep on expressing for the ingenuity, nay, greatness of Walras' analysis, should not be understood to imply agreement in every respect.

[55] The individual capitalist's loss may, of course, be compensated, in part, wholly, or more than wholly, by the gain he will then make on the stock of capital goods he owns already. This fact, however important in other respects, is not relevant here.

[56] Without mentioning Walras, Cassel adopted the same view—for him also saving *consists* in demanding capital goods or in applying productive services to their production. But he failed to understand how, on introducing genuine money, Walras shifted his standpoint radically, as we shall see in a moment. Another matter may be adverted to here. An increase or decrease in the prices of assets to be acquired is less likely to be neglected than would be a decrease or increase in the price of a service: this provides a possible argument against the view so frequently voiced at present that moderate variations in the rate of interest do not seem to have any noticeable in-

from the preceding argument that, sharply renouncing allegiance to the Turgot-Smith theory of saving, Walras' analysis agrees with Böhm-Bawerk's in yielding the result that the prices of consumers' goods and prices of capital goods will, within the assumptions of this analysis, in principle move in opposite directions.

At last, we introduce money and monetary transactions. Deferring Walras' other exploits in the field of monetary theory and policy to the next chapter, we must see right now how he fitted money into his schema of the economic process, how he determined absolute prices in money as well as in *numéraire,* and whether he was right in claiming that his monetary economy enjoys the same properties of determinateness and stability that may be attributed to his *numéraire* economy. For this purpose it will suffice to deal with the case of a money of given quantity that consists of a material of negligible use value [57] and to note briefly that Walras, who in the first edition (1874-7) of his *Éléments* had based his monetary analysis on the concept of the economy's 'monetary requirements,' [58] adopted in the second edition the concept of the 'amount of cash people desire to hold' (*encaisse désirée*),[59] which was, however, not made part and parcel of his pure theory of general equilibrium—not fully amalgamated with it—before the fourth edition (1900).[60] It is there that

fluence. Also, since the use of assets for capitalists consists in reaping their yields, the Walrasian theory leaves room for the possibility that an increase in the price of capital goods may cause demand for them to expand just as . . . [note incomplete.]

[57] As we shall see in the next chapter, Walras also analyzed the cases of monometallism, bimetallism, and monometallism 'regulated' by the issue of token money. But his fundamental analysis is carried out for the case of a government paper money of given quantity. Observe at once that this means only that the *material* money is made of has no use value but not that this money *itself* has none: this will be explained presently. But observe also that the simplification which consists in not having to attend, when discussing fundamentals, to the problems that are raised by the value, as a commodity, of the money material is bought at the price of having to postulate an arbitrarily fixed quantity of money. *In this trivial sense,* our question is answered already: since this quantity is arbitrary, absolute prices cannot be determined uniquely. But the question we ask is not this one: we ask instead whether the price level and all the other monetary and non-monetary quantities in the system are uniquely determined when the quantity of money has been fixed.

[58] *Circulation à desservir*—an old concept already familiar to Petty. Walras himself (preface, p. IX), borrowed this concept from the physiocrats. The *encaisse désirée* appeared first in the *Théorie de la monnaie* (1886).

[59] We are in the habit of associating this 'cash-balance approach' with Marshall, who developed it independently during the 1880's. See on the significance of this approach and cognate matters Professor Marget's scholarly articles, 'Léon Walras and the Cash-Balance Approach to the Problem of the Value of Money,' *Journal of Political Economy,* October 1931, and 'The Monetary Aspects of the Walrasian System,' ibid. April 1935.

[60] Or, more exactly, before he presented, in the bulletin of the Société vaudoise des Sciences Naturelles, his paper on 'Equations de la circulation' (1899). This is much later than Marshall may be assumed to have arrived at roughly similar results (see J. M. Keynes's Marshall biography, *Essays in Biography,* pp. 196-206). But not only

the whole of the Walrasian structure of pure theory appears in all its logical beauty.

The ground floor of this structure is the theory of the 'market' of consumers' goods. On the second floor we find the theory of production and the 'market' of production services, not separated from, but integrated with, the first market. On the third floor we have the 'market' of capital goods similarly integrated with the two others. And on the fourth floor there is another 'market,' integrated with the other three, of 'circulating capital,' that is, of the stocks or inventories of goods—new capital goods for sale at the establishments of their producers, and consumers' and producers' inventories of all kinds—that are necessary to keep things going.[61]

Thus, after having determined, in his theory of production, the equilibrium (*numéraire*) prices and quantities for both consumers' goods and productive services—all of which, once determined, are to remain unchanged while the goods are being produced—Walras lets actual delivery of these services and of (equivalent) goods begin at once, that is, before the program of production decided on 'in principle' has been carried out. Of course this presupposes that households and firms are from the outset in possession of stocks of goods (inventories) which are now introduced among the data of the general-equilibrium problem.[62] As we have already seen, Walras treated them formally as he had

---

did Marshall not publish these results until twenty years after Walras' paper, but also he never formulated the logic of them as rigorously and completely as did Walras. Still it should be borne in mind that, in principle, all that follows applies to Marshallian as well as to Walrasian economics.

[61] In order to facilitate the mathematical treatment, Walras extended the meaning of coefficients of production in a manner that is interesting because a similar device has been recently adopted by Professor Leontief in his input-output analysis. Briefly and concretely, if we have a product (A) which has, with respect to the capital-goods service (*K*), a coefficient of production a_k, then this a_k is to include not only the quantity of (*K*) that is necessary to produce a unit of (A) but also the quantity of (*K*) that, if the production of (A) is increased by a unit, is required for the concomitant increase in stocks held by producers (Walras, *Éléments*, p. 298; W. W. Leontief, 'Input and Output Analysis . . .' *American Economic Association, Papers and Proceedings*, May 1949, pp. 219-20).

[62] These stocks exist of course in specific forms, such as wine in cellars or handsaws in workshops. In reality, these specific goods need not at any given moment be, even approximately, what the maximizing conditions for the subsequent period would require. Here, so it seems to us now, we have the essentially dynamic problem how the economic process adapts itself to situations that are inherited from the past and are always out of date when they have to be acted upon. But Walras eliminated this problem by the heroic assumption that stocks, like capital goods, are exactly as if they had been produced in the past with a view to conditions obtaining in the present. This is the meaning of his phrase, constructing the equilibrium system *ab ovo*. We may render it by saying that he created an economic world in which every element fits perfectly into its niche, even if, owing to the fact that production takes time, it had to be produced when nobody could have known exactly what the niche would be like. There is point in such a construction. But, once more, it is but the first milestone on a long road.

treated the capital goods: there are the stocks themselves and, in addition, there are the services they render currently, namely, the *services d'approvisionnement.* Hence stocks and their services have to be priced separately, but the price of each stock stands to the price of its service in the same relation as the price of the service of each capital good stands to the price of the capital good itself.[63] Note that the introduction of stocks and the services of stocks constitutes Walras' method of synchronizing the economic process: on condition of paying the price of the service—that is, an interest charge on the circulating capital involved—households are now able to 'transform' their productive services immediately into consumers' goods. But this is evidently no mere detail but an essential feature of the general equilibrium system to which, by way of anticipation, Walras already adverted in his theory of production (*Éléments,* p. 215).

With the stocks enters money. It is simply a particular item in the list of inventories and also renders a *service d'approvisionnement,* which acquires a price, like any other service, by virtue of its marginal utility functions.[64] This

[63] This conceptual arrangement, presupposing as it does the existence of a net price of each *service d'approvisionnement,* is open to the same objection that may be raised against the postulate of the net yield of a capital good. But as soon as we admit the existence of such a *service d'approvisionnement* that is capable of having a net price (i.e. a price greater than depletion of the stock plus insurance), we cannot object to the distinction of stock and service on the ground that this spells double counting. In fact, since Walras derives the prices of stocks, via the rate of interest, from the prices of their services—i.e. in a manner equivalent to a discounting process—there is here a remarkable affinity with Böhm-Bawerk's schema although, almost tragically, those two great men completely misunderstood one another. But the affinity becomes obvious if we state the matter like this: the households receive the products they want *at once* (instead of receiving them at the end of the period of production), and they pay interest in order so to receive them. See next sentence in the text.

[64] This price must not be confused with the price of money itself. Let p' denote the price of money in terms of the *numéraire,* π' the price of its *service d'approvisionnement,* and i the rate of interest, then, according to the rule for the value of capital goods that do not wear out (such as land), we have $\pi' = p'i$. If money serves as *numéraire,* $p = 1$ and $\pi = i$.

As regards the marginal utility curves for the services of money and stocks in general, it must be observed, however, that they are not 'given' in the same sense as are the marginal utility curves for beer or bread: in Frisch's terminology, they are not as autonomous as are the latter, and they are valid only for a structure of production and for habits of payment which the economic process itself keeps on changing. Walras saw this difficulty but he comforted himself by pointing out that in practice households and firms normally know 'very approximately' how great a revolving fund of goods and money they need. This is true, but the theorist who avails himself of this fact must indeed point out, as did Walras, that he is excluding uncertainty by special hypothesis. Incidentally we may remark that Walras thus disposed, without intending to do so, of the later theory (J. R. Hicks) that there would be no need for holding cash in the absence of uncertainty of any kind and that, therefore, the phenomenon of money depends for its existence on uncertainty. Walras, within his schema, had no opportunity to do justice to the importance of the element of uncertainty. But he

price emerges in a special market, which Walras called the capital market (*marché du capital*)—in distinction to the market of capital goods (*marché des capitaux*)—and which is an 'annex' of the market of all productive services (*Éléments*, p. 245). All suppliers of services are now paid, and buy products, in money. Capitalists save no longer by exchanging productive services against capital goods but they save in money and we have a quantity called *monnaie d'épargne* in addition to the two quantities of transaction money (*monnaie de circulation*) in the hands of households and of firms. The latter *borrow* money and *buy* new capital goods. The equilibrium price of the 'commodity' in this market, namely, of money's *service d'approvisionnement*, is determined by the condition that people's demand for this service—represented by their *encaisse désirée*—be equal to the total amount of money in existence. Having determined this equilibrium price we may choose money itself for *numéraire* and then restate the condition by saying that the rate of interest should be such as to equalize the *encaisse désirée* and the total amount of money in existence.[65]

So far, the 'existence' of a unique set of solutions or of equilibrium values for the Walrasian system is not affected at all by the introduction of money: the situation in this respect remains, qualifications included, much as we found it in the case of the *numéraire* economy. This could be proved but should be intuitively clear from the fact that Walras fits in money by a device that amounts to setting up its *service d'approvisionnement* as just one more service (of no *direct* utility) to be traded in—which evidently no more changes the logic of the situation[66] than would the introduction of any other additional commodity or service. It should be added, however, that owing to the nature

---

showed that meeting uncertainty is not essential for money to circulate and to be held, so that there is no warrant for the proposition that a money economy is necessarily dynamic. This does not amount to denying that all the really troublesome problems about money arise in *evolutionary* processes.

[65] It should cause no surprise that we find ourselves suddenly in close proximity to the Keynesian theory of interest (the 'own-rate' theory, see *General Theory*, p. 223). The affinity stands out particularly well—and so does the difference—if we observe that, within Walras' schema, there is only room for the first of Keynes's three motives for holding cash, viz. the transaction motive, whereas there is no room for the other two, viz. the 'precautionary' and the 'speculative' motives (*General Theory*, p. 170). The saving schedule thus coincides with the supply schedule in the capital market. But the two other motives can be readily inserted into Walras' picture. If we do so, then the savings schedule no longer coincides with the supply schedule of loanable funds. But this does not invalidate the Walrasian theory: it only amounts to supplementing it by additional hypotheses. See on this O. Lange, 'The Rate of Interest and the Optimum Propensity to Consume,' *Economica*, February 1938, and Franco Modigliani, 'Liquidity Preference and the Theory of Interest and Money,' *Econometrica*, January 1944. The argument of these writers is not invalidated by D. Patinkin's criticisms in 'Relative Prices, Say's Law, and the Demand for Money,' *Econometrica*, April 1948, although it is open to others.

[66] This has been denied of late, precisely on the ground that Walras excluded money from the things or services of things that have marginal utility functions, i.e.

of the service that money is supposed to render, the price of its service enters the demand and supply equations that determine the prices of all the other commodities and services in a peculiar way. This may be seen most easily by observing that variations in the price of the service of money—or, choosing money for *numéraire*, interest—affect directly the values of capital goods and stocks (inventories) and through these all the other prices and quantities in the system, including those of the productive services such as wages and the quantity of labor demanded and offered. This is important to keep in mind: any variation in any price affects all other prices, offers, and demands, but variations in the price of money have an additional influence of particular importance. Hence money prices are not simply translations of prices expressed in a *numéraire* that is not money into prices expressed in another *numéraire* that is not money: money prices are not proportional to *numéraire* prices; they are prices adjusted to a new condition, that is, the condition that governs equilibrium in Walras' capital market. We may still formulate this monetary equilibrium condition as we did above, namely, that total *encaisse désirée* should be equal to the total quantity of money in existence, but we must keep in mind that the *encaisse désirée* depends, among other things, on the total *numéraire* value of transactions and that the latter also depends on the price of the service of money and cannot remain constant if this price—or the rate of interest—changes. In other words, we cannot fulfil the monetary equilibrium condition by treating as given not only the existing quantity of money but also the total *encaisse désirée*, and letting monetary equilibrium come about by appropriate variations in the rate of interest alone. If this fact is realized and acted upon, then we may aver indeed that the Walrasian argument determines a consistent set not only of relative but also of money prices or, if you wish, the price level.

Walras himself realized this situation and must therefore be credited with having created a theory of money that is complete, consistent, and perfectly adequate, within its own assumptions, to determine absolute prices in terms of money.[67] But at the critical point he failed to go through with it. On the ground that the influence of variations in the rate of interest upon the sum total of transactions, hence upon the *encaisse désirée*, is only 'indirect and feeble' (*Éléments*, p. 311) he decided to neglect it altogether and then pro-

from the set of things that qualify for commodities. But this view is based on nothing but a misunderstanding of Walras' decision to consider at first a kind of money, the *material* of which has no value as a commodity (*Éléments*, p. 303) in order to defer the problems that arise if money is made of a material that has an appreciable value in consumption or production, such as gold or silver. This question has nothing to do with two other cognate ones: (a) whether the concept of a 'service of money' is admissible; and (b) whether Walras did or did not emphasize the parallelism between monetary and 'real' processes too strongly.

[67] This theory has in particular nothing to fear from the man of straw some contemporary economists have baptized Say's Law. Nor is it affected by zero homogeneity of demand and offer functions although in Walras' theory, as in any other, it must of course remain indifferent whether people calculate in dollars or in cents.

ceeded to base much of his reasoning about applied monetary theory on the simplifying assumption of its absence. This assumption, quite apart from the question whether it is factually justifiable or not,[68] would change the whole situation if we were to take it as part of Walras' rigorous theory. Then, as Walras himself observed, the equation of monetary circulation would indeed be 'external to the system of equations that determine economic equilibrium' (ibid.), and then there would be some warrant for saying that Walras' system is essentially a 'real' or *numéraire* system, complete as such, on which he threw, as a separable piece of apparel, the 'veil of money' (see, however, next chapter).[69] Money interest and money prices would then be no longer determined simultaneously with the relative prices and would in general be inconsistent with them.[70] In view of the spirit as well as the wording of Walras' text, it is, however, much more natural to say that, for the purposes of applied monetary theory, Walras decided to abandon his method of general analysis and to adopt that of partial analysis. This means that he decided to adopt an approximation to which the standards of rigorous analysis do not apply.[71]

But the question of stability (and of the presence of a tendency in the system to realize the equilibrium values of its elements) is now much more difficult to answer than it was before. This is not owing to any change in the logical situation that the introduction of money has brought about—which is much as it was in the *numéraire* economy—but to the fact that in a money economy it is more difficult to accept Walras' general pattern of the economic process. Of this Walras was perfectly aware. Proof of it is his emphasis upon the instability of bank credit (e.g. *Éléments*, pp. 353-4). Apart from this it stands to reason that the insertion of a monetary capital market offers the economic engine new opportunities for stalling which are absent in a *numéraire* economy: we may exclude uncertainties in obedience to Walras' directions; but in the case of a 'commodity' which is as volatile as money and which can be

68 It seems to me beyond question that in general it is not. It may, however, serve some particular purposes.

69 This assumption is the second reason (in addition to Walras' careless statement on p. 303 of the *Éléments*, that money is to be considered as an *objet sans utilité propre*) that may be adduced in favor of writers who interpret Walras in that sense. There is a third one. Walras' exposition does without money as long as possible and thereby creates the impression that the theory of money is indeed something to be plastered upon the façade of a building that had been completed beforehand. Closer analysis shows, however, that this is no more than an expository device which is of a piece with his method of abstracting from the facts of production in his presentation of his theory of exchange. The great master of 'universal interdependence' should be free from suspicion on this score.

70 This is obvious. If a change in the rate of interest involves, in principle at least, rearrangements of all real and monetary magnitudes in the system, then the postulate that the *encaisse désirée* should remain untouched is equivalent to introducing another condition that will in general make the system overdetermined and, in this sense, spell contradiction.

71 The main motive seems to have been a wish to gain possession of a simple form of 'quantity theory.'

so easily redirected at a moment's notice, we cannot help thinking of them all the same. Under these conditions the practical value of the final result, at which we arrive nevertheless, is no doubt much reduced. It reads: both for a *numéraire* and for a money economy, Walras' system of the economic process is determined and stable, though he did not quite succeed in proving this rigorously; for a process which is stationary except for positive or negative investment on traditional lines, it is hitchless in the sense defined above, and full employment of resources is in fact one of its properties; conclusions other than these can be arrived at only by introducing hypotheses at variance with those of Walras.[72] If in the last analysis Walras' system is perhaps nothing but a huge research program, it still is, owing to its intellectual quality, the basis of practically all the best work of our own time.

8. The Production Function

All that remains to be said about the period's work on the higher levels of theoretical analysis may be grouped conveniently around the two sets of data that were the two pillars of the classical temple of 1900, the given tastes of consumers and the given technological possibilities within the horizon of producers. The former topic will be dealt with in the appendix to this chapter, the latter best fits in here. In both cases we shall be only supplementing what, for a lower level of analytic rigor, we have already learned before. In both

[72] This may be illustrated by the question of the possibility of underemployment of labor *in equilibrium* that has played so conspicuous a role in the Keynesian controversy. In the Walrasian system such underemployment is possible only if the Walrasian supply conditions of labor are replaced by the hypothesis that wage rates are 'rigid downwards' at a figure higher than the Walrasian equilibrium figure. But we may add the further hypothesis that, if rigidity be removed, the fall in wages that would ensue fails to attain equilibrium because this fall *may* so reduce firms' receipts or, even without doing so, create such pessimistic anticipations as to induce shrinkage of operations all round so that the falling wage rates would never catch up with the ever-falling equilibrium level. We may reach a similar result, given some wage rigidity, by assuming that capitalists, while bent on saving without any regard to returns, are unwilling to accept the current returns to investment and wish to hold whatever they have decided to save 'in the form of immediate, liquid command (i.e. in money or its equivalent)' (Keynes, *General Theory*, p. 166). Whatever we may think of the realistic virtues of such assumptions, the point to be kept in mind is that, even if accepted, they would not invalidate Walras' theory within *his* assumptions. In particular, they would not prove that the Walrasian 'condition of full employment'—which is not a postulate but a theorem—makes *his* system overdeterminate and, in this sense, self-contradictory. It should be added again that economists who wish to establish a tendency in the capitalist economy to produce perennial unemployment have nothing to fear from a proof that, on so high a level of abstraction, *perfect* equilibrium in *perfect* competition would involve full employment. Nor has this proof itself anything to fear from the ubiquity of unemployment in a world that is never in perfect equilibrium and never perfectly competitive.

cases I shall carry the story to the present situation. In both cases I shall have to be sketchy to the point of incorrectness.[1]

[(a) *The Meaning of the Concept*.] We begin by recalling the concept of a production function as it is commonly used today. Suppose that a business man A *contemplates* producing a well-defined commodity X at the rate of $\bar{x}$ per unit of time in a single plant *that is to be constructed for this purpose*. This may require a unique set of rates of inputs per unit of time—such as $\bar{v}_1, \bar{v}_2, \cdots \bar{v}_n$ of the equally well-defined services $V_1, V_2, \cdots V_n$—that are technologically fixed like the Walrasian coefficients of production and define for us economists the only 'process' or 'method' of production that is available. As a rule, however, there exist several or even infinitely many such processes or methods of production by which $\bar{x}$ can be produced. Each of them is identified by a distinct set of time rates of inputs—again, for us economists: should it happen that two or more technologically different processes use exactly the same combination of rates of inputs in order to produce $\bar{x}$, they would be the same process for us. Mr. A will choose between these possibilities with a view to minimizing the total cost of producing $\bar{x}$ and hence reject from the outset all those processes that use more of *all* the (scarce) services $V_1, V_2, \cdots V_n$ than does another. Among the rest, which we may call the eligible choices, he will choose according to the price situation he expects to prevail in the factor markets during the period for which he plans.

The complete list of all those eligible choices, with which A or his consulting engineer is fully familiar, defines A's or his engineer's technological horizon.[2] Allowing the $\bar{v}$'s to vary continuously and smoothly [3] and letting $\bar{x}$ vary continuously and smoothly also, we may express a man's technological horizon by setting up a transformation function of the form, $x = f(v_1, v_2, \cdots v_n)$, which we call the production function and which associates with any given set of the v_i's$(i = 1, 2, \cdots n)$ a definite maximum value of x which it is possible for him to produce with the given set. Any change in the technological horizon, for example, caused by the discovery of a new process or even by some known process becoming commercially available which was not so before, destroys this production function and replaces it by another. All this is quite simple, and it should be fairly obvious which properties we are to assign to the production function on the various levels of abstraction that are prescribed

[1] My inability to present an account of either topic that would be at the same time brief, elementary, and correct—an inability of which I was never fully aware before I put that appendix and this section into their final shapes—had to be stressed because it illustrates so tellingly the conditions in both fields, in which faltering advance was incessantly being undone by mutual misunderstandings between workers—attended with unnecessary peevishness—and all but universal unwillingness to pull the same way. Confusion went so far as to make it difficult, sometimes, to make sure what writers really meant e.g. by the marginal productivity theory.

[2] From this must be distinguished the firm's (or anybody's) time horizon, i.e. the time span over which it plans. The concept of a time horizon has been introduced by Tinbergen.

[3] A continuous function has no jumps, a smooth function has no kinks.

to us by the requirements of the particular problems we wish to investigate. Thus, when we are high up in thin air and hunting for the 'purest' features of the logic of production, we shall assume, as we have just done, that production functions are continuous and also that they are differentiable twice in all directions.[4] Reality very frequently fails to correspond to these assumptions. But this is no objection so long as we are concerned with the pure logic of production. It becomes an objection only when we apply results, derived by means of them, to patterns and problems for which discontinuity and non-existence of partial derivatives of the first and second order are relevant: there is no sense whatever in either asserting the presence of continuity and differentiability or denying it for all patterns and all problems. Neglect of this trivial truth has been an unbelievably fertile source of futile controversy to this day and has impeded analytic advance in a manner that is most interesting from the standpoint of the student of 'scientific progress' and of the 'ways of the human mind.' In order to bring out this aspect it will be convenient to touch first upon a number of points as they present themselves today in order to clear the ground (or part of it) for our story of the historical development and in order to supply to the reader information that may help him to appreciate it. Some modern expositions of the theory of production and cost (mainly of static aspects) are listed for reference in the footnote below.[5]

(1) We have come to distrust the idea of any well-defined commodity or service. Moreover, firms do not as a rule produce just one commodity in one quality but many commodities in many qualities, and ability to shift their production from one to the other is obviously an important consideration in the choice of a productive set-up.[6] Finally, a change in the combination of productive services will frequently affect of itself the quality or even kind of the commodity a firm produces. To some extent, this may be taken into account by admitting many commodities ($x_1, x_2, \cdots x_m$) into the production function and by writing the latter in the implicit form, $\varphi(x_1, x_2, \cdots x_m; v_1,$

[4] That is, we shall assume that, v_i and v_j being representative productive services ($i, j = 1, 2, \cdots n$), all expressions of the forms $\frac{\delta x}{\delta v_i}, \frac{\delta^2 x}{\delta v_i^2},$ and $\frac{\delta^2 x}{\delta v_i \, \delta v_j}$ exist and are continuous.

[5] R. G. D. Allen, *Mathematical Analysis for Economists* (1938); on the production function and constant-product curves, see especially pp. 284-9, which are readily understandable for non-mathematicians and reading of which would greatly facilitate the perusal of this section. J. R. Hicks, *Value and Capital* (2nd ed., 1946), especially Part II. P. A. Samuelson, *Foundations of Economic Analysis* (1947), particularly ch. 4, perusal of which, strongly recommended, requires some mathematics, but very little. E. Schneider, *Theorie der Produktion* (1934). Gerhard Tintner, 'A Contribution to the Nonstatic Theory of Production' (with an excellent summary of the static theory) in *Studies in Mathematical Economics and Econometrics* (H. Schultz memorial vol.), 1942.

[6] Louis M. Court, 'Entrepreneurial and Consumer Demand Theories for Commodity Spectra' (*Econometrica*, April and July-October 1941) has considered the case of infinitely many commodities, an idea of great importance.

$v_2, \cdots v_n) = 0$. This has been done by Allen, Hicks, Leontief, Tintner, and others.

(2) If we wish to base our theory of production on the Jevons-Böhm-Taussig theory of the 'roundabout' process, we may introduce time explicitly into the production function, that is by writing: $x = \psi(v_1, v_2, \cdots v_n; t)$. This practice is strongly suggested by Wicksell's treatment of capital problems and has been adopted by several modern authors. (See e.g. Allen, op. cit. p. 362.)[7] Evidently, however, there are other characteristics of a firm's technological pattern besides rates of inputs and time: the rates of change of these rates, lags in some of them, cumulation (integrals) of others, outputs that are expected not for the immediate but the more distant future, may all be significant. Without going into these problems, we will advert to the practice of inserting shift parameters ($\alpha, \beta, \cdots$) into the production function, which then looks like this: $x = f(v_1, v_2, \cdots v_n; \alpha, \beta, \cdots)$. This amounts to not more than a purely formal recognition of the fact that production functions do change in time. The practice may justify itself any day, of course, but so far it seems to me that this fact is equally well expressed by saying, as we said above, that an innovation destroys a production function and sets up a new one.[8]

(3) For the economist a process or method of production is defined by the independent variables in the production function, even though this may amount to throwing together what are very different processes or methods to the engineer: this practice simply means that technological differences per se are without interest for us. But it follows that we must include all the productive services that may be required for any of the eligible methods of producing a commodity, although some of these methods may require services that are not required for others. This creates a difficulty that has induced some theorists (see, e.g., Schneider, op. cit. p. 1) to include in the production function only those processes or methods that use the same services (though in different proportions) and to define the technological horizon not by one production function but by many.

More important, however, is another point. As defined, our production function refers only to a single firm—strictly, only to a single unit of production

[7] The treatment of time as an independent variable fits well also into the Marshallian system, although for other reasons. But though Marshall so treated it in his verbal statements, he did not do so in his mathematical formulations, except of course for value problems—which is a different matter.

[8] If, in the manner of Marshall and Hicks, we form a separate category of those innovations that are 'induced' by mere expansion of production—which must not be confused with simple changes to methods of production that are within the firm's technological horizon from the first but do not pay until a certain output figure has been reached—we do in fact recognize an intermediate class of cases which it is useful to separate out for some purposes. But so long as it is not possible to foresee the effects of induced innovations exactly, there is no point in introducing them into the production function or into cost curves. If it is possible to foresee these effects exactly, then induced innovations must be already within the horizon and need not be 'introduced.'

or 'plant' [9]—and not to the economy as a whole. But throughout that period and even today, it was and is common practice to reason as if there were such a thing as a social production function,[10] and it is not difficult to see the reason why: we obviously wish to speak of a 'social' marginal productivity when expounding the theory of distributive shares. And so most of the leaders of that period, among them Böhm-Bawerk, J. B. Clark, Wicksteed, and Wicksell, took the existence of an aggregative (social) production function for granted, at least by implication, without realizing that the logical right to use this concept must be acquired by proof.[11] Many modern authors, especially those of the Keynesian type, are just as careless.

(4) Mathematically, the production function enters the theoretical set-up—in order to yield demand functions for productive services, see for example Allen, op. cit. pp. 369 et seq.—as a restriction upon firms' behavior: these strive to maximize net profits *subject* to the possibilities listed in the production function. We might try to crowd into a single expression the whole of the technological facts that, for any purpose in hand, seem relevant to us. But even where this is possible, it is much more convenient to make a single relation basic—we shall of course choose one that has some primary economic significance; of this presently—and then to introduce the other facts (hypotheses) that are to be taken into account as further restrictions or, as we may say, as restrictions upon the restriction that we regard as fundamental. The best way of making this clear is as follows. Suppose we have n services [12] which define a 'production surface' in $(n + 1)$ dimensional hyperspace. In general we shall find that firms cannot move about freely over the whole of this surface and that technological conditions permit choice only within the boundaries of a certain region. Thus there may be 'limitational factors,' which must, by technological necessity, be always used in strict proportion to the quantity of product or to the quantity of some other factor (R. Frisch); there

[9] The problem of production functions for concerns that operate more than one plant will be excluded from consideration in order to save space. Some work has, however, been done on it of late.

[10] Marshall and Walras were really the only authors whose argument, carefully scrutinized, turns out to be free from any implications of this kind.

[11] To overlook this was perhaps natural for those literary economists who did not have any explicit concept of the production function at all. It was less natural for Wicksteed and Wicksell. But we must not forget that, under conditions of pure competition, the equilibrium relations between the marginal physical productivities realized in different firms and industries are easy to establish and that this is all that was required for their purposes: Marshall's 'marginal shepherd' was well qualified to represent the marginal productivity of his kind of labor in any employment, hence the social productivity of this kind of labor in general.

[12] Of course, if we consider scarce services only, account must be taken of cases in which it depends on the extent of firms' demand whether a given service is scarce or not: water may cease to be 'free' in a given spot if firms need more than a certain amount of it. We have touched upon this point already in another connection.

may be also restrictions of other types (A. Smithies).[13] We shall return to this in a moment, but must now advert to a particular short-run type of these additional restrictions, the importance of which for the theory of marginal productivity has been pointed out by Professor Smithies.

I have emphasized the fact that the full logical meaning of the concept of production functions reveals itself only if we think of them as 'planning' functions in a world of blueprints, where every element that is technologically variable at all can be changed at will, without any loss of time, and without any expense.

But whenever we apply the concept, as we certainly wish to do, to firms that own going concerns and are already committed to plant, equipment, and perhaps part of an existing administrative apparatus, then, according to the time we allow for adaptation, those elements of their existing set-up that are resistant to change will act upon technological choice as further restrictions.[14] To assume them away will bring us back into the sphere of pure logic and not alter the fact that reality will fail to correspond to the theoretical model and to the theorems, especially the marginal productivity theorems, that are derived from the model; and to allow time for full adaptation—Marshall's method of dealing with this situation—will not help us either, because during the lapse of the necessary time other disturbances will occur that will prevent correspondence to the model from ever being brought about. It is as important to realize the inevitable discrepancies between theory and fact that must result from this as it is to realize that they do not constitute a valid objection to the former; it is no valid objection to the law of gravitation that my watch that lies on my table does not move toward the center of the earth, though economists who are not professionally theorists sometimes argue as if it were.

(5) It is therefore under exceptionally favorable circumstances only that we can observe 'logically pure' production functions. This is the case particularly in agriculture, where we have not only observational but also experimental material with which to construct them. But whenever we try to do so from observations of going concerns alone, we meet difficulties similar to those that we meet in trying to construct statistical demand curves and cannot in general expect—not at any rate without taking special precautions—that we get the production functions of economic theory. Nevertheless and in spite of the errors in interpretation to which they may give rise,[15] 'realistic' production

[13] R. Frisch, 'Einige Punkte einer Preistheorie . . .' *Zeitschrift für Nationalökonomie*, September 1931. A. Smithies, 'The Boundaries of the Production Function and the Utility Function,' *Explorations in Economics, Notes and Essays Contributed in Honor of F. W. Taussig* (1936).

[14] Marshall was well aware of this fact and of its importance for the interpretation of actual business behavior. See his Pittsburgh gas case, Smithies op. cit. p. 328.

[15] One of these errors stems from the observation, in itself quite correct, that a going plant, designed for a particular output and for a particular process of production, is often very rigid and leaves little room for adaptations to new situations of the productive combination it embodies, especially to changes in relative prices of services. Consideration of these relative prices, as foreseen at the time when the plant was erected, is embodied (often subconsciously) in the set-up of the plant itself.

functions are of great importance. They help to destroy the layman's impression that production functions and marginal productivity schedules are just theorists' fictions. They confront us with new problems and shed light on the stretch of road before us. For examples I refer the reader to the report of a committee of the Econometric Society published in *Econometrica* (April 1936) by its chairman, Mr. E. H. Phelps Brown.

[(b) *The Evolution of the Concept.*] As we have seen in the preceding chapter and in Parts II and III, schedules of marginal productivity, in terms of physical and of value products, have been in use ever since the times of Turgot and even before. The production function itself appeared in 'classic' times under the name of the State of the Arts—it being recognized that certain arguments hold only if technological knowledge is assumed to be constant. The most important of these arguments was the law of decreasing returns from land, but already Ricardo, by recognizing that 'real values' of commodities are 'regulated' by the 'real difficulties' encountered by the least-favored firm, pointed toward a wider generalization. And then there was what Marshall called Thünen's 'great law of substitution.' All this had still to find its proper relation to the principle of marginal *utility*, but the rest looks to the backward glance—apart from the more difficult problems that lurk behind even the simplest case—like a fairly easy task of polishing, co-ordinating, and developing existing ideas, all of which were to be found, in one form or another, in J. S. Mill's *Principles* or, at all events, in Mill plus Thünen. The Austrians accomplished this in their way and Marshall in his.[16] In Marshall's *Principles* we find in fact, though he did not avail himself of the production function explicitly, a very complete and properly qualified marginal productivity theory of the firm and of distribution, and in addition many indications that he saw the problems beyond.[17] If we take in his treatment of the subject fully, even in the

[16] Two other contributions should be mentioned here that seem to have remained almost unnoticed for a reason that is highly characteristic for the conditions prevailing in our field—their brevity: A. Berry in a paper on the 'Pure Theory of Distribution,' read before section F of the British Association for the Advancement of Science and published in its *Report*, 1890, presented 'equations of marginal productivity' that equated prices of productive services to marginal physical productivities multiplied by the prices of products. And Edgeworth, in 1889 and then again in 1894 (see *Papers* II, p. 298 and III, 54) did the same. Both use production functions explicitly and present the equalities referred to as elements of a comprehensive equilibrium system. Neither received much credit for what must be listed as a considerable achievement. Professor Stigler, however, noticed them both (*Production and Distribution Theories*, pp. 132 and 322). Owing to their close relation to Marshall and, especially in Edgeworth's case, to all other builders in that field, it seems hopeless to try to appraise individual 'rights.' But their contributions help us to realize the breadth of the wave, at the crest of which stands Marshall's work.

[17] Professor Stigler (op. cit. ch. 12) has shown very well how Marshall, pushing his way slowly through traditional underbrush, ended up by accepting eventually the whole of the marginal productivity apparatus. If, however, he would never admit the full extent to which he actually did so, this is, I think, adequately explained by (1) his re-

form given to it in the first edition of his *Principles*, we cannot help feeling some surprise at the statements at the beginning of Wicksteed's *Essay*, to wit, that 'in investigating the laws of distribution it has been usual to take each of the great factors of production . . . to inquire into . . . the special nature of the service that it renders and . . . to deduce a special law regulating [its] share of the product' and to unify these laws on the basis of 'the common fact of service rendered.'[18] But Wicksteed, dropping Marshall's wise hesitations and qualifications and writing down the production function explicitly, did set forth boldly the naked logic of the matter and also attempted a proof of the propositions—both of them guardedly affirmed but not proved by Marshall—that every 'factor's' distributive share will under ideal conditions tend to equal its quantity multiplied by its marginal degree of productivity; and that those shares will tend to sum up to (to 'exhaust') the net product of every firm and, in the sphere of social aggregates, Marshall's 'national dividend.' Now, both propositions are equilibrium propositions and need not hold outside of the point of equilibrium, assuming that one exists. Marshall was of course aware of this but it was left for Wicksell to state it explicitly.[19] Wicksteed, however, based his proof on the sufficient but not necessary postulate that the production function is homogeneous of the first order, in which case the 'exhaustion theorem' would hold identically, that is, all along the line and not only in equilibrium.[20] He did recant later on (see *Common Sense of Po-*

---

luctance to throw in his lot with the non-English economists who did the same thing; (2) his justifiable aversion to assigning a 'causal' role to the partial coefficients of the production function; and (3) his awareness of conceptual difficulties, some of which were alluded to above.

[18] P. H. Wicksteed, *An Essay on the Co-ordination of the Laws of Distribution* (1894), p. 7. If the statements above are hardly fair to Marshall, they are strikingly unfair to Walras and even to J. B. Say. The irritation that Walras displayed in his 'Note sur la réfutation de le théorie anglaise du fermage [rent of land] de M. Wicksteed' (*Recueil publié par la Faculté de Droit de l'Université de Lausanne*, 1896, republ. as *appendice* III of the 3rd ed. of his *Éléments*, but left out in the 4th, which, however, contains the new no. 326 on marginal productivity) is therefore less unjustified than Professor Stigler declares it is. Moreover it is a misunderstanding to think that Walras claimed personal priority for the theory of marginal productivity as defined by himself. As far as this goes, the note on p. 376 of the *Éléments* is conclusive.

[19] See his *Lectures* I, p. 129. Professor Stigler's exposition of Wicksell's share in the solution of the 'modern' marginal productivity theory—I call it 'modern' in order to distinguish it from that of Longfield and Thünen—is very interesting because it shows how difficult it is, even for first-class minds, to grasp and appreciate relatively new ideas that have already been displayed in broad daylight. Wicksell might have learned all or nearly all that was to be learned from Marshall and the Austrians. But it took him another decade, after having himself adumbrated the theory in 1893, to arrive at his final view of the matter (see Stigler pp. 373 et seq.), in part, as an acknowledgment shows, with the help of Professor D. Davidson.

[20] A function of two or more independent variables is called homogeneous of the first order or 'linear and homogeneous' in all or some of these variables if, when these increase or decrease in a given common proportion—for instance when they are multiplied by a constant λ—the dependent variable increases or decreases also in the same

litical Economy, p. 373n.) but without carrying out the alterations that this recantation would have called for. Before going on we had better see what happened at about the same time in Lausanne.

Remember that Walras originally used what may be called a degenerate production function, that is, a production function restricted to technologically fixed and *constant* coefficients of production. In 1894, Barone suggested to him the idea of turning these technological constants into economic variables and of introducing, for the determination of these, a new relation, the *équation de fabrication*, which was to express the fact that, if some coefficients are decreased, output may be maintained by an appropriate compensatory increase of others: the new 'unknowns,' that is the new variable coefficients, were then to be determined by means of the condition that costs be minimized for any given output and any given factor prices. Barone himself started work on these lines and published two installments of a corresponding theory of distribution ('Studi sulla distribuzione: la prima approssimazione sintetica') in the *Giornale degli Economisti*, February and March 1896,[21] without however going on with it—we shall presently see why. Walras had already glanced at variability of coefficients of production in connection with his theory of 'economic progress,' which he defined (in contrast to 'technological progress') as progressive substitution of the services of capital goods for services of 'land.' He then reproduced Barone's suggestion in his 'Note' of 1896 (mentioned above) and in the new no. 326 of the fourth edition (1900) of the *Éléments*. There he formulated 'the theory of marginal productivity' in three propositions of which the

proportion. Call x the product as before, although now this x, standing for the total national dividend, would raise very delicate index-number problems, and $(v_1, v_2, \cdots v_n)$ the quantities of scarce factors used in producing x. Then the production function, $x = f(v_1, v_2, \cdots v_n)$ is said to be homogeneous of the first order if $\lambda x = f(\lambda v_1, \lambda v_2, \cdots \lambda v_n)$ for any point $(v_1, v_2, \cdots v_n)$ and any λ. In this particular case the relation, $x = v_1 \frac{\delta x}{\delta v_1} + v_2 \frac{\delta x}{\delta v_2} + \cdots + v_n \frac{\delta x}{\delta v_n}$, holds over the whole interval in which the x-function exists. This is Euler's theorem, or rather a special case of Euler's theorem, on homogeneous functions. Identifying the $\frac{\delta x}{\delta v_i}$'s with the various factors' marginal degrees of physical productivity, we see that their shares exhaust the social product over the whole of that interval and whatever the amount of the product, although all that we can aver in cases not linear and homogeneous is that they do so in the equilibrium point. Translating this into economic terms, first-order homogeneity means that there are neither economies nor diseconomies of scale, or that large- and small-scale production is equally efficient, or that there are 'constant returns to scale.' In itself this implies nothing, of course, about what happens when only one of the 'factors' is increased, the others remaining constant, i.e. about the shape of each 'factor's' marginal productivity curve. Note that, since λ is arbitrary, we may put it equal to the reciprocal of any of the v_i's, e.g., to $\frac{1}{v_1}$. Then the production function reads: $\frac{x}{v_1} = f(1, \frac{v_2}{v_1}, \cdots \frac{v_n}{v_1})$, i.e. the average productivities of all 'factors' are functions of the proportions but not of the absolute amounts in which they are used.

[21] See Stigler, op. cit. pp. 357 et seq.

last was omitted, without warning, or motivation, from the *édition définitive* (1926): (1) free competition brings about minimum average costs; (2) in equilibrium *and* if average cost equals price, the prices of productive services are proportional to the partial derivatives of any production function [that contains only substitutional (compensatory) services] or to the marginal productivities; (3) the whole amount of product is distributed among the productive services.[22] In 1897 (*Cours* II, §§ 714-19) Pareto criticized the marginal productivity theory—mainly on the ground that it breaks down in the case of what are now called limitational factors—and blocked out a theory that covered all the more important possibilities and which was technically improved in the *Manuel*. But he looked upon this not as an improvement—especially not as an improvement on Walrasian lines—but as a renunciation of the marginal productivity theory, which in the *Résumé* of his Paris course (1901) he declared 'erroneous.' It was necessary to inflict these details upon the reader because they serve to clarify the situation in the late 1890's.[23]

By 1900, then, the production function had established itself, as a result of the efforts of many minds,[24] in its key position, alongside the utility func

[22] In proposition (2) I have italicized the word 'and'; and I have inserted the proviso that only substitutional factors are included because this was clearly Walras' meaning, as a preceding sentence on the same page (375) shows, where he explicitly recognized the existence of other, non-substitutional ones. I think that both alterations only emphasize Walras' true meaning. But I am unable to offer an explanation why, changing his careless (and meaningless) original statement that each service's rate of remuneration is 'equal' to the partial derivative of the production function into the statement that it is proportional to it, he did not say what the factor of proportionality is, namely, in full equilibrium of pure competition, the price of the product. And I am also unable to say why, seeing that he imposed the condition that total receipts be equal to total cost, he dropped the exhaustion theorem which follows from this condition. Observe that, since firms will always try to minimize total cost, whatever their output, propositions (1) and (2) hold also for outputs other than the equilibrium output of pure competition. Then the factor of proportionality is no longer product price, but is still marginal cost.

[23] The reader finds many further details in Stigler's work (especially pp. 323 et seq.) and in H. Schultz, 'Marginal Productivity and the General Pricing Process,' *Journal of Political Economy*, October 1929. This paper contains much useful information and especially the simplest exposition in English of Pareto's theory of production. Unfortunately it is also misleading not only in individual points but also in the total impression it conveys. In this respect, perusal of J. R. Hicks's 'Marginal Productivity and the Principle of Variation,' *Economica*, February 1932, and of the subsequent controversy between Hicks and Schultz (ibid. August 1932) would provide an antidote.

[24] It is hardly possible to be more specific than that. The names of Berry, Edgeworth, Marshall, Barone, Walras, and Wicksteed all enter in some way or another when we discuss this difficult case of paternity. Remember, we are now discussing the birth of the production function as such and not the older or newer marginal productivity ideas that had more or less definitely pointed toward it for a century or more. The Walras-Barone *équation de fabrication* is of course nothing but a particular form of the production function.

tion, as the second of the two descriptive functions that I have called the two pillars of the classic theory of that time.[25] The old 'laws of returns,' properly generalized and polished, lay at hand to supply the properties which the production function was to enjoy, either generally or 'normally,' and which we shall now restate again. If we wish to define marginal productivity of a service as the partial derivative of the production function with respect to the quantity of that service, we must, as has been pointed out already, assume first of all that these partial derivatives exist. We may postulate in addition that they are positive, that is, that a small increase in the quantity of any services will increase the quantity of the product.[26] Following Turgot we may postulate further that this rate of increase itself increases at first $\left(\frac{\delta^2 f}{\delta v_i^2} > 0\right)$, then passes through a single maximum and, after having reached this point, keeps on declining $\left(\frac{\delta^2 f}{\delta v_i^2} < 0\text{; law of decreasing returns in the primary sense}\right)$. In this case two corollaries follow: (1) there exists a point beyond which the average productivity of every service (x/v_i) decreases also (law of decreasing returns in the secondary sense); (2) cross derivatives are positive, which means that if I increase the quantity of a productive service v_i by a small amount, this will not only decrease (after the point indicated) its own marginal productivity but also increase the marginal productivities of all the other productive services $\left(\frac{\delta^2 f}{\delta v_i \delta v_j} > 0\right)$

A methodological remark may be usefully inserted here. Among the properties to be assigned to the production function, there are some that follow from others and therefore may be 'proved deductively' or 'stated as theorems.' Thus decrease of average productivity (after a certain point) may be deduced from, or proved by, the decrease of marginal productivity and there is then no need for any *separate* observational or experimental proof. Thus Wicksell (see his article in the Thünen Archiv, 1909) was right in holding, and F. Waterstradt (ibid.) was wrong in denying, that the 'law' of decreasing average productivity follows from other properties of the production function which we usually assume. But, though we have in general some latitude in deciding which properties we wish to postulate and which we wish to formulate as

[25] See first sentence of this section. By using this simile, I do not mean to deny that from some standpoints, especially the Austrian one, there is reason to object to looking upon the utility and production functions as completely equal in analytic status, and something to be said for regarding utility as the one and only pillar of the building.

[26] Beyond an 'operative interval' this need not be so of course: so many workmen may be already employed in a plant that additional workers would reduce output—everybody treading on the toes of somebody else. It does not make any real difference whether this possibility is expressed by saying that after a certain point marginal productivity becomes negative or by saying that, since no employer, if a free agent and acting upon the rules of economic logic, will take on any service increments that will decrease output, marginal productivity cannot fall below zero. For certain purposes the first alternative is preferable.

theorems, this is not always so. Thus, there is no economic *axiom* that would imply the proposition that physical marginal productivity (after a point) decreases monotonically. And in any case we always have to postulate some propositions for which, within a deductive sector of our (or any) science, it is not possible to provide logical proof. This raises the question of their status or nature. Formally they enter as hypotheses (or as definitions in B. Russell's sense), which on principle we can frame at will. But when, with a view to application, we ask whether they are 'true' or 'valid,' that is, whether results arrived at by means of them may be expected to be verifiable (in general or with respect to certain phenomena or aspects of phenomena), then there are only two possibilities: they may be deductively provable in some wider system that transcends economics or its deductive sector, or they must be established by observation or experiment. This is the case of the proposition that asserts decrease (after a point) of the marginal productivities of productive services in function of the quantities of these services. This means that when we assert this proposition we are asserting a fact and this imposes upon us the duty of factual verification. Of course evidence for such a proposition may be so overwhelming that we may refuse the challenge as vexatious. But since there is no logically binding rule for deciding what is and what is not vexatious, we must on principle be always prepared to meet the challenge: we have no *logical* right to reply that the challenged proposition is 'obvious'; and we are committing a definite error, if we call it 'evident.' For us, these truths are important because they have been and are frequently sinned against in the matter of 'laws of returns': we shall presently see an interesting instance of this is the discussion on first-order homogeneity. Let us note in passing that here we are brushing against an interesting problem of general epistemology.

I take this opportunity to mention Edgeworth's analysis of the 'laws of return' (published originally in the *Economic Journal*, 1911; republished in *Papers Relating to Political Economy*, vol. I, pp. 61 et seq. and 151 et seq.), which has been rightly called one of his most important contributions to economic theory by Professor Stigler (op. cit. pp. 112 et seq. to which the reader is referred). It is as interesting to note that Edgeworth had still to struggle for the recognition of quite elementary matters such as that the 'law' of diminishing returns does not apply to land only, as it is to note that Edgeworth, whose chief merit it was to teach the distinction between decreasing marginal and decreasing average returns, had repeatedly confused the two himself and that his presentation in the paper in question is not correct in every detail. The matter was taken up again by Karl Menger (the mathematician, son of the economist) in his 'Bemerkungen zu den Ertragsgesetzen' (two articles in *Zeitschrift für Nationalökonomie*, March and August, 1936; see also a comment by K. Schlesinger, ibid.). We must be grateful to the eminent mathematician for the lesson on slovenly thinking which he administered to us and which may serve as a shining example of the general tendency toward increased rigor that is an important characteristic of the economics of our own period. But in effect, the logical crimes revealed—except the confusion between decreasing marginal and average returns—have hardly been productive of serious errors in results. Even as regards that confusion it should be mentioned that, though no less a thinker than Böhm-Bawerk committed it, it remained quite harmless in his case, for he reasoned correctly about decreasing marginal returns to his roundabout process.

The reader will have no difficulty in understanding why it was that the properties of the production function—that is, the use of a production function that constitutes the only relation between the productive services employed, all of which are assumed to be 'substitutional'—recommended themselves to theorists, particularly for classroom and textbook purposes. Such a production function is easy to handle and yields simple results. Moreover it picks up, from the mass of relevant technological facts, just those that are subject to *economic* choice and thus serves well to display the *economic* logic of production. It cannot be repeated too often that this production function is valid only on a high level of abstraction, for planned and not for existing plants, and for a limited region of the production surface at that. But on that level, and for that range, it is an advantage and not a blemish that it discards all the cases in which the economic logic is thwarted by additional restrictions of a purely technological nature. These additional restrictions exist however, even in the stage of planning an enterprise; many more impose limits upon long-run and still more upon short-run adaptations of existing concerns; and as we approach the patterns of real business life we lose that pure logic more and more from sight, especially because the restrictions prevent even immediately adaptable services—such as labor that can be hired by the week or day or hour—and their prices from behaving according to the marginal productivity rules, even apart from the facts that perfect equilibrium and pure competition are never fully realized. And the reader will also understand that some economists will express this situation by saying: 'the marginal productivity theory is of universal application on a high level of abstraction,' whereas other economists will prefer to say: 'the marginal productivity theory is erroneous.' Barring the regrettably frequent cases of failure to grasp the meaning of the theory, this is all there is to the controversy on the production side of 'marginalism' that has been carried on to this day.[27] In particular, all that Pareto

[27] Telling illustrations of this statement may be gleaned, e.g., from the controversy between Professor R. A. Lester, 'Shortcomings of Marginal Analysis for Wage-Employment Problems' (*American Economic Review*, March 1946) and Professors F. Machlup, 'Marginal Analysis and Empirical Research' (ibid. September 1946) and G. J. Stigler, 'Professor Lester and the Marginalists' (ibid. March 1947, where the reader also finds Lester's reply to Machlup and the latter's rejoinder). In this connection a warning to the reader suggests itself: in appraising an author's view on marginal productivity theory it is always necessary to make sure what an author means by this term: Pareto and Stigler, e.g., seem in places to mean only theories that *assume* all 'factors' to be connected by one relation only, this relation expressing universal substitutability. Statements may be true of *this* marginal productivity that are not true of marginal productivity theories that admit also other relations between the factors. The latter is the meaning adopted here. For instance, Walras' original theory, which worked with constant coefficients of production and admitted no substitution except the substitution of production of a product for production of another product, and Wieser's theory which did the same are still marginal productivity theories for us. This is important to remember: the circumstance that a theory includes boundary conditions, which will

can have meant by renouncing the marginal productivity theory is that we cannot be content to deal with the case of substitutable services—the case of the single substitutional relation—any more than we can be content to deal with the case of constant coefficients, but that we must take both into account and, in addition, cases in which coefficients of production vary with the quantity produced [28]—which simply amounts to saying that the fundamental analytic schema that uses nothing but the substitutional relation needs to be supplemented if we wish to approach reality more closely,[29] but remains valid within its proper sphere.

[(c) *The Hypothesis of First-Order Homogeneity.*] If, following Wicksteed, we further endow the production function with first-order homogeneity, that is, if we assume that there are no economies or diseconomies of scale, we secure further simplifications which explain why many authors cling to it,[30] even though it is generally recognized by now that we do not need it for proving that distribution according to marginal productivity rules will just exhaust the product. Again I have to report a long, inconclusive, and unnecessarily

---

prevent some factors from earning at the rate of marginal physical productivity multiplied by either the prices of the product or the marginal revenue, *does not prevent us from calling this theory a marginal productivity theory.*

[28] This led him to define the coefficients of production in a new way, which is useful only if we wish to retain these coefficients while getting rid of the assumption of their constancy. He expressed the quantities of productive services employed as functions of the quantities of products. His coefficients of production are then the partial derivatives of these functions with respect to the various services (*Manuel,* p. 607). A similar idea was used by W. E. Johnson ('The Pure Theory of Utility Curves,' *Economic Journal,* December 1913) and in some respects generalized by A. W. Zotoff ('Notes on the Mathematical Theory of Production,' ibid. March 1923, a brilliant contribution, the neglect of which might provide subject matter for another homily about the manner in which economists work). Neither author acknowledged indebtedness to Pareto.

[29] In trying to do so we discover of course that the range within which 'factors' can be substituted for one another rapidly decreases as we make factors more and more specific. With the time-honored triad of the services of land, labor, and capital, substitutability holds almost unrestricted sway. When it comes to Douglas fir lumber, dentists, and cutting tools, it almost vanishes in the short run. This merely means that we must state, in each instance, what type of factors, of periods, and of problems we have in mind, and there should be no reason for quarreling either about marginal productivity or about 'method' in general. It sounds almost incredible and yet it is the fact, nevertheless, that this has remained a source of controversy to this day—of controversy that was, in part at least, kept alive and embittered because both parties erroneously believed that there was a political interest at stake.

[30] In order to satisfy himself of this the reader need only observe the frequency with which first-order homogeneity turns up (sometimes unnecessarily) in Professor Allen's treatment of problems of production and distribution (see his *Mathematical Analysis for Economists,* passim). A still more telling instance is Professor Hicks's 'Distribution and Economic Progress,' *Review of Economic Studies,* October 1936. One of the most important of these simplifications refers to the coefficient of elasticity of substitution.

acrimonious discussion [31] which hardly deserves more than the following comments.

First of all, he who asserts first-order homogeneity of the production function asserts a fact, at least hypothetically. Since this fact is not implied in any of the other properties that, in general, normally, or for particular purposes we have previously agreed to attribute to the production function,[32] it can be established or denied only by factual evidence if at all. Edgeworth's early criticism of Wicksteed's use of first-order homogeneity is indeed disfigured by misplaced irony. But it had at least the merit of realizing correctly that it is facts and not speculations which are needed to refute the hypothesis: this is why he hunted for contradicting instances. The vast majority of participants in the discussion, however, have tried to this day to 'prove' or to 'refute' it by logical argument or by appeal to its obviousness or lack of obviousness,[33] which inevitably leads into deadlock.

Second, we must not forget that asserting (denying) the practical possibility of multiplying all 'factors' by a constant λ is one thing; and asserting (denying) that output would also be multiplied by λ, if it were practically possible to multiply all 'factors' by λ, is quite another thing.[34] Nobody denies that the

[31] It is not possible—and neither would it be profitable—to follow this discussion in detail. Therefore I shall mention here, besides Wicksteed and his earliest and most severe critic, Edgeworth, only a few modern contributions, namely: F. H. Knight, *Risk, Uncertainty and Profit* (1921); N. Kaldor, 'The Equilibrium of the Firm,' *Economic Journal,* March 1934; A. P. Lerner, *Economics of Control* (1944), pp. 143, 165-7; G. J. Stigler, *Theory of Price* (1946), p. 202n.—all of whom stand for first-order homogeneity. Strongly on the other side of the fence: P. A. Samuelson, *Foundations,* p. 84; and E. H. Chamberlin, 'Proportionality, Divisibility, and Economies of Scale,' *Quarterly Journal of Economics,* February 1948. See ibid. February 1949 for two criticisms and Chamberlin's rebuttal.

[32] Such a particular-purpose property is that all 'factors' be substitutional. Some writers seem to have believed, though more often implicitly than explicitly, that first-order homogeneity follows from this property. H. Schultz even tried to prove it ('Marginal Productivity and the General Pricing Process,' *Journal of Political Economy,* October 1929, Appendix 1). This is an error.

[33] Appeal to obviousness can of course be met by simple denial, but it should not be met by saying, as has been said by Professor Samuelson (*Foundations of Economic Analysis,* p. 84) that the hypothesis is 'meaningless' since anyone who declares it to be obviously valid will, if challenged, defend it by labeling any contradicting facts as 'indivisibilities' (see footnote 35, below), thus making the hypothesis true by definition. This is not so, though I do not deny that uncritical reference to indivisibility of some factor 'which must of course exist if the production function does not display first-order homogeneity' does give some color to the indictment: indivisibilities, too, are facts that call for, and admit of, empirical verification. Nor is it relevant (see Samuelson, ibid. p. 84n.) to point out that any function may be made homogeneous in a variety or hyperspace of higher dimension: the relevant question is whether it is homogeneous in the n factors (or a subset of these) which it is always possible to enumerate completely.

[34] Pareto for instance denied validity of the first-order homogeneity assumptions on both grounds (*Cours* II, § 714).

practical possibility is more often absent than present. Controversy should therefore be confined to theorems for which the assumption is both necessary and sufficient. Since neither assumption is necessary for the ordinary marginal productivity theorems, it is readily seen that the room for disagreement could have been greatly reduced if this distinction had been kept in mind. It is a striking illustration of the lack of rigor prevailing in economic discussion that this was not done.

Third, one obstacle to first-order homogeneity that is universally recognized by its sponsors is indivisibility or 'lumpiness' in some factor or factors—such as management, railroad tracks, rolling mills. Such factors cannot be varied by small quantities even in the blueprints of a plant that is still in the planning stage—where size of plant is a variable—and much less so within the framework of a going concern,[35] where it is only or mainly variation of output from

[35] To deny the existence or importance of such indivisibilities and their relation to often very large intervals of increasing physical returns would be absurd. The claim that they account satisfactorily for observed deviations from first-order homogeneity can therefore certainly be made good to some extent, and the theorist, especially the teacher of elementary theory, who assumes homogeneity of the production function (with proper qualification as regards a direct relation between output and the quantity of some 'factor' or 'factors'), *disturbed by indivisibilities*, may feel sure that he is covering perhaps all the ground he cares to cover. Also, indivisibilities may be reduced by taking account of the cases in which 'lumpy' factors, such as managers, may be varied by hiring the part-time services of consultants or again the cases in which the 'lumpy' units in which a 'factor' is available (units of costly machinery for instance) may be explained by the structure of the demand for it and not by technological necessity. I am not denying anything of that. All I wish to show is, on the one hand, how all this explains the duration and inconclusiveness of the debate and, on the other hand, how easy it is to slip, from the tenable assertion of these facts, into a habitual and thoughtless appeal to indivisibility in general. Indivisibility of course also interferes with the assumptions of continuity and differentiability of production functions. On this see P. A. Samuelson, op. cit. especially pp. 80-81.

Finally, reference should be made to cases where absence of first-order homogeneity (presence of economies of scale) is made to spell indivisibility (and vice versa) by definition (Stigler, Kaldor). There is no point in quarreling about definitions. In this case Professor Samuelson is right in holding that indivisibility is void of empirical content (and in this sense 'meaningless') but this is no reason for refusing to work out theories that rest on the homogeneity hypothesis, which does retain empirical content however we label the cases to which it does not apply. On the other hand the choice of the word indivisibility seems to suggest that Professors Stigler and Kaldor mean more than a definition. They may mean to agree with Professor Knight, who declared absence of economies of scale to be 'evident' if all services in a combination and the product are 'continuously divisible.' This is an assertion about supposedly unchallengeable facts and not meaningless in Samuelson's sense: we may challenge either the facts or, even if we do not challenge the facts of any particular case, we may deny that the proposition in question is universally 'evident.' If a product requires n kinds of services and if one of them is a lubricant—all of them being substitutional and as divisible as you please—it is not evident to me that the quantity of lubricant applied *must* be proportionately increased in order to increase the product in the same proportion, even if all the other services must.

a plant of given 'size' which is under discussion. We conclude by glancing at a circumstance of a different type.

Fourth, then, we note that a given hypothesis may be verified not only by observations that bear upon its validity directly but also by observations that do so indirectly by verifying consequences that follow from it: many physical hypotheses are verified in this way alone. Now, *if there were any sense in speaking of a national production function at all,* first-order homogeneity of this function would supply a very simple explanation of a remarkable fact, namely, the relative constancy of the main relative shares of 'factors' in the national dividend. For two factors, v_1 and v_2, such a 'social' production function of the form, $x = v_1^{\alpha} v_2^{1-\alpha}$, $(\alpha < 1)$, was first suggested by Wicksell (*Lectures*, I, p. 128) and has been extensively used by Douglas and Cobb.[36]

So far we have, throughout this section, defined marginal degree of productivity by means of a partial derivative, that is, our marginal product has been the increment of product which we get when adding an infinitesimally small amount to the quantity of a service employed while keeping the quantities of all other services strictly constant.[37] We have indeed seen that the latter is not always technologically possible and that when it is not, marginal productivity breaks down. But now we have to add that even where the addition of an infinitesimal amount to some service employed, all other conditions remaining the same, yields a determined increment of product, this procedure need not be the most economical method for securing this increment: it may be more economical to adjust the quantities of the other services employed as well. It is true that these adjustments may be of the second order of smallness, especially if we are very strict about the smallness of the increment we contemplate adding in the first place. But this need not be so. Furthermore it is true that there are purposes for which it is proper and useful to keep all other services constant in order to isolate the effects upon product of the one singled out for study; [38] but there are other purposes, among them

[36] C. W. Cobb and P. H. Douglas, 'A Theory of Production,' *American Economic Review*, Supplement, March 1928. This was the original paper that was to be followed by an impressive series of econometric studies, Professor Douglas' treatise on *The Theory of Wages* (1934), and further studies summed up in his Presidential address, 'Are there Laws of Production?' *American Economic Review*, March 1948. Also see V. Edelberg, 'An Econometric Model of Production and Distribution,' *Econometrica*, July 1936. Professors Cobb and Douglas inserted a second constant into the formula above so as to make it read: $x = cv_1^{\alpha} v_2^{1-\alpha}$, but this does not make much difference.

[37] See Marshall's *Principles*, p. 465.

[38] We then get the marginal productivity curves turned out, e.g., by agricultural experiment stations. Thus, a steer may be kept in strictly invariant conditions except for the number of pounds of hay he is being fed: this will isolate the effects upon his weight of successive increments of hay. Or, the wheat yield of a given plot of land may be studied in this manner as a function of the quantity of nitrogen contained in a fertilizer applied. It will be observed that this method will produce a theoretically infinite number of marginal productivity curves for each 'factor,' one for each of the theoretically infinite number of combinations of other circumstances.

the analysis of business behavior and of the behavior of distributive shares, for which it may be quite misleading to do so. This difficulty worried Marshall greatly and induced him to emphasize the dangerous concept of Net Marginal Product,[39] that is to say of the marginal product that results from an increment in the quantity of a factor, after corresponding rearrangement of the others. Marginal productivity in this sense is no longer properly expressed by a partial differential coefficient.[40]

Output being evidently measurable, the production function is not exposed to the criticism that induced economists, or most of them, to drop the utility function: you can see and count loaves of bread; you cannot see and measure satisfaction, at least not in the same sense. Technically it is however just as possible to do without the production function as it is to do without the utility function: the fundamental theorem that the marginal productivity (utility) of a dollar's worth of each 'factor' (consumers' good) must be (at least) equal to the marginal productivity (utility) to the firm (household) of the marginal productivity (utility) of a dollar's worth of any other 'factor' (consumers' good) follows in both cases, though in a different garb, whether we use production (utility) functions or simply marginal rates of substitution or transformation. This can be visualized, if we agree to admit two factors only, V_1 and V_2, and mark off their quantities, v_1 and v_2, on the two axes of a rectangular system of co-ordinates in space, reserving the third axis for output: the latter then swells up from the factor plane in a loaflike fashion, forming the production surface.[41] Sections parallel to the factor plane will cut out contour

[39] See *Principles*, pp. 585-6. The net marginal product is a value concept and the difficulty in question arises in the precincts of the cost problem rather than in the immediate neighborhood of the production function. We may, however, bring it in here by defining the marginal degree of productivity by means of an ordinary instead of a partial differential coefficient. Suppose again that there are two 'factors' only, v_1 and v_2, so that the production function reads: $x = f(v_1, v_2)$. Write the total differential

$$dx = \frac{\delta f}{\delta v_1} dv_1 + \frac{\delta f}{\delta v_2} dv_2$$

Then, dividing through, e.g. by dv_1, we can define marginal degree of productivity as

$$\frac{dx}{dv_1} = \frac{\delta f}{\delta v_1} + \frac{\delta f}{\delta v_2}\frac{dv_2}{dv_1}$$

For use to be made presently, note that if $dx = 0$, we have

$$\frac{dv_2}{dv_1} = -\frac{\delta f}{\delta v_1} \Big/ \frac{\delta f}{\delta v_2}$$

[40] Marshall also observed that, if we take rearrangements into account, marginal productivity will vary according to the time that is allowed for adaptation. See on this E. Schneider (op. cit. p. 28) and his concepts of total and partial adaptation.

[41] Readers not familiar with this construction which is by now classic had better look up Allen, op. cit. no. 11.8, pp. 284-9, and, for the derivation of (stable) demand functions for 'factors,' pp. 370-71 and 502-3.

lines that are loci of constant output. Projected on the factor plane they will cover the positive quadrant of the latter with equal-product curves or isoquants,[42] each of which depicts all the combinations of the two factors that result in a given quantity of output,[43] and isolates nicely the relation of substitutability from the other relation that enters when we proceed from any equal-product curve to a higher one, that is, increase output.[44] All this has been worked out and made fruitful—and brought into general use—only in our own time, mainly by the efforts of Professors Allen and Hicks and their followers. I mention it here to emphasize the historically important fact that it stems from Edgeworth and Pareto and that, by 1914, all the elements of the modern theory were present at least embryonically. Similarly, it should be intuitively clear that the theory of production functions and of the families of equal-product curves must have done much to improve the theory of cost. The great contribution of the period to 1914 was indeed the theory of opportunity cost—and its application to the problems of income formation—which has already been dealt with in Chapter 6 and owes little to the rigorous elaborations in the field of cost phenomena with which we are concerned here.[45] But in itself this contribution touched but peripherically upon the problems of what we now understand by the theory of cost. So far as exact aspects are concerned Pareto's was the chief performance.[46] However, instead

[42] The term 'isoquant' was introduced by R. Frisch but originally for a different concept, for which it should have been reserved.

[43] That is, along each equal product curve, $dx = 0$. The marginal rate of substitution (dv_2/dv_1) is subject to the usual restrictions (to which homogeneity of the production function may or may not be added). The 'law of decreasing returns' to any (substitutional) service is expressed by the condition that equal-product curves be convex to the origin in the operative interval.

[44] I hesitate to call this other relation complementarity because this term has by now acquired a different meaning (see Allen op. cit. p. 509). But the two-factor diagram (Allen, p. 371) is perhaps the best means of showing, on an elementary level, how services that co-operate in production may within limits compete with one another and vice versa and how the two relations stand to one another in the case of two substitutional factors.

[45] It is perhaps not superfluous to mention that a rigorous formulation of the theory of cost from the standpoint of the maximum problem of the individual firm—with the production function introduced as a restriction—is one of the best means of settling the question of the pricing of factors that have no, or no eligible, alternative opportunities of employment. From this standpoint, the opportunity-cost principle reveals itself as a special case of a more comprehensive principle. But this procedure is not the only possible one. The Austrian theory of imputation also took care of this case (the vineyards that, unless used as vineyards, could not be used at all or used only for grazing goats), and Böhm-Bawerk, in particular, said all about this that there is to be said.

[46] For a good presentation of Pareto's theory of cost, see H. Schultz, op. cit. sec. v. Along with Pareto we should again mention W. E. Johnson. For modern presentations see Allen, *passim;* J. R. Hicks, *Value and Capital* (1939), Part II; P. A. Samuelson, *Foundations*, ch. 4. Also see von Stackelberg, *Grundlagen einer reinen Kostentheorie* (1932) and L. M. Court, 'Invariable Classical Stability of Entrepreneurial Demand and Supply Functions,' *Quarterly Journal of Economics*, November 1941.

of entering into these developments, I shall conclude by noticing another development that stems directly from Marshall. In doing so we re-enter the field of partial analysis but in a region that borders upon general analysis.

(d) *Increasing Returns and Equilibrium.* Marshall himself undoubtedly did more than any other leader to pack a maximum load of business facts upon his theoretical schema. The width of his grasp shows nowhere more impressively than in his theory of production. But we may duly admire this performance and yet feel that his marvelous comprehension both of purely analytic and of 'realistic' aspects resulted in an exposition that seemed to leave many loose ends about and certainly left plenty of problems for his successors. Thus, his emphasis upon the element of time in relation to the phenomena of decreasing marginal and average cost [47] constitutes a major contribution.[48] His familiar concepts of prime and supplementary costs, of quasi-rent, of the representative firm,[49] of normal profit, and, above all, of internal and external economies, together with his attention to particular patterns of the data that individualize almost every firm's environment,[50] go far toward presenting all the clues that are needed for a satisfactory treatment of decreasing costs in all its various meanings and aspects. Nevertheless we get clues only and Keynes was right in asserting that in this field Marshallian analysis was least complete and left

[47] Throughout the discussion that we are about to survey, decreasing cost and increasing returns, increasing cost and decreasing returns, were as a rule treated as synonyms, which of course they are not. As late as 1944, Professor Lerner found it necessary to advert to this (*Economics of Control,* p. 164). But I am not aware of any error that could be attributed to this bad habit. However, it may have confused many a beginner.

[48] Modern factual investigators who keep on discovering the existence and importance of the intervals of falling average and marginal cost in the cost curves of individual firms—intervals, as we have already seen, that may cover the whole of the observable range of these cost curves—and believe that these findings shake the foundations of 'neo-classic' cost analysis, are really rediscovering Marshall: a striking illustration of the fact that the majority of economists *do not read.*

[49] The analytic intention that gave birth to the methodological fiction called Representative Firm stands out on p. 514 of the *Principles;* and so does its relation to decreasing cost. In the subsequent discussion, Professor Pigou introduced the concept of the Equilibrium Firm, which differs from Marshall's representative firm only in that the latter does, and the former does not, represent the modal conditions of the industry (see *Economics of Welfare,* 3rd ed. p. 788). This conception of a modal firm is important for more than one possible purpose of realistic theory but has never been exploited fully. (See however the study by S. J. Chapman and T. S. Ashton on 'The Sizes of Businesses, Mainly in the Textile Industries,' *Journal of the Royal Statistical Society,* April 1914.)

[50] See, e.g., *Principles,* p. 506. But chs. 10 and 11 of Book v are full of suggestive remarks—and warnings—of this kind. It should be emphasized again that Marshall made it more difficult for himself to express his meaning, and for his readers to understand him, by the false or at least misleading parallelism that he had before (pp. 397-8) set up between the 'laws' of decreasing and increasing returns which he himself disavowed repeatedly, e.g. by the statement that increasing return shows seldom in the short run (pp. 511-13).

most to do (*Essays in Biography*, pp. 225-6). This was, I think, because of Marshall's aversion to going through with pure analytic schemata and to his bent toward misplaced realism. He insisted on including internal and external economies in his (industrial) 'supply' schedules (though he noticed the objection to this, *Principles*, p. 514n.)—I suppose, in order to make these more realistic—in spite of the fact that he thereby destroyed their reversibility and rendered them useless for the purposes of static theory: they really represent pieces of economic history in the form of diagrams.[51] He thus blurred the clarifying distinctions between falling cost curves and downward shifts of cost curves and between costs that fall while production functions stay put and costs that fall in consequence of changes in production functions.[52] At any rate it is understandable that both the leads given by Marshall and the loose ends left by him must have started discussion in any environment that took any interest at all in the foundations of economic theory. The only thing to wonder at is that this discussion took so long to burst into print and to present results to the scientific public at large. For instance, Professor Viner's famous paper on 'Cost Curves and Supply Curves' that, starting from Marshall's analysis, successfully cleared up a large part of the ground, appeared only in September 1931 (*Zeitschrift für Nationalökonomie*); Professor A. A. Young's paper on 'Increasing Returns and Economic Progress' only in December 1928 (*Economic Journal*). We shall group our brief comments around the topic Increasing Returns and Equilibrium, and even so shall have to confine ourselves to but few of the many valuable contributions that ought in fairness to be considered.[53]

[51] It is only from the standpoint of static theory that Professor Stigler's strictures on Marshall's concepts of external economies are fully justified (op. cit. pp. 68 et seq.). Both internal and external economies are concepts that denote undeniable facts which deserve to be divided up in these two categories (see, however, F. H. Knight, *Fallacies in the Interpretation of Social Cost*, first publ. in 1924, that is, at a very early stage of the controversy on decreasing cost; republ. in *Ethics of Competition*, 1935). We shall understand by external economies nothing but the downward shifts in the marginal and average cost curves of individual firms that may result from the historical growth of their environments (not necessarily from the growth of their 'industries'), bearing in mind that Marshall expressed this fact by declining 'cost curves'—which are similar in nature to demand curves that may rise owing to similar causes and, like these, are simply curves fitted to the points of a histogram—and that some of his followers, Professor Robertson particularly, kept to this method.

[52] What seems to me to be overemphasis on industrial 'supply' schedules as against cost schedules may perhaps be explained similarly. We cannot go into this but shall, for the purposes of our exposition, use nothing but individual cost curves.

[53] By a stroke of editorial genius, Keynes arranged a symposium (D. H. Robertson, G. F. Shove, and P. Sraffa) on the matter ('Increasing Returns and the Representative Firm' published in the *Economic Journal*, March 1930) that is still eminently worth reading. He prefaced it by a fragmentary bibliography to which I refer the reader. I wish to add several important notes by Mr. R. F. Harrod, especially his 'Notes on Supply,' *Economic Journal*, June 1930, and his 'Law of Decreasing Costs' ibid. December 1931; also Mrs. Robinson's article, ibid. December 1932, and Professor Robbins', ibid. March 1934.

After rumblings which we must neglect, there appeared in the *Economic Journal* (December 1926) the famous paper by Professor Sraffa that was destined to produce the English branch of the theory of imperfect competition.[54] But for our present topic, his criticism was not anything like as 'destructive' as Keynes, to judge from his introductory remarks to the Symposium, seems to have considered it to be. Sraffa had simply pointed out that, *under conditions of pure competition,* a firm cannot be in *perfect* equilibrium so long as increase in its output would be attended by internal economies.[55] Partly influenced by Sraffa and partly by way of developing Marshallian teaching, Professor Pigou, in his 'Analysis of Supply' (*Economic Journal,* June 1928, inserted in the third ed. of *Economics of Welfare,* Appendix III), pointed out that, if we base declining industrial supply curves on external economies only, we may still retain rising supply curves for individual firms and thus avoid—formally at least—any conflict between 'increasing returns' and competitive equilibrium conditions, granted that we really believe in the existence of such a conflict at all. He added that if the growth of an industry or its environment induces increased specialization and this again increased size of the firms com-

54 Piero Sraffa, 'The Laws of Returns under Competitive Conditions.' But the main ideas, critical and constructive, had appeared a year before: 'Sulle relazioni fra costo e quantita prodotta,' *Annali di Economia,* 1925, which shows Sraffa's starting points and the nature of his brilliantly original performance much better than does the English article. See also his contribution to the 'Symposium.'

55 This means only that, given a market price at which any single firm is able to sell as much as it pleases, it will, so far as pure logic is concerned, always be advantageous for the firm to increase its output if this can be done at falling marginal costs in the short run and at falling average costs in the long run, and that therefore equilibrium output cannot be attained before these conditions have ceased to operate. Hence the proposition in our text above may well seem self-evident. Nor had it ever been denied by Marshall, whose equilibrium points on falling supply curves—industrial supply curves—must, as we shall see presently, be based upon the facts of external economies. Only, Marshall was so anxious to point out the many circumstances that in practice (where pure competition practically never prevails) prevent the firms we have any opportunity of observing from acting upon our proposition that it nowhere stands out clearly. His followers, especially Professor Robertson, whose common sense was impressed by the ubiquity and importance of internal economies even in industries that are considered as competitive, thought that denying the presence of internal economies amounted in these cases to denying the obvious. It is interesting to notice why: they thought so for the same reason that is at the bottom of the reluctance of so many economists to admit the proposition that there are no net profits in perfect equilibrium of pure competition (see below, footnote 56 and subsec. e). Both theorems apply to states of perfect equilibrium only and, since perfect equilibrium exists in real life still less often than does pure competition, internal economies, just as net profits, may in fact be ubiquitous without thereby impairing either the validity or the value of either theorem. But if the proviso 'in the point of perfect equilibrium' be left out and still more if our proposition be thrown into the faulty form that makes it read 'pure competition and internal economies are incompatible,' then we speedily cease to wonder how it was possible for a proposition to be considered as *obviously* wrong by some that appeared as self-evident to others.

posing that industry and increased opportunities for harvesting internal economies, we get a type of external-internal economies (as Professor Robertson called them) that may be of some analytic use. More important was his suggestion to make the costs of firms functions both of their own outputs and of the output of the industry or group—provided we can make definite sense of these concepts—to which they belong. Much has been done to put the topic into a more promising shape by Harrod, Shove, Viner, and Young, but I have said all I can say in the available space to convey to the reader this striking instance of the slowness and roundaboutness of analytic advance,[56] and to set him pondering over the question why results were established in and after 1930 that might easily have been established by 1890.

Instead of grouping our comments around decreasing costs we might as well have grouped them around Marshall's complex doctrine of Normal Profit, which survived well to the present time when it is still quite common to find teachers dividing the profit item into Marshallian normal profits and windfall profits.[57] Since we have dealt with this range of problems already (see above, ch. 6) we have only to add two points that are more easily dealt with on the higher theoretical level on which we are moving now: the one refers to the relation between production functions and cost functions in general and the other to the 'tendency toward zero profits' in particular.

[(e) *Tendency toward Zero Profits.*] But since the subject of profits is still more than are others infested by confusions, it will be well to restate first a few propositions that will serve to disentangle the points that interest us now from others with which they are habitually associated. Marshall as a rule considered the profit item of the balance sheets of business practice—and especially the balance sheets of owner-managed firms—rather than anything that

[56] The reader must not think, as he might from the brevity of my account, that this bit of housecleaning was all that resulted from the work that went into that controversy. Thus, the useful distinction between the marginal value product to the individual firm (the marginal private net product) and the marginal social net product was worked out by Pigou and Shove. In a sense this work culminated in R. F. Kahn's, 'Some Notes on Ideal Output,' *Economic Journal*, March 1935.

[57] The concept of a normal rate of profits has been refined by several modern economists, particularly by Mrs. Robinson, Mr. Shove, and Mr. Harrod. See especially Harrod's 'A Further Note on Decreasing Costs,' *Economic Journal*, June 1933. The concept of windfall profits is now mainly in use for *aggregate* profits that arise (if for this purpose we may use the terminology of Keynes's *Treatise on Money*) from a surplus of investment over saving, so that *individual* profits that are due to chance tend to drop out of the picture. It might be argued that this arrangement misses the essence of the profit phenomenon and falls below the level attained by Marshall. It might also be argued that Mr. Harrod's definition—the normal rate of profit is the rate of expected profits that leaves a firm without motive either to increase or to decrease its capital commitment—re-establishes the connection between profits and return to physical capital, which it was the main achievement of the period before 1914 to sever. But all this does not matter here where we are concerned only with the question of the surplus of receipts over payments (actual or imputed) to 'factors' that is relevant to the construction of cost curves.

has any claim to be called 'pure profit,' and he considered this profit item as it is rather than as it would be in (static) equilibrium of a stationary process. Though careful analysis, in this as in other cases, can no doubt unearth the contours of a comprehensive schema in which everything finds its appropriate place—but of a schema that is Ulysses' bow to less powerful minds—the ordinary reader simply finds a *fricassée* of such things as: earnings of management of all possible kinds, including also the earnings of better-than-common management; gains from successful risk-taking and uncertainty-bearing, that is the sort of thing that gives a favorable bias to the relation between expected and actual results; gains from advantages incident to the control of particular factors, some of which would, in other firms, not contribute as much to results as they do where they are; chance gains that go to the owner as residual claimant, due regard being paid to the wisdom of Goethe's dictum that only the able enjoy consistent luck; and, among other things, gains that accrue to a firm *as it grows*, or else, *because it has grown*, relatively to its competitors or absolutely or both; an element of monopoly entering, implicitly or explicitly, wherever required. Evidently, these items do not constitute a logically homogeneous whole, in the same sense as do for instance wages, in spite of all the qualifications that have to be added also in their case. Nevertheless Marshall created a sort of normal rate of profit out of this compound—warily treading his way through the dangers of circular reasoning—which he associated felicitously with the representative rather than with the marginal firm.[58] This normal rate of profit may be loosely defined as the rate that makes it worth while to enter, and to stay in, business (these expressions mean the same thing in the end), and thus acquires a distinction from the managerial salary that is easier to justify in a common-sense manner than in strict logic. Somehow all this has grown into the simplified normal profit of Marshall's followers and then into the marginal efficiency of Keynes's *General Theory*.

Now, nobody has ever asserted that *this* rate of profit either is or tends toward zero. Walras meant something entirely different when he set up his concept of an *entrepreneur ne faisant ni bénéfice ni perte*.[59] What he did mean

[58] Observe the wisdom of this move. Operating with the marginal firm, the theorist leaves out of account the broad fringe of 'submarginal' firms, the existence of which often dominates an industry's situation and casts doubts on the very definition of the marginal firm. This is another argument for the concept of the representative firm, to which justice has not been rendered even now.

[59] The almost violent aversion displayed toward Walras' concept, first by Edgeworth and then by a long line of economists to this day, is therefore wholly unjustified and rests on nothing but a complete failure to understand Walras. Barring this, however, I wish to repeat that two objections to it are invalid on logical grounds. First, it has been asserted, already by Edgeworth, that to speak of a zero profit, in an analysis of a capitalist economy the motive force of which is profit, is in itself absurd: but there is nothing absurd or self-contradictory in holding that the drive for profit is the motive force of the private-enterprise economy and in holding at the same time that profit would be eliminated in perfect equilibrium of pure competition. Second, it has been asserted that the zero-profit proposition is *ipso facto* disproved by economic reality. But for the analogous reason, even if the existence of net surpluses were much more of

can be most easily realized if we analyze the list of causes that produce the Marshallian rate of profit. We then also realize that the Marshallian theory, according to which profits have no tendency to vanish, and the Walrasian theory, according to which they do, not only do not contradict one another but, *referred to the same level* of abstraction, turn out to be identical. The reader can satisfy himself of this by observing, first, that Marshall's theory, as he himself presented it, is geared to phenomena of change or growth that static equilibrium excludes;[60] second, that the monopoloid elements that enter Marshall's analysis, though implicitly more than explicitly, and which are not necessarily excluded by the assumptions of static equilibrium, do violate the assumptions of pure competition; and that, if we are resolved to display the logical properties of perfect equilibrium in pure competition, Marshall's profits will in fact vanish as completely as will Walras'.

Observe that this does not necessarily exclude institutional gains such as may accrue to an innkeeper from good relations with the police.[61] Nor does it exclude the existence of net surpluses *in the system*. Only they should in good logic not be associated with profits but rather with the control of the thing that gives rise to them. Even with the most perfect competition, 'factors' will frequently receive more than is necessary to induce them (a) to offer their services for productive use and (b) to offer their services at any particular spot in the system.[62] As mentioned before, Pareto also noted, from a somewhat different angle, the surpluses that may arise from technological or institutional obstacles to optimum allocation of resources (*transformations incomplètes*) that are the cornerstone of his theory of rent. Careless handling of these surpluses may easily lead into circular reasoning or to 'meaningless' appeal to some logical necessity, according to which they 'must' be associated with some

an established fact than it is, there would be no force in such an appeal from an equilibrium proposition of the kind involved to facts culled from an evolutionary reality, which is never in equilibrium and never is, or can be, purely competitive. Observe this interesting feature of the situation: we have here a proposition that can hardly apply to reality under any conceivable circumstances; and which is nevertheless of the utmost importance in order to understand this reality.

[60] In particular it excludes the function of managing uncertainties, whose importance links up with change.

[61] Such institutional positions of vantage, if their importance is asserted, must of course be identified and established or reference to them is indeed meaningless. But since, subject to this condition, theorists can stress them as they please, I have never been able to understand why denial of the zero-profit proposition should have become the cherished badge of theorists with radical leanings. Moreover, for their comfort, there is always the monopoly element to fall back upon.

[62] These two cases are not always kept distinct. Thus, Mrs. Robinson (*Economics of Imperfect Competition*, 1933) defines such surpluses in the first sense on p. 102, and in the second sense on p. 103. But it should be noted that her distinction between cost curves that do and cost curves that do not include such surpluses (ch. 10) spelled an important advance. She called all these surpluses Rents. We have already noticed that this concept of rent (foreshadowed, as we know, by Senior, J. S. Mill, and also Marshall) comes in usefully for some purposes.

factor or other. But their existence and also this association are indubitable facts that are not difficult to establish. Because of this I feel unable to give instances from the literature that would clearly illustrate either of these mistakes.[63] Finally, it is convenient to use this opportunity to point out the relation between decreasing costs and profits, even though we have already seen that, so far as perfect equilibrium in pure competition is concerned, there is no need to worry about them.

For this purpose we cannot do better than borrow the argument of Marx. As we know, he made investment of industrial exploitation gains—which are not profits, though he called them so, but capital gains—the main motor of economic evolution. If we press this process into a schema of cost curves that fall owing to internal and external economies [64] and incidentally to increasing sizes of individual firms, we immediately realize two things. First this process, while it does not benefit the individual firms or the bourgeois class as a whole *ultimately*, is attended *at every step* by temporary gains that are profits in our sense and accrue to firms that grow in this manner more quickly or more *successfully* than do others. Disequilibrium prevails throughout, but Marx saw that this disequilibrium is the very life of capitalism,[65] and it is with this disequilibrium, on the one hand, and with decreasing costs in this sense, on the other, that pure profits are chiefly associated. Second, Marx's process, as he did not fail to notice, must in strict logic lead to monopolies or oligopolies of those firms that have once gained an initial advantage. Marshall's treatment of the same set of problems in general, and of decreasing costs in particular, really comes to the same results on both points, due allowance being made for his superior technique and his anxiety to do justice to all the facts, frictional and other, that prevent those individual trees from growing into the high heavens. We shall have to return once more to this historically important, though only 'objective,' doctrinal affinity. Having thus cleared the ground we can settle our two questions very quickly.

The emergence of the production function into explicit recognition, a development that we may for our present purpose associate with Wicksteed's *Essay on the Co-ordination of the Laws of Distribution* (1894), raised a problem of co-ordination of the theories of production and of cost that did not exist before. The old theory of production, such as we find it in J. S. Mill and even in Marshall, was simply a discussion of the 'factors of production' and fitted in easily with the 'laws of cost.' But however effectively the intrusion

[63] The difficulty of agreeing on such instances is greatly increased by the fact that authors who levy this charge, from Marshall to Samuelson, have invariably abstained from giving references. Of course there may be plenty in bad textbooks.

[64] This is not quite correct, of course. But it will do for our present purpose.

[65] An inkling of this truth must have been present in the mind of A. Smith when he wrote that it is the firm with the lowest average costs in the industry that sets the price of the product. This does not, as Marshall thought (*Principles*, p. 484), contradict Ricardo's opposite statements: Smith thought of an evolutionary and Ricardo thought of a stationary process, and there is in fact a tendency for the lowest costs to prevail in the first case and a tendency for the highest costs to prevail in the second case.

of the production function clarified other problems, it obscured for a considerable time the problem of the relation between the technology and the economics of production, or, as we may also say, between technology on the one hand and cost and distribution on the other. This may be best illustrated by Wicksteed's own attempt to derive a proposition on the distribution of the national dividend, namely the proposition that distributive shares determined according to the marginal productivity principle will just exhaust the national dividend, apparently [66] from nothing else than a property of the production function, namely first-order homogeneity. It is easy to see now that the production function alone does not determine either cost of production or distribution and in particular that, by itself, it cannot tell us much about the existence or absence of net gains to firms. Not less easy is it—now—to see how the production function fits into the cost and distribution phenomena. All that we need for this purpose is to keep in mind that, in the sphere of pure economic logic, the production problem is the problem of maximizing the difference between a firm's receipts and costs and that this maximum is subject to the technological restrictions embodied in the production function.[67] But around 1900 this was not so easy for the average economist to see, especially if he was not in the habit of throwing his ideas into the simple mathematical form which in this instance clears up everything. A center of such confusion as there may have been [68] was of course the zero-profit proposition, the meaning of which we have taken pains to make clear.

From what has been said above it should be clear that there is a perfectly good way of satisfying ourselves that, on the way toward perfect equilibrium in pure competition, with the qualifications that have been indicated—*and do not render the proposition either circular or tautological*—pure profits tend to vanish. All we have to do is to list all the sources of such surpluses over paid out or imputed costs we can think of [69] and then to show cause why they all shrink and, in the limiting case, disappear on that way. Equality between (properly discounted) planned receipts and planned costs may be legitimately inferred from this—though only with the reservation that somebody may any day present specific instances to the contrary—and is further strengthened by the consideration that firms that make less than total costs in the sense above

[66] I say 'apparently' in order to emphasize that this interpretation is unfair and not only because of his later recantation. Other conditions are partly stated and partly implied.

[67] There may be of course many other restrictions. Among them is one that is very important from the standpoint of any individual firm and that has not received the attention it merits, viz. the funds at the disposal of the firm.

[68] Again I do not wish to mention instances. For, with economists' loose ways of expressing themselves, I find it very difficult to array individuals whose statements might be amenable to more favorable interpretations.

[69] It is particularly important to keep in mind that, with correct handling of imputation, imputed subjective costs of managerial activity are *no* loophole for circularity or tautology to enter. On the contrary, it is the objector who commits these sins if he vaguely refers to unspecified possibilities of unspecified gains.

will, in the long run, go out of business and men who expect to make more than total costs in the sense above will, under the conditions assumed, be drawn into business in the long run.[70] But a more rigorous though still elementary proof has been offered and has gained some currency in classroom work.

For brevity's sake we assume away all but substitutional factors—so that the only restriction upon a firm's maximizing behavior is the ordinary or 'normal' production function as defined above—and also the problems that arise in the case of discontinuities of cost curves.[71] In perfect equilibrium and perfect competition, marginal costs to a firm will be equal to the price of the product which, like all factor prices, the firm accepts as data. In a large class of cases this condition determines output uniquely. Since, in strict logic, the firm will minimize total and average costs for any output, average costs must be at a minimum also for this output. But in the point of its minimum, the average cost curve is intersected, from below, by the marginal cost curve. Therefore marginal and average costs are equal in this point and both are equal to price. It is true that in the Cambridge theory of the early 1930's (R. F. Kahn, J. Robinson) average cost includes normal profit. But this schema applies only to situations of imperfect competition: only in imperfect competition can this normal profit contain anything besides returns to owned factors evaluated at the market prices of these factors. Hence pure profits are zero in perfect competition.[72] This may be unduly 'abstract.' But there is nothing wrong with it in logic.

Appendix to Chapter 7

Note on the Theory of Utility

In this Note we shall survey, in the briefest possible compass, the whole career of the utility theory of value, both its earlier developments which we know already and its later developments down to its metamorphoses in our own epoch. Let us keep in mind throughout that, although we shall now deal with utility theory (and its successors) as a theory of consumers' behavior, its importance extends far beyond this field into those of production and income formation as has been pointed out in the preceding chapter.

[70] Explanation of numbers and sizes of firms offers no difficulty at all, even in the case of first-order homogeneity. I mention this here once more in order to draw attention to the surprising fact that, so far as general theory is concerned and always excepting Marshall, these problems of evident interest have been almost completely neglected or declared to be insoluble.

[71] Space forbids our entering into these problems which have attracted some attention in our own period. A single reference will have to suffice: G. J. Stigler, 'Note on Discontinuous Cost Curves,' *American Economic Review*, December 1940.

[72] There is hardly any justification for Professor Samuelson's formulation of this theory on p. 83 of his *Foundations;* and none at all for his statement on p. 87 that 'net revenue'—if this means 'pure profits'—does not tend to be zero even in (perfect equilibrium of) pure competition.

[1. THE EARLIER DEVELOPMENTS]

We know that, from Aristotelian roots, this theory was developed by the scholastic doctors whose analysis of value and price in terms of 'utility and scarcity' lacked nothing but the marginal apparatus. We also know that, alongside of scholastic teaching and presumably not entirely without its influence, the utility theory of value began to be taught by laymen—Davanzati being our star instance—and that it went on developing quite normally right into the times of A. Smith—Galiani's work being the peak achievement of the epoch, though Genovesi should not go unmentioned.[1] Even the 'paradox of value'—that comparatively 'useless' diamonds are more highly valued than is 'useful' water—had been explicitly posited and resolved by many writers, for example by John Law. And there was, though standing by itself on a side line, Daniel Bernoulli's expression for the marginal utility of income (Part II, ch. 6, sec. 3b). But then this development came to a standstill: though many economists, particularly on the Continent and still more particularly in France and Italy, referred to the element of utility as a matter of course—and though Bentham formulated explicitly what was to be known as Gossen's law of satiable wants—they failed entirely to exploit it any further. Some who tried to do so did it in so very infelicitous a way as to discredit rather than to spread its use. Condillac, for instance, who may be considered its most important sponsor in the last quarter of the eighteenth century, explained the *utility* of air and water by the effort involved in breathing the one and drinking the other. A. Smith and, following him, practically all the English 'classics' with the exception of Senior [2] evidently did not realize the possibilities of the utility approach to the phenomenon of economic value and were content to turn away from 'value-in-use' with a reference to the paradox of value that should not have been a paradox any more. Let me repeat that it is quite wrong to explain this attitude, especially in the case of Ricardo, by saying that, while seeing all there is to see about utility, they did not care to elaborate so obvious an aspect of things: it is quite clear—and can, for Ricardo, be proved from his correspondence—that they did not follow up the utility clue because they did *not* see their way to using it effectively. But Senior's treatment does constitute a definite step in advance. In France and Italy the old tradition that favored the utility approach did not die out entirely. But neither did it bear fruit. J. B. Say, who made an attempt on this line, spoiled his chance by his handling of the matter that was still more clumsy than it was superficial and led nowhere.

A number of 'forerunners' began to emerge, however, though none of them received any recognition at the time. The two who achieved the largest measure of posthumous fame have been mentioned already, H. H. Gossen and J. Dupuit. There were several others, but it will suffice to mention three:

[1] [These men and their work are discussed in Part II.]

[2] Malthus should not, I think, be listed as another exception, though his criticism of Ricardo's theory of value does point in the direction of a utility theory.

Walras, the father of Léon; Lloyd, who published three years later; and Jennings.[3] The three performances are closely similar in nature and results. In particular, the marginal utility concept (Walras' *rareté* and Lloyd's special utility) [4] is clearly present with all three authors and so are those general arguments about how wants and utility are related to value that became so familiar half a century later.

[2. Beginnings of the Modern Development]

Léon Walras tells us that he started from his father's teaching. But Jevons and Menger undoubtedly rediscovered the theory for themselves. In so doing, all three of them improved and amplified it, but their historical achievement consists in the theoretical structure they erected upon it and not in these improvements. As we have already seen, they all restated Gossen's or Bentham's or Bernoulli's Law of Satiable Wants; in so doing they all treated utility (or the satisfaction of wants) as a psychological fact that is known to us from introspection, and as the 'cause' of value; they felt little or no compunction about its measurability; [1] and they all made the utility of every commod-

[3] A. A. Walras, *De la Nature de la richesse et de l'origine de la valeur* (1831). His *Théorie de la richesse sociale* (1849) adds nothing to the theory of value, so far as I can see, but contains several other points that are of interest, e.g. the definition of capital as every good that serves more than once. W. F. Lloyd—'student' of Christ Church (this admirable title which might be considered the only one fit for a scholar is at present Mr. Harrod's) and Professor of Political Economy in the University of Oxford, 'A Lecture on the Notion of Value . . .' delivered before the University of Oxford in 1833 (1834). It is strange that an Oxford professor of economics should have needed rediscovering. Nevertheless, such was the case. The merit of having rescued Lloyd's name from oblivion belongs to the late Professor Seligman ('On Some Neglected British Economists,' in *Essays in Economics*, pp. 87 et seq., the work to which reference has repeatedly been made already). Our text shows, however, that Professor Seligman was in error when he allocated to Lloyd the 'proud position of having been the first thinker in any country to advance what is known today as the marginal theory of value, and to explain the dependence of value on marginal utility' (op. cit. p. 95).

[J. A. S. did not complete this note. On Richard Jennings (*Natural Elements of Political Economy*, 1855), see the article in *Palgrave's Dictionary* and Jevons' *Theory of Political Economy* (2nd ed., ch. 3).]

[4] As everybody knows, Léon Walras retained the term *rareté;* Gossen had spoken of 'utility of the last atom'; Jevons introduced final utility and final degree of utility; the phrase marginal utility (*Grenznutzen*) is von Wieser's; Wicksteed suggested fractional utility, J. B. Clark specific utility, Pareto *ophélimité élémentaire*.

[1] Walras indeed eventually convinced himself or was convinced by J. Henri Poincaré, the great mathematician, that utility, though a quantity, was unmeasurable. But this did not induce him to delete, from the text of his *Éléments*, statements and implications to the contrary. See, e.g., p. 103 of the *édition définitive* (1926), where he *defines* his *rareté* (marginal utility) as the derivative of total utility with respect to quantity possessed, borrowing his father's analogy to velocity—the derivative of displacement with respect to time.

ity to its possessor depend upon the quantity of that commodity alone.[2]

Further work, partly induced by hostile criticism, transformed this 'psychological' or 'subjective' or 'modern' theory of value before long. In order to convey the essentials of a story that cannot be told satisfactorily in the space at our command, we shall confine ourselves to a minimum of names and reduce to a sequence of logical steps what actually was a sequence of controversies, which were sometimes as acrimonious as they were pointless.

[3. THE CONNECTION WITH UTILITARIANISM]

The first task that confronted the sponsors of the 'new' theory of value was to defend it against all the misunderstandings—some of them quite puerile—to which it had given rise.[1] Ever fuller restatements resulted—nourished by applications to particular cases, which were not valueless though they were sneered at as futile casuistry—that did something to clear the ground for further advance. For instance the Austrians, who faced German opponents of strongly anti-utilitarian tastes, pretty quickly realized the necessity of clearing their skirts of hedonism. The historical alliance of utility theory with utilitarian philosophy was obvious. We cannot blame men who were no theorists for suspecting that there was also a logical one. Moreover, some of the most prominent exponents of marginal utility were in fact convinced utilitarians: Gossen was, and Jevons, and Edgeworth. They, and others too, had used language that was apt to create the impression that marginal utility theory depended upon utilitarian or hedonist premisses—Bentham certainly thought so —and could be attacked successfully by attacking these. Jevons was the chief culprit: he even went so far as to call economic theory a 'calculus of pleasure and pain'—Verri had done so before—and elicited from Marshall the rebuke that he was mixing up economics with 'hedonics.'

It was one of the many merits of Marshall's treatment of utility that he deplored and renounced the alliance with utilitarianism (see especially his footnote, pp. 77-8 of his *Principles*, Book I, ch. 5). But in one respect he followed

[2] But, unlike Gossen, they did not postulate linearity of the marginal utility function. That this is not a harmless and insignificant detail can be shown by asking ourselves such questions as how a moderate inflation affects the marginal utility of money income for those whose money income remains constant in the process. The answers differ according to the form of the function. And since the straight-line form is certainly unrealistic (except for infinitesimal intervals), the answer derived from it is practically sure to be wrong. See R. Frisch, *New Methods of Measuring Marginal Utility* (1932).

[1] The protagonist of the Austrian group who did most of this work was Böhm-Bawerk. I shall mention only his controversy with Dietzel in the *Jahrbücher für Nationalökonomie* (1890-92), and both the text of and the appendices to the third edition of his great treatise on capital and interest (*Kapital und Kapitalzins*). A brilliant and compact survey of arguments and counterarguments has been presented by P. N. Rosenstein-Rodan in the article 'Grenznutzen' in the German encyclopedia (*Handwörterbuch der Staatswissenschaften*, 4th ed., vol. IV, 1927).

Jevons in teaching a doctrine that comes more naturally from a utilitarian although, again, the relation is one of association rather than logic. From the standpoint of a calculus of pleasure and pain, 'disutilities'—the term is Jevons' —should be in fact introduced on the same level as utilities. This is what Jevons did. Walras did not do so and the Austrians, Böhm-Bawerk in particular, were strongly opposed to doing so. But Marshall and Pigou kept to the Jevonian standpoint: Marshall developed it into his doctrine of real cost (efforts and sacrifices), which, in a way, was the olive branch presented to his 'classical' predecessors. J. B. Clark and, in Vienna, Auspitz and Lieben also accepted it. Notice that this standpoint, however independently arrived at, stands in line with old tradition (compare, e.g., what has been said above on Galiani's theory of value); and that, outside of the utility theory tradition, it had the support of A. Smith (and of many philosophers of natural law). In England, Cairnes sponsored it, but it was renounced by Wicksteed and, more effectively, by Keynes. The analytic importance of the question lies in its bearing upon the concept of supply of labor and, if we adopt an abstinence theory of interest, of capital. In all other respects it makes little difference whether we take the available amount of labor as given or insert into our system another equation (marginal utility of real wages = marginal disutility of labor) in order to determine it.

Actually it is not difficult to show that the utility theory of value is entirely independent of any hedonist postulates or philosophies. For it does not state or imply anything about the nature of the wants or desires from which it starts.[2]

[4. Psychology and the Utility Theory]

Once we recognize the purely formal character of the theorist's utility concept, we are naturally led to question the relations between the utility theory of value and psychology. Some of the early Austrians seem to have believed that their theory was rooted in psychology and even that they were developing what in essence was a branch of 'applied psychology.'

This belief was encouraged by some Austrian psychologists such as von Meinong and von Ehrenfels, who held that Menger had made a valuable contribution to psy-

[2] We have also seen above that the theory does not imply any hypothesis concerning the role of egotism in human behavior and that it is not particularly 'individualistic.' It is, however, interesting to notice, first, how difficult it is for people to realize all this whose whole thinking runs in 'philosophic' terms and who are primarily interested in possible philosophic implications; and that this difficulty is greatly increased by the presence of cases where sponsorship of the theory is actually combined with hedonist or individualist philosophies or politics or where, even in the absence of such philosophical or political preferences, the language of an author invites interpretation in a hedonist or individualist sense. In the latter case it may be next to impossible to get rid of undesired associations evoked by the words used. This explains the many attempts that have been made to replace the word utility, which seems to convey more than the fact that a thing is actually being desired, by other terms such as *desiredness* (Fisher) or *ophelimity* (Pareto).

chology which was capable of more general application. Certain applications, for instance to the psychology of religion, were in fact made which it is impossible to report without a smile though they were far from being nonsense. Thus, von Ehrenfels actually spoke of marginal piety and of the marginally pious individual. But many non-Austrian economists, who sympathized with the Austrian theory, also thought (and even think) a great deal of the importance of its psychological aspects. On this compare: Maurice Roche-Agussol, *La Psychologie économique chez les Anglo-Américains* (1918) and *Étude bibliographique des sources de la psychologie économique* (1919); also the same author's 'Psychologische Ökonomie in Frankreich,' *Zeitschrift für Nationalökonomie,* May 1929 and January 1930.

Let us note in passing a side issue that has never received the attention it deserves. If psychology is to render effective assistance to economics at all, economists must not, of course, neglect experimental psychology and especially the work that turns upon the measurement of sensations. It is, to say the least, a curious fact that one of the early exploits in this field, the one that was undertaken by E. H. Weber, has led to a result amplified by G. T. Fechner (see above ch. 3, sec. 3) into the 'fundamental law of psycho-physics,' which is formally identical with the Bernoulli-Laplace hypothesis about the marginal utility of income: it postulates that, if y be the intensity of sensation, x the physically measurable external stimulus, and k an individual constant, then $dy = k\,dx/x$.

This was in fact noticed by some economists. But it was brushed aside by the leading Austrians, Wieser, for example, declaring (*Theorie der gesellschaftlichen Wirtschaft,* § 1) that this law had nothing whatever to do with Gossen's law of satiable wants. But however that may be, the efforts of psychologists to measure psychical quantities is not a matter of indifference to any economist who is not entirely lacking in scientific imagination. For examples of recent progress in the measurement of sensation, see especially Professor S. S. Stevens' 'A Scale for the Measurement of a Psychological Magnitude: Loudness,' *Psychological Review,* September 1936, and his and J. Volkmann's, 'The Relation of Pitch to Frequency,' *American Journal of Psychology,* July 1940.

But both the Austrians and others soon came to realize that their 'psychology' was a mistake: the utility theory of value has much better claim to being called a logic than a psychology of values. Opponents, however, at first did not see this, any more than did adherents. In consequence, the sponsors of the 'psychological theory of value' had to face two additional indictments: first, that they were exploring psychological aspects of value-in-use that were irrelevant to the objective facts of the economic process; second, that their psychology was bad. The first indictment has no other basis than a failure to understand the import of the theory.[1] The second would be quite true, if any psy-

[1] It was formulated by many Marxists, e.g. by Karl Kautsky in his Preface to Marx's *Theorien über den Mehrwert:* the psychological theory describes how individuals feel about the process of valuation which, determined by hyperindividual social forces, runs its course irrespective of these feelings exactly as a railroad accident happens irrespective of what the passengers feel about it. The reader should carefully distinguish between the error in this—which consists in overlooking the measure of success with which the theory explains precisely those very objective facts that this argument holds are beyond its reach—and the perfectly sound principle that the facts of a social process must never be confused with the images of them in the individual psyches. But many non-

chology were involved in the utility theory of value *considered as a theory* of economic equilibrium. If we ask how consumers come to behave as they do in all those wider problems of human behavior for which particular psychological propositions become relevant, we must in fact appeal to all that modern professional psychology—of all varieties, from Freudianism to behaviorism—might have to give us.

As a rule, however, the necessity of such an appeal does not arise in technical economics—it is different, of course, in economic sociology. Most of us would indeed find it difficult or at least highly inconvenient to avoid entirely all reference to motives, expectations, comparative estimates of present and future satisfactions, and the like, however fervently we might hope for an economic theory that would use nothing but statistically observable facts. But such use of psychical observations must not be confused with the use of methods or results borrowed from professional psychology. Like all other research workers, whatever their field, we take our facts where we find them, irrespective of whether or not they are also dealt with by other sciences. We do not become dilettantes in physics when we use the physical facts that are implied in the classical law of decreasing returns in agriculture. No more do we become dilettantes in psychology—or borrow from professional psychology—when we speak of motives or, for that matter, of wants or satisfactions. But though this practice does not present any problems concerning the relation between economics and psychology, it does present another. Early utility theorists talked about psychical facts with the utmost confidence. They included them in the stockpot of common experience—that source of knowledge of the course of everyday life, no element of which a reasonable man could possibly call into question. But so far as these psychical facts are known to us only from observation of what goes on in our own individual psyches—from introspection—their standing evidently leaves something to desire, even though most of them, such as the satisfaction incident to quenching one's thirst, are so simple and so little problematical that he who quibbles about them might easily compromise himself in the eyes of men of less delicate methodological conscience. In any case, nobody will deny that it is preferable to derive a given set of propositions from externally or 'objectively' observable facts, if it can be done, than to derive the same set of propositions from premisses established by introspection. And, as we shall presently see, this can actually be done in the case of the utility theory of value, at least so long as we do not ask it to do more for us than to furnish the assumptions or 'restrictions' that we need within the equilibrium theory of values and prices. This is the *Leitmotiv* of subsequent developments.[2]

Marxists also held that, by its probings into the 'psychology' of value-in-use, the utility theory contributed nothing to our understanding of economic processes. For an example see the article 'Grenznutzen' by W. Lexis, in the second edition of the *Handwörterbuch der Staatswissenschaften.*

[2] Before proceeding I wish to advert to a type of pseudo-psychology which is nothing but an abuse. Keynes's well-known psychological law about the propensity to consume is an outstanding example. It avers that both individuals and societies will, if

5. Cardinal Utility

Let me repeat once more: in the beginning, utility, both total and marginal, was considered a psychic reality, a feeling that was evident from introspection, independent of any external observation—hence, to repeat this also, *not* to be inferred from those externally observable facts of behavior in the market which were to be explained by it—and a *directly measurable* [1] quantity. I believe that this was the opinion of Menger and Böhm-Bawerk. Marshall, though he spoke boldly of utility as a measurable quantity, refined upon this, in the remarkably careful argument of Sections 2-9, Chapter 5, Book I of his *Principles*, by adopting the weaker assumption that, though we cannot measure utility or 'motive' or pleasantness and unpleasantness of sensations *directly*, we can measure them indirectly by their observable effects, a pleasure for instance by the sum of money a man is prepared to give up in order to obtain it rather than go without it.[2] This was no doubt a step in advance. But we shall henceforth merge both these theories of utility measurement into one conception which we shall call (the theory of) Cardinal Utility. Both present difficulties and are open to objection. But neither is simply nonsense.

However, even on this level and apart from mere defense and elaboration, there was plenty to do. In order to illustrate, I shall mention three contributions of major importance. First, none of the founding fathers, not even Walras, had bestowed adequate care upon fundamentals.[3] The theory badly needed rigorous restatement. This was accomplished, in a manner that anticipated

they experience an increase in income, normally increase their expenditure or consumption but by less than the increase in income. Whether this is so or not, it is a statement of statistically observable fact which Keynes raised to the rank of an assumption. Nothing is gained, except a spurious dignity, by calling it a psychological law. Our experience with such 'laws of human nature,' from the seventeenth century on, is certainly not encouraging. But even Jevons would not do without them (*Theory of Political Economy*, p. 59).

[1] The meaning of direct measurability is best instanced by the measurement of length. It may be defined as the association, with every utility sensation, of a real number, unique except for the choice of a unit which is to be interpreted as a unit sensation. Nobody held that this could be done as easily as it can in the case of length. But some authors did hold that there was no difficulty of principle involved. The presence of a practical difficulty—that would reduce utility measurements to rough 'estimates'—was recognized by Böhm-Bawerk (*Kapital und Kapitalzins*, 3rd ed., Appendix).

[2] He guarded this carefully against circularity. The exact definition of measurability in this sense would run as follows: it is possible to associate, with every utility sensation, a real number, unique except for the choice of a unit, which is to be interpreted as a unit quantity of an externally observable incentive producing an externally observable reaction. An illustrative analogy, which is however not quite satisfactory, is provided by the method of measuring heat by means of a thermometer.

[3] This may surprise readers who remember the prolix commentaries of the Austrians. But then Wieser and Böhm-Bawerk were fatally handicapped by their lack of the necessary mathematics.

many a later performance, by Antonelli.[4] Second, Edgeworth did away with the assumption that the utility of every commodity is a function of the quantity of this commodity alone, and made the utility enjoyed by an individual a function of all the commodities that enter his budget. Marshall welcomed this step coldly (to say the least), perhaps because he thought of the mathematical complications involved in making the equations of utility theory partial instead of ordinary differential equations. As a third example we choose Marshall's attempt to make the measurement of utility operational by means of the concept of Consumer's Rent.

The term Consumers' Surplus or Rent is Marshall's, but the essential idea—not every detail—is Dupuit's. The reader should, if necessary, refresh his memory from *Principles*, Book III, Chapter 6, so that this space may be reserved for comments. There, Marshall does not mention Dupuit's name, and only inadequate amends are made for this by means of a statement occurring in another and far distant place (Book V, ch. 12, concluding footnote), namely, that 'the graphic method has been applied in a manner somewhat similar to that adopted in the present chapter by Dupuit in 1844 and, independently, by Fleeming Jenkin in 1871.' The idea of 'measuring' the total utility accruing to an individual from the consumption of a given quantity of a given commodity by the sum of money represented by the definite integral, taken from zero to the given quantity, of his individual demand function (the consumers' surplus is then the difference between this integral and the price actually paid times the quantity bought) is at first sight open to a number of objections, which were in fact raised but most of which rest upon misunderstandings of Marshall's meaning. Appreciation of the value of the tool will be best conveyed by a frank recognition of the limitations to which, at least in the original Marshallian formulation, it must be understood to be subject. First, it was meant to be essentially a tool of partial analysis; the price of one commodity only is made to vary, all other prices being kept constant. Second, even within this range, the concept of consumers' rent embodies a method of approximation (though it may be exact in certain cases). For it assumes that the marginal utility of income does not change if the individual, having acquired a first unit of the commodity in question for, say, $100, a second for, say, $99, a third one for, say, $90, goes on spending more and more money on additional units as they are offered to him at decreasing prices. Strictly, this is inadmissible. But if this expenditure is but a small part of his total expenditure—so that his other expenditures are not perceptibly affected by this one —we may neglect, as of second order of magnitude, the variations in the marginal utility of income that actually occur. Of course, this limits the method severely: it cannot be applied to such things as food in general or house room or it can be applied only to small ranges of variations in the prices of these, and Marshall knew why he used tea as an example by which to display it. But within these limits the method is neither incorrect nor valueless. Even the sum of all consumers' rents *enjoyed by an individual*—a concept that looked absurd to some critics—and the sum of all consumers' rents enjoyed by all individuals *buying an individual commodity* may be made to carry meaning by means of further assumptions that are not worse than others we habitually make. However, consumers' rent had a bad reception from the first, and Professor Pigou, who developed Marshall's teachings so faithfully in other respects, did not throw the weight of his authority into its scale. But of late, Professor Hicks, impressed by its usefulness in welfare economics (see below, sec. 8), recalled it—or something

[4] G. B. Antonelli, *Sulla teoria matematica della economia politica* (1886).

like it—from the limbo of dead issues to what looks like another lease on life. See his note to Chapter 2 of *Value and Capital* and his articles 'The Rehabilitation of Consumers' Surplus' (*Review of Economic Studies,* February 1941); 'Consumers' Surplus and Index Numbers' (ibid. Summer 1942); and 'The Four Consumer's Surpluses' (ibid. Winter 1943). [Cf. also R. L. Bishop, 'Consumer's Surplus and Cardinal Utility,' *Quarterly Journal of Economies,* May 1943.]

6. Ordinal Utility

Of course, if measurability were the only stumbling block in the way to acceptance of the marginal utility theory, critics could be satisfied by a reformulation that retains the concept of utility or satisfaction but makes it a nonmeasurable quantity.[1] For there is in fact no compelling necessity of insisting upon measurability so long as we are interested only in a maximum problem: there are means of telling whether or not we are on the top of a hill without measuring the elevation of the place where we stand. And since the objection to measurability was the most serious of the objections that were raised from the first by nonmathematical opponents of the nonmathematical exponents of the marginal utility theory, some of these, Wieser especially, soon discovered that they could afford to yield the point,[2] at least with respect to total, as distinguished from incremental, utility. Pareto, who, after having at first accepted the marginal utility theory in the Walrasian form, turned against it around 1900,[3] also raised primarily this objection which then was anything but new, to wit: 'show me a utility or satisfaction that is, say, three times as great as another!' But nobody questioned people's ability to compare satisfactions expected from the possession of different sets of goods without measuring them, that is to say, people's ability to array such sets in a unique 'scale of preference.' This is what we mean by Ordinal Utility.

Only the briefest reference can be made to a point on which economists have not been able to reach agreement to this day. We can, as has just been stated, array hypo-

[1] A quantity or magnitude (the Greek μέγεθος) is defined as anything that is capable of being greater or smaller than some other thing. This property implies only transitivity, asymmetry, and aliorelativity (the last term meaning that no thing can be greater or smaller than itself). It also covers the relation of equality, which is however symmetrical and reflexive (the latter term meaning the opposite of aliorelative). Now, quantity in this very general sense does not imply measurability, which requires fulfillment of two more conditions: (1) that it be possible to define a unit; (2) that it be possible to define addition *operationally,* i.e. so that it can be actually carried out.

[2] This is, I suppose, what Wieser meant when he said that utility had no 'extension' but only 'intensity.' If my interpretation be correct, this turn of phrase was no doubt highly infelicitous.

[3] Pareto's publications during the nineties, the *Cours* in particular, are substantially pristine utility theory (or ophelimity theory, as he called it). I *think* that his change of heart was first revealed in the lectures he gave in 1900 at the *École des Hautes Études* in Paris. The first publication on the new line that I know is his 'Sunto di alcuni capitoli di un nuovo trattato di economia pura,' in the March and June numbers of the *Giornale degli Economisti,* 1900.

thetical sets of goods ordinally. Suppose that an individual tells us that he prefers a set of goods (B) to a set of goods (A) and a set of goods (C) to the set of goods (B); therefore he prefers (C) to (A) (transitivity). But can we go further and assume that the increase in satisfaction which, on the showing of the experiment, he must experience when, having been promised (A), he is then promised (B), is capable of being greater or less than, or equal to, the increase of satisfaction he would experience if, having been promised (B), he is then promised (C)? This question is by no means otiose because it has been asserted by some and denied by others that admissibility of this assumption opens a way back to measurability (*even though, by itself, it is not sufficient to insure it*). We cannot go into this question and must content ourselves with a reference to the three most important papers about it. They are: O. Lange, 'The Determinateness of the Utility Function' (*Review of Economic Studies*, June 1934); P. A. Samuelson, 'The Numerical Representation of Ordered Classifications and the Concept of Utility' (ibid. October 1938); and especially F. Alt, 'Über die Messbarkeit des Nutzens' (*Zeitschrift für Nationalökonomie*, June 1936). For readers who can muster sufficient interest in questions of this kind, I shall however add this: the merit of having *seen* the importance of this assumption is Lange's. But he failed to see that it was only necessary, but not sufficient, in order to prove the possibility of measurement. Samuelson's argument points this out correctly. Alt's argument, however (which was not known to Samuelson), is logically adequate and reduces the problem satisfactorily to one of empirical verification of the seven assumptions involved (which it is true has not been attempted so far).

Pareto proceeded to develop the idea of ordinal utility and eventually worked out what must in fairness be considered the fundament of the modern theory of value.[4] He was not quite consistent about it and slid back again and again into the habits of thought he had acquired in his formative years. Further advance was made, however, by Johnson and Slutsky although it was not until 1934 that the job was completely done by Allen and Hicks.[5] Additional prob-

[4] See the Appendix to his *Manuel* in its entirety. But the later article in the French edition of the encyclopaedia of mathematical sciences (*Encyclopédie des sciences mathématiques pures et appliquées*, 1911), contains several improvements (the earlier article in the German ed. is of no importance).

[5] W. E. Johnson, 'The Pure Theory of Utility Curves,' *Economic Journal*, December 1913. This important paper contains several results that should secure for its author a place in any history of our science. But, having apparently been written in ignorance of Pareto's work, it aroused not unnatural resentment on the part of Italian economists because of its failure to acknowledge Pareto's priority in most essentials. The Russian economist and statistician Eugen Slutsky, Professor in the University of Kharkov, published in the *Giornale degli Economisti*, July 1915, an article entitled 'Sulla teoria del bilancio del consumatore,' the complete neglect of which outside of Italy may perhaps be excused on account of the conditions prevailing in that year. It keeps to the idea that utility is a quantity, though an unmeasurable one; posits certain assumptions about its properties; and then develops the theory of consumers' behavior with which little fault can be found so long as that view of utility is accepted. Ample amends for that neglect were made by Henry Schultz ('Interrelations of Demand, Price, and Income,' *Journal of Political Economy*, August 1935); by R. G. D. Allen ('Professor Slutsky's Theory of Consumers' Choice,' *Review of Economic Studies*, February 1936); and by J. R. Hicks, who in *Value and Capital* gave Slutsky's name to the

lems cropped up in the process, some of them in several different forms, but the familiar outcome may be briefly stated as follows.[6] Cardinal utility had been conceived as a uniquely determined [7] real function of the quantities of commodities (per stated period of time) at the disposal of the individual or household. Ordinal utility cannot be so conceived. But it is still possible to *describe* its behavior by means of any real function of the same quantities that increases whenever we proceed from any given set of commodities to another which the individual prefers, decreases whenever we proceed from any given set of commodities to another which is less acceptable to the individual, and assumes constant values (does not change) whenever we proceed from any given set of commodities to one which is equally acceptable to the individual—just as the two bundles of hay were to Buridan's ass. Such a function will represent the individual's 'scale of preference' mentioned above but, unlike the function that represents cardinal utility, it will not do so in a uniquely determined way, because all it is devised to tell us is whether there is increase, decrease, or equality of utility. Everything else about it, any further algebraic or numerical features it may display, is entirely arbitrary and has in fact no economic meaning. Hence, if φ be any such function,[8] any monotonically increasing function of φ, call it $f(\varphi)$, will do just as well. Pareto called such a function an Index Function (*funzione-indice*). They were to play the same role in the value theory that works with ordinal utility as had been played by the utility function in the value theory that worked with cardinal utility—in fact, we might call them utility functions that obviate the objection against measurability.

As a matter of fact, however, it was not the index function as such, but another construct that became characteristic of this stage of value theory, namely, the indifference surfaces or, in the case of two commodities, the indifference curves (curves of equal choice, *curve di scelti uguali*). It is very interesting to notice that historically these were independently 'discovered,' for purposes that

---

fundamental equation of the modern theory of value. Perusal of Professor Allen's article, a shining example for what in this book is considered correct behavior in the case of unexpected discovery of predecessors, will tell readers unfamiliar with Italian all there is to know about Slutsky's performance. No comment is, I trust, necessary on the famous 'Reconsideration of the Theory of Value' by Allen and Hicks (*Economica*, February and May 1934), which marks substantial advance beyond Slutsky.

[6] I cannot do more than indicate the most important milestones on the main road. Many other things must go by the board. For instance, part of the development I am trying to describe in the text was paralleled by the thought of the later Austrians, though, owing to the inefficiency of their nonmathematical method, they did not get very far. On these Viennese developments, see A. R. Sweezy, 'The Interpretation of Subjective Value Theory in the Writings of the Austrian Economists,' *Review of Economic Studies*, June 1934.

[7] This must of course be qualified in two directions: we are always free to choose a unit and we are always free to choose our zero point. In these two respects cardinal utility is also arbitrary—but not more so than is any other method of measurement.

[8] For technical reasons, we do, however, require certain other properties, such as continuity and differentiability.

had nothing to do with ordinal utility, by Edgeworth,[9] who fully accepted the doctrine of cardinally measurable utility. Let us for a moment return to this doctrine. Confining ourselves to the two commodity case, we can then lay off the quantities of these commodities on two of the co-ordinates of a three-dimensional diagram and represent by the third co-ordinate the varying amounts of total utility enjoyed that correspond to all the possible combinations of the two commodities. The result is a utility surface that rises from the origin as the quantities of the two commodities increase, and possibly flattens out later on, presenting a shape not unlike that of a loaf of bread (Pareto called it *la colline du plaisir*). A succession of horizontal planes—that is, of planes parallel to the plane of the two commodity co-ordinates—will cut out from this loaf curves along which total utility is constant, the quantities of the commodities varying in such a way that the increase of one just compensates the individual for the corresponding decrease of the other. These curves, the whole meaning of which seems to rest upon the assumption that utility is measurable, are what Edgeworth called indifference curves. If we project them on the commodity plane, we get the familiar 'indifference map.' Edgeworth used it very elegantly in his theory of barter, particularly in order to delimit the range of possible barter terms or exchange ratios.[10]

But so soon as we project the indifference lines on the commodity plane, the utility dimension vanishes from the picture so that their meaning is no longer dependent on any hypothesis of measurability. They then tell us no more than (1) that the individual considers certain combinations of the two commodities as equally eligible and (2) that he prefers combinations represented by any 'higher' indifference curve to combinations represented by any 'lower' one. The first man to see the implications of this was Irving Fisher.[11] He had no objection to measurability. On the contrary, he tried to make it operational (see below editor's note between sections 7 and 8). But in doing so, he encountered certain difficulties when, in the second Part of his work, he discarded the untenable assumption that the utility of each good depends on its own quantity only ('independent goods').[12] At this point doubts were bound to arise not only about the measurability but also about its very existence. Accordingly, Fisher presented an analysis completely free from utility assumptions that worked only with indifference maps in the modern sense. With him—as later

[9] They put in appearance in his *Mathematical Psychics* (1881) and therefore antedate ordinal-utility analysis of the Pareto type by about twenty years.

[10] Marshall was sufficiently impressed with this brilliant piece of work to reproduce the gist of it in a note in the appendix to his *Principles*. But this is all he had to do with indifference curves. It is incorrect to say that he anticipated the idea by the apparatus of curves which he used in his *Pure Theory of Foreign Trade* (1879).

[11] *Mathematical Investigations* (see above, ch. 5, sec. 7b). It is not sufficiently recognized that, partly explicitly, partly by implication, this book anticipated the better part of modern value theory.

[12] The nature of these difficulties will be indicated in the next footnote. It is my guess—not, I think, a very hazardous one—that it was these difficulties which motivated Marshall's adherence to the conception of independent goods.

on with Allen and Hicks—indifference curves were the starting points of the analysis; they were not, as with Edgeworth, derived from a utility surface.

However, the indifference curves are part of index functions and can also be derived from these. This is what Pareto did. But they are just as independent of the particular index function chosen as they are of the particular form of the cardinal utility function, being uniquely determined by the scale of preferences. This suggests the idea of doing also without index functions, especially because they give rise to difficulties similar to those that Professor Fisher met in the case of utility functions.[13] But it took until 1934 to give full effect to it and to develop a theory that is nothing but a logic of choice: the theory of Allen and Hicks that was published in that year was, so far as I know, the first to be completely independent of the existence of an index function and completely free from any lingering shadows of even *marginal* utility, which is replaced in their system by the marginal rate of substitution.[14] In consequence, elasticities of substitution and complementarity are defined exclusively from the scales of preference and likewise divorced from utility. Beyond this we cannot go. It must suffice to mention the most important of the problems that are as yet unsolved within the range of this theory of choice: so far, indifference curves are satisfactorily defined for individual households only; the question remains what meaning is to be attached to collective indifference curves—for example, indifference curves of a country—which have been used in some of the most brilliant theoretical work of our time.[15]

[The first six sections of the Note on the Theory of Utility had been substantially completed and had been typed. The next few paragraphs were found in manuscript, incomplete, with shorthand notes to indicate the argument contemplated. See editor's note at end of this section.]

7. The Consistency Postulate

As the reader knows, indifference-curve analysis has at long last become part of current teaching. The profession has got used to it, and even the controversy concerning its suitability for a sophomore course has died out. But it should have been clear from the first that things would not stop at indifference varieties and that they are after all but a midway house. They are more elegant and methodologically safer than was the old utility analysis but they

[13] Though we can always proceed from given index functions to indifference curves, we cannot always proceed from given indifference curves to index functions. For the latter to be possible, i.e. for an index function to 'exist,' it is necessary that the differential equation of the indifference curves be integrable. In the case of only two variables (two commodities), there is always an integrating factor; in the case of three or more there need not be one. This question of integrability was very serious for Pareto's approach. Later developments have deprived it of its importance.

[14] It may be well to point out explicitly that this involves discarding Gossen's law of satiable wants.

[15] See, e.g., Professor Leontief's paper on 'The Use of Indifference Curves in the Analysis of Foreign Trade,' *Quarterly Journal of Economics*, May 1933.

have not helped us to results that the latter could not have reached; and no result of the latter has been proved definitely wrong by them. Moreover, if they 'assume less' than does the utility analysis, they still assume more than, for purposes of equilibrium theory, it is necessary and comfortable to assume. And if they use nothing that is not observable *in principle*, they do use 'potential' observations which so far nobody has been able to make *in fact*: from a practical standpoint we are not much better off when drawing purely imaginary indifference curves than we are when speaking of purely imaginary utility functions.[1] Accordingly, it has been pointed out, as early as 1902, by Boninsegni, and a few years later by Barone,[2] that for the purposes of writing the equations of equilibrium theory we do not need either.[3] What then do we need for this purpose if we leave every other out of account? A little reflection shows that even the early utility theory of value never actually used any other postulate than this: faced with a given set of prices and a given 'income,' everybody chooses to buy (or sell) in a uniquely determined way. Everything else is idle decoration and justified, if at all, by such interest as may attach to it from the standpoint of other purposes. Barone had seen this but he had failed both to formulate this postulate exactly and to prove its sufficiency. This has been done by Samuelson,[4] who formulated the consistency postulate: if

$$\psi_i = h^i(P_1, \cdots P_n, I) \quad (i = 2, \cdots n),$$

$$\sum_{i=1}^{n} \psi_i P_i - I = 0,$$

[1] On the possibilities of 'The Empirical Derivation of Indifference Functions,' see the paper with this title, by W. Allen Wallis and Milton Friedman, in Lange *et al.* editors, *Studies in Mathematical Economics and Econometrics*, 1942 (Henry Schultz memorial volume)—though here again we must never say never; see, e.g., Professor Wald's important paper, 'The Approximate Determination of Indifference Surfaces by Means of Engel Curves,' *Econometrica*, April 1940. Of course, this must not be allowed to obliterate the logical difference: it does make a difference whether or not a certain construct has, to use the phrase of Immanuel Kant, a 'relation to possible experience' (*Relation auf mögliche Erfahrung*). Also, it can of course be shown just as in the case of the utility analysis that indifference-variety analysis is not open to any indictment on the score of circularity or emptiness.

[2] P. Boninsegni, 'I Fondamenti dell' economia pura,' *Giornale degli Economisti*, February 1902; and E. Barone, 'Il Ministro della produzione,' ibid. September and October 1908 (see above, sec. 5).

[3] They realized, of course, the necessity of restrictive assumptions about consumers' behavior from which the properties of demand functions would follow. This distinguishes their views from G. Cassel's, who simply advocated the scrapping of everything behind demand functions to make these the ultimate data. See his 'Grundriss einer elementaren Preislehre,' *Zeitschrift für die gesamte Staatswissenschaft* (1899), which deserves to be mentioned because it was the first uncompromisingly radical attack upon the whole structure of the utility theory of value made by an economist trained in mathematics. In his *Theory of Social Economy*, Cassel substantially repeated the argument.

[4] In his 'A Note on the Pure Theory of Consumer's Behavior,' *Economica*, February 1938; see also 'The Empirical Implications of Utility Analysis,' *Econometrica*,

and proved brilliantly that this gives all the restrictions we need for our

$$\sum_{i=1}^{n} P_i d\psi_i = 0 \quad \text{and} \quad \sum_{i=1}^{n} dP_i d\psi_i < 0 \quad (\text{not all } d\psi_i = 0).^5$$

[Editor's note: The plan for the remainder of this Appendix to Chapter 7 (Note on the Theory of Utility) is not quite clear. There is no doubt that J. A. S. intended to make his treatment of welfare economics a part of this Appendix, which is described as a digression or note on utility (see the first paragraph of section 5 of this chapter, The Theory of Planning and of the Socialist Economy) and there is some evidence that it was to be sub 8 (section 8). The section on Welfare Economics which follows was a preliminary treatment probably written in 1946 or 1947. The first six sections of the Note on the Theory of Utility were apparently written at the end of 1948. This material had been typed and read by J. A. S. Sometime later he sketched out section 7 (The Consistency Postulate) and put down notes for a section 8 (The Corpse Shows Signs of Life). It is conceivable that welfare economics would have been discussed here. 'The Corpse' is so fragmentary, however, that I have simply presented it in the next two paragraphs as part of this note and have made Welfare Economics section 8 of the Appendix to Chapter 7.

'8. *The Corpse Shows Signs of Life.* We have surveyed what in spite of backslidings and detours looks like a very definite line of development to a goal that seems to have been definitely reached by Samuelson. However, the picture would be incomplete if we failed to notice a number of symptoms which seem to be at variance with that line and to point in another direction. If these symptoms could all be interpreted as survivals of old views, they would not be worth while mentioning. It is but natural that a concept like utility, so deeply rooted both in century-old tradition and in the habits of everyday thought and parlance, should not give way easily. But there is more to it than this. It is true that it has by now been cogently proved that the concept of utility is superfluous in the theory of equilibrium values—which is in fact not only the strongest but the only needful argument against it. But it has not been proved—and cannot be proved in the nature of things—that the concept can never be useful for any other purpose. However we may feel about it, we cannot deny the heuristic service it has rendered in the past—historically it was the discovery of the very theory which now can do without it—and there is no saying whether its fertility is exhausted for all time. In this connection it becomes relevant to note that *some* arguments against it have no weight and others have gone too far. It is even possible that the argument against measurability is among the latter. Of course, as far as this goes, if we ever come to devise methods of measurement, it would not be the old psychic reality: there is the possibility that we might wish for a potential; there is even a possibility that we might measure without subjective reality [shorthand notes].

'And in this connection [shorthand notes] whatever objections against them [shorthand notes]'

[J. A. S. then jotted down the following references, which he obviously intended to discuss.]

'1. Irving Fisher, *Mathematical Investigations in the Theory of Value and Prices* (1925), his doctor's thesis first published in the *Transactions of the Connecticut Academy of Arts and Sciences*, 1892.

October 1938. Cf. N. Georgescu-Roegen, 'The Pure Theory of Consumer's Behavior,' *Quarterly Journal of Economics*, August 1936.

5 [J. A. S. did not finish this section or fill out the mathematical symbols for the Samuelson postulate; the mathematical formulation above was supplied by R. M. G.]

2. Aupetit [not certain, writing illegible].

3. Irving Fisher, 'A Statistical Method for Measuring "Marginal Utility" and Testing the Justice of a Progressive Income Tax,' in *Economic Essays Contributed in Honor of John Bates Clark* (1927).

4. Ragnar Frisch, 'Sur un Problème d'économie pure,' *Norsk Matematisk Forenings Skriften*, 1926.

5. Ragnar Frisch, *New Methods of Measuring Marginal Utility* (1932).

6. Paul A. Samuelson, 'A Note on Measurement of Utility,' *Review of Economic Studies*, February 1937.

. . . is not true [shorthand notes] welfare economics [shorthand notes] consistency [shorthand notes] parameter, *features* [shorthand notes]

Potential, [shorthand notes] Engel Curves.'

8. Welfare Economics *

The reader is presumably familiar with the distinction made in current teaching between 'positive' and 'welfare' economics. Little beyond convenience of exposition can be adduced for this distinction so far as it means not more than that positive economics is to explain and welfare economics is to prescribe. For all propositions of welfare economics can be formulated in the indicative mood just as well as any propositions of positive economics can, by the insertion of the appropriate axiological postulates, be turned into an imperative. Since, however, modern welfare economics has, as a matter of fact, acquired a distinct status of its own, it is convenient to notice its development separately. We have also an additional motive for doing so since the subject bears an obvious relation to the subject of interpersonal comparison of satisfactions that has not yet been touched upon.

We know the hallowed antiquity of welfare economics: a large part of the work of Carafa and his successors as well as of the work of the scholastic doctors and *their* successors was welfare economics. We also know that the welfare point of view was much in evidence in the eighteenth century and that, in Italy, the phrase *felicità pubblica* appeared very frequently on title pages. For Bentham and the English utilitarians generally this point of view was, of course, an essential element of their creed. Hence, the positive spirit of Ricardian economics notwithstanding, we find it also in the English 'classics,' particularly in J. S. Mill. So far as this goes, modern welfare economists merely revive the Benthamite tradition.

The temporary victory of the utility theory naturally gave a new impulse. We can see this already with the forerunners, such as Dupuit and Gossen. But current work in welfare economics harks back to Marshall's teaching, as developed by Pigou, and to Edgeworth and Pareto. Marshall made two contributions, besides offering many of those general considerations that were so con-

* [There were two treatments of welfare economics (one typed and one in manuscript), which had many points in common. The manuscript version is presented here. Both treatments were preliminary and were written earlier than the preceding seven sections of this Appendix on the Theory of Utility.]

genial to his propensity to preach. First, as has been mentioned above, he rediscovered Dupuit's consumers' surplus or rent, and thus presented welfare economics with an analytic tool that is, or was thought to be, particularly adapted to application in this field. Second, he formulated several propositions of the kind that is typical of modern welfare economics. The most famous one is noticed in the footnote below.[1] Its importance consists not so much in the proposition per se, but in the fact that it spelled a new departure: the virtues of the perfectly competitive equilibrium state—what Marshall called the *doctrine of maximum satisfaction*—had indeed been questioned many times before from a variety of standpoints; but this was the first time that this was done within the range of the pure theory of that state, the first time that, *on the theoretical plane*, the possibility was considered of turning individual actions into channels more conducive to general welfare than those of laissez-faire. Edgeworth's many contributions are perhaps best exemplified by that part of his theory of taxation which is concerned with justice. The treatment is in the spirit of his *New and Old Methods of Ethics* (1877), that is, in the spirit of hedonism or utilitarianism. The main points are the distinction between, and the rigorous definition and quantification of, the concepts of equal, proportionate, and minimum sacrifice, the equalitarian implication of the last-mentioned idea coming duly into view.[2] Mainly, Edgeworth's efforts were directed against popular errors of reasoning such as are implied, for instance, in the widespread belief that decreasing marginal utility of income is all that need be assumed in order to make progressiveness of taxation follow from the postulate of equal sacrifice.[3]

All this is simply revived Benthamism—or rather, Benthamism in the armor of a better technique—and implies not only a quantitative conception of utility or satisfaction or welfare but also the further idea that satisfactions of differ-

[1] Marshall (*Principles*, pp. 533 et seq.) averred that the sum total of satisfaction in a society *might* be increased beyond the maximum attainable under laissez-faire in a state of perfect equilibrium in perfect competition by taxing the production of commodities subject to decreasing returns and using the proceeds in order to subsidize the production of commodities subject to increasing returns. This proposition, which we cannot discuss here, has been much amplified by Professor Pigou and especially by Mr. R. F. Kahn, the chief authority on the subject. See the latter's paper 'Some Notes on Ideal Output,' *Economic Journal*, March 1935.

[2] The decisive proposition was that, in order to minimize the total sacrifice involved in raising a given sum, taxation should, to the requisite amount, wholly absorb, first, the excess of the highest income over the second highest one, then the excess of these two over the third highest one, and so on.

[3] This error can be found, as a witness to our loose habits of thinking, in the writings of quite reputable economists, though it should be obvious that, given the intention to take away from taxpayers equal 'amounts' of satisfaction, nothing follows from the 'law' of decreasing marginal utility of income except that higher incomes should pay higher absolute sums than smaller incomes: whether a tax devised to give effect to that intention is to be progressive, proportional, or regressive depends on the particular form we choose to adopt for that law of decrease.

ent people can be compared and, in particular, summed up into the General Welfare of society as a whole—the idea of 'interpersonal comparability of utility.' This idea, which few economists will care to defend nowadays [4] although many use arguments that presuppose it, has had a chequered career. It has been challenged almost from the first, for example, by Jevons, and then again and again both by writers who raised no difficulty about measurability and by writers who did. But it kept on intruding, the chief reason being, of course, that it seemed so useful in welfare economics. Marshall himself evidently did not object to it,[5] and Wicksell actually went to the length of saying that parliamentary discussions on questions of taxation would be meaningless if it were impossible to compare the utilities of different persons.[6] This is going rather far, but on the other hand it is also going rather far to state unconditionally that interpersonal comparison of utility [7] is meaningless in every sense and for all purposes.

However, from the standpoint of those economists who are steadfast opponents both of interpersonal comparison *and* of measurement of individual utilities, any attempt at either is of course no better than walking on clouds. Nevertheless, they were in no mind to give up welfare economics. It is here that Pareto enters again to save the situation, at least in part. He and, following him, Barone pointed out that objection to interpersonal comparisons (or measurability) does not invalidate those propositions of welfare economics which refer to events that benefit or injure some members of society without injuring or benefiting others.[8] This principle will also enable us, in a more restricted sense, to speak of an event's being 'socially beneficial' when some people are injured (lose something), but when those who are can be fully indemnified (so that they no longer prefer their old situation to the new one)

[4] See L. Robbins, 'Interpersonal Comparison of Utility,' *Economic Journal*, December 1938.

[5] It is true that he wrote (*Principles*, Book I, ch. 5, p. 76): 'We cannot directly compare the pleasures which two persons derive from smoking; nor even those which the same person derives from it at different times.' But the emphasis is upon the word 'directly'; and the sentence means not more than that, exactly as measurement of the desires of a given person is always an indirect one in the sense explained above, so interpersonal comparison must resort to indirect methods. Marshall's reasoning in fact repeatedly implies the possibility of interpersonal comparison.

[6] See, e.g., his article on Cassel's system, republished as Appendix I to the English edition of the *Lectures*, vol. I, p. 221.

[7] Perhaps I should explain, as I have explained before with respect to measurability and integrability, that this need not amount to more than saying that it may be possible to frame hypotheses concerning the relation between the significance of a dollar to the poor man, A, and the significance of a dollar to the rich man, B, that yield none but reasonable results.

[8] This means, of course, that such events, rearrangements, or measures can be called 'beneficial' or 'injurious' irrespective of any interpersonal comparison and irrespective of the question by how much the beneficiaries or victims are benefited or injured. The case where *all* individuals are benefited or injured is evidently covered by our formulation

at the expense of those who have been benefited and when, after this has been done, the latter are still better off than they were before.[9]

The standard work from which the new Anglo-American welfare economics stems, Professor Pigou's *Economics of Welfare* (1920; 3rd rev. ed. 1929),[10] though it does take some account of the point of view just referred to, goes much beyond the limits drawn by the Paretian suggestion, especially as regards transfers of wealth from the relatively rich to the relatively poor. But the new Anglo-American welfare economics itself tries to respect those limits, though trespass on forbidden ground is still frequent. That is to say, it tries to confine itself, on principle, to propositions that can be established without the aid of either interpersonal comparison or measurement of utility. Such self-restraint might seem surprising in view of the fact that its main result is to deprive of their scientific or pseudoscientific foundations many equalitarian articles of faith to which most modern economists are emotionally attached. But not much self-restraint is actually needed, for a device has been discovered that enables welfare economists to elude those restrictions. It is called Social Valuation and consists in replacing the conception of social welfare defined as the sum of individual satisfactions by the dictate of some agent who decides what relative weights are to be attached to the (unmeasurable) desires of the members of society.[11] That this agent is nothing but the *volonté générale* of the eighteenth century should be clear; so should the danger that this agent become but a name for the interests and ideals of the analyzing individual.

Under these circumstances, the question arises once more in what way modern welfare economics differs from that of the English 'classics.' [12] It dif-

[9] The reader will realize on reflection that this is more than what it seems to be at first sight, viz. a very artificial definition of what is meant by making 'society' better off.

[10] Originally *Wealth and Welfare* (1912).

[11] This may be illustrated by the parliamentary discussions on questions of taxation envisaged by Wicksell. According to the modern view, neither parliaments nor anyone else can compare the utilities of the persons who are to pay the taxes and the utilities of the persons who are to receive the proceeds or to benefit in other ways by the corresponding public expenditure. But this does not really matter: the parliamentary majority itself simply puts a comparative (ordinal) value upon the sacrifices and benefits involved. And similarly, the reader will no doubt put the value he pleases both on the comparative and on the absolute merits of the two procedures.

[12] Since it is impossible for us to enter into the methods and results of modern welfare economics, readers may welcome a few references: A. Burk (Bergson), 'A Reformulation of Certain Aspects of Welfare Economics,' *Quarterly Journal of Economics*, February 1938; H. Hotelling, 'The General Welfare in Relation to Problems of Taxation and of Railway and Utility Rates,' *Econometrica*, July 1938; N. Kaldor, 'Welfare Propositions in Economics and Interpersonal Comparisons of Utility,' *Economic Journal*, September 1939; J. R. Hicks, 'The Foundations of Welfare Economics,' *Economic Journal*, December 1939; T. de Scitovszky, 'A Note on Welfare Propositions in Economics,' *Review of Economic Studies*, November 1941; O. Lange, 'The Foundations of Welfare Economics,' *Econometrica*, July-October 1942; G. Tintner, 'A Note on Welfare Economics,' *Econometrica*, January 1946. Professor Hotelling's paper is of particular interest because it contains what is perhaps the most famous

fers, first, by a better technique. Second, partly because this better technique yields better results but much more because the preconceptions and affiliations of the modern radical differ from the preconceptions and affiliations of the old radical, it also differs by its attitude toward business and laissez-faire. But third it also differs by a circumstance that is not to its credit. Classic welfare propositions—including those of Jeremy Bentham—display a remarkable awareness of the qualifications to which considerations of instantaneous welfare maxima become subject as soon as we take account of the future. Not less remarkably, such considerations are almost completely absent from the writings of modern welfare economists. Practically their only topic is the administration of the means afforded by an existing industrial structure. This is no objection so long as welfare propositions remain exercises in pure theory and are frankly described as such. It is a fatal objection as soon as the welfare economist, repeating a long-exploded methodological error, proceeds to 'prescribe.' The chief objection to the most popular of all welfare precepts—equality of incomes—is not that it has no rigorously defensible foundations; the chief objection is that, *even so far as tenable*, it is completely uninteresting by comparison with the question of its effects upon cultural and economic evolution.

'practical' proposition of modern welfare economics, namely, that maximizing general welfare (in a particular sense) requires that all goods and services should be produced and consumed in quantities such as to equalize marginal costs and prices even where, owing to the presence of decreasing average costs, this involves losses to the producing industry—a proposition that is of great theoretical interest. Another excellent example for 'modern welfare economics at work' is Professor Samuelson's 'Welfare Economics and International Trade,' *American Economic Review*, June 1938, supplemented by 'Gains from International Trade,' *Canadian Journal of Economics and Political Science*, May 1939, and *Foundations* (1947), ch. 8.

[When originally written, the latest reference in this section was to Tintner's article in *Econometrica*, January 1946. The reference to Samuelson's *Foundations* (1947) was added later in pencil.]

CHAPTER 8

Money, Credit, and Cycles

1. Practical Problems

Once more the bulk of the vast literature on money and related subjects, which the period under survey produced, grew out of the discussions of current problems. It contained, as the literature on money always did and does, a large quantity of completely worthless publications and a still larger quantity of publications which, though more or less meritorious within their range, are uninteresting from the standpoint of a history of analysis. It is nevertheless necessary, recalling what has been said in Chapter 2, section 3, to restate a few of those practical problems that induced discussions of some importance.

(a) *The Gold Standard.* The literary reflex of the tendency that dominated the monetary policy of the period, the maintenance or adoption of the gold standard, merits more careful analysis than it is possible for us to offer. There were in all countries, among those who discussed actualities of national monetary policy in a practical spirit, very many unconditional 'pro's.' They included, as does every party to every practical controversy, narrow-minded fanatics without a trace of intelligence, but on its higher levels this was a respectable group. I shall mention, by way of example, Bamberger, Giffen, de Parieu, though a dozen other such trios would do just as well.[1]

In view of the superficial sentence that some of us are in the habit of passing on the monetary thought of that time, it should be noticed, first, that the opinions and recommendations of the unconditional 'pro's' were incessantly under fire—so that nothing could be farther from the truth than the idea that the economists of that period as a body worshipped the golden calf—and, second, that these opinions received but qualified support from those leaders of scientific economics *who actually worked in the field.* As we shall see, neither Jevons, nor Walras, nor Marshall, nor Wicksell, nor Wieser, nor Fisher can, without qualification, be called either theoretical or practical gold monometallists. Later on, moreover, the depressions of the eighties and nineties raised the question of gold's responsibility either for falling or for cyclically fluctuating prices. And the emergence of the gold-exchange standard raised the

[1] Ludwig Bamberger (1823-99) was a typical doctrinaire liberal of the German type—a revolutionary in 1848, a staunch enemy of socialism, protection, and even social insurance ever after. As a member of the Reichstag he established himself as its authority on money, and his great aim was to get Germany on the gold standard and to keep her there. He was a violent anti-bimetallist (see subsec. b), disposing of the bimetallist argument by pointing to the silver interests behind it. But the particular task he manfully strove to accomplish and the particular historical conditions in which this task posited itself to him must be taken into account before we condemn his views on the score of theoretical inadequacy. The more important of his speeches and articles (*Ausgewählte Reden und Aufsätze über Geld- und Bankwesen*) have been edited by K. Helfferich (1900).

Sir Robert Giffen (1837-1910), an economic journalist and civil servant, belongs to that category of meritorious or even eminent economists to whom this book cannot do justice. His *Progress of the Working Classes in the Last Half Century* (1884) and his *Growth of Capital* (1889) are landmarks in the history of economic statistics. Here we have to notice his valiant defense of the gold standard (*Case against Bimetallism*, 1892; *Evidence before the Royal Commission on Gold and Silver*, 1886-8) and his almost ferocious hatred of Fancy (i.e. non-gold) Monetary Standards.

F. E. de Parieu (1815-93) was by far the most important of the three. A public man—half politician, half civil servant—he specialized in the fields of taxation (income tax and related matters) and monetary policy. From 1857 on, perceiving the ineluctable drift of things, he advocated the gold standard—but with due respect to the French silver problems—and international monetary co-operation (see subsec. c below). His work on money is in his various reports. His works on public finance have been noticed already. [J. A. S. intended to but did not do this in the unfinished sec. 6 of ch. 6.]

question of the merits of actual gold circulation to which, as we know, Ricardo had already returned a negative answer.[2]

(b) *Bimetallism.* This was, throughout that period, the most fertile source of 'practical' controversy. The popular and political literature of the silver men—justice to silver; dollar of our fathers; You shall not crucify mankind upon a cross of gold—contains many arguments that kept on a much lower level than anything that can be found in the writings of the sponsors of gold. In particular, it is infested by products of a semi-pathological nature, for at that time bimetallism was the chief hunting grounds of monetary monomaniacs. Nevertheless, it is the fact—a fact that these semi-pathological products and also the victory of the gold party tend to obliterate—that, on its highest level, the bimetallist argument really had the better of the controversy, even apart from the support that a number of men of scientific standing extended to the cause of bimetallism.[3]

(c) *International Monetary Co-operation.* The various international monetary unions and conventions, such as the Latin Union, the Scandinavian Union, the German Union (before the foundation of the empire), naturally suggested more comprehensive schemes. On the initiative of France, an international currency conference was held in Paris, 1867, that under the leadership of de Parieu succeeded to a surprising extent in keeping clear of the bimetallist hornets' nest, considered the question of a uniform world coinage of gold, and adopted what were so far the boldest proposals ever made for a world-wide monetary union. But at the subsequent international conferences of 1878, 1881, and 1892, pressure by the United States diverted discussion and proposals to bimetallism and thereby killed the original idea.[4] However, at the conference of 1892, the German economist, Julius Wolf, proffered a new idea, namely,

[2] The gold-exchange standard was essentially a practitioner's idea. Scientific analysis had little if anything to do with the 'discovery.' There are, however, a number of critical interpretations of the exchange standard by scientific economists of which it must suffice to mention: L. von Mises, 'The Foreign-Exchange Policy of the Austro-Hungarian Bank,' *Economic Journal,* June 1909; J. M. Keynes, *Indian Currency and Finance* (1913); Fritz Machlup, *Die Goldkernwährung* (1925); C. A. Conant, 'The Gold-Exchange Standard,' *Economic Journal,* June 1909; and a series of important papers and reports by E. W. Kemmerer, see, e.g., his analysis of the case of the Straits Settlements in *Political Science Quarterly,* XIX and XXI (December 1904 and December 1906).

[3] It is, however, quite impossible to sample that torrent of publications. Instead, I shall mention two works of undoubted scientific standing that may serve as an introduction to the popular literature also: J. S. Nicholson, *Treatise on Money and Essays on Monetary Problems* (1888), and F. A. Walker, *International Bimetallism* (1896). There was a Bimetallic League whose many publications are recommended to readers desirous of going further into the subject. Additional material is to be found in the reports and other writings of S. Dana Horton, next to Walker the leading American advocate of international bimetallism. The outstanding purely analytic performance on bimetallism is that of Walras (*Éléments, leçons* 31 and 32).

[4] On these conferences, whose reports contain many contributions of analytical merit, see H. B. Russell, *International Monetary Conferences* (1898).

that an international gold reserve be deposited in a neutral country and that international banknotes be issued on the basis of this reserve—the idea that, though in an entirely different form, was to be partly realized by the International Fund of Bretton Woods fame.

(d) *Stabilization and Monetary Management.* The chief appeal of the bimetallist argument, at least for people not directly interested in silver production, was of course in the prospect it held out of *rising* prices. Officially, however, bimetallists preferred to speak of *stabilizing* the price level. But other schemes of stabilization, unconnected with silver, were also produced, for example, schemes that proposed to divorce circulation entirely from gold and to use paper money. And though, during three decades of falling prices, it was primarily the price level people thought of stabilizing (as always, there was intentional or unintentional confusion of this aim with the aim of keeping up individual prices, especially those of agricultural products), broader aims were by no means absent. Even mere stabilization of prices implies—as its main purely economic motive—concern with stabilization of a country's economic situation. But stabilization of employment was often mentioned explicitly. Further, especially in connection with discussions of the gold-exchange standard, there was much talk about stabilizing money rates.[5]

All this already meant monetary management of one kind or another. For instance, bimetallism spells management whenever, in order to make it work, it is necessary to regulate the price of silver—that is to say, to peg it by purchases in order to keep silver from driving gold out of circulation—for in this case the monetary system no longer works automatically. All schemes that

[5] The 'comedy of errors' present in almost any discussion of economic policy may be instructively illustrated by one particular instance pertaining to that range of problems. When Austria, in the nineties, adopted the gold-exchange standard, it was urged by politicians and in the press that one of the advantages of this arrangement would be to secure lower interest rates than would prevail in the case of a fullfledged gold currency. Truth and error in this should be easy to disentangle. A central bank that is to keep exchanges within gold points must, in the long run, do pretty much all that a central bank does under the fullfledged gold standard, and refrain from doing what such a bank must not do. Therefore, interest rates in a money market that works under the gold-exchange standard cannot be normally lower than they would be in a money market that works under a fullfledged gold standard. But, first, the total amount of gold necessary in order to start a gold-exchange-standard system is smaller than the total amount of gold that is necessary to start a system with actual gold circulation. Hence money rates in the initial period need not be kept on so high a level for so long in the former case as would be necessary in the latter case. Second, with the central bank in control of the whole of a nation's monetary gold stock, it is easier in the former case to avoid the necessity of varying bank rate in passing spells of difficulty than it is in the latter. However, politicians and the daily press claimed that interest rates would normally be lower with a gold-exchange standard than they would be with a fullfledged gold standard. And in their zeal to refute this erroneous proposition, professional economists usually failed to admit the two true ones—so that, as so often happens in our field, both parties to the controversy were, in effect, right and wrong at the same time.

went further than this involved, of course, still more management. As an example, I shall mention a proposal that commanded some support: the proposal of an inconvertible paper currency to be regulated by a government department that was to buy government bonds for this currency—to increase liquidity—whenever the price level fell, and to sell government bonds—to decrease liquidity—for this currency whenever the price level rose. This proposal may be considered as one of the many precursors of the open-market operations of the Federal Reserve System. But the idea of open-market operations was familiar in other forms also. For monetary management was not confined to management of the currency. It extended to management of the foreign exchanges and, more important, of bank credit.[6] Nor did it remain in the realm of 'plans.' It was increasingly practiced by all the great central banks.[7] And it is not true that monetary management of this and other types knew no other purpose than to safeguard a nation's gold stock. It was practiced for therapeutic purposes. These purposes differed from ours and the full-employment purpose was not the dominating one. But it is as misleading to overstress the importance that was then attached to playing the gold standard game for its own sake as it is to speak of the monetary systems prior to 1914 as 'automatic.'[8] Unless this be clearly understood, it is impossible to appreciate the doctrinal developments of that age either in themselves or in their relation to the thought of our own time.

For the rest we must be content to notice a few of the performances, in the field of 'monetary reform,' of the scientific leaders. Jevons sketched out what seemed to him 'An Ideally Perfect System of Currency'[9] in which gold, while retained as means of exchange and common denominator of values, was to cease to be the standard for deferred payments, 'the amounts of debts, although expressed in gold, being varied inversely, as gold varies in terms of other commodities.' This revived the 'tabular-standard plan' of Lowe (see above, Part III, ch. 7, sec. 3) and is also the keynote of Marshall's suggestions.[10] The

[6] Thus, the issue of control of credit *vs.* control of money, which carries over into more recent times, was already discussed.

[7] For England, in particular, see W. T. C. King, *History of the London Discount Market* (1936).

[8] They looked more automatic than they were because they functioned so smoothly. Moreover, if the Bank of England seems (statistically) to have reacted, in its discount policy, mainly to the inflow or outflow of gold, it must not be forgotten that, in the conditions that prevailed roughly until 1900, reacting to the inflow and outflow of gold involved essentially the same behavior as would have reacting to the domestic business situation, in nine cases out of ten. When this ceased to be so, central banks increasingly resorted to 'gold devices,' i.e. increasingly abandoned the orthodox gold standard game.

[9] Written about 1875 but first published in his important *Investigations in Currency and Finance*, posthumously edited by Mrs. Jevons and Professor Foxwell in 1884. Attention is called to Foxwell's Introduction.

[10] In order to save space, I neglect the other features of Jevons' scheme, which are in the direction of an international note issue and clearing system based upon gold. Marshall's exploits in the role (as he styled it) of 'amateur currency-mediciner' saw the

latter include, however, a novel idea. Adopting Ricardo's ingot plan, he proposed that these ingots should consist of both gold and silver and that silver bars of a certain weight should be legally 'wedded' to gold bars of a certain weight so that the monetary unit would constitute a claim to quantities of both gold and silver in fixed proportion (Symmetallism). Irving Fisher's proposal,[11] the Compensated Dollar, combined adoption of the gold-exchange standard with the device of varying the gold content of the monetary unit according to the variations of an official price index so that a dollar should represent, instead of a constant quantity of gold, a constant quantity of purchasing power. Finally, Walras advocated a plan that linked up with actual practice in France in a manner that was as ingenious as it was simple. Gold was to remain the standard monetary metal and to be coined for private account without limit. Silver was to be the material of token coins (*billon*) which, however, were not only to provide small change (*billon divisionnaire*) *but also a type of legal-tender money that was to be used for the purpose of controlling the price level* (*billon régulateur*): government was to expand its circulation when prices were falling and to contract its issue when prices were rising. The modern ring of this proposal needs no emphasis. Walras added another, which makes him one of the precursors of our own '100 per cent plans.' He recognized, though only in the case of banknotes, the fact that banks create means of payment or, as he put it, that banks can lend to entrepreneurs without borrowing the same amount from capitalists (savers). But he disapproved of it. And he proposed that the silver surplus be used in order to coin additional silver tokens in the amount of banknotes outstanding—minus the amount of legal-tender cash held by the issuing banks—and to suppress the latter.[12]

The merits or demerits of these plans are not in question here. They have been mentioned for two reasons: first, because they show how utterly unfounded is the belief that scientific leaders did not attend to problems of monetary reform until our own day; second, because all those plans rested upon a basis of analytic work, the fundamental importance of which must be recognized quite independently of whether or not we like the plans themselves.

---

light in a paper he read at the Industrial Remuneration Conference in 1885, significantly entitled 'How far do remediable causes influence prejudicially (a) the continuity of employment, (b) the rates of wages?' (see Keynes's biography of Marshall, *Essays in Biography*, p. 204); in his evidences before the Royal Commission on the Depression of Trade and Industry (1886), before the Gold and Silver Commission (1887-8), and before the Indian Currency Committee (1899), published in *Official Papers* (1926); and in his article 'Remedies for Fluctuations of General Prices' (*Contemporary Review*, March 1887). See also F. Y. Edgeworth, 'Thoughts on Monetary Reform,' *Economic Journal*, September 1895.

[11] See Irving Fisher, assisted by Harry G. Brown, *The Purchasing Power of Money* (1st ed., 1911).

[12] *Études d'économie politique appliquée*, I and V.

2. Analytic Work

The story of the period's purely analytic work—to which henceforth we shall confine our attention almost exclusively—is a story of successful advance.[1] Though, as we have just seen, most of the leaders participated with zest in the discussions on the practical problems of their day, their work was less dependent upon this stimulus than had been the work of their predecessors: more than before analysis forged ahead, as it were, under its own steam, and the purely scientific filiation of ideas—doctrinal change that is not simply reaction to changing facts and changing political humors—is more in evidence than it was in the preceding period. And more than in other parts of economics new and valuable methods and results grew out of the pre-existing stock of knowledge: in 'general theory' it is possible, if we so choose, to speak of revolution; in monetary theory there was only vigorous evolution. No break occurred with the work that J. S. Mill had thrown into an imperfectly systematic form. Yet most of the ground on which the structure of monetary analysis stands today was actually conquered.

The general picture I am about to present suffers from the impossibility of giving an account, except on rare occasions, of the factual work of that period which is at least as important for our own as are the 'theories.' But all that can be done in a sketch like this is to mention types and give one or two examples of each. There are, first, some really excellent official reports: besides the English ones, which as usual hold first place, I will again refer to those of the international monetary conferences and of the U.S. National Monetary Commission (1911-12). Second, there are the histories of currencies and of banking—such as W. A. Shaw's *History of Currency, 1252-1894* (1895) or W. G. Sumner's classic, *A History of American Currency* (1874). Third, the period produced repertoires of materials that are still of value—Adolf Soetbeer's (1814-92) *Materialien zur Erläuterung und Beurteilung der wirtschaftlichen Edelmetallverhältnisse* (1885; English trans. from 2nd ed., 1887, the seventh part of which contains his famous Table of Prices) is the outstanding performance of this genus. A fourth type is exemplified by Sir R. H. Inglis Palgrave's statistical work on central banks, especially the Bank of England (most of it summed up in his *Bank Rate and the Money Market*, 1903, which is a masterpiece of the art of making figures speak): it is very difficult to formulate particular results but he who peruses this book page by page suddenly discovers that he understands its subject. Fifth, we should note the infiltration of modern statistical methods into the field—the earliest example known to me being J. P. Norton's *Statistical Studies in the New York Money Market* (1902).

[1] Four references will suffice: Professor Marget's work (*Theory of Prices*, 1938-42), though not primarily written from the historical point of view, is yet by far the best guide to the history of monetary analysis during that period; Professor Rist's *History of Monetary and Credit Theory* (English trans., 1940) must also be mentioned again; Professor Howard Ellis' *German Monetary Theory, 1905-1933* (1934; together with authorities there quoted or mentioned in the Bibliography) presents an exhaustive treatment of the work within its field; V. F. Wagner's *Geschichte der Kredittheorien* (1937) usefully supplements Professor Rist's work.

Why is it, then, that the work of that period is sometimes referred to so slightingly and that many of us construct an entirely unrealistic cleavage between it and our own? One answer is precisely that the evolutionary quality of those new methods and results make them look like mere reformulations of old stuff. But there is another answer, one that is highly interesting for the student of the mechanisms of scientific 'progress.' That period failed to develop and systematize its conquests in a form readily accessible to all economists, with all implications and applications nicely worked out and displayed on a silver platter. These conquests therefore did not penetrate into the common run of literature, especially into the textbooks, so that derogatory criticism, while it arouses just indignation in scholars like Professor Marget, is at the same time in a position to justify itself by quotations from the common run—even from such well-known, successful, and (in their way) meritorious books as Karl Helfferich's *Das Geld* (1903), or J. L. Laughlin's *Principles of Money* (1903), or Horace White's popular *Money and Banking* (1st ed., 1895; 5th ed., 1914), or David Kinley's *Money* (1904), or Alfred de Foville's *La Monnaie* (1907). Even Adolf Wagner's *Sozialökonomische Theorie des Geldes* (1909), which takes a higher flight and contains several original points, is not in much better case, and Karl Knies's *Geld und Credit* (1873-9), important though it is in other respects, added but little to the topics covered by its title.

In conscience, we must, however, mention at least a few more of those textbooks that stand out from the rest for one reason or another: Jevons' *Money and the Mechanism of Exchange* (1875), which ran into many editions—a charming book in which rather trite elements are sometimes glorified by original sparks; J. Shield Nicholson's *Treatise on Money and Essays on Monetary Problems* (1888)—a work that has never got its due; F. A. Walker's famous textbook, *Money* (1878), perhaps the best means to familiarize oneself with the current doctrine of those times at its best; Tullio Martello's *La Moneta* (1883), the value of which is but slightly impaired by some liberalist vagaries on free coinage; A. Messedaglia's *La Moneta* . . . (1882-3), one of the best performances of the scientific literature on money that preceded the Walras-Marshall-Wicksell-Fisher achievements. In addition, the parts, books, or chapters on money of the general treatises—such as Pierson's, or Divisia's, or Colson's—ought to be mentioned.[2] But we must confine ourselves to the Third Book of G. Cassel's *Theoretische Sozialökonomie* (1918, 4th ed. rev. 1927; English trans., 1923, new ed., 1932). This work deserves to be singled out because it presents, with a clearness that does not admit of doubt, an instance of the view that the fundamental logic of the economic process is entirely independent of the monetary phenomenon, the theory of which fundamentally consists merely in the theory of the price level—by which relative prices (exchange ratios) are turned into absolute money prices on quantity-theory lines—and therefore *really* and not only *apparently* stands outside the body of general economic theory. In this respect, Cassel entirely missed the import of Walras' message, which in other respects he followed so closely. But if we take his treatment as an outstanding instance of what is indeed a completely antiquated view of the matter, we must add that he represents this view extremely effectively and that his treatment therefore retains importance. Nor is this importance merely historical. We may well use Cassel whenever we wish to find out what our own advance really amounts to.

[2] On Pierson, Divisia, and Colson, see above, ch. 5.

A brief description of the nature and fate of the chief analytic performances of the period will explain this paradoxical state of things.

(a) *Walras.* First, by far the greatest of those performances was that of Walras.[3] In the same sense in which it is true to say that he created economic statics, the modern theory of economic equilibrium, it is also true to say that he created the modern theory of money. In fact, his theory of money and credit is simply part of this general theory of economic equilibrium. He therefore substantially fulfilled the great desideratum which has been so much stressed during the last twenty years, namely, the desideratum that the analysis of money should be built into the system of general theory instead of being developed independently and then plastered upon it. And, *so far as monetary statics is concerned,* all propositions developed about money and monetary processes are either contained in his system or may be derived from it by introducing additional assumptions. Thus, as has been shown by Lange,[4] the Keynesian analysis of the *General Theory* (not of the *Treatise* of 1930) is but a special case of the genuinely general theory of Walras. But, as we have seen, Walras did not come into his own until the twenties. Such influence as he exerted during the period under discussion was mainly through Wicksell and Pantaleoni. And even these two did not fully appreciate the importance of his work on money. His immediate successor, Pareto, was altogether blind to it and slid back rather than advanced in this particular field. Two excellent followers Walras did find. But they remained almost completely unknown, Aupetit and Schlesinger.[5]

So far as the period under survey is concerned, the Walrasian theory of money simply did not exist for the overwhelming majority of economists. I take, however, the opportunity to advert to the original work of Del Vecchio, which, in part from Walrasian bases, started in the last years of that period.[6]

Another body of original work on money, related to that of Walras, may be conveniently mentioned here, namely, Irving Fisher's. Most of it came too late to exert influence within the period. And when it did appear, professional attention was too much concentrated on one book, *The Purchasing Power of*

[3] It is only in the 4th ed. of the *Éléments d'économie politique pure* (1900) that we find Walras' pure theory of money fully developed. His slow progress toward this most important piece of monetary analysis covered the years 1876-99, the starting point and the individual steps being reflected in the first three editions and in a number of memoirs on applied problems which eventually went into the *Études d'économie politique appliquée* (see above, ch. 7, sec. 7e).

[4] See O. Lange, 'The Rate of Interest and the Optimum Propensity to Consume,' *Economica*, February 1938.

[5] A. Aupetit, *Essai sur la théorie générale de la monnaie* (1901); Karl Schlesinger, *Theorie der Geld- und Kreditwirtschaft* (1914). These two books, especially the latter, are striking instances of the fact that in our field first-class performance is neither a necessary nor a sufficient condition for success.

[6] Gustavo Del Vecchio, Professor at the University of Bologna, began publishing his important series of papers in 1909. They were summed up in his *Grundlinien der Geldtheorie* (1930) and more completely in his *Ricerche sopra la teoria generale della moneta* (1932).

Money (1911), the success of which obscured the fact that it presented only one aspect—and not the most important one—of its author's monetary theory *as this phrase is understood now.* Ever since the publication of this book Fisher has been classed as a sponsor of a particularly rigid form of quantity theory (see below, sec. 5) and all his other contributions to monetary analysis of the economic process as a whole—monetary analysis in the sense in which Keynes's *General Theory* is monetary analysis—have been neglected. This was and is because he did not call them monetary or income analysis but chose other titles, such as *Theory of Interest* or *Booms and Depressions.* In consequence, his readers never got a full view of his work on money and in particular never noticed the Walrasian streak in it.[7]

(b) *Marshall.* The second great performance of the last three decades of the nineteenth century was Marshall's.[8] Like Walras, though less explicitly, he saw the monetary problem as part of the general analysis of the economic process and as one of the doors to the theory of employment. More clearly than Walras, though less emphatically than Wicksell, he taught the importance of the distinction between the 'real' and the 'monetary' rate of interest and of attending to the details of the mechanism by which changes in the amount of money act on the economic system. And there were many hints that suggest future developments though only a few of them will be mentioned in this chapter. He held all the elements required for a decisive step forward though he did not himself take this step. Unlike Walras he was indeed in a position of effective leadership. From 1885 on, the whole world's population of economists would have listened had he addressed it. But only glimpses of his views on

[7] Practically all of Professor Fisher's numerous books and papers are relevant for the scholar who may some day attempt the task of co-ordination. I mention here only the most important of those books that have not been mentioned above, ch. 5, sec. 7b. *Appreciation and Interest* (*Publications of the American Economic Association*, August 1896); *The Purchasing Power of Money* (with H. G. Brown, 1911; rev., 1913); *The Money Illusion* (1928); *Booms and Depressions* (1932). But the *Rate of Interest* (1907), fully developed into *The Theory of Interest* (1930), which has been mentioned already, is really still more important for *monetary* theory in the present-day sense. Fisher's work on index numbers will be mentioned later.

[8] Marshall's final presentation of his contributions, to be mentioned presently in the text, was preceded by a number of communications, mainly to official committees of inquiry, that were republished in his *Official Papers* and may be supplemented by a number of passages in the *Memorials.* But the *Principles* also contain important elements of an imposing total. The reader finds a survey of most of the essential points in Keynes's biographical memoir (*Essays in Biography*, pp. 195-206), but must be warned again that this memoir was written by a (then) fervent disciple. In some points the large claims made by this disciple on behalf of the originality and priority of the master must certainly be discounted. For the rest, Keynes's statement that Marshall developed the whole of his monetary theory during the seventies should be accepted unreservedly—though without prejudice to the claims of Walras and Wicksell. Another point is interesting to note: Marshall's monetary analysis, like his economic analysis in general, clearly started from J. S. Mill's and must be understood as a development of the latter's teaching.

monetary problems were vouchsafed to it until the publication, in his extreme old age, of his *Money, Credit, and Commerce* (1923), when nothing in it seemed novel any more. His Cambridge pupils and other followers of his did listen. As a matter of historical justice, it should be emphasized that, in developing the English monetary theories of our own time, Hawtrey, Lavington, Keynes, Pigou, and Robertson developed Marshallian teaching—though on lines of their own.

It is unnecessary to comment upon works that are in every student's hands. All that is necessary to point out here are the links with Marshall. Professor R. G. Hawtrey should perhaps not be called a pupil in the same sense in which this term applies to the others. But most of the propositions that individuate his teaching—which, as the reader knows, is mainly geared to the problems of business cycles—may be traced to Marshall (and some to Wicksell). The best way of putting it is perhaps to say that Hawtrey's analysis is an original development, in a certain direction, of Marshall's analysis. Of his numerous works, it will suffice to mention here *Good and Bad Trade* (1913), *Currency and Credit* (1st ed., 1919), *The Art of Central Banking* (1932), *Capital and Employment* (1937). Frederick Lavington's works are not so well known as they deserve to be: *The English Capital Market* (1921) and *The Trade Cycle . . .* (1922). They are unconditionally Marshallian. So is Professor Pigou's article, 'The Value of Money,' in the *Quarterly Journal of Economics*, November 1917, his chief contribution to monetary theory per se. Other contributions are to be found in his *Industrial Fluctuations* (1927). Of all the rest, I will mention only his monetary analysis of the economic process, *Employment and Equilibrium* (1941). The theoretical skeleton of Lord Keynes's first book, *Indian Currency and Finance* (1913), was also Marshallian, and in his *Tract on Monetary Reform* (1923) he wrote that his 'exposition [of monetary theory] follows the general lines of Prof. Pigou and Dr. Marshall' (p. 85n.), though notes of his own are sounded at critical points. His most ambitious book, *A Treatise on Money* (1930), may be described as a development of (though also away from) Marshallian and Wicksellian lines—the Wicksellian elements were rediscovered, however, not taken from Wicksell. It was only in *The General Theory of Employment, Interest, and Money* (1936) that allegiance to Marshall was formally renounced. This makes it all the more important to note that it was not so much theoretical differences which produced this posthumous break with Marshall as the difference in social vision—in the diagnoses Marshall and Keynes formed about the economic situation of their times. As far as points of theory and not factual assumptions or practical recommendations are concerned, there was one important difference only—about the mechanism of saving and investment—but even this one could have been reduced to a matter of shift of emphasis, had it not been essential for Keynes to divorce himself from what he styled the 'classic theory.' Professor D. H. Robertson's strikingly original *Banking Policy and the Price Level* (1926) went really further beyond Marshall than any of the works mentioned in this paragraph. If it stood alone, it would not be appropriate to pigeonhole Robertson with the Marshallians. Nor can he be so pigeonholed on the strength of his theory of business cycles. But the rest of his publications on money (including his well-known elementary textbook), the most important of which have been republished in his *Essays in Monetary Theory* (1940) may be said to have grown from Marshallian roots.

But this success of Marshall's teaching on money was to come later, so late that he lost part of the credit for it. Up to 1914, monetary theory outside of Cambridge was practically untouched by Marshallian influence.

(c) *Wicksell.* The third great performance to be mentioned is that of Wicksell.[9] Posthumously he acquired even greater international reputation as a monetary theorist than either Marshall or Walras. This better fortune is due to the facts that his Swedish disciples never ceased to call themselves Wicksellians, even when they criticized and surpassed him, and that his message became accessible in German at a relatively early date and in a form that was not so forbidding as was that of Walras. But it took him decades to reach the Anglo-American sphere.

Again it is hardly necessary to mention such well-known names as Myrdal, Ohlin, Lindahl, Lundberg. Gunnar Myrdal's *Monetary Equilibrium* (Swedish, 1931; German, 1933; English, 1939), Bertil Ohlin's Swedish essay on the theory of expansion, 'Penningpolitik, offentliga arbeten, subventioner och tullar som medel mot arbetslöshet' published in a report on Monetary Policy to the Swedish Unemployment Commission, 1934), and Erik Lindahl's English summary of his contributions (*Studies in the Theory of Money and Capital,* 1939). Erik Lundberg's *Studies in the Theory of Economic Expansion* (1937) will represent the post-Wicksellian development. It is an interesting fact to note in a history of economic analysis that, until about ten years ago, this development paralleled and in some important points anticipated, the English (Keynesian) one without becoming known to English economists. Some mild protests naturally resulted from this state of things and also some discussions about the differences between, and the relative merits of, the two bodies of thought. See Ohlin's 'Some Notes on the Stockholm Theory of Savings and Investment,' *Economic Journal,* March and June 1937, and the subsequent discussions in the same Journal (see below, Part v, ch. 5). Professor D. Davidson, the contemporary and helpful critic of Wicksell, should not go unmentioned. The reader finds all he ought to know about Davidson's monetary doctrines in the excellent article, 'The Monetary Doctrines of Professor Davidson,' by Mr. Brinley Thomas (*Economic Journal,* March 1935). In the latter's *Monetary Policy and Crises* (1936) there is a brief but useful sketch of Swedish monetary theory since Wicksell.

(d) *The Austrians.* In the fourth place, there were the contributions of the Austrian group. They all started from Menger,[10] who did not, however, strike out on a line for himself: his theory, though a masterly performance so far as

[9] Wicksell's chief contributions are in his *Geldzins und Güterpreise* (1898). R. F. Kahn's trans., *Interest and Prices,* with an introduction on the evolution of Wicksell's thought by Professor Ohlin, appeared in 1936, but some of the essential ideas, especially the famous Wicksellian 'cumulative process' *were* presented to the English public in the article on 'The Influence of the Rate of Interest on Prices,' *Economic Journal,* June 1907, and in vol. II of his *Lectures on Political Economy* (Swedish original, 1906; English trans., 1934). Very important, because emphasizing certain points that do not stand out so strongly in those two books is also his (Swedish) article on the obscure point in the theory of money, 'Den dunkla punkten i penningteorien,' *Ekonomisk Tidskrift,* December 1903. As in the case of Marshall, it should be observed that Wicksell started from Mill and that his monetary theory developed from a criticism of the latter and the English authors behind him, Tooke in particular.

[10] See *Collected Works* (4 vols., London School Reprints, 1933-6). Menger's chief pieces on money were the chapter on the theory of money in his *Grundsätze* and the article 'Geld' in the 3rd ed. of the *Handwörterbuch* (1909).

it went, was simply a descendant from Davanzati's. It was Wieser who attempted a new departure.[11] In trying to do justice to it we meet with the same difficulty that confronted us when we were trying to define his place in the history of general theory. Wieser's spacious vision of the monetary phenomenon is not adequately rendered by calling him a sponsor of the 'income-approach' [12] or a sponsor of the consumption standard. It comprised much more than that, in particular the conception of a monetary theory of the economic process as a whole. But he was so deficient in technique and so little able to coin his metal that nothing of this came out as it should have. And so his influence touched only a few individuals. The author of the group's standard work on money, von Mises,[13] who was also its foremost teacher in the field —in fact the founder of a school of his own—was no doubt one of them. But he was only partly in sympathy with Wieser's views.

3. Fundamentals

(a) *Nature and Functions of Money.* Discussions on the nature and functions of money and hence on the question of definition were carried on throughout the period. But, with the exception to be noticed under (b), they did not excite much interest and, without any exception, they did not produce very interesting results. I believe that a majority of writers accepted, or would have been willing to accept, Roscher's definition.[1] Menger and his followers did so with particular emphasis—without any intention to commit themselves thereby to all its implications. Others, Americans especially, accepted Walker's neat phrase—'Money is that Money does'—in an equally non-com-

[11] Wieser's ideas on money, like those of Walras, developed when his original work on general theory had been done. His first publication in the field was his inaugural lecture delivered on his appointment to Menger's chair in Vienna ('Der Geldwert und seine geschichtlichen Veränderungen,' *Zeitschrift für Volkswirtschaft, Sozialpolitik und Verwaltung,* 1904). An improved version was presented in an address to the Verein für Sozialpolitik at its Vienna meeting in 1909 and published in the Verein's *Schriften,* vol. 132, and another in the article 'Geld' (Allgemeine Theorie des Geldes) in the 4th ed. of the *Handwörterbuch,* 1927.

[12] On Wieser as a sponsor of the income approach, see below sec. 6b.

[13] Ludwig von Mises, *Theorie des Geldes und der Umlaufsmittel* (1st ed., 1912, 2nd ed., 1924, English trans. under the title, *Theory of Money and Credit,* 1934).

[1] 'The false definitions of money divide up into two main groups: those that consider it to be something more, and those that consider it to be something less, than the most salable commodity' (Roscher, *Grundlagen,* Book II, ch. 3, § 116 [trans. by J. A. S.]). As an example of the contrary opinion, I quote Richard (son of the more important Bruno) Hildebrand, *Theorie des Geldes* (1883), where we learn that money, far from being a commodity is 'the very opposite of a commodity.' In *Interest and Prices* Wicksell quoted both these authors. And his comments upon the issue illustrate well how little such general pronouncements really mean to the serious worker. But the contradictions between them help to discredit economics in the eyes of all those laymen and historians who take them too literally and believe that everything else follows from them.

mittal spirit. Most writers distinguished between money or primary money (meaning coin and government fiat, often but not always, also banknotes or at least notes of central banks) and 'credit' or fiduciary money (meaning means of payment arising out of credit transactions), a distinction to which some attached great importance [2] and which, in certain cases to be noticed, was in fact indicative of something more significant than terminological preference. We have seen above that the leading authorities on money were not addicted to any uncritical gold standard fetichism. Where they did stand for the gold standard, as in Italy, there were good and sufficient practical reasons for their doing so. But practically all must be classed as theoretical metallists in our sense of the term.[3] It seems worth our while to advert to the following points.

First, the practice continued to prevail of developing the theory of money from its old four functions: medium of exchange, measure of value, store of value, standard of deferred payments—many authors insisting both on the separability of these functions and on the practical reasons why we actually find them combined. Walras, anticipated of course by all those authors who—like A. Smith and Malthus—had used labor as a standard of value, introduced the useful fashion of keeping distinct the *numéraire*—a commodity whose unit is used in order to express prices and values but whose own value remains unaffected by this role—and *monnaie*—the commodity that actually serves as means of exchange and whose value is consequently affected because its monetary role absorbs part of its supply.

Second, many writers went out of their way to emphasize the store-of-value function of money. This is important because it raises the question how far the economists of that period were aware of the phenomenon that is called Liquidity Preference in the Keynesian economics of our own day. Marshall spoke of a law of hoarding according to which people's demand for gold hoards increases as its value rises (see *Official Papers*, p. 6). Occasionally he seems to have given thought to the fact that people sometimes fail to spend though they have the power to do so.[4] Von Mises noticed in passing that money is sometimes held as an asset (*Vermögensanlage*). Going further, Kemmerer averred (*Money and Credit Instruments*, p. 20) that 'large sums of money are continually being hoarded' and that 'the proportion of the circulating medium which is hoarded from time to time . . . varies with all the influences which affect . . . business confidence.' Moreover, Marshall and others, especially Fisher, were aware of the role that hoarding, in the sense of unwillingness to

[2] See, e.g., Laughlin, op. cit. or Mises, op. cit. In our own time no less an authority than Professor Rist (op. cit.) may be cited in support of the opinion that neglect of that distinction has been the source of many errors, theoretical and practical. But the errors can be avoided even if we include 'credit' with money, and committed if we do not.

[3] Pareto, evidently disgusted by Italian currency troubles, went even so far as to call paper money 'false money' (*moneta falsa*). Other Italians also, such as Pantaleoni, considered it as a pathological case. Equally strong metallism, though differently motivated, we can find only in Marx.

[4] So already in *Economics of Industry*, see J. M. Keynes, *General Theory*, p. 19n.

spend, plays in the mechanism of depressions. But only outsiders, such as Hobson, attached 'critical importance' to it as a cause of disturbance in general and of unemployment in particular.[5] Since it is this feature that constitutes the theory of Liquidity Preference, we must, I think, credit—or debit—the introduction of the theory to Lord Keynes (see, however, below, sec. 6).

Third, the theory of money of that period was not monetary analysis either in the sense of Becher and Quesnay [6] or in the modern sense; that is to say, it was not the general theory of a monetary economy. We have indeed seen that Walras' theory of money is fully integrated with his general theory of value and distribution. We have noticed and shall notice again other advances in that direction, in particular the one associated with Wicksell's name. On the whole, however, monetary theory remained in one separate compartment and the 'theory of value and distribution' in another. Prices (including rates of income) remained primarily exchange ratios, which money reduces to absolute figures without affecting them in anything except for clothing them with a monetary garb. Or, in other words, the model of the economic process was in all essentials a barter model, the working of which inflations and deflations might disturb but which is logically complete and autonomous. Practically all the most valuable work of the period—so far as it was not concerned with specifically monetary problems—was Real Analysis, even where it expressed its concepts in terms of money.[7]

This situation found expression in the creation of an interesting concept that emerged and vanished with it. If, on the one hand, the facts of value and distribution are logically so independent of money that they can be set forth with only a passing reference to it, but if, on the other hand, it is recognized that money may act as a disturber, then the problem arises of defining how money would have to behave in order to leave the real processes of the barter model uninfluenced. Wicksell was the first to see the problem clearly and to coin the appropriate concept, Neutral Money. In itself, this concept expresses nothing but the established belief in the possibility of pure 'real' analysis. But it also suggests recognition of the fact that money *need* not be neutral. So its creation induced a hunt for the conditions in which money is neutral. And this point eventually led to the discovery that no such conditions can be formulated, that is, that there is no such thing as neutral money or money that is a mere veil spread over the phenomena that really matter—an

[5] J. A. Hobson, *Physiology of Industry*, p. 102, approvingly quoted by Keynes; see preceding footnote.

[6] On Becher and Quesnay in this connection, see above, Part II, ch. 6.

[7] This statement may cause some difficulties for the beginner which an example will remove. Böhm-Bawerk's Fund of Subsistence is a real concept denoting all sorts of consumable goods. Nevertheless, he speaks of it in terms of money. But this does not mean either that he adopts a monetary concept of capital or that he attributes to money any influence on the process he describes. His money—like Ricardo's so far as the general theory of the *Principles* is concerned—is nothing but a homogeneous expression for a medley of quantities of physical goods.

interesting case of a concept's rendering valuable service by proving unworkable.[8]

Fourth, so long and so far as the theory of money actually did dwell in a separate compartment, its central—and practically only—problem was the exchange value or purchasing power of money. In the analytic work of the period this stands out much more clearly than it did before. Hence the popularity of the book title, Money and Prices, which persisted into postwar times.[9] No doubt influenced by the progress of the index-number method, most authors, especially in the United States, did not hesitate to define the value of purchasing power of money as the reciprocal of the price level. The Austrians distrusted index numbers,[10] and felt more theoretical qualms concerning the nature of the value of money.

A brief comment on these qualms seems justified. From the first, the Austrians entertained a wish, not unnatural from their standpoint, to apply their marginal utility theory to the case of money—which both the enemies of this theory and some of its foremost sponsors, Wicksell for instance, declared to be impossible. Now it was easy to apply the marginal utility theory to the significance that individuals attach to their monetary income. Daniel Bernoulli (see above, Part II, ch. 6, sec. 3b) had already done this. But this significance for the individual of a unit of his money income—its subjective exchange value as Menger called it—does not help us at all when we wish to explain the purchasing power or exchange value of money—Menger's objective exchange value of money. For the latter must be known to the individual—the individual must know what his money will buy—before he can put any subjective value upon his money. On the face of it, it is therefore impossible to do in the case of

[8] See J. G. Koopmans, 'Zum Problem des "neutralen" Geldes' in *Beiträge zur Geldtheorie* (1933). The problem in question must, of course, not be confused with such problems as stability of price level or stability of employment and the like. As soon as we hold that a monetary system or policy insures such stability, we admit precisely that it exerts an influence and hence that it is *not* neutral. The outstanding example, next to Wicksell's, of an economist's development from belief in the barter model and the possibility of a neutral money toward the belief that nothing can be averred about economic processes without specific reference to some given behavior of money, is afforded by the series of Professor Pigou's works. The turning point is to be found, I think, in his *Theory of Unemployment* (1933).

[9] A few examples in addition to others mentioned elsewhere: Antonio De Viti de Marco, *Moneta e prezzi* (1885); L. L. Price, *Money and its Relations to Prices* (1896); Richmond Mayo-Smith, 'Money and Prices,' *Political Science Quarterly* (June 1900); E. W. Kemmerer, *Money and Credit Instruments in Their Relation to General Prices* (1907)—a brilliant performance that had the misfortune of being overshadowed by the greater one of Fisher; J. L. Laughlin, *Money and Prices* (1919) and *A New Exposition of Money, Credit, and Prices* (1931); Albert Aftalion, *Monnaie, prix et change* (1927).

[10] They were, of course, not the only ones to do so. An American instance is Laughlin. Generally speaking, index numbers imposed themselves upon the profession as a whole by a slow process of infiltration which wore out opposition rather than convinced it (see below, sec. 4).

money what can be done in every other case, namely, to deduce its exchange value from curves or schedules of marginal utility: to attempt to do so seems to spell circular reasoning. We cannot stay to discuss the efforts of Wieser and especially of Mises to overcome this difficulty or the objections raised against their solution by Anderson.[11] But it should be pointed out that, quite independently of this question, the Austrian way of emphasizing the behavior or decision of individuals and of defining exchange value of money with respect to individual commodities rather than with respect to a price level of one kind or another has its merits, particularly in the analysis of an inflationary process: it tends to replace a simple but inadequate picture by one which is less clear-cut but more realistic and richer in results.

Most economists agreed—or would have agreed if asked—that marginal utility analysis does not apply to the case of the exchange value of money. But the question whether the supply and demand apparatus applies to it was answered affirmatively by most. This was the natural position to take for those who were prepared to treat money like any other commodity, as were the Austrians and E. Cannan. But it is curious that many of those who, by adopting a special formula for money such as the equation of exchange or the cash-balance formula (see below, secs. 5 and 6), testified to their belief that money cannot be so treated, should also have taken that position. In fact, both friends and foes of the 'quantity theory' agreed in describing it as an application of the demand and supply apparatus to the case of money.[12]

[(b) *Knapp's* State Theory of Money.] In Germany what may be described as a tempest in a teapot was raised by Knapp's *State Theory of Money*.[13] This book presented a theory of money that turns upon the adage: Money is the Creature of Law. Had Knapp merely asserted that the state may declare an object or warrant or ticket or token (bearing a sign) to be lawful money and that a proclamation to this effect or even a proclamation to the effect that a certain pay-token or ticket will be accepted in discharge of taxes must go a long way toward imparting some value to that pay-token or ticket, he would have asserted a truth but a platitudinous one. Had he asserted that such action of the state will *determine* the value of that pay-token or ticket, he would have asserted an interesting but false proposition. But he did neither. He explicitly denied that he was interested in the value of money. His theory was simply a theory of the 'nature' of money considered as the legally valid means of payment. Taken in this sense it was as true and as false as it is to say, for example, that the institution of marriage is a creature of law.

[11] See von Mises, *Theorie des Geldes* (2nd ed., p. 100); B. M. Anderson, *The Value of Money* (1917).

[12] This idea was actually carried out by Professor Pigou in his paper on the 'The Exchange Value of Legal-Tender Money' (see *Essays in Applied Economics*, 1923).

[13] This is the title of the English (abridged) translation (1924) by H. M. Lucas and J. Bonar of G. F. Knapp's *Die Staatliche Theorie des Geldes* (1905). I shall not go into the copious Knapp literature, about which the reader finds more than enough in Professor Ellis' *German Monetary Theory*, 1905-1933 (see above, sec. 2). There he also finds a more generous appraisal of Knapp's performance than I feel able to present

If this be so, however, how are we to account for the success of the book which, though substantially confined to Germany, was spectacular? An attempt to answer this question might make an interesting study in the social psychology of economic analysis. First, Knapp's exposition was extremely effective. His forceful dogmatism and his original conceptualization of his theory [14] impressed laymen and those economists who were laymen in economic theory. Second, many people and especially politicians at that time welcomed a theory that seemed to offer a basis for the growing popularity of state-managed money —during the First World War it was in fact widely used to 'prove' that the inflation of the currency had nothing to do with soaring prices. Third, in almost complete ignorance of both the literature and the logic of the subject, Knapp believed that his theory offered not only an alternative to theoretical metallism—his pet aversion—but the only possible one and that it alone was capable of explaining why such a thing as paper money can exist at all. *And this absurd claim was widely accepted*, although Knapp entirely failed to work out a non-metallist theory of the value of money.[15] Fourth, leaders such as Wieser and Hawtrey, who were themselves advancing toward such a theory, felt some sympathy for the work that bore a superficial resemblance to their own. He who is interested in the question 'what it is that succeeds and how and why' and who believes that the answer to this question is more revealing than anything else can be of the conditions prevailing in a field of human endeavor will do well to ponder this.

4. The Value of Money: Index Number Approach

Much more important than the theoretical discussion on the purchasing power of money was its statistical complement: the vigorous developments in the field of price index numbers during that period constitute indeed one of the most significant facts in the entire history of economics and one of the most significant strides toward an economic theory that is to be not only quantitative but also numerical. Index numbers of production followed with a considerable lag upon those of prices but the foundations for their postwar developments were also laid. And there was a beginning in the construction of wage and employment indices. But precisely because the subject expanded to vast dimensions, no attempt can be made here to survey its growth. I shall merely mention the outstanding efforts at systematization of what was becoming a semi-independent specialty or science, and then offer a few comments

[14] He was a master in the art of coining new concepts and naming them felicitously. It should be observed that the Greek words borrowed for the purpose served very well: the German economists of that time were not as a rule good theorists, but most of them had had a classical education and knew Greek.

[15] To some extent this was done by one of his critics who deserves to be mentioned: Friedrich Bendixen, *Wesen des Geldes* (4th ed., 1926) and numerous other publications.

that may help the reader to link up the subject with the rest of economic analysis and to see its more general bearings.[1]

[(a) *Early Work.*] Index numbers having attracted the attention of the British Association for the Advancement of Science, Edgeworth, acting as secretary of the committee that was appointed for the study of the subject, wrote his two famous reports (1887 and 1889),[2] remarkable not so much on account of the recommendations proffered as regards practical methods of index making as on account of the comprehensive analysis of meanings and purposes—labor standard, consumption standard, question of all-purpose index, and so on. In 1901, C. M. Walsh published his *Measurement of General Exchange Value,* which also based discussion of statistical technique upon a comprehensive economic theory of index numbers elaborated in his important book, *The Fundamental Problem in Monetary Science* (1903). Next must be mentioned Professor W. C. Mitchell's monograph on wholesale price index numbers, *Index Numbers of Wholesale Prices in the United States and Foreign Countries* (Bulletin 173 of U.S. Bureau of Labor Statistics, 1915, to be used in its revised edition, Bulletin 284, 1921). But the American century in index numbers was to be ushered in by Professor Irving Fisher's monumental work on *The Making of Index Numbers* (1922),[3] the fountainhead of almost all the best later work. But all that can be noticed here of the wealth of its results is this: Fisher analyzed, classified, and 'rectified' existing and possible index number methods by means of certain previously established 'tests'; that is to say, he formulated certain conditions which index numbers ought to satisfy; and ever since most of the theory of index numbers has really been the theory of these tests. This is much more important than is the search for an 'ideal index number' per se, though of course the tests were devised in order to rationalize this search.

[(b) *The Role of the Economic Theorists.*] The point about index numbers that is most relevant to a history of economic analysis is the dominant role played by economic theorists in their development. On the face of it, index

[1] The reader will find what he needs in the way of background in C. M. Walsh's article on 'Index Numbers' in the *Encyclopaedia of the Social Sciences.* On production indices, see A. F. Burns, 'The Measurement of the Physical Volume of Production,' *Quarterly Journal of Economics,* February 1930. The best reference on wage and employment indices is to the outstanding work of A. L. Bowley, especially *Statistics of Wages in the United Kingdom during the Last Hundred Years,* fourteen articles in the *Journal of the Royal Statistical Society,* 1898-1906 (partly with G. H. Wood, whose work on 'Real Wages and the Standard of Comfort since 1850,' ibid. March 1909, complements this investigation) and 'Measurement of Employment,' ibid. July 1912.

[2] They are most easily accessible in his *Papers Relating to Political Economy* (vol. I, sec. III), where they have been reprinted under the title 'Measurement of Change in Value of Money.'

[3] The links with monetary theory are more in evidence in the parts of the *Purchasing Power of Money* (1911) that are devoted to index numbers. These parts should be perused together with the book mentioned above.

numbers pertain to the province of the statistical technician and their theory should accordingly be part of the theory of statistics, just as is, for example, the theory of sampling. A great part of the work on index numbers was in fact done by statisticians or by economists who cared little for 'economic theory.' For instance, the formula that of all displayed the most indestructible vitality is due to a man who cannot without qualification be called an economist at all, Laspeyres.[4] But almost all the decisive impulses and ideas came from economic *theorists* as they had in the eighteenth century and in the first half of the nineteenth. In order to establish this point it is enough to mention the names Jevons, Edgeworth, and Fisher, to which should be added that of A. A. Young.[5] But these were not isolated cases. An ever-increasing number of economists whom everyone would class primarily as theorists took an interest either in developing the method or in elucidating, critically and constructively, the meaning and purposes of index numbers. Marshall suggested the chain system.[6] Lexis, Walras, Wicksell, Wieser, Pigou, to mention but a few leaders, contributed substantially to the theoretical foundations.[7] Their work was continued, on an enlarged scale, during the twenties and thirties. Unfortunately, we shall not be able to notice in any detail the developments since 1920. But three performances of this period will, nevertheless, be mentioned in what follows—those of Divisia, Haberler, and Keynes.

Before going on let me restate the reason why I thought it necessary to insist on the share of economic theorists in developing the index number

[4] E. Laspeyres published the formula $\frac{\Sigma p_1 q_0}{\Sigma p_0 q_0}$ (prices weighted by quantities in the base year), which secured him immortality—a student can no more go through any complete training in economics without hearing of Laspeyres than he can without hearing of A. Smith—in the *Jahrbücher für Nationalökonomie und Statistik*, 1864; also 1871.

[5] Jevons' two papers that gave indeed a decisive impulse but do not justify Fisher's statement that he 'may perhaps be considered the father of index numbers' or the concurring statement of Keynes, are: 'A Serious Fall in the Value of Gold . . .' (1863) and 'The Variation of Prices and the Value of the Currency since 1782' (1865), both included in *Investigations in Currency and Finance*. Splendid work of seminal importance but, for a theorist, surprisingly unmindful of the theoretical questions involved. Edgeworth's work, which partly remedied this shortcoming, and Fisher's have already been mentioned. Allyn A. Young's work in the field is in less danger than is the rest of his work of being entirely forgotten because some of it is embodied in his contribution to H. L. Rietz's well-known *Handbook of Mathematical Statistics* (1924).

[6] In the article on 'Remedies for Fluctuations of General Prices,' *Contemporary Review*, 1887.

[7] W. Lexis was, of course, not primarily an economic theorist. But his paper 'Über gewisse Wertgesamtheiten . . .' in *Zeitschrift für die gesamte Staatswissenschaft* (1886) was a piece of theoretical reasoning of great importance, though it attracted little notice. Walras' contribution (1874, 1885) has been included in his *Études d'économie politique appliquée* (*ed. définitive*, 1936, pp. 20 et seq.); Wicksell's is in *Interest and Prices*, ch. 2; Wieser's—'Über die Messung der Veränderungen des Geldwerts'—in *Schriften des Vereins für Sozialpolitik* (vol. 132, 1910); Pigou's in *Economics of Welfare* (1920; and earlier in *Wealth and Welfare*, 1912).

method. Some statisticians and some economists of anti-theoretic bent seem to think that this piece of 'realistic' analysis is something to set against the flimsy structures of theory, something that has been created, in the true scientific spirit, for the purpose of replacing mere speculation. It seemed important to correct this opinion. The subject of index numbers affords a good example of the manner in which theoretical research and statistical research are really related and in particular how statistical methods may grow out of the theorist's work.

[(c) *Haberler, Divisia, and Keynes.*] With the exception of Wieser, most of the leading Austrians took a critical, not to say hostile, attitude toward the idea of 'measuring' variations in the purchasing power of money (reciprocal of price level) by index numbers. They were inclined to refuse citizenship to the concept of price level and, in any case, to deny its measurability on principle.[8] In view of the fact that so many economists placed and place an uncritical trust in index figures without troubling themselves about their meaning,[9] this attitude provided a much needed antidote. And not only that. The criticism, at first merely negative, eventually turned constructive in Professor von Haberler's book on the meaning of index numbers.[10]

The core of his analysis is an interpretation of price index numbers that turns upon the following proposition: *for a given individual of unchanging tastes,* the price level has fallen (risen) between the points of time t_0 and t_1 if, his money income remaining the same, the individual is able to buy at t_1 a collection of goods which he prefers to the collection he was able to buy at t_0 (is unable to buy at t_1 a collection of goods which he prefers to the collection he bought at t_0). This interpretation connects index numbers with welfare economics. But its chief importance is in the fact that it bases them upon the theory of choice and thus makes them come to anchor in the very center of modern value theory.[11]

Whereas Haberler abandoned the idea of an 'objective' price level and replaced it by what may be termed a subjective one, Divisia produced the theory of the objective price level or monetary parameter, or monetary index (*indice monétaire*), an achievement of first-rate importance. An attempt at a simple explanation of the essential idea is made in the footnote below.[12]

[8] This attitude found its strongest expression in Professor von Mises' *Theory of Money and Credit.*

[9] This applies to any index figures, including those of physical output. In the last ten years or so a reaction has set in of which the most important symptom is that Lord Keynes, who in the *Treatise on Money* (1930) evidently attached much importance to price indices as tools of theoretical analysis, entirely avoided their use in his *General Theory* (1936).

[10] G. von Haberler, *Der Sinn der Indexzahlen* (1927).

[11] Pareto's suggestion in a similar direction (*Cours,* vol. I, pp. 264 et seq.) and a number of related ones (of which one is contained in Edgeworth's reports mentioned above) were much less convincing. We cannot stay, however.

[12] If expenditure upon all goods and services, E, changes by a (positive or negative) increment ΔE, then it is evidently possible, in a purely formal way that does not imply

It stands to reason that the idea of an over-all price level, even if admissible, is for many purposes much less useful than is the idea of sectional price levels, for example, of a price level of consumers' goods (Consumption Standard) and services as distinguished from a price level of producers' (or else investment) goods, or of a price level of finished products as distinguished from a price level of productive services and so on. The over-all price level in particular hides the relative movements as against each other of these sectional levels, and these relative movements are of pivotal importance for certain cycle theories, especially for that of Professor von Hayek. They are also of pivotal importance for the 'monetary dynamics' of Keynes's *Treatise*, Book II of which, entirely devoted to this subject, is the chief reference for this type of analysis. [This section was left unfinished.]

5. The Value of Money: the Equation of Exchange and the 'Quantity Approach'

We have seen that, so far as the large majority of writers on money are concerned, there is some truth in the statement that monetary analysis of that period dwelt, as it were, in a separate compartment. It is also true—though we have noticed exceptions such as Walras and the Austrians—that the furniture of this separate compartment was designed for the special purpose of explaining the value or purchasing power of money and not intended for any other use. Now, whenever we propose to explain the behavior of a single variable of the economic system, it is evidently convenient to bundle up all the others

anything about causation, to divide up ΔE into three parts: one that is 'due' to the changes in prices that have occurred—this part is equal to the quantities previously bought each multiplied by the changes in the respective prices or, symbolically, to $\Sigma q \Delta p$, another part is 'due' to the changes in the quantities bought and is equal to the prices previously obtaining each multiplied by the changes in the respective quantities or, symbolically, to $\Sigma p \Delta q$; and the third part is 'due' to the fact that the increments of the quantities have also been bought at the changed prices and is therefore equal to those increments of the quantities each multiplied by the increments in the respective prices or, symbolically, to $\Sigma \Delta q \Delta p$. Now, if the changes in prices and quantities (the Δq's and Δp's) are small fractions of the quantities and prices themselves (the q's and p's)—which can be the case only if we consider a very short period of time—then their product will be still smaller, so small that we may neglect it for practical purposes. But then we are left with two terms only, the one expressing that 'effect' upon expenditure that we should observe if prices had remained unchanged and therefore free from the 'effects' of any changes in prices; the other expressing that 'effect' upon expenditure that we should observe if quantities had remained unchanged and therefore free from the 'effects' of any changes in quantities. And the latter figure ($\Sigma q \ \Delta p$), expressed as a percentage of the original expenditure ($E = pq$), then serves to define the change that has occurred in the price level or monetary index—which thereby acquires an unambiguous and analytically important meaning. This theory, which had been partly anticipated by Lexis (op. cit.), was published by Professor François Divisia in several numbers of the *Revue d'économie politique*, 1925-6, under the title 'L'Indice monétaire et la théorie de la monnaie,' and again in his *Économique rationelle* (1928), ch. XIV.

into a few big aggregates and to consider these as the 'causes' that determine the one to be explained. The so-called Equation of Exchange is certainly the simplest possible system of such aggregates that contain the value of money or the price level at all. And if the latter be the thing to be explained, the others drop naturally (though illogically) into the role of its 'causes'—and the Equation of Exchange, in itself nothing but the statement of a formal relation without any causal connotation, then turns or may turn into the Quantity Theory. This is why during that period both the equation of exchange and the quantity theory enjoyed another lease on life and why so much of the discussion on the theory of money took the form of arguments for and against the quantity theory. We must therefore try to find out what the quantity theory of these writers really amounted to. To accomplish this in the way most useful to the reader, we shall concentrate on the outstanding achievement in this line, Professor Fisher's theory of the purchasing power of money.[1]

In itself there is nothing new about what has come to be called the Fisher or Newcomb-Fisher equation. It simply links the price level (P) with (1) the quantity of money in circulation (M); (2) its 'efficiency' or velocity (V); and (3) the (physical) volume of trade (T). Let us express this by writing $P = f(M, V, T)$. To this functional relation the Fisher equation imparts the particular form: $P = f(M, V, T) = \frac{MV}{T}$ or $MV = PT$. Again, this equation is *not* an identity but an equilibrium condition. For Fisher did not say that MV is the same thing as PT or that MV is equal to PT by definition: given values of M, V, T tend to *bring about* a determined value of P, but they do not simply *spell* a certain P. But the really interesting monetary analysis begins behind the façade of the equation. Two sets of questions arise.

[(a) *The Definition of the Concepts.*] First, what are the precise meanings of P, M, V, T? Whatever may be urged against the quantity theory approach, one virtue it certainly has: the obvious vicinity of its concepts to statistical material forces theorists to do what without this compulsion they often fail to do, namely, to define their concepts accurately and operationally. We cannot discuss or even list, but can only point to, all the problems that lurk behind the question which prices should, for the general purposes of the equation of exchange, be included in P, and consequently which transactions in T.[2] Fisher

[1] In doing so, we take quantity theory analysis at its highest. On the whole, the cost we incur thereby in terms of information about numerous other formulations is not great. But it must be stated that, though overshadowed by Fisher's performance, Kemmerer's (*Money and Credit Instruments in Their Relation to General Prices*, 1907) would serve our purpose nearly as well. Fisher gave generous credit to Simon Newcomb's treatment of Societary Circulation (*Principles*, 1885; see above, ch. 5, sec. 7a) which is in fact an important contribution. But we cannot go into the merits peculiar to it.

[2] An idea of these problems may be derived by perusal of the Appendices to Fisher's *Purchasing Power of Money* (1911). The notion of giving up altogether the concept of a general price level of everything that is bought and sold for money (an idea that was to be carried in the twenties to its extreme by Carl Snyder's general price-level concept;

himself, although in his introductory considerations he defined T as the amount of 'goods' bought by money, adopted a wider concept—that included securities—in his statistical work. But attention must be called to some problems concerning the definition of M.

Most writers on money displayed reluctance to calling checking deposits money—at least to doing so without qualification. As we have seen, they usually stressed the difference between money and 'credit' (see below, sec. 6) or 'primary' and 'fiduciary' money. But when it came to working the equation of exchange, the majority—especially the Americans, who did by far the greatest part of the statistical work—included the quantitatively most important type of 'credit instruments,' checking deposits, as a matter of course, often going so far as to call them 'deposit currency.' The M of their equation of exchange, then, meant substantially coin, government fiat, banknotes, demand deposits. Since this means including practically 'everything that buys,' it might seem that they should have, on the one hand, taken account of barter (and also of the fact that part of the social product is consumed directly by its producers) and, on the other hand, excluded non-circulating money (the cash reserves of banks and hoards). The first difficulty was, so far as I can see, not taken very seriously; as regards the second I shall simply quote Kemmerer's opinion (op. cit. p. 23): 'it makes no difference to the truth of the quantity theory whether new money is offered for commodities all at once, slowly, or not at all,' because money that does not circulate has simply the velocity zero.

In Europe, especially on the continent of Europe, this conceptual scheme was much less popular, in part, because most Europeans did not face up to the statistical task. To give a front-rank example for an alternative scheme: Wicksell (as Rodbertus before him) confined M to metallic money (and, I suppose, fiat paper money that does not carry any title to redemption in metal), and interpreted banknotes and deposits as devices for increasing the velocity of 'money'—so that bank reserves instead of having the velocity zero, would have a very high one (Fisher's 'virtual velocity'). The reader should observe that there is no intrinsic merit or demerit in either arrangement: convenience alone is the criterion for choosing between them. This criterion, of course, tells heavily for the 'American alternative.' But there is another point to attend to. Fisher introduced the checking deposits (M') with a distinct velocity (V') separately into his equation so as to make it read: $MV + M'V' = PT$. But he introduced two additional hypotheses. First, he assumed that there exists a very stable relation between the primary money (the hand-to-hand cash) people carry in their pockets or keep in their chests or vaults and the amounts of liquid means they keep on checking account. Second, he assumed

---

see 'A New Index of the General Price Level from 1875,' *Journal of the American Statistical Association*, June 1924) and of replacing it by several sectional price levels (consumers' goods, investment goods, and so on) was not, so far as I know, discussed during that period except that it was implied in the Austrian group's hostility to the price-level concept. The trend of opinion in favor of the idea of multiple price levels eventually triumphed conspicuously in Lord Keynes's *Treatise* of 1930, Book II.

that, *in equilibrium,* and for periods that are not too long, there exists a very stable relation between the reserves of the banking system and the sum total of checking deposits. Let us consider what this means. By virtue of these two hypotheses Fisher's position lies somewhere between the position of those who simply include in *M* demand deposits along with 'currency outside of banks' without making any distinction between these two categories (so far as purchasing-power problems are concerned) and the position of those who, like Wicksell, include only coin and irredeemable paper. For that part of the quantity of money which Fisher called 'primary' and which, envisaging Anglo-American conditions of 1911, he identified with gold acquires a position not shared by the checking deposits. These remain indeed 'deposit currency,' but the idea is suggested that the variation in the amount of *this* currency is governed by the variation in the quantity of the 'primary currency' or, under those conditions, of gold. The reader will see how well this links up with the compensated-dollar plan, which aims at controlling the price level by appropriate variations of the gold content of the monetary unit.

Two additional points must be mentioned about the V—additional, that is, to the observation made above that the velocity concept depends upon the quantity concept we choose to adopt. First, no great advance beyond Mill was made in the analysis of the factors behind the velocity of money.[3] In fact, it was not before the publication of Pigou's *Industrial Fluctuations* [4] that the various types of velocity were clearly distinguished and that the most important of them, the now familiar Income Velocity, was brought home to the profession at large. But it should not be said that the economists of that period habitually considered velocity to be a constant. Kemmerer's [5] emphasis on its variability as a function of the general business situation should suffice to refute an accusation that is constantly being repeated and that has created, in many minds, an entirely unrealistic impression to the effect that it is the chief merit of modern analysis to have recognized this variability. Second, we must pay our respects to some pioneer efforts in statistical measurement of velocity—landmarks, even though only partly successful, on the road toward numerical economics, principally associated with the names of des Essars, Kinley, Kemmerer, and, above all, Irving Fisher.[6]

[3] On the fortunes of the concept of velocity of goods, see Marget, op. cit. *passim.* Kemmerer introduced it into his equation of exchange.

[4] A. C. Pigou, *Industrial Fluctuations* (1st ed., 1927), Part I, ch. 15. Prior to this work, there is not much besides Wicksell's contribution (*Interest and Prices,* ch. 6).

[5] See above, sec. 3a.

[6] Pierre des Essars in 'La Vitesse de la circulation de la monnaie,' *Journal de la société de statistique de Paris,* April 1895; David Kinley, Doc. No. 399 in *Reports of National Monetary Commission,* 'The Use of Credit Instruments in Payments in the United States,' and also two papers in *Journal of Political Economy,* 'Credit Instruments in Retail Trade,' March 1895, and 'Credit Instruments in Business Transactions,' March 1897; Kemmerer, op. cit.; Irving Fisher, op. cit., but originally in 'A Practical Method of Estimating the Velocity of Circulation of Money,' *Journal of the Royal Statistical Society,* September 1909. Having derived his figures for velocity, Fisher

[(b) *Distinction between the Equation of Exchange and the Quantity Theory.*] The second set of questions turns upon our distinction between equation of exchange and quantity theory. How far did the writers of that period *actually* go beyond the statement of the formal equilibrium relation $MV = PT$? The task of answering this question is rendered more difficult by the fact that those writers themselves did not make that distinction but often described themselves as adherents of the quantity theory when all they meant was that they saw some advantage in the use of the equation of exchange or its equivalents. However, so far as the majority of first-flight authors are concerned, we may well take as typical the opinion that Pigou was to express a little later ('The Value of Money,' *Quarterly Journal of Economics*, November 1917):[7] 'The "Quantity Theory" is often defended and opposed as though it were a definite set of propositions that must be either true or false. But in fact the formulae employed in the exposition of that theory are merely devices for enabling us to bring together in an orderly way the principal causes by which the value of money is determined.' This statement, in which the words Quantity Theory should be replaced by Equation of Exchange, certainly holds true for Marshall himself and all Marshallians: they did not go at all beyond using their variant of the equation of exchange. The same applies to the Wicksellian treatment of the influence upon price levels of autonomous variations in the quantity of money: Wicksell put so much emphasis upon the role of the rate of interest as to leave little room for *direct* influences of autonomous variations in the quantity of money. Of course, from the standpoint of those extremist opponents of the quantity theory, presently to be noticed, who denied that autonomous variations in the quantity of money have *any* influence upon its value, he—and Marshall—would have to be classed as quantity theorists.[8] The case of Walras was different, at least on the surface.

actually proceeded (*Purchasing Power* . . . and papers there quoted, p. 492) to present the whole equation of exchange in numerical terms—a truly Napoleonic victory even though more like Borodino than Austerlitz.

[7] See also *Essays in Applied Economics* (1923; 'The Exchange Value of Legal-Tender Money').

[8] Wicksell was so preoccupied with driving home his point that autonomous increases in the quantity of money act on the economic process, via the rate of interest on bank loans, by expanding bank credit that he often came near to denying the direct influence. But he always recovered himself. For instance he showed that an increase in the gold stock must have a direct influence on prices, at least to the extent to which it increases the incomes and the expenditure of gold producers. On this see below sec. 6b.

The position taken by von Mises illustrates to perfection the difficulties with which we have to contend. He is the foremost critic of the price-level concept. He denied that there is sense in holding that an increase in money will *ever* increase the price level proportionately. All he averred was (op. cit. 2nd ed., p. 111) that there is 'a relation' between changes in the value of money and changes in the proportion of demand for to supply of money. This he called the useful element in the quantity theory—which, moreover, he defends against many objections. I think we had better take the clue proffered by himself and pigeonhole him with the opponents of the quantity theory in the historical sense, i.e. the quantity theory opponents meant to combat.

Walras' position is extremely difficult to understand. His purely analytic work upon the problem (see his treatment in the *Éléments* and in the 'Note sur la "Théorie de la Quantité" ' in the *Études d'économie politique appliquée*, pp. 153 et seq.) presents first of all a most interesting feature: he did not simply posit that the value of money is inversely proportional to its quantity, but he tried to deduce it rationally from the marginal utility principle, going so far as to say that one would have to reject the latter in order to have a right to reject the former. Another interesting feature is that he lets the quantities of fixed and circulating capitals be determined beforehand as a function of a given rate of interest. But, proved under these restrictions, the theorem in question, while of course true, is extremely weak and fully open to the objection we so often meet, that the quantity theory is true only under assumptions that render it trivial and quite valueless. For Walras' theorem really amounts to not more than that, all other things being *strictissime* equal, a given amount of transactions could be effected as well by means of a smaller amount of monetary units if all prices were reduced in the same proportion. However, not only did Walras call *this* the *théorie de la quantité*—which in itself would entitle us to class him with its *opponents* for, if this is really its *formule exacte*, then there is certainly nothing to it—but he also seems to have been a victim of the delusion that this theorem was all the analytic basis needed for his plan of currency reform, that is, he identified this theorem with the proposition that practical control of the price level can be achieved by controlling the quantity of money, a proposition which, right or wrong, has certainly little to do with the theorem proved.

Kemmerer's proposition that the amount of the circulating medium that is being hoarded varies widely in the short run amounts to renunciation of the quantity theory in the strictest sense and reduces so much of it as we may impute to him to the statement that P is determined by the three variables M, V, and T, whereas we cannot say *just as well* that M is governed by P, V, and T, or V by P, M, T, or T by P, M, V. Fisher expressed this by saying (*Purchasing Power*, p. 172) that 'the price level is *normally* the one absolutely passive element in the equation of exchange.' [9] But he went further than this. He also held, not indeed as a matter of general theory but as a matter of statistical fact, that in practically all cases of substantial fluctuations of price levels it was M only, and neither V nor T, which varied sufficiently to be considered as the explaining variable, in other words, that M was normally the most important 'active' variable as P was normally the passive one. This seems

[9] The reader will realize that the words 'just as well' in the first formulation and the word 'normally' in the second are quite essential. To repeat a comment made on this point in Part III, ch. 7, nobody ever has denied or can deny that a rise (fall) of the price level will induce a fall (rise) in gold production and an outflow (inflow) of gold so that, in the case of a free gold currency, the price level *cannot* be 'absolutely passive.' Moreover, Fisher's assertion applies only for states in the neighborhood of equilibrium, not to states of disequilibrium ('transitional periods') as we shall presently see—a fact which, and the implications of which, the unwary reader is practically certain to overlook.

to come as near to teaching quantity theory in its boldest acceptance as any front-rank economist's teaching ever did.[10] If in addition we remember the rigid assumptions that Fisher made concerning the relation between total checking deposits and gold, by virtue of which the total quantity of the circulating medium is (under the Anglo-American conditions of 1911) governed by gold production and gold exports or imports, we seem to get not only a quantity theory of the value of money but (for those particular conditions) a gold-quantity theory of it.

All the more important is it to realize that those critics were wrong who classed Fisher as a sponsor of the most rigid and most mechanical type of quantity theory and who on the strength of this see a well-nigh unbridgeable gulf between the monetary theory of the period under survey, as represented by Fisher, and the monetary theory of the twenties and thirties. They are wrong for two reasons: (1) the monetary theory of the twenties and thirties is much more under quantity theory influence than is generally realized;[11] (2)

[10] It is interesting to compare Fisher's presentation with that of the only other front-rank economist who went equally far, Cassel (see, e.g., his *Theory of Social Economy*, Third Book). He first expounds a strict quantity theory but only for the imaginary case of two disconnected states of the economy exactly equal in every respect except for a difference in M—and hence in P. He then stresses what nobody else had ever stressed with such energy, that this proves *nothing whatever* concerning the effect which a change in M, introduced in a real economy, would exert—adopting at this point the view usually held by opponents of the quantity theory. But then, having stated that nothing can be said a priori about the effects of actual changes of M in real life and that we must simply look at the facts, he finds for 1850-1910 (and, with less confidence also for the first half of the nineteenth century) that the quantity theory holds after all, not as a theory but as a statistical fact. Boldly generalizing from this, he then puts forth his famous 'Law of 3 per cent': the Sauerbeck index number having been approximately equal in 1850 and 1910 and the world's gold stock having approximately increased during that period at the rate of 2.8 per cent per annum, the T must have a tendency to increase at approximately that rate—and price level will hence increase or decrease according to whether gold production increases the world's gold stock by more or less than this per year. This is indeed unconventional theory. But it is interesting not only in itself but also on account of its methodology. The reader should observe that a physicist would have much less objection to the latter than most economists had. On the facts, see e.g. J. T. Phinney, 'Gold Production and the Price Level . . .' *Quarterly Journal of Economics*, August 1933.

[11] This most important fact unfortunately cannot be fully displayed here. I shall give a mere pointer toward the bridge between the old quantity theory analysis and more modern works. All those, especially American, writers on money who, e.g., in connection with the open-market operations of the Federal Reserve System, reasoned in a manner involving belief in the possibility of controlling ('stabilizing') business by controlling the quantity of the circulating medium were quantity theorists with a vengeance, a fact partly obscured because, faced by a different institutional set-up, they naturally expressed themselves in ways different from the authors of the Currency School. Particularly interesting in this connection is the theory that banks are *normally* 'loaned up,' that is to say, that banks will normally extend their loans as far as regulative legislation will permit them to go. The theoretical importance of this proposition is that it

it should be clear, not only from all the other writings of Fisher but especially from his *Theory of Interest,* that he cannot be classed with quantity theorists except in a special sense.

First, he stopped short of the quantity theorem in its fullest possible sense by admitting the influence of *T* on both *V* and *M* (*Purchasing Power . . .*, ch. 8, § 6)—this weakens the theorem considerably, at least as a long-run proposition, because it introduces a relation between the 'independent variables' that interferes with the direct effects of variations in *T* on *P*. Second, since the quantity theorem holds only in a state of equilibrium, it is of course neither a qualification nor an objection to say that it does not hold in what Fisher calls 'transition periods.' But actually, since the economic system is practically always in a state of transition or disequilibrium, phenomena that *seem* incompatible with the quantity theorem and have in fact furnished many of their arguments to its opponents are almost always in evidence. By paying careful attention to them—especially to one type of them, namely, the tendency of the interest rate to adjust itself to both rising and falling prices with a lag (see below, sec. 8) [12]—Fisher entirely changed this situation. In strict logic, of course, he thereby merely supplemented the information that the quantity theorem conveys. But for practical purposes and, especially, if we place ourselves on the standpoint of naïve friends and foes of the quantity theorem, we might say with almost equal justice that, in a large and particularly valuable part of his work, he shelved it. Third, Fisher untiringly emphasized that *M, V, T* were only the '*proximate* causes' of *P*. Behind them there are almost a dozen indirect influences on purchasing power (op. cit. chs. 5 and 6) which act on price levels through *M, V, T*. All quantity theorists of all times would have accepted this, at least under critical fire. But there is a point beyond which emphasis upon those indirect influences begins to impair the status of the proximate causes, which then easily degenerate into intermediate causes and finally into mere names for what we are then led to label 'real' causes. And this point Fisher seems to have reached: particularly in dynamic analysis (his analysis of 'transitional periods'), which is really the thing that matters, those indirect causes become much more interesting than

makes the quantity of 'money' (deposits) strictly dependent upon the action of 'monetary authorities'—i.e. that, from the standpoint of the economic process, *M* becomes a datum or a strictly independent variable. For a characteristic example of this type of neo-quantity theory, see L. Currie, *The Supply and Control of Money in the United States* (1934). But even the Keynesian group, which more than any other emphasizes antagonism to the quantity theory, is not free from its influence. Lord Keynes himself at first professed to accept it. (See *Tract on Monetary Reform,* p. 81.) But, like Pigou, he actually only accepted the equation of exchange. In the *General Theory* he professed to renounce it. But he did not succeed entirely in freeing himself from its shackles. Whoever treats *M* as an independent variable inevitably pays some tribute to it.

[12] Reference must be made in passing to one of Fisher's most original contributions, viz., his work on the problem of Lag Distribution. See his papers in the *Journal of the American Statistical Association,* 'The Business Cycle Largely a "Dance of the Dollar,"' December 1923, and 'Our Unstable Dollar and the So-Called Business Cycle,' June 1925.

the question whether or not they can be forced into the straitjackets of *M, V, T*.

But why should that great economist have insisted on adopting what on closer scrutiny turns out to be a particularly narrow and inadequate, if not actually misleading, form of his own thought? I will hazard a hypothetical answer: he had conceived a scheme—the compensated-dollar plan—which he believed to be of great and immediate practical utility; for the success of a practical scheme simplicity is essential; [13] hence it was the simplest aspect of Fisher's analysis, the quantity theory aspect, which presented itself to his mind and dominated his exposition. The theory in the *Purchasing Power of Money* is conceived as a scaffolding for statistical work that in turn was to serve a piece of social engineering. This is what pushed aside all other considerations. But they were there and by virtue of their presence his quantity theory, if quantity theory it must be, is something quite different from other quantity theories.

As the argument above amply shows, it is not easy to draw a convincing boundary line between economists who adhered to, and economists who rejected, the quantity theorem. But there were all the time many professed enemies of it—in Germany [14] and in France they were in the majority—who held that that theorem was untenable or else completely valueless. Compared with Fisher's performance and indeed with the performances of any of those leaders who may be credited (or debited) with having used the quantity theorem in some sense or other, the arguments of those professed enemies do not show up very well. This is due to the fact that, so far as those top-flight quantity theorists are concerned, opponents were really fighting windmills: as is so often the case in economics they were trying to knock down a creation of their own fancy; they were trying to refute what had never been held—for example, that the amount of money in circulation is the sole regulator of its value—or to urge what, unknown to them, was fully taken into account by any of the better expositions of the obnoxious theorem. They thus often raised objections that asserted nothing but what was factually and theoretically correct but were nevertheless incorrect *qua* objections. Vice versa, where their arguments would have constituted valid objections—for example, the argument that quantity of money has nothing at all to do with its value—they were often patently wrong. Finally, they sometimes made points that were

[13] That simplicity was a major consideration may be inferred from two facts: first that he stowed away all the most important things into the compartments labeled 'transitional periods,' a label that suggests the desire to focus the reader's attention upon the simple equilibrium proposition; second, that he expressed the latter in an equation instead of expressing it much more satisfactorily in a system of equations which could have been easily 'dynamized' so that the equilibrium proposition would have naturally taken its true place as a special case. In another author, the failure to adopt the latter course would be easily understandable. In the case of an expert mathematician like Fisher, only the intention to simplify can account for it.

[14] See S. P. Altmann, 'Zur deutschen Geldlehre des 19. Jahrhunderts' in *Festgabe für Schmoller*, 1908, I.

both valid and relevant but not decisive: this holds for Anderson's criticism, which otherwise stands out brilliantly from the rest.[15] These shortcomings also impair the critical implications of the factual research, very valuable in itself, that was done with a view to 'refuting the quantity theory.' Again and again such phenomena as that in the earlier phases of an inflation prices rose less than *M*, and in the later phases more than *M*, were adduced against its validity—a shot that completely fails to hit the target.[16] Fisher's attempt at verification, though open to certain criticisms concerning the correlation of time series, is greatly superior to anything done by opponents.[17] Nevertheless, these

[15] B. M. Anderson, *Value of Money* (1917). A sample of his criticism may be useful. Suppose that the wages of domestic servants be increased (without any servant being dismissed) and that these servants use their additional income exactly as their employers had used the same sum before. Therefore nothing has changed except that the price of directly consumed services that should be included in the price-level index has gone up: *M* and *T* have remained constant, yet *P* has risen. In his review of Anderson's book in the *Economic Journal*, March 1918, Edgeworth replied to this by pointing out that though *M* and *T* have remained constant, V has been increased. But, obviously, an increase in V which *occurs automatically in certain cases of price changes* cannot be set against Anderson's objection. Hence he was right. But while his objection stands, it would not tell heavily against any quantity theory that does not pretend to be more than a broad approximation.

[16] The following small sample from this literature may be welcome to some readers: H. P. Willis, 'History and Present Application of the Quantity Theory,' *Journal of Political Economy*, September 1896; Alfred de Foville, 'La Théorie quantitative et les prix,' *L'Économiste Français*, April and May 1896; D. Berardi, *La Moneta nei suoi rapporti quantitativi* (1912); J. L. Laughlin, 'A Theory of Prices,' *Publications of the American Economic Association*, 3rd series (February 1905); W. C. Mitchell, *Gold Prices and Wages under the Greenback Standard* (1908) and 'Quantity Theory of the Value of Money,' *Journal of Political Economy*, March 1896; J. Lescure, 'Hausses et baisses générales des prix,' *Revue d'économie politique*, July 1912; B. Nogaro, 'Contributions à une théorie réaliste de la monnaie,' ibid. October 1906; E. Dolléans, *La Monnaie et les prix* (1905). For Germany, I will mention two of the period's best men on money and monetary policy, though they do not present themselves favorably in their arguments against the quantity theorem—which were in part developed for the particular purpose of showing that the fall in prices, 1873-98, had nothing to do with gold production or with the extension of the area of the gold standard: Erwin Nasse ('Das Sinken der Warenpreise . . .' *Jahrbücher für Nationalökonomie*, July and August 1888) and W. Lexis (the famous statistician), numerous papers, see, e.g., his criticism of Walras' plan in his review article, 'Neuere Schriften über Geld- und Edelmetalle' (ibid. July 1888); see, however, Rist (op. cit. p. 253n.) for quotations to the effect that Lexis accepted the quantity theory in principle. Their inability to handle properly what after all was not a very complicated argument is astounding. So is K. Marx's failure to see that the cost of producing money (however defined) must act on commodity prices through its effect upon the supply of money: he denies any influence of quantity of money upon prices, *Capital* (English trans., Kerr ed., vol. I, p. 136).

[17] Another attempt that corroborates Fisher's result is conspicuous for excellence of workmanship: Oskar Anderson, 'Ist die Quantitätstheorie statistisch nachweisbar?' in *Zeitschrift für Nationalökonomie* (March 1931). One of the reasons why both verifica-

did not yield. And they were justified in refusing to do so. For they had a case.

A simple example will elucidate this apparently paradoxical situation. Consider a case of war inflation that runs its course like this: disturbance of domestic production and of export and import trade first raises most prices, the government's war demand being financed by means that would without the war have been spent by private individuals; this rise in prices together with an increase, at an increasing rate, in war demand *in physical terms* then enforces resort to the manufacture of 'money' (or credit instruments that do not have, in this case, the properties of the ordinary credit instruments of commerce); and finally there develops an increasing demand for loans by producers—a credit expansion in the commercial sense but incessantly fed by ever-increasing prices. Now, historians, politicians, businessmen will certainly describe such a process in terms of the war itself and of the disturbance on the one hand and the excess demand on the other which the war entails. They will be surprised to learn that, instead of war and war disturbance and war demand, it is just M, V, and T that 'cause' inflation and that it is only M and V that really matter. And if they are told that these are the 'proximate causes' whereas war, war disturbance, war demand are 'indirect' ones—the quantity theorist will always have to admit the 'direct' role of variations in T—which are operative but only at one remove, they will not be content. If anything, they will be annoyed, especially, if they suspect that more is at stake than a mere theoretical argument. In this they were right, of course: in the nineteenth century as well as in the twenties and thirties of the twentieth a rigid quantity theory, one that attributed to M an altogether unjustifiable role in economic therapy, had a way of suddenly emerging from more careful formulations. Especially in the United States, the sound-money men—and all those economists who felt quite rightly that currency troubles are but the reflex of deeper things—had plenty of reason for distrusting the possible practical implications of the quantity theorem, a distrust that then extended, however unfairly, to the quantity theory analysis itself. But they could have urged purely scientific reasons also. What I have described as straitjackets may be useful for certain restricted purposes exactly as are all such oversimplified set-ups, for example, the Keynesian system. Outside of the range of these purposes, they become inconvenient and impediments to more fundamental analysis. If, moreover, we admit cyclical variability of V and stress the importance of such 'indirect' causes as the rate of interest, the rate of change of P (vs. P itself), and so on, they become in addition useless. And it is hardly an exaggeration to say that

tions and refutations from statistical material failed to convince should be noted in passing: to a large extent, the decision to accept, or to refuse to accept, given statistical evidence, is a highly subjective matter. Since no material can ever bear out the quantity theory with a 100 per cent accuracy and no material that covers, say, at least ten years can ever fail to show some relation between P, T, and M, there must in most cases be room for fair difference of opinion as to what given statistical findings really mean. It is the merit of more refined methods, such as those of O. Anderson, that they offer criteria that are more reliable than is simple 'impression.'

the chief progress of monetary theory in more recent times has been the result of a tendency to tear up the straitjackets and to introduce explicitly and directly all that the best presentations of the quantity theory relegated into the limbo of indirect influences. Lesson: in economics more than elsewhere, a good cause and one that will win out eventually may be so inadequately defended as to appear to be bad for decades together.

[(c) *Purchasing Power Parity and the Mechanism of International Payments.*] Before going on, let us touch upon two other matters. In that period, more definitely than before, we find in the neighborhood of the quantity theorem its old ally, the purchasing-power-parity theory of foreign exchange, that is, the proposition that, if left to itself, the price of a country's monetary unit in terms of foreign currencies tends to be inversely proportional to the relations between the respective price levels. It was repeatedly stated, for example, by Marshall and Schlesinger, but when, in the discussion on the exchange troubles that arose during and after the First World War, Cassel pressed it energetically into service, it struck most people like a new discovery.[18] As I have stated it, the proposition does not seem very exciting. Both Marshall and Schlesinger noticed it as they went along, without putting much emphasis upon it. And we may discern, in the torrent of publications which 'purchasing power parity' was to produce, a quiet little inlet of discussions about the merits of that proposition as a tool of analysis.[19] The excitement sprang from the fact that Cassel linked it up with a strict quantity theory and, in application, with the problems of war inflation. In consequence of this, the purchasing-power-parity theory turned into the so-called 'inflation theory' of foreign exchange, which reads: increase in M raises the price level; the rise in a country's price level decreases the value of its monetary unit in terms of non-inflated foreign currencies. Opposing arguments were marshalled under the flag of a 'balance-of-payment' theory, which often, though not always, went so far as to make the causal nexus run from exchange rate to price level instead of from price level to exchange rate. We cannot go into this controversy in which opponents never met each other's arguments on the same plane of fact and of abstraction and which, though better things were not lacking, on the

18 Cassel's many publications on the subject started in 1916. The references that are likely to be most useful to the reader are to Cassel's *Theory of Social Economy* (ch. 12) and to Professor H. Ellis' work on *German Monetary Theory* (Part III), which goes far beyond the German discussion and will prove helpful to those readers who wish to enter more fully into a subject to which I can only draw attention.

19 This inlet was mainly fed from English sources. See especially A. C. Pigou, 'The Foreign Exchanges,' *Quarterly Journal of Economics*, November 1922, and J. M. Keynes, *Tract on Monetary Reform* (ch. 3, glorified by an excellent treatment of forward trading in exchange). The discussion had the merit of raising several worth-while questions, but ended in the anaemic result that the purchasing-power-parity theorem, when properly qualified, was of hardly any value at all. As a matter of fact, this is not true, and Lord Keynes might have arrived at a better definition of the equilibrium rate of exchange than he produced when preparing his Clearing Union and Bretton Woods plans, if he had not disposed so lightly of what is a quite valuable starting point.

whole presents a sad example of the futility—largely due to inadequate analytic power of the participants—of so many economic controversies.

I take this opportunity of noticing another controversy (or set of controversies) that proved more fruitful: the controversy on the mechanism of international payments. It ran its course and produced its results in the twenties and thirties, but its sources are in the work of the nineteenth century and some of the most important participants drew inspiration from the contest between Thornton and Ricardo (see above, Part III, ch. 7, sec. 3).[20] We have before us what is indeed a typical case of normal scientific development. The older authors had, more or less explicitly, noticed all the essential elements of the problem. But when J. S. Mill summed up their work, it was nevertheless an incomplete and one-sided picture that emerged, namely, the schema of the mechanism of unilateral international payments (tributes, or loans, or repayment of loans), according to which the paying country first transfers gold, thereby increasing the price level of the receiving country and reducing its own so as to acquire an export surplus, which then takes care of the subsequent payments. The glaring inadequacy of this account, which not only puts the whole burden of adjustment on the price level but also neglects the phenomena inevitably associated with such an adjustment, was indeed felt and noticed by Bastable ('On Some Applications of the Theory of International Trade,' *Quarterly Journal of Economics*, October 1889) and others, but the theory proved a hardy plant and survived in current teaching right into the twenties, in spite of protests (e.g., Wicksell's in 'International Freights and Prices,' *Quarterly Journal of Economics*, February 1918). When the problem of German reparations drew everybody's attention to these questions of mechanism, relatively rapid progress was made in building up an organon of analysis that was new as such though none of its elements were. Ohlin's performance (*Interregional and International Trade*, 1933) supplies a convenient landmark in this as it does in other respects. The role of Taussig's teaching should be particularly noticed. He started from Mill's schema and, in spite of a number of improvements he added, personally never abandoned it. But by virtue of the criticism he elicited and of the work of his pupils, whom his leadership inspired, he helped the new analysis into existence almost as effectively as if he had created it himself. On the one hand, much of the most significant theoretical work developed from his teaching, Viner's especially. On the other hand, he started off an important sequence of factual researches.[21]

[20] The following brief and inadequate comments that cannot do more than indicate another 'bridge' between our own work and the past may be supplemented by J. Viner's treatment of the subject in *Studies in the Theory of International Trade* (chs. VI and VII). It is a pleasant duty to criticize the author for having impaired his picture by stressing inadequately the importance of his own contribution in *Canada's Balance of International Indebtedness* (1924). Relying once more on this reference, I shall in what follows mention contributions with great brevity.

[21] In general, that period's factual research on international capital movements is among its major titles to our gratitude. C. K. Hobson's *The Export of Capital* (1914) will serve as an example.

6. The Value of Money: the Cash Balance and Income Approaches [1]

The Newcomb-Fisher equation of exchange and expressions closely similar to it were indeed widely used (or implied by verbal circumlocutions) but not universally. We are now going to glance at two other important formulae. In both cases, it is as important to grasp that they were fundamentally equivalent to the Newcomb-Fisher equation as it is to understand the nature of the differences that induced many economists to prefer them. Or to put the same thing from a different angle: the important thing to understand is why those formulae, in spite of their fundamental equivalence with the Newcomb-Fisher equation, nevertheless suggested advance in a different direction.

(a) *The Cash Balance Approach.* Walras often spoke of the quantity of money. But the central concept of his analysis of money is the *encaisse désirée*, that is, the amount of cash that people individually desire to hold at any moment. Similarly, the Cambridge economists, following Marshall's lead and in obedience to the Petty-Locke-Cantillon tradition, adopted a formula that expressed the same idea. Let n be the amount of 'cash in circulation' with the public, p the index number of the cost of living, k the number of 'consumption units,' also an index figure, representing the physical complement of the public's holdings of hand-to-hand cash, k' the number of consumption units representing similarly the physical complement of the public's checking deposits, and r the fraction of k' that banks keep as a cash reserve against k', then we have [2]

$$n = p(k + rk')$$

[1] Specific reference should again be made to Professor Marget's treatment of these subjects (op. cit., vol. I, chs. 12-16).

[2] See, e.g., J. M. Keynes, *Monetary Reform*, American ed., 1924, pp. 82-6. Three things should be observed with respect to this particular formulation. (1) The 'public' includes the business world; though business does not spend on consumers' goods, the physical complement of its holdings of cash in hand and at banks is nevertheless measured in 'consumption units,' exactly as is the physical complement of consumers' cash and balances. (2) In the chapter in which this exposition of the Cambridge theory occurs, Keynes confused—as did so many others—use of the equation of exchange and acceptance of the quantity theory; as a matter of fact, he did not mean to accept the quantity theorem in any strict sense. (3) In particular, he emphasized, already in *Monetary Reform*, the wide variability of k, k', and r, and he also protested, though mildly, against the uncritical assumption that 'a mere change in the quantity of the currency cannot affect k, k', and r'—statements that foreshadow certain features of the analysis of the *General Theory*. The *Treatise* takes up an intermediate position, the main features of which are the breaking up of the general price level into sectional price levels, and the explicit introduction of Saving and Investment among the variables. The equations of the *Treatise* (Book III) must be looked upon as developments of the equation above. They illustrate the meaning of my statement to the effect that progress of monetary analysis in the twenties and thirties largely consisted in brushing aside the comprehensive aggregates of equation-of-exchange analysis and in introducing explicitly the variables expressive of the 'indirect influences.'

This is the so-called Cambridge equation, which is to embody the Cash Balance Approach. It assumes and asserts exactly what the Newcomb-Fisher equation assumes and asserts. In particular, it is not more and not less of an identity. The feature that at first sight may seem to constitute a substantive difference, namely, the absence of velocity, is not very important: for all the problems that, in the Newcomb-Fisher equation, are treated under the heading Velocity turn up in much the same form when we try to work with the Cambridge equation. But there is nevertheless something about it which deserves notice because it sheds light on an important aspect of the Filiation of Scientific Ideas. In expressing the Cambridge equation in words, it is natural to say—and all Cambridge economists did say—that 'the public choose' or 'elect' to keep $p(k + rk')$ in cash and balances, and this manner of speaking constitutes a psychological bridge to later, especially Keynesian, opinions: for it *points* toward the individual decisions that are behind the public's behavior in the matter of holding liquid assets and *suggests* analysis of the motives that prompt them. Especially, if we express the matter by saying that there is such a thing as a 'balance of advantage' as between holding money and holding other forms of wealth, we cannot help seeing the signpost that points toward the Liquidity Preference Theory of Keynesian fame. But once more we have to add that this does not amount to the liquidity preference theory. It is clear, especially in the case of Walras' *encaisse désirée,* that we need additional assumptions concerning people's attitude toward holding cash to carry us from the one to the other.

(b) *The Income Approach.* We have noticed that Tooke, in his '13th thesis,' had suggested that the explanation of money prices should start from consumers' incomes. As we know, he offered this as an alternative to the explanation of price levels by the quantity of money which he rejected. Ever since, the Income Approach has appealed to analysts—though it was also adopted by others—who disliked the quantity theory or even the equation of exchange.[3] But it is easy to see that, in itself, the former is nothing but another way of writing the latter. Moreover, the amendment might seem to be of doubtful value since incomes evidently 'determine' prices in the same sense only in which prices 'determine' incomes. Yet Wieser's[4] and Hawtrey's preference for this approach is quite understandable, though it yields no result that cannot be obtained via the equation of exchange: like the cash balance ap-

[3] This holds for A. Aftalion (*L'Or et sa distribution mondiale,* 1932), or for R. Liefmann (*Geld und Gold,* 1916), who said categorically: incomes determine prices, and also for Tooke's follower, Adolf Wagner, but not for the most eminent of the sponsors of the income approach, R. G. Hawtrey (*Currency and Credit,* 3rd ed., 1928), who starts from Consumers' Outlay, which is 'proportional jointly to the unspent margin [equivalent to *encaisse désirée,* J. A. S.] and the circuit velocity of money.' He calls this 'a form of the quantity theory' (p. 60). Several German writers, however, refused to see this and had to be taught by Hans Neisser, *Tauschwert des Geldes* (1928) that there is no contradiction between the income and the quantity theory.

[4] See his *Social Economics* or his article 'Geld' in the *Handwörterbuch* (4th ed., 1927).

proach, it points to individual behavior; more than the cash balance approach, it removes mere quantity of money from the position of a proximate 'cause of the price level' and substitutes for it one that is still nearer to prices—income, or even consumers' expenditure;[5] finally it relieves the theory of money prices from such questions as what is to be considered as money. The effect of an increase of money upon prices is indeterminate so long as we do not know who gets the additional money, what he does with it, and what the state of the economic organism is on which the new money impinges. The income formula does not in itself take account of all these questions but it directs our attention toward them and thus helps monetary analysis to step out of its separate compartment. This advantage is particularly obvious in analyzing an inflationary process. Though there is really not much more sense in quarreling over the question whether it is the increased quantity of money or the increased pay roll that 'causes' inflation than there would be in quarreling over the question whether it is the bullet or the murderer's intention that 'causes' the death of the victim, there is still something to be said for concentrating on the mechanisms by which the increased quantity of money becomes operative—not to speak of the additional advantage which counts for so much in economics, namely, that the income-expenditure formula does not meet with some of the prejudices that the equation of exchange encounters.

7. Bank Credit and the 'Creation' of Deposits

The important developments that occurred during that period in the banking systems of all commercialized countries and in the functions and policies of central banks were, of course, noticed, described, discussed. We cannot survey the vast literature which performed this task and of which reports of official commissions and the articles of the best financial journals, the London *Economist* in particular, formed perhaps the most valuable part. It was written by businessmen, financial writers, business economists of all types who knew all about the facts, the techniques, and the current practical problems of banking but who cared little about 'principles'—except that they never failed to refer to established slogans—and cannot be said to have had any very clear ideas about the meaning of the institutional trends they beheld. Considered from the standpoint of scientific analysis, these works were, therefore, raw material rather than finished products. And since the 'scientific analysts' of money and credit largely failed to do their part, namely, to work up this material and to fashion their analytic structures to its image, we might almost—though not quite—characterize the situation by saying that that literature on banking and finance was as much of a separate compartment within the litera-

[5] The reader will recall that this particular advantage does not amount to a great deal if, when using the equation of exchange, we pay proper attention to the factors that govern the variations, especially the cyclical variations, in velocity. On the other hand, it might be said that if we do this we have really accepted what the income approach is meant to convey.

ture on money and credit as the latter was a separate compartment within the literature on general economics.

There are a number of books for England, in particular, such as W. T. C. King's *History of the London Discount Market* (1936) and the various histories of the Bank of England (e.g., the recent one by Sir John Clapham, *The Bank of England*, 1944), which will supply part of the information that cannot be given here. For other references, see the little bibliography attached to the article on 'Banking, Commercial' in the *Encyclopaedia of the Social Sciences* (especially the books of the following authors: C. A. Conant, A. W. Kerr, A. Courtois, E. Kaufmann, A. Huart, J. Riesser, O. Jeidels, C. Supino, C. Eisfeld, H. P. Willis). This bibliography contains two items which, owing to their high quality, should be particularly mentioned: C. F. Dunbar's *Theory and History of Banking* (5th ed., 1929, but essentially a work of the nineteenth century) and F. Somary's *Bankpolitik* (1st ed. 1915; 2nd ed. 1930). Perusal of *A History of Banking Theory* by L. W. Mints (1945) will show the reader how far the descriptive literature 'spilled over' into the books on monetary and banking theory, though the author's presentation of his huge material is somewhat impaired by undue emphasis on the shortcomings of a particularly narrowly defined commercial theory of banking (the 'real-bills doctrine').

The situation described above by the separate-compartment simile accounts for the emergence of a special type of book which was written not only for the general reading public but also for economists in order to enlighten them on the facts and problems of banking or finance. The success of these books proves, better than anything else could, how far the separation of those departments, between which they sought to establish connection, had actually gone. Two famous instances call for notice. The one is W. Bagehot's *Lombard Street: A Description of the Money Market* (1873), one of the most frequently and most admiringly quoted books in the whole economic literature of the period. No doubt it is brilliantly written. But whoever now turns to that book with its fame in mind will nevertheless experience some disappointment. Barring a plea for the reorganization of the management of the Bank of England and for a reform of English practice concerning gold reserves, it does not contain anything that should have been new to any student of economics. Obviously, however, it did teach many economists things they did not know and were glad to learn. Our other instance is the not less brilliant book by Hartley Withers, *The Meaning of Money* (2nd ed., 1909), whose chief merit consists, as we shall presently see, in having boldly spoken of the 'manufacture' of money by banks. But this should not have surprised anyone. Yet it was considered as a novel and somewhat heretical doctrine.

Thus, academic analysis of credit and banking—including the contribution of writers who, without being academic economists themselves, conformed to the academic pattern, as did some bankers—went along on the stock of ideas inherited from the preceding period, refining, clarifying, developing no doubt but not adding much that was new. Substantially, this meant the prevalence of the commercial theory of banking which made the commercial bill or, somewhat more generally, the financing of current commodity trade the theoretical cornerstone of bank credit. We shall, of course, trace this position to Tooke and Fullarton. But the currency school influence was stronger than appears on the surface. Toward the end of the period, it asserted itself particularly in the precincts of the theory of cycles (see below, sec. 8).

As regards central banking, economists enlarged indeed their conception of the functions of central banks, especially the controlling and regulating function of the 'lender of last resort.' But most of them were surprisingly slow in recognizing to the full the implications of Monetary Management, which as we have seen was developing under their eyes. Adherence to the commercial theory was, of course, partly responsible for this. Because of it, control continued to mean—not wholly but primarily—control by 'discount policy.' The economics profession was not even sure whether it was in the power of central banks to regulate market rates or whether bank rate was merely 'declaratory.' [1] Votaries of both opinions then discussed the effects of bank rate in terms of the two classic *modi operandi:* on the one hand, pressure on prices by restriction of credit (*almost* equivalent to amount of commercial bills presented for discount); on the other hand, attraction from abroad of foreign funds or recall from abroad of domestic funds.

As regards banking in general, it is quite true that strict adherence to the commercial theory caused economists to overlook or misconceive some of the most important banking developments of that time. Nevertheless, the derogatory criticism leveled at it in our own day is not entirely justified. To begin with, it was not so unrealistic for England, and English prestige in matters of banking tended to make English practice the standard case. But, quite apart from this, it should be emphasized that acceptance of the commercial theory does not necessarily involve uncritical optimism about the working of the discounting mechanism. Economists stressed the 'elasticity' of the system that turns on financing commodity trade. But they had grown out, or were growing out, of the opinion that if banks simply finance the 'needs of trade,' then money and production will necessarily move in step and no disturbance will arise—which is the really objectionable thesis. On the one hand, most of them realized, as Ricardo and Tooke had done before them, that there is no such thing as a quantitatively definite need for loans or discounts and that the actual amount of borrowers' demand is as much a question of the banks' propensity to lend and of the rates they charge as it is a question of borrowers' demand for credit. On the other hand, they realized more and more that the practice of financing nothing but current trade—discounting good commercial paper—does not guarantee stability of prices or of business situations in general or, in depression, the liquidity of banks.[2] And it was Wicksell's achieve-

[1] The futility of this discussion, which could have been settled by a glance at the facts, should be obvious. We shall, however, think more kindly of it if we observe that the technique of 'making bank rate effective' was only slowly developing during that period and that economists were still slower in discovering what was actually being done. Without this technique it is indeed a fair question to ask whether central banks can do much more than follow the market—which is what is meant by the phrase that their rates are 'declaratory.'

[2] In other words—putting the matter from the standpoint of the policy of credit control—it was being increasingly realized that attention to the purpose to be financed (*current* commodity transaction) and to the quality of the credit instruments involved (*good* commercial paper) did not enable central banks to dispense with attention to

ment to introduce both facts into the general theory of money by means of his famous model of the Cumulative Process (see below, sec. 8).

Finally, there is another point, quite independent of all this, that must be noticed: the curious narrowness and lack of realism in that period's conception of the nature of bank credit. In order to make this point stand out clearly, let us restate how a typical economist, writing around 1900, would have explained the subject of credit, keeping in mind, however, all the limitations and dangers inherent in speaking of typical views. He would have said something like this. In the (logical) beginning is money—every textbook on money, credit, and banking begins with that. For brevity's sake, let us think of gold coin only. Now the holders of this money, so far as they neither hoard it nor spend it on consumption, 'invest' it or, as we may also say, they 'lend' their 'savings' or they 'supply capital' either to themselves or to somebody else. And this is the fundamental fact about credit.[3] Essentially, therefore, credit is quite independent of the existence or non-existence of banks and can be understood without any reference to them. If, as a further step in analysis, we do introduce them into the picture, the nature of the phenomenon remains unchanged. The public is still the true lender. Bankers are nothing but its agents, middlemen who do the actual lending on behalf of the public and whose existence is a mere matter of division of labor. This theory is satisfactory enough in cases of actual 'lending on account of others' [4] and of savings deposits. But it was also applied to checking deposits (demand deposits, the English current accounts). These, too, were made to arise from people's depositing with banks funds that they owned (our gold coins). The depositors become and remain lenders both in the sense that they lend ('entrust') their money to the banks and in the sense that they are the ultimate lenders in case the banks lend out part of this money. In spite of certain technical differences, the credit supplied by deposit banking—the bulk of commercial credit in capitalist society—can therefore be construed on the pattern of a credit operation between two private individuals. As the depositors remain lenders, so bankers remain middlemen who collect 'liquid capital' from innumerable small pools in order to make it available to trade. They add nothing to the existing mass of liquid means, though they make it do more work. As Professor Cannan put it in an article in *Economica* ('The Meaning of Bank Deposits') which appeared as late as January 1921: 'If cloak-room attendants managed to lend out exactly three-quarters of the bags entrusted to them . . . we should certainly not accuse the cloak-room attendants of having "created" the number of bags indicated by

the quantity of credit outstanding: this is implied, though perhaps not adequately, in the theory of the bank rate.

[3] We know that leading theorists described the process in terms of the commodities that credit operations were in the last analysis intended to transfer. But for our present purpose it is not necessary to go into this again.

[4] By this is meant a contractual arrangement by which an owner of large funds which he does not immediately need, e.g. an industrial corporation that has just received the proceeds of a bond issue, employs the services of a bank to lend out these temporarily idle funds in the money market, to stock brokers or bill brokers.

the excess of bags on deposit over bags in the cloak rooms.' Such were the views of 99 out of 100 economists.

But if the owners of those bags wish to use them, they have to recover them from the borrowers who must then go without them. This is not so with our depositors and their gold coins. They lend nothing in the sense of giving up the use of their money. They continue to spend, paying by check instead of by coin. And while they go on spending just as if they had kept their coins, the borrowers likewise spend 'the same money at the same time.' Evidently this phenomenon is peculiar to money and has no analogue in the world of commodities. No claim to sheep increases the number of sheep. But a deposit, though legally only a claim to legal-tender money, serves within very wide limits the same purposes that this money itself would serve. Banks do not, of course, 'create' legal-tender money and still less do they 'create' machines. They do, however, something—it is perhaps easier to see this in the case of the issue of banknotes—which, in its economic effects, comes pretty near to creating legal-tender money and which may *lead* to the creation of 'real capital' that could not have been created without this practice. But this alters the analytic situation profoundly and makes it highly inadvisable to construe bank credit on the model of existing funds' being withdrawn from previous uses by an entirely imaginary act of saving and then lent out by their owners. It is much more realistic to say that the banks 'create credit,' that is, that they create deposits in their act of lending, than to say that they lend the deposits that have been entrusted to them. And the reason for insisting on this is that depositors should not be invested with the insignia of a role which they do not play. The theory to which economists clung so tenaciously makes them out to be savers when they neither save nor intend to do so; it attributes to them an influence on the 'supply of credit' which they do not have. The theory of 'credit creation' not only recognizes patent facts without obscuring them by artificial constructions; it also brings out the peculiar mechanism of saving and investment that is characteristic of fullfledged capitalist society and the true role of banks in capitalist evolution. With less qualification than has to be added in most cases, this theory therefore constitutes definite advance in analysis.

Nevertheless, it proved extraordinarily difficult for economists to recognize that bank loans and bank investments do create deposits. In fact, throughout the period under survey they refused with practical unanimity to do so. And even in 1930, when the large majority had been converted and accepted that doctrine as a matter of course, Keynes rightly felt it to be necessary to re-expound and to defend the doctrine at length,[5] and some of its most impor-

[5] *Treatise on Money*, ch. 2. It is, moreover, highly significant that, as late as June 1927, there was room for the article of F. W. Crick, 'The Genesis of Bank Deposits' (*Economica*), which explains how bank loans create deposits and repayment to banks annihilates them—in a manner that should have been indeed, but evidently was not even then, 'time-honored theory.' There is, however, a sequel to Lord Keynes's treatment of the subject of credit creation in the *Treatise* of 1930 of which it is necessary to take notice in passing. The deposit-creating bank loan and its role in the financing

tant aspects cannot be said to be fully understood even now. This is a most interesting illustration of the inhibitions with which analytic advance has to contend and in particular of the fact that people may be perfectly familiar with a phenomenon for ages and even discuss it frequently without realizing its true significance and without admitting it into their general scheme of thought.[6]

For the facts of credit creation—at least of credit creation in the form of banknotes—must all along have been familiar to every economist. Moreover, especially in America, people were freely using the term Check Currency and talking about banks' 'coining money' and thereby trespassing upon the rights of Congress. Newcomb in 1885 gave an elementary description of the process by which deposits are created through lending. Toward the end of the period (1911) Fisher did likewise. He also emphasized the obvious truth that deposits and banknotes are fundamentally the same thing. And Hartley Withers espoused the notion that bankers were not middlemen but 'manufacturers' of money. Moreover, many economists of the seventeenth and eighteenth centuries had had clear, if sometimes exaggerated, ideas about credit creation and its importance for industrial development. And these ideas had not entirely vanished. Nevertheless, the first—though not wholly successful—attempt at working out a systematic theory that fits the facts of bank credit adequately, which was made by Macleod,[7] attracted little attention, still less favorable attention. Next came Wicksell, whose analysis of the effects upon prices of the rates charged by banks naturally led him to recognize certain aspects of 'credit creation,' in particular the phenomenon of Forced Saving.[8] Later on, there

---

of investment *without any previous saving up of the sums thus lent* have practically disappeared in the analytic schema of the *General Theory*, where it is again the saving public that holds the scene. Orthodox Keynesianism has in fact reverted to the old view according to which the central facts about the money market are analytically rendered by means of the public's propensity to save coupled with its liquidity preference. I cannot do more than advert to this fact. Whether this spells progress or retrogression, every economist must decide for himself.

[6] In consequence, there may be merit and even novelty in a piece of work which can be proved to say nothing that has not been said before in some form or other—which in fact we have had occasion to observe many times. It seems to me that Professor Marget's account of the development of the doctrine of credit creation (op. cit. vol. I, ch. 7) does not attach sufficient weight to this consideration.

[7] Henry Dunning Macleod (1821-1902) was an economist of many merits who somehow failed to achieve recognition, or even to be taken quite seriously, owing to his inability to put his many good ideas in a professionally acceptable form. Nothing can be done in this book to make amends to him, beyond mentioning the three publications by which he laid the foundations of the modern theory of the subject under discussion, though what he really succeeded in doing was to discredit this theory for quite a time: *Theory and Practice of Banking* (1st ed., 1855-6; Italian trans. 1879); *Lectures on Credit and Banking* (1882); *The Theory of Credit* (1889-91).

[8] In itself the idea was not new, see F. A. von Hayek, 'Note on the Development of the Doctrine of "Forced Saving,"' *Quarterly Journal of Economics*, November 1932, republ. in *Profits, Interest and Investment* (1939). But it now appeared in a larger con-

were other contributions toward a complete theory, especially, as we should expect, in the United States. Davenport, Taylor, and Phillips may serve as examples.[9] But it was not until 1924 that the theoretical job was done completely in a book by Hahn, and even then success was not immediate.[10] Among English leaders credit is due primarily to Professors Robertson and Pigou not only for having made the theory palatable to the profession but also for having added several novel developments.[11] Elsewhere, especially in France, resistance has remained strong to this day.

The reasons why progress should have been so slow are not far to seek. First, the doctrine was unpopular and, in the eyes of some, almost tinged with immorality—a fact that is not difficult to understand when we remember that among the ancestors of the doctrine is John Law.[12] Second, the doctrine ran up against set habits of thought, fostered as these were by the legal construction of 'deposits': the distinction between money and credit seemed to be so obvious and at the same time, for a number of issues, so important that

---

text and with a new emphasis. During the last decade, the concept has fallen into unmerited disfavor. But it has its merits. In particular, it clears up a point that has caused difficulties to many. Banking operations, so Ricardo had said, cannot create 'capital' (i.e. physical means of production). Only saving can do this. Now, whenever the expenditure from deposits that are created by banks increases prices, i.e. under conditions of full employment (and also in other cases), a sacrifice of consumption is imposed upon people whose incomes have not risen in proportion, which achieves what otherwise would have to be achieved by saving, and there is point in calling this, metaphorically, Involuntary or Forced Saving and in contrasting it with what is usually called Saving (Voluntary Saving). That under conditions of unemployment and excess capacity no such sacrifice need necessarily be imposed upon anyone is no reason for discarding the concept.

[9] Davenport's contribution merely consisted in hints which he threw out in his *Value and Distribution* (1908) without making much of them: he emphasized, e.g., that it is not correct to say that banks 'lend their deposits.' W. G. L. Taylor, in a book which (like Davenport's) never received the recognition it deserved, went much further (*The Credit System,* 1913). A great stride was made by C. A. Phillips (*Bank Credit,* 1920), who not only did much to clear up the theoretical questions involved but in addition pointed out the difference between the expansion of loans and investments that is possible for an individual bank which competes with others and the expansion that can be performed by a system of competing banks, considered as a whole.

[10] Albert Hahn, *Volkswirtschaftliche Theorie des Bankkredits* (3rd ed., 1930). One reason why this book left so many economists unconvinced was, however, the fact that the theory of bank credit there presented was wedded to certain highly optimistic views about the possibility of achieving permanent prosperity, which prejudiced some economists against its essential achievement.

[11] D. H. Robertson, *Banking Policy and the Price Level* (1926). Forced saving figures there under the name of Imposed Lacking. A. C. Pigou, *Industrial Fluctuations* (1927), Part I, chs. 13 and 14.

[12] Thus Walras saw the phenomenon of credit creation quite clearly (though he confined himself to banknotes). But he considered it as an abuse that ought to be suppressed and refused for this reason, to make it a normal element of his general schema (*Études d'économie politique appliquée,* ed. of 1936, p. 47 and pp. 339 et seq.).

a theory which tended to obscure it was bound to be voted not only useless but wrong in point of fact—indeed guilty of the elementary error of confusing legal-tender money with the bookkeeping items that reflect contractual relations concerning this legal-tender money. And it is quite true that those issues must not be obscured.[13] That the theory of credit creation does not necessarily do this seemed small comfort to those who feared its misuse.

8. Crises and Cycles: the Monetary Theories

We have seen on the one hand that, broadly speaking, the monetary analysis of that period centered in the problems of Value of Money (or price level) but on the other hand that some leading economists were working their way toward monetary analysis of the economic process as a whole in which mere price-level problems fall into secondary place. This tendency has been illustrated by the implications of the cash balance and income approaches but it asserted itself also in many other ways. It is significant, for instance, that Marshall originally intended the volume that appeared as *Money, Credit, and Commerce* to carry the title *Money, Credit, and Employment:* and there are in fact many things in it that come within the range of recent Income and Employment Analysis. Much more significant was it that Wicksell, in his somewhat hesitating way that is so engaging, eventually made up his mind to the effect that we need a concept of monetary demand for output as a whole.[1] This revived the Malthusian idea and anticipated, though in an incompletely articulate manner, the consumption function of Keynes's *General Theory*.

But the most considerable advance in the direction of monetary analysis in the present-day sense occurred within the precincts of the problems of interest and business cycles. We have already noticed symptoms of a growing inclination of economists to recognize and to use a monetary concept of capital. Nothing came of this, nor did the few attempts that were made to interpret

[13] One of them is the old issue: control of 'money' vs. control of 'credit.' Considerations of the kind alluded to explain the aversion of many French authorities to the credit-creation idea. For instance, one of the leading purposes of Professor Rist's *History of Monetary and Credit Theories* is to combat the 'confusion' of money and credit.

[1] The reference that will be most useful to the reader is to Myrdal's *Monetary Equilibrium* (Swedish ed. 1931, English trans. 1939; see above, sec. 2c). Once more, the point to grasp is this: demand schedules are defined for a single commodity. According to 'classical' theory (Say's law), there would be no sense in speaking of a demand schedule for all goods and services (or all consumers' goods and services) taken together. If we do so, nevertheless, we are for a special purpose doing something that is not covered by the ordinary theory of demand and are taking therefore a step beyond it. This special purpose may or may not be meaningful. It may or may not be well served by the aggregate-demand technique. But in any case, it should be recognized as a thing *sui generis* that carries its own particular problems. Wicksell's adoption of it spelled renunciation of Say's law. He is, therefore, the patron saint of all those economists who renounce Say's law at present.

interest as a purely monetary phenomenon meet with any success.[2] Throughout the period, the rate of interest remained, for practically all economists, a rate of return—however explained—to physical capital and the money rate a mere derivative of the real rate.[3] It had long been recognized, of course, that the two may diverge from one another: Ricardo's explanation of how new money inserts itself into circulation implies recognition of this fact, and writers on banking must always have been aware of it. But nobody attached much importance to it until Wicksell made it the center of his theory of the value of money and the subject of an elaborate analysis that produced the Wicksellian Cumulative Process: he pointed out that, if banks keep their loan rate below the real rate—which as we know he explained on the lines of Böhm-Bawerk's theory—they will put a premium on expansion of production and especially on investment in durable plant and equipment; prices will eventually rise; and if banks refuse to raise their loan rate even then, prices will go on rising cumulatively without any assignable limit even though all other cost items rise proportionally.[4]

The analytic situation created by this argument may be described like this. In itself the Wicksellian emphasis upon the effects of possible divergences between money and real rates of interest does not constitute a compelling reason for abandoning the position that the fundamental fact about interest is a net return to physical goods, a position from which Wicksell himself never departed. However, it does constitute a good and sufficient reason for treating the money rate as a distinct variable in its own right that depends, partly at least, upon factors other than those that govern the net return to physical capital (natural or real rate). The two are related, of course. In equilibrium they are even equal. But they are no longer 'fundamentally the same thing.'[5]

[2] They were so little noticed or so completely forgotten that they were not even mentioned in the discussion on this topic in the 1930's. One of them, Silvio Gesell's, was however rescued from oblivion by Lord Keynes, see *General Theory*, ch. 23, VI.

[3] This meaning of real or 'natural' rate must not be confused with the wholly different meaning in which Marshall used the phrase (*Principles*, Book VI, ch. 6, concluding note), namely, the meaning of money rate (or 'nominal' rate) corrected for price-level changes. The two are related but not identical and Marshall has, so far as I can see, no share in the Wicksellian idea I am about to discuss. His own merit in emphasizing what may be termed the distinction between nominal and actual rate is shared by Irving Fisher (*Appreciation and Interest*, 1896).

[4] Böhm-Bawerk's comment on this argument was: 'Wicksell must have been dreaming when he wrote that.'

[5] The following paraphrase of the paragraph above may prove helpful. Into the Walrasian system enters just one rate of interest, which is a rate of net return on physical 'capitals.' Strictly, this implies that the money rate of interest is not only equal to this rate of net return in equilibrium but identical with it, in the sense that the money rate is merely the monetary expression of the rate of net return on physical 'capitals.' If we want to recognize explicitly that instead of being identical with this rate of net return (equivalent to saying that it is 'fundamentally the same thing') the money rate has some measure of independence, we must introduce it as another variable and posit equality with the 'real rate' as an additional equilibrium condition. This

And so soon as we recognize this, they will drift further and further apart and *we* shall drift further and further away from the position that the net return to physical goods of one kind or another is the fundamental fact about the interest rate of the loan market—the position which we have traced to Barbon and which Lord Keynes was to condemn on the ground that it involved 'confusion' between rate of interest and the marginal efficiency of (physical) capital.[6] Other factors, such as the loan policy of banks, will then seem to us to be just as fundamental, and the road opens toward the purely monetary theories of interest that emerged later and of which the Keynesian was to attract more attention than any other. Let us, however, keep in mind three things. First, we have been sketching a most interesting line of doctrinal development, which starts with Barbon and runs a course that, for the moment, ends with Keynes. But it is not suggested that the individuals who made themselves responsible for the newer monetary theories of interest consciously arrived at their conclusions by working out the implications of the situation created by the Wicksell analysis: this may have been the case with his Swedish disciples—though I do not wish to question *anyone's* subjective originality—but it was certainly not so with the others. Second, it is not suggested that, by retracing Barbon's steps, the economists of our epoch have simply returned to the monetary theories of pre-Barbonian times: though similar to them in important respects—and especially to those of the scholastics—theirs are unquestionably novel in others. Third, by defining the new variable of our economic system, money interest, as a thing that is monetary in nature and not only in form, we do not eliminate from the problem of the loan rate the 'real' factors as completely as some modern economists seem to think: the rate of net return to physical investment remains, at the very least, a factor in the demand for loans and therefore cannot vanish from any complete theory of the money rate.[7]

---

is what Wicksell did. His investigations into the conditions of monetary equilibrium were not entirely successful. They made history of analysis, however, through the impulse they gave to contemporaneous and later research, especially by his Swedish followers (see e.g. Myrdal, op. cit.).

[6] Wicksell's real or natural rate of interest is the marginal productivity of (physical) capital (more precisely, the marginal productivity of Böhm-Bawerk's roundabout process). It is, therefore, not identical with Keynes's marginal efficiency, which is the same as Fisher's marginal rate of return over cost (*Theory of Interest*, p. 169) and means marginal productivity of current investment. But the two concepts stand in a unique relation to one another so that, for the purpose in hand, they may nevertheless be used interchangeably. Lord Keynes may hence be said to have condemned the 'confusion' between money and real rate of interest or, better, the habit of nineteenth-century economists to link them together too closely. It then appears that Wicksell was the first to undermine this habit.

[7] This fact is important precisely because it is so often denied and because Keynes's exposition in the *General Theory* tended to obscure it, although it is not less essential for his monetary theory of interest than it is for any other. It comes in by way of the condition that the equilibrium amount of current investment is the amount for which 'marginal efficiency' is equal to the money rate. The statement that interest is the

Wicksell's position in the development of modern monetary cycle theories is quite similar to his position in the development of modern monetary interest theories. He himself no more held a monetary cycle theory than he held a monetary interest theory. But he opened the road for the former as he opened it for the latter. In fact, the Cumulative Process itself need only be adjusted in order to yield a theory of the cycle. Suppose that banks emerge from a period of recovery or quiescence in a liquid state. Their interest will prompt them to expand their loans. In order to do so they will, in general, have to stimulate demand for loans by lowering their rates until these are below the Wicksellian real rate, which, as we know, is Böhm-Bawerk's real rate. In consequence, firms will invest—especially in durable equipment with respect to which rate of interest counts heavily [8]—beyond the point at which they would have to stop with the higher money rate that is equal to the real rate. Thus, on the one hand, a process of cumulative inflation sets in and, on the other hand, the time structure of production is distorted. This process cannot go on indefinitely, however—there are several possible reasons for this, the simplest being that banks run up against the limits set to their lending by their reserves—and when it stops and the money rate catches up with the real rate, we have an untenable situation in which the investment undertaken on the stimulus of an 'artificially' low rate proves a source of losses: booms end in liquidation that spell depression.

This theory has been sketched out by Professor von Mises,[9] who, while extending critical recognition to Wicksell, described it as a development of currency school views. It was further developed by Professor von Hayek into a much more elaborate analytic structure of his own,[10] which, on being presented to the Anglo-American community of economists, met with a sweeping success that has never been equaled by any strictly theoretical book that failed to make amends for its rigors by including plans and policy recommendations or to make contact in other ways with its readers' loves or hates. A strong critical reaction followed that, at first, but served to underline the success, and then the profession turned away to other leaders and other interests.[11] The social psychology of this is interesting matter for study.

factor that limits investment is as true as to say that the price of motor cars is the factor that limits the demand for them, and is equally incomplete.

[8] Obviously the rate of interest, a minor factor in short-run investment, is a major one in long-run investment such as investment in durable machines, railways, utilities, the capital value of which increases rapidly as the interest rate is reduced. [J. A. S. intended to expand this—he penciled 'This is obscured by risk—otherwise.']

[9] *Theorie des Geldes* . . . 1924, Third Part, ch. 5, secs. 4, 5. This reference is to the 2nd ed., in which the line of reasoning above is presented as an essentially complete explanation of cycles. The fundamental ideas, however, are already contained in the original edition of 1912.

[10] *Geldtheorie und Konjunkturtheorie* (1929); *Prices and Production* (1931). A new version that altered the argument in several important respects appeared in 1939: *Profits, Interest, and Investment;* and a further installment that covered much new ground, in 1941: *The Pure Theory of Capital.*

[11] Other successes of 'theoretical' books, in our time, for example, the success of Professor E. H. Chamberlin's *Monopolistic Competition* and Hicks's *Value and Capital,*

Hawtrey's [12] analysis makes business cycles, as he himself put it, a purely monetary phenomenon in a sense in which the Mises-Hayek cycle is not. Hawtrey makes no use of the element of disturbance (or maladjustment) in the time structure of plant and equipment; fluctuations in the flow of money income, themselves caused by exclusively monetary factors, are the only cause of general cyclical fluctuations in trade and employment. But he does use the Cumulative Process and traces it like Mises to the inherent instability of the modern credit system. Banks, then, are again supposed to start abnormal activity by easy conditions for loans. Only the main link of this with general booming conditions is not increase in orders for new plant or equipment but increase in the stocks held by the wholesale trade that also react to small changes in loan rates. Expansion leads to further expansion, hence to increased money incomes and to loss of hand-to-hand cash by the banks, whose inability to go on expanding loans indefinitely then leads to a rise in rates which reverses the process—which is why the central bank rate plays so great a role in this analysis. Thus, similarities are sufficiently pronounced to entitle us to speak of a single monetary theory, the votaries of which disagree on one issue only: whether bank-loan rates act primarily on 'durable capital' or via the stocks of wholesalers. Throughout the twenties, Hawtrey's theory enjoyed a considerable vogue. In the United States, especially, it was the outstanding rationalization of the uncritical belief in the unlimited efficacy of the open-market operations of the Federal Reserve System that prevailed then.

Nor is the fundamental unanimity of the votaries of the monetary theory of cycles [13] seriously disturbed by those economists who place responsibility for the phenomenon with the vagaries of gold. This idea commanded more assent when it was used to 'explain' those longer spans of prevalent prosperity or prevalent depression that are in fact associated (more or less) with significant changes in the rate of gold production, such as, roughly, 1849-72 or 1872-91. But it has also been used to 'explain' business cycles proper. In this case, since an accession of gold acts on bank reserves and hence makes banks more will-

---

were more enduring and therefore greater in the end. But they lacked the spectacular quality of Hayek's. The much greater success of Keynes's *General Theory* is not comparable because, whatever its merit as a piece of analysis may be, there cannot be any doubt that it owed its victorious career primarily to the fact that its argument implemented some of the strongest political preferences of a large number of modern economists (see below Part v, ch. 5). Politically, Hayek's swam against the stream.

[12] R. G. Hawtrey, *Good and Bad Trade* (1913), and many later works. Perusal of *Capital and Employment* (1937) will show the extent to which Mr. Hawtrey modified his earlier views.

[13] When we speak of monetary theories of cycles, a double meaning of the word theory (see Part I) leaps to mind. A monetary theory of cycles is an explanatory hypothesis of cycles that runs in terms of money and lending. But nobody denies that *any* explanation of the phenomenon must take account of its monetary features. We may, therefore, use the word monetary theory also for the sum total of propositions about the ways in which money and credit behave in the cycle. And, considered as contributions to monetary cycle theory in this sense, many arguments, such as Hawtrey's, retain importance even for those who do not accept them as adequate in the role of explanatory hypothesis.

ing and able to lend, we have a particular reason for expecting expansion instead of the more general reason formulated by Mises and Hawtrey but, for the rest, the argument will be much the same: again credit inflation owing to low money rates, again the point at which interest catches up with prices, and reversal of the process. The most eminent sponsor of this type of monetary theory, Professor Irving Fisher, at first stated it in this unsophisticated manner in his *Purchasing Power of Money*, 1911 (ch. 4).[14] But, though he continued to emphasize the monetary aspects of the phenomenon, he so broadened the basis of his analysis as to end up with the Debt-Deflation Theory, which, contrary to his unduly restricted claim, applies to all recorded business cycles and is in essence not monetary at all. Ostensibly, the burden is chiefly laid upon the fact that in the atmosphere of prosperity debts are accumulated, the inevitable liquidation of which, with the attendant breaks in the price structure, constitutes the core of depression. Behind this surface mechanism there are the really operative factors—new technological and commercial possibilities chiefly—which Fisher does not fail to see but which he banishes to the apparently secondary place of 'debt starters' (*Econometrica*, October 1933, p. 348), so that, exactly as in the case of his general monetary analysis (see above, sec. 2), the true dimensions of what is really a great performance are so completely hidden from the reader's view that they have to be dug out laboriously and in fact never impressed the profession as they should have done.

9. Non-Monetary Cycle Analysis

It will be convenient to go on in order to glance briefly at some analyses of cyclical phenomena other than Hayek's that are non-monetary *in the sense defined*,[1] although we shall have to cross the frontiers of this chapter's subject in doing so. But we shall go no further than is necessary in order to establish one important proposition, namely, that *all* the essential facts and ideas about

[14] The version presented in *Purchasing Power* had been published before, in summary, in *Moody's Magazine* under the title 'Gold Depreciation and Interest Rates,' February 1909. The main stepping stones to the Debt-Deflation Theory are the articles: 'The Business Cycle Largely a "Dance of the Dollar,"' *Journal of the American Statistical Association*, December 1923, and 'Our Unstable Dollar and the So-Called Business Cycle' (ibid. June 1925), both of which concentrate on fluctuations of prices and interest rates that are traced to purely monetary conditions, and the book *Booms and Depressions* (1932) partly summarized and partly complemented in 'The Debt-Deflation Theory of Great Depressions,' *Econometrica*, October 1933, to which reference is made in the text.

[1] The italicized words should be kept in mind because, in view of the fact noticed in the preceding section, namely, that the demand for money and especially for bank credit must always play *some* role, and mostly an important one, in explanations of fluctuations, any less strict definition of 'purely monetary theories' would result in the inclusion of many more. But even so dividing lines are very much a matter of subjective judgment and cannot be drawn sharply. Not all historians will, e.g., call the Mises theory purely monetary or the Hayek theory non-monetary.

business-cycle analysis had emerged by 1914: the subsequent thirty years brought forth, indeed, a flood of statistical and historical material, and many new statistical and theoretical techniques; by clarification and elaboration they may be said to have expanded the subject into a recognized branch of economics; but they added no principle or fact that had not been known before.[2]

(a) *Juglar's Performance.* As we have seen, it was the spectacular phenomenon of 'crises' and the less spectacular but still more irritating phenomenon of depressions ('gluts') which, in the preceding period, first attracted the attention of economists. We have also seen, however, that some of them did look beyond depressions: such men as Tooke and Lord Overstone fully realized that crises and gluts were but incidents or phases of a larger process; many more displayed symptoms of a vague awareness of this fact. Nevertheless, it was only during the period under survey that the 'cycle' definitively ousted the 'crisis' from its place in economists' minds and that the ground was cleared for the development of modern business-cycle analysis, though practically all workers in the field continued to use the old phrase—an interesting case of 'terminological lag.' This is why the decisive performance is considered here although it was published in 1862. It was the work of a man who was a physician by training, but must be ranked, as to talent and command of scientific method, among the greatest economists of all times, Clément Juglar.[3] This evaluation rests

[2] This statement and my failure to make the (impossible) attempt to survey the achievements of this later literature on cycles must not be interpreted in a derogatory sense. On the contrary, I believe the work embodied in this literature to be as valuable as any ever done by economists. This much at least will be evident from what I shall say about it in Part v. It is nevertheless essential to realize the extent to which this work rests upon bases laid before 1914. Attention is called to Professor R. A. Gordon's 'Selected Bibliography of the Literature on Economic Fluctuations, 1930-36,' *Review of Economic Statistics*, February 1937, and to the list of *books* about Business Cycles published by the Bureau of Business Research, University of Illinois, College of Commerce and Business Administration, 1928. Professor von Haberler's masterly presentation of the modern material (*Prosperity and Depression*, 1937; 3rd enlarged ed., 1941) is recommended as an introduction to the subject: reliance on the fact that few if any students of economics fail to consult this work is my main excuse for keeping my own comments upon it as brief as possible. The reader will understand, however, that my admiration for it does not involve agreement in every point. Work prior to 1895 is fairly well covered by a history that appeared in that year: E. von Bergmann, *Geschichte der nationalökonomischen Krisentheorieen.* From a lengthy list of other historical and critical publications, I will mention only: Alvin H. Hansen, *Business-Cycle Theory* (1927); then, once more, F. Lutz, *Das Konjunkturproblem in der Nationalökonomie* (1932); and W. C. Mitchell's *Business Cycles . . .* (1927), especially ch. 1.

[3] Clément Juglar (1819-1905) abandoned medicine for economics in 1848. He had no formal training in the latter subject and cared even less than he knew about formal theory. His was the type of genius that walks only the way chalked out by himself and never follows any other. Many people do this in a subject like economics. But then they mostly produce freaks. The genius comes in where a man produces, entirely on his own, truth that will stand. Of his many publications it is only necessary to mention the principal one: *Les Crises commerciales et leur retour périodique en France, en*

upon three facts. To begin with, he was the first to use time-series material (mainly prices, interest rates, and central bank balances) systematically and with the clear purpose in mind of analyzing a definite phenomenon. Since this is the fundamental method of modern business-cycle analysis, he can be justly called its ancestor. Second, having discovered the cycle of roughly ten years' duration that was most obvious in his material—it was he who discovered the continent; islands near it several writers had discovered before—he proceeded to develop a morphology of it in terms of 'phases' (upgrade, 'explosion,' liquidation). Though Tooke and Overstone had done the same thing, the modern morphology of cycles dates from Juglar. And so does, in the same sense, 'periodicity.' This morphology of a 'periodic' process is what he meant when he proudly claimed to have discovered the 'law of crises' without any preconceived theory or hypothesis.[4] Third, he went on to try his hand at explanation. The grand feature about this is the almost ideal way in which 'facts' and 'theory' are made to intertwine. In themselves, most of his suggestions concerning the factors that bring about the downturn (loss of cash by banks, failure of new buying) do not amount to a great deal. But all-important was his diagnosis of the nature of depression, which he expressed with epigrammatic force in the famous sentence: 'the only cause of depression is prosperity.' This means that depressions are nothing but adaptations of the economic system to the situations created by the preceding prosperities and that, in consequence, the basic problem of cycle analysis reduces to the question what is it that causes prosperities—to which he failed, however, to give any satisfactory answer.

Economists were at first slow to follow up Juglar's lead. Later on, however, most of them, even those who were more inclined than he was to commit themselves to particular hypotheses concerning 'causes,' adopted his general approach—so much so that today Juglar's work reads like an old story very primitively told. And at the end of the period stands a work that, on the one hand, was entirely conceived in his spirit and, on the other hand, ushered in a most important part of the cycle analysis of our own time: Wesley C. Mitchell's *Business Cycles*.[5]

Angleterre et aux Etats Unis ('crowned' by the Académie des Sciences Morales et Politiques in 1860, publ. as a book in 1862, 2nd ed. 1889, English trans. by W. Thom, from 3rd ed., 1916). There is a *Notice* of his life and work by Professor Paul Beauregard, in the *Comptes rendus* of the Académie des Sciences Morales et Politiques (1909).

[4] Juglar seems not to have considered the implications of the fact that his 9-10 year cycle could not be expected to be the only wavelike movement in his material. Later workers naturally discovered others. At least the names of N. D. Kondratieff (1922) and Joseph Kitchin (1923) should be mentioned (on these and predecessors, see Mitchell, op. cit. pp. 227 and 380). But we can do no more than advert to this line of advance. Juglar's merit is hardly diminished by these developments—in fact, they only serve to enhance his historical position.

[5] *Business Cycles* (1913); entirely re-written version, *Business Cycles: the Problem and Its Setting* (1927); *Measuring Business Cycles* by A. F. Burns and W. C. Mitchell (1946). I do not mean to suggest, however, that Professor Mitchell derived his approach from Juglar, any more than I would suggest that the inventors of the 'Harvard

(b) *Common Ground and Warring 'Theories.'* That period, then, established a method, at least the fundamental principle of a method, on which, by the end of the period, a majority of business-cycle analysts agreed and which was to serve the bulk of the work of our own time. Agreement went further than this however. By the end of the period the lists of the features or symptoms that characterize cyclical phases—which different economists did draw up or would have drawn up—looked much alike. And not only that: by the end of the period most workers agreed—or tacitly took for granted—that the fundamental fact about cyclical fluctuations was the characteristic fluctuation in the production of plant and equipment. Now, how is this? We seem to be discovering a lot of common ground that should have assured much parallelism of effort and much agreement in results. Yet this is not at all what a survey of that literature reveals. On the contrary, we seem to behold nothing but disagreement and antagonistic effort—disagreement and antagonism that went so far as to be discreditable to the science and even ludicrous. The contradiction is only apparent however. Agreement on the list of features, even if it had been complete,[6] does not spell agreement as to their relations with one another, and it is the interpretation of these relations and not the list per se which individuates an analytic scheme or business-cycle 'theory.' Even agreement to the effect that it is the activity in the plant-and-equipment ('capital goods') industries which is the outstanding feature in cyclical fluctuations does not go far toward ensuring agreement in results since it leaves the decisive question of interpretation wide open. And, in order to avoid misunderstanding, we must emphasize at once that the outstanding feature of cyclical phases, whatever it is, need not contain within itself the 'cause' that explains why cyclical fluctuations exist: this 'cause' may still lie somewhere else, for example, in the sphere of consumption. But in spite of all this, it remains both true and important that agreement went further than the troubled surface suggests and that most of the analysts of the business-cycle phenomenon who produced theories, which look so different, really started from a common basis.

1. The fact that the 'relatively large amplitude of the movements in constructional, as compared with consumption, industries' is one of the most obvious 'general characteristics of industrial fluctuations' [7] can hardly fail to ob-

---

Barometer' were subjectively dependent on him. All I want to point out is the objective contour line of the development of that method—Filiation of Scientific Ideas is an objective process which may, but need not, involve any subjective relation. Similarly, Menger had not heard of Gossen until long after he had developed his version of the marginal utility analysis. Yet Menger's work stands in an objective sequence in which Gossen stands, in time, above him.

[6] It was substantial but not complete. An example will illustrate: nobody can fail to recognize that prices move characteristically in the course of a cycle; but their behavior is not quite regular and there are prosperities in which they failed to rise; this left room for difference of opinion on whether or not they should be included in a list of 'normal' features.

[7] Pigou, *Industrial Fluctuations* (1927), Part I, ch. 2.

trude itself upon anyone [8] who has learned to look at a cycle as a whole, though it may escape attention so long as one looks merely at the depression phase. Nevertheless, it took time for it to be recognized consciously and with full awareness of its pivotal importance. Speaking very roughly, we may associate this achievement—or a decisive share in this achievement—with the work of Tugan-Baranowsky.[9] It is, however, only the emphasis upon the pivotal importance of that fact which constitutes the historical merit of the work. His own interpretation of it—that is, his distinctive theory—which runs in terms of alternating accumulation and release of liquid saving, is valuable only as an example of how short the way is from a promising starting point into a blind alley, even for an able and serious worker.

II. The outstanding work in the line under discussion is Arthur Spiethoff's.[10] His analytic schema first lists a number of possible starters of a process of expansion of plant and equipment, which process then accounts without difficulty for all the other observed phenomena of booms, great care being taken to account for the individual peculiarities of every historical instance. This em-

[8] Walras, it is interesting to note, treated as common knowledge the fact that the *production des capitaux neufs* goes on in alternating high tides and low tides—characterized by respectively high and low rates of discount and of prices—and identified it (in 1884) with what we call business cycles of about 10 years' duration. He does not quote Juglar but Jevons. (*Études d'économie appliquée,* 1936, p. 31.)

[9] Mikhail Ivanovich Tugan-Baranowsky (1865-1919) was the most eminent Russian economist of that period and should perhaps have been mentioned also in other connections. The methodological aspect of his work is particularly interesting: he did much historical work of high quality; but he was also a 'theorist'; and he combined, or welded into a higher unit, these two interests in a way which he had learned from Marx and which was by no means common. From Marx, too, he had learned to theorize, though he experienced the influence both of the English 'classics' and of the Austrians with the result that his theoretical work in the end amounted to a 'critical synthesis.' But neither his *Theoretische Grundlagen des Marxismus* (1905) nor his *Soziale Theorie der Verteilung* (1913) made any mark. This was but natural in view of the deficiency in rigorous thinking both displayed, which is as deplorable as it is curious in a man of his ability. More important were his work on the history of industrial capitalism in Russia (1st Russian ed., 1898; German trans. 1900) and *Modern Socialism in Its Historical Development* (1906; English trans. 1910). The only other item that need be mentioned out of what no doubt was an imposing total is the most important of all, for this did make a mark and did exert influence far and wide, viz., his history of commercial crises in England (first in Russian, 1894; German version, 1901; French, 1913). Again, the first and theoretical chapter is a distinctly poor performance. The rest stands in the history of our science.

[10] On Spiethoff, see above, ch. 4, sec. 2d. The main reason why his work developed so slowly was his heroic resolve to carry out a vast program of minute factual research single-handed—practically without any research assistance at all. Though he began to publish fragmentary results in 1902 (in Schmoller's *Jahrbuch*), a provisional presentation of the whole—really a preview only—was not published before 1925 in vol. VI of the 4th ed. of the *Handwörterbuch der Staatswissenschaften,* article 'Krisen.' I understand that preparations are being made for the publication of a fuller version in English.

phasis upon the expansion of plant and equipment is reflected in the choice, for the role of fundamental index, of iron consumption (production plus imports minus exports). The problem that remains, namely why this expansion eventually runs into a general condition of production at a loss ('overproduction'), is then solved by means of several factors, such as shortage of working capital and temporary saturation of demand in particular directions. This schema, which at every step leaves plenty of room for alternatives, is admirably suited for absorbing, into their proper places and without exaggerating their importance, many other factors that are worked up into unique motors of the cyclical movement by other theories, such as 'psychological' factors, monetary factors, acceleration, undersaving. Spiethoff's analysis, therefore, comes nearest to an organic synthesis of relevant elements and to full utilization of the co-ordinating power of that starting point. And it has still another virtue: with the possible exception of Marx, Spiethoff was the first to recognize explicitly that cycles are not merely a non-essential concomitant of capitalist evolution but that they are the essential form of capitalist life. Also he was one of the first to observe that there are long periods during which prosperity phases of cycles are accentuated by favorable conditions ('spans of prosperity') and other long periods during which depression phases are accentuated ('spans of depression'). He refused, however, to combine these drawn-out spells of predominant prosperity and depression into 'long cycles' and he reserved judgment as to their causation.

It would be extremely interesting to compare Spiethoff's work on cycles with the work of Robertson, which though independent of Spiethoff's, displays affinity in important respects.[11] There is no similarity in method. Spiethoff

[11] Professor D. H. Robertson's publications start in January 1914 with an important but all but unknown article ('Some Material for a Study of Trade Fluctuations') in the *Journal of the Royal Statistical Society* that presented historical material in support of the promising idea—which Robertson failed to exploit but which never vanished completely from his horizon—that cycles have something to do with the impact upon the economic process of *new* industries, some booms being connected, e.g. with railroad building, others with inventions in steel production, electricity, the explosion motor, and so on. Next came his *Study of Industrial Fluctuation* (1915), which drew a picture closely similar to Spiethoff's. The monetary complement (saving, forced saving, credit creation, and so on) was added in his famous *Banking Policy and the Price Level* (1926; 3rd ed., 1932) and elaborated in various papers most of which are reprinted in *Essays in Monetary Theory* (1940). A passage in *Banking Policy* . . . (p. 5) is so important for the *histoire intime* of the monetary analysis of our day that quotation is imperative: 'I have had so many discussions with Mr. J. M. Keynes on the subject-matter of Chapters v and vi [containing the monetary analysis], and have re-written them so drastically at his suggestion, that I think neither of us now knows how much of the ideas therein contained is his and how much is mine.' This, of course, was J. M. Keynes of the *Treatise* and not of the *General Theory*, but there were in Robertson's book some pointers also toward the latter. In view of the later disagreements between these two eminent men, it is desirable to notice that, whatever their immediate cause, there was always this fundamental difference: Keynes concentrated on monetary aspects and monetary policy from the first, whereas Robertson emphasized 'real factors'—

started, in the spirit of Juglar, from minute investigations of available statistics; Robertson worked first and last as a 'theorist,' taking only the broadest and most obvious facts as a base and concentrating on forging tools of interpretation. Therefore, their work is complementary rather than competitive. But their general visions of the cyclical process and its causation were closely similar.[12]

III. A few examples will suffice to display the fact that most theories of cycles are nothing but different branches of that common trunk, 'plant and equipment.'

First, the reader will realize without difficulty that even the purely monetary theories of cycles may be included among the 'investment theories.' For although they locate the *causes* of the cyclical movement in the monetary sphere, *effects* upon the plant-and-equipment industries are bound to play some role. If, in particular, explanation pivots on the money rate of interest, disturbance in the structure of 'physical capital' must always be a factor in cyclical situations though, especially from a short-run point of view like, for example, Hawtrey's, it need not be made the decisive one. If we do make it the decisive one, we get the non-monetary or semi-monetary theory of Hayek—increased production of durable plant and equipment ('lengthening of the period of production') through a fall of the money rate of interest below the marginal rate of profit.

Second, writers who agree to interpret business cycles primarily as investment cycles—in the physical sense of the term investment—may still differ as to the 'starter' and such differences will then individuate their theories. Thus, what may be termed the *perpetuum-mobile* theory contents itself with the fact that depression itself will in its course produce conditions favorable, first, to revival and, then, to the construction of new plant and equipment. To give another example, Mrs. England, with a keener sense of the necessity for a more convincing cause, pointed to the activity of promoters or, more generally, to the intrusion into the horizon of entrepreneurs of new technological or commercial possibilities.[13]

Third, whatever it is that gives the prosperity impulse, we may derive a dis-

---

as against both monetary and psychological ones—from the first. There were thus wide stretches of ground that were Robertson's own and into which Keynes's analysis never penetrated. Within this wider frame, monetary propositions acquire a meaning—and one that is very relevant for practical applications—that is wholly different from the meaning and implications which the *same* monetary propositions convey if taken by themselves.

[12] Robertson repeatedly expressed awareness of this fact, regretfully hinting at the prohibitive barrier of language. It can, I believe, only happen in economics that a scientific worker would leave it at that. I do not say this in reproach. I say it because the case illustrates a state of things that is very general and explains much in the history of economics.

[13] Of the interesting papers by Minnie Throop England, we note especially 'Promotion as the Cause of Crises,' *Quarterly Journal of Economics,* August 1915, and 'An Analysis of the Crisis Cycle,' *Journal of Political Economy,* October 1913.

tinctive theory by emphasizing the indubitable fact that the plant and equipment, construction of which is undertaken in reaction to such an impulse, takes time to get into existence and working order—time during which there is nothing to blunt the edge of that impulse. Consequently, when later on the stream of additional products impinges upon consumers' goods markets, something like 'general overproduction,' that is, a price fall that turns expected profits into actual losses, may result. If we trust this explanation sufficiently, we can speak of a 'lag theory' of the cycle. We get another version if we put the main emphasis, instead of on the fall in the prices of consumers' goods, on the rise in the price of cost items. The former version may be exemplified by the works of Bouniatian and Aftalion, the latter by that of Lescure, though there is much in all three of them to relieve the pressure on the factor primarily stressed.[14] Incidentally, we may infer from this that he who says that business cycles are primarily cycles in prices *may* mean exactly the same thing as he who says that they are primarily cycles in investment.

Fourth, there was again, as there had been in the preceding period, a crop of those theories which, in one way or another, impute responsibility for depressions to the inadequacy of money incomes in general—more precisely their failure to expand *pari passu* with the production, actual or potential, of consumers' goods[15]—or to people's saving habits or, finally, to inadequacy of the incomes of some classes and the saving habits of others. I have had occasion already to comment on the indestructible vitality they owe to their popular appeal. It was to this appeal—particularly strong in prolonged periods of predominant depression—and not to any great improvement in their analytic foundations that they owed their survival. Leading scientific opinion, however, continued to be unfavorable to them and they continued, to borrow Lord Keynes's felicitous phrase, to live in a scientific underworld. So much was this the case that leading economists did not even bother to make the concessions that were obviously indicated. For though the argument against oversaving

[14] Mentor Bouniatian, *Wirtschaftskrisen und Ueberkapitalisation* (1908), enlarged as *Les Crises économiques* (Russian original, 1915; French trans. 1922); A. Aftalion, *Les Crises périodiques de surproduction* (1913); J. Lescure, *Des Crises générales et périodiques de surproduction* (1906; 3rd ed., 1923). All three of these authors, but especially the two last, are particularly notable for strict adherence to Juglar's methodological principles.

[15] This was sometimes called 'the flaw in the price system' and may also be expressed by saying that the expansion of production in capitalist society is normally attended by a long-run tendency in prices to fall ('deflation'). It is highly characteristic of the mental habits that prevail in economics that this fact, which received much attention, was hardly ever seen in its organic significance. Some economists—I think that Marshall was among them—noticed it with approval much as A. Smith had approved of 'cheapness and plenty.' For others, it was just a 'flaw.' The best that can be reported was that some writers pointed out that falling prices did not spell disturbance where they were a consequence of cost-reducing improvement; and that others pointed out that monetary remedies for falling prices would create disturbance of their own (profit inflation).

theories may be strong so long as they aver that saving is an ultimate and independent 'cause' of disturbance, it should never be denied, on the one hand, that there are plenty of hitches in the saving-investment mechanism and, on the other hand, that saving, in a depression that has already set in for reasons other than saving, may make things worse on balance than they otherwise need be, especially if saving takes the form of hoarding as it is likely to do in a depression. But the leaders of prevailing opinion, though they had occasional glimpses of all this,[16] completely failed to go into the matter properly—a fact that explains much in the recent history of economics. They evidently attached but little importance to these possibilities of disturbance. They did not even emphasize the role in the cycle of that saving which is being used for the repayment of bank loans. Thus a considerable tract of open country was left unguarded in which, to the backward glance of the economist of today, there seems to stand, in something that to many looks very like a halo of glory, the figure of J. A. Hobson. Actually, his was not a solitary figure. Nor did he come very near to having anticipated the doctrines of present-day Keynesianism. But we shall confine ourselves to him.[17]

In most cases, there is no sharp dividing line between underconsumption theories and others. Some, though not all of them, might just as well be couched in terms of overproduction or overinvestment, monetary or 'real'—whereupon it becomes easy to see that they are but another branch of the plant-and-equipment tree. This is particularly clear in the case of the type of oversaving argument that was espoused by Hobson. Today most writers who see saving in the role of villain of the piece aver that the mischief arises from savers' not spending at all, either on current consumption or on 'investment goods': the problem then is to show why, having saved, people refuse to invest, thereby creating unemployment and pools of idle money.[18] But though Hobson notices this aspect of the matter he based, not quite logically, his explanation of cyclical fluctuations and of the incident unemployment upon an entirely different argument. With him saving produces alternating prosperities and depressions precisely because savers do invest promptly and thereby increase the productive powers of the economic engine beyond the possibility of sale at cost-covering prices. This line of reasoning may be labeled Overproduction-through-Saving and is certainly not Keynesian. But Hobson, like Tugan-Baranowsky before him, went on to point out that most saving is done by the relatively rich, and he used this fact to arrive at the proposition that the ultimate cause of cyclical disturbance and of the incident unemployment is the

[16] For such a glimpse, in the case of Marshall, see Keynes's *General Theory*, p. 19n.

[17] See above, ch. 5, sec. 2a. The two books that bear most directly on the subject of this section are: *The Industrial System* (1909) and *Economics of Unemployment* (1922).

[18] This way of looking at the matter is, of course, related to the fact that present-day analysis is primarily short-run analysis. In the short run, saving can create trouble only if savings are hoarded; if they are quickly disbursed in acts of investments, they sustain activity in the first instance; and their long-run effects do not enter into a short-run picture.

inequality of incomes. Therefore, we shall understand why economists who are interested in nothing but politically relevant results will hail Hobson as a forerunner of Keynes.[19]

Fifth, it is only for the sake of convenience that I put Marx at the end of our list of examples. In justice, he ought to have been put first because more than any other economist he identified cycles with the process of production and operation of additional plant and equipment.

Both followers and enemies have experienced difficulty in attributing to Marx any clear-cut theory of cycles. The obvious reason for this difficulty is that Marx did not live to systematize his ideas on the subject: his theory remained the great 'unwritten chapter' of his work. But there is another and more fundamental reason. His topic was capitalist evolution. Everything he ever wrote, even his scheme of a stationary society, was written to elucidate this topic. Capitalist evolution was to end in the breakdown of the system. But he early adopted the idea—it is already in the *Communist Manifesto*—that the current crises were previews of this breakdown, that is to say, the same kind of phenomenon that need only intensify itself in order to bring about definitive breakdown (the economic complement of the Revolution).[20] Therefore, *all* the elements of capitalist reality were, directly or indirectly, relevant also to his vision of the cyclical phenomenon. The 'unwritten chapter' would have had to sum up the *whole* of his analysis of capitalism. And the whole of this analysis in turn centered in (1) the production of 'real capital' and (2) in the factors that change its composition (relative increase of constant compared with variable capital[21]). These are the unifying conceptions to which must be referred what otherwise may easily appear to be disjointed and even contradictory hints. There are, of course, many of these, such as: capitalists' ineluctable craving for accumulation (regardless of return) that is to motivate bursts of investment activity—the weakest point, though buttressed by various suggestions about more substantial factors; the ever-present impulse that produces manias and crashes (vividly but superficially described by

[19] As Lord Keynes himself has pointed out (*General Theory*, ch. 23, VI), Gesell's claims to that honor are much stronger.

[20] This is why it was essential for Marx to assume, and if possible to prove, that crises would increase in intensity as time went on, a thesis that was abandoned by Hilferding (1910) and eventually also by Kautsky, who had put up the most elaborate defense of it in 1902. Most other cycle analysts of that period either did not pronounce upon the subject—which means, I take it, that they did not see any reason why depressions should grow either more or less severe—or were inclined to take the opposite view. It is important to bear in mind that this opposite view may mean two different things: first that the *fundamental* movement would decrease in amplitudes or, second, that people would learn to handle surface phenomena and effects (speculation, swindling, bank failures, shrinkage of expenditure owing to unemployment) so that the *observed* amplitudes would grow smaller though the underlying process remains the same. No such distinction was explicitly made, however, so far as I know, in any of the more influential writings.

[21] Constant capital is, of course, not the same as plant and equipment, but the relative increase in the latter is the salient point about that process.

Engels); the tendency of the rate of profit to fall (whether or not satisfactorily motivated); overproduction and anarchy (uncertainty) of capitalist decision; recurring periods of reinvestment (renewal of the physical apparatus of production) with periods of reduced activity to follow. There were others, among them a clear pointer toward underconsumption by the laboring masses as the 'last cause of all real crises' (*Capital*, vol. III, p. 568) and toward the consequent inability of capitalists to 'realize' the surplus value that 'exists' in the commodities that have been produced. Conflicting evidence makes it impossible, however, to impute to Marx an underconsumption theory of *cycles* though it remains possible to attribute to underconsumption a role in conditioning an ultimate state of stagnation.[22]

But none of these hints, taken by itself, nor their sum total amounts to a theory of cycles. So far as Marx himself is concerned, the historian of analysis, after having noticed the basic conception and also perhaps the particularly unsatisfactory handling of money and credit, must leave it at that. All the same, there are a number of Marxist cycle theories. But they should be attributed not to Marx but to their authors—Marxists who, either selecting hints that appealed to them more than others or trying to develop, from the Marxist basis, ideas of their own, provided substitutes for the 'unwritten chapter' rather than reconstruction of it—fully believing, no doubt, that they were interpreting Marx and always keeping in mind the cherished relation between the crises of experience and the ultimate catastrophe of capitalism. It is not possible to survey them in a sketch like this.[23]

(c) *Other Approaches.* Though it is impossible to survey all the other ideas that emerged during that period about the nature and causation of economic fluctuations, it is both possible and necessary to point out that most of them, besides being suggested by untutored observation, were bound to appeal to economists who had developed economic statics as the centerpiece of their science. As we have seen above, they naturally exaggerated the importance of their central achievement. They saw more in it than do we, that is, more than a logical schema that is useful for clearing up certain equilibrium relations but is not in itself directly applicable to the given processes of real life. They did not realize how many and how important the phenomena are that escape this logical schema and loved to believe that they had got hold of all that was essential and 'normal.' Now, from the standpoint of this type of

[22] The conflicting evidence is widely scattered. But see, e.g., *Capital*, vol. II, p. 476, where Marx avers that the share of the working class in the consumable product increases in the period preceding a crisis. The weight of this passage is enhanced not so much by the fact that Marx, a few lines before, declared the proposition that crises were caused 'by the scarcity of solvent consumers' to be 'purely a tautology,' as by the fact that the proposition follows logically from his own scheme.

[23] P. M. Sweezy's work, though in this matter somewhat impaired by an evident desire to turn Marx into a Keynesian, will again prove extremely useful as a help for further study. I will merely repeat names already mentioned: O. Bauer, Bukharin, Grossmann, Hilferding, Kautsky, Luxemburg, and Sternberg. The best analysis of Marx's own views that I know of is that by H. Smith, 'Marx and the Trade Cycle,' *Review of Economic Studies*, June 1937.

analysis, it is natural to locate the 'causes' of observed disturbances *either* outside of the economic system [24] *or* in the fact that the economic engine, like any engine, never works with precision. And this attitude toward observed fluctuations was the common root—or common characteristic—of another group of theories that also seem at first sight to have nothing to do with one another.[25] We shall notice three examples.

First, the most exogenous of all factors that influence economic life is variation of harvest in so far as due to weather, a factor pressed into service for the purpose of explaining business fluctuations by W. S. Jevons, H. S. Jevons (his son), and H. L. Moore.[26]

Second, the fact that the economic engine is likely to stall may be exploited for the purposes of business-cycle analysis in various ways. The most direct one is to attribute responsibility to uncertainty in general, which will result in 'erroneous' decisions. But since this uncertainty is, in many respects, due to the fundamental properties of the private enterprise economy, we may also directly accuse the latter's institutions.[27] And since individual errors cannot con-

[24] Factors that act upon the economic system from outside are called external or exogenous factors, theories that work with such factors, exogenous (as distinct from endogenous) theories. It should be borne in mind, however, that this concept does not carry as definite a meaning as it might seem to do. On the one hand, its content will vary according to what we include in the economic system: everybody excludes uncontrollable natural events, but not everybody will also exclude 'politics.' On the other hand, even if we exclude from the concept everything that is not covered by the theory of 'business behavior'—difficult though this is in such cases as central bank action and the like—the content of the concept will still vary according to whether we mean by endogenous processes such processes only as are uniquely determined by an initial situation (Tinbergen's meaning) or also such processes as are influenced by factors not present in the initial situation, e.g. unexpected introduction of new methods of production.

[25] Another group of theories that would overlap with ours also may be related to the unduly great confidence that the best theorists of the period placed in the equilibrium analysis. This group may be called the Disproportionality Theories and comprises theories that locate the source of cyclical troubles in 'maladjustments' as between different groups of prices and quantities. This idea comes naturally to anyone who accepts Say's law as a starting point of his analysis of cycles (*not* necessarily his general theory of the economic process) and is moreover easy to substantiate from observation of certain very obvious facts. A large number of economists could be quoted—though principally economists who were not specialists of business-cycle analysis—who were content to accept it. But I have not chosen this point of view for discussion, because Disproportionality remains an empty phrase so long as it is not linked with definite factors that are to account for it and because, so soon as it is so linked, those factors and not disproportionality per se will individuate an author's theory. As an example of an analysis that stresses certain types of disproportionalities—that are mainly due to lags—E. Lederer's *Konjunktur und Krisen* (in *Grundriss der Sozialökonomik,* Part IV, XI, 1925) may, however, be mentioned.

[26] W. S. Jevons' papers were reprinted in *Investigations in Currency and Finance* (1884); H. S. Jevons, *The Sun's Heat and Trade Activity* (1910); H. L. Moore, *Economic Cycles: Their Law and Cause* (1914).

[27] The reader will realize that this 'explanation' may easily degenerate into generali-

vincingly be held to produce *big* disturbances, unless they are overwhelmingly one way, we may put our trust in 'waves of optimism and pessimism,' a version that was quite common and later on was to appeal to such authorities as Pigou and Harrod.[28] There are many other variations of this theme, none of which is entirely void of a modest element of truth and all of which are unequal to the burden put upon them.

Third, so long as we do not see much ground for believing that the economic system produces general fluctuations by virtue of its own logic, we may easily conclude that these fluctuations arise simply whenever something of sufficient importance goes wrong, no matter for what reason. Roscher had already delivered himself to this effect, and no lesser man than Böhm-Bawerk once expressed the opinion [29] that there was no general explanation of either cycles or crises: they belong in a 'last chapter' of an economic treatise where all their possible causes should be listed. There is more in this opinion—I am inclined to believe that Marshall would have agreed with it—than appears at first sight, though Juglar's achievement suffices to show up its inadequacy. It takes account of, though it overstresses, the fact which is so often neglected by ardent 'theorists,' namely, that every cycle is a historical individual *to some extent* and that unique combinations of circumstances must enter largely into every analysis of a particular case. Moreover, it bars effectively all those single-factor explanations that rest on nothing but their author's pet aversions—such as saving or exploitation. Finally, it invites detailed study of individual mechanisms, which carries us a long way, though not the whole way. The bulk of what has been done on this line belongs, however, to the postwar period: the necessary analytic techniques were slow to develop.[30] [On these postwar developments, see below Part v, ch. 4, Dynamics and Business Cycle Research.]

All this—together with what has been said above in section 8—seems to establish our thesis: the essentials of both the methods and the explanatory principles that serve in today's business-cycle analysis, barring refinements of

---

ties that are as indubitable as they are empty. A classical example of this is the statement that 'the "cause" . . . of business cycles . . . is to be found in the habits and customs [institutions] of men which make up the money economy. . .' (L. K. Frank, 'A Theory of Business Cycles,' *Quarterly Journal of Economics*, August 1923).

[28] See Pigou's *Industrial Fluctuations* (1927) and Harrod's *Trade Cycle* (1936). In justice to both authors it must, however, be added that their important contributions to our understanding of cyclical phenomena are entirely independent of, and but little impaired by, their partiality to that theory. In England, Professor Robertson is its most eminent opponent.

[29] I am sure of this but am unable to provide the reference. If my memory serves me, he said it in a review. [Professor Haberler, who read this work in manuscript, suggests that J. A. S. is referring to Böhm-Bawerk's review of E. von Bergmann's *Geschichte der nationalökonomischen Krisentheorieen* (1895), *Zeitschrift für Volkswirtschaft, Sozialpolitik und Verwaltung* (vol. VII, 1898).]

[30] Several authors of the period under survey made, however, use of the 'principle of acceleration' (see Haberler, op. cit. pp. 85 et seq.). And there were several contributions that, though they passed unnoticed, foreshadow later developments. The 'hog cycle,' e.g., was discovered by S. Benner as early as 1876 (*Benner's Prophecies of Future Ups and Downs in Prices*).

technique, date from before 1914—an instance of continuity in development or of filiation of ideas that is all the more interesting because conscious effort was all the other way. Fairly satisfactory synthesis that would have left no major fact unaccounted for and would have constituted an excellent basis for further research was 'objectively' possible by then. Why was it not attempted? The answer seems to be that objective possibility is one thing and its realization quite another thing: no more than any other history can the history of research afford to neglect the personal element. Entangled in controversy that was often petty, enamoured of their own ideas and particular emphasis, economists plodded along successfully enough. But nobody rose to what would indeed have been a most difficult feat of leadership.[31]

In view of an entirely unfounded criticism that many of us are in the habit of directing against the work of that time, it should be added that economists did not fail to offer explanations of unemployment that were certainly not obviously inadequate. By going once more over the contributions that have been mentioned and scrutinizing them for their implications concerning unemployment, the reader can easily satisfy himself of this. Sectional and general, technological and 'monetary,' temporary and 'permanent,' types of unemployment were all in the picture that would have resulted from an effort at balanced synthesis—even our own mistakes were there. The indictment that the economists of that time disposed of all unemployment as merely frictional is true only if we adopt so wide a definition of friction as to render the indictment tautological.[32]

But another indictment stands against the vast majority of the economists of that period if it be indeed proper, considering the analytic situation in which they worked, to call it an indictment: with few exceptions, of which Marx was the most influential one, they treated cycles as a phenomenon that is superimposed upon the normal course of capitalist life and mostly as a pathological one; it never occurred to the majority to look to business cycles for material with which to build the fundamental theory of capitalist reality.[33]

[31] In the postwar period, Pigou (op. cit.) came perhaps nearest to accomplishing that feat.

[32] The indictment may be made more tenable by reformulating it to the effect that, without denying persistence of unemployment as a fact, the analysts of that period, and Marshall in particular, treated full employment as the 'norm' toward which the system incessantly 'tended.' If by the term 'norm' we mean a property of the logical schema of perfect equilibrium under perfect competition, the indictment fails, because it can be proved that within this logical schema there would in fact exist no involuntary unemployment. If by the term 'norm' we mean a property of reality, namely, a tendency of the capitalist system, as it actually works, to approach full employment and to stay there until something occurs to drive it off the full-employment state, then it becomes true to say that the economists of the Walras-Marshallian type were inadequately aware of the qualifications subject to which existence of such a tendency may be asserted. At the same time, the indictment does not amount to more than this.

[33] [This, of course, is what J. A. S., himself, attempted in his monumental *Business Cycles: a Theoretical, Historical, and Statistical Analysis of the Capitalist Process* (2 vols., 1939) and much earlier in his *Theorie der wirtschaftlichen Entwicklung* (1912; 2nd rev. ed. 1926; English trans., *Theory of Economic Development*, 1934).

Part V

CONCLUSION

A Sketch of Modern Developments

CHAPTER 1

[Introduction and Plan]

1. Plan of the Part

Once more we change our rules of procedure. The surveys presented in the three preceding Parts were indeed far from complete. But though incomplete, they aimed at conveying fairly *comprehensive* pictures. So far as scientific economics in the usual sense is concerned, no significant man or work or movement was left out—not intentionally, at least—and I have done what I could do within this volume to touch upon the more important framework and frontier questions. In this Part, we shall not go on with this plan. In a sense, our inquiry ends, at the foothills of the Marshall-Wicksellian mountain range, with the last glance at the classical situation around 1900. If we go on at all, it is with a different and much more restricted purpose. It seemed desirable, first, to show how the work of that period fared in our own time; [1] second, to point out some roads that are leading away from and beyond it; and, third, to attempt diagnosis and prognosis of contemporaneous efforts. This will at best give us a bird's-eye view of just a few great contours with all the details and all the frontier districts left out. More than that, this view will have to be highly selective.

I cannot even list all that I am going to leave out. But I will illustrate it by mentioning two men: Gottl and Spann. The widely different messages of these men, as is indeed obvious from the considerable body of literature produced by their followers, have shaped many a mind. In this sense, they are possibly

[1] [To a considerable extent, J. A. S. had already done this in Part IV. It will be recalled that, when outlining the plan of the book in Part I, he wrote: 'Part IV will present an account of the fortunes of analytic or scientific economics from the end of the "classic" period to the First World War though the history of some topics will (for the sake of convenience) be carried to the present time. . . . Part V is merely a sketch of modern developments, relieved of some of its cargo by the anticipations in Part IV that have just been mentioned, and aims at nothing more ambitious than helping the reader to understand how modern work links up with the work of the past.']

more important than any two high-powered technicians of economic theory. But they are not important for us. We are concerned with the technicians. He who writes a history of, say, agricultural technology does not thereby prove that he thinks it more important than the history of religion. Only so far as those authors—or any other of the same type—actually attempted analytic work *in the sense adopted for the purposes of this book*, does our failure to deal with them carry implications to which they or their adherents could object. Is this quite understood?

[J. A. S. never finished this introduction to the Conclusion nor did he cover some of the topics he planned to include. In place of the introduction he would have written, there is presented in the next section a summary of five lectures, which were outlined at the same time that he was planning Part v and the last two or three chapters of Part iv and which presumably summarize what J. A. S. considered to be the main lines of advance in the recent period.

What he actually intended to cover in the Conclusion (in addition to chs. 2, 3, 4, and 5 below) can only be guessed at from two pages of abbreviated notes (mostly in that maddening shorthand), which are reproduced in the Appendix. Among the 'things still entirely lacking in (Part) v' he listed:

(1) Morgenstern and von Neumann, *Theory of Games and Economic Behavior* (1944)
(2) *Leontief's Linear Programming*
(3) Income Analysis—Social Accounting
(4) . . . Chenery (Engineering Production Functions) . . . Frisch
(5) (Several lines of shorthand notes)

From the second paragraph of section 3 (this chapter), it is obvious that J. A. S. also intended to comment on the 'unprecedented wealth of statistical facts' and on Econometrics, 'the new relation between economic theory and statistical methods.']

2. The Progress of Theoretical Economics during the Last Twenty-Five Years [1]

(a) *Introductory Lecture on the Scope of the Course.* The First World War caused a complete change in the economic policies of all nations which has persisted ever since. This was due, first, to the fact that all nations have had to face new problems arising out of political and economic situations in which they had never found themselves before. But, second, this change in policies was due also to the fact that the war had thoroughly upset the previous distribution of political weights. Thus, we observe not only new problems and new situations but also new attitudes toward them.

[1] [J. A. S. delivered a course of five lectures in January 1948 at the School of Economics, University of Mexico, on this subject, which coincides roughly with what was intended for Part v (partly anticipated in Part iv). What follows is a brief summary of those lectures, written in advance for translation into Spanish and presented here in place of the Introduction and Plan, which were never completed. The summary is printed in full despite certain repetitions; references in square brackets show where the subjects are treated in the *History*. These lectures were, of course, planned for a mixed audience and were of necessity rather general and elementary.]

Economics and Political Economy. Economists moved with the times and a significant change occurred in their views about practical questions. The sum total of these views together with the schema of social values that underlies these views we shall call Political Economy. Accordingly, we say that a new Political Economy arose after 1918. But, however interesting it would be to describe this new Political Economy and to inquire into its sociological roots, this is *not* our task in this course. The new views on economic policy will be considered only so far as they are relevant to the development of scientific economics.

By Scientific or Analytic Economics, in contrast to Political Economy, we shall mean the stock of facts and methods that economists collect with the purpose of *explaining* the phenomena of economic life. The difference between this analytic economics and political economy can be illustrated by analogy with the difference between the subjects that are taught at a faculty of medicine. Such a faculty has professors of surgery, internal medicine, and so on who teach the practical art of treating patients. But there are also professors of chemistry, physiology, biology who teach the scientific foundations of that art but not that art itself. It is with the analogues of the latter that we are concerned.

Economics and Economic Theory. We shall restrict our subject still further. Perhaps the most important progress that has occurred in scientific economics is the vast increase in our command over facts. All types of information about facts have increased beyond the boldest dreams of past generations but our epoch has been particularly characterized by an increase of *statistical* information which was so great as to open up quite new possibilities for scientific research. In step with this increase of statistical *material*, there has been an equally important development of statistical *methods*. But we shall disregard all this and concentrate our attention on the developments in that restricted field which is called Economic Theory.

So many misunderstandings still prevail about the nature, use, and limitations of Economic Theory that it is necessary to explain our conception of it. There was a time when Economic Theory meant precisely what we have called Political Economy above: there was a 'liberal' or 'socialist' or 'mercantilist' theory, and all those theories more or less meant political *doctrines* or at least practical recommendations. This is not the modern view. The modern economist considers theory simply as an instrument of research. This *instrumental character* of economic theory will be illustrated by examples which will also explain the relation that nevertheless exists between economic theory and economic policy.

Precisely because economic theory is only an instrument of research, it cannot produce concrete results without the facts that are supplied by statistics or non-statistical description. This had been realized already by the Spanish economists of the sixteenth and seventeenth centuries. But the alliance between statistics and theoretical economics was not complete until the emergence of modern Econometrics.

The Main Lines of Advance within Economic Theory. The most obvious way in which sciences advance is by *new departures*, that is, by the discovery of new facts, or new aspects of old facts, or new relations between facts. Examples will be given from the history of physics and of economics. But there is another way. When we use the concepts and theorems that we have inherited from our predecessors, these concepts and theorems—which we call the *analytic apparatus* of a science—change in our hands. We add here and correct there and so this apparatus slowly develops into a different one. It will be our first task to describe how, approximately between 1890 and 1914, a system of economic theory consolidated itself and how this system formed the basis of later work, which started in the early 1920's and transformed it without intending to do so [Part v, ch. 2 of this *History*]. Then we shall see how a new analytic apparatus developed which is known as economic dynamics [Part v, ch. 4 of this *History*]. Another new departure, mainly associated with the name of Lord Keynes will be considered next [Part v, ch. 5]. And, finally, we shall sum up what has been accomplished and what might be expected for the near future.

(b) *The Marshall-Wicksell System and Its Development.* Scientific economics found its systematic form in the eighteenth century (Beccaria, A. Smith, Turgot) and, after various 'revolutions,' in the *Principles of Political Economy* of J. S. Mill. This system was in turn revolutionized by the introduction of the marginal utility principle (Jevons, Menger, Walras). But another process of consolidation took place between 1890 and 1914, and a theoretical system of apparatus emerged which is embodied in the standard works of A. Marshall and K. Wicksell. A few minutes will be devoted to describing the salient characteristics of this system and the extent to which it was accepted by the professional theorists of all countries [Part iv of the *History*]. We shall then proceed to discuss the main lines of advance that started from this system.

The Theory of the Individual Firm and Monopolistic Competition. Neither Marshall nor Wicksell had neglected the task of analyzing the behavior of individual firms. But their theorems, except in the case of monopoly, referred mostly to a whole group of firms (industry) or even to the whole organism of the social economy. They hardly realized the necessity of investigating more closely the behavior of the individual units that combine to produce the phenomena which we associate with an industry or the social economy. In analyzing this behavior theorists soon discovered that the case of perfect or pure competition was a rare exception rather than the rule, and that the economic organism, especially in cases of decreasing average cost, does not function as it would under perfect or pure competition. From this a new body of theorems arose, the theory of Imperfect (Robinson) or Monopolistic (Chamberlin) Competition, the main features of which will be briefly characterized [Part v, ch. 2 of the *History*].

Indifference Varieties. In spite of the protests of Pareto and others, the theorists of the Marshall-Wicksell generation used uncritically the concept of marginal utility. During the 1920's and 1930's this concept was rapidly discarded in favor of the 'indifference-curve' approach. The reasons for this and the advantages of the indifference-curve approach will be discussed briefly (See Hicks, *Value and Capital*, 2nd ed., 1946) [Part iv, ch. 7, sec. 8 and App. and Part v, ch. 2]. The consequences of the passing of the old marginal-utility theory for *Welfare Economics* can only be touched perfunctorily [Part iv, ch. 7, Appendix: Note on the Theory of Utility].

Other Improvements of the Marshall-Wicksell Apparatus. With increasing scientific rigor and especially with the increasing use of mathematics in economic theory, the theorists have in the last twenty-five years been able to develop many of the doctrines taught by Marshall and Wicksell and to correct others. An example of these developments is the theory of substitution which created the concept of elasticity of substitution. This conception is useful in settling in a few lines many problems that filled pages and even volumes in the past (for instance the problem of the influence of the introduction of machines upon the interests of labor). Corrections have been mainly applied to the old theory of production by means of a closer analysis of the properties of Production Functions [Part iv, ch. 7, sec. 8].

(c) *Economic Dynamics.* We call a relation *static* if it connects economic quantities that refer to the same point of time. Thus, if the quantity of a commodity that is demanded at a point of time (t) is considered as dependent upon the price of this commodity at the same point of time (t), this is a static relation. We call a relation *dynamic* if it connects economic quantities that refer to different points of time. Thus, if the quantity of a commodity that is offered at a point of time (t) is considered as dependent upon the price that prevailed at the point of time ($t - 1$), this is a dynamic proposition. These definitions of the terms 'static' and 'dynamic' must be carefully distinguished from others that have been used and are still used sometimes. The Marshall-Wicksell system was essentially static.

The Importance of a Dynamic Theory. The necessity of developing a dynamic theory rests upon three facts: (1) It is obvious that most quantities demanded and offered, both of finished commodities and of factors of production, as well as prices and incomes are in reality related to other economic quantities that belong not to the same moment but to the past or to the expected future. It is particularly obvious that monopolists want to maximize gains not for the moment but over a stretch of time. (2) It is not so obvious but it is nevertheless true that this makes a great deal of difference to results. If we drop the hypothesis that each element of the economy depends only on the other elements as they are at the same point of time, quite different results and quite new phenomena emerge, for instance the phenomenon of *endogenous fluctuations.* (3) Finally, the task of developing a dynamic theory is very difficult and cannot be accomplished simply by adding dynamic qualifications to static theory. It requires new techniques and raises fundamental problems of its own. An example of the new techniques required is the theory of difference equations. An example of the new fundamental problems is economic equilibrium, which, if considered from a dynamic standpoint, appears in a new light.

An Illustration: the Cobweb Problem. When farmers observe current prices of, e.g., pork and fodder, they will decide to produce more or less hogs according as hog production is or is not profitable at this current relation between the prices of pork and fodder. But this decision cannot take effect before a certain period has elapsed. The resulting supply of pork will then impinge on the market and change the pre-existing relation between the prices of pork and fodder. This will induce new decision by the farmers and so on. This 'cobweb problem' or 'hog cycle' will be discussed, under simplifying assumptions, by means of a simple diagram. A similar problem is the so-called shipbuilding cycle studied by Tinbergen (*Weltwirtschaftliches Archiv*, 1931). [All the problems outlined for this lecture on Economic Dynamics are treated in Part v, ch. 4 of the *History*.]

(d) *Income Analysis.* We have a strong scientific interest in reducing the number of the economic variables with which we have to deal. If we tried to write down the equations that determine the static equilibrium of millions of firms and households, we should never accomplish the task. In particular, we could never marshal the statistics that would be the necessary complement of such a system. This suggests the idea of reducing the number of variables to a few great social aggregates. This idea is very old. From the first economists have tried to reason on national income, national sum total of wages, and the like. But it was only during the last quarter of a century that this idea has been systematically followed up. It is clear that we should be in a much better position to apply theory to statistics and statistics to theory if we could, for some purposes or for all, confine ourselves to such variables as National Income, National Consumption and Investment, Quantity of Money, Employment, and Interest Rates. Analysis which attempts to do so is called *Macroanalysis* (R. Frisch). Because the National Income is the central variable in which we are particularly interested, it is also called *Income Analysis.*

The Keynesian Theory. The most successful of all the theoretical systems that have been inspired by this wish to simplify the structure of economic theory is the static system that is associated with the name of the late Lord Keynes. Many others have also been constructed, for example, by Amoroso, Frisch, Kalecki, Pigou, Tinbergen, Vinci. Lord Keynes used only four variables explicitly: quantity of money (deposits), consumption, investment, and interest rates. Income enters also, but is simply identical with consumption plus investment. The price level is eliminated by the use of 'wage-units' or labor hours in which all quantities are expressed. Employment is wedded to income by the assumption that it is strictly proportional to income expressed in wage-units. The variables are linked together by three relations: the liquidity-preference function, the consumption function (which implies the famous 'multiplier'), and the investment function, all of which will be briefly explained.

Discussion of the Keynesian Theory. Keynes presented his theory as a *macrostatic* system. But it is possible to turn it into a macrodynamic system without great difficulty.

It is much more serious that Keynes assumed not only that methods of production remain unchanged but also that the amount of industrial equipment does not vary. This restricts his analysis to very short periods of time (3-10 months). Moreover, since technological change is the essence of the capitalist process and the source of most of its problems, this assumption excludes the salient features of capitalist reality.

The novelty in Keynes's theory of saving consists simply in this. Before Keynes, economists used to take it for granted that, normally, savers invest whatever they save. Keynes assumed that people save without having any definite intention to invest and that, when they have saved, they may decide not to invest at all but to keep their savings in the form of money (*General Theory of Employment, Interest, and Money,* 1936, pp. 165-6). On this alone rests the peculiar features of his theory of interest. But saving without investment occurs only in deep depressions, that is to say, in about one year out of every ten on the long-time average. The concept of marginal efficiency of capital is not the same as the old marginal productivity of capital, but essentially it expresses the same facts.

Keynes's theory of wages is interesting because it seems to supply an explanation of permanent unemployment as distinguished from cyclical unemployment. But it does so only by means of the assumption that monetary wage rates are rigid. And nobody has ever denied that unemployment may persist indefinitely in this case.

The Success of the Keynesian Theory. We have seen that fundamentally Keynes accepts the Marshallian apparatus of economic theory and that he only adjusted it in a number of points. But these points were very important for the explanation of the depression of the 1930's and therefore rightly attracted attention. Moreover, his simple system that considers only a few aggregates was easy to master and to manipulate. From these factors of scientific success we must, however, distinguish a much more potent factor of *political* success. Keynes seemed to present an argument that saving, the great virtue that the majority of bourgeois economists from A. Smith on had always extolled, was really a vice that was the cause not of capital formation but of unemployment and capital destruction. This attracted many people who had for other reasons renounced allegiance to the values of capitalist society, and thus made Keynesian doctrine—not quite logically—the banner of economic radicalism. [All the salient points of this Lecture on Income Analysis will be found developed in Part v, ch. 5, 'Keynes and Modern Macroeconomics.']

(e) *Summary of the Course.* It is impossible to foresee what future generations will think of the work in economic theory from 1920 to 1945. We can survey the points which posterity will have to judge but we cannot pronounce upon their value. One thing must be kept in mind, however. The economic theory of our own time and of all future times can never again be so fascinating to the wider public as it had been in the times when it was understandable to every educated person and when it seemed to establish directly 'eternal laws' and practical rules. Everyone can understand A. Smith. Only specialists can understand the matrix calculus and functional equations. Everyone is interested in free trade or protection. Only specialists are interested in questions of determinateness and stability.

The Progress in Technique. The one thing that can be confidently asserted about the work of the period we have been surveying is that the theory of 1945 is greatly superior to the theory of 1900 as regards technique. Results are more reliable, proofs are more rigorous. This in itself also means *more* results and more *specialized* results that fit better the endless variety of the configurations of economic reality. At the same time it must be admitted that fundamentally new ideas have been almost wholly absent. We make much more of the ideas which we have inherited from the preceding period and often present them in a new light, but we have added little to them. As a conspicuous example, the theory of Business Cycles will be briefly discussed in order to show that all the essential ideas were developed before 1914 [Part v, ch. 4].

Economic Theory in the Service of Economic Policy. Modern theory no longer undertakes to show that free trade is the right policy for all times and places. But it shows much better than could have been shown by Smith or Mill what will be the effects of a particular measure of protection on the interests of all classes of society. Modern theory no longer undertakes to prove that perfect competition is an ideal. But it can show what the effects of given deviations from competition will be. Modern theory no longer recommends saving under all circumstances. But it gives to economic policy a complete description of the process of saving and of the effects that different kinds of saving will exert upon the economic situation of a country. Many other examples could be cited in order to show that modern theorists are developing an apparatus that is indeed no longer simple but will render in the end the same service to economic policy which theoretical physics renders to engineering.

Planning and Socialism. What has just been said may be applied to any kind of economic planning. Economic theory is slowly developing the *mental instruments* that are necessary in order to 'rationalize' planning and to tell planners what they must do and avoid in order to attain certain given ends. If a socialist society is defined as the perfectly planned society, then we may further say that modern theory is building the foundations of a truly 'scientific' socialism [Part iv, ch. 7, sec. 5]. To say that pure theory is of no interest for practice is as unreasonable as to say that pure mechanics is of no interest for building the machines we want. The ends themselves, that is to say, the kind of society or culture we want, we must choose ourselves. No science can do more than indicate the means of attaining whatever it is we want.

[3. Background and Patterns] [1]

Very roughly, the beginnings of what I believe to be a new period in the history of economic analysis date from the First World War. But this was a coincidence. Causally, that world war had little to do with the new tendencies, which in fact were discernible before 1914. The public, of course, was under the impression, as it always is in any epoch of striking events, that the economic phenomena it observed were entirely novel, unheard-of, and of a na-

[1] [Apparently J. A. S. intended to do here very briefly what he did for the preceding period in Part iv, ch. 2.]

ture to upset completely the schemata of analytic economics. And it was a new experience for some people to be poor instead of rich and for others to be rich instead of poor, for some to see their interests championed by politicians instead of ignored, for others to see their interests attacked by politicians instead of defended as they used to be. But no economic fact or process observable during that war and its aftermath had anything new to teach to the scientific economist. The inflationary processes in particular fitted beautifully into the oldest of old schemata. Nor is this anything to wonder at. Economics is a very unsatisfactory science. But it would have to be much more unsatisfactory than it is if such an event as a war, however extensive and destructive, sufficed to upset its teaching.

The fundamental independence from war influences of the developments that brought about a new period of economic analysis can be easily established by listing them. First, there was the unprecedented wealth of statistical facts. Second, there were new results that grew out of working the old apparatus. Third, there was the development of dynamics. Fourth, there was the new relation between economic theory and statistical methods (Econometrics). It is these four—obviously interdependent—aspects of contemporaneous work that will be discussed in the chapters that are to follow. The rest of this chapter will be devoted to the discussion of a matter of 'atmosphere.'

Our time is one of transition, not only in the sense in which any time is of necessity transitional, but also in the specific sense defined by rapidity, and by universal *awareness* and expectation, of actual and impending social change of a fundamental nature. Few will deny this. It will be convenient to state at once the two ways in which that fact bears upon the scientific work in our field.

The first things to occur to most of us are the new patterns and the new problems. But so far as these are concerned, it is more important to realize the extent to which they are but old friends in new sociological garb than it is to realize the extent to which we are really facing new *scientific* problems. For to begin with, we may repeat for recent economic history what was said a moment ago for the economic history of the First World War. Social patterns, economic and other policies, economic situations are all quite different, but this does not in itself imply that new economic principles are either suggested by them or required in order to understand them. Thus foreign policies, economic and other, that strike the good old liberal as novel heresies and more enthusiastic observers as great discoveries would, as we have seen, have looked very familiar to Malynes and Misselden. The labor contract is no longer 'free,' but not only has it never been so except during comparatively short spells of history but also this does not mean a novel problem to the analyst—all he has to do is to take a different model from his box of tools. Political rents—payments from public funds to particular groups to which no specific economic service corresponds—are a salient feature of modern society; but they were not less important in the society of Louis XV: the fact that the recipients carried different class connotations is, for purposes of purely economic analysis, less important than it might seem. Friends and foes of the New Deal agreed in looking upon it as new. So it was in more than one sense. But not in our sense: practically every measure that is covered by that slogan had been observed and fully analyzed before. Nor is this all. There are possible events that would create historically novel situations. Fullfledged (not bolshevist) socialism, adopted by modern industrial society, is an example. But to the economist it would not present a new problem. The theory of a socialist economy lies ready at hand, fully worked out in part by thoroughly bourgeois economists at a time when there was no hope or danger of that exercise in pure theory ever being put to practical use. In this respect, economists were better than was their repute.

Nevertheless, there are patterns and problems that are *analytically* novel. Among the examples, I might have mentioned 'going off gold,' devaluation, depreciation, exchange control, and other features of monetary management as instances of time-honored devices—only they were not always 'honored' and hence they were known under uncomplimentary names. But this would be only substantially, and not quite, correct. We do see other sides of them that were not seen before, and we have learned to reason about them in different ways. Moreover, theory tends to become—in part intentionally, but still more unintentionally—specialized when, by tacit agreement, theorists look for a long time at the same social and economic pattern. Its features are then taken for granted, and many propositions are framed to fit even the least persistent of them. If central banks are practically treasury departments; if other banks have almost lost all functions but the clerical ones of cashing checks and buying government bonds; if the market rate of interest does not mean a thing and money-market and stock-exchange mechanisms are well-nigh paralyzed; if the profit motive of the industrial family is rapidly vanishing; if salaried employees administer the most important concerns; if private thrift and private investment have ceased to function, and income generation through government expenditure is looked upon as a normal element of the economic process, in which taxation absorbs the higher incomes; and so on—then the relative importance of the various pieces of the capitalist engine is so thoroughly affected (many of the pieces do not work at all, whereas others that could be justifiably neglected before assume a dominant role) that all the 'applied' fields will naturally acquire an entirely different complexion. And theorists will redistribute their emphasis upon their various models and work out some of them more fully while shelving others. But it is important to realize that this is all and that from the standpoint of analytic technique it means much less than the layman is inclined to believe.

[Unfinished; many shorthand notes and then a sentence, which began: 'The other way in which awareness of actual and impending change influences scientific work . . .']

CHAPTER 2

[Developments Stemming from the Marshall-Wicksell Apparatus]

[1. The Modern Theory of Consumers' Behavior and the 'New' Theory of Production]

The modern theory of consumers' behavior developed almost wholly during the last quarter of a century so far as the doctrine is concerned that is actually used and taught by the sector of the economics profession that is primarily interested in theory in this sense. But what was and is being developed consists in methods and results, mainly associated with the work of Fisher, Pareto, Barone, Johnson, and, if we do not mind adding a paper that remained practically unknown for a decade or more after its publication, Slutsky. This means that the fundamental ideas were present before the close of the First World War, not in the form of embryonic suggestions only, but well worked out, mainly by authors of international reputation, in forms accessible, so we should think, to every professional theorist. They had only to sink in and to be clarified, amplified, applied, and occasionally straightened out in the process. But little had to be added to them that was fundamentally new. The situation was much as it was in the automobile industry: in spite of all the improvements and new gadgets, a modern motor car is still much the same kind of thing as the motor car of 1914.[1] Exactly the same holds for what may still be called the new theory of production. And the concept of

[1] While I think it necessary to emphasize this fact because it is quite essential in order to understand the present situation, I do not wish it to be misunderstood. Such a misunderstanding would be involved for instance in any impression the reader might conceive to the effect that emphasis upon that fact implies derogation either of the performance of our age or of the talent that went into it: a physicist writing in 1730 might have been equal in mental stature to Newton; but it was 'objectively' impossible for him to produce another work like the *Principia Mathematica* (1687): he would have had to bend to 'objectively' and 'relatively' lesser tasks. Similarly, it is no reflection upon either Frisch or Samuelson to include their performances in the category of elaborating or continuing work. On the contrary, both performances illustrate well the types of originality that were possible in the field of the theory of consumers' behavior at the time they wrote: both performances produced novelties but novelties like the self-starter and not like the Otto motor.

elasticity of substitution illustrates well not only what has been done but also what could be done in this field under the given circumstances.[2]

A historian, inspired by his observations about similar events in the past, might have expected that Walras would have missed the boat, that is, that his work, in an epoch that was able to understand him at last, would have been thrown into the limbo where dwell the works that, inadequately appreciated in their own time, were condemned on technical inadequacies of their apparatus when their real time had come. This was not so, however. The work on consumers' behavior and on production that can be fitted into his system and that, in part, was fitted in by Pareto, instead of preventing him from taking his proper place, produced rather a modernized Walrasian system. This process extends from 1924, when Professor Bowley's *Mathematical Groundwork of Economics* made Walras' equilibrium system internationally accessible —already modernizing it in many spots—to 1939 when Professor Hicks's *Value and Capital*, or the first two parts of it, completed the task.[3] To some extent this book was particularly successful in unearthing Walrasian problems of which Walras himself had not been aware. And, partly in its wake and partly independently, a rich stream of contributions was released from which I shall merely 'read by name' the works of Lange, Metzler, Mosak, and—only alphabetically last—Samuelson. Much or most of this work pivots around questions of determinateness and around stability conditions and thus constitutes the bulk of the work of our day in the field of fundamental theory or even *Grundlagenforschung*.

[2] For a general survey of the nature and uses of total and partial elasticity of substitution, see again Allen, *Mathematical Analysis*, pp. 341-5, 372, 504, and 512. The concept, first introduced in its simplest form by Hicks (*Theory of Wages*, 1932) and Joan Robinson (*Economics of Imperfect Competition*, 1933), was immediately put to good use by both authors in the formulation of propositions that acquire delightful simplicity thereby (e.g., see also J. R. Hicks, 'Distribution and Economic Progress: A Revised Version,' *Review of Economic Studies*, October 1936). For a time the concept was therefore deservedly popular but this popularity was soon impaired by the related facts that it ceases to be so simple so soon as there are more than two goods or 'factors' under consideration and that it works with difficulty when applied to statistical data. I regret my inability to survey the results of the considerable literature to which the concept has given rise. See however the discussions in *Review of Economic Studies*, February 1934 and February 1936). Another example of this type of gadget is A. P. Lerner's measure of monopoly power ('The Concept of Monopoly and the Measurement of Monopoly Power,' *Review of Economic Studies*, June 1934).

[3] Even in those two parts, Hicks did much more than modernize Walras. So far as mere modernization goes, he also modernized Marshall, and I do not mean to suggest that 'modernization' describes those two parts of *Value and Capital* adequately. On the other hand, Hicks's treatment is much too brief to accomplish the modernization of Walras and Marshall *completely*; it should be said rather that he produced essential material for it.

[2. Theory of the Individual Firm and Monopolistic Competition]

Equally important, however, and much more important as regards direct applicability to practical questions and hence for the economic profession as a whole, is another development that objectively stems from Marshall—the Theory of the Individual Firm and in connection with it, the Theory of Monopolistic or Imperfect Competition.[4] Everyone knows that this new arm of the economist's analytic engine was added, in different forms, by English and American authors who worked independently of one another—a striking proof of the intellectual, still more than practical, need for this type of theory and a not less striking illustration of how the logic of the scientific situation may drive different minds along similar lines of advance.[5] In the United States, *The Theory of Monopolistic Competition* sprang, without any warning, fully armed from Professor E. H. Chamberlin's head in 1933 [6] and met with a

[4] Still more than in other cases, I am anxious in this one to divest my emphasis upon a historical filiation from any semblance of derogation. This emphasis seems imperative because of two different sets of facts. First, Marshall, on the strength of his frequent use of the concept of the (small) individual *industry*, to which in particular most of his diagrams refer, has been sometimes accused of having neglected the economics of the individual *firm*. But as we have seen, and as analysis of his argument (and of such concepts as a firm's special market or internal economies) could prove, he gave, on the contrary, quite unusual attention to the problems of the individual firm and offered suggestions that indeed called for development but force us, precisely because of this, to look upon later work, especially by Marshallians, as an offshoot from his. Second, Marshall's concepts and treatment of the individual industry and of increasing returns invited criticism: their very shortcomings were fertile; they spoke with so certain a voice that the critic's constructive task was cut out for him.

[5] This and the fact that we have here to do with a broad movement in which many participate, though only few make the decisive hits that history records, stand out still more clearly if we take account also of the related literature on oligopolistic patterns. We then discern a similar movement in the Northern countries (see especially F. Zeuthen, 'Mellem monopol og konkurrence,' *Nationaløkonomisk Tidsskrift*, 1929, and *Problems of Monopoly and Economic Warfare*, 1930) and in Germany (see von Stackelberg, *Marktform und Gleichgewicht*, 1934, who noticed and discussed most of the German as well as the non-German contributions).

[6] Chapter 8 (on distribution), the contents of which were first presented in a paper read before the American Economic Association (at the meeting in Philadelphia, 1933) and which was then published *in extenso* in *Explorations in Economics* (in honor of F. W. Taussig, 1936), was added to the 2nd ed. of the book (1937). Chapter 7—the second chapter on selling costs—was omitted from the Ph.D. thesis handed in at Harvard on April 1, 1927 in order to meet the time limit, although it was fully worked out by then. The thesis does not differ in any essential from the 1st ed. of the book and, since it was in the stage of final revision for several months before, does not owe anything to Sraffa's article ('The Laws of Returns under Competitive Conditions'), which appeared in the *Economic Journal*, December 1926. The author proposed the subject for a Ph.D. thesis as early as 1921, when he was a student at the University of Michigan (author's communication). In spite of subconscious influences that may have come from early Marshallian training, we therefore have here a striking instance of

corresponding success, which was as much due to the force and brilliance of his exposition as it was to the maturity of the scientific situation. The work claimed to reconstruct the whole of value theory by blending or fusing the hitherto separate theories of monopoly and competition. Nor was this all. It also claimed to teach a new economic *Weltanschauung* from the standpoint of which practically all economic problems appear in a new light. In any case the most important original contributions of the work—mainly contained in Chapters 4-7 on product differentiation and selling costs—met with very little fundamental dissent, if indeed with any. But a whole literature that amplified and applied these contributions followed in its wake.

In England, Mrs. Joan Robinson's *Economics of Imperfect Competition*, also in 1933, impinged upon a less unprepared profession and, for this and other reasons, was less spectacularly successful. As we know, Piero Sraffa, in 1926, had thrown out the idea that appeal to the theory of monopoly was the remedy for the difficulties about equilibrium that had arisen in connection with increasing returns. In doing so he had already suggested that actual conditions in industry will in general lie in the intermediate zone between monopoly and competition and that, since it was the competitive theory which held the field, it was then necessary 'to turn towards monopoly.' Finding monopoly thus released 'from its uncomfortable pen' (Robinson, op. cit. p. 4) in which it had existed, in seclusion from the main corpus of economic analysis, Mrs. Robinson proposed to reconstruct the theory of value by allowing monopoly to 'swallow up the competitive analysis'—every firm being a monopolist, that is, a single seller of its own product, and competition coming in by bits until we reach the limiting case where a large number of such single sellers of perfectly substitutable products sell in a perfect market, and the demand for the product of each of them becomes perfectly elastic, the case usually described as perfect competition (op. cit. p. 5).[7] It should be observed that this concept

subjective and objective originality—and of originality of the purely theoretical type that owed nothing to 'the collection of direct empirical evidence,' though a 'guiding principle' certainly was to create a theory that would fit facts better than what Chamberlin conceived to be the theory of competition current at that time (author's communication). It seemed worth while to abandon, in this case, the principle of sketchiness that governs our exposition, especially in this Part, not only because of the importance of the book that—next to Keynes's *General Theory* and with Hicks's *Value and Capital* and Hayek's contribution—must certainly be considered as one of the most successful books in theoretical economics that the period since 1918 has produced, but also because its author is not, like most authors mentioned in this book, beyond reach of personal interview. And personal contact, though only one of several methods for studying the ways of the human mind and especially the manner in which original work emerges and takes effect, is an important one and particularly useful in providing a check on the others. Three elements of scientific achievement are particularly obvious in this case: the maturity of the scientific situation; the ability to grasp an important idea with force and enthusiasm; and the ability to stay with it and to shut oneself off from the disturbing effects of other scientific ideas or aspects.

[7] In her Foreword and Introduction, Mrs. Robinson not only acknowledged obligation to Marshall and Pigou but gave ample credit to Sraffa, to whose papers—both the

of monopoly is not the traditional one. In fact the traditional concept can be satisfactorily defined only by the criterion that it admits the application of the Cournot-Marshall theory of monopoly. But this theory in turn presupposes the existence of a demand curve that is independently given and immune to influences from other firms upon the behavior of the one under consideration. Hence the traditional theory of monopoly is constitutionally unable to 'swallow up' any cases where these influences cannot be neglected, and hence the traditional concept of monopoly becomes inapplicable.

English and the Italian contribution mentioned in Part IV, ch. 7, sec. 8d—it is therefore necessary to recur in all questions that touch upon her fundamental analytic intentions. This is rendered more difficult by the fact that Sraffa (see next sentence in our text) did not use the word Monopoly in the Robinsonian but in the usual sense. But she also acknowledged indebtedness to, or a sort of partnership in the spirit with, a number of other fellow economists of whom we must in particular notice three. There was Harrod, whose share in the analysis of impurely or imperfectly competitive patterns must be valued more highly than his papers (including his 'Doctrines of Imperfect Competition,' *Quarterly Journal of Economics*, May 1934; 'Imperfect Competition and the Trade Cycle,' *Review of Economic Statistics*, May 1936; and 'Price and Cost in Entrepreneurs' Policy,' *Oxford Economic Papers*, May 1939) would in themselves indicate, especially considering the dates of their publication. And there were Shove and Kahn, whose names may, at some future time, owe the greater part of their recognition to Mrs. Robinson's generous tributes. These tributes were fully deserved (as was Keynes's tribute to Kahn, see below ch. 5). Both are scholars of a type that Cambridge produces much more readily than do other centers of scientific economics or rather of science in general. They throw their ideas into a common pool. By critical and positive suggestion they help other people's ideas into definite existence. And they exert anonymous influence—influence as leaders—far beyond anything that can be definitely credited to them from their publications. I take this opportunity to mention a point on which Mrs. Robinson lays great emphasis in her Foreword and indeed throughout her book, the 'marginal revenue curve.' She gives credit, for both the thing and the word, to several of her contemporaries, particularly to Mr. Harrod and Professors Yntema and Viner. It is quite natural that use of this convenient tool suggested itself at that time to many (including Chamberlin), especially to those who had previously struggled with the clumsier Marshallian total curves. We must not, however, forget that the tool was first used by Cournot, and no author of the 1920's or 1930's can have any *objective* claim to it.

CHAPTER 3

[Economics in the 'Totalitarian' Countries] *

NO EXPLANATION SHOULD be needed of what to some readers may seem to be an unjustifiable neglect of 'totalitarian' economic literatures. However I do wish to state that such neglect has nothing to do with political prejudice. I have no intention of neglecting any analytic work that has been done or is being done in 'totalitarian' countries, and the mere fact that such work is presented in the wrappings of a 'totalitarian' philosophy *or even intended to serve and to implement it* is no more reason for me to neglect it than my strong personal aversion to utilitarianism is a reason for neglecting the analytic work of Bentham. The various totalitarian philosophies themselves, however, are excluded—just as has been the utilitarian philosophy qua philosophy—not because they are 'totalitarian' but because they are 'philosophies,' that is, speculations that live outside the sphere of empirical science. In this respect we are merely carrying out a principle that has been followed all along and has been fully discussed in Part I, where the distinction between analytic economics and political economy was introduced mainly to give effect to it. Since this view is at variance with deeply rooted beliefs, the reader is invited to refresh his memory about what was said there.

The principle above does not, however, fully explain why the economic literature introduced in totalitarian countries will not figure greatly in the sketch that is to follow. There are two other reasons for this: first, some of the most important contributions, such as von Stackelberg's *Marktform und Gleichgewicht* (1934), or part of Del Vecchio's work on money, have already been mentioned in Part IV, where we carried the histories of a number of topics down to the present; second, material of the kind that belongs in a history of economic analysis has not been plentiful under totalitarian regimes. For the rest, the cases of the three main totalitarian countries, Germany, Italy, and Russia,[1] are too different to be covered by a single generalization.

* [This is the only chapter written for Part V, the subject matter of which is not mentioned in the Mexican lectures (ch. 1, sec. 2 above).]

[1] Japan and Spain never were 'totalitarian' in any meaningful sense of the term. But as regards Japan, it should be observed that the interruption of contacts during the war and my ignorance of the language have created a lacuna which, in the time at my disposal, I have been unable to fill. All that prewar contacts enable me to say is that the importance of this lacuna is certainly not negligible and may be considerable. [In the two years since his death, former Japanese students have published translations or arranged for translations of *all* the books and long essays of J. A. S. This includes

1. Germany

In Germany, methods of teaching and research had been rapidly improved in the period of the Weimar Republic (1918-32). Historical work and work on current problems (of the kind cultivated by the Verein für Sozialpolitik) went on as before; as noticed in Part IV, chapter 4, these types of work gradually lost their anti-theoretical methodological bent, and both interest and competence in 'theory' increased, the spreading use of Cassel's treatise [2] being equally significant as an effect, a cause, and a symptom; in addition there were the autochthonous messages of such teachers as von Gottl, Liefmann, Oppenheimer, and Spann, to which even their most severe critic cannot deny the merit of having stimulated many minds; and there were, more accessible to Anglo-American understanding (and to my own), the performances of Diehl, Eucken, and others and, above all, those of Spiethoff and Sombart. The Viennese group, under the leadership of Professor L. von Mises, though it retained a vital individuality until it was, for the time being at all events, dispersed in the 1930's, entered into closer relations than before with the rest of German economists and was thus in a position to assert its own distinctive doctrines.

Two tendencies toward Americanization cannot be left out of this sketch. One was the inexorable progress of specialization. Though the comprehensive courses on general economics, economic (and social) policy, and public finance remained in their dominant positions, specialized groups began to acquire more and more definite existence; in a more significant sense than before, it

---

the early work in German and this *History*. *Das Wesen und der Hauptinhalt* . . . (1908) and *Theorie der Wirtschaftlichen Entwicklung* (1912) were translated in 1936 and 1937.]

[2] Gustav Cassel has repeatedly been mentioned before. It seems appropriate, however, to recall in this place the stages in the career of the most influential international leader of our science in the 1920's—for such he was, whatever his critics (including myself) may say. We recall first the three pieces of work by which he established himself (his sketch of a theory of prices in the *Zeitschrift für die gesamte Staatswissenschaft*, 1899; the paper, not yet mentioned, on the causes of the variations in the general price level, 'Orsakerna, till förändringar i den allmänna prisnivån,' *Ekonomisk Tidskrift*, 1905; and *The Nature and Necessity of Interest*, 1903). Partly owing to the advantage he held as a 'neutral,' he rose into international fame during and after the First World War—chiefly as an expert on money and international relations and as an assiduous participant in international conferences on these subjects (I mention only, as a sample, *Money and Foreign Exchange after* 1914, 1922: today's monetary experts could do worse than study this book). Finally, he made a great success, at least outside the sphere of orthodox socialism, by his treatise, *Theoretische Sozialökonomie*, which, guided by chance or else very shrewd insight, he published in German (1918). I am myself the author of a review of the 4th ed. (1927) that was as far from favorable as was Wicksell's review appended to the English ed. of vol. I of the latter's *Lectures*. I do not think that either Wicksell or I said anything that ought to be retracted. But we overlooked something, viz., that the book was exactly what German economists needed.

was possible, after 1918, to speak of agricultural, or labor, or industrial economists. Again, research institutes like the National Bureau of Economic Research or the Bureau of Agricultural Economics grew up both inside and outside the government departments concerned with economic problems. It will suffice to mention the Institut für Weltwirtschaft at the University of Kiel, founded by one of the most efficient organizers of research who ever lived, Professor Bernhard Harms, and the Institut für Konjunkturforschung, the foundation of a similarly efficient organizer, Professor Ernst Wagemann in Berlin[3]—both of which added new economic journals to the existing ones. There is only one point in this picture of considerable advance and still more considerable promise that, from the standpoint taken in this book, must be registered as of sinister import. As the Weimar Republic settled down, the governments of the individual states—there were neither federal nor private universities, only state universities—yielded increasingly to the demand of political parties, mainly the Social-Democratic and the Centrist parties, that the appointments to professional office in economics should take account of the politics of candidates. The argument, discussed quite openly, ran as follows: economics, unlike physics and like philosophy, is a *Weltanschauungswissenschaft*, that is, a 'science' into the research and teaching of which necessarily enter the ultimate beliefs and allegiances of the investigator or teacher. These ultimate beliefs and allegiances were embodied in the socialist and the centrist (Catholic) parties and in an agglomeration of all other parties defined by the negative characteristic that they were neither socialist nor Catholic; hence, professorships should be divided up, as equally as possible, between members of these three political groups, though nobody advocated, to be sure, that this should be done irrespective of qualifications. There is no need to discuss this matter again. Less openly, the tendencies verbalized by the theory of the *Weltanschauungswissenschaft* make themselves felt under any circumstances and in all countries. Also they never prevail fully anywhere—except in modern Russia. In the Weimar Republic the resistance of the faculties and of upright members of the bureaucracy kept them in relatively narrow bounds.

Under these circumstances the advent of National Socialism did not mean quite as great a break and did not cause all the damage that a foreign observer might expect. The National Socialist regime was intolerant not only of criti-

[3] The latter started frankly from the Harvard barometer curves, though its work, mainly statistical, soon expanded—much as did the work of the Harvard Economic Society—far beyond what these curves imply. This institute was perhaps the most important single influence in spreading knowledge of modern statistical methods (as then understood). Its methodological work is therefore of historical importance. It is mainly contained in supplements to the institute's journal, the *Vierteljahrshefte zur Konjunkturforschung;* see e.g. supplements no. 4 on *The Analysis of Economic Curves* (H. Hennig); no. 6 and 11 on *Seasonal Variations* (O. Donner); no. 9 on *Trend* (P. Lorenz); and no. 12 on *Russian Contributions* (A. L. Wainstein, S. A. Perwuschin, M. W. Ignatieff). There was close co-operation with the Federal Bureau of Statistics (*Statistisches Reichsamt*), which published a series of monographs in addition to its current publications.

cism of its policies but also of any display of lack of sympathy with the party philosophy. It promoted party members and demoted Jews. If it did not insist on acceptable professions of faith, it welcomed them. In individual instances, the party or groups within the party and even the authorities went much further than all this implies. And in addition, the disturbing effects of the general conditions then prevailing upon research and study must be taken into account. However, though less so than in the field of the physical sciences, the bulk of professional work went on. In particular, nobody would have got into trouble in consequence of having worked out new theoretical or statistical tools. A work like Keynes's *General Theory* could have appeared unmolested—and did.[4] It must not be forgotten that the creed of National Socialism was not primarily or essentially economic and that, hence, it was compatible not only with all kinds of technical economics but also with the advocacy of widely differing policies.

2. Italy

In Italy we find a similar situation, only much more pronounced. The Fascist regime resented criticism of its measures as much as or, since individual policies were much more closely associated with the leader personally, still more than was the case in Germany.[5] It also insisted either on a sympathetic attitude of economists or else on neutrality—perhaps the best way of expressing the situation is to say that what the government insisted on was absence of active hostility to Fascist principles. A few leading men—such as Ricci and Bresciani-Turroni—expatriated themselves, but most were not seriously disturbed. Purely scientific work was not interfered with at all.[6] Under these

[4] See Carl Föhl, *Geldschöpfung und Wirtschaftskreislauf* (1937). The author tells us in the preface that his manuscript had been completed in December 1935. All the more interesting is the far-reaching though not complete parallelism between his argument and *Keynes's* (see below ch. 5).

[5] Hitler left individual measures, and especially economic measures, to his lieutenants, who stayed in positions of leadership for relatively long spells and were allowed to acquire reputations with the public and to develop policies of their own. Mussolini did not permit this. In consequence the economic policies of Fascism, even as regards details, tended to become in the public eye his own personal measures.

[6] It is important to emphasize that even in treatises that took a professedly sympathetic attitude to the *città corporativa* the analytic parts did not differ from generally accepted economic doctrine and could have been written just as well by enemies of Fascism. As an example I mention Professor Luigi Amoroso's *Principii di economica corporativa* (1938). The first two parts deal respectively with the theories of money and of equilibrium and are completely free from political implications, Fascist or other. Only the third part develops what might be termed the economic philosophy of Fascism—much of which, as formulated by Amoroso, would command the hearty approval of the modal American economist. As another example, I mention a course of lectures on economic policy or political economy that did not keep to the ivory tower of what we call here 'purely scientific work' and still displays not much constraint: Professor Giovanni Demaria's *La politica economica dei grandi sistemi coercitivi* (1937).

conditions, scientific economics continued to move at what we have seen in Part IV was a high level, both within and without the Pareto school, until the war. Barring war effects there was no break and neither was there one after the fall of the regime.

3. Russia

But the case of Russian economics [7] in the Stalinist period differs from the German and Italian cases, not in degree but in kind. In the decade preceding that period—roughly between 1917 and 1927—this was not quite so. Opponents of the Soviet regime or even neutrals were indeed dealt with much more ruthlessly than were opponents of the National Socialist or Fascist regime. Scientific research itself, not only discussion of policies, was regimented in a manner unheard of in Germany or Italy, not only because of the nature and methods of the bolshevist administration but also because of two other reasons that contradicted and, nevertheless, reinforced each other. On the one hand, the Soviet creed, ideologically at least, was essentially an economic creed and slight deviations from the holy books, even if of a purely theoretical kind, acquired an importance that is difficult for us to understand; on the other hand, the bolshevist government very naturally exploited to the full the naïve emotionality of the 'revolutionary people,' who necessarily believed that, the millennium having arrived, there were no longer such things as 'economic laws' and hence no need for any economic analysis at all. In this situation discussion tended to be geared exclusively to the momentary wishes of the men who were, or were believed to be, at or near the helm, and such arguments as that a certain view was 'reactionary' or 'leftist'—in fact, pure denunciation—began to replace scientific views. Nevertheless the break was not complete. Conversion to Soviet orthodoxy was made easier by the facts that Marxism, now the prescribed creed, had had a strong hold on Russian economists even before 1917 and that there is plenty of room for scientific analysis within the limits set by allegiance to its principles. So long as genuine Marxist stalwarts like Bukharin played some role, we might have still to state that, qualitatively more than quantitatively, genuinely analytic work was at an ebb, but there would be no reason to question that there was genuinely scholarly work—as the mere existence of the Marx-Engels Institute suffices to show. However there were other institutes, for example one for research in agricultural economics and another for business or cycle research, which for the time being enjoyed some freedom not only in collecting but

[7] I repeat that I do not know Russian. The following remarks are based upon (a) such Russian works as are available in languages I know, especially English and German; (b) conversation with colleagues who do know Russian but must not be held responsible for the impression I received from it; and (c) secondary literature of very unequal value, of which most, though not all, has an anti-bolshevist bent. I mention only the item that I have found more useful and, so far as I can judge, more correct than any other: A. Zauberman, 'Economic Thought in the Soviet Union,' *Review of Economic Studies* (vol. XVI (1), 1948-49 and vol. XVI (2) and (3), 1949-50). [J. A. S. had apparently read only the first of the three articles by Zauberman.]

also in interpreting economic data. Kondratieff's work, already mentioned, caused a great stir [8] and constitutes, so far as I can make out, the peak performance of the work produced by a considerable number of competent economists (Perwuschin, Oparin, Sokolnikoff, and others); this work, in spite of the sinister implications of the fact that some of the authors have not been heard of since, may be taken as proof that serious economics survived until the rigors of the Stalinist regime fully asserted themselves. Then the break occurred after all, and teaching as well as the work of the Institute of Economics of the U.S.S.R. was more and more reduced to descriptive treatment of the practical problems of the Soviet government and to mutual recriminations of slaves incessantly in fear for their lives.[9] We confine ourselves to two points that promise better things for the future. First, Soviet Russia inherited from pre-Soviet times an excellent tradition of work in statistical methods and their mathematical—mainly probabilistic—background. This work, much less exposed than economics to political attack, survived and continued to produce internationally recognized contributions. Second, it is evidently impossible to 'plan' investment without developing an apparatus, however primitive, for comparing alternative methods of carrying it out, even if the purpose itself is given by dictatorial command, and for comparing alternative investment purposes if there is some freedom of choice. But into any attempt to do so, actuarial norms and the concepts of value, marginal productivity, and interest enter by logical necessity. The task of Soviet economists was and is not to improve these concepts but to smuggle them in in such a manner as to hide their fundamental identity with the corresponding 'capitalist' concepts.[10] Advance

[8] N. D. Kondratieff's long-cycle theory has been published in several books and articles, some of which are available only in Russian. An abbreviated translation by Professor W. F. Stolper of a German article that Kondratieff himself believed to give the gist of his theory can be found in the *Review of Economic Statistics*, November 1935, and a survey by Mr. George Garvy of the controversy that arose about it ('Kondratieff's Theory of Long Cycles') in the same journal, November 1943. This survey shows very well, on the one hand, the venomous ferocity with which controversies were carried on in that atmosphere and, on the other hand, the facts that scientific points of view were not absent and that scientific work was still possible. Kondratieff was exiled to Siberia in 1930.

[9] The bulletins of the Academy of Sciences of U.S.S.R. (Department of Economics and Law) contain comments on this state of things (though not in the terms above) that waver between condemnation and recommendation of a sterilized Marxism. But it seems questionable whether analytic work of the kind that is being turned out, with its childish attempts at rediscovering elements of economic logic without running into heresy, is really preferable to total suspension of such work. The importance of these attempts seems to be greatly overestimated by C. Landauer, 'From Marx to Menger,' *American Economic Review*, June 1944. Also see John Somerville, *Soviet Philosophy* (1946).

[10] An almost pathetic example has been presented by Holland Hunter, 'The Planning of Investments in the Soviet Union,' *Review of Economics and Statistics*, February 1949. Professor Hunter there translated a chapter of a textbook by Professor Khachaturov on the *Economic Principles of Railroad Transportation* (1946), and ana-

on this line is difficult and slow owing to the incessant threat of denunciation that lurks behind the unfavorable reviews that publications of this kind seem to have received so far. However, there is in these publications some promise for the future, especially because it is safe to predict that denunciations of this type will go out of fashion: bolshevist economists are bound to discover in the end what Pareto and Barone realized half a century ago, namely, that there is an economic logic that has nothing specifically 'capitalist' about it. Nor is this all. National income accounting and budgeting techniques are rapidly developing in non-bolshevist countries—they can hardly be called 'capitalist' any more—and traditional economics will have to adapt itself to them. [J. A. S. intended, but did not actually write, a section on national income accounting in this concluding Part.] These techniques and corresponding methods of analysis are still more obviously needed in the Soviet state. There thus exist two tendencies that, born of similar needs, have begun to assert themselves independently in Russia and elsewhere, especially the United States, and now tend to converge—as do so many others. Still, beyond this there is nothing to report for a history of economic *analysis*, and only he can wonder at this who, even at this point, has not grasped the purpose of this book.[11]

lyzed the Coefficient of Relative Effectiveness of Investment under the aspect mentioned in the text in a most instructive manner. The reader finds other examples, though less completely worked out, in the [first of the three] articles by Zauberman, who gives prominence to the work of S. G. Strumilin. He also mentions (vol. XVI (1), p. 3n.) an early attempt made by Mrs. B. Khmielnitskaya to secure room for economic theory by defining it—quite sensibly—as the science of the norms of rational management of a socialist ('organized') society. It is amusing to note that in doing so she seems to have adapted for her purposes the German von Gottl's concepts of idiography (the description of individual facts, 'ideographic' must be a misprint) and nomothesis (the generalizing statement of laws, which she changed into 'normography,' wisely replacing von Gottl's 'nomos' by 'norm').

[11] One of the causes of the scientific sterility of Russian economics in the period under survey was, of course, the fact that some of the rulers, in particular Lenin, Trotsky, and even Stalin, wrote so extensively and authoritatively on questions that ordinarily belong in the sphere of professional economics. Therefore even a reader who does grasp the purpose of this book and who knows how to distinguish economic analysis from political economy might still object that I do not report on the works of those three men or at least on the voluminous works of Lenin. The answer has been given already: however great their historical importance in other respects, as contributions to economic analysis they are negligible.

CHAPTER 4

Dynamics and Business Cycle Research

Let us recall once more that here, as throughout this book, Dynamics means exclusively analysis that links quantities pertaining to different points of theoretic time—in the sense that has been repeatedly explained before—and not the theory of evolutionary processes that run their courses in historic time: it is practically coextensive with sequence analysis and includes period analysis as a special case, but it is not coextensive with the theory of economic growth or development, or 'progress.' [1] Thus defined dynamics is a genuinely new departure. We have indeed seen at various turns of our way, particularly in the case of Sismondi, that dynamic considerations in our sense intruded into economic analysis times out of number, chiefly by implication but also explicitly. But the exact core of economics was nevertheless static and was believed to constitute a self-contained body of doctrine, a body moreover that embraced all or almost all of the essential insights. This is obvious in the case of Walras. But it also applies to Marshall.[2] He no doubt added plenty of extra-static considerations, chiefly about growth but also about sequences, so much in fact that he may be said to have posited the task of future dynamic theory (see e.g. *Principles*, p. 519), just as he posited the task of future econometrics; but though he presented material, viewpoints, and desiderata, he did not cross the Rubicon. For the rest, we have noticed the suggestive pointers of Pantaleoni and Pareto, but there was no advance toward the goal to which they pointed.

By the phrase, 'crossing the Rubicon,' I mean this: however important those occasional excursions into sequence analysis may have been, they left the main body of economic theory on the 'static' bank of the river; the thing to do is not to supplement static theory by the booty brought back from these excursions but to replace it by a system of general economic dynamics into which statics would enter as a special case. The realization of the fact that even a static theory cannot be fully developed without an explicit dynamical schema

[1] This is repeated here because many modern authors do identify dynamics with the theory of growth. The chief authorities for our terminology are Frisch and Hicks. Prominent examples of another terminology are Harrod (see especially *Towards a Dynamic Economics*, 1948) and Stigler. An intermediate position is held by many, e.g. by Charles F. Roos (*Dynamic Economics*, 1934). I also repeat that my insistence on this distinction is due not to any wish to quarrel about words but merely to a wish to avoid confusion.

[2] But not to Böhm-Bawerk, see above, Part IV, ch. 6, sec. 5.

(Samuelson),[3] which we have noted before, is a first step in this direction, and if space permitted, a few others could be mentioned.[4] However, no attack on the whole front of Walrasian theory has as yet developed and the analogy with a building plot is still painfully apposite: an increasing number of workers see the new goal; but for the time being this is practically all, since H. L. Moore's effort did not go substantially beyond comparative statics. More positive success has attended the efforts to 'dynamize' aggregative theory.

[1. Dynamizing Aggregative Theory: Macrodynamics]

This is understandable. On the one hand, aggregative theory that reduces truly innumerable arrays of variables to half a dozen or even less can evidently stand up much better than could a Walrasian system under the complications that are inseparable from even the simplest dynamic schema. As an illustration, consider so simple a dynamizing device as the introduction of lags. Offhand and until more powerful methods are invented than are available now, there is very little we can say when we give different time indices to all the quantities that enter the Walrasian system, except that it becomes unmanageable thereby. But this is no longer so if the only variables we have to take care of are 'consumption,' 'investment,' and a national income that is identically equal to current consumption plus current investment. Suppose we postulate arbitrarily that the consumption (C_t) of some period (t) equals a constant proportion (α) of the income of period ($t-1$), αY_{t-1}; and that the investment (I_t) in period t equals a constant proportion (β) of the difference between current consumption and the preceding period's consumption, $\beta(C_t - C_{t-1})$ or $\beta(\alpha Y_{t-1} - \alpha Y_{t-2})$. Remembering that $Y_t \equiv C_t + I_t$, we get as, on the strength of grammar-school mathematics, it is easy to see:[5]

$$Y_t = \alpha(1+\beta)Y_{t-1} - \alpha\beta Y_{t-2}.$$

This is a homogeneous second order difference equation with constant coefficients, which is very easy to solve by an elementary technique that lies ready at hand and yields certain economically interesting results. The tempta-

[3] See *Foundations*, Part II, especially ch. 11. I take the opportunity to submit that there and in Appendix B, also in 'Dynamic Process Analysis,' his contribution to *A Survey of Contemporary Economics* (H. S. Ellis, ed.), Professor Samuelson has performed a most meritorious pedagogical task; there is no better introduction to the meaning and techniques of modern dynamics.

[4] Pressing considerations of space are, however, not the only reason for refraining: on the one hand, I do not wish to blur the main contours by details; on the other hand, I do not wish this sketch to degenerate into a bibliography. Going over the volumes of *Econometrica* is almost all that the reader needs in order to find the ropes.

[5] This is (the gist of) the Hansen-Samuelson equation; see P. A. Samuelson, 'Interactions between the Multiplier Analysis and the Principle of Acceleration,' *Review of Economic Statistics*, May 1939, reprinted in *Readings in Business Cycle Theory* (selected by a Committee of the American Economic Association, G. von Haberler, chairman, 1944).

tion to avail oneself of so tremendous a simplification is almost irresistible and impervious to the objections that might be raised on theoretical grounds.[6] No wonder, then, that the early 1930's were fertile in such aggregative schemata —R. Frisch's macrodynamics.[7] Not all of them were mathematically exact of course—a fuller survey would have to mention several important ones that were presented by non-mathematical economists such as Professor von Hayek. It should be carefully observed that this drive toward macrodynamics was in itself quite independent of any wish for a closer alliance of economic theory with statistical figures: macrodynamics would have asserted its claims even if theorists' attitudes to statistics had not changed at all as compared with the preceding period, and as a matter of fact several writers who displayed no symptoms of such a change in attitude were just as anxious as anyone can be to secure the advantages of aggregative simplification.

[2. The Statistical Complement: Econometrics]

But, on the other hand, the equally strong drive toward a numerical economics, an economics that would be statistically operational, is also a dominant factor in our scientific situation. And this factor, however independent of the desire for a simplification of the pattern of economic theory per se, also favors macrodynamic methods. For with few exceptions the aggregative variables—particularly if their number be augmented by price levels and interest rates—are easy to identify with our most important time series. As an outstanding example, which displays both tendencies closely united and which constitutes so important an element in the economic research of our time that it cannot be omitted from any sketch of it, however brief, I mention the work of Tinbergen.[8] His numerous aggregative schemata, most of which use many

[6] It is convenient to defer consideration of these objections and of an important qualification that should be added to them. But let us note at once that our example also illustrates the fact that economists are prone to yield to the further temptation to improve upon the situation by introducing additional simplifications: in our example, it is not only the reduction in the numbers of variables which simplifies things but also the postulate that the coefficients are constant; if they were not, the equation would not be so easy to handle.

[7] We mention here only one example, namely Professor Frisch's own schema presented in his powerful paper, 'Propagation Problems and Impulse Problems in Dynamic Economics,' *Economic Essays in Honour of Gustav Cassel* (1933). The reader will find many others in Tinbergen's survey article quoted in the next footnote.

[8] In the long list of Professor J. Tinbergen's publications the one that is perhaps most suitable to serve as an introduction, to American and English readers, of his theoretical and statistical methods is his *Statistical Testing of Business-Cycle Theories:* I, *A Method and its Application to Investment Activity;* and II, *Business Cycles in U.S.* 1919-32 (League of Nations, 1939). Still more useful as a survey of what may be called now the earlier work in dynamics is his article 'Suggestions on Quantitative Business Cycle Theory,' *Econometrica*, July 1935. Both titles are unduly unassuming. Just now the reader should ignore the specific reference to business cycle research—the reason for which will be explained presently—and accept the first as a treatise on, and the latter as a survey of, general dynamics.

more variables to start with than do those of other authors, are in the first instance set up on the basis of purely theoretical considerations that are extremely simple—so much so that it is perhaps more enlightening to speak of common-sense considerations: they embody, in a system of (almost always) linear equations with constant coefficients, the definitions of obviously important aggregates (definitional equations); the relations that common sense suggests should subsist between them (balance equations); and relations that are supposed to describe the behavior of classes of households and firms (behavior or 'decision' equations).[9] This involves the fundamental principle that construction of the theoretical set-up should *precede* the statistical work: the relations themselves are not suggested by statistical observations; they are postulates and not results.[10] Statistical figures are to 'explain' the numerical values of some variables by given numerical values of others by the method of multiple correlation—a process which also eliminates those 'explanatory' variables whose partial regression coefficients *indicate* the insignificance of their influence. The system is then, by process of successive substitutions, reduced to 'final' equations that are held to depict the economic mechanism.[11] In itself, every step in this procedure is open to serious criticisms, about which no more can be said than that they should not blind us to the greatness of this pioneer effort. Since most of these criticisms are of a statistical nature, the statistical work of Frisch—partly taken account of by Tinbergen—and his group should at this point be mentioned again, particularly the work of Haavelmo, who during his brief sojourn in the United States, without holding a teaching position, exerted an influence that would do credit to the lifetime work of a professor.[12] In any case, however, the economist who accepts macrodynamics as it stands, with or without its statistical complement, may speak of conquest already achieved—and not only of a developing attack and of the increasing clearness of a goal, which is all that we are able to record in the matter of dynamizing the Walrasian or Paretian system.

[3. The Interaction of Macrodynamics and Business Cycle Research]

Exactly as macrodynamics has been and is being propelled by the specifically econometric drive—the tendency toward reasoning in terms of statistical figures—so both the theoretical and the numerical components of macrodynamic work have been propelled by the preoccupation with business cycle

[9] For examples, see the work cited in the preceding footnote. It should be remembered that Tinbergen's publications *of this type* begin (so far as I know) in 1934.

[10] This is the fundamental difference between the methods of Tinbergen and those of W. C. Mitchell, whose methods will be touched upon below.

[11] I feel in duty bound to offer my apologies to Professor Tinbergen for this sort of report. But I hope that he and the reader will prefer even these jejune sentences to the bare reference to his works which not every reader can be trusted to follow up.

[12] The bulk of his teaching has been embodied in a number of papers published in *Econometrica*. But see especially Trygve Haavelmo, 'The Probability Approach in Econometrics,' Supplement to *Econometrica*, July 1944 (Cowle's Commission Papers, New Series 4).

problems. This preoccupation is, as we have already seen, a salient characteristic of our time. From the foregoing analysis of the factors that produced macrodynamics and in particular statistical macrodynamics, we may infer that this development would have occurred even if there were no such thing as the particular kind of fluctuations that are commonly identified as business cycles. From what has been said earlier in this Part and in Part IV we may infer that preoccupation with the phenomena of business cycles would have increased, as compared with the times before 1914, even if modern macrodynamics had not emerged. But it is obvious that both developments were bound to reinforce one another and that, on the one hand, the methods, materials, and results of business cycle research encompassed more and more of general economics and, on the other hand, the methods, materials, and results of modern macrodynamics evolved principally with a view to serving business cycle research,[13] so much so that reference to business cycles intrudes even into the titles of many macrodynamic publications of much wider range.[14] It is now easy to formulate more precisely the nature and results of this interaction.

We have seen in Part IV, Chapter 8, that all the fundamental ideas concerning the phenomenon of business cycles were present before 1914.[15] What our period added, besides critical development of these ideas, was in the first instance the new wealth of data and new statistical methods of handling them. Even the econometric program, barring the 'higher' mathematics, had been carried out by such outstanding students as Juglar, Mitchell, and Spiethoff.[16] But incomparably greater possibilities have offered themselves since 1919. Some writers were content to use whatever figures the arms of their analytic apparatus could grasp. An outstanding example is Professor Pigou, whose *Industrial Fluctuations* (1st ed. 1927), though remaining a 'theoretical' work, nevertheless, owing to the new material, differs greatly from the kind of work that an economist of the same type would have produced before 1914. Others displayed a tendency to plunge into the statistical material directly and to

[13] A simple way for the reader to realize this is to glance over Professor H. M. Somers' 'Classified Bibliography of Articles on Business Cycle Theory,' appended to the volume of *Readings in Business-Cycle Theory*, to which reference has been made already, or to some of the other bibliographies mentioned there (p. 444), particularly the one by Professor R. A. Gordon.

[14] This is why, speaking of macrodynamics per se and not intending to speak of business cycle research specifically, I had, nevertheless, in a previous footnote, to quote two of Tinbergen's works whose titles carry this connotation. The reason why, with what might seem uncalled-for pedantry, I insist on this point is simply that it is essential to a correct diagnosis of the modern scientific situation.

[15] This also applies to Professor von Hayek's theory, if it is permitted to link it up with that of Professor von Mises. If it is not, I apologize.

[16] Spiethoff's preliminary presentation of his business cycle analysis as a whole did not, it is true, appear before 1923, and his comprehensive work, as well as its translation into English, is still expected. But this delay was and is caused by the heroic attempt to master vast materials single-handed. As regards Mitchell, the reference above is to his book of 1913.

scrap the existing apparatus as well as the existing explanatory hypotheses. We may illustrate this tendency by two instances that in other respects have very little to do with one another, namely the work of the Harvard Committee (W. M. Persons) and the work of Mitchell.

The Harvard University Committee on Economic Research, presided over by Charles J. Bullock and chiefly directed by Warren M. Persons and W. L. Crum, embarked upon extensive historical-statistical investigations and developed important time series, but owes its international renown—its methods being discussed, copied, and further developed almost everywhere, especially by E. Wagemann's Berlin Institute—to the 'three-curve barometer,' a revised version of which the reader finds authoritatively described in the April 1927 number of the *Review of Economic Statistics* ('The Construction and Interpretation of the Harvard Index of Business Conditions'). No analysis of its method is possible here. We must confine ourselves to indicating the fundamental principle and to adding three remarks which the reader is urgently requested to bear in mind. The principle is to correlate time series which common sense indicates to be particularly relevant, after having 'eliminated' from them seasonal variations and the 'secular trend,' so that cycles are given as a residual (for details see W. M. Persons, 'Correlation of Time Series,' Rietz's *Handbook of Mathematical Statistics*, 1924, ch. 10).

The remarks I wish to add are these: (1) The statistical methods used by the Harvard Committee are in the light of later, and even of contemporaneous, developments of 'higher' statistics exposed to serious objections. But this must not induce us to overlook the impulse that both further compilation of statistical figures and the development of statistical method derived from that pioneering venture; or to overlook the fact that there was a rough common sense about those methods that would go some way toward justifying their results as approximations, if anyone cared to undertake the task.

(2) If critics erred in failing to give due weight to the historical importance of that venture, they erred still more in that part of their criticism which was directed against the forecasting value of the barometer. The fact is that the barometer curves indicated the approaching break in 1929 clearly enough—the trouble was that the interpreters of the curves either would not believe their own methods or else would not take what they believed to be a serious responsibility in predicting depression.

(3) The constructors of the Harvard Barometer emphasized for the benefit of their readers and also believed themselves that they were not using any of that discredited and discrediting monster, economic theory. Professor Persons was quite prone to reply to theoretical objections by pointing to the hundreds of correlation coefficients that had been figured out under his direction. As a matter of fact, however, they did use a theory that was all the more dangerous because it was subconscious: they used what may be termed the Marshallian theory of evolution. That is to say (if we neglect the important but in this connection secondary correction for seasonal variations, one of their most lasting contributions) they assumed that the structure of the economy evolves in a steady or smooth fashion that may be represented (except for occasional changes in gradient, 'breaks') by linear trends and that cycles are upward or downward deviations from such trends and constitute a separate and separable phenomenon. This is an error which we shall have to mention again presently. But though erroneous, this view constitutes a theory, or the backbone of one. The little methodological controversy on the subject of 'business cycle research without theory,' which flared up occasionally, was of a nature similar to the one that arose about the work of Mitchell and

the National Bureau of Economic Research and will hence be touched upon together with the latter.

The importance of the work of Wesley Clair Mitchell and the National Bureau of Economic Research, which he led and inspired, has been emphasized already. Just as Professor E. Wagemann said somewhere that the publications of his Institut für Konjunkturforschung were simply the second volume of his *Allgemeine Geldlehre* (1923), so Mitchell might have said that (most of the) publications of the National Bureau formed all together a huge second volume to the first he had published in 1913. And his volume of 1927, *Business Cycles: The Problem and its Setting*, was, like Wagemann's *Konjunkturlehre* of 1928, an organizing survey of problems, viewpoints, and materials—for work which it was given to him to carry, if not to completion, at least as far as his (and A. F. Burns's) monumental *Measuring Business Cycles* (1946). We cannot enter into a discussion of what is known as the National Bureau method of depicting cycles statistically. All we can do is to point out that this effort of establishing and of marshalling a vast amount of (primarily) statistical material essentially continues the plan that was partially executed in the book of 1913 and owes nothing to macrodynamic theory, though it may eventually set problems and provide important checks for it: the work of Mitchell and his group aims primarily at showing what it is we have to explain and, beyond this, suggests viewpoints from which to do so.

I use this opportunity for a brief comment on the little controversy about methodology adverted to above. Mitchell might have done something toward preventing it, had he distinguished more clearly between theory in the sense of explanatory hypothesis and theory in the sense of analytic apparatus. Most of us would agree with him if he felt that the formulation of explanatory hypotheses should wait upon acquisition of a fuller command of the facts and that the explanatory hypotheses, so far offered, old and new, lacked proper substantiation and might be unable to stand up in the light of the facts he was going to assemble. Even so he displayed no active hostility to the many 'theories' of business cycles which he listed in his book of 1927 with perfect detachment. But in addition he cared little for the technical refinements of 'theory' in the instrumental sense of the term, just as he cared little for the modern refinements of statistical method. His early associations with Veblenite tendencies did the rest to make him appear, in the eyes of the profession, as more of an anti-theorist than he was—and still more so in the eyes of those votaries of macrodynamics for whom economic theory and the mathematical model tend to be synonymous. But actually, in intention as well as in fact, he was laying the foundations for a 'theory,' a business cycle theory as well as a general theory of the economic process, but for a different one. Similarly, the Harvard Committee, in professing to proceed without theory, really meant no more than that they did not intend to be guided in their factual work by preconceived explanatory hypotheses.

But business cycle research is research into sequences of business situations which are also the subject matter, or part of the subject matter, of macrodynamics. Co-operation between the two was thus obviously indicated. All students of business cycles, not debarred by mathematical disabilities, should have recognized this from the first. The formal logic of lags, rates of change, cumulations, and of the oscillations they may produce is bound to be helpful in the interpretation of the observed behavior of time-series material. Macrodynamics should be not less helpful in any attempt to put the existing theoretical material into a more promising shape, for instance, in deciding questions of determinateness and in formulating conditions of damping or explosiveness and the like. Problems of the mechanisms by which impulses are propagated through the economic system may be cleared up by macrodynamic methods, which therefore may contribute substantially, among other things, to our understanding of cyclical turning points.[17] The star example by which to demonstrate the usefulness of these methods is the theory of oscillators, that is, of factors that create fluctuations in the system, although they are perfectly steady—free from fluctuations—themselves.[18] 'Literary' students of business cycles will not easily see the possibility of this. They will be prone to argue that no factor can contribute to cyclical fluctuations unless its own time series is oscillatory. And so they might be expected to show some signs of gratitude to macrodynamics for thus widening their horizon as they should in other instances for having their arguments sharpened and corrected. If they do not always do so, this is no doubt primarily owing to mathematical disabilities. But there is also another reason which it is important to state.

It has been said above that macrodynamics helps us to understand mechanisms of propagation. It will perhaps assist the reader if he will look upon the economic system as a sort of resonator, which reacts to the impact of disturbing or 'irritating' events in a manner that is partly determined by its physical structure. Think for instance of a violin that 'reacts' in a determined manner when 'irritated' as the player applies the bow. Understanding the 'laws' of this reaction contributes to a complete 'explanation' of the phenomenon that we call a violin concert. But evidently this contribution, even if reinforced by the contribution of the neurophysiologist, does not explain the whole of it: aesthetic evaluation and the like apart, there is a range of purely scientific ground that acoustics and physiology are constitutionally unable to cover. Similarly macrodynamics, while quite essential to an explanation of cyclical phenomena, suffers from definite limitations: [19] its cyclical models are what acous-

[17] An instructive example of this type is the discussion between Professors R. Frisch and J. M. Clark concerning the relation between the turning points of consumption and the production of capital goods in the cycle ('The Interrelation between Capital Production and Consumer-Taking,' 'Reply,' 'Rejoinder,' and 'A Further Word,' *Journal of Political Economy*, 1931-2).

[18] A mechanical model will illustrate this phenomenon. Let an electric clock be placed upon a somewhat rickety table. The electric current that keeps the clock going is perfectly steady. Yet it may produce an oscillatory movement of the table.

[19] The simile limps, of course, like all similes. And so does the following suggestion which is not a simile. Cycles run their courses in the *historical* evolution of the capitalist economy. Even neglecting all the economic sociology that must therefore inevitably enter into their explanation, we cannot help recognizing that their theory or, to avoid this word, their analysis must be largely bound up with the theory or analysis of evolution rather than with dynamics, which is the theory or analysis of sequences that do not carry any *historical* dates. No doubt there are certain mechanisms that played as great a part in 1857 as in 1929. And these must be taken account of in any observed

tic models of resonators are for the violin concert. But its votaries will not see this. They construct macrodynamic models that are to explain all there is to explain, for economists, in the cyclical phenomena. The very attempt to do so involves several definite errors of fact.[20] And flimsy structures based upon arbitrary assumptions are immediately 'applied' and presented as guides to policy, a practice that of course completes the list of reasons for irritation in the opposite camp. One sometimes has the impression that there are only two groups of economists: those who do not understand a difference equation; and those who understand nothing else. It is therefore a hope, rather than a prognosis to be presently fulfilled, which I am expressing if I venture to say that this entirely unnecessary barrier—but one which is no novelty in our science—to fertilizing interaction will vanish by virtue of the logic of things.

I have still to advert to a promising branch of dynamics that is not indeed microeconomics, because it does not reach the individual deciding agents, but is not macroeconomics either, because its models do not embrace the whole of the economy: it is akin to Marshall's partial analysis and is (mostly) concerned with individual industries. The famous corn-hog cycle is the best-known instance: if farmers, under the influence of a favorable relation between the price of hogs (pork) and the cost of rearing them (price of corn), all decide at roughly the same time to increase their hog production and if, as will be the case in this instance, they all come out at roughly the same time with an increased supply of hogs, this may cause a sharp drop in the price of pork (and also a rise in the price of corn), which might induce a majority of them to contract their production, which would recreate favorable conditions that would in turn lead to another expansion in hog production. The resulting cycle may of course be damped, explosive, or stationary, and a very simple general model can be set up to describe this mechanism that is indeed observable, not only on the hog market but in a large class of cases.[21]

---

cycle by more or less generally applicable macrodynamic schemata, just as must, on a lower level of technique, the ordinary theory of supply and demand. But they are only tools and do not in themselves suffice, even if supplied with all conceivable time series, to reconstruct the phenomenon as a whole and, of course, still less its long-run outcomes.

[20] Three of these may serve as illustrations. They will at the same time show why the respective objections do not tell against the models themselves but only against the claim alluded to. (1) Macrodynamic models, presented with that claim, involve the proposition that the 'causes' of business cycles must be found in the interaction between the social aggregates themselves, whereas it can be proved that business cycles arise from sectional disturbances. (2) With the same proviso, macrodynamic models carry the implication that the structural changes that transform economics historically have nothing to do with business cycles, whereas it can be proved that cycles are the form that structural changes take. (3) Constructors of macrodynamic models, almost always, aim at explaining all the phases of cycles (and the turning points) by a single 'final' equation. This is indeed not impossible. But it spells error to assume that it must be possible and to bend analysis to this requirement.

[21] The reader is referred to M. Ezekiel, 'The Cobweb Theorem,' *Quarterly Journal of Economics*, February 1938 (reprinted in the volume, *Readings in Business Cycle*

Another famous instance, displaying the phenomenon for durable goods, is Professor Tinbergen's shipbuilding cycle.[22] On the one hand, it stands to reason that no great confidence can be placed in the results that such schemata yield—more apparently than really—and that extreme care is imperative in applying them, if indeed they be applicable at all to any practical cases at all. Thus, readers of Professor Tinbergen's paper will note with concern the formidable list of assumptions contrary to fact that they are asked to accept. But even if they accept them all, they will find it difficult to reconcile themselves to the complete neglect of all the influences upon shipbuilding that other industries and general business conditions are bound to exert; and they may see in the basic graph (op. cit. p. 154) more traces of the business cycle than of the mechanism that the schema isolates. On the other hand, however, schemata of this kind are first steps toward a more perfect dynamic theory and must therefore be listed as pioneer ventures of first-order importance: the same reader who is impressed with their shortcomings—much as he would be in reading a description of Columbus' flagship—should be also impressed with the fact that an element of the mechanism they describe is undoubtedly present in almost every practical case and, furthermore, with the host of well-defined tasks that they suggest for further work on the same line. Such work cannot at present claim to be more than exploratory. But it explores the ground on which a new structure will stand some day.

Theory), where he will find all that is necessary including almost all the relevant literature.

[22] J. Tinbergen, 'Ein Schiffbauzyklus?,' *Weltwirtschaftliches Archiv*, July 1931. The model is very interesting. Let currently available tonnage of freight-carrying vessels be represented on a time axis. Call it $f(t)$ and assume, as a first approximation, that it varies only in consequence of new tonnage produced, which we can therefore denote by $f'(t)$. Postulate that freight charges will be high (low) when tonnage is low (high) relatively to its trend which will stimulate (discourage) orders for new tonnage, the execution of which will discourage (stimulate) further orders and so on. Increase of tonnage at any point of time will thus depend upon the relative scarcity or abundance of tonnage some time (say ϑ years) before: $f'(t) = -af(t - \vartheta)$ where a is a constant that represents the intensity of reaction. This is a mixed difference and differential equation, the first of its type to enter economic theory. Its solution will describe the development in time of the tonnage (theoretically ever after), if the development in an initial interval be given. According to a standard method much used by physicists, we get the solution by means of the (tentative) substitution, $f(t) = e^{\alpha t + \beta}$. Mathematically trained readers will notice that this solution will be periodic if we make α an imaginary number (Euler's relation: $e^{i\alpha t} = \cos \alpha t + i \sin \alpha t$). [See J. A. S., *Business Cycles* p. 533.]

CHAPTER 5

[Keynes and Modern Macroeconomics] [1]

In a history of economic analysis, it is from the standpoint of modern macroeconomics that we must look upon the greatest literary success of our epoch, J. M. Keynes's *General Theory of Employment, Interest and Money* (1936), and it is from this standpoint only that we can attempt to do justice to it. From any other view, this inevitably spells injustice. Like most of the great economists whose messages reached the general public, especially like A. Smith, Lord Keynes was much else besides being a worker in the field of economic analysis. He was a forceful and dauntless leader of public opinion, a wise adviser to his country—the England that was born in the First World War and that afterwards kept, with deepening lines, the social physiognomy then acquired—and a successful representative of her interest, a man who would have conquered a place in history even if he had never done a stroke of specifically scientific work: he would still have been the man who wrote *The Economic Consequences of the Peace* (1919), bursting into international fame when men of equal insight but less courage and men of equal courage but less insight kept silent.[2]

His *General Theory*, in a sense, was a similar feat of leadership. It taught England, in the form of an apparently general analysis, his own personal view of her social and economic situation and also his own personal view of 'what should be done about it.' In addition, impinging as it did upon the moral atmosphere created by the depression and upon a rising tide of radicalism, the message of the book, issued from the vantage ground of Cambridge and propagated by many able and faithful disciples, met with equal success elsewhere and particularly in the United States. Considering that Lord Keynes's attitude

[1] [This was the last thing written by J. A. S. for his *History*. It was left behind to be typed when he departed from Cambridge for the Christmas vacation, December 1949. It was not typed until after his death. Hence there was no opportunity for corrections or modifications.]

[2] In Parts II, III, and IV, I have occasionally attempted to sketch personalities as personalities. This cannot be done in this brief survey. Therefore I shall merely add that the tribute above fails to convey a picture of the man or even the wealth of his interests. Even his purely scientific work will not enter our picture in all its aspects. I have described the words above as a tribute. But behind this tribute there is a much ampler one that remains unwritten here. [See 'John Maynard Keynes (1883-1946),' written by J. A. S. for the *American Economic Review*, September 1946, reprinted in *Ten Great Economists* (1951).]

was rather conservative in many respects, especially in matters touching freedom of enterprise, this might seem surprising. But it must not be forgotten that he rendered a decisive service to equalitarianism in an all-important point. Economists with an equalitarian bent had long before learned to discount all other aspects or functions of inequality of income except one: like J. S. Mill they had retained scruples concerning the effects of equalitarian policies upon saving. Keynes freed them from these scruples. His analysis seemed to restore intellectual respectability to anti-saving views; and he spelled out the implications of this in Chapter 24 of the *General Theory*. Thus, though his scientific message appealed to many of the best minds of the economic profession, it also appealed to the writers and talkers on the fringes of professional economics who gleaned nothing from the *General Theory* except the New Economics of Spending and for whom he brought back the happy times of Mrs. Marcet (see Part III, ch. 4) when every schoolgirl, by learning the use of a few simple concepts, acquired competence to judge of all the ins and outs of the infinitely complex organism of capitalist society. Keynes was Ricardo's peer in the highest sense of the phrase. But he was Ricardo's peer also in that his work is a striking example of what we have called above the Ricardian Vice, namely, the habit of piling a heavy load of practical conclusions upon a tenuous groundwork, which was unequal to it yet seemed in its simplicity not only attractive but also convincing. All this goes a long way though not the whole way toward answering the questions that always interest us, namely, the questions *what* it is in a man's message that makes people listen to him, and *why* and *how*. However, our only task is to insert into our survey Keynes's contribution to our analytic apparatus. But the importance of his work seems to impose the duty, before doing this, of presenting a few comments on its wider aspects.

[1. Comments on the Wider Aspects of Keynes's Work]

First, Keynes's work presents an excellent example for our thesis that, in principle, vision of facts and meanings precedes analytic work, which, setting in to implement the vision, then goes on hand in hand with it in an unending relation of give and take. Nothing can be more obvious than that in the beginning of the relevant part of Keynes's work stood his vision of England's aging capitalism and his intuitive diagnosis of it (which he followed up without the slightest consideration of other possible diagnoses): the arteriosclerotic economy whose opportunities for rejuvenating venture decline while the old habits of saving formed in times of plentiful opportunity persist. This vision was clearly formulated in the first pages of the *Economic Consequences of the Peace* (1919) and adumbrated with increasing clearness in successive works, especially in the *Tract on Monetary Reform* (1923) and the *Treatise on Money* (1930), Keynes's most ambitious purely scholarly venture. This *Treatise*, though no failure in the ordinary sense of the term, met respectful but damaging criticism and, above all, failed to express Keynes's vision adequately. Thereupon, with admirable resoluteness, he determined to throw away the impeding pieces of apparatus, and bent to the task of framing an analytic system that would express his fundamental idea *and nothing else*. The result, given to the world in 1936, seems to have satisfied him completely, so much so that he felt himself to have led economics out of 150 years of error into the land of definitive truth—a claim that cannot be put to test here but was as readily accepted by some as it discredited his work in the eyes of others.

Next, we must record Keynes's acknowledgments of indebtedness, which in all cases can be independently established, to Mrs. Joan Robinson, Mr. R. G. Hawtrey, Mr. R. F. Harrod, but especially to Mr. R. F. Kahn, whose share in the historic achievement cannot have fallen very far short of co-authorship. I take this opportunity to rescue from threatening oblivion, in addition to his share in Keynes's *General Theory* and in the theory of imperfect competition, another contribution of Kahn's. Marshall, though offering plenty of material about the theory of short-run processes, always emphasized primarily the properties of the long-run normal without, perhaps, making it sufficiently clear that what he really meant was the pure logic of the economic process rather than any state of things that will actually emerge at any future time. It was necessary to realize that what in fact emerges and can be observed is the result of a succession of short-run events and short-run responses to them and will in general bear little resemblance to the perfect equilibrium that *would* emerge if time were given for everything to work itself out without any further disturbances occurring meanwhile. This point of view, obviously very important for the improvement of economic analysis, has been taken consistently by Mr. Kahn, more consistently and consciously than by anyone else, I believe, although I am unable to put my finger on any particular publication of his that would substantiate this assertion. (On the possible relation of this *scientific* contribution to the short-run *philosophy* of our age, see above Part IV, ch. 7.)

Third, Keynes must be credited or debited, as the case may be, with the fatherhood of modern stagnationism. In itself stagnationism is practically as old as economic thought. In any prolonged period of economic *malaise* economists, falling in like other people with the humors of their time, proffer theories that pretend to show that depression has come to stay. We have had instances before. But so far as our own epoch and scientific literature are concerned, this attitude can be traced as we have seen to Keynes's *Economic Consequences of the Peace*. In the United States, very naturally, it did not 'catch on' until the crisis of 1929-32, but in the aftermath of this crisis it caught on with a vengeance. A group that might almost be called a school and that found resonance in almost all the strata of public opinion—the opinion of the harassed business community included—rose to scientific importance under the brilliant leadership of Professor Alvin H. Hansen, who amplified and expanded the doctrine of the mature or stagnating economy in part on different grounds than Keynes. We cannot attempt a critical analysis of it and shall confine ourselves to noting that it stood up better than might have been expected in the face of apparently contradicting evidence for three reasons: (1) because the new economic opportunities that are unfolding themselves may be, in part with justice, attributed to the consequences of the Second World War and thus be interpreted as an intermezzo that is irrelevant to questions of fundamental trend; (2) because every span of prosperity, however prolonged, displays setbacks that it will always be possible to interpret as manifestations of that trend; (3) because some workers who are not 'stagnationists' in either Keynes's or Hansen's sense nevertheless arrive at a similar result for reasons of their own.[3] It sometimes looks as if we ought to speak not of stagnationists and anti-stagnationists but rather of two different lines of a single stagnationist argument—at least if we neglect all those anti-stagnationist writers who confine themselves to criticizing individual stagnationist arguments.

Finally, fourth, let us note the significant fact—significant in that it shows the extent to which Keynes's *General Theory* was a response to widely accepted ideas—that in the 1930's other works appeared that, each in its own way, attempted to express views that were similar to Keynes's in important points. An enthusiastic Keynesian has for instance spoken of 'Swedish stepping stones to Keynes' and, if we neglect the value judgment which this phrase implies, we may indeed agree that the leading Swedish economists, in particular Lindahl, Myrdal, and Ohlin, developing certain pointers of Wicksell's, built with similar materials according to a similar plan. However, I shall merely mention two works that will illustrate what I mean.

Erik Lundberg's *Studies in the Theory of Economic Expansion* (1937) appeared a year after Keynes's *General Theory*, took full account of the latter, and contains explicit acknowledgment of its 'stimulating influence.' But no work of this range and depth can, within a single year, be *formed* by an out-

[3] Thus, it is possible to feel unconvinced by Keynes's and Hansen's arguments and nevertheless to predict that capitalist evolution tends to peter out—i.e. to settle down into a condition that might be just as well described as 'stagnation'—because the modern state may crush or paralyze its motive forces. Modern taxation is only an example of the numerous factors which work that way, all of which can be established by an analysis of the present state of England. And inhibitions of this kind—which moreover can also be shown to be the inevitable outcome of capitalist history—will do as well as the factors emphasized by Keynes and Hansen: evidently it comes to the same thing, in a profit economy, whether the objective opportunities for gainful enterprise decrease or the profits after having been made are taxed away. Let us note in passing that there is, in some points, a strong affinity between the Keynes-Hansen and the Ricardo-J. S. Mill argument concerning the advent of a stationary state. This is particularly clear in the case of Keynes, who in his earlier writings repeatedly spoke of a 'decreasing response of nature to human effort'—on the eve of a period of unsaleable foodstuffs and raw materials—and of pressure of population. This element is not only absent from Hansen's argument but has been by him actually turned into its opposite. But the notion that opportunities for investment will in the future tend to decline as compared with people's propensity to save, though handled in a manner different from Ricardo's, is present with both authors [Hansen and Keynes]. The main difference is that they predicted difficulties in the process of the economy's settling down to a stationary state that did not occur to Ricardo. [J. A. S. in his *Capitalism, Socialism, and Democracy* (1942) put forward the point of view 'that capitalist evolution tends to peter out because the modern state may crush or paralyze its motive forces.']

side influence unless its author has arrived at somewhat similar conclusions by himself. In addition, Wicksell's influence is much more obvious than Keynes's, and Lundberg's work, both in methods and results, differs sufficiently from Keynes's to put his fundamental independence from the latter beyond doubt. Indeed, except for effectiveness of presentation, we might well speak of superiority, especially (but not only) because Lundberg tackled from the first the problem of sequence which had to be done for Keynes by followers. For us the book is particularly interesting because it displays the micro- and macrodynamic roots of current Keynesianism much better than did Keynes himself. And for the post-Keynesians of our day it should be particularly interesting because of the enlightening experience that it may afford of seeing 'Keynesian' propositions in a different light and in different connections.

Carl Föhl's book, *Geldschöpfung und Wirtschaftskreislauf* (1937), owes nothing to Keynes's *General Theory* because, as the author stated in the preface, his manuscript had been completed in December 1935 so that he was not able to do more than to add references to the *General Theory* here and there. All the more striking are a number of parallelisms between his and Keynes's propositions though, for English and American readers, the full extent of actual agreements will not be obvious at first sight. This is owing to two facts: Dr. Föhl used a different conceptual apparatus and arrived at his conclusions by methods that tend to obscure those agreements; and writing in a different environment he gave much space to problems that are no longer interesting to the American profession. Precisely because of this, the study of this book would be extremely instructive to American economists: precisely because of its apparently un-Keynesian approach, it reveals (objective) doctrinal relations and sheds what amounts to new light on several Keynesian problems, especially the problem of equilibrium underemployment. This book has had some influence in Germany and, so I have been informed by a Danish fellow economist, a considerable influence in Denmark.

[2. The Analytic Apparatus of the General Theory]

The analytic apparatus of the *General Theory* is, first, essentially static. We shall explain presently the apparent paradox that its place in the history of analysis is nevertheless bound up with the impulse it gave to macrodynamics. Nor do I mean to deny that large parts of the book—some would say, its most valuable parts—are devoted to dynamic considerations. But these were added to a skeleton [4] that was severely static, so much so as to neglect, on principle, all sequences and periods.[5] Second, this static theory is not the statics of long-run normals but the theory of short-run equilibria. Third, the most important point in this connection is that, of all the aspects of the investment proc-

[4] This skeleton has been exactly formulated many times. We content ourselves with mentioning O. Lange 'The Rate of Interest and the Optimum Propensity to Consume,' *Economica*, February 1938, and L. R. Klein, *The Keynesian Revolution* (1947).

[5] The outstanding example of this is the Kahn-Keynes multiplier. [J. A. S. planned to discuss this in the later portion of this chapter which was not finished.]

ess, it is only the expenditure effect of new investment which enters the *model* (not the *book*): as Keynes himself rightly emphasized, physical capital (equipment) is assumed to remain constant throughout, both in kind and quantity. This limits the theory to an analysis of the factors that determine the higher or lower degree of utilization of an existing industrial apparatus. Those who look for the essence of capitalism in the phenomena that attend the incessant recreation of this apparatus and the incessant revolution that goes on within it must therefore be excused if they hold that Keynes's theory abstracts from the essence of the capitalist process.[6] Fourth, though aggregative, Keynesian analysis—no doubt for the sake of simplicity—presupposes 'free,' if not actually 'pure,' competition in all commodity and factor markets. Fifth, everybody is supposed to react to a particular kind of 'real' values, namely, to prices expressed in wage-units or prices divided by an average money wage per unit of labor, which is determined by bargains between employers and employees—a well-nigh desperate measure of simplification that makes results incomparable as between two different points of time unless wage rates are the same in both. But there is an important exception to this postulate that people calculate in terms of real values in this sense: workmen do so only in so far as they save and invest but not in their bargains about their labor; when they negotiate wage contracts they consider exclusively money wage rates.[7]

Within the framework set by these five points, Keynesian analysis—the analysis of current national income—works five endogenous variables, that is, variables which the system is to determine: national income itself, employment, consumption, investment, and the rate of interest; and one exogenous variable that is given to the system by the action of the 'authorities,' quantity of money.[8] Employment may be allowed to drop out on the strength of the

[6] This does not preclude us from finding several points of contact between Keynesian and Marxian analysis. Fundamentally, however, they are opposites.

[7] This raises three questions: (1) the question of the realism of this postulate per se; (2) the question of the warrant for making this exception from the rule that is adopted for all other transactions; (3) the question of the effects upon Keynes's wage theory of this postulate. In the available space we cannot answer any of them—beyond pointing out that it was by virtue of this postulate that Keynes rejected the usual theory of the supply function for labor, which is based on the opposite postulate. Slightly exaggerating the importance of this point, Keynes calls it 'our point of departure from the classical system' (op. cit. p. 17). But it is true that, as his argument is laid out, it is this postulate which enables him to defend what is for his system a fundamental proposition, namely, that the wage contract *does not in principle determine real wages.* Followers have, gradually and tacitly, receded from this untenable position, which is less essential for his argument than Keynes himself thought. Observe, however, the tenable element in it: any increase or decrease of wage *rates, if* it increases or decreases wage *incomes* in a sufficiently important sector of the economy (or even locality), will have some influence upon prices and this influence may, in part or wholly, offset the effect of the change in money wage rates—a nexus which is of course worth emphasizing.

[8] One of the many inadequacies of our exposition, which cannot aim at more than calling up a few essentials in the minds of readers who are supposed to be familiar with the *General Theory,* is that we must follow the practice of many Keynesians in

hypothesis, perhaps permissible in the very short run, that it is uniquely determined by national income. The latter's current value is by definition identically equal to current consumption plus current investment, all three quantities being expressed in wage-units.[9] And, with all the 'givens' implied, current value of national income may be said to be 'determined' by three functions or schedules that Keynes dignified with the title of 'psychological laws': [10] the consumption function, the investment function, and the liquidity-preference function, the three great simplifiers, which are to implement Keynes's vision of the economic process, in particular the intention to prove the existence of underemployment equilibria and, to put it with perhaps inadmissible emphasis, his conviction that saving (or, alternatively, the rate of interest) holds the role of villain of the piece that impoverishes nations.[11]

In a sense similar to that in which the Marshallian demand curve descends from Cournot (and, objectively, also from Verri), the Keynesian consumption function descends from Malthus and Wicksell [12] but received added pre-

---

assuming the quantity of means of payment to be externally given, i.e. of being freely malleable by governments and *central* banks. This assumption brings us, all protests notwithstanding, dangerously near to a crude quantity theory of which an externally given quantity of money is, as we have seen, an outstanding feature. It would be unbearably unrealistic, even for modern England, unless, as Arthur Smithies has pointed out, we define the quantity to mean legal tender outside of banks plus the maximum of deposits the law and the 'authorities' permit banks to create.

[9] Since savings are defined as the difference between income and consumption, this identity yields the familiar identity between current savings and current (rate of) investment. But for the latter identity to be valid, current investment must not in turn be identified, as has been done by Keynes, with the rate of production of new capital equipment. See on this P. A. Samuelson, 'The Rate of Interest under Ideal Conditions,' *Quarterly Journal of Economics* (February 1939), pp. 292-5.

[10] They have of course no claim to this title, not even in the sense in which, at a push, it is admissible so to call Gossen's law of satiable wants.

[11] Those who are of the opinion that economic facts and Keynes's analysis do not bear out this conviction and that the element of truth in it reduces to so much of it as had been recognized by J. S. Mill, W. Roscher, and A. Marshall (see Keynes's and even Hobson's grudging admission of this, op. cit. p. 19n.), will naturally look for a non-analytic explanation. They may find it, first, in England's situation in which many difficulties were capable of being solved by the expropriation of 'rentiers' which, for political reasons, were practically insurmountable in any other way; and, second, in the kind of man Keynes was—he, the unattached intellectual, who abhorred bourgeois virtues but was much too civilized to like violent measures, had a not unnatural preference for the 'euthanasia' of the creditor interest.

[12] There is, however, this difference between the cases of Marshall and Keynes. They would be exactly similar if the historian could say that Marshall *saw* his demand curve in the less rigorous presentation of Mill and added rigor and 'edge' to it. But Marshall *must* have found all the rigor and edge that anyone could desire in Cournot. Keynes, had he even been inspired by Malthus (Wicksell he then hardly knew), would have had still to do all that remained for a disciple of Mill to do in the case of the Marshallian demand curve. However, the (objective) affinity between Keynes and Malthus stands out with particular clearness at the beginning of the *General Theory* (p. 25),

cision at the hands of Keynes. As everybody knows, it represents current total national consumption (total expenditure on 'consumption' in terms of wage-units) as a function of current national income (in wage-units) and expresses the arbitrary postulate that any increase in the latter is always attended by an increase in the former but by a smaller one.[13] The investment function is less easy to convey in a few words because of its connection with the very important dynamical considerations of Keynes's chapters 11 and 12, which do not enter into its explicit statement. It relates the rate of aggregate investment to the marginal efficiency of (physical) 'capital in general which that rate of investment will establish' (op. cit. p. 136), the marginal efficiency of capital being defined as the relation between the expected yield of one more unit (properly chosen) of any capital good and the cost of producing this unit.[14] This, as Keynes pointed out, is the same as Fisher's 'marginal rate of return

---

where Keynes worked out his concepts of Aggregate Supply and Aggregate Demand Functions and of *effective demand.* Whatever weight we may attach to Keynes's warnings, we are inevitably driven to considering these functions, which are capable of intersecting once (or several times) but are in any case not identical, as generalizations of the genuine concepts of supply of and demand for individual commodities. Keynes, aware of the pitfall, makes little use of this notion later on. But it is the Malthusian notion. And if valid it would of itself suffice to establish the possibility of an equilibrium of which full employment would not be a property. I repeat that the arguments that Keynes set forth against what he conceived to be the classical theory (in his sense) are entirely irrelevant against any correct statement of the full-employment equilibrium theory and that his indictment that the classical theory knows no unemployment except a frictional one is true only if the term frictional is defined so widely as to rob the indictment of all significance.

[13] This 'psychological law' of the propensity to consume must of course refer to individuals. But the postulate in question refers to social aggregates. I have called it arbitrary merely to emphasize the fact that it formulates only one of several possibilities. We can express the consumption function by writing $C = f(Y)$, then the postulate reads that the marginal propensity to consume, dC/dY, is always smaller than unity. But let us note at once that, since instead of this consumption function, we might just as well write a savings function, $S = \varphi(Y)$. It has become usual with many Keynesians to insert into both functions a second variable, namely the rate of interest, i, the importance of this concession being minimized by postulating that the influence of i is negligible.

[14] The investment function is usually written $I = F(Y, i)$, which expresses the marginal efficiency of capital by the form of the function F. The marginal propensity to invest at a given rate of interest is then $\delta F/\delta Y$. But we may also leave out the i in order to emphasize the cases where investment is 'autonomous,' i.e. either imposed upon the system by an external factor, such as government, or else entered into without any regard to current conditions. Or we may, on the contrary, consider investment as wholly 'induced' by consumers' buying and then write the investment function $I = \varphi(C, i)$ as has been done by Lange (see note 4 above). These and other expressions suggest themselves for the purpose of underlining this or that possibility but none of them, taken by itself, does full justice to the thought of Keynes, who wisely refrained from presenting any of them himself.

over cost.' [15] But there is this difference between the two: whereas with Fisher this marginal rate of return over cost—which implies a discounting process of the series of expected yields—constitutes the basic fact about the interest phenomenon, Keynes broke away at this point from what I have termed the Barbon tradition and, in intent at least, established a monetary theory of interest, according to which interest is not derived from, or expressive of, anything that has, in whatever form, to do with the net return from capital goods.[16]

This brings us to the third of Keynes's basic functions or schedules, the liquidity-preference function. In Chapter 13 of the *General Theory* Keynes seemed to accept the theory that makes the rate of interest 'depend on the interaction of the schedule of the marginal efficiency of capital with the psycho-

[15] *Theory of Interest* (1930), p. 168. I can, however, testify to the fact that Keynes, whose knowledge of economic literature and particularly of contemporaneous and non-English literature was not of the first order, arrived at his concept quite independently and that he inserted the acknowledgment in question upon his attention's having been drawn to Fisher's formulation. When he received the information, Keynes possibly acknowledged too much. Such, at least, is Professor Lerner's opinion. On the other hand, it may be argued that both concepts are indeed improvements upon the concept of marginal productivity of capital as developed by Marshall and especially Wicksell—and this again points back to Böhm-Bawerk—but not more than that. The 'prospectiveness' of marginal productivity of capital and its relation to its replacement costs, few if any authors who used it would have denied.

[16] Since this is, speaking from the standpoint of theoretical analysis alone, perhaps the most important original contribution of the *General Theory*, a few comments are in order. First, Keynes's monetary theory of interest was subjectively original *qua* monetary theory of interest but not objectively so. From the scholastics through their Protestant successors to several pre-Keynesian modern writers, explanations of the interest phenomenon have been offered that link it to money and whose authors would all agree to the divorce that Keynes pronounced between the yield of non-monetary capital and interest. The objective importance of Keynes's work, so far as this goes, was the success that his teaching met with: he actually converted a large number of fellow economists who twenty years or so before considered a monetary theory of interest hardly worth serious attention. Second, we must again recall the fact that Wicksell, without adopting a monetary theory, made such an important stride toward it as to inspire Swedish followers of his to do so. This Wicksellian line of advance is most easily accessible, for the English reader, in Professor Erik Lindahl's *Studies in the Theory of Money and Capital* (1939) and Professor Bertil Ohlin's two articles 'Some Notes on the Stockholm Theory of Savings and Investment,' *Economic Journal*, March and June 1937. The articles gave rise to a discussion between Keynes, Ohlin, Robertson, and Hawtrey that was followed by a number of articles by other economists. But we must be content to add, third, that the particular form that Keynes gave to his monetary theory was original both subjectively and objectively. It may differ much or little from the Swedish one or from the one sponsored by Professor Hicks (*Value and Capital*, ch. 12), which perhaps comes nearest to holding the field in that part of Anglo-American literature that accepts the monetary theory of interest at all; but it differs a great deal from other forms—so much so that it is a mere question of temperament whether one wishes to see in them any affinity at all with the Keynesian form.

logical propensity to save' (time preference). For he stated as his only objection that it is impossible to deduce the rate of interest *merely* from these two factors bcause it will also depend on the form in which the saver wishes to hold whatever he saves. Having decided how much he will 'reserve in *some* form of command over future consumption' (p. 166; note the classical ring of this phrase), he has still to decide whether and to what extent he will part with immediate command for a specified or indefinite period, that is, on his liquidity preference.[17] On the face of it this clearly amounts to not more than an amendment. Later on, however, even in the *General Theory*, Keynes himself and still more some orthodox followers of his, especially Professor Lerner,[18] went much further than that in the direction of the propositions that interest is nothing but a payment for overcoming one's reluctance to part with the one ideally liquid asset in existence (own-rate theory of interest) and that the quantity of money, considered relatively to the amount of it that is absorbed by transactions, is the sole directly governing factor in its determination.[19] Current saving and current investment, being identically equal, cannot determine anything. Planned (ex ante) saving and planned (ex ante) investment determine income (total net output) but not interest. And a number of paradoxes follow for which some verification can be found in the freakish situations of deep depression.[20]

[17] In the exact formulation, this liquidity preference is usually introduced in an equation of the form $\overline{M} = L(Y, i)$, which compares the available amount of money (see note 8 above)—I bar the M in order to indicate that it is given—with a 'demand' for money that is partly determined by the volume of transactions, represented by Y, and partly by people's expectations about the future behavior of the various interest rates (the 'speculative motive'), which is represented by i.

[18] On Professor Lerner's argument see Franco Modigliani, 'Liquidity Preference and the Theory of Interest and Money,' *Econometrica*, January 1944, p. 79. I take this opportunity to recommend this paper as a general commentary on this whole range of questions.

[19] Observe that, among many other things, interest must indeed also equalize the advantages of holding cash and other assets. This is another instance of Keynes's Ricardian way of reasoning: the fact that the rate of interest must be such as to compensate savers for their marginal 'abstinence'—if it did not, it could not be what it actually is—is obviously insufficient to establish the abstinence theory of interest. Observe further that, like everything else, both propositions—the own-rate and the abstinence theory—can be made formally true by a sufficient number of 'givens,' with the added advantage that the tables can be turned upon the objector with the utmost ease on the ground that he does not understand the assumptions of the argument. See in this connection W. Fellner and H. M. Somers, 'Alternative Monetary Approaches to Interest Theory,' *Review of Economic Statistics*, February 1941.

[20] To mention one example: the Keynesian theory, taken literally, yields the conclusion that an increase in the inducement or the propensity to invest, or in the propensity to consume, will only increase employment but have no *tendency* to raise the rate of interest. The opposite in any normal situation is evident and has been stated as a theorem by Professor Samuelson, not as an objection to Keynesian doctrine but as part of it (see *Foundations*, p. 279, and compare J. R. Hicks, 'Mr. Keynes and the "Classics"; A Suggested Interpretation,' *Econometrica*, April 1937, pp. 152-3).

[3. The Impact of the Keynesian Message]

By means of those three basic functions or schedules a system of three equilibrium conditions (equations) and one identity can be written that will, with the quantity of money as an externally imposed datum, and under proper assumptions, uniquely determine interest, investment, and either savings or consumption and can be extended to include also other variables such as Keynes's wage rates.[21] But it was not this exact and crippled rendering of Keynes's message which fascinated, but the resplendent whole of it. Particularly in its bearings upon saving, interest, and underemployment, this message seemed to reveal a novel view of the capitalist process not only, as we saw before, to the public and 'writers on the fringes' but also to many of the best minds in the sphere of professional analysis—a novel view that was as attractive to some as it was repellent to others.[22] This created almost immediately an atmosphere

[21] The identity is either $Y \equiv C + I$ or $S \equiv I$. In the first case we may use the equations $C = f(Y, i)$ and $I = \Phi(C, i)$, in the latter case the equations $S = \varphi(Y, i)$ and $I = F(Y, i)$. For an extension see Modigliani, op. cit. p. 46. But the system, especially any extended system, is not so simple a matter as it might seem to the layman. This is the reason why, though I cannot go into the problems involved, I have tried to save my conscience by inserting the words, 'under proper assumptions.' It is not difficult to draw up a system that will display inconsistencies and fail to define an equilibrium or even multiple equilibria. This is important to observe because such disequilibrium systems play a role in the Keynesian discussion: for the Keynesian they may be a means for showing that, without government expenditure ('fiscal policy'), the economy may be incapable of hitting upon an equilibrium state, in particular a full-employment equilibrium state.

Let us note, in passing, another important point. If we speak not of current but of planned consumption and investment, then a condition of stability of the system is that the sum of the marginal propensity to consume and the marginal propensity to invest—the marginal propensity to spend—be smaller than unity. If it is equal to or greater than unity, the system will still be determined but it will 'explode' instead of converging toward equilibrium when displaced. Now several writers are prone to argue as if this stability condition could be used to 'prove' that the propensity to spend is actually smaller than unity because, so they hold, in capitalist reality the economic system does not explode. This argument is quite inadmissible on logical grounds of which I mention only one: a short-run theoretical system may be explosive while the corresponding long-run system is not; and a long-run theoretical system may be explosive while the corresponding reality is not.

[22] The division of professional opinion cannot be described in the same terms for every country: in some it amounted to not more than a ripple on the surface. But in England and the United States it went deep, and here a phenomenon asserted itself unmistakably that deserves passing notice. Keynesianism appealed primarily to young theorists whereas a majority of the old stagers were, more or less strongly, anti-Keynesian. One aspect of this fact is too obvious to detain us and has, in addition, often been emphasized: *of course* it is true that part of the resistance which every novel doctrine meets is simply the resistance of arteriosclerosis. But there is another. The old or even mature scholar may be not only the victim but also the beneficiary of habits of thought formed by his past work. I am not referring now to that deeper understanding

that was ideally suited for a struggle full of zest—as much so, in principle, as was the atmosphere created by Ricardo in 1817, but more so, in fact, owing to the temperature produced by the vastly increased number of professional economists. All that can be done in this sketch is to list the three types of tasks that were undertaken and together account for the torrent of more or less Keynesian literature that is so characteristic of the decade after 1936.

The first task of course proceeded from the need felt by almost every economist to find out and to tell how he stood in relation to a message that nobody could ignore. The bulk of the profession's work went on as usual and was but little affected by that message. But for all theorists, general economists, and workers in the fields of money, banking, and business cycles, that need could be satisfied only by laborious analysis, criticism, development. Since we cannot survey the literature of this type satisfactorily,[23] we merely note two facts. The one is that to have created such a response is, in and by itself, an achievement, frank recognition of which is the greatest and most deserved of the compliments that may be paid justifiably to the memory of Lord Keynes. It was not the analytic performance which did it; nor was it the attraction of the practical issues raised. As in the case of Ricardo, it was the intellectual performance spiced by the—real or putative—relevance to burning questions of the time which achieved what, in our field, neither could have achieved by itself. The very blemishes of the intellectual performance and the very objections that may be raised against Keynes's practical answer were instrumental in bringing about spectacular success and in extending controversy over the whole field that lies between, and includes, recommendations and purely logical questions of method. The other fact is the cumulative property of success of this kind, which can be best conveyed with reference to teaching. Any successful work of scientific standing must be mentioned in courses on the subject to which it is relevant. But a teacher, as soon as he discovers that students will take to a work independently of his teaching or can be trusted to have become acquainted with it before they entered his course, will also discover the pedagogical advantages to be reaped from referring to, and building upon, such previous knowledge; and he will, whatever his own opinions, deal much more intensively with such a work than he would merely on its merits. Thus as in banking or insurance, growth induces further growth merely by increasing reserves, success engenders success. Literature produces further literature.

The second task that the *General Theory* presented was the development, critical or constructive, theoretical or factual, of a large number of individual

---

of things that can hardly be acquired except by the labor of decades: apart from this and the difference in attitude to 'policy' that results from this, there is such a thing as analytic experience. And in a field like economics, where training is often defective and where the young scholar very often simply does not know enough, this element in the case counts much more heavily than it does in physics where teaching, even though possibly uninspiring, is always competent.

[23] A sample of it, though heavily weighted 'in favor,' the reader will find in *The New Economics*, edited and introduced by S. E. Harris (1947).

points.[24] There were the questions of Keynesian underemployment equilibrium, of the 'own-rate' *versus* the 'loan-fund' theory of interest, of the principle of aggregative (macroeconomic) theory, of the relation between money and real wages, and many others, all of which produced 'special literatures' of their own. But one example must suffice, the work that has been and is being done on the consumption function. No theorist worthy of the name can accept as an *exact* statement the postulate that links expenditure on consumption (in terms of wage-units) with income (in terms of wage-units) alone. Still less is it possible to accept the Keynesian property of this function (dC/dY, see note 13 above) as universally valid. We have therefore an approximation before us. But how close is this approximation and, in particular, precisely *how* imperative is it to add a term to allow for shifts of the function in time? And how seriously are we sinning if we decree that the function be linear? Or must we take in sails and admit independent variables other than income—for instance, the amount of assets or at least liquid assets that individuals happen to have already? All these questions are theoretical questions in the first instance to be answered with reference to the autonomy of the function [25] and to its consistency with other relations that we mean to accept on the same plane of argument. But evidently they have also a most important factual aspect.

[24] It should be observed that, so far as effects upon the content of a theory are concerned, criticism or elaboration and even apologetics come to much the same thing: irrespective of the worker's intention, his work gradually changes, and in the end annihilates, original meanings. But this is not so as regards the renown of a work and the position it will ultimately occupy in the history of a science. Here, the worker's attitude and value judgments are much more important, even for the opinion of future theorists but, of course, still more so for the future opinion of the profession and the reading public. For instance, it would be easy to compile a list of arguments (all of them valid) from the writings of, say, Hicks, Lange, Modigliani, and Samuelson that in hands less friendly than theirs would sum up to a very damaging criticism. But they had no intention to damage. In Keynes's case, merit and luck combined to blunt the edges of the criticism of some of those who were most competent to inflict injury—compare Marshall's attitude to Ricardo.

[25] The concept of the autonomy of a function or equation is due to Professor Frisch. In a system of relations (mathematical or not) that are supposed to hold simultaneously in a given framework of data, there may be some that hold individually only if the others do and perhaps also if the given framework of data remains unchanged, and others that retain individual validity even if some do not hold (and in another framework of data). The latter we call autonomous, though we use this term also in other senses (as in 'autonomous investment'). The property is not absolute: a relation may be more or less affected by a failure of the others. Therefore we had better speak of higher or lower degrees of autonomy. Frisch's paper on the subject (not published to my knowledge) is one of the most interesting contributions of our time to the pure logic of modern theory. [In reply to a query by the editor, Professor Frisch stated that the idea of autonomy of a function or equation is explained at great length in several of his mimeographed lectures in Norwegian and that in printed form it is mentioned only briefly in a note 'Repercussion Studies at Oslo,' *American Economic Review*, June 1948.]

And it is not surprising but a matter for congratulation that a dozen or so econometricians have devoted, and are devoting, attention to it.

The third task springs from the necessity of 'dynamizing' the Keynesian system either on the lines suggested by Keynes himself or on others. This necessity became obvious as soon as people began to 'work' the Keynesian system seriously, for, as we know, even the mere question of the stability of a static system quickly leads into dynamic considerations. But in addition many Keynesians set about introducing into their models the usual 'dynamizers,' especially lags. As examples I mention Professor Smithies' model [26] and then again the Hansen-Samuelson equation which we have already met. Thus, Keynesian equilibrium analysis gradually gave way to Keynesian 'process analysis,' and at present this Keynesian process analysis tends to merge with the older and broader macrodynamics, the development of which we have glanced at before. Here, at long last, we are at the point from which it is possible to define and locate the historical importance of Keynes's purely analytic contribution to economics. This being important and, owing to the brevity of our exposition, not easy to grasp, the reader's attention is requested for the following résumé.

So far as the exact core is concerned, Keynes's system is essentially static. This static theory sufficed for the purposes he had most at heart, particularly for his doctrine of underemployment equilibrium. However, partly because it was inevitable that he should have had to add dynamic considerations to that core, partly because his work impinged on a situation in the field of pure theory that was dominated (independently of him) by the novel interest in macrodynamics, this macrodynamics absorbed his work. But, owing to the position Keynes's work conquered in the thought of the profession, it was not simply swamped by macrodynamics but in turn helped to mold and to propel the latter—for which Keynes's model was particularly qualified by virtue of its simplicity. Professor Hicks was obviously right in saying that 'the *General Theory of Employment* . . . is neither the beginning nor the end of Dy-

[26] Arthur Smithies, 'Process Analysis and Equilibrium Analysis,' *Econometrica*, January 1942. It has been pointed out already that most Keynesians (or writers who use the Keynesian or a similar apparatus) introduced *planned* (or ex ante) savings and investments so as to be able to make equality of savings and investments an equilibrium condition instead of the *identity* it is in the case of savings and investments actually performed. This is in agreement with Keynes's position for he surely emphasized the gulf that exists between saving and investment *decisions* strongly enough. Nor does it, in itself, involve leaving the precincts of Keynesian statics. But it does so as soon as we connect savings and investments explicitly with some quantity of the past, e.g. with yesterday's income. And then we are led away easily, though not by logical necessity, not only from Keynesian statics but also from the Keynesian structure as a whole. Take for instance the concept of idle savings. Laymen sometimes believe that the Keynesian argument implies that there must, somewhere in the economy, exist savings that are idle in the sense that they are not being invested. But this notion is meaningless within the Keynesian argument. However, it immediately acquires meaning if we introduce lags. Nor is it difficult to tell where the introduction of lags tends to lead us, if it leads us away from Keynes: it leads us toward Robertson and Lundberg.

namic Economics.' [27] But it is also true that, unintentionally and perhaps even against his will,[28] Keynes gave a mighty impulse to it—almost all work in macrodynamics now starts from a 'dynamized' form of his model. In a history of analysis this is the point to stress.[29] In a history of economic thought Keynes's policy recommendations—time-bound as they were—and certain characteristically Keynes's doctrines—which are losing their hold already—may be much more important.

[The manuscript breaks off at this point; there are brief notes, partly in shorthand: 'Other points to be added . . . Macroeconomics will need a new conceptual apparatus . . . new general objects . . . multiplier . . . accelerator . . .']

[27] 'Mr. Keynes and the "Classics,"' *Econometrica*, April 1937, p. 159.

[28] 'Forget all about periods,' he once said to a pupil.

[29] An interesting instance of a macrodynamic model of inventory cycles that makes use of Keynes's consumption function and thus illustrates well what I was trying to convey is Lloyd A. Metzler, 'The Nature and Stability of Inventory Cycles,' *Review of Economic Statistics*, August 1941.

Editor's Appendix

THIS APPENDIX is written for the specialist who is interested in the order in which the various parts of the *History* were written and to what extent they were completed. I have already touched briefly upon these problems in the Editor's Introduction and in editorial notes (in square brackets) throughout the book. The ordinary academic reader will find everything he needs to know in the introduction. As I stated there, everything had been written out in longhand originally; some of the chapters had been written early and rewritten later; most of them had been typed and corrected in pencil by J. A. S.; a few sections had been typed toward the end and the typescript had been read very hastily or not at all; and, finally, there was some material still in manuscript. There were even alternative versions of some of the manuscript in the chapter on Equilibrium Analysis (ch. 7 of Part IV).

The reader is reminded that the original manuscript, the alternative versions, many bits of discarded manuscript, the notes (some of them on those little pieces of yellow paper with which every student and close associate was so familiar), and the first typescript with corrections and suggested revisions in the hand of J. A. S., will all be deposited in the Houghton Library at Harvard University, where they may be consulted by the interested scholar. Although I attempted to present as complete and accurate a version as possible of what was actually written, there are undoubtedly some places where a different interpretation would be possible. It is, therefore, a great source of satisfaction to me that the original manuscript and the notes for revision will be available in the Houghton Library.

In my anxiety to show that the author would not have sent his *History* to the publisher without further work upon it, it may be that I have overemphasized the degree of its incompleteness. In reality, the *History* was substantially finished. The three main Parts (II, III, and IV) needed a little polishing here and there, a few additional pages to complete some of the sections, a few titles and subtitles, and, of course, the references needed to be checked. The chapters on The 'Mercantilist' Literature (Part II) and on Sozialpolitik and the Historical Method (Part IV), which date from the early period, would have been revised. This was also true of the section on Senior's Four Postulates in Chapter 6 of Part III. A little more work remained to be done on some of the sections in the chapter on Equilibrium Analysis. On the whole, however, Parts II, III, and IV were all but completed. As for the rest, the introductory Part I and the concluding Part V were being written at the very end and were somewhat less complete. These two parts, however, were distinctly subsidiary and not absolutely necessary to the main plan, the divisions of which were based on those of the *Epochen der Dogmen- und Methodengeschichte* of 1914. Part I was to be a brief exposition of methodological problems of which all but the last two sections of the final chapter had been written; Part V was to be an equally brief treatment, relating the present state of economics to the work of the past as described in the three main parts. The photostats of the plans of Part V (which appear below in this appendix) indicate that perhaps two-thirds of the conclusion must have been written. There is another way of indicating the relative importance in the whole work of the introduction and the conclusion, namely, by comparing the relative amount of space allotted to them with the total. The copy which eventually went to the publisher consisted of 1919 typed pages —about 20 per cent of it in single space. Had the *History* been completed, there might have been 2000 typed pages, of which the introduction would have occupied a little more than 100 pages or 5 per cent of the total and the conclusion another 100 pages or 5 per cent of the total. Thus the two together would have taken up only about 10 per cent of the total space.

It has already been stated in the Editor's Introduction that J. A. S. probably began writing the *History* in 1941 or 1942 and that substantial portions were typed in 1942 and 1943. At that time he intended merely to translate, revise, and bring up to date the *Dogmengeschichte*. Subsequently most of this early work was rewritten—so completely rewritten that often only a page or two (much crossed out and written over) of an early version was used in a final version. A question naturally arises at this point: how do we know when various chapters and sections were written? For the most part we do not know the actual dates of writing, but we do know in many cases either the actual or approximate dates of typing. The date of typing may be considerably later than the date of writing, since J. A. S. often accumulated a large amount of manuscript before sending it off to be typed. He did not have even a part-time secretary until the fall of 1948, and the typing was done by at least five different people using different typewriters and having distinctive typing styles. Mrs. Thorpe, who did much of the typing between 1943 and the middle of 1948, often put the date of typing on the carbon copy. (It was a great pile of these carbon copies, in the attic of the Acacia Street house, which first indicated to me just what had been written and kept me searching until I found manuscripts and first typescripts for all the carbon copies.) One young woman typed manuscript only in the summer of 1948, a second in the academic year 1948-9, and a third in the fall of 1949. Other means of determining the approximate time and order of writing are two reports of progress, which were made to me in the second half of 1947 and the first half of 1948, and the dates of some of the references quoted. The following outline of dates of typing will help the reader to understand the detailed explanation of the order in which the *History* was written and the extent to which various parts were rewritten. Many of these bits of manuscript were without a title. Where there was a title provided by J. A. S., I have enclosed it in quotation marks. Otherwise the headings are merely descriptive of the material covered. The references in parentheses at the end of each description indicate the part, chapter, and section in which this subject matter was eventually treated. Items dated 1950 (and after) were typed after the death of the author.

KNOWN OR APPROXIMATE DATES OF TYPING [1]

1942 (?)	'The Beginnings.' Early version of Graeco-Roman Economics, The Scholastic Doctors and the Philosophers of Natural Law, and The Consultant Administrators and Pamphleteers. (II, chs. 1, 2, 3)
Jan. 10, 1943	The Historical Method.[2] Final version (IV, ch. 4, sec. 2)
Feb. 19, 1943	Equilibrium Analysis. Early version (IV, ch. 7)
March 15, 1943	Wages, Unemployment, Poverty. Early version (II, ch. 5, secs. 3 & 4)
June 19, 1943	'Consultant Administrators and Pamphleteers.' Intermediate version (II, ch. 3)
June 19, 1943 – July 10, 1943	'The "Mercantilist" Literature.' [2] Final version (II, ch. 7)
July 13, 1943	Population, Increasing and Decreasing Returns. Early version (II, ch. 5, secs. 1 & 2)
Dec. 1, 1943	'The Political and Intellectual Scenery.' Early version (III, ch. 3)
1943 (?)	'Scope and Method.' Early version (III, ch. 5)
Dec. 12, 1943	Senior's Four Postulates.[2] Final version (III, ch. 6, sec. 1)
Dec. 17, 1943	Sozialpolitik.[2] Final version (IV, ch. 4, sec. 1)
March 26, 1944	Value and Money before 1790. Early version (II, ch. 6)
March 27, 1944 – April 4, 1944	The Scholastics and Their Successors. Intermediate version (II, ch. 2)
Aug. 23, 1945 – Sept. 17, 1945	'Graeco-Roman Economics' and 'The Scholastic Doctors and the Philosophers of Natural Law.' Final version (II, chs. 1 & 2)
Feb. 21, 1946	'Unemployment and the "State of the Poor."' Final version (II, ch. 5, sec. 4)
Summer 1948	'Money, Credit and Cycles.' Final version (III, ch. 7)
1948-9	'Some Questions of Principle.' Early version of Introduction (I)
1948-9	'Fundamental Unity of the Period's Economic Theory.' Final version (IV, ch. 7, sec. 1)
1948-9	'Cournot and the "Mathematical School": Econometrics.' Final version (IV, ch. 7, sec. 2)

[1] Known dates give month, day, and year; approximate dates (especially after mid-1948) are based on the typewriter used and the typing style. The term 'final version' means the last version, the one actually used. Sometimes, of course, there was only one version. In such a case, even if unfinished, it became the final version.

[2] These four portions of the manuscript were never revised; the final version was also the early version. There is ample evidence that the author intended to revise them.

<table>
<tr><td>1948-9</td><td colspan="2">'Statics and Dynamics. Determinateness. Stability. Equilibrium.' Early version (IV, ch. 7, sec. 3)</td></tr>
<tr><td>1948-9</td><td colspan="2">'The Competitive Hypothesis and the Theory of Monopoly.' Early version (IV, ch. 7, sec. 4)</td></tr>
<tr><td>1948-9</td><td colspan="2">'The Theory of Planning and of the Socialist Economy.' Final version (IV, ch. 7, sec. 5)</td></tr>
<tr><td>1948-9</td><td colspan="2">'Partial Analysis.' Early version (IV, ch. 7, sec. 6)</td></tr>
<tr><td>1948-9</td><td colspan="2">'Note on the Theory of Utility.' Final version (IV, ch. 7, App. secs. 1-6)</td></tr>
<tr><td>1948-9</td><td colspan="2">'Welfare Economics.' Early version (IV, ch. 7, App. sec. 8)</td></tr>
<tr><td>Late 1949</td><td colspan="2">Introduction: Scope and Method. Final version (I, chs. 1, 2, 3, 4)</td></tr>
<tr><td>Late 1949</td><td colspan="2">'Partial Analysis.' Final version (IV, ch. 7, sec. 6)</td></tr>
<tr><td>Late 1949</td><td colspan="2">'The Walrasian Theory of General Equilibrium.' Final version (IV, ch. 7, secs. 7a, 7b, 7c)</td></tr>
<tr><td>Late 1949</td><td colspan="2">'The Production Function.' Final version (IV, ch. 7, sec. 8)</td></tr>
<tr><td>Late 1949</td><td colspan="2">Developments Stemming from the Marshall-Wicksell Apparatus. Final version (V, ch. 2)</td></tr>
<tr><td>Late 1949</td><td colspan="2">Economics in the Totalitarian Countries. Final version (V, ch. 3)</td></tr>
<tr><td>Late 1949</td><td colspan="2">'Dynamics and Business Cycle Research.' Final version (V, ch. 4)</td></tr>
<tr><td>1950</td><td colspan="2">Walras' Theory of Production. Final version (IV, ch. 7, sec. 7d)</td></tr>
<tr><td>1950</td><td colspan="2">Keynes and Modern Macroeconomics. Final version (V, ch. 5)</td></tr>
<tr><td>1950</td><td colspan="2">'Value and Money.' Final version (II, ch. 6)</td></tr>
<tr><td>1950</td><td colspan="2">'The Contribution of the Applied Fields.' Final version (IV, ch. 6, sec. 6)</td></tr>
<tr><td>1950</td><td>'The Concept of Equilibrium.' Discarded</td><td rowspan="3">(IV, ch. 7, sec. 3)</td></tr>
<tr><td>1950</td><td>'Statics, Dynamics, the Stationary State, Evolution.' Final version</td></tr>
<tr><td>1950</td><td>'Determinateness and Equilibrium. Stability.' Final version</td></tr>
<tr><td>1950</td><td colspan="2">'The Competitive Hypothesis and the Theory of Monopoly.' Final version (IV, ch. 7, sec. 4)</td></tr>
<tr><td>1950</td><td colspan="2">'Welfare Economics.' Final version (IV, ch. 7, App. sec. 8)</td></tr>
<tr><td>Sept. 1951</td><td colspan="2">Walras: The Introduction of Capital Formation and of Money. Final version (IV, ch. 7, sec. 7e)</td></tr>
<tr><td>April 1952</td><td colspan="2">Adam Smith and the Wealth of Nations. Final version (II, ch. 3, sec. 4e)</td></tr>
</table>

The outline above is, of course, not complete. For many portions of the *History*, we have no specific information about the dates of typing. The outline does serve, however, to show what was written at the very beginning and at the very end. The manuscript typed in 1942 and 1943 was all completely rewritten with the exception of those items commented on in footnote 2. This was probably accomplished with respect to Part II (with the exception of the chapter on value and money) by the end of 1945.[3] It is my impression that Chapters 1-5 of Part III and Chapters 1-5 of Part IV were written next. The chapters on pure theory in Parts III and IV and the chapters on money in these parts were written relatively late. The money chapters were written at roughly the same time, but not in chronological order, the latest chapter having been written first. The earliest chapter on Value and Money (in Part II) had not been typed by January 1950, and I am frankly puzzled as to when this chapter was rewritten.[4] This knowledge of the order in which some of the later chapters were written I owe to two brief interviews with J. A. S. in which he outlined for me the state of the *History*. This he did somewhat reluctantly, at my request, because publishers' agents were attempting to find out from me when the book would be finished. I jotted down a rough outline but unfortunately I did not put down the dates. I believe the first interview may have been in the fall of 1947 and the second in early 1948 because J. A. S. had a Sabbatical half year in the fall term 1947-8. During this period he worked steadily at the *History*. On the first occasion he told me that Part II was complete except for the chapter on Value and Money; that Part III was complete except for Chapters 6 and 7, which remained largely to be done; and that in Part IV, Chapters 1-5 and Chapter 8 (Money, Credit, and Cycles) [5] were typed but that Chapters 6 and 7 remained to be done. The Note on Utility (appendix to ch. 7) was written but not typed. On the second occasion he reported that Chapter 6 of Part IV could be used substantially as it then stood.

Chapter 6 of Part III was typed before the summer of 1948 and Chapter 7 of the same part—the money chapter—during that summer. Finally, J. A. S. began to work on the chapter on 'higher pure theory' (Part IV, ch. 7, Equilibrium Analysis). Sections 1-6 and the Appendix (Note on Utility, which had been written for some time) were typed in the fall of 1948.

During 1949, the last year of his life, J. A. S. apparently wrote the introductory and concluding Parts I and V, revised sections 3-6 in Part IV, Chapter 7 (Equilibrium Analysis), and wrote section 7 of this chapter on The Walrasian Theory of General Equilibrium and section 8, the Production Function. All of these were typed during the last quarter of 1949 or were found in manuscript and typed after the death of the author. References in several of these sections

[3] The final version of ch. 5 (Population, Returns, Wages, and Employment) was typed in February 1946, and ch. 7 was left as it had been written in 1943. Ch. 6 on Value and Money was rewritten very late (possibly in 1948).

[4] This problem will be discussed below.

[5] I have here used the final numbering of the chapters as later determined by J. A. S. At that time he was thinking in terms of ten chapters. Sozialpolitik and the Historical Method were to be treated in two separate chapters (chs. 4 and 5) and the Note on Utility was to have been a chapter (ch. 9). This naturally changed the numbering of the other chapters (the money chapter becoming ch. 10).

or chapters to articles in periodicals which were published in February and May 1949 confirm these impressions as to the date of writing.

Part I was found with a pile of notes, manuscript, and reprints in the Cambridge study. It was to have been in six chapters, which I reduced to four. The first three chapters were so very short that I made them three sections of Chapter 1, retaining the original chapter titles as section titles. Two sketchy plans for Part I found among the notes indicate that J. A. S. was at work on the final chapter of the introduction. (See also editorial notes on pp. 43-5 above.)

There was an earlier introduction typed the previous year by the part-time secretary who worked during the academic year 1948-9. It consisted of 38 pages of typescript as compared with 87 pages in the final unfinished version. It was labeled 'Chapter I: Some Questions of Principle.' There were six subheadings, some of which appear as section titles in the final version:

> Why Do We Study the History of Economics?
> But Is Economics a Science at All?
> The Historical Character of Our Subject Matter
> Is Economics an Ideology?
> Economic Thought and Economics
> Economics and Economic Theory.

Very little of this earlier introduction is embodied in the final one. Typed pages 1 and 6-8, much crossed out and revised, were used in Chapter 1 (J. A. S. chs. 1, 2, and 3) and typed pages 15-17 in Chapter 4 (J. A. S. ch. 6). Otherwise the material in the final manuscript of Part I was completely new.

I do not know why J. A. S. entitled Chapters 2 and 3 (originally chs. 4 and 5) 'Interlude I' and 'Interlude II.' I added the titles and subtitles in square brackets, as I have done throughout wherever J. A. S. failed to supply detailed titles. He had indicated the six divisions in Chapter 2. The title supplied by me (The Techniques of Economic Analysis) is not quite accurate since strictly speaking there are only three such techniques (Economic History, Statistics, and Theory) with Economic Sociology as a *possible* fourth (see above, pp. 12 and 20-21). The last unfinished chapter in Part I (The Sociology of Economics) is concerned with many of the problems treated in 'Science and Ideology,' the author's presidential address before the American Economic Association in December 1948, and I am sure that he worked on both simultaneously. As was his custom, J. A. S. spoke from rather detailed notes and wrote up the address for publication afterward.

Part II was complete except for the money chapter, which was written but not typed, and the inevitable revisions. The manuscript, notes, and discarded manuscript for Part II, Chapters 1-4 and 7 (2-5 and 8) were found in a pile in the closet of the Taconic study.[6] The first typescript for Chapters 1-5 and 7 (2-6 and 8), read and corrected by J. A. S., were in a file box labeled by the author. The manuscript for Chapter 5 (6) was also in this file box apparently

[6] The numbering of chapters in parentheses was the original numbering which was changed at the very end. Since it occurs in many places in the manuscript, it is put in here for the convenience of people who may use the material in Houghton.

because the author had not yet read the typescript of section 4, the concluding section. The carbon copies were with all the others in a room on the third floor of the Cambridge house. The manuscript of Chapter 6 (7), Value and Money, with numerous notes and discarded bits of manuscript, including some pages from the early version typed in March 1944, were found in a separate file box.

Until the last year or so J. A. S. had planned to have eight chapters in Part II. He then reduced the number to seven. There was a fragment of a Chapter 1 entitled 'From the Beginnings to the First Classical Situation' beginning with '1. Plan of the Part.' The first two paragraphs of this plan have been used at the beginning of the chapter on Graeco-Roman Economics (see above, pp. 51-2), since it is obvious that J. A. S. had not made the necessary revisions at the beginning of this chapter when he made it the first instead of the second in the Part.

Part II was written earliest and rewritten more than any other. It is here that we see most clearly how the original plan (to translate, revise, and bring up to date the early sketch of doctrines and methods) grew and changed almost beyond recognition. It will be recalled (Editor's Introduction, p. v) that the *Epochen der Dogmen- und Methodengeschichte* was divided into four parts or chapters, which in turn were divided into sections. These sections were given titles in the table of contents but were merely numbered as they occurred in the text.

This practice of numbering his sections, without titles, J. A. S. followed when he began writing the *History of Economic Analysis*. It was mainly in the chapters which were written early and not subsequently revised (chs. 1 and 7 of Part II and ch. 4 of Part IV) that the editor had to supply section titles. Later the author gave titles not only to sections but even to subsections, for example, in Parts III and IV. This last was not done at all in Part II. Where the sections in Part II were long, the editor divided them and supplied titles for subsections.

The first part or chapter of the *Dogmengeschichte* (The Development of Economics as a Science) treats very briefly the sources of economics in the writings of the philosophers (from ancient times down to the eighteenth century) and in the popular discussion, subjects that are covered in considerable detail in Chapters 1-3 of Part II of the *History;* the second part or chapter (The Discovery of the Circular Flow of Economic Life) includes roughly those authors (the physiocrats, Turgot, and Adam Smith) and topics that are discussed in Chapters 4-7 of Part II of the *History*. The *Dogmengeschichte* devoted 32 pages—somewhat large pages, to be sure—to what required 326 pages (pp. 51-376) in the *History*.

A glance at the outline (pp. 1187-8) of the Known or Approximate Dates of Typing various portions of the *History* will be most helpful in tracing the evolution of the chapters in Part II. Most chapters went through at least two stages but Chapters 2 and 3 (The Scholastic Doctors and the Philosophers of Natural Law and The Consultant Administrators and the Pamphleteers) went through no less than three stages—an early, an intermediate, and a final treatment.

The early version of Chapters 1-3 (entitled 'Chapter I: Beginnings') consisted of 77 typed pages divided into 17 sections without titles. It starts with a description of the author's concept of Classical Situations and ends with a short account of the Consultant Administrators and of Public Finance. It must have been typed not later than 1942, since a few pages of it are embodied in an intermediate version of Chapter 2 typed June 19, 1943. Several pages of this early version were used in the final manuscript of the first chapter, Graeco-Roman Economics. For example, typed pages 5-6, 14-16, and 19-21 became manuscript pages 2-3, 42-4, and 52-4 of the final version. I believe the date of typing in this case is somewhat misleading, and that this chapter was kept back and sent off to be typed only when Chapter 2, which was revised in 1944 and again in 1945, was ready. There were no section titles, although the sections were numbered.

Chapters 2 and 3 were revised and expanded twice. There is no trace of the early version in the intermediate treatment of the Scholastics and only four pages (39-42) of the early version appear in the intermediate treatment of the Consultant Administrators. A few pages from both the early and intermediate versions are used in the final manuscripts of Chapters 2 and 3 but most of the material is entirely new. Chapters 1 and 2 were typed finally in August and September 1945, and it seems probable that Chapter 3 was typed about the same time, but we have no definite date. The editorial note on page 181 above explains how Chapter 3, section 4e (Adam Smith and the *Wealth of Nations*), which had been discarded by the author without ever being typed, was restored by the editor.

Chapter 4 (The Econometricians and Turgot) was entirely new except for two typed pages taken from the intermediate treatment of the Consultant Administrators and the Pamphleteers. J. A. S. was somewhat in doubt about the title. It was originally 'The Econometricians.' He added 'and Turgot?' in pencil on the first typescript.

Chapter 5 (Population, Returns, Wages, and Employment) had a rather full early version which was typed in two sections on March 15, 1943, and July 13, 1943. It was almost completely rewritten with only two typed pages from the early version used in the final version, the last section of which was typed on February 21, 1946. This last section of typescript had not been read and corrected by J. A. S.

Chapter 6 (Value and Money) was found in manuscript, obviously not quite finished, with the pages unnumbered and slightly mixed up. The order of pages in such cases was determined by Arthur W. Marget, who put this chapter together and did much of the work of editing it. Some of the manuscript was much crossed out and written over, but it seemed to be divided into seven sections, of which 1, 3, 6, and 7 had titles. In the file box with this manuscript, there were voluminous notes (largely in shorthand) and many discarded bits of manuscript—also the manuscript of the early treatment of money typed in March 1944. Several typed pages from the early manuscript were used in sections 2 and 3 of the later version. Among the notes was a plan of the chapter, which is reproduced on the opposite page. This plan confirmed the impression that seven sections were intended and supplied the missing section titles. This page, as well as the three others reproduced in this appendix, will give the reader a more vivid impression than mere words could convey of the appearance of many of the notes and the difficulty of deciphering them.

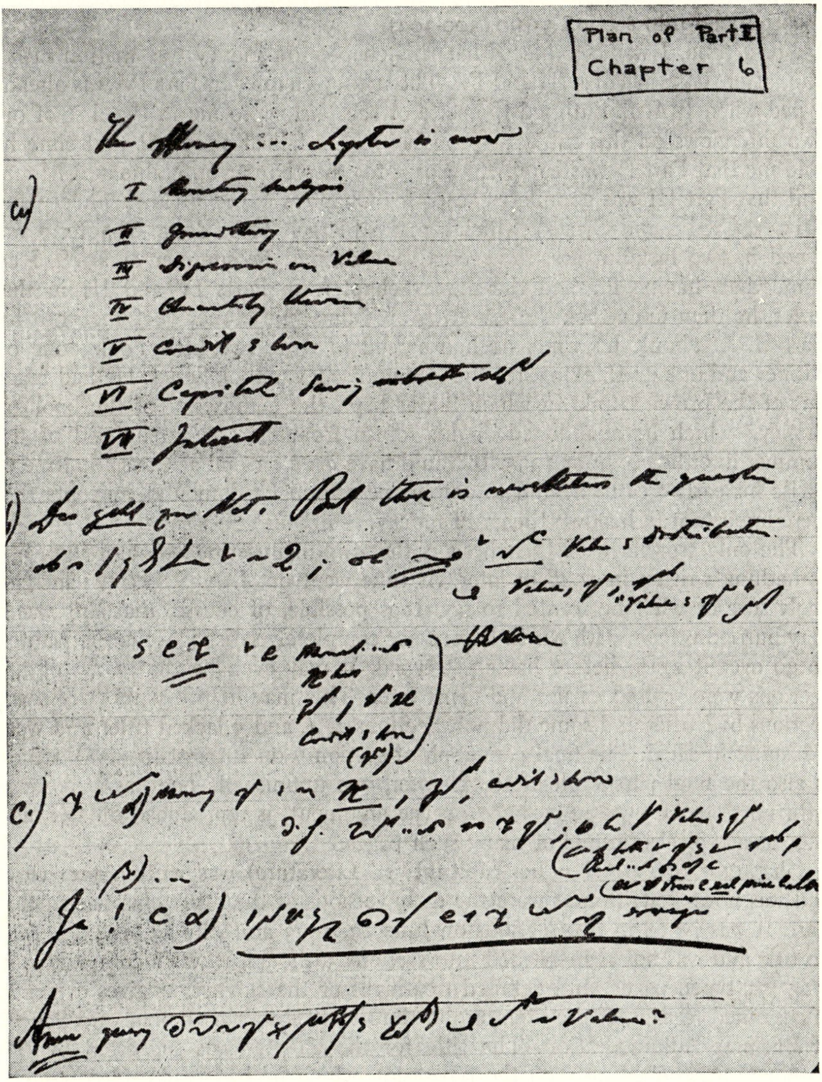

As I have said already, I am frankly puzzled as to when this revision of Value and Money in the early period was written. I have some reasons for feeling that it might have been done rather early, as I stated in my note on page 276 above. If that was so, however, I do not understand why it was never typed, unless J. A. S. wanted to do a good deal more work on it and decided to wait until he was working on the money chapters in Parts III and IV. We do know that the early version, which consisted of 31 typed pages, was typed on March 26, 1944. Pages 1-12 of this early version were incorporated into section 2 of the later version (see above, pp. 289-98) and pages 14-18 on Galiani were incorporated into section 3 (pp. 300-302).

For a time, I was convinced that this chapter on money was written rather late, after those in Parts III and IV. The money chapter in Part IV was already typed when J. A. S. outlined the state of the *History* to me in the first of our two interviews on this subject—probably in the fall of 1947. At that time he told me that Part II was complete except for the chapter on Value and Money and that Part III was complete except for Chapters 6 and 7 (Pure Theory and Money, Credit, and Cycles), which remained largely to be done. Chapter 7 was typed in two installments, the second one during the summer of 1948. I assume that, having finished the money chapters in Parts IV and III in that order, he then undertook the rewriting of Value and Money (before 1790) for Part II. At about this time, he had agreed to write two little books, one on Money and one on Banking, for the Economics Handbook Series. He had taken out of the brown trunk, in which it was kept, the manuscript of the book on money,[7] which he abandoned on his return from Europe at the end of the summer in either 1934 or 1935. It would have been natural at the same time to revise his early treatment and to emphasize certain fundamental concepts that were important to his own theory of money.

The only trouble with this thesis is that the manuscript does not look like something written in 1948 or later. As time went on, J. A. S. became increasingly sure of what he wanted to say. It is possible, of course, that this was a very hurried version with which he was not completely satisfied—that he wanted to go over it again before having it typed. It may even be that some of the sections were revised earlier and some later. This may help explain why some sections had titles and some did not. Sections 2, 4, and 5 lacked titles and were not quite finished. The final paragraph of section 7 on Interest (p. 334), which is also the final paragraph of the chapter, was unfinished. The page, crowded with notes to be used in carrying on the argument, is reproduced on the next page as a typical example of many such pages.

Chapter 7 of Part II (The 'Mercantilist' Literature) was written very early and was never rewritten as were the early versions of the other chapters in this Part. It was typed in two sections on June 19, 1943 and July 13, 1943. It had no title and was not even divided into sections, although it was a comparatively long (71 typed pages) and detailed treatment of the subject. It gives evidence of sustained reading of the literature in the Kress Library at the Harvard School of Business Administration. The title for the chapter was suggested by the author in a penciled note on the typescript, which he had read and corrected. The editor divided the chapter into sections and subsections and supplied titles.

Part III presented no such problems as those we have just reviewed. It was apparently written in a perfectly straightforward way and was complete except

[7] This manuscript, written in German, is now being translated and edited by Arthur W. Marget in the hope that eventually it may be published.

for the first section of Chapter 6. It corresponds to the third part or chapter of the *Dogmengeschichte* (The Classical System and Its Offshoots). All of Part III was assembled in Taconic. The manuscript of the first four chapters with notes

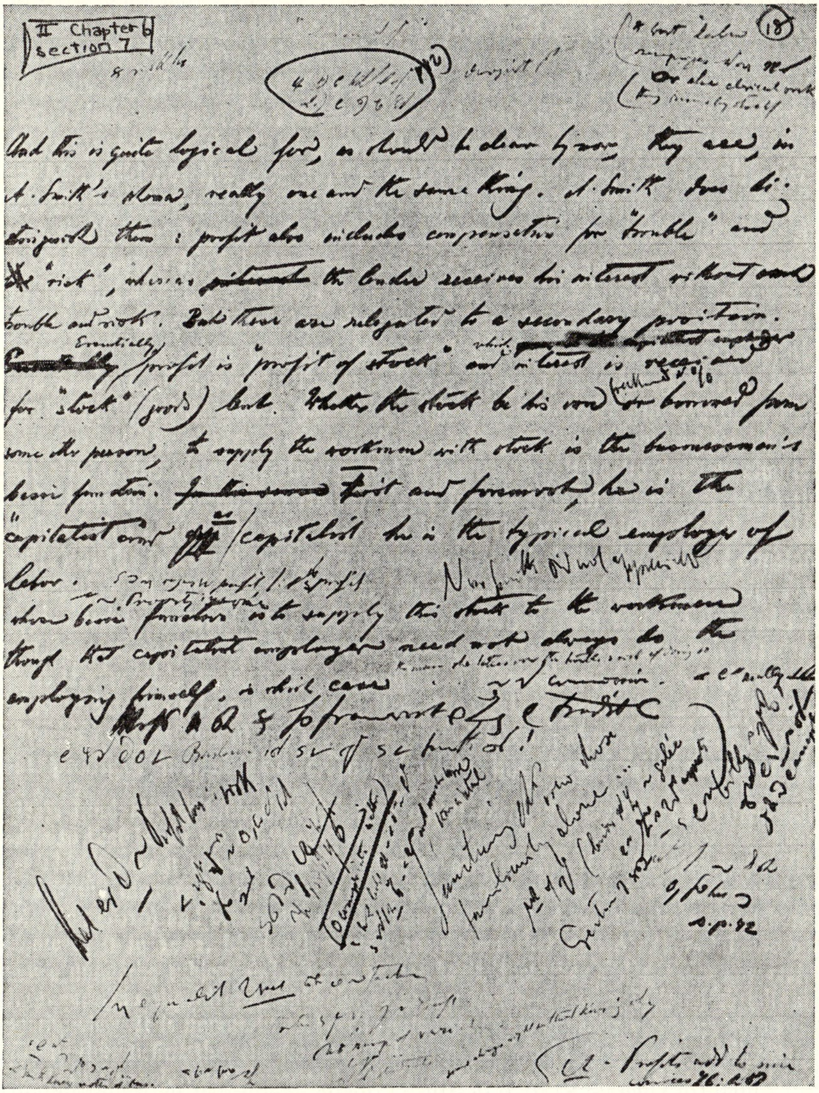
II Chapter 6
section 7

And this is quite logical for, as should be clear by now, they are, in A. Smith's scheme, really one and the same thing. A. Smith does distinguish them: profit also includes compensation for "trouble" and "risk", whereas the lender receives his interest without trouble and risk. But these are relegated to a secondary position. Essentially profit is "profit of stock" while interest is recompense for "stock" (goods) lent. Whether the stock be his own or borrowed from some other person, to supply the workmen with stock is the businessman's basic function. First and foremost he is the "capitalist" or capitalist he is the typical employer of labor.

and discarded material was found in a heap in the closet of the Taconic study. The first typescript of these chapters was in two folders on the desk. The manuscript and typescript of Chapters 5 and 6 were in one file box, and there was another box of notes and bits of discarded manuscript for these chapters. The manuscript and the typescript of the two chapters on Money, Credit, and Cycles (Part III, ch. 7 and Part IV, ch. 8) were in the same file box.

All the typescript of Part III had been read and corrected by the author in pencil except the last two sections of Chapter 6—section 5 (Capital) and section 6 (The Distributive Shares). It should be noted, however, that these were two very long and important sections consisting of 103 typed pages. Some of the other chapters had been read very rapidly and superficially, especially the middle portion of the money chapter. A few days before his death, on his return from the meetings of the American Economic Association toward the end of December 1949, J. A. S. began to go through Part III systematically. In addition to penciled corrections on the typescript, there was a little pile of notes on several sheets still attached to a pad with the heading 'Reading III ? 30.xii.49.' These were undoubtedly suggestions for changes. Then or earlier he had also removed some pages from the end of Chapter 5 (sec. 5c, The Model, and sec. 6, The 'Classic' Conception of Economic Development). Clipped to the first of these pages was a sheet of shorthand notes with the comment 'Ch. 5, sec. 5 becomes quite loose!'

There were not so many 'early versions' for Part III as for the preceding part. There was a 'Chapter II: The Political and Intellectual Scenery,' a few pages of which were used in the final version of Chapter 3; there was a 'Chapter III: Scope and Method,' a few pages of which were used in the final version of Chapter 5; and there was the material (with no title) on Senior's Four Postulates which, without being rewritten, became the first section of Chapter 6. The first and last of these three were typed in December 1943.

The editorial note on page 575 explains that J. A. S. would have revised the material on Senior's postulates and integrated it with the rest of the chapter. But how do we know this? The rest of this chapter was written rather late—probably in 1948. There were 161 typed pages, but it began with section 2 (Value). The first page of section 2 was page 1 of the typescript. The material on Senior's postulates in a folder was put at the beginning of the chapter. In discussing the plan of Part IV on page 758, J. A. S. wrote 'Chapter 7 (Equilibrium Analysis) corresponds to Chapter 6 of Part III and assigns the same piloting function to Walras that was assigned to Senior in Part III.'

There was also another problem—that of a title for Chapter 6. All the other chapters in Part III were complete with titles, section titles, and in many cases subsection titles. All of Chapter 6 from section 2 on was complete with section titles and subsection titles. But section 1, not having been revised, lacked a title and so did the chapter, since the chapter title appears at the beginning of section 1. Here again the Plan of the Part provided a solution. This time it was the plan of Part III on page 383 where J. A. S. explained that he proposed 'to draw a picture of analytic *developments* with reference to a cross section . . . represented (in Chapter 5) by J. S. Mill's *Principles*' and that he would simplify matters 'by reserving the details of pure theory and of money . . . for two separate chapters (6 and 7).' Hence the titles for Chapters 5 and 6—General Economics; A Cross Section and General Economics: Pure Theory.

Part IV may be considered a development of the fourth part or chapter of the *Dogmengeschichte* (The Historical School and the Marginal Utility Theory) but only so far as the broad subject matter is concerned. In the early sketch, this material required only 27 pages; in the *History*, it required nearly 400 pages.

At one time this Part was to have consisted of ten chapters; then the number was reduced to nine and finally to eight. This was not the result of any elimination of material but rather the result of the consolidation of Chapters 4 and 5 into Chapter 4 and of Chapters 8 and 9 into Chapter 7, the intervening chapters having changed their numbers. Because this confused me at first and because it may confuse others using the manuscript and notes deposited in the Houghton Library, I shall quote from Chapter 1 of Part IV as it was originally written—before being edited. Probably the first three chapters of Part IV and the parallel chapters in Part III had been written and typed not later than early 1947. After commenting on the first three chapters, the outline for the Plan of the Part on page 758 read as follows:

> Then follow comments on two allied groups of men and ideas that lend themselves to separate treatment, the group whose work centered in the contemporaneous interest in social reform and whose leaders were with singular infelicity dubbed 'socialists of the chair' (*Kathedersozialisten*); and the group that was called, and called itself, the historical school (Chapters 4 and 5). The much-debated question of economists' value-judgments will conveniently be touched upon in connection with the former and the famous 'battle of methods' (and its American counterpart, the institutionalist controversy) in connection with the latter. To some extent, this arrangement impairs our picture bceause when we go on to a brief survey of the men, groups, and developments in 'general economics' (Chapters 6 and 7), we shall have already eliminated two of the most important influences upon this 'general economics.' Let me hence entreat the reader to peruse these chapters in their order. The last three chapters of the Part deal with sets of topics that it has seemed best to reserve for separate treatment. Chapter 8 corresponds to Chapter 6 of Part III and assigns the same piloting function to Walras that has been assigned to Senior in Part III. It aims at presenting the emergence of the elements of modern pure theory in a manner that will, I am afraid, prove as unsatisfactory to the modern theorist as it will seem overloaded to the non-theorist. The latter may be right in contenting himself with what he will have read on these matters in Chapters 6 and 7. Chapter 9, on the fortunes of utility theory and its successors to the present day, stands by itself or almost so and should only be read by those who take special interest in the matter. Segregation of the topics of money, credit, saving and investment, business cycles in the last chapter (10) calls but for this remark: segregation imposed itself for reasons of exposition as it did in Part III.

The manuscript and typescript of Chapters 1-5 were found in a file box. In the folder with Chapter 4 were notes and reprints to be used in the rewriting of this chapter. The manuscript, typescript, notes, and discarded bits of manuscript for Chapters 6 and 7 were found in another file box. There were also a few bits from Chapter 7 found in the desk at Littauer. After mid-1948, the carbons were no longer deposited in the attic on Acacia Street so that it was somewhat more difficult to find out just what had been done and where it belonged. J. A. S. had glanced over the typescript of most of the chapters in this part very hastily and made small corrections in pencil. He certainly had not read through the early chapters systematically as he was approaching the end of his work. For example, he had not corrected the numbering of the chapters in the Plan of the Part quoted above.

Part IV presented no real difficulties except with reference to Chapter 4 (Sozialpolitik and the Historical Method), Chapter 7 (Equilibrium Analysis), and the concluding section of Chapter 6 (sec. 6: The Contribution of the Applied Fields), all of which were unfinished. Chapter 4 as printed consists of two early versions typed in 1943, which would have been extensively revised. The long editorial note on pages 800-801 says all that is necessary about this chapter. Chapter 6 was written and typed relatively late but seems complete except for the final section on the applied fields which was only sketched out. Of the five subsections, two had headings only and another—that on public finance—was unfinished. This material was found in manuscript and typed after the death of the author.

Chapter 7 (Equilibrium Analysis) aimed 'at presenting the emergence of the elements of modern pure theory,' assigning the piloting function to Walras. There is a brief early treatment typed in February 1943. It consists of 29 typed pages with many blank spaces for footnotes to be filled in later. The concluding paragraph, summing up and appraising the contribution of Walras to scientific economics, breaks off in the middle of a sentence. J. A. S. had read the first typescript [8] and made many penciled notes in the margins and other blank spaces. These were not corrections but suggestions for elaboration of the argument. The final version is a long chapter of over 200 typed pages (123 printed pages) which covers essentially the same topics as those discussed in Economics 203, the course in Advanced Economic Theory given by the author.

Much of this chapter was written a few pages at a time during the second half of 1948 and the whole year 1949—possibly after a return from a classroom discussion of the subject. This last fact explains to some extent the existence of a number of abandoned 'early versions' for some sections and the existence of alternative versions for other sections. It was a little confusing in the beginning to choose from among these, but the choice was made easy in some cases by the fact that an early version was revised and extended to form a final version (sections 4 and 6, for example). The plan of the chapter and the numbering of the sections was always perfectly clear with the single exception of the position of the material on Welfare Economics which will be explained below.

The first six sections of Chapter 7, the first six sections of the Appendix to the chapter (Note on the Theory of Utility), and the section on Welfare Eco-

[8] This typescript together with the manuscript will be deposited in the Houghton Library at Harvard. This arrangement had not been made in the late spring of 1950 when Richard M. Goodwin read the various sections of this chapter. He wished to incorporate it at the end of section 1.

nomics were typed during the academic year 1948-9.[9] Sections 1, 2, and 5 were left as they had been typed with minor corrections and revisions in pencil on the typescript. The typed version of section 3 was abandoned by the editor, two alternative versions in manuscript being used in its place. Sections 4 and 6 were revised and added to by the author. The final version of section 6, part of section 7 (sub a, b, and c), and section 8 were typed in the last quarter of 1949. The version of Welfare Economics typed in 1948-9 was abandoned by the editor for another found in manuscript, which became section 8 of the Appendix (Note on Utility). (It may be a little confusing that both Chapter 7 itself and the Appendix to the chapter have eight sections.)

We now comment on the sections in their numerical order, omitting sections 1, 2, and 5, which—as has been stated—presented no particular problems. Section 3 (The Concept of Equilibrium) presented several problems. There were no less than four different versions with four different titles—the typed version of 1948-9 and three alternative versions in manuscript to which J. A. S. had clipped a page of shorthand notes with the comment 'There are now *three* alternative formulations of [section] 3 [undecipherable shorthand] for the purpose of inevitable rewriting of 3.' The title of the typed version was '3. Statics and Dynamics. Determinateness. Stability. Equilibrium.' I labeled the three alternative formulations (3a), (3b), and (3c). Their titles were as follows: (3a) The Concept of Equilibrium; (3b) Statics, Dynamics, and the Stationary State, Evolution; (3c) Determinateness and Equilibrium. Stability. There was a great deal of repetition of the problems discussed in these four versions, and yet no single one of them was complete. I abandoned the typed version for reasons to be discussed in the next paragraph but one. I decided to use alternative formulations (3b) and (3c), which were roughly complementary, whereas (3a) tended to repeat what was treated more comprehensively in (3b). At first it was my intention to publish (3a) and some other early and alternative versions in this appendix. The arrangement whereby they will be deposited in the Houghton Library at Harvard makes this unnecessary.

In the editorial note at the beginning of the chapter on Equilibrium Analysis, I explained that it had first been put together with the assistance of Richard M. Goodwin. This was done in the late spring and early summer of 1950 before Parts II and III and the preceding chapters of Part IV had been edited because Goodwin was leaving for Europe. In dealing with section 3, he used parts of all four formulations, arranging them so as to give as much coherence and continuity as could be achieved. Later, after much work on the earlier portions of the *History*, I decided to present it as nearly as possible as it had been written. This meant, of course, no mixing and rearranging of different

[9] At this point, I should like to correct certain implications as to dating made in the editorial notes on pp. 951-2, 983, and 1068-9. The first four sections of Chapter 7 were written, I believe, during 1948 and not 'long ago' as stated. The Note on the Theory of Utility was *typed* in 1948-9 but *written* earlier. Section 8 of this Note (Welfare Economics) was written at about the same time as the first six sections of the Note. These corrections are based partly on a careful study of the typing; to some extent they are due to the realization that the Appendix on utility was once Chapter 9.

treatments of the same subject, even in the interest of more complete coverage.

I found no manuscript for the typed version of section 3, which was so general and so completely lacking in specific footnote references that I began to wonder if it could have been dictated. Later on I had the same feeling for the same reasons about the typed version on Welfare Economics. As I have pointed out on more than one occasion, J. A. S. first wrote all the *History* in his own hand. Occasionally he bemoaned the fact that there was so much to do and so little time in which to do it. When during 1948-9 he had adequate secretarial assistance for the first time, I remember encouraging him to attempt to dictate some of the material he knew so well with the idea that he could revise it later. He reported that the experiment was not successful.

Section 4 (The Competitive Hypothesis and the Theory of Monopoly) affords an example of the difficulties encountered when the manuscript pages were not numbered at all and several bits of typescript were each numbered independently with no hint of their order. The final version of this section consisted of four different installments, written at different times. Three (the first two and the last) had been typed in 1948-9 and one existed only in manuscript. Actually the first two followed directly after one another despite the fact that the pages were numbered 1 to 8 and 1 to 5 respectively. First J. A. S. read and revised in pencil these two typed installments; then he added several pages in manuscript with the last paragraph of the typescript continued on the first page of the new manuscript. Finally the fourth installment (3 typed pages) seemed to follow the last paragraph of the new manuscript installment although this last is not absolutely certain (see note, p. 983). To further confuse the situation, there was found among the notes another treatment in manuscript entitled 'Monopoly, Oligopoly, Bilateral Monopoly.' This was apparently a brief first attempt that had been discarded without ever being typed.

There were three versions of section 6 (Partial Analysis), all typed from manuscript, two in 1948-9 and one in the last quarter of 1949. The first of these (5 typed pages) had obviously been discarded; typescript and manuscript were found folded up together in the closet of the Taconic study. The other two versions were found in the file box with the rest of the material for this chapter. The second version (8 typed pages) was read and revised and had several pages of new manuscript added to it. It was then retyped and became the third version (12 typed pages). This last version had not been read and corrected by the author after it was typed.

Now we come to section 7 (The Walrasian System of General Equilibrium), which was unfinished and most of which had not been typed. Fortunately, since this was to be the pivotal section of the chapter, a good deal of it was found in manuscript. Perhaps it would not be out of place to recall here the comments made on the work of Walras on page 827 above: 'His system of economic equilibrium, uniting, as it does, the quality of "revolutionary" creativeness with the quality of classic synthesis, is the only work by an economist that will stand comparison with the achievements of theoretical physics. . . It is the outstanding landmark on the road that economics travels toward the status of a rigorous or exact science and, though outmoded by now, still stands at the back of much of the best theoretical work of our time.'

The editorial note on page 998 explains how this chapter was put together from six different installments, two of which were typed and four of which existed only in manuscript. For the most part there were no subsection titles. The two typed installments (of 9 pages each) were found with their manuscripts. They had not been read by J. A. S. These are now subsections 7a, 7b, and 7c. Five different installments were found in manuscript with pages unnumbered. I numbered them 1-3, 4-7, 8-24, 25-36, and 37-55. The first 3 pages were used as the introduction to the section, pages 4-7 were discarded, pages 8-36 became subsection 7d (Walras' Theory of Production), and pages 37-55 became subsection 7e (The Introduction of Capital Formation and of Money). The discovery of this last important section of manuscript was rather dramatic. It had been overlooked when the section was first put together. I was going through the file box in September 1951 in the hope of finding a few discarded paragraphs on this subject. I did find a few preliminary pages and I was having them typed when suddenly I came upon pages 37-55. These last subsections must have been written in the second half of 1949. There is a reference on page 1021 to Leontief's 'Input and Output Analysis,' *Papers and Proceedings, American Economic Association*, May 1949.

Section 8 (The Production Function) was typed in the last quarter of 1949. It must have been written during that year—possibly in the summer—since there is a reference (p. 1040) to a controversy in the *Quarterly Journal of Economics* for February 1949. (The February number probably appeared in March.) J. A. S. had scarcely more than glanced at the typed copy and had not made the usual corrections in pencil. He had been very busy in December 1949—writing the article on Mitchell for the *Quarterly Journal*, putting down notes for 'The March into Socialism' for the December meeting of the American Economic Association, preparing an outline of the Walgreen Lectures to be given in Chicago in January, along with the usual lectures and consultations at Harvard. It is for this reason that none of the material typed in late 1949 was read carefully and corrected.

Finally we arrive at the appendix to the chapter. The first six sections of the Note on the Theory of Utility and the version of Welfare Economics (printed above as section 8 of the Note) had been written earlier than other parts of the chapter. It will be recalled that the account of 'the fortunes of utility theory and its successors to the present day' (which at one time was to have been ch. 9) had been written but not typed when I had my first interview with J. A. S. on the state of the *History* during the latter part of 1947. The six sections of the Note were numbered, but the first four did not have titles. Section 7 (The Consistency Postulate) and the beginnings of a new section 8 (The Corpse Shows Signs of Life) were apparently written later and had not been typed at all. For reasons given in the editorial note on page 1068, I believe that Welfare Economics was originally to have been section 8 of the Note on Utility and I have placed it in that position. Since the new section 8

(The Corpse) consisted of only a single paragraph and a few notes, I have put it in the editorial note already mentioned.

The version of Welfare Economics actually used was not the one typed in 1948-9. The latter was rather general and lacked specific footnote references with one exception. Moreover, I could find no manuscript corresponding to this treatment. As I have already explained, I had the impression that, like the early version of section 3, it might have been dictated. There was another version in manuscript, which had never been typed. It was writtten in ink and corrected in blue pencil and lead pencil as were the first six sections of the Note on Utility; it certainly looks as though it had been written at the same time as the latter. The section numbers for the Note (1-6) were in parentheses; there was a pair of parentheses with no number inserted before the title, Welfare Economics. Finally, the latest reference in this version of Welfare Economics, as originally written, was to an article by Tintner in *Econometrica*, January 1946. Later a reference to Samuelson's *Foundations* (1947) was added in pencil. This is consistent with the probable time of writing of the first six sections. The manuscript version was more specific than the typed version; each version had certain things the other lacked. Goodwin suggested a composite version, using some pages from both treatments; but, as a matter of editorial policy, for reasons already given, I had ruled against this solution. I finally decided—with qualms, to be sure—to use the manuscript version.

Chapter 8 (Money, Credit, and Cycles) was probably the first of the money chapters to be completed; it was certainly the first to be typed. Apparently when J. A. S. sent it off to be typed he was not happy about it. (Of course, he was never really satisfied with his own work; if only there were time, he felt, it could be improved in so many ways.) Clipped to the first typescript, which had been hastily read and corrected by the author, were a number of small pieces of paper with names, outlines, and shorthand notes. On the outside was the comment 'Now this was reserved as containing necessary additions and corrections—they are not carried out and were thus left when I sent the chapter off in despair.' For this chapter, I supplied some titles for subsections which will be easily recognized from the fact that they are enclosed in the usual square brackets. I also divided section 8 on Crises and Cycles into two sections (8 and 9) so that I could preserve the subtitles under Non-Monetary Cycle Analysis.

Part V (Conclusion: A Sketch of Modern Developments), like the introductory Part I, was intended to be brief. Its function was to help the reader understand how modern work links up with the work of the past. J. A. S. was working on Parts I and V at the time of his death. There was a file box in the Cambridge study containing 'Notes and Brief Plan for Part V.' It is from the two pages of notes reproduced on the next two pages that we know what were to be the main lines of discussion. Unfortunately the plan itself is mostly in shorthand. It indicates eight items of which at least the last three—Developments from Marshall, Business Cycles and Dynamics, and Keynes—had actually been written up. The list of 'Things still entirely lacking in V' is perhaps more revealing because more of it is in longhand.

Only a fragment of an introduction to the Part existed. It was for this reason that a summary of the Mexican Lectures (see editorial note, p. 1140) on the

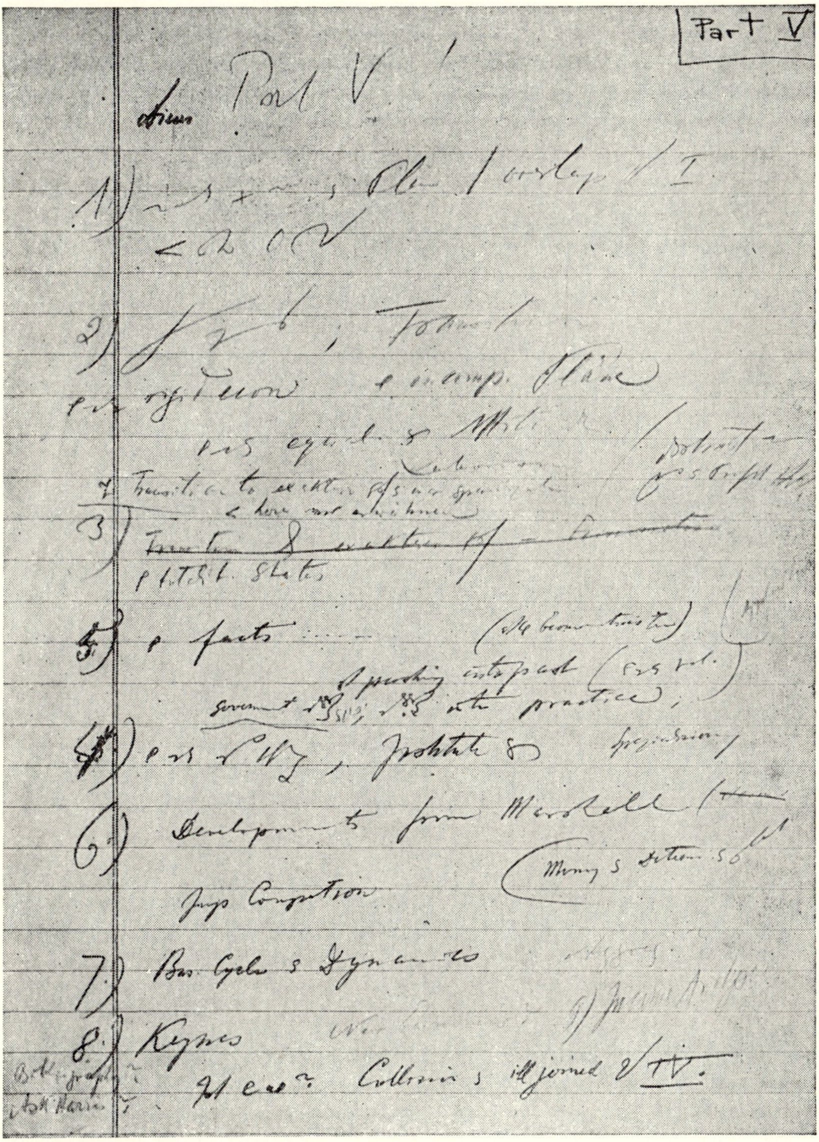

Progress of Theoretical Economics during the Last Twenty-five Years was published in Chapter 1.

Chapters 2-5 were written in 1949. Chapters 2-4 were typed in late 1949, but Chapter 5 (Keynes and Macroeconomics) was not finished and was not typed until after the author's death. Of these chapters, only Chapter 4 (Dynamics and Business Cycle Research) had a title. This seems also to have been

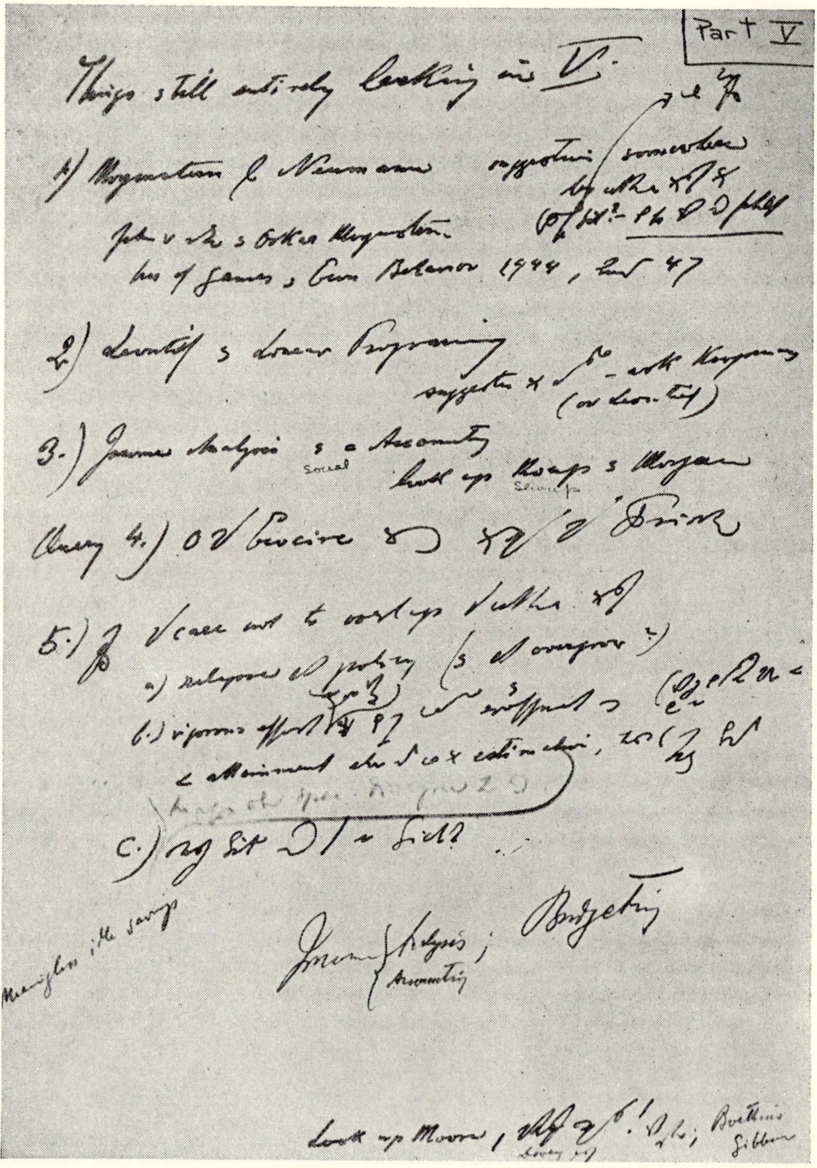
Part V

Things still entirely lacking in V.

1) Morgenstern & Neumann

2) Leontief's Linear Programming

Budgeting

the only one of these chapters read by the author after it was typed. The other chapter titles and all the section titles were supplied by the editor.

E. B. S.

List of Books Frequently Quoted

(WITH EDITIONS USED)

WHAT FOLLOWS is by no means a complete list of the books quoted in the *History* or even a list of the books quoted several times. The list is confined to books which are quoted repeatedly or to books for which the edition used is important and where specific information about the edition is not given on each occasion the book is quoted.

Allen, R. G. D., *Mathematical Analysis for Economists*, London, 1938.

Aquinas, Saint Thomas, *Summa Theologica* [Latin, 6 vols.], Turin (Italy), Libraria Marietti, 1932.

Böhm-Bawerk, Eugen V., *Capital and Interest: A Critical History of Economical Theory* [1st German ed. 1884; English trans. 1890], Reprint, New York, 1932.

Böhm-Bawerk, Eugen V., *The Positive Theory of Capital* [1st German ed. 1889; English trans. 1891], Reprint, New York, 1923.

Bowley, A. L., *The Mathematical Groundwork of Economics: An Introductory Treatise*, Oxford, 1924.

Cairnes, J. E., *Some Leading Principles of Political Economy Newly Expounded*, London, 1874.

Cannan, Edwin, *A History of the Theories of Production and Distribution in English Political Economy from 1776 to 1848* [1893], 3rd ed. 1917; 4th printing, London, 1924.

[Cantillon, Richard], *Essai sur la nature du commerce en général* [1755], Reprinted for Harvard University, Boston, 1892.

Chamberlin, Edward Hastings, *The Theory of Monopolistic Competition: A Re-orientation of the Theory of Value* [1933], 5th ed., Cambridge, Mass., 1946.

Cournot, Augustin, *Researches into the Mathematical Principles of the Theory of Wealth* [1st French ed., 1838; English trans. by Nathaniel T. Bacon, 1897], New York, 1927.

Custodi, Pietro, *Scrittori classici italiani di economia politica* (50 vols.), Milan, 1803-16.

Fisher, Irving, *Mathematical Investigations in the Theory of Value and Prices* [1892], New Haven, 1926.

Hayek, Friedrich A., *The Pure Theory of Capital*, London, 1941.

Heckscher, Eli F., *Mercantilism* [1st Swedish ed. 1931], London, 1935.

Hicks, J. R., *Value and Capital: An Inquiry into Some Fundamental Principles of Economic Theory*, Oxford, 1939.

Jevons, W. Stanley, *Investigations in Currency and Finance* [papers written 1862-82], ed. with introd. by H. S. Foxwell, London, 1884.

Jevons, W. Stanley, *The Theory of Political Economy* [1871], 2nd ed., rev. and enlarged, London, 1879.

Keynes, John Maynard, *Essays in Biography*, London, 1933.

Keynes, John Maynard, *The General Theory of Employment, Interest and Money*, London, 1936.

Keynes, John Maynard, *A Tract on Monetary Reform*, London, 1923. *Monetary Reform* (American ed. of above), New York, 1924.

Keynes, John Maynard, *A Treatise on Money* (Vol. I, *The Pure Theory of Money;* Vol. II, *The Applied Theory of Money*), London, 1930.

Malthus, T. R., *Principles of Political Economy Considered with a View to Their Practical Application*, London, 1820.

Marget, Arthur W., *The Theory of Prices*, New York, 1938-42.

Marshall, Alfred, *Principles of Economics* [1890], 4th ed., London, 1898.

Marx, Karl, *Capital: A Critique of Political Economy.*

Vol. I, *The Process of Capitalist Production* [1867], original English trans. by Moore and Aveling, rev. and amplified according to 4th German ed. by Ernest Untermann, Chicago, Charles H. Kerr & Co., 1906.

Vol. II, *The Process of Circulation of Capital* [1885].

Vol. III, *The Process of Capitalist Production as a Whole* [1894].

Vols. II and III, trans. by Untermann, Chicago, Charles H. Kerr & Co., 1909.

Mill, James, *Elements of Political Economy*, 1st ed., London, 1821.

Mill, John Stuart, *Autobiography*, London, 1873.

Mill, John Stuart, *Principles of Political Economy with Some of Their Applications to Social Philosophy* [1848], 7th ed. 1871; ed. with introd. by Sir W. J. Ashley, London, 1909.

Pareto, Vilfredo, *Cours d'économie politique*, Lausanne, 1896-7.

Pareto, Vilfredo, *Manuel d'économie politique* [Italian ed. 1906], Paris, 1909.

Ricardo, David, *The Principles of Political Economy and Taxation* [1817], 3rd ed. 1821, Everyman's Library ed., London and New York, 1912, reprinted 1917.

Rist, Charles, *History of Monetary and Credit Theory from John Law to the Present Day* [1st French ed. 1938], New York, 1940.

Robinson, Joan, *The Economics of Imperfect Competition*, London, 1933.

Roscher, William, *Principles of Political Economy* [1st German ed. 1854], New York, 1878.

Samuelson, Paul Anthony, *Foundations of Economic Analysis*, Cambridge, 1947.

Say, Jean Baptiste, *A Treatise on Political Economy; or The Production, Distribution, and Consumption of Wealth* [1st French ed. 1803], trans. from 4th French ed. by C. R. Prinsep, Boston, 1821.

Seligman, Edwin R. A., *Essays in Economics*, New York, 1925.

Sempere y Guarinos, Juan, ed., *Biblioteca española economico-politica* (4 vols.), Madrid, 1801-21.

Senior, Nassau William, *An Outline of the Science of Political Economy* [1836], Library of Economics Reprint, London, 1938.

Smith, Adam, *An Inquiry into the Nature and Causes of the Wealth of Nations* [1776], ed. by Edwin Cannan from text of 5th ed., Modern Library, New York. [The Modern Library ed. is the one referred to throughout except in Part II, ch. 3, sec. 4e, where the page references are to the Everyman's Library ed., London and New York, 1910, reprinted 1917.]

Stigler, George J., *Production and Distribution Theories*, New York, 1941.

Sweezy, Paul M., *The Theory of Capitalist Development: Principles of Marxian Political Economy*, New York, 1942.

Tagliacozzo, Giorgio, *Economisti napoletani dei sec. XVII e XVIII*, Bologna, 1937.

Thornton, Henry, *An Enquiry into the Nature and Effects of the Paper Credit of Great Britain* [1802], Library of Economics Reprint, London, 1939.

Tooke and Newmarch, *A History of Prices and of the State of the Circulation from 1792 to 1856* [6 vols., 1838-57], reproduced from original with an introd. by T. E. Gregory, New York, 1928.

[Turgot, Robert Jacques], 'Réflexions sur la formation et la distribution des richesses,' *Éphémérides du citoyen*, 1769, vols. 11 and 12; 1770, vol 1. [Republished in *Oeuvres* ed. by Dupont de Nemours, vol. V, Paris, 1808.]

Viner, Jacob, *Studies in the Theory of International Trade*, New York, 1937.

Walras, Léon, *Éléments d'économie politique pure (Théorie de la richesse sociale)* [1874-7], 5th ed., Paris and Lausanne, 1926.

Walras, Léon, *Études d'économie politique appliquée (Théorie de la production de la richesse sociale)* [1898], Paris and Lausanne, 1936.

Walras, Léon, *Études d'économie sociale (Théorie de la répartition de la richesse sociale)* [1896], Paris and Lausanne, 1936.

Wicksell, Knut, *Lectures on Political Economy* [1st Swedish ed. 1901-1906], English trans., ed. with introd. by Lionel Robbins, London, 1934.

Index of Authors

Subject Index

To facilitate use of the subject index, reference is made throughout to the three important periods of economic analysis in the following manner:

From 1790 to 1870—Classical Period
From 1870 to 1914—Neo-Classical Period
From 1914 to Present—Modern Period

The first and third terms correspond to J. A. S.'s usage. For the second period, it was believed to be preferable to retain the term 'neo-classical' because of its general usage in the profession, in spite of J. A. S.'s explicit rejection of the term. For his objections, see page 919.